THE RANGER IDEAL VOLUME 2

Texas Rangers in the Hall of Fame, 1874–1930

by
Darren L. Ivey

University of North Texas Press
Denton, Texas

©2018 Darren L. Ivey
All rights reserved.
Printed in the United States of America.

10 9 8 7 6 5 4 3 2 1

Permissions:
University of North Texas Press
1155 Union Circle #311336
Denton, TX 76203-5017

The paper used in this book meets the minimum requirements of the American National Standard for Permanence of Paper for Printed Library Materials, z39.48.1984. Binding materials have been chosen for durability.

Library of Congress Cataloging-in-Publication Data

Ivey, Darren L., 1970- author.
　The Ranger ideal / Darren L. Ivey.
　　pages cm
　Includes bibliographical references and index.
　ISBN-13 978-1-57441-690-9 (cloth : alk. paper)
　ISBN-13 978-1-57441-701-2 (ebook)
　1. Texas Rangers in the Hall of Fame, 1823–1861 2. Texas Rangers—Biography. 3. Texas—History, Military.

F385 .I94 2017
363.209764–dc23
　　　　　　2017027901

The electronic edition of this book was made possible by the support of the Vick Family Foundation.

Cover image: J. B. Gillett's Winchester Model 1873, loaned by Lou, Lee and Beulah Evans/ Catalog #0217; Texas Ranger Badge, c. 1880s, gift of Dan Ragsdale/Catalog #2584.1-2. Courtesy Texas Ranger Hall of Fame and Museum, Waco, Texas.

Cover photographs (L to R): John B. Jones, courtesy Texas State Library and Archives Commission, Austin, Texas; Ira Aten, courtesy Castro County Historical Museum, Dimmitt, Texas; and William J. McDonald, courtesy Library of Congress, Washington, D.C.
Typeset by vPrompt eServices.

For Dusti

"She walks in beauty, like the night"

The Ranger

Once along the border, like the drift of autumn leaves,
Thronged the Indians, desperadoes and the cattle-lifting thieves
Until there came swift-riding over the valley, hill and flat
The Law in dirk and derringer and tall—white—hat.

Rip Ford and old Buck Barry—there is glamor in the names
Of the men who made the Rangers, as the record still proclaims:
The lifter left the cattle and the outlaw hid his gat
When they thought about the rider in the tall—white—hat.

As tall as he his story from the borderland uncouth—
Some of it is legend but most of it is truth ...
For fact stands out of hard fought fight, or years
of stand-up strife—
The Ranger rode the border and the outlaw rode for life.

His is a tale unended. Still riding down the years
Come the hoofbeats of the Ranger and his stalwart form appears ...
Though dark may be the danger, he has no care for that,
Riding on into the future in his tall—white—hat.

—William B. Ruggles
Trails of Texas (1972)

Contents

Preface and Acknowledgments   vii
Introduction   xiii
Timeline of Texas Ranger History (1874–1930)   xv

Chapter 1   John B. Jones: "Transformed His Indian Fighters into Lawmen"   1

Chapter 2   Leander H. McNelly: "No Quarter Given"   49

Chapter 3   John B. Armstrong: "The Strong Right-Hand of Two Ranger Captains"   99

Chapter 4   James B. Gillett: "Unflinchingly Faced both Indians and Outlaws"   121

Chapter 5   Jesse L. Hall: "An Enviable Record of Courage and Action"   153

Chapter 6   George W. Baylor: "A Life of Adventure and Conflict"   203

Chapter 7   Bryan Marsh: "A Fearless Law Officer"   243

Chapter 8   Ira Aten: "A Code of Duty and Service"   281

Chapter 9   James A. Brooks: "A Resolute, Steely Nerved Lawman"   315

Chapter 10   William J. McDonald: "Faced Death with a Calm Certainty"   361

Chapter 11	John R. Hughes: "A Relentless Manhunter and Intrepid Lawman" 411
Chapter 12	John H. Rogers: "A Man of Conviction and Faith" 457

Endnotes   501
Bibliography   685
Index   743

Preface and Acknowledgments

The Texas Rangers are one of the most iconic law enforcement agencies in the world. Like Scotland Yard and the Royal Canadian Mounted Police, they have a rich history of highs and lows, triumphs and failures. Similar to those venerable organizations, the Rangers were born out of necessity. From its earliest days, the expanding borders of Texas endured raids from hostile Indian war parties and Mexican *bandidos*. In response, Texian volunteers, bearing such diverse titles as "mounted riflemen," "mounted spies," and "mounted rangers," rode forth to meet them. This military era of the Ranger service was depicted in Volume 1 of this trilogy.

With Volume 2, we witness the Texas Rangers transforming from state-funded soldiers to professional lawmen. In *Texas Rangers: Lives, Legend, and Legacy*, Bob Alexander and Donaly Brice identified a few attributes that ensured the Frontier Battalion's continuing fame: skillful leadership, dedication to duty, personal courage, and a growing professionalism. Separate from the battalion both organizationally and doctrinally, the Special State Troops on the Rio Grande battled their Mexican foes as warriors, rather than policemen, and the trend toward a law enforcement mentality in that command developed more gradually. Through the late nineteenth century, the members of the Frontier Battalion and the Special State Troops, which merged into the battalion in 1881, progressed from being manhunters and keepers of order, although those remained core assignments, to investigators of livestock theft, armed robberies, fence-cutting, homicides, and numerous other felonies.

In chronicling the service's history, Byron Johnson, director of the Texas Ranger Hall of Fame and Museum in Waco, has devised the phrase "The Ranger Ideal." The core tenets of his thesis include moral clarity, the placing of society above self, and the certainty that one can indeed make a difference. He cites as vital to the Rangers' ongoing mission the principles of "honor, self-sacrifice, perseverance, dedication, valor, duty and humility." Serving the state following the Civil War, the men found in these pages were on the forefront protecting citizens from the Comanche's knife or the outlaw's bullet. Johnson rightfully declared: "Many of their names and deeds have been lost to history, but Texas is their legacy. It would not exist without their sacrifice."

The legislative act of 1874, which established the Frontier Battalion and the state troops on the border, offered Texas, for the first time, a permanent Ranger force to quell the significant crime wave plaguing the state. With the lawmakers' accomplishment, and subsequent actions by the governor and adjutant-general, the Texas Ranger tradition was finally incorporated into a complete organizational structure with a clear chain of command, while still allowing for individual resourcefulness. To operate efficiently, company leaders had to master administrative duties such as recruitment and retention, maintaining headquarters and detachment camps, obtaining equipment and supplies, deploying personnel to specific locales, and composing reports to superiors. Writing on the Frontier Battalion, Doctor Harold J. Weiss observed, "Centralized police work had to be meshed with the Ranger tradition of duty, initiative, and the ability to outlast opponents."

Supporting the new loose hierarchy were legal tools and protections available to both peace officers and American society in general. In a letter written to me, Bob Alexander, a veteran of forty years in law enforcement, remarked: "What is not novel to that movement into the Texas Rangers' newfound sphere of activity were particular written guarantees common to the population at large: The United States Constitution. Not infrequently blood and thunder writers and/or scholarly authors seem to overlook or at least underplay this incontestable and concrete truth." In reading these pages, one will see the daily work of nineteenth-century Texas Rangers was subject to a well-established Constitutional system, doubtless familiar to the modern observer, involving probable cause, affidavits and search warrants, complaints and arrest warrants, grand juries, and appellate courts.

Organizational schemes and legal code notwithstanding, the key to the service's long existence continues to be adaptability. When new weapons technology emerged, such as the six-shooter or the lever-action rifle, Texas Rangers were quick to realize the potential. The same holds true for law enforcement techniques that improved their professionalism. Since the days of Eugène-François Vidocq, considered the father of modern criminology, police agencies have employed to varying degrees intelligence-gathering, confidential informants, undercover operatives, clandestine surveillance, crime scene reconstruction, and the collection of physical evidence. The Rangers followed this still-rudimentary trend, with the earliest example being the lists of fugitives published by the adjutant general's office, sometimes known as the "Book of Knaves" or "Bible II." From the sweep through Kimble County in 1877 to the use of undercover agents in the 1880s and 1890s to the elementary use of dactylography in 1905, the Ranger service accepted and improved upon modern police practices to accomplish its central mission.

The twelve men featured in this volume served from 1874 to 1930, ten in front-line supervisory positions, and two as first sergeants—the senior enlisted man of their companies. They stamped the Texas Rangers with their unique character, and ensured the fame of the service would endure. John B. Jones and L. H. McNelly initiated the traditions of the modern service, albeit using differing methods. Building upon their foundation was John B. Armstrong, James B. Gillett, Jesse Lee Hall, George W. Baylor, Bryan Marsh, and Ira Aten—the men who made the Rangers world renowned. Even though the "Four Great Captains"—James A. Brooks, William J. McDonald, John R. Hughes, and John H. Rogers— received their commissions in the 1880s and 1890s, they embodied the service's flexibility and provided critical leadership in a transformative time.

Although thirty-one men have been inducted into the Texas Ranger Hall of Fame, I continue to maintain some have since been neglected by history. They have been overlooked in favor of others, although they may, from time to time, be briefly mentioned in a book. The lives of Texas Rangers in the middle of the nineteenth century, which was covered in Volume 1, were fitting examples of my assertion. Rangers who served in the era of the Wild West have been researched and chronicled in great detail, but, nevertheless, some of these men have been overlooked. The lives of Jones, McNelly, Armstrong, Aten, Brooks, McDonald, Hughes, and Rogers have been examined by five award-winning authors in the past few years, with nearly all these books being published by the University of North Texas Press. However, no biography is ever complete and new information or interpretation is always possible. More to the point, Gillett wrote his autobiography in 1921, but a more recent work has not been produced to examine his life anew. Similarily, Lee Hall's story, last covered in 1940, is in severe need of a modern analysis, and neither George Baylor nor Bryan Marsh have been the subjects of full-length profiles. When Volume 3 reviews the twentieth-century Rangers, one will again notice an absence of books on worthy men, including, but not limited to, Tom Hickman, Jim Riddles, and Stanley Guffey. Having noted the absence of up-to-date biographies on a significant number of these men, I have decided to help fill the void. This series of three books, the second of which you hold in your hands, seeks to introduce men unfamiliar to all but the more knowledgeable students of Ranger history, while honoring those who are already known.

To that end, the ability to turn words into sentences is a small skill dependent entirely on the author. Transforming those sentences into a full-length non-fiction book requires, not only the writer, but also a legion of generous people who lent their time and expertise to the endeavor. I recognize the contributions of those people here, and thank them profusely.

Christina Stopka, Christina Smith Claridy, Amanda Crowley, and Shelly Crittendon, Texas Ranger Hall of Fame and Museum, Waco, Texas; Sergeant Joe B. Davis, Texas Rangers (Ret.), James M. McCrae, and Jean Eckstein, Former Texas Rangers Foundation and Association, Fredericksburg, Texas; Sharon Yglecias, Texas Ranger Foundation Association, Waco, Texas; Sergio Velasco and Halley Grogan, Texas State Library & Archives Commission, Austin, Texas; David S. Turk, Historian, U.S. Marshals Service, Washington, D.C.; Anita Tufts, Historical Research Center, Texas Heritage Museum, Hill College, Hillsboro, Texas; the reference staffs at the Manhattan Public Library, Manhattan, Kansas, Kansas State University Libraries, and Midwest Genealogy Center, Independence, Missouri; Jacquelyn Slater Reese, Western History Collection, University of Oklahoma Libraries; Joy Pitts, East Texas Research Center, Stephen F. Austin State University; Geoff Hunt, The Texas Collection, Baylor University; Dr. John R. Lundberg, Tarrant County College;

Preface and Acknowledgments   **xi**

Nancy Sherbert, Kansas State Historical Society, Topeka, Kansas; J. P. "Pat" McDaniel and Cathy Smith, Haley Memorial Library and History Center, Midland, Texas; Lisa Struthers, San Jacinto Museum of History, La Porte, Texas; Catherine Wusterhausen, Texas Legislative Reference Library, Austin; Sam Kidd and Tiffany Wright, Smith County Historical Society, Tyler, Texas; Janell Appleby, Mason County Historical Commission, Mason, Texas; Maurine Liles and Royal W. Munro, Wilson County Historical Society, Floresville, Texas; Leta Dennis, Castro County Historical Museum, Dimmitt, Texas; Dawn L. Resanovich, Lebanon County Register of Wills and Clerk of Orphans' Court, Lebanon, Pennsylvania; Mike Miller, Grace Mcevoy, and Rusty Heckaman, Austin History Center, Austin, Texas; Dana Stubbs and Ines Waggoner, Genealogy Department, Corsicana Public Library, Corsicana, Texas; Linda Merryman, West Waco Library & Genealogy Center, Waco; Stephanie Arage Bennett, Dallas Public Library, Dallas, Texas; Danny Gonzalez, El Paso Public Library, El Paso, Texas; Mandy Roane, Marfa Public Library, Marfa, Texas; Coi E. Drummond-Gehrig, Denver Public Library, Denver, Colorado; Rogers R. Bardé, John Fox, Jr., Genealogical Library, Paris, Kentucky; Dewey Snider, Lexington Public Library, Lexington, North Carolina; Arthur Erickson, Greensboro Public Library, Greensboro, North Carolina; Professors Morgan J. Morgan and Charles W. Sanders, Jr., Kansas State University; Bob Alexander, Maypearl, Texas; Donaly Brice, Lockhart, Texas; Sarita Armstrong Hixon, Armstrong, Texas; Charles Temple, Tyler, Texas; Ross J. Cox, Sr., San Saba, Texas; Will Teague, University of Arkansas at Fayetteville; Robert Morehouse, Superior, Wisconsin; Bill Holland, Dimmitt, Texas; Larry J. Walker, The Magazine House, Bend, Oregon; Professor Charles David Grear, Central Texas College; Dina Thomas, Carthage, Missouri; Cheraux Hampton, Sonoita, Arizona; Bob Brown, Big Horn Galleries, Cody, Wyoming; and Joe Grandee and Christy Davis, Pantego, Texas.

    Once more, I thank the excellent team at the University of North Texas Press in Denton: Ronald Chrisman, Elizabeth "Bess" Whitby, Karen DeVinney, and April Eubanks. Their commitment to producing quality literature is only exceeded by their willingness to shepherd a "young" writer through the process.

Special thanks to Chuck Parsons, Luling, Texas, and Dr. Paul Spellman, Wharton County Junior College, for reviewing the manuscript and for their valuable recommendations. My profound gratitude goes to Byron Johnson for his continued generosity and support, and for loaning me the expression that became this book's title.

My wife, Dusti, has been an inspiring constant in my life for the past thirty years, and she was no different regarding this book. She proofread every chapter, corrected the numerous grammatical mistakes, offered insightful suggestions, and generally made the final version better. My graditude to her, and my love, is limitless.

Introduction

The Homer Garrison Texas Ranger Museum, located at historic Fort Fisher on the banks of the Brazos River, officially opened to the public on October 25, 1968. The fulfillment of a desire to honor Texas Rangers, past and present, took years, and its guiding force was Senior Captain, and later U.S. Marshal, Clint Peoples. While the project was his brainchild, Peoples had the assistance of the Fort Fisher Committee, the Fort Fisher Ranger Museum Committee, the Texas Ranger Commemorative Commission, the Texas Ranger Commemorative Foundation, and scores of other dedicated and civic-minded individuals. As part of the agreements the project required, the museum's management was turned over to the City of Waco. At the same time, the facility was certified by the Texas Department of Public Safety as the Official Museum of the Texas Rangers. Presently, the museum showcases exhibits related to the Rangers and pioneer history of Texas, and has grown to include, but is not limited to, firearms, badges, clothing, saddles, equipment, and an extensive art collection. Starting in 1978 and continuing through the 1980s, several additions were built to expand the museum space.

The Texas Ranger Commemorative Commission, established by the legislature in June 1971, was appointed to oversee the celebration of the famed service's sesquicentennial anniversary in 1973. A subsidiary organization, the Texas Ranger Commemorative Foundation, chaired by Captain Peoples, became responsible for building and financing a Texas Ranger Hall of Fame. During a banquet that followed the groundbreaking ceremony at Fort Fisher on August 4, 1973, a film, entitled *The Texas Rangers: A Certain Kind of Man*, was shown to the audience. The program portrayed several historical events involving the Texas Ranger service, including the deaths of outlaws Sam Bass and Bonnie and Clyde. Country western singer Johnny Rodriguez, a good friend of the late Ranger Joaquin Jackson, sang "They Took It Up," which had been composed specifically for the occasion by Tom T. Hall and Allan Pace. In addition, the future facility was named the

Official Hall of Fame of the Texas Rangers by the Texas Ranger Commemorative Commission. After months of construction that cost the taxpayers not one cent, the Hall of Fame was dedicated at high noon on February 7, 1976. An integral component of the Hall of Fame and Museum, the Moody Texas Ranger Memorial Library was established to house an ever-growing collection of service records, case files, correspondence, photographs, microfilm, periodicals, and books.

Twenty Texas Rangers were initially inducted, including Jones, McNelly, Armstrong, Gillett, Hall, Baylor, Aten, Brooks, McDonald, Hughes, and Rogers. Marsh was installed on May 23, 1979. The inclusion of some men has later stirred debate, but as Byron Johnson commented to me in an email, "The serving Rangers who make induction decisions for the Texas Ranger Hall of Fame have a unique perspective on the service—*at their point in the continuum* ... We have urged them to consider candidates based on criteria: who made major contributions to the development of the service, displayed exceptional valor—outside that normally expected of their contemporaries, or gave their lives in the line of duty under extraordinary circumstances. We think these adapt well to changing times, mores and mindsets."

On May 29, 1997, the Seventy-fifth Legislature passed House Concurrent Resolution No. 55, which designated the Texas Ranger Hall of Fame and Museum as the official state repository, library, and archives for the service. As well, the Moody Library was renamed the Texas Ranger Research Center. Governor George W. Bush, later to become the nation's forty-third president, signed the measure into law. With the archival collection growing too immense for the available space by the mid-2000s, the family of the late Tobin and Anne Armstrong, descendants of Texas Ranger John B. Armstrong, headed a fundraising campaign for the renovation and expansion of the Research Center. The facility was dedicated on June 7, 2012, as the Tobin and Anne Armstrong Texas Ranger Research Center.

Timeline of Texas Ranger History (1874–1930)

1874	John B. Jones is appointed major and commanding officer of the Frontier Battalion; L. H. McNelly is named captain of Company A, Washington County Volunteer Militia; Jones and a party of Rangers engage hostile Indians in Lost Valley; McNelly deals with the Sutton-Taylor Feud.
1875	John B. Armstrong enlists in McNelly's company; McNelly is ordered to the border; McNelly and Armstrong engage *bandidos* at Palo Alto Prairie; James B. Gillett enlists in Company D, Frontier Battalion; Jones deals with the Mason County War; McNelly creates international incident at Las Cucharas and Las Cuevas.
1876	McNelly attempts to deal with King Fisher; the Washington County Militia reorganizes as Special State Troops; Lee Hall is appointed second-in-command of McNelly's company; Hall witnesses the end of the Sutton-Taylor Feud.
1877	McNelly discharged from service; Hall named commander of Special State Troops; Jones orders his Rangers to focus on law enforcement; Armstrong arrests John Wesley Hardin and extradites him to Austin; Jones initiates the "Kimble County Clean-up"; Jones negotiates an end to the Horrell-Higgins Feud; Jones meets with failure in the El Paso Salt War.
1878	Jones and Hall involved in catching Sam Bass; Gillett occupied in breaking up the Pegleg Crossing gang.

1879	Jones appointed adjutant-general; George W. Baylor is commissioned into the Frontier Battalion; Baylor and Gillett assigned to El Paso; Baylor and Gillett pursue Victorio.
1880	Bryan Marsh is appointed captain of Company B, Frontier Battalion.
1881	Baylor engages Indians in the Sierra Diablo; Marsh keeps the peace at San Angelo and in railroad camps; Gillett creates an international incident; Jones dies; Gillett leaves the service; Marsh is dismissed from the battalion.
1883	James A. Brooks enlists in Company F, Frontier Battalion; Ira Aten enlists in Company D.
1884	John H. Rogers enlists in Company F.
1884–1888	Baylor, Aten, Brooks, and Rogers deal with fence-cutters.
1885	Aten involved in shootout at San Ambrosia Creek; Brooks and Aten are present at *Las Ysles* parley.
1887	Brooks and Rogers wounded in fight with Conner family; John R. Hughes enlists in Company D.
1888	Brooks appointed captain of Company F.
1889	Aten and Hughes investigate the Williamson family murders; Aten deals with Fort Bend County feud and leaves the service.
1891	William J. McDonald is commissioned captain of Company B.
1891–1892	Brooks and Rogers involved in the Garza War.
1893	Rogers is commissioned captain of Company E; Hughes is appointed captain of Company D; McDonald is involved in gun battle with Sheriff John P. Matthews.
1895–1896	The entire Frontier Battalion deals with the Fitzsimmons-Maher boxing match.
1896–1897	McDonald breaks up the San Saba Mob.
1899–1906	All four companies of the Frontier Battalion deal with the Reese-Townsend Feud.
1899	Rogers enforces the quarantine during the Laredo smallpox epidemic.

Timeline of Texas Ranger History (1874–1930)   **xvii**

1901	Rogers apprehends Gregorio Cortéz; the Frontier Battalion is reorganized into the Ranger Force.
1906	Brooks resigns from the service; McDonald investigates a "riot" in Brownsville; Rogers writes his "Rules and Regulations."
1907	McDonald resigns from the Ranger Force.
1911	Rogers resigns from the service.
1911–1914	Hughes deals with cases originating in the Mexican Revolution.
1915	Hughes dismissed from the service.
1919	Rogers testifies in front of the Ranger investigation committee.
1927	Rogers returns to the Ranger Force as captain of Company C.
1930	Rogers dies while serving as a Ranger

John B. Jones. #1/102–333. *Courtesy Texas State Library and Archives Commission, Austin, Texas.*

Chapter 1

John B. Jones: "Transformed His Indian Fighters into Lawmen"

John B. Jones is the "father" of the modern Texas Ranger service. While Stephen F. Austin laid the foundations of the Ranger tradition, Jones transformed his Indian fighters into lawmen. To accomplish this task, he mastered the administrative, logistical, financial, and political details inherent in forming any new military organization. He instituted an enduring system of personal discipline, organizational accountability, and admirable performance. Not merely a bureaucrat, the major commanded his Rangers both from his first-floor office in the state capitol and in the field, personally inspecting the line of companies several times each year. Writing on the Frontier Battalion, Dr. Harold J. Weiss, Jr. observed that Jones "presided over its transformation into a state law-enforcement agency. More than any other man, the rangers owed their march toward institutional continuity to him." The force he created has survived through multiple reorganizations and name changes, and continues to serve the citizens of Texas today.

He was born on December 22, 1834, in Winnsboro, Fairfield District, South Carolina. Henry Jones, his father, had been born in the same area on August 22, 1807. His mother, Nancy Elizabeth (Robertson) Jones, the daughter of a prominent planter and officer in the War of 1812, was born on November 16, 1812. They married on September 16, 1832. In addition to John, their children included Polly R. Jones, born on August 30, 1833; Caroline Robertson "Carrie" Jones, born on February 1, 1837; Francis E. "Fannie" Jones, born on April 17, 1839; Ann P. Jones, born on December 5, 1840; Benoni Robertson Jones, born on December 10, 1842; and Mickle C. Jones, born on December 20, 1844.[1]

The family moved to the Republic of Texas in 1838, settling on 1,143 acres near Gilleland Creek in Travis County. Henry Jones became a prominent figure in the early days of the Republic. He served under Colonel Edward Burleson at the actions of Brushy Creek and Plum Creek, and commanded a militia regiment before and during the Vásquez Invasion. He was military commander of Austin in 1842, and, in the affair known as the "Archives War," prevented the removal of the official documents from that city. The Joneses moved to Matagorda County that same year, settling on 1,120 acres near Caney Creek to farm sugar, cotton, and tobacco. For over a decade, thirteen to twenty-eight slaves were forced to work the land. Starting at age twelve, Jones, affectionately known to his sisters as "Bud," attended school in Matagorda, and at Old Baylor Baptist academy in Independence, Washington County; Rutersville College near La Grange in Fayette County; and Mount Zion Collegiate Institute in Winnsboro.[2]

Founded on January 9, 1777, the Mount Zion Society was granted a charter to operate its public school as a college in 1785, but never functioned above the preparatory level. With its strict rules and discipline, the academy was quite different from the rough and tumble environment that had characterized John's earlier school life. James Wilson Hudson was the revered president of the institution, which offered the sons of prominent Upcountry families the foundations for a classical education. Homesick and miserable, Jones felt little appreciation for Latin, Greek, English, or mathematics, and he wrote his father numerous times begging to be allowed to return home. Colonel Jones finally yielded and gave his son permission to leave the school. Following his father's instructions, John stopped in Macon, Georgia, where his sisters were attending Wesleyan Female Academy. There he learned his sister, Polly, had recently died of typhoid fever. Another tragedy awaited him after he arrived home when Nancy died on February 5, 1848, due to complications in birthing her seventh child. To make matters worse, the baby girl also perished.[3]

By 1856, Colonel Jones had purchased four separate tracts of land in Navarro County situated along Richland and Pin Oak Creeks. Encompassing 4,746 acres, the property became known to the family as "the Rancho." John obtained another five hundred acres on Richland Creek in his own name. After Henry completed his acquisitions, he moved onto his lands with his children and twenty-three slaves. South of the confluence of Richland and Rush Creeks, the colonel built his plantation house atop a hill surrounded by "good land" and numerous trees. John and his father decided to go into business together and divided their responsibilities. The colonel raised cotton, hogs, and cattle, and operated a saw mill.[4] John devoted himself to the raising of the partnership's blooded horse herd. "As a horseman, I have never seen his equal," wrote his niece, Helen Halbert Groce. "His steed and himself seemed to be one—in perfect rhythm and harmony in every movement. He was simply irresistible on horseback."[5] The business arrangement proved profitable as John's ranch increased to eleven hundred acres by 1860. He also owned one lot in Corsicana and one slave. Henry's holdings in the same year totaled 4,774 acres, thirty-two slaves, four hundred horses, and twenty head of cattle. The real estate was valued at $41,820, and his personal estate at $68,266.[6]

Despite his commitment to the ranch, Jones decided to become a Mason, and was initiated into the Dresden Lodge No. 218 on October 3, 1857. Active in lodge affairs for two years, Jones was elected Worshipful-Master for the years 1859 and 1860. He then turned his interest to the Masonic organization at the state level. He attended the meeting of the Masonic Grand Lodge at La Grange in June 1860, where he was elected Grand Lecturer for the central portion of the state. He was also appointed to the committees on petitions, credentials, and charter lodges.[7]

Standing five feet, eight inches in height and weighing 135 pounds, Jones had a slightly protruding forehead over large, dark eyes, and a narrow face boasting a thick, drooping moustache. Mrs. Groce remembered: "I can see him now, the perfection of neatness; dark well-kept suit, white shirt, black bow tie, heavy black moustache and hair, smooth olive skin, piercing, twinkling, sparkling, penetrating black or brown eyes that seemed to see through your soul." A true gentleman in speech and manner, Jones spoke with a soft, measured voice. Furthermore, he abstained from tobacco and liquor and, while a temperate man in his comportment, he loved sponge cake, fresh buttermilk, and strong, black coffee. He was a devoutly religious man who declined to curse and seemed bereft of a sense of humor, although he was never perceived as stodgy.[8]

The Navarro County Agricultural & Mechanical Association, of which Jones served as secretary, sponsored the county's first fair. The event opened on October 16, 1860, and lasted two days. Among the exhibits were showings of livestock, farm implements and products, sewing, and various items of domestic manufacture. While hailed as a success, the fair would be the last one for some years because of the coming war.[9]

As the secession crisis swept through the southern states, Jones and his father actively supported Texas severing her ties to the Union. Indeed, Henry had been a founding member and vice president of the Matagorda chapter of the Southern Rights Association over a decade previously. On February 21, citizens of the county chose overwhelmingly by a vote of 631 to thirty-eight in favor of separation. After the surrender of Fort Sumter, Jones journeyed to Virginia to join the assembling army of the new Confederacy. He supposedly discovered a regiment of Texas cavalry, under Colonel Benjamin Franklin Terry, was organizing in Bowling Green, Kentucky, and he went to join his fellow Texans there. If such a scenario occurred, Jones remained only a short time in Terry's camp, too brief to have been added to the September 26 muster-in roll. Although virtually every account on Jones asserts he was a member of the Eighth Texas Cavalry ("Terry's Texas Rangers"), the rolls in the Compiled Service Records of Confederate Soldiers confirm he was never formally enlisted in that regiment.[10]

Traveling to Galveston, he enlisted as a private in Captain Marcus Delafayette Herring's company, Joseph Warren Speight's Texas infantry battalion on January 4, 1862. Speight's battalion of three companies, of which Herring's became Company B, was organized and mustered into Confederate service as the First Texas Infantry Battalion on February 18. In a letter to Brigadier-General Paul Octave Hébert, dated March 16, Speight noted his men were armed as best as circumstances would allow, but the weapons were of inferior quality. Indeed, some had no arms at all. By April 16, while at Camp Speight near Millican on the Central Railroad, another seven companies had been added to the battalion, which was then reorganized into the Fifteenth Texas Infantry Regiment. Speight was appointed colonel, James Edward Harrison lieutenant-colonel, and John W. Daniel major. That same day, Jones was appointed regimental adjutant with the rank of first lieutenant. His monthly base pay was set at ninety dollars while he received another ten dollars for acting in his staff role. Incidentally, commanding Company K was Captain Richard Coke, a man who would play a significant role in Jones's life twelve years later.[11]

On June 29, Speight's troops began their march from Millican through East Texas and finally arrived at Austin, Arkansas, near Little Rock, where they established Camp Nelson on October 17. Brigadier-General Henry Eustice McCulloch was ordered to organize an infantry division, and the Fifteenth was assigned to the division's Second Brigade under Colonel Horace Randal. The regiment marched to Camp Bayou Meto near Pine Bluff, Arkansas, on November 23.[12]

Lieutenant-General Theophilus Hunter Holmes, newly appointed commander of the Trans-Mississippi Department, planned to defend all of Arkansas. To that end, he posted one corps to take a position near the Boston Mountains to deter any possible invasion from Missouri. He also dispatched one brigade of Texans and one of Arkansawyers to the unfinished stronghold of Arkansas Post to defend the Arkansas River line. The balance, including McCulloch's division, was kept in reserve at Little Rock. The immediate danger appeared to be a large Union army assembling at Helena. Holmes sent McCulloch's division to DeVall's Bluff on the White River to dissuade any contemplated offensive. Heavy, freezing rains ensured any engagement with the enemy would be impossible. When the Federal advance failed to appear, the division was recalled to Little Rock.[13]

On December 15, McCulloch's men were ordered west to reinforce Major-General Thomas Carmichael Hindman's troops retiring from Prairie Grove. After marching about four miles, the Texans were instead directed to a new camp near Little Rock. The next day, the Fifteenth was detached and instructed to report to Brigadier-General William Steele, who had assumed command of the Indian Territory at Fort Smith.[14]

Before undertaking the journey, Speight was assigned to command a brigade, on January 7, 1863, made up of his own regiment, as well as the Twenty-second, Thirty-first, and Thirty-fourth Texas Cavalry Regiments

(Dismounted) and Captain Henry Clay West's Arkansas battery. Jones was placed on detached service from the regiment to be acting assistant adjutant-general of Speight's brigade on January 10. His appointment would be confirmed on April 2, to take rank from April 18. After a grueling march through eight to twelve inches of snow, the brigade arrived at Fort Smith and established its camp on January 15. The ranks were thinned by desertions, illness, and losses from enemy actions. From there, the Confederates went into winter quarters at Camp Kiamichi near Doaksville in the Choctaw Nation.[15]

In April, Jones and his fellow soldiers were redirected to hinder the forward movement of Union troops from New Orleans. The brigade marched to Shreveport, Louisiana, arriving on May 14. Appalled at their condition and lack of discipline, Lieutenant-General Edmund Kirby Smith sent the Twenty-second and Thirty-fourth Texas dismounted regiments to a camp of instruction to receive further infantry training. The Fifteenth and the Thirty-first were ordered to Grand Ecore two days later to reinforce Major-General Richard Taylor. After garrisoning Simmesport for two weeks, the two regiments were paired with Brigadier-General Jean Jacques Alfred Alexandre Mouton's brigade. Participating in an offensive in the Bayou Lafourche country, undertaken to reduce pressure on besieged Port Hudson, Mouton swiftly drove the Yankees out of Thibodaux and dashed to seize Raceland, Des Allemands, and Boutte Station. Despite the campaign's limited success, Port Hudson ultimately surrendered on July 9. The brigade went into camp at Vermilionville and Speight returned to Texas on sick leave. In his absence, Lieutenant-Colonel Harrison of the Fifteenth Texas assumed temporary command of the brigade.[16]

On September 28, the Rebels received orders to prepare for a two-day march across the Atchafalaya to commence at four p.m. The battle plan envisioned an encirclement of the Federal position at Mary Catherine Stirling's Botany Bay Plantation on Bayou Fordoche. Brigadier-General Thomas Green's dismounted cavalry troopers were to attack the enemy front, Mouton's and Speight's brigades were to cut off any Yankee withdrawal along the Morganza road, the Third Cavalry Regiment, Arizona Brigade was to do the same at Baton Rouge, and James Patrick Major's brigade was left in reserve at the river crossing to secure the Confederate line of retreat.[17]

Richard Taylor. Wet collodion glass plate negative. Civil War Photograph Collection. *Courtesy Library of Congress, Washington, D.C.*

The following day, Speight's six hundred men assaulted the rear of the enemy position at Stirling's Plantation. They advanced through high sugar cane under heavy fire and took cover in a ditch in front of the Federal line. Meanwhile, Major Hannibal Honestus Boone's two hundred mounted troopers dispersed the Yankee cavalry, then supported the infantry by attacking the enemy in the front. The entire Texan line discharged their rifles, and Lieutenant-Colonel Harrison ordered a charge. The Rebels rushed four hundred yards across a field, shouting wild Texas yells. While the Yankees were pushed out of the sugar house and the slaves' quarters, the Texans could not dislodge them from their breastworks by frontal assault. Harrison ordered Jones to take fifty men and make a demonstration on the enemy's left flank. Jones's detachment clambered over the levee and opened fire on the bluecoats who were retreating down the works and into the woods. Enemy reinforcements appeared over the levee and the Texans again climbed to the other side to escape the Yankees' fire. The two sides fought at close quarters for an hour before the Union troops were driven from their positions; 462 were forced to surrender. The Rebels lost twenty-six killed, eighty-five wounded, and ten missing, of which the Fifteenth Texas lost fifteen killed, fifty-two wounded, and one missing.[18]

General Green, commanding the Confederate forces on the Atchafalaya, wrote a report on the engagement and commended, by name, the brigade's senior officers, as well as its adjutant:

> The heavy loss maintained by Speight's brigade shows the desperate nature of the conflict, and it is not out of place to mention here even where all distinguished themselves, the gallant bearing and activity of Lieutenant John B. Jones, Assistant Adjutant-General of Speight's Brigade.[19]

Jones received further praise for his actions at Stirling's Plantation. Lieutenant-Colonel Harrison wrote to Colonel Samuel Smith Anderson, Kirby Smith's adjutant general:

> I wish to call the attention of Lt. Gen'l Smith through you to Lt. Jno. B. Jones, adjutant of the Regt. Lt. Jones has been Adjutant of this

Regt. from its organization until Speight's Brigade was organized about ten (10) months since. He has since that time acted as Brigade Adjutant, and aid [sic] to Col. Speight. Lt. Jones is a young man of high moral and intellectual worth. A good disciplinarian and drill officer. I know of no young man of superior merit. In our recent engagement on the Farouche, being in command of the Brigade, he was most efficient rendering me invaluable services, and bore himself with daring gallantry throughout, worthy of all praise and after the enemy had fled, he mounted Maj. Boone's horse (who had been severely wounded) and led a cavalry charge upon the routed enemy capturing two field officers and from one hundred & fifty (150) to two hundred (200) others. There was no other officer present and the surrender was made to Lt. Jones. He had with him in this charge not exceeding twenty privates of Maj. Boone's command, whom I induced to follow him. Knowing his merit, I respectfully recommend and ask his promotion to the rank of captain.[20]

Green endorsed Harrison's recommendation: "Lt. Jones is one of the most gallant young officers in our army and is well worthy of the promotion asked for." General Mouton also concurred with the application. Although no formal approval of his promotion can be found in the official records, his advancement to captain did, nevertheless, occur shortly thereafter.[21]

On October 18, 1863, Speight's two regiments were folded into the Second Texas Brigade commanded by Brigadier-General Camille Armand Jules Marie, Prince de Polignac. Even though he had just returned on the thirteenth, Speight, incensed at losing his brigade, cited poor health and returned to Texas; Harrison took his place as regimental commander. The Southerners were suspicious of Polignac and unable to pronounce the dapper Frenchman's surname. Taylor informed the men if they were still unhappy after Polignac had led them in battle, he would be relieved. Mollified, the rank and file took to mockingly calling their new brigadier "Polecat." In response, Polignac earnestly strove to win his troops' trust. Constituting the new brigade was the Fifteenth Texas Infantry, Seventeenth Texas Consolidated Cavalry (Dismounted), Twenty-second Texas Cavalry (Dismounted),

Thirty-first Texas Cavalry (Dismounted), and Thirty-fourth Texas Cavalry (Dismounted).[22]

Meanwhile, Major-General Nathaniel Prentice Banks, commanding the Union Army of the Gulf, was planning another invasion, this time up the west bank of Bayou Teche to Vermilionville and Alexandria, then overland to Texas. Major-General William Buel Franklin was selected to lead the operation, with two divisions each from the XIII and XIX Corps, and with a cavalry division, totaling some 19,500 men in all. Franklin left Bisland on October 3, and reached Opelousas and Washington by the twenty-fourth. Rather than moving toward Texas, though, he became concerned with the lack of direction from his superior, the difficulty in navigating roads after recent stormy weather, the shortage of transportation on Bayou Teche, and his insecure supply line. In the end, Franklin abandoned the expedition on November 1, and began countermarching south.[23]

Taylor followed and, on November 3, Harrison's regiment was detached to join with the Eighteenth Texas, commanded by Colonel Wilburn Hill King, and the Eleventh Texas, under Colonel Oran Milo Roberts, at Opelousas. Their mission was to make an assault in conjunction with General Green's cavalry on the Federal rearguard at Bayou Bourbeau. The infantry element was placed on the left flank under the overall command of Roberts, with the Eleventh on the extreme left, the Eighteenth in the middle, and the more experienced Fifteenth to the right. Charging under enemy artillery fire and taking heavy casualties, the Fifteenth Texas drove the Union troops from their positions. Captain Richard Coke fell near the Opelousas Road with a chest wound. Jones cautioned Harrison of flanking Federal cavalry preparing to strike the Confederate rear, and the colonel swiftly mounted a counterattack. However, Union reinforcements arrived on the field and pushed the Texans back. Franklin continued the withdrawal, frequently skirmishing with Confederates, and reached New Iberia on November 17. Three days later, the Fifteenth Texas received orders to rejoin Polignac's brigade.[24]

Following a cold and monotonous winter spent in camps around Monroe, the brigade readied itself to raid lightly defended Vidalia, situated across the Mississippi from Natchez, on February 6, 1864. Assaulting the town the next day, the 550 Texans were ultimately repulsed by Union reinforcements from

Natchez and four Yankee gunboats. Polignac led his troops from the front, shouting, "Follow me! Follow me! You call me 'Polecat,' I will show you whether I am 'Polecat' or Polignac!'" Professor Ella Lonn, writing of foreign soldiers in the Confederacy, observed: "Polignac, by his judgement and coolness under fire, gained the confidence and respect of his men, as he soon gained their affection by his care and attention." His battle prowess proven, and his foragers having acquired four hundred head of cattle, horses, and mules, the French general disengaged and led his men back to the Confederate lines at Harrisburg.[25]

After patrolling the Red, Atchafalaya, and Mississippi Rivers, Jones and Harrison took a leave of absence to visit Navarro County. While they were away, Polignac's brigade was ordered to Carroll Jones's plantation on Bayou Boeuf as part of the effort to block Banks's forthcoming advance. The French general's men arrived on March 19 and were assigned to an infantry division commanded by General Mouton. Taylor had been informed of Banks's arrival in Alexandria, and was urgently assembling troops to meet the enemy. According to a letter written by his sister Fannie, Jones and Harrison left for the front on April 4. While they were en route, the brigade fought Federal troops at Mansfield and Pleasant Hill. Mouton was killed in the former action, and Polignac replaced him as division commander. Speight had returned from sick leave and rejoined the command on February 18. Issued a surgeon's certificate of disability, he resigned on April 15, and Harrison officially succeeded him as colonel. In addition, Harrison was named to temporarily take over the brigade until he was succeeded by Colonel Robert Dillard Stone of the Twenty-second Texas.[26]

The Confederates engaged the retreating Yankees in almost continuous fighting throughout the rest of April and into the following month. They met again on the morning of May 16 at Mansura, thirty miles south of Alexandria. Polignac, Colonel Xavier Blanchard Debray, and thirteen field pieces held the left flank, while Colonel Arthur Pendleton Bagby and Brigadier-General James Major were on the right with nineteen guns. The Federals deployed forty-two cannons and the battle opened at six a.m. with a lively, four-hour exchange of artillery fire. Meanwhile, the enemy infantry marched through the scorching heat several times in an attempt to strike the Rebel center, and to turn Taylor's right.

Each effort was repulsed. Once the small arms fire began, Polignac advanced to charge the Yankees, but Major-General John Austin Wharton stopped the movement and signaled his intention to crush the enemy the next day at Samuel James Norwood's plantation near Yellow Bayou and Bayou De Glaize. By ten o'clock, outnumbered and in danger of being flanked on the left, the Confederates withdrew toward Evergreen. Despite Wharton's plans, the opposing sides met two days later on Norwood's property, but, this time, the Confederates achieved victory. Polignac's battered division was forced back by superior numbers but reformed, counterattacked, and held the field by the end of the battle. Colonel Stone was killed, and Harrison resumed temporary command of the brigade, which had lost thirty-two killed, eighty-seven wounded, and eighty-eight missing in action.[27]

The rumor circulating through the camps of Polignac's division was that they would be transferred across the Mississippi to fight there. The soldiers found the idea of marching away from the defense of Texas to be unacceptable, and troop morale worsened. Possibly to counter declining spirits, the division was instead ordered north on August 30 to join Major-General John Bankhead "Prince John" Magruder's forces in Arkansas. They established camps at Monticello, Walnut Hill, Poplar Bluff, Camden, and Camp Bragg near Washington in September and October. Amid these moves, Wilburn King was named to take permanent command of the Texas brigade. Polignac's division was beset with rampant desertion, illness, and supply problems. The following month, the men erected a new camp near Minden, Louisiana, where the morale crises continued to the point where Polignac ordered the execution of three deserters by firing squad. In January 1865, the Texans marched to new winter quarters at Grand Ecore on the Red River, where the troops were kept busy building fortifications. Making a gradual withdrawal back toward home, most of the Texas troops that had fought in Louisiana, including King's men, were bivouacked at Camp Groce, east of Hempstead in Waller County, by the end of March.[28]

On February 16, King's veteran regiments were ordered to reorganize and form cadres for two new infantry brigades. King was to oversee one and newly promoted Brigadier-General James Harrison the other. After some delay, the Fifteenth and Twentieth Texas Infantry Regiments, the Seventeenth

Texas Dismounted Cavalry, and Peter Hardeman's dismounted First Arizona Cavalry were assigned to Harrison's First Brigade the following month; Jones continued as adjutant. On April 17, the brigade moved to Camp Rogers, four miles from Houston, and Major-General Samuel Bell Maxey assumed command of the division on the twenty-fifth. On May 14, Harrison's brigade was ordered to Richmond, Texas, which would prove to be their last duty station.[29]

Jones had been recommended the previous year by Harrison, Green, and Polignac for promotion to the rank of major in the Fifteenth Texas. The appointment was supposed to have been approved, but Jones did not receive his new commission in time "owing to irregularities in the mails." On May 24, he completed his last official act as brigade adjutant when he issued General Order No. 13, which directed the regimental commanders to march their men as near to home as possible and discharge them from the Confederate service.[30]

Once the Trans-Mississippi Department had surrendered to the Federal army, Jones returned home to his ranch. He was thirty-one years old, but his health had been ravaged by the rigors of campaigning. After almost a year spent recuperating, he was approached with a remarkable task. Friends in Navarro County asked him to travel to Mexico and discover a suitable place for a colony of expatriates. Conditions in Reconstruction-era Texas, including ruined farms and ranches, a wrecked economy, political persecution, and freedmen exercising their newly won rights and entering the workforce, had convinced these people to try building new lives in foreign lands. Indeed, some three million would leave the vanquished Confederate states and emigrate west of the Missouri River, to Northern cities, to Canada, to Egypt, and to Latin America. An estimated eight to ten thousand Southerners trekked to countries south of the Rio Grande, and possibly half that number went to Mexico. Jones agreed to make the trip, but after touring the country for "nearly a year" he reported his failure in finding a suitable location. The Texan's assessment would prove farsighted. Ultimately, Confederate colonies in Mexico would fail after the collapse of Emperor Maximilian I's empire, but their demise was also hastened by the emigration of too few farmers and builders, by the influx of ne'er-do-wells and paupers, by the lack of capital, by a fixation on the leaders' lost status, and by an inability to adjust to the Latin culture.[31]

Undeterred, Jones's friends and other parties in Louisiana requested he next find a site for a colony of three hundred families in Brazil. His father emphatically approved of the idea, seeing the financial opportunities in raising horses there, and convinced Jones to agree. In 1867, Jones departed Texas for Brazil where he was heartily received as the agent of potential colonists. Through books, such as those written by oceanographer and explorer Matthew Fontaine Maury, the country was attracting Southerners due to an abundance of available land for sugarcane and cotton farming, cheap labor, religious and political acceptance, and government subsidies personally authorized by Emperor Dom Pedro II. Along with emissaries from other colonization societies, Jones was the honored guest of government engineers, interpreters, and guides as they conducted him on an eighteen-month tour of the country. He made a detailed study of the climate, economy, and agricultural resources and facilities, and weighed the pros and cons of immigration. In the end, though, he reported back to his principals that, in his opinion, Brazil would not be "congenial" for American expatriates. Unlike his appraisal in Mexico, Jones would be proven incorrect regarding Brazil. While the true number is unknown, many Southerners successfully settled in rural towns such as Santa Barbara (later called Villa Americana), Paraná, or Santarém, or in the cities of São Paulo and Rio de Janeiro. Presently, the descendants of these *Confederados* still living in Brazil are scattered throughout the country.[32]

The decision to remain in Texas was followed by Jones immersing himself once more in the business of stock farming. Before John left to explore foreign climes, Henry Jones had granted his son power of attorney over his affairs. By 1866, he owned 2,424 acres and John possessed 1,600. In 1869, the colonel acquired 2,500 acres near the village of Cross Roads and raised a similar number of horses. The same year, he deeded to John more than five hundred acres located seven miles west of Dresden. He also gave his son a one-half interest in a herd of six hundred horses. In 1870, Henry's real estate was valued at seven hundred dollars and his personal assets at fourteen hundred. John was assessed with $2,200 in real estate.[33]

Jones likewise pursued his Masonic duties, serving as the Worshipful Master of the Dresden lodge in 1865, 1869, and 1870. He was demitted from the Dresden lodge and affiliated with the Corsicana Lodge No. 174 in 1872. He went on to hold nine committee memberships, three appointive positions, and four elective offices in the Grand Lodge of Texas.[34]

Diversifying his business interests, Jones, his future brother-in-law Arthur Farris Robbins, and several other partners founded a private bank in 1870. In May 1871, he was chosen as director of the county's Agricultural and Mechanical Association. Serving as a delegate from Navarro County the following month, he attended the state Democratic Party convention in Houston for the purpose of nominating a candidate for the Third Congressional District. In April 1872, he acquired a town lot in Corsicana and established the banking and mercantile firm of John B. Jones & Company in partnership with Robbins. The energetic business climate in town the following year proved a boon to the new business. However, by May 1876, while Jones was commanding the Frontier Battalion, liabilities had mounted and the banking house failed, leaving depositors to experience personal losses.[35]

Following the end of the Civil War, four thousand Federal troops had been deployed to Texas, but the majority were stationed in the interior counties. Major-General Philip Henry Sheridan, commander of the Fifth Military District, instructed them to protect freedmen and white Republicans from unreconstructed Confederates, organized terrorist groups, and outlaw gangs. For more than a year, depredations raged unchecked in the frontier counties until infantry and cavalry companies began advancing westward. The reasons for the delay were the belief that reports from the borderlands were exaggerated and that the Texas state government, under Governor James Webb Throckmorton, was conspiring to remove U.S. soldiers from the interior. Consequently, calls for mounted state troops raised along the frontier were refused. In November 1866, elements of the Fourth and Sixth Cavalry Regiments were ordered to proceed to posts in the northern and western counties.[36]

On January 26, 1874, in his first address to the Fourteenth Legislature, newly inaugurated Governor Richard Coke spoke to the issue of the frontier:

> Every citizen of Texas is entitled to demand of the State government protection of life, liberty, and property, in return for his homage to the government ... Every consideration of humanity, justice and interest,

demands protection for the people of the frontier ... The tomahawk and the scalping knife must be stayed in their bloody work, and the lives and property of our people made secure.[37]

On April 10, the legislature enacted an amended House Bill No. 128 introduced by Representative Robert Bean of Grayson County. Section 19 of "An Act to Provide for the Protection of the Frontier of the State of Texas against the Invasion of Hostile Indians, Mexicans, or other marauding or Thieving Parties" authorized the governor to create a "battalion of mounted men" comprised of six companies of seventy-five men each. Despite its generic official designation, the contingent was being called the "Frontier Battalion" in correspondence as early as June. Although the new force was intended primarily to combat the rising tide of Indian raids, Section 28 stated: "Each officer of the battalion ... herein provided for, shall have all the powers of a peace officer, and it shall be his duty to execute all criminal processes directed to him, and make arrests under *capias* properly issued, of any and all parties charged with offense against the laws of this State." Like Ranger groups of the past, the battalion was envisioned as a temporary formation, to be disbanded or reorganized as the governor deemed fit, but the executive was also directed to keep the men in the field as long as necessary. The consequence was that, for the first time in the state's history, Texas possessed a permanent Ranger force.[38]

The battalion commander received a monthly wage of $125; captains, $100; lieutenants, $75; sergeants, $50; corporals and privates, $40. Pay was to be issued quarterly. The men enlisted for a term not to exceed four years, but could readily obtain early discharges if they so desired. According to long-standing tradition, the Rangers provided their own horses, personal equipment and sidearms, while the state provided ammunition, camp gear, rations and forage, and a breech-loading carbine (although the cost of the latter was deducted from the first month's pay). The battalion's operating budget for the first year was set at $300,000, but $23,776 would be used for the support of minute companies on the Mexican border.[39]

The Rangers fell under the auspices of the state adjutant general, who in turn answered to the governor. Former Confederate general William Steele was the first adjutant general to oversee the new Frontier Battalion, and he offered steady support to the men in the field.[40] On May 2, General Steele chose Jones, the governor's old comrade in the war, to command the battalion with the rank of major. The choice was controversial, to say the least. Many felt the command should go to a proven frontiersman, but Jones's admirers quickly took pen in hand to urge support for his appointment. Colonel Clinton McKamy Winkler, a fellow Mason at the Corsicana lodge, wrote the editor of the *Houston Telegraph* to inform him of Jones's qualifications. He began by recalling Colonel Henry Jones as an "old time Indian fighter" from whom his son would have learned of "the character and habits of the Indians." He went to summarize Jones's record in the late war and his "cool bravery under fire, and soldierly bearing," as well as his friendship with Coke stretching back to their days in the army. He concluded with his belief that soon "Maj. Jones will command and enjoy the confidence and respect of the best and bravest of [the Indian fighters]; and that the people of the frontier will learn to sleep soundly whilst he keeps watch, and directs the operations of the battalion."[41] Even while his appointment was debated in the press, Jones appeared before a notary on May 19 to sign his oath of office, swearing he would bear "true allegiance to the State of Texas, and ... serve her honestly and faithfully against all her enemies or oppose whatsoever."[42]

William Jeff Maltby had been among those recommended for the battalion command, and he particularly resented losing out to Jones, a man he believed received the job only because the governor "was his personal friend and that [Coke] had seen his bravery tested many a time on the battle field in the Confederate war." Years later, after having served under Jones as commander of Company E, the captain generously amended his opinion: "He was a man endowed with excellent judgment, his bravery was unquestioned, and he soon proved himself in every way qualified to fill the responsible position to which Governor Coke had appointed him."[43]

Distributed on May 6, General Order No. 2 detailed the battalion's order of battle, formally assigned officers to their companies with instructions to begin organizing their commands, and specified that periods of service were to be twelve months. Steele further stated: "As it is expected that this force will be kept actively employed during their term of service only

William Steele. From Clement A. Evans's *Confederate Military History*.

sound young men without families and with good horses will be received. Persons under indictment or of known bad character or habitual drunkards will be rejected." In addition to Maltby, the other original captains of the battalion were John R. Waller, Company A; George Washington Stevens, Company B; Elisha Floyd Ikard, Company C; Rufus Cicero "Rufe" Perry, Company D; and Cornelius Vernon "Neal" Coldwell, Company F. The first battalion quartermaster and paymaster was Abner Pickens Blocker, Sr. He resigned shortly afterward and was replaced by Martin McHenry Kenney. Doctor E. G. Nicholson was named the battalion surgeon and served intermittently until April 10, 1878.[44]

Jones's talent for quick action allowed the six Ranger companies authorized in the legislation—some 450 men—to take the field by July 10. As he positioned the battalion in the most exposed frontier counties, the major detailed six men from each company to serve as his personal escort under the command of Lieutenant J. Thomas "Tom" Wilson. Achieving twenty-five miles per day, Jones would regularly tour the line of companies in an army ambulance (a type of light wagon) with his horse trailing behind. Two Rangers rode as an advance guard a half-mile ahead, while two more would serve as flankers on either side. The balance of the detachment followed the major's wagon in a file of two abreast with the supply wagons bringing up the rear.[45]

On July 12, 1874, Jones, at the head of twenty-five Rangers from his escort and ten from Company B, cut the fresh trail of fifty Kiowa raiders heading down Salt Creek near Fort Belknap. They followed the scattered sign fifteen miles into Lost Valley in present Jack County. Novices in Indian fighting, the Rangers rode straight into the ambush prepared by Lone Wolf (Gui-päh-go), the principal chief, and Maman-ti, a war chief and medicine man. Jones coolly ordered a countercharge, then extricated his men from the trap and led them to a shallow, brushy gully at the head of the valley. Private William A. "Billy" Glass was mortally wounded, Rangers Lee Corn and George Moore were injured, and thirteen horses were lost in cutting through the Kiowa circle. From their position, the Texans faced warriors to their front, their right flank, and their left. The Rangers and the Indians then engaged in long-range rifle fire until dusk. While the besieged Texans lay prone under the hot sun, Jones boldly remained on his feet, walking up and down the firing line, issuing orders and offering inspiration to his men. Three hundred yards away, the Indians made the mistake common to inexperienced riflemen firing from a higher elevation, and their bullets passed over the Rangers' heads. The Texans were more accurate in their shooting, carefully making every round count. They would account for between three and fifteen Indians depending on the source of the estimate.[46]

Although assailed by thirst, Jones had refused to allow any of his men to ride the one mile to Cameron Creek. Shortly before four p.m., he reluctantly permitted David W. H. Bailey and Mel Porter to fill the canteens. Bailey was taken in another ambush and tortured to death, but his companion escaped. With only eighty rounds of ammunition remaining, Jones directed the Rangers to hold their fire, and the Indians seemingly moved off in a westerly direction with their dead and wounded. John P. Holmes volunteered to ride for Fort Richardson and bring back reinforcements. No stranger to violent death, but sickened by Bailey's grisly end, the major was unwilling at first, then relented. At five o'clock, the Rangers quietly slipped away to James Carroll Loving's ranch some twelve miles from their previous position. Holmes returned at three a.m. with Ninth Cavalry troopers in tow, but the Indians had left the valley in every direction before concentrating once more twenty miles to the northwest. The combined party of soldiers and Rangers did find the remains of Bailey and buried him. The same day as the fight with the Kiowas, another scouting detachment of the Frontier Battalion found the Indians' reserve camp on the Big Wichita, where they captured forty-three pack mules and horses, a variety of packsaddles and blankets, and other equipage. Although the five-hour skirmish at Lost Valley was a draw, and Jones disregarded basic fieldcraft in approaching the valley, he earned praise for his "cool conduct" and "unmistakable, determined courage" in saving his men from complete massacre.[47]

Believing large bodies of Indians would be raiding into Texas from the Fort Sill reservation, Jones ordered Companies B and C to coordinate their scouting operations. Ikard moved into southwestern Clay County, nearer to Stevens's camp in northwestern Young County.[48] Following the battle of Adobe Walls on June 27, where a party of twenty-eight buffalo hunters and one woman held off superior numbers of Cheyennes and Comanches, the United States Army mobilized an extensive campaign into the *Llano Estacado*. By the following spring, the Comanche and Kiowa menace on the Southern Plains was effectively ended at Palo Duro Canyon. With Indian fighting seemingly at an end, General Steele, on February 4, 1875, ordered the state troops to allow the peaceful movement of tribal parties from Mexico to the reservations in Indian Territory.[49]

By October 1874, Jones had completed three tours of the frontier, and had gently but firmly introduced a sense of discipline and order to the battalion. On the twenty-seventh, he reminded company commanders that the rations and forage provided by the state government were for the sole purpose of feeding the men and the horses, and not for the "camp followers and loafers" who loitered at the camps. The major also prompted the officers and men to remember that "we are in the employment of the Government, being paid for our time and services." He continued, "Company Commanders will require of the men all the service that can be performed with justice to their horses, in scouting up and down the line, or on such larger scouts or expeditions against the Indians as it may be expedient for them to make." Three days earlier, he had written to the adjutant general: "I am happy to report that the Battalion is now in good working order, the officers and men in fine spirits are doing their duty in protecting the frontier of the State from the depredations of the Indians as well as it can be done by so small a number of men."[50]

Hostile warriors were not the only trial the Frontier Battalion faced. In his December report, the major wrote:

> Besides the scouting for Indians, the battalion has rendered much service to the frontier people by breaking up bands of desperadoes who had established themselves in those thirty settled Counties, where they depredate upon the property of good citizens, secure from arrest by the ordinary processes of law, and by turning over to the civil authorities many cattle and horse thieves, and other fugitives from justice in the older Counties.[51]

Unfortunately, the severest handicap came not from Indians or law breakers but instead from the legislature. The appropriation authorized in the act of 1874 for frontier defense was nearly exhausted by December of that same year. To keep the battalion from being completely disbanded, Jones was directed to reduce manpower from 470 to two hundred. Steele issued General Order No. 8 on November 25, which decreased Companies A, B, C, D, and E to one lieutenant, two sergeants, three corporals, and twenty-five privates. Company F was cut to one captain, one lieutenant, three sergeants, three corporals, and thirty-seven privates. Jones considered the staffing shortage so critical that he was reluctant to grant leaves of absence. Although he did allow Lieutenant Wilson a few days for personal business, the major reminded his subordinate that "it is more necessary than ever that every officer and man should remain constantly at his post of duty." Captain Kenney resigned the office of quartermaster, effective February 10, 1875, and Jones assumed his duties and those of commissary for the battalion on March 17. Additionally, Company C was mustered out on March 31. After Company A was disbanded on April 30, the remaining four companies were composed of one lieutenant and thirty men each. Throughout its existence, the battalion often found itself the victim of budget cuts, usually mandated by representatives from the eastern counties. Thus, the Rangers never fielded the full strength authorized by the legislature.[52]

On another tour of inspection, Jones and his escort were at the Company B camp in Lost Valley on May 8, 1875, when they received word of horses being stolen from the Loving ranch. Jones and five of his escorts, Captain Ira Long and ten men from his company, and four Rangers from Company D set out to trail the raiders. They found evidence of the Indians' presence five or six miles south of the ranch and followed further into the valley. Jones and Long spotted seven Indians fleeing on horseback, and the Rangers galloped after them for three or four miles over the rocky hills and through woods. With Long in the lead, the Rangers engaged the hostile Indians and killed five, including one woman who "handled her six-shooter quite as dextrously [sic] as did the bucks." One Ranger was wounded, and one of the battalion's horses was killed and two wounded.[53]

The leading criminal challenges Jones and his Rangers faced in the first years originated in cattle rustling. Following the Civil War, and with the advent of trail-driving stock to the Kansas railheads, ranching spread along the Rio Grande valley, through the Llano, Concho, and Pecos countries, and into the Panhandle. As cattle-raising expanded, so too did thievery. Rustlers either willfully altered brands and sold the cattle to legitimate stockmen or slaughtered the beeves for their hides. However, county lawmen, court officers, and witnesses were often intimidated or bribed by the thieves. Sometimes, the officials were full-fledged members of the rustling gangs. Such weak county authority led the affected ranchers to take the law into their own hands. Writer and researcher Frances Mayhugh Holden observed: "The basic cause of the struggle was the same: where civil authority for law enforcement, not yet well established, could not adequately protect life and property, outlawry flourished and citizens organized to stamp it out." While vigilantism could sometimes be employed in a sincere desire to rid the community of evildoers, just as often the practice was used to further private agendas. In such a climate, the Rangers, while making numerous arrests, were many times unable to secure convictions. Apprehended rustlers could be released by sheriffs unwilling to receive them, by juries for lack of evidence, or by their compatriots. In response, lynch mobs would occasionally remove the accused from their jail cells and, without benefit of due process, string them up from the nearest telegraph pole or tall tree.[54]

The violence and lawlessness born of civil war and reconstruction, and exhibited in family feuds, political rivalries, and range wars, was an endemic problem in Texas. Jones himself contended with one such in Mason County. The county, situated in the upper Llano River country, was excellent range for stock-raising and the vast majority of its inhabitants were ranchers. Only approximately 25 percent were Anglo-Americans whereas the remainder were of German heritage. At first, the two ethnic groups were united by the necessity of opposing Indian raids. However, once the secession crisis swept the state, the Anglos of the county supported leaving the Union and the German majority favored Texas remaining. Indeed, while most of the state voted to secede, Mason County voted seventy-two to two to stay. Following the war, separated by language, religion, and political differences, stock raisers in Mason County and the surrounding Hill Country, regardless of their ethnicity, became careless of the ownership of "stray" cattle as they drove them to market.[55]

In retaliation for suspected Anglo stock thefts, the German faction began the shooting phase of the feud with two murders in mid-February 1875. Following this initial violence, Lieutenant Daniel Webster Roberts, commanding Company D, stopped in Mason on the eighteenth to procure grain for the company's horses. Roberts was getting ready to retire for the night in the hotel when Sheriff John Clark barged in calling for the Ranger to help quell a lynch mob. Roberts armed himself, and the two lawmen rushed to the county jail. Presently, Roberts, Clark, and cattleman James Trainer confronted more than five dozen armed men intent on taking five suspected rustlers out of their cells for the purpose of hanging them. Outnumbered and outgunned, Clark ran to get help while the other two could only watch as the mob took the doomed men away. Roberts, Clark, and a posse of citizens soon pursued the throng on the Fredericksburg road. Approximately a half-mile south of town, they discovered the mob lynching three of the men from the jail and a fourth lying dead with a bullet in his head. As the crowd scattered, the fifth victim freed himself from the noose and escaped. The hanging men were cut down and one was found to still be alive. The grand jury convened and probed the recent events, but no indictments were handed down. Clark was believed to have ties to the German mob and his efforts in this episode were judged by the Anglos to be highly suspicious.[56]

The feud was waged in the court system for a few months, but the next killing changed the conflict from one for "control of the cattle range to a war of vengeance." On May 13, Deputy Sheriff Johann Anton "John" Wohrle rode to Karl Friedrich "Charley" Lehmberg's Llano County ranch, which employed Timothy P. Williamson as a foreman. Williamson had been arrested in Mason County the year before for selling a yearling not his own. The matter had never gone to trial, but Williamson was told he had to post a new bond. Lehmberg offered to guarantee the surety right then and there, but the deputy informed him the matter would have to be settled in town. Once on the trail, the party was surrounded by a dozen masked gunmen near Willow Creek. Williamson begged Wohrle for permission to flee, but the deputy refused and killed the former's horse. One of the nightriders then shot the ranch foreman down. Popular opinion, supported by the killing of the horse, believed Wohrle was likely a co-conspirator in the slaying.[57]

Tim Williamson had been the best friend of ex-Ranger William Scott Cooley, late of Company D. In fact, the two had together twice driven cattle herds up the trail to Kansas, an experience certain to forge lasting bonds.[58] Upon learning of the murder, Cooley left his Menard County farm for Mason, where he compiled a list of Williamson's alleged killers. His first victim, John Wohrle, having since left the sheriff's office, was fatally shot on August 10 while cleaning out a well. According to sensationalized newspaper reporting, Cooley then allegedly scalped the corpse. His next target was Peter Bader, the man thought to have murdered Williamson. Cooley rode to his quarry's farm nine days after Wohrle's slaying only to kill Peter's brother, Karl, in a case of mistaken identity. In an unrelated act, which further intensified the feud, Clark and a German posse ambushed adversaries Moses Baird and George W. Gladden, killing the former and seriously wounding the latter. Needing allies to further his personal vendetta, Cooley joined forces with John R. Baird, the murdered man's brother, and John Peters Ringo at the village of Loyal Valley (also known as Cold Springs). Baird was able to draw on scores of supporters from the cattlemen of Llano and Burnet Counties.[59]

Meanwhile, the term of enlistment for the Rangers had ended on June 1, but Jones convinced the men to serve without pay through September 30, when the legislature next met. On September 1, five companies of one lieutenant, three sergeants, three corporals, and thirty-four privates each were enlisted for twelve months. One of the new units, Company A under Lieutenant Ira Long, was formed to serve as the major's escort company.[60]

Even before reorganizing the battalion, Jones had decided to lead a major expedition into Mason County and quell the troubles occurring there. On August 27, Jones ordered Roberts to ready Sergeant Nelson Orcelus "Mage" Reynolds and twenty men for an "important scout." The Rangers were further directed to each pack twenty days' rations and fifty rounds of ammunition, and the captain was to ensure the detachment was well mounted. The date for the rendezvous at Captain Coldwell's camp was set for September 14. However, the scout, originally scheduled to commence the next day, had to be delayed one week due to Lieutenant Long's company being unable to make the assembly in time. Instead, the major ordered Roberts, on September 6, to take a detachment and reach Coldwell's camp by the twenty-second. Setting out, Jones and twenty Rangers from Companies A and D traveled through Loyal Valley on September 28, crossed the Llano, and rode up to Charles Keller's store on the north bank. There they were greeted by a heavily armed posse of fifteen to twenty Germans led by the sheriff, who anticipated an attack from Baird and Cooley's followers. Jones rode back up the trail to Cold Springs and confirmed that all was quiet for the moment. He went on to Mason on the twenty-ninth and learned that Cooley, Baird, and the recovered Gladden had visited town while the sheriff's posse was at Keller's establishment. While there, the three outlaws had murdered county hide inspector Daniel Hoerster while he was riding down the street. The killers then made their escape, and Jones dispatched three scouting detachments in pursuit without success.[61]

The Rangers searched for the fugitives over the next several weeks. A number of those conducting the manhunt were former colleagues of Cooley, and some proved unwilling to pursue their friend. Indeed, Sergeant Reynolds and Private James P. Day accepted honorable discharges on October 7 rather than continue the chase. Ranger Paul Durham did the same four days later. Despite the loss in manpower, the sweep through the county brought "a perfect quiet" to the area, even if the Rangers failed to capture their quarry. After conducting an ill-conceived raid on Loyal Valley, Sheriff Clark, already under indictment in Mason and adjacent counties, feared he would be the next victim and wisely took his leave on October 14. Gladden and Baird found Peter Bader in Llano County and killed him. The Rangers ultimately arrested twenty-two men, twelve for offenses committed in the county and the others from neighboring locales. Although murders had been committed in broad daylight, in front of witnesses, the grand jury refused to indict. The Rangers were forced to release their prisoners.[62]

In mid-October, Cooley and Gladden were rumored to be on the loose in Menardville, possibly hiding at the residence of "Old Man Jackson." Cooley was supposedly threatening his enemies, and Jones declared "There will be no quiet in [Mason] while he is at large." Roberts reported neither outlaw was actually in the area, and opined Jackson was more likely to inform the law as to Cooley's whereabouts than protect him. Having concluded his role in the disturbance, Cooley was briefly incarcerated in Burnet and Lampasas Counties on unrelated charges, and died in Fredericksburg on June 10, 1876, of "congestion of the brain," or "brain fever." Author Clifford R. Caldwell observed his symptoms as described by eyewitnesses matched those of meningitis or encephalitis. By the end of October 1875, Jones decided that the county had calmed sufficiently for him to attend to other matters. He left in Mason twenty-six men of Company A, who stayed until April 16 of the following year. Fifteen men had been murdered in a span of eight months, and more would die in the years to come, but the Frontier Battalion played no further role in the Mason County War.[63]

Financial shortages continued to plague Jones. On October 25, 1875, he ordered the five company commanders to reduce their ranks to two sergeants, one corporal, and seventeen privates per company, effective November 30. The major amended his instructions on November 12, and allowed Company B to retain its complement of three sergeants. Jones continued to establish a practice of accountability when he further directed that company monthly returns would be submitted in triplicate, and a second monthly report stating the operations and condition of the companies would be written on the fifteenth of every month. On March 8, 1876, Jones reported that the battalion had fought nineteen engagements with hostile Indians, and killed twenty-seven, wounded fourteen, and captured one. Another ten or twelve were believed to have been killed or wounded. The Rangers recovered one captured Mexican boy, one hundred horses, and two hundred head of cattle. The battalion also fought white thieves six times, arrested 110 fugitives, and recovered fifteen to twenty thousand dollars' worth of stolen stock. In the same time, two Rangers were killed and six were wounded. Jones posted General Order No. 9, which instructed the company commanders to recruit their respective units on April 1, 1876, to include three sergeants, three corporals, and twenty-six privates. Rather than disband the battalion the following summer, the legislature decreased the annual appropriation. Effective September 1, each company was comprised of one lieutenant, two sergeants, two corporals, and sixteen privates. Company A continued to be Jones's escort, while Company B was stationed on the Brazos in northeastern Throckmorton County; Company D, the San Saba River in Menard County;

Company E, on Jim Ned Creek in southwest Coleman County; and Company F, on the Nueces in northwest Uvalde County.[64]

After the Army crushed the last of the Southern Plains bands in the Red River War, the focus of the Frontier Battalion began to shift more completely from Indian fighting to peacekeeping. On March 20, 1877, Major Jones issued General Order No. 15, which instructed the companies to cease Indian scouting and concentrate on "the suppression of lawlessness and crime." This new mandate did come with a set of limitations, in that both Governor Coke and Adjutant General Steele firmly believed in the primacy of the county sheriffs. The two officials repeatedly stated that the Rangers could only operate when requested by county authorities, and only then in a supporting role.[65]

The still-simmering troubles in Mason contributed to the rise of organized livestock theft in neighboring Kimble County. Lives and property ceased to be respected, and ordinary citizens armed themselves. As Ranger H. B. Waddill later recounted, "Everyone that is not known is looked upon as the enemy." Indeed, the outlaws had achieved complete mastery of the county, and even sought to keep Seventeenth Judicial District Judge William Allen Blackburn from convening court on April 30. Jones organized a military-style campaign to break the gang's dominance. "Our business is to enforce the law and keep the peace," he wrote on April 8. "We must have no personal quarrels or feelings in the discharge of our duty, and should carefully guard against strife or ill feeling against either good or bad people."[66]

The operation began when Jones infiltrated Private Waddill of Company C into the county as an undercover operative. The Ranger spy quickly unearthed details on significant criminal activities and described Kimble as "a thiafs [sic] stronghold." On April 2, Sergeant Lamartine Pemberton "Lam" Sieker and seven Rangers arrested Sheriff J. M. Reynolds and escorted him to the Menard County jail. The sheriff was believed to be an accessory to the illegal activities occurring in the county and removing him from the scene increased the chances for success.[67]

On April 19, the major took thirty-five Rangers from Companies A and F to Paint Rock Spring in northeastern Edwards County and detailed five-man detachments to arrest every man of dubious character they encountered.

Two parties were to sweep down the South and North Llano Rivers, while a third was to clear Cedar Creek, and the fourth Johnson's Fork to the main Llano. The following day, they converged on the county seat of Junction and rendezvoused with Company D, which was already in place. Beginning on the twenty-first, the Ranger force, in five ten-man squads, probed the Llano valley and, disregarding the presumption of innocence, took anyone into custody who could not adequately account for themselves. Not one arrest ended in bloodshed. The prisoners were transported back to Junction and shackled to a tree, as the town possessed no jail. A log-and-cedar-post structure was built sometime during the Rangers' assignment in Kimble County, and those captured were shackled in "the bull pen." By April 23, twenty-one fugitives had been apprehended, and Jones increased that number to forty-one over the next several days. Transferred to Fredericksburg to await trial, thirty of the prisoners were known to be wanted in eighteen other counties.[68]

Judge Blackburn and the district attorney requested Jones provide protection for the court, as well as for jurors and witnesses. The grand jury handed down twenty-five indictments, including several for Sheriff Reynolds and County Judge William Potter, both of whom resigned on May 3. Since Kimble County had only been organized the year before, the jury list contained the names of only nine qualified men. The jury commissioners composed a new list so the pending cases were continued until the next court session. Few of the indicted men would be tried, let alone convicted. Occasional returns by the Rangers would be necessary, but law-abiding citizens could breathe easier as the outlaws' stranglehold had been broken.[69]

Range wars and feuds were all too common in the West, nowhere more so than the Lone Star State. Texans, seasoned by war and Indian fighting, were quick to solve their own difficulties—usually with violence. Lampasas County was one such place and the scene of the next major operation of the Frontier Battalion. One side of the feud was the five Horrell brothers; the other was John Calhoun Pinkney "Pink" Higgins. The Horrells—James Martin "Mart," Thomas, Merritt, Benjamin Franklin, and Samuel, Jr.—were no strangers to trouble. On March 14, 1873, in Jerry Scott's Matador Saloon in Lampasas, Mart, Tom, Merritt, and several cronies opened fire on a detail of state policemen attempting to arrest a friend of the brothers. Captain Thomas Howard Williams and three officers were gunned down, and three more fled. Having been wounded, Mart and two of his friends were taken to the Williamson County jail in Georgetown, but they were soon released by a crowd of supporters. The five brothers packed up their families and left for seemingly healthier climes on the Ruidoso River in New Mexico. They quickly found themselves at the center of the "Horrell War," which is regarded by historians as being the first phase of the Lincoln County War. Ben was killed, and the remainder returned to Texas. Standing trial for the murders of Captain Williams and his policemen, Mart, Tom, and Merritt were acquitted in October 1876.[70]

Rancher and Indian fighter Pink Higgins was an equally dangerous individual, and he was backed by his brothers-in-law, Robert Mitchell and William R. Wren, both tough fighting men. While the traditonal version holds that Higgins blamed the Horrells for rustling his cattle, author David Johnson has uncovered evidence that suggests Pink was convinced Merritt Horrell had engaged in an extramarital affair with Mrs. Higgins. Regardless of whether the dispute was over stolen livestock or a wayward wife, Higgins stalked into Wiley and Toland's Gem Saloon on January 22, 1877, and fatally shot an unarmed Merritt four times. When they heard the news, the surviving brothers swore vengeance on the killer.[71]

Higgins was determined to remain on the offensive. On March 26, he, Wren, and several friends ambushed Mart and Tom five miles east of Lampasas. Mart was hit in the right shoulder and Tom in the back. They escaped and raced for town. Arrest warrants for Higgins and Bob Mitchell were filed soon after the incident. Captain John C. Sparks, commanding Company C of the Frontier Battalion, was in Lampasas attending district court, and promptly conducted an unsuccessful search for the culprits. On April 22, the two fugitives entered the Rangers' camp and surrendered. Higgins and Mitchell each posted a ten-thousand-dollar bond and returned home. All seemed calm afterwards, and Sparks and his men were shifted to another area in May.[72]

On June 7, Higgins, Mitchell, Wren, Ben Terry, another brother-in-law, and Frank Mitchell, Bob's younger brother, encountered the three Horrell brothers and four of their allies—John Dixon, Rufus Overstreet, Bob McBee, and Jim "Buck" Waldrup—in the town square. The ensuing gun battle spilled into the streets and two stores until town leaders could establish a cease-fire. Frank Mitchell and Waldrup were killed in the fracas. Seven days later, an ailing Major Jones arrived with fifteen Rangers under Sergeant Reynolds, who had rejoined the battalion on September 1, 1876. Since the feud had so divided the county and kept witnesses and jurors from stepping forward, the major knew that only unconventional methods would prove successful. He decided to proceed "in the interest of peace and quiet, rather than in accordance with the strict dictates of the law." In fact, he intended to personally intervene and resolve the difficulty between the two factions.[73]

Reynolds and six or seven Rangers surrounded Mart Horrell's ranch house on Mesquite Creek at five o'clock on the morning of July 28. Moving through a heavy rain, they slipped into the house with their Winchesters at the ready, surprising eleven sleeping men, women, and children. Jolted awake, the three Horrell brothers found themselves looking down rifle barrels. Reynolds loudly identified himself, and the feudists reluctantly surrendered. The sergeant and his men then escorted Sam, Tom, and Mart back to camp.[74]

Having been charged with assault with intent to kill, they were taken to Lampasas where Jones warned them the fighting would have to stop. He drafted a long letter, dated July 30 and addressed to Higgins, Mitchell, and Wren. The message promised a cessation to hostilities if the Higgins party also agreed to peace. Mart, Tom, and Sam all signed. The following day, the major personally arrested the three Higgins leaders and wrote a corresponding letter to the Horrells dated August 2. This second missive accepted the peace overture and agreed to end the fighting and bitter feelings. Higgins, Mitchell, and Wren signed as well. Jones submitted the two letters to the *Lampasas Dispatch* for publication in the August 9 edition. A tenuous peace took effect and, while animosity existed well into the next century, never again did the feud erupt into violence. Jones would later apologize for not adhering strictly to the law, but his pragmatic approach succeeded where normal methods would have likely prolonged the conflict.[75]

The triumph of peacefully settling the Horrell-Higgins feud would fade in the embarrassment of the "El Paso Salt War." Five hundred miles west of Austin, El Paso shared more similarities with Old Mexico than with the rest of Texas. Americans by chance rather than choice, *Paseños* paid little attention to which side of the Rio Grande they happened to be on. The Anglo minority, some eighty individuals, was preoccupied with personal and political feuds dating from the Civil War and Reconstruction. By 1877 the factions' leaders were Charles Henry Howard and Don Luis Cardis. Emigrating from Virginia in the 1850s, Howard served in the famed Eighth Texas Cavalry, and as district attorney and district court judge, before arriving in El Paso in 1872. His many friends and supporters greatly admired him, while his numerous enemies loathed him. The Italian-born Cardis was the *patrón* of the *mexicano* electorate. El Paso County's representative in the Fourteenth and Fifteenth Legislatures, he was able to deliver the vote of his constituents, regardless of citizenship, in any local election. Immersed in a struggle for wealth and power, both men possessed an ambitious and unscrupulous nature. Historian Paul Cool remarked on the atmosphere in El Paso County: "Every political alliance represented a potential personal hatred. Enemies lost all sense of proportion. When honor was at stake, a rival's defeat was seldom enough. His personal ruin or death became the preferred solution."[76]

The catalyst that caused the situation to explode into outright violence was salt. For about fifteen years, *Paseños* had utilized large deposits below Guadalupe Peak one hundred miles east of El Paso. Financier and former Travis County sheriff George B. Zimpelman, Charles Howard's father-in-law, located the lakes based on Memphis & El Paso Railroad land certificates he held, and received a patent for three sections. Following a survey of his claims, he appointed his trusted son-in-law "salt agent" for the tract. Howard proclaimed that the salt was now available only to paying customers, even though Mexicans had long considered the *salinas* a public resource. Seizing the prospect to promote *mexicano* interests and enhance their political power, both Cardis and Father Antonio Severo Borajo, the sinister former parish priest in San Elizario, assured them that the will of the people would always transcend laws written far away in Austin.[77]

On September 29, 1877, Howard had two *salineros* arrested for merely intending to take salt from the deposits, and a mob of fifty to sixty *Paseños* proceeded to "arrest" Howard and his agent, John McBride. The two men were held in San Elizario for three days while Howard negotiated for his life with *metizo* Francisco "Chico" Barela and approximately a dozen other junta leaders. The judge was forced to sign a pledge stating on pain of death he would cede the *salinas* to public usage, take no legal action against his abductors, post a twelve-thousand-dollar surety bond, and forever quit the county within twenty-four hours. Released on October 3, he rushed to Mesilla, New Mexico. Resenting his disgrace, Howard returned to El Paso exactly one week later. Armed with a double-barreled shotgun, he killed Cardis in Solomon Schutz's store on the corner of San Francisco and Santa Fe streets, then fled back to Mesilla leaving the earlier peacemaking in tatters.[78]

Governor Hubbard concluded that citizens of both the United States and Mexico had displaced lawful authority in the upper valley with mob rule. On October 24, 1877, he dispatched Major Jones to El Paso to restore order. Jones arrived in town on November 5 after traveling by train and stagecoach through Kansas and New Mexico. The scene was tense as the mob had again gathered in San Elizario furious over the murder. The sheriff had only two possemen, and Jones had come alone, so he decided to employ the same methods that had quieted the Horrell-Higgins feud. He met on two occasions with a ten-man committee representing the junta. He stated firmly that he had come to the county to restore the peace, not to resolve the question of ownership of the saline lakes. He told them the matter would be decided in the courts, as would Howard's fate. The committee responded with their belief that they had the authority to arrest Howard and compel him to sign papers and post bond. They also had the right to seize the money forfeited by Howard when he broke his word. Their self-awarded powers were derived from the conviction "they were the people and the people were the law."[79]

Back in El Paso, Jones raised a detachment of Company C. Local Anglo citizens, including Howard, urged Jones to appoint the capable Captain Gregorio Nacianceno García as commander. The major wanted no one involved in the local disturbances, though, so he chose John Bernard Tays, an honest and sincere man who, nevertheless, had absolutely no experience that would allow him to deal with the crisis. Continuing the chain of poor decisions, the new lieutenant recruited twenty Anglos who were of uneven quality at best, "a mixed bag of young and old, of Anglos and 'law and order' *Paseños*, of community pillars and man-killers." Retired lawman and prolific author Bob Alexander commented on Jones's arrangements: "Perhaps, pure economics or a burdensome workload did invalidate the wisdom of sending a whole company, but taking along two or three or four proven law-enforcement veterans, men capable of taking charge during troublesome times teetering at the brink of anarchy, wouldn't have been imprudent."[80]

Jones next proceeded to make a choice that would have severe repercussions. Fulfilling his promise to arrest Howard for murder, the major persuaded the judge to return to El Paso and surrender himself. Jones brought Howard before the justice of the peace late in the evening on November 16. Several decisions were made in the hearing contrary to Texas law, but were undertaken in a failed effort to avoid more turmoil. The magistrate allowed the accused to waive examination and placed him under a bond of four thousand dollars to appear in district court in March 1878. Howard pledged to leave the county in the interim, a vow many, including Jones, believed. The major reported to General Steele that, despite "much excitement and many threats," the mob had disbanded and promised to submit to the law. Consequently, he did not foresee a confrontation. Jones finalized details with Tays on November 22, before beginning the long journey home via Coleman and Kimble Counties. If he could have stayed in El Paso for another month, his well-honed skills in persuasive negotiation could have kept the inevitable violence from occurring, but a scheduled court appearance in Austin on December 3 prompted him to return.[81]

Shortly thereafter, a party of forty *Paseños* with carts went to the lakes, either to force a confrontation or to gather salt for sale in Mexico. Howard sued in district court in Ysleta on December 12, and served a writ in San Elizario restricting the transaction pending the final resolution of the case. Leaving Sheriff Charles Kerber to follow the next day, Tays sent four of his men along as an escort. *Mexicanos* from both sides of the border began gathering in San Elizario, soon numbering more than five hundred. After brutally murdering local merchant Charles E. Ellis, the mob besieged Tays's adobe headquarters, where Howard had sought refuge. The two forces traded a sporadic fire that resulted in three or four Mexican casualties; Sergeant C. E. Mortimer was mortally wounded. In his Austin office, far from the scene, Jones received a telegram that conveyed, according to "reliable" reports, Ellis and six Rangers had been slain. The two sides agreed to a cease-fire on December 16, and, the following morning, Howard yielded to Chico Barela and the other *Paseño* leaders at the junta's headquarters. While keeping the judge and Tays in one room, the junta tricked the other Rangers into surrendering and confined them in a corral. Howard, Charles McBride, and John G. Atkinson were put before an eight-man firing squad and executed. The Rangers were released on December 18, and returned unarmed to El Paso. The state property—arms, ammunition, forage, and food—seized by the Mexicans was later valued at $2,500.[82]

Federal troops of the Ninth Cavalry and civilian volunteers from Silver City—the latter described as "hard-faced and battle-scarred"—also marched to El Paso, the first elements arriving on December 20. The worst of the volunteers were hired killers led by renegade John Kinney. Under the overall direction of Sheriff Kerber, they arrested two men in Ysleta (who were later shot "while attempting to escape") and fought two brief engagements in Socorro. The bloodthirsty civilian volunteers, and some of Tays's Rangers, continued their rampage of vengeance with numerous acts of murder, assault, robbery, rape, and attempted rape. The Silver City posse became a political liability for Governor Hubbard, and the adjutant general discharged them on January 10, 1878.[83] Even while he refused to condone the actions of the sheriff's posse, Jones did make allowances for their behavior. He also subtly shifted responsibility away from Tays's detachment and placed it firmly on Kerber:

> In times of profound peace and quiet it might be proper to characterize these occurrences as [wanton outrages] ... from the evidence it appears that on the 23d December the sheriff considered it his duty to make the arrests of several parties, leaders of and active participants in the mob, who were known to be in Socorro, and to search certain houses for arms. In doing this several men were killed and one woman wounded; and on the same day two prisoners were killed; but these occurences, transpiring in the wake of a wild, fanatical, and brutal mob, in a period of excitement, closing up a reign of terror by the mob which is said to have been "brutal and atrocious," though not justifiable, were probably unavoidably incident to the duties which the officer in charge conceived that he was called on to perform.[84]

The governor requested that the Texas congressional delegation demand a federal investigation into the role played by Mexican citizens in the crisis. On December 31, President Rutherford Birchard Hayes ordered the army to conduct the inquiry. The next month, Jones appeared before the Senate Committee on Foreign Affairs in Washington and testified on border conditions. In discussing the Salt War, he described how Mexicans on the other side of the river were drilling in preparation for a war to retake the lands lost thirty years previously. By the middle of January 1878, Colonel John Haskell King, Ninth Infantry, and Lieutenant-Colonel William Henry Lewis, Nineteenth Infantry, arrived at the abandoned post of Fort Bliss and began to take statements. First Lieutenant and Adjutant Leonard Hay, Ninth Infantry, acted as the recorder. Only then did Hubbard learn the federal government had started its work. He ordered Major Jones on February 8 to proceed to El Paso and assume his place on the commission as the state's representative.[85]

Jones was still in Washington when the board of inquiry convened on January 22. Once he arrived on February 18, the major learned that the probe's scope had expanded to include the conduct of the Rangers and other state and local officials. After seating himself on February 19, Jones lodged a formal protest regarding the new line of questioning. The actions of the volunteers and the Rangers were not the concern of the military, he contended, but rather matters for the civilian courts. The other two commissioners ignored Jones's objection, wrote their majority report, and left El Paso. Jones's minority summary focused on addressing perceived inconsistencies, including the evidence that the mob had acted under discipline with near military precision, and repeating his exception to the wider range taken by the investigation. He laid the blame for the trouble on Cardis for hindering Howard in his legal interests. Jones went on to criticize the United States Army and the Mexican government for failing to control the border; he estimated one hundred Mexican nationals had come over the river to participate in the riots. He agreed with the majority that Fort Bliss should be garrisoned once more, and advocated the extradition from Mexico those members of the mob who had fled across the Rio Grande.[86]

As district court would soon convene, Jones authorized an additional thirty men for Tays's company and extended their terms of enlistment. The grand jury returned indictments on approximately one hundred men who were named as members of the mob that had executed Howard and the others. All had fled to Mexico, and promises from Mexican officials to return them went unfulfilled in violation of the extradition treaty between the two countries. John Tays resigned on March 31, 1878, and was succeeded by his older brother James. Over time, *Paseños* under indictment quietly returned to their homes and resumed their normal lives. George Zimpelman appointed another agent, John C. Ford, a former member of Tays's company, who enjoyed better relations with the local population than had Howard. He dealt with the Mexicans cordially, and they paid him reasonable fees for the salt.[87]

While Jones was dealing with insurrection in El Paso and its aftermath, Sam Bass was emerging as front-page news. Since his preferred targets, banks and railroads, were institutions unpopular with the ordinary citizen, this desperado became a hero in Texas folklore. The victims of his crimes likely did not sing his praises, but to the general public Bass became one of the best-known Texas outlaws and the most admired. Many anecdotes were later written of his generosity and devil-may-care spirit. Following his death, he became the subject of a ballad, which declared, "A kinder hearted feller you seldom ever see."[88] The young Indiana-born cowboy had made the ominous decision to default on a loan in 1875, squander the eight thousand dollars, and begin robbing stagecoaches with several friends. Their success was lackluster until they held up a Union Pacific train at Big Spring, Nebraska, on September 18, 1877. The robbery secured the gang sixty thousand dollars in newly minted twenty-dollar gold coins. Their illicit gains attracted nationwide attention, and the railroad and express companies posted substantial rewards. Riding southward, the outlaws tangled with federal soldiers and Kansas peace officers, and two gang members were killed. Twenty thousand dollars of the stolen money was recovered by the authorities.[89]

Escaping into Texas in November, Bass and his gang, the members of which changed often, held up two stagecoaches west of Fort Worth, and four trains near Dallas. None of their heists came even close to equaling the return of the Big Spring robbery, but the multiple losses provoked the political and corporate powers into taking action. Governor Hubbard had earlier issued an arrest warrant for Bass on behalf of the state of Nebraska. Following the holdups in North Texas, the governor posted a one-thousand-dollar bounty for the capture of each train robber.[90] Lured by the reward money, federal and county lawmen, undercover Rangers, Pinkerton operatives, railroad detectives, bounty hunters, militiamen, and eager citizens flooded the region surrounding Dallas. With so many searching for a single objective, the manhunters often collided with one another. To impose some sort of order on the situation, Governor Hubbard directed Major Jones take charge of the pursuit on April 11, 1878.[91]

Very soon the major came to possess the solution to the Bass problem. James Murphy, a friend of the outlaw leader, had been swept up in the mass arrests of known Bass associates and indicted as an accessory. In the course of their robberies, the fugitives had taken U.S. mail bags and were thus wanted by federal as well as state authorities. Utilizing an approach common in modern American law enforcement, Jones secured the cooperation of Andrew Jackson Evans, the U.S. attorney for the Western District of Texas, to offer Murphy a deal. If Murphy would join the Bass gang and keep Jones informed on the outlaws' movements and plans, the federal charges would be dropped. Murphy signed a contract with Evans on May 21, despite the dangerous position into which he was placing himself.[92]

Bass and his chief lieutenants, Seaborn "Sebe" Barnes and Francis M. "Frank" Jackson, would kill Murphy without hesitation if they suspected him of being an informant. Indeed, Barnes was immediately suspicious and advised eliminating Murphy. The spy was able to assuage Jackson's doubts, but Barnes continued to urge Bass to murder Murphy.[93] The gang reconnoitered banks at Ennis, Waco, Belton, and Round Rock during the early weeks of July, while the various posses scoured the brush country north of Dallas. Once in Belton and again in Georgetown, Murphy managed to mail letters identifying Round Rock as the next target. Bass nearly caught him in the Georgetown post office.[94]

Once Jones received the messages on July 17, he scrambled to assemble an adequate number of Rangers to meet the gang in Round Rock, a town on the old Chisholm Trail twenty miles north of Austin. The major had a three-man detachment of Rangers at the state capitol, while the nearest full complement was Company E under Lieutenant Mage Reynolds at Lampasas, seventy miles to the northwest. Jones dispatched Corporal Vernon Coke Wilson to direct

Jim Murphy, Sam Bass, and Sebe Barnes (L to R). Photograph by Hamilton Biscoe Hillyer, Austin, Texas. *Courtesy Hardin-Simmons University Libraries, Abilene, Texas.*

Reynolds and his men to Round Rock. He then ordered his detail—Richard Clayton "Dick" Ware, Christopher Reyzor Connor, and George Herold —to proceed to the town and await his arrival. Boarding the International & Great Northern train, Jones himself reached Round Rock on July 18, flanked by Maurice B. Moore, a Travis County deputy sheriff and former Ranger.[95]

The following day, Jones added stable keeper Henry Highsmith, and Williamson County Deputy Sheriff Alijah W. "Caige" Grimes, both ex-Rangers, to his small force. At the same time, Adjutant General Steele sent Captain Lee Hall to the scene. Unbeknownst to Jones, Lieutenant Reynolds had taken his company to San Saba where the messenger found him. Reynolds mounted up eight of his men and rode hard for Round Rock. On the fateful day of July 19, they were still forty-five miles from their destination.[96]

Jones dispersed his men around town and made his way to the telegraph office at the railroad depot. The streets were nearly empty as the day was extremely hot. Bass knew Lee Hall by sight, so the Ranger officer stayed in his room at the Davis Hotel. Bass, Barnes, and Jackson arrived in Round Rock at four p.m. with the intention of buying tobacco and making another reconnoiter. Murphy was able to loiter at a store on the outskirts of town. Once their scouting was completed, the three robbers resolved to take the Williamson County Bank the next day.[97] They then tied their mounts in an alley and walked up Main Street toward Henry Koppel's store. The lawmen were seemingly loafing in the afternoon sun, but they were watching the outlaws, albeit without knowing their identity. Deputy Sheriff Moore observed the bulge of a handgun hidden under clothing and informed Deputy Grimes, who was under orders to see that all strangers' weapons were checked while in town. Backed by Moore, Grimes followed the outlaws into the store and asked Sam Bass if he was carrying a pistol. Bass replied, "Yes," and the bank robbers whirled around and opened fire. Grimes dropped dead in the doorway, and Moore took a bullet through his lungs while shooting Bass in the hand. The outlaws raced through the gunsmoke filling the store and out into the street.[98]

The quiet of Round Rock exploded into a cacophony of gunfire, shouts, and plunging horses. Dick Ware raced from the barber shop where he had been getting a shave. Reaching the store before the others, he was also the first to return the outlaws' fire. Moments later, Jones dashed up Main Street triggering his pistol and dodging a bullet as he ran. Chris Connor and George Herold joined the fight in the yard of the livery stable as the surviving gang members raced for their horses. The wounded Bass was trying to get astride his rearing gelding when Herold put a rifle bullet into the outlaw's back where it lodged in his kidney. Barnes was mounting his horse when Ware killed him with a carefully aimed shot to the head. Jackson managed to get atop his steed and assisted Bass into the saddle. The two raced out of town while several lawmen retrieved their horses, then galloped in pursuit.[99]

Lieutenant Reynolds and his weary men arrived in town two hours too late. The next morning, Sergeant Charles Liborn Nevill led a detachment of nine Rangers and one county deputy after the fleeing robbers. They found the mortally wounded Bass lying at the base of an oak tree. Unable to travel further, the outlaw had convinced the reluctant Jackson to leave him behind, and the latter rode away into obscurity. Bass surrendered and was taken back to Round Rock. From his death bed, the bandit was talkative about trivial matters, but he refused to divulge the whereabouts of Jackson or his other confederates. "It's agin my profession to blow on my pals," he told Jones. "If a man knows anything, he ought to die with it in him." He succumbed to his wounds on the afternoon of July 21, forty-eight hours after the fight. Following an inquest, Bass and Barnes were both buried in the local cemetery.[100]

Even though the outlaw gang had been eliminated, the situation was not entirely resolved. The participants of the fight argued as to who had killed Bass and Barnes, which county lawmen should receive a portion of the credit, and how the one thousand dollars in reward money was to be divided. In addition to having the charges against him dropped, Jim Murphy was given fifty dollars in compensation. He believed he should have gotten more, and spent several months demanding a larger share from Jones. He died on June 5, 1879, after accidentally ingesting an eyewash containing belladonna—a toxic substance. Jones gave Bass's horse to Deputy Grimes's widow.[101]

Adjutant General Steele resigned in January 1879 for health reasons, and Governor Oran M. Roberts nominated Jones to succeed him on the twenty-second. Several state senators were critical of the submission, and the Senate went into executive session on the same day to discuss the matter. Their chief complaint was that Jones, during his tenure as commander of the Frontier Battalion, had also held the position of quartermaster and drew pay for both offices. The major wrote a letter to Senator Charles Stewart explaining the matter. When the battalion was first established in May 1875, Captain Martin Kenney was appointed the quartermaster and drew a salary of $250 per month; $1,500 per annum was earmarked for traveling and other contingent expenses.[102] Once Kenney had resigned, Jones met with the governor and adjutant general, and the three officials decided Jones would assume the duties of quartermaster. He would also receive the same monthly compensation for traveling expenses. The arrangement specified Jones would not handle monies, and claims for all supplies would be reimbursed by the adjutant general, who was a bonded officer. The accounts were regularly approved by General Steele and Comptroller Stephen Heard Darden under the advice of Attorney General H. H. Boone. Jones estimated he had been able to save the state treasury five thousand dollars. He appeared before the committee on frontier defense, chaired by Senator John S. Ford, and explained the policy. As the governor, adjutant general, attorney general, and comptroller had already endorsed Jones's actions, the opposition in the Senate was thought to have originated from disappointed seekers for commissions in the battalion. Steele certified the correctness of Jones's statement to Senator Stewart, and proved instrumental in removing opposition to Jones's appointment.[103]

The Senate confirmed the nomination on January 25, and an editorial in the *Galveston Daily News* hailed the decision:

> The new Adjutant General, Major John B. Jones, whose nomination by Governor Roberts was confirmed by the Senate yesterday, is a citizen of Navarro County. He was selected by Governor Coke to command the Frontier Battalion on the formation of the corps, and in the discharge of his duties and responsibilities has won golden opinions from all sorts of persons in the sections in which he had been engaged. He also gained special distinction and credit for shrewdness and vigor in the operation against the Sam Bass gang, and in other services requiring executive ability and prompt and decisive action. He will doubtless bring to the new office the same zeal and capacity that marked his conduct in the old.[104]

Taking his oath of office on the twenty-seventh, and giving his bond of ten thousand dollars the following day, Jones's first general order instructed the company commanders to continue reporting directly to him. While remaining in command of the battalion, his expanded duties curtailed his earlier habit of visiting every company in the field. Instead, he appointed Neal Coldwell battalion quartermaster (and *de facto* executive officer) on May 9, to date from the fourth, and delegated personnel, inspection, payroll, and logistical responsibilities to him. Despite its recent successes, though, the Frontier Battalion saw its funding reduced from $150,000 to $100,000.[105]

Under the new militia law that went into effect on September 1, 1879, Jones held the rank of brigadier-general and assumed the *ex officio* duties of chief of staff, quartermaster-general, commissary-general, inspector-general, paymaster-general, and chief of ordnance. In addition to the frontier forces, Jones commanded a state militia of six regiments comprised of forty-seven companies and 20,092 officers and men.[106]

The year 1879 continued to bring momentous change to Jones's life. Following four committee memberships in the Grand Lodge, his service climaxed with his election to the office of Most Worshipful Grand Master of Texas. Jones was also a regular attendee at the Baptist Church in Austin, and there he had met Ann Eloise (Holliday) Anderson, the widow of Thomas J. H. Anderson. Described as "beautiful and accomplished," Mrs. Anderson had been born in Aberdeen, Mississippi, on November 20, 1838, and was educated at the Judson Female Institute in Marion, Alabama. Her late husband had been a planter in Robertson and Milam Counties, and their children were Reuben T. Anderson, born on March 19, 1859; Attilia Aldridge Anderson, born on December 14, 1859; Elizabeth Anderson, born in 1862; Anna Eloise Anderson, born on August 17, 1863; Mary E. Anderson, born on August 1, 1866; Eleanor Lena Anderson, born on August 4, 1869; and Thomas J. H. Anderson, born in 1871. After the senior Thomas's death, Ann moved to Austin and built a two-story frame house for her family on San Jacinto Street. She and the children became popular among Austin's elite, and her home was the center for much of the city's social affairs. From there, she also oversaw her various successful business interests.[107]

Even at the age of forty-five, Jones was considered an extremely eligible bachelor. The friendship he formed with Ann turned to love, and they married on February 25, 1879. Since Jones had never purchased a home in Austin, the couple decided the new family would live in Ann's house. Her children grew to regard Jones as a father figure, and he whole-heartedly reciprocated their feelings. Reuben was particularly devoted to his step-parent. Indeed, he had served in Companies D and B of the Frontier Battalion from September 1, 1878, to January 31, 1880.[108]

In a letter written to the governor in early 1880, Jones detailed the accomplishments of the Frontier Battalion in the preceding six years. He pointed to the fact that settlement of frontier counties, previously stagnant or depopulated for twelve years, had advanced to encompass twenty-one new counties. Since 1874, the Rangers had pursued ninety-seven Indian bands, fought in twenty-six engagements, killed seventy-seven warriors and wounded twenty-nine, captured another three, and killed twenty-three Mexican bandits and wounded three. In addition, 6,871 horses and head of cattle had been recovered. He did concede depredations continued, but to a lesser extent.[109]

In August 1880, the Sheriff's Association of Texas convened its annual meeting at the Dallas Opera House. Duval County Sheriff Eugene A. Glover offered a resolution that the Frontier Battalion and the Special Force be recognized as "an auxiliary to the regular constabulary force of Texas indispensable at present to the frontier counties, and in General Jones and Captain Oglesby we recognize the right men in the right place." The sheriff's motion was unanimously adopted.[110]

During the months of October and November 1880, the adjutant general undertook a tour of inspection and observation along the frontier. He traveled from Fort Elliott, in Wheeler County, to the head of the San Saba River in Menard County. Since his last trip to the frontier two years before, the line of settlements had advanced from fifty to one hundred miles westward. The tier of border counties, which was once populated only by independent stockmen living in dug-outs and picket houses, was now filling with farmers, townsmen, and cattle barons supported by foreign investment. The cattle raisers moved farther west to a line stretching from the Canadian River to the Rio Grande, by way of the headwaters of the Red, Brazos, Colorado, and Concho Rivers. More work would remain for Rangers in the Panhandle, but the tour allowed Jones to see the fruits of his labors. On December 31, 1880, he made his annual report to the governor.[111]

Governor Roberts addressed the legislature on January 13, 1881, and praised the efficiency of the Frontier Battalion and the Special State Troops in protecting the frontier counties while operating with nearly one-half the expense formerly appropriated. He also commended the efforts of the Texas congressional delegation in the passage of a law that barred officers of the United States, excepting the president, from granting reservation Indians the right to enter Texas for any purpose. Jones was reappointed on January 24. On February 28, the Frontier Battalion consisted of five companies and four captains, one lieutenant, eleven sergeants, nine corporals, eighty-seven privates, and three teamsters. The following month, Jones reorganized the Special Force once commanded by L. H. McNelly and Lee Hall into Company F, and transferred its members to the battalion. The officers and men of the six companies now numbered five captains, two lieutenants, six sergeants, thirteen corporals, eighty-nine privates, and five teamsters. In the last months of Adjutant General Jones's tenure, though, the battalion's appropriation for the year ending February 28, 1882, was slashed from $100,000 to eighty thousand dollars.[112]

Jones's health had never been robust, but by the summer of 1879, he had become noticeably frail. In early 1881, his already delicate condition began to seriously deteriorate. On March 6, Doctor Wade Allen Morris, his family physician, made a house call to the Jones residence in Austin, and found the general in severe pain and suffering from nausea. He had been ill for about a week. Diagnosed with acute hepatitis involving the stomach, Jones's symptoms lessened by the next morning. At noon, he experienced "severe rigor" and presented with vomiting and acute discomfort across his abdomen. By evening, he was feeling better, but the symptoms periodically returned over the next month. By the twenty-third, he could not take food or medicine by mouth, and had to be "nourished and medicated per rectum." Through his entire ailment, much of the administration of the department fell on the shoulders of Henry Orsay, the clerk in Jones's office, while Quartermaster Coldwell supervised the Frontier Battalion.[113]

The Galveston *Daily News* reported on April 7: "Adjutant General Jones continues in a precarious condition, his disease having culminated in abscess of the liver, from which in his debilitated condition, it is extremely doubtful if he can recover." His condition was reported as improved on April 9, but there remained grave concerns about his recuperation. He was rallying by April 16, but his long and painful recovery lasted through the summer. In early July, he traveled to San Antonio to see Dr. Ferdinand Ludwig von Herff and undergo surgery for his abscess, which left him greatly weakened. Following a second surgery performed by Dr. Thomas Dudley Wooten on July 18 in Austin, complications set in and Jones died at four a.m. the next day. On the twentieth, his funeral service was held at the Baptist Church with the Reverend G. W. Rogers delivering "an eloquent and impressive funeral oration." The *Statesman* noted the procession included the governor, state departmental heads, a military escort, and "a large cortege of friends and citizens." Jones was buried at Oakwood Cemetery with full Masonic rites.[114]

An essential figure in his son's life, Colonel Henry Jones remained on the Rancho where he was successfully engaged in planting and stock raising. In 1888, he helped to found the Henry Jones School near Frost; Miss Frankie Long was the original teacher. He died on December 26 of the same year.[115]

Already twice a widow, Ann married Alexander Watkins Terrell, a distinguished jurist, Confederate veteran, politician, and diplomat, on April 26, 1883, in Austin. While Terrell served as Minister to Turkey from 1893 to 1897, Ann's charm and grace, evident as an accomplished hostess in Austin, proved a benefit to her husband in diplomatic social settings. She died on November 25, 1908, and was buried in Oakwood Cemetery near General Jones.[116]

Reuben matriculated at the Texas Military Institute in Austin in 1873, but left to attend the Preparatory Department of Roanoke College in Salem, Virginia, in 1875. He then studied Latin, English, and mathematics at Richmond College in Richmond, Ohio, from 1876 to 1877. He subsequently worked as a real estate agent and a stock raiser. He married Mary Shirley Gregg on December 15, 1891, in Austin. He died in Amarillo on December 12, 1932, of chronic myocarditis and was buried in Oakwood Cemetery in Austin.[117]

Attilia graduated from the Hollins Institute in Botetourt Springs, Virginia, in June 1877, with a degree in English literature and a proficiency award in history. She married banker and real estate dealer Lewis Hancock on

January 4, 1883, in Austin. They raised one son and three daughters. Lewis died on February 11, 1920, of myocardial ischemia. Suffering from diabetes, Attilia died while in a diabetic coma at Seton Hospital on December 9, 1944. She was buried in Oakwood Cemetery.[118]

Elizabeth graduated from the Hollins Institute in June 1878. She married stockman Alonzo Millett on July 2, 1884. She died in San Antonio on December 16 of the same year of typhoid malaria. The funeral procession that escorted her casket to the train depot was reported as being three-quarters of a mile long. Her remains were transported to Austin where she was buried in Oakwood Cemetery.[119]

Annie married lawyer and stockman Thaddeus Austin Thomson, Sr. on June 14, 1883, and bore him three daughters and a son. In 1913, Thaddeus was appointed U.S. ambassador to Columbia, where they served for three years. He died on January 18, 1927, of apoplexy. She died on November 18, 1931, in St. Louis, Missouri.[120]

Mary wed banker Walter Bremond on June 10, 1886, in St. David's Episcopal Church in Austin. They had two daughters and a son. Walter died on January 10, 1925. Mary died on May 6, 1951, of a cerebrovascular accident and was buried in Oakwood Cemetery.[121]

Eleanor married physician Matthew Mann Smith on November 20, 1894. They had two sons. Matthew died on January 10, 1924. She later married widower and retired postmaster Grant Gregory Campbell, and they lived in Dallas. Grant died on December 31, 1956, of a cerebral hemorrhage, and Eleanor succumbed to congestive heart failure on March 13, 1957, both deaths occurring at St. Paul Hospital in Dallas. She was buried in Oakwood Cemetery.[122]

Thomas died on June 8, 1905, at his mother's home; he had been ill for several months. He was buried in Oakwood Cemetery in Austin.[123]

A slight, frail man physically, John B. Jones is a colossus in the annals of the Texas Rangers. He established the basic organization and administration, he demanded high standards in terms of performance and accountability, and he adopted a strategic outlook that encompassed the entire frontier. His legacy is a Ranger service that still bears his imprint and has endured to the present day.

Leander H. McNelly. Cabinet card photograph by James Inglis, Montreal, Canada. *Courtesy Albert and Ethel Herzstein Library, San Jacinto Museum of History, La Porte, Texas.*

Chapter 2

Leander H. McNelly: "No Quarter Given"

Leander Harvey McNelly stands at the crossroads of the soldiers Texas Rangers had been and the lawmen they were becoming. Faced with uncontrolled mayhem on the Rio Grande, he approached the battlefield determined to neutralize the enemy by any and all means at his disposal. With no quarter given, his methods have been questioned as being brutal and extralegal, but, amid the blood-drenched chaos of the border country, they proved effective, albeit with a price. In aggressively recovering stolen livestock and punishing *bandidos*, he gained a heroic reputation among Anglos, and one of infamy amid *mexicanos*. The contradiction remains intact to this day. Whatever success he enjoyed came from an innate drive that belied his sickly frame and from leadership abilities forged in the crucible of war. Indeed, the only practical training or experience he possessed in law enforcement came from three years in the hated Texas State Police. Professor Michael Collins wrote: "McNelly was a hard man to know, even harder to understand—especially if you were a bandit or a rustler. The way he moved, the way he spoke, his quiet strength; unlike so many leaders who simply exuded confidence, there was something else about him, something about his manner that distinguished him from others, something intuitive and difficult to define."

He was born on March 12, 1844, near Follansbee, Brooke County, in what is now West Virginia. His father, Owen McNelly, was born in Newry, County Down, Ireland, in approximately 1810, while his mother, Mary Katherine (Killian) McNelly, was born in 1815. The two married in 1830. Seeking to escape the strife of Ireland's troubles, the family had immigrated to the United States in about 1832, and settled in Brooke County to raise sheep. Owen and Mary's other children were Owen McNelly, Jr., born in 1831; Peter John McNelly, born in 1833 or 1834; Margaret McNelly, born in 1835; Clarinda (or Clorinda) McNelly, born in 1837; Thomas McNelly, born in 1839; James McNelly, born in 1845; and Mary McNelly, born in 1847. The 1850 federal census records the two Owens and Peter as being laborers. In his youth, Leander spent two years in Missouri with Peter's family before returning to Virginia.[1]

In 1859, Peter traveled to Texas to locate better land for his family's sheep. The following year, he loaded his wife and children, Leander, and the livestock on flatboats and floated them down the Ohio and Mississippi Rivers. Reaching New Orleans, the two brothers drove their flocks overland to Washington County, arriving in the autumn. At the same time, Peter's family sailed aboard the steamship *General Rusk* to Galveston, and disembarked on the last day of October 1860. During the family's relocation, the younger McNelly was already showing signs of the tuberculosis that would eventually kill him. For the short term at least, the time spent in the warmer climate was said to have invigorated and strengthened him. In the year before the outbreak of the Civil War, McNelly tended sheep for Travis J. Burton, whose pioneer father was the namesake for the settlement to be established in 1862.[2]

As the nation fractured into civil war, John Robert Baylor had led a Confederate invasion force into the Mesilla Valley of New Mexico. Months later, Brigadier-General Henry Hopkins Sibley traveled to Richmond to seek permission from President Jefferson Davis for the completion of the territory's conquest. Sibley was a West Point graduate and career U.S. Army officer who had been posted to Fort Union before his resignation. He argued, once Santa Fe was taken, secessionists in New Mexico and California would flock to the Confederate banner and assist in winning the entire Southwest. Sibley's plan was authorized, and he traveled to San

Antonio to raise a cavalry brigade of twenty companies and a battery of howitzers. However, his efforts were delayed by difficulties in securing recruits, arms, and ordnance stores. Despite orders to offer him every assistance, Sibley had not been advanced any funds, and was forced to purchase supplies on his private account and on the credit of the Confederate government.[3] According to the expedition's chief of artillery, Major Trevanion Theodore Teal, other objectives in Sibley's scheme may have been the seizure of the Colorado and California silver and gold mines, and the annexation of New Mexico/Arizona, Colorado, Utah, Nevada, and California, as well as Chihuahua and Sonora.[4]

At the same time, Brigadier-General Edward Richard Sprigg Canby had been organizing the Union army in New Mexico for several months. Martial law was established, *habeas corpus* was suspended, several regiments of New Mexican volunteers were raised, and Forts Union and Craig were made important centers of the Federal military strategy.[5]

Desiring to enlist in the Confederate army, McNelly falsified his age as eighteen and enrolled in the Sibley Brigade on August 27, 1861. Traveling to Camp Manassas on Salado Creek near San Antonio, he was mustered into Captain George Washington Campbell's Company F, Fifth Texas Mounted Volunteers on September 5 as a private. The regimental field and staff officers included Colonel Thomas Green, Lieutenant-Colonel Henry Cameron McNeill, and Major Samuel A. Lockridge.[6]

Men go to war for a multitude of reasons, and Professor Donald S. Frazier has noted the Sibley Brigade numbered few recruits who were substantial landowners or slaveholders. The majority of the enlisted men were stock raisers, tradesmen, laborers, or those who did not identify with a particular occupation. Most were young, impressionable men, sometimes with relatives also serving in the outfit. In addition to directly defending the Lone Star State's borders, Professor Charles David Grear suggested these Texans went to New Mexico because of their "backgrounds as Indian fighters, the opportunity to serve with kin and friends, the effects of the institution of slavery, personal background and place of birth, and notions of manifest destiny." McNelly's exact motivations remain unknown.[7] Some twenty years after the conflict ended, Private William Lott Davidson of Company

Thomas Green. Crayon portrait of albumen photograph. *Courtesy Austin History Center, Austin, Texas.*

A, Fifth Texas Volunteers would put pen to paper and record his military experiences. Speaking with more than a touch of the romantic, he offered a possible explanation:

> this brigade was composed of volunteers from the very flower of the chivalry of Texas and ... when Texas called on them, these men left their

homes, property and loved ones, their wives, children, mothers, [and] sweethearts and went into the ranks of their struggling countrymen to uphold their honor and sustain their cause. No selfish motives actuated them but they enlisted for the war solely for their country's good.[8]

Even after the brigade's organization was complete, the men were allowed to remain idle for six weeks. On November 8, Colonel Green was finally ordered to move his regiment from San Antonio to El Paso; the other two regiments and the brigade headquarters departed by November 18. Anticipating the arid wilderness of the Trans-Pecos, with its scarce water holes and springs, Sibley divided his troops into smaller detachments that marched a day apart. Every company was assigned three six-mule wagons, and the brigade and regimental staffs, quartermaster, and medical corps were each likewise well-supplied with transportation and teams. Despite the abundance of equipment, the march was complicated by lack of water and lax discipline that led to the loss of horses, mules, and cattle. Moreover, much of the seven-hundred-mile journey was spent facing a bitter north wind. Before the column had traveled three-fourths of the distance, the provisions were nearly exhausted, with only poor-quality beef remaining. The unruly soldiers, mainly recruited from frontier counties, also disregarded proper camp sanitation, which contributed to disease and several deaths. Once in El Paso, Sibley "assumed command of all the forces of the Confederate States on the Rio Grande at and above Fort Quitman and all in the Territory of New Mexico and Arizona" on December 14. His new command, known as the "Army of New Mexico," included his Fourth, Fifth, and Seventh Texas Mounted Volunteers, and two batteries of four 12-pound brass howitzers. While Sibley would take over field operations, Colonel Baylor continued in his role as civil and military governor of Arizona Territory.[9]

On January 1, 1862, McNelly was assigned to detached service with Sibley's mounted escort. The duties of this body of soldiers were to act as the general's orderlies, bodyguards, and couriers. According to Confederate Army regulations, "At the opening of a campaign, the commander of an army determines and announces in orders the number of orderlies ... and the corps or regiments by which they are to be supplied, and the periods at which they shall be relieved. In marches, the mounted orderlies follow the Generals, and perform the duty of escorts." Two days later, Sergeant W. J. Bullard was appointed orderly to the general and placed in charge of the couriers, or "expressmen" as the orders termed them. On the fifteenth, McNelly and his comrades paraded before Sibley's headquarters, and the general furnished them a "basket of champagne." After consuming their gift, the men were treated to a speech by First Lieutenant Thomas Peck Ochiltree, the commander's aide-de-camp.[10]

In the first week of January, the army marched up the Rio Grande Valley toward the deserted Fort Thorn. During one rest stop twenty miles from Doña Ana, the escort was vaccinated, although the inoculations proved ineffective. Arriving at their destination on January 21, Sibley incorporated Major Charles Lynn Pyron's four companies of the Second Texas Mounted Rifles and Captain John G. Philip's company of New Mexican volunteers into his forces; Captain Sherod Hunter's independent company was sent to occupy Tucson. Having reached Mesilla, the designated base of operations, on the eleventh, Sibley commenced the invasion of New Mexico on February 7. His brigade, reduced by pneumonia, smallpox, and measles to number approximately 2,600, began marching from Fort Thorn across the *Jornada del Muerto*; Green's regiment was the army's lead element. The march was grueling as cold mountain winds, freezing rains, and snow battered the column. The critical shortage of feed corn and the poor grass along the axis of advance had left the brigade's livestock in poor condition. This setback was compounded by weakened draft animals being able to pull only half the supply wagons, which created a deficiency in food and ammunition. Since the available Confederate commissary stores only consisted of ten days' half-rations of corn meal, flour, and beef, the Texans were compelled to first move on the depot at Fort Craig.[11]

When he learned of Sibley's approach, Canby concentrated his forces at Fort Craig and Fort Union, including five companies of the Fifth Infantry, three each of the Seventh and Tenth Infantry Regiments, two of the First Cavalry, four of the Third Cavalry, one battery of six guns, and another of two. His regular troops were supported by ten companies of the

First New Mexico Volunteers under famed frontiersman Christopher "Kit" Carson, ten companies of the Second New Mexico Volunteers and eight of the Third, three companies from other New Mexico infantry regiments, Captain James "Paddy" Graydon's independent spy company, a company of the Second Colorado Infantry, and approximately one thousand unorganized militia. In all, Canby's forces totaled approximately 3,800 men, of which twelve hundred were regulars.[12]

The Texan brigade went into camp twelve miles south of Fort Craig on February 13. Over the next week, Sibley, or Green when the general was incapacitated, tried repeatedly to entice Canby into a full-scale engagement, but the Union commander refused due to a distrust of his volunteers' mettle. By the early morning of February 21, the Confederates were encamped east of Mesa del Contadero, and Sibley sent Pyron's companies to reconnoiter the Valverde ford, seven miles above the post. While the remainder of the brigade broke camp and followed Pyron to the crossing, the Texan scouts reached the east bank of Valverde and watered their horses in the river. Shortly thereafter, a force of 850 Union cavalrymen appeared several hundred yards downstream. Anticipating an attack, Pyron formed his dismounted troopers in a defensive line among the cottonwood groves near the river. As four companies of the Fourth Mounted Volunteers and two 12-pounders rushed to reinforce Pyron, the Federal troops crossed the river under fire and drove the Confederates back seven hundred yards to some sand embankments. When Lieutenant-Colonel William Read "Dirty Shirt" Scurry arrived, he deployed his regiment to Pyron's right and the cannons to the far left. Reaching the river, Canby pushed his infantry and artillery across to the eastern side. The opposing forces continued to skirmish while reinforcements rushed to the battlefield, including the rest of the Fourth Texas, all but one company of the Fifth, three companies of the Seventh under Lieutenant-Colonel John Schuyler Sutton, and the brigade's remaining four howitzers.[13]

Later that afternoon, an inebriated Sibley turned over command once more to Green. The colonel ordered two consecutive assaults—Captain Willis Lang's lancer charge on the Union far left, and Major Henry Raguet's attack on the enemy's right—that were both repulsed, but they did disrupt the

Union advance. By four p.m., Canby moved to enfilade the Confederate left, but the realignment of his battalions opened a gap of eight hundred yards in his center. Exploiting that hole in the Union line, Scurry led 750 dismounted Texans on the Confederate right in a charge, and seized six unsupported Union cannons in fierce hand-to-hand fighting, the Rebels' shotguns and pistols performing deadly execution. In the resulting confusion, Canby ordered a general retreat across the Rio Grande. The Federals suffered sixty-eight killed, 160 wounded, and thirty-five missing. The Confederates lost thirty-six killed, including Major Lockridge, 150 wounded, and one missing. Company F, McNelly's permanent billet, sustained two killed and six wounded in the battle. The captured field pieces were subsequently used for the newly organized "Valverde Battery" under the command of First Lieutenant Joseph Draper Sayers.[14]

Returning to Fort Craig, Canby blamed his defeat on the supposed incompetence of his volunteers. Sibley realized the post was too strongly defended to be easily taken, so he led his crippled brigade up the Rio Grande and seized Socorro on February 25, Albuquerque on March 2, and Santa Fe on the fourth. Regrettably for the weary Confederates, the Yankees had destroyed what supplies they could not take with them in a withdrawal to Fort Union. Fortunately, provisions were discovered at a Federal depot at Cubero, and a Union supply train of forty wagons was taken at Carnuel Pass. The captured stores were estimated to be adequate for another forty days of campaigning.[15]

By March 1862, Confederate fortunes in New Mexico were deceptively encouraging. When he had reached Albuquerque, Sibley established his headquarters and left his more capable subordinates to prosecute the campaign in the field. Their final objective in the territory was Fort Union, the last obstruction to a Southern offensive into Colorado. Unbeknownst to the Rebel commanders, though, the First Colorado Volunteers from the Pike's Peak mining district was making forced marches through heavy snow to reinforce the threatened post. Additionally, a full brigade under Colonel James Henry Carleton was approaching from Fort Yuma, California. Simultaneously, Lieutenant Ochiltree was named to lead a delegation of dispatch bearers to Richmond. Captain Campbell decided he would accompany the party east and resigned his commission on March 8. At the captain's insistence, Benton Bell Seat was elected the new company commander two days later.[16]

The beginnings of the Confederate defeat in New Mexico were to be found at the southern tip of the Sangre de Cristo range, southeast of Santa Fe. On March 26, Major Pyron's and Major John Samuel Shropshire's five hundred Rebels skirmished with four hundred soldiers of the Colorado advance guard in Apache Canyon. Two days later, Colonel Scurry and seven hundred to one thousand reinforcements united with Pyron's command, then moved down the canyon to its eastern entrance at La Gloriéta Pass. Seven hundred of the "Pike's Peakers" under Colonel John Potts Slough moved to engage the Rebels. The two sides battled feverishly at close quarters for six hours before the Federals withdrew to Kozlowski's Ranch. Four days later, Slough retreated toward Fort Union to protect that post. After Major John Milton Chivington's detachment destroyed sixty Confederate supply wagons containing spare ammunition, rations, forage, medical supplies, and baggage, the Texans were forced to withdraw to Santa Fe. Sibley and Green rapidly advanced from Albuquerque with six companies of the Fifth Texas, and arrived at the territorial capital on April 4. Some provisions were captured from the Yankees, but these were reserved for the wounded.[17]

The destruction of the supply train made Sibley's position untenable and, down to only two thousand effectives, the general began withdrawing his battered and bloodied troops from Santa Fe in preparation for an evacuation of the territory. Although two new regiments were being raised in San Antonio to assist in holding New Mexico, the regulars and volunteers with Canby at Fort Craig, Carleton's Californians then at Tucson, and five thousand Union soldiers preparing to leave Fort Riley, Kansas, were an immediate threat to the outnumbered Texans. Plagued by a shortage of adequate transportation, Sibley also reported an absolute lack of ammunition and supplies, and that nothing could be purchased from Mexico with Confederate currency. While New Mexico remained a crucial military and political goal, the Rebels were faced with either starvation or defeat at the hands of a numerically and logistically superior enemy.[18]

Learning Canby had left Fort Craig for Albuquerque on April 1, Sibley dispatched troops to protect the supplies stored at the depot there. The Union force was before the town by the ninth, and the two armies skirmished for two days before Canby moved off to Tijeras, where he linked up with the Colorado volunteers. On April 12, the Confederates abandoned Santa Fe and Albuquerque and moved down either side of the Rio Grande. Sibley's Texans were able to assemble two wagonloads of Enfield rifles, but they were forced to leave behind several hundred sick and wounded men who were subsequently captured by the Federals. With the chain of command falling into anarchy, the Rebels exhibited inadequate march and camp discipline, and the column spread out for miles. On the fifteenth, Canby attacked Green at Peralta, but the Texan, aided by Scurry's reinforcements, utilized the terrain to evacuate the village with few losses. That same night, Sibley crossed the river at Los Lunas, and the entire army marched downstream for two days, parallel to Canby's force on the opposite bank. On the night of the seventeenth, Sibley avoided Fort Craig by recrossing the Rio Grande, passing the Magadalena Mountains, and escaping into the rugged San Mateo range. The Confederates reached the river on April 25, thirty miles below the Yankee post. In the last week of the month, they rambled southward past Fort Thorn and Mesilla.[19]

On April 30, McNelly's assignment to Sibley's escort ended, and he returned to the ranks of the Fifth Texas. By this time, less than eighteen hundred men of the tattered Army of New Mexico remained, and most of them were scattered along the Rio Grande. The Rebels were fatigued, malnourished, and ravaged by disease. Discipline had dwindled and morale plummeted. Their excess baggage and equipment had been abandoned or destroyed, while sixty to seventy horses and mules died in the arduous retreat. However, they refused to forsake the guns of the Valverde Battery, which were viewed as symbols of their service and sacrifices in New Mexico. One week after leaving the mountains, the Texans straggled into camps near Fort Bliss in order to rest and refit. By June 17, the Fourth and Fifth Texas Regiments of the Sibley Brigade departed El Paso and were en route to San Antonio across the scorching Chihuahua desert of West Texas. Four hundred soldiers of the Seventh Texas remained behind at Doña Ana.[20]

A woman known simply as Mollie had ridden the Overland stage east from El Paso, and passed the Fourth Texas on the road. She later wrote to the *San Antonio Herald*:

> The men were suffering terribly from the effects of heat; very many of them are a-foot, and scarcely able to travel from blistered feet. They were subsisting on bread and water, both officers and men; many of them were sick, many ragged, and all hungry; but we did not see a gloomy face—not one! They were all cheerful, for their faces were turned homewards.[21]

Carleton's "California Column" reached Fort Thorn on July 4, and the last remaining Confederate troops evacuated New Mexico four days later. Elements of the once proud brigade staggered into San Antonio from mid-July through late August. Having once mustered ninety-six soldiers, Company F numbered only forty men by this point in time.[22]

Sibley was recalled to Richmond to face charges of drunkenness and cowardice, while James Riley of the Fourth Texas, the senior colonel, took over the brigade. Members of that regiment assembled at Cypress City, and those of the Fifth and Seventh Texas rendezvoused at Hempstead. The dearth of provisions continued to plague the Texans, and many of the new recruits remained untrained. The three regiments were reorganized into a new brigade on October 28. The soldiers were given a sixty-day furlough, which was extended through December due to a lack of supplies and arms.[23]

Anticipating imminent action, the regiments underwent increased discipline and drill as they bivouacked along the Galveston, Houston & Henderson Railroad. Major-General John Bankhead "Prince John" Magruder was planning a joint land and naval campaign to retake Galveston, which had been captured the previous October. Captain Leon Smith of the Confederate Navy was placed in command of a flotilla of four steamships that had been refitted as "cottonclad" rams. William Scurry, promoted to brigadier-general on September 26, was to lead the land forces with Magruder commanding the entire expedition.[24]

On the early morning of December 25, the brigade entrained to Harrisburg where they sat idle for five days. Tiring of the delay, Colonels Green and

Arthur Pendleton Bagby, the latter commanding the Seventh Texas, went to Magruder in Houston and volunteered their troops to act as sharpshooters aboard the steamships. Magruder, after some brief reluctance, agreed, and the two colonels quickly returned to Harrisburg to gather their men. Meanwhile, the Fourth Texas had already boarded the train for Virginia Point. Informing Colonel Riley of the change in orders, Green and Bagby gathered the prospective volunteers. The response to the mission was so enthusiastic that every captain had to choose just fifteen men from their companies. McNelly was among those chosen for the special mission, while the remainder marched to join the Fourth Texas.[25]

Provided by the First Texas Heavy Artillery, one 32-pound rifled gun was mounted on the *Bayou City*, and two 24-pound howitzers were put aboard the *Neptune*. Green's dismounted cavalry boarded the first steamer, and Bagby's the second. The *John F. Carr*, *Lucy Gwinn*, and *Royal Yacht* were placed in supporting roles. Scurry, his remaining cavalry, the Twentieth Texas Infantry, the Twenty-first Texas Infantry Battalion, detachments of the Twenty-sixth Texas Cavalry under Colonel Xavier Blanchard Debray, and the Second Texas Cavalry, supported by six siege pieces, a railroad ram mounted on a flat car with an eight-inch Dahlgren gun, and fourteen smoothbore and rifled cannons, were to cross the railroad bridge from Virginia Point to the island and take Kuhn's Wharf and the Strand. Opposing the Confederate expedition in the harbor were six Union gunboats—the *Westfield*, the *Clifton*, the *Harriet Lane*, the *Owasco*, the *Sachem*, and the *Corypheus*—mounting a total of thirty heavy cannons. Three companies of the newly arrived Forty-second Massachusetts Infantry occupied the wharf and the town.[26]

The Texan soldiers entered Galveston shortly after midnight on New Year's Day, 1863, positioned twenty-two cannons on the corners of Twentieth and Twenty-first Streets, and opened fire at four a.m. The Massachusetts soldiers on Kuhn's Wharf at the north end of Eighteenth Street stayed behind their barricades. Meanwhile, broadsides of shot and shell from the *Sachem*, *Corypheus*, and *Owasco* slashed into the Confederate infantry and forced them to take cover. Rebel shore batteries near the wharf and on the west end of the Strand were likewise driven back. Steaming out of the morning fog, Commodore Smith's cottonclads smashed into the rear of the Union squadron.

Federal naval fire sank the *Neptune* after she rammed the *Harriet Lane*, but Green's "horse-marines" and the gunners on the *Bayou City* boarded the Union vessel despite significant damage to their own riverboat. After desperate hand-to-hand fighting that killed or wounded every Union officer onboard, the Confederates captured the craft. The *Owasco* steamed in close to both ships and poured in a barrage with its eleven-inch guns before a volley of Rebel rifle and shotgun fire swept her deck. The Yankee flagship, the *Westfield*, ran hard aground on Pelican Spit, and Commander William Bainbridge Renshaw, the fleet commander, ordered her scuttled rather than surrender her; Renshaw and twelve crewmen were accidentally killed in the explosion. Once news of Renshaw's demise reached the Union fleet, the surviving ships put to sea, despite having raised the white flag of surrender.[27]

While McNelly was a member of the boarding party, he did not lead the seizure of the *Harriet Lane*, although some would incorrectly give him that honor years later. According to his great-nephew, Charles B. McNelly: "Lee McNelly was the first Confederate Officer to board the Union Flagship, 'Harriet Lane' and accept its surrender in Galveston waters on January 2 [*sic*], 1863." James Harvey McLeary, a member of Sibley's brigade, positively identified Sergeant James Carson of Company A, Fifth Texas as the first man aboard the vessel, "followed closely by Captain Leon Smith and others." Other sources point to Captain Smith and General Green as being the first to capture the *Harriet Lane* with the other men close behind.[28]

In six hours, Magruder had retaken Galveston with a butcher's bill of twenty-six killed and 117 wounded. The casualties of the Sibley Brigade totaled seventeen killed and twenty-eight injured. Union losses included 51 sailors dead, wounded, and missing, as well as Colonel Isaac S. Burrell and 258 men of the Forty-second Massachusetts who surrendered. Magruder, Green, Smith, and the rest of the expedition would receive the Thanks of Congress for their exploits. Although the Yankee blockade persisted, the port continued under Confederate control for the remainder of the war.[29]

McNelly and his comrades had a fortnight to enjoy their victory before they would be called upon again. On January 16, Riley's brigade was ordered to Hempstead and, four days later, was directed to join Major-General Richard Taylor's forces at Opelousas, Louisiana. The general planned to use the Texans along Bayou Teche and Bayou Lafourche to distract Federal forces from investing Port Hudson. On February 18, they were instructed to march to Cheneyville. At New Iberia, they were reunited with Sibley, who had been cleared of the charges against him.[30]

By March 1863, Taylor, commanding the District of Western Louisiana, was facing a Federal land and naval assault of overwhelming numbers. In turn, his small army was composed of only two brigades, one of sturdy Louisianans commanded by Brigadier-General Jean Jacques Alfred Alexandre Mouton, and the other Sibley's Texans. The latter had arrived at Berwick Bay on April 7, still hurting from their campaign in New Mexico. Although the troops possessed a large number of horses, additional soldiers had to be recruited to fill the depleted ranks. At least half the Texans held a serviceable firearm, while the rest owned weapons of an insufficient nature. Taylor would perceive a noticeable absence of discipline within the brigade. In addition, he suffered from a lack of watercraft and sufficient heavy artillery to defend the interconnecting network of rivers and bayous. Thus, the Union held the strategic initiative, and Taylor could only fortify his position at Camp Bisland and wait. The existing defenses were improved and expanded to include additional earthen or wooden strongpoints.[31]

Major-General Nathaniel Prentice Banks planned to concentrate sixteen thousand men at Brashear City on Berwick Bay, then advance up Bayou Teche as far as Alexandria, crush Taylor's army, and remove the threat to the Federal communication lines. With his right flank secured by the *Clifton*, Banks pressed forward on April 11 and skirmished with Confederate cavalry pickets between Pattersonville and Centerville. The Texans were pushed back repeatedly by the fire from the Federal gunboat, but continued to impede the Union advance. At the end of the day, Sibley's brigade was forced to withdraw, as the Yankees occupied Pattersonville, five miles from the Confederate line.[32]

The following day, Banks ordered eight thousand troops to march across the cane fields against the Rebel line at Bisland. Taylor had deployed his six hundred Texans and their twelve guns along the west bank of the Teche, and the six hundred Louisianan infantrymen and six guns on the east side. The Confederate gunboat *Diana* provided riverine fire support.

Company F was positioned to the right of a battery of six 12-pounders, which was in continual action throughout the day. During the hard fighting, the Confederates were steadily pushed back until they were forced behind their works. The furious exchange of artillery fire allowed the Federals to determine the size and location of the Rebel guns. As evening fell, Banks moved his forces back as he received word his reinforcements were steaming up the Atchafalaya. Taylor learned of the approaching Federal flotilla, and deployed cavalry and two 6-pound guns to oppose any troop landings. The general also ordered Sibley to undertake a surprise dawn attack on the Union left. As the sun rose on April 13, though, the Texan horsemen remained in place as Sibley made no effort to follow his orders, effectively ceding the tactical advantage to the enemy. Enraged at Sibley's failure, Taylor had to reorder his dispositions. The Fifth Texas Cavalry, under the aggressive Colonel Green, was assigned to secure the right flank and defend the coastal swamp.[33]

By seven a.m., Confederate pickets began reconnoitering the enemy lines, then a reinforced skirmish line of the Eighteenth and Twenty-fourth Louisiana and Seventh Texas moved five hundred yards forward of their works. After a half-hour, the skirmishers were pushed back and, once the fog lifted, the Federals renewed the attack. Artillery fired furiously on both sides while the Union troops struggled through the fields. The *Diana* was struck in the superstructure by a thirty-pound Yankee shell, which exploded in the engine room. The gunboat moved out of cannon range in order to effect repairs. By early afternoon, the Federal columns closed to within rifle range of the Southern works. The Union troops then deployed into lines of attack and pushed the Rebels back. Sibley's Texans were securing each flank of the Confederate position. On the right, the Fifth Texas was locked in combat with two New York regiments, and drove them back across rows of sugar cane. The Union attack failed to break the Confederate line, and the Federals withdrew to engage the Rebels in an artillery duel that lasted until nightfall. Taylor learned the Union flotilla had landed ashore on Grand Lake and eight thousand enemy troops were now in his rear. The Yankees were marching on Franklin, threatening the general's line of retreat. As the sun set, in danger of being surrounded, Taylor began making plans to evacuate Bisland. Sibley was relegated to supervising the supply train.[34]

While details were destroying bridges, Confederate cavalry fought delaying actions, and Taylor executed a skillful withdrawal through a heavy rainstorm. The Fifth Texas was placed at the end of the column as rearguard. The pursuing Federal troops failed to seize the road that was the Rebel line of retreat, instead taking one that ran parallel. Once he realized the Union failure, Taylor ordered a holding action at Irish Bend on April 14. Green also stubbornly impeded the Federals at Centerville, Jeanerette on the fifteenth, New Iberia the next day, and Vermilion Bayou on the seventeenth. In one instance, McNelly and other troopers of Company F ambushed their pursuers two miles above New Iberia. The Texans dismounted in the trees along the north side of the curving, sunken road and waited for the Yankee cavalry. "We had just taken our position when here they came, in full tilt, with banners flying," Captain Seat wrote. "As they came to the corner I gave the order to fire." With several of their number dead on the ground from the unexpected volley, the shocked Union soldiers retreated down the road. Rather than pursue the broken enemy, Seat led his men in mounting and racing past Green's next position. The rearguard actions of Green's regiment allowed the Confederate evacuation to reach safety. The Texas horsemen were then sent to pasture near the Sabine.[35]

Disgusted with Sibley's failure to attack at Camp Bisland, Taylor was further angered when the latter continued to neglect his duties during the retreat. Taylor preferred charges against Sibley and, although the court-martial later acquitted him, the disgraced general was never offered another assignment. On May 20, Green received promotion to brigadier-general for his valiant leadership and the permanent command of the brigade.[36]

Banks's army continued its advance along Bayou Teche, and marched into Alexandria on May 8, while the outnumbered Taylor was retreated to Natchitoches. On the thirteenth, Banks abandoned his recent conquest in order to besiege Port Hudson. Taylor reoccupied Alexandria, and instructed Mouton, Green, and James Patrick Major to return to the Teche country. With Banks engaged at Port Hudson, Taylor was determined to retake the Lafourche region, then New Orleans.[37]

On June 19, Taylor sent Major's brigade across the Atchafalaya, down the west bank of the Mississippi to Donaldsonville, then to Bayou Lafourche and Bayou Boeuf east of Brashear City. Major's orders were to cut off the enemy's line of retreat from Brashear City, while the balance of the army attacked the town. Taylor positioned his brigades under Green and Mouton on the lower Teche near Berwick Bay, while 325 volunteers under Major Sherod Hunter started across Grand Lake at six p.m. on the twenty-second to "turn the enemy's stronghold at Brashear City." In position at dawn on the twenty-third, the Valverde Battery commenced a fierce bombardment of the Yankees on the other side of Berwick Bay. Federal gunners in the defensive works around the town returned a desultory fire. After becoming lost in the swamps, Hunter's party reached their destination and charged the enemy positions on either side of the railroad depot. Once Green and Mouton crossed the bay, they found Hunter had taken nearly seventeen hundred prisoners. Earlier that same day, Major's brigade had gone west to Bayou Boeuf and reached the railroad bridge there, where they could cut off the retreat of the Federals entrenched on the west bank. By this time, McNelly had been promoted to captain and volunteer aide-de-camp on Green's personal staff. That evening the general sent him and a party of men to Bayou Boeuf. The "intrepid scout" arrived around midnight and met with the Yankee commander at daybreak on June 24. Accepting that further resistance would be futile, the Union colonel surrendered his sword and the 435 officers and men of his command later that morning.[38]

Receiving orders from General Mouton on June 26, General Green took his and Major's brigade to capture Fort Butler, a Federal stronghold established at Donaldsonville on the junction of Bayou Lafourche and the Mississippi River. Arriving on the twenty-seventh, Green prepared his dismounted Texans to storm the redoubt late that night. Starting at two a.m. on June 28, the Rebels breached the entrenchments, but the assault stalled under a storm of musketry and thrown bricks. Salvos fired by a Federal gunboat finally pushed the attackers back. Green noted in his report that McNelly rendered "good service" in the assault and performed with predictable "coolness and courage." More setbacks spelled disaster for the Southern Cause as Taylor received word on July 10 that Port Hudson and Vicksburg had each fallen. With these losses, the Mississippi River was now completely under Union control, and the Confederacy was split in two.[39]

The reduction of Port Hudson released Banks's army to continue field operations, and Taylor was forced to abandon the Lafourche campaign. On July 13, while the Confederates were evacuating, Green's and Major's fourteen hundred cavalrymen ambushed a Federal force at Cox's Plantation. The approximately six thousand bluecoats had been marching south from Donaldsonville along Lafourche Bayou. Badly mauled, the Federals fell back to their starting point. On July 21, Taylor marched his forces up Bayou Teche toward Vermilionville, and the Yankees reoccupied Brashear City and Berwick Bay the next day.[40]

After the failed attempt to capture Sabine Pass, Banks concentrated his forces near Camp Bisland on the lower Teche in preparation for another offensive into Texas. Due to his inferior numbers, Taylor was reluctant to bring on a general engagement and risk defeat. Instead he contented himself with hit-and-run attacks on smaller forces detached from Banks's main body, and beyond the prompt reach of the Union army. The Federals marched to take the Confederates near Washington in the rear, but were repulsed by Green on September 7 at Morgan's Ferry on the Atchafalaya River. The Yankees retreated to an area between Morganza and Fordoche, made camp, and worked to ready themselves for another attempt. On September 12, McNelly and another scout captured three Union soldiers of the XIII Corps within four hundred yards of their camps at Morganza.[41]

After waiting three weeks for the Billy Yanks to move, Tom Green, now commanding a cavalry division comprised of his old brigade led by Colonel Bagby and Major's brigade, conducted a reconnaissance to determine the enemy's strength. Green's cavalry and a portion of Colonel Joseph Warren Speight's infantry crossed the Atchafalaya at Morgan's Ferry on September 29, and routed the enemy at Stirling's Plantation. Major Hannibal Honestus Boone and McNelly led the charge through a shower of Minié balls that wounded Boone and killed Lieutenant William F. Spivey of the Thirteenth Texas Volunteers. The Rebels captured 450 Yankees, two 10-pound Parrott guns, and two stands of colors. Following another defeat at Bayou Bourbeau, the Federals retired to New Iberia.[42]

McNelly's continued gallantry in action won him the esteem of his superiors. Upon the recommendation of General Green, he was authorized by Lieutenant-General Edmund Kirby Smith, on January 21, 1864, to raise a company of scouts. Once he completed organizing his new command, McNelly was to be attached to Bagby's brigade headquarters. In his endorsement, Green observed McNelly "displayed more ability, greater activity, and more daring than any officer of [his] command as a scout." The captain spent several months recruiting for his company in Brenham and Galveston, and mustered three officers, nine non-commissioned officers, and sixty privates into service on February 1. They were posted to La Grange that same month.[43]

Meanwhile, fearing General Banks was mounting an overland invasion of Texas, Magruder urgently requested General Green and his hard-fighting division be transferred to the Lone Star State. Beginning on December 14, the eight Texan regiments marched by way of Niblett's Bluff to Houston and Virginia Point, where they bivouacked and prepared defenses for a month. In the meantime, Green was nominated for the rank of major-general on February 14, 1864. The anticipated attack had not materialized by the middle of February, instead having taken place on the Rio Grande. Colonel John S. Ford was tasked with repelling the invaders. Green's troops were sorely needed in Louisiana, so, on March 5, they were ordered to retrace their steps to General Taylor's army.[44]

After conducting a scout in the Simsport area, McNelly rode to Marksville on March 12, and reported to Major-General John George Walker the presence of six gunboats and two transports landing at the former place. On Carroll Jones's plantation, Taylor established a depot at the junction of the roads leading to Burr's Ferry and Natchitoches, approximately thirty miles north of Alexandria. Desperately in need of more cavalry, Taylor ordered Green's horsemen to meet him at Beasley's Plantation. The Fifth Texas, numbering 250 men under Lieutenant-Colonel McNeill, arrived on the thirtieth. The Seventh Texas, with 350 troopers, followed the next day. By March 23, Green's division numbered 2,500 men. Bagby and Green both reached Pleasant Hill on April 1.[45]

Green was appointed to lead the newly organized cavalry corps comprised of the assembling Rebel horsemen. Major succeeded him as division commander, while Brigadier-General Hamilton Prioleau Bee was to command the second division; both were ordered to screen the Rebel army gathering toward Mansfield. Bagby's brigade—the Fourth, Fifth, and Seventh Texas Cavalry Regiments, and the Thirteenth Texas Cavalry Battalion—remained in Major's division.[46] Taylor's infantry consisted of Walker's Texas Division and Mouton's two brigades of Louisianans and Texans. In total, at this time, Taylor commanded nine thousand men of all arms. Major-General Thomas James Churchill's Arkansawyers and Brigadier-General Mosby Monroe Parsons's Missourians, totaling 4,400 strong, were soon ordered from Keatchie to Mansfield, arriving on the night of the eighth.[47]

Assembling at Berwick Bay, the Federal army numbered two divisions of the XVI Corps, one of the XVII Corps, two divisions each of the XIX and XIII Corps, one cavalry division, four regiments of black troops, and thirteen artillery batteries. Their axis of advance was along the Teche through Opelousas to Alexandria; the last elements arrived on March 25. As Kirby Smith advised President Davis, "The only true line of operations by which the enemy can penetrate the department is the valley of Red River, rich in supplies; with steam-boat navigation for six months in the year, it offers facilities for the co-operation of the army and navy, and enables them to shift their base as they advance into the interior."[48]

Returning to Bagby's brigade with his new recruits, McNelly was on hand when Taylor made his stand at Mansfield on April 8. After the battle was joined at four p.m., Mouton ordered his Louisianans and Texans on the left flank to charge the enemy. Securing the Creole general's extreme left was Major's dismounted cavalry division. Mouton was killed while his men were assaulting Honeycutt Hill, and his men showed signs of weakening under the Union fire. Green mounted his troopers and rode to assist their flagging comrades. Mouton's infantrymen were reinvigorated and both bodies of soldiers charged the Federals who had taken cover behind a rail fence. The Yankees were driven back three miles where they made a brief stand before fleeing once more. McNelly was seriously wounded in the day's fighting, and command of the scouts passed to Lieutenants William D. Stone and Thomas T. Pitts. Under their leadership, the company did "noble duty" at Pleasant Hill the next day. While McNelly was recovering, Green was killed by a shell at Blair's Landing on April 12, and General Bee assumed command of the cavalry corps for a few days. He was soon replaced by Major-General John Austin Wharton.[49]

On the twenty-second, Banks evacuated Grand Ecore and marched south through Natchitoches to Alexandria. Taylor dispatched Bee to the Cane River, forty-five miles to the south, to cut off the Federals' retreat. When Bee reached Monett's Ferry on April 23, he placed his men in a strong hilltop position that protected his flanks. The Union vanguard, commanded by Brigadier-General William Hemsley Emory, feinted on Bee's right flank, while several regiments forded the river and attacked the Rebels' left. McNelly's scouts informed Bee of the enemy's crossing, but the outnumbered Bee was forced to withdraw. The company remained constantly in the saddle during the entire Federal retreat, which ended in the battle of Yellow Bayou. McNelly rejoined his command several days after the May 18 action.[50]

On June 4, while reconnoitering the west side of False River with fifty to sixty scouts, McNelly was attacked by three hundred Union cavalry troopers under Lieutenant-Colonel John Montgomery Crebs. Four of McNelly's men were killed or wounded and seven were taken prisoner, including one lieutenant. The Federals lost one killed and two wounded. On July 6, McNelly was ordered to take a detachment of scouts and cross the Atchafalaya and gather intelligence on the Federals' movements. Riding into the Lafourche country, they "betook themselves to the swamps and canebrakes, where they confined their operation until the enemy commenced their retreat, when his men were again assembled and once more were at work on their rear."[51]

In the closing months of the war, the captain and his company of scouts were assigned the mission of "hunting up jayhawkers on the Calcasieu." These lawless men—draft dodgers, deserters, common brigands, and escaped slaves—infested the thick oak groves and dense pine forests and preyed equally on Union and Confederate soldiers, as well as innocent civilians. Shortly thereafter, the Texans were attached to General John Walker's cavalry corps. When Walker's command was relocated to Hempstead, Texas, McNelly, three other officers, and seventy-eight men were likewise transferred. On April 26, 1865, he was ordered to take his company to Washington County and scout for deserters there and in adjacent counties. He camped on Mill Creek and, according to naturalist Gideon Lincecum, "stirred up the lag-behinds and the disloyal rascals fearfully." On May 23, in addition to his other duties, he was directed by Walker to take charge of railroad trains in Washington County.[52] Five days later, General James Major wrote a testimonial that extolled McNelly as an officer who "remained true to his colors to the very last and by his determination and other soldierly qualities retained his company intact when those around disbanded." The general went on to describe the captain as a "true soldier" and paid tribute to his "gallant and meritorious conduct" and "daring courage and consummate skill."[53]

Apparently paroled sometime that same month, McNelly returned to farming and worked eight hundred acres near Brenham that had once belonged to Richard Thomas Matson; among his holdings were two horses and 125 head of cattle. He married Matson's step-daughter, Carey Cheek Matson, on October 16, 1865. McNelly's new bride had been born on June 24, 1848, and was the daughter of the late John Cheek and Sarah A. (Hall) Cheek Matson. Following Matson's death at the battle of Pine Bluff, Arkansas, and the death of her mother on January 1, 1865, Carey had inherited a portion of the estate, including the farmhouse and the surrounding eleven hundred acres on Mill Creek. McNelly and Carey soon brought two children into the world: Leander Rebel, born on July 26, 1866, and Irene Mary, on April 29, 1868.[54]

Crime ran rampant in Texas in the years following the "War of the Rebellion." In July 1865, a military presence was established in Brenham, and Federal troops were bivouacked at neighboring Camptown. The local citizenry and their occupiers clashed on September 7, 1866, and one Union soldier was killed and two were wounded; a number of buildings were burned in retaliation. Throughout the eastern counties, extensive violence was directed at emancipated freedmen by embittered, likely racist, whites and, surprisingly, other former slaves. Other acts of aggression were perpetuated by Unionists and Secessionists refighting the war, as well as those who made their living through robbery and murder. Professor James M. Smallwood observed: "Reconstruction really amounted to a Second Civil War, one that pitted whites who had supported [the] Confederacy against loyal white Union men, the freedmen, and the Northern forces who occupied Texas." Statistics commonly accepted at the Constitutional Convention of 1868 indicated 939 homicides occurred between May 1865 and June 1868. Four hundred and sixty of these murders were perpetrated by whites against whites, 373 by whites against blacks, fifty-eight by blacks against other blacks, and ten by blacks against whites. The total figure was later increased in a supplementary report to 1,035. In the four years following the war, a mere 279 indictments were handed down, which resulted in only five convictions. Much of the trouble in general was blamed on rootless men and women who emigrated to Texas after the war. Noticing a certain trend, lawmakers passed prohibitions on the public consumption of alcohol, gambling, and the carrying of firearms in areas other than the frontier counties. Some locales were overrun with outlaws who were organized well enough to openly defy law officers. In these and other places, authorities were unable to execute civil process. Furthermore, the large numbers of men who had not taken the amnesty oath meant that jury pools were often too small to hold trials. Secretary of State James Pearson Newcomb reported to the state senate on June 18, 1870, that approximately 590 murders had been committed between January 1869 and March 20, 1870.[55]

With local lawmen unable to bring criminals to justice, county officials requested military assistance. Brevet Major-General Joseph Jones Reynolds, commanding general in Texas, reported to the War Department:

> For the suppression of bands of desperadoes, which have infested nearly every part of the State, and the arrest of parties indicted for murder, it has been necessary to furnish military aid to civil officers. These parties have usually met with armed resistance, and in the encounters which ensued several persons have been killed. With very few exceptions indictments had been found against these persons, and in every case they invited their fate by refusing arrest, and in resisting by force of arms the legally constituted authorities of this State and of the United States.[56]

On May 10, 1870, "An Act to establish a State Police, and provide for the regulation and government of the same" was introduced in the state senate. The bill was hotly debated in both houses, and finally enacted in late June; the governor signed the measure into law on July 1. Formed under the auspices of Adjutant General James Davidson, the State Police's authorized personnel included four captains, eight lieutenants, twenty sergeants, and 125 privates. Appointed to four-year terms, the captains were to receive a wage of $125 per month. Moreover, every local law officer was enrolled as an auxiliary member and fell under the authority of the adjutant general.[57]

Opponents to the legislation believed law enforcement should remain under the purview of local authorities. They feared the accumulation of excessive powers, as well, in the hands of the governor and other state officials. Indeed, the law granted state policemen the ability to search private dwellings and arrest persons without the benefit of a warrant, and seize an offender in one part of Texas and transport him to another for trial in complete defiance of the state constitution. This extralegal authority, coupled with the fact that the ordinary citizens of Texas had not approved of the establishment of the police force, but instead had it imposed upon them, would cause a great deal of resentment.[58]

By this time, McNelly's farm encompassed 966 acres, and he was running a herd of six horses and seventy-five head of cattle. The total value of McNelly's real and personal property was assessed at $10,700.[59] Despite his commercial achievements, McNelly accepted a commission of captain in the State Police on July 12, and was assigned to command the Third Police District on the twenty-fifth. McNelly's bailiwick encompassed Limestone, Freestone, Anderson, Cherokee, Nacogdoches, Shelby, Robertson, Leon, Houston, Angelina, San Augustine, Sabine, Madison, Trinity, Newton, Jasper, Tyler, Polk, Walker, Brazos, Grimes, Montgomery, Liberty, Hardin, Orange, Harris, Chambers, Jefferson, Fort Bend, Brazoria, and Galveston Counties.[60]

While McNelly was arranging to take on his new role, John Wesley Hardin, soon to become infamous as Texas's deadliest *pistolero*, was hiding out at his uncle's farm near Brenham. Even with the blood of six or seven men on his hands by that time, Hardin respected the new captain enough to intentionally avoid him. Years later, the outlaw commented: "The State Police had been organized and McAnelly [*sic*] had been placed on the force, so on consultation with friends, it was thought best I should leave Brenham."[61]

Although he had earned a reputation that would give even a prolific man-killer pause, McNelly was taking on an intimidating challenge. Out of 137 counties, 108 reported some 2,790 wanted fugitives were at large during the summer of 1870. Seven hundred and two were charged with murder, 413 with assault with intent to kill, and 1,137 with various other felonies. Nevertheless, the captain quickly set to work. Mat Banks, a convicted horse thief, and Randall Lightfoot and Charles Hine, both incarcerated for theft and attempted murder, had escaped from the Travis County jail in early 1869. They remained at large until McNelly was ordered to find the fugitives and take them into custody. The captain, doubtless with a posse, cornered the three outlaws near Sand Fly in northern Bastrop County on July 23, 1870. Hine resisted arrest and was shot dead; the other two wisely surrendered.[62]

Edward "Ed" Pierce (or Pearce) was another dangerous bandit, one who was reputed to have killed several men, both black and white, in Grimes and Anderson Counties. As the *Houston Daily Union* opined of the notorious outlaw: "Pierce and his gang must be taken." Pierce was charged with murdering a man in Grimes County on July 24, 1869. The governor offered a reward of five hundred dollars for the apprehension and delivery of the killer to the Grimes County sheriff. On September 8, 1870, McNelly and a squad of state policemen went to the Bush plantation on Cedar Bayou, where Pierce's gang was reported to be hiding. Entering the cedar thicket, McNelly and his men surprised the fugitives and succeeded in capturing two, but Pierce was able to escape. He remained at large until he was finally captured by Judge Edwin Waller in Hempstead on May 24, 1872. The accused was tried in Anderson on October 16, and the jury deliberated for only ten minutes before acquitting him. Ironically, McNelly's old comrade-in-arms, H. H. Boone, defended Pierce in court.[63]

While McNelly and a number of his fellow policemen were performing valuable service to the citizens of Texas, others were perpetrating acts that would ensure the force was reviled as a whole. Perhaps chief among the latter was Captain John Jackson Marshal "Jack" Helm, who led the posse that killed brothers William and Henry Kelly, sons-in-law of Pitkin Barnes Taylor, while they were "attempting to escape." Prior to his appointment, Helm, as deputy sheriff of Lavaca County and sheriff of DeWitt County, had been authorized by General Reynolds to make war upon members and associates of the Taylor family, who were branded in official reports as "horse thieves or desperadoes." He engaged in this reign of terror alongside Captain Charles S. Bell, a "special officer." Helm was dismissed from the State Police in the aftermath of the Kelly murders, and later became a leader of the Sutton party in DeWitt County. He was killed by James Creed "Jim" Taylor and John Wesley Hardin on July 18, 1873, in Albuquerque, Gonzales County. The ex-captain's murder did not halt the violence in DeWitt, and McNelly would soon be drawn into the bloody events occurring there.[64]

In the first days of December, General Davidson ordered the State Police to close the "gambling hells" in each district, arrest the gamblers, and turn them over to local authorities for trial. Obeying theses instructions, McNelly and Captain George Washington Farrow were dispatched to Robertson, Limestone, Galveston, and Harris Counties. In his year-end report for 1870, Davidson declared to the governor: "The effect of this action is already beneficially felt, and receives the sanction and hearty co-operation of all good citizens in the State."[65]

On December 5, 1870, Sam Jenkins, a sixty-eight-year-old freedman, was murdered in Huntsville. He had recently testified before a Walker County grand jury that he had been flogged by four white men. McNelly traveled to the scene of the crime with a squad of policemen to investigate the slaying. He quickly accumulated sufficient evidence to arrest four men—Nathaniel A. Outlaw, John Wright, Fred Parks, and John McKinley Parish—on January 6, and bring them before Judge James Russell Burnett of the Thirtieth Judicial District for a preliminary hearing. Beginning on the eleventh, the well-attended proceedings in Huntsville lasted for three days, and resulted in Parks being acquitted, and the others being bound over for trial at the next district court term. McNelly was instructed to return the three perpetrators to the sheriff's custody in the interim.[66]

Outlaw, Wright, and Parish had obtained pistols from friends at some point prior to the end of the hearing and concealed them on their persons. Strictly as a precaution, McNelly and policeman Tom Keese started to search the three men before escorting them from the courtroom. The captain had just finished disarming Outlaw when the other two prisoners produced their weapons and opened up on the two officers. Even though a bullet to the thigh knocked him down, McNelly was able to return fire and hit Wright in the arm. Parish shot Keese in the face and neck, but the injured policeman's own round struck him in the hand. The unarmed Outlaw wisely threw himself to the floor and stayed there until the shooting stopped. However, his fellow prisoners escaped into the street and out of town with the aid of their armed associates. Altogether an estimated thirty shots were fired in the space of seconds.[67]

Governor Davis declared martial law in Walker County on February 15, the order being dated as January 20, and General Davidson convened military tribunals for approximately twenty persons twelve days later. Most of the defendants were charged with aiding and abetting the escape of Wright and Parish, or failing to assist in their capture, and a number were fined. Once he recovered from his wound, McNelly set out after the two fugitives, but they escaped justice. Outlaw would receive five years' imprisonment for his role in Jenkins's murder, but the governor pardoned him on March 11. Martial law was lifted nine days later.[68]

By the end of 1870, 978 persons had been arrested—109 of them for murder, 130 for assault with intent, and 394 for additional offenses. Stolen property worth nearly thirty thousand dollars was returned to rightful owners. Seven people had been killed and two wounded while violently resisting arrest, and three killed as they attempted escape. The police force was reorganized on May 2, 1871, to comprise eight captains, twelve lieutenants, thirty sergeants, and 210 privates. The officers were entitled to receive an additional thirty dollars per month for the use of their horses and arms. Three days later, McNelly was transferred and placed in command of the restructured Fourth Police District. His new jurisdiction encompassed Brown, Comanche, San Saba, Lampasas, Hamilton, Coryell, Hays, Travis, Williamson, Bell, Falls, McLennan, Limestone, Freestone, Leon, Robertson, Milam, Brazos, Burleson, Bastrop, Fayette, and Washington Counties.[69]

In the summer of 1872, McNelly encountered an event that would be seen time and again in the history of the Texas Rangers: the labor strike. On or around June 1, the Houston & Texas Central Railroad issued a new wage increase to its workers that came with stipulations. In return for the higher pay, employees were to sign an agreement that stated that, as a condition of employment, the company would no longer be held liable for any injuries suffered on the job. The contract was accepted by only a few, while the remaining work force refused, calling the document a "Death Warrant." Employees hurriedly met on June 4, reiterated their pledge to not sign the agreement, and called for a walk-out. The next day, the strike began in earnest when two trains, one en route to Houston and the other to Hempstead, were stopped. All the passenger cars were moved to sidings, and only the engines and the mail cars were allowed to continue. Some additional engines were disabled, but the strikers were careful to avoid any property damage, the use of violence, or breaking any federal laws regarding the U.S. mails. All the same, the presence of McNelly and a detachment of state policemen might well have encouraged railroad employees to practice peaceful protests. In the end, nearly half the labor force was fired and replaced by new workers, but management withdrew the Death Warrant after demonstrating they would not simply capitulate to employee demands.[70]

Since the end of the war, Anglo and *tejano* ranchers in South Texas had been plagued by cattle rustling raids emanating from Mexico. Likewise, Tamaulipas suffered from savage depredations as bands of armed ruffians swept through *ranchos*, robbing and murdering at will. Beginning in 1871, many of these outrages were carried out at the behest of Juan Nepomuceno "Cheno" Cortina. Levi English, Sr., a prominent and influential Dimmit County cattleman, convinced the governor to send a force to South Texas to halt cattle rustling, and protect English's property and that of his neighboring ranchers. Assigned to command the campaign, McNelly was ordered to scout from Brownsville to Eagle Pass "for the purpose of arresting criminals and breaking up the cattle and horse stealing prevalent in that locality." The Rio Grande Expedition proved short-lived, and McNelly returned to Burton within one month. The captain's full report on the expedition, dated July 25, has disappeared and only the summary remains. This abbreviated statement mentions only the Indian raids that had occurred along the line of march, and does not explicitly state whether he engaged any hostile forces. The trip to the border did allow him, however, to survey the country over which he

Juan N. Cortina. #1/102-105. *Courtesy Texas State Library and Archives Commission, Austin, Texas.*

would operate in the future. His return three years hence would be followed by more dramatic results.[71]

That same year, Congress appointed three commissioners to inquire into depredations on the frontier of Texas. The officials held public sessions in Brownsville, Ringgold Barracks, Corpus Christi, Santa Gertrudis, San Diego, Laredo, El Sauz, Eagle Pass, Brackettville, Fort Clark, Uvalde, and San Antonio from July 1872 to June 1873. Their two reports amassed a considerable amount of testimony, petitions, and claims to present a detailed record of events on the border from 1866 to 1872.[72] The Mexican government responded to the congressional probe by establishing their own special investigation into cross-border raiding in September 1872. The report of their findings took issue with the American accounts, determined depredations were conducted by disaffected Confederates, Indians, and Mexican nationals based south of the border, as well as those living in Texas. The commissioners denounced Mexicans who preyed on their countrymen and drove stolen stock into Texas. They also censured Texans who purchased the animals at bargain prices.[73]

In November 1872, James Davidson, after resigning as adjutant general and losing a legislative election, accompanied Secretary of State Newcomb on a trip to New York City to market state bonds. While the pair were gone, officials discovered Davidson had been embezzling monies earmarked for the frontier defense fund and the State Police, the total amount being over $37,000. The governor ordered McNelly to pursue his former superior and bring him back to face justice. By the end of the year, McNelly was in New York City on Davidson's trail. He checked the register of the lavish St. Nicholas Hotel and found the fugitive had checked out on November 26. The captain received a letter from Acting Adjutant General Francis L. "Frank" Britton instructing him to send photographs and descriptions of Davidson to the authorities in Canada. Once this was accomplished, McNelly was to return home. While he was reported to have fled to Belgium, Davidson remained at large and reemerged in New Zealand.[74]

Once more in Texas, McNelly continued to serve in the State Police even as the force's days appeared numbered. Perhaps wanting to build a financial cushion against that time, he was commissioned a deputy U.S. marshal in the Western District of Texas on April 4, 1873. Later in the month, he went to Hill County to apprehend former postmaster Richard R. Booth and ex-deputy postmaster R.C. Doss for stealing sixteen dollars from a registered letter. Returning to Austin on April 30, McNelly lodged Doss in the county jail and handed Booth over to the federal marshal. Booth appeared before U.S. Commissioner W. D. Price for a four-day preliminary hearing, and he was bound over for the federal grand jury. Once indicted, Booth's trial in federal district court began on July 1, and lasted three days. He and Doss each blamed the other for the theft, and both claimed they were not present while the crime was being committed. Evidently, the legal strategy created sufficient reasonable doubt, as the jury brought in a verdict of not guilty.[75]

In the thirty-three months of its existence, the State Police arrested approximately ten thousand wrongdoers, including 696 for murder and thirteen hundred for other violent crimes. Also included in the tally were twelve hundred apprehensions for livestock theft or illegally slaughtering cattle, nineteen hundred for illicit gambling, and twelve hundred for various property crimes.[76] Nevertheless, opposition to the force remained widespread. The Thirteenth Legislature enacted a bill that repealed the Police Act of 1870, which, in turn, abolished the State Police. Governor Davis vetoed the measure, but his objection was overridden on April 22, 1873, with a vote of fifty-eight to eighteen in the House and eighteen to seven in the Senate. The law took effect immediately upon passage. Closing up his accounts with the government, McNelly returned to his family and his farm. By this time, he possessed some 880 acres of good land, but his time as a farmer would prove short-lived.[77]

Once he entered office, Governor Richard Coke was forced to deal with, among other issues, the problems of extensive crime and frontier depredations. He resisted a reemergence of a state police force and believed local government was best suited to provide law and order. "The sheriff is the mainspring of the law in his county, its right arm, as the district attorney is in his district," he declared to the Fourteenth Legislature.[78] The first seventeen sections of the frontier protection act passed on April 10, 1874, authorized the governor to raise a company of twenty-five to seventy-five minutemen in any frontier county that was being ransacked by hostile Indians, Mexicans, or Texan outlaws. The length of service was set at between three and twelve months. When the crisis passed, or the executive made the decision, the company was to be discharged. While the provisions found in the new law matched Coke's view, other politicians managed to insert legislation creating the Frontier Battalion.[79]

As with the Frontier Battalion, the men of the minute companies were to provide their own mounts, six-shot pistols, clothing, and camp equipage. The State would provide a breech-loading carbine, ammunition, and provisions for both men and horses. The wages were fixed at one hundred dollars for captains, seventy-five dollars for lieutenants, fifty dollars for sergeants, and forty dollars for corporals and privates. The minute companies raised under the act remained subject to the State of Texas, but operated according to the rules and regulations of the U.S. Army. Section twenty-eight of the new law vested these men with the powers of peace officers, and required them to execute criminal process and apprehend lawbreakers anywhere in the state.[80]

With the recent lynching of three men near Clinton, Governor Coke ordered the raising of a minute company to "assist the civil officers of DeWitt County in enforcing quiet and obedience to law in that desperado ridden section." McNelly's distinguished military and police record led him to be commissioned its captain on July 14, and Company A, Washington County Volunteer Militia was organized eleven days later. His clearly defined orders were to subordinate himself and his company to DeWitt County Sheriff William Jordan Weisiger, to be accompanied by Weisiger or other local law officers when making arrests, to possess a valid and legal warrant when taking suspects into custody, to respect the limits of his authority under the law, to maintain the strictest discipline among his men, and to preserve public order. Making his recruiting depot in Burton, McNelly's company of one lieutenant, four sergeants, three corporals, and twenty-five privates was enlisted from residents of Washington and Travis Counties, individuals with no personal stake in the Sutton-Taylor dispute. The company was issued fifty Sharps .50-caliber carbines, a matching number of cartridge belts and shoulder slings, and three thousand rounds of ammunition.[81]

Napoleon Augustus Jennings, a Ranger who rode with McNelly, and later became a newspaperman in the East, described his former captain as "under the average height and slimly built, but he sat so erect in the saddle and had such an air of command that he seemed like a cavalry officer at the head of a company of soldiers." Jennings further recalled upon their first meeting, McNelly was "not more than thirty years of age, although he wore a heavy, dark brown moustache and 'goatee,' which at first glance, made him look slightly older." He went on to describe the captain as "a very quiet, reserved, sedate sort of man, but he always had a pleasant word for those under him and was greatly loved by all the men."[82]

On August 1, the Rangers rode into Clinton, the seat of DeWitt County, with instructions "to report to the Sheriff, and under the orders of that officer, to execute process of the courts, for arrest of criminals, to preserve the peace, and render such assistance as might be desired by the local authorities, in conformity with the law."[83] McNelly's later report to Adjutant General William Steele of conditions in DeWitt County stated that,

> A perfect reign of terror existed in this and adjoining counties, armed bands of men were making predatory excursions through the country, overawing the law-abiding citizens, while the civil authorities were unable, or unwilling to enforce the laws framed for their protection. The lives of peaceful citizens who had given no cause of offence to either party, were in jeopardy, as neutrals were considered obnoxious to both factions ... The action of the District Judge and states [sic] attorney, or rather their inaction, has been the cause of trouble which might otherwise have been nipped in the bud, and I am satisfied that if a Judge and attorney of probity, ability and nerve, were sent down to hold court in December, they could effectually prevent a continuation of disgraceful scenes in and out of the halls of justice. With the present incumbents there is no hope; fearful of giving offense they have passed over in silence infringements on the law which have transpired under their immediate observation, and have given just cause for bringing the majesty of the law into contempt among a class of men who at best have but a slight regard for it.[84]

The bad blood between the Sutton and Taylor families had begun when William "Bill" Sutton led a posse that killed Charley Taylor and James Sharp in Bastrop County on March 25, 1868. The open fighting phase of the feud commenced the following Christmas Eve with the murder of William P. "Buck" Taylor, and reached its peak with the murder of Bill Sutton in Indianola on March 11, 1874. By the time the Rangers arrived, the Sutton party numbered between one hundred and 150 supporters in DeWitt, Karnes, and Gonzales Counties. Their Taylor enemies, whose adherents were mostly found in Gonzales and Lavaca Counties, could muster an equal number of fighting men. In recent years, two interpretations, one revisionist and one based more in tradition, have emerged regarding the struggle in DeWitt County. For some time, James Smallwood has developed a thesis that argues "there was no feud," and portrays the Taylors as the pro-Confederate ringleaders of a vast, loosely organized criminal conspiracy that "spread chaos and lawlessness into at least forty-five Texas counties." According to the professor, the wrongly named Sutton party was in reality a collection of loyal Unionists and Reconstruction-era lawmen who were duty-bound to bring the Taylors to justice. Taking the opposite position, author Chuck Parsons maintained both factions "realized completely that the actions they took to eradicate their enemies were for revenge ... [the conflict] became the archetype of what a blood feud was, a model for other groups to follow. Texas men who carried on a feud did not have to have a model to follow; carrying on a blood feud came naturally to those who believed revenge was obligatory."[85]

On August 3, district court convened, and the grand jury was expected to return murder indictments on men of both factions. McNelly's company had its first brush with the feudists three days later, when approximately fifteen to twenty-five Sutton partisans attacked Sergeant Charles M. Middleton and three privates eight miles from Clinton. The four men were escorting rancher John Milam Taylor, who had been subpoenaed to furnish testimony in district court, from Yorktown to the county seat. The gun battle lasted approximately fifteen minutes, and ended with one Ranger injured and two horses killed; one Ranger was briefly missing in action. The Suttons later parleyed, apologized, and explained they assumed they were firing on their Taylor foes. McNelly believed they were attempting to assassinate the witness. Leading the Sutton party was Captain Joseph "Old Joe" Tumlinson, veteran ranger in the days of the Texas Republic.[86]

Throughout the fall and early winter, McNelly deployed constant patrols, especially targeted saloons, harried fugitives, secured the court while in session, and prevented members of the opposing factions from meeting. To aid him in his mission, the captain wangled a commission of special deputy U.S. marshal on November 10. He developed a system of espionage to keep him informed of the feudists' plans, and tried to establish friendly relations with both sides. The Rangers' tour of duty in DeWitt County can be considered a success. Parsons commented: "the public's attitude was in favor of just enforcement of the law, not mob violence; the public remembered the quality of McNelly—that no prisoners in his custody were murdered 'attempting to escape'—and that his constant patrolling prevented much bloodshed. They also appreciated that he did not turn over prisoners to lynch mobs." However, he was not able to take John Wesley Hardin or the less dangerous Jim Taylor into custody. McNelly's Rangers did not bring a permanent end to the feud, but for six months "De Witt County [enjoyed] a greater degree of quiet, and of immunity from terrorism and violence, than has been known there for several years."[87]

Meanwhile, the endemic bloodshed in the Nueces Strip was once more on the rise. Well-organized bands of Indian, Mexican, and American cattle and horse thieves were prowling every range between the Nueces River and the Rio Grande, and driving stolen stock to eager buyers in Mexico. Some brigands engaged in the bloody, albeit less profitable, business of killing cattle, skinning the carcasses, and moving the hides over the border. The most vicious looted stores and ranch houses, burned them, and murdered the occupants, as well as innocent travelers. From 1865 to 1873, an estimated 100,000 head of stolen cattle were driven across the Rio Grande. South of the river in Tamaulipas and Coahuila were several *ranchos* that provided an organized rendezvous for the Mexican butchers, stock-dealers, and ranchers who profited from the raids. An article of faith among Texas cattlemen was that many civil and military authorities in Matamoros, Mier, Bagdad, Camargo, and other border towns were fully aware of the situation, encouraged the raiding, and, indeed, shared in the proceeds.[88]

In March 1875, 150 Mexican *bandidos* crossed the border near Eagle Pass. North of the border, they divided into four groups and rode off in separate directions. Three of the bands were intercepted and repelled by U.S. cavalry troopers posted at San Diego. The fourth was able to reach Corpus Christi.[89] The various accounts of the subsequent raid differ on several details, but all agree on certain points. On the morning of March 26, the fourth gang of bandits, numbering some thirty Mexicans and three Americans, was riding toward the tiny village of Nuecestown. As they traveled north, the brigands robbed eight to thirteen travelers and took them prisoner, burned down Thomas John Noakes's store in town, and killed three people. The robbers quickly fled back into Mexico, leaving a wounded comrade behind. The infuriated townsmen lynched the abandoned bandit, and numerous "minute companies" of volunteers throughout South Texas took their revenge on known wrongdoers and innocent *tejanos*. Concealed within the reprisal campaign were those Anglos who used the anarchic conditions to settle old scores with *mexicanos* in Nueces and Encinal Counties. Folklorist J. Frank Dobie claimed the number of Mexicans indiscriminately killed in the aftermath of the Nuecestown Raid exceeded the figure slain at San Jacinto.[90]

The governor and adjutant general responded to the appeals for aid by sending for McNelly. The Washington County company, which faced disbandment due to depleted appropriations, was nevertheless mustered out on March 31, and mustered back in the next day, with an authorized strength of forty men. General Steele ordered McNelly to the Rio Grande "for service against the armed bands of Mexican marauders infesting the region between the Nueces and the Mexican Boundary."[91]

The company started for the border on April 10, and arrived in Corpus Christi by the twenty-fourth. After establishing his headquarters camp at Las Rucias near Edinburg on May 16, the captain developed an extensive network of paid informants who provided intelligence on the movements of the bandits. He then ordered the disbandment of all unofficial bands of armed men that had formed for the purported reason of self-defense. As Jennings recollected: "Large parties of mounted and well-armed men, residents of Nueces County, were riding over the country, committing the most brutal outrages, murdering peaceable Mexican farmers and stockmen who had lived all their lives in Texas." While professing they were serving the cause of law and order, these vigilantes were often indistinguishable from common marauders, and only added to the chaotic situation.[92]

Testifying before the House Committee on Foreign Affairs the following year, McNelly said of *tejano* ranchers:

> I do not know of any Mexican who owns a ranch on this side of the river and who lives in Texas whom I do not consider to be a good citizen. I believe they are all good citizens. They all want to see the laws enforced, and they all want to have this raiding broken up; but very few of them dare take an active, open stand in the matter. They are very right, too, for it would be very dangerous for them to do so.[93]

Faced with a criminal element that played by merciless rules, McNelly chose to act accordingly. Author Frederick Wilkins called him "a hard commander in a harsh time." Unquestionably, the Rangers executed bandits in retaliation for their bloodletting, or as object lessons for others who might think of marauding across the border. Few prisoners were turned over to local authorities as they were sometimes summarily hung or "shot while attempting to escape." According to Jennings, "the more we were feared, the easier would be our work in subduing the Mexican raiders." From the captain's standpoint, such extralegal methods also meant he did not need concern himself with the feeding and guarding of outlaws caught in the act, and having to depend on the vagaries of the court system for their punishment. Anglos from Corpus Christi to Brownsville knew of McNelly's methods, as did army officers stationed in the region. Artist Frederic Remington summarized the prevalent attitude: "The bandit never laid down his gun but with his life; so [*la ley de fuga*—"the law of flight"] was in force in the chaparral, and the good people of Texas were satisfied with a very short account of a Ranger's fight."[94]

McNelly also sanctioned harsh measures in wresting information from the captives they did apprehend. His principal interrogator was Jesús Sandoval (known to his comrades as "Old Casuse"), a Cameron County *ranchero* who was regarded by his enemies across the river as "Americanized and consequently criminal—a traitor to Mexico." The *bandidos* burned his Estero

Grande ranch house and drove off his *remuda*. Surviving numerous assassination attempts, Sandoval withdrew into the chaparral and there nursed a burning desire for vengeance. His pursuit of retribution may have led him to be indicted for murder in Starr County in March 1873. On December 17, 1874, two suspected *bandidos* were lynched on the Point Isabel road, three miles from Brownsville. Casuse was one of three *rancheros* suspected of the deed, and a warrant was issued for his arrest. He was cleared of the charges the following month, but the dead men's relatives vowed to take the law into their own hands. Despite his legal difficulties, Casuse was added to the rolls in McNelly's company on May 1, 1875, as a private, and the captain found him to be an excellent scout and interpreter, as well as an enthusiastic inquisitor. Sandoval's favorite technique was to place a noose over a prisoner's head, throw the rope over a tree limb, and repeatedly lift him off the ground until he confessed everything. After the captive had been wrung of all intelligence, Casuse sometimes lynched him.[95]

Jennings wrote that Sandoval's wife and fourteen-year-old daughter were raped, and his ranch destroyed. George Durham, another member of the company, concurred and regarded Sandoval as "the most vicious, merciless killer that ever has come to my notice." The purported family tragedy was theorized to have been the reason for his implacable hatred for bandits, but Sandoval's subsequent testimony to Congress does not lend credence to this assertion. Furthermore, the 1850 federal census reveals Sandoval had four sons in that year and no daughters. He might have had other children subsequently, but, for whatever reason, Sandoval does not appear in later censuses. Jennings's work was published in 1899, and possibly the memory of the elderly Durham had been influenced by the earlier work. This suspect claim has since found its way into numerous accounts on McNelly.[96]

Captain Richard King, once a steamboat pilot on the Rio Grande, and now an affluent rancher on Santa Gertrudis Creek, made the Rangers welcome by furnishing them with beef and good horses. The cattle baron and other citizens of Nueces County also raised money to fund the company's operations. After they recovered some of King's stolen stock months later, King presented the Rangers with Winchester lever-action rifles as a token of his thanks.[97]

McNelly's principal enemy on the lower Rio Grande was "Cheno" Cortina, the same individual who had opposed "Rip" Ford in the border war of 1859. Following the insurrection that bore his name, Cortina resided in Mexico where he served as a general in both the Imperial and the Republican armies, governor of Tamaulipas, and *alcalde* of Matamoros. By 1875, he had become one of the largest *rancheros* in Northern Mexico, mainly by stealing thousands of head of Texas cattle. After personally inspecting the situation on the border, General Steele noted: "Cortina is the recognized head and protector of all of the cattle thieves and murderers, from Camargo to the mouth of the Rio Grande ... His armed adherents are said to number over two thousand." On McNelly's orders, First Sergeant George A. Hall infiltrated Cortina's camp at Bagdad and provided his captain with intelligence on bandit activities.[98]

On June 5, McNelly learned from his informants that a party of Mexican rustlers had crossed the river eight miles below Brownsville. He immediately ordered Lieutenant Thomas C. "Pidge" Robinson and eighteen men to the crossing of Arroyo Colorado to search for the raiders. The lieutenant apprehended one of the Mexicans, Rafael Salinas, on June 8. From the prisoner Casuse learned Cortina had apparently sent eighteen men under Camillo Lerma and José Maria Olguín (known as *El Aguja,* or "The Needle") to the La Parra area to steal eighteen hundred head of cattle. The bandit chieftain needed the stock to fulfill a contract with a Cuban buyer.[99]

On the evening of June 11, Encarnacion García, another interrogated prisoner, allowed Casuse to confirm the bandits would be crossing the arroyo that night en route for the Rio Grande with three hundred stolen beeves. McNelly positioned his men in a motte until two a.m. when a scout reported the outlaws had passed four miles east of the ambush earlier in the night. The company set out in pursuit across the Palo Alto Prairie. At seven o'clock, the hell-for-leather captain and his Rangers swooped down on the sixteen *bandidos* and the pilfered cattle. The Mexicans ran the stock for three miles before gathering the herd on a small island in the Laguna Madre salt marsh. Crossing to the other side, the rustlers spread out and readied themselves for a fight. The Texans held their fire and advanced toward the Mexicans in a skirmish line. "As soon as we struck the water, the raiders commenced firing

McNelly's Rangers. Oil on canvas by John Wade Hampton. *Courtesy Cheraux Hampton.*

on us with Spencers and Winchester carbines," the captain later reported. "We advanced at a walk (a more rapid gait being impossible) and not firing a shot or speaking a word and keeping our line well-dressed."[100]

Once the Rangers were within seventy-five to one hundred yards, the Mexicans wheeled their horses and withdrew at a slow pace. Reaching solid ground, McNelly ordered the company to increase its gait, and they were soon within striking range. The Mexicans fell back more swiftly and the Rangers' horses could not match their speed. The captain instructed his three best mounted men to race to the enemy's right flank and attempt to force them to accept action. "And as I had anticipated," McNelly recounted, "the Mexicans turned to drive my men off, but they held their ground, and I got up with four or five men, when the raiders broke." In a series of individual combats that stretched over six miles, the Rangers cut down every rustler, except Olguín who escaped into the tall grass. The Rangers suffered one fatality, sixteen-year-old L.B. "Berry" (or "Sonny") Smith, who was later buried at Fort Brown with full military honors. Several of the dead were identified as Matamoros policemen and the rest as known followers of Cortina. McNelly had the bodies stacked in the Brownsville town square "like cordwood" as examples to would-be raiders.[101]

The same afternoon, the captain sent a telegrammed report, with some errors, to the governor in Austin:

> This morning I came up with a band of twelve raiders, after a forced march of twenty-five miles. They attacked me when I overtook them. It was a running fight. After that I got seven of them engaged and killed all. They fought desperately. I lost one man, Benj. Smith, and two horses killed and two wounded. I took 250 beeves. Tonight I go for another party. My men are all trumps.[102]

Two days later, the captain wired the adjutant general from Camargo, "Had a fight with raiders, killed twelve and captured two hundred and sixty beeves. Wish you were here."[103]

Whether the Rangers' activities played a role, the situation on the border experienced an improvement in at least one respect. In May 1875,

Cortina had been arrested by the order of President Sebastián Lerdo de Tejada. Charged with smuggling, levying import and export duties without authority, insubordination, and the theft of government property, he was incarcerated in the Prisión Militar de Santiago Tlatelolco in Mexico City. The *caudillo* escaped from the capital and declared for Porfirio Díaz and the Plan de Tuxtepec. Once Díaz assumed the presidency, he ordered Cortina be detained and, after a second stay at Santiago Tlatelolco, the bandit chieftain was held under house arrest until his death on October 30, 1894.[104]

In mid-October 1875, McNelly received word at his camp near Santa María that two hundred head of cattle had been stolen in Cameron County and crossed over to Monterrey. The rustled stock was said to be for Juan Flores Salinas, a prominent *ranchero* and general of *rurales*, who held a contract for eighteen thousand head. On November 16, sixteen or seventeen raiders drove a herd of approximately seventy-five head of cattle toward the Las Cuevas Crossing of the Rio Grande. The captain arrived on the river at a point opposite Camargo by noon of November 18; his thirty men joined him that evening after riding fifty-five-miles in five hours. McNelly found D Company of the Eighth Cavalry already on the scene negotiating with the *alcalde* for the return of the rustled Texan cattle. McNelly had no desire to discuss matters and declared his intention to cross the border. Captain James Franklin Randlett, the troop commander, urged McNelly to wait, but the ranger officer would not be dissuaded. He also expected the army to support him.[105]

The deep mud on the river banks allowed only five horses to cross, and, beginning at one a.m. on the nineteenth, McNelly was compelled to ferry the remaining men across two at a time in a small dugout canoe. Amid a heavy night fog, the mounted Rangers rode ahead of those forced to walk. After traveling three miles along a cattle trail through brush and scattered trees, the Texans came upon what was believed to be Flores's Rancho Las Cuevas. Sergeant John B. Armstrong cut down an alert sentry, and the mounted Rangers charged the *vaqueros* working on morning chores. The captain later reported killing four of the Mexicans, but other sources estimated as many as five or six times that number. In the aftermath of the fight, McNelly learned he had struck Las Cucharas (also known as

Rancho Cachattus) rather than Las Cuevas. The intended target site lay a half-mile distant.[106]

The common perception among border Texans was that all Mexican males living close to the river were potential cattle rustlers, so the Rangers did not pause to question whether they had killed innocent men. Instead, even though the gunfire had alerted everyone within hearing distance, they boldly moved on to Las Cuevas. They found a force of Mexican militia numbering approximately one hundred mounted and 150 dismounted present at the ranch. The Rangers took the defenders under fire for ten minutes, and their Sharps carbines proved deadly before McNelly called for a withdrawal to the Rio Grande.[107]

The Rangers reached the river, and the captain deployed pickets in the brush to his front. While his men dug in, McNelly walked up and down the line giving orders. At about seven o'clock, General Flores and twenty-five horsemen galloped into view, driving the pickets before him. "Charge them, boys! Open up on them as fast as you can," the captain cried. The Texans formed a line on top of the river embankment and smashed Flores's charge, killing the general in the process.[108]

Soon the Rangers were faced with a greater number of Mexican soldiers and irregulars massing just out of effective rifle range. Captain Randlett, awaiting McNelly's return, dispatched forty of his troopers to support the Rangers. McNelly requested the balance of the horse soldiers be sent across to again attack Las Cuevas, but the cavalry captain refused to take further action until Major Andrew Jonathan Alexander, his immediate superior, arrived. Throughout the afternoon, the Rangers and regulars fended off several weak assaults. When a flag of truce was raised among the Mexicans around five p.m., Randlett crossed the river and met with representatives of the Camargo *alcalde*. In this and in two more discussions, the Mexicans demanded the immediate recall of all American forces from Mexico, and promised to do everything possible to capture the rustlers and the stolen cattle. Randlett agreed to a ceasefire until nine o'clock the following morning.[109]

While the two parties parleyed, Major Alexander arrived on the scene and assumed command of the federal forces. Captain Randlett returned to Texas and rendered his report. Alexander ordered the Americans to retire to the Texas side of the river. The regulars obeyed, but McNelly refused to comply until the thieves and stolen stock were produced.[110]

On the morning of November 20, Major Alexander was directed to urge McNelly to return to Texas, and was forbidden to support the Rangers if they were attacked. McNelly held his position until late in the afternoon when he delivered a brash ultimatum: guarantee the thieves and stolen stock would be delivered up in Rio Grande City at ten o'clock the following morning, or the Rangers would attack in one hour's time. The Camargo delegation assured the Ranger captain that his terms would be met, and McNelly led his men back across the river. However, the next day, the Mexicans proved reluctant to honor their promise, and McNelly led a dozen heavily armed Rangers back into Mexico. After the Texans brandished their weapons and promised to shoot the Mexican officials, sixty-five head of cattle were driven across the river, but no thieves were turned over to face American justice.[111]

The public was enthusiastic in its praise of McNelly's Rangers, even though only one-third of the rustled stock was recovered, no thieves were apprehended, and the Texans were nearly annihilated. Bold action was more prized than the lengthy negotiations and weak response that epitomized most federal responses to border incursions. The "Las Cuevas War" did not end raids into Texas. Instead, internal developments in Mexico proved to be the solution, although one that occurred after McNelly's tenure.[112]

Along with Colonel John S. Ford and other luminaries, McNelly traveled to the nation's capital and appeared before a House committee on Texas border troubles on January 24 and 29, 1876. Following his testimony, he returned to Texas, and was in Austin by February 20.[113] While their captain was in Washington, a detachment of the company discovered a slaughter house for stolen beeves on December 28, some forty miles north of Las Rucias. The *ranchero* in charge of the house was arrested. The Mexican made a failed attempt to bribe the detachment's sergeant, then tried to escape. He was killed in the attempt.[114]

As they moved their camp from Santa María to Laredo, the company was within five miles of Edinburg on May 17, when they discovered a party of four Mexicans crossing stolen stock. In the subsequent fight, the Rangers killed two of the thieves and severely wounded another. The Texans recovered seven head of cattle and six horses. McNelly noted that General Mariano Escobedo was dining with American military officers in Edinburg at the same time. The Ranger commander called on Captain Henry Joseph Farnsworth, Eighth Cavalry, to aid in recovering the rest of the stolen cattle. As the situation did not fall within the definition of "hot pursuit," the army officer refused. McNelly and three men went into Mexico themselves and searched to within one-and-a-half miles of Escobedo's lines. The Rangers did not find any livestock, and McNelly demanded the *alcalde* of Reynosa produce the cattle and thieves. The *alcalde* promised his assistance, but no action was taken. McNelly believed the cattle were intended for Escobedo's *soldados*.[115]

The Rangers next turned to the problem of Anglo outlawry in the Nueces Strip. Chief among the cattle rustlers was John King Fisher, a flamboyant gunfighter and rancher on Pendencia Creek near Eagle Pass. Fisher, described as "the most colorful and notorious outlaw who ever operated on the Texas border," provided his ranch as a sanctuary to fugitives and stock thieves operating on both sides of the Rio Grande. Leading his own gang of desperadoes, Fisher personally backed his control with his six-shooter. A sign posted next to the trail leading to his ranch proclaimed, "This is King Fisher's Road—Take the other."[116]

Since county authorities had proven unable to bring Fisher to justice, McNelly decided to apprehend the outlaw king himself. On June 4, 1876, the captain and fifteen Rangers quietly surrounded Fisher's headquarters and entered the ranch house with pistols drawn. Fisher and nine of his men were taken into custody without incident and turned over to Maverick County Sheriff C. J. Cook in Eagle Pass. The Rangers also gathered some six to eight hundred head of stolen cattle and horses. McNelly then personally undertook a forty-mile round trip through the *brasada* to secure witnesses. To facilitate his endeavors, he was appointed a special deputy sheriff of Maverick County. Returning on June 6, he encountered Fisher and his men, seven of whom could have been indicted for murder, on their way home. The outlaws' lawyer had fabricated numerous legal technicalities and pressured the sheriff to release his clients on bond. McNelly disgustedly sent the witnesses home and ordered the release of the seized stock.[117]

Still smarting from Fisher's release, McNelly wrote state senator "Rip" Ford requesting his assistance. The captain appeared before a legislative committee on June 21, and testified on the difficulty of enforcing the law in counties with weak local authorities controlled by the criminal element. On July 22, the legislature responded by passing "An Act to suppress lawlessness and crime in certain parts of the State, and to make an appropriation therefor," mustering out the Washington County Volunteer Militia on the twenty-fifth, and mustering them back in as "Special State Troops" the following day. Colonel Ford was a driving force behind the bill, and would later describe his relations with McNelly as "of the most amicable character."[118]

The legislation gave McNelly and his new company of fifty-two men the mission of pursuing "bands of criminal and lawless men too strong to be suppressed by the civil authorities." The captain was to be paid $166 per month; the first lieutenant, $133 per month; the second lieutenant, $125; the sergeants, fifty dollars each; and the corporals and the privates, forty each. Section 6 declared each member of the company,

> shall be clothed with the powers of peace officers, and shall aid the civil authorities in the execution of the laws. They shall have authority to make arrests, and ... be governed by laws regulating and defining the powers and the duties of Sheriffs when in discharge of these duties, take an oath before some authority legally authorized to administer the same, that each of them will faithfully perform his duties in accordance with law.

The legislature also appropriated forty thousand dollars to McNelly's new company.[119]

Despite the greater authority given him, McNelly's time in command was running out. His unconventional methods, his disregard for muster rolls and vouchers, and his lack of regular, detailed reports irritated many in the state house. In addition, as his tuberculosis worsened, his doctor in San Antonio twice signed a certificate of disability.[120]

Governor Richard Bennett Hubbard responded by appointing Jesse L. Hall second-in-command of the company, over the heads of several proven

Rangers. Hall was the legislature's choice for McNelly eventual replacement. For a time, the captain supervised the company from a hotel room bed in Austin or San Antonio, or from his farm, while Hall acted as the field commander.[121]

When the company's term of service ended on January 31, 1877, the governor issued orders for the Rangers to be mustered out and reconstituted the next day as a new twenty-four-man company. General Steele explained that McNelly's health, budget cuts, and the reduced company being too small for a captain's command forced the Ranger's discharge. He was severely criticized in the press for his actions concerning the dying officer. He responded to his detractors by pointing to the fact that McNelly had not performed field service for nearly six months, and his medical bills accounted for nearly one-third of the company's operating budget.[122]

Leander McNelly retired to his farm and died of tuberculosis on September 4, 1877, at the age of thirty-three. He was buried at Mount Zion Cemetery near Burton. Speaking of the captain's service on the Rio Grande, Colonel Ford eulogized him as "an energetic officer of great ability, who had availed himself every opportunity to promote the interests of that section, in fact of all Texas."[123]

Needing regular employment after her husband's death, Carey was a clerk in the State Land Office for many years. She joined William Sidney Johnston Chapter 105 of the Texas Daughters of the Confederacy in 1901. After three decades of widowhood, she married merchant William Thomas Wroe on April 15, 1909, in San Antonio. Her new husband had served in Company I, Fifth Texas Cavalry during the war. William died in Austin on January 3, 1933. Carey was admitted to the Women's Confederate Home in Austin on September 28, 1937. She died there of pneumonia and influenza on October 29, 1938. After a funeral service at St. David's Episcopal Church, she was buried in Oakwood Cemetery in Austin next to her son. She was the namesake of the Carey McNelly Wroe Chapter of the Children of the Confederacy, which organized in San Antonio on October 30, 1945.[124]

Denied the captain's steadying hand at a crucial age, Rebel lived up to his name as an adult. He worked as a clerk, but was jailed in Brenham in late 1891 on charges of robbery and assault with intent to murder a man named

Frank Broescho. The subsequent court proceedings resulted in a mistrial. In the second hearing, Rebel's defense counsel, Major H. H. Boone, entered a plea of guilty on March 23, 1893, and the young McNelly drew a two-year sentence at Huntsville. Entering through the gates of the penitentiary on April 24, he received a full pardon from Governor James Stephen Hogg on December 6, 1894. Suffering from tuberculosis like his father, Rebel succumbed to the disease in Tombstone, Arizona, on January 1, 1907. His body was transported to Austin, and he was buried in Oakwood Cemetery.[125]

Irene attended Baylor College in Washington, Texas. While attending school, she died of an accidental injury on May 8, 1884. She was buried near her father in Mount Zion Cemetery.[126]

Outwardly a quiet and reserved man who, according to some, resembled a Methodist preacher, McNelly was a tenacious soldier who brooked no obstacles to the completion of his mission. Faced with a cruel and bloodthirsty enemy, he participated in illegal executions, and extracted confessions from prisoners by extreme methods. However odious to the modern observer, his actions proved effective in bringing a measure of peace to the Rio Grande country. He broke the stranglehold thieves and murderers had placed on the border counties, and paved the way for his successors to finish the work using more civilized and legal means.

John B. Armstrong. #P.80.336. *Courtesy Texas Ranger Hall of Fame and Museum, Waco, Texas.*

Chapter 3

John B. Armstrong: "The Strong Right-Hand of Two Ranger Captains"

John Barkley Armstrong III is best known for his pursuit and capture of John Wesley Hardin, the most notorious gunfighter in the state of Texas. The Ranger's intrepid manner and leadership abilities were honed in the best McNelly tradition. Walter Prescott Webb said: "One does not have to follow John Armstrong's career very far to recognize that he was a man after McNelly's own heart. His methods were McNelly's methods and he never hesitated to administer extreme unction to those who could not be handled in a more gentle manner." Even before his famous apprehension, his exploits in Mexico, and elsewhere along the border, earned Armstrong the nickname "McNelly's Bulldog." In all, he was the strong right-hand of two Ranger captains. However, he was more than a simple peace officer and manhunter. Once he laid down his guns, he became an entrepreneur aspiring to build something greater than himself. To that end he established one of the great cattle ranches of South Texas, introduced the railroad into the region, and played a pivotal role in the commercial development of the lower Rio Grande.

He was born on January 1, 1850, in McMinnville, Warren County, Tennessee. His parents were Doctor John Barkley Armstrong, Jr. and Maria Susannah (Ready) Armstrong. His father had been born on January 20, 1819, in Giles County, Tennessee. After attending Clinton College in New Middleton, and the Medical Institute of Louisville, Kentucky, for the 1841–1842 session, he moved to Readyville and married Maria at the Stone's River Church in Rutherford County on May 23, 1842. A lady known for her "high culture and unusual literary gift," she had been born on March 2, 1813, in Readyville. Within a few months of the younger John's birth, the family was residing in the town of Nichols in Cannon County. In addition to a successful practice, the elder Armstrong possessed real estate valued at four thousand dollars. He also owned one slave, a twelve-year-old black male. John's siblings included Thomas Temple Armstrong, born February 7, 1843; Mary "Mollie" Ready Armstrong, born November 18, 1844; William Francis Armstrong, born September 12, 1846; Laura Maria Armstrong, born September 16, 1847; Lavanda "Van" Martin Armstrong, born September 10, 1852; and Betavia "Beta" Jane Armstrong, born November 13, 1854.[1]

As the sectional crisis loomed, Doctor Armstrong, a staunch Southern Unionist, decided to return his family to Eastern Tennessee where his political views were more acceptable. The seeming incongruity of supporting the Union and being a slaveholder was nevertheless common in the Border States. The men in the upper South who fell into this category typically defended slavery, but denied secession would protect the institution. Instead, they saw the Union and Constitutional guarantees as shields from abolitionist sentiment. In late 1854, the Armstrongs and their slave moved to a house on College Street in McMinnville. Shortly after arriving at his new home, young John began attending the private school of Reverend James Waller Poindexter. Except for some interruptions caused by the war, Armstrong received a classical education from Poindexter, the pastor of Cumberland Presbyterian Church, until 1868.[2]

By the eve of the war, the Armstrongs' financial situation could be considered comfortable. The elder John owned three thousand dollars worth of real estate, and a personal estate of two thousand. Regrettably, he had also increased the number of slaves working his lands and in his household to seven: one woman aged forty, one man aged thirty-five, one woman aged twenty-two, one man aged seventeen, two girls aged five and one, and one boy aged four.[3]

The question of whether Tennessee should secede from the Union was settled, for the time being, on February 9, 1861, when voters decided to forgo even holding a convention on the matter. The doctor was among those who attended a meeting of "Union men of Warren" in McMinnville on April 13. The object of the assembly was to prepare the Southern Rights Union Party for the state convention, and nominate a candidate for governor in the August elections. Armstrong was appointed as a delegate to the state convention, but the shelling of Fort Sumter and President Abraham Lincoln's calling for 75,000 volunteers to put down the "insurrection" overshadowed other events. The secession of Tennessee is more involved than space allows, but, suffice to say, the state severed its ties to the Union in a June 8 referendum. Eastern Tennessee continued to oppose separation.[4]

During the war, McMinnville sat astride the battle lines of the state. Indeed, Confederate raider and general John Hunt Morgan and his new bride spent their honeymoon in the Armstrong residence. He also made the house and McMinnville his headquarters before embarking on his Ohio raid. When Major-General Joseph Wheeler raided Federal communication lines during the Chattanooga campaign, Confederate cavalry under Major-General John Austin Wharton destroyed the depot at McMinnville and forced the city's surrender on October 1, 1863. Throughout the conflict, the local economy struggled as commercial merchandise and valuable personal property were kept hidden from looters. McMinnville would change hands several times, and the teenaged Armstrong would befriend soldiers on both sides. Once the state was firmly under Yankee control, Unionists held a convention in Nashville that, among other items, appointed county officials to register voters in preparation of the upcoming presidential election. Doctor Armstrong was one of four men in Warren County chosen for the duty.[5]

In March 1868, Doctor Armstrong was elected to the board of directors of the Southwestern Railroad, which was anticipated to run from McMinnville to Danville, Kentucky. He was reappointed to the post in June 1870. Later the same month, Armstrong claimed three thousand dollars in real estate and another two in personal property. He also employed one domestic servant.[6]

Despite his belonging to a respected and prosperous family, young John Armstrong made the decision to leave Tennessee. Whether he ran afoul of

Reconstruction authorities, or simply decided to join the great westward migration is unknown. After spending two or three years in Missouri and Arkansas, he traveled to Texas, and settled in Austin. His name does not appear in the available city directory for 1872–1873, and the occupation he pursued while living in the state capital remains unknown.[7]

Sometime in early 1873, Armstrong became a member of the Travis Rifles militia company commanded by Captain M. D. Mather and First Lieutenant Albert S. Roberts. As was the case with many such military organizations, the Travis Rifles was a social club in addition to its martial purposes.[8]

At 11:50 a.m. on January 15, 1874, after being called to arms, the Travis Rifles marched to the capitol. In the aftermath of the previous month's contested gubernatorial election, circumstances in Austin were fast becoming a crisis. Lieutenant Roberts had been summoned by Sheriff George B. Zimpelman, an ally of Governor Richard Coke, to ready the company for peacekeeping duties. Shortly thereafter, the company received orders from Adjutant General Francis L. "Frank" Britton to protect Governor Edmund Jackson Davis. Instead, the lieutenant allowed the assembled men to choose between obeying the general's orders or acting as a *posse comitatus* for the sheriff. The Travis Rifles, to a man, voted to support Coke. Visiting the armory, the company equipped themselves in order to safeguard the upper part of the statehouse occupied by Governor Coke and the legislature. City Marshal Minas Long and members of the police force had taken possession of the staircase connecting the upper and lower levels of the building. The policemen were relieved by the Travis Rifles, and Armstrong was placed at the bottom of the steps leading into the building; he remained on post for about twenty hours while the town teetered on the brink of anarchy. Governor Davis received word from President Ulysses S. Grant he could expect no federal assistance, and the erstwhile executive vacated his office.[9]

On June 20, 1874, Armstrong was requested to run for the office of city marshal on the Democratic ticket. In a primary on the twenty-fourth that featured eleven candidates, Jeff Johnson received 193 votes, the largest share, while Armstrong garnered seventy-two. When the general election was held the following month, Ed Creary, an Independent, was chosen to be city marshal.[10]

Perhaps finding Austin too tame, Armstrong enlisted in Captain L. H. McNelly's Washington County Volunteer Militia on May 20, 1875. His enrollment in McNelly's company would insure Armstrong saw plenty of action. He participated in the fight at Palo Alto where McNelly's Rangers destroyed a gang of *bandidos*, except for one survivor. He was promoted to the rank of fifth sergeant on August 20. In October, Armstrong and a detachment brought in sixteen suspicious men, and the sheriff in Brownsville refused to take custody or sign a receipt. The officer indignantly demanded to know the charges or the nature of the evidence. Growing exasperated, Armstrong tore up the list of the prisoners' names, released them, and stormed out of the jail. Demonstrating the level of cooperation between state and county officers, the sheriff warned the Rangers not to get drunk in town, or he would arrest all of them. Refusing to be dismayed by the lack of support, Armstrong followed his captain across the Rio Grande to recover stolen cattle and attacked two *ranchos* suspected of involvement in the rustling. The incursion sparked an international incident.[11]

Cattle Raid on the Texas Border. Wood engraving from *Harper's Weekly* (January 31, 1874). *Courtesy Library of Congress, Washington, D.C.*

As a member of McNelly's company, Armstrong was acquiring a reputation as a brave and resolute law officer. He was described as "tall and graceful, with an impressive face set off with a sweeping blond moustache ... His voice was pleasing and he had the bearing of the knightly gentleman he was."[12]

On July 25, 1876, the Washington County company was discharged from state service, and the Special State Troops were mustered back in the following day. Armstrong was among those who reenlisted. In San Patricio County, the Garner and Means families had been feuding since the beginning of the year. On August 26, Edward Rufus Garner, the former sheriff, was killed while attending church in Meansville, and the community grew furious with the entire Means family. The next day, Armstrong and a squad arrived to investigate the slaying. Armstrong's contribution to closing the case is unknown, but eighteen-year-old Alley Means was indicted by the grand jury for the homicide. One member of the Means family later claimed John Helms Means, the accused's older brother, was the actual shooter, but Alley took the blame due to his age and unmarried status. Once the court granted a change of venue to Nueces County, Means was convicted of first-degree murder in May 1880, and sentenced to life imprisonment at Huntsville. He appealed the case, but the conviction was upheld on January 22, 1881. Despite the life sentence, Governor John Ireland granted Means a pardon on May 9, 1885. Oral tradition maintained San Patricio residents feared the Means clan's wrath, and no light appeared in any home for two years. Finally, Rangers were said to have ordered the family to sell their property, pack, and leave the county.[13]

Captain McNelly had earlier tried to get a conviction on John King Fisher in June 1876, but the wily outlaw leader managed to evade prosecution. Several months later, on September 22, Armstrong led a detachment into Fisher's domain. Once the Rangers had arrived at Carrizo, Armstrong learned a gang of outlaws were encamped on the shores of Espantosa Lake ten miles to the northeast. A second band was supposed to be stopping for the night at Fisher's ranch. On September 29, the sergeant detailed Corporal M. H. "Polly" Williams with ten men and "a number of civilians" to the Pendencia, while he led the remainder to the lake. Armstrong and his squad drew near the camp about midnight and, dismounting and assigning two men to guard the horses, advanced on foot. They also left one outlaw who had been captured along the way. As the state officers drew within twenty yards of the camp, two desperadoes began shooting. "We responded promptly and a lively little fight ensued, resulting in the death of three of them and the wounding of another in five places," the sergeant wrote. Armstrong learned from the injured man that the four outlaws were the only ones in the camp, as the remainder had left that morning. When Armstrong and his squad returned to their horses, the two men left behind related how the prisoner had attempted to escape, refused three times to obey the order to halt, and was killed.[14]

Once Corporal Williams arrived at the Pendencia, he found that everyone had departed after having been warned of his approach. Hearing of a "bad" Mexican at Whaley's ranch, some eight miles away, Williams sent three men to apprehend him. "He refused to surrender and fought desperately until our men were obliged to kill him in self-defense," Armstrong later reported. The Rangers also recovered a total of fifty stolen horses and eighty-two head of cattle from both locations.[15]

Armstrong and Private T. W. Deggs were ordered to apprehend John Lewis Mayfield, who stood accused of murder in Parker County. He had been convicted of the crime and sentenced to hang, but he escaped while his case was being appealed. Governor Coke offered a five-hundred-dollar reward for his arrest and his delivery "inside the jail door" of Parker County. On the evening of December 5, Armstrong and Deggs found the fugitive in his corrals and attempted to take him into custody. Armstrong had no more identified himself and his fellow Ranger then Mayfield cursed them and pulled his pistol. He fired two shots at the lawmen before they killed him. The dead man had been popular, and his friends in the community came swiftly to the scene. Armstrong and Deggs were obliged to leave in the face of the angry crowd to avoid further bloodshed. They went back to San Antonio, but returned to Wilson County for the inquest. Besides the two Rangers, the only witness to the shooting was the dead outlaw's wife who had been inside the house. Surprisingly, the verdict declared that Mayfield "had been murdered by one Armstrong and another man, both claiming to belong to McNelly's Rangers." The promised payment for Mayfield would not be forthcoming as the reward stipulated the fugitive had to be delivered to the Parker County jail. Mayfield's body was buried in a secret grave by his friends, and the money was never paid. Armstrong did receive the gift of a fine horse, and possibly five hundred dollars, from the original murder victim's son.[16]

After McNelly was discharged from the Ranger service, Lee Hall took over as the first lieutenant commanding, and Armstrong was promoted to second lieutenant on January 25, 1877. While the men were reticent in welcoming their new leader, Armstrong left no indication of his feelings on being passed over for the command. Six days later, he, Hall, and seven men conducted a scout along the Nueces and Frio Rivers all the way to the Atascosa County line. The detachment then divided with Armstrong taking four men to Pleasanton, the county seat at that time. Hall and the rest of the detachment went to Dog Town in McMullen County, where they arrested two men wanted for cattle theft. Armstrong apprehended John Parker, wanted for murder in Goliad County, on February 2. On the nineteenth, Armstrong's squad arrested William Creswell in Frio County and Fred Eastwinger in La Salle County. The next day, they took into custody Frank M. Drake in McMullen County, and J. H Drake and F. M. Franklin in Atascosa County. All of the prisoners were delivered to the authorities in Atascosa County.[17]

In May, Lieutenant Hall organized a "roundup" in the Eagle Pass area similar to the one Major John B. Jones had directed in Kimble County. Armstrong arrived on the ninth, Sergeant A. L. Parrott the next day, and Hall on the thirteenth. Desperadoes fled across the Rio Grande, but some were captured before they could escape. Armstrong arrested four outlaws on the Texas side, and persuaded Mexican authorities to apprehend three more. Riding with Hall and Parrott to Piedras Negras, the officers took a man named Williams (also known as Jim Jones) into custody for horse theft, and on suspicion of being involved in the Blanco stage robbery.[18]

Even though he possesed a solid record of service, Armstrong achieved everlasting fame for one act: the capture of John Wesley Hardin, "more dreaded than any desperado in the State of Texas." While he likely slew far fewer than the forty-two men he claimed to have killed, Hardin's reputation for gun handling was nevertheless well-deserved.

At the time of his final arrest, he was credited in the newspapers with twenty-seven homicides. The correct number may never be absolutely established, but author Bill O'Neal has documented nineteen specific gunfights in which Hardin dispatched eleven antagonists and possibly one more. Exhaustive research subsequently conducted by Chuck Parsons and Norman Wayne Brown indicates the tally could perhaps be increased to include eleven to sixteen additional victims. Naturally, the possibility exists that Hardin shot men in the course of further altercations to which he has not been linked.[19]

John Wesley Hardin. #1235. Noah H. Rose Photograph Collection. *Courtesy Western History Collections, University of Oklahoma Libraries, Norman, Oklahoma.*

Hardin was a cousin to the Emanuel "Mannen" Clements family, which was allied to the Taylors of DeWitt County, and had aided his relatives in their feud with the Sutton faction. He was forced into hiding by his murder of Brown County Deputy Sheriff Charles M. Webb while in Comanche on May 26, 1874. Heretofore, Hardin had enjoyed a considerable measure of sympathy and support from the general population of Texas. Unfortunately for the gunfighter, Webb had been a sincere, well-liked peace officer, and, with this most recent slaying, the goodwill bestowed on Hardin evaporated. Governor Coke initially offered an eighteen-hundred-dollar reward for the killer's capture. Hardin fled Texas with his wife, Jane, and infant daughter, Molly, and traveled to Florida. There he assumed the alias of "John H. Swain," operated saloons, caroused and gambled, fathered a son, then moved to Alabama one step ahead of the Pinkertons. On January 20, 1875, the legislature authorized the governor to offer another reward of four thousand dollars for Hardin being "delivered within the jail house door of Travis County."[20]

Doubtless to his chagrin, Armstrong had accidentally shot himself on May 29, 1877, and was walking with the aid of a cane. Nonetheless, he still requested permission to work the Hardin case. On July 15, John Riley "Jack" Duncan, a Dallas policeman, was recruited to assist him as a Ranger private. Adopting the guise of a Taylor partisan, Duncan was sent to work undercover in DeWitt and Gonzales Counties. He cultivated a relationship with Neill Bowen, Hardin's father-in-law, and discovered the gunfighter's location in Alabama. On August 18, the two manhunters set out in pursuit aboard an eastbound train from Austin. Adjutant General William Steele endeavored to secure arrest warrants for Hardin under his given name and his alias, which he promised to forward to Armstrong. While in Montgomery, Armstrong waited for the legal documents from Steele. Duncan went on ahead to Pollard, Alabama, then to Pensacola, Florida. He telegraphed Armstrong to hurry as he had found their quarry. Once Armstrong arrived in Pensacola, the two Rangers enlisted the assistance of Escambia County Sheriff William Henry "Hutch" Hutchinson to aid them in the apprehension, although they did not reveal Swain's true identity.[21]

On August 23, while planning the arrest, the officers were informed that Hardin was set to take the afternoon train to Pollard. Armstrong,

Duncan, Sheriff Hutchinson, and eight deputized citizens decided to take the outlaw into custody once he was on the train. After Hardin and three of his friends were aboard the smoking car, Armstrong took up his position in the adjacent express car. Duncan, Hutchinson, and a deputy were poised to enter the smoker on the end behind Hardin and opposite from Armstrong, while the remaining deputies secured the station and platform. Duncan and the county officers boarded the car at the same moment Armstrong entered, facing Hardin. The fugitive saw the long-barreled Colt .45 in Armstrong's hand and whispered that something "smelt of Texas business." The sheriff seized Hardin, who struggled and tried to reach for his own weapon. The gun tangled in his suspender strap. Twenty-one-year-old James W. "Jim" Mann, one of Hardin's friends, pulled his pistol and fired at Armstrong but missed. Armstrong shot back several times, and the assailant jumped through the window. Once the Ranger fired more accurately, Mann collapsed dead on the platform. As Duncan, Hutchinson, and the deputy struggled to restrain Hardin, Armstrong demanded the killer's surrender, but he replied, "Shoot and be damned, I'd rather die than be arrested." Armstrong smashed his gun barrel over the outlaw's head, which allowed the officers to manacle the stunned man.[22]

The Escambia County lawmen were sent home with thanks, while the two Rangers, their prisoner in hand, ordered the train to continue to Whiting. Armstrong placed Hardin in the jail while he and Duncan waited for General Steele to forward them the necessary rendition papers. On August 23, Armstrong sent a telegram to General Steele: "Arrested John Wesley Hardin, Pensacola, Florida this P.M. ... Hurried aboard the train then leaving for this place. We are waiting for a train to get away on. This is Hardin's home and his friends are trying to rally men to release him. Have some good citizens with [me], and will make it interesting."[23]

Concerned about the possibility of a breakout, the two lawmen moved Hardin to Montgomery, where he was again placed under heavy guard in the local lockup. There they waited two long days for the needed extradition warrants. On August 24, Armstrong sent a second telegram to the adjutant general: "Arrived this A.M. Prisoner in jail. No Papers whatsoever received by the Governor. What is the matter?"[24]

Hardin secured the services of an attorney who petitioned the court for a writ of *habeas corpus*. Appearing before the local judge, Armstrong identified himself as a sworn law officer from Texas and produced the copy of the telegram requesting the proper warrants. The magistrate was sympathetic to the Rangers' plight and continued the case for five days. Anxious the whole affair was being doomed by a slow-moving bureaucracy and mail system, Armstrong sent two telegrams. The first was again to General Steele: "Hardin taken out on writ of Habeas Corpus. Case continued until Wednesday. Send another requisition by man or express. Am afraid it will miscarry by mail as did the first. Answer." He then sent another message to Governor Hubbard: "Please telegraph the Governor of Alabama that you have forwarded requisition for John Wesley Hardin alias John Swain. They were trying to release him on writ of habeas Corpus."[25]

Governor Hubbard contacted George Smith Houston, his counterpart in Montgomery, the same day and the matter was settled. Armstrong sent one final message to General Steele: "If requisition does not come tonight Gov. Houston will issue warrant on Gov. Hubbard's telegram so I can leave here at six tomorrow morning ..."[26]

Armstrong, Duncan, and Hardin left Montgomery on August 25, followed by a throng of curious spectators. As they passed through Memphis on the twenty-sixth, and Little Rock and Longview the following day, each train station was packed by a large crowd. Indeed, word of Hardin's capture had raced ahead, so when they arrived in Austin on August 28, a multitude of people had already gathered in front of the Travis County jail. The Rangers were forced to lift Hardin and carry him over the heads of the assembled onlookers to the jailhouse door. In an interview with the *Statesman*, Armstrong credited Duncan with working up the arrest. Hardin stood trial in Comanche for Deputy Webb's killing beginning on September 28. Once the case was handed to the jury two days later, the defendant was convicted of second-degree murder after three hours' deliberation. Following a failed appeal, Judge James Richard Fleming of the Twelfth Judicial District sentenced Hardin to Huntsville Penitentiary for twenty-five years at hard labor. While the notorious gunman became Convict No. 7109, Armstrong and Duncan received the promised reward from the legislature, and the former was promoted to first lieutenant on December 1, 1877.[27]

For four years, Armstrong had been enchanted by Mary Helena "Mollie" Durst, a young lady known for her "loveliness, amiability of manners, accomplishments and talent." He may have first met her, on June 5, 1874, when she presented a flag to the Travis Rifles on behalf of the ladies of Austin. With the Hardin business complete, he decided the time had come to call upon her. Born in Austin on March 22, 1855, the object of his affections was the daughter of Major James H. and Mary Josephine (Atwood) Durst. The elder Durst had commanded a company of mounted riflemen in 1838 and 1839. The courtship was brief, and Armstrong and Mollie married at St. David's Episcopal Church in Austin on February 20, 1878.[28]

The following month, Armstrong returned to duty. Hall telegraphed him to bring any available men to Round Rock in anticipation of apprehending stage and train robber Sam Bass. The careers of the outlaw and his gang came to an end in a wild shootout in Round Rock's streets before Armstrong could reach the scene. Despite missing the gun battle, the lieutenant remained active. On December 5, a stagecoach robbery, perpetrated by two masked men, occurred one and a half miles from Marion. Armstrong arrived on the Luling stage the following morning, and surveyed the crime scene. He was able to follow the thieves' sign only a short distance through the thicket before losing the trail on the prairie. Witnesses to the robbery, and the Ranger, were of the same opinion: the suspects were not professional criminals. One local "bad character" was suspected, but no evidence existed with which Armstrong could take immediate action. By this point in time, Armstrong may have decided, with a new bride to support, he needed a more financially beneficial occupation. Regardless, he resigned his commission in the Special State Troops on December 30, 1878.[29]

Armstrong and Mollie first resided at Mary Durst's boardinghouse on Hickory Street in Austin. His rangering days now fully behind him, Armstrong entered into the business of real estate investments and land development projects with an office on the corner of Congress Avenue and Bois d'Arc Street (present Seventh Street).[30] While his commercial interests expanded, the Armstrongs experienced a growing family. To the couple were born Maria Josephine, on April 5, 1879; Jamie Durst, on January 5, 1881; John Barclay, Jr (IV), on July 7, 1884; and Charles Mitchell, on November 8, 1886.[31]

In December 1852, Mollie's father had purchased from the José Francisco Ballí family the lower fourteen leagues of the La Barreta land grant in what is now Kenedy County. After Major Durst's death in 1858, his widow took their two young children to Austin. Over the course of five or six years, Charles George Lovenskiold and John Solomon McCampbell, two Nueces County lawyers, defrauded the family of ownership of the land. Once Armstrong learned of the scheme, he, Mollie, and James William Durst, her brother, brought suit in 1883 to regain title to the property. Unfortunately, the already complex web of conflicting rights grew even worse in September 1886. John W. Mackay held seventy-six land certificates, each for 640 acres, and claimed land that was part of the La Barreta grant. Asserting the tract was vacant public land, Mackay sued Armstrong and the others in court. The defendants, aided by their attorneys, Bethel Coopwood and James Babbage Wells, Jr., gathered depositions and official documentation from Mexican archives to prove the validity of the grant. After a lengthy legal process, their claim was established in Nueces County District Court on March 26, 1889, but the judge failed to publish the law and facts he used in his decision. On appeal, the state supreme court reversed the judgement and sent the case back to the lower court. Based on this decision, and with the passage of the Confirmation Act in 1901, the State of Texas sued Armstrong and his fellow defendants the following year, claiming the land to be public. The case was finally resolved on October 26, 1904, in favor of the Durst/Armstrong family. The confirmation patent was signed on January 18, 1907.[32]

While the case worked its way through the courts, Armstrong, James, and rancher Mifflin Kenedy developed La Barreta into a successful cattle spread. In 1883, James began to live on the ranch in order to authenticate the family's claim. Two years later, Armstrong and his family, including his mother-in-law, joined James on the property. While living in a one-room shack, Armstrong and "don Fermín," an elderly Mexican carpenter, spent eighteen months building a new, more spacious ranch house in the Chicago pasture. Their new home became known as Las Agujas (The Needles), or the Chicago Ranch. By 1887, Armstrong's nearly 32,000 acres boasted two horses; the next year, eight horses and 144 head of cattle. In 1889, he was assessed for fifty thousand acres, twelve horses, and six hundred head.[33]

Despite his achievements in business, Armstrong remained interested in the profession of arms. On April 3, 1888, he was mustered into the Brownsville Rifles as a private. Likely due to the immense expanse of Nueces, Cameron, and Hidalgo Counties surrounding the ranch, and its distance from any county seat, Armstrong was also appointed a Special Ranger attached to Company D, Frontier Battalion on June 5. Adjutant General Wilburn Hill King had initiated the practice early in his tenure after legislatures began to regularly slash appropriations. Provided the total number never exceeded the legally mandated 450 men, the unpaid position allowed the individual in question to legitimately carry a firearm and possess arrest powers. These appointments were typically held by stock association and railroad detectives, local law officers, and prominent citizens such as Armstrong.[34]

Meanwhile, Armstrong worked to develop his ranch holdings at the same time his family grew. Julia Katherine was born on February 5, 1889; Elliott Ropes "Tim" arrived on October 9, 1890; and Thomas Reeves on September 5, 1892. By 1891, Armstrong was running fifty horses and fifteen hundred head of cattle. The following two years, his herd numbered twenty-four horses and 850 head. In 1893, the ranch headquarters was moved approximately seven miles northwest to its present site where a new house, also called the "Chicago Ranch," was built. The old building was moved to the grounds of the newer headquarters and renamed "the Cottage."[35]

Armstrong's twin interests in business and military affairs continued on a track of success. On January 2, 1891, he was appointed to the headquarters of the Second Brigade, First Division, Texas Volunteer Guard as a quartermaster with the rank of major. In compliance with General Orders No. 2, dated February 21 of the same year, Armstrong returned his Special Ranger commission on March 6. In his letter to Adjutant General Woodford Haywood Mabry, he listed his occupation as manager of the Corpus Christi & South American Railway Company. Indeed, on April 30, Armstrong was elected to the railroad's board of directors. On January 10, 1893, he traveled to Brownsville, where he was appointed to the open position of assistant inspector general on the brigade staff. Brigadier-General Rawleigh Portues Smyth became the new brigade commander on the same day. By the following year, Armstrong was involved in the San Antonio & Aransas Pass Railroad as the land and tax agent. On May 1, 1895, he was promoted to lieutenant-colonel and appointed to the First Division staff in Alice as assistant chief of ordnance. For reasons of his own, even though he held a higher grade, Armstrong always preferred to be addressed as "Major Armstrong." He retired from the Volunteer Guard on July 13, 1900.[36]

In December 1897, while playing with Julia's pet dog in their comfortable house at 2610 Whitis Avenue in Austin, Mollie received a scratch that had tragic consequences. The family belatedly discovered the Newfoundland was rabid, and Mollie became ill ten days after the incident. She died in terrible agony on December 25. Armstrong had been away from home on ranch business and arrived two days later. The funeral was held on December 28 at St. David's Church, the scene of their wedding nineteen years earlier, and she was laid to rest in Oakwood Cemetery. Armstrong took his children back to Austin, where Mary Durst cared for them until her passing in 1912. Tragically, Elliott died of diphtheria on the evening of May 30, 1898, and was also buried in Oakwood Cemetery. The deaths of his wife and son were a serious blow to Armstrong, ones from which he never fully recovered.[37]

Finding solace in civic affairs, he directed his energies into the economic development of South Texas. For years, citizens on the lower Rio Grande had sought to bring the railroad to Brownsville, and the recent drilling of artesian wells and successful experimenting with cash crops promised rich opportunities for commercial farming. With the support of his fellow ranchers, Armstrong petitioned the Southern Pacific, which controlled the San Antonio & Aransas Pass Railroad, to lay tracks from Alice to Brownsville. The Southern Pacific declined despite frequent requests due to the undeveloped status of the region. Influential citizens in Cameron, Hidalgo, and Nueces Counties were determined to acquire a rail line and approached railroad promoter Uriah Lott, who proved enthusiastic about the project.[38]

In 1899, Lott partnered with railroad executive Benjamin Franklin Yoakum in a syndicate to raise the necessary capital. After acquiring financing from the St. Louis Union Trust Company, the construction firm of Johnston Brothers, owned by Benjamin Franklin and Presley Morgan Johnston of St. Elmo, Illinois, was contracted to build the entire railway. On June 6, 1903, the St. Louis, Brownsville & Mexico Railway Company was granted a charter from the state. Among its original incorporators were many of the prominent ranchers and business leaders of the region, including Robert Justus Kleberg, Sr., Caesar Kleberg, John Gregory Kenedy, Richard King II, Robert Driscoll, Sr., Jim Wells, and John Armstrong. Lott was named the company's first president. After the contracts were signed, the company secured the right-of-way, managed land donations and cash bonuses, and located new town sites. The railroad's principals established real estate firms and irrigation companies, converted some of their ranch acreage into farmland, and promoted townsites. The major formed the Armstrong Town and Improvement Company of Corpus Christi, with a capital stock of 3,200 acres worth $500,000. The first segment of the line was built from Corpus Christi to Brownsville, followed by the second from Robstown to Bay City, and the third from Bay City to Houston. The St. Louis, Brownsville & Mexico arrived at the town of Katherine on March 4, 1904, which served as Armstrong's shipping point on the railroad. The first passenger train arrived in Brownsville on July 4, amid a great celebration. The venture proved visionary as the trains brought in waves of farmers eager to plant cotton and corn, land speculators, irrigation engineers, and produce wholesalers. Later in the year, Armstrong united with Kleberg, Driscoll, and Kenedy in pledging to spend $20,000 for the planting of orange groves on each man's ranch.[39]

In the aftermath of a substantial commercial and social triumph, tragedy once again struck the Armstrong family. Having studied engineering at the University of Texas and Texas A&M, John Jr., was thrown from his horse while working cattle and died from a broken neck on May 6, 1905. Major Armstrong was on hand and could only watch helplessly as his son perished.[40]

Despite suffering crushing personal losses, Armstrong carried on for over a decade before he died at three p.m. on May 1, 1913, in Kingsville. He had been attended by Doctor Martin Emmett Miles since April 26,

B. F. Yoakum. #1975/070-5451. William Deming Hornaday Collection. *Courtesy Texas State Library and Archives Commission, Austin, Texas.*

before succumbing to "uremia due to chronic intestinal nephritis." Following a service at St. David's church in Austin, he was buried beside Mollie at Oakwood Cemetery.[41]

In his last will and testament, dated September 26, 1912, Armstrong had divided his assets evenly between his five surviving children "as nearly as practicable, share and share alike." In addition, a monthly stipend of $150 was advanced to Julia and Tom, the youngest siblings, until she married and he turned twenty-three. Charles, Tom, and Jamie's husband were named as executors of the estate.[42]

Josephine attended Washington College in Chestertown, Maryland, in 1896, and H. Sophie Newcomb College in New Orleans. She married cotton broker Andrew Stewart, Jr. on April 18, 1906, at St. Mark's Episcopal Church in San Antonio. They lived in New Orleans, where Andrew maintained his office. In 1925, the couple purchased the Oak Alley Plantation near Vacherie in St. James Parish. They refurbished the ramshackle house, first built in 1836, which was later given a National Historic Landmark designation. Andrew died on October 28, 1946, and was buried in the plantation's cemetery. Josephine died on October 3, 1972, and left the manor and twenty-five acres to a non-profit foundation she had created. She was laid to rest next to her husband.[43]

Jamie attended Washington College in Chestertown, Maryland, Sophie Newcomb College in New Orleans, and the University of Texas at Austin, where she graduated in 1901 with a bachelor of science degree. She married John Mirza Bennett at St. David's on April 26, 1905. Her husband was a banker at the National Bank of Commerce in San Antonio, and a cattle rancher. Together they raised three daughters and one son. Jamie died of cerebral thrombosis at Nix Memorial Hospital on April 22, 1963. She was cremated two days later.[44]

Charles attended Yale University Law School from 1905 to 1908, graduated with a bachelor of laws (LL.B.) degree, and was a member of the legal fraternity of Phi Delta Phi. He was successful in the real estate business in Brownsville before succeeding his father in managing the ranch. He married Lucie Tobin Carr at St. Mark's on January 23, 1918, and fathered three sons and one daughter. While ably managing his ranching interests, Charles was also an avid polo player and introduced the sport to South Texas. He was involved in a fatal car crash on September 13, 1941, and was buried in Oakwood Cemetery.[45]

Julia attended Hollins Academy in Botetourt Springs, Virginia, in 1904, and later Sophie Newcomb in New Orleans. She married lumber merchant Zeb Mayhew on December 31, 1913, at St. Mark's. They lived on Great Neck, Long Island, New York, and raised one son and two daughters. She divorced Mayhew in 1925 and married lumber company manager George Allard Kaufmann in New Orleans on February 25, 1936. Her second husband died on August 1, 1956. She died in New Orleans on December 26, 1991.[46]

Of all the Armstrong children, Thomas might have been the one most similar to his adventurous father. He graduated with a bachelor of letters (B.Litt.) degree from Princeton University in 1913, and from Harvard Law School with a LL.B. degree three years later. After a short stint at the Andrews-Kurth law firm in Houston, Tom volunteered for army service and was sent to the Officer Training Camp in Leon Springs, Texas, in May 1917. Commissioned a captain of Field Artillery on August 15, he was assigned to Battery F, 345th Field Artillery, 90th Division on August 29. He embarked with the American Expeditionary Forces to France on June 30, 1918. Fighting in the Meuse-Argonne Offensive, he was promoted to major on October 6, and commanded the Second Battalion. He remained with the Army of Occupation in Germany from December 1918 to May 1919 before returning home to be discharged on June 11. Unenthusiastic about returning to the practice of law, he wound up handling Standard Oil of New Jersey's South American operations for the next twenty-four years. After service with the War Production Board in Washington, D.C., and Charles's death, Tom returned to Texas and managed the ranch. On June 4, 1949, he married the widow Henrietta Rosa (Kleberg) Larkin, granddaughter of Richard King, at the Church of the Holy Trinity in New York City. Interestingly, Armstrong had been a good friend and Princeton classmate of Henrietta's late husband, John Adrian Larkin. Indeed, he had introduced them and had served as best man at their wedding thirty-four years earlier. In addition to being his brother-in-law and neighbor, Armstrong was lifelong friends with Robert Justus "Bob" Kleberg, Jr., the chief executive of the King Ranch, and they were said to have "shared great and trying adventures." Henrietta died in October 23, 1969, and the major followed her in death on March 3, 1986.[47]

John B. Armstrong was a man who brought modernity to the border country. As a Texas Ranger, he rooted out the lawless characters infesting the region, then returned as a pioneering cattleman. While he could have been content as a large land owner, he recognized the necessity of transforming the lower valley into an agricultural center. To that end, he welcomed both the railroad and the farmer. Even with all his later achievements, the capture of John Wesley Hardin remains his most celebrated feat.

James B. Gillett. *Courtesy Marfa Public Library, Marfa, Texas.*

Chapter 4

James B. Gillett: "Unflinchingly Faced both Indians and Outlaws"

James Buchanan Gillett served six years with the Frontier Battalion. While not a lengthy career, his tenure was longer than most at that time, and he unflinchingly faced both Indians and outlaws. After a stint as marshal of the one of the toughest towns in the West, he played a pivotal role in the ranching industry of the Big Bend. Author Leon Metz called Gillett "a man of courage, intelligence, and resourcefulness. Within his limitations, he epitomized the near perfect lawman, and set standards equaled but never exceeded to this day." His contributions to the Ranger service did not end with his resignation from the Frontier Battalion, though. In his twilight years, he penned a revealing first-hand account of life as a Texas Ranger in the Old West.

He was born in Austin, Travis County, Texas, on November 4, 1856. His parents were James Shackleford and Elizabeth Jane "Bettie" (Harper) Gillett. The elder Gillett had been born in Lincoln County, Kentucky, on April 1, 1810, and lived in Missouri, Santa Fé, and Van Buren, Arkansas, before settling in Paris, Texas, in 1839. Trained as a lawyer, he also commanded ranger companies under John C. "Jack" Hays and Peter Hansbrough Bell during the Mexican War, and rose to the rank of major. He later served as adjutant general of Texas in the Bell and Elisha Marshall Pease administrations with the rank of colonel. Born on August 5, 1825, Bettie was the daughter of a planter who had emigrated from North Carolina to Washington County, Texas. The two married on November 8, 1850, in the same locale. Five children were born to the couple, but only James, Mary Harper Gillett, born in August 11, 1854, and Eva Gillett, born on December 24, 1858, survived into adulthood; two brothers died in infancy. During the Civil War, the elder Gillett was mustered into Captain William H. D. Carrington's company of mounted troops on March 16, 1864. Further details of his service are unknown. The three children attended local pay schools in Austin. Gillett started at a German school and endured two tedious years until classes closed in the summer of 1868; he never returned. By 1872 the family had moved to Lampasas due to Bettie's ill health. Gillett soon started working on ranches in Lampasas, Coleman, and Menard Counties. By the time of his last riding job, he was making thirty dollars a month, which was considered top wages for a cowhand at that time.[1]

On June 1, 1875, Gillett went to the Little Saline near Menardville and enrolled in Lieutenant Daniel Webster "Dan" Roberts's Company D of the Frontier Battalion. He later recalled, "This was probably the happiest day of my life, for in joining the rangers I had realized one of my greatest ambitions." Once the enlistment process was completed, the company shifted its headquarters to Camp Las Moras, five miles southwest of Menardville. Gillett's skill and commitment to duty impressed his commander and his comrades. In return, the new recruit thought his lieutenant was "the best of company commanders." Furthermore, Sergeant Nelson Orcelus "Mage" Reynolds acted as the young Ranger's mentor, and Gillett likewise held the highest respect for him. On June 23, Major Jones instructed Roberts to scout north of Bear Creek on the Llano River to the Colorado, while Captain Cornelius Vernon "Neal" Coldwell was to do the same south of the Llano. Roberts reported Reynolds's detachment, sent to the North Llano, found no sign of Indians, as did another which scouted the Colorado.[2]

Under the dynamic Roberts, Company D held a reputation for being a tough outfit of Indian fighters.[3] Gillett's first action occurred in August 1875. A band of fifteen warriors raided the John Gamble ranch on Honey Creek and stole horses that were hitched within twenty-five steps of the ranch house. Private Lamartine Pemberton "Lam" Sieker was sitting in the lobby

Dan W. Roberts. From James B. Gillett's *Six Years with the Texas Rangers*.

of the Frontier Hotel in Mason when he received word of the raid. He saddled up and rode all through the night fifty miles west to Camp Las Moras. After Sieker arrived about eight o'clock in the morning and reported to Roberts, the captain ordered Sergeant Newton Harris "Plunk" Murray to assemble eleven men with ten days' rations and one hundred rounds of ammunition each for a scout; novice Ranger Gillett was one of the detachment. He wrote, "As can be imagined, I was delighted with my good fortune in getting on the party and looked forward with intense satisfaction to my first brush with the Indians."[4]

Crossing the San Saba River, Roberts deployed two scouts, and the Rangers quickly found the trail of the Indians on Scalp Creek on August 20. Thought to be approximately thirty-five to forty miles ahead, the raiders continued on into the flat country between the head of the South Concho River and the Pecos. They were finally spotted early on the fourth day of the pursuit, and Roberts advised his men to "tighten their cinches, leave their coats and slickers, and make ready to fight." Giving last-minute orders to the detachment, the lieutenant led the double file of Rangers to within four to six hundred yards of the enemy before they were noticed. The Indians, presumed to be Lipans, raced to their horses and positioned themselves on nearby elevated ground fifteen or twenty feet apart using their mounts as shields.[5]

Once within one hundred steps of the enemy, the Rangers dismounted and began to shoot the enemy's horses. The battle was joined, and within minutes the Indians had mounted in order to escape. Roberts ordered the Rangers to pursue. After finally getting astride his nervous horse, Gillett, along with Edward Armon Sieker, Jr. set out after an Indian who first ran on foot and then rode double with another warrior. In the running fight, the Indian riding behind dropped his rifle and a "fine rawhide rope," hoping to distract the two Rangers; when that failed, he began shooting arrows. Following the braves into a mesquite grove, Gillett closed to within twenty steps of the Indians, dismounted, and shot the fleeing horse. The first Indian hit the ground running and fled into the tress, and Gillett remounted to continue the chase. As he passed the dead horse, the private noticed the other warrior was pinned underneath and that he was actually a white boy with red hair. Sieker was credited with overtaking and killing the fleeing brave. The white boy was not found in the aftermath of the fight even after the area was searched. The Rangers did not lose a man, while they killed one Indian and three horses, wounded another warrior, recovered a stolen Mexican boy, and captured fifty-eight horses and mules. Numerous enemy saddles, bridles, and trinkets were seized. The red-haired youngster and Gillett were reunited forty-nine years later at an annual meeting of the Old Time Trail Driver's Association in San Antonio. Gillett learned the now-grown man was actually Herman Lehman, and he had been captured by Apaches to be raised as one of their own.[6]

As a private, Gillett was not mentioned by name in any of the early reports submitted to the battalion commander. His involvement in individual apprehensions is unknown, but Company D operated from Camp Las Moras and Camp Jones, a later bivouac five miles above Menardville. Active in Menard, Mason, Kimble, and McCulloch Counties, noncommissioned officers reported various arrests in the first month of 1876, including those of Kimble County Sheriff J. M. Reynolds for intentionally allowing prisoners to escape, R. M. Johnson for swindling, William Gentry and Albert Gambe for handling stolen cattle, Luke Hamilton for rustling, Reuben Hornsby "Rube" Boyce for murder, Black Bush and Sam Monroe for cattle theft, and James Moore for the same crime.[7]

During the summer of 1876, Major Jones planned a campaign to strike the Lipans and Kickapoos on the Pecos. On June 18, the battalion commander assembled twenty men of Company D, including Gillett, and all thirty men of Captain Ira Long's Company A, and rode into Kerr County. There he also gathered to his force a portion of Captain Coldwell's Company F. After ten days of scouting, the column reached Fort Lancaster, then marched up to the head of Live Oak Creek. From that point, they rode to the South Concho and returned to Camp Jones near Menardville on July 14.[8]

By this time, Company A, which served as Major Jones's escort, had several vacancies in its ranks, including the position of company commander. Lieutenant Long had resigned on August 15. Rather than oversee operations strictly from an office, the major had established a mobile command post in the form of a wagon—generally referred to as an ambulance—and personally visited each company in the field. His escort primarily provided protection to Jones, but they were also available to pursue any Indian trails discovered along their route, support beleaguered areas, and undertake special assignments.[9] Gillett recalled several Company D members were anxious to apply for the open positions:

> They wanted me to go with them, but I hesitated to leave Captain Roberts. My friends then explained that we could see a lot more country on the escort than we could in a stationary company; and that we would probably be stationed down on the Rio Grande that winter, and going up the line in the spring would see thousands of buffalo. This buffalo proposition caught me, and I went with the boys.[10]

His decision to remain or go to Company A was made easier when Roberts chose to resign, effective August 31. Accordingly, Gillett, Charles Liborn Nevill, and "Mage" Reynolds, as well as three others, transferred to the escort company on September 1, 1876. First Lieutenant John M. Denton was appointed the company commander.[11]

Spending September in camp on the Salado, the company accompanied the major in October on his last inspection tour for the year. Gillett later wrote of the escort's dispositions when on the march:

> Each morning at roll call the orderly sergeant detailed a guard of nine men and one non-commissioned officer to guard for twenty-four hours. When ready to begin our day's journey, the company was formed in line and the men counted off by fours. On the march Major Jones and Doctor [E. G.] Nicholson [the battalion surgeon] rode in front, followed by the captain of the company, the orderly sergeant, and the men in double file. Following these came the wagons. An advance guard of two men preceded the column about one-half mile. Four men, known as flankers, two on each side of the company, paralleled the column at a distance of one-half to a mile, depending on the nature of the country ... The non-commissioned officer with the remaining guard covered the rear and brought up

the pack-mules. Thus protected, it was almost impossible for the command to be surprised by Indians.[12]

At the end of the tour, effective December 1, Lieutenant Denton resigned his commission for health reasons, and he was succeeded by Captain Coldwell the same day. Nevill was promoted to the rank of first corporal, but he was discharged at the request of his father on December 15.[13]

Over the winter, Company A made their headquarters at Camp Hubbard in Frio County. Early in 1877, Sergeant Reynolds was directed to position himself and five men thirty miles up the Sabinal and watch from there to D'Hanis on the Seco for the approach of raiding Indians. Corporal Jackson was to take four men to Woodward's pasture on the Llano, eighteen miles from camp, and likewise keep vigil. The balance of the company remained in camp ready to respond to any depredations, or conducted daily patrols. In April, citizens of the county circulated a petition requesting Company A be retained in the vicinity. Major Jones noted that the petition was the thirteenth such in the last month from as many different quarters that were demanding assistance. He further observed the impossibility of responding to each call due to the limitations of manpower and budget. Indeed, Coldwell's men were soon thereafter on the trail to Kimble County before returning to Frio on June 23.[14]

At the same time, the stagecoach running from San Antonio to Fort McKavett had been robbed on January 19, 1877, near the relay station at the Pegleg Crossing of the San Saba River. The hold-up was not the first, nor the last, and occurred at the usual location—a draw where the horses had to strain to climb the west bank. Bandits had a hideout nearby called the "roost," from which they could observe the coach and determine whether it was too well protected. In the past, Captain Roberts had assigned a Ranger to ride shotgun on the stage in an effort to halt the repeated holdups. Invariably, when the guard was removed, the robberies resumed. Posses usually lost the trail in the rough country to the south.[15]

One of the suspects in the robbery was William Allison, who had familial ties to the Dublin clan. James "Jimmy" Dublin, patriarch of the family, operated a ranch in Kimble, which offered sanctuary to outlaws, including Allison, who was his son-in-law, and his three sons, James Roland, also known as

"Roll," John Sheldon, or "Dell," and Richard, or "Dick." On April 16, Dell and Lewis "Luke" Cathey, likely accompanied by Roll, Allison, and Mack Potter, murdered a man near the South Llano over the ownership of a cow. Four days later, members of Company A attempted to arrest Dick and Dell Dublin and Potter, but the apprehension seems to have been unsuccessful. According to his autobiography, Gillett had known the Dublin brothers while working as a cowhand for rancher Joseph Franks in 1873.[16]

Three days later, Major Jones quietly led Company A and thirteen men from Company F down the North and South Llano Rivers and its tributaries, methodically searching the countryside and arresting every suspicious person. The four groups were then to rendezvous with the major and the main body on the nineteenth at Junction in Kimble County. Gillett accompanied one scout to Fort McKavett and arrested several hardcases there. His horse was injured and, once Coldwell's men rode north, Gillett was forced to remain with Company D until the escort returned six weeks later. Roll and Allison were arrested as accomplices to the April 16 killing, while Dell, Dick, Potter, and Cathey escaped the dragnet.[17]

Later in the summer, Company A was ordered to break up an insurgent expedition into Mexico being raised by Colonel Pedro Advíncula Valdés, also known as "Winker," near Eagle Pass. Traveling to the Rio Grande, and cooperating with Lee Hall's Special State Troops, Sergeant George Washington Arrington and nineteen men arrested more than fifty revolutionaries. While Major Jones was addressing the Horrell-Higgins trouble, he instructed Coldwell to send Gillett to Lampasas to reinforce the Ranger presence in the county, and to visit his widowed mother.[18]

On August 24, Sergeant "Mage" Reynolds was promoted to second lieutenant and given command of Company E, then in Coleman County. As the outfit was being organized, Reynolds specifically requested Gillett and Charles Nevill be added to the company rolls. Gillett had been working the border country, and he arrived at Reynolds's camp decked out in a wide sombrero, fringed buckskin jacket, and large-roweled Mexican spurs. He soon changed his appearance to clothes more appropriate to Central Texas. All three Rangers were mustered in on September 1, 1877, with Nevill becoming the first sergeant.[19]

Nelson O. Reynolds. From James B. Gillett's *Six Years with the Texas Rangers.*

Following the capture of the infamous John Wesley Hardin in Florida, and his subsequent extradition to Austin, every member of Company E was detailed to escort the gunfighter to Comanche for his murder trial, and to protect him from mob violence. The Rangers left with their heavily shackled prisoner on September 19, and delivered him to the Comanche County jail five days later. The mood of the outraged townspeople prompted Nelson to keep his men guarding Hardin inside the jail while twenty-five deputized citizens were positioned outside. In his autobiography, Hardin claimed that "the brave Reynolds told me that if the mob attacked me or the jail he would arm me and let me out to rough it with him and his men." There exists only Hardin's word for Reynolds's alleged promise, but the fact remains the "intrepid" Ranger lieutenant was determined to protect his prisoner from a lynch mob. The trial convened in Judge James Richard Fleming's courtroom on the twentieth-eighth and the proceedings lasted until the thirtieth. Once Hardin was convicted of murder in the second degree, he appealed the verdict and was taken back to the Travis County lockup, arriving on October 6.[20]

While the Hardin case moved through the court system, Company E broke camp on October 23, and conveyed prisoners Bill Allison and Wes Johnson the 180 miles to Kimble County. For the first four days of November, they assisted the sheriff in guarding the jailed outlaws. With their protection duties completed, Corporal Warren and three men escorted District Court Judge William Allen Blackburn to Menardville, while Gillett and six men were sent to pursue a party of Lipans who had raided into Junction. After an uneventful round-trip of seventy miles, Gillett's detachment returned the same day. He was dispatched with three Rangers on the seventh to McIvers's ranch on the Saline to apprehend Ben Allen, a fugitive from Mason County, but the officers failed to find their quarry. Another scout was ordered on November 11, with Gillett and two men being sent to Runnels County to capture Tom Runnels and George McReynolds. While on the Concho, they apprehended another man who was charged with assault and battery in Limestone County. The detachment returned to camp on the seventeenth.[21]

While Gillett and his men were gone from camp, the captains of Companies B, C, and E were instructed to each discharge four men from their respective commands on November 12, effective at the end of the month.

Whether due to their friendship with Reynolds, or their excellent records as lawmen, Gillett and Nevill were retained in the service. The company moved its headquarters to Camp Bear Creek in Kimble County. On November 21, Reynolds and two men captured Dell Dublin at a cow pen four miles from Junction. The fugitive was easily taken, but warned his brother Dick, who had just ridden up as Dell was being placed into custody. Kimble County did not possess a jail at that time, so Gillett and five Rangers took the prisoner to Llano County two days later. Through the remainder of the year, the state officers conducted several scouts looking for Starke Reynolds and Dick Dublin. Corporal Gillett commanded one such excursion on December 8, another the next day, and a third on December 24. At the same time, more stage holdups occurred at the Pegleg Crossing on December 14, and on July 5, 1878. Once more, the unidentified robbers escaped capture.[22]

On January 16, 1878, Gillett and five Rangers rode out in pursuit of the remaining Dublin brother and fellow murderer Ace Langford. On the fourth day of the manhunt, the officers reached Thomas Potter's ranch on Packsaddle Creek and crept up on the house where they believed the killer to be hiding. "Old Man" Potter was outside doing chores and, once the posse moved into the open, he shouted, "Run, Dick, run! Here come the Rangers!" The officers spurred their horses forward and Dublin, cut off from the corral, raced into the brush. Galloping after him, Gillett called for the outlaw to halt, then fired a warning rifle shot when he failed to comply. Dublin vanished down into a ravine with Gillett hot on his heels. Catching sight of the fugitive, Gillett again ordered him to halt, but Dublin moved to run. Gillett immediately cut him down. The other members of the scout rode up and, before he could be stopped, Private Ben F. Carter shot Dublin's corpse twice more. The Rangers returned to camp having marched some ninety miles.[23]

On January 24, Sergeant Nevill led another scout for fugitives that captured Rube Boyce, once more wanted for murder, and delivered him to the Kimble County jail. The following month, Lieutenant Reynolds, Gillett, and five other Rangers took five prisoners captured in Kimble and Menard Counties to Austin; Boyce was one of those manacled. Riding along the Junction and Mason road, ten miles from Camp Bear Creek, on February 21, the detachment passed near fugitive Starke Reynolds's ranch. Always before, the outlaw had escaped apprehension, and the lieutenant declared another attempt would only be a waste of time. The officers were barely a half-mile beyond the house when they came face to face with Starke himself on the road. The outlaw and the Rangers were about four hundred yards apart when they saw each other in the same instant. Starke at once turned his horse and raced for the Llano bottoms three miles away. The Rangers chased the fleeing criminal through the dense and scrubby live oak and mesquite brush. Privates Ware, Carter, and Dave L. Ligon dropped out, and Reynolds and Gillett closed on the outlaw as they neared the river. Gillett spurred his horse past the lieutenant and raced ahead. Seeing that he was being pursued by only one man, Starke dropped to the ground and shielded himself behind his horse. He warned Gillett to "Stop or I'll put a load of buckshot into you." Gillett was not able to rein in his horse until he was within twenty-five yards of the shotgun. He then dismounted and moved to engage the outlaw. Starke broke from behind his horse to flee into the thicket, and Gillett fired a shot at him. The fugitive ducked back behind his mount, and Gillett attempted to draw a bead on him. Suddenly, Ligon dashed up and, seeing he was outnumbered, Starke threw down his gun and surrendered. Starke was added to the shackled prisoners and turned over to the Travis County sheriff.[24]

The crackdown on the Pegleg gang continued when thirteen head of stolen cattle were recovered on the South Llano near the Dublin and Allison ranch on March 22. The same day, Mack Potter was arrested on a charge of rustling cattle in Menard County. On the twenty-fourth, Gillett and several other Rangers escorted Potter to Menard County and delivered him into the custody of the sheriff. Nevill and three men took Dell Dublin from Austin to Kimble County on April 11 for trial. They returned to camp with their prisoner on the twenty-ninth. Meanwhile, on April 24, Gillett and two Rangers escorted state witnesses from McKavett to Junction to appear in the Dublin trial. Dublin's friends had threatened any who should testify against him. Gillett's detachment returned on the twenty-seventh. The next day, Lieutenant Reynolds moved the company into Junction to better assist the sheriff in guarding the prisoners. The Rangers remained in town until May 5. Two days later, Corporal Warren and five men escorted the prisoners back to the county jail in Austin. On May 13, the company headquarters was relocated to Camp Barton in Burnet County.[25]

On June 1, Lieutenant Reynolds moved the company to a pecan grove on the San Saba River, two miles from the town of the same name. On July 18, Reynolds received a message from Major Jones that Sam Bass was planning to rob the bank in Round Rock. The battalion commander's orders were to respond to the scene and assist in capturing the outlaw. The lieutenant was too ill to ride a horse and would instead travel by hack. Sergeant Nevill selected a detail of seven men, including Gillett, and, within thirty minutes, the Rangers were ready. Leaving camp at sunset, the Rangers traveled 110 miles in an overnight marathon ride to Round Rock. They made camp on the banks of Brushy Creek on the afternoon of the nineteenth, and Reynolds went into town to report to Jones. As the lieutenant approached Round Rock, he was met by posses pursuing Bass and Francis M. "Frank" Jackson, both of whom had survived the recent shootout with Rangers, local officers, and civilians. The mortally wounded Bass had escaped, but Sergeant Nevill's detachment found him the following morning and returned the outlaw to Round Rock. Reynolds and the company were back in San Saba by July 26.[26]

With the notorious train robber in his grave, the company moved to Camp Stockbridge where more routine assignments awaited Gillett. On August 25, he and five Rangers were sent to assist the San Saba County sheriff in capturing unknown parties for shooting in the streets and disturbing the peace. The monthly return reported "nothing accomplished," and the detachment returned to camp on the twenty-sixth. The Frontier Battalion was reorganized on September 1. In addition to a commanding officer, each company was ordered to be composed of two sergeants, two corporals, and twenty privates.[27]

Having spent a year-long incarceration in Austin, John Wesley Hardin's appeal was denied on June 5, 1878. With the jury's decision upheld, Reynolds and twenty Rangers left camp on September 11, and arrived at the Travis County jail nine days later. They then took the gunfighter to Comanche for sentencing. On September 28, Judge Fleming imposed a term of twenty-five years' imprisonment at hard labor. Gillett was among those who escorted the twenty-six-year-old man-killer to Comanche, then to Huntsville, arriving at the penitentiary on October 5.[28]

On October 23, Company E was ordered to escort Bill Allison and Wesley Johnson to Kimble County for their court dates. Once the trial ended, the Rangers set out to apprehend Caleb Hall and assorted other bandits, rustlers, horse thieves, and murderers hiding out in the brush. Arriving on the North Llano, they established Camp Contrary below the mouth of Bear Creek. Immediately starting to scout the country, they arrested several outlaws wanted on minor charges. Gillett's "good and meritorious conduct" in the recent breakup of the Pegleg gang, among other cases, resulted in his promotion to first corporal on November 24. Meanwhile, Rube Boyce escaped the Travis County jail by using a pistol his wife had smuggled into his cell. Based on the testimony of Allison, who turned state's evidence, the two surviving Dublins and Mack Potter were indicted and convicted by August 1880. Each of them received a ten-year sentence. Allison was found guilty of cattle theft and entered Huntsville penitentiary on May 29, 1881; he served three years. Boyce was captured in Socorro, extradited to Austin, and stood trial in federal district court in February 1882 for the stage robberies. He was convicted, but his attorneys appealed, citing improper conduct on the part of the prosecution and some jurors. Boyce was released on an eight-thousand-dollar bond, pending a new trial.[29]

After Reynolds left the battalion on February 28, 1879, First Sergeant Nevill assumed command and moved the company to Camp Swenson. Gillett resigned from Company E on August 31, and reenlisted in Company C on September 1. He was promoted to the rank of first sergeant on September 12.[30] Being assigned to the detachment posted in Ysleta, Gillett traveled to San Antonio to meet his new commander, Lieutenant George W. Baylor. Once arrived in the Alamo City, Gillett found a new mentor in the older, more seasoned man. The lieutenant was preparing to take his family to Ysleta, and the sergeant joined the escort. The cavalcade traveled for forty-two days through hostile territory before they reached their destination. Despite being under her father's watchful eye, Gillett's attentions were drawn to Lieutenant Baylor's pretty sixteen-year-old daughter Helen, and the two were soon courting.[31]

Gillett found he had little time for romance as the detachment, and indeed El Paso County itself, were still dealing with the aftermath of the Salt War. The authorized strength for Baylor's outfit was twenty men, and nine were held over from the previous commander's tenure. Most of the administrative details were handled by Gillett as first sergeant, and he was likewise required to lead his Rangers in the field.[32]

Around the same time, eighteen Mescalero warriors attacked a hay-cutting camp near the La Quadra stage station, and allegedly massacred the five Mexicans working there. The lieutenant learned of the depredation on October 4, and, shortly after midnight, led Gillett and four other Rangers to the scene of the raid. Finding that none of the Mexicans had been killed, but each had instead fled into the night thinking his companions had been slain, Baylor's detachment followed the raiders' trail, which led into Mexico. Receiving permission to cross the border from the *alcalde* of Guadalupe, the Rangers and twenty-three Mexican townsmen and *vaqueros* rode in pursuit of the Apaches. The Texans and their allies cornered their prey in the Sierra Ventana at ten a.m. on October 6. Certain the Indians planned an ambush, Baylor sent men along the ridges of the Cañada de los Marranos. They sprang the trap, and the pursuers charged up a slope to the Apaches' hidden position at the base of a cliff. Gillett killed one Indian, and another was slain in the first few moments, but then the two sides settled down to an ineffective exchange of fire. The pursuers could only fire at the enemy's puffs of powder smoke, since they rarely caught sight of the Apaches. The Rangers and Mexicans silently withdrew at six o'clock in the evening.[33]

The detachment was active in the pursuit of Victorio, the Chihenne (or Mimbres) Apache chief, and his followers after they jumped the San Carlos Reservation in Arizona the following month. The Indians ferociously raided settlers on both sides of the border, and eluded American and Mexican soldiers and posses for months. In response, the governor of Chihuahua placed a bounty of two thousand pesos on Victorio's head. Baylor, Gillett, and the rest of the detachment (renamed Company A at the same time Baylor was promoted to captain) rode alongside military forces of the two countries in pursuit of the Apaches.[34]

On September 17, 1880, Baylor, Gillett, and a dozen Rangers were invited to join over one hundred volunteers from the Mexican towns of Guadalupe, San Ignacio, Tres Jacales, Paso del Norte (changed to Ciudad Juárez in 1888), and from the Texan towns of Ysleta, Socorro, and San Elizario, to cross into Mexico. The following night, they found Indian sign north of the Rancheria Mountains, but bad weather obscuring the trail made determining enemy numbers difficult. The Rangers and seventy-three volunteers conducted a night march to Carrizal in response to a report of Apaches being sighted there. Regrettably, the Indians had already left by the time the column arrived. Instead, the posse rode east toward El Cobre Mountains, then to the Candelarias. Having located Victorio's band, the Rangers and volunteers fell back to San José to await Colonel Joaquin Terazas, the Mexican commander.[35]

Unfortunately, the Rangers were denied a role in the final campaign, as Terazas ordered the United States and Texas troops to return north of the Rio Grande. The general instead assaulted the Apache stronghold with his own five hundred *soldados*, and scored a smashing victory, killing most of the Indian warriors, including Victorio. A small number of survivors under the leadership of seventy-three-year-old Nana, Victorio's capable lieutenant, eluded capture and fled into Sonora. The next year, Nana led fifteen warriors of his own band, and twenty-five Mescaleros, in cutting a bloody swath through New Mexico for six weeks before escaping into the Sierra Madre.[36]

The lack of advancement and the meager wages were beginning to be a concern to a young Ranger with a girl and a possible future together. His monthly salary was fifty dollars, which was insufficient to support a family in any reasonable degree of comfort. Gillett's apprehension of how to provide for a wife led him to make a fateful decision that resulted in an international incident.[37]

On Christmas Eve of 1880, an intoxicated Abran and Enofre Baca murdered newspaper editor A. M. Conklin at a church meeting in Socorro, New Mexico, before fleeing across the border. The indignant members of the Socorro Committee of Safety, and the territorial governor, each offered a five-hundred-dollar reward for the capture of the two killers.

Wanted posters were disseminated throughout the Trans-Pecos region. Gillett had paid little attention to the slaying, but his interest quickened when he learned in February 1881 that two men matching the Bacas' descriptions were in Ysleta. He arrested the two suspects on February 24 before they could leave town, spurned a one-thousand-dollar bribe to release them, and delivered his prisoners to the authorities in Socorro three days later. Unfortunately, while one was Abran Baca, the other was a cousin, innocent of any wrongdoing. The townsfolk and the governor each paid Gillett half the promised rewards, but even that was more than he had earned at any one time. Eager to collect the balance, he stayed alert for news of Enofre Baca.[38]

In March, an informant told Gillett that the brother still at large was clerking in a store in the Mexican town of Zaragoza, across the river from Ysleta. The spy confirmed the information within the week, whereupon Gillett recruited Ranger George Lloyd and crossed over the border into Mexico. Risking dishonorable discharges or worse, the two lawmen apprehended Baca in the store at gunpoint on March 28, and took him back to Texas under fire from the fugitive's countrymen. They rode into Ysleta unhurt, but Captain Baylor, a stickler for the rules, was furious at the flagrant violation of the law. After Gillett explained the situation, the captain reluctantly gave him permission to transport his prisoner to New Mexico. Baylor did specify Gillett would escort Baca to Santa Fe, rather than Socorro, because of the danger from vigilantes there. Citizens of Socorro, learning of the murderer's return to the territory, boarded the train on March 31 when it made a scheduled stop in their town. A deputy sheriff leading twenty-five to thirty armed men forced Gillett to relinquish Baca. The outlaw was promptly hung kicking and screaming from the crossbeams of the gate in the courthouse yard. However, the deputy did present a notarized receipt so the Ranger sergeant could still claim the reward. He received his money from Governor Lewis "Lew" Wallace in late April.[39]

Baylor was hard-pressed to contain the affair, which was rapidly becoming a diplomatic firestrom. An angry Governor Oran Milo Roberts demanded an explanation, while equally furious Mexican authorities issued strongly worded complaints over the violation of their sovereignty, as well as the kidnapping and murder of a citizen of their country. In the end, the matter was seemingly resolved officially, and Gillett received no disciplinary action. Unofficially, a rumor spread that Judge José Baca was prepared to pay a handsome sum if a certain Ranger sergeant was bushwhacked. According to the possibly apocryphal story, Baylor visited with the judge, and the reward was quickly recinded.[40]

In January 1881, a detachment led by Captain Baylor participated in what is called the last fight between Texas Rangers and hostile Indians. After a pursuit of Apaches who had attacked a stagecoach, the Rangers surprised the enemy camp, killing six, including women and children, capturing a woman and two children, and scattering the rest of the band into the mountains. Gillett took no part in the action, as he and three men were left in camp at Ysleta.[41]

His immediate future secure both professionally and financially, Gillett and Helen Baylor married on February 10, 1881. The union was troubled from the beginning. The groom was a mature, experienced lawman while the bride was a sentimental and childish young woman. She was also, reportedly, an indifferent housekeeper who preferred church and civic activities to maintaining the home. Gillett and Helen welcomed their first son, Baylor, who was born later in the year, but he would tragically die at the age of three.[42]

On December 26, 1881, Gillett resigned from the Ranger service to accept the position of captain of guards for the Atchison, Topeka & Santa Fe Railroad. He was responsible for security on the main line between El Paso and Rincon, New Mexico. Despite the monthly salary of $150, he stayed with the railroad for only several months before being appointed assistant city marshal of El Paso. His boss was Marshal Dallas Stoudenmier, a gunslinging Confederate veteran from Alabama, and an ex-Ranger.[43]

The previous year, George Washington Campbell had been appointed marshal, but he resigned after a salary dispute with the city council. Amid rumors ruffians in town were planning to riot, Baylor had sent Gillett and five men to keep the peace. Problems with crime, health and sanitation, public transportation, flood control and drainage, and utilities continued to plague the town's leaders. Stoudenmier was hired to police El Paso, and the Rangers would return several times to assist him.[44]

Dallas Stoudenmier. *Courtesy El Paso Public Library, El Paso, Texas.*

On April 14, 1881, the atmosphere in town was tense following the murders of two *vaqueros* who were killed while looking for rustled cattle. Standing in the street, Campbell and rancher John Hale were arguing with Constable Gus Krempkau, whom they considered overly friendly with the Mexicans, when Hale suddenly shot Krempkau through the lungs. The dying Krempkau managed to return fire and wounded Campbell. Stoudenmier was in the nearby Globe Restaurant when the shooting started and came at a run. Unlimbering his pistols, he missed his intended targets, and killed an innocent bystander named Ochoa by mistake, but his next two bullets caught Hale in the forehead and Campbell in the stomach. The former marshal died the next day. The shooting has become known as "the Four Dead in Five Seconds gunfight."[45]

Stoudenmier was held blameless by most of the respectable citizenry, but the sporting crowd did bear a grudge for Campbell and Hale's deaths; chief among them were James, John, and Frank Manning. In addition to a ranch, the brothers owned the two-story Coliseum, a combination saloon and variety theater, at the rear of the El Paso Hotel. Shortly thereafter, a botched attempt was made on Stoudenmier's life, and his brother-in-law, Stanley M. "Doc" Cummings, was mysteriously killed in the Coliseum. Gillett suspected the establishment's bartender as having taken a hand in the deed. Both events were believed to have been instigated by the Mannings, and the nervous town leaders struggled to fashion a truce between the belligerents.[46]

Stoudenmier was forced to resign on May 29, 1882, due to his uncontrollable drinking and feuding with the town council. Immediately, Gillett was unanimously named to fill the vacant office. He was cautioned by his ex-boss, "Young man, I congratulate you on being elected city marshal, and at the same time I wish to warn you that you have a man's size job on your hands." By this time, the El Paso police force included Edgar H. Scotten, William P. Raynor, W. H. Wheat, George Harris, and James Henry Comstock. To commemorate the new appointment, Gillett received a gold badge from the Manning brothers and "Colorado" Charlie Utter. The badge was a shield engraved with "City Marshal of El Paso" and hanging from a scroll that was inscribed with "J. B. Gillett."[47]

In the early 1880s, El Paso, sometimes mockingly known as "Hell Paso," was one of the roughest frontier towns in Texas. The new marshal equipped himself with a brace of .45-caliber pistols mounted with pin-headed screws and slid onto slotted plates riveted to his gun belt. In addition to the pair of six-shooters, Gillett stashed two sawed-off shotguns in strategic locations throughout town. "I'll bet I've stopped a dozen killings in El Paso by presenting one of those guns," he later recalled. In his time as the city's chief lawman, he never backed down from a challenger nor had to kill a man.[48]

Wangling a commission of deputy U.S. marshal, Stoudenmier continued his quarrelsome ways and, while drunk in Neal Nuland's Acme Saloon on July 29, got into a shooting scrape with ex-deputy William Page. After a few harmless shots were fired, Marshal Gillett arrived in time to break up the fight. He arrested both of the participants and they were taken before the court the next morning. Stoudenmier and Page were each fined twenty-five dollars, and the former was placed under a $250 peace bond. Trouble flared up again between Stoudenmier and the Manning brothers in the Coliseum on September 18, 1882. A misunderstanding led to heated words, and Stoudenmier and Doctor George Felix Manning, the eldest of the brothers, both pulled their pistols and started shooting. The physician was shot in his hand—a potentially career-ending wound—and the lawman was struck in the chest and the left arm. Stoudenmier was killed when Jim Manning approached from the rear and fatally shot him behind the left ear. Gillett responded to the sounds of the gunfire and placed the Mannings under arrest. They were acquitted in the subsequent trial.[49]

In 1881 and 1882, the railroads were slowly crossing the Trans-Pecos country. Surveyors and construction crews of the Texas & Pacific made their way north of the Davis Mountains, while those of the Southern Pacific moved to the south. With the state becoming connected by rail, stockmen on the crowded ranges to the east of the Pecos began to look reflectively at the abundant cattle country to the west. The Big Bend was a cowman's paradise with the country "rich in grama grasses, shrubs, trees, and edible cacti for hungry cattle. The soil is good; the rainfall limited but timely. Water is scarce, but plentiful enough in the springs and the creeks for ranching." With the once-hostile Indians on reservations, the progress of the railroads, and the drought plaguing the eastern counties, enterprising cattlemen began in 1880 to drive their herds westward. Five years later, the migration was complete, and the Big Bend was fully stocked by 1890.[50]

Aspiring to benefit from the expanding opportunities, in November 1882, Gillett entered into a cattle-raising partnership with his old comrade Charlie Nevill, now sheriff and tax collector of Presidio County. The partners bought one hundred head of cattle from George Gaither of El Paso, and pastured them at Mitre Peak, then situated in Presidio County. In either 1883 or 1884, the outfit became known as Nevill & Company, and they moved their herd to Calamity Creek, twenty-five miles south of Alpine. They also acquired four sections on Alamito Creek and the Presidio del Norte road. The two ex-Rangers would welcome John M. Dean, the former Presidio County attorney, as a third partner in 1885 or 1886. By this time, their herds numbered eighteen horses and seven hundred cows. As Gillett worked to build his cattle interests, his and Helen's second son, James Harper Gillett, was born on September 5, 1884, in Ysleta.[51]

Possibly under the strain of an unhappy home life, Gillett fell into a political dispute with alderman and mayor *pro tem* Paul Keating. Keating blamed Gillett for a rumor that stated the mayor was often too drunk to attend to city business. In turn, Keating implied Gillett had been lax in his accounting of assessed fines. The two adversaries met in the street on March 23, 1883, and Gillett clouted the alderman several times with his fist. He then threatened to shoot the politician. Keating swore out a warrant for the marshal's arrest, alleging "assault and battery and threats of shooting." The marshal was placed under a $750 peace bond. By his actions, Gillett had put himself in a difficult position, but he enjoyed the support of the decent citizens of El Paso. Nevertheless, he submitted his resignation to the town council on April 1, effective on the thirty-first. The weeks before he stepped down allowed Gillett's accounts to be examined. The committee appointed to conduct the audit endorsed the marshal's bookkeeping, and their report was unanimously adopted. Despite tendering his badge, Gillett did not fully depart the El Paso police force, as he instead became assistant marshal to new appointee Samuel Watson Boring on August 24.[52]

He left the marshal's office completely on April 1, 1885, to become manager of the G4 Ranch located in southern Brewster County. The 55,000-acre spread set in survey block G4 was owned by the Estado Land and Cattle Company operated by Brigadier-General Richard Montgomery Gano and his two sons. The Ganos furthered their holdings by leasing water rights that gave them control of an immense area stretching from "the Agua Frio on the north to the Rio Grande on the south, and from the Terlingua Creek on the west to the Chisos Mountains on the East." Gillett commented, "At that time not one single human was living in the country mentioned, and not one head of cattle grazing in that territory. The Ganos had it all to themselves."[53]

In May, the company purchased two thousand head of cattle in Dallas and Denton Counties. The herd was shipped to Toyah, then driven to the ranch. At about the same time, two herds of two thousand head each were acquired in Uvalde County and likewise moved west. With six thousand head on the Estado range, Gillett established the headquarters camp near Ojo de Chisos on the west side of the Chisos. He also placed line camps on the upper Terlingua and at the mouth of that same creek. Thus, the cattle were held inside a triangle with twenty-five miles to thirty miles between each camp. Under Gillett's management, the G4 proved a profitable enterprise. Unlike the overstocked and overgrazed ranches that suffered during the droughts of 1885 and 1886, not one Gano cow died from lack of water or grass. In June 1886, Gillett was able to boast that he had overseen the branding of 950 calves.[54]

In addition to his ranching duties, Gillett was elected county commissioner for Precinct No. 13 in November 1886. The following year, he sold his one-third interest in the partnership with Dean and Nevill in return for seven hundred yearling steers. Over the next several years, he increased his operating capital through the shrewd purchase and sale of several cattle herds. In 1889, he purchased the E. M. Powell range eight or ten miles south of Alpine, and moved his seven horses and 560 head of cattle there. At the same time, he bought the neighboring Altuda ranch from a mortgage company in Fort Worth.[55]

Gillett and Helen's marriage had been worsening for years. In 1889, she filed for divorce, charging he spent an inordinate amount of time in brothels. The split was finalized on March 2, and Helen was awarded custody of Harper. She immediately changed her son's name to Harper Baylor Gillette as she wanted nothing more to do with the name James. She also believed the addition of the extra "e" made the surname more refined.[56]

In the same year, Mary Lou Chastain came to Alpine to visit her brother's family and met the young lawman-turned-rancher. Born on March 29, 1867, Lou, as she was known, was the daughter of Joseph T. and Martha Chastain. The introduction led to friendship, then quickly blossomed into courtship. They married on May 1, 1889, at the bride's home in San Marcos.[57]

Gillett resigned from the Estado company after six years to devote himself to his own developing ranch interests. During his stewardship, the G4 herd had increased to thirty thousand head of "fat and sassy" cattle. Over the next six years, his own herds fluctuated between ten to fifteen horses and five hundred to eight hundred head. He also acquired four town lots in Alpine. Even as Gillett expanded his business, his family was also growing larger. He and Lou welcomed Beulah, born on October 24, 1890; Pansy Elizabeth, born on December 22, 1891; Mary Eva, born on January 10, 1894, but she died seventeen days later; James Stuart "Jeb," born on March 2, 1895; Lucile Chastain "Lou," born on June 20, 1896; and Leota, born on August 26, 1898.[58]

Gillett was elected sheriff of Brewster County on November 4, 1890, and served one term. Days after he took office, two bandits attempted to rob the Texas & Pacific train at Van Horn in present Culberson County. Following a gun battle with guards, one of the bandits was captured immediately, while the other, E. L. Vandegriff, raced the fifty miles to Marfa. The would-be robber boarded an eastbound train on November 19. The conductor identified Vandegriff and sent a telegram up the line to Alpine. Sheriff Gillett and Private Walter W. Jones of the Frontier Battalion's Company D boarded the train and took the suspect into custody. Fresh from this apprehension, the sheriff was appointed to the additional post of county tax collector. He had already given his bond on November 17, and swore his oath one week later.[59]

On December 19, following an argument earlier in the evening, cowboy Finus "Fine" Gilliland attempted to murder one Albert Cockrell in front of the latter's Alpine home. Despite firing five shots, the erstwhile assassin missed his target and immediately fled. Captain Frank Jones, a party of Rangers, and Sheriff Gillett started out after the fugitive and cornered him the next day in Musquiz canyon. Dodging gunfire, Gilliland was pressed closely and forced to abandon his horse in his escape into the mountains. The fugitive reappeared shortly thereafter "repping" for the Dubois & Wentworth ranch. On January 28, 1891, during a roundup, he fell into an argument with cattleman Henry Harrison Powe over an unbranded brindle bull yearling. The dispute turned violent, and Gilliland mortally wounded the rancher. Gillett's deputy, Thalis Tucker Cook, a former Ranger himself, and Private James Mitchell "Jim" Putman of Company D rode in pursuit. Three days later, the two lawmen overtook their prey in the Glass Mountains northwest of Marathon. When the outlaw saw his hunters approaching, he opened fire. In the flurry of bullets, Deputy Cook was shot in the right knee, his horse and that of Gilliland were both killed, and Putman's mount was gravely wounded. In another exchange of gunfire, the Ranger decisively ended the affair with a bullet between Gilliland's eyes. Sadly, Putman was forced to put his horse down as its wound was too great. The Ranger got his companion aboard the packhorse, and they both began the long walk into Marathon.[60]

After leaving the sheriff's office on November 8, 1892, Gillett held other public positions in Alpine, including being elected county tax assessor on November 6, 1894. He was also commissioned a deputy U.S. marshal for the Western District of Texas on April 7, 1894. His appointment was renewed on October 5, 1896.[61]

In this stage of his life, Gillett developed a desire to join the Masons. In the middle of January 1889, Masonic Lodge No. 596 relocated from Fort Davis to Marfa. Gillett petitioned the lodge, was accepted, and received his Entered Apprentice Degree on February 5, 1892, his Fellowcraft on March 8, 1892, and his Master Mason Degree on April 12, 1892. He demitted on April 12, 1894, to become a charter member of Lodge No. 766 in Alpine. Gillett continued to rise in the Masonic hierarchy, and served as Worshipful Master of the Alpine Lodge from 1896 to 1900. He was appointed and served as a District Deputy Grand Master in 1899.[62]

The family moved from their home in Alpine to the Powell ranch on September 8, 1897. On October 16, Gillett wrote in his day book, "Bought the entire ranch interest [sic] and half interest [sic] in the registered Durham Cattle from J. M. Sedberry, Consideration $500,000." The additional stock bearing the SED brand increased his herds by fifteen head.[63] As Gillett recalled, in 1887 or 1888, "the NH outfit south of Alpine" pioneered the raising of Hereford cattle in the Big Bend country. Once barbed wire fences went up across the Trans-Pecos range in the 1890s, enterprising cattlemen, including Gillett, further imported Herefords and introduced Shorthorn and Durham breeding stock into their herds. These strains began to replace the Texas Longhorn. In particular, the Hereford became favored for its quality of beef and its resilience; the resulting Highland Hereford lifted "the Big Bend to high rank among the cattle-raising regions of the nation."[64]

The family moved back to town in the late summer of 1900, so the children could attend school. They returned to the ranch the following summer. By 1901, in addition to the home ranch, Gillett was controlling another eight tracts of 640 acres each. The herd had increased to twenty horses and twelve hundred head of cattle. On February 21, 1902, Gillett acquired the "O Six" pasture south of Alpine from Herbert Lee Kokernot, and moved his family there the following month. He ran his herd on these twenty-eight sections that were adjacent to the Altuda ranch. He sold his entire interest in the Powell range to Alfred S. Gage in October for a sale price of $364. In the meantime, the Gilletts' second son, Milton E., was born on December 3, 1900.[65]

Gillett joined the Christian Church of Alpine on February 28, 1904, a decision he considered the best act of his life. Selling the Altuda ranch on May 2, he moved his family to New Mexico in August, and settled on the Leland Farm, a 126-acre alfalfa farm near Roswell. They made several arduous trips back to Alpine to manage their ranching interests, staying for a period of time so the children could start school in October 1905. On December 21, 1905, Gillett sold all of his ranch holdings in Texas, including nineteen horses and five hundred head, for thirty thousand dollars. He did retain his ten town lots in Alpine. The family then returned to Roswell in April 1906.[66]

Later the same year, Gillett and Lou decided to sell the Leland Farm due to the colder temperatures, the inconvenience of the children attending different schools, an inability to adjust to farming life, and for financial reasons. The sale was completed on April 1, 1907, for $25,000, and the family moved back to Texas in May. They rented a house in Marfa until Gillett bought the 29,000-acre Barrel Springs Ranch from George W. Medley in July for $57,000; the herd of 1,768 head of cattle was delivered by September 15. The proud rancher wrote,

"This is one of the best equiped [*sic*] ranches in the country and one of the best herds of Hereford Cattle. Just the place I have always wanted." Once settled at the ranch, Gillett hired a tutor to teach the children at home, except for Beulah and Pansy, who began attending the San Marcos Baptist Academy in January 1909. Desiring to attend a house of worship closer to home, the family transferred their memberships to the First Christian Church in Marfa. Four neighboring families joined the Gilletts for Sunday school meetings that were regularly conducted on Sunday afternoons at the ranch.[67]

The ex-Ranger's happiness was shattered on August 19, 1908, when his son Jeb was killed while herding cattle. His pony had stepped in a prairie dog hole, and the resulting fall broke the youngster's neck. The horse was so crippled in the accident that Gillett was forced to kill it the next day. Tragedy continued to strike the Gillett family when Pansy grew ill from ptomaine poisoning on May 4. Her parents took her to Corpus Christi, and remained by her bedside for over two months. Gillett then brought his wife and still-ailing daughter to Marfa in late August, where they planned to stay until she was sufficiently recovered to return home. Pansy developed typhoid fever and her heart, already damaged from a childhood bout of scarlet fever, was not strong enough. She died on the morning of October 20.[68]

Despite personal tragedies, the demands of a cattle ranch remained. Presidio County ranchers were adversely affected by the scarcity of rain in 1917 and 1918. Gillett observed the drought was the worst in twenty-five years, and the cattle losses were significant. On November 12 of the latter year, due to his interest in the Hereford breed, he joined with his ranching colleagues in forming the Highland Hereford Breeders' Association; he would serve as vice-president in 1919, then director and president in 1925 and 1926. He also held membership in the Texas and Southwestern Cattle Raisers' Association.[69] Gillett was one of the founding members of the Texas Ex-Rangers' Association, which was organized at the Weatherford courthouse on August 10, 1920. He was repeatedly elected to the office of captain during the 1921, 1922, and 1923 meetings. At the second annual gathering, Gillett announced his memoirs, *Six Years with the Texas Rangers*, would be released later in the year, and the book has remained in print ever since.[70]

On September 28, 1923, Gillett leased his ranch for a term of five years to Milton and sold his son all of the registered Hereford cattle, horses, and work mules. Moving with Lou to a house in Marfa that they had purchased two years previously, he spent his retirement by being active in service clubs, performing as a public speaker at the Bloys Camp Meetings in the Davis Mountains, and helping to organize the West Texas Historical Association. He was elected to the board of directors of the Marfa National Bank in 1926, and served until at least 1931. When the new Christian Church was dedicated on April 18, 1926, Gillett was appointed an elder. In October 1928, he was elected first vice-president of the Texas Trail Driver's Association at the annual meeting. He was appointed a Special Ranger on February 23, 1931, but there is no indication Gillett served in an active law enforcement capacity, and the warrant expired one year later.[71]

The renowned Ranger's heart began to fail in the spring of 1937, and he went to Temple for medical treatment. He died of coronary sclerosis and coronary thrombosis at Scott and White Hospital on June 11. He was buried in the Marfa cemetery the following day with Masonic honors conducted by the Alpine lodge, as well as two others.[72]

Following Gillett's death, Lou remained at the Barrel Springs Ranch before moving to El Paso in 1945. She died on May 3, 1948, at Southwestern General Hospital of arteriosclerotic heart disease. Her funeral services were held at the First Christian Church in Marfa, and she was buried next to her husband.[73]

James Harper Baylor Gillette and his father had a strained relationship. The two did not see each other for twenty-four years after the divorce, and rarely after that. Instead, Harper was raised by his mother and grandparents in El Paso and Guadalajara, Mexico. He attended high school in Guadalajara, where he came to appreciate the sport of bullfighting. Shortly after his mother's death, he entered the first of dozens of *encerronas* as an amateur *teroro* before becoming an apprentice to the legendary matador Francisco Gómez ("El Chiclanero"). Making his professional debut in July 1908, he achieved in two years the distinction of becoming the first American-born *matador de toros* in the history of the sport. He appeared in fifty-two *corridas* in twenty-four Mexican cities and killed one hundred bulls. Deciding to retire in December 1911, he drifted from job to job before he returned to the United States three years later. He married Roxa Dunbar on April 21, 1915, in San Antonio. He was a construction superintendent at Camp Travis, sold insurance, and worked in the censorship office in San Antonio, and for an oil company. After Gillett disinherited him, Harper and Roxa established a five-acre poultry ranch in San Antonio. He died on June 26, 1941, in San Antonio of respiratory failure. His remains were cremated and he was interred at Mission Burial Park.[74]

Beulah married George Wesley "Dub" Evans, Jr. on June 7, 1911, at the First Christian Church in Marfa. She bore him one daughter and three sons. In 1919, they moved to Grant County, New Mexico, where George was the co-owner of two ranches. Eleven years later, he became one-third owner and manager of Augustine Plains Ranches, Inc. of Socorro and Catron Counties. The Augustine Plains ranch was divided in 1943, and George's seventy sections near Magdalena were renamed the Montosa Ranch. Both George and Beulah were active in the New Mexico Cattle Growers Association and the American National Cattleman's Association. Beginning in 1944, he served two terms in the state senate. He died on May 3, 1967, of a heart attack while inspecting his cattle. He was buried in Sunset Memorial Park. After George's death, Beulah became active in the Magdalena Community Church where she served as an elder. She was also a substantial supporter of the Montosa Camp Meeting and Bloys Camp Meeting Associations, and the New Mexico Boys Ranch. Beulah died in Albuquerque on October 19, 1988, and was buried at her husband's side.[75]

Lucile attended the Bonn Avon School for Girls in San Antonio in September 1913. She married cattleman Lee S. Evans, Dub's older brother, at the Barrel Springs ranch in 1915. They lived on a spread north of Laguna, New Mexico, and raised two daughters from his first marriage. Lee was a past president of the New Mexico Cattle Growers Association. He died in El Paso on June 22, 1962, of a heart attack. Lou moved to Fort Davis and later died on July 10, 1988, at Baptist Memorial Hospital in San Angelo.[76]

Leota attended Bonn Avon with her sister, then the Alamo Business College in San Antonio in January 1919. She married rancher William Kellum Colquitt on December 29, 1920, in Marfa, and bore him two sons. He died of an acute appendicitis on April 21, 1927, at the El Paso Masonic Hospital.

She married motel owner Monroe Lee Wilson on November 3, 1932, in Las Cruces, New Mexico. Lee, as he was known, had a son and a daughter from a previous marriage. Lee and Leota lived in Harlingen, where he operated Wilson's Sporting Goods Store and Wilson's Pier, a fishing outfitter and shrimping company along the Arroyo Colorado. He died on October 31, 1973, in San Angelo after an illness. He was buried in Cedar Hill Cemetery in Ozona, Crockett County. Leota died at Baptist Memorial Hospital in San Angelo on April 19, 1992. She was buried next to Lee two days later.[77]

Milton attended military school in San Antonio in September 1913, and the Alamo Business College at the same time as his sister. He married Freida Burns in Kansas City, Missouri, on November 26, 1930. Following his father's retirement, he oversaw the Barrel Springs Ranch, and he was running 1,200 head of cattle on 30,000 acres by March 1940. He also grazed high-grade sheep on his land as early as 1927. Milton died on November 27, 1949, in a Marfa hotel room. His cause of death was listed as unknown, but contributory causes included the consumption of alcohol and paraldehyde; the latter was used for the treatment of alcoholism and several nervous disorders.[78]

James B. Gillett served in the early years of the Frontier Battalion—a period when the Rangers faced dangers at every turn. He fought Indians and outlaws, guarded John Wesley Hardin, initiated an international incident, and, upon his resignation, served as city marshal and county sheriff. After leaving the service, he pioneered the cattle industry in the Big Bend. Even with all these accomplishments, perhaps his greatest gift to historians and Ranger aficionados was to write one of the most enduring descriptions of service in the Frontier Battalion.

Jesse Lee Hall. From Dudley G. Wooten's *Comprehensive History of Texas*.

Chapter 5

Jesse L. Hall: "An Enviable Record of Courage and Action"

Jesse Lee Hall was among the first of the professional lawmen who were entering the Texas Rangers. Even before Major Jones's formal order shifting the Frontier Battalion's focus to civil policing, Hall understood the battle for law and order did not end with a shooting or an arrest. The struggle continued in the courts with rules of evidence, attorneys, and juries. While he amassed an enviable record of courage and action, his skills at persuasion convinced many an outlaw to surrender and a feudist to lay down his guns. Most importantly for the continuation of the Ranger service, he understood political conditions in Austin, and excelled in earning and retaining the good will of citizens and, especially, lawmakers. A bold fighting man, he was sadly out of his depth when removed from that sphere. Frederic Remington pronounced him "a gentleman of the romantic Southern soldier type, and he entertained the highest ideals, with which it would be extremely unsafe to trifle."

He was born in Lexington, Davidson County, North Carolina, on October 9, 1849. The original spelling of his middle name was "Leigh," but Hall would change it soon after arriving in Texas. Doctor James King Hall, his father, had been born on January 13, 1816, in Iredell County, and Frances Mebane

(Rankin) Hall, his mother, on November 19, 1827, in Guilford County. They were married by the bride's father, a Presbyterian minister, at Weston in Davidson County on January 4, 1849. Jesse's younger siblings were Richard Moore Hall, born November 17, 1851; William Paisley Hall, born December 13, 1853; James King Hall, Jr., born April 5, 1856; Francis Rankin Hall, born September 9, 1859; and Charles Wharton Hall, born August 15, 1864.[1]

Between October 1849 and July 1850, the family moved to a plantation in Iredell County. The doctor owned five female slaves ranging from age thirty to one. Additionally, he was ordained an elder in Bethany Church on April 17, 1853, and "as a physician and a citizen, no one was held in higher esteem than Dr. Hall."[2]

In early 1858, the family moved to Greensboro in Guilford County. The elder Hall had been persuaded to resettle in order to absorb the practice of Doctor Algernon Sidney Porter, father of William Sydney Porter, who would become better known to the world as the writer "O. Henry." Doctor Hall established his office on West Market Street in a house purchased from Congressman John Adams Gilmer. Two years later, the former's real estate holdings were valued at $4,500, while his personal estate was assessed at $22,000. He owned fifteen slaves. On August 7, 1861, the doctor was appointed the regimental surgeon of the Twenty-second North Carolina Infantry. While his father was away serving the Confederacy, their home was burned, and Leigh, his mother, and his brothers were forced to take refuge with relatives. Doctor Hall resigned his commission on June 19, 1862, on account of ill health.[3]

Lee was tutored by his grandfather, Reverend Jesse Rankin, at Finley High School in Lenoir. The Presbyterian minister's strict discipline and Calvinistic worship did not agree with the precocious and adventurous Hall, who was frequently punished for his infractions. While he found much to contemplate in the works of Robert Burns, Tom Moore, and Lord Byron, he eventually pleaded to be sent home.[4]

Although his father wanted Leigh to be a physician, Hall instead developed a desire to go west. So, in 1869, he traveled to Grayson County, Texas, where he used his education to become a schoolteacher in McComb. In addition to changing the spelling of his middle name, Hall acquired the nickname of "Red" due to the coloring of his wavy hair. Sadly, his teaching career did not prove financially rewarding, as his personal estate in 1870 was valued at one hundred dollars.[5]

Having occasionally assisted local peace officers, Hall accepted the appointment of constable for Precinct No. 1 in Sherman sometime in 1871. Before the early–1870s, the constable was regularly the most engaged local law officer in Texas. Regrettably, in the turmoil of Reconstruction, they often proved too inexperienced to cope with rising levels of crime and violence, were frequently unable to deputize enough citizens for assistance, and lacked adequate funding and the accommodations to detain their prisoners. The construction and subsequent improvements of roads and rail lines, the establishment of telegraph lines, and the need to lodge offenders in county jails would see constables focus on civil process, and the county sheriffs emerge as the state's preeminent lawmen. Even as these responsibilities were changing, Hall was in the forefront of handling several cases in Sherman. Robert Moore and members of the outlaw McDonald family had been at large for a year since breaking out of the Bonham jail. Hall and a party of Dallas policemen discovered them on the East Fork of the Trinity River on June 30, 1872. After a wild exchange of gunfire, the wounded Moore was captured, while the rest of the gang escaped. On December 14, a railroad tie contractor was killed in the town of Denison, likely for the seventy or eighty dollars in his pockets. Hall arrested a suspect who had been seen with the victim, but Justice of the Peace William Shackelford released the prisoner for unknown reasons.[6]

Hall's stint as a constable proved brief when he was offered the position of Grayson County deputy sheriff. His primary responsibility was to police Denison, which had been founded at the terminus of the Missouri, Kansas & Texas Railroad. Following a pattern demonstrated throughout the West, the rowdy boomtown of tents and shanties saw the establishment of whorehouses, gambling parlors, saloons, and dance halls on Skiddy (present-day Chestnut) and Main Streets. As author Wayne Gard noted, "Brawls and holdups were everyday events. Cowboys shot up the streets, and Indians full of firewater filled the night with their whoops." Murderers, thieves, and other lawbreakers were able to operate with impunity as the nearby Indian

Territory offered them sanctuary from North Texas lawmen. "Arming himself with a Winchester rifle, and with his belt garnished with navy revolvers," Hall was determined to apprehend these desperadoes. For three months, until the town's incorporation on March 7, 1873, and election of the first city officials six days later, he and fellow deputy J. C. McDowell worked from an office on the corner of Skiddy and Rusk Streets. The pair combined the responsibilities of deputy sheriff, constable, recorder, and town marshal. During his tenure of slightly less than two years, seven men were killed, although not by Hall's hand, and he made 1,060 arrests. On March 31, 1873, he returned to Denison from a pursuit to Little Rock, where "he got his man." Horse theft was already rampant in Grayson and the adjacent counties by the spring of 1873, when Hall faced a notorious practioner of that trade and two comrades, all heavily armed, on the banks of the Red River. The two companions threw down their weapons and fled, while the horse thief surrendered rather than test Hall's marksmanship. On May 15, Hall, already known as "one of the hardest working deputies in the county," announced his candidacy for sheriff, but the Democratic county convention chose another aspirant on August 16. The loss had no negative effect on Hall's career, as he obtained an additional commission of deputy U.S. marshal later in the year. On February 25, 1874, Grayson County Sheriff James Williamson Vaden led a six-man posse, including Hall, to the W. L. Holder farm, located between Sherman and the Georgetown settlement, where they peacefully arrested Holder, three of his sons, and a son-in-law on charges of murder in connection to an ongoing feud. The lawmen returned with their prisoners the next day. Hall made two trips to Pilot Grove, twenty-five miles southeast of Denison, in February and April, and arrested one man for attempted murder, and another two for stealing horses. Leading five possemen in June, Hall engaged Mike Gormley's band of desperados on the Teshimingo road, twenty miles from the Red River. Gormley was wounded in the skirmish, but his confederates were able to carry him away. In August, Hall apprehended two horse thieves in Jack County, and took them to Sherman. He was relieved of his position with the sheriff's office on September 19 for unknown reasons; whether he retained his position as a federal officer is also unclear. By the following year, Hall was working as a special deputy sheriff, and, on September 17, he and a constable took two individuals charged with murdering a Cherokee Indian into custody near Elizabethtown. Hall received one thousand dollars in reward money for the arrest. He and J. W. Holt pursued John A. Purnell, the former sheriff of Hill County, into Kansas in March 1876, and captured him near Baxter Springs. The disgraced lawman, a fugitive from justice for the past three years, was under indictment for embezzlement, and the state had offered a reward of six hundred dollars for his apprehension.[7]

Having acquired a reputation as a capable officer, Hall traveled to Austin, and was elected the sergeant-at-arms for the House of Representatives of the Fifteenth Legislature. In July 1876, the lawmakers voted to reorganize Captain L. H. McNelly's militia company into Special State Troops. Twenty-six legislators requested the governor appoint Hall as second lieutenant and second-in-command under McNelly on July 23. The choice was based on Hall's past accomplishments, as well as his warm relationship with various members of the house. The appointment was also made due to McNelly's declining health and the captain's general distaste for administrative duties. Hall was supposed to bring greater accountability to what was perceived by many as an out-of-control outfit.[8]

After receiving his commission on August 10, 1876, the Rangers in the company gave Hall a chilly reception, as they preferred Sergeant John B. Armstrong. The new lieutenant, by affording respect to McNelly and performing his duties in an exceptional manner, soon gained their grudging respect. Wilburn Hill King, who would later serve as adjutant general, described him as "a man of daring and almost reckless courage, of fine physique and resistless energy."[9]

For the next six months, Hall led from the company's camp near Oakville, and reported to his captain who had taken to his sickbed. When McNelly had taken his men to the Rio Grande in 1875, his efforts focused primarily on combating Mexican bandits raiding across the border. By the summer of 1876, the Special State Troops were pursuing Anglo outlaws in the Nueces Strip: a territory covering some thirty counties from San Antonio to Eagle Pass to Brownsville to Corpus Christi. South Texas was infested with cattle rustlers, horse thieves, and killers, both Anglo and Mexican.[10]

On August 24, Hall was informed of a bank robbery in Goliad and took an eleven-man detachment to investigate. Upon reaching town the next day, he was told by citizens that the alleged outlaws were also guilty of stock theft and murder. Sheriff C. P. Miles was reportedly protecting the robbers and unlikely to arrest them. To make matters worse, a gang of stockmen and their hired gunmen had ridden in from neighboring counties intent on ridding the area of nesters. The regulators ordered all men who did not own property to leave, and killed two who challenged their authority. Hall first ordered the paid warriors to disperse, then set about tracking down the bank robbers who had fled toward Mexico. Sheriff Miles was suspended from duty, and the lieutenant acted in his stead though October 4, arresting twenty men. Hall remained in Goliad during the October court session to insure the county was orderly. On the fifteenth, he arrested William Dumman, who was wanted for attempted murder in Bee County, and Frank Callison on the thirtieth for the Goliad bank robbery. Turning state's evidence, Callison implicated his brother Thomas Callison, William Cavett, James T. Trumble, Lark Ferguson, Alfred Day, John Green, John Pabler, and Thomas Jasper as active participants. The suspects were prominent among a group of twelve to fifteen young men known as troublemakers. Placed in the San Antonio jail, Callison also accused William Brooking, William Riley "Bill" Taylor, and John King Fisher of aiding and abetting.[11]

Serving other warrants in Goliad County, Hall and a squad of Rangers, accompanied by Deputy Sheriff A. A. Herriman, attempted to arrest Henry Hoff, Jr. and Henry Luterbacker for murder on November 20. Unfortunately, the peaceable apprehension that was foreseen turned into a deadly shootout. The officers failed to capture the two fugitives, and John Schweitz, a friend of Hoff, shot at Private George W. Talley. The Ranger returned fire and killed his assailant.[12]

Following the deaths of William "Bill" Sutton and James Creed "Jim" Taylor, the Sutton-Taylor feud in DeWitt County seemed to be sputtering to an end with only an occasional incident. The shocking murders of Doctor Phillip H. Brassell and his eldest son George on September 19, 1876, would spell the culmination of the quarrel's murderous phase. After Brassell, a well-regarded physician living near Shiloh, had been dragged from his sickbed at around ten p.m., he and George were taken several hundred yards from their house by a party of seven or eight masked men. They were then inexplicably and cold-bloodedly executed. The double homicide stunned the community, and Hall and his company arrived in Clinton on November 23. They were opposed by hostile feudists, an antagonistic sheriff, and fearful citizens. Amid such an atmosphere, witnesses were prejudiced against stepping forward to identity the killers.[13]

Nevertheless, Hall set to work and secured enough evidence for the grand jury, which convened in December. On the twentieth, the empaneled members handed down fourteen murder indictments on seven men, one each for the doctor and his son. Two days later, in a cold rain, Hall and approximately a dozen Rangers crashed a wedding dance at a house near Cuero and served arrest warrants on the accused. "We came very near having a fight in the house, but finally talked them into a surrender which was very fortunate, as it would have been a very bloody affair," the lieutenant wrote. Judge Henry Clay Pleasants, presiding over a courtroom guarded by hard-eyed Rangers, refused bail, and ordered the defendants bound over for trial. The prisoners were held in the Galveston County jail.[14]

The feud quieted as the surviving ringleaders were dispersed. By May 1877, no murders had occurred in DeWitt County for eight months. Judge Pleasants distrusted the sheriff to safely transport the seven prisoners indicted for the Brassell killings to the new county jail in Cuero. Instead, Lieutenant John Armstrong was detailed to deliver them. The trials of the defendants commenced on December 18; one had his case dismissed, and two were tried and acquitted. Three others were convicted of first degree murder, but later released on a technicality. The case of the last meandered through the court system until his conviction in 1899. Sentenced to twenty-five years, he promptly received a pardon from Governor Joseph Draper Sayers.[15]

John Wesley Hardin, the most wanted of the feudists, remained at large. Hall aspired to be the one responsible for his capture, but that achievement would belong to Lieutenant Armstrong. However, the apprehension and imprisonment of the notorious gunfighter would allow the company to continue, despite budgetary overruns and lack of support from certain lawmakers. After he succeeded McNelly as company commander on

January 25, 1877, Hall's Rangers had been in danger of being disbanded the following spring. Legislators from East Texas, whose constituents did not require Ranger protection, advocated such a measure in order to save funds. Citizens throughout South Texas flooded General Steele's office petitioning him to retain Hall's company. One example of the state officers' continued significance occurred on March 28, 1877, when Hall and three Rangers captured noted stagecoach robbers Ham White and John Vaughan in Bastrop. The officers also recovered most of the stolen money from the outlaws' last hold-up, and Hall and federal marshals were able to accumulate sufficient evidence to see White convicted. The *Goliad Guard* editorialized: "to disband Hall's company at this time would endanger the life of every man who had advocated law and order and it would place the outlaws of the West in a position to undo all the work of the past year." As a result, prominent members of the West Texas Stock Association met in Goliad on June 11, and voted to donate seven thousand dollars for the company's maintenance. Due to their generosity, Hall and his men remained in the field.[16]

For years, residents along the lower Rio Grande had been plagued by deserters from the French and Mexican armies. Having few marketable skills and needing to make a living, these former *soldados* often turned to violent crime. By the late 1870s, the border saw a new influx of raiders, this time troops serving in the Lerdo and Díaz forces, *rurales*, or renegade revolutionaries. The *Zona Libre* continued to make the northern borders of Tamaulipas and Nuevo Leon a safe haven for smugglers. Bandits persisted in driving rustled Texas stock across the Rio Grande, and Mexican officials still ignored their activities, or were active accessories in the outlawry.[17]

At the same time, Lieutenant-Colonel William Rufus "Pecos Bill" Shafter, commanding the Twenty-fourth Infantry at Fort Clark, was dealing with Lipan and Kickapoo depredations. He suggested to Brigadier-General Edward Otho Cresap Ord, the departmental commander, that soldiers be allowed to cross into Mexico while in hot pursuit of either Indian or Mexican raiders. Ord recommended this change in standing orders to his superiors at the same time President Rutherford Birchard Hayes became "convinced that the invasion of our territory by armed and organized bodies of thieves and robbers, to prey upon our citizens, should not be longer endured."

On June 1, 1877, Ord was granted the authority "when in pursuit of a band of the marauders, and when his troops are either in sight of them or upon a fresh trail, to follow them across the Rio Grande, and to overtake and punish them." As the policy effectively ignored Mexico's sovereignty, President Díaz issued the order to his troops to "repel with force the insult that is sought to be inflicted on Mexico by the invasion of her territory."[18]

One piece of unfinished business was the "King of the Strip," King Fisher. After McNelly's unsuccessful attempt to put the outlaw leader away for cattle rustling, Fisher had ruled the *brasada* uncontested. Hall also tried to bring Fisher to justice, but he could never secure enough concrete evidence for a conviction. Instead, he resorted to the extralegal and unorthodox strategy of burying Fisher under an avalanche of indictments. As many as twenty-two charges of murder, cattle rustling, horse theft, and other offenses kept Fisher and his lawyers preoccupied in seemingly endless trials, dismissals, acquittals, and changes of venue. In just one trip to Laredo in November 1878, Hall and four men arranged for testimony in the Fisher cases. The lieutenant was even able to get the gunfighter denied bail and held in San Antonio's infamous "bat cave" jail for four months. While being escorted by three Rangers to a cell in Laredo, Fisher escaped on September 3, 1879, eight miles from the intended destination, but his bid for freedom proved short-lived. By July 1881, Fisher was finally cleared of the last charges, and decided to pursue strictly legitimate business activities.[19]

While Hall was forcing Fisher to spend his time in courtrooms, the lieutenant planned a move on the rest of the criminal element infesting the Eagle Pass country. He departed Castroville on July 30, 1877, with a thick sheaf of warrants. He stopped near Frio City the next day, and added to his force Sergeant George Washington Arrington and nineteen men from Captain Cornelius Vernon "Neal" Coldwell's company. When the Rangers reached Eagle Pass on the third, they surrounded the town and moved in to make their arrests. Outlaws scattered for distant locales. The largest number of apprehensions occurred on August 4, when Hall and his men caught up with forty-eight of Colonel Pedro Advíncula Valdés's band. The Rangers also arrested four murderers and three horse thieves for whom Hall held warrants. Their prisoners in hand, the lawmen moved on to Laredo and Corpus Christi.

John King Fisher. #2152. Noah H. Rose Photograph Collection. *Courtesy Western History Collections, University of Oklahoma Libraries, Norman, Oklahoma.*

By the middle of the month, the lieutenant and his Rangers had filled the Eagle Pass jail to capacity. He reported to the adjutant general that he had as many prisoners as Rangers, and he planned to send the former to the Castroville lockup.[20]

Events occurring in Rio Grande City compelled General Steele to send Hall there. On August 12, Segundo Garza, a notorious outlaw who had been charged with murder, was sprung from the jail by his brother, Rafael, and a band of fifteen to twenty fellow revolutionaries. The jailer and his wife, three guards, and the county attorney were wounded in the breakout. Rudolfo Esproncedo, a former captain in Mariano Escobedo's forces who was indicted for horse-theft, also escaped, and all of them fled for Camargo, pursued by a detachment of the Eighth Cavalry under Major William Redwood Price.[21] A stipulation of the "hot pursuit" order of June 1 had been that American troops would not cross the border if Mexican forces were present to intercept retreating raiders. Whether the order applied to jail breaks was in some doubt.[22]

Price and the Starr County deputy sheriff crossed a few hours later to demand the surrender of the fugitives and the punishment of those involved in the escape. The Mexican officials in Camargo obfuscated and delayed until the officers returned to Texas. The major apprised General Ord and Governor Richard Bennett Hubbard of the situation, and the latter sent a telegram to the Tamaulipas authorities. Hubbard then notified President Hayes of his intention to demand the return of the culprits under the standing treaty of extradition between the U.S. and Mexico. Assistant Secretary of State Frederick William Seward assured Hubbard that measures would be taken to resolve the international incident. Seward then instructed John Watson Foster, the U.S. minister to Mexico, to urge extradition and demand reparations from the Díaz regime. Meanwhile, Mexican troops massed in Camargo, and announced their intention to protect the country's sovereignty and citizens.[23]

Hall was still in Eagle Pass with a detachment of nine Rangers. He and his men were recuperating from the rigors of their sweep through the county. Indeed, several of the Rangers were ill, and many of the hard-ridden horses were not fit for service. Receiving the order to proceed to Rio Grande City, Hall replied he and six men would depart the following morning.

The remainder were to join him on the border as soon as possible. While the Rangers were en route, President Díaz attempted to take matters into his own hands. He ordered the extradition to proceed without further difficulty, and offered a reward for several men who had escaped to Matamoros. Opposition to his command, and to his rule, rose in that city. [24]

Having ridden 240 miles in five days, Hall and his detachment arrived in Rio Grande City on August 21. He reported that one of the escaped prisoners and two of his rescuers had been detained by Mexican authorities and taken to Matamoros. Four other raiders were known to be in the Camargo vicinity. The lieutenant and Major Price conferred on the course they should pursue the next day. Price was restricted from acting, and had been instructed to turn the matter over to state authorities.[25]

The two officers crossed over to Camargo to meet with Colonel José Maria Gomez, the military *commandante*. The Mexican officer assured them everything possible was being done to cooperate with the Americans. Hall disbelieved Gomez, and set a deadline of four days for the delivery of the fugitives. Gomez later reported Hall had threatened him with an invasion force of 25,000 Texas militiamen. No evidence supports his claim, but General Ord and Governor Hubbard, nevertheless, believed Hall had made such a statement. The governor responded by ordering Hall to confine his activities to the Texas side of the river until he was advised of the necessity to take drastic action.[26]

Needing to balance placating his people's resentment of American intransigence with demonstrating his authority, Díaz ordered a fifteen-hundred-man force to Matamoros to enforce his earlier command. General Servando Canales, *commandante* of Matamoros, complied and surrendered the three wanted men in the dead of night to a Brownsville officer. Hall was informed the other four raiders were still in Camargo, untouched by the authorities. A detail from Fort Brown escorted the prisoners to Hall's detachment in Webb County, and the Rangers returned them to the Rio Grande City jail. Hall himself remained in Matamoros, and unsuccessfully attempted to extradite five murderers indicted in Duval and Hidalgo Counties.[27]

The three men surrendered to American justice went on trial in late September. As a large number of Camargo citizens were present in the

Rio Grande City courtroom, Rangers were likewise on hand to maintain the peace. The rumor of an attempt to rescue the prisoners was widely believed. Despite the tense atmosphere, all three were convicted and sentenced to five years' imprisonment. Following the trial, in open disregard for the extradition agreement, Matamoros authorities released the murderers Hall had recently tried to bring back to the United States.[28]

Despite any treaty violations, Ord called attention in his 1879 annual report to the efforts by Mexican authorities in curbing depredations. He likewise stated that border conditions had improved in the previous two years. Wishing to recognize the Mexican government's endeavors, the president rescinded the "hot pursuit" order, and Secretary of War Alexander Ramsey issued the formal instructions on February 24, 1880.[29]

Meanwhile, on November 23, 1877, Hall returned to Sherman and found Grayson and Cooke Counties full of "Chicago detectives" searching for outlaw Sam Bass. The following month, Union Pacific detective J. H. Gaines requested that Hall, who had been promoted to captain on December 1, assist in tracking down the elusive train robber. Hall, Sergeant A. L. Parrott, two other Rangers, Gaines, and Sheriff William Calvin Everheart of Grayson County began their manhunt in Castroville. They tracked the Bass gang to Uvalde, then followed a false trail to Fort Clark, but picked up the outlaws' scent in Frio City.[30]

As the Brassell murder case had entered the trial stage, Hall was needed at Cuero. He passed command of the pursuit to Parrott, and remained in DeWitt County until after Christmas. Parrott, Gaines, and one other Ranger continued the chase for Bass. Meanwhile, the gang robbed the Concho stagecoach at Mary's Creek, nine miles west of Fort Worth, then another between Fort Worth and Weatherford. Bass recruited additional manpower, including Seaborn Barnes, and held up the Houston & Texas Central No. 4 train in Allen, twenty-four miles northeast of Dallas, on February 22, 1878. The governor immediately posted a five-hundred-dollar reward for each of the train robbers. The Texas Express Company and the H&TC followed suit the following day. On the day of the robbery, Hall was in Austin; the next morning he traveled to Houston. Visiting the H&TC offices, he arranged for Parrott, James E. Lucy, and three other officers to be provided transportation.

Parrott and the others joined him in Houston, and together they entrained to Allen to investigate the crime. Hall and his detachment then went to McKinney and obtained horses from the Express Company.[31]

Although he had captured the attention of the public and Texas officialdom, Sam Bass was not the only outlaw at large. For three months, Hall and his men waited for a chance to nab a gang of rustlers in Calhoun County. Suspects included Frank Hartman, Gordon Frank, and Charlie Ernst, all of whom were residing near Long Mott. On February 23, the trio robbed the C. M. Holden store in Fulton. Corporal William Lawrence Rudd and two Rangers maintained a surveillance, while a fourth infiltrated the gang. The next day, Ernst surrendered to authorities, and Gordon Frank was taken into custody on February 24. On March 1, Ranger A. S. Mackay reported he had arrested Hartman the previous night.[32]

As the Rangers continued to search for Bass and his gang, North Texas became inundated with marshals, sheriffs, Pinkerton detectives, and private citizens seeking the promised rewards. Since Bass had freely spent his loot in a variety of saloons, gambling halls, and brothels in Fort Worth and Dallas, he had no shortage of discreet sympathizers and active supporters. Allegedly, he also donated money to honest citizens who were down on their luck. Ironically, due in part to Bass's largesse, many innocent and not-so-innocent people were arrested on suspicion of aiding the fugitives. Even as the dragnet swept through the northern part of the state, the Texas & Pacific railroad was struck at Eagle Ford on April 4. The same line was again robbed at Mesquite. However, Major John B. Jones of the Frontier Battalion had accepted an offer from James Murphy, a member of Bass's gang who wanted to turn informant. The major lessened the pace of the manhunt, and wagered on this new approach to finally apprehend the outlaws.[33]

Murphy got a message to Jones alerting him to a planned bank robbery in Round Rock. On July 19, Hall was serving as sergeant-at-arms at the state Democratic convention when the governor informed him of Jones's departure to the scene of the forthcoming crime. The executive ordered the Ranger captain to follow and assist the major. Having arrived by train at two o'clock, Hall telegraphed Lieutenant Armstrong to bring several men to Round Rock. The captain met with Major Jones, and both decided Hall should stay in a hotel room, as several members of the gang knew him by sight. The robbers were expected the next day.[34]

Fifteen minutes later, Hall heard gunfire in the street and, grabbing his Winchester and pistol, raced downstairs to enter the fray. Finding the shooting already over, he saw Deputy Sheriff Alijah W. "Caige" Grimes dead on the ground in front of Henry Koppel's store, Deputy Maurice Moore wounded but still standing, and the body of Seaborn Barnes in the street. Bass and Francis M. "Frank" Jackson had escaped. Hall unhitched Grimes's horse and, together with Rangers Christopher Reyzor Connor and George Herold, dashed after the desperadoes. They followed a blood trail some six miles into the rocks and cedar brakes. As the sun set, the pursuers turned their fatigued horses toward town, intending to resume searching the next morning. Once in Round Rock, Hall discovered Armstrong, one or two other Rangers, and scout James Lucy had arrived, as well as Hall's brother, Richard, and Netteville Devine of San Antonio. Sam Bass was found mortally wounded the next morning, barely three miles from town.[35]

With the manhunt completed, Hall and twelve Rangers stationed themselves at Collins, forty-five miles from Corpus Christi, while Armstrong and a half-dozen men remained in Cuero. By the end of the fiscal year, the company had arrested sixty persons for murder, twenty-two for assault with intent to kill, and ninety-nine for various forms of robbery and theft. Funds became so meager that the captain was ordered, on September 21, to slash his command to two sergeants and fifteen privates. The reductions were not enough, and the company was slated to be disbanded. Concerned citizens wrote editorials, letters, and petitions protesting the company's imminent discharge. Despite the turn of events, the men continued making arrests in Nueces, DeWitt, Live Oak, McMullen, and San Patricio Counties, and recovered more than seven hundred head of rustled cattle. Corporal Rudd was sent to Brownsville on November 17, to arrange for the arrest and extradition from Matamoros of Martine Rodriguez, wanted for murdering a Nueces County deputy thirteen months previously. The fugitive was apprehended, but Mexican authorities refused to release him to Rudd's custody, despite his status as a naturalized American citizen who had voted in Nueces County for years.[36]

On December 21, Hall was ordered to transport all state ordnance and public property to Austin, and the company was mustered out on January 2, 1879. Any chance for Hall re-assembling his command lay with the Sixteenth Legislature, but the captain might have been losing some influence. He was defeated for the office of sergeant-at-arms, although he contended his loss lay more with the "active and energetic work of his competitor."[37]

In his annual address to the legislature, Governor Oran Milo Roberts reminded the lawmakers that citizens on the frontier had volunteered to financially support the company if it was retained by executive authority. He imparted to the assembled body, "I would continue this company 'for a longer period than six months,' on the condition that the State, by my said act, should in no wise become responsible either to the men or those who advanced them supplies; and that they must look alone to the Legislature for a just recognition of their claims."[38]

On April 22, the legislature authorized the formation of "a special force for suppression of lawlessness and crime" in south and southwestern Texas.[39] The following month, the legislature appropriated $46,000 for the expenses of Hall's company in the last seven months of 1878. When the bill was placed on his desk, the governor swiftly vetoed the measure. On June 10, the lawmakers convened in special session and made another appropriation, which this time was approved by the executive on July 4. Whether Hall would remain in command was apparently a matter of concern for the Ranger officer, as he telegrammed Adjutant General John B. Jones inquiring of the governor's intentions.[40]

In the end, Hall's worries were unwarranted. The officers and men of the new company were mustered into service on August 1, 1879, with Hall as captain and Thomas Lindsey "Bose" Oglesby as lieutenant. Hall arrived at Carrizo Springs on the eighteenth, and completed the company's organization two days later. He then traveled to Eagle Pass on the twenty-second. Averaging a strength of twenty-seven men, the Rangers were soon permanently headquartered at San Diego in Duval County. They covered some thirty counties in South Texas in small detachments, attending court, assisting local civil authorities, arresting numerous offenders, and recovering scores of stolen cattle and horses. In one instance, beginning on September 17, Hall, Sergeant Rudd, and five Rangers scouted Frio County for fugitives from justice. On the nineteenth, they arrested one individual wanted for cattle rustling in Uvalde County, and another man six days later for sheep theft in Maverick County. The first prisoner was lodged in the Atascosa County jail while the second was still in custody at the end of the month. They returned to camp on September 29, having ridden some five hundred miles.[41]

The residents at Santa María petitioned for protection from rustlers headquartered across the river at Bolza Ranch. Hall sent a detachment of five men to the area on October 21, and followed by stage two days later. He arrived on scene on the twenty-sixth as the bandits were plotting a raid. He stayed three days, then returned to San Diego, leaving the five men to keep watch. Before he departed, Hall telegrammed General Jones and reported "everything quiet."[42]

On November 1, while at Santa María once more, Hall learned of another robbery scheme, this time at John Campbell's store, approximately twenty miles southeast of Pleasanton. The captain and two men arrived on scene on the fifth to find a posse of citizens guarding the mercantile. The trouble had started when three strangers had earlier patronized the store and their behavior had aroused suspicion. The lawmen and the posse quickly hid themselves to await the return of the suspects. Just ten minutes after the Rangers' arrival, five men rode up, two of them seized the clerk while the others began pulling goods off the shelves and stowing them on their pack horses. Hall, his men, and the citizens rushed from their places of concealment and ordered the robbers to surrender. The thieves opened fire, and one was killed in the answering hail of bullets; a second was mortally wounded and a third seriously wounded. One member of the posse was wounded in the leg. Using the clerk as a shield, the last two bandits were able to escape. The outlaws' horses were discovered to have been stolen, and were returned to their rightful owners.[43]

In the early days of 1880, Hall was visiting Corpus Christi where he met Elizabeth Cook "Bessie" Weidman in the home of Captain Richard E. Halter, her brother-in-law. The veteran Ranger captain was quickly smitten with the twenty-one-year-old Pennsylvania beauty. She returned his affections, but when he proposed marriage, she accepted on one condition: he had to leave the Rangers. On May 24, Hall retired from the service, to take effect on June 1, and turned over command of the company, and all public property and funds, to Lieutenant Oglesby.[44]

Before he left his command, Hall was involved in one final tragic controversy. According to newspaper accounts, Corporal Charles Brown McKinney and a squad of Special State Troops were searching for a horse thief near old Fort Ewell on February 25. Believing they had cornered their man, the state officers called on him to halt. Since the Rangers wore no badges or other symbols of authority, the suspect could not visually confirm the armed contingent confronting him were lawmen. When he began to run, they opened fire, killing him. The dead man was later identified as Manuel Martinez, a law-abiding citizen of Atascosa County, and not the Wilson County outlaw of the same name. He left behind a wife and four children. The press was swift to condemn the shooting. In reviewing the matter, a *Galveston Daily News* editorial declared: "One of the most dangerous attributes of a peace officer is too much zeal, which is frequently the cloak for reckless ruffiansim." Hall was in Austin on March 6, waiting for Governor Roberts to arrive in town for the annual department head meeting. The following day, he explained the actions of the detachment. According to the captain, one of his men had posed as a horse thief, and Martinez had agreed to sell the undercover officer thirty head of cattle stolen from the ranch of Santos Benavides on the Rio Grande. When the Rangers attempted to make an arrest, Martinez produced a pistol and loosed several shots. The officers fired in self-defense, and Hall firmly absolved his men of any blame. With no witnesses able to refute Hall's statement, the case seems to have been dropped.[45]

After formally leaving the Rangers, Hall went into the sheep business. On May 7, he had sold twenty-three bags of shorn wool in San Antonio. Along with Edward Buckley, a well-known wool buyer from Corpus Christi and several other men, he traveled to Crockett County on July 22 to scout locations for sheep grazing. They also planned to sink artesian wells. The machinery required for the task preceded the party by several days. The following month, Hall and Buckley were riding through a rainstorm when they reached Sycamore Creek, west of Brackettville. As they stopped to water their horses, they suddenly heard a roaring sound, and were shocked to see a forty-feet-deep surge of water rushing at them, knocking down trees and everything else in its path. The pair barely had time to spur their horses out of the creek bed and up the nearby hill before the flash flood swept by. In early October, Hall took eleven bags to market in San Antonio, with another eleven held on consignment at the Losoya Street warehouse of Major Alcee J. Toutant Beauregard. By the middle of the same month, Hall completed the last monetary details resulting from his tenure as Special State Troops commander. In a letter to General Jones, he reported he was "getting along first-rate in the sheep business."[46]

The press in Galveston observed his passage through the city on November 10, 1880, and noted he was traveling east. Indeed, he married Bessie at the Lutheran Church in Lebanon, Pennsylvania, on November 25. The happy couple arrived in Galveston by train on January 4, 1881. Later in the summer, Hall purchased the W. P. Crary ranch in La Salle County for ten thousand dollars. He stocked the property with approximately 2,400 Angora goats that were valued at $3,600; he also owned one horse worth thirty dollars.[47] On January 9, 1882, Hall purchased land certificate no. 1152 for eight hundred dollars. Surveys No. 41 and No. 42 were patented five days later, entitling him to 1,280 acres along the Green Branch, a tributary of the Nueces River in McMullen County. The county tax rolls of the same year reveal he owned two wagons and two hogs. Twelve months later, he was running twenty-five horses and 175 head of cattle. Although he had attended the woolgrowers' convention in San Antonio in 1882, he seems to have divested himself of his sheep. On December 11, 1883, he purchased for one hundred dollars a tract of land in La Salle County, authorized by veteran donation land certificate no. 139, which totaled 160 acres on Spear Creek, also a tributary of the Nueces River. On February 5, 1884, Survey No. 2001 was patented, and Hall took possession of 1,280 acres along Johnny Creek, yet another tributary of the Nueces. By that year, his herd had increased to 250 horses. By 1885, he owned a total of 6,720 acres in La Salle County, but claimed no livestock.[48]

Even while he built his own spread, Hall was employed by James Junkin Dull, and his younger sibling Andrew Jackson Dull, of Harrisburg, Pennsylvania, in early 1882 to manage the 250,000-acre Dull Ranch in

La Salle and McMullen Counties. On April 14, he acted as agent for the brothers, and purchased two hundred acres of vacant public land along the Rio Frio for the sum of one hundred dollars. Additional property was purchased by the Dulls from William Alexander Waugh, the first white settler in La Salle. Beginning with twenty-one horses, nine head of cattle, 7,500 sheep, and 1,300 goats, the ranch's holdings would grow to encompass 400,000 acres, and support a herd of twelve thousand head of cattle and an unknown number of wild mustangs that were broken and used as saddle stock, or sold to the army as remounts. Hall's agreement with the Dull brothers guaranteed him a percentage of the increase in the herds. Lawless men were infesting the entire region, and Hall strove to bring to a halt the unbridled rustling and fence-cutting occurring on his range. To that end, he ordered barbed wire to enclose the ranchland, imported a crew of tough cowboys and ex-Rangers to work the ranch, and received an appointment as a special deputy U.S. marshal on June 15. As Sheriff William O. "Bill" Tompkins was considered a friend to the outlaws, Hall supported the candidacy of his old corporal Charles McKinney for the county office. The ex-captain even led a body of armed men to the polls on February 3, 1883, to guard the balloting from voter fraud. The bitterness between Hall and Tompkins extended past McKinney's electoral victory. Both were attending the Bexar County Wool-Growers Association meeting on June 5, when they had a "personal encounter" in which Tompkins was knocked down. Although he would be murdered only three years later, McKinney stamped out much of the rampant crime during his tenure. On February 7, Hall was appointed to the executive committee of the Texas Live Stock Association at the convention in Austin, while he was chosen as marshal at the convention at Krisch's Hall in San Antonio on January 26, 1884. Two daughters would be born to Lee and Bessie in those years in La Salle: Jessie Lee, on October 3, 1882, and Sarah Elizabeth, on December 23, 1883, both births occurring in San Antonio. The Hall family lived in a log and adobe house measuring thirty-five feet in length and twelve feet in width, and surrounded by a twenty-foot-wide gallery where they gathered often in the fresh air. Hall was also appointed postmaster of the post office located at the ranch headquarters on August 6, 1883, but was replaced by Nicholas R. Miller one year later.[49]

Hall's brothers, Richard and Frank, came to manage a sheep ranch that ran approximately 2,750 head, and was a division of the overall Dull outfit. In March of 1882, his parents made a visit to Texas, and joined their sons on the ranch. They brought with them eighteen-year-old Will Porter, who would spend two years in Richard's home. There the tubercular youth would amass material for his later writing career as the novelist "O. Henry." Indeed, he modeled his character Ranger Lieutenant Sandridge in "The Caballero's Way" on Hall.[50]

By 1885, the Dull brothers were becoming discouraged with their ranching properties, and Hall's days as ranch manager were winding down. In one of his last acts of company business, he sold two thousand head to a buyer from Colorado. By late March, the entire Hall family was registered at the Hutchins Hotel in Galveston. James Dull was noted as being in San Antonio on May 9, and both he and his sibling were registered as guests at the Menger Hotel on May 11, and once more on the twenty-eighth. Hall was likewise at the Menger the following day. Whether they had journeyed to Texas to discuss with Hall his future in their employment is unknown, but the probability remains strong the brothers met with him at least once in this time frame. In any event, the Dulls reneged on their agreement with Hall regarding his percentage of the livestock increase, and instead offered him a flat rate of five thousand dollars for each of the three years he had supervised the ranch. Sometime in this period, Hall apparently sold off his personal real estate, as his name does not appear in the La Salle County tax rolls of 1886.[51]

Hall did not remain unemployed for long. On July 28, 1885, he received a commission as agent of the Comanche, Kiowa, and Wichita Reservation at Anadarko, Indian Territory. His appointment had been endorsed by the Texas congressional delegation and by the governor of North Carolina. He took up his new duties on September 1, assisted by a chief clerk and two or three assistants. The three-room administration building from which they conducted government business was a crude affair built of native cottonwood and lumber hauled from Wichita, Kansas. One room was designated as the agent's office, another for chief clerk Wells Clifford Morrill, and the third served as a file room for the reservation's books and papers. The surrounding structures included a commissary, a doctor's office, a sawmill, and a corral.

Trading posts licensed by the federal government were arranged along the main road through the agency. The government's Comanche, Kiowa, and Apache wards lived mainly south of the Washita River, while the Taovayas, Wacos, Tawakonis, Kichais, Delawares, and Caddos were to the north—more than four thousand Indians in total.[52]

Certain complications, which would affect Hall's tenure, had their origins in events occurring years before. The Kiowa and Comanche Agency at Fort Sill had been merged with the Wichita reservation on September 1, 1878, and the headquarters was placed at Anadarko. Beginning with the consolidation of the reservations, and continuing for the next twenty-three years, the Wichitas and the Caddos north of the Washita were mostly ignored in favor of their Comanche, Kiowa, and Apache neighbors. The latter outnumbered the former, and their recently free existence of raiding and hunting convinced the bureaucrats that they needed extra attention in order to adopt the white man's "civilization."[53]

The Comanches had once roamed the Southern Plains as autonomous bands with purposefully weak institutional leadership. After their surrender and confinement to the reservation, the People were pressured to choose a principal chief for the entire nation. In no small part to his leadership abilities and personal integrity, Quanah Parker of the Kwaharʉ band gradually acquired the influence necessary to secure the position. Seeking to secure a level of prosperity for his tribe, and a food supply more reliable than government-issued rations, Parker joined with Charles Goodnight and other pioneer stockmen in the cattle and horse raising business. By 1885, Parker had completed negotiations for the leasing of the rich grazing lands on the north banks of the Red River to the "Big Five" cattlemen—Samuel Burk Burnett, Daniel Waggoner, Eli Calvin Sugg, Cornelius Taylor Herring, and James Preston Addington—as well as the Harrold & Ikard Ranch and the Francklyn Land & Cattle Company. The stockmen's objective was accomplished, in part, by the bestowing of generous gifts and other inducements upon the Comanche leader. Soon, the Texans were running 75,000 head of cattle on one-and-a-half million acres of lush grasslands, while paying only six cents an acre per year. Although the "grass" payments totaled $55,000 annually, and were below fair market value, the agreement provided the agency's residents with a much-needed infusion of cash money in the form of twice-yearly installments. In the same year, Comanches across the reservation individually owned cattle herds ranging from one animal to two hundred head. One year later, twenty-seven families lived in houses while the rest continued a nomadic existence on the reservation. At the same time, only forty-eight families were involved in farming. Those who became affluent were able to employ Anglo laborers to work their fields, but the annual agricultural output was never sufficient to achieve subsistence levels.[54]

The leases did not keep the reservation Indians from levying cattle from herds moving up the Western Trail. In one instance, complaints were made against two Kiowas, Polant and Komal-ty, for the killing of stock trespassing on the reservation. On September 18, 1885, a federal marshal arrived at Anadarko with a warrant for the pair. Hall called the two Kiowas into his office and informed them he was going to arrest them. The agent and Morrill then tried to stall until a military detail from Fort Sill could arrive to support them. Unbeknownst to the two officers, the message never reached the post. After three hours, the two restless Indians tried to leave Hall's office, and the agent and the clerk attempted to block their exit. While the four struggled, several Kiowas joined the fray and chief Lone Wolf had to be curbed from cutting Hall's throat. Polant and Komal-ty escaped in the confusion, but they were quietly apprehended two days later in their camp. Hall harbored no hard feelings and, believing their earlier actions in killing stray cattle harmless, he soon gained their release.[55]

In October, Hall traveled to Sherman to collect his family and bring them to Anadarko. The reservation became a veritable playground for his adventuresome daughters. A third girl, Martha Dorothy Kline, was born to the family on May 2, 1887. While outward appearances may have looked blissful, a darker tone began to color Hall's personal life. The Reverend John Jasper Methvin, a Methodist missionary who knew him as a reservation agent, later commented: "He was generous to a fault, full of hospitality, of fine physique, vigorous of mind and body, a great man in ruins on account of drink."[56]

Alcohol would prove to be a recurring theme in Hall's life, and several reports surfaced of excessive drinking among reservation personnel. In addition

Quanah Parker in citizen's garb. Studio photograph from original glass negative by William J. Lenny and William L. Sawyer, Purcell, Indian Territory. *Author's Collection.*

to Hall's "intemperate habits," Reverend Methvin noted the school superintendent had been dismissed for drunkenness, although later reinstated, and an employee had accidentally shot himself while intoxicated. Meanwhile, Hall noted the amount of time the Indians spent in horse racing and card playing, especially monte. During the issuing of government rations or the semiannual disbursement of the grass payments, gambling was conducted openly around the traders' stores and in an arbor constructed especially for that purpose. Hall ordered public gaming to cease, but the vice proved impossible to completely eliminate. The wagering sometimes involved Anglos, but more often was conducted between Comanches or with other Indians. The agent also had deep concerns, which he first raised in the summer of 1886, regarding the peyote rituals that were spreading through the Comanche and the Kiowa communities. Conducted in tipis at night, safe from the prying eyes of outsiders, the quiet and dignified peyote meetings provided the Indians with social interaction and a redefined access to their traditional belief system after the Sun Dance and other pre-reservation ceremonies had been suppressed. As in the older rites, personal visions and medicine, curing practices, and the symbiology of earth, sun, and moon were important to peyote gatherings. More practical was the fact leaders in the new rituals were able to achieve political power within Comanche society. Indeed, Quanah Parker was a prominent figure in peyote circles, and he used his status to forge alliances and cement his primacy as the main spokesman for his people. Hall and his successors attempted to eradicate peyotism on the reservation, but the practice flourished in spite of them.[57]

When Hall took over the agency, the Kiowa school, the only one on the reservation, was plagued with high turnover in personnel and an inferior quality of appointees. He supported the Comanches' request for a school of their own, as did several of his successors and inspectors of the Indian Rights Association. Finally, a school would be established near Cache Creek and open its doors in October 1892.[58]

Alleged irregularities in Hall's accounts for the second and fourth quarters of fiscal year 1886 brought queries from the office of the Comptroller of the Treasury. A voucher, signed by Hall, and dated August 26, 1886, authorized a payment of $319 for plow work. Apparently, the voucher contained "a material misrepresentation of fact in regard to the service rendered." Citing section eight of the Act of July 4, 1884, chapter 180, the Comptroller questioned whether Hall should be held liable for the funds paid out to the contractors. In December 1886, Hall signed a voucher that paid an individual sixteen dollars for eight days' work on a grist mill. The submitted receipt was not an original document but one that was an abstract of several vouchers. The Comptroller believed Hall to have inadvertently committed fraud and referred the matter to the secretary of the treasury. The secretary decided Hall would not be credited for the sixteen dollars and decreed the issue closed.[59]

In the same month, an inspector from Washington advocated in his report abolishing the current reservation system in favor of allowing Indian reservation inhabitants private ownership of land; Hall concurred. Aspiring to further the assimilation of Indians into American culture, Congress passed the Dawes Severalty Act, which was signed into law on February 8, 1887. The measure approved dividing commonly held tribal lands and distributing the tracts to individual Indians. The excess acreage was to be sold to squatters, "boomers," ranchers, and railroad and oil companies. Furthermore, the leases of the cattle barons were voided, and both they and most of the Anadarko reservation Indians contested the legislation that threatened their mutual livelihood. Rising in opposition, Caddo Jake, the headman of the tribe of the same name, convinced his followers to raise money to hire an attorney. Hall responded by threatening to remove from the reservation any lawyer the tribe retained to fight allotment. Years after Hall's departure, the bipartisan Jerome Commission negotiated the settlements authorized by the Dawes Act. In the end, the allotments proved too small for any meaningful ranching, and the land was unsuitable for farming.[60]

Such injustices were to happen in the future, though. In the spring of 1887, Pa-ingya (In the Middle) rose among the Kiowas and called for his fellow tribesmen to join him at Lone Wolf's camp west of Elk Creek. The prophet claimed he could raise the dead, including the buffalo, slay his enemies with fire and whirlwinds, and free all Indians from the white men. Except for chief Stumbling Bear, the Kiowas flocked to Pa-ingya's side. Hall and the other government officials on the reservation observed the proceedings with some trepidation. The agent requested a military presence from Fort Sill in March, and led a cavalry troop to Elk Creek to investigate. They found the Kiowas assembled for the doomsday, and Hall persuaded the Indians to return to their homes and wait there. Once his medicine failed to produce the desired results, Pa-ingya was discredited. Later in the spring and summer, the reservation was again beset with white rustlers who were preying on the Indians' cattle herds. On April 1, Hall requested the commanding officer at Fort Sill dispatch two cavalry troops to aid him in deterring cattle thefts and to recover stolen stock. The mounted element, Troops D and H, Third Cavalry, returned to Fort Sill on May 10 and 22, respectively.[61]

By this time, Hall held between $60,000 and $75,000 of lease money in the Comanches' name, and he advised the Commissioner of Indian Affairs to authorize the procurement of cattle for the tribe. With permission granted, the agent advertised for the purchasing of 2,500 head each of yearling heifers, two-year heifers, and cows with their calves. According to Professor Charles Cornelius Painter, an agent of the Indian Rights Association, traders and cattlemen with business on the reservation saw their livelihoods threatened and protested to the commissioner. The latter wrote Hall and informed the agent that permission had not been conferred, and forbade him to purchase cattle. The commissioner avoided officially recognizing the existence of the leases, and cited a recent opinion by the Attorney General questioning a legal basis for the practice. Instead, thirty thousand dollars was spent on trivial items that did little to improve conditions at the agency.[62]

In addition to the wasted monies, Hall became discouraged with a change in the policy regarding meat rations. First, the amount for 1887 was 500,000 pounds below the level of the preceding year. Second, the contractor had previously made a weekly delivery of locally raised cattle with the weight being accessed at that time, but now a six months' supply of Mexican beeves was to be issued beginning on November 1. They were weighed at delivery, and Hall had to issue them every week. All the while, the herd was expected to decrease over the winter by an estimated 30 to 60 percent due to death, weight loss, and straying. The savings for the department was to be a few dollars, but the Indians were the ones to suffer, as there would be a deficiency of beef before the winter was half over.[63]

When he had completed an inspection tour of the reservations headquartered at Anadarko and Darlington, Professor Painter wrote a report to his superiors in which he gave his opinion of Agent Hall:

> I found in Capt. Hall the best Agent in this part of the Indian field, so far as his work among and for the Indians is concerned ... He came here, as he told me, not for his salary, but to get rich. He would not be mean enough to rob the Indian, but hoped to be on hand to get a big grab when these Indians were either bounced, or the country opened in some way. He fought the unruly elements among them at the imminent peril of his life. He has disarmed their hatred of him, except in a few cases. He has heartily espoused their cause, as against cattle men. He fights their battles for them on every hand: perhaps obeys orders in regard to keeping cattle off more perfectly than is desired by the Bureau—he sometimes thinks so. He has driven out some of the most worthless appointees, and will keep it up until he or they go. I am satisfied that either this Agent will have to go, or the Department will have to reform its management of affairs; for he is too independent to submit to the conditions imposed, and, as I believe, too earnest in his efforts to advance his Indians ... [64]

Hall spent the summer of 1887 attending federal court in Fort Smith and, upon his return to Anadarko, cooperating with an inquiry headed by Special Indian Agent Eugene E. White. Ordered by Bureau of Indian Affairs headquarters, the probe was looking into Hall's management of the reservation. White asserted Hall had presented fraudulent vouchers in his accounts, spent public funds for his personal use, and appropriated the monies in his charge from cattlemen leasing Indian pastures. He also cited periods of intoxication and frequent absences without leave. Since the case was becoming a criminal matter, Hall retained Judge Robert R. Hazelwood of Henrietta as his legal counsel.[65]

He was formally suspended from his position on October 18, 1887, by Indian Inspector Thomas Damron Marcum. The following month, a federal warrant was sworn out charging Hall with presenting false vouchers and attempting to defraud the United States government. Dora Raymond, his first biographer, asserted Texas stockmen, resenting Hall's policies concerning the grazing of Indian lands, had influenced events behind the scenes in order to remove the troublesome agent. On the same day, Special Agent White was temporarily placed in charge of the agency, and even his tenure was marked by abuses of authority and conflicts of interest.[66]

The Hall family traveled to Waco, where, on February 23, 1888, Lee surrendered himself to Major Charles Baer Pearre, the U.S. attorney. Accompanied by a deputy federal marshal, Hall went to Dallas the next day and posted a bond of five thousand dollars. The following month, Hall was charged in U.S. district court in Graham with one count of embezzling $14,800. In April, the federal grand jury in Waco returned three indictments for embezzlment, and two for presenting false claims. The case was scheduled to be heard in Graham, but was continued on March 13, 1890. After his dismissal from the bureau, Hall settled in San Antonio. There he worked as a wholesale coal merchant, a cattle buyer for Mexican stockmen, and a traveling freight agent for the Houston & Texas Central Railroad. Even while the case meandered through the courts, another Hall daughter, Mary Weidman, was born in San Antonio on September 13, 1889. Virginia Derr was born during a visit to Lebanon, Pennsylvania, on November 29, 1890. The next year, Hall worked for Richard's unsuccessful gubernatorial campaign against James Stephen Hogg.[67]

In federal court in Graham, Colonel William Lyne Crawford, another member of Hall's legal team, filed a motion on October 20, 1891, to quash the charges against his client. The request was granted on three indictments, but denied on two others. Hall's trial began on the twenty-third, and he was acquitted the same day. On December 27, 1892, a government auditor ascertained that Hall had not been given credit or a receipt for eighteen thousand dollars worth of property he turned over to his successor. The recommendation was that no criminality should be attached to Hall; rather the fault lay in erroneous bookkeeping. In addition, Hall had hired day laborers rather than contractors for certain improvements on the reservation, and the department had disallowed the payments. Despite his exoneration, Hall's reputation was tarnished, and he was not reinstated to his former position.[68]

Meanwhile, in early January 1892, unionized employees of the San Antonio & Aransas Pass Railway went on strike over low wages. Hall was deputized by the SAP to keep the peace during the labor dispute. On the third, the watchman guarding railroad property in Yoakum was held up, and several engines were stripped of essential parts. The following day, Hall and twelve heavily armed railroad policemen shepherded the first passenger train through Cuero to Yoakum, which was also the headquarters of the striking workers. The captain noted the strikers were "uniformly courteous" to him along the way, and the only incivility he witnessed was directed at the "scabs" who had been recently hired to fill vacated positions. Once at the depot, Hall and some of his men remained to protect company property, and the former Ranger commented he "intended to talk peace" to the disgruntled employees. His guard force was increased to fifty tough men, and two more passenger trains passed though on January 6 without incident. The same day, two of Hall's deputies arrested a striker for loose talk, and the captain promptly ordered the man's release. On January 7, Deputy William Taylor arrested John M. Edwards for interfering in the management of the railroad. Edwards was charged with contempt of court and tried on the thirteenth. The strike ended after a few weeks, at which time Hall's services were no longer needed.[69]

Once the frontier closed, Hall found himself ill-suited to make a living in fields other than law enforcement. Disenchanted with his financial failures, and possibly with his heavy drinking, Bessie began to make more frequent and prolonged visits to her mother and older sister in Pennsylvania. When she and the girls went to Lebanon in 1894, her stay there became permanent.[70]

With the outbreak of the Spanish-American War in 1898, Hall was able to return to the profession of arms at which he had proven so successful in the past. In fact, his name was mentioned for the command of a regiment in the coming conflict. Such a position would offer opportunity for promotion and financial security. Hall's plan was to raise a force of five hundred former Rangers and frontiersmen, and offer them to the War Department. He received no reply from Washington. Undeterred, Hall spoke to Theodore Roosevelt, who was organizing his First U.S. Volunteer Cavalry (the "Rough Riders"), but the future president declined his services.[71]

Denied a chance to serve with the Rough Riders, Hall found another way, in May 1898, to get into the war. With tropical diseases, especially yellow fever, being a real concern, officials sought to recruit men who had already been exposed to the virus and had built immunities. On May 11, Congress authorized the creation of ten "immune" regiments for service as federalized volunteers. An advertisement in San Antonio newspapers informed readers that Hall was recruiting a company for the First U.S. Volunteer Infantry, although, unofficially, the army was not particular if a man did not have the requisite resistances. Indeed, the ex-Ranger received permission to raise two companies for service in the regiment, being commissioned a captain on May 25. The Immunes were mustered into service at Camp Hawley in Galveston between the twenty-fifth and June 4. First Lieutenant Charles Swift Riché, an officer of the Corps of Engineers posted in Galveston, and a graduate of the West Point Class of 1886, was elected colonel.[72]

In June, Hall submitted to a medical inspection, but he failed to pass. The reason was due to a hernia he had suffered in 1872, when he stayed in the saddle atop a bucking horse. As he was following an Indian trail at the time, he had been obliged to ride without medical attention for a hundred miles. The soldiers in his company had noticed his vitality, despite his age, and were crestfallen to be denied his leadership. Personnel of the regiment and citizens of Galveston called on military authorities to commission Hall, regardless of the surgeon's findings. Their petition was granted on June 21, when Hall was appointed captain of Company M. He accepted his new rank on July 2.[73]

On July 13, Brigadier-General Henry Clark Corbin, Adjutant General of the U.S. Army, directed the regiment make ready to depart for Cuba and report to Major-General William Shafter at Santiago for garrison duty. The Texans entrained for New Orleans on the twenty-second, and disembarked in Algiers the next day, but their subsequent stay in the Crescent City proved problematic. Bessie arrived in town from Pennsylvania to visit Hall on July 25, but, even though they had not seen each other in two years, his duties prevented him from spending much time with his wife.[74]

On August 15, the Immunes were ordered to cease preparing for Santiago and, instead, ready themselves for a return to Galveston. While the entire regiment was keen to see action, the adjutant general had remarked the soldiers lacked discipline, ignoring the endless delays, the rampant illness among the men, and the squalor they had been forced to live in at the fairgrounds camp. Hall obtained a leave of absence and traveled to Washington on August 17 to plead the regiment's case. The next day, the First U.S. Volunteers traveled aboard Southern Pacific railcars to Galveston to await orders. After much commotion, the Immunes, including Hall, were mustered out on October 28. The war with Spain was ended by the Treaty of Paris on December 10. Among other territorial gains, the United States acquired sovereignty over the Philippine Islands and its seven million inhabitants in return for twenty million dollars.[75]

Peace did not long endure, and hostilities between members of the Filipino independence movement and U.S. troops broke out in Manila on February 4, 1899. As the fighting spread along the American outpost line, Major-General Elwell Stephen Otis, commanding general of the VIII Corps and the Department of the Pacific, ordered his eleven thousand regular and volunteer troops to engage Emilio Aguinaldo y Famy's army of forty thousand Filipinos. After two weeks of fighting, Aguinaldo withdrew from Manila toward Malolos and attempted to conduct a conventional campaign typified by trench warfare and the seizing of territory. In the meantime, President William McKinley was authorized, on March 2, 1899, to maintain the army at a strength not greater than 65,000 men, and to recruit a force not exceeding 35,000 volunteers. In raising twenty-seven infantry and three cavalry regiments, all enlistments were set at twenty-eight months, unless sooner discharged. This increase was to continue only for the duration of the war, or until July 1, 1901.[76]

After the release of the Immunes from duty, Hall wasted no time in attempting to obtain another commission. He returned to Washington to secure a position in one of the new infantry regiments. His determination was rewarded with a commission of first lieutenant in the Thirty-third U.S. Volunteer Infantry on July 5, 1899, and Hall accepted his appointment on the twenty-second. Detached for recruiting service in Galveston from August 6 to the seventeenth, he traveled to Camp Allyn K. Capron on the grounds of the San Antonio Jockey Club. There, Hall was assigned to Company L as the acting commanding officer on August 25.[77]

Despite his prior military service, Hall remained a civilian at heart, and eschewed the manual of arms or parade ground drill. Colonel Luther Rector Hare, the regimental commander, agreed and emphasized open-order tactics, marching, and riflery in the regiment's training. The Third Battalion, to which Company L belonged, was posted to Fort Clark from September 4 to the seventh for rifle training and squad- and company-sized instruction. The regiment broke camp on September 16 and entrained for San Francisco. The first to leave, the Third Battalion, under Major John Alexander Logan, Jr., arrived on September 19, and went into camp at the Presidio.[78]

On September 30, the Thirty-third boarded their ship, the U.S. Army Transport *Sheridan*, and set sail for Manila. The voyage to the Philippines was a wretched experience for the soldiers. Rough seas and seasickness, rotting food due to a broken refrigeration system, and petty thefts all contributed to a generally unpleasant transit. Hall was relieved from command of the company on October 25 and, based on a surgeon's certificate of disability, granted ten days' leave, likely to his sickbed. Two days later, the *Sheridan* docked in Manila, and Hall remained determined to see action.[79]

The central plain of Luzon was comprised of Pangasinan, Pampanga, Bulacan, Tarlac, and Nueva Ecija provinces. This region had been the seat of war since fighting began in Manila in February. The American VIII Corps originally numbered fifteen thousand regular and volunteer soldiers, but their ranks soon swelled to sixty thousand. The division and brigade commanders were all senior officers who had campaigned in the Civil War and in Indian fighting. The junior officers had seen routine service on the western frontier, or action in Cuba the previous year. Before the summer monsoon began, U.S. troops had driven a wedge between the poorly armed and ill-disciplined Filipino revolutionaries in the central and southern provinces and, with the onset of drier weather, were ready to capitalize on their gains. The strategy was relatively simple: crush the Army of Liberation in the north and capture Emilio Aguinaldo. To that end, three separate columns would take the field in October. Elements of Major-General Henry Ware Lawton's First Division were to push up the Rio Grande de la Pampanga, across the northwestern and northern borders of the plain toward the Gulf of Lingayen, garrisoning the towns along the axis of advance, and occupying the eastern mountain passes.[80]

Contributing to the overall strategy, First Lieutenant Matthew Arlington Batson, Fourth Cavalry, had proposed to recruit one hundred Macabebe tribesmen from Pampanga Province into a company of scouts. The officers and the sergeant were to be detailed from American line companies, while the corporals and privates from the native warriors. The Tagalogs, who primarily composed the senior revolutionary leadership, were the heredity enemies of the Macabebes, and the latter could be expected to fight them aggressively. General Lawton endorsed the plan and forwarded it to General Elwell Otis. On September 1, 1899, Batson was assigned to organize and command a company of Macabebe scouts. These men were not enlisted in the U.S. military forces as no provision had been made for such an occurrence. Rather, they were paid and equipped as civilian employees of the Quartermaster's Department. Their first action resulted in a victory over the Filipino revolutionaries, and Otis was suitably impressed. Over the next two months, Batson received authorization to enlist four more companies; the first, second, fourth, and fifth companies were assigned to the First Division, and the third to the Second Division. Nearly all the older veterans who had witnessed the successful utilization of Indian scouts understood the need for native irregulars who could travel light through the flooded rice plains and the dense undergrowth of the higher ground, and perform reconnaissance in advance and to the flanks of the American forces. The indigenous fighters would detect ambushes or hold enemy insurgents in place until the main element could maneuver to attack the exposed flanks and rear.[81]

General Lawton, a hard-charging career officer and recipient of the Medal of Honor, had directed his assistant adjutant-general to find "three or four good officers for duty with Batson's scouts—men who want to come, and are the right stuff." On October 28, Hall was offered a billet with the Battalion of Macabebe Scouts in Lawton's division, which the lieutenant readily accepted. Two days later, he received orders to report to Lieutenant Batson at San Isidio for duty with the Macabebes.[82] For unknown reasons, General Lawton disapproved Hall's reassignment and revoked the order. The lieutenant went to the headquarters of the First Division to meet with Major Clarence Ransom Edwards, Lawton's assistant adjutant-general. The general apparently changed his mind, and the original directive was

Macabebe Scouts. From *Harper's History of the War in the Philippines*.

confirmed the same day. Subsequent monthly muster rolls show Hall absent from his regiment and on detached service with the Scouts beginning November 4. "The Fighting Thirty-third" would be assigned to Brigadier-General Lloyd Wheaton's division, and subsequently win themselves a reputation in the Philippines for quick-marching and hard-fighting.[83]

Even before Hall received his new posting, the fall campaign had commenced. Chosen to spearhead Lawton's operation, Brigadier-General Samuel Baldwin Marks Young was given the immediate command of the Northern Expedition, and his troops began marshalling at San Fernando de Pampanga on September 20. The organization of Young's provisional brigade included eight companies of the Twenty-fourth Infantry, eight troops of the Eighth Cavalry, nine troops of the Fourth Cavalry, two companies of the Thirty-seventh Infantry, "Lowe's Scouts," and Batson's Macabebe companies. Young commenced his campaign on the morning of October 12, and engaged the enemy at Arayat, Cabiao, San Isidro, Taboatin River, Cabanataun, Aliaga, Talavera, and Saragossa. Meanwhile, a supply base was established at Calumpit, and advance depots were established at Arayat and San Isidro. Although the advance exceeded expectations, the primitive transportation network of narrow, unpaved trails and fragile bridges hindered the rapid movement of troops and wagons, and progress became delayed by unseasonable rains, flooding, and mud. Needing to press forward after the withdrawing *insurrectos*, Young, a hell-for-leather cavalry officer, gave the order, on November 6, for the brigade to cut loose from its unwieldly supply train. Instead, the American and allied troops would live off the land until the completion of the campaign. Beginning the rapid advance two days later, the Macabebe battalion was first in the line of march.[84]

On the morning of the eighth, the Macabebe battalion, the brigade headquarters, and Captain George Francis Chase's troop of the Third Cavalry made a forced march on the eastern trail, by way of Hacienda de Valle, to San José. The cavalry arrived at one-thirty p.m., the Macabebes a half-hour later, and the Americans captured an enemy commissary carrying two hundred dollars, some important dispatches, and a large hoard of ammunition. From the seized documents, Young learned Aguinaldo was evacuating his forces through San Nicolas Pass, and the Americans would need to move rapidly in order to intercept the enemy.[85]

Reporting to Batson at San José on November 8, Hall was given command of the first company of Macabebe Scouts. He took the place of Second Lieutenant Henry Moss Boutelle, Third Artillery, a popular officer who had been killed in action on November 2 between Santiago and Saragossa. First Lieutenant Dennis Patrick Quinlan, Eleventh Cavalry, commanded the second company; First Lieutenant Albert C. McMillan, Thirtieth Infantry, commanded the fourth company; and First Lieutenant Harry R. Chadwick, Thirtieth Infantry, commanded the fifth company.[86]

On the eleventh, at eight a.m., the column began to advance over ten miles of demanding mountain trails to Lupao, which they reached by one-thirty. The next morning, at six o'clock, they moved on toward Humingan. After a five-mile march, they arrived at eight-twenty and found two hundred enemy soldiers formed up in front of the town. The Filipinos opened fire on the Scouts at a range of five hundred yards. Hall deployed to the left of Humingan to cut the Rosales road, Quinlan to the right to seal the enemy's escape route along the Tayug road, and Batson and the other two companies charged the Filipino position. The two sides skirmished for fifteen minutes before the *insurrectos* dispersed and escaped. The Macabebes remained in Humingan for one day of garrison duty.[87]

Joined by four mountain guns and Chase's troop, Batson and his men marched to Tayug, arriving the evening of the thirteenth. The next morning, the Macabebes rejoined Young's command at Asingan on the Agno River. The general ordered them to move toward Urdaneta, where they fought a brief action, and Villasis. Early on the sixteenth, Batson received orders to redeploy to Binalonan; he then pushed on to Pozorrublo.[88]

In his headlong dash, General Young's column had accomplished Lawton's goals of outflanking Aguinaldo's army, sealing escape routes into the mountains, and forcing the enemy forces to fragment into smaller bands. American elements situated on the railroad were now able to move forward unopposed. The one disappointment in the overall operation was due to General Wheaton. Tasked with commanding an amphibious landing at Lingayan Gulf, his natural caution caused him to miss uniting with the fast-marching Lawton and blocking Aguinaldo's line of retreat to the north. As a result, the opportunity to capture the revolutionary leader was squandered, but Young commenced rapid movements designed to prevent the Filipinos from uniting. "Aguinaldo is now a fugitive and an outlaw, seeking security in escape to the mountains or by sea," the general reported.[89]

Due to their reverses while operating as a conventional force, Aguinaldo and his chief lieutenants held a council of war on November 13, and disbanded the Army of Liberation. The rebels' shift to classic guerrilla tactics—raids, "bushwhacking," and close-quarters skirmishing—increased hardships and casualty rates for American forces throughout the archipelago. The Filipino independence movement possessed clear goals, such as prolonging the war until public support in the States withered, avoiding set-piece battles, and disrupting American governance, but the revolutionaries lacked a comprehensive strategy to achieve their objectives. The U.S. Army responded with a combination of "benevolent pacification" policies—municipal governments, public works, education, and sanitary reforms—and "hikes," or what would be become known in modern military parlance as search-and-destroy operations. This style of warfare depended greatly on the small-unit commanders—captains and lieutenants—in order to succeed.[90]

Even as the combatants altered their respective tactics, Batson learned of the enemy's presence on the Aringay River during the evening of November 19. Facing two hundred Filipino partisans, Hall, situated on the left flank, and Quinlan, on the right, led their companies in fording the swift-running river through a heavy fire. Batson brought the rest of the battalion to the water's edge and covered the advance. Having crossed, Hall and Quinlan's warriors struck the *insurrecto* entrenchments on the opposite bank and carried them by assault. Meanwhile, Chase and his dismounted troopers fired on sharpshooters positioned in the hills on the left and drove them off. One Macabebe tribesman was mortally wounded, while Batson was shot through the left instep, an injury that took him out of any subsequent action. After a sharp fight lasting twenty minutes, the guerrillas fled from their upstream works, and the Americans pushed into the town of Aringay in the rear of the trenches meant to defend the coast road.[91]

With Batson on medical leave, Lieutenant-Colonel Wilbur Elliott Wilder, an officer on Young's staff, was placed in charge of the Scouts and led them to Naguiliang. Being informed Aguinaldo himself was fleeing in front of them, Wilder ordered Hall to pursue from Naguiliang over the mountain trail to San Fernando. The lieutenant arrived in the latter place after midnight on the twenty-first without sighting his quarry. The depleted American forces were in desperate want of supplies, and the cavalry mounts required shoeing. The Macabebes were also dismayed at the loss of their adored commander Matthew Batson, and many were sick and exhausted. The general was able to provide some relief by ordering badly needed reinforcements and rations be sent to his column.[92]

On November 23, Hall and Quinlan, with seventy-five effective Macabebes, accompanied Young's column to Namacpacan, but Aguinaldo was safely away toward the province of Abra. On December 5, the American soldiers and the Scouts were at Narvacan, where they drove a strongly entrenched enemy force into San Quintin canyon east of the town. Fighting over rough terrain, Young's troops killed twenty-five *insurrectos* in the trenches before the remainder was pushed back into the mountains; six hundred prisoners were recovered. The American casualties numbered one killed and twelve wounded. The same evening, the general halted his campaign and established his headquarters at Vigan. General Otis ordered medical supplies and quartermaster's stores be sent to Young's depleted troops. The Macabebes had been dispersed across the area by the needs of the campaign, and all but one hundred were too ill or demoralized to continue any further. Generals Young and Lawton approved their relief from further duty in northern Luzon, and evacuation to Manila for rest and refit.[93]

Even though Young had suspended his operation, the pursuit of Aguinaldo continued. On November 26, Major Peyton Conway March and his four-company battalion of the Thirty-third Infantry, Hall's parent regiment, had been ordered to follow the fugitive president. They caught up with his sixty-man rearguard, under Brigadier-General Gregorio del Pilar, at Tirad Pass on December 2. After failing to take the heights by direct assault, March sited sharpshooters on a hill overlooking the enemy works and sent another detachment to outflank the *insurrectos*. Five hours after the battle began, in the scorching heat, the entrenchments were finally taken. Fifty-two Filipinos were killed, including General del Pilar, but their sacrifice enabled Aguinaldo to escape. March called the battle the "insurgents' Thermopylae." Ten days later, Hall was scouting the front of Tirad Pass when he accidentally stepped over the edge of a bluff. Admitted to the First Reserve Hospital in Manila on December 20, he was diagnosed with a double oblique inguinal hernia. Evidently, Hall was determined to get back into the fight as he returned to duty on December 24.[94]

While Hall had been convalescing, the American cause received a blow on December 19, when General Lawton was killed in action on the west bank of the San Mateo River. On January 4, 1900, Major-General John Coalter Bates assumed command of the First Division, and promptly introduced his plans for a campaign in southern Luzon. The same day, Brigadier-General Wheaton and Brigadier-General Theodore Schwan were given temporary command of two expeditionary brigades.[95] Wheaton, commanding the first brigade, was ordered to offer battle to the enemy and pin him down in the Cavite area. Schwan, commanding the second brigade, was given the assignment of clearing Cavite and Laguna provinces, as well as portions of Batangas and Tayabas. In addition to cutting Filipino general Mariano Trias's line of retreat, Schwan was to also leave garrisons at each town along the route of march, rather than have them reoccupied by the guerrillas. Once Trias was contained, Wheaton was to launch a frontal assault on the trapped enemy forces. The units assigned to Schwan's provisional brigade included the Thirtieth Infantry, Forty-sixth Infantry, five troops of the Fourth Cavalry, four troops of the Eleventh Cavalry, and a three-gun battery of the Seventh Artillery. A detachment of Macabebe Scouts under First Lieutenant William C. Geiger, Fourteenth Infantry, was assigned to Schwan's column. The detachment consisted of five officers and 140 men divided into two companies; one commanded by Hall and the other by First Lieutenant James H. Blount, Twenty-ninth Infantry.[96]

After assembling at San Pedro Macati, the detachment commenced its march on the afternoon of January 5 for Muntinlupa; the brigade had left earlier that morning. The Macabebes passed Pateros and camped for the night. The next morning, the command resumed its march and arrived in Muntinlupa at approximately five p.m. Geiger's detachment rejoined the brigade, which split into dual columns and continued on to Biñan by way of two parallel roads. The Scouts were attached to the column that took the inland road at the foot of the hills. One and a half miles from town, the advance guard, consisting of the Scouts and detachments of the Fourth and the Eleventh Cavalry, found two to three hundred of the enemy entrenched in the rice fields to the front and atop a high hill to the right. The Americans immediately attacked. Hall and his company were sent to the left of the road to engage the enemy who were situated in an irrigation ditch in the rice field. Concealed behind thick bamboo, the guerrillas resisted bravely, but the Macabebes and dismounted cavalry fought their way through the thickets to drive the rebels from their position. Blount's scouts likewise assailed the insurgents on the hill. The skirmish lasted a half-hour, and the enemy was forced to flee, leaving fifteen killed or wounded and twelve rifles behind. Sweeping forward, the column crossed open rice fields. When the Macabebes were within eight hundred yards of Biñan, they discovered a line of guerrillas in the woods on both sides of the road. Hall's company deployed to the right of the road and Blount's to the left. The Scouts and a battalion of the Thirtieth Infantry routed the 250 Filipino fighters after thirty minutes of combat. In both engagements, the enemy's losses were estimated at eighteen killed and three mortally wounded.[97]

On January 7, at seven o'clock in the morning, Schwan led the expedition out of Biñan, save one battalion left behind to garrison the town, and began the march for Silang. Geiger's detachment reconnoitered to the west of Carmona, but found no trace of the enemy. Passing around the town, they discovered hostile forces on a high hill to the southwest. Ordered to dislodge the *insurrectos*, the Macabebes encountered no resistance. The detachment reached Silang later in the day, and remained for two days.[98]

On the morning of January 9, Hall and a picked detachment of fifteen Macabebes were ordered to report to Colonel Cornelius Gardener, Thirtieth Infantry. A dispatch from division headquarters had related that seven insurgent battalions, some fifteen hundred strong, were retreating toward Alfonso and Bailen. Gardner's regiment, Hall's Scouts, and a mountain gun were detached to meet the reported movement of the enemy. Departing town, the Scouts marched to Indang, arriving at ten a.m. At five o'clock that same day, Hall and his men commenced a three-hour march with the Third Battalion of the Thirtieth to Alfonso. The Scouts and infantrymen left at ten the next morning for Magallanes. Approximately three miles east of Magallanes, the Americans surprised and seized two enemy outposts, taking three guerrillas and their arms prisoner. Three hundred yards further, they discovered insurgent forces advancing rapidly in column. Hall's scouts and the rest of the advance guard deployed into a front line without halting, supported by an infantry company on either wing, and fired on the Filipinos. After returning a volley, the enemy troops broke and fled. Colonel Crisostomo Riel, commander of the Second Regiment of the revolutionary forces, was captured, along with three partisans, two horses, and one rifle. A short distance later, the Americans engaged the advance guard of Riel's regiment and scattered them after a short fight. Two miles farther, Gardner's command came into contact with the enemy's main body deployed on the other side of a deep gorge outside Magallanes. Hall's scouts and a company of the Thirtieth maneuvered through the gorge under covering fire, and dispersed the *insurrectos* with a few well-aimed volleys.[99]

Leaving Magallanes on the morning of the twelfth, Hall's scouts marched to Bailen, from where they guided three companies of the Thirtieth to Alfonso, arriving there at noon. They took to the road at three o'clock for

Bayuyungan where they rejoined Colonel Gardner's command after a march of thirty-three miles. The column departed for Talisay on the morning of the thirteenth where they were joined by General Schwan. From there, they traveled to Santo Tomas, then to Tanauan where Hall's men were reunited with the balance of Geiger's detachment.[100]

On January 15, Schwan again split his brigade into two supporting columns for the move on Batangas. While one cavalcade made a flanking movement through San Pablo, Tiaon, and Rosario, the main column, comprised of brigade headquarters, two infantry battalions under Gardner, Hall's detachment, and an artillery battery, marched directly to Ibaan, then on Batangas the following day, where they met slight resistance and drove the enemy in the direction of San José and Rosario. Departing Batangas on the nineteenth, Schwan's main column marched to Rosario and San Pablo. At noon the next day, they marched from the latter town and engaged guerrillas entrenched on both sides of the road at the crest of some hills four miles to the north near San Diego. In two hours of fighting, eighty-two of the enemy were killed, and a large number wounded. One American enlisted man was slain and eleven were injured. Two Macabebes were wounded: one severely and one slightly. On January 22, the column marched to Majayjay, where they encountered three small hostile detachments, defeating them with little effort.[101]

Entering Majayjay on the twenty-third under desultory fire, the column left almost immediately for Luisiana, where they came under fire. Scouting the surrounding countryside, the Macabebes moved on to Cavinti, Pagsajan, Santa Cruz, San Antonio, and Pieta before returning to Pagsajan, Lumbang, Cavinti, and Santa Cruz. The campaign concluded in the latter town on February 8. The Scouts had captured eighteen weapons, twelve hundred rounds of ammunition, and fourteen horses. General Schwan wrote, "The Macabebe scouts were well handled by their officers; were always with the advance, and performed excellent service as scouts in locating and searching out the enemy and his trenches."[102]

Schwan transferred command of the garrisons created in the course of the expedition to General Wheaton, and returned to Manila. In departing, he asserted that since the "march was done on steep and rocky mountain trails, through deep gorges over bridgeless streams, it must be conceded that the performances were remarkable, and reflect the highest credit upon the American soldier, regular or volunteer." The Macabebe detachment was ordered to take a boat from Santa Cruz to Manila, then a train to Calumpit.[103]

With two arduous campaigns under his belt, Hall took sick leave, perhaps with the intuition his good fortune was soon to end. According to his friend, First Lieutenant Charles Pelot Summerall, Fifth Artillery, Hall confessed: "Every day, I have been going along these trails with the insurgents shooting and killing some of my men, and some day it will be my turn. I am not going to let that day come. I will never go out there again." He was invalided to the hospital in Manila on March 7 with remittent malarial fever. Two days later, he was transferred to the Convalescent Hospital on Corregidor, and returned to duty on March 19. The hernia that had reappeared after his fall the previous December had grown much larger. Going on sick call at the detachment's hospital on April 5, Hall sought treatment in Manila two days later, and was fitted with a truss on the seventeenth. He was transferred to the Corregidor hospital on April 23, before returning to duty on June 5. Hall was relieved of duty with the Macabebe Scouts on June 8, and ordered to report to his regimental commander at Vigan.[104]

Hall's poor health continued to place him on the sick list. Colonel Marcus Daniel Cronin, who had recently taken command of the Thirty-third, ordered him to report to the regimental surgeon on June 18 for medical attention. He was placed on bed rest in his quarters two days later. On June 22, he transferred to the First District Hospital in Vigan with a diagnosis of acute dermatitis on both calves and both thighs. The next day, he experienced another bout of malaria, but returned to duty on the twenty-fifth. On July 1, Hall received a leave of absence and traveled to San Francisco. He was honorably discharged from the service for physical disability on September 26, to take effect on October 6, 1900.[105]

While Hall had been fighting on Luzon, Emma Roberts Weidman, his mother-in-law, died in late March 1900. Her will was to have a profound effect on Hall and his marriage. The terms stated that Bessie and her sister, Martha Kline, would receive the maternal estate, the home and furnishings, and income from an eight-thousand-dollar trust if they lived together until

Virginia turned fifteen years old. If the conditions were not met, the estate would be divided into six equal portions. Bessie's reduced share would be too small to support her and their daughters. Thus, Hall and his wife lived apart, but she and the girls enjoyed a reasonable measure of comfort.[106]

Hall returned to Texas by way of El Paso, and arrived in San Antonio by late October 1900. Nearly two years later, he traveled to Washington and testified before the Senate Committee on the Philippines, better known as the Lodge Committee. Chaired by Henry Cabot Lodge of Massachusetts, the group had been established in December 1899 to review U.S. policies in the archipelago. One matter the senators investigated was the charge that American forces had engaged in the killing of civilians, the burning of barrios, villages, and towns, the executions of prisoners, and the use of torture. On the morning of May 15, 1902, Hall appeared before the committee and testified that he personally knew of only one instance where a Macabebe under his command had utilized the "water cure." One or two days before Hall left the Philippines, the sergeant in question had extracted information from two or three prisoners using the technique, thereby uncovering a cache of sixty to seventy firearms. Hall stated the water cure was a part of the local culture practiced by many of the tribal groups, and he did not punish the sergeant or order him to cease. He further claimed American officers had to keep a firm handle on the Macabebes, but their discipline was satisfactory and abuses were rare. Excused by the committee, Hall returned to Texas.[107]

His health broken by campaigning, the aging Hall was also growing desperate to leave a legacy for his family. As always, his ambitious dreams for financial security exceeded his grasp. The Texas road he peddled to the Missouri Pacific and the Rock Island railroads, the rice lands he tried to sell in St. Louis, the work he did as a secretary for the Texas building at the World's Fair, and the real estate and oil investments all failed. He stood surety for the notes of friends, which further impoverished him, and worked as a traveling agent for a sewing machine company.[108]

Finally, in 1906, he was presented another opportunity to put his true talents to good use. Recently, Yaqui Indians had been ransacking the Carbo gold and copper mining district in Sonora and ambushing bullion and supply trains, killing the teamsters. Giroux Consolidated Mining Company's La Sultana mine, which had just experienced a particularly rich ore strike, had been one of the hardest affected by the raids, and the company's superintendent and assayer were both slain. In addition to armored motor cars, William R. Bassett, business manager of the Giroux mines, responded to the depredations by deciding to hire veterans of Cuba and the Philippines to act as guards. Hall received a telegram offering him a one-year contract to recruit and command the company's security force. The firm agreed to an annual salary of five thousand dollars and allowed him *carte blanche* in selecting and leading six men "who can pull a trigger quickly and who hold life cheaply but will sell it dearly in defense of other people's gold." Before heading to Mexico, Hall met Bessie at Washington, D.C.'s Metropolitan Hotel in May, and the two enjoyed a second honeymoon. He was also able to visit with Elizabeth, Dorothy, Mary, and Virginia in Philadelphia, and present them with a portion of his retainer. After visiting his mother in Greensboro, he went to San Antonio to begin recruiting. Assembling his squad from 160 applications, Hall purchased tickets for himself and his "band of daredevils" to Carbo on the Guaymas branch of the Southern Pacific. Once there, they rode some thirty miles to La Sultana mine.[109]

For nearly a year, Hall supervised the safe transport of ore from La Sultana to the Carbo railhead. On horseback, he and his force, increased to twenty guards, escorted the armored car carrying the bullion. Three of Hall's men paid the ultimate price to ensure every shipment was successfully conveyed to the waiting trains. When not safeguarding the gold, they spent their time in the mountains hunting Yaquis. The *Galveston Daily News* reported that the "La Sultana rangers" had "more than half a hundred encounters with the Indians ... but have come off victorious in every instance." Despite their hard-won triumphs, the company was to be disbanded when the rail spur from Carbo to the mine was completed. Hall resigned from the mining company's employ on May 1, 1907.[110]

In the last years of his life, Hall promoted several projects in Texas and Mexico involving mining concessions, oil leases, real estate, and colonization proposals. As each scheme failed, he fell deeper into depression, turned more and more to drink, and his health suffered.[111]

The discouraged and sickly ex-Ranger was admitted to Santa Rosa Hospital in San Antonio on March 1, 1911. In his last days, he confessed his sins to Father James Martin Kirwin of the Galveston diocese, received absolution, and was baptized into the Catholic faith. Lee Hall died on March 17, of fatty degeneration of the heart. He was buried in the National Cemetery at San Antonio three days later.[112]

Bessie continued to live at the home of her sister, Martha Kline. After Martha's death in 1925, she went to stay with Jessie and her family. Bessie died of heart failure on October 11, 1926, at Jessie's home in Warrenton, Virginia. She was laid to rest next to her husband five days later in San Antonio.[113]

Jessie Lee married coal mine operator and gentleman farmer Isham Keith III on October 24, 1906, in Lebanon, Pennsylvania. She bore him one son and one daughter; both of her children predeceased her. The couple lived in Clarksburg, West Virginia, and Warrenton, Virginia. Isham was an influential man in Fauquier County, serving as chairman of the county Board of Supervisors and chairman of the local Democratic Party committee. Jessie was active in the Warrenton Garden Club, the Garden Club of Virginia, the Garden Club of America, and the Woman's National Democratic Club. Having suffered heart trouble for several years, Isham died suddenly on September 13, 1936. Sometime after Isham's death, Jessie moved to New York City. There, on March 30, 1946, she married Colonel Simon de Korsakoff, Chevalier de Malte. Her new husband had been a Russian Imperial Army aviator in World War I, and later held the same rank in the White Army. In the post-war years, he was a sportsman, yachtsman, big game hunter, and well-respected marine painter. She died on September 3, 1958, at her home in Warrenton, and was buried at the Warrenton Cemetery.[114]

Elizabeth worked in Lebanon, Pennsylvania, as a private secretary. She married Albert Couden Whitaker on April 28, 1928, in Jessie's Warrenton home. The newlyweds lived in Wheeling, West Virginia, and Elizabeth helped to raise Albert's one daughter and three sons from a previous marriage. Her husband worked in the steel industry as a company president and director. Diagnosed with paralysis agitans (Parkinson's Disease) five years previously, Albert died on October 7, 1951. After suffering from arteriosclerosis for a year, Elizabeth died at Ohio Valley General Hospital on September 23, 1959, of a ruptured abdominal aorta. She was buried next to Albert in Greenwood Cemetery three days later.[115]

Dorothy lived with her sister, Jessie, in Pennsylvania before she married her first cousin Frank Kerr Hall on August 9, 1911, at Luther Place Memorial Church in Washington, D.C. She bore him two sons, one of whom died while a toddler. Frank was involved in mahogany cutting and the sugar planting business in Camaguey, Cuba, beginning in 1902, and Dorothy maintained a second home in Houston. Following Frank's death in Cuba on October 20, 1918, Dorothy returned to Pennsylvania. In 1925, she lived with her surviving son and became a file clerk in the War Department in Washington, D.C. She retired in 1955. Dorothy died on October 21, 1970, at the National Lutheran Home in Washington. She was buried in Mount Lebanon Cemetery.[116]

Mary worked as a governess before she married Paul Grass Adams in Lebanon, Pennsylvania, on April 12, 1913. She bore him two daughters and two sons. He was a well-known lawyer, district attorney, county solicitor, chairman of the county Republican committee, and state legislator. Mary was also involved in Republican politics and several women's interest groups, and was a member of the Salem Lutheran Church. Paul died on October 12, 1952, at Marshal Square Sanitarium in West Chester. He was buried in Mount Lebanon Cemetery. Mary died suddenly on April 23, 1963, at St. Clair Hospital, and was laid to rest next to her husband.[117]

Virginia lived in Lebanon, Pennsylvania, where she worked as a trained nurse. On November 12, 1918, she was issued a passport in order to accompany her uncle Frank, who was ill, to Cuba. While residing in Camaqüey, she married First Sergeant Siebert "Bert" Pearson, U.S. Marine Corps, on May 11, 1919. Bert was assigned to the Sixth Provisional Brigade at the U.S. Naval Station, Guantánamo Bay. She ultimately bore him three daughters. They returned to the United States in July 1919, and Bert was assigned to the Philadelphia Navy Yard. After his separation from the service on January 15, 1920, they lived in Michigan and in Myrtle Point, Oregon, where Bert was the chief of police. Virginia was a member of District No. 17, Coos County Nurse's Association. Bert died on March 31, 1964, of prostate cancer, and was buried in Myrtle Crest Memorial Gardens. Virginia died on

June 20, 1972, in Camarillo, California, and her remains were interred at her husband's side.[118]

Guarding an immense territory that stretched from the mouth of the Rio Grande to the headwaters of the Nueces, Lee Hall was highly successful in bringing law and order to South Texas. He further burnished his laurels with gallant and honorable service in the Philippines. Unfortunately, when uninvolved in law enforcement or military roles, he seemed unable to find his way, and his forays into business and public office invariably resulted in failure. He loved his wife and daughters, but was not always able to care for them as he wished.

George W. Baylor. *Courtesy The Texas Collection, Baylor University, Waco, Texas.*

Chapter 6

George W. Baylor: "A Life of Adventure and Conflict"

G eorge Wythe Baylor did not epitomize the professional law officers who were enlisting in the Ranger service in the late 1870s. Instead, he was reminiscent of the citizen-soldiers of the 1850s. Before entering the Frontier Battalion, he had experienced a life of adventure and conflict in conventional war and on the frontier. Similar to Rip Ford, he was both a daring fighter and a learned scholar. Wilburn Hill King, adjutant general and historian, would observe Baylor "served the State long and well, and [was] noted for excellence of personal character and conduct, and soldierly courage and zeal." He was eloquent, highly educated, and a prolific writer, but his fiery temper would lead him into a grievous choice.

He was born at Fort Gibson in the Indian Territory on August 24, 1832. His father, Doctor John Walker Baylor, had been born in 1783 in New Market, Virginia, and appointed an assistant surgeon in the Seventh U.S. Infantry on July 24, 1824. He was dismissed May 28, 1825, but reinstated on July 11. Doctor Baylor was finally dropped from the rolls on May 20, 1833. George's mother, Sophie Marie (Weidner) Baylor, had been born in Baltimore, Maryland, in 1784. They raised seven children besides George: Sophie Elizabeth Baylor, on October 1, 1807; John Walker Baylor, born in December 1812;

Mary Jane Baylor, born in 1814; Henry Weidner Baylor, born on June 9, 1818; John Robert Baylor, born on July 27, 1822; Charles Gano Baylor, born on June 19, 1825; and Frances Norton "Fanny" Baylor, born in 1828.[1]

Having moved to Second Creek near Natchez, Mississippi, following his discharge, Doctor Baylor died on January 28, 1835. Sophie and her adolescent children relocated to the Taylor plantation near Pine Bluff, Arkansas, which had been recently purchased by her son-in-law, James Low Dawson. Dawson went bankrupt in the Panic of 1837, and the family lived in Little Rock before returning to Fort Gibson to open a boarding house for officers. There, George attended grammar school. He moved to Texas in December 1845 to live with his brother, John Robert, at Ross Prairie near La Grange, Fayette County. His brother's homestead proved to be a happy time for him.[2]

Baylor was sent to Rutersville College where he studied under Professor William Halsey. Upon completing his matriculation, he attended Baylor University, founded by his uncle, Judge Robert Emmett Bledsoe Baylor. The college was then located in Independence, Texas, and George lived with his brother, Henry, in town. After graduating, he moved to San Antonio, possibly in September 1852, where his mother had settled. He worked as a clerk for the army's Commissary Department at the Alamo, and spent his spare time escorting visitors around the site of the famous siege.[3]

In the spring of 1854, Baylor caught "gold fever." He departed New Orleans on March 22 aboard the steamship *Daniel Webster*, bound for San Juan del Norte, Nicaragua. He navigated the transisthmian route to the Pacific port of San Juan del Sur, and embarked on the wooden side-wheel steamer SS *Cortes* on the thirty-first. Arriving in San Francisco on April 16, Baylor worked for wages in Grass Valley and Placerville while he learned the business of mining. However, he would have to wait an entire year for the next great rush. Reports swept the northern mining camps in the early spring of 1855 of "rich auriferous discoveries" in the Kern River country of the southern Sierra Nevada. Five thousand eager prospectors, Baylor among them, descended on the valley. In an area stretching twelve miles, the placer miners worked the streams, gulches, and ravines from Democrat Hot Springs to Hobo Hot Springs, and were reportedly earning seven to fifty dollars a day. The alluvial deposits ebbed after a few months, and placers departed, looking for the next bonanza. The hard rock miners remained, intent on digging to the quartz veins containing gold.

Working on La Mismo Gulch, Baylor was not one of those fortunate enough to locate a viable claim. Instead, he partnered with Zeke Calhoun and Moses Kirkpatrick, and built a mill and a smelter on Green Horn Gulch.[4]

Baylor did not acquire much in the way of riches, but he was occasionally at the center of events. In May 1856, William Tell Coleman, a successful merchant in San Francisco, reformed the Committee of Vigilance, which would boast some 2,600 members. Having returned north, Baylor joined this second organization soon after its founding. In addition to participating in several extralegal hangings, he stood guard at the committee's headquarters, "Fort Gunny Bags," a converted liquor warehouse. At this location, he first met Chief Justice David Smith Terry of the state supreme court. On June 21, the judge, a fiery opponent of the Committee, had been "arrested" for stabbing a vigilante leader. He would be tried by the Committee and found guilty of the charges, but was inexplicably released on August 7.[5]

While hunting with three companions in Anderson Valley on August 11, Baylor volunteered to assist an uncle of William Coleman in tracking a party of ruffians who had bushwhacked and wounded the elder Coleman the previous month. Baylor, William, and the other three men tracked the desperadoes to a house on the side of the mountain. Ignoring a call to surrender, the outlaws opened fire and wounded Baylor on the thumb, and Coleman through the arm. After a quick flurry of shots, two of the renegades were killed, one of them by the shotgun-wielding Baylor. The latter and his compatriots surrendered themselves to the authorities in Santa Rosa, and were indicted by the grand jury for murder. On October 28, the trio were arraigned, pled not guilty, and requested trials. In Baylor's hearing, held on November 7, he was acquitted after the jury deliberated for three hours.[6]

Despite receiving a nomination as delegate to the Democratic state convention in July 1858, the disenchanted Baylor quit California and headed home to Texas. The mail steamer SS *Sonora*, carrying $2,225,000 in treasure, left San Francisco on November 5. Upon arrival in Panama City on the nineteenth, the 650 passengers traversed the Isthmus route to Colón (or Aspinwall). They then embarked on the steamship SS *Granada*, reaching Havana, Cuba, on November 24. The last leg of the journey was aboard the *Philadelphia*, which departed the next day, and arrived in New Orleans on November 28. While Baylor cannot be definitively placed on any of the aforementioned vessels, the timetable is consistent with his first confirmed presence in New Orleans when he signed the City Hotel's guest book on November 29. On December 17, he and two servants checked into the St. Charles Hotel. Baylor left the Crescent City aboard the steamship *Charles Morgan* two days later, and arrived in Galveston on the twentieth. From there, he sailed to Powder Horn near Indianola, then rode the stagecoach through thick swarms of mosquitos to Victoria. While visiting his mother in San Antonio, he learned of the provocative activities of his brother John in Parker County.[7]

George's elder sibling had been elected leader of the "Frontier Army of Defense," a committee of men intent on eliminating Indian depredations. Two hundred fifty of these vigilantes went on to the Brazos Reservation on May 23, 1859, and demanded the surrender of Indians involved in the raids. When confronted by Captain Joseph Bennett Plummer and two companies of the First Infantry, John and his men retreated, murdering and scalping an elderly Caddo as they withdrew. Enraged Reserve Indians followed the vigilantes to William Marlin's abandoned ranch house, opened fire on their antagonists, and drove them from the agency after a three- to four-hour fight. The incursion accomplished nothing, except to get six men killed, but forced the issue to the forefront. In late July, Indian Agent Robert Simpson Neighbors shepherded 384 Comanches from the Clear Fork agency, and eleven hundred Wichitas and Caddos from the Brazos reservation, across the Red River to the Wichita Agency.[8]

Despite the removal of the reservation tribes to the Indian Territory, depredations continued to plague the northwest frontier. George was living on John's ranch outside of Weatherford when one raid, occurring on June 12, 1860, claimed the life of Josephus Browning, a good friend of the Baylors. John and George; John's sons, John William and Walker Keith Baylor; and a slave were on Hubbard's Creek hunting cattle when they heard the news. Upon arriving at the Browning ranch on the Clear Fork of the Brazos near the mouth of the creek, the sight of their friend's mutilated corpse drove the Baylor brothers into a seething rage. Three days after the killing, John R. and George Baylor led four other men after the guilty party. Crossing the Clear Fork, they found two of the raiders on June 20, and the Baylors quickly killed them. The following morning, the manhunters found seven more Indians running a herd of fifteen stolen horses near Paint Creek. All the Comanches were dispatched, five of them falling before George's shotgun, and the horses were recaptured. Driving the recovered stock the next day, the white men encountered another band of six Indians with thirty-five head of horses. After a short *mêlée*, three Indians were killed and the rest, most bearing wounds, managed to escape. The victorious posse returned to Weatherford bearing the scalps of nine dead raiders, as well as that of a white woman taken by the Indians in their earlier foray. Besides these grisly trophies, the Baylor party recovered bows and arrows, shields, lances, and tomahawks. Large barbecues were held in their honor in Young, Palo Pinto, and Parker Counties. Relishing his newfound notoriety, George informed the enumerator working on the 1860 federal census for Parker County that his occupation was "Indian Killer."[9]

In January 1861, George was elected the captain of a party of men from Palo Pinto, Parker, and Young Counties for another expedition against hostile Indians. Termed a "buffalo hunt," the campaign of 250 volunteers was under the overall command of John Baylor, and left camp on the twenty-sixth. Riding up the Big Wichita and over to the Pease River, the Texans traveled south to the headwaters of the Salt Fork of the Brazos before returning home. In the end, the expedition failed to engage any Indians in a meaningful fight and accomplished little except to harden some of the men, George included, for the rigors of war.[10]

Indeed, the sectional crisis was fast approaching, and Baylor enlisted in Company H, Second Texas Mounted Rifles on April 13, 1861, at Weatherford. His captain was Harris A. Hamner, and his colonel was legendary ranger John S. Ford. Possibly due to his past fighting experience, Baylor was elected to the rank of first lieutenant. The regiment was mustered into the Texas State Troops on May 8 at San Antonio before being transferred to the Confederate States Army on May 23. On that same day, Baylor was appointed regimental adjutant.[11]

While the state organized for war, the situation in far-off New Mexico also occupied the attention of Texas officialdom. Despite the lack of resources and population, the territory allowed the Confederacy access to the Pacific Ocean and the mineral wealth of California. However, the reception to any invasion was expected to be mixed. The Anglo residents of southwestern New Mexico, mostly from the Southern states, supported an annexation bid by Richmond, but the *mexicano* population further up the Rio Grande mistrusted the Texans, no matter which government held the allegiance of the Lone Star State. Additionally, the Federal military presence in the region was centered in nine major forts, and Union garrisons were positioned closer to the vulnerable arms and matériel at unoccupied Fort Bliss than any Southern force. Apprehensive of the post being seized, Colonel Earl Van Dorn, commanding the Confederate Department of Texas, instructed Colonel Ford to dispatch a battalion of the Second Texas and six artillery pieces to secure Bliss and protect the western frontier from invasion. John, the regiment's lieutenant-colonel, and Major Edwin Waller, Jr. were assigned to command the expedition with six companies. George was to accompany his brother as adjutant.[12]

The Union War Department ordered the transfer of all regular infantry in New Mexico. Forts McLane, Buchanan, and Breckinridge in the western part of the territory were abandoned, $500,000 worth of commissary stores were destroyed, and the garrisons marched to Forts Craig, Fillmore, and Union prior to leaving. The Regiment of Mounted Riflemen and four companies of dragoons were to stay and protect the interests of the United States. Colonel Edward Richard Sprigg Canby, the new Federal commander in New Mexico, was authorized to call volunteer companies into the service.[13]

Lieutenant-Colonel Baylor's command—Companies A, B, D, and E, Second Texas Mounted Rifles, and Company B, First Texas Artillery—began converging on the upper Rio Grande in early July. The main body of Texans captured Fort Bliss and its vital armory and commissary stores. Meanwhile, Companies C and F of Baylor's battalion were assigned to garrison Forts Davis and Lancaster respectively. On the evening of July 23, John Baylor marched north from El Paso before Federal troops could arrive from western New Mexico. Major Isaac Lynde, the Union commander of the southern district, had been authorized to seize Fort Bliss, but he feared an attack on his own command and made no real effort to oppose Baylor. Three hundred fifty Confederate horsemen forded the San Tomas crossing, one mile below Fort Fillmore, and occupied Mesilla on the twenty-fifth. The major responded by concentrating his forces at Fillmore.[14]

The Federals finally launched a halfhearted attack against Mesilla on July 26, but were severely trounced. Lynde lost three killed and nine wounded, while Baylor had six Texans wounded and twenty horses killed. The major abandoned Fort Fillmore, and marched over five hundred men toward Fort Stanton. During the retreat, George and two other men captured nineteen Yankees who had stopped at a small spring. Not to be outdone, Colonel Baylor overtook and caught all of Lynde's exhausted command at San Augustín Springs, twenty miles from Fort Stanton, without firing a shot. Ironically, among the Union troops captured were those of the Seventh Infantry, Doctor John Baylor's old regiment. In addition, a sizeable amount of beef cattle, flour, rice, coffee, hay, and other stores was seized. As the country south of the *Jornada del Muerto* was now cleared of the Federal military, the colonel proclaimed the establishment of the Confederate Territory of Arizona on August 1, which encompassed all of New Mexico below the thirty-fourth parallel. He then assumed the powers of civil and military governor at Mesilla and appointed officials to staff his administration.[15]

The force the governor had at his disposal to hold the region south of the *Jornada* was a small one. Canby planned a counter-offensive to reclaim the territory from the Confederates. A mounted Rebel brigade under Brigadier-General Henry Hopkins Sibley was slated to secure the remainder of the territory from a Federal presence. Unfortunately, the first elements of Sibley's command did not leave San Antonio until October. Governor Baylor learned Canby possessed 2,500 men—eleven companies of experienced U.S. regulars, thirteen companies of poorly trained New Mexican volunteers, and a battery of artillery—at Fort Craig, approximately 117 miles upriver, and planned to advance on the Confederate-held region. Outnumbered, the governor sensibly responded by preparing to transport supplies to more secure locations in Texas, destroy those that could not be moved, and evacuate the territory. However, the anticipated Federal offensive never materialized as Canby discovered that the first elements of the Sibley Brigade had arrived at Fort Bliss.[16]

Riding east from California, Colonel Albert Sidney Johnston had by this time reached Mesilla, where he met George Baylor. The young lieutenant must have impressed the veteran officer as he offered Baylor a position on his staff. While en route to Richmond, the fifty-eight-year-old Johnston had been appointed a full general on August 31, to date from May 30. Having become the subject of tremendous expectations, he reached the Confederate capital on September 5. There he was given command of the Western Department, which encompassed Confederate territory from the Appalachians to the Great Plains. Baylor was appointed aide-de-camp to General Johnston on October 17, with the rank of lieutenant. He followed his new superior from Columbus, Kentucky, to departmental headquarters in Bowling Green on December 12.[17]

The military situation Johnston faced was grim as he struggled to acquire the essential recruits and arms, while still maintaining a defensive line over three hundred miles long from Columbus to Bowling Green to the Cumberland Gap. With multiple axes of advance from which to choose, Union generals Henry Wager Halleck and Ulysses S. Grant commenced offensive operations in February 1862. Johnston's outnumbered and frequently inexperienced subordinates were defeated at Logan's Cross Roads, Forts Henry and Donelson, and Elkhorn Tavern. In quick succession, the Confederacy's western front collapsed, and Missouri, Kentucky, and the western two-thirds of Tennessee, including Nashville and Memphis, were soon lost. With portions of the Tennessee River either undefended or under Federal control, the Middle South was opened to invasion.[18]

Johnston received reinforcements from New Orleans, Mobile, and Pensacola, and concentrated 43,000 men at Corinth, Mississippi. He then assumed the post of commanding general of the new field force—the Army of Mississippi—on March 29. General Pierre Gustave Toutant-Beauregard was designated second-in-command. Major-General Braxton Bragg was named chief of staff, while Baylor was formally appointed Johnston's senior aide-de-camp on April 3. The army was soon organized into four understrength corps under majors-general Leonidas Polk, Bragg (in addition to his staff assignment), and William Joseph Hardee, and Brigadier-General John Cabell Breckinridge. Despite the presence of Regular Army veterans at the highest levels, the vast majority of the brigade commanders, regimental officers, and recruits were inexperienced soldiers who had never waged a sustained campaign or fought in a major battle. The lack of sufficient uniforms, arms, ammunition, and equipment was another obstacle to be overcome.[19]

Having marshaled his forces, Johnston now needed to strike the scattered enemy before they could similarly unite. On April 3, the Army of Mississippi departed Corinth and marched for Pittsburg Landing, Tennessee, where Grant's army of forty thousand was encamped. Heavy rains slowed the struggling train of supply wagons, cannons, and caissons to a laborious crawl. Aggravating the delay was the knowledge Major-General Don Carlos Buell's 35,000 troops were also on the move and could be expected within days. Johnston kept his own counsel as to his plans, but he did reveal he "was going to hit Grant, and hit him hard." By sundown on April 5, the Rebels were drawn up within a mile of the three-mile wide Federal camp situated between Owl Creek on the north and Lick Creek on the south near Shiloh Church.[20]

Johnston planned a frontal assault on Grant's position while simultaneously turning the Yankee left flank. By placing Bragg, Hardee, and Polk on the right, center, and left respectively, such a move would hopefully push the Federals from Lick Creek, roll up the line, and throw it back onto the junction of Owl Creek and the Tennessee River. The commanding general allowed Beauregard to draw up the dispositions for the army, but his Creole subordinate produced an overly complicated formation that called for the army's three corps to be deployed in three parallel lines that would attack *en echelon*. Either Johnston became aware of the new plan too late to make changes, or he merely accepted the situation, but both generals share responsibility for the arrangement that sent their gray-coated battalions into the fray.[21]

As Hardee's skirmishers commenced the fight on Sunday morning, April 6, Johnston and his staff rode to "where the firing was heaviest" and were soon near enough to hear the bullets as they whizzed by. One of the general's staff officers cautioned him to not expose himself needlessly, but Johnston only smiled and moved closer to the front. After braving massed Yankee volleys for almost an hour, the charging Confederates struck the crumbling Federal line, one hundred yards in front of the Union tents, and a gap opened in the Rebel ranks through which Johnston passed. The cheering Southerners marched at the double-quick, and were swiftly into Brigadier-General Benjamin Mayberry Prentiss's camp. As the Johnny Rebs pressed home the attack all along the front, the flawed battle formation Beauregard had ordered grew compacted in the swampy woods, and officers became unable to maneuver their men.

Instead, all they could do was push forward in uncoordinated assaults. Johnston had intended to turn the Union left before rolling up the line. Unfortunately, the Billy Yanks were forced into Pittsburg Landing instead of away from the river as Johnston's original plan had envisioned.[22]

At ten o'clock, alerted to the threat of a Union division preparing to turn the Confederate right flank, Johnston directed Baylor carry an order to Brigadier-General James Ronald Chalmers to "sweep round to the left and drive the enemy into the river." Positioned on the extreme right, the latter general's Second Brigade was part of the Second Division of Bragg's II Corps. After delivering the instructions, Baylor found Johnston had moved closer to the right, and located him on a high hill overlooking the Second Texas Infantry's position. Orders were given for the regiment and the rest of Brigadier-General John King Jackson's Third Brigade to advance. Baylor obtained permission to join his fellow Texans in the charge, and Colonel Calhoun Benham, whom Baylor had known in San Francisco, accompanied him. By ten-thirty, Chalmers's and Jackson's men were in attack positions on the heights above the confluence of Lick Creek and Locust Grove Branch. Thirty minutes later, preceded by an artillery barrage that hammered the Federal line, the two Confederate brigades attacked, and Jackson's troops captured the retreating enemy's camp. They then swept aside a light Yankee skirmish line and smashed into the two Union brigades in the wooded ravines to the west and north. Jackson's attack became part of the massive assault on the Federal line deployed in the Peach Orchard. Although they inflicted heavy casualties, the Southerners stalled for a time in the ravines to the south. Finally, with five Confederate brigades attacking the Union position front and flank, the Federals retired to the north side of the orchard where they regrouped. Baylor would never receive an actual wound in the war, but he was scratched on the nose by a Minié ball sometime during this attack. He and Benham rode back to where they had left Johnston, and found he had moved in the direction of Sarah Bell's old cotton field. Riding that way just behind the line of battle, Baylor followed the sounds of the heaviest fire and soon learned the general had been shot, perhaps seriously.[23]

Baylor rode a short distance, crossed a ravine near a log cabin, and, beyond, found Johnston and several staff officers in a depression that emptied into the gulch. The dying general was lying on the ground after a bullet had severed the popliteal artery below his right knee. The blood that had filled his boot was leaking out in a stream that ended in a pool eight feet away. Johnston had sent his personal surgeon to care for some wounded Union prisoners and, despite a search, no doctor could be found. Those gathered around the general, who tragically exsanguinated in fifteen minutes, did not possess the medical knowledge to even administer a tourniquet. Baylor went to look for an ambulance wagon, without success, and upon returning to the ravine, he found Johnston's body had been removed to headquaters.[24]

The revered Johnston's death stole the impetus from the Confederate effort. After taking the Hornet's Nest in a dozen desperate assaults, Bragg and the other corps commanders marshaled their divisions for the final push on Grant's fortified line at the Landing. However, as the Rebel soldiers made contact with the enemy, Beauregard, who had assumed command, ordered them to halt the attack and withdraw out of range of the Federal guns. The general compounded this controversial move by not ordering a reconnaissance of the Union lines during the night. Once darkness fell, two Union gunboats, moored at Dill Branch, continually shelled the Rebel bivouacs, which, together with a cold, driving rain, ensured an uncomfortable rest for Federal and Confederate soldier alike.[25]

At first light on April 7, Beauregard granted Baylor and his fellow staff officers permission to escort Johnston's body from the field to Corinth. During the night, Grant had reorganized his forces at Pittsburg Landing and, reinforced by Buell's 35,000 soldiers, attacked Beauregard later in the morning. The previous day's fighting had disrupted Confederate unit organization and cohesion, and ammunition reserves had not been supplied to the troops. The 28,000 Rebels able to fight were relentlessly driven back across the hard-won ground they had taken the day before, losing men with every retrograde step. Finally, by midafternoon, Beauregard ordered a retreat, and the battered Confederate army staggered back to Corinth.[26]

While in Corinth at the same time, Baylor applied for an order to rejoin his regiment, and informed the Confederate high command he would await instructions in New Orleans. The following day, he was relieved from duty with the Army of Mississippi, and ordered to report to his regiment. On April 24, his orders were changed and he was directed to report to Beauregard at Corinth. He was further instructed to return to his regiment if the general should have no need for his services. Baylor learned his brother John was recruiting troops for Arizona and, on July 15, he applied to Secretary of War George Wythe Randolph for a commission of lieutenant-colonel of the Battalion of Partisan Rangers. Meanwhile, Baylor discovered his old outfit was without a captain and, being the senior officer on the company's rolls, requested permission to rejoin the Second Texas Cavalry on September 7.[27]

Despite the reverses suffered by Sibley's column in New Mexico, John Baylor continued to believe the Confederate occupation of the territory was vital to the war effort. He secured the permission of the War Department to raise a brigade to once more invade. The former governor established a recruiting depot along the Colorado River at Columbus, Texas, for what was to be called the Arizona Brigade. George Baylor was appointed major on the brigade staff. As the outfit remained in camp throughout the winter of 1862 and 1863, he was in charge of the recruiting endeavors, and was promoted to lieutenant-colonel and commanding officer of the Second Battalion in late 1862. The brigade was ordered to La Grange on January 8, 1863, and the following day to Virginia Point. Baylor's command was subsequently consolidated with John W. Mullen's cavalry battalion, and reorganized as the Second Texas Cavalry Regiment, Arizona Brigade. Baylor was appointed colonel on February 1; Mullen, lieutenant-colonel; and Sherod Hunter, major. The new regiment was mustered into Confederate service on the thirteenth for the duration of the war. In addition to Baylor's command, the Arizona Brigade was composed of Peter Hardeman's First Regiment, Joseph Phillips's Third Regiment, and Spruce McCoy Baird's Fourth Regiment. Fifteen days later, the brigade was ordered to West Bernard in Wharton County.[28]

While organizing the brigade, Baylor met Sallie Garland Sydnor in Houston. Born on February 13, 1843, she was the daughter of John Seabrook Sydnor, a prominent Galveston slave dealer and former mayor. They married on April 22, 1863, at Christ Church. Two days later, rather than an assignment to the southwest territories, the Arizona Brigade was broken up, and Baylor and his men were sent to James Patrick Major's cavalry brigade in the District of West Louisiana. They crossed the Sabine at Niblett's Bluff on May 6, and proceeded to Lieutenant-General Richard Taylor's headquarters along the lower Bayou Teche. Major's brigade also included the First Texas Partisan Rangers, Colonel Walter Paye Lane; Second Texas Partisan Rangers, Colonel Benton Warren Stone; and Phillips's Arizona regiment.[29]

By the spring of 1863, the Union controlled the Mississippi River from its mouth north to Baton Rouge, as well as the Gulf of Mexico as far west as Berwick Bay. While General Grant laid siege to Vicksburg, Major-General Nathaniel Prentice Banks, commander of the Federal Department of the Gulf, was ordered to open the Mississippi from New Orleans to Vicksburg. Rather than immediately engage in costly and time-consuming siege operations at Port Hudson, Banks decided to first bypass the fortress and clear the Mississippi's west bank of the Confederate threat to his line of communications. Sharp fights at Camp Bisland and Irish Bend saw Taylor's forces dispersed, and Banks departed Alexandria on May 13. He moved his army east, crossed the Mississippi on the twenty-third, and invested Port Hudson. Taylor reached Alexandria on June 1, where he found Major's brigade newly arrived.[30]

Reinforced by additional troops from Texas to number about five thousand, Taylor was determined to capture Berwick Bay, seize the Lafourche country, and plant his artillery batteries on the west bank of the Mississippi in order to threaten New Orleans. Despite the subsequent Confederate victory at Brashear City, the fall of Vicksburg and Port Hudson forced Taylor to evacuate on July 21, and withdraw to west of Berwick Bay and Bayou Teche. The Confederates finally concentrated in the Red River Valley south of Alexandria.[31]

Seeking to enforce the Monroe Doctrine and respond to the French occupation of Mexico, President Abraham Lincoln ordered Banks to gain a foothold in Texas. Beginning on October 3, 19,500 soldiers under Major-General William Buel Franklin marched northwest from New Iberia and the Berwick Bay country toward the Lone Star State. Brigadier-General Thomas Green's Confederate cavalry troopers undertook a scouting mission to learn the Federals' intentions, and battled Union forces at Carencro (or "Carrion Crow") Bayou on October 14, and Buzzard's Prairie the next day. The Rebel general surmised the Yankees numbered between twelve and fifteen thousand men. Having reached Opelousas on October 21, Franklin decided to withdraw due to scarce provisions and forage in the pine barrens of western Louisiana. On November 3, Green's horsemen and three infantry regiments from Major-General John George Walker's Texas division struck Franklin's northernmost camp near Grand Couteau on Bayou Bourbeau, three miles south of Opelousas. Major's brigade comprised the right wing of Green's battle line. Baylor's men galloped across an open prairie in what Green regarded as "the most brilliant charge on record." The Texans raced around the left flank and surprised three Federal regiments encamped on Carencro Bayou. Capturing nearly six hundred Federal troops and one cannon, the Confederates pursued the enemy until they were stopped by Yankee reinforcements from the south. The Union troops fell back, and Green followed with some of his cavalry.[32]

The Federals withdrew to New Orleans, regrouped, and launched an expedition of six thousand soldiers that seized Brownsville and portions of the lower Rio Grande Valley. Departing Vermillion Bayou on December 17, Major's brigade marched through the icy cold for Texas. Over the winter, Baylor's men manned the coastal defenses at Virginia Point where they rested and refit for the coming campaign. Placing recruiting notices in the newspaper, the colonel offered prospective newcomers thirty days' furlough and a fifty-dollar bounty, but they were required to provide their own weapons and horses.[33]

In the spring of 1864, the Union War Department changed their strategy from an inconclusive coastal invasion to a combined army-navy offensive ascending the Red River through Louisiana for a strike into either Texas or Arkansas. General Banks, leading the Army of the Gulf, was placed in overall command of the land operations. Rear Admiral David Dixon Porter commanded the riverine force, which boasted 104 vessels: ten ironclads, two stern-wheeler river monitors, an older monitor, ten tinclads, one timberclad, one ram, twenty-one steamboat troop transports, and numerous tenders, tugs, supply ships, and dispatch boats. Despite some personal differences, the general and the admiral cooperated effectively in advancing up the river. Leaving New Orleans on March 22, the nearly fifty thousand Federal troops occupied Fort DeRussy, Alexandria, Natchitoches, and Grand Ecore by early April.[34]

General Taylor had too few men to successfully oppose the Federal advance, and wrote his commanding officer, Lieutenant-General Edmund Kirby Smith, to send reinforcements. Kirby Smith advocated for a Fabian strategy using interior lines and drawing the Yankees deeper into Rebel territory. Facing superior enemy numbers, Taylor withdrew two hundred miles, continually taking all horses and matériel, and destroying any cotton his troops discovered along their line of retreat. On April 3, the Confederates prepared fortified positions three miles southeast of the vital crossroads town of Mansfield.[35]

Meanwhile, on Kirby Smith's orders, Major-General John Bankhead "Prince John" Magruder, senior commander in Texas, dispatched Green's cavalrymen to Alexandria on March 6. Major's brigade had been paired with Green's command at Galveston, and the Texas horsemen started for Louisiana on March 11. One night while traveling through the piney woods, Baylor had hung his cavalry saber, a gift from his father-in-law, on a bough at the head of his bedding. Breaking camp the next morning, Baylor forgot to take the sword along and only remembered it several miles later. He sent a soldier back to the bivouac, but the weapon was gone. The loss of the colonel's saber was a trifling matter, though, as Union forces moved swiftly and took Alexandria on the fifteenth. Green redirected his route of march north to Hemphill, and, struggling through the Sabine River swamps, crossed over into Louisiana at Logan's Ferry on April 6.[36]

Travelling ahead of their general, Baylor and his men reached Mansfield on April 5, while the foot soldiers of Walker's and Major-General Jean Jacques Alfred Alexandre Mouton's divisions had done the same four days earlier. Two understrength cavalry divisions and four horse artillery batteries were formed into a corps under Green when he arrived. After Major was promoted to the division command, Colonel Walter Lane was named to take charge of the brigade.[37]

On April 6, Lane's brigade deployed around Ten Mile Bayou to screen Taylor's positions and skirmish with probing Federals. The same day, Banks separated from the naval component at Grande Ecore and marched overland toward Shreveport with three infantry divisions and one of cavalry. The necessity of protecting his flanks and line of communications and supply had reduced his ranks to approximately seventeen thousand. He was also fifteen miles beyond any fire support offered by Porter's flotilla.[38]

At seven-thirty the next morning, the enemy vanguard of three cavalry brigades and three batteries skirmished with Lane's pickets at Wilson's Farm. Baylor's dismounted men were posted to the left wing on the crest of a hill. Major dispatched the Fourth and Fifth Texas Cavalry Regiments to support Lane, then moved to the front to assume command. Green similarly sent Brigadier-General Hamilton Prioleau Bee's cavalry division forward. The Yankees charged to within fifty yards of the position, but the gray-coated horsemen stood their ground. Baylor later wrote, "This close work soon became too hot for the enemy, and when we charged them with a yell they broke in confusion." The brigade pushed the Union troops back nearly one mile, but they had to withdraw in the face of Northern reinforcements that threatened to flank them. At two p.m., Major ordered his men to move back five miles to Green's defensive line near Carroll Jones's mill. Four hours later, the Federals twice brought up infantry to envelop Colonel Arthur Pendleton Bagby's brigade on the right, but were repulsed by enfilade rifle and artillery fire. The Fourth Texas sortied across the creek, brushed aside the enemy picket line, and drove the confused Federals back nearly one-quarter of a mile. As the growing darkness brought an end to the day's fighting, Major brought up wagons to resolve the shortage of ammunition and water, and to provide care for the wounded.[39]

In the early morning of April 8, Green retired with the bulk of his corps to where Taylor was holding his position at Henry Moss's plantation, three miles south of Mansfield. Bee's cavalry troopers were left to delay the Federal advance and allow time for Taylor to assemble his 8,800 men along Sabine Crossroads. Once the army commander stood ready to meet the massing Union troops, which would number some twelve thousand, Green was placed in charge of Mouton's two brigades on the left flank and Major's troopers on the extreme left. Walker's three brigades were on the right. Once they arrived at the plantation, Bee's horsemen were sent to anchor Walker's right flank. Federal skirmishers and artillery probed the Confederate positions until four p.m., when a general attack upon the Yankees was ordered. Charging through canister and musket fire, Walker's infantry smashed the Union left, while Mouton's foot soldiers pinned the right, and Major's dismounted cavalry rolled up the flank. Baylor's regiment led the charge and, when a wounded

Colonel Lane was carried from the field, the former assumed command of the brigade. The routed Yankees fell back through the pine forest as their ranks were overrun, until they halted at Pleasant Grove at six o'clock, three miles from the initial point of contact. The Union wagon train left abandoned on the road temporarily distracted the deprived Johnny Rebs before they continued on. Baylor had remounted his men, and they joined in the advance. Once the Confederate army halted, Major once again placed his troopers on the left. The Yankees were deployed in front of a small creek known as Chapman's Bayou. Another half-hour of relentless fighting continued with the Federals being pushed beyond the water, until nightfall brought an end to the battle. The Union troops repositioned themselves on a low ridge above the bayou. During the night, Taylor unsuccessfully attempted to turn the refused Federal right, and Banks withdrew twenty miles to Pleasant Hill, arriving at dawn. The encounter had been costly for both sides. The Federals lost approximately 113 killed, 581 wounded, and 1,541 captured or missing. Taylor reported Confederate casualties to be one thousand killed and wounded.[40]

The next morning, Bee's cavalry was ordered to continue the pursuit, while the rest of the corps was to follow. The Texans rode past dead or wounded Union soldiers and burning wagons before they caught up with the Federal rearguard approximately three miles northwest of Pleasant Hill. The Confederate horsemen rode on until they sighted the main body of the Union force situated on the heights one mile from the town. The troopers of Baylor's brigade dismounted and pressed forward as skirmishers in an attempt to coax the enemy artillery to fire. The Texans continued through the afternoon, while the rest of the Confederate army arrived on the field of battle.[41]

At five o'clock, the Southern artillery opened fire with great effect, and the cannons on both sides dueled for a short time. Once the enemy batteries fell silent, the Confederate infantry advanced at the double-quick. Thomas James Churchill's and Mosby Monroe Parsons's divisions drove into the brigade on the Union left flank in a "desperate clash of arms." The Yankee right held fast against the attacks of Walker's three brigades. Once the infantry was fully engaged, the entire force of Rebel cavalry charged the Federal infantry situated in a thick brush on the extreme left. The attack was repulsed with moderate loss. As Baylor observed, "We were not strong enough to dislodge them or flank them." The horsemen were ordered to fall back to a wood, dismount, and continue the fight on foot. Major moved around the enemy's far right flank, and Baylor's troopers ousted the Federals from a wooded ravine. The entire division drove the bluecoats back into their works, but the Yankees refused to withdraw any farther. The Union center was threatened by the collapse of their left flank, but, as darkness fell, a counter-attack on the Southern right and center drove the Confederate line into retreat. The Federals held the field, but soon after fell back to Grand Ecore. Confederates losses were estimated at 1,200 killed and wounded and 426 missing. The Union suffered 150 killed, 844 wounded, and 375 missing.[42]

As Banks withdrew, Churchill's, Parsons', and Walker's divisions were shifted to Arkansas on April 14, leaving Taylor the cavalry and Brigadier-General Camille Armand Jules Marie, Prince de Polignac's division. Major-General John Austin Wharton was ordered to succeed Tom Green, who had been slain at Blair's Landing, and his troopers skirmished daily with the Federals along the Red over the next several weeks, including at Natchitoches, Lecompte's Plantation, Monett's Ferry (or Cane River Crossing), and Rapides Bayou Road. At David's Ferry, on May 4, Baylor captured the transport *City Belle* and approximately three hundred Ohio infantrymen. The following day, he forced the Union to scuttle the gunboat *Covington No. 25*, and seized the gunboat *Signal No. 8* and the troop transport *John Warner*.[43]

On May 18, Taylor moved to prevent Banks from crossing the Atchafalaya, and his five thousand Rebels engaged the retreating Union troops at the Norwood Farm near Yellow Bayou. General Wharton exercised field command of the Confederate forces. From left to right, William Henry Parsons's Twelfth Texas Cavalry and the divisions of Major, Bee, and William Steele comprised the right wing of the Southern line; Polignac's infantry held the left. Confederate artillery batteries commenced the battle with a "fierce fire," and the fighting quickly became general. Supported by the First Texas Cavalry, Baylor's brigade rode toward a stand of timber at eleven a.m., where enemy pickets were hidden. The colonel led his men forward, and they charged into the woods with a wild Texas yell. Pushing the Federal cavalry back through the trees, the Confederate horsemen faced Union infantry and artillery deployed in an open field. The brigade drove the gun crews from their pieces, but Baylor found himself flanked by Union cavalry, with enemy infantry still to his front. Outnumbered and at risk of being cut off, Baylor's men slowly withdrew in good order. He had a horse shot from under him. The entire Confederate line reeled under the onslaught of the Union army, but the Federals declined to press home the attack. Instead they resumed their retreat the following day, crossing the river while unopposed by Rebel cavalry.[44]

Decades later, Baylor would write his troubles with Wharton began on the Yellow Bayou battlefield when the general rudely questioned the colonel's decision to retire before superior numbers. The next day, Wharton reprimanded Baylor and his regimental commanders for criticizing the management of the campaign. Soon after, Baylor was informed his wife Sallie was deathly ill, and he obtained a thirty-day furlough to return to Houston. Sallie soon recovered, but the colonel requested a twenty-day extension. The request was approved by Generals Lane, Walker, Magruder, and Kirby Smith, but Wharton seemed to imply Baylor had lied about his wife's condition in his request. The insult was not forgotten.[45]

After the brigade was briefly in Arkansas, General Wharton requested Baylor return with his regiment to Texas in December 1864, and reinforce the coastal defenses from an anticipated Federal invasion. Baylor was then preparing to confer with President Jefferson Davis about the possible promotion of two colonels, David S. Terry and Alexander Watkins Terrell, who were junior to him. Wharton gave Baylor his word the matter would trouble him no more, and the Second Arizona took its station near Hempstead. The colonel was disgusted when his outfit was later dismounted, and further incensed when he was ordered to report to Colonel Terry. Terry was the same individual Baylor had met in San Francisco, while the former had been in the custody of the vigilance committee. Baylor told the courier "you go back to General Wharton and tell him I'll see him in Hell first."[46]

Baylor left his camp on April 6, and rode the train immediately to Houston where General Magruder had established his headquarters. On the city streets, he chanced to meet Wharton and Brigadier-General James Edward Harrison sitting in a carriage. Wharton demanded to know the location of Baylor's command. When Baylor identified his regiment's bivouac,

John A. Wharton. From Clement A. Evans's *Confederate Military History.*

Wharton stated, "You had better be with it." Baylor replied he was going to Magruder to "have justice." Wharton ordered Baylor to consider himself under arrest. The two men exchanged additional angry words. Baylor called his superior "an infernal demagogue" and attempted to strike him, but Harrison moved the carriage to prevent the blow landing. The two antagonists parted with the promise to wait to settle their differences until the war's end.[47]

Upon reaching Magruder's private suite in the Fannin Hotel, Baylor was forced to impatiently wait for the general's return. A still enraged Wharton then entered the same room, called Baylor a "damned liar," and slapped him across the face. Baylor answered these two mortal insults by shooting the unarmed Wharton in the heart, killing him instantly. The colonel was arrested and detained in the courthouse awaiting court-martial proceedings. Sallie bravely joined her husband in his cell and repeatedly refused to leave his side, likely saving the colonel from retribution. While Baylor was incarcerated, his regiment was assigned to Jerome Bonaparte Robertson's Third Brigade of Samuel Bell Maxey's infantry division.[48]

After General Kirby Smith surrendered the Trans-Mississippi Department, Baylor was released and signed his parole in Galveston on June 21. The disintegration of the Confederacy meant Baylor would not be tried by military authorities for the killing. Released on bail, he was brought before the civilian courts in Houston three years later. After a mistrial, Baylor was eventually acquitted on December 6, 1868. For the rest of his life, Baylor would express profound sorrow and regret for Wharton's murder.[49]

While his case worked its way through the courts, the ex-colonel established George W. Baylor & Company, a general forwarding and commission firm located on Avenue B, or "the Strand," in Galveston. Later known as the Wall Street of the Southwest, the Strand offered Baylor substantial opportunities to build his business as a cotton and wool factor and commission merchant. Journalist Kimber Fountain, who explored the island, commented: "Cotton production in Texas verifiably boomed after the Civil War, and the sale and export of the fiber through the myriad commission houses and merchants along Galveston's Strand Street lined the pockets of local businessmen." The business district began as wood-framed buildings, but prosperity, and the fire of 1869, would produce the opulent Victorian architecture for which the Strand became famous. Eight newspapers, an entire block of insurance companies, five of the state's largest banks, and the finest restaurants in town were among Baylor's neighbors. Baylor also became a director of the Planter's Cotton Press Company, which was incorporated on November 10, 1866. The partnership was formed to build and operate cotton presses, cotton pickers and cleaners, and establish cotton yards throughout the city and county.[50]

The last commercial advertisement for Baylor's firm appeared in the July 25, 1868, issue of the *Galveston Daily News*. The reasons for his departure from the commission business on the Strand are unknown. Perhaps it was his restless nature that could not abide remaining in the same occupation, or perhaps his business acumen was not sharp enough for the cutthroat trade in which he engaged. The cotton industry was not a "genteel profession. Cotton traders were shrewd, hard-headed, intensely competitive, secretive, and, by profession, hagglers." Additionally, the unregulated cotton market of the late 1860s and early 1870s was characterized by rough-and-tumble trading practices. Farmers and inland gin operators competed with factors, who, in turn, vied with buyers, each attempting to maximize their own individual profits. Eventually, enterprising and ambitious capitalists would rise to prominence and bring organization to the business world of Galveston, but Baylor, while a gallant and courageous fighting man, may have simply been unable to measure up; or perhaps there was another reason altogether that will never be known.[51]

Instead, he turned to the insurance business as an agent for the Guardian Fire Insurance Company of Philadelphia in the winter of 1869. The following year, Baylor was hired by the Fire Insurance Company of Baltimore as the manager for Texas, and, by 1872, he was working for the Life Association of America in Dallas. In addition, with Francis Ernest Guedry, he opened the firm of George W. Baylor & Guedry, Real Estate and Insurance Agents. He sat on the board of directors for the Dallas Homestead Building Association, and was elected president *pro tem*. The partnership with Guedry was dissolved on September 24, 1874, by mutual consent. Baylor continued in the business as the sole proprietor. While he dickered over the price of cotton, bartered tracts of land, or offered his clients the finest insurance for their needs, he and Sallie welcomed into the world Helen, born on December 10, 1865; Sophie Marie, who died in infancy; and Mary Courtenay, born on June 15, 1875.[52]

On August 21, 1875, the *Statesman* reported Baylor was preparing to establish a sheep ranch on the Leona River near Uvalde. He instead settled on thirteen acres at Chalk Bluff in the Nueces Canyon, and engaged in "farming in a small way, raising mostly game chickens." Like many a warrior before and after him, Baylor's stint as a businessman ultimately proved lackluster. By February 1879, he had been reduced to "raising cabbages and onions." His request of Governor Oran Milo Roberts for a captaincy in the Rangers cited his record on the frontier and as a brigade commander in the war. The letter was accompanied by the endorsements of eight San Antonio citizens, the state speaker of the house, the lieutenant-governor, and a state senator. Adjutant General John B. Jones promised to approve the application and recommend the appointment when a vacancy opened, or if the Frontier Battalion expanded.[53]

Fortunately for Baylor, in the wake of the Salt War, the governor desired to consolidate the state's authority in faraway El Paso County, and believed Baylor would perform that chore well. Baylor was commissioned second lieutenant effective August 1, 1879, and ordered to take command of the detachment of Company C posted in El Paso.[54]

The following morning, the lieutenant set out for his new command along the six-hundred-mile San Antonio–El Paso Road. He was accompanied by Sallie, Helen and Mary, his sister-in-law Kate Sydnor, and an escort of five Rangers commanded by First Sergeant James B. Gillett. The sergeant described his commander as "a perfect specimen of a hardy frontiersman" and "a high-minded Christian gentleman." But he also recalled that "Baylor cared nothing for discipline in the company." Where the Rangers were concerned, Gillett observed that Baylor was a bit of a soft touch: he would accept any excuse, forgive any infraction, and take on any recruit who asked to join. Captain Cornelius Vernon "Neal" Coldwell, the battalion quartermaster, noted a lack of self-restraint or basic fieldcraft among the men. The one regulation Baylor rigidly enforced was that of no alcohol in camp or on the trail. He quickly discharged anyone who broke that rule.[55]

Baylor was a man in his prime. He was six feet two inches in height, older than his new colleagues, better educated, more experienced, and possessed of a wider reputation. He had a talent for newspaper writing, and a fondness for adding historical references to his reports. During their overnight stops, Sallie, a "splendid musician," entertained the party by playing the piano that was loaded in the wagon; Baylor accompanied her on the violin he had purchased twenty-odd years previously in California. He was greatly admired by his men and the public, but he remained in his temperament the aggressive "Indian killer" of his youth rather than a professional peace officer. Upon arriving in Ysleta, he assumed formal command of the detachment from First Sergeant Marcus Humphrey Ludwick on September 15. In time, Baylor settled his family in a house in town and developed an adjacent orchard. While he made his domestic arrangements, the lieutenant was faced with several issues. Cattlemen and sheepherders had moved beyond the Pecos seeking better grazing, the best of which was found in the Davis Mountains. Towns surrounded the military posts of Forts Davis and Stockton. Alongside this wave of settlers came the twin problems of outlaws fresh from the Salt War and the Lincoln County troubles, and Apaches raiding from New Mexico.[56]

The last major Indian uprising in the El Paso area was instigated by Victorio, the able chief of the Chihenne (or Mimbres) band of the Chiricahua Apaches. Through a combination of war and diplomacy, he resisted the federal government's attempts to relocate his people to the barren San Carlos Reservation in southeastern Arizona. He finally accepted a compromise in June 1879, to settle his followers on the Ojo Caliente Agency near Fort Stanton, New Mexico. However, Victorio soon learned of plans by Grant County authorities to arrest him on charges of horse theft and murder. He jumped the reservation on August 21 with forty Chihenne and Mescalero warriors, escaped into the Black Range of southwestern New Mexico, fought off pursuing cavalry detachments, and crossed over into Chihuahua in October.[57]

Fifteen Mexicans from San José and Carrizal were searching for hostile Indians in the Candelaria Mountains when they were massacred in a canyon by Victorio and his warriors. Once the scouting party was declared missing, a thirty-five-man rescue force set out on November 7 only to fall into the same ambush and lose eleven more. One hundred sixty-five volunteers from Paso del Norte and other Mexican border towns assembled to ride to the battle site and bury the bodies. Having secured his reputation locally

Victorio. #X-32937. *Courtesy Western History Collection, Denver Public Library, Denver, Colorado.*

as an Indian fighter, Baylor was invited to join the expedition. He declined the offered command, since the burials would be occurring on Mexican soil, but he did accept the position of second-in-command. Baylor, nine Rangers, and four American volunteers left Ysleta on the seventeenth and arrived at the scene three days later. Even though the burial proved to be a grisly chore, it did offer a chance for Baylor and his men to develop connections. Upon their return, the Mexicans voiced their appreciation and vowed they would ride with Baylor anytime. These alliances would pay dividends later.[58]

On August 2, 1880, Baylor and his men departed Ysleta and reached Fort Quitman two days later. The fourteen Rangers, along with war captain Mariano Culmanaris and twenty-seven Pueblo Indians, joined Colonel Benjamin Henry Grierson's Tenth Cavalry troopers in blocking Victorio from entering Texas, and further denying him access to crucial water holes. In all, Baylor and Detachment C were in the field for twenty-five days in August and September. The lieutenant received orders via the telegraph from Grierson who was near Van Horn Wells. Baylor's men were "to scout towards Eagle Springs and look close for Indian trails." Victorio was thought to be intending to head for the Guadalupe and Sacramento Mountains in order to recruit warriors from the Tularosa or Fort Stanton reservations. Unable to send a reply message, Baylor led his Rangers and Indian auxiliaries down the old stage road to the Eighteen Mile Water Hole, where they found sign of a fight between U.S. regulars and Apaches. Between Bass Canyon and Van Horn Wells, they struck Victorio's trail. Baylor's detachment overtook the American troops thirty miles beyond at Rattlesnake Springs. Victorio was at a rock water tank on the west side of the Sierra Diablo, and, when he observed the Rangers and soldiers approaching, he retreated toward Mexico. Baylor's detachment and Captain Nicholas Nolan's Company A, Tenth Cavalry had ridden to the left of the mountains and were positioned at Carrizo Springs, while other cavalry troopers had gone to the right. Learning that Victorio was on the run, Baylor and Nolan, with their respective outfits, followed the Indians through the night, and reached the stage road by morning. Victorio's band raced down the road to Eighteen Mile Water Hole, where they left the stage route, but they returned and ambushed the stagecoach on the ninth. The Apaches mortally wounded Brevet Major-General James J. Byrne, chief engineer of the Texas & Pacific railroad, killed a sheepherder working for Don Jesús Cobos, and stole sixty head of cattle. Successfully evading the trap set by the Army, the raiders then crossed the border on August 12, and made for the Boracho Mountains.[59]

In the midst of the hunt, the detachment was discharged on September 1, and immediately mustered back into service as Company A. Baylor was also promoted to the rank of captain.[60]

The new spirit of cooperation that existed on both sides of the upper Rio Grande was independently duplicated in Washington and Mexico City. President Rutherford Birchard Hayes had rescinded his order of June 1, 1877, authorizing U.S. soldiers to cross the border in "hot pursuit" without Mexican approval. With this change in policy, an American force was invited to conduct a joint operation with Colonel Joaquín Terrazas, a veteran Indian fighter, in the Candeleria Mountains. Colonel Eugene Asa Carr, commanding the Sixth Cavalry, rode south out of Arizona into Chihuahua, while Colonel George Pearson Buell and the Fifteenth Infantry marched from New Mexico. In addition, ten troops of Grierson's regiment were still deployed along the Texas border to block Victorio from entering the United States. Baylor also received an invitation to join the campaign, and he departed Ysleta with fifteen Rangers on September 17, 1880.[61]

Scouts located Victorio's camp in the Tres Castillos Mountains, and the columns of Buell, Carr, and Terrazas, including Baylor's Company A, moved in to seal the enemy's escape routes. Unexpectedly, Terrazas informed his American counterparts, on October 9, that their presence in Mexico had been found "objectionable" by the central government. The presence of two *norteamericano* forces deep in Mexican territory was apparently disconcerting to the politicians and their constituents. Despite his impolite dismissal from the country, Baylor later spoke well of the consideration he received from Terrazas and the other Mexican officers.[62]

After the American troops returned home, Terrazas surrounded the Apache camp and attacked on the early morning of October 14. The battle was over by nine o'clock, and resulted in the deaths of Victorio, sixty other warriors, and eighteen women and children. Sixty-eight women and children and 180 animals were captured. Terrazas reported that only a few had escaped.[63]

Victorio's death did not end the Apache Wars in Texas. After some survivors of his band—twelve warriors, four women, and four children—evaded Terrazas, they slipped into Texas. In January 1881, they attacked a stagecoach in Quitman Canyon, and killed the driver and the single passenger.

Initially, there was belief that white renegades may have been responsible for the crime. Depredations had also been occurring since the sixth between El Paso County and the Candelaria Mountains. Baylor received a letter from Adjutant General Jones, dated January 6, regarding the matter. He replied to the general on January 16, and indicated he was ready to take the field that very day in pursuit of the Quitman raiders.[64]

Following the trail from Quitman through the icy, rough country along both sides of the Rio Grande, Baylor, Corporal Nat Harrison, fourteen privates, and three Pueblo scouts found the raiders' *ranchería* on the south side of the Eagle Mountains. Along the way, Baylor had been able to read the sign, and confirm the marauders were Indians. The Apaches were alerted to the Rangers' presence and deserted their camp, leaving supplies on the frozen ground and their breakfast on the fire. Hoping to strike a new trail, Baylor led his men down the west side of the mountains, and rendezvoused with Lieutenant Charles Liborn Nevill's Company E at Eagle Springs on January 24. Under orders from General Jones, Nevill had left his camp three days before and had found the trails left by the fleeing Apaches. The lieutenant shared his detachment's rations with Baylor's men, who had exhausted their own supplies. The combined party had only enough for another five days, but Baylor believed they could overtake the Apaches within that time frame, replenish their supplies at the Pecos settlements, or, as a last resort, live off the land.[65]

The following day, the twenty-six Rangers followed the freshest trail north through the Sierra Diablo in present Hudspeth County. By the evening of January 28, they were within five miles of their quarry. The Rangers made a cold camp in a canyon in the northwest portion of the Diablo range, and reconnoitered after nightfall. The Rangers could not see the Indians' campfire in the dark. Before daybreak, they crossed the snowy mountain and rode one mile before, at seven o'clock, they spied the Apaches' morning fire another mile ahead. Leaving five men to guard the horses, the Rangers advanced on foot to within two hundred yards of the enemy camp. Baylor divided the Ranger force, sending Sergeant Lavoizare Blair Caruthers of Company E and seven men to the left flank, and taking Nevill and eleven Rangers to the other. Walking in single-file, the Texans concealed their approach behind Spanish Dagger plants and moved to within one hundred yards of the Apaches. The Indians were eating their breakfast when the Rangers quickly deployed into a line, knelt, and raised their rifles. They delivered two withering volleys of fire, then charged the survivors with a Texas yell. The Apaches broke and ran, only to come under fire from Caruthers's men. Four warriors, two women, and two children were killed. One woman and two children were captured; all three were wounded. The remainder, most of them injured, escaped, but the wind and bitterly cold weather made their survival uncertain. Nine horses, seven mules, two Winchester carbines, and one Remington rifle were seized. Baylor was not hurt in the skirmish, but he had felt the wind caused by several near-misses. His force suffered no losses, except for a horse that had been killed by the accidental discharge of a private's rifle.[66]

All the Apaches' loot and camp equipage was piled on the ground and set on fire. The Rangers then settled down to enjoy a hearty breakfast of horse meat, venison, and roasted mescal plant. They did not remain long afterwards, as their horses had not been watered since eleven o'clock the previous day, and there were only two miniscule pools of water nearby; one of those had been contaminated with blood during the fight. They reached Apache Tank, some thirty miles distant, where they were able to water the footsore stock. Returning to Eagle Station on February 1, the two companies separated. On Baylor's orders, Nevill transported the captured woman and the children to Fort Davis for medical treatment. All the captured horses and mules were left behind, except the four best pack mules. While Baylor continued to pursue Apache raiders, he was never able to bring them to battle. The engagement of January 29 marked the last fight between the Texas Rangers and a band of hostile Indians.[67]

Despite the Apaches' defeat, authorities in Texas and Chihuahua remained concerned with continuing depredations further west. On May 10, Baylor warned Mexican officials that six Mescaleros had been allowed to leave the Fort Stanton reservation for two months. "As the scope of the country they are authorized to travel over is nearly 500 miles," he continued, "they will very likely cross into Chihuahua and depredate on the people there ... They left on foot; but no one acquainted with Apaches will doubt their riding back, and likely with a drove of horses."[68]

While depredations shifted from West Texas to New Mexico and Arizona, Baylor found his bailiwick was not yet free of turmoil. As the Texas & Pacific and Southern Pacific Railroads neared El Paso, the town transformed from a sleepy, adobe village into a boom town inundated with bankers, merchants, cattlemen, gamblers, thieves, and murderers, all of whom scented ripe pickings. Saloons, gambling parlors, dance halls, and brothels became a common sight. On January 7, 1881, the mayor and board of aldermen had requested the presence of state troops, and Company A was soon ordered to relocate its headquarters to El Paso. General Jones also authorized Baylor to increase his strength to twenty men. Regardless of the railroad's approach, Baylor indicated on May 8 that he was moving his company from Ysleta due to the exorbitant rents. The "Great Day" of the Southern Pacific's arrival occurred on May 19, amid much fanfare. Once the Texas & Pacific arrived in El Paso, Baylor was obliged to post squads of Rangers to the numerous small towns that had sprouted along the tracks.[69]

Even as the captain's responsibilities grew, the size of the Frontier Battalion did as well. Jones's successor, Adjutant General Wilburn Hill King, appointed to the office on July 25, 1881, issued General Order No. 2 on August 4, which enlarged the battalion to a total of six captains, six sergeants, twelve corporals, ninety-nine privates, and five teamsters. From November 1, 1880, to December 31, 1881, Company A conducted forty-six scouts and made sixty-two total arrests, which included seven for murder, sixteen for theft, and thirty-five for miscellaneous offenses. The Rangers also guarded one jail, and rendered assistance to civil authorities on eight occasions. The company returned its headquarters to Ysleta on April 24, 1882.[70]

While still in the state service, Baylor campaigned on the Democratic ticket for sheriff of El Paso County later in 1882. He lost to Benito Gonzales on November 7 by a slight margin. Due to insufficient appropriations, each company of the battalion was reduced that same month to one commanding officer, one first sergeant, two corporals, one teamster, and ten privates, effective December 1. Rustlers plagued the Texas-New Mexico line in the first part of 1883. Major Albert Jennings Fountain, commanding the New Mexico Volunteers, was charged by Governor Lionel Allen Sheldon to pursue stock thieves, and he requested the assistance of Baylor in apprehending any who escaped into

Wilburn H. King. #1997/001-35-04. *Courtesy Texas State Library and Archives Commission, Austin, Texas.*

Texas. The Rangers had already been able to assist Fountain's militiamen on March 1 by capturing Doroteo Saius, a leader in John Kinney's extensive criminal empire. Having already arrested some fifteen gang members, the major was especially desirous to apprehend Pablo Gomez and Mauro Saius, both of whom were under indictment. Fountain believed they were hiding out in Concordia or Ysleta. Baylor replied he was willing to extradite any fugitives from New Mexican justice. He did, however, caution the major that any arrests of Texas citizens in New Mexico required warrants, as they would certainly be released under a writ of *habeas corpus* otherwise. Except for Colonel George Bushrod Stevenson, the captain was unable to locate any ranchers willing to swear out complaints for their rustled stock. In addition, Margarito Sierra, a jailed member of Kinney's gang, informed on his fellow bandits, but did not provide the names of those who had fallen prey to the thieves. Regardless, the matter was soon resolved when Kinney was taken into custody on the Gila River later in March. With the rustlers standing trial and receiving prison sentences, a nine-man detachment was assigned to Carrizo Springs in July 1883, while five Rangers were sent to Toyah in newly created Reeves County. Lycurgus S. "Kirk" Turnbo was appointed first sergeant on September 1. By February 1884, eight Rangers were stationed in Pecos, another six in Toyah, and a like number in Murphysville.[71]

Throughout the early 1880s, barbed wire spread across the cattle ranges of Central Texas. The fences—built "pig tight, horse high, and bull strong"—not only allowed land owners to enclose their properties and keep herds from straying, but also permitted ranchers to better manage the breeding process. In addition to any positive uses, cattle trails, public grasslands, roads, and water sources could now be fenced off from common usage. This state of affairs ran counter to the tradition of free grass and open range that had existed for decades, and ended the need for the multi-county roundup. On unfenced ranges, cattle could be worked by an average ratio of three cowboys for every thousand head, with more hired for roundups. Once the pasturage was enclosed, the work load was lessened, and fewer hands were needed. Large cattle ranchers controlling prime range approved of the newfangled technology, but homesteaders who wanted acreage, smaller stockmen who owned herds but no land, cowboys threatened with unemployment, and rustlers hindered by the wire preferred the status quo. Thus, fence cutting—popularly called "nipping"—became a wide-scale problem.[72]

Governor John Ireland codified the transformation into law when he called the Eighteenth Legislature into special session. Convening on January 8, 1884, the lawmakers passed legislation, amid contentious debate, that made fence-cutting a felony punishable by up to five years in prison. The governor signed the act on February 6. Additional laws demanded every three miles of fence possess an unlocked gate, and forbade the fencing of land not privately owned or leased. The legislators also appropriated fifty thousand dollars to fund the state's enforcement of the new laws.[73]

General King named Baylor temporary battalion commander on March 6, 1884, with the rank of major. While Baylor was on detached duty, and First Sergeant Turnbo was absent on a scout, Sergeant Francis William "Frank" DeJarnette commanded Company A. Baylor moved the companies to locations where they could best combat fence-cutters, assist undercover operatives, and aid local authorities. Company A was stationed in Murphyville with detachments at Ysleta and Toyah; Company F was placed in Pearsall with detachments at San Diego, Helena, Rio Grande City, and Waelder; and Company C was located in Wichita Falls with detachments in Wilbarger, Clay, Montague, Jack, and Parker Counties. Company B was posted to Coleman County, Company E to Brown, and Company D to Menard. The last-named station was selected due to its central location to the affected areas. Detachments of the latter three companies were rotated through Llano, San Saba, McCulloch, Runnels, Lampasas, Hamilton, Erath, and Comanche Counties as needed. Baylor and nine men traveled to Runnels City on April 29.[74]

In present Coke County, the "Fish Creek crowd" was a group of "nesters" squatting on the ninety-thousand-acre ranch of Representative Thomas Lawson Odom near Fort Chadbourne. After they refused to vacate Odom's range, he sought legal action in court, and soon began to suffer cut fences. William Carlton, an operative for Farrell's Commercial Detective Agency, recruited Benjamin Goodin Warren, a forty-two-year-old resident of Nolan County, to infiltrate the Fish Creek gang and gather evidence. Warren became a member of the bunch, and even swore an oath of allegiance. He was able to provide the state with the names of those involved in wire-nipping in the area, and offered to testify at trial. Baylor and twenty-five Rangers from Companies A, B, and E left Runnels City on May 3, and rushed to Abilene by train. They then rode to Fort Chadbourne, arriving the next day. Baylor enlisted Warren in Company E, and received a membership list of the Fish Creek outfit from the new private. The Rangers arrested eight men the same day and, one week later, a grand jury in Runnels City indicted another fifteen men on the roster. With the governor determined to end the practice of nipping, General King authorized Baylor to employ "some capable and determined lawyer to assist in the vigorous prosecution of these fence cutters." Once the need for the emergency measures ceased, Baylor rejoined his command in Presidio County on August 13, and reverted to his permanent rank at the end of the month.[75]

The Fish Creek arrests proved to be the only success in the fence-cutting episode, and even that ended in tragedy. The case meandered through seemingly endless court sessions, and the defendants brought suits for false imprisonment against Baylor and Odom. Indeed, the captain left for Sweetwater on January 17, 1885, to stand trial for the specious charge. Odom and Warren were sitting together next to a stove in the lobby of Sweetwater's Central Hotel on February 10, when someone fired one shot through a window from outside. Odom was only grazed by the bullet, but Warren was struck in the face and killed instantly. With the prosecution's primary witness murdered, the fence-cutting cases were dropped. Two of the Fish Creek leaders were indicted for Warren's murder. Their cases were given continuance after continuance until they disappeared from the docket in 1887.[76]

The appropriation for the battalion had been increased to $100,000 in fiscal year 1884, and the authorized strength was raised to 120 officers and men. However, by the end of the 1885 legislative session, the annual budget was reduced from $75,000 to sixty thousand. General King responded by reducing Company B to eighteen officers and men, and Companies C, D, E, and F to seventeen each. He also issued General Order No. 21 on March 31, which disbanded Company A, effective April 15, 1885. Captain J. T. Gillespie of Company E was detailed to transfer the public property under Baylor's charge from Murphysville to Toyah, and to arrange for its disposition to "the best advantage of the State."[77]

Free from the demands of the Rangers, Baylor immersed himself in the political arena. His attempt to become U.S. marshal for the Western District of Texas failed, but he was elected to the Twentieth Legislature in 1886. Representing the Eightieth District, he took his seat on January 11, 1887, and served until January 8, 1889. Composed of ten organized and eight unorganized counties, the district was the largest in the state. Baylor served on the committees for Counties and County Boundaries, Federal Relations, Indian Affairs, Internal Improvement, Public Lands and Land Office, and Stock and Stock Raising; he also chaired the Military Affairs committee. He introduced pieces of legislation that ultimately created Brewster, Jeff Davis, and nine other counties, as well as the Forty-first Judicial District. After his reelection bid failed, Baylor was appointed clerk of the U.S. district court in May 1889. The following year, he was named to the same position with the federal circuit court. He resigned in 1892 to run for county assessor and collector, but his support for Governor James Stephen Hogg led to his defeat.[78]

Once the United States was embroiled in a war with Spain, Baylor offered his services to President William McKinley through the efforts of the Honorable Joseph Draper Sayers, to Major-General Fitzhugh Lee through Senator Horace Chilton, and finally to Governor Charles Allen Culberson personally. He cited his experience as an Indian fighter, cavalry commander, and Texas Ranger, his fluency in Spanish, and his lack of concern with regard to yellow fever. All declined his overture, likely on account of his age.[79]

Helen had married Jim Gillett on February 10, 1881, then divorced him on March 2, 1889. Together they had two sons, one of whom did not survive infancy. She then walked down the aisle with Texas Ranger Captain Frank Jones on October 3, 1892. The couple lived in Colonel Baylor's home, along with Jones's daughter. Frank was killed in a skirmish with a band of outlaws the following year. By her second husband, Helen was left another son, Frank Baylor Jones, who was born with a congenital heart defect. She continued to live with her parents and, during her father's occasional bouts of unemployment, worked as a district court stenographer, notary public, postmistress of Ysleta, and *El Paso Herald* correspondent for hotel and depot news. Despite her martial misfortunes, Helen wed Captain Samuel Merwin Lee at St. Clement's Episcopal Church on November 14, 1895. Lee was head clerk for the railroad contracting firm Hampson & Smith, and he soon took his wife and step-sons to Cuernavaca, Mexico, where he worked as a superintendent on a construction project. Helen would change both her children's surnames to Lee.[80]

In 1899, Baylor, Sallie, and Mary moved to Cuernavaca and lived with Helen and Lee. On August 18, 1900, Mary relocated to the American colony in Guadalajara. Baylor and Sallie joined her there on December 25, 1901, and the Baylor women founded a private school known as *Colegio de Estudios Altos*. The years following were filled with some joy and much sorrow. Baylor was unable to secure steady employment, and the school struggled at first. He did take to writing some fifty-two articles for the *El Paso Daily Herald*, as well as others for the *Galveston Daily* and *Semi-Weekly News* and the *Confederate Veteran* magazine. One of the bright spots in his daily life was playing his violin in the evenings, while Mary accompanied him on the piano. Mary adopted Arthur Bridges, born in Anaconda, Montana, on February 9, 1901, after the boy's mother had died of yellow fever, and his father had abandoned him. She also took in Marguerita Velasco, an orphaned student. After a brief illness, Helen died in Monterrey on May 25, 1903. Following a short bout with pneumonia, Sallie passed away at their home in Guadalajara on April 3, 1904, and was buried there. Helen's son, Frank, contracted scarlet fever and, his heart further weakened by the infection, died on December 24, 1908.[81]

The Mexican Revolution brought changes for Baylor, Mary, Arthur, and Marguerita, and their life in Guadalajara. On November 3, 1910, Antonio Rodríguez was accused of murdering the wife of a respected rancher in Edwards County, Texas. Shortly afterward, a mob dragged him from his Rocksprings jail cell out into the street, beat him severely, then drenched him in kerosene and set him on fire. Upon learning of the immolation, many of the Mexican residents of Guadalajara, Rodríguez's hometown, rioted outside the U.S. consulate, chanting "death to gringos." The protests grew more violent, and numerous American-owned businesses were destroyed. Whether the Baylors were in any immediate danger during the rampage is unknown. Just weeks later, Francisco Ignacio Madero González launched an abortive attack on Ciudad Porfirio Díaz, which would begin a decade of internecine warfare. When Victoriano Huerta overthrew *presidente* Madero on February 19, 1913, and had him executed three days later, the violence threatened to spiral further out of control. In response, President Woodrow Wilson appeared before Congress on August 27, and urged all Americans to leave Mexico. Heeding the warning, the Baylors left behind ten thousand dollars in property and took passage on the SS *Yucatan* out of Veracruz on September 25. They arrived in New Orleans four days later. Reaching San Antonio, all four refugees settled in a house located at 901 Avenue B.[82]

On June 1, 1914, Baylor applied for a state pension citing his Confederate service. His request was granted the same day retroactive to the first day of April. Baylor fell ill on March 1, 1916, and he died on March 27. The primary cause of death was listed as "senility" while the contributing cause was "exhaustion." He was buried in the Confederate Cemetery in San Antonio.[83]

By 1914, Mary had become a teacher at St. Mary's Hall in San Antonio, and the family was living at 109 West Quincy. Over time, Marguerita and Arthur moved out of her household. In 1921, she was working for the Schermerhorn Advertising Company as a clerk. By 1930, she was operating a small stock farm. Mary moved to La Vernia sometime prior to 1940 to run a dairy farm, and died of pulmonary tuberculosis on February 4, 1942. She was buried in City Cemetery #1 in San Antonio.[84]

In his own mind, George Baylor was first and foremost an Indian fighter. Many historians have seconded this notion, but he did perform admirably as a peace officer, and accrued a respectable number of arrests. While he hated Indians, although to a lesser extent than his brother, he achieved a greater rapport with the *mexicanos* in his jurisdiction than any other captain at the time. In his temperament, he was the last of the old-style Texas Rangers.

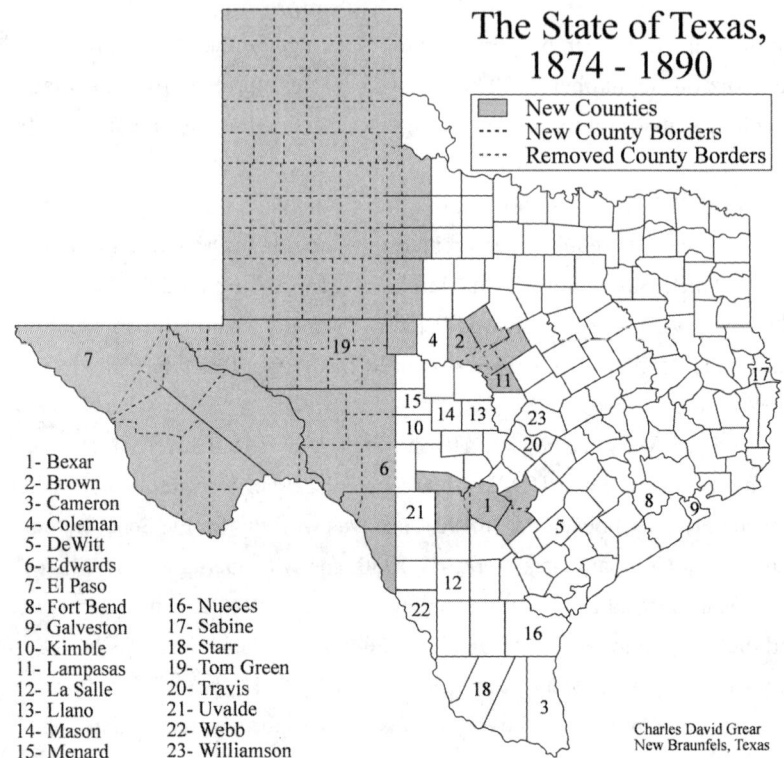

Map of Texas, 1874–1890.

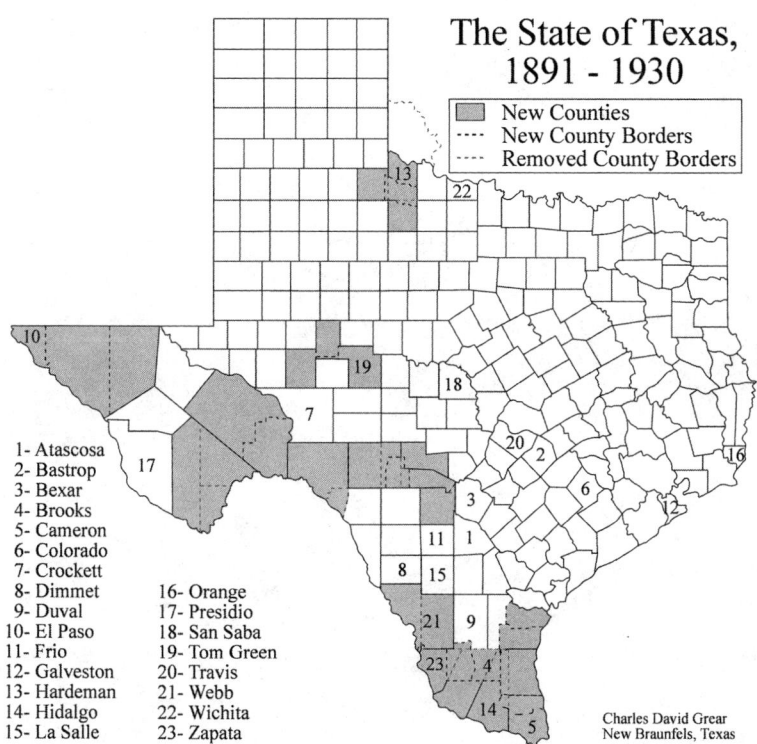

Map of Texas, 1890–1915.

Bryan Marsh. *Courtesy Haley Memorial Library and History Center, Midland, Texas.*

Chapter 7

Bryan Marsh:
"A Fearless Law Officer"

Bryan Marsh III was a fearless law officer who commanded the respect of lawbreakers and law-abiding persons alike. These solid characteristics, admirable in a Texas Ranger, were exhibited despite debilitating injuries. After harrowing yet honorable service in the Civil War, he subdued an explosive confrontation between civilians and soldiers in San Angelo and brought law and order to railroad construction camps. However, his successful eight months as a Ranger captain were sadly undermined by reports of alcoholism, a seemingly volatile nature, and an indifference to the protocols of command. Ranger Jefferson Davis Milton famously described his captain: "he would drink a right smart and scrap right smart. He was an old Confederate war colonel with one arm shot off at the shoulder and the other hand almost gone. But he would fight his shadow; wa'n't afraid of anything. Give him two drinks and he would spit in a tiger's eye." Like McNelly, the difficulties Marsh caused his superiors ultimately outweighed his continued worth to the State of Texas. That same attitude did not extend to the voters of Smith County as he served five terms as sheriff, and remains an honored figure in Tyler more than one hundred years after his death.[1]

He was born in Gaston, Sumter County, Alabama, on February 9, 1833. His father, Bryan Marsh, Jr., had been born on May 13, 1808, in Sumter

County, and worked as a merchant in Prairie Bluff, Wilcox County. Rebecca Waller (Jones) Marsh, his mother, had been born in November 11, 1804, in North Carolina. They married on January 4, 1830, in Clarke County. The younger Bryan's siblings were Martha Marsh, born on October 27, 1830; Darius Marsh, born on October 17, 1831; Edmund Marsh, born on November 10, 1834; Isabella Marsh, born on February 22, 1836; William Marsh, born on September 13, 1837; Sarah E. Marsh, born on June 6, 1839; and Peter Marsh, born on December 30, 1841. The 1840 federal census presents the Marsh household as having twelve white persons and fifteen slaves. Ten years later, Bryan, Jr. was a planter whose real estate was valued at $7,500. He also owned two male slaves, ages thirty-seven and eleven, and six females, aged between three and seventeen.[2]

The promise of unlimited opportunities encouraged many to travel west, and Bryan, Jr. joined the droves of settlers emigrating to stake land claims in East Texas. In 1851, he purchased 1,476 acres along Mud Creek in Smith County, nine miles southeast of the county seat of Tyler. Two years later, he bought another 320 acres on Harris Creek, northeast of town. The elder Marsh died on February 17, 1854, and his namesake was obliged to take charge of the family's financial affairs. In addition to the land, Bryan, Jr. left behind fourteen slaves and four horses. In time, Bryan III's acute business sense helped to establish him as one of the county's leading entrepreneurs. He joined William Tell Odd Fellow Lodge No. 27 sometime after January 16, 1852, and was elected warden in 1856. He also became a member of the Old Dover Baptist Church in 1855. By the beginning of 1859, he was partnered with Franklin Newman Gary and Augustus O. Erwin in F. N. Gary & Co., a dry goods and grocery firm located on the southwest corner of the public square.[3]

Marsh married Araminta "Mittie" Shuart, "a pretty and accomplished young woman," on December 21, 1858, in Smith County. She had been born on December 21, 1840, in Alabama, the daughter of Colonel Henry Shuart, a prominent farmer. Their son, Henry Bryan Marsh, was born on October 28, 1859, at Mt. Carmel, near Tyler.[4]

The 1860 federal census indicates Marsh declared his occupation as "farmer." His real estate holdings were valued at three thousand dollars, and his personal estate at twenty thousand. By this time, Rebecca and his brother

Peter were living with his family. Marsh personally owned fourteen slaves, fourteen more as his mother's trustee, and another three as his brother's guardian. The non-population schedule for the same year specified that Marsh claimed 320 acres of improved land, 670 acres of unimproved land, livestock valued at $1,250, 150 bushels of wheat, 1,600 bushels of Indian corn, and fifty bales of cotton.[5]

In November 1861, Colonel Middleton Tate Johnson received authorization from the Confederate War Department to raise a cavalry brigade for twelve months' service. Over the next several months, the fifty companies who answered Johnson's call to arms would be organized into the Fourteenth, Fifteenth, Sixteenth, Seventeenth, and Eighteenth Texas Cavalry Regiments.[6]

On February 26, 1862, Marsh enrolled in Captain John Charles Robertson's company in Tyler as a private. Ten companies were organized as the Seventeenth Texas Cavalry at Jamestown on March 15, and mustered into Confederate service for one year. Robertson's command was designated as Company C. On the same day, George Fleming Moore was elected colonel, Sterling Brown Hendricks lieutenant-colonel, and John McClarty major. The organization of the Seventeenth Texas complete, the Texans marched to Camp McKnight near Clarksville to join their sister regiments in Johnson's brigade.[7]

On April 10, Johnson was instructed to march his brigade from Clarksville to Little Rock, Arkansas. The Seventeenth Texas took up the march on the twenty-second, reached Camden, Arkansas, on May 13, and proceeded to cross the Ouachita River the same day. The companies were not faring well as many of the men were sick with the measles. Those affected had fallen out every day since they started from Shreveport. Marsh himself contracted pneumonia the day after his regiment marched through Camden, and he stayed in Holly Spring to convalesce while his fellow soldiers continued on toward Little Rock.[8]

On May 22, in accordance with the Confederate Conscription Act of April 16, 1862, the regiment reorganized for three years, or the duration of the war, and held elections for all officers. Because of the decision, many company officers resigned, including Captain Robertson. James Rather Taylor was chosen as the new colonel, Sterling Hendricks and John McClarty retained their ranks, and Marsh became captain of Company C. In the aftermath of the election, Colonel Moore was formally relieved of duty on May 24. Two days later, the regiment marched for Searcy, forty miles north of Little Rock.[9]

After his health was entirely recovered, Marsh started out after the regiment, and arrived in Austin, Arkansas, on June 4. His entire company, less twenty men still sick with the measles, had accompanied Colonel Taylor on a scout up the Little Red River, where they engaged an enemy foraging party. Marsh was ordered to bring up the supply train to Searcy on June 6, and arrived the next day at eleven p.m. He was just sitting down to dinner when one of the pickets reported they had been fired on at the Little Red four miles from town. Two Confederate soldiers had apparently been killed. The company was immediately ordered to saddle their mounts and form into a line of battle. Ten men from each of the regiment's companies were detailed to compose an advance guard under Taylor's command. Joined by the Twelfth and Sixteenth Texas Cavalry Regiments, the Seventeenth was ordered to the river and, after fording the Little Red, they were apprised of two Federal battalions being formed four miles ahead. They also learned the two men thought killed had instead been taken prisoner. Taylor's detachment followed the Union battalions for approximately six miles before overtaking them. They found the Federals drawn up in a line in the woods to the right of the Confederate regiment. The Rebels rode to within two hundred yards of the enemy position before they began taking fire. At that point, Colonel Taylor ordered the men, mostly armed with double-barreled shotguns, to fire only one barrel and leave the other for the charge. The Confederates galloped toward the Union troops and scattered them into a wheat field. Five men and five or six horses were taken in the retreat. Fifteen Federal soldiers were reported killed. The Texans were within six miles of the Union camps, and the regiment remained in place until midnight. They then returned to Searcy.[10]

Despite promises made to Colonel Johnson, the five Texas cavalry regiments he had raised were placed under the command of Brigadier-General Albert Rust in mid-June. While in camp at Searcy, the brigade received orders on July 4, to advance to Duvall's Bluff in Prairie County and reconnoiter the White River for Federal gunboats. The Texans soon discovered the enemy had landed troops near Batesville, fourteen miles below the Confederate position, and were moving to attack by both land and water. As the brigade prepared to march downriver and meet the Federals, one of the Rebel pickets from the opposite bank came in with an intercepted dispatch from the gunboat commander to Major-General Samuel Ryan Curtis. The message revealed the Yankee general would be unable to reinforce the waterborne force and would be compelled to fight his way to the boats with his three thousand men.[11]

General Rust ordered his regiments to immediately start for Des Arc with all available men and horses. The Rebel force amounted to about two thousand soldiers. Colonel Taylor ordered Marsh to take command of the 250 men detached from the regiment on account of being sick or without weapons. The brigade reached Des Arc on July 7, and attacked the enemy with the expectation of surprising fifteen hundred Union troops. William Henry Parsons's and William Fitzhugh's cavalry regiments met the enemy head-on, while Taylor's Texans maneuvered left to take the Federals in the rear. Unfortunately, Parsons and Fitzhugh were repulsed before Taylor could get into position. The Seventeenth then had to race back to the Confederate lines some fifteen to twenty miles to avoid being cut off.[12]

While bivouacked at Camp Crystal Hill, the regiment was dismounted on July 13 on account of a shortage of feed for the horses; additionally, less than half were fit for duty. Shortly thereafter, the Fifteenth, Seventeenth, and Eighteenth were combined with the Tenth Texas Infantry to form a brigade under Colonel Allison Nelson. Bad water and provisions contributed to widespread sickness among the brigade members. Marsh himself was down with bilious fever for ten or twelve days before he could resume command of his company. Following the brigade's move to Camp Hope, which began on August 19 and ended on the twenty-seventh, the health of the soldiers began to improve due to the better water quality.[13]

Colonel Nelson was promoted to brigadier-general on September 12, but he fell ill with typhus on the twenty-seventh. The following day, Nelson was named the commander of the Second Division, which was comprised of his brigade and that of Colonel George M. Flournoy. He had little time to enjoy his advancement as he died on October 7. The name of the brigade's bivouac was changed from Camp Hope to Camp Nelson in his honor. Major-General Theophilus Hunter "Granny" Holmes, commanding the Trans-Mississippi

Department, named his chief of artillery, Colonel James Deshler, to succeed Nelson as brigade commander. Furthermore, Major John McClarty resigned on October 22.[14]

The fall of Forts Henry and Donelson, New Madrid, Island No. 10, New Orleans, and Memphis left Vicksburg and Port Hudson as the only Confederate strongholds on the Mississippi. Rebel territory along the Cumberland, Tennessee, and Mississippi Rivers was at once vulnerable to Yankee invasion. In October 1862, while Major-General Ulysses S. Grant besieged Vicksburg, General Holmes ordered the construction of garrisons on the Arkansas and White Rivers. The principal fortification was the Post of Arkansas, a fortress being constructed near the village of Arkansas Post on the Arkansas River. Called Fort Hindman by the Federals, the stronghold was a square fortress whose exterior parapets were each one hundred yards in length. The emplaced artillery included two 9-inch Columbiads and another of eight inches, four 10-pound Parrot rifled guns, and four 6-pound smoothbore cannons.[15]

On November 21, Deshler's brigade broke camp and traveled by foot and steamship from Camp Nelson to the Post of Arkansas. They arrived seven days later, and joined Colonel Robert Rice Garland's Texas brigade and Colonel John William Dunnington's Arkansas brigade. In addition to leading two Arkansas infantry regiments, Dunnington, also a lieutenant in the Confederate Navy and former commander of the gunboat *Pontchartrain*, supervised the river defense. Brigadier-General Thomas James Churchill was assigned to the Trans-Mississippi Department on December 10, and given command of the post's five thousand-man garrison.[16]

Once the fort was complete, General Churchill proceeded to undertake offensive operations. Utilizing the Arkansas and White Rivers, Confederate troops raided Federal supply shipping along the Mississippi between Helena and Milliken's Bend, Louisiana. Major-General John Alexander McClernand, commanding the newly formed Union Army of the Mississippi; Major-General William Tecumseh Sherman, commanding the XV Corps of that same organization; and Rear-Admiral David Dixon Porter, commanding the Mississippi Squadron, responded on January 4 by making plans to reduce Arkansas Post.[17]

The following day, a fleet of sixty to eighty transports, nine gunboats, and three ironclads carried thirty thousand foot soldiers, one thousand cavalrymen, and forty guns from Young's Point, below Milliken's Bend, up the Mississippi.[18] General Churchill learned the Federal convoy had reached the cut-off between the White and the Arkansas on the afternoon of January 9. He ordered his three brigade commanders to ready their men for the anticipated assault. They were further instructed to take defensive positions at rifle pits two miles below the fort. Deshler's Texans occupied the fort's defensive works on the right, and Colonel Dunnington's Arkansawyers were on the left. Garland's brigade was held in reserve, except for five companies of skirmishers positioned several hundred yards in front of the Confederate line. Captain William Hart's Arkansas battery was placed to the right of the rifle pits by the river.[19]

As the Federal troops advanced by land and water on January 10, the Confederates marched out of the post and manned the line of entrenchments. The Union gunboats began shelling the fort and the rifle pits at eight a.m. while the Yankee troops landed with Sherman's corps in the lead. Becoming surrounded by superior numbers at three o'clock in the afternoon, the Confederates fell back into the post and erected makeshift breastworks. The unrelenting naval fire continued even after nightfall, and the Rebels could do nothing but endure the shower of iron.[20]

The next morning, McClernand deployed four gunboats and his artillery to fire on the Confederates. In a deafening three-hour barrage, the Rebel cannons inside the fort, except for one 6-pounder, were overwhelmed and eventually silenced. The enemy foot then charged across the open, level ground. When the Union line was within eighty yards, the Johnny Rebs let loose a "deadly volley" and the bluecoats withdrew, reformed, and charged repeatedly without success. At one p.m., the intense bombardment was renewed, which soon detonated the magazine. Once two Federal gunboats passed the post, the flotilla was able to bring fire directly to bear on the Rebels and rake their right flank, front and rear. One soldier of the Sixth Texas Infantry recounted, "Great gaps were torn in [the fort's] earthen sides and in some places they were almost leveled to the ground by the immense shells from the heavy cannon of the enemy's gunboats." Deshler's brigade—the Confederate left wing—was hard-pressed until General Churchill ordered every other company on the right to reinforce the beleaguered flank. Once the left was strengthened, the carnage between the opposing lines was horrific but the Southerners could not long endure the pressure. The Texan continued, "the roar of the artillery, the rattle of musketry, the hideous shrieking of the shells, the thunder of the bursting bombs, and the howling of their fragments ... made the place seem more like one of the pits of the infernal regions than a part of this fair earth." At four o'clock, as the Union troops were forming four ranks deep for an eighth charge, white flags of surrender began to appear without orders over Garland's brigade. The Federals lost 134 killed and 898 wounded, but the Confederates suffered only sixty-five killed and eighty-three wounded. Regardless, the entire garrison of seven thousand officers and men yielded along with eight thousand stands of arms, twenty cannons, and a considerable volume of stores. With Arkansas Post safely in Yankee hands, the Federals could concentrate on reducing Vicksburg and securing control of the Mississippi River.[21]

Meanwhile, Marsh and 313 other men of the regiment were gathered on the riverbank and placed under guard. They were herded aboard Federal steamboats on the evening of the twelfth, and began their journey up the Mississippi the next day. The officers, including Marsh, arrived at Camp Chase, near Columbus, Ohio, on January 30, while the enlisted men were delivered to Camp Butler near Springfield, Illinois, or Camp Douglas, south of Chicago. The fighting of the previous two years had produced an immense number of prisoners of war that stretched the resources of both belligerents, and threatened soldiers with deprivation, disease, and death. Therefore, on July 22, 1862, Major-General John Adams Dix, representing the Union army high command, and Major-General Daniel Harvey Hill, his Confederate counterpart, had ratified an agreement to create a cartel for the exchange of prisoners. Under the terms, paroled captives were prohibited from participating in military activity until released. Among the accord's nine articles was a "scale of equivalents" stipulating man-for-man trades of officers and enlisted personnel. Additionally, officers could be exchanged for specified numbers of enlisted men based on rank. Since August 1862, Camp Chase had been a temporary holding facility for prisoners, pending their parole and formal exchange.

The cartel existed for ten months until the Union War Department suspended the compact in May 1863, following reports the Southern government was treating captured black soldiers as runaway slaves and executing their officers. Fortunately for Marsh, pursuant to the established protocols of the Dix-Hill cartel, he was transferred to Fort Delaware, near Delaware City, Delaware, on April 10, nearly a month ahead of the Yankee change in policy. He waited at the depot until his parole became official on the twenty-fifth, then was forwarded to City Point, Virginia, for exchange four days later. He arrived on May 2, and was joined by much of the regiment. From September 1862 to June 1863, the prisoner population of Camp Chase ranged between 756 and 1,367. Perhaps because of the reduced number of detainees, the time Marsh spent in prison had not been exceptionally arduous, except for the monotony, rotten food, and being at the mercy of capricious guards. Not so fortunate were 111 of his fellow prisoners who had died in captivity, including fourteen from Company C.[22]

Formally returned to Confederate service, Marsh and the other ex-prisoners of his outfit were hurried to Petersburg on May 5 to oppose Major-General George Stoneman's cavalry raid. After serving as skirmishers on the outskirts of town, and only briefly engaging the enemy, the Texans left for Richmond the following day. They departed the Confederate capital on the eleventh by train, reached Chattanooga, and received orders to proceed to General Braxton Bragg's Army of Tennessee at Tullahoma, attaining their destination on May 19. Colonel Taylor was ill during this time, and Marsh assumed command of the regiment as the ranking officer. Many of the newly arrived Rebel soldiers were frustrated at not being allowed to return to the Trans-Mississippi Department. They also had to endure near-constant harassment from veterans in the army who questioned the surrender at Arkansas Post, and each man's personal courage. Once the Texans demonstrated their mettle in battle, though, the comments of naysayers would cease.[23]

Due to depleted troop strength, those soldiers of the Seventeenth Texas who had been captured at Arkansas Post were consolidated with similar remnants of the Eighteenth, Twenty-fourth, and Twenty-fifth Texas (Dismounted) Cavalry Regiments to form the Seventeenth, Eighteenth, Twenty-fourth, and Twenty-fifth Texas Cavalry (Dismounted) Regiment. The Sixth and

Tenth Texas Infantry Regiments were merged in a similar fashion, and all were brigaded together under the command of Thomas Churchill; out of the 120 officers once belonging to Deshler's brigade, only the thirty best were retained for the consolidated regiments. Churchill's reorganized brigade was assigned to Major-General Patrick Ronayne Cleburne's division in Lieutenant-General William Joseph Hardee's corps. Marsh was named commander of the reorganized Company I composed of the past Companies C, I, and K. "The old 17 [sic] regiment is no more," Marsh wrote his wife. "She was buried at Tulahoma [sic] on the 23 of last month by Parson C. C. Gillespie of the 25." Colonel Clayton Crawford Gillespie of the old Twenty-fifth Texas Cavalry, Lieutenant-Colonel John Taylor Coit of the former Eighteenth Texas, and Major William A. Taylor of the onetime Twenty-fourth Texas were designated the field officers of the merged regiment. In a complicated, and potentially confusing, policy, despite the fact the officers from the four regiments were now assigned to a new unit, any potential promotions remained as if they were still on the rolls of their original outfits.[24]

The surplus officers and those soldiers of the Fifteenth, Seventeenth, Eighteenth, Twenty-fourth, and Twenty-fifth Texas Cavalry Regiments, and the Sixth and Tenth Texas Infantry Regiments, not captured at Arkansas Post were re-formed into the Seventeenth Consolidated Texas (Dismounted) Cavalry. Assigned to the Trans-Mississippi, Colonel Taylor, Lieutenant-Colonel Hendricks, and Major William Aurelius Ryan were assigned to this particular outfit on June 8. Hendricks quit the service on October 29, and Ryan succeeded him on February 10, 1864, to take effect from the day of Hendricks's resignation. Unfortunately for Ryan, Lieutenant-General Edmund Kirby Smith questioned his rank in the Eighteenth Texas, and the promotion went unconfirmed. The issue remained in an administrative limbo until the final days of the war. In the meantime, Sebron Miles Noble officially filled the vacant office of major, and was addressed in reports as the regiment's lieutenant-colonel. His service record does not indicate a formal elevation to the higher rank.[25]

Marsh and his fellow Texans arrived at a time when the strategic outlook seemed secure. Following the costly and tactically indecisive second battle of Murfreesboro (or Stones River), Bragg took up position to oppose a

Patrick R. Cleburne. Engraving from glass plate negative. Civil War Photograph Collection. *Courtesy Library of Congress, Washington, D.C.*

Union advance southeast toward Chattanooga. Cleburne's division, situated at Wartrace and Bellbuckle, held the center of Bragg's defensive line, and guarded both the wagon road through Liberty Gap and the railway through New Fosterville. William Starke Rosecrans and his Army of the Cumberland occupied Murfreesboro, and the Union commander frustrated his superiors with his reluctance to commence active campaigning. As General Halleck reported, "the winter and spring were passed in raids and unimportant skirmishes."[26]

In early June, Bragg's army was composed of two infantry corps commanded by Hardee and Lieutenant-General Leonidas Polk, as well as two cavalry corps under Major-General Joseph Wheeler and Brigadier-General Nathan Bedford Forrest. Rosecrans made a demonstration with two corps in front of Polk's forces at Shelbyville on June 24, then sent two more in a lightning strike through Hoover's Gap to Manchester behind Bragg's right flank. Yet another marched along the Murfreesboro–Shelbyville Pike against the highly contested Liberty Gap that led to Hardee's position around Wartrace.[27]

By June 26, Bragg finally understood the actions on his left were only a feint, and Union troops at Manchester were the real danger. While Rosecrans had completely outmaneuvered his opponent, and forced him to withdraw from fortified positions, Bragg received little assistance from his subordinate generals as a continuing lack of communication and trust plagued the army's high command.[28] Amid heavy rains, Bragg moved the Texas Brigade to Liberty Gap and kept them in line of battle for two days and nights. By June 27, the army began its retreat from Middle Tennessee. At sundown of the twenty-eighth, after deploying three or four companies as skirmishers to deceive the enemy, Churchill's men followed through the mud as the rear-guard. The Eighth Texas Cavalry provided mounted support. Although Marsh expected the Confederate forces to make a stand at the otherwise indefensible Tullahoma, Bragg kept his troops marching as Rosecrans feinted against the Confederate left once more, struck the right, and took Manchester. The Texans had several skirmishes with the enemy before the Confederates, their flank threatened, crossed the Bethel Bridge on Elk River on June 30. Marsh was briefly detached from his company to act as the brigade provost marshal. In his absence, his men aided in delaying the Federals until the bridges could be burned. The Texans received orders to retreat across the Elk, and the bridges were destroyed at approximately nine o'clock in the evening. The division crossed the Tennessee River on July 8, and made its way to Tyner's Station, nine miles east of Chattanooga.

The Rebels had eaten little but green apples and green corn scavenged from the muddy roadsides since leaving Tullahoma. Once bivouacked, they were treated to a feast of more green corn—seven roasting ears for each man. When the shortage of supplies occasioned by the retreat was resolved, and the bacon and the corn meal began appearing once more, morale improved in the camps.[29]

The Confederates established a new defensive line along the Tennessee River, while the Yankees rebuilt the wrecked bridges and secured their lines of communication and supply. Cleburne's division was assigned to picket duty around Harrison's Landing in late August to defend the fords and ferries. The troops, poorly positioned to meet the enemy, covered an area from ten to twenty miles above Chattanooga and skirmished with the Federals nearly every day. On August 16, Rosecrans had moved to cross the river west of Chattanooga and turn the Rebels out of the city. While a single Union brigade kept Bragg's attention to his front and to the east, Rosecrans's forty thousand soldiers crossed the mountains into the Confederate rear. Bragg remained ignorant of the Federals' true intentions until September 5, when a copy of the *Chicago Times*, revealing the Yankee battle plans, appeared at his headquarters. With his line of communication to Atlanta threatened, the Confederate general quit Chattanooga, the river, and the crucial railroad. Instead, on the eighth, he marched south in a desperate gamble to catch the Army of the Cumberland as they emerged from the passes of Lookout Mountain. Meanwhile, Cleburne had sent Marsh to Georgia to hunt down various deserters and stragglers. He returned from his mission in early September, after an absence of eight days. In addition to the changed tactical conditions, he learned that, during his time away, Churchill had returned to Arkansas, and James Deshler, recently promoted to brigadier, had resumed command of the brigade. Meanwhile, General Hardee had requested a transfer to Mississippi, and General Daniel Hill was assigned to take command of the corps.[30]

By September 9, the two armies began to arrive at the foot of the mountain, and the commanding generals maneuvered their elements into position amongst the rocky terrain. With the division commander sick, and the mountain passes blocked by fallen trees and other obstacles, Cleburne's men were unable to attack the enemy at McLemore's Cove.

The Confederates were finally able to reach the scene on the eleventh, and skirmish with the Yankees as they were retiring. In addition, confusion and internal bickering at Bragg's headquarters, as well as in those at the corps- and division-levels, prevented the Confederates from destroying exposed Union forces in detail.[31]

The two armies began concentrating in preparation for a major engagement. Rosecrans deployed his troops along the left bank of Chickamauga Creek, while Bragg arranged his men on the opposite side. Being informed that reinforcements were on the way that would swell his ranks to 68,000, the Southern commander decided to go on the offensive. On September 19, while the remainder of the army struck first the Union left flank, then the center and right, Hill's corps was held in reserve near Glass Mill. By one p.m., as the Federals intensified their pressure on the Rebel right flank, Cleburne's five thousand soldiers were dispatched to march six miles behind the arrayed Confederates, cross Chickamauga Creek at Thedford's Ford, and reinforce that part of the line at the Youngblood farm. They arrived at five-thirty, just in time to prevent the enemy from driving the Confederate forces back across the creek. On the left flank of Cleburne's line of brigades, shouting wild Texas yells, Deshler's men broke through the dense, smoke-filled woods and poured a heavy fire into the Federals. The Yankees steadily retreated, grimly trying to hold until the coming darkness would end the fighting. As one Confederate participant wrote, "it was war to the knife and a fight to the finish." Just before sundown, the Texans made a final desperate charge through the burning field, captured a battery of six guns, overran one line of bluecoats, and drove a second back one-half mile to Kelly Field. Colonel Franklin Collett Wilkes of the old Twenty-fourth Texas, who had replaced Gillespie as regimental commander, was slightly wounded in the engagement, and Lieutenant-Colonel Coit assumed temporary command. The regiment lost four killed in the battle and seven or eight wounded. Cleburne ordered his brigades to halt at nine o'clock, and they made a cold camp.[32]

During the night, Bragg reorganized the command structure of his army. The left wing was assigned to Lieutenant-General James Longstreet, who had just arrived with eight fresh brigades from the Army of Northern

Virginia. The right was commanded by Polk, who was given Hill's corps, Benjamin Franklin Cheatham's division, and William Henry Talbot Walker's Reserve Corps.[33]

On the twentieth, after some delays, the fighting began at nine a.m. and continued throughout the day. Deshler's brigade was again on the left flank of Cleburne's division as Hill's corps faced Major-General George Henry Thomas's six divisions along the Lafayette road. On a ridge in front of Thomas's *abatis*, the Texas brigade was exposed to the hottest portion of the enemy's withering fire for four hours with little protection. "The enemy's fire was terrific," a Texas private remembered. "Besides the infantry fire, eighteen Napoleon guns poured a deadly shower of grape and canister fire into our ranks as we advanced." Colonel Wilkes's Texans suffered approximately two hundred killed and wounded while enduring the fusillade. While walking the line, encouraging his men, Deshler was killed by a shell that tore through his chest. Wilkes was wounded by shrapnel, and once more taken out of action. Deshler's three regiments stubbornly held their positions within 250 yards of the Union lines until they were ordered to withdraw at two o'clock, having suffered fifty-two killed and 366 wounded.[34]

Between two and three p.m., Cleburne's battered division was directed to support a renewed attack on Thomas's fieldworks. With Hill's corps on line by five o'clock, the Rebels charged through a galling fire and drove the Federals from their salient. At the same time, Longstreet launched an attack on the Federal right, and Major-General John Bell Hood's division spearheaded a charge through a gap in the Union line. The Yankees fled before the general assault in a panic, except for troops who consolidated atop Horseshoe Ridge and Snodgrass Hill under Thomas's command. Withstanding repeated attacks, Thomas retreated in good order and saved the Army of the Cumberland from complete disaster. The entire Confederate army pursued, taking numerous prisoners, until nightfall ended the advance. Wilkes's regiment lost twenty-eight killed, 150 wounded, seven mortally, and one captured. Of those, Company I lost two killed and eighteen wounded.[35]

On the afternoon of September 21, Bragg ordered Cleburne to pursue the retreating Yankees, and the Rebels were halfway to Chattanooga by sunset.

The division commander had his men on the march early the twenty-second, and reached Missionary Ridge outside of Chattanooga that same afternoon. Rather than carrying the Federal works by direct assault, Bragg decided to lay siege to the city. He placed his left flank atop Lookout Mountain, with the line running across Missionary Ridge to the Tennessee River. Cleburne's division was posted in the center near the crest. Although Bragg had intended to starve the Yankees out of their fortifications, his men instead found themselves on short rations as the weather grew colder.[36]

Marsh and his men held a position at the foot of Missionary Ridge by October 5. At one time, he was on picket duty within 175 yards of the Union lines. The captain wrote his wife that he had ninety-six men present for duty, two wounded, and another two on an unspecified absence. Wilkes and Coit were still away, and Major Taylor was evidently unavailable, so Marsh was once again the regiment's ranking officer. As the Confederates settled into the siege, Major-General John Cabell Breckinridge succeeded Hill as corps commander, and Brigadier-General James Argyle Smith was placed in command of Deshler's brigade. At the same time, Coit fell ill, and Taylor succeeded him as acting commander.[37]

Bragg began losing the tactical advantage when two corps from the Army of the Potomac were sent to reinforce Chattanooga. Furthermore, President Lincoln appointed General Grant commander of the newly created Military Division of the Mississippi on October 16; among the forces under his direction was the Army of the Cumberland. Five days later, Grant arrived in Chattanooga, replaced Rosecrans with General Thomas, and began formulating a new strategy to break the stalemate. The Federals went on to capture Brown's Ferry on October 27 and secure a supply line, known as the "Cracker Line," across Raccoon Mountain and Lookout Valley. With provisions and matériel entering the city, Union troops were able to effectively lay siege to the cold and hungry Confederates in the mountains.[38]

Shortly after this setback, "Old Reliable" Hardee returned to the Army of Tennessee and took over Polk's corps. Cleburne's division was then transferred to Hardee's command, which occupied the right of the Confederate line along the ridge. Breckinridge corps was on the left.[39]

On November 23, in response to the movement of Cleburne's division from the line toward Chickamauga Station, Grant ordered two divisions forward to capture Orchard Knob, a solitary Rebel outpost one mile in front of Missionary Ridge. Bragg cancelled Cleburne's assignment, and ordered him to a new position behind the center of the Confederate line to act as the army's principal reserve. After the seizure of Orchard Knob, Grant moved at mid-morning on the twenty-fourth to attack Bragg's left atop Lookout Mountain. Scrambling up the slopes through a thick mist, the Federals fought their way toward the entrenched Confederate positions in what became known as the "Battle Above the Clouds." Shortly after nightfall, the mountain was in Federal hands.[40]

Earlier that same day several Union divisions began maneuvering against the Confederate right. By two p.m., with Smith's Texans in the van, Cleburne's division was sent to reinforce that flank, and deployed along Tunnel Hill and the adjacent Billy Goat Hill. Three Federal divisions under General William Sherman were also advancing on the same position. Cleburne knew this was too much ground to cover with the three brigades at his disposal, but Union skirmishers were already ascending the far side of Billy Goat Hill. At three o'clock, Smith and his troops were ordered to charge the hill and repel the bluecoats. The Texas brigade dashed across the valley and up the hill, but the three Yankee regiments on the crest poured a galling fire down the slope. General Smith realized his lone brigade could not hope to take the heights, and Cleburne pulled the Texans back to the crest of Tunnel Hill. The Union soldiers followed them up the hillside, and Smith's men easily repulsed the assault. Sherman declined to press home the attack in the growing darkness, which gave Cleburne the opportunity to organize his regiments and place Taylor's men on the right flank.[41]

The Federal attack came at eleven a.m. on November 25, when two of Sherman's brigades assaulted Tunnel Hill from the north and northwest. Under the cover of trees, Confederate skirmishers fired for an hour until they steadily withdrew to the main battle line. The Union troops advanced to within fifty yards of the Confederate positions before canister fire forced them to retire behind some abandoned breastworks further down the slope. Receiving permission to counter-attack, General Smith sallied forth with elements of the Sixth, Seventh, and Tenth Texas Infantry Regiments and the Fifteenth Texas dismounted cavalry. He and Colonel Roger Quarles Mills led the charge on horseback, and both were quickly downed with serious wounds. Colonel Hiram Bronson Granbury of the Seventh Texas shortly thereafter assumed command of the brigade. Two more times the Union troops reformed and advanced into the teeth of the Rebel volleys. A private of the Tenth Texas Infantry wrote in his diary: "the enemy [loss] was heavy for we shot them like cutting hay." By noon, the Federals decided to not resume the attack, but settled for harassing the Rebels from the bottom of the hill. At three-thirty that afternoon, Cleburne organized a counter-attack employing troops from Georgia, Arkansas, and Texas. The Federals broke and the Texans pursued them to the foot of the hill before Cleburne recalled them. The attack was complete by five o'clock, and the battle was finished.[42]

Although Cleburne's division had held its ground for seven hours against determined Union assaults, the rest of the army did not fare as well. The Confederate center had collapsed and the enemy was in possession of Missionary Ridge. General Hardee ordered a withdrawal across the Chickamauga, and ordered the destruction of the bridges. Smith's brigade acted as the rearguard.[43]

Marsh and his comrades reached Chickamauga Station on the morning of the twenty-sixth. Shortly after midnight, Cleburne received orders for his division to hold Ringgold Gap "at all hazards" until the army's supply train was safely traveling south. Brigades filled the entirety of the narrow pass in a double line, and the Seventeenth, Eighteenth, Twenty-fourth, and Twenty-fifth Texas was posted to the right on the north slope of the defile. As the last of Cleburne's regiments arrived, the Federal columns attacked, only to be met by enfilade artillery fire and rifle volleys. In the midst of the fight, Marsh was ordered to redeploy Company I to a hill on the brigade's right, assume command of the two companies already there, and secure the flank from Yankee skirmishers. When he reached the crest of the ridge, known locally as White Oak Mountain, the captain observed a Federal force thirty yards from his position. He led a charge "with a shout in gallant style" and routed the enemy, taking one battle flag and forty-six prisoners. By noon, the wagon train was secure, and, two hours later, Cleburne began quietly withdrawing his troops from their positions toward the rendezvous at Dalton. The Seventeenth suffered eight killed and twenty-nine wounded, of which Company I's losses were two killed and eight wounded. General Cleburne and the division later received the Thanks of the Confederate Congress for their six-hour holding action at Ringgold Gap.[44]

In the wake of the Chattanooga debacle, Bragg tendered his resignation to President Jefferson Davis on November 29, which the executive at last accepted. Hardee temporarily took over the army until General Joseph Eggleston Johnston was named the permanent commander; the latter assumed his duties on December 27. Meanwhile, Cleburne's division went into winter quarters six miles north of Dalton at another place called Tunnel Hill. They built "comfortable huts," but were ordered to Taylor's Ridge three miles to the west in late February. On March 1, 1864, the Texas Brigade moved to Mill Creek and entrenched along the Middle Springs Place Road three miles east of the town. The hours spent in camp were consumed by division and corps drills. The winter proved bitterly cold for the Confederate soldiers, and the men were short of adequate clothing. As her husband endured the harsh weather, Araminta died on December 23 of typhoid fever, but Marsh did not learn of his wife's passing for several months.[45]

Popular with the rank and file, Colonel Granbury was promoted to brigadier-general and permanent command of the brigade on March 5, to date from February 29. In his first command decision, Granbury ordered a reorganization of the consolidated regiments, which had long been a source of discontent among the men. Consequently, the companies of the old Seventeenth and Eighteenth Texas Regiments were separated from those of the Twenty-fourth and Twenty-fifth Texas and formed into the Seventeenth and Eighteenth Texas Cavalry (Dismounted) Regiment. In March, Captain George D. Manion of the old Eighteenth Texas Cavalry signed the field and staff muster roll as commanding officer of the regiment. The same month, Marsh was also acting regimental commander.[46]

Once Grant was appointed general-in-chief of the Union armies on March 2, he implemented a coordinated offensive strategy that combined maneuver with brute force across multiple theaters. While three smaller columns targeted Mobile, Richmond from the James River, and the Shenandoah

Valley, George Gordon Meade's Army of the Potomac made ready to confront the Army of Northern Virginia. Simultaneously, Sherman, the new Federal commander in the west, began his advance into northwest Georgia on May 4. Seizing the initiative and constantly keeping Johnston on the defensive, Sherman used the 100,000 men under his command to fix the Rebels in place while outflanking them. Sherman had no liking for the costly frontal assaults that characterized Grant's Overland Campaign in Virginia, and neither Sherman nor Johnston fought their engagements to decisive conclusions. Nevertheless, the Yankee drive forced the 55,000 Confederates to abandon Dalton and Resaca, and conduct a fighting withdrawal toward Atlanta. Professor John R. Lundberg commented: "In the fierce fighting the Texans again began losing strength due to battle casualties, but the survivors carried on in spite of their odds. The Confederate war effort weakened, but continued for Granbury's Brigade because of a devotion to the Confederacy and effective leadership on the part of Hiram Granbury, Patrick Cleburne, and others."[47]

Union troops crossed the Etowah—"the Rubicon of Georgia"—on the twenty-third, west of the position Johnston had taken at Allatoona Pass, a gorge south of the river through which ran the Western & Atlantic Railroad. Johnston had hoped to draw the Union forces into making an assault on ground favorable to the Southern cause. The wily Sherman realized the Confederate position was too strong and, instead, chose to strike the crossroads at Dallas, then at Marietta, Johnston's base of supply. After General Joseph Wheeler led a raid on the enemy left, Johnston ordered his infantry commanders to deploy their men. Hood's corps remained near Allatoona, Leonidas Polk's moved to a commanding position near Lost Mountain, and Hardee's marched eight miles toward Dallas. On May 24, Major-General James Birdseye McPherson's Army of the Tennessee and Thomas's Army of the Cumberland marched toward Dallas. Major-General John McAllister Schofield's Army of the Ohio was positioned at Burnt Hickory in support of Thomas's left flank.[48]

The Confederates concentrated on Dallas, and entrenched to defend the town the same day. Hardee's corps constituted the left flank, Polk's troops were in the center along the Dallas–Atlanta road, and Hood's were around a small Methodist church called New Hope on the right. On May 25, while the other Federal armies were still some distance from Dallas, Major-General Joseph "Fighting Joe" Hooker's XX Corps made repeated attempts to seize the vital crossroads at New Hope Church, all of which were beaten back until a driving rainstorm and the early arrival of nightfall ended the fighting. Later in the evening, Cleburne was ordered to shift his division to the extreme right at Pickett's Mill and reinforce Hood's corps. Sherman occupied himself with arranging his scattered elements around the broken and mountainous battleground for most of the twenty-sixth.[49]

Cleburne's division fought one of the bloodiest actions of the war on May 27, when Thomas ordered an attack to envelop the exposed Confederate right flank. While the rest of the Federal line made demonstrations to avert the Rebels' attention, two Union divisions set out at eleven a.m., and were in position to attack the entrenched Southern line by three-thirty. Some thirty minutes later, Cleburne became aware of the Federal presence on the right, and sent Granbury's men at the double-quick to extend and strengthen the line. Taking up a position in the open along the edge of a steep ravine, soon to be immortalized as "the hell hole," the Texas Brigade and the Eighth Arkansas Infantry were assailed by Brigadier-General Thomas James Wood's three Federal brigades. Striving through thick undergrowth and across rough ground, the Yankees lost five hundred men in the first few minutes, and were repeatedly driven back by storms of rifle balls and enfilading grapeshot, canister, and shrapnel. The bloody Union assaults finally ended at sundown. After a nighttime bayonet charge forced the enemy in the ravine into a panicked retreat, the brigade returned to their original position with over two hundred Union prisoners. By the end, the Federal casualties had risen to roughly 1,600 killed and wounded, while Cleburne's division lost approximately 450 men.[50]

The next morning, the fallen enemy lay thick at the bottom of the defile. "One could walk upon dead Yankees for a long distance down our front," observed one Tennessee soldier. Later in the day, two brigades of Cleburne's division were ordered to the left flank as the Yankees were attempting to turn the Confederate position. While the two forces continued to maneuver for the most advantageous position, the Texans "kept on fighting … sleeping, when [they] had a chance to sleep, with gun in hand, without removing belts or cartridge boxes, sleeping in harness as it were, with bullets and bombshells constantly flying over and around [them]." Johnston was a brave and inspirational leader, and his strategy of trading space for time preserved his army's strength in the face of a numerically superior foe. However, he was already distrusted by the administration in Richmond, and his refusal to make a decisive stand intensified political opposition to his tenure. Sherman's constant flanking movements compelled Johnston, on June 4, to pull his army back to a line of fortifications near Marietta. The network of breastworks and emplaced batteries stretched from Lost Mountain northeastward to the small Baptist chapel known as Gilgal Church, to Pine Mountain and Brush Mountain. One mile forward of the main Confederate positions, Pine Mountain became a salient in the center of the Rebel line. At the same time, Granbury took a leave of absence due to poor health, and admitted himself to an Atlanta hospital. General James Smith again assumed command of the brigade.[51]

Following General Polk's death by cannon fire on June 14, the Confederates evacuated the Pine Mountain salient and shifted their line to run the twelve miles from Brush Mountain to Gilgal Church to Lost Mountain. Hardee's corps was placed on the left flank from Lost Mountain to Gilgal Church, with the late Polk's corps in the center and Hood on the right. With these redeployments, Gilgal Church, surrounded by Cleburne's division, had become the angle in the Confederate line. Sherman deployed his forces with Schofield on the right, Thomas in the center, and McPherson on the left.[52]

By May 5, Marsh had become the senior captain of the Seventeenth Texas Cavalry, and he wrote to Johnston on June 9, requesting he be promoted to the vacant colonelcy. Marsh referred the general's attention to the fact the regiment had been without any field-grade officers since Colonel Taylor and Lieutenant-Colonel Noble both died at the battle of Mansfield the previous April. Furthermore, the vacancy caused by Major McClarty's resignation had never been filled. Marsh requested he be commissioned major to date from McClarty's resignation, and colonel from April 8. The letter was first sent to Colonel Mills, commanding Granbury's Brigade, then "respectfully forwarded" to Brigadier-General Lucius Eugene Polk, temporarily commanding Cleburne's division, to Hardee, the corps commander, and finally to Johnston, who approved the promotion. No general or special order has been discovered to indicate an advancement beyond his captaincy, but Marsh revealed his new rank to one of his sisters in a letter dated June 20, 1864. Furthermore, his signature officially appeared as early as August 6, with the rank of colonel. Despite this correspondence, he may have been premature in his announcement. In the margin of the cover page of Marsh's letter, there is a faded note, dated July 25, 1864, that states "Roster called for before action could be taken." Lundberg speculated, "It may be that Granbury, who had just taken command of the brigade in March, preferred [William A.] Ryan ... Ryan must have come back, and that is why the promotion never went through. Of course that late in the war, it is tough to tell whether it was lost or denied." Several sources correctly name Thomas F. Tucker as the last official colonel of the Seventeenth Texas, but, in keeping with the regiment's peculiar status, he was actually commanding the Seventeenth Consolidated Texas Cavalry (Dismounted) operating west of the Mississippi; he assumed that position effective April 9. Rightly or wrongly, Marsh remained in public a colonel, and was addressed as such for the rest of his life.[53]

On June 15, Sherman resumed his attempts to turn the Confederate flanks. The Union commander ordered an assault on the Rebel fortifications at Brush Mountain and at Gilgal Church, the latter held by Cleburne's division. Beginning at five p.m., divisions of Hooker's XX Corps attacked the section of the line that ran from Gilgal Church to Pine Knob. Major-General Daniel Butterfield's division drove in the Southern skirmishers, but wavered under the withering fire of Cleburne's men. Repulsing the bloody frontal assault that stretched into the late afternoon, and anticipating another attack, the Texans dismantled the walls of the church to strengthen their breastworks. Shortly after they finished, John Geary's division charged the Confederate line, only to be pinned down without cover by heavy musketry and artillery fire. The Federal troops dug in for the night where they lay and the opposing lines were unusually close when night fell. The Yankees had lost 650 men while Cleburne's casualties were approximately 250.[54]

On the morning of the sixteenth, Cleburne's division was subjected to intense rifle fire. At six o'clock, while moving his men from one line of entrenchments to the next, Marsh was caught in the open and struck by a Minié ball one or two inches above his right elbow. The projectile exited his arm three inches higher on the opposite side, shattering the bone in the process. In addition, his left hand was badly mangled by another bullet, and two or three fingers were shot off. While his men sought cover, the injured Marsh sank to the ground and began bleeding to death. Seeing the fallen man in mortal danger, Private Marquis de Lafayette "Pal" Price, a member of Company I detailed as a brigade sharpshooter, exposed himself to the hail of Yankee fire and dragged his commander to safety. The treatment of Marsh's wounds required an amputation; his right arm was removed below the shoulder two hours later in the regimental field hospital. He was then sent to Camp Kingston Hospital in Atlanta.[55]

Later, in the afternoon, Schofield's commanders discovered the line around Gilgal Church, manned by Granbury's troops, was vulnerable to enfilade fire. Several Federal batteries were deployed three hundred yards from the brigade's position, and opened up with canister and solid shot. As the sun set, Johnston directed Hardee's corps to abandon Lost Mountain, and retire to new positions east of Mud Creek. As Cleburne withdrew, the Federals shelled the retreating Confederates. The casualties were light, but Lucius Polk lost his leg, and his active service was concluded.[56]

Unlike Polk, Marsh's war had not yet ended. Rather than accept a discharge, he was granted a sixty-day medical leave of absence on August 11. The order was signed by General Hood, who had taken command of the army after Johnston was relieved on July 17. No official record could be located for Marsh between August 11 and the Confederacy's demise the following spring. Judging by his parole of honor signed at Meridian, Mississippi, on May 14, 1865, he had, at some point, returned to active duty and been assigned to Lieutenant-General Richard Taylor's Department of Alabama, Mississippi, and East Louisiana. The general surrendered the forces under his command on May 5, under the same terms as those given to General Robert Edward Lee at Appomattox. Marsh's exact role in Taylor's organization remains undetermined. Despite his injuries, either a staff position or another field command is not outside the realm of possibility. According to journalist and author Sidney Smith Johnson, shortly before the cessation of hostilities, Marsh was nominated for the rank of brigadier-general. The fighting was over before his commission reached him, although he had supposedly commanded a brigade for a time. No evidence was found in the Compiled Service Records or *Official Records* to support this assertion.[57]

Having sacrificed much for the Lost Cause, Marsh returned home to his farm, which by now encompassed one parcel of 480 acres and another of 117 acres. Over the next two years, his herd increased to five horses and seventy-five head of cattle. He married Lucy Mary Portis on September 18, 1866, in Clarke County, Alabama. A "bright-minded, attractive woman," she had been born on January 8, 1844, in Mississippi. Her father was Colonel Edmund Marsh Portis, a substantial planter and prominent citizen of Alabama. In 1867, Marsh purchased a home at 522 South Broadway Avenue in Tyler. Situated on a 480-foot by 450-foot lot, the original residence had possessed only three rooms, but, once he assumed ownership, Marsh expanded the house into eight rooms, three porches, and a bathroom. In December 1870, he acquired a tract to the east that added an additional eighty-five feet to his property.[58]

Even as he reentered civilian life, Marsh continued to serve, and was elected county sheriff on June 25, 1866. He received the room in the southwest corner of the courthouse as his office in early 1867, provided the district court jury could also use the space when needed.[59] However, Marsh's term was cut short by Reconstruction politics. Major-General Joseph Jones Reynolds, the Federal military commander in Texas, entered into an agreement with Republican leaders to exclusively appoint members of that party to local and state offices, in exchange for a recognition of the army's supremacy in the state. On October 28, 1867, the general named thirty-three men to vacant positions. Reynolds then issued Special Order No. 195 on November 1, which removed four hundred Democrats from office and installed 436 Republicans in their place. One of those affected by the order was Sheriff Marsh.[60]

In September 1868, Marsh became a partner in the wholesale grocery and commission merchant firm of Jessup, Marsh & Wiggins in Shreveport, Louisiana. The offices of Marsh and his associates, John M. Jessup and John Marsh Wiggins, were located on the levee near the railroad depot. The business also represented the Carolina Life Insurance Company of Memphis, Tennessee. While Marsh was in Shreveport, Lucy remained in Tyler, and their first daughter, Mitty Rivers, was born on December 9, 1868. Wiggins sold his interest in the firm to Edwin Daniel McKellar on February 17, 1870. The same month, Marsh became a trustee for the Life Association of America's Louisiana and Texas Department.[61]

Announcing the dissolution of the partnership on July 19, 1872, Marsh relocated to Tyler. State and local elections were held throughout Texas on December 2, 1873, and Julius A. Robinson was elected sheriff of Smith County. However, by May 1874, Robinson was on trial in district court for either malfeasance or nonfeasance regarding eighteen thousand dollars in railroad bonds. When he was shortly thereafter unseated, Marsh took office as sheriff for the second time, presumably through an appointment by the commissioners' court. Nevertheless, Captain Richard Brown Long, also a Confederate veteran and prominent merchant, filed a petition of notification in district court on June 13, 1874. The captain contested the election on the grounds Marsh had not met the requirement of twelve months' residency in the county, or being a registered voter, nor he had taken the oath. Thus, he was constitutionally ineligible. Long further argued the election had not been held in accordance with the state constitution. Testimony was first heard in the case on September 7. Long moved to amend his original notice of contest, but the court refused and dismissed the case. Marsh remained the county's chief lawman.[62]

On October 30, 1874, three prisoners overpowered the jailer and escaped from the county lockup. The fugitives were quickly apprehended by the sheriff and a small number of citizens. Although a few shots were fired during the recapture, no one was injured. In all his time as a peace officer, Marsh never carried a sidearm or rifle. According to legend, when asked the reason, he replied, "What would a one-armed man do with a gun anyway?" Local tradition also called attention to the respect he engendered as a lawman: "The sheriff would often yell out his name to some desperate law violator and ask him to come out of his place of hiding, and the violator never failed to obey him."[63]

By the beginning of 1875, Marsh was being hailed as a "gentlemanly, polite, and efficient" peace officer. On May 28, his deputy, John W. Herrin, and Asbury Forston, a prisoner wanted in Smith County for murder, were aboard a Houston & Texas Central train bound for Tyler. During a stop at the Palmer station, twenty-seven miles from Dallas, two or three armed men, accompanied by two women, entered the car, leveled their guns at the surprised deputy, and took Forston away. The escaped outlaw was quickly recaptured, and Marsh traveled to Dallas on June 1 to reclaim the prisoner and finish the trip back to Tyler. Three men alleged to have participated in freeing Forston were arrested a few days later, while eight other suspects remained at large. Regardless of the escape, Marsh was elected to his own term on February 15, 1876. After the witness in a bootlegging trial was murdered in front of the City Hotel on December 3, 1877, Marsh and a deputy marshal were quickly able to capture the killer. The next few years were relatively quiet for Marsh. His second daughter Mary had been born on March 6, 1877. He continued to serve the county until November 5, 1878. By 1880, the family home was surrounded by a four-acre lot, and Marsh kept two horses and four cows on this tract. He was also a mail contractor in June of the same year.[64]

Following the resignation of Ira Long, commander of Company B of the Frontier Battalion, Marsh was appointed the outfit's new captain at Hackberry Springs on December 15, 1880.[65] He barely had time to get settled before his first command challenge occurred the following month. Marsh had given Sergeant John W. Adams a draft in the amount of $150, with the instruction to have the instrument cashed. Adams followed his orders, then went on a gambling spree at Fort Concho with the money. The captain charged the sergeant with embezzlement, and Adams was lodged in the Tom Green County jail.[66]

In early 1881, elements of the Tenth Cavalry Regiment, comprised of black soldiers and white officers, were stationed at Fort Concho. Across the North Concho River from the post was the town of San Angelo, which boasted an abundance of saloons, gambling houses, and brothels. While diversified, the town's economy depended greatly on nearby cattle ranchers and the garrison. Fueled by resentments originating in the war and Reconstruction, as well as racial prejudice, soldiers and civilians had long held contempt for one another. Four years previously, Captain John C. Sparks and some of his Rangers had abused their authority in dealing with black troops in town, leading to that officer's dismissal. In February 1879, Captain George Washington Arrington, Sparks's successor, had demanded an army sergeant be remanded to his custody following a saloon shooting in town. Several soldiers led by the noncommissioned officer had retaliated for insults received earlier in the day. Colonel Benjamin Henry Grierson, the post commander, had refused the Ranger captain, and informed him he had no jurisdiction on a military post; the sergeant avoided trial by deserting.[67]

Benjamin H. Grierson. Civil War Photograph Collection. *Courtesy Library of Congress, Washington, D.C.*

On January 31, 1881, Thomas J. McCarty, a local sheepman, shot and killed Private William Watkins, an unarmed Company E trooper, outside Charley Wilson's saloon. The rancher fled town, but he was apprehended by sentries from the fort as he tried to cross the river. After spending the night in the guardhouse, McCarty was turned over to Sheriff James Daniel Spears. Watkins had been the second black soldier killed in San Angelo by a white man that month, and the troops of the garrison were livid.[68]

McCarty appeared at an examining trial in Justice of the Peace William Russell's court on February 2. During the proceedings, black soldiers from the post invaded the courtroom and demanded the prisoner. Denied their request, they then served notice that if the defendant was allowed bail, they would kill him and put the town to the torch. McCarty was taken to Ben Ficklin, the county seat, where deputies and a detachment of Tenth Cavalry troopers saw him confined in jail. Whether the threat factored into his ruling on the fourth, Justice Russell found sufficient probable cause to charge McCarty with first-degree murder, and ordered him held without bond awaiting the grand jury.[69]

Copies of a handbill soon appeared on the streets of San Angelo. The ultimatum was later found to be the work of both black and white soldiers who, regardless of race, had been mistreated by the townspeople they were sworn to protect:

Fort Concho, Texas, Feb. 3, 1881

We, the soldiers of the U.S. Army, do hereby warn the first and last time all citizens and cowboys, etc., of San Angelo and vicinity to recognize our right of way as just and peaceable men. If we do not receive justice and fair play, which we must have, some one will suffer—if not the guilty the innocent.

It has gone too far, justice or death.

Signed U.S. Soldiers[70]

On the afternoon of February 4, McCarty's brother, John, who closely resembled the jailed man, arrived in San Angelo. Watkins's comrades were irate that his murderer should supposedly be allowed to go free. Arming themselves, a party of thirty to forty soldiers left the fort that night and went into town. The embittered cavalrymen fired a fusillade of shots into the Nimitz Hotel and Sterling Clack Robertson's store. Despite the heavy volume of fire, nobody was killed and only one person received a minor wound. Colonel Grierson ordered the guilty troopers confined and charges prepared. The three noncommissioned officers who led the raid were reduced to the ranks.[71]

Even before the shooting, Judge Thomas A. Falvey of the Twentieth Judicial District, District Attorney William Herman Lessing, and Sheriff Spears dispatched a rider to Hackberry Springs on February 4 to summon Captain Marsh. The citizens also telegraphed the governor. Twenty-two Rangers rode the eighty miles from their camp, and arrived in San Angelo on February 5. Establishing their headquarters in John Richard "Sarge" Nasworthy's wagon yard, the captain then deployed five men to secure the jail in Ben Ficklin and others to take up strategic positions around San Angelo. The remainder accompanied Marsh to a meeting with Colonel Grierson. Marsh sent a Ranger to a rooftop overlooking the approaches, and allegedly instructed Jeff Milton, "Get your Winchester. Throw a shell into it. Kill the first man that bothers me."[72]

The Ranger captain and the army colonel talked in private, and neither left a detailed, written record of the meeting. In a composed and professional report, Marsh informed Jones that he asked Grierson for "assistance to help preserve the peace, which was granted." Grierson stated to his superiors: "The Captain at once came over to consult with me, and we have been cooperating to insure quiet and order and to prevent further disturbance." Perhaps utilizing copious amounts of dramatic license, J. Evetts Haley, Milton's biographer, and/or Milton himself, asserted the fire-eating captain informed Grierson, "I am going to kill the first man that comes across the river without a pass—[Negro] or anyone else. Keep these troops on this side of the river. If they cross, we'll kill every one of them." Supposedly stunned, the colonel reminded Marsh that Company B's numbers were few. The Ranger captain reportedly replied, "Yes, but enough to kill every one of these [Negroes] if you don't obey my orders." Depending on the version, the discussion between the two battle-tested officers either ended in collaboration or a stalemate.[73]

On the seventh, Marsh reported "all quiet" to the adjutant general, but, on the same day, Judge Falvey requested of Jones that the captain "remain here for some time longer." Claiming Watkins's death had been accidental, Tom McCarty was taken to the Travis County jail on February 10 or 11, and arranged bail on the twenty-fifth. With peace restored, Company B departed the county on March 5. At the April court term in Ben Ficklin, McCarty's case was postponed until the autumn. In the same month, the grand jury took no action against any of the soldiers involved in the shooting of February 4.

Once the October term began, a change of venue was granted in McCarty's case, and the trial was held in Junction. After quick deliberations, the jury returned a verdict of not guilty.[74]

While Marsh had been contending with a powder keg in San Angelo, the Texas & Pacific Railroad was racing its Southern Pacific competitor across West Texas. Since April 1880, the railroad company had laid 505 miles of track, with 425 miles' worth of construction occurring in 1881. When the tracks of the two companies united at Sierra Blanca on December 1, 1881, the entire state became connected across its breadth, and the nation possessed its second transcontinental railway. The converging rails advanced the transformation of the Texas Rangers into state law officers, and enabled them to more quickly traverse the territories to which they were assigned. In the meantime, as Texas & Pacific construction progressed west from the Concho country, Company B became responsible for policing the towns that sprang up along the right-of-way. The populations of these ramshackle communities were largely transitory, although some settled by upstanding townsfolk survived. Colorado City in sparsely populated Mitchell County was one such notorious location.[75]

Sergeant Richard Clayton "Dick" Ware, the man who had killed Seaborn Barnes in Round Rock three years before, decided to run for sheriff of Mitchell County. W. P. Patterson, a cattle rancher and editor of the *Colorado City Courant*, opposed him for the office. Patterson was described as an amiable man when sober, but a terror when under the influence. He lost the election on January 10, 1881, then proceeded to get himself arrested by the Rangers twice for the careless discharge of his pistol while drunk. Since the county did not yet possess a jail, prisoners were shackled to a mesquite tree, at least until they were clear-headed. Patterson, still smarting from his defeat at the polls, objected to this public humiliation, and nursed a burning resentment for Ware and his Ranger comrades. Indeed, the rancher made insulting remarks about the state officers, and, on one occasion, the one-armed Marsh "lit into Patterson when a good fisticuff followed."[76]

Bitterness and excessive alcohol created a deadly encounter on May 17. The pugnacious Corporal James Martin "Jim" Sedberry, Private Milton, and greenhorn Ranger Louis Benjamin Wells were patrolling the streets of Colorado City at two a.m. The three lawman heard gunfire coming from the direction of the Nip and Tuck Saloon, and hurried toward the sound of the shots.

Richard C. Ware. *From Texas Ranger Sketches. Courtesy Robert W. Stephens.*

In front of the rowdy establishment, the Rangers found Patterson and his friend Ab Adair, and questioned them about who had been shooting. Clearly inebriated, the rancher-editor claimed he knew nothing. Sedberry requested to see Patterson's pistol, thinking to inspect the weapon to confirm whether it had been fired, and Patterson retorted, "Damn you, you will have to go examine somebody else's pistol." Sedberry and Wells immediately responded by seizing Patterson's arms but the muscular rancher struggled free. He pulled his handgun and fired at Sedberry's belly. The bullet missed its intended target, but the muzzle blast scorched the Ranger, leaving him with powder burns. Milton ended the altercation with a single shot from his .45 pistol, and Patterson dropped into the street. Wells, who had been a Ranger for only three months, then pumped another bullet into the fallen man. Inside the Nip and Tuck, Patterson's friends, who also belonged to the political bloc opposing Sheriff Ware, denounced the three Rangers. The patrons threatened to work themselves into a lynch mob in a short amount of time. Milton boldly walked into the saloon and informed the loudest accuser of the crowd to stop his haranguing or join Patterson in death. The state officers then surrendered to the sheriff, but retained their arms.[77]

The following day, Justice of the Peace —— Smith of Precinct No. 1 toyed with the idea of holding the three Rangers without bond until the examining trial. Captain Marsh, who had ridden from his headquarters at Hackberry Springs, bluntly told the magistrate that "the boys are going to camp with me tonight whether you make their bonds or not, and they will be in court tomorrow." The justice wisely set bail at fifteen hundred dollars each, and two local residents signed as sureties. The captain and the three Rangers then returned to camp and their regular duties to await the grand jury. General Jones sent Captain Daniel Webster Roberts to conduct an internal investigation of the episode. After interviewing several witnesses and local citizens, including Patterson's brother, Roberts's report cleared the Company B members of any wrongdoing. On the other hand, James Henry Calhoun, the prosecutor for the Twelfth Judicial District, filed murder charges against them. The case would be delayed by a number of continuances until November 1883, when it finally came to trial in Abilene. In the end, the jury acquitted them of all charges.[78]

Foreshadowing events some eighteen years in the future, attorneys for the defense questioned whether privates in the Frontier Battalion had the legal authority to make arrests. In response, General King recommended the legislature modify the May 10, 1874, law establishing the battalion, and endow all members with the powers of law officers, similar to the legislation that had given the same authority to McNelly's company in 1876.[79]

More mundane duties awaited Marsh in June 1881. He and seven Rangers pursued the Dan Crary gang, which was charged with the theft of a portable water tank and six head of cattle. The lawmen finally cornered their prey on the Pecos River where they recovered the stolen stock and took the fugitives into custody. The prisoners were turned over to Sheriff Ware. Similarly remanded to the county officer was William Hendricks on a charge of land forgery, but the latter was immediately and inexplicably released. On August 5, Marsh and thirteen Rangers left his camp at Big Springs and rode the fifty-five miles to Pecos City. Two days later, he left five men in town and took the remainder after horses stolen by Indians. The lawmen rode fifty miles to the northwest and scouted until the ninth. They then returned to Pecos City, arriving the next day.[80]

Even before the death of General Jones, Marsh and his men were the subject of citizens' complaints describing poor leadership, excessive drunkenness, and other improper conduct. Indeed, there exist several references to Marsh's overindulgence in alcohol. At the same time, he enjoyed the support of respectable businessmen in Mitchell County. An editorial, written by "Amicus Popull," appeared in the *Galveston Daily News*, and emphatically declared: "Captain Marsh is the right man in the right place." While attempting to evaluate an individual's physical, mental, and emotional health solely through an incomplete historical record is mere speculation at best, the state of his intemperance may well have been produced by valid reasons. Naturally, any medical explanation would be hampered by a lack of documented examinations and the deficiency of clinical knowledge at a time when psychiatry was in its infancy. Nevertheless, the diagnosis currently classified as post-traumatic stress disorder has its roots in the malady called "soldier's heart," which was first observed among Union veterans by Doctor Jacob Mendes Da Costa in 1871. While he never treated a Southern patient, Da Costa noted "it would be strange indeed, if men of the same race, transformed into soldiers under much the same circumstances, and, though oftener on interior lines, enduring on the other hand generally more privations, should have escaped" the same afflictions. Symptoms comparable to the doctor's diagnoses that presented decades after the war were termed "melancholy" or "nostalgia." In the same postwar period, physician Silas Weir Mitchell studied the neurology of battle-related amputations and the ghostly pain patients endured in non-existent appendages; he coined the term "phantom limb." In reviewing Mitchell's work, Professor Shauna Devine observed he "learned of the psychological effects of suffering wounds of this nature, helping to establish a foundation in which theories and treatment of posttraumatic stress disorder could develop."[81]

Like many of his fellow veterans, Colonel Marsh, once of the Confederate Army, endured for years the rigors of campaigning, grueling months in prison, the emotionally agonizing death of a loved one while far from home, the physically painful loss of extremities, the anxieties of facing crude surgery and of life afterward, and the pervasive death and devastation of war. Given the sum total of these traumas, the notion he would later rely on liquor as a coping mechanism for potential neuralgia, flashbacks, nightmares, and other psychological wounds is not inconceivable. Additionally, Marsh was a successful businessman and law officer before and after his state service, and references to his alcoholism seem restricted to the time he spent as a Ranger. While a functioning member of society in a civilian setting, operating in the paramilitary environment of Ranger camps and field work may have resurrected painful memories and aggravated his personal "nostalgia." Sadly, the historical record is unable to provide definitive answers.

Regardless of any unspoken and, at this stage, completely hypothetical reasons as to Marsh's behavior, Captain Cornelius Vernon "Neal" Coldwell, the battalion quartermaster, arrived in Colorado City on June 22 to inspect the company. He subsequently rendered a written report declaring Marsh unfit for command, but no action was taken due to General Jones's illness. Persuaded by Coldwell's account, Wilburn Hill King, Jones's replacement, contemplated convening a court-martial. However, owing to the "peculiar character" of the battalion, the distances between the various company headquarters, and the resulting difficulty, expense, and delays in holding a hearing, he opted to forgo that alternative. Instead, he summarily discharged Captain Marsh and his entire complement on August 31, reenlisted the men he wanted to retain, and promoted Samuel Alexander "Soft Voice" McMurry to take command of the new company the next day.[82]

Marsh left no indication of his sentiments on being dismissed. Instead, he returned to Tyler and, over the next several years, he bought and sold at least seven properties. While he was engaged in his various business affairs, Marsh also served as a deputy for Sheriff Francis Brownlee "Frank" Clinkscales. When Clinkscales died unexpectedly on June 9, 1885, the commissiners' court named Marsh sheriff on the fifteenth to fill the vacancy. The *Galveston Daily News* had "every reason to expect an efficient sheriff in Colonel Marsh." The court's choice and the newspaper's opinion notably belie the image of Marsh as an out-of-control alcoholic. Indeed, he was elected to his own term on November 2, 1886. Along with his local duties, Marsh served on the finance committee of the Texas Sheriff's Association, and later as the organization's vice-president. He was additionally bailiff of the state supreme court during its term in Tyler. He was re-elected November 6, 1888, and November 4, 1890, and served until November 8, 1892.[83]

On July 29, 1895, Marsh was one of ten former Confederates appointed by Governor Charles Allen Culberson to represent Texas at the ceremony dedicating the Chickamauga and Chattanooga National Military Park the following September. In 1898, Marsh was stricken with paralysis, and lost the power of speech. Despite his malady, likely a stroke, he reportedly remained cheerful and retained the same personality and manner as in his prime. The following year, he was able to attend a reunion of his old Confederate company "to the delight of all the old veterans," and received an ovation upon his appearance. He died on March 25, 1901, and was buried at Oakwood Cemetery in Tyler.[84]

Following her husband's death, Lucy boarded at Mary's house with her family. On December 26, 1930, she filed an application to receive a pension based on Marsh's Confederate service, which was approved. Living with her grandsons at 508 South Broadway by this time, Lucy died of a coronary embolism on November 2, 1934. She was buried next to her husband in Oakwood Cemetery.[85]

Henry attended Texas A&M University and passed the bar in 1881. Becoming one of the leading lawyers in Tyler, he was named city attorney in 1882 and Assistant Attorney-General in the administration of Governor James Stephen Hogg, his good friend and former law partner. He married Sarah E. "Sallie" Portis on October 7, 1889, in Clarke County, Alabama, and they raised three daughters and one son. Sallie was the younger half-sister of his step-mother. In the late 1890s, Henry partnered with Archibald Graham McIlwaine in the law firm of Marsh & McIlwaine. Later, James W. Fitzgerald joined the firm. Henry was an original director of Citizen's National Bank, and relinquished much of his law practice to become chairman of the board in 1930. He died at Mother Frances Hospital on September 28, 1940, of pneumonia. He was buried in Oakwood Cemetery.[86]

Mitty never married, and she boarded with Mary's family in Tyler. By 1927, she and Lucy moved down the street to the old house at 522 South Broadway. She died there on November 14, 1941, of gallstones and uremia. She was buried in Oakwood Cemetery.[87]

Mary married grain and feed dealer Isaac Henry Crutcher on October 21, 1897. Together with their two sons, they lived at 628 South Broadway. Suffering from heart disease, she died of paralysis on November 5, 1912, and was buried in Oakwood Cemetery the following day.[88]

Bryan Marsh remains a popular figure in his adopted hometown of Tyler. Built in 1889, the North Side School, an eight-room elementary school, was located on the northwest corner of North Bois d'Arc Avenue and West Bow Street. The building was later renamed in his honor. A granite marker was placed at the site in 1965. The facility operated until 1970, when it was converted to a church. Another historical marker honoring the Texas Ranger and sheriff was dedicated on Tyler's Main Street in 2016.[89]

The case of Bryan Marsh remains a puzzle. He was a determined fighter, and that quality may have cost him his position as a Ranger captain. On the other hand, he was able to make his way in civilian life with great success. One may only speculate whether his foibles were inherent in his nature, attributable to wartime experiences, or a failure to distinguish his law enforcement role from military service.

Ira Aten. *Courtesy Castro County Historical Museum, Dimmitt, Texas.*

Chapter 8

Ira Aten: "A Code of Duty and Service"

Austin Ira Aten was the quintessential frontier lawman. Beginning with his childhood and stretching into his middle years, he bore witness to many stirring events in Texas history. From the Rio Grande to the Caprock, and beyond, he lived a code of duty and service to his fellow citizens. His time as a working Texas Ranger and as sheriff of two counties was spent performing typical peacekeeping functions: hunting desperadoes, testifying in courtrooms, operating undercover, and investigating felonies. Author Allen G. Hatley noted Aten "seems to have fit better than most men into the new law enforcement duties of the Frontier Battalion." He became so successful that, for a time, he received assignments directly from the governor's office. Despite beholding the worst humans could do to each other, Aten remained at his core an honorable and morally upright man committed to his family and his community.

He was born in Millbrook, Peoria County, Illinois, on September 3, 1862. His parents were Austin Cunningham and Katherine Eveline (Dunlap) Aten. His father had been born in Eaton, Preble County, Ohio, on August 4, 1832, while his mother was born on March 19, 1833, in Augusta County, Virginia. They married on May 19, 1853, and moved to Peoria County shortly thereafter. Austin was educated at the Rochester Seminary in Peoria and preached at Elmore in 1854, in addition to farming. Ira's siblings included

Margaret Angeline Elizabeth "Angie" Aten, born on March 12, 1854; Thomas Quinn Aten, on February 16, 1856; Clara Isabell "Belle" Aten, on June 8, 1858; Frank Lincoln Aten, on August 26, 1860; Calvin Grant Aten, born on December 7, 1868; and Edwin Dunlap Aten, on September 5, 1870.[1]

By 1860, the Atens' homestead was valued at $2,100, and Austin's personal estate was worth $987. He enlisted in Company I, Seventy-seventh Illinois Infantry on August 16, 1862, and mustered into service on September 2. Austin served throughout the war, and mustered out on July 10, 1865, as a corporal.[2] Returning home, Austin once more moved his family, this time to Indian Point Township in Knox County. He farmed but also worked in the hardware business. The Atens relocated to Abingdon two years later.[3]

Desiring to give his family the limitless opportunities afforded by the West, Austin moved his wife, his mother and mother-in-law, his young children, and Angie's family to the Texas Hill Country. Setting out in October 1876, they arrived at their new homestead near present Pflugerville on the twenty-ninth. While the farm was in Travis County, Round Rock in Williamson County was the closest town. In addition to working his farm, Austin became a "fire and brimstone" Methodist circuit-preacher.[4]

Aten was in Round Rock with his father and Frank shortly after the Sam Bass gang attempted to rob the town's bank. In the wake of the gun battle between lawmen and the outlaws, Reverend Aten was requested to offer spiritual comfort to the mortally wounded Bass. Together with Frank, he went inside the tin shop to pray over the dying outlaw. Aten was left outside to peer through the window.[5]

The demise of Sam Bass, and the exploits of the Texas Rangers who brought him down, planted the idea in Aten's mind that he would one day join those legendary lawmen. His father, however, wished him to become a farmer or cattleman. On April 26, 1883, through the assistance of Lonnie Carrington, Aten enlisted in the Frontier Battalion in Austin. He was sent to Camp King near Uvalde to join Company D under the comand of Captain Lamartine Pemberton "Lam" Sieker. In June, Sieker decided to shift the camp to a site five miles southeast of Uvalde to utilize the fresh water offered by the Leona River. The new bivouac was titled Camp Leona.[6]

Aten was first mentioned in the monthly returns on January 11, 1884, when he rode out alone to apprehend Tom Rickerson, who had allegedly stolen a horse in Llano County. The journeyman Ranger found his quarry at Taylor, northeast of Round Rock in Williamson County, and made his first solo arrest. Aten took his prisoner to Austin, then to the Llano County sheriff. He returned to Camp Leona after an absence of nine days. On February 14, the company moved to Camp Johnson, near the Pegleg Crossing of the San Saba River. From there, the Rangers handled persistent fence cutting and brand altering cases in Menard, Mason, San Saba, and McCulloch Counties.[7]

While keeping order during the spring roundup in Menard County, Sieker was requested to provide protection to the Kinney County deputy sheriff and tax collector working the rough Devil's River country. On April 12, Aten and novice Ranger John Louis Bargsley, leading a pack mule with thirty days' rations, were detailed to meet the county officer at Beaver Lake, one hundred miles to the southwest. Arriving at their destination the following evening, the two Rangers set out the morning after to escort the collector on his yearly rounds. The people in the area were sheep and cattle ranchers squatting on state or railroad land; none had paid taxes on their livestock before, and none wanted to start now. The only enforcement mechanism the deputy sheriff had at his disposal was to threaten to round up the herds or flocks and sell them for the delinquent taxes. While the taxman had been run out of the area the year before, he now had two armed Rangers with him. When several ranchmen looked ready to make trouble, the presence of Aten and his companion proved to be the difference in the collector having a successful trip. In all, he separated between four and five thousand dollars, most of it in gold, from the reluctant stock-raisers. After a month of riding the rough country, the two Rangers left the county officer at Pontoon Crossing on the Pecos. They then rode the 150 miles to their camp near Menardville, arriving on May 11.[8]

Early the next month, Aten was part of a squad, commanded by Lieutenant Frank Jones, that kept order at the district court session in Llano. Partnered with Ranger William Wallace Collier, Aten arrested noted pistoleer and fugitive stagecoach robber Reuben Hornsby "Rube" Boyce on the thirteenth for being drunk and disorderly. The two Rangers brought him before a Llano County justice of the peace. Five days later, Aten and Private J. A. Puckett served a *capias* on Tom Moore, and committed him to the custody of the sheriff. On June 23, Aten arrested Jim House on a charge of forfeiting his bond. While Lieutenant Jones's men were busy in Llano County, Company D moved its headquarters back to Camp Leona.⁹

Wanted in Llano County for murder, and horse theft in Blanco County, fugitive C. C. Davis was rumored to be running for Mexico. Captain Sieker gathered a detachment of Rangers and headed to the border. After searching the country around Eagle Pass and Del Rio, the exhausted Rangers returned to Uvalde without having found the outlaw. On July 9, Aten made his own foray after Davis, and scouted southeast to Johnson City in Blanco County. Failing to find the killer there, Aten continued the hunt by questioning potential witnesses along the trail. His dogged investigation led him to Brady City, where he arrested Davis. Aten took his prisoner back to Llano County and turned him over to the sheriff. The Ranger had been on the trail nine days and covered 242 miles. On July 22, Davis was being led from his cell to make a court appearance when he seized the weapon of Deputy Sheriff James B. O'Bannon and shot the lawman in the chest and neck. With a second homicide on his record, Davis reportedly fled in the direction of Brady City. Sieker tapped Aten to recapture him. The Ranger private left Llano on July 24, and rode to Uvalde for a quick meeting with the captain. Ordered to cooperate with Maverick County Sheriff Thomas Lindsey "Bose" Oglesby, Aten was to set up at the head of the Nueces and keep watch over the country from Eagle Pass to Del Rio. Davis was believed to be heading for the border, but he was instead apprehended in Grayson County.¹⁰

Aten remained in Eagle Pass through the months of August and September, and arrested a total of seventeen fugitives. In the first of these pursuits, he and several officers scouted for Robert Dow, wanted for murder, and Pedro Pedraza, charged with theft, approximately forty miles east of Eagle Pass. The outlaws willingly surrendered at a ranch situated on the Rio Grande, and the lawmen took them back to Sheriff Oglesby. Before starting out, the county officer had informed Aten a man wanted on a misdemeanor charge was in the same area. Even though Rangers normally did not trouble themselves with petty crime, Aten decided to accommodate the sheriff, and told his men to continue while he would go capture the crook. He rode into the wanted man's camp early in the morning, just as breakfast was being served.

The Ranger spotted the fugitive at the head of the table and took a seat next to him. Aten then told him he was wanted on a charge in Eagle Pass and he needed to come along to clear up the matter. The man agreed, but appeared nervous. Aten noticed he was unarmed, and was determined to keep him from getting ahold of a gun. The man finished his meal before Aten did, and rose to stand near the stove. Aten took a drink of coffee and put the cup down, only to find himself covered by a gun in the outlaw's hand. The Ranger prepared to dive under the table and shoot from cover, but the man said, "I don't want to kill anyone; all I want is to get away." Aten answered, "You have the best chance in the world to get away." Still covering the Ranger, the fugitive retreated into the brush and disappeared. Aten left the camp and caught up with his men and the two prisoners. The officers agreed there was no use in pursuing the escaped man, as he likely had left Maverick County. Presently they heard he had ridden into New Mexico, and still later they found out he was a "bad man" wanted in Indian Territory on three charges of murder. He was reported to have been killed in New Mexico. Aten returned to Camp Leona on September 22.[11]

Earlier in the month, on the third, five armed robbers held up the Fredericksburg biergarten of fifty-five-year-old Johann Wolfgang Braeutigam. When the proprietor attempted to defend his establishment, the thieves shot and killed him. The murderers fled down the Colorado to the northwestern corner of Travis County near the Burnet County line. There, they holed up near Travis Peak. Setting out in pursuit on October 5, Corporal Philip Cuney Baird's detachment, including Aten, arrested William "Bill" Allison at Oatmanville near Austin for the homicide. After a "long chase," Jackson "Jack" Beam and Charles Wesley Collier, two more of the alleged killers, were apprehended at New Braunfels. The detachment returned to Fredericksburg on the seventeenth, and, following a preliminary hearing, the three suspects were bound over to await the grand jury. When Corporal Baird questioned the security of the Gillespie County jail, the Rangers, with Sheriff John Walter's consent, transported Beam and Collier to the lockup in San Antonio. However, the sheriff and the townspeople refused to allow Allison to be taken out of the county.[12]

On November 18, Aten and Private James V. Latham were scouting in Kimble County when they arrested a fourth suspect for the Braeutigam homicide. After the apprehension, the two lawmen took their prisoner, known as Ed (or Ede) Jones, to a location several miles southeast of Fredericksburg, where he was turned over to Sheriff Walter. Unfortunately, certain parties were not willing to allow the justice system to work. The Fredericksburg jail was torched on January 7, 1885, and Allison perished in the flames.[13]

Once Corporal Baird resigned to accept the position of chief deputy sheriff of Mason County on November 30, 1884, Aten was promoted to fill the vacancy. The advancement in rank proved to be short-lived. Aten was logged as a corporal in December, but following reports recorded him as a private once more.[14]

On May 31, 1885, Aten was part of Sergeant Benjamin Dennis Lindsey's detachment that was searching the country around their bivouac at San Ambrosia Creek for a pair of escaped Mexican convicts. Twelve miles southeast of camp, the seven Rangers spotted two men on horseback a half-mile away leading a spare horse toward the river. Once the officers and the unknown riders spotted each other, the pair suddenly galloped away. Aten and fellow private Ben C. Riley were leading the pack mule some distance behind the rest of the detachment, which galloped in pursuit. The chase covered two miles, and Lindsey and the three men with him were slowed by the muddy creek bed. Aten and Riley continued, and caught up to within one hundred yards of the Mexican riders on a hillside. The two Rangers demanded their quarry's surrender. The mystery pair were not the escapees, but the Rangers suspected they could be horse thieves. Regardless, as they had run, they still fell under suspicion. Riley moved to disarm the duo, but they opened fire instead, hitting him in the left shoulder and the thigh. Riley, even though he was badly wounded, and Aten returned fire, and Frank Edward Sieker, the captain's younger brother, rushed onto the scene, his pistol blazing. About fifteen shots were fired, and both Mexicans were struck, one in the shoulder and the other through the hand. Unfortunately, one of them shot Frank Sieker above the heart, mortally wounding him. The injured Mexicans then raced over the hilltop just as Lindsey and two other Rangers arrived, the fourth having broken his collarbone in a fall from his horse.[15]

Aten and the unwounded Rangers followed the trail to the Loyas Ranch, where they were met by Pendincia Herrera, a Webb County deputy sheriff,

"Texas Rangers on the Border After Outlaws and Bandits." *Art courtesy of Joe Grandee, Historical Western Artist, www.joegrandeegallery.com.*

and fifteen armed Mexicans. Herrera identified the two wounded men as Apolonio Gonzales and his thirteen-year-old son Pedro. They had reportedly come from Laredo for a horse at a nearby sheep camp. Lindsey intended to arrest the pair and take them to Carrizo Springs for resisting arrest and attempted murder. The deputy countered that he would transport the men to Laredo where the sheriff would decide matters. Outnumbered, the sergeant was forced to accept the solution. While Lindsey tended to the now deceased Sieker, Riley, and the other man injured in the chase, Aten and two Rangers escorted the cavalcade to the county seat eighty miles up the river. The state officers saw the culprits turned over to Sheriff Dario Gonzales on June 1. The sheriff turned out to be a relative of the two suspects, and released his kinsmen within thirty minutes of taking them into custody. He proceeded to arrest the Rangers on charges of assault with intent to murder. The father and son were allowed to flee into Mexico. Sergeant Lindsey, having arrived in Laredo by this time, argued that the pair had fired on lawmen, and his Rangers had been obliged to use deadly force to defend themselves. Nevertheless, they were held for twenty-seven days in the Webb County jail before being released on bond. The governor ordered an assistant attorney-general to Laredo, and the Rangers' cases were ultimately dismissed. To prevent further trouble with the local Mexican population, Company D was ordered to move from San Ambrosia to Uvalde, then to Menardville.[16]

As required by law, the battalion reorganized on September 1. Financial deficiencies in the state budget caused Adjutant General Wilburn Hill King to decrease the number of officers and men in the battalion. On September 25, orders were issued to reduce each company to number one captain, one sergeant, and eight privates, effective October 5. Exactly ten days later, Captain Sieker was promoted to the post of battalion quartermaster, and Lieutenant Jones succeeded him as company commander. While the company's command structure was preparing to change, Aten and Private Lemuel Kenneth Henderson of Company F worked together on October 6 to bring in Thad Willmore, who was wanted in Nolan County for murder. The two Rangers arrested the suspect the same day, delivered him to the sheriff in Uvalde, and returned to camp on the eleventh.[17]

Captain Jones and Company D. #P.6.246. Front Row (L to R): Frank Jones and Baz Outlaw. Back row (L to R): Unidentified, Unidentified, T. F. Sellers, Unidentified, Arthur Jones, and Unidentified. *Courtesy Texas Ranger Hall of Fame and Museum, Waco, Texas.*

On March 14, 1886, Aten received orders to report to the Adjutant General for detached duty. Following their capture, Wesley Collier and Jack Beam, the suspected killers of John Braeutigam, had been transferred to the Mason County jail, but they escaped on September 11, 1885. The two fugitives were reportedly on the Colorado, and Aten was to apprehend them. On March 24, 1886, the Ranger and two citizen possemen apprehended Beam at a ranch on the Pedernales Creek in Travis County. Continuing the hunt for Collier, Aten tried to take him at George Wells's ranch on Long Hollow on April 29. While the Ranger succeeded in wounding him in the hand, the fugitive evaded capture. Aten recruited area rancher John R. Hughes to assist him in capturing Collier. After several weeks on the trail, they found the accused murderer at the home of stockman Nicholas Dayton in Williamson County. The outlaw's hiding place was actually near Liberty Hill, not far from Hughes's old Long Hollow Ranch. The pair waited hidden all day on

May 24, watching the house, and waiting for their chance to catch the alleged killer without bloodshed. The opportunity never arose, and they stayed in place through the night.[18]

In the morning, Hughes managed to creep to the west door of the house, while Aten entered through the front entrance. Collier happened to be awake in bed and was alerted to Hughes's presence by some slight noise or motion. Distracted, the outlaw was unprepared when Aten stepped into view with his pistol in hand and said, "Hold up, Wesley." Collier opted to make his play and reached under his pillow for a gun. Aten shot him once through the heart. The following year, Captain Jones wrote: "Aten is deserving of both credit and reward for his work after these murderers."[19]

In the late 1870s, Texas cattle ranges began to see the use of barbed wire. The wire was mostly employed in the central part of the state as cattlemen increasingly fenced in the grass and water once thought to be open to all. Erected by stock raisers, fences penned herds onto one's own property while keeping others out. Used by homesteaders who moved into the areas between ranches, the wire kept cattle from straying into cultivated fields. When the effects of the 1883 drought became fully realized, the fencers with viable pasturage and water holes were determined to protect their assets, while those without were anxious to gain entry to them.[20]

Desperate men, usually grangers or small-scale stockmen one step away from ruin, gathered together in secret societies. These nightriders targeted the fences of those who incurred their wrath: either cattle raisers who enclosed their own property as well as acreage leased from the state, or those who illegally fenced in public lands. Conditions such as these bred an atmosphere of fear and suspicion. Public sentiment favored the "nippers" over the fencers. Citizens refused to identify neighbors as fence-cutters or speak out against them. Local law enforcement authorities, dependent on public goodwill to retain their jobs, were reluctant to investigate, much less prosecute. Since the local justice system was rendered ineffective, the victims of fence-cutting pleaded for assistance from the state. General King was disinclined to involve the Rangers in pursuing shadowy groups that commanded widespread public support. Instead, he lectured supplicants for his aid that they were responsible for their own problems.[21]

Governor John Ireland disagreed with his adjutant general, and called for legislative action in October 1883. When the representatives convened in January 1884, the governor offered a large list of solutions, including prohibiting the fencing of unleased public land, ensuring free access to privately held property, and making fence-cutting a felony punishable by one to five years in prison.[22]

Once he signed the legislation into law, the governor turned to the use of undercover agents to bring the nippers to justice. Rangers operating openly could not hope to secure convictions in a community where the ordinary, hard-working individual was either directly involved or sympathetic to the problem. Instead, Ireland hired Pinkerton's National Detective Agency from Chicago, Farrell's Commercial Detective Agency from New Orleans, and numerous private operatives throughout Texas to scour the affected counties for evidence. After three months, the investigators had identified many of the fence-cutters, but failed to gather enough evidence for a conviction, even if a grand jury would have been prepared to indict. In addition, the members of the Frontier Battalion were instructed to make curtailing fence-cutting their sole mission. In Brown County alone, the damages cost ranchers one million dollars.[23]

On August 1, 1886, Aten was summoned to Governor Ireland's office in Austin where he was assigned to special duty. The lawman was to assist Lampasas City Marshal Nelson Orcelus "Mage" Reynolds, a well-regarded former Ranger, in apprehending those responsible for fence-cutting. Walter P. Webb noted "the crime was particularly hard to handle because the fence-cutter carried no evidence of his deed. The horse thief was caught with the horse and the cow thief with the cow, but the fence-cutter rode away from the curling steel tendrils with no evidence upon him. He had to be caught on the job through detective work." The Ranger corporal's investigation quickly pointed to two young perpetrators who committed the crime more for the notoriety than for any unethical reasons. During the trial, the defense attorney questioned whether Aten had lied to the suspects in order to catch them. After Aten admitted he had, the lawyer asked if Aten was still lying. The insulted Ranger nearly jumped over the table to teach the attorney a lesson; instead, he settled for issuing a verbal rebuke.

Despite Aten's restraint, Judge William Allen Blackburn fined him fifty dollars for using intemperate language.[24]

Aten was to display a talent for secret service when dispatched to Brown County on August 26. He went to Coleman by train, purchased a horse and saddle, and rode into the Jim Ned Creek country, sixteen miles north of Brownwood, posing as a cowhand looking for work. Upon arriving in the county, Aten reported to local ranchers Washington Morgan Baugh and Levin Powell Baugh, who referred him to Joe Copeland, an area farmer hired by the brothers as a spy. With Copeland's assistance, the Ranger infiltrated the local gang of cutters after only three weeks. The undercover operatives accompanied the gang on their nocturnal forays to gain their confidence and surreptitiously secure evidence. In the course of their work, Aten and Copeland learned that the Baughs' fence would be cut on November 9. Captain William Scott and a detail from Company F were sent in to provide support. At eleven o'clock that night, four nippers, whom Aten had previously identified, were cutting fence wires when Captain Scott, Aten, Sergeant James A. Brooks, and Rangers John H. Rogers, Francis Powell "Frank" Carmichael, James Allen Newton, and William "Billy" Treadwell rose from concealment and called on them to surrender. Two cutters fled into the darkness without their horses, while the other pair—Amos Roberts and Jim Lovell—responded with gunfire. The Rangers shot back and killed them both. Experienced by now in clandestine work, Aten avoided being openly tied to the gun battle by slipping out of the county. He remained detached to the adjutant general through November 27. He then assisted Sheriff Oglesby in Maverick County before returning to Company D, now headquartered at Camp Sieker in Edwards County, on December 22.[25]

Accompanying Captain Jones into the upper reaches of Edwards County on April 5, 1887, Aten was on the trail of Alvin C. and Walter P. "Will" Odle. Alvin and Will were wanted for horse theft in Burnet County, and the two Rangers found them on the seventh at a house in the upper end of the county. The captain wanted to apprehend the pair that night, but Aten counseled waiting until the early morning and taking the outlaws by suprise. Moving into position at sunrise, the two lawmen entered the house and had the outlaw brothers, and accomplice Henry Cavius (also known as Henry Wilson), covered before they could react. On April 14, Aten recovered three horses stolen by Cavius and the Odles. Four days later, the Ranger met the Burnet County sheriff in Uvalde, where the prisoners were placed into that officer's custody. The Burnet jail proved unable to hold Will Odle, and he escaped on August 21. Remaining incarcerated, Alvin was transferred to the jail in Kerrville. On October 11, Captain Jones and two men set out on Will's trail, but they turned back after an unsuccessful two-day search.[26]

From June 28 to September 10, 1887, Aten was on detached duty and participated in the pursuit of train robbers John Barber and William Henry "Bill" Whitley. He was joined in the chase by new recruit John R. Hughes, but the two could never catch their prey. Aten separated from Hughes at Cisco on September 10 in order to attend court in Brown County as a witness in the ongoing fence-cutter trial. He was occupied with the proceedings until the end of the month when the state granted a change of venue to Bell County. Aten was once more on the trail of Barber and Whitley from October 1 to November 14, with the same lack of results. He then attended federal court in San Antonio as a witness in a smuggling case from the fourteenth to the twenty-first. More court duty followed, this time in Leakey in Edwards County, for a murder case that lasted until November 27. For the fence-cutting cases in Bell County, Aten once more attended court as a witness. On December 28, the judge ruled the change of venue was improper, and sent the case back to Brown County for trial. At the same time, Sheriff John Thomas Olive of Williamson County received a telegram from the Indian Territory that Barber and Whitley had been sighted, and a request for Olive to dispatch a "sufficient force to capture them." Aten accompanied the sheriff to the Nations, but the outlaws had already departed, leaving no clues as to their next location. The fugitive pair had not heard the last of the Texas Rangers, though, for soon another, John H. Rogers, would be on their trail. Despite any personal disappointments, Aten returned to Texas and attended court at Georgetown as a prosecution witness in the Alvin Odle case; he was occupied with this duty until January 21, 1888. General King then ordered him to rejoin his company, and Aten was present in Camp Savage,

Company D's headquarters in Duval County, by February 2. He was later present to witness a joyous event. Nineteen-year-old Calvin Aten, Ira's younger brother, desired to follow in his sibling's footsteps and enlisted in Company D on April 1, 1888.[27]

While he was pleased with Calvin's decision, Aten hated undercover duty, labeling it "the most disagreeable work in the world." Ironically, his success would ensure he remained in the role. Even after his promotion to first sergeant of Company D, he continued to work up fence-cutting cases at the behest of General King.[28] On July 30, 1888, Governor Lawrence S. Ross personally sent Aten to Navarro County to "Stop that fence cutting at all costs." Having learned in Brown County, Aten cited the dangers of working covertly alone, and received permission to take Private James W. King with him on August 4. The two Rangers took the train to Waco, and there purchased a one-eyed mule and a broken-down wagon for the trip to Navarro. Camping for the night at crossroads stores along the way, they adopted the guise of vagabonds looking for cotton-picking work; King's fiddle-playing helped reinforce that illusion. When the pair reached Richland, they "accidentally" broke a rear wagon wheel and managed to make their way to the blacksmith's shop. Since they claimed to have no money for repairs, the wheel stayed broken, and the two operatives camped nearby. Picking up his fiddle, King soon drew a crowd and, before long, they had landed jobs in the cotton fields. Aten and King soon discovered their fellow workers were part of the fence-cutting crowd, but as they were busy picking cotton, no fences were being cut. Many of the nippers were "cowboys or small cow men" forced by economic conditions to work as wage laborers. When the season ended, they planned to resume their nocturnal sorties.[29]

After two months, Aten tired of picking cotton while waiting for the nippers to act. In addition, the fence-cutters were cautious of involving outsiders, and the Ranger was unable to secure any reliable information. This blend of exasperation and an urge to prompt the suspects into action led Aten to develop an unconventional tactic. Initially, his idea appears to have been only a joke, but, as time went on, he began to treat it more seriously. The plan was to mount an explosive device on a fence that would detonate if the wire was cut. The bomb consisted of a long wooden box, a shotgun charged with gunpowder, dynamite sticks, and detonation caps.[30] He explained his reasoning to Captain Sieker:

Dear Sir:

I have only one more chance with any hopes of stopping fence-cutting in this section & that is with my dynamite boom as I call it. I have had the law examined and it dont [sic] say any-thing about a man having the right to protect his property by the use of dynamite or by the use of a shotgun either. So I have come to the conclusion if it was not against the law to guard a fence with a shotgun to protect the property, it certainly would not be against the law to use dynamite for the same purpose. There-fore I have invested some money in dynamite & will in a few day's [sic] set my dynamite boom's upon the few fences that have been put up recently to protect them. Should the Gov. or the Genl. disapprove of this, all they have got to do is to notify me to that effect, & [etc]. They sent me here to stop fence-cutting any way I could, and to use my own judgement [sic] &c. how to do it. And that is what I am doing and if they will let me alone the balance of this month I will have my boom's set and when the fence is cut, why they will hear of it in Austin …

Dont [sic] be uneasy about my actions for I will use the greatest precaution with my boom's and see that no innocent men get's hurt with them. They are dangers in setting them unless a man is awfull [sic] carefull [sic]. However, if I get blowed up, you will know I was doing a good cause …[31]

Aten was ordered to cease further work on the bombs, and transferred back to his company at Camp Leona on November 4, much to the relief of both the Ranger and his superiors. Before he left, he exploded the bombs, which were heard for miles around. Rumor spread that more devices were planted on all the fences. Even if there were no further detonations, popular lore relates how fear of the "booms" decreased the amount of fence-cutting in Navarro County. Turning to more routine duties, Sergeant Aten and five Rangers were detached to Edwards County on February 1, 1889, and made their camp at Barksdale.[32]

The following month, Aten received a message from Captain Jones ordering him and Corporal Hughes to investigate a brutal quadruple homicide near Eagle Pass. "I want you and Hughes to take hold of the matter and stay with it, regardless of time and trouble, just as long as you believe there is hope of accomplishing anything toward identifying the murderer," the captain instructed his subordinates. Four unidentifiable corpses, three female and one male, had been retrieved from the Rio Grande between February 26 and March 1. One woman was approximately fifty years of age, the next roughly thirty, and the third about seventeen. The man was in his early twenties. All had been discovered with their skulls crushed by a blunt instrument, and the bodies tied to heavy stones with new rope.[33]

Once they arrived in Eagle Pass, the two Rangers consulted with Maverick County Sheriff William Navarro Cooke. Hughes recalled having encountered Richard H. "Dick" Duncan and his brother, George Taplin "Tap" Duncan, on February 7, near the Nueces River. The Duncans were accompanied by a man who identified himself as "Picnic" Jones, who related how they were riding escort for three women and a young man driving a wagon. In the course of the conversation, the Rangers had observed the wagon was green in color, had appeared almost new, and been stamped with "J. S. Clark, San Saba" on the side. Aten remembered having arrested the same three young cowboys on March 1 for suspicion of horse theft, although the actual charge was unlawfully carrying pistols. The offenders had been allowed to post bond.[34]

While Hughes searched for the murder scene, Sergeant Aten decided to ride to San Saba and attempt to trace details of the wagon, especially the seller and the purchaser. Once arrived, Aten spoke to Sheriff Sewell B. Howard, and learned that Mary Ann Williamson was approximately fifty; her "grass widow" daughter, Levonia Williamson Holmes, was about thirty; her other daughter, Beulah, was around sixteen, and her son, Ben, twenty-one. Several items matched the physical descriptions of the bodies found in the Rio Grande, such as the oldest woman possessing dentures and the man having buck teeth. In almost certainly identifying the murder victims, Aten had achieved a significant break in the case, as he could now track their final days. Career lawman Bob Alexander confirmed that "working backwards—reconstructing a victim's last known whereabouts and movements—is the typical and time-tested technique for conducting the vast majority of homicide investigations." Positive identification of the exhumed bodies, coupled with other admissible physical and circumstantial evidence, led Aten and Hughes to view the Duncan brothers, and "Picnic" Jones, as the prime suspects in the murders. By this time, Jones had been positively identified as H. Walter Landers. The growing suspicion was shared among the community, and Dick, proclaiming his innocence, opted to surrender himself to the sheriff.[35]

On March 11, the Rangers arrested the Duncans on four counts of murder in the first degree, and the accused appeared at a *habeas corpus* hearing in Burnet on April 11. Aten and Sheriff Cooke were responsible for locating witnesses and confirming they were on hand to testify. Tap Duncan was subsequently released for lack of evidence. After being indicted for the killings, Dick was brought before District Judge Winchester Kelso in Eagle Pass in early December 1889. He was tried, convicted of all charges, and sentenced to hang. Duncan appealed the verdict in state and federal criminal appeals courts, and even petitioned Governor James Stephen Hogg for clemency. He failed to avoid his appointment with the hangman, and the death sentence was carried out on September 18, 1891. Walter Landers, alias "Picnic" Jones, was indicted as an accessory, but, despite a two-hundred-dollar reward for his arrest and conviction, he remained at large. He was believed to have been murdered by Duncan, who ensured his body would never be found.[36]

Aten's stint as a homicide investigator proved to be the penultimate act of a superb Ranger career. His final undertaking took place in the town of Richmond, Texas. When Richard Coke was inaugurated as governor in 1874, the Southern Redeemers gained power and repealed the Reconstruction policies instituted at the end of the so-called "War for Southern Independence." The last holdout of Radical Republicanism, Fort Bend County had a population that was 80 percent black. After the war, several Republican carpetbaggers had united with area scalawags to energize the freedman vote into a powerful political machine that placed blacks in county offices. By the late 1880s, the wealthier white Democratic minority began to regain political control from the Republican-black majority. The situation became more complicated when the Democrats split into the Young Men's Democratic Club, known informally as "Jaybirds," and the Cleveland and Thurman Club, or "Woodpeckers." The three factions engaged one another in true Texas political fashion, escalating from threats toward open violence.[37]

The killing of James Madison Shamblin, the Jaybird leader and a justice of the peace, on August 2, 1888, and the wounding of Henry H. Frost, another member, on September 3, prompted the Jaybirds to drive the most prominent black Republicans out of the county. The latter's constituents promised retaliation, and the election scheduled for November 1888 proved to be a watershed event. Remarkably, the voting occurred without incident, as an all-white roster of Woodpeckers soundly defeated their Jaybird opponents. Personal rivalries were exacerbated, though, and, on June 21, 1889, county tax assessor Jefferson Kyle Terry killed Jaybird leader Levi Eden "Ned" Gibson with a double-barreled shotgun in neighboring Wharton County. Volney M. Gibson, Ned's brother, and other fellow Jaybirds, vowed vengeance as both sides readied themselves for a fight.[38]

Governor Ross did not wait for the situation to worsen, and ordered Rangers to the scene. Sheriff James Thomas Garvey and Judge James Weston Parker, both Woodpeckers, declined to cooperate with the state officers. Departing their camp at Realitos in Duval County, Captain Frank Jones, Aten, and six Rangers reached the county seat of Richmond on June 28. The captain opened a dialogue with both factions, and brought about a dubious calm. Aten was ordered to Wharton with half of the detachment to keep the peace during Terry's preliminary hearing. After the defendant was bound over for trial, Aten and his men returned to Richmond. Desiring to attend to his dying wife in Boerne, Jones and three Rangers returned to camp on July 10, leaving Sergeant Aten and Privates Frank Louis Schmid, James R. "Jim" Robinson, and David Seth Roberson to monitor the situation until the district court convened in September. Unfortunately, the captain had been misled by the seemingly peaceful appearance. Aten witnessed the worsening situation, but he could do little except maintain friendly relations with the adversaries and maintain a visible presence in the streets.[39]

On August 16, at approximately six p.m., the anticipated violence exploded as Volney Gibson and his brother Guilford traded a barrage of bullets with Judge Parker and his nephew Deputy Sheriff William T. Wade. Having heard the gunfire from camp, Aten saddled up, leaving an ailing Private Robinson behind, and raced into town. Jaybird members responding to the shooting took position behind an iron fence surrounding the courthouse, where they faced an armed Woodpecker mob. Aten, Schmid, and Roberson placed themselves between the two factions and tried to calm them, but the feudists were determined to wage war. The sergeant was told by Volney to clear the street or they would be killed. Aten called to his men, "Save yourselves, boys, it's not our fight." They moved off the street, but, at that moment, gunshots rang out and Schmid was severely wounded. Sheriff Garvey, ex-sheriff Jacob W. "Jake" Blakely, H. H. Frost, and an innocent girl were killed in the fierce exchange, the latter by a stray bullet.[40]

Aten wired Governor Ross, and twenty-four officers and men from the Houston Light Guard militia company were on hand the following morning to enforce the peace. Ross himself arrived that evening with an assistant attorney-general. Twenty-three men, including Volney Gibson, were arrested on charges of murder and disturbing the peace. The governor attempted to arrange an accord between the factions concerning an interim sheriff to replace the slain Garvey. He failed to achieve a consensus so Ross, the former ranger captain and Confederate general, demanded they accept Sergeant Ira Aten, or he would declare martial law. The leaders of the two sides agreed, and Aten reluctantly consented to serve. He was discharged from Company D on August 20, and appointed sheriff and tax collector the next day; he would swear his oath on September 2.[41]

Despite Aten being a stranger to Fort Bend County, a dozen prominent citizens, including Clement Newton Bassett, Sr., John Harris Pickens Davis, Thomas Walter Jones, and John Matthew Moore, signed on his behalf three surety bonds worth forty thousand dollars on August 29. The governor released the Volunteer Guard troops to return home, and the Rangers to their camp. A quiet replaced the turmoil that had plagued the county. After the August 16 street fight, the power of the Woodpeckers was broken as they began to quit their offices in favor of safer climes. On October 22, white citizens signed the charter of the Jay Bird Democratic Association, which dominated county politics for the next sixty-nine years. While a good officer and a better man, Aten was nevertheless a product of his times. His name was seventh on the original membership list.[42]

The Christmas season would bring a reminder of the recent past. On December 24, U.S. Marshal James Jones Dickerson of the Eastern District of Texas, and a party of heavily armed deputies, arrived at the Richmond depot bearing arrest warrants. In the past several weeks, the federal grand jury, impaneled at Galveston, had indicted fifty-four Fort Bend County residents, all of them Jaybirds, on a total of nearly five hundred charges. The marshal and his deputies were in town to execute the warrants. Twenty-two of the indictments were for murder and, surprisingly, Sheriff Aten was one of those charged. Allegedly he was an accomplice in the killings of Garvey and Blakely. He was also accused of subornation of perjury.[43]

The astonished Jaybirds were taken by train to Galveston, where their cases were heard by U. S. Circuit Court Judge Chauncey Brewer Sabin. With the assistance of Houston and Galveston businessmen, bail totaling $21,000 was posted. After a change of venue to Galveston, Kyle Terry was brought to trial in early 1890 for the murder of Ned Gibson. Aten was standing near Sheriff Patrick Tiernan's office on January 21, with several Jaybirds, including Volney Gibson. Gibson allegedly told Aten he did not want to meet Terry, as the defendant had made death threats and a fight might break out. Aten left Gibson and his allies and went upstairs in search of the district attorney. He wanted to make arrangements to keep the factions apart. At the same time, Kyle Terry walked into the courthouse and crossed the rotunda. As the Woodpecker leader climbed a staircase to the courtroom, Volney Gibson took deliberate aim and killed him with a bullet to the heart. While indicted for the murder, Gibson was never convicted, instead dying of tuberculosis the following year. Meanwhile, the legal farce against Aten languished on the docket. Finally, all the charges against him, as well as the other defendants, were dismissed on April 4.[44]

Aten resumed his duties as sheriff and tax collector, and life took on a more normal direction. He attended the annual Texas Sheriffs Association convention in Abilene in June, then the first meeting of the Jay Bird Association in

October. Even before his term ended on November 4, 1890, Aten had begun to look for new opportunities in West Texas. The county commission granted him a thirty-day furlough in August.⁴⁵

Desiring to start a new life in farming and stock raising, Aten relocated to the Panhandle on December 1, where he settled in Castro City, fifty miles south of Amarillo. He acquired 640 acres, and initially ran six horses and five head of cattle. As the livestock industry had exploded over the previous decade, he had come west at a most opportune time. Indeed, the number of cattle in the region had grown from 97,236 head in 1880 to 250,046 (not including oxen or milk cows) ten years later. Along the way, Aten had stopped in Austin and enlisted as a Special Ranger in Company B on November 19, 1890. He applied for a renewal of his commission on May 2, 1891, which was granted three days later. Diversifying his commercial interests, Aten partnered with R. A. Roberts in a land and insurance business. He also pledged his support for the Chicago World's Fair in his capacity as commissioner for the Texas Exhibit.⁴⁶

In November 1891, Castro County, which had been attached to Oldham County for administrative purposes, was organizing, and the location of the county seat was being hotly contested. The two towns under consideration were Castro City and Dimmitt, separated from each other by two and one-half miles. Aten was promoting the former, while attorney Andrew McClelland and his land speculator brother, Hugh, were supporting the latter. Some "two or three months before [the] election," many of the proponents for Castro City, including Aten, were persuaded to change their minds, in exchange for town lots in Dimmitt. Once the issue of the county seat became moot, the question of school trustees took center stage. Aten had acquired some enemies in the contentious debate, chief among them James W. Carter, and they goaded the McClelland brothers into a confrontation with the ex-Ranger.⁴⁷

Aten was speaking at a public meeting before the elections when Andrew called him a liar, a deadly insult in those days. However, Aten let the slur pass, due to the crowd in the room. On December 21, the county elections were held, and the new officials were sworn into office in Tascosa. Two or three days later, Aten strapped on his gun and came to town to settle his differences with Andrew McClelland. Spotting his foe outside a dry goods store at the intersection of Broadway and Jones Street, across from the courthouse, Aten dismounted from his wagon and confronted the attorney, "Andrew, you called me a liar [the other] night. Can you still say it?" McClelland held fast to his words. Aten cursed him, and McClelland replied he was unarmed. Aten told him to get a gun as he would wait. While Andrew entered the store to get heeled, his brother Hugh suddenly emerged from his office immediately to the west and opened fire, missing Aten and hitting the ground. Hugh dodged around the corner of the building as Aten shot back, the slug inflicting a flesh wound on McClelland's back. Hugh cried out, and harmlessly fired two or three more times. The former Ranger shot through the corner of the structure, and the bullet hit his opponent in the back of the neck, causing him to flee.[48]

Andrew McClelland came back down the street firing two pistols, but the bullets missed. As the lawyer ran to hide behind some nearby mules, Aten carefully returned fire—bystanders said he calmly used both hands to hold his gun—and shot Andrew in the left shoulder. McClelland fell underneath the rearing mules, and snapped off more wild shots before Aten shot him through the hands, ending the fight. Aten surrendered to the authorities, and was indicted for assault with intent to kill. He quickly made bond, and waived any preliminary hearing. The McClelland brothers recovered from their wounds. They were also charged, but moved back to Tennessee before their case came to trial.[49]

During the McClelland episode, Aten was courting Imogen Boyce, who lived in Austin with her family. He may have known her since their school days in the late 1870s, and possibly began walking out with her in 1889 or 1890. Her feelings about marrying a man with a badge are more certain. If Aten wanted to wed, he would need to find another line of employment, hence his move to West Texas. Although they had planned to wait another year before marrying, Imogen insisted they tie the knot before his trial. He was living in a dugout while getting the ranch and house ready, but the living conditions made little difference to her. They married on February 3, 1892, at the Central Christian Church in Austin. Immediately afterward, the couple entrained for their home in Castro County.[50]

Aten's case received a change of venue to Tulia, about thirty miles east of Dimmitt. Although pregnant with the couple's first child, Imogen attended the trial and offered enormous encouragement to her husband. As Aten knew no one in Swisher County, he was understandably nervous about the outcome. Even while attempting to free himself of legal entanglements, Aten was able to settle down to enjoy his flourishing ranch interests and growing family. He and Imogen had acquired 160 acres of school land for the sum of $250 on April 28, 1892. In addition to his acreage, he owned eleven town lots in Dimmitt, a number that would increase to twenty-one by the following year. Aten would soon find he need not have worried, as he was acquitted on December 20, 1892. Perfecting the happy news was the birth of his first son, Marion Hughes, two days later.[51]

In the spring of 1893, Sheriff Perry G. Cox of Castro County was failing to suppress the cattle rustling and horse theft occurring in his jurisdiction. The law-abiding voters expressed their dissatisfaction by demanding his resignation. The county officer's bondsmen withdrew their financial support, and he was forced to resign. In choosing the sheriff's successor, the county commissioners looked to the ex-Texas Ranger living quietly on his ranch. Aten had promised Imogen his days as a lawman were over, but he felt duty-bound to help his neighbours, and accepted the appointment on May 9. For the second time, on June 13, he swore his oath of office as a county sheriff. Imogen was in Austin with Marion visiting her parents and in-laws, and wrote she would not return home until Aten resigned. He replied in a letter that if she returned, assessed the situation, and still wanted him to quit, he would do so. Reverend Aten and Imogen's father convinced her to go home. After a few days back in Castro County, Imogen understood the trouble honest citizens were facing, and gave her blessing. In fact, Mrs. Aten often belted on a six-gun and acted as the jailer for her husband. Further mixing business with family, Imogen's brother, John Ely Boyce, was employed as a deputy.[52]

The rustlers had grown so bold as to commit thefts in broad daylight. Their victims were too intimidated to testify or render a guilty verdict if a case happened to be tried in court. The sheriff observed defense lawyers could invariably "get one or two men to hang the jury in every case." Since a jury could not be counted on to convict, Sheriff Aten employed a tactic similar to one used by Lee Hall in his dealings with King Fisher: arresting the leaders of the criminal gangs on any and every charge acceptable to the courts. He determined to "send them to the penitentiary or break them up with lawyers' fees."[53]

His principal targets were Fred and Oscar Cordel, two brothers who operated a ranch located six miles northeast of Dimmitt. The Cordel spread was a known hangout for the shadiest characters in the Panhandle country. Frequently, a hanging beef would be ready for butchering, but the animal's hide was never seen. The altering of a brand was readily seen on the inside of the skin, and popular opinion grew that the brothers did not want the evidence on display. Growing weary of paying their lawyers, the Cordels gathered their ill-gotten livestock, and pushed the herds out of the county. People professed not to know where the ringleaders had gone, but they were rumored to have moved to New Mexico, to the Cimarron River north of the Canadian, or east off the caprock. Although sympathizers tried to obscure their passage, Aten, Swisher County Sheriff Frank W. Scott, and JA Ranch foreman Bob Bishop followed the outlaws' trail east through Swisher, Briscoe, Armstrong, Donley, Collingsworth, and Greer Counties. The lawmen found the herd on the Washita River, approximately forty miles north of the Red River in Oklahoma Territory. Aten and his assistants crept up on three rustlers who willingly surrendered. The thieves were lodged in the Cheyenne jail in Roger Mills County.[54]

William "Bill" Burkett and Bob Dixon, two of the prisoners, agreed to return to Texas without the necessity of extradition papers; the third rustler, a man named Howard Thatcher, refused. Aten made a proposal to one of the cooperative outlaws, the twenty-one-year old Dixon, to give him his freedom if the rustler offered testimony. Sending his companions to round up the stolen stock, Aten took the recalcitrant Thatcher to Guthrie to place him in a more secure jail. The sheriff met with Governor William Cary Renfrow, and requested thirty days to return to Texas and bring back extradition warrants. The governor agreed, as Oklahoma Territory had enough outlaws without adding more from the Lone Star State.[55]

Riding back to the Washita, Aten ordered his men to drive the nearly three hundred head home, while he went to Cheyenne to collect the two prisoners. He caught up to the herd the following day. The cattle had been taken from ranches in Castro and Swisher Counties, but also those along the trail to the Washita, including the JA, the XIT, and the T Anchor. The law officers and their captives returned over the trail and restored the stolen cattle to their rightful owners.[56]

Aten secured an indictment from the Donley County grand jury for cattle theft against Thatcher, and obtained extradition papers from Governor James Stephen Hogg. The sheriff returned to Guthrie one day before the thirty-day time limit expired. The rustler had tried to gain his release through a writ of *habeas corpus*, but Governor Renfrow refused to allow it. Thatcher was a dangerous man who was wanted on other charges. Taking extreme precautionary measures with his prisoner, Aten traveled through Vernon to Amarillo by train, then drove the fifty miles to Dimmitt in a buggy.[57]

Back at home, Sheriff Aten continued working the case. "I arrested the Cordels at their ranch," he later reminisced. "They made no opposition; they just figured on beating their case, which was easily done in that country at the time." Because a conviction was doubtful in Castro or Swisher Counties, Aten had his prisoners indicted in Armstrong County. Bob Dixon, the young rustler-turned-witness, testified against his partners in crime and was subsequently released. The other two were found guilty. Although Aten was unable to secure any convictions against the Cordel brothers, his tactic of "breaking them up on lawyer's fees" ensured one of the worst gangs in the Panhandle was no more. By January 1895, stock theft in Castro County had ceased, and rustlers steered clear of Aten's territory.[58]

As the birth of Ira and Imogen's second child drew near, Imogen chose to have the delivery at her parents' homestead in Williamson County. Their second son, Albert Boyce, was born on March 7, 1894. Aten's blessings were increased that year by the fall county elections. Having made diligent efforts to end the rustling epidemic and assorted other crimes, his neighbors rewarded him with a full term as sheriff on November 6.[59]

Colonel Albert Gallatin Boyce, Imogen's cousin, was the general manager of the XIT Ranch, and he tendered Aten an intriguing job offer in late 1895. The Escabarda division in Deaf Smith County was being plagued by cattle rustlers, and Boyce needed someone to stop them. Although he had been retained in office only one year previously, the sheriff resigned to work for the ranch as division superintendent. Deputy Sheriff John Boyce was appointed on November 12 to complete the unexpired term. Aten acted as one of his brother-in-law's bondsmen.[60]

The XIT, owned by the Capitol Freehold Land and Investment Company of England, and leased to its American partners, the Capitol Syndicate of Chicago, possessed over three million acres of land in the Panhandle, complete with over 150,000 head of cattle, 325 windmills, and ten dams. Beginning with the Texas Longhorn, the ranch improved its breeding program over the years with the inclusion of Hereford, Shorthorn, and Angus stock. With six thousand miles of barbed wire, the XIT was the largest enclosed property in the world. The name of the ranch was said to have stood for "Ten in Texas," allegedly referring to the ten counties the home range was supposed to have encompassed. In actuality, the name was suggested by famed trail boss Abner Pickens "Ab" Blocker, Jr., as the brand would be easy to make but difficult to burn or alter. Additionally, the ranch covered only nine counties.[61]

Branding on the XIT, 1904. Gelatin silver print photograph by W. D. Harper. *Courtesy Library of Congress, Washington, D.C.*

The Escabarda division was situated in the center of the ranch along the New Mexican line. The 600,000-acre pasture featured the "Canadian [River] breaks, with their creeks, canyons, hills, and scrub timber." Enemies of the XIT prowled along the eastern and western sides of Deaf Smith County, and Colonel Boyce had decided a six-shooter response was the suitable answer. The manager's orders were to shoot first and ask questions later. When he accepted the job of superintendent, Aten likewise assumed the substantial personal risks. He doubled his life insurance, and kept his pistol ready. He never used the same trail twice in a row while riding about the ranch, always slept away from the camp fire, and treated every new arrival as a potential assassin until the stranger could be identified.[62]

Given *carte blanche* to handle the situation, Aten imported Jonathan Woodard "Wood" Saunders, formerly of the Frontier Battalion's Companies F and D, and serving Ranger Edward Fulton "Big Ed" Connell of Company B to ramrod the fight against rustlers. The manager believed in the effectiveness of taking a hard line with the criminal element that plagued his division. "I controlled them through fear," he would later remark. Saunders was positioned at Trujillo camp on the south end of Menneosa Pasture near the New Mexico line, while Connell was placed at the Tombstone camp to watch for rustlers from the Cherokee Strip.[63]

Every day, a cowboy, bearing a Winchester and a pistol, would ride from the two camps along the fences looking for individuals who had no legitimate reason to be on the ranch. The line-riders went everywhere armed, and were ordered to maintain an attitude of perpetual vigilance. The western range became tense as XIT employees began taking potshots at any man found near the fence line. The thieves frequently pulled the fences down in a manner that resembled damage done by the cattle, then pushed cows and calves into New Mexico. The Canadian River country, with its hills, draws, canyons, and plentiful running water, was good range for holding and concealing stolen stock. In response, Aten, along with Saunders, Connell, and a party of armed riders, would venture across the state line and scout the country for the stolen stock. Working fast, the superintendent was typically successful in recovering the cattle before the rustlers could brand the calves or move the herd away. As Aten recalled, Connell and Saunders were quite active until "finally it got too quiet for these daring old Rangers. They found no thrills in routine cowpunching and camp work, so they quit to hunt a new field."[64]

Aten's life outside of ranch business was equally busy. He continued to run his own spread in Castro County, and managed his extensive real estate interests in Dimmitt. He also purchased 160 acres from Lewis Epps. In 1896, his livestock numbered forty-one horses and twenty-four head of cattle. The following year, he traded to Allan Grafton Bell the home ranch, the Epps property, his town lots, four mules and two horses, and thirty-eight head of cattle in exchange for the latter's 180-acre ranch at Brushy in Williamson County. Aten retained his herd of sixty-one horses. His household continued to grow as Ira Dunlap was born on March 30, 1896, and his first daughter, Imogen, on April 4, 1898. He was elected a constable and a Deaf Smith County commissioner for Precinct No. 3 in 1896. As most of his constituents were XIT cowboys, he was handily reelected in 1898 and 1900. Diversifying his business interests, he became a director of the Hereford National Bank.[65]

The 1900 federal census disclosed the family living on the XIT with eighteen ranch hands and one farming family. In 1901, Aten purchased land near Hereford and established a small ranch on which he ran seventy-five horses and ten head of cattle. The number of his stock soon increased to one hundred horses and fifteen head. Even though it was a small town of only three blocks, Hereford, situated along the Pecos & Northern Texas Railroad, provided more conveniences for his family than the isolated Escabarda division headquarters, including three general stores, a meat market, a restaurant, the post office, two drug stores, a grocery store, a barber shop, and a blacksmithy. Following the move, Aten continued to be involved in civic affairs. In January 1903, he was chosen as a director of the Hereford Board of Trade. After the city incorporated the following month, he was elected an alderman on April 10.[66]

For much of its existence, the XIT had operated at a loss because of deficits from predators and rustlers, adverse weather, prairie fires, fluctuations in the cattle market, and its sheer size. Farmers and developers were looking for land and, wanting to recoup their losses, the ranch's investors began to liquidate their holdings in 1901. The last head of cattle would be sold eleven years later, and the final thirty-nine acres in 1963.[67]

With his division's operations winding down, Aten resigned, and the family relocated to California in November 1904. In preparation for the move, he had sold his cattle herd earlier in the year; he would later sell his one hundred horses. Imogen's health was suffering, and her husband thought several years in a more salubrious climate would benefit her. After brief stays in Los Angeles and San Diego, he purchased 160 acres north of El Centro in the Imperial Valley in October or November 1905. On his land, which was called the Home Ranch, he planted eucalyptus trees in May 1906, and six one-hundred-yard rows of Myers cotton in November 1907. He later filed on a section of government land two miles west of Calipatria and, through subsequent purchases, established a "model stock ranch" of seventeen hundred acres. He planted flax and alfalfa on 320 acres for livestock feed, but the chief commodity of the property was cattle. Due to the lush pastures irrigated by overflow from the Colorado River down the New River channel, the Calipatria Ranch was able to support five thousand feeder steers from October 1 to June 15 of each year. Aten bestowed eighty acres of the Calipatria Ranch to each of his children as they came of age. Later he would raise hogs and dairy cows, and cultivate fruit trees.[68]

Despite being newcomers to the valley, Aten and his family quickly established themselves as involved residents. Aten offered to trade his ranch holdings in Deaf Smith County, advertised as "6,946 acres of good ranching and farming land," for deeded land in Imperial Valley. He entered into a partnership with Francis Bartow Fuller to form the real estate firm of Fuller & Aten; their offices were located west of the old Franklin Hotel. In mid-June 1906, Aten acquired his partner's interest in the business, and advertised under the name of the Ira Aten Land Company. He became vice-president of the first El Centro Chamber of Commerce on August 1, 1906, and continued to serve on the board of directors in September or October 1907. He was elected as district school trustee on October 1 of the same year, and acted as director of Fuller's El Centro National Bank and the Imperial Valley Oil and Cotton Company. Delving into local politics, he worked on the campaign committee advocating for the separation of Imperial Valley from San Diego County in May 1907. Aten's efforts bore fruit. In an election held on August 6, Imperial County was created with El Centro being named the county seat.

Aten was elected Imperial Township's second constable. Another girl, Eloise, was born to the Atens on December 12, 1908. As the first Aten child born in California, she was known by her parents and siblings as the "Golden West Baby." When a local chapter of the Farmers' Union was formed on August 8, 1909, Aten was appointed doorkeeper.[69]

Aten's son, Boyce, attended Stanford University at Palo Alto from 1912 to 1914, and returned to school in 1915. When the United States entered World War I in April 1917, he left college and enlisted in the Army. He promptly applied for admission into the officer's reserve corps training school at the Presidio. After earning his commission of second lieutenant, he fervently requested active service at the front, and, on March 1, 1918, was assigned to Company D, 129th Machine Gun Battalion, 69th Infantry Brigade, Thirty-fifth (Missouri-Kansas) Division at Camp Doniphan, Oklahoma. On May 2, Boyce and his fellow doughboys embarked on the HMS *Leicestershire* at Long Island, New York, and sailed for France. They reached La Havre on the eighteenth, and were assigned to the U.S. First Army under the command of General John Joseph "Black Jack" Pershing. Beginning on September 26, the division assaulted the Vanquois Hill sector of the Hindenburg Line. As the Americans took the hill, Boyce commanded his four Hotchkiss machine guns with "fearless bravery and coolness" and captured Hill 239 (Bois de Rossignol) on the right flank. Company D then provided direct fire support to the infantry and armor assaulting the German fortifications at Cheppy, Charpentry, and Montrebeau Wood. On September 28, Boyce assumed command of the company due to the deaths of the ranking officers. While attacking the village of Exermont on the twenty-ninth, the division's right flank became exposed to an enemy counterattack. Company D directed eight machine guns to fire into the densely packed Germans, inflicting tremendous casualties. Boyce went to liaise with his infantry counterpart, received a severe head wound from shrapnel, and died on October 2 after being transported to a base hospital. Once the American Legion post in El Centro organized on July 31, 1919, the building was named in his honor. His remains were returned home on October 4, 1921, and buried in Evergreen Cemetery in El Centro with full military honors.[70]

Filled with equal measures of pride and sorrow, Ira was appointed to the board of directors of the Imperial Irrigation District from February 1923 to March 1939. In the first year of his tenure, he was named that body's president. He helped to bring water and electricity to the once-arid valley, and transform it into a fertile agricultural paradise, primarily through the use of the Boulder Dam and the All-American Canal. Dispute over the project created two opposing factions, and Aten and his four fellow directors were accused of malfeasance in spending assessment funds to advocate legislation. The quartet were indicted by the grand jury in 1924, and the case remained in the courts until a new district attorney was elected. The indictments were then ordered to be quashed. In 1938, the board received a federal grant for $2,760,000 for the electric power plants on the canal.[71]

As he entered his golden years, Aten refused to slow his demanding pace. He was one of the founders of the Imperial Valley Pioneer's Association (presently the Imperial County Historical Society), and a charter member of the Imperial Valley Texas Association. He was involved in capitalizing the Home Telephone Company to provide phone service to the valley. The Home Ranch house was often the popular scene of barbecues, and family and group picnics, and Aten was an honorary member of the Sheriff's Posse of Mounted Deputies.[72]

Following an attack of pneumonia, Ira Aten died on August 6, 1953, at his vacation home in Burlingame. The last rites were held at his ranch, and he was interred in the family plot at Evergreen Cemetery.[73]

While Aten had been alive, the health of his wife declined, and she lived in the cooler town of Burlingame, where the family had a second residence. After his death, Imogen was involved in the Women's Christian Temperance Union on the county- and state-level. She died on March 3, 1957, in Burlingame, and was buried at Evergreen Cemetery.[74]

When American involvement in the Great War began, Marion unsuccessfully attempted to join the U.S. Air Service in San Francisco. Undaunted, he went to Toronto, Canada, and enlisted in the Royal Flying Corps on November 20, 1917, as an aviator cadet. On April 23, 1918, he was discharged from the RFC and accepted a permanent commission in the Royal Air Force the following day. He received his aviator's certificate on

November 12, 1918. Having missed the chance to see action in France, he volunteered for No. 47 Squadron, a British unit supporting General Anton Denikin's White Russian forces in that country's civil war. Reporting for duty on August 19, 1919, with the rank of Flying Officer, he participated in several ground attack sorties, and received the Distinguished Flying Cross on October 27. The White Russians awarded him the St. George's Cross 4th Class and the Order of St. Vladimir 4th Class with Swords. Following the conclusion of British involvement in the conflict, he transferred to Egypt and No. 70 Squadron in July 1920. Following a flying instructor's course in England, he returned to 70 Squadron in late 1921, and was posted to Iraq. In June 1924, Marion was mentioned in dispatches for distinguished service in Kurdistan. After a stint with No. 12 Squadron in England, he resigned from the RAF on November 25, 1927. Returning home, he was employed by the newly organized El Centro Flying Club, where he worked as an instructor "on the fields he was refused enlistment." Thereafter, he managed the El Centro farm, and filed a patent on a braking device for aircraft on June 12, 1928. He co-wrote *Last Train Over Rostov Bridge*, a semi-fictional account of his experiences in Russia, shortly before his death on May 10, 1961.[75]

After Imogen graduated from Stanford University, she became secretary-treasurer of the Athletics Department at the college. She took a similar position with the San Mateo County Stanford Alumni club in March 1934. She died on January 11, 1987, in Contra Costa County, California.[76]

Eloise graduated from the University of Wisconsin in June 1932, with an English degree. She had met advertising major Roland William Radder in college, and they married in 1934. They had one son. The family lived in Green Bay, where Roland was a salesman, before moving to Burlingame in 1938. He became the owner of Radder Dallas food brokers. Roland died on October 7, 1974, at Peninsular Hospital of an unspecified illness. Eloise died on August 16, 1976, in San Mateo.[77]

Ira Dunlap attended Stanford from 1915 to 1917. When his father began working with the Irrigation District, Ira D. was delegated management of the Calipatria Ranch. Indeed, his siblings leased their interests to him, and he assumed control of the entire operation. Becoming highly regarded as a cattleman, he later leased a 400,000-acre cattle ranch at Vermejo Park in northern New Mexico, sixty-two miles southwest of Trinidad, Colorado. He married Mabel Ella Hoffman on October 28, 1919, and they divided their time between Imperial County and Albuquerque. He was appointed acting postmaster of Vermejo Park on November 3, 1937, and was confirmed in the position on January 6, 1938; he resigned on July 30, 1940. Mabel died on December 8, 1957, in Los Angeles. Ira married Sigrid E. McBain on May 18, 1959, in Las Vegas, Nevada. She had replaced him in the post office, so they likely had known each other for some time. He died in October 1984, in Albuquerque.[78]

Ira Aten was devoted to God and to his family, and lived his life according to a strict moral compass. While wearing a badge, he was a dedicated public servant who brought law and order to wild areas of the Lone State Star. As a private citizen, he remained a man who believed in service, and his reputation enabled him to take a leading role in community affairs.

James A. Brooks. #P.80.342. *Courtesy Texas Ranger Hall of Fame and Museum, Waco, Texas.*

Chapter 9

James A. Brooks: "A Resolute, Steely Nerved Lawman"

James Abijah Brooks was the first of the "Four Great Captains." As such, he provided steady leadership while the Frontier Battalion transitioned though the dawn of the twentieth century to become the Ranger Force. Robert M. Utley commented: "Tall, lean, and tough, he was also modest, quiet-spoken, and courteous, and possessed of a high sense of duty fortified by determination, courage, and a mind that grasped both the larger mission and the immediate task." The reputation Brooks justly acquired over twenty-three years as a Texas Ranger was one of a resolute, steely nerved lawman, but, like any man, he was not without his flaws. He was a notably excellent shot with rifle and pistol, but equally quick to pull a cork. His record as a peace officer, state legislator, and county judge was superb, but his track record as a husband and father was less than idyllic. Despite his failings, he was a faithful public servant who, with his guns, and later his law books, helped to build a land of law and order, representative government, and industry.

He was born on his family's farm near Paris, Bourbon County, Kentucky, on November 20, 1855. His father, Doctor John Strode Brooks, was born in Winchester in Clark County on September 26, 1802, and his mother, Mary Jane (Kerr) Brooks, on October 10, 1818, in Bourbon County. John graduated from Transylvania University Medical Department in Lexington in 1825. He and Mary Jane married in Bourbon County on March 11, 1838. James's older sisters were Annie E. Brooks, born May 16, 1839; Jane Marie "Jennie" Brooks, born January 18, 1842; Mary Adeline "Ada" Brooks, born February 1845; Sally Kenny Brooks, born February 18, 1848; and Francis "Fannie" Breckinridge Brooks, born July 8, 1850; while his younger siblings were Lillie Belle Brooks, born November 11, 1860; and John Clarence Brooks, likely born October 2, 1863. On May 1, 1839, the elder Brooks purchased ninety-five acres along the Hutchinson Road "on the waters of Houston Creek," and an adjacent twenty-one acres on December 1, 1846. By 1860, the property, worked by eight slaves, was valued at $23,000. At the same time, his personal estate was assessed at ten thousand dollars. As a successful physician, Doctor Brooks enjoyed a large measure of respectability, and, as early as 1841, the family's members were regular attendees of the Hopewell Presbyterian Church, in nearby Hutchinson. James began a common school education at the Hutchinson Academy in 1862, and continued until age seventeen.[1]

With the onset of the Civil War, Doctor Brooks worked in the hospitals situated around Lexington. Discussing the role of doctors from Brooks's alma mater in the city, Joshua and Karen Leet noted, "Transylvania's physicians faced the same hardships the troops faced ... Doctors faced almost impossible odds as they tried to save lives, heal injuries, make quick and difficult decisions about which men could be helped and which could not and do their best to prevent the spread of devastating diseases under dreadful living conditions during a bloody and terrible war." James's father, sixty years old by this time, was rarely home, and drove himself into a state of exhaustion. Hospitalized in the spring of 1863, the doctor passed away on April 3, and was interred in the Lexington Cemetery the following day.[2]

Brooks's widowed mother was forced to subdivide the homestead and sold 110 acres to Anne's husband, James H. Kerr, on April 15, 1867. The 1870 federal census revealed the reduced state of the Brooks family, with the remaining property valued at $9,620. Ten years later, Mary was a boarder in her daughter Jennie's home.[3]

In late 1876, Brooks boarded the train in Lexington, and traveled to Chicago before entering Texas on January 1, 1877. He journeyed to Collin

County where he went to work on a cousin's farm, then for area ranchers through the summer and fall of 1877. With his saved wages, he purchased 116 acres of land on the headwaters of Wilson Creek in the spring of 1878. His livestock holdings included one horse, forty-nine head of cattle, and four hogs. Enticed by the lure of new lands, though, he sold his farm after only six months.[4]

In the spring of 1879, Brooks gathered his small number of cattle and added them to a larger herd owned by William Bartlett of Clay County, Missouri. With John R. Brown acting as trail boss, Brooks and his fellow cowboys drove 3,400 head up the Chisholm Trail to Caldwell, Kansas. Some of the herd was purchased by the U.S. government to feed the Cheyennes and Arapahos on the Darlington Agency in the Indian Territory, and Brooks helped drive the cattle to the reservation. He became ill in the autumn, and was nursed back to health at the Boston & Billings Ranch, fifty miles from Caldwell. Obeying doctor's orders, he returned to Texas, arriving in San Antonio on January 1, 1880.[5]

Brooks spent the next four years engaged in several mostly failed business ventures in San Antonio and throughout South Texas. One of his more successful endeavors was the investment of his funds from the cattle sale in Kansas into a drive of 3,100 Mexican sheep from Duval County to San Antonio. The least profitable may have been a futile effort to find gold in the Shafter mining district. Sadly, Brooks would develop a life-long dependence on alcohol, and possibly the disappointments of these early years fueled his drinking. In 1881, he was reportedly "liquoring up" in a Cotulla saloon, and witnessed Lee Hall back down six badmen. The ex-Ranger's bravado was not lost on young Brooks.[6]

Discouraged by his lack of success, Brooks enlisted in Company F of the Frontier Battalion in Cotulla on January 15, 1883. The outfit was commanded by Lieutenant Charles Brown McKinney, but the time Brooks spent under his leadership proved brief. The "well known and highly respected" McKinney, who had first entered the service under L. H. McNelly, soon resigned to become sheriff of La Salle County. Lieutenant Josephus "Joe" Shely replaced him as company commander on March 1.[7]

Brooks and the rest of the company were kept busy pursuing lawbreakers throughout South Texas for the remainder of 1883. The International & Great Northern Railroad had reached La Salle County the previous year, and Cotulla had gained a subsequent population boom and a reputation for being a tough town. Many of Brooks's early assignments were routine in nature, as evidenced by his search for a stolen buggy on March 28. The novice private found the item the same day, and returned it to the proper owner. On the twenty-ninth, he arrested one of the two thieves involved, and delivered him to the Cuero jail; he apprehended the second the following day. On April 12, Brooks went on a scout with stockmen to recover stolen cattle in Karnes County. Two days later, they captured ten head and delivered them to their rightful owners. The company headquarters was relocated to Pearsall on June 11, but, in late November, Shely decided to make Cotulla the site for his winter quarters. The lieutenant was promoted to the rank of captain, effective May 1, 1884. Twenty-four days later, the company headquarters returned to Pearsall.[8]

Brooks first met John H. Rogers in the spring of 1884. Although a lapsed Presbyterian who indulged a thirst for good whiskey, Brooks took a liking to the staunch and temperate Methodist. Despite differing personalities and having nothing in common, except their Ranger service, the two men would remain good friends until Rogers died forty-six years later.[9]

The company made fifty-two arrests in the month of May 1884, which ranged from carrying a concealed weapon, to property theft, to murder. Operating as a member of Lieutenant William Scott's detachment in Gonzales County on July 4, 1884, Brooks arrested a suspect charged with assault with intent to kill in DeWitt County. The private delivered his prisoner to the sheriff the same day. Based on his solid performance, Brooks was advanced to the rank of corporal on November 25. He then promoted to sergeant on December 1, to replace William Taylor "Brack" Morris, who had resigned. Brooks and four men departed Yorktown the same day, and traveled to Cuero to attend district court. On the second, the sergeant took one Ranger and investigated fence-cutting in the eastern portion of DeWitt County, but they were unable to acquire any viable information on suspects. The two state officers returned to Cuero on the fourth. When notified of the murder of Karnes County Sheriff Edgar Leary, Brooks, Lieutenant Scott, and Private Abraham Lincoln Shely, the captain's brother, rode to Helena on December 27. Leary had been mortally wounded the day before by a drunk and unruly Emmett Butler, the nineteen-year-old son of a wealthy local cattleman. As Leary lay dying, Butler attempted to flee on horseback, but he was shot from the saddle by the crowd in the street. The young killer breathed his last the following morning. The three Rangers remained in Helena, ensuring the peace, then Scott returned to Yorktown on December 31. Together with Captain Shely, he organized the transfer of his detachment and equipment to Helena.[10]

On January 6, 1885, the lieutenant sent Brooks and another Ranger after a herd of stolen horses. By the ninth, the pair were in DeWitt County to meet up with Scott, and he and Brooks traveled by rail to Victoria the following day. After an interview with the local sheriff, they returned to Cuero, seemingly without success in recovering the livestock. On January 11, the entire detachment made a sweep of Goliad County, and returned to Helena three days later. On the twenty-third, Scott and Brooks received an invitation to attend the annual meeting of the Guadalupe and San Antonio River Stock Association, which was held at Yorktown. They returned to Helena the next day. On January 25, the entire detachment, plus wagon, team, and equipment, were ordered to report to company headquarter near Cotulla, arriving on the thirtieth.[11]

In the same month, Dimmit County was quickly becoming an international flashpoint. After horses were stolen from area ranchers on the night of December 30, 1884, Sheriff Joseph Tumlinson and a posse followed the trail across the Rio Grande. Riding approximately two miles into Mexico, they were chased back into Texas by thirty *bandidos*. On Febuary 6, 1885, one hundred Mexicans crossed the river with the intention of releasing four comrades jailed in Carrizo Springs for horse theft. Fourteen were killed in clashes with local lawmen and vigilance committees before retreating south. Other brazen raids were reported throughout the border country, which prompted Governor John Ireland to send Adjutant General Wilburn Hill King and Ranger detachments to Dimmit County.[12]

Renderings of the following episode have relied in the past on the recollections of participants, often composed decades after the fact. Including those of Brooks and Ira Aten, these reminiscences seem to have conflated two separate incidents into one. On the other hand, the monthly reports were written by Shely and Brooks when their memories were presumably still fresh, and offer a clear sequence of events. On February 5, Sheriff Charles McKinney and ten men rode through a "lonely and desolate country of mesquite bushes and cactus," and arrived at William Votaw's ranch, eight miles from the border, the following day. Brooks and two men accompanied the posse. They then proceeded to the Ainsworth ranch where Brooks was joined by members of the Company F detachment stationed there. Together with McKinney's posse, First Lieutenant Silas Hay of the Texas Volunteer Guard, and a detachment from Company D, commanded by Lieutenant Frank Jones, Brooks's Rangers rode to the Almita Crossing of the Rio Grande. The thirty Texans continued to an island, known as *Las Ysles* to local residents, in the middle of the Rio Grande, arriving on February 8. The next day, at sunrise, fifty Mexicans emerged on the other side of the border. While both banks of the river were lined with armed men, McKinney and ex-Ranger Lee Hall composed the Texas delegation to an arranged parlay, while the Mexicans were represented by two unidentified Mexican officers and Doctor Owen Clinton Pope, a Baptist missionary and future president of the institution that would become known as Hardin-Simmons University. Ira Aten's memoirs recount his presence there acting as a messenger for the Texans. For a time, an accord seemed unlikely and a fight imminent. However, the impromptu diplomacy finally resulted in the release of the four Mexican prisoners at the Dimmit County jail, and a pledge that Americans guilty of raiding south of the border would be delivered to Mexican authorities. In return for these concessions, the Mexicans promised to provide protection to Americans in Mexico, disperse *bandido* gangs on the river, and deliver, to Texas, prisoners being held in Mexican jails. According to Brooks, "matters seemed to be amicably adjusted," but a rumor gained credence for a time that Maverick County Sheriff Thomas Lindsey "Bose" Oglesby, Shely, and Hall had been killed in retaliation for the fourteen *bandidos* slain days before.[13]

Meanwhile, Captain Shely and Lieutenant Scott escorted General King to Encinal on the eighth, then to the Votaw ranch and the crossing the next day. Shely and Scott found that Brooks and the rest of the assembled lawmen had gone to *Las Ysles*, but the two officers discovered, upon their arrival the next morning, that the others had already returned to the Votaw ranch.

Finding their subordinates there, Shely and Scott traveled on to the Ainsworth ranch and reported to General King. On the eleventh, Shely, Brooks, and two men made a scout of eastern Dimmit County, and returned to Votaw's ranch the next day. On February 13, Shely, Captain Lamartine Pemberton "Lam" Sieker, Votaw, a few local stockmen, and three Rangers (one of them likely Brooks) proceeded to *Las Ysles*. The following day, the Texans went over the river to meet with local officials and citizens and obtain information regarding the recent unrest. The Texans returned to *Las Ysles* the same day, and Shely and his men to their headquarters camp on the fifteenth.[14]

Although long acknowledged as cow country, Dimmit County began to see an increasing number of sheep in the late 1870s. An estimated thirty thousand were grazing by 1880, and the cattlemen and the *pastores* soon clashed. Eight men rode to David Leval's sheep camp on February 28, 1885, and took overseer Manuel Flores away. Five of the party then went to another ranch three miles distant and seized two other Mexicans. The next day, the bodies of all three were found hanging from the limb of a tree. The perpetrators were apparently never found. Tensions were already running high, when, on March 7, Jose Maria Mendiola killed G. M. Hodges, the station agent in Encinal, without apparent provocation. The murder was initially believed to be in revenge for the recent lynching, and a mob attempted to get to the suspect, but the investigation ultimately proved Hodges had no connection to the hangings. The same evening, Jesus Sanches was shot to death at Raymond Martin's sheep camp by four men described as "Americans." The gunfire attracted the attention of Simon Perez, another shepherd who worked for the adjacent McDonald & Urbahn ranch. The innocent bystander-turned-witness was also murdered. After trailing the killers and gathering evidence, Sheriff McKinney and Captain Shely apprehended four men, on March 12, suspected of the murders. On the sixteenth, by order of the captain, Brooks and Private Joe B. Donegan went before the court in Encinal to make an affidavit for the four arrests. The following day, the two Rangers secured the horses ridden by the suspects on the day of the murders. Perhaps feeling the noose tightening, Felix Taylor, the youngest of the quartet, offered to turn state's evidence against his accomplices. Brooks and Donegan escorted Taylor to one of the murder scenes to collect evidence, then back to the jail. The subsequent convictions helped to calm passions in the county, and, once the free range was enclosed in barbed-wire fences, landless stock-raisers were forced to search for grazing pastures elsewhere.[15]

Captain Shely resigned effective June 15, and was succeeded by William Scott. Brooks would later credit Scott as his mentor in the trade of law enforcement. The company also transferred its headquarters camp to Uvalde County on the twelfth of the same month. Brooks spent much of July, August, and September in scouting Edwards, Uvalde, and Crockett Counties, recovering stolen horses, pursuing jailbreakers, and arresting suspected stock thieves.[16]

Once more, appropriations from the legislature forced a change in the number of Frontier Battalion personnel. On October 5, Company A was disbanded, and all the remaining companies were reduced by six men each. Brooks was promoted to first sergeant, and the company was posted to Vernon in Wilbarger County on November 24. In the first three weeks of December,

Captain Scott and Company F. #P.97.77 Front row (L to R): Ed Randall, Billy Birdwell, Kid Rogers, Allen Newton, and a Ranger known only as Hinds. Back Row (L to R): Frank Carmichael, John Rogers, William Scott, J. A. Brooks, Bob Crowder, and Jim Harry. *Courtesy Texas Ranger Hall of Fame and Museum, Waco, Texas.*

they worked with federal officers and Indian agents in the Chickasaw Agency to apprehend two fugitive Texas rustlers.[17]

On March 1, 1886, emboldened by the Knights of Labor union, three hundred workers on the Texas & Pacific and the Missouri, Kansas & Texas ("the Katy") railroads went on strike to protest the unscrupulous business practices of financier Jason "Jay" Gould and his associates. Consequently, rail traffic in North Texas ground to a halt. On April 3, Katy officials instructed a mail train, bearing seven lawmen and five railroad guards, to force their way into Fort Worth. Timothy Isaiah "Longhaired Jim" Courtright, the gunfighting ex-city marshal, oversaw the posse. When the train reached Buttermilk Junction at the city limits, strikers, concealed in high grass, threw the switch and opened fire; Deputy Sheriff Richard W. "Dick" Townsend was killed, and two other officers were wounded. Two of the bushwhackers were thought to have been injured in the fifteen-to-twenty-minute gun battle. Historian Richard F. Selcer would call April 3 "the single bloodiest day in Fort Worth law enforcement history." Brooks and four Rangers arrived in the city the next day to keep the peace. The governor also called for federal troops to intercede. The officers closed the gun shops and patrolled the streets making arrests. The strike ended by April 22, and the national organizers left town. The lawmen soon followed. Brooks would later remember the Fort Worth strike as one of his most dangerous assignments.[18]

The next few weeks would twice bring Brooks to the brink of death. On May 10, he and Privates Dee Caldwell and Henry Putz were directed to cross the Red River into the Indian Territory and hunt for a gang of horse thieves. The Rangers followed the trail for fifty miles, then called on Indian Agent Robert Latham Owen at the Union Agency in Muskogee. Requesting assistance, the Texans were partnered with Lieutenant Thomas Rogers Knight of the U.S. Indian Police, who held several warrants for the rustlers. The four officers learned the stolen horses and mules had been sold to settlers in Smith Pauls Valley. A man named Guthrie had reportedly purchased the mules, and Brooks was to either recover the stock or persuade the buyer to pay fair market value to keep them. Riding southwest from Muskogee, the lawmen crossed the Canadian River, and passed Cherokee Town before arriving in the valley located alongside the Washita River in the Chickasaw Nation. They found the horses, but could not locate the mules. Explaining the situation to the area ranchers, the officers drove the recovered horses west to William Vinson "Red" Alexander's store on the Washita, arriving on May 19.[19]

After securing the horses, Brooks and his party talked with the citizens congregated around the store. Learning one of the suspects had been seen in the vicinity, the law officers sat on the front porch to wait. Shortly thereafter, three cowboys rode up to the store, dismounted, and went inside. One of them, later identified as Albert St. John, was armed with a pistol and resembled the description they had been given earlier. The Cherokee Strip Live Stock Association had previously called him a "notorious desperado and reputed cow thief." Lieutenant Knight had three weeks earlier warned St. John about carrying firearms inside the Territory, and now felt duty-bound to disarm him. The Indian policeman requested backup from Brooks, and the sergeant agreed. Caldwell stayed outside while the other three officers walked into the store and saw St. John sitting on the counter at the opposite end.[20]

Knight strode down the narrow aisle toward the suspect, whose back was turned to the policeman. Brooks moved to the right and Putz stood a step behind. In a low, firm voice, Knight said, "I'll take that pistol from you now." Startled, St. John slid off the counter to the floor, and his hand dropped to his weapon. Brooks shouted, "Hold up! Hold up!" Knight grabbed the leveled pistol, and the three peace officers pulled their own guns. St. John seized Brooks's pistol with his left hand and cried, "Let 'er pop!" The occupants in the store were deafened by four gunshots. Two of Brooks's bullets and one of Putz's struck St. John, who staggered backward and fell to the ground on his side. As one of the projectiles had struck him in the heart, St. John died almost instantly. The witnesses ran outside, followed by the lawmen moments later. Brooks called for a doctor, but the alleged rustler was beyond the skill of any sawbones.[21]

The four lawmen rode out of town before dusk with the stolen horses. During the night, they were passed by sixteen armed men who failed to see them. It is unknown if this party was a posse searching for Brooks and his colleagues or outlaws simply moving in the darkness. Riding on, they returned the horses to their legal owners and arrived at the I. B. Ranch near

Fort Sill. There they wrote reports on the events of three days prior, and the Rangers returned to camp on May 25.[22]

Six days later, Monte Hines Sandels, the federal attorney in Fort Smith, charged Knight, Brooks, and Putz with murder. The grand jury indicted the trio on August 2, and Knight was jailed in Fort Smith on the twelfth. Brooks and Putz surrendered to U.S. Marshal John Carroll and joined Knight on September 1. They were kept under house arrest through the autumn before being released in early November under their own recognizance. Their court date was set for March 10, 1887.[23]

Meanwhile, Captain Scott had positioned Company F at Brownwood on September 30, 1886. Brooks returned from Fort Smith and joined the company there. Ira Aten of Company D had infiltrated the community the month before to secure evidence of fence-cutting. The Ranger detective began accumulating the names of those involved, and soon discovered where the nippers planned to strike next. On the night of November 9, Scott, Brooks, Aten, and Privates John H. Rogers, James Allen Newton, Francis Powell "Frank" Carmichael, and William "Billy" Treadwell prepared to catch the suspects in the act. The lawmen were accompanied by brothers Washington Morgan and Levin Powell Baugh, the owners of the fence in question, and five or six civilians.[24] The *Statesman* published a telegram the next day describing the attempted apprehension:

> At 11 o'clock the cutters were heard coming up the line of the fence. They were permitted to pass a few of those in ambush, but on arriving opposite him, Capt. Scott demanded their surrender, stating they were rangers. His only answer was a pistol shot, then the firing become [*sic*] rapid on both sides ... When the firing ceased one wire cutter was found killed and one mortally wounded, while two made their escape on foot, their horses being captured.[25]

The dead man was recognized as Jim Lovell, a constable in the neighboring precinct, who, despite his official position, was under indictment for fence-cutting. The wounded nipper, Amos Roberts, was taken into town, but he later died following an operation to remove the bullet from his chest.

Roberts had been charged with the same offence as his late partner. Scott identified the two who escaped as Charles Johnson and John Matthews; the latter was thought to be wounded. Brooks attempted to find the fugitives on November 20, but he returned to camp later in the day without his quarry. He and the rest of the company lingered in Brown County for the remainder of the year and conducted scouts into Concho, Lampasas, San Saba, and McCulloch Counties. Following the gun battle, instances of wire-nipping became fewer. The grand jury indicted five fence-cutters in February 1887, and the defendants were granted a change of venue to Bell County. Enjoying popular support, their cases drifted through the court system until the charges were dismissed two years later.[26]

By the end of the year, the Ranger service had lost a valuable friend to the risks inherent in law enforcement. Sheriff Charles McKinney, in his second term in office, had subsequently become entangled once more in an old feud with George W. "Bud" Crenshaw and James Eli McCoy. On December 26, 1886, the sheriff was ambushed and assassinated by his two enemies while responding to a false complaint near Twohig. Two days later, Governor Ireland issued a five-hundred-dollar reward for the killers' capture, while the county court and local ranchers offered additional funds. Crenshaw was hunted down and killed by Captain George Heinrich Schmitt's Rangers, while McCoy surrendered and stood trial for murder. He was convicted and executed by hanging.[27]

On March 22, 1887, Captain Scott and five men were sent once more to the Piney Woods. While Brooks had been in court in Arkansas the previous year, Willis Jackson Conner and his sons—John Willis, Frederick M. "Fed," Charles Wilson, William E. "Bill," and Alfred Horton "Alfie"—had allegedly murdered two neighbors over the ownership of land in the Holly Creek bottom. The bodies had been discovered in the swamps of the disputed property in December 1883. By virtue of the Rangers' earlier efforts, Charles and Alfie Conner were imprisoned in Huntsville while "Uncle Willis," as he was known, and his other sons were indicted. They escaped into the swamps and woods, and gathered together a gang of fearsome cutthroats.[28]

Once the Rangers arrived, Scott called upon some of the citizens to volunteer for a scout into the rough country south of Hemphill. They located the Conner camp at two a.m. on the thirty-first, and planned their raid. At five o'clock, the posse moved to a point three hundred yards from the camp. As the captain waited for daylight, they formed into two squads with Rangers James B. Harry and James Newton, and deputized possemen Judge James Polly, Judge William Wallace Weatherred, Henry Harris, John Toole, and Milton Anthony on the left flank. Scott and Brooks, John Rogers, Frank Carmichael, Billy Treadwell, and James H. "Jim" Moore were on the right. The lawmen deployed forward into a steep descent near Lick Branch, then Scott's detachment came under a relentless fire when Willis, Fed, John, and Bill sprang an ambush from the brush and trees. At a distance of twenty to thirty feet, the first volley killed Moore; the remaining Rangers each fired two or three shots, then the second volley swept over the lawmen. Brooks had three fingers on his left hand shot off and another bullet hit his right hand between the second and third fingers, while Scott was struck in the left lung and Rogers in the left side and arm. Treadwell's rifle jammed after a few shots, while Carmichael covered his wounded comrades with a rapid fire from his Winchester. His fusillade wounded Fed and killed a pack horse. Harry and Newton began to move toward Scott's position, but were stopped by Judge Weatherred, who ordered them to remain in place. The other members of the squad similarly refused to enter the fight and instead took cover nearly eighty yards away.[29]

The Conners did not escape unscathed as Brooks killed Bill in the exchange. The remaining outlaws fled, but Fed would later die in another shootout with lawmen. Leander Jackson Conner, another of Willis's sons, hid in Louisiana until he was tracked down and captured. John rode away from Sabine County and his family's troubles into an unknown fate. Willis and his eight-year-old grandson were killed by a private detective seeking the one-thousand-dollar reward. In the concluding act of the feud, Charles received a pardon from Governor Lawrence S. Ross on March 18, 1889.[30]

At daybreak, the seriously wounded Scott issued several orders, then relinquished command to Brooks. The sergeant and Rogers's injuries were bandaged, and doctors were summoned from Hemphill and San Augustine to treat the wounded. Scott did nearly perish, while Brooks lost three fingers and had the bullet removed from his right hand. The slain Jim Moore was buried at the scene, but, several days later, his body was disinterred and taken to the Hemphill Cemetery.[31]

The three wounded men convalesced and returned to duty, but Brooks was subpoenaed to appear before the federal court in Fort Smith. The legal proceedings stemming from Albert St. John's death had been originally scheduled for March, but two postponements had pushed the case back on Judge Isaac Charles Parker's docket. Elias Cornelius Boudinot, an attorney and full-blooded Cherokee Indian, offered his services to Brooks, Knight, and Putz *pro bono*. Fort Smith lawyers Thomas Harris Barnes, William Moore Mellette, and Wayman Crow Jackson completed the legal defense team. The defendants entered pleas of not guilty on July 15, 1887, and testimony began the same day. Sandels, the prosecuting attorney, called over a dozen witnesses to the stand, including four bystanders in the store that fateful day. After the prosecution rested on July 22, the defense called just three witnesses: Knight, Brooks, and Putz. Closing arguments were heard on the twenty-fourth. Two days later, Parker instructed the jury, and the panel members withdrew to deliberate. Shortly thereafter, they returned to the courtroom and read the verdict: the three were found not guilty of first-degree murder, but guilty on the charge of manslaughter. While the lawmen had acted in self-defense, the jury were perhaps persuaded by the argument they had no official authority to arrest St. John.[32]

The judge must have been as surprised as Brooks, Knight, and Putz. After issuing the sentence on July 28, Parker had them lodged in the Fort Smith jail for three weeks of house arrest. He then called them into his office in late August and suspended their sentence effective immediately.[33]

As Brooks and his fellow defendants returned to their respective homes, a drive to secure a presidential pardon for them began. Captain Scott asked Captain Lam Sieker to assist in gaining exoneration. An application was sent to U.S. Attorney General Augustus Hill Garland, who forwarded this and all subsequent documents to President Grover Cleveland. Letters and telegrams from friends and admirers of Brooks, members of the congressional delegations of Kentucky and Texas, Adjutant General King, and Governor Ross, as well as two dozen petitions with over seven hundred signatures, were also received. On September 13, 1887, the president issued pardons for Knight, Brooks, and Putz based on "mitigating circumstances showing no criminal intent."[34]

Appreciative of the outpouring of support he had received, Brooks returned to Texas. He reported to Captain Scott in Cisco, then went on to the Ranger camp at Ballinger in Runnels County. He arrived on September 15, and learned his pardon had been granted. Having been discharged from the battalion on July 31 following his conviction, Brooks reenlisted in Company F on September 20, and receieved his old rank of sergeant. One day after his thirty-second birthday, the company moved its headquarters to a site near San Angelo in Tom Green County. Commanding a detachment at Barksdale, Brooks spent a good deal of his time scouting the rough terrain of Edwards County, as well as attending district court there, before returning to Tom Green County to apprehend three rustlers on December 13. The following month, he was back in Edwards County where he arrested two suspects charged with stock theft. Brooks and his detachment rejoined the company on January 23, 1888.[35]

On March 26, the Rangers returned to their old camp near Ballinger. The following month, Scott resigned his commission and went to work as a railroad contractor in Mexico. Brooks was promoted to first lieutenant on May 1, 1888, and assumed command of the company. He shifted the company headquarters from Ballinger to Bear Creek and the Taylor Ranch near Kerrville on June 7 and June 13 respectively, then Laredo on September 30.[36]

Brooks had ordered the entire company to Kerr County on May 31, to hunt for suspected fence-cutters. While he was there, Captain Cornelius Vernon "Neal" Coldwell, having resigned as quartermaster of the Frontier Battalion on February 15, 1883, introduced the lieutenant to his "niece," Virginia Willborn, who lived on the edge of Center Point. Captivated by the plucky young lady, Brooks would take a leave of absence in September 1889 to court her. They eventually married at the Center Point ranch on September 16, 1890.[37]

Even amid Brooks's burgeoning romance, the lieutenant and his men were occupied with keeping the peace on an increasingly troubled border. Turmoil erupted in Starr County when Abram Recéndez, a *mexicano* prisoner arrested by Sheriff Warren Washington "Wash" Shely in May 1888, was killed by Private Jim Dillard of Company D while making a purported escape attempt. Sheriff Shely, the brother of Joe Shely, had been accused of participating in previous lynchings of Mexicans, and smoldering Hispanic resentments toward Anglos were enflamed. Based on subsequent events, Customs inspector Victor Sebree has traditionally been blamed for the Recéndez shooting. Drawn into the ensuing political brawl, Catarino Erasmo Garza, newspaper editor and persuasive orator, moved to Rio Grande City and wrote several editorials criticizing area Anglo lawmen in rather unpleasant terms. At one point, he was charged with criminal libel. Sebree was apparently one of those Garza maligned, and the stage was set for a showdown.[38]

Like many stories of gunfights occurring decades ago, descriptions of the incident do not agree. The accepted version was that Sebree met Garza, who was seated in the doorway of a barber shop, on the afternoon of September 21. Sebree called for Garza to fight him, but the editor declined. Garza's companion, a man by the name of Federico Lopez, reportedly fired the first shot. The alternate account, the one embraced by the Mexican consul at Rio Grande City, asserted that after Garza refused Sebree's challenge, the federal officer then dismounted and shot at his enemy several times. The revolutionary had time to return fire even after he was hit twice.[39]

Regardless of which account was more accurate, Sebree feared the reaction of the Mexican quarter, and sought refuge in the guardhouse at Fort Ringgold. Hot on his heels, some two hundred armed men demanded Sebree be turned over to them, but they were ordered to leave the military reservation. The mob, many of whom were characterized as smugglers and bandits in the Anglo press, seized control of the streets and began rioting. Frantic telegrams poured into the statehouse, and newspapers reported lawless conditions in the county. More than 150 deputies and possemen from Cameron, Hidalgo, San Patricio, and Uvalde Counties rushed to Rio Grande City by the twenty-fourth. In addition, 135 troopers of the Third Cavalry were stationed at the fort, and Ranger Companies D and F were on hand to present an aggregate of over three hundred peacekeepers. On October 22, the state officers arrested twenty-three men for conspiracy to commit murder, and another two for assault with intent. All the prisoners were housed in the county jail. Fortunately, Garza was expected to live and was reported as resting comfortably. Further unrest was avoided when the county judge, the justice of the peace, and the sheriff convinced the protestors to end the riot in exchange for their promise that Sebree would face justice. The crowd dispersed, but Sebree was never arrested or indicted for the shooting.[40]

With hostilities calmed for the moment, Lieutenant Brooks maintained his headquarters in Rio Grande City in October 1888 to suppress stock thieves. From there, the Rangers went to Santa María on October 21, 1889, then Cotulla on May 10, 1890. The latter town became the company's permanent station for the better part of the next ten years. The Rangers had been given a daunting task in La Salle County. The adjutant general reported: "Large bodies of organized, well-armed and desperate characters were raiding the ranches and driving away stock in droves, and bidding defiance to the citizens and peace officers." Amid the moves, Brooks was appointed captain in May 1, 1889.[41]

The simmering racial tensions exploded into outright violence on the early morning of June 24, 1891. The previous evening, Jim Trent and Floyd Gardiner, two black men, were drinking and carousing in Encinal. They went to a house where a *fandango* was being held, and proceeded to disturb the other guests with their obnoxious behavior. Albert Johnson, a local constable, was called, and he came to the dance with the intention of arresting the two inebriated men. Instead, he was met with a fusillade of bullets and driven away. Johnson assembled a deputy and a civilian to aid him in making an arrest, and returned to the house in question around three o'clock in the morning. There they were fired upon by Trent and Gardiner, and Edward Reinbolt, a white carpenter who had joined the two offenders. The lawmen returned fire and a furious gun battle ensued for several minutes. The perpetrators were finally taken into custody, but with a "fearful cost." An innocent bystander who had been attending the *fandango* was killed outright. Two members of the posse were casualties: one gutshot, and the other shot in the leg. Reinbolt was also killed. Trent and Gardiner were unwounded in the "Negro riot," as the *Statesman* labeled the affray. Throughout the morning, the enraged populace of Encinal were working themselves toward a lynching when the decision was made in the afternoon to move the two suspects to Cotulla for safekeeping. When the shooting occurred, Brooks, Rogers, and Private Tupper Harris had been in Pearsall attending the trial of ex-deputy sheriff Alfred Young Allee, who had shot and killed Walter C. Bowen, editor of the *Cotulla Ledger*. On the twenty-fifth, the state officers returned to Cotulla to guard the jail. The next day, Brooks left four Rangers on protection detail and went to Encinal with Rogers and two other men to acquire details of the incident. The captain returned to Cotulla on June 26, leaving Rogers in charge of the investigation. On the twenty-ninth, Brooks consulted with Judge Robert Weir Hudson and District Attorney Marcellus French Lowe, both of the Thirty-sixth Judicial District, in Pearsall on the three killings. He returned to Encinal the following day escorting Adjutant General Woodford Haywood Mabry and Lowe. The prisoners remained under Ranger protection until July 3.[42]

Passions had barely cooled when yet another revolutionary uprising troubled the Rio Grande country in the autumn of 1891. Now recovered from his wounds, Catarino Garza opposed the Mexican government of *presidente* Porfirio Díaz which had been in power since 1876, and advocated for the restoration of the country's 1857 constitution. The insurrectionists also resisted the modernizers from both sides of the border who wanted to turn South Texas into a commercial center, which had the unhappy consequence of economically and socially dispossessing poorer *mexicanos*. On September 15, Garza gathered together an armed force of twenty-eight men, later reinforced by twelve more, to invade Mexico. Crossing near Mier, he stayed nine days in Tamaulipas, raiding along the river between Reynosa and Camargo, before returning to Texas. Seventy-odd *Garzistas* crossed into Mexico near the Agua Negra ranch on November 7 and were defeated by Federal forces at Derramadero de las Ovejas on the eleventh. Ninety-two *insurrectos* invaded on December 19, near Guerrero, and skirmished with Mexican customs guards and soldiers at Las Tortillas ranch, and again at Arroyo del Bagre the next day.[43]

Following the third failed incursion, U.S. army troops and federal marshals were sent to enforce American neutrality. Unlike the Cortina War of thirty years previous, the Garza uprising was not the sole province of one demographic group, but instead drew assistance from a wide range of social and economic classes. The *Garzistas* were dispersed across the *brasada* of South Texas, and benefited from widespread sympathy and support among the *mexicano* population in the border country, as well as from some Anglo sheriffs, deputy marshals, Customs officials, judges, businessmen, and landowners. However, in addition to being revolutionary patriots, the insurgents were accused of acting as traditional *bandidos*. Political bosses, such as James Babbage Wells, Jr., and wealthy merchants and ranchers, some with Spanish surnames, called on the governor to provide them protection. Testimony obtained from the Mexican side of the border seemed to indicate the insurgents forcibly seized food, supplies, and horses from some *rancheros* and rebuffed appeals for reimbursement. In the end, Garza's three invasions achieved little save compelling Mexico City to demand Washington enforce the neutrality laws. The Garza war became the talk of the nation, and reporters descended on the border country and telegraphed sensationalist stories to their newspapers.[44]

The situation grew worse when a skirmish between U.S. regulars and *Garzistas* at Retamal Springs on December 22 resulted in the death of Corporal Charles H. Edstrom, Third Cavalry. Having committed murder on Texas soil, the insurgents became a matter for the Rangers. Brooks was ordered by General Mabry to the scene on December 25, the captain arriving at Laredo the next day.[45] Mabry was insistent Brooks and Captain James S. McNeel of Company E focus on the breaking of state laws such as the soldier's slaying or the ongoing occurrences of horse theft. He instructed Brooks:

> You have nothing to do with any violation of the neutrality laws, as they are international questions which Texas must leave to the Federal authorities. Your command is not to be employed in the capacity of scouts for the United States troops, but will act independently in the performance of your duties. Such action ought to be most effective, because of the nature of the service your command is accustomed to.[46]

Brooks arrived at the Salennia Ranch on the twenty-eighth where he joined Captains John Gregory Bourke and Francis Hunter Hardie. That evening,

Garza Revolutionists in the Texas Chaparral. Photomechanical print by Frederic Remington. *Courtesy Library of Congress, Washington, D.C.*

they departed to scout for the *Garzistas*. Brooks was in the company of Zapata County Sheriff Robert Anderson Haynes and Deputy U.S. Marshal William H. Van Riper when they exchanged shots with enemy sentinels. As the sun set, they located Garza's camp in a dense thicket on the Soledad Ranch. Commanded personally by Garza, the Mexicans were estimated to number two hundred men. Sheriff Haynes sent a message to Captain Hardie requesting assistance. Brooks's dozen Rangers, and Troops A and G, Third Cavalry, rode to the scene and engaged the revolutionaries on the evening of December 29, but the Mexicans slipped away in the night. The morning of the thirtieth, Brooks and his companions trailed the band north and captured Garza loyalist Sisto Longorio at Colorow Ranch. The evening of the same day, they were near Rendado Ranch and fought a brief skirmish with one of Garza's outposts. The Americans trailed the fleeing *insurrectos* the morning of December 31 until they were dispersed.[47]

The state officers' pursuit was made even more difficult by the poor grazing found in the *brasada* and by an erratic logistical system. On January 4, 1892, Brooks, Sheriff Shely, Captain McNeel's company, and Captain James Ormond Mackay's troop engaged fifty *Garzistas* on La Havana Ranch, twenty miles south of Fort Ringgold. The revolutionaries once more proved difficult to apprehend, although a few saddles and horses were captured. Captain Bourke, senior military officer in the pursuit, reported a conversation with Longorio, who said Garza was "feeling very despondent and his band has been disintegrating for some days. Don't like being followed by U.S. troops and Texas Rangers." General Mabry arrived in San Diego to personally inspect the crisis. He was met by Brooks and McNeel at Corpus Christi on January 21. From there, Brooks took his superior to Laredo on the twenty-seventh, then Gatta Creek on February 3. Mabry and Brooks were encamped in the field when they were visited by journalist Richard Harding Davis. The famous New York-based reporter described the Rangers' bivouac: "The Rangers' camps look much like those of gypsies, with their one wagon to carry the horses' feed, the ponies grazing at the ends of the lariats, the big Mexican saddles hung over the nearest barb fence, and the blankets covering the ground and marking the hard beds of the night before." Davis shared a breakfast of bacon and coffee with the Texans, and the adjutant general treated him to "some very thrilling stories of their deeds and personal meetings with the desperadoes and 'bad' men of the border." Even when pressed, Brooks refused to speak of his own accomplishments, and the journalist concluded, "big men cannot tell of the big things they do as well as other people." Perhaps to make up for a reluctance to boast of their feats, the Rangers provided their guest a "most wonderful" demonstration of their shooting skills. According to Davis, Brooks placed eight rifle bullets into a target at sixty feet in one continuous roll of sound. Garza finally went into exile in Costa Rica in February 1892. Those he left behind were stripped of their revolutionary identity and began to behave more and more as common bandits. One of the last skirmishes of the Garza war occurred near the Bennett Ranch on March 22, and resulted in the death of Ranger Robert E. Doaty of Company E.[48]

Brooks moved his headquarters to a camp near Realitos on April 7, but maintained a presence at Cotulla. Over the next several months, the Rangers of Companies E and F scoured Frio, Starr, Duval, Encinal, La Salle, Zapata, Hidalgo, and Webb Counties for revolutionaries and fugitives from justice; Lee Hall accompanied several of the patrols. By June 1893, Brooks and his men had returned to Cotulla. After Rogers was promoted to the command of Company E, Daniel Lynch Musgrave was appointed first sergeant in his stead. The entire Garza affair had proven a fiasco not only for the *insurrectos*, but also the regulars and the Rangers. The inconclusive clashes and paltry captures could not compensate for the financial cost and physical hardships suffered during the campaign. The complicated state of affairs in South Texas regarding support for or opposition to Garza among federal marshals, army officers, and county sheriffs only intensified as they fell into bickering with each other.[49]

On July 13, 1894, Brooks and four Rangers were sent to Temple to keep order during a violent railroad strike instigated by the Brotherhood of Locomotive Firemen. Captain John R. Hughes and four of his men were likewise in town. Their joint assignment was to protect the trains and other property of the Gulf, Colorado & Santa Fe Railroad that ran between Gainesville and Galveston. Reinforcements in the form of Corporal Tom M. Ross and two more men from Company E reported to Brooks on July 15, as did Private Adolphus Asbury Neely and four men of Company B the next day. While there were a few minor disturbances, the federal troops deployed to the town and the various court injunctions did much to keep the peace. On the twenty-second, Brooks went to Austin to consult with General Mabry on the situation. The following day, Mabry ordered Hughes and eight Rangers to return to their respective stations, while Corporal Ross was placed in charge of seven men in Temple. Brooks returned to Cotulla on July 24, and Hughes and his men reached their headquarters camp on July 27.[50]

Virginia had given birth to their first child on June 28, 1894, a girl they christened Mary Vernon Brooks. The captain was on a scout when his daughter was born, but he quickly returned to Cotulla. Five months later, on December 12, Mary died. Brooks never discussed his daughter's death, but the tragedy likely affected his marriage and his relationships with his other children in the years to come.[51]

In early 1895, Company F was reduced to eight Rangers. Sergeant Musgrave resigned in late February and was replaced by John Natus. For the years 1895 and 1896, the battalion scouted 173,381 miles, arrested 676 offenders, recovered 2,856 head of stolen stock, assisted the civil authorities on 167 occasions, and guarded jails thirteen times.[52]

Rather than combatting an Indian raid or a gang of train robbers, the Ranger service was next entangled in a piece of political theater when they were called upon to stop a boxing match. In 1894, James John "Gentleman Jim" Corbett, recently crowned world heavyweight champion after defeating John Lawrence Sullivan, had considered a challenge to fight middleweight titleholder Robert Prometheus "Ruby Bob" Fitzsimmons. After a series of lengthy delays during which time they waged a venomous war of words in the press, the two fighters agreed to a bout. However, their managers found more and more states, including the former boxing havens of Florida and Louisiana, were following the national trend in enacting anti-prizefighting legislation. With the number of potential sites dwindling by May 1895, Dallas sportsman Daniel Albert Stuart believed he could produce a significant fight and offered a venue in the North Texas town.[53]

Organizing a syndicate of businessmen to raise capital, Stuart prepared to erect a coliseum in Dallas at great cost. Moralists were outraged, but state laws regarding boxing matches were ambiguous at best. In 1889, legislation had been enacted that allowed prizefights, bullfights, and "other dangerous contests" in Texas following the purchase of a five-hundred-dollar license. Two years later, Governor James Stephen Hogg and the legislature made boxing an offense under the criminal statutes, but whether the later criminal law superseded the earlier civil code was left unanswered. In July 1895, State Comptroller Newton Webster Finley declared the 1891 law had repealed the 1889 act, and Governor Charles Allen Culberson concurred in an executive proclamation. Undeterred, Stuart and his backers vowed to fight the ruling in the courts. Judge James Mann Hurt, chief justice of the Court of Criminal Appeals, ruled, due to the conflicting nature of the existing statutes, prizefighting was not a felony. Religious associations, reformers, and other special interest groups supported Governor Culberson's call for a special session of the Twenty-fourth Legislature on September 26. Five days later, the state's chief executive and the legislators made prizefighting illegal in Texas. Once the law became effective, the governor instructed the adjutant general to take all steps necessary to halt the bout. Mabry ordered Captain Rogers to have an undercover Ranger follow Fitzsimmons, while Brooks was to send two men to do the same with Corbett.[54]

While Corbett and Fitzsimmons established training camps in San Antonio and Houston respectively, Stuart canvassed Arkansas and Indian Territory for a venue, but he was unable to find officials agreeable to the event. The promoter and his financial backers decided to hold the bout in Texas, despite the law. At the same time, Stuart abandoned his plans for Dallas and instead considered proposals to hold the match in the El Paso area. The locale offered a setting far from Austin, and one serviced by numerous railroads to accommodate the anticipated rush of sports reporters and aficionados. The promising location had its own share of opposition to a prizefight, though. The town had already seen a contest between the city fathers who seemingly turned a blind eye to the local vice trades and the El Paso Ministers' Union that championed public virtue. The proposed bout was yet another source of contention between the two groups.[55]

Late in the year, the vain and conceited Corbett dropped out and quit Texas to become a stage actor. The redoubtable Stuart telegraphed Irishman Peter Maher to take the place of the departed boxer. Maher had lost an earlier bout with Fitzsimmons and was eager for a rematch. While Maher was not in the same league as Corbett, the fight for the diamond-studded Police Gazette Championship belt and ten-thousand-dollar purse still had potential.[56]

As El Paso teemed with ministers and women's church groups, and journalists and boxing enthusiasts, the two contenders established their training camps in the vicinity by mid-January. Nearly the entire Frontier Battalion and the adjutant general were soon in El Paso to prevent the match. Brooks and three men of Company F were in San Antonio on February 7 to meet Mabry, and together they proceeded to El Paso the following day. Arriving on the ninth, Brooks was joined by four more Rangers over the next two days. The captain later reported the Rangers "guarded trains and shadowed Fitzsimmons and other pugilists for the purpose of preventing them from fighting on Texas soil." The site for the prizefight was to be on Mexican soil near Langtry, almost four hundred miles down the Rio Grande. The fighters and their entourages, the dozens of reporters, and half of the Frontier Battalion were aboard the train on the evening of February 20. After morning stops at Marathon and Sanderson, the seventeen-hour journey came to an end amidst a pouring rain. A narrow wooden bridge stretched from the bank of the river to the sandbar where the ring had been constructed. With the scene of the fight outside their jurisdiction, Mabry and the Rangers observed the proceedings from the high bluffs on the north side of the Rio Grande. Refereed by Chicago newsman George Siler, the bout, and the absurdity that epitomized the entire episode, ended abruptly when Fitzsimmons knocked out Maher in, according to Siler, one minute and forty-three seconds.[57]

Brooks and Company F returned to their home station at Cotulla on February 22, where the captain supervised his Rangers as they conducted several routine arrests. On April 5, he was ordered to Laredo to keep order during the municipal elections. He was joined the next day by W. A. Evetts, who had promoted to first sergeant, and they arrested three men who had perjured themselves before a grand jury investigating irregular voting practices, and three more for illegal voting. With the situation in hand, Brooks and Evetts returned to Cotulla on April 8. The two Rangers testified in Laredo before the same grand jury on June 23 and 24.[58]

Fitzsimmon-Maher Fight. #1731. Noah H. Rose Photograph Collection. *Courtesy Western History Collections, University of Oklahoma Libraries, Norman, Oklahoma.*

Samuel Vaughan "Pete" Edwards, the La Salle County animal and hide inspector, was appointed sheriff on December 21, 1896. The campaign had been contentious and stirred up unresolved hostilities. Ten years previously, Edwards was deputy to Sheriff Charles McKinney, and had been wounded in the course of the latter's murder. Sheriff William L. Hargus had abruptly resigned shortly after being elected to his second term, and Edwards's selection proved to be an unpopular choice.[59] The citizens of La Salle County took sides in the argument, and Company F was called in to keep order. James Richard Devenport of the Armstrong Ranch was a particularly vocal opponent of Sheriff Edwards. The latter would resign in June 1898, and Will Burwell would take his place.[60]

As mounting tensions between the United States and Spain led to open warfare in April 1898, officials in Austin grew concerned that Mexico would become involved in the conflict. General King assigned Company B to Langtry and Company D to Valentine, while Company E remained at Alice. Company F was sent to Laredo briefly before going to Alice and Brownsville. After going to Laredo again, Brooks went to Cotulla where he investigated a recent murder. On the night of May 21, attorney William Jerry Bowen was shot five times in front of his home. Leaving behind a wife and two young daughters, he expired before he could name his killer. Brooks and twelve Rangers worked the case and quickly arrested A. J. Poteet for the crime. During the investigation, Brooks discovered Poteet had earlier lost his claim to school land and blamed Bowen, who had represented the opposite party. Poteet had solicited E. A. McCurry for his assistance in the murder, but the latter refused; he did, however, loan his pistol to Poteet. The defendant was indicted for murder and denied bail during his *habeas corpus* hearing. He was then remanded to the county jail. Poteet was subsequently granted a change of venue, and details of the subsequent trial in Brownsville are unknown. Professor Paul Spellman, Brooks's biographer, noted items in the captain's personal papers indicated he apparently remained "agitated that the case never came to any resolution." His inquiry in Cotulla completed, Brooks hurried to Brownsville once more in May, and served alongside Troop D of the First Texas Cavalry in patrolling the coast. The regiment did not go overseas or see any action.[61]

While Brooks was still in Brownsville, his daughter Corrinne Kenny was born on December 7, 1898. His son John Morgan would be born the following year on August 17. The captain's descendants concur Brooks was never a capable husband and father. His children's formative years were marked by his long and frequent absences from home, as well as his continuing addiction to alcohol. In the coming years, he would dote on his son and virtually ignore his daughter, except for the occasional disparaging comment about her "fat, ugly arms" or some other trait he deemed undesirable. One episode illustrates this unhappy inclination. When Virginia was six months pregnant with Morgan, as he was known, Corrinne was severely hurt by a mule kick to the face. Virginia spent months caring for her daughter even after Morgan's premature birth. For reasons known only to himself, Brooks seems to have blamed Corrinne for his son's untimely entry into the world.[62]

On the day of Corrinne's birth, Captain Brooks entrained to Hidalgo to contend with another spell of political turmoil. Twenty-five years before, the resurgent Democratic Party had spread its influence into the Rio Grande Valley and secured the Hispanic *peón* vote. By exploiting that bloc, Anglo *patróns*, prominent businessmen and stock raisers led by Stephen Powers, gathered political power in Cameron County. These men were members of the "Blue Club," or Club Azul, so-called because of the color of the ballot they used. Succeeding Powers, Judge Jim Wells would form similar clubs in Hidalgo, Starr, Webb, San Patricio, and Duval Counties, and consolidate his political control over the Lower Rio Grande by 1892. In opposition, James Leal Haynes, collector of customs at Brownsville, and the Republicans established their own voting clique, known as the "Red Club," or Club Colorado. The two groups were often at odds, both at the voting booth and in the streets. Hidalgo County Sheriff John Closner was an affluent sugarcane farmer and one of the first to employ irrigation systems in the valley. He was also a steadfast Democrat who was backed by Judge Wells. In the aftermath of the November 1898 elections, allegations surfaced of voter fraud. The Republican club in the county scheduled a meeting for December 11 to address the situation. Captain Brooks was instructed to monitor the potentially explosive situation. Arriving in town, he calmed the club's fuming leaders before leaving for Cotulla on the thirteenth.[63]

Throughout the summer of 1899, Company F remained stationed at Cotulla, but fielded detachments throughout the lower valley with camps near Brownsville and Hebbronville. On August 31, Brooks was directed to proceed to Colorado County and take over from Captains Bill McDonald and John Rogers in preserving the peace there. The Reese-Townsend troubles had kept the Rangers of Companies B and E busy earlier in the year. Brooks, First Sergeant Winfred Finas Bates, Private Anderson Yancey "Ancey" Baker, two other men from Company F, and one each from Companies B and E attended the autumn term of district court and insured a trouble-free session by disarming the citizens. The state officers were so successful in calming the situation that the feud was not mentioned in the newspapers until the following year. On January 12, 1900, Brooks was placed in charge of keeping order in Bastrop during the trial of James Gaither "Jim" Townsend. The defendant had been charged with the murder of Burrell Green Whittington "Dick" Reese. After their arrival, the captain, Bates, and Privates Will, and J. T. Armstrong began to confiscate weapons from members of both factions in the streets and the courthouse.[64]

The trial began calmly on the fifteenth at one o'clock as District Judge Edward R. Sinks granted a continuance and adjourned at four-thirty. The partisans of both factions drifted into the saloons, and anger over damaged family honor quickly mixed with alcohol to produce trouble. Concealed within the Golden Rule Saloon, John Walter Reese, James Henry "Jim" Coleman, Thomas Barnette Daniels, and Leslie Wilkinson "Les" Reese opened fire on some of their enemies in the street. Howard Asa Townsend, son of the late Sheriff James Light Townsend, escaped unscathed. Deputy William D. Clements was hit in the lungs as he rushed to cover, while Colorado County Sheriff William Thomas Burford's son, Arthur, was shot between the eyes, killing him instantly. Within twenty minutes, Brooks, Scurry, and Armstrong, and Rangers William L. Wright and Creed Taylor of Company E, had arrested and jailed seventeen members of the Reese party. Sergeant Bates, Winchester rifle in hand, was placed in the courthouse door to prevent any of the Townsend faction from exiting the building. Brooks and Sheriff George W. Davis, assisted by Rangers and deputies, combed the town's hotels and saloon for hidden weapons. Adjutant General Thomas Scurry dispatched reinforcements to

Bastrop, including Captains McDonald and Rogers, which brought the total number of Rangers in town to approximately twenty.[65]

The trial of Jim Townsend was set aside for the moment, and the four alleged shooters were indicted for murder and assault with intent to kill. Their *habeas corpus* hearing was held on February 17, but the actual trial was continually delayed. Three days before the initial court date, Brooks was in West Point, a small rail stop between Bastrop and Columbus, inspecting and disarming travelers on the westbound trains. He continued to Bastrop and joined General Scurry, Rogers, Bates, and five Rangers in keeping the peace during the proceedings.[66]

In a subsequent questionable decision, Walter Reese and Jim Coleman were hired as Fort Bend County law officers, and were standing on the Rosenburg depot platform on July 31. While awaiting an arriving train, they spotted passengers Marcus Harvey Townsend, Will and Jim Clements, Augustus Bruce "Gunger" Wooldridge, and Frank Walker "Red" Burford. Reese and Coleman fired into the railcar, and, in the exchange, the former was struck in the hip and the latter was severely wounded by three bullets. The train had started moving even as the first shots rang out, and the fight was quickly over. Burford and Clements were arrested in Houston and remanded to Richmond. They waived examination and each submitted a bond of $250. Reese and Coleman were not charged. When the matter of the Bastrop shooting was finally heard in San Antonio on November 4, 1904, the charges against all the defendants were dismissed. Hard feelings festered for several more years, and Captain Hughes's Company D would have a direct role in the feud's conclusion.[67]

On March 19, 1900, Brooks dispatched Sergeant Bates, Privates A. Y. Baker and Alonzo W. "Lon" Livingston, and Special Ranger John Francis Dunn to scout the pasture of Alice rancher Francis Smithers for cattle thieves. Two days later, they encountered Segundo Perez, Santiago Garcia, and an unidentified Mexican after dusk; the three had roped a steer and were trying to remove it from the ranch. The rustlers forcibly resisted, and Perez was mortally wounded and Garcia received a non-fatal gunshot wound. The third man managed to escape with Garcia into the darkness. Baker sent to Alice for a doctor, and Perez was taken to Corpus Christi, where he died of his wounds.

On the twenty-fifth, a complaint was made against the officers for the shooting, and Brooks went with his men to Corpus Christi where they waived an examination trial and gave bond. He returned to Alice the next day.[68]

The following month, the Wall-Broocks-Border feud, festering for the past six years, erupted into physical violence in San Augustine County. Author Joseph F. Combs, who lived in the area during the feud, believed the trouble began much earlier: "The feelings of both factions were fed by the fires of hate and distrust from the childhood of the young men involved until the parents of these young men also became involved through political difference and the desire to stand by their sons in what they believed to be their duty under the circumstances." Others contend the trouble started while C. Lycurgus "Curg" Border and his partner, Archibald "Arch" Price, were either running a protection racket on area cotton farmers, or aggressively collecting overdue debts for a local storekeeper. More provocative than Border's violent tendencies was Curg's longtime friend, Price, who was a black man, a fact that did not sit well with many people in the red-dirt East Texas country. In both versions of the story, Border and Price fell into conflict with the Wall family during the local elections of 1894. Border was the scion of the powerful Border-Broocks family of landowners, who were loyal Southern Democrats. The patriarch of the latter clan, W. A. "Uncle Buck" Wall, and his sons, George Washington, Lopez "Pez," Ney, Brune, and Eugene Beauharnais, were solid adherents of William Jennings Bryan's People's Party and equally important in the community. Curg and George were particularly bitter enemies, and that hatred only deepened when the Walls led a successful grassroots challenge to the Democrats' hegemony. The Populists carried the race, and Buck was elected county commissioner and George county sheriff.[69]

Regardless of whether the quarrel was started by childhood animosities or political arguments, the young hotspurs of the two factions did provide the impetus toward open hostilities. On April 17, 1900, George, who was thought by his enemies to be an aggressively overbearing officer, jailed the ill-tempered and unbalanced Curg on a charge of disorderly conduct. The sheriff purportedly refused to allow him to post bail, and local legend does not explain how Wall could legally decide on bond, normally a function of the courts. In any event, Curg exacted retribution for the insult four days later when he mortally wounded Wall with a shotgun. The sheriff's brother, Eugene, evened the score by shooting to death Benjamin Carlo Broocks, Curg's cousin, on the courthouse square on June 2. A boisterous mob composed equally of normally law-abiding citizens and troublemakers gathered in town and threatened to lynch the killer. George Wall's replacement in the sheriff's office was Noel Gill Roberts, Eugene's nephew, and he allowed his uncle to remain under house arrest at Uncle Buck's farm. Two days after the latest shooting, Curg, two of Ben's brothers, and a brother-in-law waylaid Sheriff Roberts, his brother Sidney, and their uncle Felix in the courthouse. The fracas left Sidney and Felix dead and the sheriff wounded.[70]

The county was poised to descend into all-out war as both the Wall and Broocks-Border clans threatened to wipe out their respective foes. The state government was called upon to restore order, and the governor dispatched Rangers and militiamen to San Augustine. Arriving in the troubled area with their respective commands on June 6, Captains Brooks and Rogers restored order, arrested belligerents, and guarded and transported prisoners. Sheriff Roberts resigned on the twenty-eighth, and Winfred Bates, recently promoted to lieutenant of Company B, was temporarily appointed in his stead. Lieutenant D. L. Lynch and Private Livingston were named as acting deputies. The Stone Fort Rifles deployed from Nacogdoches, and Judge Thomas C. "Tom" Davis of the Second Judicial District arrived from Center to assist in the disposition of cases. Under the state officers' steadying hands, Eugene and Brune Wall answered for Ben Broocks's murder, and Curg Border was tried for Sheriff Wall's killing. All were acquitted, and the Rangers moved on to their next assignment. Once they left, though, Lopez was bushwhacked on May 30, 1901, as was Eugene on October 25. Uncle Buck, having now lost three sons to violence, led his surviving family members to safer locales. Once passions cooled, Curg was elected sheriff in December 1902, but he abused his authority and his constituents, and was removed from office after less than two years. In May 1904, drunk and swearing to kill his replacement, he was shot through the head while resisting arrest.[71]

In 1899 and 1900, two judges—both unfriendly to the Rangers—separately interpreted the 1874 act authorizing the Frontier Battalion as exclusively giving arrest powers to the major commanding the battalion and the captains and lieutenants. Attorney General Thomas Slater Smith handed down a legal opinion that supported the jurists' contentions. At the behest of the governor, the adjutant general ruled the Rangers would reorganize until the legislature could remedy the situation. The battalion was altered to a paltry four companies of six men each; three of them officers who were the sole personnel accorded the ability to make arrests. In his biennial report, General Scurry recommended the existing regulations be changed to grant all Rangers, regardless of rank, the powers necessary to make arrests and execute criminal process. The force he envisioned would not exceed four companies of twenty privates each and the monthly wages would be increased to attract better personnel for longer periods of time. The adjutant general's suggestions would be incorporated into the forthcoming legislation. The reduced battalion existed from June 1, 1900, to July 8, 1901, when the new Ranger Force was established.[72]

Before Brooks and the rest of the battalion reorganized, another controversy that involved boxing arose in Galveston in early 1901. Members of the local sporting establishment, and that of Chicago, had paired Joseph Bartlett "Chrysanthemum Joe" Choynski, a nationally ranked Jewish light-heavyweight, with an up-and-coming black fighter named John Arthur "Jack" Johnson in an "exhibition bout." In the wake of the Fitzsimmons-Maher match five years earlier, promoters had discovered a loophole in the law banning prizefighting. As long as no money was spent toward the boxers' purses, in wagering, or for admission fees, bouts were classified as exhibitions. Naturally, the expenses and profits of fights were simply handled under the table. The smart money was on Choynski, who had gone the distance with boxing legends Fitzsimmons, Gentleman Jim Corbett, and James Jackson Jeffries. The hard-hitting pugilist's skills were on the decline, but, ironically, some of his greatest fights were still to come. Johnson, a future heavyweight champion who would beat the previously undefeated Jeffries in the 1910 "battle of the century," had heretofore won several contests against relative unknowns. His bout with the veteran Choynski promised to be a boost to an auspicious career. The fight was to be held at Harmony Hall on the night of February 25.[73]

In January 1899, Captain McDonald and members of his company, along with Galveston County law officers, had worked to prevent a match between Choynski and Australian fighter Jim Hall. Two years later, the Rangers returned to the Island for a similar purpose. Captain Brooks, Lieutenants Bates and Baker, and Private John Jesse Sanders first arrived in Houston by train on February 20. They immediately gathered with General Scurry, then went to Galveston on the twenty-first. Meeting District Attorney John Lovejoy at the Tremont Hotel, Brooks and Baker collected information on the prizefight, and the prosecutor agreed to try the contenders once the law was broken. Thereafter, Brooks employed two undercover detectives to search for the sports book believed to be operating in the city. The captain stayed overnight at the Tremont, two more nights at the Washington Hotel, and another two at the Grand Hotel, but was unable to find the wagering exchange. Sanders, Private E. W. Machen, and Private Creed Taylor of Company E joined the rest of the detachment in Galveston on February 24.[74]

The following evening, a large crowd packed Harmony Hall to watch Choynski and Johnson. Brooks and his men were also spectators and succeeded in finding positions at ringside. In the third round, Choynski feinted with his right and hit Johnson—later to be known as the "Galveston Giant"—with a devastating left hook to the head that dropped the younger man senseless to the mat. The Rangers made their way into the ring and arrested both fighters for violating the old law. Amid a booing and jeering crowd, the officers escorted their prisoners to the county jail, where they were held for twenty-four days, although they were released nightly. Brooks left town for other duties on February 27, but returned on March 4 to serve as a witness in the case. Despite the political theater and the convening of three grand juries, no indictments were ever returned against Choynski or Johnson.[75]

Finally, the day of reorganization occurred on July 8. The Frontier Battalion was restructured into the Ranger Force, and dispersed throughout the state in a fashion similar to the earlier outfit. Brooks officially became captain of Company A on July 12, 1901, with his station remaining at Alice. He moved his family into a new home, which also served as company headquarters. The appropriation to field the thirty-two officers and men of the new force was set at thirty thousand dollars.[76]

On August 19, A. Y. Baker and Lon Livingston rode from Alice to Palito Blanco to arrest Pablo Flores. They had apprehended two suspects the day before and left them under the watch of Private Sanders. Once the two Rangers found Flores, he barricaded himself in a house and opened fire on the officers. Baker's rifle jammed, but he merely grinned and began whistling a tune. He then calmly extracted a pocket knife from his pocket and used it as a screwdriver to repair his weapon. With the lieutenant otherwise occupied, Livingston killed their quarry and saved Baker's life.[77]

In May 1902, Brooks and his company were dealing with depredations on the southern ranges of the King Ranch. The captain delegated much of the field work to the tough, experienced Ancey Baker. At the same time, the lower Rio Grande Valley was again ignited by political turmoil. Federal Customs officers, supporters of the Republican "Reds," mobilized the Mexican vote against the Democratic "Blues." The collector of customs castigated the Rangers in his Spanish-language newspaper and incited the existing anger into open violence. Baker and his equally outraged Rangers reacted by intimidating their critics.[78]

On the morning of May 16, Baker, Rangers Harry Wallis and William Emmett Robuck, and Jesse Miller, a King employee, were scouting the seventeen-thousand-acre El Sauz Ranch along the Arroyo Colorado when they encountered Ramón de la Cerda. The latter had tied up several calves and was rebranding one of the animals. Baker and de la Cerda both pulled their weapons and fired. The rustler's bullet struck Baker's horse in the head. While the steed was falling, the Ranger shot de la Cedra above the right eye, killing him instantly. Justice of the Peace Estévan García Osuña and seven witnesses investigated the scene. They noted the calf, the dead horse, and de la Cedra's pistol with one spent shell. With the evidence supporting Baker's plea of self-defense, García filed a record of inquest which ruled the incident a justifiable homicide.[79]

The situation took a dramatic turn at Baker's examining trial when the unsubstantiated results of a second inquest were presented. Justice Encarnacion Garza and another seven witnesses had exhumed de la Cerda's body six days after the killing. They determined the deceased had been bound and dragged before being fatally shot, but their evidence was never entered into the official record. Nevertheless, the three Rangers and Miller were charged with murder. Baker posted a ten-thousand-dollar bond with the aid of prominent supporters, including Captain Richard King and Major John B. Armstrong. The "Blues" and the Rangers considered Garza's work as an effort to portray Baker as a murderer, while "Reds" and other Ranger detractors enthusiastically accepted the findings.[80]

The strong anti-Ranger sentiment in the area only increased the tension and soon led to serious trouble. At ten o'clock on the evening of September 9, Baker, Ranger Robuck, and Jesse Miller were riding from Brownsville on the Santa Rosalia Road toward camp when several shotgun blasts fired from ambush ripped into the group. Baker was severely wounded in the back, Robuck was killed, and Miller's horse was felled. Brooks had earlier learned of a rumored plan to kill Baker, and he subsequently gathered enough evidence to arrest Ramón de la Cerda's brother, Alfredo, and five co-conspirators, including Justice Garza. After Alfredo was jailed, a lynch mob began to gather, and the Rangers were required to protect the man who had allegedly murdered one of their own.[81]

After he was released on bond, Alfredo publicly threatened to kill Baker. The de la Cerda family even offered one thousand dollars for his death. On October 3, the Ranger sergeant inadvertently encountered Alfredo in the Gerónimo Fernández & Brothers dry goods store in Brownsville and shot him. Alfredo would live for another hour before succumbing to his wounds. Baker promptly made his way to Fort Brown, where he stayed for the night. The sergeant was charged with murder and released on bond. Brooks and Baker then traveled by stagecoach to Alice, while the balance of Company A stayed in Brownsville. Claiming self-defense at his February 1903 trial, he insisted Alfredo had attempted to pull a weapon, and he had been forced to respond. The jury believed Baker and he was acquitted. A second jury in September found him not guilty in the death of Ramón de la Cerda.[82]

The volatile de la Cerda incident caught the attention of the administration in Austin. The governor dispatched General Scurry to Brownsville to investigate. Scurry determined Brooks and his men were only guilty of being too sensitive to partisan slurs. He also concluded Company A could no longer remain and effectively perform their duties. Scurry summoned Company D to take over in the lower valley, and Brooks and his men were dispatched to Laredo. Despite the commotion, Company A's service had been notable.

From November 1, 1900, to August 1, 1902, Brooks's Rangers had conducted 289 scouts, and performed 134 arrests, including twelve for murder, six for assault with intent to murder, two for conspiracy to murder, nine for aggravated assault, and forty-five for livestock thefts. They killed three men in the same number of armed encounters, while suffering no casualties themselves.[83]

The Batson oil field in southwestern Hardin County hit its first gusher in 1903, and, in January 1904, Governor Samuel Willis Tucker Lanham directed Brooks to survey the scene. The captain found the town wide open with local officers negligent in enforcing the law, instead willing to let the captain shoulder the burden. Brooks traveled to Austin and delivered his report personally to the governor on February 15. Lanham then instructed the captain to return to Batson in force. Brooks, Sergeant Bates, and Privates Lott Tumlinson and Clyde McDowell arrived in town on February 20. After setting up camp in a grove near town, the Rangers went to work. Since Batson had no proper or even makeshift jail, they shackled their prisoners to trees with chains and locks. Brooks personally arrested fifteen men during the month on charges ranging from disturbing the peace to assault with intent to murder. On busy days, up to a dozen men, usually inebriated to some degree, could be fettered until they were transferred to the county lockup in Kountze. The more civic-minded citizens of Batson would in time pay for a suitable jail.[84]

For the remainder of the year, Brooks and Bates would return time and again to Batson, supplant corrupt local authorities, apprehend numerous criminals, and keep order with steady resolve and the threat of physical force. Such an approach set a pattern in oil boom towns for the next three decades. The company also aided local law enforcement in Hempstead, an eventful railroad town in Waller County known as "Six Shooter Junction," and patrolled Crockett, Dimmit, Kinney, La Salle, Pecos, Val Verde, and Webb Counties. In the midst of his numerous trips to Batson throughout 1904, Brooks was in the coal town of Minera on June 28 and 29. His mission there was to impose order during a volatile labor strike. The town, twenty-five miles northwest of Laredo, had a population of about one thousand immigrants from northern Mexico, most of whom worked in the mines. The walkout was organized by labor union leaders, but did little to produce better working conditions for the miners. Instead, Captain Brooks and a detachment of Rangers arrived in town, and the miners returned to their jobs. The agitators were fired and ordered to leave company property.[85]

In June 1903, developers Carl Frederick Groos and Edwin J. Buckingham had surveyed the land north of Carrizo Springs and purchased the 100,000-acre Cross S Ranch in Zavala County. The ranch was one of the largest in the Southwest until the partners divided it into parcels, and sold lots to create the town of Crystal City. One year later, Brooks would purchase 640 acres less than one mile south of the San Antonio Road and next to an artesian well. Shortly thereafter, while working in Starr County, Brooks met rancher Edward Cunningham Lasater, and the two became fast friends. Lasater established the Falfurrias Immigration Company and invited investors to purchase tracts. The resulting land sales led to the founding of the town of Falfurrias in November of that same year. Brooks made a down payment of $240 for eighty acres, the balance of $960 to be paid in four annual installments at 7 percent interest. Over time, he would purchase five separate tracts in the immediate area that totaled more than fourteen hundred acres.[86]

Thirty-five miles south and west of Batson, oil was located on Moonshine Hill in northeastern Harris County in May 1904. A similar discovery was made two miles west at the small railroad town of Humble. By the end of the year the Moonshine Oil Company and the Higgins Oil Company were sinking wells in the area. On January 9, 1905, the first gusher blew in on Moonshine Hill and led to a tent community bearing the same name. Thirty-one wells were producing an estimated 87,775 barrels per day by March 1905, and some ten thousand people were living in the town where stores, hotels, boardinghouses, saloons, and livery stables were being established. In 1905, the Humble field became the largest in southeast Texas. Similar to Batson, the boomtown attracted unsavory characters, and Brooks went to the Hill on January 25 to restore order. He completed his work by the end of the month and returned to Laredo.[87]

Effective June 1, Adjutant General John Augustus Hulen increased Company A's area of operations to include Kimble, Menard, Tom Green, Kent, Irion, Midland, and Mitchell Counties. Still based in Laredo, Brooks focused his attentions to the north and west of his home station. He and his men would work cases in Abilene, Odessa, San Angelo, and Midland, among other locales, over the following two years.[88]

The lower Rio Grande Valley would still require his attention, as was proven in Brownsville. William Thomas Eldridge, a prominent sugar planter in Eagle Lake, had been embroiled in a feud with William Meriwether. Eldridge had been the victim of a botched assassination attempt, and Brooks traveled to Brownsville to investigate. The captain mediated what he believed was a truce and returned to Laredo. However, Meriwether and a companion were murdered, and Eldridge was arrested for the crime. He was later acquitted due to the lack of concrete evidence.[89]

In quiet times, Brooks returned to his ranch in Starr County, where he had moved his family earlier in the year. In addition to the earlier land purchases, he began working with Ed Lasater on political matters. Brooks quickly ran afoul of County Commissioner Manuel Guerra, the political boss of the county for a decade, and an ally of Democrat *jefe político* Jim Wells. A tense peace had existed between the political factions of Guerra, then-Sheriff Wash Shely, and County Judge John R. Monroe. The truce would end with Shely developing a debilitating mental disorder and leaving office on November 6, 1906, and with the arrival of Lasater. The latter, a formidable Republican, developed his own influence in the northern reaches of Starr County, while a fuming Guerra watched from his powerbase in Rio Grande City.[90]

The November 1904 elections had proven contentious. Lasater arrived at the county seat the day before the polls opened and chided Guerra for the numerous armed "deputies" roaming the streets. Guerra responded the only trouble would be started by the Falfurrias rancher's partisans. In front of a growing number of spectators, Lasater then suggested a unique solution:

> Tomorrow on election day, suppose we de-deputize every deputy sheriff in Starr County, and as the polls open at seven in the morning you will sit in your chair on one side of the entrance of the voting place and I will sit in my chair on the other side. We will each hold a cocked .45-automatic pistol pointed at the other. Should any of my men get out of line in any way whatsoever, you will shoot me; if any of your men get out of line in any way whatsoever, I will shoot you.

With the crowd watching, Guerra had no choice but to accept the challenge. The two power brokers sat in their chairs for twelve hours the next day without any trouble or need for gunplay.[91]

With the truce over, the 1906 elections promised to be even more antagonistic. Guerra supported his cousin Deodoro Guerra in the race for sheriff, and Lasater put up Deputy Sheriff Gregorio Duffy, a Democrat who had broken with the Guerra machine. Two other members of Manuel's family were campaigning for other county offices, which made the sheriff's contest vital. The Democratic political bosses in the lower valley were alarmed at the prospect of a Republican victory in Starr County, and all were determined to block any disruption to their control.[92]

District Judge Stanley Welch, a fervent Democrat and crony of the Wells-Guerra machine, came to Starr County to supervise the election, and influence the results. The nine special deputies already on duty were supplemented by forty-one more whose task was to shepherd Democratic voters to the polls. Once the estimated fifty Lasater partisans arrived in town, the atmosphere became even more ominous. The night of November 5 proved raucous with a number of drunken brawls that left one of Lasater's men near death. Indeed, the commotion drowned out the sound of the gunshot that killed Welch while he lay in his bed. When the jurist was missed on the morning of the election, District Attorney John I. Kleiber went to his room and found him dead. Even the judge's murder could not change the inevitable outcome of the election as the loyalist Democratic candidates were swept into office. Deodoro Guerra won the sheriff's office by sixty-three votes.[93]

On November 14, 1906, Brooks submitted his letter of resignation to take effect the following day. He referred to pressing "private business" that required his personal attention. The high regard he enjoyed was reflected in the letter he received from the adjutant general:

> The Governor, as well as myself, deeply regrets that it becomes necessary for you to leave the Service ... You have made an enviable record, and the loss of your experience to the State cannot be estimated. You have always most faithfully and excellently performed your duties, and you

can and doubtless will, look back upon your long service as an officer of the State with pride and satisfaction.[94]

By the summer of 1908, Brooks and Lasater were thoroughly engaged in the struggle for political dominance in northern Starr County. The two spent hours in discussion with other allies, and all came to realize the best option was not to fight the seat of power to the south. Instead, they had to create a new county encompassing the Falfurrias area. The first step in achieving this goal was to elect someone to the state legislature who could then wield their influence. Brooks did not consider himself a politician, but he was accorded a wide measure of respect due to his two decades of public service. He announced his decision to run for the seat in the Ninety-fifth Legislative District. He campaigned primarily in the northern part of Starr County and in Hidalgo County, both of which comprised the district. Brooks was elected to the Thirty-first Legislature and took his seat on January 12, 1909, determined to get the bill passed that would create a new county. Among his legislative appointments were assignments to the Public Building and Grounds Committee, the Commerce and Manufacturing Committee, and, demonstrating the reach of his political backers, the chairmanship of the Committee on Counties.[95]

On January 25, Brooks presented House Bill No. 238, "An Act to create and establish the county of Falfurrias." The bill was read for the first time and referred to his own Committee on Counties. The committee did not recommend the proposal pass, and Brooks wrote the minority report on February 9. The Speaker laid the bill before the House for a second reading on February 17. Franklin Oliver Fuller of Cold Springs offered an amendment that defined the county as an area comprising nine hundred square miles taken from Starr, Hidalgo, Nueces, and Duval Counties. The bill passed a third reading on March 2 and to engrossment on March 9, but the regular session adjourned on March 13 before any further action was taken.[96]

Even while he pushed his personal agenda, Brooks was one of seven legislators who introduced House Bill No. 409 on February 12 that provided for the Ranger Force's organization, proscribed its duties and powers, and regulated its compensation. The measure received a favorable report, but died on the Speaker's table. Two special sessions then followed in the spring, and two more in the summer of 1910, but Brooks's county bill was never placed on the House's agenda. He continued to lobby for his proposal in Starr County and in Austin, even during adjournments.[97]

Running for re-election, Brooks defeated Finis Lafayette Marshall in the July 1910 primary before being returned to the House by his constituents in November. He answered the roll call on January 10, 1911, as he took his seat for the Thirty-second Legislature. On January 19, he sponsored House Bill No. 94, which was read and referred to the Committee on Counties. Brooks did not serve on this body in the new session. The bill narrowly survived the committee debate and was amended on February 7 to designate the proposed county's limits. It passed the House by a vote of 103 to two, and was sent to a committee run jointly with the state senate. The bill passed the Senate on March 2, and a conference committee of five members was appointed to ready it for final passage. Five days later, the completed legislation came out of committee bearing the name of Brooks County, grateful admirers having entitled the county made from portions of Starr, Hidalgo, and Zapata Counties after him. The House voted 107 to one for its passage, and the Senate unanimously approved the measure. Governor Colquitt signed the bill into law on March 11.[98]

Brooks resigned his House seat after the regular session adjourned in order to focus on getting the county officially organized on September 1. The elections for local offices were held the next day, and Brooks was chosen as county judge. In his new role, Brooks dealt with misdemeanor crimes, the setting of bonds, the issuance of search warrants, appeals from justice of the peace and municipal courts, marriage licenses, and motor violations. Among his other responsibilities was chairing the county commissioner's court and serving as *ex officio* superintendent of the public school system. He also managed the building of the first county roads and bridges.[99]

In his twenty-eight years on the bench, Brooks held office through the terms of six county attorneys, five sheriffs, and three county clerks. After Brooks County was organized, Ed Lasater switched to the Democratic Party, which would reign supreme until 1992. Judge Brooks was supported in his election bids by Lasater's political machine, but he seems never to have been a minion of the county boss. After his first reelection in 1913, he ran virtually unopposed for the next nineteen years. In 1932, Lee Allison Dickey managed a serious campaign, but Brooks prevailed in the July primary by a comfortable margin. He won the November election running as the only candidate. In the campaign for his fourteenth and ultimately last term, the venerable judge met three challengers for his office. He handily beat his opponents in the August primary and the November general election.[100]

While Brooks was in the forefront of the county's political and social elite, his life in Falfurrias experienced at least one terrible shock. Virginia died on January 3, 1928, due to complications from an acute intestinal obstruction. She was buried in the Alice City Cemetery.[101]

Even before his last electoral victory, Brooks's health had begun to fail. After he resumed his place on the bench on January 1, 1939, his left ear grew cancerous and a portion had to be removed. The combination of his years in the Rangers and his decades-long alcoholism left him physically unable to continue in office. Thirty days after assuming office for the fourteenth time, he stepped down from his post. In his last years, Brooks lived in his son's home. He died peacefully in his sleep on January 15, 1944, of acute cardiac dilatation as a result of "nephritis chronic servility." He was interred in Falfurrias Burial Park.[102]

Corrinne never married and worked as a bookkeeper for the First National Bank of Falfurrias. She also refused to forgive Brooks for the manner in which he had treated her or for his alcoholism. She died at Brooks County Hospital on January 29, 1980, of cardiac arrest after a prolonged illness. Curiously, she was buried next to her father.[103]

Morgan graduated from Falfurrias High School, then enlisted in the U.S. Army at Fort Sam Houston on August 7, 1917. He served in the Army Motor Transport Corps during World War I, and was assigned to Motorcycle Company No. 301. Morgan sailed from Hoboken, New Jersey, to France aboard the *Cedric* on September 29, 1917. His unit saw action on the Western Front with the Quartermaster Corps. Brooks debarked St. Nazaire aboard the USS *Mongolia* on June 26, 1919, and arrived in Boston on July 6. After his discharge on July 15, he attended Texas A&M University for two years before returning home to manage the ranch. He served as a deputy sheriff for many years. He married music teacher Gladys Opal Spark on September 7, 1933, and they adopted an infant girl in 1941. When Captain Brooks became ill, Morgan assisted him in the office. He replaced his father as county judge, and served until December 31, 1970, when he retired for health reasons. Gladys died of pneumonia on May 3, 1978, and he followed her in death on December 13, 1983. They were both interred in Falfurrias Burial Park.[104]

James Abijah Brooks was, without a doubt, a flawed man. Sadly, his fondness for a bottle contributed to his failings as a husband and father. However, in twenty-three years as a Texas Ranger, he achieved an impressive record of apprehendeding lawbreakers and safeguarding the lives and property of honest citizens. As the twentieth century dawned, he offered firm leadership while the Frontier Battalion transformed into the Ranger Force. His continued undertakings for the State of Texas as a legislator and county judge remained consistent with his earlier contributions. A faithful public servant, he was the first of the "Four Great Captains."

William J. McDonald. Portrait from glass plate negative. George Grantham Bain Collection. *Courtesy Library of Congress, Washington, D.C.*

Chapter 10

William J. McDonald: "Faced Death with a Calm Certainty"

William Jesse McDonald was the best known of the Four Captains. His deserved reputation as a law officer was enhanced by his self-assured nature, his flair for showmanship, his demonstrable marksmanship, and the publicity he received for his abundant and colorful exploits. Paul N. Spellman commented: "McDonald never saw a reporter or a photographer he didn't like, and his exploits, though not necessarily more exciting or dramatic than the others, nevertheless became the stuff of which legends and myths are made." Indeed, folklore credits him with inspiring the often-repeated "one riot, one Ranger" mythos. Regardless of his theatrics and his gift for coining a phrase, McDonald faced dangers with a calm certainty and a deadly aim. However, more important than any manhunting or gunfighting, McDonald made significant contributions toward refashioning the Rangers' law-enforcing methods. He understood the modern requirements for evidence collection, report writing, and courtroom testimony that were becoming necessary in a changing Ranger service.

He was born in Kemper County, Mississippi, on September 28, 1852. His father, Enoch McDonald, had been born in Georgia in 1826, and Eunice (Durham) McDonald, his mother, in 1831 in North Carolina. "Bill Jess," as his family called him, had one older sister Mary, who was born on August 2, 1849.

The family worked a 160-acre cotton farm valued in 1850 at fifteen hundred dollars. While Albert Bigelow Paine, McDonald's first biographer, wrote the land was worked by "half a hundred slaves," only three men and three women were kept in 1850, and five women and three men ten years later.[1]

The issue of slavery, the secession crisis, and the resulting civil war would profoundly impact the young Bill Jess McDonald. In the national debate over the Compromise of 1850, Enoch, although a slaveowner, identified as a member of the Union Party in Mississippi. Favoring Senator Henry Clay's proposal, the organization drew strength from both Whigs and Democrats who denounced secession as unconstitutional. Later in the decade, Enoch returned to the Democratic Party, and was named a delegate for Kemper County to the state convention that convened on July 4, 1859. His views on secession shifting, he attended a local meeting in the county courthouse on November 19, 1860, and sat on a committee that drafted resolutions favorable to severing ties with the Union. Once the state seceded, Enoch enlisted in the Fortieth Mississippi Infantry at Meridian, and was elected major on July 22, 1862, to take rank from May 14. Serving in Sterling Price's Army of the West, he was killed at the battle of Corinth on October 4, 1862.[2]

Once she learned of her husband's death, the newly widowed Eunice McDonald set to managing the family's three farms, complete with gin house, and raising her young children in a war-torn Mississippi. A woman of iron will, she convinced her former slaves to stay and work the land. As hostilities ended, she was able to sell a cotton crop for twenty-five cents per pound. In 1867, Eunice decided to take Mary and Bill and move to her brother Thomas's 156-acre farm near Henderson in Rusk County, Texas, where she kept the house. A shooting affray occurred in Henderson between a man named Tutt and another named Durham on December 28, 1866. Durham was wounded in the leg and required an amputation to save his life. Whether this was Thomas J. Durham is unknown, but Eunice's brother was reportedly an ailing man, and he died within a year or two of the McDonalds' arrival. Ownership of the farm then passed to another brother, David D. Durham. Although Paine wrote that the McDonalds lived in genteel poverty, Eunice was a shrewd businesswoman who had sold some of her Mississippi property and livestock while renting out other lands.[3]

On April 3, 1869, Colonel Peter V. Green stopped at the widow Griffin's cabin near Millville in Rusk County for a meal. Drunk and offensive, Green was taken by a gang of five freedmen outside where he was severely beaten, then lynched from a hickory tree. Seeking vengeance three days later, Captain Charles M. Green, the colonel's brother, and fifty armed accomplices seized five black men, who had been arrested for the crime, from the county jail. The masked vigilantes dragged their prisoners to the town square where they were hung from the limbs of shade trees. Shortly afterward, federal troops arrived to investigate.[4]

As he was related to the Green family, McDonald was allegedly involved in the affair to some extent. Whether he was present at the storming of the jail and the hanging of the five prisoners is unknown, but he did participate in a running fight between Captain Green and Yankee soldiers at Henderson. Taking cover in the courthouse, the bluecoats were able to capture and disarm Green when he attempted to carry the building. McDonald withdrew, but he resolved to rescue his kinsman. Before the release could be organized, though, the regulars moved Green to the military stockade at Jefferson. McDonald persisted in gaining Green's liberation, and was arrested while "nosing" around the enclosure holding the captain. Charged with murder, Green was eventually tried, convicted, and sentenced to prison; McDonald was acquitted.[5]

Whether his recent choices had stemmed from wartime sufferings, the death of his father, or the travails of Reconstruction, McDonald's narrow escape from a prison sentence, or worse, seems to have led him to choose a different path. Resolving to pursue a career in business in 1871, he borrowed funds from his mother and enrolled in George Soule's Commercial College, a New Orleans business school established in 1856. In addition to the commercial curriculum, Soule taught his students mathematics, science, and languages. Following graduation and a short stint of teaching penmanship, McDonald acquired capital from relatives, and purchased a ferry business and a store at Brown's Bluff on the Sabine River in Gregg County. Restless for new opportunities, he moved to Mineola in Wood County in 1873, to open the dry goods and grocery firm of W. J. McDonald & Company on South Johnson Street. Borrowing more money from his mother, he went into partnership with a

Durham cousin. Additionally, McDonald diversified his commercial interests to include 105 acres in land and thirteen town lots.[6]

While McDonald was developing his business, he was also active in community affairs. During the congressional convention at Sulphur Springs on September 2, 1874, he was a member of the Committee of Platform and Resolutions. Moreover, he was an officer in Lodge No. 502 of the Ancient Free and Accepted Masons, and built McDonald Hall, the first opera house in Mineola, in 1877. Located on Front Street, the structure was two stories, with the Masonic hall and entertainment amenities upstairs. In June 1878, he was a delegate to the Tenth District's senatorial convention.[7] One of the prominent citizens of Mineola McDonald befriended early in his residence was District Attorney James Stephen Hogg. The relationship between the two men was often volatile with disagreements over politics, but Hogg did introduce McDonald to his future bride. Indeed, the latter married Rhoda Isabel Carter on January 13, 1876, in Quitman. A local girl, she had been born on January 22, 1858, the daughter of a successful attorney and land owner.[8]

Throughout its existence, the grocery firm struggled financially, and had become insolvent by 1877. McDonald's debts amounted to eighteen thousand dollars while his assets, including goods, notes, and real estate, totaled sixteen thousand. On September 1, fifteen creditors, who were owed $13,712, agreed to receive all assets owned by W. J. McDonald & Company as payment for the debt. Other individuals who had outstanding claims declined to accept this resolution, but before they could take legal action the company's holdings were yielded to a receiver. McDonald unloaded some of his assets, while others were sold at discount prices in a sheriff's sale. To extricate himself from his financial entanglements, McDonald sold off personal property, including real estate, to reimburse several creditors, including his uncle and his brother-in-law. Other parties sued McDonald to recover the monies owed them. By the summer of 1885, the various court cases were settled, with one winding its way through the legal system to the state supreme court.[9]

Albert Paine related how McDonald made the gradual choice to pursue a life in law enforcement. Apparently, George Gordon, a local bully, came into town with a bulldog that attacked and injured McDonald's "prized pointer." McDonald threatened to shoot the dog, and a chastened Gordon swore to keep the animal at home. As he had backed down the intimidating man, McDonald decided to apply for a job as a deputy sheriff of Wood County.[10]

No primary evidence could be found to either confirm or refute the story, but McDonald was working for Sheriff Fielden P. Dowell when he confronted criminal James "Jim" Bean in Smith County. Bean had been convicted of burglary and scheduled to be transported to the penitentiary when he escaped from the Tyler jail in June 1881. On August 13, McDonald had business in the area, and, making inquiries at a cabin, learned the fugitive was hunting in the Sabine River bottoms. The deputy soon found Bean, and approached to within fifty yards before he was noticed. Ignoring the command to halt, Bean attempted to raise his shotgun to fire, but McDonald was too quick, and shot first. The outlaw dodged behind his horse, then a tree, before fleeing into the brush. McDonald followed the trail on horseback, and came across the fugitive's boots, shotgun, and blood-covered shotbag. Afoot, Bean could cross the sloughs of the Sabine easier than the mounted officer and thus made his escape. While returning from a manhunt for Jim Bean and his brother Edward (or "Ed"), the newspapers noted McDonald and a fellow deputy named Reeves passing through Palestine on August 29, 1882. The lawmen had followed two suspects across Anderson, Leon, and Robertson Counties. When they finally confronted their quarry in Brazos County, McDonald and Reeves discovered that, while the descriptions matched those of the brothers, they had followed the wrong men. In any event, justice prevailed two months later when Jim was seriously wounded by a posse near Sunset in Wise County. He was extradited to Kansas to face charges of murdering Caldwell City Marshal George S. Brown, but died of his injuries in Wellington on November 5. Back in Texas, Ed Bean was arrested and charged with the May 21, 1883, murder of farmer and ferry-owner Charles Stevens in Gregg County. First prosecuted by District Attorney Hogg in June 1884, Bean was twice convicted and granted new trials based on technicalities before he finally pled guilty in June 5, 1885.[11]

The business environment of Mineola waned in the early 1880s, and McDonald decided he would seek his fortunes in other locales. In 1884, he and Rhoda drove a cattle herd across the state to Wichita County. He later sold some of his cattle, purchased four town lots in Wichita Falls, and established lumber yards in Wichita Falls and Harrold. After about a year, McDonald sold out and moved his stock to Hardeman County to start ranching on 640 acres along Wanderers Creek; his herd averaged between two to forty horses and twenty-seven to three hundred head of cattle. McDonald experimented with the raising of goats, which ultimately failed, grew wheat, and advanced a prosperous irrigation project that involved the damming of the nearby creek. Beginning in 1887, he would also own three to eight lots in town, and entered the local Masonic Lodge. By 1891, he had acquired four more properties totaling 1,283 acres, which he owned for almost a decade. Even when they lived elsewhere in the coming years, the McDonalds would continue to call Hardeman County and the town of Quanah their home.[12]

Early in 1887, McDonald became a deputy for Sheriff James Milton Allee, and he often rode with Company B of the Frontier Battalion in pursuit of malefactors. Sheriff Allee's office was understaffed, and the county and state officers cooperated in manhunts. Sometimes the Rangers, under Captain Samuel Alexander "Soft Voice" McMurry, remanded their prisoners to the care of the county jail. On February 20, the Rangers went to Greer County and captured Jink Williamson, an alleged horse thief. Given into McDonald's custody, the prisoner struck the deputy and bolted. McDonald shot at the fleeing outlaw, but missed, and Williamson escaped. When not chasing desperadoes together, McDonald and some of the men of Company B eagerly played small-stakes poker, "a ranger obsession of courting the sense of personal luck while enjoying the fickle play of fate."[13]

The deputy sheriff soon became known as "the avenging angel of the Hardeman frontier" and "the most feared lawman in a 3,500 square mile region." On March 25, he arrested four men in possession of the same number of possibly stolen horses, and apprehended alleged horse thief Frank Grissom on April 8. Riding to Kirkland five days later, he and Ranger Dennis A. Peal (or Peale) arrested R. R. Blankenship, who was wanted in Coryell County for stealing horses. On September 10, McDonald and three Rangers left Quanah and rode approximately seventy-five miles to Cottle County in search of William "Billie" Trumble, a dangerous horse thief, fence-cutter, and murderer. They returned three days later without having sighted the fugitive. Another scout on the fourteenth, looking for suspected rustler Lee Hickman, covered 120 miles in a drenching rain and was similarly unproductive. As further proof of his commitment to the law, McDonald preferred to spend the Sabbath searching the county for signs of cattle rustling. He quickly discovered one indication was the presence of cowhides missing the area that should have been marked with a brand. If a cow was suspected of having its brand altered, an irrefutable method to prove the charge was to kill the animal, remove the skin, and inspect the underside. The legitimate owner's original mark would show plainly, unlike the thief's newer brand. Any rustler who wanted to conceal evidence of his wrongdoing after skinning the cow would cut away the brand entirely, but, ironically, this only served to demonstrate his guilt. As for McDonald, Professor John Miller Morris observed he "excelled at the detection of altered brands and hides, approaching it as a deductive challenge to his mind."[14]

Bill and Bood Brooken, known as "two wild and crazy brothers," led a band of violent horse thieves in stealing stock along the Wichita River. Hiding out in the cedar brakes, they sold their stolen horses in Hardeman, Greer, and Wilbarger Counties, and rewards for their arrest totaled two thousand dollars. In addition to usurping other men's property, they ambushed and murdered William Turner, an old gang associate, near Seymour on March 14, 1887. Paine credited McDonald with personally arresting Bood and forcing Bill to run for Mexico, where he was later captured. The deputy may have accompanied the posse that struck an outlaw hideout in the Wichita brakes near Seymour on July 10, but the objects of their manhunt—Bill Brooken and Pete Rose—were alerted to the lawmen's presence and fled. In actuality, though, beginning on April 6, 1887, Wilbarger County Sheriff W. N. Barker and Captain McMurry directed the lengthy effort that ended the Brooken gang by the middle of 1888.[15]

Regardless of whether he had led the chase, McDonald was granted a commission as a Special Ranger on March 18, 1889, which enabled him to pursue fugitives across county lines. As such, he worked up cases with Company B, or on his own.[16] McDonald shortly thereafter received another badge when he became a deputy U.S. marshal for the Northern District of Texas. According to one story, U.S. Marshal George A. Knight asked McDonald the nature of his politics, and the latter responded, "I am the damndest, hell-roaringist, all-firedst Democrat you ever saw; if politics has anything to do with this appointment, I'd just as well go back." The marshal responded, "Well, you're pretty emphatic but your kind of politics seems to suit the job well." As a federal officer, McDonald developed a particular technique for catching outlaws. Going undercover, he assumed various false identities in order to collect information on the criminals in his jurisdiction. For instance, in the guise of a fruit tree salesman, he collected orders that would go uncompleted, but he also gathered intelligence on perpetrators, their associates, and the locations of stolen property. In late February 1890, McDonald went into the Indian Territory with a number of warrants. Near Kingfisher, he encountered seven men, four of whom he sought for violation of federal laws. The band quickly had the marshal covered and forced him to withdraw. McDonald promised to return and, two weeks later, he fulfilled his vow; two of the outlaws soon found themselves in jail.[17]

In addition to his achievements in the field of law enforcement, McDonald enjoyed a long-standing friendship with Jim Hogg, who was elected governor in 1890. McDonald had chaired the Hardeman County Democratic Convention, which supported Hogg in the recent campaign. He likewise backed his old friend for reelection two years later. Once McMurry retired on January 31, 1891, McDonald's loyalty, and his well-earned reputation as a peace officer, led to his being appointed captain of Company B, effective February 1. He joined his new command in Amarillo on January 29. Disembarking from the Fort Worth & Denver train around midnight, the captain rented a hotel room and went to bed. He was just falling asleep when a messenger awakened him with an important telegram: hostile Indians were depredating in Hall County, approximately one hundred miles southeast of Amarillo. McDonald initially thought his new subordinates were playing a trick on him. After all, raiding Indians had ceased to be a concern ten years ago. Instead, McDonald returned to bed until more messages arrived, all claiming the same news as the first. Not crediting the alarm, but still obliged to investigate, McDonald dressed and made his way to the telegraph office. After receiving more information, he arranged for a special train ride to Salisbury in Hall County.[18]

When the captain and his men reached the town, they found Salisbury seemingly abandoned and its citizens hiding. McDonald soon found that an

Eastern tenderfoot had been unnerved by a pack of drunken cowboys carousing around their campfire. While the rumors had raced across the Panhandle, so much so that newspapers took them seriously, the Rangers only lost sleep, and returned to Amarillo.[19]

The Rangers of Company B, and the citizens of the Panhandle, soon learned a new kind of leader was in charge. Slightly under six feet tall with dark mustache and muttonchops, Captain McDonald was lean with an air of authority. Eugene Cunningham recalled him as, "tall, angular, at once awkward-seeming and cat-quick on his feet, his lined face was weathered to the rich red-brown of saddle leather, and made notable by prominent nose and gray-blue eyes of a live, alert directness." James Ransler "Jim" Gober, the first sheriff of Potter County, observed: "McDonald was altogether a different kind of character than McMurry. McDonald was seeking a reputation as a notorious general and was somewhat boastful of his adventures in capturing or killing outlaws, but he seemed to be friendly with me." Although arrogant, courageous, and tenacious, McDonald's greatest weakness was his inability to admit when he was wrong. Any man who did not adopt his point of view was viewed as an enemy. Historian Ben H. Procter commented: "Ranger Captain Bill McDonald was an uncomplicated man, unwilling—or unable—to view life in complex form. To him no shades of gray existed." On the other hand, while other captains were able to impartially enforce the law in the numerous feuds that wracked Texas, McDonald sometimes became part of the problem.[20]

McDonald was assuming his command at an uncertain time. Members of the legislature proposed abolishing the Frontier Battalion in January of 1893. The *Dallas Morning News* reprinted an *Amarillo Northwestern* editorial on February 2, 1893: "We think such action at present by that honorable body would not be prudent, from the fact that the ranger force is of great service in aiding to capture outlaws who have been forced out of more thickly settled portions of the state to the territory and many of the sparsely settled counties of northwest Texas."[21]

Frequently headquartered in Quanah or Amarillo, his company ranged across the breadth of the Texas Panhandle. The size of the region, coupled with the limited number of local law officers, compelled the Rangers to deal with every type of crime, ranging from misdemeanors and minor felonies, including disturbing the peace, public drunkenness, adultery and bigamy, and larceny, to major offenses, such as assault, bribery, embezzlement, forgery, burglary, train robbery, stock theft, rape, and murder. A recurring problem in the Panhandle was the conflict between the cattle barons, such as Charlie Goodnight and Murdo Mackenzie, and small-scale ranchers, nesters, and Grangers. McDonald was often called upon to keep the peace between the large cattle ranchers and those who built towns, organized counties, and represented an end to the old ways. In the first three years of his tenure, the Rangers worked with local sheriffs and judges, testified in court, served criminal process, guarded jailed prisoners, and generally kept the peace. One particularly troublesome area was the tier of counties adjoining New Mexico, which was a haunt for cattle rustlers and horse thieves. He also dealt with outlaw gangs who congregated in the sand hills along the Red River in Greer and Hardeman Counties before fleeing into Oklahoma Territory, and provided protection to the Texas & Pacific rail line out of Fort Worth.[22]

In July 1893, Sheriff John Pearce Matthews of Childress County paid a visit to McDonald in Quanah. The county officer requested the assistance of a Ranger to apprehend Joseph Preston "Joe" Beckham, the fugitive sheriff and tax collector of Motley County, and an enemy of Matthews. Ordered to halt his pursuit at the Red River, Ranger Robert B. McClure accompanied Matthews, Childress County Commissioner George W. Cook, another of Beckham's foes, and Sheriff Jeff Davis Harkey of Dickens County. When the officers reached the state line, Matthews convinced McClure to continue, even though they had no legal authority in the Indian Territory. Beckham was subsequently captured, and turned over to the sheriff at Cloud Chief. Matthews pinned the blame for the illegal arrest on McClure, and McDonald was compelled to go to the Territory and secure his subordinate's release. Despite their chicanery, Matthews and Cook were unable to hold onto Beckham, as the latter successfully filed a writ of *habeas corpus*.[23]

The renegade lawman hurried to Quanah and surrendered himself to McClure on August 14. He begged the Ranger to escort him to Matador and protect him from Matthews and Cook. The two took the train for Motley County the next day and, when they stopped in Childress, Matthews appeared and demanded McClure hand over Beckham. The Ranger refused, and Matthews organized a mob to force the issue. McClure returned Beckham's pistol, and instructed him to defend himself. The Childress County sheriff was forced to back down, and the Ranger and his prisoner reached Matador on August 16. Several days later Matthews was in Quanah demanding in "very severe language" McDonald discharge McClure. The captain refused, which only served to enrage the sheriff even more.[24]

This was not the first time Matthews had run afoul of the law, or confronted a law officer. In 1890, he had fled a murder charge in Franklin Parish, Louisiana, where he had killed a riverboat captain. In Amarillo, working as a ranch foreman, he clashed with two Rangers in a saloon brawl and developed an intense loathing for the entire service. This grew to include McDonald who had had no role in the fracas. Notwithstanding his dealings with state officers, Matthews was elected sheriff on November 4, 1890, and again on November 8, 1892. In the latter year, McDonald and Matthews were both attending the annual sheriff's convention in Houston where McDonald took umbrage at an insulting remark Matthews made about the governor. Beginning with Paine, some accounts have depicted Matthews as a renegade killer with a badge. This is both erroneous and biased. Matthews did possess a temper, and reportedly hated to be thwarted in his wishes, but he also provided effective service to his constituents.[25]

After a night of hard drinking, Matthews and deputies Cal Dykes and D. S. Smith were in Quanah on December 9 for two appointments with Hardeman County Sheriff Richard Poteet Coffer. Following time spent in a saloon and a restaurant, the men from Childress County, and Coffer, headed for the Fort Worth & Denver train depot just before six o'clock that evening While en route, they encountered McDonald in the middle of Main Street between the depot and the opera house. Angry words between Matthews and McDonald led to an exchange of gunfire at point-blank range. McDonald was hit in both shoulders with one bullet exiting his neck and the other breaking ribs and puncturing a lung. In his subsequent monthly report, McDonald stated his belief that someone besides the sheriff shot him. Matthews was struck twice over the heart, but the bullets were stopped by a "big plug of tobacco" and a "book of papers" in his pocket. At the end of the shooting,

Matthews bore two mortal wounds on his back caused by firearms of different calibers. He may have been accidentally shot by his own deputies. The sheriff expired on December 30 of blood poisoning.[26]

In the aftermath of the shooting, McDonald received a letter from Motley County Sheriff William Moses requesting three or four Rangers join a manhunt along the line between King and Stonewall Counties. The sheriff was pursuing seven or eight outlaws wanted for robbery and horse theft, including Joe Beckham, who was free on bail and awaiting trial. Unable to respond himself, the captain sent Sergeant William John L. Sullivan to join Moses on December 20. The posse conducted an unsuccessful ten-day scout through Motley, King, Stonewall, and Dickins Counties. Meanwhile, McDonald slowly and painfully recovered from his wounds, especially the damage to his lungs and bones. He was forced to stay in bed for months, and a blood clot in his brain caused a temporary bout of blindness and delirium. McDonald was indicted for his role in the gunfight with Matthews, and pled not guilty at his preliminary hearing; he posted bail and continued his convalescence. His defense attorney argued at trial the fatal bullets had been fired by other persons at the depot, and McDonald had only acted in self-defense. On May 16, 1894, he was acquitted of the charges. Even as his case moved through the court system, the McDonalds went on a short vacation to Shreveport and Austin. Once he had mended, the captain returned to duty.[27]

In March 1894, Colonel Robert Dickey Hunter, president of the Texas & Pacific Coal Company, had reduced the wages of his coal miners in the company town of Thurber. In response, the miners threatened to strike, and Hunter requested assistance from Adjutant General Woodford Haywood Mabry. McDonald and three men arrived in Thurber, seventy-five miles west of Fort Worth, on June 8. He quickly discovered Knights of Labor activists—known as "walking delegates"—from Oklahoma Territory were agitating for a strike. The union firebrands were headquartered in "Jimmie Grant's" saloon three-quarters of a mile from Thurber. Since the building was in Palo Pinto County, the agitators remained safely outside the jurisdiction of the Erath County authorities. Miners were lured to the watering hole on Saturday and Sunday afternoons with the promise of free beer. After a sufficient amount of time, Messrs. Bruce and D. W. Stewart, the proprietors, and the union men addressed the now tipsy miners on the evils of the company. Several days later, Hunter enforced mine safety policy by dismissing every miner who was still under the influence of alcohol. In return, he and his foremen were subjected to death threats, pamphlets were distributed, and rumors circulated that dynamite would be dropped into the pits if the entire work force did not quit.[28]

Consulting with Hunter, and attending a union meeting, McDonald calmed the commotion and advised mine management, workers, and strike advocates that he meant to keep the peace. The union speaker was attempting to convince the miners to dynamite the mines when McDonald intervened and told the assembled workers they were being led into trouble that would land them in prison. The majority of the miners merely wished to return to their jobs, and for the union interlopers to leave them alone. The laborers requested Ranger protection when they went to the mines, and McDonald assured they had nothing to fear. The activists admitted defeat and peaceably returned to Oklahoma.[29]

The following month, another labor dispute flared in Texas when the American Railway Union, organized by socialist labor activist Eugene Victor Debs, called for a nationwide strike against the Pullman Palace Car Company of Chicago. The immediate catalyst was the cutting of wages for workers while the company attempted to adjust to the ongoing Panic of 1893. Between June 26 and August 2, the boycott closed rail traffic in twenty-seven states from Illinois to California. The movement of agricultural products, raw materials, and finished goods halted, while tracks and switches were sabotaged and train cars were burned. President Grover Cleveland ordered federal troops and U.S. marshals to put down the strike, which outraged union supporters throughout the entire railroad industry. Mabry proactively dispatched Companies B, D, and F to ride trains from Galveston to Fort Worth to the Red River. McDonald himself went to Wichita Falls to keep order in the rail yards there. There were several small outbreaks of trouble, but the further use of federal soldiery and court actions finished the strike. The American Railway Union did not survive the end of the labor crisis.[30]

Following in the footsteps of Sam Bass, scores of Texas outlaws set their sights on the numerous railroads crisscrossing the state. On October 19, 1894, one such gang struck the Texas & Pacific line near Gordon in Palo Pinto County. Sam Baker, Ben Hughes, and two other desperadoes forced the locomotive to stop, and robbed the express car of thousands of dollars. Local posses and McDonald's Rangers were quickly on the trail. Beginning on the twentieth, Sergeant Sullivan and a detachment scoured Palo Pinto, Jack, Erath, and Young Counties for six days without success. However, on November 15, Sullivan's squad captured three men who were suspected in the robbery, and another the following day. Theorizing Hughes would go to his brother in the Indian Territory, McDonald crossed the Red River, but to no avail. Meanwhile, federal officers eventually wounded and captured the fugitive at Checotah on February 27, 1895. Another robber was taken into custody without incident, and the fourth surrendered himself to the U.S. marshals. Baker was killed in a personal altercation.[31]

While Sergeant Sullivan's detachment was engaged in their manhunt for the Hughes gang, they were informed of a group of suspicious characters encamped on Sid Webb's ranch near Bellevue in Clay County. The Rangers tracked the men to a house on November 14, 1894, and surrounded the building. The suspects blazed away at the lawmen, and Sullivan and his men returned fire. The fusillade forced the outlaws into the loft, and Sullivan and Private William J. McCauley (the captain's nephew) kicked down the door and threatened to burn the house. Four members of William Tuttle "Bill" Cook's gang—Thurman "Skeeter" Baldwin, William Farris, Jess "Buck" Snyder, and Charles Turner—surrendered and were taken into custody. The Rangers and other law officers later escorted the prisoners to Fort Smith, where three of them received long prison sentences.[32]

Cook fled across Texas into New Mexico. He was captured by Sheriff Thomas Decatur Love of Borden County, Texas, and Sheriff (and Deputy U.S. Marshal) Christopher Columbus "Charley" Perry of Chaves County, New Mexico, at a sod house near old Fort Sumner on January 11, 1895. Love, Perry and Sheriff Young Douglas McMurry of Mitchell County, Texas, escorted their prisoner to Fort Smith, where he was convicted and received a forty-five-year prison sentence at Albany, New York.[33] Sullivan claimed credit for supplying Perry with the crucial information necessary to take Cook. The monthly return supports his assertion he was in New Mexico, but he seems to have been left out of the capture. For years, he remained bitter over the perceived slight and the loss of any reward money.[34]

Even with the Cook gang eliminated, the Panhandle country was still overrun with desperate criminals. In the mid–1890s, George "Red Buck" Weightman was one of the most wicked outlaws at large in Texas and Oklahoma Territory. In addition to committing armed robbery and horse theft, the "foul-mouthed, evil minded, vicious" Red Buck was a hired killer with a standing fee of fifty dollars. A complete badman, he had allegedly been expelled from Bill Doolin's gang for murdering a preacher. Red Buck and his gang were spotted on West Cache Creek near the Wichita Mountains and, after murdering a Waggoner Ranch cowhand and bungling a robbery of the Hightower Brothers store in Altus, they left the Indian Territory one jump ahead of the law. The outlaws crossed the Red River and committed another failed robbery, this time at the D. Waggoner & Son General Merchandise Store on the Fort Worth & Denver rail line near the present town of Electra. McDonald dispatched Sergeant Sullivan and five Rangers to pursue and capture the brigands; Wichita County Constable Tom Pickett, Wilbarger County Deputy Sheriff Johnny Williams, City Marshal Charley Landers of Vernon, and Special Ranger Bud Hardin of Harrold accompanied the state officers. The posse faced Red Buck, Elmore "Kid" Lewis, Hillary "Hill" Loftis, and ex-sheriff Joe Beckham at a dugout on Suttle Creek twenty miles north of the Red River on December 27, 1895. In the ensuing stand-off amid blizzard conditions, Weightman was wounded, but he, Lewis, and Loftis escaped. The body of Beckham, who had been fatally shot through the eye, was left behind by his companions. Sullivan hauled the slain fugitive lawman to Harrold in a buckboard and buried him in the local cemetery.[35]

In February 1896, virtually the entire Frontier Battalion was sent to El Paso to prevent a boxing match. The prizefight, featuring pugilists Robert Prometheus "Ruby Bob" Fitzsimmons and Peter "the Galway Giant" Maher, was promoted by Dallas gambler Daniel Albert Stuart and the members of El Paso's sporting community. The city was selected as a venue due to its proximity to Juárez and the empty lands of New Mexico and Arizona, as well as for its well-deserved reputation for being a rowdy, wide open town.[36]

Operating under London Prize Ring Rules, the sport of bare-knuckle boxing in Europe and America had possessed a sordid reputation for decades. Associations with the urban criminal underworld, gambling, ringside riots, and accusations of fight fixing had discouraged acceptance by society. Even after the London code had given way to the Marquis of Queensberry Rules, which introduced five-ounce gloves, three-minute rounds, referees, and the ten-second knockout rule, prizefighting still did not achieve respectability. The practice had been prohibited in Texas the year before, and Governor Charles Allen Culberson directed Mabry and his men to enforce the law. The adjutant general, McDonald, and Company B arrived in town on February 9. Captains John H. Rogers, John R. Hughes, and James A. Brooks, and members of their respective companies were also present. In all, thirty-two Rangers had been dispatched. Sergeant Sullivan recalled, "We ... had to put down the tough element of the town, as thieves, robbers, pickpockets, and other classes of criminals were giving a great deal of trouble." One instance included Sullivan and his colleagues arresting twenty-six burglars in a single night. He continued, "I can safely say that I saw more tough characters in El Paso at that time than I ever saw before in my life, or ever expect to see again." Among the throng in town for the fight was sportsman and gunfighter William Barclay "Bat" Masterson. He and five experienced gunmen had been imported by Stuart from Denver to oversee the bout's security.[37]

While progressive reform normally called for government and citizens to work together for social change, the unilateral decisions by the governor and the legislature became more statist in nature when faced with limited community support. In El Paso, the townspeople were divided over the governor's move to prohibit the match, but many more resented the sudden invasion of Texas Rangers. Together with General Mabry and the other captains, McDonald watched as the ring paraphernalia was unloaded. As Stuart, Fitzsimmons, and Maher went about town, they were followed by a captain and one or two Rangers. McDonald was assigned to personally watch the movements of the match's promoter. The lengthy delays before the fight commenced caused many spectators to leave town until there were fewer than five hundred left on the nineteenth. After having combed for a venue, including Ciudad Juárez, Stuart finally settled on a sandy island in the middle of the Rio Grande near

Langtry—a piece of land technically owned by Mexico. He was aided in his search by Judge Roy Bean, the saloonkeeper and justice of the peace, who promoted himself as "the law west of the Pecos." Just before midnight on February 20, a Southern Pacific train with two engines and ten passenger cars departed the El Paso depot and headed east. While waiting for the train, at least twenty people in the crowd had been relieved of their valuables by diligent pickpockets. The Rangers were unaware of Stuart's plans and, still determined to halt the bout, joined the growing multitude of promoters, newspaper reporters and fight enthusiasts on the train. The twenty-six state officers watched the match two days later from a bluff on the Texas side of the border. The *Chicago Dispatch* succinctly described the conclusion of the nine-month spectacle: "As we understand it, Mr. Fitzsimmons walked up to Mr. Maher yesterday, pushed his hands down and struck him violently on the jaw. There isn't anything else to tell."[38]

According to Paine, the train trip to Langtry possessed the most exciting event of the whole affair. In his book, McDonald's first biographer related a story, almost certainly invented, of events that occurred during the lunch stop in Sanderson. McDonald was in a Chinese restaurant when Bat Masterson became impatient with the slow service of his waiter. Even though the food was later described as a "diabolical meal of greasy boiled cabbage, half-cooked ham, hot bread, cheese, pie and a vile imitation of coffee," Masterson decided to correct his server's lethargy with a table caster. McDonald, who had been sitting quietly nearby, rose and took the gambler by the arm. "Don't you hit that man," he ordered. "Maybe you'd like to take it up," retorted Masterson. McDonald gave him a cold look and answered, "I done took it up." Fortunately, neither man was a hot-headed fool, and the matter ended without gunplay.[39]

The story became widespread and has been echoed numerous times.[40] Some years after the Fitzsimmons-Maher bout, Masterson became a sportswriter, and he categorically denied being involved in any altercation with McDonald. In several of his columns in the *New York Morning Telegraph*, Masterson asserted that he had seen no Chinese waiters and denounced the tale as "a brazen, cowardly lie." He further accused Paine of being "an accomplished liar, a hack writer who eked out a precarious living peddling his goulash to magazines at so much a word."[41]

William Barclay (Bat) Masterson. # 216222. *Courtesy Kansas State Historical Society, Topeka, Kansas.*

Interestingly, in his *Frontier Times* magazine, J. Marvin Hunter seems to have given Masterson the benefit of the doubt while still wanting to tell a good story. The venue was changed to Roy Bean's Jersey Lilly saloon, the nationality of the waiter became Mexican, and the impatient diner was recast as an anonymous member of the sporting crowd. The gambler loudly demanded the server bring the food and "do it damned quick." McDonald objected to the tone and told the tough that was no way to speak to a man, even if he was a Mexican. The challenge to take up the fight was the same as told in the earlier version. When the captain responded, the desperado finished his meal while carefully watching McDonald, and wisely took his leave.[42]

While the Frontier Battalion was engaged in the Fitzsimmons-Maher fight, two men robbed the City National Bank of Wichita Falls on February 25. The thieves took six hundred dollars in gold and silver, and left cashier Frank Dorsey dead and vice-president Doctor O. J. Kendall and bookkeeper P. P. Langford wounded. Deputy Sheriff Frank B. Hardesty wounded one of the bandits' horses, forcing them to ride double to escape town. The robbers later changed horses twice. The same day, McDonald and most of the company entrained from El Paso to Fort Worth. While stopped in Bellevue, the captain received a telegram describing the holdup. He arranged for horses to be waiting for the company at the Wichita Falls depot and boarded the next train. The Rangers arrived that evening, then rode out of town to overtake a posse that had already started out in pursuit. The Rangers met the party of local officers and citizens as they were returning, having failed to apprehend the bank robbers. McDonald informed them he and his men would continue the chase. The posse members were motivated by the captain's resolve, and agreed to accompany the Rangers. Later in the night, McDonald and two of his men found the suspected robbers resting under a tree near the Red River. Elmer "Kid" Lewis and Foster "Bill" Crawford both clutched cocked pistols, but decided surrender was preferable to exchanging gunshots with the more numerous Rangers and possemen. The law officers returned to Wichita Falls and placed their prisoners in the county jail. McDonald and his men kept vigil at the building, and they dispersed a gathering crowd of angry citizens.[43]

Feeling local officers and twenty-five deputized citizens had the situation well in hand, McDonald again departed for Fort Worth on the twenty-sixth. Subsequent events proved the captain wrong. That same night, the jail was surrounded by an orderly yet determined mob numbering three to five hundred people that overpowered the one deputy guarding the prisoners, trussed Lewis and Crawford, and dragged them from their cells. Outside the bank where the robbery had occurred were two ropes hanging from a telegraph pole. Lewis cursed the unmasked vigilantes as they placed nooses over the killers' heads while Crawford begged for mercy. Undeterred, the crowd hoisted the robbers into the air, and the bodies were not taken down until early February 27.[44]

Penning a scathing complaint to Governor Culberson, Judge George E. Miller of the Thirtieth Judicial District rebuked McDonald for failing to protect the prisoners while the chance of a lynching was to be expected. The governor referred the matter to General Mabry. McDonald insisted he had fulfilled his "whole duty" and, once Lewis and Crawford were confined, his responsibilities had ended. In addition, his company was needed elsewhere. He further defended himself by blaming Judge Miller for blocking an attempt to move Lewis and Crawford to the Fort Worth jail. Except for the other cases awaiting his attention, the captain's excuses were ridiculous. McDonald had promised Lewis and Crawford his personal protection and spent the first night safeguarding the jailhouse. Secondly, the judge was quite vocal in objecting to the Rangers' departure from Wichita Falls hours before the lynching, appealed to the mob to spare the prisoners, and vigorously instructed the grand jury to pursue the matter. Five murder indictments were returned, but, while Miller was indisposed, the vigilantes escaped justice through a clever act of legal maneuvering. In another example of his inability to admit a mistake, McDonald was likely embarrassed by the entire episode, and reluctant to further expose his blunder to public scrutiny.[45]

The Wichita Falls incident was one example, however brief, of the recurring problem of vigilantism. Historian and folklorist Charles Leland Sonnichsen observed a pattern that often transpired when people took the law into their own hands over the course of years: "At the start, a vigilance committee might enroll only the best citizens; but as time went on, bad men crept into the ranks. Inevitably these tough birds made mistakes and hurt or scared good people, who immediately took the other side. In the end there was complete confusion and hell to pay." McDonald dealt with members of such an organization, one more insidious than the norm, in San Saba County in 1896. The Buzzard's Water Hole Mob (the name was taken from their preferred meeting place) was believed to have descended from a vigilance committee that had plagued Brown, Comanche, Hamilton, and Lampasas Counties in the 1870s. The association's victims were cattle rustlers, horse thieves, blacks, and sheepherders at first, but grew to include men with valuable property, those who had not heeded a warning to leave the area, and a brave few who criticized the group in public. Once the railroad's arrival ushered in the rule of law, the vigilantes relocated to San Saba, Mills, and McCulloch Counties in 1884. For the next twelve years, the San Saba Mob grew to approximately several hundred members, and they murdered between twenty and fifty men in ambushes, their signature trademark being nine bullets to the body. Despite secrecy rituals, the identities of the leaders were common knowledge, and included prominent stock-raisers, clergymen, the sheriff, and other local officials. Those who were not active members were too cowed to resist the Mob's rule. Beginning on May 15, 1888, Sergeant John H. Rogers of Company F spent two days investigating a "notice to leave" addressed to William Madison "Matt" Ford, John Harris, and other citizens of San Saba and Mills Counties. Rogers's inquiry appears to have ended after he was unable to pierce the wall of silence.[46]

With two more homicides, the vigilantes' reign of terror was exposed to the public, and the course of San Saba County was forever transformed. Thomas Elijah "Lige" (or "T. A.") Henderson refused the Mob's order to leave, and was murdered on June 22, 1896. William Alexander James followed him in death on July 28. In response, Judge William Mack Allison of the Thirty-third Judicial District was pressured to request General Mabry to post a Ranger detachment north of the county seat on the Colorado River. Only four men could be spared from other duties: Edgar Thomas Neal and Allen R. Maddox sent from Rogers's company on August 10, and Sergeant Sullivan and Ranger Dudley Snyder "Dud" Barker from McDonald's. Sullivan was placed in command of the detachment, which was stationed at Hannah's

Crossing in Mills County, twenty miles from San Saba. From the beginning, county residents who were members of the Mob made clear their opposition to the Rangers' mission.[47]

Sergeant Sullivan was cut from the same cloth as his captain. He was brave, active, clever, and skilled at gathering evidence. Unfortunately, his tall, burly physique and thick beard complemented his towering ego. His role as detachment commander, and his direct access to the adjutant general, made his usual arrogance even more pronounced. Initially focusing on the William James homicide, Sullivan turned to the murder of James R. Turner, an elderly man who had been bushwhacked on his Knob Ridge farm on July 19, 1889. The Ranger sergeant pinpointed three of the killers in a few weeks and, moving his detachment into town on October 16, amassed evidence and the testimony of 339 witnesses for the prosecution; the process lasted into January of the following year. Walter Courtney Linden, the recently elected district attorney, worked enthusiastically with Sullivan's detail and decided to take the case to trial. On October 23, he convinced the grand jury to return indictments for murder on William Ford and George Washington Trowbridge, two of the men Sullivan had identified. Judge Allison granted a change of venue to Austin, but Ford's trial resulted in a hung jury in March 5, 1897. He was tried a second time with over two hundred people attached by the state as prosecution witnesses, but the jury deadlocked once more and was discharged on June 24. Following his indictment, Trowbridge's case was continued until June 9, and his trial ended on the twenty-second with the jury members also unable to agree.[48]

At the same time, Sullivan's conceit brought him down. Sheriff Andrew Jackson Hawkins, a pawn of the Mob, was ordered to instigate a confrontation with the aggressive Ranger sergeant. Obeying his instructions, Hawkins met Sullivan inside the courthouse in March 1897, and goaded the latter into pulling his sidearm. Ranger Neal interceded, and Judge Allison ordered the state officers out of the courthouse. In the street, they continued to be disruptive, and the judge, possibly sympathetic to the vigilantes, requested Mabry remove Sullivan from the county. McDonald and Ranger Robert McClure arrived in San Saba on May 4 to assess the situation. The captain warned his sergeant about his haughty attitude and alcohol consumption,

W. J. L. Sullivan. #1975/070-4530. William Deming Hornaday Collection.
Courtesy Texas State Library and Archives Commission, Austin, Texas.

but he convinced Mabry to return Sullivan to San Saba. The adjutant general agreed, but he also directed McDonald take personal command of the detachment. The criticism and being superseded caused Sullivan to feel slighted. Growing resentful through June 1897, he shirked his duty in favor of fishing trips and poetry writing, and asserted that he, not McDonald, was personally responsible for the company's successes. He then turned to bouts of heavy drinking with the Mob leaders, including the sheriff. He staggered drunk into camp on July 2, after having first become lost. The next day he returned to the saloon to once more imbibe with his new companions. The captain demanded his resignation.[49]

However, McDonald was equally contentious in his dealings with the factions of San Saba County. His belligerent canvass for witnesses, and his scornful attitude toward Sheriff Hawkins, did nothing to defuse the situation. He did, nevertheless, accumulate evidence and secure testimony through the summer and fall. The district attorney believed McDonald overenthusiastic, but also acknowledged the captain was ably carrying out his mission.[50]

Some of the alleged vigilantes the captain was investigating were friends of Judge Allison. The jurist attempted to have the Rangers returned to the Colorado, and later to Richland Springs, sixteen miles up the San Saba. These two locations guaranteed the finding of witnesses would prove impossible. McDonald countered that the county seat, where the Mob was headquartered, was where he needed to be. Whatever his faults, McDonald was a relentless detective. Thanks to the efforts of the captain and his company, District Attorney Linden was able to secure indictments from the grand jury in December 1897 for seven of the Mob's members. They were promptly released on bail by Judge Allison, but the organization had become so unnerved that they could do little besides hurl empty threats. Yet, the Mob was not broken and, indeed, only William Alvin "Bill" Ogle, convicted in Llano County of first-degree murder in May 1898, went to prison. After losing his appeal on June 20, 1900, Ogle entered Huntsville on November 12 to begin his life sentence. The cases of the remainder, including Ford and Trowbridge, were continued from one court session to the next until they were finally dismissed.[51]

McDonald and his Rangers did not subdue the San Saba Mob, but they did provide the means for Linden to ultimately do so. The seven Mob members whom Linden had indicted attempted to threaten the prosecutor on April 27, 1899, but he met them in the streets with a pistol. Linden instructed them to leave the county or face a harrying in the courts so severe he would financially ruin them all. The malefactors sold their assets and fled. Authoritatively chronicling the entire episode, San Saba historian Ross J. Cox, Sr. concluded: "The San Saba Mob was ... the most unique mob or vigilante organization ever known ... The Mob was also the most unusual, as it combined assassination with all of the trappings of secret fraternalism. Nowhere else was there such a strange mix of prayer, ritual and murder. Despite its original intent to protect property and lives and expel criminals, it developed into the most violent, destructive and destabilizing force the state ever knew. Although broken, it was never completely eradicated."[52]

Later in 1899, McDonald was sent to Colorado County to keep order during the Townsend-Reese feud. The quarrel had originated in a contest for prominence between the Stafford and Townsend families, who were once the two most politically powerful blocs in the county. Competing for cattle grazing rights and elected offices, both clans courted the decisive black vote. In December 1871, the war of words briefly flared into outright violence with a non-fatal shooting involving cattleman Robert Earl "Bob" Stafford and Sumner Townsend, a brother of Sheriff James Light Townsend. Four days following the clash, Captain L. H. McNelly of the State Police, accompanied by a private, arrived in Columbus and arrested the participants of the fight. The subsequent court proceedings resulted in nothing more severe than a levying of fines.[53]

Despite the gunplay, the dispute smoldered for nearly twenty years before blood was once more spilled. On the evening of July 7, 1890, City Marshal Larkin Secrest Hope, a nephew of Sheriff Townsend, escorted a drunk and disorderly Warren Decatur Stafford from a county-wide barbecue being held at The Grove, a park near Columbus. On the way to a holding cell, the marshal intentionally led the manacled youth down Spring Street, past his mother's house, in a seemingly provocative manner. Soon after, Warren's father, Bob Stafford, by now a wealthy cattle baron, and his uncle John confronted Larkin and Samuel Marion Hope, the latter's brother and chief deputy, outside the Nicolai saloon. Having previously arranged for the marshal's discretion regarding his alcoholic son, Bob was enraged the agreement had been broken in such a publicly insulting fashion. As he angrily shouted invectives at Larkin, the officer suddenly pulled his pistol. Three bullets mortally wounded Bob, and an unarmed John received a gunshot from Marion. Larkin ensured Bob was dead, then finished off the dying John, who had fallen into the saloon. Larkin stood trial for killing the Stafford brothers and, despite strong circumstantial evidence of premeditation, was eventually acquitted of the charges; the indictments against Marion were later dismissed.[54]

Several years later, Larkin Hope, having lost the marshal's office due to the Stafford killings, was serving as a constable. He was running against the incumbent sheriff, Samuel Houston "Sam" Reese, in the 1898 election when he was bushwhacked by an unidentified, shotgun-wielding rider on August 3. James Henry "Jim" Coleman, a close friend of Reese's two sons, was strongly suspected of committing the murder, and Reese was believed to have masterminded the deed. The sheriff was never charged, although he lost the election to newcomer William Thomas Burford, who was a brother-in-law of political boss Marcus Harvey Townsend. The latter was nephew to Light Townsend and one of the youngest men elected to the legislature. After several continuances and a change of venue to San Antonio, Coleman was acquitted due to lack of evidence.[55]

The Larkin Hope homicide was the true genesis of the Reese-Townsend feud, which grew out of the earlier Townsend-Stafford quarrel. Interestingly, unlike other vendettas, the extended Reese and Townsend factions were largely related to one another by blood and marriage, which created a peculiar alignment of conflicted loyalties. On March 16, 1899, Sam Reese, still fuming over losing the election, was on Main Street when he intervened in an argument between an acquaintance and Deputy Sheriff William D. Clements. Heated words led to a clash between Reese and Clements (Reese's nephew and a first-cousin, once removed, to Light Townsend), and Mark Townsend, Augustus Bruce "Gunger" Wooldridge, and Marion Hope quickly became involved. City Marshal William Robert "Bob" Walker and several citizens ran to support Reese. In the ensuing shootout, the ex-sheriff went down with a severed carotid artery. Local farmer Charles Boehme, an innocent bystander, also lay dead. Johnny Williams, a six-year-old boy, had been standing in his yard nearby when the bullets began flying. He was struck in the hip, which left him crippled for life.[56]

Governor Joseph Draper Sayers ordered McDonald and two Rangers from Hughes's company to investigate the shooting and restore order in Columbus. The captain's party reached town on March 22, and two Company B privates from San Saba soon also arrived. "The district judge and district attorney both informed [McDonald] that it was impossible to handle the situation," Adjutant General Thomas Scurry noted in his annual report. "But he told them that he could make the effort, and he gave the members of each faction a limited time in which to get rid of their weapons, stating that he would put those in jail who refused to comply. His orders had the desired effect." McDonald mostly persuaded the participants to cease and desist, although Will Clements narrowly escaped being murdered on the night of March 28. Clements, Hope, and Townsend were arrested on a charge of manslaughter, and, although the Reese killing bore indications of a premeditated and staged altercation, they were never prosecuted. The captain left town at the end of the month. Unfortunately, peace in Colorado County would prove an illusion. McDonald returned several times in the next year, working in conjunction with captains Brooks and Rogers to quell the bloodshed.[57]

San Saba and Colorado Counties were not the only examples of an inclination for private justice. Even as the new century neared, various parties in Texas were still determined to settle differences in the frontier style. On the evening of May 23, 1899, a band of armed men assembled in western Henderson County and rode toward the home of James Knox Polk Humphries. Early the following morning, the nightriders pushed their way into the farm house and, professing to be lawmen, questioned Humphries on the location of a suspected killer of a constable. They then forced the farmer outside, and all rode to the neighboring homes of his sons, John Samuel and George Washington. The three Humphries were taken to the Cedar Creek bottom and hung by the neck from the stooping trunk of a hickory tree. After the lynching, the victims were buried in a common grave.[58]

One of the ringleaders of the lynch mob was Joseph L. Wilkinson, a long-time resident of the county who worked as a farmer. In his memoir,

Wilkinson justified his actions by claiming he and his followers were upholding law and order and stopping dangerous criminals controlled by the Humphries family. In this particular case, the vigilantes were certain Jim Humphries and his boys were harboring James Patterson, who was suspected of murdering Constable John Rhodes. Actually, Patterson was at large in another state and read of the hangings in a newspaper. He returned to Henderson County and was arrested for the Rhodes murder. Wilkinson claimed another reason for the lynching was the stealing of his hogs. A grand jury had indicted the Humphries brothers and Patterson on a charge of theft. George and John posted bond, but Patterson absconded. The perceived leniency of the court supposedly induced the vigilantes to take drastic steps. Writing in 1989, Jim Monaghan, who married into the Humphries family, disputed Wilkinson's claims of selflessly serving the law. The former compiled the details of the case, and observed in Wilkinson's book the two most obvious reasons for the lynching: "First, that [the Humphries men] knew of Wilkinson's bootlegging activities and were a threat to reveal these facts ... Second, that they knew Wilkinson had sold the hogs ... to someone in Corsicana while they were still obligated as collateral on a loan held by a bank in Athens that Wilkinson had not paid off." Justice of the Peace Elihu H. Green conducted a two-week inquest into the triple homicide, and took sworn statements from witnesses. Also arriving in the Trans-Cedar area to investigate, Sheriff Knox Richardson and his deputies arrested John Greenhaw, Joe Wilkinson, and Wilkinson's son, Walter, for their role in the mob violence.[59]

One or two weeks after the lynching, Governor Sayers offered a two-hundred-dollar reward for the capture and conviction of each participant in the crime. The executive ordered Assistant Attorney General Ned Bradford Morris, on May 31, to give his "earnest and undivided attention" to cooperating with local officials in closing the case. To aid Morris and County Attorney Stephen Faulk, Sayers also requested, on June 3, that District Attorney Jeremiah Mitchum Crook of the Third Judicial District come to Henderson County. Two days later, McDonald and Private Augustus Yardley "Augie" Old of Company E were ordered to proceed to Athens and work with the prosecution team. McDonald arrived on June 7, and immediately traveled to the Trans-Cedar country in a buggy drawn by two horses. The captain and

Old worked up the case by collecting evidence, securing witness statements, taking suspects into custody, and guarding their prisoners in jail and at the examining trial. They brought a sense of comfort to the county residents, as they promised to remain until the killers were apprehended.[60]

In the course of the investigation, three of the vigilantes, John and Arthur Greenhaw and Polk Weeks, confessed and turned state's evidence. In addition, members of the Humphries family identified the voices and unmasked faces of some of those culpable. The analysis of physical evidence, such as the ropes used in the hangings and the tracks of the horses, were also instrumental. By the end of the month, Joseph and Walter Wilkinson, W. B. Brooks, Edward Cain, John Gaddis, Sam Hall, W. A. Johns, and Bob Stevens were arrested and charged.[61]

As the case moved into the trial phase, McDonald and Old assisted the local lawmen in maintaining the peace, escorting the defendants to and from the courtroom, and summoning witnesses. They also arrested other lawbreakers for crimes not pertaining to the trial, including carrying a pistol, public fighting, being drunk and disorderly, and disturbing the peace. Beginning in December 1899 and finishing the following August, the trials of each of the eight defendants ended in guilty verdicts. They were sentenced to life imprisonment at hard labor in the state penitentiary at Rusk. The Greenhaws and Weeks had their cases dismissed in return for their testimony. McDonald completed his role in this sad affair by escorting the convicted men to prison on August 22, 1900.[62]

Long debated by newspaper editorials and the legislature, the battalion's necessity and indeed its legal status was to come under the most intense scrutiny in its existence. While continuing to work in the Trans-Cedar, McDonald, Sergeant W. J. McCauley, and Privates Eugene Bell, T. Lawrence Fuller, and Nat B. "Kiowa" Jones were sent to Orange County on September 23, 1899, to halt a violent mixture of partisan politics, labor disputes, and racial bigotry. The perpetrators were a gang of "whitecappers" who were attempting to drive black laborers from their jobs at the local lumber mill. Joining Augie Old, who had been in town for a month, the company arrested five individuals in September, twenty-five in October, twenty-three in November, and twenty in December on charges that included murder and conspiracy to commit murder, adultery, aggravated assault, arson, disturbing the peace, robbery, and theft.[63]

On December 21, a man assaulted Fuller with a knife while attempting to free a prisoner. The Ranger shot and killed his assailant who turned out to be Oscar Poole, son of County Judge George Franklin Poole. Fuller was arrested and, on January 13, 1900, finally allowed to post a three-thousand-dollar bond by Judge Stephen P. West of the First Judicial District. The shooting was ruled justifiable homicide, but the grand jury surprisingly indicted Fuller for false imprisonment. The charge stemmed from Fuller and Private Andrew Lawrence "Lou" Saxon jailing five men for disturbing the peace in November. Judge Poole, considered a leader of the whitecapping mob, had instructed the jury that the Rangers did not possess legal authority to make the arrests. Saxon had pistol-whipped one of the drunken cowboys, and was charged with the same misdemeanor offense as Fuller. [64]

On May 21, 1900, Saxon was also found guilty of false imprisonment in Memphis, Hall County. He was fined fifty dollars and sentenced to thirty days in jail. While adjudicating the case, County Judge William Merritt Pardue, Jr. ruled on the 1874 frontier protection law that created the Frontier Battalion. He interpreted the wording of the statute to invest only the commissioned officers with the power of arrest. Enlisted Rangers did not possess that authority and thus, he charged, Saxon was guilty of making illegal arrests. Fuller and Saxon were assigned to other locales while their cases progressed through the courts. The latter would be pardoned by Governor Sayers on June 8. Nevertheless, the matter was a source of concern to state officials. The governor requested that Attorney General Thomas Slater Smith render an opinion on the issue of whether enlisted Rangers held arrest powers. On May 26, the attorney general declared, "Non-commissioned officers and privates ... referred to as 'Rangers' have no authority ... to execute criminal processes or make arrests." With one stroke of the pen, only four men in the entire battalion enjoyed the authority of peace officers, although the rank and file could assist them.[65]

General Scurry responded with General Order No. 24, which reorganized the battalion until the legislature could rectify the defective law. Beginning on June 1, four companies consisted of a captain, a first lieutenant, a second lieutenant, and three privates, while two companies were comprised of a first lieutenant, a second lieutenant, and two privates. Six of the old battalion's privates were promoted to first lieutenants, and another five were made second lieutenants. The new officers had to agree to serve for less pay: fifty dollars a month for first lieutenants, or the monthly wage of a sergeant, and thirty dollars for second lieutenants, the same wage as privates. Scurry also discharged all the Special Rangers and ordered them to return their warrants of authority.[66]

Even as their organization was undergoing a historically significant change, Fuller's trial on the false imprisonment charge was finally scheduled, and McDonald, Fuller, and Saxon went back to Orange on October 14, 1900. The captain had not been in favor of returning, and subsequent events proved him correct. Fuller, who had recently been promoted to lieutenant, and Saxon were in Adams's Barbershop the next afternoon. Saxon was sitting in a chair for a shave while Fuller was washing his face in a basin. As the barber applied a straight razor to Saxon's lathered face, a man bearing a Winchester rifle appeared in the front door. The man raised his weapon and shot Fuller in the temple. The Ranger dropped to the floor and his twitching legs soon stilled. The killer, still armed, fled to the butcher's shop next door. Local officers soon arrived, and they took Thomas F. Poole, brother of the man Fuller had killed the previous year, into custody. Fuller was the only Ranger under McDonald's command who would lose his life in the line of duty.[67]

Although he rushed to the scene upon hearing the shot, McDonald was not the one who would apprehend Tom Poole. He later expressed regret for being unable to kill Fuller's murderer. Indicted for first-degree homicide, Poole was predictably acquitted of the crime on May 4, 1901. On March 12, 1902, he was killed by City Marshal James A. Jett, who was in turn murdered by George H. Poole, Tom's brother, exactly two months later.[68]

As the Frontier Battalion was disbanded on July 8, 1901, and the new Ranger Force took its place, McDonald continued to serve as commander of Company B at Amarillo. The first few years of serving in the Ranger Force were routine. Company B and its captain performed 150 scouts in their jurisdiction and made 211 apprehensions, including thirty-eight cattle rustlers and horse thieves, five murderers, twelve robbers and burglars, and 118 minor offenders. They escorted prisoners, guarded five jails, testified at trials, assisted twenty-five district courts, aided other civil authorities on five other occasions, intervened in labor disputes, and enforced local liquor option laws. In a general reshuffling of company headquarters following the Barker-de la Cerda incident in Brownsville, McDonald and his men were transferred from Amarillo to Fort Hancock in West Texas. The captain and four of his men left for their new station on December 17, 1902. The rest soon followed.[69]

Despite being assigned to West Texas, McDonald and Private Manoah George "Blaze" Delling were sent to Walker County the next year to assist the sheriff in investigating a murder in Kittrell's Cut-Off. The captain's experience in East Texas would see him working cases in that region for the next several years. On December 4, 1903, farmer Bob James was waylaid and killed while driving a horse-drawn vehicle near his home. The sheriff responded to the scene, and employed bloodhounds to track the bushwhackers. Unfortunately, the trail was obliterated by hunters. McDonald and the sheriff labored to obtain witnesses and break down alibis in spite of intimidation from the guilty parties. On the fourteenth, the two lawmen arrested ringleader Buck Shaw, Charley Rhoden, and Plummer Clark. The prisoners were sometimes held at the prison at Huntsville for "safe keeping." The cases against Shaw and his accomplices, some of whom were held without bail, continued through the courts for several years. In the end, all were acquitted.[70]

According to McDonald's monthly return for March 1904, Paine's book, and later accounts, Mary Jane Touchstone was brutally murdered near Groveton in Trinity County in 1903. Rumored to possess a large stash of money, the elderly lady was seized by a group of relatives who attempted to force the location of the secret hoard from her. When they failed, they beat her with a stick, cut her throat, and discarded her remains in a doorway for the hogs. Touchstone's killers then searched her dead body and ransacked the house and found only one dollar. Trying to disguise the murder as an accidental death, the guilty parties scattered, with the understanding two would return to dispose of the body. Unfortunately for them, the corpse was discovered first. The two major issues with this version are that the monthly return for Febuary 1904 names the victim as "Mrs. Thomas," and, secondly, no record of a woman named Touchstone living in Trinity County at the time has been uncovered. There was a Mary Jane Thomas, who was described by the 1900 federal census as a sixty-eight-year-old widow living in Pennington. The same lady died on September 6, 1903, but her death certificate lists the reason for her demise as being an "accidental fall." The possibility the wrong name was recounted in McDonald's report and Paine's book is open to discussion. Equally debatable was that Mrs. Thomas's cause of death was erroneously entered into the official record before suspicions were raised, and the ruling was never changed.[71]

Regardless of the victim's true identity, Trinity County authorities opened an investigation into her death. Company B became involved on February 3, 1904, as the inquiry was going cold. Working the case, McDonald and Delling collected physical evidence, including burnt matches found under the house that had been used in a futile search for the supposed money. Their labors culminated in the arrest of Albert "Ab" Angle on the eighth in Walker County. On February 16, the grand jury indicted six other men as accessories, and all but one were arrested by McDonald and Delling the same day. Other suspects scattered, and McDonald was compelled to apprehend one in Shreveport, Louisiana, on March 14. Angle initially confessed to McDonald and District Attorney A. M. Campbell, County Attorney Howard Leonidas Robb, and Ned Morris, who had been hired to assist in the prosecution. Angle also implicated several friends and family members. He had been told by the prosecution team that he would be granted immunity if he admitted his role. In a hearing, Angle contradicted his earlier statement, to the extent his testimony became worthless. Coerced by his family, Angle then recanted his confession during a grand jury session. McDonald and the prosecutors obtained an indictment of Angle for giving a false statement. He pled guilty, was convicted on October 10, 1904, and received a three-year sentence. As Convict No. 24625, Angle entered Huntsville on the same day, but was released on June 22, 1907, a few months early. The remainder of Mary Jane Touchstone/Thomas's murderers escaped justice.[72]

In April 1905, President Theodore Roosevelt paid a visit to Texas. He traveled by train to Dallas and Austin, then San Antonio. One significant item on his schedule was attending a reunion of the Rough Riders in the latter city. Once the president had finished gathering with his wartime comrades, he traveled to Fort Worth to meet those who would accompany him on a hunting trip to the Big Pasture of Oklahoma Territory. Invited by Comanche chief Quanah Parker, Roosevelt's presidential party were the five most prominent cattle ranchers who were leasing 300,000 acres of lush grassland on the Comanche reservation, as well as famous wolf hunter John R. "Jack" Abernathy, Dr. Alexander Lambert, the president's personal physician, former Rough Riders, and Captain McDonald, who would act as the chief executive's bodyguard. The Dawes Amendment, which opened unused Comanche lands to white settlement, had been signed into law a few years before, and the secretary of the interior had instructed the cattle barons to vacate the reservation in 1900. In response, they directly approached Roosevelt, and convinced him to extend the order's deadline to 1902, and later to 1905. The hunting excursion was the last in a series of personal appeals to the president.[73]

Ordered to escort the president, McDonald, a staunch Democrat, was initially reluctant to carry out his instructions. After meeting the Republican Roosevelt on April 7, and spending six days with him, McDonald came to admire the man. In turn, the chief executive called the Ranger captain "a game and true man." Seventeen wolves were bagged, a few were caught by Abernathy with his bare hands, and numerous raccoons and rattlesnakes were snared.[74]

When the presidential tour ended, McDonald returned to the duties of a Ranger company commander. In the summer of 1905, he and his seven men transferred their headquarters to Alice in Jim Wells County. At the same time, the legislature reduced the Ranger Force's appropriation from $28,000 to $25,000 for the fiscal year beginning September 1905. The decrease in funding would coincide with several challenging cases.[75]

On the afternoon of September 28, at a rented rice farm near Edna in Jackson County, Henry "Monk" Gibson, a black hired hand, informed his employer, Joseph Fagan Conditt, that Conditt's wife, Lora, and two of his children had been slain. As the two men returned to Conditt's home, some six miles distant from the farm on which they were working, they were stopped by county officers who arrested Gibson for the murders. At this time, the grieving husband and father learned that another two of his five youngsters were dead. The killer had smashed Lora's skull with an adz, raped her twelve-year-old daughter and cut the child's throat, and beaten or stabbed her three young sons to death. Only the infant boy, who had also been battered, survived.[76]

Two days later, while being transported to Hallettsville for his personal safety, Gibson escaped. Deputies and vigilantes, both groups out for blood, searched the area for the fugitive. On October 3, two infantry companies and two cavalry troops from the National Guard arrived in Edna to prevent potential trouble. The governor also dispatched Captains McDonald and Hughes, and several Rangers to the scene, among them were Sergeant McCauley and Privates Samuel McKenzie and Carl T. Ryan of Company B. Gibson was recaptured on October 9, and Rangers and Guardsmen were on hand until the fervor to lynch the suspect abated. The Rangers also investigated the crime scene and reviewed the evidence. McDonald concluded the young Gibson could not have acted alone. The teenager was so exhaustively interrogated by local officers Rangers had to intervene to protect the suspect from being tortured. He still refused to incriminate another person.[77]

Meanwhile, in McDonald's own investigation, the captain suspected Felix Powell, a black male in his thirties, of being Gibson's accomplice in the murders. Despite possessing only circumstantial evidence, McDonald arrested Powell for murder on October 13. The grand jury—as well as the sheriff and most of the public—believed Gibson acted alone, and refused to charge Powell. Gibson was indicted on six counts of murder and one of criminal assault. Judge James C. Wilson of the Twenty-fourth District ordered a change of venue to San Antonio. Sheriff Albert Egg, Captains McDonald and Hughes, and Rangers from Companies B and D escorted Gibson onto the train and accompanied him all the way to the Bexar County jail.[78]

The trial opened in the courtroom of Judge Edward Dwyer of the Thirty-seventh District on December 10. The confession earlier wrung from Gibson was excluded, due to the illegal methods with which it was obtained. Since there were no eyewitnesses to the crime, the remaining evidence was circumstantial. The case resulted in a hung jury, with seven members voting for conviction and five for acquittal. Most of the jurors believed Gibson had "guilty knowledge of the crime," and none believed he was the sole actor in the case.[79]

In addition to various other people, McDonald questioned Powell throughout the next year. Finding traces of blood on Powell's folding knife, the captain had him rearrested. McDonald convinced the suspect to press his right hand, the little finger of which was "abnormal," to a camphor-soaked paper, but the resulting handprint did not match a bloody one left at the scene of the crime. With a sudden insight, McDonald handed Powell an object the same size as a folded knife and asked him to again place his hand on the paper. This time the print matched. By the end of June, McDonald obtained arrest warrants for Powell on charges of rape and murder. Over the next month, the captain also arrested five other individuals for being an accessory, aiding and abetting the murders, or murder. By the end of 1906, McDonald obtained a bench warrant for Gibson and returned him to Edna.[80]

The trial of Felix Powell began on December 5, 1906, in the courtroom of Judge Wilson in Victoria. The evidence McDonald uncovered, and the witnesses who finally came forward, sealed Powell's fate. He was convicted of murder in the first degree. After the appellate court affirmed the verdict in January, Powell was hanged in Victoria on April 2, 1907. Gibson was retried in June, and convicted of first-degree murder. The verdict was upheld by the court of appeals in April 1908, and the sentence was carried out in Cuero on June 28, 1908. In attendance at both executions was Captain McDonald.[81]

Even while he secured justice for the Conditt family, McDonald's beloved wife Rhoda had accompanied her husband from their ranch near Quanah to Alice. Already in poor health, she died on May 21, 1906, at the Santa Rosa Infirmary in San Antonio. The primary cause of death was listed as "exhaustion" while the contributory cause was a surgical operation she had undergone in the spring. She was buried in East Mount Cemetery in Greenville.[82]

The highly anticipated railroad line from Corpus Christi to Brownsville had finally arrived in the summer of 1904. Using the new connection, settlers flocked to the lower valley in what has been described as "the greatest land movement in the history of the West." Quickly developing irrigated truck and citrus farming, newcomers also wasted no time in accepting local Anglo prejudices regarding their black or *mexicano* neighbors, if they did not already display such sentiments. Despite the influx, the population of Brownsville stayed 80 percent Hispanic with Anglos comprising the remainder; only ten black families were among the town's residents. While "southern racism" did play a role in tensions on the lower Rio Grande, Professor James N. Leiker took note of several other factors concerning the numerically greater Hispanics, including "the region's political and class structure, a resented American military presence, competition and resentment between minority groups, and a turbulent transition to a developing commercial economy." Doctor Charles D. Thompson, Jr. observed a few white Texans feared blacks might ally with Hispanics and challenge the hegemony of the local Anglo-dominated establishment. Other points of contention throughout the region involved discord between new arrivals and old-timers, farmers and ranchers, Yankees and Southerners, responsible government advocates and machine politicians, and Democrats and Independants.[83]

Entering this imminent flashpoint, the First Battalion—Companies B, C, and D—of the Twenty-fifth Infantry, with nine white officers and 183 black enlisted men, were posted to Fort Brown on July 28, 1906. Although their previous duty assignment in Nebraska had been free of conflict with the civilian populace, the rank and file were subjected to acts of discrimination from Brownsville Anglos and Hispanics who were united in their opposition to black soldiers. Indeed, police officer Victoriano Fernandez was heard to remark, "I want to kill a couple of them when they get here." Contrary to later statements, these combat-hardened veterans of Cuba and the Philippines almost certainly resented the slights offered by the area residents, including their general hostility, incidents of physical assault, the Jim Crow policies of prominent saloon owners, and the unsubstantiated charge of an attack on a respectable white woman. The atmosphere was strained, but not considered tense enough to threaten unrest. In retrospect, this judgement proved faulty.[84]

Shortly before midnight on August 13, gunshots rang out beyond the short brick wall that fronted Garrison Road and separated Fort Brown from the town. The gate sentry, believing the post was under attack, alerted the garrison by firing two signal shots into the air. The barracks emptied as the troops, rifles in hand, rushed out in answer to the bugler's "call to arms." Ten to twenty individuals dashed up the dark Cowen Alley that ran between Elizabeth and Washington Streets and began shooting into buildings showing

Buffalo Soldier, 25th Infantry. Cabinet card photograph by Orlando Scott Goff, Fort Custer, Montana. William A. Gladstone Collection. *Courtesy Library of Congress, Washington, D.C.*

a light. Major Charles Wilkinson Penrose, the commander of Fort Brown, immediately ordered a roll call of his garrison, and all personnel were listed as present or accounted for. The gunmen disappeared ten minutes later, but not before killing Frank Natus, the bartender at John Tillman's Ruby Saloon, seriously wounding police lieutenant M. Ygnacio "José" Domínguez, riddling homes and businesses with bullets holes, and generally spreading chaos and mayhem throughout the town. No one positively identified the offenders in the darkness, but in the morning, spent cartridge casings and clips used by the military-issue Springfield were found in the alley. The evidence was submitted to Major Penrose, while an inspection revealed the soldiers' rifles were clean and seemingly unfired, and every round of ammunition was inventoried and certified as being on hand. Despite the conflicting evidence, telegrams deluged Austin and Washington with petitions to remove the battalion, demands that such an incident never happen again, and calls for an inquiry to identify and punish the guilty. From the moment the first shots were fired, the prevailing belief that black soldiers had been solely responsible influenced every aspect of the incident's aftermath.[85]

A citizens' committee of fifteen leading townsmen was appointed on the fourteenth to hear the unsworn testimony of twenty-two eyewitnesses. The committee further requested Governor Lanham order units of the Texas National Guard to Brownsville to provide protection. Instead he directed Captain McDonald, Sergeant McCauley, and Private Ryan to join Rangers Delling and McKenzie who were already in the city. Believing the incident to be a federal matter, the governor and the adjutant general delayed taking more positive action until they and the Texas congressional delegation could consult with the military. President Roosevelt ordered an immediate investigation, and Major Augustus Perry Blocksom, assistant inspector general of the Southwest Division, reached the scene on August 18. The army also pledged to exchange the Twenty-fifth Infantry for another regiment composed of white troops.[86]

When ordered to Brownsville, McDonald had been serving as sergeant-at-arms at the state Democratic Party convention in Dallas. Arriving by train on August 21, the captain quickly discovered that Majors Penrose and Blocksom had been collaborating with the citizens' committee, without any progress, in learning the exact identity of the perpetrators. McDonald was certain he himself could locate them quickly. The members of the committee welcomed the captain's assistance and conferred upon him the authority to conduct the investigation in their name. Setting to work immediately, he interviewed Mack Hamilton, a black ex-cavalry trooper who had been detained on suspicion following the shooting. From his cell at the county jail, Hamilton claimed to possess no knowledge of the incident, and McDonald concluded, "He was evidently lying to shield himself."[87]

While a brave and dedicated peace officer, McDonald remained a product of the antebellum South and the son of a slave-owner. In acknowledging this point, the captain's biases should be viewed in that context as he began his probe in his customary tenacious style. To his preconceived thinking, black soldiers, whom he believed unequal to white men, had destroyed private property and terrorized citizens. The officers at Fort Brown, for whom he held little regard, had mishandled the investigation and he, McDonald, knew that if he could question the troops he would get to the guilty party. Early on the morning of August 22, armed with an automatic shotgun, he and McCauley brazenly strode to the Elizabeth Street gate, ordered the guard detail to lower their arms and stand aside, and confronted the two majors. Even though the Ranger lacked legal authority on federal property, Major Blocksom later declared that McDonald "would not hesitate to 'charge hell with one bucket of water.'" With their grudging permission, the captain interrogated soldiers of the battalion and, according to Paine, found their answers "confused, contradictory and full of guilt." At the conclusion, he had compiled the names of thirteen people he believed to be guilty despite a lack of confessions or hard evidence tying the suspects to the crime. Indeed, he deemed the entire garrison to be full accessories to the crime, before or after the fact, including the white officers. Brigadier-General William Spencer McCaskey, commanding the Department of Texas, later reported to Washington: "The mode by which the civil authorities selected these special names is not known, but is believed to be guesswork." Despite the general's opinion, McDonald must have possessed sufficient probable cause to convince Judge Stanley Welch of the Twenty-eighth Judicial District to issue arrest warrants for murder and conspiracy to commit murder on August 23.[88]

McDonald found executing the warrants to be a more challenging task since Penrose and Blocksom could not, themselves, positively identify any culprit. Eyewitnesses who were initially certain black soldiers were the perpetrators equivocated in later interviews. The uniforms of the city police force resembled those of the army, and, in the dim alley on a moonless night, skin tones might have been hard to classify. Several witnesses spoke of hearing pistol shots, which would have come from a weapon unavailable to enlisted troops, but common among townspeople. Although the inspector general's inquiry did point to twelve members of the post, Blocksom believed the matter to be an internal one for the army to settle. On the evening of August 24, McDonald twice delivered the warrants to Penrose and insisted the major release the thirteen soldiers into his custody. Both times Penrose denied the request stating uneasiness regarding their physical welfare. The major also reiterated he had not personally found "any one, or party, in any way connected with the crime."[89]

McDonald was further displeased when he discovered Penrose had been directed to transfer the battalion to Fort Reno in Oklahoma Territory. The major planned to leave the thirteen suspects at Fort Sam Houston in San Antonio to await the disposition of the case. McDonald refused to accept the army's decision, and resolved to thwart the battalion's movement until the thirteen had been arrested. The train bound for San Antonio was ready to depart by midnight, but the captain ordered it to remain. He stood ready to defy the town leaders who simply wanted an end to the whole incident, Judge Welch who rescinded the bench warrants, and even President Roosevelt who had ordered away the soldiers. "It is possible McDonald might have fought the entire battalion with his four or five rangers were their obedience as blind as his obstinacy," Blocksom later testified. Threatened with a contempt of court citation, McDonald did not stop until he received a direct order from the governor via the adjutant general. At last, he realized the pointlessness of further persistence, and, early on August 25, the battalion entrained for Fort Reno. The thirteen men were detained in Fort Sam Houston on military charges, while a Cameron County grand jury failed after three weeks to find enough evidence to return any indictments.[90]

Despite his grudging acquiescence, McDonald was convinced "at least a score of them were murderous 'thugs' who were guilty of the bloody outrage against Brownsville." For his part, Major Blocksom maintained the battalion had closed ranks to shield the twelve actual culprits. His findings were based on circumstantial evidence, and the men continued to be denied a presumption of innocence or a formal hearing. Nonetheless, Blocksom recommended, all the way to the president, that the rank and file be presented with an ultimatum: name the offenders or face separation from the service. All 167 men of Companies B, C, and D continued to profess ignorance, and Roosevelt ordered their immediate discharges "without honor," effective November 16, 1906. Eleven had already left the army either honorably or dishonorably. Famed American educator, author, and orator Booker T. Washington, a friend and advisor to the president, was troubled by Roosevelt's rush to judgement, but continued to support him even after the order was given. Washington's peers, especially W. E. B. DuBois, criticized him for his stance, and the civil rights activist's biographer, Louis R. Harlan, declared Brownsville "the grossest single racial injustice of that so-called Progressive Era." Whether Roosevelt's actions were based in prejudice or in politics is open to debate, but the decision, with its casual rejection of due process, was indeed a controversial one, and quickly became a partisan issue. Although the Senate Military Affairs Committee convened hearings between February 4 and June 14, 1907, and November 18 through March 10, 1908, the evidence provided in the process changed little. Senator Joseph Benson Foraker of Ohio eloquently defended the battalion, but the presidential order stood. Major Penrose's court-martial for "neglect of duty, to the prejudice of good order and military discipline" was heard in San Antonio from February 4 to March 23, 1907. During a recess, he publicly vilified McDonald as a "contemptible coward." The captain continued to assert the major, who was acquitted of the charges, had shielded the guilty soldiers.[91]

Published in 1970, journalist John Downing Weaver's book, *The Brownsville Raid*, was not an unbiased piece of reporting, but, rather, a work of unapologetic advocacy. Indeed, Weaver declared unambiguously the discharged soldiers were completely innocent, and likened their plight to that of Captain Alfred Dreyfus in France. Denouncing the official findings with all their investigatory and statutory missteps, he accepted the assertion that the soldiers had harbored no ill will for the treatment they received prior to the shooting and implied a plot by the Brownsville residents:

> The mood of the barracks was drowsy, good-natured, relaxed. On the opposite side of the garrison wall, white Southerners had spent the summer day rehashing the story of an attack on a white woman by a black soldier. The angry, hard-drinking, pistol-packing Southerners had a motive for violence; the soldiers had none.[92]

Professor Ann J. Lane wrote her own book the following year in which she conceded:

> It is possible that some of the black soldiers of the Twenty-fifth Infantry were guilty of the attack upon the community of Brownsville. The Jim Crow restrictions they found undoubtedly rankled many of the men who had been born in a part of the country where such restrictions did not then exist. Among the soldiers were probably several who found accommodation to their newly prescribed place in society bitter and difficult. These were men, too, of a kind to be found in a peacetime army, that is rough, essentially rootless, accustomed to much drinking and carousing for release from the dreariness of army routine.[93]

Based on Weaver's efforts, and the resulting public interest in the case, President Richard Nixon pardoned the entire battalion in 1972; at the same time, Congress changed the status of their discharges to that of honorable. The lawmakers also authorized $25,000 pensions, without back pay or allowances, to the former soldiers, although only eighty-six-year-old Private Dorsie W. Willis was still alive at the time to collect. Willis commented, "None of us said anything because we didn't have anything to say. It was a frameup through and through."[94]

The separate investigations of McDonald and the War Department were both predicated on the soldiers' involvement, and the Ranger captain's investigation was labeled a "dragnet proceeding" by General McCaskey. Moreover, the suspects were consistently refused the opportunity to speak in their own defense under oath, or cross-examine their accusers in open court. Weaver has been justly commended for his part in rectifying this egregious violation of their Constitutional rights, but he did not consider any dynamics, other than racism, that may have contributed to the episode in Brownsville. Lane touched on a possible financial motive on the part of the town's saloonkeepers, but kept her arguments brief and rhetorical in nature. Expanding on the earlier work, Doctor Garna L. Christian contemplated the probability of townspeople staging the attack for the sole purpose of seeing the black soldiers reassigned. He wrote, "Considering the lack of harmony in any community, the fact that no one ever stepped forward with information to settle a score or draw public attention is as striking as the soldiers' sustained silence." Christian further observed the townspeople who testified were upright, responsible pillars of the community who seemed not to possess the brand of treacherous cunning needed to successfully accomplish a conspiracy of such magnitude. Similarly, the men of the First Battalion were honorable, decorated soldiers who had faithfully served the Republic in war and in peacetime. He concluded both communities had motive to commit the shooting, and both shared a reasonable measure of credibility. After examining past clashes between Texas civilians and federal troops, both white and black, Leiker observed the Rio Grande was a volatile blend of racial, ethnic, and class interests, and further noted a worrisome trend in deteriorating relationships between black soldiers and border communities around the turn of the century. As Brownsville was predominantly Hispanic, he speculated on the possibility of the shooters being *mexicanos* who were opposed to the Anglo social and political class, which included the garrison of federal troops regardless of their skin color. Whether the guilty parties were Brownsville residents intent on framing the black soldiers and ensuring their removal, Mexicans striking at American dominance on the lower Rio Grande, or, indeed, a small number of battalion members who sought retribution against unfriendly townspeople, the unjust manner in which the inquiries were conducted has forever tainted the case. Additionally, contradictory eyewitness testimony, a lack of conclusive physical evidence, and the ever-growing span of time will likely ensure the true identity of the perpetrators remains unknown.[95]

In the early morning hours of November 6, 1906, Judge Welch was assassinated while sleeping inside the *Casa de los Abogados*, the accommodations set aside for visiting jurists and attorneys. The judge had been in Starr County supervising a contentious local election. Political boss James Babbage Wells, Jr. requested Ranger assistance, and McDonald, McCauley, McKenzie, recently appointed Ranger Crosby Marsden, and Delling, now a federal Customs inspector, traveled to Rio Grande City. While en route on the night of November 7, they were ambushed on the old Casitas military road. McDonald's new Winchester semi-automatic rifle jammed after the first shot, but his men were carrying the more reliable Winchester Model 1895s. When the firing stopped, four Mexicans were dead, one was wounded, and three were taken into custody. None of McDonald's party received a scratch. The assailants were later identified as supporters of Gregorio Duffy, the independent candidate for county sheriff. Evidently, they had believed McDonald and his men were Democratic partisans bringing election results from La Grulla. Within a few days, the Rangers' actions were vindicated by a coroner's inquest, which ruled they had acted in self-defense.[96]

Once in Rio Grande City, McDonald was joined by the adjutant general, a cavalry troop, and Captain Hughes and his company. The town was quiet with few arrests required. His presence needed elsewhere, McDonald left Rio Grande City on November 14, before Welch's killer could be found. The closure of the case would be made by Hughes's men.[97]

Newly elected Governor Thomas Mitchell Campbell appointed McDonald to the position of state revenue agent on January 15, 1907. The aging captain, weary and still grief-stricken from Rhoda's death, was hesitant to leave the Ranger service, but he accepted nevertheless. With an annual salary of two thousand dollars, his budget consisted of two thousand dollars for a small staff of one office assistant and one clerk, another five hundred for travel and other expenses, and $175 for office supplies. His new duties consisted of enforcing the state's tax laws that dealt with individuals, businesses, and property. Although McDonald no longer served in the Rangers, he was still the same man. As Paine noted, "It was rumored that, though a civil officer, he still wore a 'forty-five' in a holster and carried an 'automatic' in his hip-pocket."[98]

In his first term, the state revenue agent handled the enforcement of the Baskin-McGregor liquor law. McDonald supervised the collection of fees owed for the issuance of licenses for saloonkeepers. He paid particular attention to country clubs and other social organizations, such as the Eagles and the Elks, who held federal liquor licenses but not retail permits to sell alcohol in the state. He traveled to San Antonio in September 1907, and to Houston the following month, to personally enforce the law in those cities.[99]

McDonald also had to contend with circus owners who constantly attempted to avoid the required taxes. They did so by contesting the tax on each performance, alleging their day and night shows were one uninterrupted presentation; and by evading a sliding scale of taxation based on admission prices. One notable case that had to be adjudicated in court involved famed scout and showman "Colonel" William Frederick "Buffalo Bill" Cody. McDonald convinced the attorney general's office to hold that Cody's Wild West show was a circus and, thus, liable to taxation as one. Buffalo Bill asserted his performances were actually an exhibition that depicted the drama of the American West. Failing to convince the celebrity to pay the occupation tax on circuses rather than the lesser toll for an amusement license, the state and Travis County brought a civil suit to recoup several hundred dollars for two performances staged in Austin. Judge George Calhoun of the Fifty-third Judicial District heard the case and, in the end, ruled in Cody's favor. The state appealed the decision, and, on April 28, 1909, the defendant again prevailed. The Court of Appeals ruled that Cody's show "portraying actual incidents that had happened in the West, and lacking most of the essentials which by common understanding a present-day circus includes, is not a circus."[100]

In 1908, McDonald took a vacation to New York City and, while there, met with Albert Paine, who was writing his authorized biography. The project was the brainchild of "Colonel" Edward Mandell House, a leading figure in the state Democratic Party and the captain's friend for years. At the time, Paine was also compiling his four-volume work on Mark Twain, and McDonald spent time at the famed writer's home in Redding, Connecticut, playing billiards. From there, he went to Washington, D.C. to visit President Roosevelt.[101]

In January 1909, Governor Campbell reappointed McDonald to a second two-year term. McDonald continued to enforce the state's tax laws, including those regarding circuses, wholesale and retail malt and liquor dealers, and social clubs, but this stint was his last as state revenue agent. Oscar Branch Colquitt, newly elected governor of Texas in 1911, appointed Edward Byron House of San Saba County to replace McDonald in the office.[102]

Offered employment by numerous sources, McDonald opted to remain on his ranch, although he was "transacting business" in Houston in late March. He returned to the Magnolia City on September 30, when twelve to fifteen hundred skilled workers in the Sunset Central repair shops went on strike. The walkout was part of a national effort aimed at Edward Henry Harriman's railroad empire. One day prior, McDonald had been engaged by the Southern Pacific, the parent company, to oversee the line's security. On October 2, his guards were escorting a body of scab employees from the No. 9 passenger train to the shop enclosure when shots rang out. One guard was killed and a replacement worker was wounded by the gunfire, while two guards were injured in the ensuing scuffle. The ex-Ranger was involved in the investigation, but conflciting eyewitness accounts were divided over whether the guards or the strikers opened fire. U.S. Marshal Calvin George Brewster was urged to deputize McDonald, but no offer seems to have been made. With violence escalating, the Southern Pacific's attorneys filed suit in federal court requesting a writ of injunction to disperse the picket lines, which was granted on October 5. Public opinion grew in opposition to the strikers, and the railroad held firm until the walkout withered away by 1914.[103]

Meanwhile, on August 9, 1911, McDonald was elected sergeant-at-arms of the Texas Senate committee investigating elections in the state. In this political post, McDonald came into close contact with his confidant Edward House. Indeed, following an assassination attempt on Theodore Roosevelt during the 1912 presidential race, House, one of Woodrow Wilson's campaign managers, arranged for McDonald to be hired as the candidate's bodyguard. On October 15, House telegrammed McDonald, "Come immediately. Important. Bring your artillery." The captain replied simply, "Coming." Thinking his mentor was in danger, McDonald borrowed a shirt from a friend and boarded the train at Quanah without taking any money. Borrowing funds along the way, he arrived in New York City two days later. House took him to campaign headquarters where the captain met Governor Wilson. Ellen Axson Wilson, the candidate's wife, told House the next day "she had slept better [that night] than at any time since T.R. was shot." The ex-Ranger and the future president quickly became friends. House wrote, "Bill said the Governor was the finest fellow in the world, and the Governor seemed equally pleased with Bill and said he was taking good care of him." Wilson's staff was also captivated by the flamboyant Texan and told the governor that McDonald could shoot from the hip and "hit the eye of a mosquito at 500 yards range." The presidential hopeful asked if the boast was true to which McDonald calmly replied, "Which eye?"[104]

Wilson won the presidency on November 5, and McDonald returned home when the U.S. Secret Service took over protection duties. Once the president-elect assumed office, he appointed McDonald as U.S. Marshal for the Northern District of Texas, effective March 28, 1913. As a federal officer, Marshal McDonald worked cases involving violations of the federal liquor laws, the national banking laws, and the White Slave Traffic Act. He also arrested lawbreakers who transported stolen property across state lines, smuggled illicit goods into the country, counterfeited the currency, and used the U.S. mails for the purposes of fraud.[105]

McDonald had first met thirty-year-old bookkeeper Pearl Wilkirson (sometimes spelled Wilkerson) when he frequented her merchant father's business in Quanah in 1911. They courted and exchanged letters while he worked as a presidential bodyguard and a federal marshal. Bill thought Pearl was too young for him, but she assured him such was not the case. On December 27, 1914, they married in Quanah. After a stop in Wichita Falls, they honeymooned in New Orleans. Upon their return, Pearl worked as a stenographer in her husband's office. He was appointed to a second term on April 24, 1917.[106]

While home in Quanah, Bill McDonald contracted pneumonia on January 5, 1918. He traveled to his sister's residence in Wichita Falls for treatment before succumbing to his illness on January 15. He was buried at Quanah Memorial Park cemetery. On his tombstone is carved the following motto: "No man in the wrong can stand up against a fellow that's in the right and keeps on a-comin'."[107]

Pearl married Louis Alva Williams, a public accountant. He died on November 25, 1925, in Dallas of a cerebral hemorrhage brought on by hypertension. He was buried in Oakland Cemetery in that city. Pearl stayed in Dallas for at least five years. She was living in Houston with a brother's family by 1940. She died on July 21, 1966, in La Porte. She was buried next to Bill in Memorial Park.[108]

William J. McDonald knew his audience, and he played to them in spectacular fashion. His robust personality, lively speech, and originality endeared him to the public, and to prominent state and national figures. He possessed more showmanship and received greater publicity than his peers, and was always able to provide color to any situation. More importantly, he mastered the administrative and investigative roles that developed into a fixture of twentieth century law enforcement.

John R. Hughes. #1975/070-5342. William Deming Hornaday Collection.
Courtesy Texas State Library and Archives Commission, Austin, Texas.

Chapter 11

John R. Hughes: "A Relentless Manhunter and Intrepid Lawman"

John Reynolds Hughes best personified the popular image of a Texas Ranger captain. He was honest, he had an agreeable personality, he spoke softly, he carried a secret heartache and bore it well, and he was a relentless manhunter and intrepid lawman. Retired federal agent and author Bob Alexander said of him: "John R. Hughes was an esteemed man of unchallenged integrity … In a six-shooter crisis, John R. was standup." While working for the State, Hughes was reticent in discussing himself, perhaps thinking it unseemly. After retirement, though, he became more open to newspapermen and writers, but not to the point of being boastful. His record spoke for itself.

He was born in Cambridge, Henry County, Illinois, on February 11, 1855. His father, Thomas Forster Hughes, had been born in Hamilton County, Ohio, in July 1812, and educated at Miami University before turning to school teaching and farming. His obituary noted he was a "deep thinker and a fluent writer." John's mother, Jane Augusta "Jennie" (Bond) Hughes, was born in Venice, Ohio, on December 29, 1827. Married on April 5, 1846, the couple and their growing family lived in Butler County before relocating to Henry County in Illinois in 1855. They moved once more to Marion County the next year. There they farmed two tracts of eighty acres, each worth $480 in 1860, and $320 two years later. John's siblings were Louise Hughes, born on October 14, 1847; Bond Hughes, born on August 1, 1850; Emery Sargent Hughes, born on February 28, 1852; William Parker Hughes, born on October 14, 1857; and twins Thomas Forster, Jr. and Ellen "Nellie" Hughes, born in June 1860. In 1865, the family moved to Mound City, Kansas. In addition to farming, Thomas purchased the Mound City House, a hotel, in 1867. Eight years later, his real estate was valued at five thousand dollars, and his personal property at one thousand.[1]

Sometime after June 1870, Hughes left home and drifted southward into the Indian Territory, living for several years on the Choctaw and Osage Indian Reservations. He accompanied at least one buffalo hunt, returning in time to hear of the Great Chicago Fire. In 1872, he received his first and only wound from a violent encounter with another person. Details are scant, but a 1938 interview related how Hughes "was shot ... by an Indian when he was 17, and he suffers from the wound to this day. His right arm was shattered and is weak and smaller than his left. He had to learn to do everything with his left hand, even shoot." In another account, writer William Cx Hancock related how Hughes had tangled with a "feared breed rustler" named Big Nig Goombi who had tried to steal the stock the former was herding. Hughes killed his man while sustaining the aforementioned wounds to the arm. One more article written by Mrs. O. L. Shipman in 1923 described the injury as having resulted from an accident. Whatever the cause, the right-handed Hughes was forced to learn how to use his left arm and hand as his dominant. He ultimately became so skilled with firearms that most thought him naturally left-handed.[2]

Moving on, he was employed at a trading post on the Comanche and Kiowa Agency near Fort Sill. Although Hughes's employers at the reservation have gone unnamed, the post sutlers were John S. Evans and John J. Fisher until 1876, then Captain F. R. Rice and Joseph K. Beyers. Moreover, Evans was a licensed Indian trader, and he constructed a satellite house, known as the "Lower Store," near the west bank of Cache Creek. Another Indian trader who might have hired Hughes was William "Buffalo Bill" Mathewson; his establishment was situated along the same stream. While on the reservation, Hughes met Quanah Parker and was friendly enough with the renowned chief to be presented with several photographs of Parker and his two wives.³

In the spring of 1877, the firm of Powers, Bulkley & Company lost their government beef contract, and Hughes was hired to help drive the remaining cattle to the Kansas Pacific Railway's shipping point in Ellis. Although Dodge City was closer, David Whitehead Powers and Fernando Cortez Bulkley were being compensated by the railroad to favor its company town with their business. Trail boss Mike Dalton led his crew, including Hughes, and the herd of twelve hundred head north over the state line and through Comanche County. There, they strayed across the "dead line," which banned Texas cattle, possibly carrying fever ticks, from more settled Kansas counties. The resident farmers came out in force, and Dalton was compelled to pay a small fine and damages for violating the quarantine law. Undeterred, Hughes and his fellow cowhands arrived in Dodge City on May 9, with the cattle "in fine condition, having found plenty of grass and water along the trail." Leaving the "Queen of the Cowtowns," Dalton guided the herd around Ness County and approached the dead line between Ellis and Trego Counties, approximately two miles west of the KP stockyards. Unlike his earlier encounter with the grangers, though, Dalton delivered the cattle to the railhead on May 22 without trouble. In a letter to the *Hays City Sentinel*, he reported, "I lost not a single head on the whole route and the stock were in good condition when I reached Ellis. Plenty of water and feed west of Ness County." The cattle were herded nearby until November, then sold. Evidently, Hughes found the experience agreeable, as he went up the trail to Dodge the following year. This time he was working for the U Ranch, which leased 150,000 acres situated between the Medicine River and the Salt Fork of the Arkansas River in the Cherokee Outlet. The herd was owned by prominent rancher Major Andrew Drumm and Andy J. Snider, a Kansas City livestock commission merchant.⁴

By February 1, 1879, Hughes and his brother Emery were in Texas raising horses near Liberty Hill on the line between Williamson and Travis Counties. Their operation was called the Long Hollow Ranch and their brand was the Running H. Their first horse, Tom McKinney, was purchased on January 7, 1879, for cash. In addition to some fifty horses, the brothers also ran a small herd of eleven cows by 1883. Evidently the ranch's stock was sufficient to attract the attention of John and James Craven, a pair of horse thieves who had taken the alias of Johnson and swept through the area in August 1883. The two bandits relieved the Hughes brothers, and their neighbors, of seventy to seventy-five horses. The Long Hollow outfit personally lost sixteen head, including their prized bay stallion, Moscow. As recounted numerous times, Hughes displayed the grit that would make him legendary when he decided to track the robbers down and retrieve his horses. He also agreed to recover his neighbors' property if they would tend to his ranch while he was away. Hughes departed on his first manhunt approximately two weeks after the thefts. Contrary to the prevalent legend, though, the *Galveston Daily News* reported Emery accompanied his younger brother.[5]

As the two neophyte manhunters doubtless learned, tracking men on the dodge was more than simply a matter of following a trail of hoofprints, manure, trampled grass, broken twigs, and dislodged pebbles. Knowledge of the surrounding country, especially available water holes, streams, and rivers, was also vital, as was the ability to ask perceptive questions in settlements along the way. Most important, though, the hunters needed to enter the minds of their prey and predict the fugitives' needs, be they food, whiskey, women, fresh horses, or shelter. The Hughes brothers "followed the thieves month after month," acquiring knowledge and skills through necessity, until the following winter when they learned the whereabouts of their horses from a boy living on a ranch near Cisco. Returning home to attend to business, the two stockmen found the neighbors had kept their promise in the interim and maintained the ranch. Emery remained behind, while John left once more on May 15, 1884. The younger Hughes arrived at Hillsboro in Sierra County, New Mexico Territory, in the second week of July. There he discovered the Craven/Johnsons had been apprehended on charges of cattle theft on June 10; Toppy Johnson (no relation) and eleven other men were also taken into custody. With the Craven brothers' arrest, sixty head of horses remained on their ranch north of Grafton. The herd was attached due to an unresolved debt, and forty head were placed into the care of Deputy Sheriff Joe Thorne; the other horses stayed on the range. By August 26, Hughes had recovered all his horses and began the drive back to Texas. The other stock was left in the custody of the Socorro County sheriff until they could be returned to their rightful owners. Hughes finally returned home after a journey of roughly three thousand miles that lasted 350 days.[6] Decades later, an article in the *Houston Chronicle* quoted Hughes as recalling: "The band of men was all broken up. Two of them were convicted for stealing my horses, and sent to the New Mexico penitentiary."[7]

In 1911, while Hughes was still a serving Ranger, author and journalist George Washington Ogden wrote a piece for *Everybody's Magazine* detailing the search for the horse thieves. Although the interview has been considered a reliable account of the manhunt, several details are present that go unmentioned in the brief newspaper articles originally describing the episode. The first, and most obvious, is that Hughes went after the stolen stock on his own. Secondly, rather than just the two Craven brothers, there was a third robber who mysteriously left the group at some point in the chase. Third, once he had tracked them down, Hughes confronted the thieves and called on them to surrender, but they resisted. The rancher killed one of them, and the other wisely fled. The researcher is left to draw the conclusion either Ogden used some dramatic license to make the tale even more exciting, or Hughes had remembered events differently by 1911. More contradictory versions would be published in the years to come.[8]

In his classic book, *Triggernometry*, Eugene Cunningham claimed Hughes tracked six horse thieves to their camp in New Mexico and faced them single-handedly; only two of the robbers survived the fight to be delivered to the authorities. Similarly, novelist Dane Coolidge recounted how Hughes, with the aid of an unnamed sheriff, "jumped them; and when the smoke had cleared away four horse-thieves were stretched out dead." Writing under the pen name Paul Havens, and later his own, Jack Martin, Hughes's first biographer, identified the sheriff as Frank Swafford and related how Hughes, Swafford, and an unknown deputy rode to the ranch where the horses were being held and confronted the two "Renald" brothers who claimed to be the owners. When the sheriff informed the pair he intended to cut the herd, shots rang out from the corral. Hughes disarmed the Renalds and two other men, while Swafford and his deputy killed four men in the corral. In total, nine men supposedly surrendered to the officers. However, according to professor emeritus Larry D. Ball, no man named Frank Swafford ever served as a sheriff for any county in New Mexico Territory.[9]

The customary story of John Hughes's manhunt has thrilled readers for decades, but, rather than the Renalds, the horse-thieving brothers have been positively identified as the Cravens, both of whom operated under the *nom de plume* of Johnson. John and Emery together tracked them for months before the former single-handedly recovered the stolen stock. The elder Hughes's exclusion from the tale might have been due to modesty or, as conveyed at the time, he was genuinely troubled by reports "a searcher for stolen property [in western New Mexico] carries his life in his hands." Regardless, the standing of his lawman brother was heightened. Despite the lack of dramatic gunplay amid a final showdown, the year-long hunt for the horses would prove to be a boon to Hughes's subsequent career and reputation as a lawman.[10]

On July 18, 1885, the brothers' partnership was dissolved, and John sold his interest in the livestock to Emery. In the spring of 1886, the younger Hughes was approached by Texas Ranger Ira Aten who needed assistance. Fredericksburg businessman Johann Wolfgang Braeutigam, who owned the land that encompassed the site of old Fort Martin Scott, had been murdered two years previously. Two of the killers had escaped from the Mason jail by digging "out through the floor, under the foundation, and to the outside." Aten's lack of success in finding them led to a sense of discouragement, and mutual friend George Wells suggested he contact Hughes who lived in the area.[11]

In his memoirs, Aten described their first meeting:

> I had never seen Hughes before and don't think he had ever seen me. He had the usual cowman's frankness and hospitality, and although I was so dejected that I felt I had lost my last friend, his presence seemed to react upon me. I liked his looks and it seemed that I could see a spark of sympathy in his eyes, so I just opened up and told him my whole story. After I had finished, Hughes said in his quiet, mild, sympathetic manner, "I will go with you and help you."[12]

Aten was delighted with Hughes's response, and the two quickly became fast friends. Aten formally deputized his new assistant, then planned how they would take the fugitive. The pair of manhunters engaged in fruitless searching for weeks before they located their quarry. On May 25, near Liberty Hill, Aten and Hughes "met and killed Collier who resisted arrest." For whatever reason, Jack Martin transformed Collier into the character Judd Roberts, a member of Butch Cassidy's Wild Bunch, and "a relative of a couple of those men who died in New Mexico." According to the myth, Roberts was intent on taking his vengeance on Hughes.[13]

Their developing friendship cemented by the hunt for Collier, Aten convinced the rancher to join the Frontier Battalion. Thinking he would only serve a few months, Hughes agreed, and he enlisted as a private in Company D at Georgetown on August 10, 1887. Setting to work almost immediately, the two Rangers pursued train robbers John Barber and William Henry "Bill" Whitley until Aten was needed in Brown County for court. Hughes continued the manhunt until, on October 1, he was ordered to the company headquarters at Camp Ross in Edwards County; he reported to Captain Frank Jones on the sixteenth. He was later described as, "A great, brown man, tanned and toughened by desert sun and wind, a slender black mustache, drooping at the corners of his mouth, he seems a figure from some seasoned old Flemish canvas." In obedience to Adjutant General Wilburn Hill King's orders, the company departed Edwards County on the thirtieth for Camp Shely, located three miles from Rio Grande City; they arrived on November 20.[14]

On March 15, Corporal Joseph Walter Durbin and a detachment of three men, including Hughes and Bazzell Lamar "Baz" Outlaw, were dispatched to Wharton per the orders of General King; they arrived four days later. Over the next two months, the four Rangers scouted the area and arrested sixteen men charged with murder and assault with intent to murder. While the others continued their sweep, Hughes was dispatched to Navarro County on May 12, and ordered to report to District Court Judge Samuel Romulus Frost. However, his efforts in combating fence cutters proved futile, and he was back in camp on June 18, having "Failed to accomplish anything, out 34 days. Marched 1000 miles." Softening the harsh suggestion of inadequacy, the monthly report read, "Hughes was unsuccessful in locating fence cutters by the indiscretion of one of the stock men, who gave the chase away."[15]

In August 1888, Hughes was thrust into a situation that had the potential to explode into a major incident. The previous May, Sheriff Warren Washington "Wash" Shely of Starr County had apprehended Abram Recéndez, a Hispanic resident of Rio Grande City, on a robbery charge. Although the arrest was peaceful, Recéndez was shot and killed by Jim Dillard, a Company D Ranger, on the sixteenth while allegedly trying to escape. The *mexicano* community of Starr County erupted in outrage to another possible example of the *ley de fuga* (law of flight). Their wrath was directed in particular at the sheriff, due to the two Mexicans who had recently been lynched while in his custody. The anti-Shely faction was not content to merely issue protests; instead, they organized a campaign to have him removed from office. To this end, they employed Catarino Garza, the editor of the *El Comercio Mexicano* in Corpus Christi. Garza was engaged in opposition to the regime of Mexican dictator Porfirio Díaz, even openly plotting the overthrow of the *Porfiriato*. The fiery newspaperman turned his journalistic attentions on Customs inspector Victor Sebree, whom he blamed for the Recéndez shooting, and found himself charged with criminal libel. Hughes went to Realitos to make the arrest on August 19. Although the would-be *insurrecto* was surrounded by his sympathizers, Hughes approached Garza and took him into custody without incident. The following day, Garza was taken to Rio Grande City, where he posted a fifty-dollar bond and was released.[16]

During this time, Hughes met the young lady to whom he would soon propose marriage. His intended bride has been an enigmatic woman, as Hughes never mentioned her in either the interviews he granted later in life, or in his personal papers. Ira Aten described her in his memoirs as hailing from Corpus Christi, and that Hughes and Aten had met her and her two sisters at a cattle ranch twenty miles from Company D's camp at Realitos. The two Rangers escorted the young ladies on a fox hunt the following Sunday, and again one week later. Hughes fell deeply in love with one of the girls. Jack Martin, the captain's first biographer, supposedly knew her real name but only referred to her as "a gay, spirited brunette of twenty, whom we shall know as Elizabeth Todd." In his article on Hughes, William Hancock identified her as "Ann." Further obscuring the issue, Martin related how Hughes had met his sweetheart, the daughter of a Corpus Christi banker, before the investigation into the Williamson family murders in 1889. Tragically, she died of an unidentified malady while he was investigating Dick Duncan's role in the killings. According to Martin, friends tried to contact Hughes with the solemn news, but were unable to reach him. Her body was purportedly interred in a small cemetery on the Gulf Coast, and Hughes made annual pilgrimages to her grave. In an interview with author Chuck Parsons many years ago, Captain Hughes's grand-nephew, Doctor Louis B. Hughes, recalled accompanying his uncle as a youth to the cemetery at Rockport in Aransas County. Unfortunately, he stayed in the car, so he never saw the headstone, and was unable to recall the young lady's name in later interviews. Martin credits Aten with stating that "the tragic death of Elizabeth Todd was largely responsible for [Hughes] remaining a bachelor."[17]

In his biography on Captain Hughes, Parsons believed he had uncovered evidence that her real name was Elfrieda Gertrude Wuerschmidt. Photographs of Hughes and a woman the author identified as Elfrieda appear in Maude Gilliland's two books, *Wilson County Texas Rangers* and *Horsebackers of the Brush Country*. Gilliland claimed she was "the girl [Hughes] planned to marry" and that both photos were taken by Ranger Herff Alexander Carnes in 1904, one in Ysleta, and the other in Rockport. However, research for this chapter revealed Elfrieda was, unfortunately, not the lost love of John R. Hughes. Instead, marriage records indicate she wed Lynn Smith Kennicott in El Paso on October 14, 1909. Federal census records from 1910 to 1940 indicate the Kennicotts lived in El Paso and Yuma, Arizona. Lynn worked for the U.S. Bureau of Reclamation for thirty years before retiring. He died of a cerebral blood clot in Tucson on July 18, 1956. Elfrieda died in Arlington, Virginia, on May 12, 1973, and was buried in Evergreen Memorial Park in Tucson. During an exchange of emails, Parsons graciously reviewed these findings and concurred with the conclusions.[18]

In an attempt to uncover the real identity of "Elizabeth Todd," this author, with few other clues available, was forced to assume her approximate age, her permanent residence, and her father's occupation as described by Martin were all true. Consequently, Mary A. Sutherland's *The Story of Corpus Christi* was consulted for the names of local businessmen, who were then cross-referenced with the 1880 and 1900 federal census records for Corpus

Christi. Those gentlemen with daughters were scrutinized for the appropriate criteria. Several electronic newspaper archives were also searched using relevant keywords, and the Aransas County Historical Commission's expert on Rockport Cemetery was consulted. None of these avenues of research proved successful, and so "Elizabeth Todd" will, for the time being, remain a lady of mystery.[19]

Hughes may still have been grief-stricken and consequently needed a change in May of 1889. That month, William "Bill" O'Grady, Captain Jones's brother-in-law, and the manager of the Fronteriza Mines in Sierra del Carmen, Coahuila, was looking for three good men to guard ore shipments departing the mines. Jones recommended Hughes, Baz Outlaw, and Walter Durbin for the job. All three accepted, and Outlaw resigned on May 16, the other two the next day. Undoubtedly, Hughes and Durbin had some concerns with Baz Outlaw. Durbin would later write: "This man was with me two years in [a] Ranger company and went to Mexico with me and I must say of all the bad men I have knew [sic] he was one of the worst and most dangerous. He never knew what fear was." Outlaw was an easygoing man when sober. In a shootout occurring in the line of duty, he was an effective gunslinger. When he was drunk, though, that fighting instinct turned into something dark and ugly, and he became a terror who was always on the lookout for trouble.[20]

The Texans' responsibility consisted of protecting the silver bullion consignments on their way to the railhead in Barroteran. As Fronteriza's monthly output had increased from fifteen thousand to twenty thousand dollars in May, the three heavily armed guards slept in shifts and kept a constant watch, their Winchesters close at hand. No robberies occurred during their tenure, and the only difficulty came not from *bandidos*, but from a labor strike that was resolved without violence. The trio eventually returned to the United States with Outlaw reenlisting in Company D on September 1, and Hughes on December 1.[21]

Shortly after rejoining the company, Hughes was placed in charge of a detachment in Edwards County, and helped to end a long-standing matter originating in Burnet County. An informant had notified Edwards County Sheriff Ira Lewis Wheat that Walter P. "Will" and Alvin C. Odle, on the run from the law for the past four years, were taking a herd of stolen horses to a rancher near the small town of Vance. Deputy Sheriff Will Terry raised a posse of four men and welcomed the inclusion of Hughes, Outlaw, and Calvin Grant "Cal" Aten (Ira's younger brother). Riding some twenty-five miles, the lawmen positioned themselves approximately one mile above Vance, near the eastern side of Bullhead Mountain, and settled in to wait for the Odle brothers to show. Shortly after midnight, on December 25, the fugitives appeared, but when the demand for their surrender was issued, they foolishly opened fire. Caught without cover, the two brothers were swiftly cut down.[22]

Charles Henry Vanvalkenburg "Charley" Fusselman was the first sergeant of Company D, and a good friend to Hughes. Even though regulations prohibited a Ranger from simultaneously holding another office, Fusselman was a Presidio County deputy sheriff, and a deputy U.S. marshal. When informed of the federal appointment, Captain Jones had turned a blind eye as "the two positions 'dovetail' very nicely." On April 17, 1890, Sergeant Fusselman was in El Paso to testify in federal court. John H. Barnes, a local rancher, rushed to the sheriff's office and reported that Mexican rustlers had killed one of his calves, then stole some of his *remuda*. Fusselman, Barnes, and El Paso policeman George Herold, a former Ranger involved in the Round Rock shootout with the Sam Bass gang, set out after the thieves. The pursuers overtook the Mexicans in a canyon in the Franklin Mountains and charged the rustlers, regardless of the inferior numbers. Fusselman and his companions quickly came under fire, and bandit leader Gerónimo Parra purportedly shot the Ranger sergeant twice in the head. As Fusselman fell from his horse, Barnes and Herold, realizing they were outnumbered, wheeled their mounts and rushed back to town for reinforcements. The sheriff and Deputy U.S. Marshal Bob Ross formed a party of ten tough men and a supply wagon, and sent them after the killers. The posse returned without any bandits in tow, but they did recover Fusselman's body, and Barnes's stolen horses from where they had been abandoned near the Rio Grande.[23]

After Hughes was informed of his friend's death, he took the next train to El Paso. Once there, he and a posse followed the trail of the bandits for six days and covered 390 miles, but had to return empty-handed, except for one man arrested on an unrelated robbery charge. Baz Outlaw took Fusselman's place as the new first sergeant. Hughes assumed additional responsibilities

Ambush on the Bandit Trail. Andy Thomas. *Courtesy of the artist.*

as corporal on April 18, but he never stopped trying to track down his friend's killer.[24]

Due to the mass migrations of the previous twenty years, the superintendent of the Census Bureau declared in 1890 that the United States once had "a frontier of settlement, but at present the unsettled area has been so broken into by isolated bodies of settlement that there can hardly be said to be a frontier line." Despite the Census Bureau's findings, in the Trans-Pecos region at least, remnants of the Wild West were alive and well. From December 1, 1888, to October 31, 1890, Company D performed 117 scouts over 22,243 miles, and conducted 133 arrests—forty-seven of them for murder, fourteen for assault with intent to kill, and forty for theft. Corporal Hughes was placed in charge of a detachment stationed in Presidio on May 7, 1890. At the end of the month, Captain Jones transferred the company headquarters to Marfa. On August 11, Hughes made a scout near Stockton, with Deputy U.S. Marshal Thalis Tucker Cook, in search of a herd of stolen horses. They were unable to find the stock, but they did strike the trail of four Mexicans who had murdered a man in Upton County on July 21. Hughes and Cook followed the tracks toward the Rio Grande until rain washed them away, and the corporal was back in camp by the twenty-second.

Ten days later, he and another Ranger were once more searching for stolen livestock. Captain Jones moved the entire company to Camp Hogg, situated five miles from Alpine, on October 1.[25]

On August 24, 1891, Hughes and another man conducted a scout to the Rio Grande, then up to Tornero Creek where they arrested Marselo Ortega Chargeo for murder and horse theft. Delivering their prisoner to jail, they were out for two days and marched eighty miles. Late in the year, silver ore from the Shafter mines was being stolen after the pack trains left for the smelters; the dollar loss was extreme. Hughes was assigned to command a detachment at Shafter in November. The corporal convinced mine employee Ernest "Diamond Dick" St. Leon, a former Ranger discharged for drunkenness, to become his confidential informant.[26] On January 12, 1892, based on St. Leon's information, Hughes and Ranger Alonzo W. "Lon" Oden attempted to arrest Matildo Carrasco, José Veleta, and Guintino Chavez on charges of theft of silver ore. The three suspects resisted arrest and were killed by the officers.[27]

On June 20, Hughes, with Privates James Mitchell "Jim" Putman and Lon Oden, arrested fugitive thief Desedario Durán near the San Antonio Colony, a Mexican settlement on the Rio Grande. Riding for Marfa with their prisoner, the Rangers chanced upon Florencio Carrasco and two other men at Jim Windham's store two days later. Florencio, the brother of Matildo Carrasco, had been charged with an assortment of crimes, including horse theft and murder, and the lawmen were under standing orders to arrest him. Hughes and Oden rode toward the three Mexicans, two of whom quickly mounted and charged the Rangers, firing their guns as they galloped closer. Carrasco dismounted and began to pull his rifle from its scabbard until one of the Rangers' bullets dropped him dead in his tracks. The other two *bandidos* were able to escape. Aware that both Durán and Carrasco had friends in the area, Hughes led his party out of the settlement and turned onto the road to Valentine. The trip was longer, but the chances for an ambush were less. Durán was safely remanded to the jail in Marfa.[28]

By the fall of 1892, Baz Outlaw's struggle with the bottle finally got the best of him, and Captain Jones reluctantly discharged him on September 18. Hughes was promoted to first sergeant in his stead the next day.[29] On May 28, 1893, Hughes arrested E. Cook and Jesús Garza for disturbing the peace, and delivered them to Deputy Sheriff A. B. Cline. Receiving orders from General Mabry, Jones relocated the company headquarters to Ysleta on the first day of June. Three days later, Hughes again arrested Garza, this time for horse theft, and turned him over to Presidio County Sheriff Denton Gibbon Knight. Five days later, he apprehended Canuto Leva at Shafter on the same charge.[30]

On June 29, Captain Jones, Corporal Carl Kirchner, and Privates Thalis Cook, Jonathan Woodard "Wood" Saunders, Robert Edward "Ed" Bryant, and Edwin Dunlap Aten (another of Ira Aten's brothers) traveled to Pirate Island—a small isle some thirty miles below El Paso. Created by a change in the Rio Grande's flow, this no-man's land was partly in Texas and partly in Mexico with no clear line of delineation. With neither country possessing genuine legal authority, some three hundred desperadoes resided on the island. The Texas lawmen were intent on serving writs on American-born outlaws Jesús María Olguin and his son Severo for horse and cattle theft, and assault to commit murder. The captain also wanted to locate Antonio Olguin, a convicted rapist and escapee from the state penitentiary at Huntsville.[31]

The Rangers camped opposite La Quadrilla, five miles below San Elizario on the east bank of the existing river channel, so they could begin the search the next day. Shortly after four a.m., the officers entered the Olguins' adobe house on the east side of the old river bed, but found only Jesús María's elderly wife, two other women, and a young boy. Moving next to search nearby homes, they sighted two riders who galloped away as the lawmen drew near. Jones unknowingly led his men across the international boundary and entered the village of *Tres Jacales*. The escaping horsemen spurred three hundred yards to the first house on the right side of the road, dismounted, and entered the structure. Almost at once, the Americans came under fire from the fleeing Mexicans and a large number of their friends. Jones alighted to the ground thirty feet in front of the building and was immediately shot through the thigh. He fell, but managed to sit up and return fire. Ranger Tucker, who was the nearest to the captain, asked Jones if he was injured. Jones replied, "Yes, shot all to pieces." Another bullet slammed into the captain's chest. "Boys, I am killed," he said as he sank to the ground dying. In the exchange of shots, Severo suffered a broken arm and Jesús María a bullet wound to his right hand.[32]

Still taking intense fire, the surviving detachment members stood fast until they were forced to withdraw, leaving their captain's body behind. Corporal Kirchner raced to San Elizario where he wired for assistance. Upon hearing their commander had fallen, Hughes and his detachment gathered their weapons and equipment, and took the next train to San Elizario, arriving at nine-thirty a.m. on July 1. Earlier that same morning, Kirchner had returned to Pirate Island, where he and El Paso County Sheriff Frank B. Simmons recovered the captain's body, and arranged for the return of his rifle, spurs, watch, and money. Jones was buried in American soil at six o'clock that evening. The Mexican government protested the presence of armed *gringo* lawmen in its territory. The U.S. Army and General Mabry separately investigated the incident, and each concluded the violation of Mexican sovereignty had been nothing but an accident. The adjutant general did note the fleeing horsemen, and the subsequent ambush of Captain Jones and his entire detachment, had been quite deliberate. Labeling their sergeant a "honest, brave, and efficient officer with sober and industrious habits," the nine men of Company D petitioned Mabry to promote Hughes to the vacant captaincy. The adjutant general concurred, and Hughes took command of the company, effective July 4. Kirchner advanced to the rank of sergeant.[33]

By the time of his promotion, Hughes was possessed of exceptional fieldcraft, robust physical strength and endurance, and a quick intelligence. In the tradition of the best Ranger captains, he would lead from the front. His talents in rangering commanded the respect of federal law officers, county sheriffs, district court judges, his ranger colleagues, and numerous other officials. His agreeable personality and modest bearing further earned him a high regard from the general public. He was an enthusiastic reader and markedly frugal. Despite his years of working the dangerous border country, he was never wounded. He also never lost a prisoner in his custody, either in an escape or to a vigilante mob. While never to the extent John H. Rogers practiced his faith, Hughes was a deeply religious man. Throughout his time in El Paso County, he often held the position of Sunday school superintendent in Ysleta. The captain also banned drinking and gambling in his company. He himself abstained from alcohol, tobacco, and card playing.[34]

The new captain lost his first subordinate the following year, not from an outlaw's bullet, but instead at the hands of an old friend. Private Joseph W. "Joe" McKidrict was in El Paso on April 5, 1894, to testify before the federal grand jury. Shortly after five p.m., he was visiting with friends at a print shop when he heard a piercing police whistle originating from the red-light district. Running to the source of the noise, he discovered Baz Outlaw, now a deputy U.S. marshal, behind Tillie Howard's brothel, inebriated and menacing people with a pistol. McKidrict attempted to pacify the intoxicated officer. The drunken man snarled, "You want that, don't you?" and shot McKidrict in the head. After the Ranger fell to the ground, Outlaw shot him again. Constable John Selman, the man who would kill John Wesley Hardin the next year, appeared, and Outlaw turned his pistol on him. The bullet missed, but Selman's face was burned by the spent powder. Temporarily blinded, the constable fired back and hit Outlaw above the heart. Mortally wounded, the killer shot Selman twice in the right leg before he surrendered to Ranger Francis Marion "Frank" McMahan. Baz Outlaw died from his wound four hours later.[35]

Having lost a valuable man, the new captain faced the budget reduction of 1895, which left him with only one sergeant and six privates to cover the vast Trans-Pecos. In the meantime, Sergeant Kirchner resigned on July 24, and was succeeded by Ed Aten. The following years would see the company endlessly responding to appeals in Pecos, Fort Stockton, Shafter, Presidio, Terlingua, Marfa, Fort Davis, El Paso, Fort Hancock, and throughout the border country. They contended with feuds and ethnic troubles, stock theft, and banditry. At times Hughes was forced to respond that he had no men to spare.[36]

Rather than customary acts of wrongdoing, Hughes was next involved in a case initiated by Governor Charles Allen Culberson. Catering to prize-fighting enthusiasts, promoter Daniel Albert Stuart planned to hold a boxing match between James John "Gentleman Jim" Corbett of San Francisco and Cornish-born New Zealander Robert Prometheus "Ruby Bob" Fitzsimmons during the Texas State Fair and Dallas Exposition. As part of his grand spectacle, he was in the process of erecting a 52,500-seat coliseum in town.[37] A vocal minority of reformers in Texas believed pugilism to be an immoral activity, and found a champion in the state's chief executive. On October 1, Governor Culberson called the Twenty-fourth Legislature into special session to deliberate the matter. Each house considered a measure prohibiting professional prizefighting, and Senate Bill No. 3 was signed into law on October 3. In expanding the reach of the state, a common theme of the Progressive Era, the governor was ready to ignore the will of the people and impose a rigid morality not shared by the majority of his constituents. Even his wife questioned this violation of democratic principles: "I don't see why one man would have the power to say what the next would do. One man's judgment is no better than another."[38]

Stuart, who had indebted himself to build the coliseum, had no intention of surrendering, and searched for the right venue to hold the event. Culberson was equally determined to stop him. Hughes was directed to follow Corbett, while some of his men were ordered to shadow Stuart. The captain trailed his quarry from Dallas to Texarkana on October 30, to Hot Springs, Arkansas, on November 2, and to Little Rock in the early morning of the fourth. Discovering Corbett did not intend to return to Texas, Hughes left him late that afternoon and retraced his steps back to Ysleta, arriving three days later. Before the year ended, Corbett pulled out of the bout, and Stuart later announced that, on February 14, 1896, Bob Fitzsimmons and Irish boxer Peter Maher would meet in El Paso. The story appeared on the front pages of newspapers across the country, and hundreds of fight enthusiasts entrained for the border town.[39]

Hughes, his three fellow captains, and nearly all their men also came to El Paso; Company D arrived on February 10. Adjutant General Mabry took personal charge of the matter, and the Rangers kept the bout's principals, managers, and trainers under constant surveillance. Hughes, Mabry, and McDonald even visited the cheerfully rough Fitzsimmons in Juárez, where he was preparing for the bout, and watched the fighter give an impromptu exhibition. Days before he was to step into the ring, Maher developed an acute case of ophthalmia from the wind-driven alkali or adobe dust prevalent at his Las Cruces training grounds. Stuart needed the reprieve, as he

Dan Stuart. Sketch from *Galveston Daily News*, February 22, 1896.

and his colleagues found Texas officialdom to be continually inhospitable, and the governor of Chihuahua also barred the fight from occurring there. Stuart had been further stymied by the Fifty-fourth Congress and President Grover Cleveland, both of whom were responsible for a February 7, 1896, law that prohibited "pugilistic encounters" in the territories and the District of Columbia. Federal marshals were dispatched to keep the fight out of the public lands of New Mexico Territory.[40]

Roy Bean, the justice of the peace who was the self-titled "law west of the Pecos," offered the solution of moving the bout to a sandbar in the middle of the Rio Grande near Langtry. Shortly before midnight on February 20, fight aficionados, newspapermen, and Rangers boarded overcrowded railcars and traveled four hundred miles down the Southern Pacific line. Upon arriving in Langtry, they found another train, with two hundred passengers from Eagle Pass, had already arrived. The following day, the match began at approximately four-thirty in the afternoon, but proved rather anticlimactic when Fitzsimmons knocked Maher out in the first round.[41]

The following month, the governor received a telegram from Van Horn stating Mexican raiders had crossed the Rio Grande, stolen 2,500 head of sheep from local rancher Stephen W. Pipkin, and driven them across the border. Hughes and Privates Cook, Bryant, and Joseph Russell "Joe" Sitter left Ysleta on March 11, and took the train to recover the stolen livestock. Charles Davis, the federal collector of customs at El Paso, was likewise requested to lend support. The captain later reported his detachment's success, although he was vague on the details. As he had been previously instructed to refrain from pursuing the thieves into Mexico, the presumption was that the *rurales* (Díaz's dreaded mounted constabulary) had provided the Texans some assistance. With the sheep returned to their rightful owner, the Rangers returned to camp on the fifteenth.[42]

More pursuits awaited Hughes later in the year. On September 24, former Ranger James B. Gillett sent a telegram to William R. Martin, the division superintendent of the Galveston, Houston & San Antonio Railroad, warning him of a gang of horse thieves encamped fifteen miles north of Altuda. The ex-Ranger sergeant further informed the superintendent the outlaws were planning a train robbery. The railroad executive requested Captain Hughes break up the plot. Hughes and Privates Ed Bryant and Thalis Cook, Presidio County deputy Jim Pool, guide Wilson C. Combs, and volunteer Arthur McMaster responded to the tip. Hughes later reported, "We struck their trail in Glass Mountains and trailed them about 80 miles and found them in the Star pasture in the Davis Mountains. They would not surrender but fired on us. When we charged on them returning the fire killing two of them, the third man escaped. The names of the parties killed are Jube Frier and Arthur Frier." In addition to the slain desperadoes, the lawmen returned with five horses after having been on the trail eight days and covering 625 miles.[43]

The man who had absconded was later identified as Burke Humphreys, a "general hard character," who was fleeing north to friends in Abilene. Hughes caught the fugitive, and by mid-October he was safely lodged in the El Paso jail, awaiting extradition to Tom Green County. On October 17, the captain helped escort Humphreys to San Angelo for trial. The hearing opened on December 23, and Hughes and Private Cook were attached as witnesses. The defendant was found guilty of horse theft and sentenced to six years in prison.[44]

As active as he was, Hughes used any free moment to work toward the apprehension of Frank Jones's killers, and those of Charley Fusselman. In early July 1893, the Olguins were taken to the Juarez jail, but efforts to extradite them to the United States failed; the outlaws subsequently disappeared from history. However, rumors persisted that sixteen to eighteen men suspected of involvement in Jones's murder were "brought to justice in one way or another." The second effort was more successful. After having been jailed in Las Cruces for horse theft and attempted murder, Gerónimo Parra had been convicted for a house burglary in 1891, and imprisoned in the territorial penitentiary at Santa Fe. He escaped twice and, following recapture, his sentence was increased to seven years.[45]

Hughes wanted the outlaw tried in Texas for the murder of Fusselman, where he was likely to be convicted and sentenced to death. Once the captain learned of his quarry's whereabouts in the fall of 1898, Hughes submitted extradition papers to Miguel Antonio Otero, the territorial governor of New Mexico, on October 25. The request was approved, and Hughes started for Santa Fe on March 7, 1899. Six days later, Hughes and Sheriff Patrick

Floyd "Pat" Garrett of Doña Anna County boarded a train with Parra in the territorial capital, and escorted the prisoner to Las Cruces, then El Paso, arriving on the thirteenth. The grand jury in El Paso indicted Parra for murder on October 6, and an arrest warrant was issued the same day. Parra was convicted of Fusselman's murder and sentenced to death. He remained defiant to the end. On January 5, 1900, at one p.m., on the way to the gallows, he and another condemned prisoner attacked their guards with knives fabricated from smuggled wire. They only managed to injure Ranger Ed Bryant before they were restrained and hung within the same hour.[46]

Following the reorganization of the battalion in June 1900, the governor and the adjutant general urged lawmakers to amend the existing law and enable all Rangers, regardless of rank, to make arrests. "This body of men cannot be too highly commended for the manner in which they have discharged the many dangerous and delicate issues incident to their employment," the governor wrote in his annual address to the Twenty-seventh Legislature. "Their services ... have been invaluable, and may be regarded as an absolute necessity to the State." Representative Ferguson Kyle of Hays County introduced House Bill No. 52 four days later: "An Act to provide for the organization of a 'Ranger Force' for the protection of the frontier against marauding and thieving parties, and for the suppression of lawlessness and crime throughout the State; to prescribe the duties and powers of members of such force, and to regulate their compensation." Senator William Ward Turney of El Paso County proposed Senate Bill No. 31 the same day in the state senate. Intense debate ensued over the issue of whether Rangers should be required to post bonds similar to county and municipal officers. Such guaranties were decided to be unnecessary, and the House approved the measure by voice vote on May 27, 1901. The Senate quickly followed suit by a twenty-three to three vote, and the governor signed the bill into law on March 29, taking effect on July 9.[47]

The new Ranger Force was authorized one quartermaster and four mounted companies consisting of one captain, one first sergeant, and twenty privates each. The governors would appoint the company commanders and the quartermaster. The latter also held the rank of captain, and additionally performed the duties of paymaster and commissary. Captains received a monthly wage of one hundred dollars; sergeants, fifty dollars; and privates, forty dollars. On July 8, 1901, Hughes was reappointed captain of Company D, which was transferred from Ysleta to Fort Hancock. From November 1, 1900, to August 31, 1902, Company D conducted 205 scouts and effected five arrests for murder, fourteen for theft, nine for robbery and burglary, and sixty-three for minor offenses. They recovered and returned to the proper owners seventy-one articles of stolen property, including horses and cattle.[48]

Sergeant Anderson Yancey "Ancey" Baker of Company A, and by extension his comrades-in-arms, had become involved in a feud between local political factions in Brownsville. To preclude any further tensions, Company A was removed from the district, while Company D was transferred from Fort Hancock to Alice, arriving on Christmas Day, 1902. A detachment was sent to Brownsville to deter stock theft in the area.[49]

Hughes was to have a significant role in a criminal case taking place in New York City. In early 1904, Abraham Henry Hummel, partner in the Manhattan law firm of Howe & Hummel, was under indictment for conspiracy to use false affidavits and extorting extravagant fees from a client. The state's chief witness was Charles Foster Dodge, who was himself being prosecuted for perjury during his divorce. Before his case was brought to trial, Dodge skipped town on a ten-thousand-dollar bond. An investigator for the district attorney traced the fugitive to New Orleans, then to Brownsville. Before Dodge could get to Laredo and over the Rio Grande, Hughes, alerted by the New York authorities, arrested him in Alice on February 15. The captain took his prisoner to Houston two days later, and waited for the politicians to settle the matter. While the governor of New York sent an extradition request to Texas Governor Samuel Willis Tucker Lanham, the scrupulous captain refused several generous bribes to release his prisoner. Hughes finally handed Dodge over to a federal marshal, who took him back to New York City. Based on Dodge's testimony, Hummel was convicted of suborning perjury, and the latter was sentenced to one year in prison and forfeiture of his law license.[50]

John Augustus Hulen had been appointed adjutant general on June 1, 1903. In the months following, he stationed the four Ranger companies in strategic locations to maximize their availability. Company D's headquarters was moved from Harlingen to Austin on June 20, 1905, and Hughes's new territory encompassed the portion of the state east of a line that stretched through Clay, Jack, Palo Pinto, Erath, Hamilton, San Saba, Mason, Gillespie, Kerr, Bandera, Medina, Atascosa, Live Oak, and San Patricio Counties. Once in Austin, Hughes was to "arrange to dismount his command as no mounts for it will be foraged at the State's expense after July 1, 1905, except for one mount for commanding officer." In his report covering 1905 and 1906, Hulen acknowledged, "The strength of the force that we are able now to maintain, owing to the small appropriation for the purpose is by far inadequate, and the pay to the men is not sufficient to bring into the service and keep there the best material."[51]

With their expanded area of responsibility, Hughes and his men were kept extremely busy responding to an overwhelming number of appeals for aid. The captain went to Groveton on July 10, and Lampasas on August 8. He then returned to Lampasas on August 22. Hughes, with Privates James Campbell "Doc" White and W. O. Dale, accompanied General Hulen to Edna on October 2 to protect suspected murderer Henry "Monk" Gibson from a lynch mob. Hughes left on October 20, and arrived in Port Lavaca six days later to assist the state fish and oysters commissioner in resolving a tax dispute. He was back in Austin by October 27, having left Dale in Port Lavaca to finish working with the commissioner. In late January of 1906, Rangers Herff Carnes and Milam Harper Wright were called to Humble, north of Houston, to maintain order during a labor strike.[52]

Later in the year, on July 17, Colorado County Sheriff Walter Eldridge "Dickie" Bridge telegrammed Governor Lanham requesting Ranger assistance in keeping the peace as the Reese-Townsend feud finally drew to a close. Earlier, on the fifth, Samuel Marion Hope, a Townsend supporter, and Spencer Herbert "Hub" Reese had engaged in a fistfight at the skating rink in Columbus that left the latter beaten and humiliated. Hub went home to find his brother, John Walter Reese, and fetch his gun. The siblings returned armed, and walked along Milam Street looking for their enemy. As they passed in front of the Franz saloon, Hope threw down on them with a shotgun. Additionally, he had been reinforced by other armed members of his faction, including Hiram Clements. Brother to William D. Clements, another Townsend partisan, Hiram had previously taken no part in the quarrel. In the course of the shootout, Walter and Hub were both wounded. Hiram was slain by Reese's brother-in-law, dentist Joseph Franklin Lessing, Jr. Indicative of the feud's complex web of familial ties, Lessing was a nephew of deceased Sheriff Light Townsend, and stepbrother to Marion Hope. The surviving participants were taken into custody by Sheriff Bridge and released on bond on the fourteenth; they never stood trial. Hughes, Sergeant Tom M. Ross, and Privates Carnes and White reached Columbus the night of July 18. The next day, the Rangers attended a public meeting designed "to express the disapproval of the citizens of the town of the existence of the feud and to devise means to prevent further fighting within the limits of the town."[53]

Hughes was recalled to Austin, but he directed Ranger Wright, working in Navasota, to join the rest of the detachment in Columbus. Sergeant Ross remained in town until July 21, and Private Carnes until the twenty-sixth, before returning to Austin. Hughes was aware the trouble in Colorado County had not ended, so he dispatched Ranger White to Columbus on August 23. Carnes and Wright joined him on September 9 to keep the peace during the district court session. White remained until October 10. For the Rangers, the affray in Columbus was the end of their involvement in the feud. The last act in the tragic drama occurred on May 17, 1907, when Marion Hope assassinated James Henry "Jim" Coleman, a Reese ally, in a San Antonio saloon.[54]

While in Hempstead during an election, Hughes was ordered to Rio Grande City to investigate the assassination of District Court Judge Stanley Welch. The jurist had been overseeing the elections when he was murdered while sleeping on the night of November 5. The captain, with Privates White and Ivan Murchison, arrived in town on November 8. Hughes traveled to Austin on December 7 to complete his monthly returns, then returned to Starr County. He was back in Austin on December 29. Ranger White and new recruit Desiderio Perez stayed behind to work up the case. The two Rangers scouted throughout Starr and Zapata Counties for five days, simultaneously obtaining information on the judge's assassination and breaking up a troublesome gang of horse thieves. Lonnie Bates, a detective and former Treasury Department agent employed by James Babbage Wells, Jr., also investigated the Welch case, and the evidence implicated José Sandoval and Alberto

Cabrera in the murder. Cabrera, a Republican bartender, fled Starr County and crossed over the border into theoretical safety.[55]

Hughes moved the company headquarters camp from Austin to Marfa in May 1907, completing the relocation by the twenty-fourth. While Sandoval was never apprehended, Hughes and Sheriff Deodoro Guerra secured Alberto Cabrera's extradition in July, and had him remanded to the Nueces County jail. There he was charged with Judge Welch's murder. Hughes transferred his headquarters to Ysleta in December. but he traveled to Rio Grande City on March 17, 1908, to testify in Cabrera's trial. The court case was transferred to Cuero on a change of venue. Hughes returned to Ysleta, but he, Tom Ross, and A. Y. Baker traveled to Cuero on June 9 to testify. In total, the prosecution called eighteen witnesses out of a pool of seventy-five. Testimony ended on July 1, and, after deliberations, the jury found Cabrera guilty and sentenced him to life imprisonment. Hughes left town the following day, and returned to Ysleta on July 6, having been gone twenty-eight days and traveling a total of 1,824 miles. Ultimately, Cabrera would escape from prison in 1912, and disappear into Mexico. Three years later, he was thought to have been killed leading a party of bandits into the United States.[56]

Since 1876, Mexico had been ruled by *presidente* Porfirio Díaz through a combination of alliances with state governors, *hacendados*, the Church, financiers, industrialists, and foreign capitalists. Under his regime, internal social instability and the protracted violence along the Rio Grande decreased, albeit at the cost of civil liberties and political rights. The U.S. Army responded to Mexico's pacification of the border by closing all military posts stretching from San Diego to El Paso, except for Fort Huachuca in Arizona. Forts Bliss at El Paso, Clark near Brackettville, Duncan near Eagle Pass, and McIntosh at Laredo continued to operate, while Forts Hancock, Quitman, Ringgold, and Brown were shut down.[57]

President William Howard Taft met with Don Porfirio in El Paso and Ciudad Juárez on October 16, 1909. During this landmark summit, Hughes was a member of the local Committee of Public Safety, which was tasked with providing security for the two chief executives. Indeed, Charles R. Moore, one of Hughes's privates, and Major Frederick Russell Burnham, head of a private security force, foiled a plot by a Mexican activist to eliminate Díaz.

The Ranger arrested the would-be assassin, who was armed with a "pencil pistol," before he was able get close to the Mexican dictator.[58]

Turmoil in Mexico would increasingly demand Hughes's attentions, but he first dealt with domestic troubles. Starting in January 1907, Captain Frank Johnson's Company A, and later Captain Tom Ross's Company B, enforced the local liquor option in dry Potter County to such an extent that relations between them and local law enforcement and saloon operators deteriorated to outright violence. Adjutant General James Oscar Newton had opposed sending Rangers to enforce county laws, but he was overruled by the governor. By October 1909, the Rangers' prohibition assignment had become so controversial that Newton sought a way to extricate them from the shambles. His solution was to withdraw Ross and dispatch Hughes to Amarillo to mediate a peace. Transferring his headquarters, the force's senior captain arrived in town on November 10, and met with officials from the police and sheriff's departments. He informed them that as long as they performed their duty in enforcing the law, even if it was unpopular, he would take no action. His firm but judicious diplomacy proved successful, and allowed the Ranger service to free themselves from a public relations nightmare. With relations with local law enforcement repaired, the captain and his men were engaged in arresting bootleggers, pimps, and gamblers, many of them for misdemeanor offenses. The Rangers were often in district court to either keep the peace or serve as witnesses. They were also on hand during elections at Fort Hancock and Ysleta, among others.[59]

On August 12, 1910, the Rangers received an appeal for assistance from Martin Luther Harkey, the Garza County attorney. In the picturesque town of Post City, founded by cereal magnate Charles William "C. W." Post three years earlier, vigilantes and mob rule were in control, while the local authorities were powerless to act. Post had wanted to build an ideal town where brothels and alcohol were not tolerated; instead, citizens were being assaulted and forced from their homes with death threats. Harkey had been enthusiastically performing his duties when some of the local criminal element decided to directly express their displeasure. While returning to town from bird hunting on August 10, the attorney was waylaid by six men wearing white hoods. They dragged their victim from his car, and bound and blindfolded him.

The leader of the gang informed Harkey they were going to whip him until he could not stand, and if he remained in town, they would kill him. Two of the hooded men restrained the attorney, a third held a pistol to his head, and the remainder took turns thrashing him until the blood poured down his back and legs. They then pistol-whipped him into unconsciousness. The frightened Harkey stole out of town the next day, bolted to Big Spring, and contacted the governor.[60]

Hughes met Harkey in Big Spring on August 13, and found him to be a severely unnerved man. The Rangers escorted the county attorney the sixty miles north to Post City while hearing of the county's troubles. Hughes, with Rangers Charles Moore and Harry Moore (no relation), investigated the matter and ultimately arrested six prominent citizens. As the captain had announced he was prepared to stay in Post City until he was convinced the unrest was over, the examining trial proceeded without incident. Even though he was under constant Ranger protection, Harkey, still traumatized by his experiences, chose to conclude his affairs, resign his position, and leave the county, never to return.[61]

Revisiting the area on September 21, Hughes, Privates Moore and Moore, and Sergeant Joseph Lee Anders of Company C tended to the town of Coahoma, ten miles east of Big Spring. For the last month, a nasty feud had been waged there between the Black, Johnson, and Echols families, and four people had been shot. Men of all factions went everywhere armed, witnesses were threatened, and an innocent girl had been wounded with birdshot to the face. After the Rangers had brought peace to the town, the upstanding citizens of Coahoma signed a heartfelt letter of appreciation for their efforts. Hughes and his men left Big Spring on October 6 to police a local liquor option election in Amarillo.[62]

From 1906 to 1908, the entire Ranger Force of four captains, four sergeants, and eighteen privates had executed 1,017 arrests, (458 of them for felonies), traveled a total of 277,871 miles, and recovered thousands of dollars in stolen property. Considering the immense number of appeals for Ranger assistance, General Newton urged the legislature, on August 31, to increase the 1910–1911 appropriation to fifty thousand dollars, or double the previous amount. He also asked for an increase in the size of the organization to at least fifty officers and men. Unfortunately, the lawmakers denied the Rangers additional funds and manpower. Indeed, they disbanded Company A on September 30, 1910. In the reorganization that followed, Company D became responsible for all North and West Texas.[63]

Hughes and two of his Rangers were in San Benito on November 4 for the trial of Charles Archer Craighead, who was one of their own. On October 1, Craighead, Ranger Dee W. Cox, and Deputy Sheriff Earl West were in the house of their laundress, Paula Treviño. As Craighead was talking to the woman about his clothes, Valentín Noyola was sleeping in a nearby bed with a hat pulled over his face. Several months previously, Charles's brother, James Patterson Nelson "Pat" Craighead, and Ranger Quirl Bailey Carnes had arrested Noyola on a drunk and disorderly charge. Hearing Charles's voice, Noyola leaped to his feet and slashed at the Ranger with a knife, cutting the front of his shirt. Craighead leaped back and pulled his pistol. His five shots hit Noyola in both shoulders, in the left side of his chest, in the abdomen, and in the inner thigh, killing him instantly.[64]

Craighead surrendered to the local authorities, and was bound over for the grand jury on a five-thousand-dollar bond. Desiring to positively resolve the case, he asked to be indicted. He was represented by Judge Jim Wells, the powerful long-time political boss of Cameron County, at the examining trial in Brownsville. The trial proved to be anticlimactic, as the district attorney requested that the judge instruct the jury to return a verdict of "not guilty." On July 31, Pat Craighead and Deputy West had been wounded in a firefight at San Benito with an unidentified party from Mexico that left Ranger Carnes, Special Deputy Sheriff Henry Boomer Lawrence, and one informant dead. Some in the community theorized Charles had come to believe Noyola was involved in the San Benito affray, and had gone looking to exact vengeance. One of Noyola's brothers menaced Craighead, but nothing came of the threat.[65]

The company had been headquartered in Amarillo for a short time, even though Hughes was rarely there. In October, he was ordered to relocate the company back to Ysleta. The *El Paso Herald* noted Hughes would return to Amarillo "preparatory to moving his camp here. He and his rangers will reach here about Oct. 10." The transfer was postponed until mid-November because "owing to strenuous times in other parts of the state he was delayed." The captain reached Amarillo, and the *Herald* reported the company would "arrive soon."⁶⁶

The same month, Hughes turned to monitoring the volatile electoral race in Cameron County between the Democratic "Blue" ticket, supported by the Wells machine, and the Independent "Red" party, made up of Republicans and disaffected Democrats. The scene was tense as the county authorities belonged to the Blue faction and the city officials supported the Reds. Hughes intended to leave two of his men in Brownsville to reinforce other Rangers already there. The district attorney and the district court judge, both loyal Democrats, urged Adjutant General Newton to observe the elections. With such a highly charged setting, General Newton did travel to Brownsville, accompanied by Captain Rogers. The two met with Hughes and Ranger Captain Marvin Eugene Bailey, commanding Company B. The Rangers of Hughes's and Bailey's companies were deployed to the voting precincts that seemed to have the most potential for trouble. Despite the poisonous partisan environment, the only disturbances were some boisterous drunkenness and hurled threats.⁶⁷

In 1910, in order to give his regime the illusion of democracy, Porfirio Díaz permitted a presidential election to occur in Mexico. However, the iron-fisted dictator had no intention of relinquishing power. Francisco Ignacio Madero González, an intellectual reformer, scion of a wealthy Coahuila *hacendado* family, and leader in the *antireeleccionista* movement, began making strides in unseating the eighty-year-old Díaz, and was thrown into prison prior to the election. With Madero's campaign quashed, Don Porfirio was "elected" to his seventh consecutive term in June. After his family secured his release, Madero learned he was to be rearrested and executed, and departed San Luis Potosí for the United States on October 5, 1910. Traveling to San Antonio, he soon delivered his *Plan de San Luis Potosí*. The Plan was backdated to the day he left Mexico to avoid charges under U.S. neutrality laws, and called for a general uprising against the *Porfiriato* to commence on November 20.⁶⁸

Opposition protests to Díaz and the United States commenced in Mexico City and throughout the country on November 10. The demonstrations were provoked by the extralegal execution of Antonio Rodríguez, who had murdered a rancher's wife in Edwards County, Texas. In retaliation for his crime, the Mexican national had been burned at the stake in Rocksprings on November 3. While Rodríguez's death was a catalyst, Mexico's political unrest was due more to a general discontent among the country's population. Grievances included the failure of Díaz to champion his citizens' interests both at home and abroad, the presence of extensive foreign capital in the economy, and the *Porfiriato's* preferential treatment of American entrepreneurs, the largest single group of investors in Mexico. On the eleventh, the U.S. consulate in Ciudad Porfirio Díaz (present Piedras Negras), opposite Eagle Pass, became the target of an angry mob hurling rocks.[69]

As a precaution, Governor Thomas Mitchell Campbell directed his Ranger captains to evaluate the developing events. Madero's proposed attack on Ciudad Porfirio Díaz on November 20 had ended in failure, but the revolutionary movement remained intact. Hughes left El Paso and entrained to Marfa. He reported from there that a deputy sheriff at Ruidosa, situated on the Rio Grande above Presidio, had crossed over into Mexico and encountered a band of 117 *insurrectos*. The rebels had assured the deputy their fight was with Díaz, and they would not raid into Texas. On November 26, Hughes traveled on to Presidio, where he found anxious townsmen readying themselves for hostilities from the Mexican side of the river. For the moment, the scene was peaceful.[70]

The tense quiet was broken when Madero's *insurrectos* attacked Mexican federal troops on December 15. From a rooftop, Hughes and the county sheriff observed through binoculars the two forces maneuver four miles upriver from Ojinaga, across the river from Presidio. Indeed, rather than Ciudad Porfirio Díaz, the revolution would find its first victories in Chihuahua as guerrilla chieftains Pascual Orozco and Francisco "Pancho" Villa overwhelmed small parties of the Mexican federal army.[71]

Following his inauguration on January 17, 1911, Governor Oscar Branch Colquitt fulfilled a campaign promise on February 1, and reduced the manpower of the Ranger Force to two captains, two sergeants, and eight privates— a total of twelve Rangers policing nearly four million citizens and some 268,820 square miles. His command reorganized as Company A, Hughes carried on with one sergeant and five privates. The same year, the governor set a dangerous precedent by introducing a spoils system for commissioning Rangers. His example would be followed by three of his successors, all of whom abused their appointive power to pay political debts. Such practices reduced morale and effectiveness, since sometimes the choices were utterly unqualified for the job.[72]

Even as the governor was slashing the Rangers' budget and manpower, the revolution in Mexico was gathering impetus, particularly in Chihuahua. El Paso became the central point for the acquisition of arms and ammunition by the revolutionary movement. The Shelton-Payne Arms Company, a sporting goods dealer in town, served as a facilitator in smuggling the matériel across the river to all combatant factions of the revolution. In the month of January, Rangers from Hughes's company supported federal officers in patrolling along the Rio Grande near El Paso, and in enforcing the neutrality laws. Pascual Orozco, Madero's senior commander in Chihuahua, marched on Ciudad Juárez, opposite El Paso, on January 30. The news alarmed the residents of El Paso, who feared the battle would spill across the river. After a tense week, the news was received that Orozco was falling back from the border as Mexican federal troops were reinforcing Ciudad Juárez.[73]

Despite Orozco's withdrawal, the War Department dispatched four troops of cavalry from Fort Meade, South Dakota, to El Paso to patrol the Rio Grande. Another troop was sent from San Antonio to Presidio. The U.S. government went one step further and charged Madero, on February 13, with violating the federal neutrality laws. The revolutionary evaded the arrest warrant by departing San Antonio unnoticed, traveling secretly to El Paso, and stealing across the border into Chihuahua on February 14. There, he took personal command of his insurgent forces of one hundred men. Madero remained a wanted man in Texas, where Governor Colquitt ordered Hughes to keep watch for the *insurrecto* leader and be ready to arrest him if he returned to United States soil.[74]

Hughes remained in El Paso, although he sent two men each to Van Horn and Kent on the governor's orders to maintain order during local elections. The captain continued with the U.S. cavalry troopers in patrolling the Rio Grande. To the army's consternation, some several hundred Mexicans had crossed the border downriver from El Paso to enlist in the revolutionary forces. As the recruits were not armed while on American soil, the military was powerless to intervene. Hughes and his Rangers alternated between El Paso and their headquarters in Ysleta, able to move quickly on the thrice-daily trains.[75]

On May 8, Orozco's *maderistas* attacked the federal garrison in Ciudad Juárez from the north, while Villa's men advanced from the south. The Rangers deployed along the riverbank to apprehend any fugitives from American justice who might try to cross over during the battle. One man, wanted for murder, was captured. Standing atop tall houses and boxcars, Hughes and many El Pasoans observed the struggle across the river. "Wish you and all the force could be here to enjoy the fun," the captain lightheartedly informed the adjutant general. The Rangers tried to keep the spectators back, as stray Mexican bullets flew across the river into El Paso. But five American citizens were killed and sixteen wounded from the gunfire. The battle in Juárez, involving bitter house-to-house fighting, concluded two days later with a Madero victory, and the city was declared Mexico's provisional capital. The rebels had killed approximately one hundred federal *soldados*, while their own losses amounted to fifteen dead.[76]

Governor Colquitt was incensed the U.S. government took no significant action in responding to the firing across the border. Believing Washington lacked a coherent foreign policy regarding the upper Rio Grande valley, the governor decided to take matters into his own hands. He ordered Hughes to remain in El Paso on May 15 as his personal representative, and report on whether hostilities seemed likely to resume. The captain also assisted the sheriff in scrutinizing the movements of the revolutionary groups in the city.[77]

After suffering similar reverses elsewhere, the thirty-five-year *Porfiriato* collapsed. The once-invincible Díaz met with Madero and signed the Treaty of Ciudad Juárez on May 21. The dictator stepped down four days later and, with his wife and vice-president, went into exile in Paris, where he would die in 1915. As he boarded the steamer, Don Porfirio observed: "Madero has unleashed a tiger; let's see if he can tame it."[78]

Even though the Mexican Revolution seemed to be waning by the summer, Hughes and his company were still hard-pressed in responding to the countless requests for their assistance. In June, the Ranger captain had three men in Big Spring answering an urgent summons from the sheriff; one man assisting the El Paso County sheriff; and another stationed in Valentine. He retained one private in Ysleta. The following month, Hughes and Privates Craighead, Moore, and Charles H. Webster were in Pecos in response to an appeal from District Court Judge Samuel Jackson Isaacks. Leon Cárdenas Martínez, a young Mexican aged either sixteen or eighteen years old, had admitted to slaying schoolteacher Emma Brown on July 22, in Saragosa, after she had resisted his romantic attempts. However, he later recanted his confession. Tensions in town were high, and a lynching seemed likely. The presence of the state officers kept any violence from occurring, and Martínez was convicted of murder on July 29 and sentenced to death. After the trial, two of the Rangers accompanied the sheriff in transporting the killer to the Midland jail for his safety. Due to his age, Martínez was the subject of an intense legal battle and public opinion campaign waged to save his life. The effort proved futile, and he was hanged in Pecos on May 11, 1914.[79]

The low wages afforded the Ranger Force continued to ensure the service lost experienced men. Private Harry Moore and Sergeant Herff Carnes resigned from Company A on July 5 and August 8, respectively. Both became mounted Customs inspectors, and their one hundred-dollar-per-month salaries equaled that of a Ranger captain.[80]

Realizing the undermanned and underfunded Rangers could not adequately patrol the border, Governor Colquitt continued his quest to seek another source of funding. The governor wrote to President Taft on September 14 requesting a conference. The two executives met in Hutchinson, Kansas, on September 26. Colquitt came away from the discussion with a presidential promise that Congress would reimburse the additional expense of maintaining an enlarged Ranger Force. The governor's campaign rhetoric made doubtful by recent events, the legislature passed legislation on October 1, 1911, authorizing three mounted companies of one captain, one sergeant, and twelve privates each, for a total of forty-two Rangers. The monthly wages were set at one hundred dollars for captains; fifty dollars for sergeants; and forty for privates. Even though the Service's total manpower was reduced, one significant improvement was that all Rangers were to be once again mounted.[81]

Hughes reported that Company A had made 377 arrests from September 1, 1909, to June 30, 1911, the offenses including murder, rape, robbery and burglary, highway robbery, kidnapping, felony theft, and numerous others. The Rangers also stood watch at district court sessions, kept order at elections, assisted local authorities, guarded jails, and recovered stolen property (not including livestock) worth over $550. They conducted 273 scouts and covered a total of 88,637 miles, much of them on horseback.[82]

Hughes, his sergeant, and six privates returned to El Paso on November 23, 1911, to work up several cases of neutrality violations. The Rangers coordinated with American federal officers and *maderista* agents in the investigation of the El Paso-based revolutionary junta that supported General Bernardo Reyes's planned rebellion. Considered Díaz's successor, the general had been in Europe when the dictator was driven from office. Presently in San Antonio, Reyes plotted to overthrow *presidente* Madero, who had been elected to office in October. The law officers discovered, on November 26, that Doctor Rafael Limón the *reyista* paymaster, had gone to San Antonio to acquire funds, and planned to return on November 30. At the same time, the junta in El Paso was procuring dynamite, and had rented a room in which to construct bombs. The Rangers were able to obtain an adjacent room, and conducted surveillance on the bomb makers. The investigation climaxed on November 30 when Hughes and his Rangers, Deputy U.S. Marshal (and ex-Ranger captain) John H. Rogers, Special Agent Louis E. Ross of the U.S. Bureau of Investigation, and a Mexican special agent raided the *reyista* junta, arresting fourteen men for neutrality law violations. Reyes and thirty-seven co-conspirators were indicted by a federal grand jury. The wider Reyes conspiracy had been smashed in Laredo on November 20 by the army and the Customs service, with support from Rangers of Company B. Hughes left town on December 2, but frequently returned to work on revolutionary cases.[83]

Several unintended consequences of the Reyes conspiracy's unraveling included the Rangers' contributions to neutrality enforcement being overlooked, federal officials contending such matters were the province of the federal government, and the belief in Washington that the border was now peaceful and subsidizing the Ranger Force unnecessary. The president notified the governor that federal aid would soon cease, and asked for a list of the total expenditures so Congress could reimburse the state. Federal assistance to Texas ended on January 31, 1912. The state's claim for the supplemental expense incurred in the three months was calculated at $9,639.41.[84]

Insulted over Washington's haughty attitude, Governor Colquitt instructed his Ranger captains to cease enforcing neutrality laws in cooperation with federal officials. Colquitt was quickly able to get satisfaction when the garrison of Ciudad Juárez mutinied on January 31, and declared for Emilio Vázquez Gómez. The garrison members arrested their commander and the city chief of police, freed prisoners from the jail, looted stores and saloons, and erratically discharged their weapons. They then proceeded to isolate themselves by wrecking the telegraph office, demolishing bridges on the two rail lines into the city, and obstructing traffic with El Paso. Hughes reported that Orozco was marching on Juárez to put down the mutiny, but the general's loyalty to the Madero administration was in doubt.[85]

Colquitt promptly telegraphed Taft and urged immediate action. The president replied he had taken steps to respond and brought the matter to the attention of the secretary of war. The governor requested he be kept informed. His major point was the recurrence of stray gunfire into El Paso. Colquitt instructed Hughes to impress that fact on the leader of the *vazquista* rebels, and the captain ordered Ranger Charles Moore to deliver the message. Hughes also prepared an identical message for the commander of the Mexican federal forces. Unfortunately, no such officer was present in the Juárez area. The episode was resolved when Orozco arrived on February 3 and spoke to the mutineers. The general's status was so great the rebels promptly surrendered, and Orozco seized the leaders.[86]

President Madero quickly faced another crisis when Orozco and Pancho Villa, two of his senior military commanders, took up arms against him and each other. Given the American casualties resulting from the fighting in Juárez, the governor was concerned renewed combat would place more citizens in danger. He ordered the majority of the Ranger Force to El Paso, and instructed Adjutant General Henry Hutchings to assess the situation and deliver a report. Perhaps with some hyperbole, the *El Paso Herald* declared: "The rangers are prepared for anything from a fight to a barn dance frolic and the seasoned campaigners along the River Grande are itching for a taste

Francisco "Pancho" Villa. Portrait from glass plate negative. George Grantham Bain Collection. *Courtesy Library of Congress, Washington, D.C.*

of trouble." The alarm proved to be exaggerated after Orozco's forces took Ciudad Juárez on February 27, 1912, with only minimal struggle. Nevertheless, the Rangers were involved in assisting federal authorities to stem the flow of weapons smuggled from Texas to Mexico. They played active roles in large seizures in El Paso and Laredo.[87]

Moreover, on March 3, General Orozco renounced his allegiance to Madero and formally joined the rebel cause. This proved to be a watershed moment, not only because of his military capabilities and his fame in Chihuahua, but also because he quickly supplanted Emilio Gómez as the movement's leader. The new *orozquista* rebels were well-funded and believed they could import arms, ammunition, and supplies through El Paso. The revolutionaries were destined to be disappointed, though. The United States had diplomatically recognized Madero as the legally elected president of Mexico, and, on March 14, the Taft administration enacted a ban on munitions transfers to Mexico. The embargo was revised eleven days later to allow weapons deliveries to the *maderista* forces. To acquire matériel, Orozco's rebels were forced to smuggle shipments across the border, but the paltry amounts could not adequately supply the revolution.[88]

Thus, the Rangers found themselves once again enforcing federal neutrality laws, as well as the arms embargo. The ever-active Hughes arrested three men who were employed by Enrique C. Llorente, the Mexican consul in El Paso, to recruit troops for the Madero government. The captain consulted with a Bureau of Investigation agent who advised him that no case could be made against the three suspects, although one was detained and charged with illegally carrying a firearm. Hughes was accused by Manuel Esteva, the Mexican consul general in San Antonio, of favoring the *orozquistas*. The governor responded by repeating his order that the Rangers remain politically neutral in their duties. Insulted, Hughes, a consummate professional, scorned the accusation and asserted his company had worked well with the Madero secret service in El Paso for the past month. Indeed, Llorente, the chief of that network, was willing to state that fact in writing. In March, a Ranger aided in the capture of two Americans for breaking neutrality laws, and in confiscating fourteen thousand cartridges intended for Orozco's rebels. Throughout that month, Company A assisted federal authorities in making fifteen arrests for neutrality violations, and in seizing 18,761 rounds of rifle ammunition.[89]

Civilians and soldiers alike in El Paso were tempted to realize significant profits in smuggling arms and ammunition across the border to Ciudad Juárez. Hughes accompanied Bureau of Investigation agents in raids, which were followed by the arrests of Sabino and Abelino Guaderrama on charges of conspiracy to smuggle 52,000 cartridges. The captain and his Rangers were involved in seizing 390 rifles and 83,760 rounds of rifle ammunition throughout the month of April. In addition to numerous independent operators, major arms dealers, such as Krakauer, Zork and Moye, Douglas Hardware Company, and Shelton-Payne, managed hugely lucrative businesses selling ammunition to *orozquista* and *maderista* agents. Indeed, in a two-year period, forty thousand rifles, ten million rounds of ammunition, and five hundred tons of dynamite were transferred across the border. The law allowed the purchasing of matériel, but not the exportation. The federal grand jury indicted the Krakauer firm with conspiracy to smuggle munitions in October 1912. With a change of venue to Phoenix, the jury acquitted the defendants of all charges.[90]

Between instances of smuggling suppression, Hughes spent a portion of his time testifying in the federal trials of *reyista* conspirators he had arrested the previous year. He also responded to the constant appeals for Ranger assistance. He assigned two men to the Panhandle to investigate rustling in Dickens County, one Ranger to testify in Galveston liquor trials before joining two others to enforce the peace in Sweetwater during the court session, and two more Rangers to quell more feuding in Big Spring and Coahoma, where one man had been killed.[91]

On May 21, Rangers Charles Moore and Charles Webster, and A Troop of the Fourth U.S. Cavalry, faced a large party of mounted *orozquistas* gathered on Pirate Island, the same ground where Captain Frank Jones had lost his life. The rebels had positioned themselves atop two adobe houses and in skirmish lines on either end of the buildings. The American regulars fell back to approximately five hundred yards from the international boundary, but Moore and Webster held their ground, some one hundred yards from the border. One of the Mexicans fired a shot, and the two Rangers unsheathed their rifles, rode into the brush, and dismounted. The cavalry troopers withdrew another hundred yards. Suddenly, approximately thirty-five *orozquistas* charged. The screaming, rifle-armed riders were closing on the Rangers, when the two law officers stepped from cover and walked toward them. Moore signaled the charging Mexicans to halt with an upraised hand. "This is Texas," he warned in Spanish. The surprised *insurrecto* commander dispatched several of his men to parley with the Rangers. Moore informed them their cause was not his concern, but, if they crossed into Texas, they would be arrested. Even though his force outnumbered the Rangers and soldiers, the rebel captain decided not to engage the Americans in battle. Instead he withdrew his men back to the Mexican side.[92]

As spring turned to summer, General Victoriano Huerta, the *maderista* field commander, crushed the *orozquistas* in several decisive battles. The rebel forces repeatedly fell back toward the city of Chihuahua. As the renewed hostilities neared Juárez, the citizens of El Paso were again concerned about the fighting spilling over into Texas. The sheriff notified the adjutant general that the Mexican garrison had been reinforced with *soldados* and artillery. He also passed on a rumor that the *maderistas* had secretly organized a force in El Paso to launch an assault across the international bridge when the federal troops attacked Juárez. The governor responded by placing General Hutchings and the entire Texas National Guard on alert and ready to move to El Paso by special trains. The executive intended to protect the city if the U.S. troops at Fort Bliss could not. The adjutant general arrived in El Paso on June 20, but again the alarm proved false, and he returned to Austin three days later.[93]

Hughes and Private Moore traveled to Brownsville in June for "special duty." While they were gone, the Orozco insurrection continued to crumble throughout the month of July, until Juárez was the only city remaining in rebel hands. The two Rangers returned to Ysleta on August 7, reporting that "everything in that section was quiet." Madero's forces finally entered the beleaguered city on August 16. Five hundred refugees, both civilian and military, staggered over the border into El Paso. The revolution was seemingly at an end, but bands of *orozquistas* turned to guerrilla warfare or brigandage in northern Chihuahua. Customs agents, U.S. marshals, and federal troops positioned themselves along the border. Returning to El Paso, Captain Hughes and his company joined the sheriff in deterring the irregulars from raiding into Texas.[94]

Early the next year, Moore informed the captain of heavily armed Mexicans crossing the border on Pirate Island. He and Webster, along with an El Paso deputy sheriff, went to the scene on January 28, 1913. The following day, the officers had another encounter with *insurrectos* when they discovered six revolutionaries on the Texas side of the island. Once the Mexicans fired on the lawmen, the Americans defended themselves and killed two mounted rebels, one of whom was carrying a battle flag. Two more were wounded, and the survivors fled back to Mexico. Prior to departing to report the confrontation, Moore retrieved the enemy standard. He and Webster posed with the flag for a photograph in El Paso before Hughes sent it to the adjutant general.[95]

Hughes submitted an incident report to the governor, and Colquitt responded, "Keep me advised of the situation and shoot straight if necessary." He later wrote, "I think the time has come when the State of Texas should not hesitate to deal with those marauding bands of rebels in a way which they will understand. I instruct you and your men to keep them off of Texas territory if possible, and if they invade the State let them understand they do so at the risk of their lives."[96]

By early February 1913, the border crisis had seemingly quieted to the point where Hughes could disperse his eight Rangers to Marfa, Valentine, Hebbronville, Dickens, and Fort Stockton, in addition to Ysleta and El Paso. However, General Huerta, chief of the Mexican army, overthrew President Madero on February 18 and placed him under arrest. On February 22, while the deposed leader and José María Piño Suárez, his vice-president, were being moved from Lugumberri prison to the Federal District, they were assassinated. The general-turned-provisional-president publicly declared the two had been killed in a failed rescue attempt. Huerta moved to consolidate his position, but opposition to his regime quickly emerged—mainly in the person of Venustiano Carranza, the governor of Coahuila. Carranza issued a revolutionary manifesto, raised an armed force he called the Constitutionalist Army, and took his place at its head as "First Chief." Among the *insurrectos* who rallied to his banner was Pancho Villa, who had been living in exile in El Paso. Romanticized by the American press, Villa developed his followers, the *División del Norte*, into the foremost fighting force in the Constitutionalist

Army. The Revolution would now enter its bloodiest phase on the border as the fighting spread across the entire northern tier of states.[97]

As the Mexican foreign minister was a *huertista*, Carranza opened a direct dialogue with Governor Colquitt on matters affecting Texas and Coahuila in May 1913. Washington refused to recognize Huerta as the rightful leader of Mexico, which, in time, proved beneficial to the Constitutionalist cause. Border towns, such as Nuevo Laredo, Ojinaga, and Matamoros, were rallying to the Huerta banner, while rural areas were supporting the Constitutionalists. *Insurrecto* activity increased, weapons smuggling across the border intensified, and some Hispanic Texans were slipping into Mexico to join the struggle. Additionally, England, France, and Germany—all maneuvering for influence on the eve of World War I—dispatched material support to the Huerta regime. The Rangers suffered from too few numbers and too many appeals for aid to cover the border effectively. Governor Colquitt answered the protests of the *huertista* consul in San Antonio by pointing to the federal government which had the lead in enforcing neutrality.[98]

In April 1913, Hughes and his men were on hand at El Paso's Union Station to welcome famed novelist Zane Grey. The former dentist had traveled to the border town to conduct research for his next book. Hughes's Rangers provided the author of *Riders of the Purple Sage* with firsthand material regarding conditions on the border. Grey was impressed by the Texas lawmen. His subsequent book *The Lone Star Ranger*, published in 1915, was dedicated to Hughes and his company with "the hope that it shall fall to my lot to tell the world the truth about a strange, unique, and misunderstood body of men—the Texas Rangers—who made the great Lone Star State habitable, who never know peaceful rest and sleep ... who will surely not be forgotten and will some day come into their own."[99]

Relations between management and the predominately Hispanic labor force at the smelter near El Paso became increasingly tense in late April. Approximately three thousand workers went on strike, and the two sides skirmished twice, resulting in one man killed and one wounded. Ranger Grover Scott Russell of Hughes's company was on duty in rowdy Smeltertown. On June 23, the captain assigned him to assist Deputy Sheriff William Henry Garlick in serving an arrest warrant for rustling on Manuel Guaderrama.

The suspect's family was well-known to El Paso lawmen as being involved in thefts, smuggling, and murder. Hoping to locate the suspect, the officers went to the combination grocery store and saloon Manuel and his brother Juan owned in Smeltertown. Russell and Garlick casually entered the establishment and asked to purchase ten cents worth of tobacco from Juan, who was minding the counter. The lawmen watched Juan closely, as well as the door that led to the neighboring saloon. Unfortunately, they did not consider Juan's elderly mother, Marina, who edged behind Russell and struck him over the head with an axe handle. As the poleaxed Ranger began to drop, Juan yanked a Luger pistol from under the counter and fatally shot Russell and Garlick. He then dashed around the counter, drew the window shades, and slashed at the murdered officers' heads with a hatchet. After ensuring the lawmen were indeed dead, he then apparently realized he had shot his mother in the stomach with a stray round. She would die after an hour of agonizing pain. In the meantime, Juan called the city police and reported the two lawmen had entered his store drunk and belligerent, and had assaulted his mother. The police informed him the sheriff's office had jurisdiction in Smeltertown. Word of the shooting reached El Paso only a few minutes later.[100]

Hughes rushed to El Paso from his Ysleta headquarters and assisted the chief deputy sheriff in investigating the murders. The captain was positive the killings had been premeditated and in response to the slain officers having earlier arrested several Guaderramas for rustling. Thirteen Guaderrama men were taken into custody, six of whom were indicted for murder. Only five were still under indictment when the trial began on January 13, 1914. After the case was handed to the jury, they deliberated for forty-two hours and cast 116 ballots before announcing to the judge they were hopelessly deadlocked. In the second trial, which began in June 1915, Juan Guaderrama was convicted of second-degree murder and sentenced to five years' incarceration.[101]

In May 1913, Hughes, accompanied by two Rangers, went to Valentine in order to curtail cattle rustling. Despite his plan to spend several months in the area, events in Chihuahua forced him to leave his men in Valentine and Marfa, and return to El Paso. The momentum in the ongoing struggle in northern Mexico was now with the Constitutionalists, although the cacique warlords who composed the leadership were divided by personal ambitions and agendas. Small bands of men claiming to support the Constitutionalist cause were gathered downriver from Ysleta in the town of Guadalupe. They boasted of their intentions to attack Ciudad Juárez in early July. Hughes doubted the success of such an endeavor, but he was still obliged to patrol the Rio Grande, sometimes in concert with mounted Customs inspectors. While the would-be revolutionaries from Guadalupe were less of a threat, four columns of the Constitutionalist Army were maneuvering toward Juárez by late June. Captain Hughes, El Paso's mayor, army officers, and city police detectives all reconnoitered the river in order to form contingency plans in case of an attack.[102]

The Ranger captain scouted downriver as far as Fort Hancock, and came to view the likelihood of an attack on Juárez as remote. He also reported the Constitutionalists were not raiding into Texas and, indeed, seemed friendly to Americans. With the situation appearing normal, Hughes left the border and headed for Valentine to combat the rustlers wreaking havoc on the ranchers in that region.[103]

On November 15, Hughes was in San Antonio on another task when Villa captured the Juárez rail station, caught the garrison by surprise, and took the city by subterfuge. Later the same month, Hughes was assigned to investigate potential subversive activity in San Antonio. The governor was receiving threatening letters warning of Hispanic dissidents arming themselves in the Alamo City, and he wanted Hughes to investigate the matter. The captain obtained the names of various arms dealers, personally questioned a portion of them, and arranged for the sheriff to interview the remainder. Hughes subsequently reported there were no suspicious purchases of munitions, and the sheriff would be notified if there were in the future. The Ranger captain also pursued leads in San Marcos and other locales in the area, and located several signers of the hostile letters. As a result, Hughes concluded there existed no Hispanic plot, and the letters were merely a feeble gesture by one of the minor revolutionary factions.[104]

In April 1914, the Ranger Force consisted of eighteen officers and men. Company A, under Captain Hughes, had seven privates covering West Texas and the lower Rio Grande valley from stations at Ysleta, El Paso, Dickens, Uvalde, Hebbronville, and Raymondville. By the summer, Hughes had been a part of the Ranger service for twenty-seven years, but, as he neared his sixtieth birthday, the captain began to look at other prospects. He checked into the San Carlos Hotel in Brownsville on June 7, and proceeded to discuss the possibility of running for sheriff with influential citizens of Cameron County. These gentlemen wanted the Ranger to enter the race as a compromise candidate before the Democratic primary on July 25. He agreed and allowed his name to be added to the ballot. However, within days, he changed his mind and withdrew from the contest on June 17. The reason Hughes would consider other opportunities was that James Edward Ferguson, Jr. was emerging as the Democrats' gubernatorial candidate. The captain was uneasy about what a potential Ferguson administration would mean to the Ranger Force and to his own career.[105]

Hughes's suspicions were well-founded. Once inaugurated on January 19, 1915, Governor Ferguson immediately used the Ranger Force to reward his supporters. The tradition of Ranger captains hiring their own men was long-standing, and Hughes could be counted on to resist any meddling in the recruitment process. However, Ferguson needed to pay his political debts. Thus, the new governor chose not to reappoint the non-political Hughes in order to replace him with a more compliant officer. The veteran Ranger captain stepped down from his post on January 31.[106]

Through the years, Hughes had wisely invested his paltry salary in real estate around Ysleta, along with a generous gratuity he had received from mine owners in Shafter for services rendered. By the time he left the Ranger service, his investment portfolio was showing a healthy return. After he retired, he operated an alfalfa farm near Ysleta. The same year, he was once more the superintendent of the local Sunday school. Wishing to devote time to his business ventures, Hughes purportedly refused the appointment of El Paso police chief. He purchased stock in the Citizen's Industrial Bank in Austin in 1929, and was the chairman of the board and majority shareholder by the 1940s. He was later chairman of the Motor and Industrial Finance Corporation.[107]

Although a self-described "horseback Ranger," Hughes satisfied his love of travel by purchasing a brand-new 1924 Model T Ford. Even as he advanced into his seventies and eighties, he drove twice to California to visit his old friend Ira Aten, to Austin numerous times, to Corpus Christi, to Hot Springs, Arkansas, and to Hot Springs, New Mexico. When his nephew, Emery H. Hughes, son of his brother Emery S. Hughes, indicated a desire to own his uncle's "antique" automobile, Hughes gave the car to him and purchased a new Ford V-8.[108]

In his retirement, Hughes was accorded numerous accolades, and became a symbol for a bygone era of gunfighting lawmen, desperate outlaws, and the Texas frontier. He was included in Eugene Cunningham's classic book *Triggernometry*, which was first published in 1934. The chapter covering his career was entitled "Bayard of the Chaparral," suggesting Cunningham saw Hughes as a "knight without fear and beyond reproach." Hughes served as grand marshal of the Sun Carnival parades of 1936 and 1942. Along with Jim Gillett, he was a guest of honor at the Texas Centennial Exposition in Dallas. In addition, an oil portrait of the captain by professional artist Leola Freeman was unveiled at the celebration. Mrs. Freeman named her work "Lone Star Ranger" after the book of the same name written by Zane Grey. In July 1942, Jack Martin published *Border Boss* that purported to tell his life story.[109]

The iconic Ranger captain received one last honor on May 21, 1947. Both houses of the Fiftieth Legislature passed resolutions inviting Hughes to be their guest, and extended to him the privileges of the floor for that day.[110]

However, between the end of May and the beginning of June, Hughes was experiencing increased signs of declining health, and he was reportedly despondent. On June 3, 1947, he took his Colt .45 pistol into the garage of his niece's home in Austin and shot himself in the roof of the mouth. He did not leave a note. Apparently, no one heard the gunshot, and he was found only after his relatives missed him at dinnertime and searched for him. An inquest held the same day by Justice of the Peace Mace Thurman ruled the fatal injury to have been self-inflicted. He was buried with full honors in the State Cemetery on June 5. At the time of his death, he was the oldest living Ranger captain.[111]

John R. Hughes was not a man given to self-aggrandizement. While he granted interviews in his later life, he remained reluctant to discuss many aspects of his daring life. To a public nostalgic for a Wild West in the recent past, he was a perfect model of a heroic yet modest captain. His reputation for winning every gun battle and never losing a prisoner was mostly true, with some measure of journalistic exaggeration. What cannot be disputed is his status as one of the Ranger service's greatest manhunters.

John H. Rogers. #P.80.342. *Courtesy Texas Ranger Hall of Fame and Museum.*

Chapter 12

John H. Rogers: "A Man of Conviction and Faith"

John Harris Rogers was a man of conviction and faith. Indeed, he resembled more a preacher than the stereotypical Ranger captain. In fact, he was a staunch Presbyterian who never swore or used alcohol. An elder in his church, he was a quiet and modest man. His understated manner in enforcing the law led many a criminal to erroneously assume the captain was weak. These miscreants found, to their sorrow, this notion was false. Rogers was a proven veteran of several gun battles, and bore the scars to prove his strength. To the men of the Ranger service, he offered steady leadership and a moral authority that would see the Frontier Battalion transition into the Ranger Force. Brigadier-General Pleasant Blair Rogers, his son, wrote: "I am now a retired soldier who served over thirty years in the United States Army and fought in two wars. I have seen many good men die, but my father was the best man I ever saw live."

He was born on the family homestead near Kingsbury, Guadalupe County, Texas, on October 19, 1863. Born in 1844, his father, Pleasant William Miles Rogers, grew up on the family farm along the Chickasaw Trail in Tennessee and Mississippi. His mother, Mary Amanda (Harris) Rogers, had been born in Wilson County, Tennessee, on February 6, 1845. In the fall of 1856, John's Grandpa Rogers decided to join the westward migration and traveled to Texas, where he acquired 162 acres in Guadalupe County. In the subsequent sectional conflict, Pleasant and four of his brothers cast their lot with the Southern Confederacy. Pleasant joined the Third Texas Infantry on November 25, 1861, was discharged on July 12, 1862, and enlisted in the Thirty-sixth Texas Cavalry on July 15, 1863. Three of the brothers would survive the war; the other two were not so fortunate. Pleasant married Mary, who had since moved to Texas, on January 8, 1863. Following the war, the couple lived on the Guadalupe County farm. Besides John, Pleasant and Mary raised Laura Henrietta Rogers, born on March 25, 1866, and Curren Lee Rogers, born on April 2, 1869.[1]

Pleasant grew ill and died on December 18, 1875. The widow Rogers was left to care for three small children. She married "stock driver" William Carey Crier on March 1, 1876, and he took over the management of the farm. Except for scattered fenced-in cultivated fields, all of Guadalupe County was open range suitable for the grazing of livestock. As the leading industry of the area was cattle raising, most farmers also engaged in that pursuit. To William and Mary was born Maggie Amanda Crier, on September 27, 1877, and Haywood Crier, on September 21, 1883.[2]

As a teenager, John Rogers devoted himself to the teachings of the Christian faith, and remained true to his beliefs for the rest of his life. Carrying both a pocket Bible and a gun in the years to come, this career lawman would read Scripture to youthful prisoners in an attempt to lead them onto a better path. Walter P. Webb wrote: "There was just one quality that the Borderlands held against Rogers, and that was one which would have added to his reputation in another portion of the state. He was a bit too much the Presbyterian—the Sunday School man—to wholly please the Border."[3]

After spending the fall session of 1880 studying agriculture at Concrete College near Cuero in DeWitt County, Rogers journeyed to recently organized Mitchell County to work as a cowhand for a ranch on Lone Wolf Creek. Following the events that saw Captain Bryan Marsh of the Frontier Battalion relieved and his company disbanded, Rogers enlisted in the reorganized Company B on September 5, 1882, as a private. His early duties included taking the train to El Paso on October 30 to observe the state and local elections occurring there. The polls were quiet, and the company returned in

November. He then helped keep the peace in the rail towns on the Texas & Pacific line from Midland to Big Spring to Abilene.[4]

On November 18, Adjutant General Wilburn Hill King issued General Order No. 8, which reduced each company to fifteen men, leaving the battalion with only ninety officers and men. The order was effective from December 1, through the remainder of the fiscal year ending February 28, 1883. Rogers found himself the victim of more budget cuts when he was discharged, effective October 31. He spent four months at home in Guadalupe County, then traveled to Cotulla to enlist in Company F on March 1, 1884, under Lieutenant Josephus "Joe" Shely. The first mention of Rogers in the official reports occurred relatively soon after he joined the company. On April 24, he and another Ranger were sent to La Salle County to search for stolen livestock. Unfortunately, the pair failed to find any and returned to camp on May 6. The Frontier Battalion boasted a field strength above customary levels in 1884, with 136 officers and men. From December 1, 1883, to November 30, 1884, Company F made 340 arrests, including eleven for murder and 181 for cattle, horse, or other thefts. Their number of apprehensions was three times as many as the next highest figure.[5]

In August, Shely, recently promoted to captain, and a detachment of six Rangers, including Privates John Rogers and James A. Brooks, were sent to Anahuac in Chambers County to break up the rampant cattle rustling occurring there. The local cattlemen's association had requested assistance, and Governor John Ireland personally ordered in Shely. The thieves had run roughshod without fear of the consequences, but once the Rangers arrived they were quickly put to flight.[6]

Rogers was assigned to work with a Karnes County deputy in apprehending Cotulla resident Richard Jones on September 2, 1884. Feuding with another individual, Jones had assaulted his nemesis the previous day with the intent to murder. Rogers captured Jones on the third, and remanded him to the custody of the county sheriff. The private was later assigned to Lieutenant William Scott's detachment in Cuero. He arrested Joseph Megler on December 13, on a charge of forgery in DeWitt County, and deposited him in jail the same day. On December 19, the entire detachment relocated to a camp one mile north of Yorktown.[7]

Joe Shely. *Courtesy Wilson County Historical Society, Floresville, Texas.*

As Cotulla seemingly began to settle down, General King contemplated shifting Company F to another locale in need of assistance. The Nineteenth Legislature reduced the battalion's appropriation, which forced the adjutant general to put his thoughts into action. Rogers was discharged on January 20, 1885, but allowed to reenlist on May 5. While one company was left to watch over the lower valley, Company F was transferred to Uvalde County in June. Captain Shely resigned, and Lieutenant William Scott replaced him as the company commander. On July 10, Rogers and Private William Terry were sent into the eastern portion of Edwards County to apprehend Reinhart Mingus and Peter Mingus for cattle theft. The two Rangers captured their prey the next day and returned to camp. The pair of rustlers were delivered to Edwards County Sheriff Ira Lewis Wheat on the twelfth. Sergeant Brooks, Sheriff Wheat, and one other Ranger set out on July 19 to locate horses stolen in Taylor and Runnels Counties. They recovered the stock in Edwards County the following day, and arrested Tony Mingus for cattle theft, finishing the work Rogers and Terry had started. In November, Company F moved from Uvalde to Wilbarger County, where they established camp near the town of Vernon.[8]

The Piney Woods of Sabine and San Augustine Counties lay alongside the Red River across from Louisiana. The country possessed its own version of open range as stock-raisers ran hogs on unfenced land. As with cattle, questions concerning ownership of land and swine were often settled with violence. One such episode occurred near Hemphill where Willis Jackson "Uncle Willis" Conner, and his sons, had claimed all the acreage around their cabin, regardless of the actual legal title. After two men who had purchased the land on which the Conner home stood turned up dead on December 8, 1883, Willis and four of his sons surrendered peacefully to the law. Charles Wilson Conner and his brother Frederick, also known as "Fed," were tried for the crime the following year. Both were convicted, and Charles received a twenty-five-year sentence on October 15, 1884, while Fed appealed and received another trial. He was again found guilty and sentenced to life imprisonment. Fed would never serve his time, though. He was still in the San Augustine jail with his father and his brothers William and John when fifteen family members and friends staged a jailbreak on March 25, 1885. For months, the Conners evaded posses by moving from one improvised camp to the next while sending messages to relatives proclaiming their innocence. According to future Ranger captain and adjutant general William Warren Sterling, they were "the most audacious band of desperadoes in deep east Texas [who] lived like savages in the dense thickets, trapped, stole livestock, and defied the local authorities."[9]

In February 1886, those same officials called on Governor Ireland for assistance. In the company of Nacogdoches County Sheriff Andrew Jackson "John" Spradley and Deputy William Muckleroy Burrows, Lieutenant Scott briefly reconnoitered the area and educated himself on a territory vastly different from the plains and deserts Rangers usually worked. Scott, recently promoted to captain on May 1, retrieved his company and returned to the hostile environment of Sabine County, arriving at Hemphill on July 15. Scott and his men established camp near town and began hunting for the fugitives.[10] They were able to get word of Alfred Horton "Alfie" Conner, another of Willis's sons, on August 1. Alfie had been among the mob that broke his family out of jail. The Rangers trailed him across the Sabine into Calcasieu Parish, Louisiana, and apprehended him on the sixth. After a brief scrap, the fugitive was shackled and taken back to Hemphill. He drew a two-year sentence for the jailbreak, and was imprisoned at Rusk from September 18, 1886, to July 14, 1888. Even with the task of finding the rest of the Conners unfinished, Company F was withdrawn from East Texas and returned to Brown County. There they fought a gun battle with fence-cutters on November 9, 1886, that resulted in two perpetrators mortally wounded.[11]

The company broke camp at Brownwood and returned to Sabine County, arriving on March 29, 1887. The Conner family was still hiding in the wilds of the piney woods. After the two attorneys who had prosecuted the murder case were threatened, local authorities requested assistance in apprehending the notorious gang. The officers were able to persuade one of the Conners' neighbors to reveal the location of the family's lair. The outlaws were away on a hunt with the informant when the lawmen arrived at the hideout ten miles south of Hemphill so they settled down to wait.[12]

On March 31, at approximately two o'clock in the morning, the mole arrived and directed the Rangers toward the Conners' camp situated on top of a knoll. The officers chose those who would stay behind to guard the horses, and the remainder crept quietly through the stand of pines. The area immediately around the campsite had been cleared of all the trees, leaving no cover for anyone approaching. At daybreak, Captain Scott divided his company into two squads, and the Rangers proceeded toward the encampment. One of the Conners was alerted to the advancing lawmen, and the outlaws opened fire. Ranger James H. "Jim" Moore was killed outright, Scott was shot through the left lung, and Rogers was wounded in the left side and arm. One of the Conners, one packhorse, and four dogs were killed, and another outlaw was wounded. The surviving fugitives escaped into the woods.[13]

Rogers stayed in San Augustine for two weeks recovering from his wounds. In late April, he traveled to his mother's ranch to convalesce. Returning to the company, now posted near Weatherford, one month later, he was accompanied by his younger brother, Curren "Kid" Rogers, who enlisted in the Frontier Battalion on June 1.[14]

In Rogers's absence, Sergeant John McNelly (nephew of Captain L. H. McNelly) had been detached from Company B on April 3, and ordered to work the aftermath of the Conner fight. Captain Scott was still recovering from his wounds, and Sergeant Brooks was dealing with legal entanglements in Fort Smith, Arkansas. After several weeks in the piney woods, McNelly returned to his own bailiwick on the sixteenth. The captain returned, and the company headquarters was shifted on June 10 to the town of Cisco.[15]

On June 17, six or seven men held up the Southern Pacific No. 19 train one mile east of Flatonia, and robbed the express and mail cars, as well as the passengers, not even sparing the conductor, brakeman, and porter. The combined value of the looted money and valuables was estimated to be ten thousand dollars, eight thousand of which belonged to Wells, Fargo & Company. Witnesses later reported the leader of the thieves, the only one unmasked, was addressed by his confederates as "Dick." After delaying the train for more than an hour, the bandits mounted their waiting horses and rode off. Once word reached Flatonia, a posse set out after the gang, but the robbers had too great a lead. Three men suspected of the train robbery were in the custody of U.S. Marshal John Rankin by the twenty-first. A fourth was apprehended in San Antonio by the Harris County sheriff on June 22, and the Bexar County sheriff arrested a fifth the same day. Two days later, two of the suspects were discharged for lack of evidence. The other three were released on the twenty-seventh. Deputy U.S. Marshal William H. Van Riper suspected train robber John Barber was behind the crime and recruited Rogers on July 10 to assist him in catching the fugitive. The two lawmen tracked Barber toward Doan's Store and the Indian Territory, but ultimately lost the trail. Rogers returned to camp on July 13.[16]

Despite the unsuccessful manhunt, Rogers supervised another detachment on August 4, this time to Callahan County to pursue horse thieves. Once more, the search was unproductive. On the seventh, Company F broke camp.

While the Rangers were en route to Ballinger in Runnels County, Rogers led four men on August 9 in scouting northern Brown County for several suspects charged with assault with intent to murder Joe Copeland, a local man who had assisted authorities in fence-cutting cases the previous year. The following day, Rogers and his detachment arrested four of the wanted men, and delivered them to the sheriff; the Rangers returned on the twelfth. While Scott traveled ahead to locate a new campsite, Rogers supervised the company's movements. The men reached Ballinger on the fourteenth, and Rogers resumed his place in the ranks. However, the brief tastes of command he had experienced would serve him well, as chances for advancement awaited him in the near future.[17]

On October 3, the stagecoach was held up near San Angelo. Rogers, along with Brooks and three other Rangers, arrived in town the following day. While Brooks led the sheriff and one of the men north along the stage road to search for signs of the highwayman, Rogers took the other two south. On the fifth, Rogers and his companions received word that horse thief George Bright had been spotted outside of town. Leaving the trail, the three Rangers followed the outlaw to a motte of trees near the Concho River. Choosing to resist arrest, Bright pulled his pistol, but Rogers beat him to the draw. The gunshot wound proved non-fatal, and Bright was lodged in the county jail. The officers continued to hunt for the stage robber, and Brooks caught up to him by the ninth. The fugitive was turned over to the U.S. marshal.[18]

The rest of the company followed Rogers and Brooks to Tom Green County on November 11, establishing headquarters two miles east of town along the Concho. Five days later, Rogers and Private T. S. Crowder undertook a one-day scout for fugitives in the southern portion of Tom Green County. Beginning on December 6, the two Rangers twice performed similar duty in the northern and eastern parts of the county. They were joined by Frank Carmichael on a fourth outing on the ninth, this one into the county's western reaches, and a fifth on December 12. The patrols resulted in a total of eight arrests, all for stock theft.[19]

While outlaws were being brought to justice by the Rangers, Braxton "Brack" (or "Captain Dick") Cornett, a suspect in the Flatonia robbery, was killed by Alfred Young Allee, grandfather of the Ranger captain of the same name, at a ranch in Frio County on February 12, 1888. Meanwhile, train robber John Barber was still at large and reportedly last seen riding south. Company F got on his trail, but returned to camp on April 29 without their quarry. Later, on September 22, Barber robbed the train near Harwood as a member of the Cornett-Whitley gang, which now included William Henry "Bill" Whitley, Samuel Dawson "Kep" Queen, and Kep's nephew Victor Queen. Most of the outlaws were either captured or killed by pursuing lawmen near Floresville on September 25. Barber was slain the following year in the Indian Territory by deputy U.S. marshals Captain Gideon White and Barney Connelly.[20]

Being unable to catch Barber himself was to have no effect on Rogers's career. After Captain Scott resigned, he was succeeded in command by Lieutenant Brooks. Rogers was promoted to sergeant on May 1, 1888, and placed in command of a detachment in Mills County. Rogers moved his men to Ballinger on the twenty-fifth, and the entire company moved to Kerr County six days later. On June 15, Rogers commanded a detachment near Barksdale, and later Leakey, from where he made numerous arrests for cattle rustling, horse theft, the blotching of brands, and fence-cutting. Brooks moved the company headquarters to Rio Grande City on October 6, and Rogers commanded a detachment at Brownsville and Edinburg from May 3, 1889 to June 15. Company F relocated to Santa María the following October, while Rogers was ordered to take command of a detachment in Rio Grande City on January 5, 1890.[21]

Between 1889 and 1891, the entire Frontier Battalion was quite active. The Rangers of the four undermanned companies conducted 394 scouts covering 89,472 miles, guarded twenty-five jails, and engaged outlaws with deadly force nine times, killing three men and wounding two. Two state officers lost their lives and one was wounded. The battalion members arrested 597 men, including seventy-six for murder, sixty-one for assault with intent to kill, thirty-nine for aggravated assault, 160 for livestock theft, and 201 for misdemeanors. On May 20, 1890, Rogers and his men reunited with the rest of the company at a new camp one mile from Cotulla. Budget cuts had compelled Company D to shift its focus to the Big Bend on April 28, and Company F was assigned to cover the whole expanse of South Texas. At first, the honest citizens and the criminal element of wild and wooly

Cotulla looked askance on the soft-spoken, modest and deeply religious Ranger sergeant. Once Rogers apprehended a sufficient number of cattle rustlers, horse thieves, murderers, and other troublemakers, the townspeople became believers.[22]

In the fall and winter of 1891, unfinished business threatened to once more plunge the borderlands into war. On September 15, Catarino Garza and his armed followers crossed the Rio Grande at Mier and proclaimed their *Plan Revolucionario*. The basic tenets of the *pronunciado* called for the overthrow of Porfirio Díaz, the restoration of the 1857 Constitution, the redistribution of "vacant" land, and the promise of restored civil liberties, fairer trade policies, and the end of outside investors infringing upon local autonomy. Garza flamboyantly announced to his fellow citizens, "The last of the independent journalists, the most humble of all, today abandons the pen to seize the sword in defense of the people's rights." The *Garzistas* remained in Mexico for nine days and skirmished with military forces there before returning to Texas.[23]

The U.S. government responded to the flagrant violation of federal neutrality laws by sending several cavalry troops to apprehend the insurrectionists. The country that became the scene of the "Garza War" encompassed an area from Eagle Pass to Brownsville to Corpus Christi. According to captured documents from Garza's camp, his force totaled sixty-three commanders, 186 officers, and 1,043 soldiers. Generally, Garza's movement enjoyed support from local politicians and elected officials, while state and federal authorities were determined to suppress the insurgents. On December 12, Rogers was informed that a party of Mexicans was camped on Gatta Creek in Encinal County, and engaged in killing cattle. The sergeant found camps the next day where twenty-five head of cattle had been slaughtered, and located 150 of Garza's men along the same stream. On the fourteenth, he left four Rangers on the creek, and, accompanied by a fifth, traveled to Laredo to notify the local authorities. After informing Brooks of developments on the fifteenth, Rogers returned to his four men on the Gatta, and they followed the trail of the *Garzista* band through the brush. On December 16, the Ranger detachment was joined in the pursuit at Los Angeles in La Salle County by two U.S. marshals and Captain Francis Hunter Hardie's G Troop, Third U.S. Cavalry. The combined force tracked the *insurrectos* to the point above Carrizo

Springs where the latter crossed the Rio Grande into Mexico. Rogers and the other Rangers returned to Cotulla on Christmas Day.[24]

On March 5, 1892, Rogers and seven men joined Captain James S. McNeel at Realitos, and together they scouted for bandits for three days, although without any success. The Rangers were later reported to have located two hundred rebels near Las Cuevas and requested army assistance. Captain John Gregory Bourke, Third Cavalry, and his troops undertook a forced march of over fifty miles to reach the scene. The Americans made contact with the *insurrectos*, but the latter were able to slip away and blend into the local populace.[25]

José and Pancho Ramirez, the accused killers of Corporal Charles H. Edstrom, Third Cavalry, remained at large, and Rogers was informed of their presence on Black Creek near Palo Blanco on March 27. He and two Rangers, accompanied by former Ranger Lee Hall and cattleman John William Baylor, both riding as volunteers, took the two brothers in their camp on the thirtieth. José was killed in the gun battle, and his brother vanished into the brush on foot. Brooks, Rogers, Baylor, and a detachment of Rangers captured Pancho two days later and took him to the Starr County jail.[26]

With his force being reduced, Garza quit the fight and left his revolution to wither away. The American lawmen continued to run the insurrectionists to ground. On April 26, Rangers from Companies E and F delivered four *pronunciados* to Deputy U.S. Marshal Antonio Paulino Santos Coy in Nueces County. The suspects were charged in U.S. district court and found guilty of violating the neutrality laws. In 1892, over one hundred *Garzistas* were tried in federal court in San Antonio. By February of the following year, a total of 150 men were indicted. The final disposition of the cases varied according to the financial resources and quality of the legal representation of the defendants.[27]

When not in the field tracking outlaws or revolutionaries, Rogers was a dutiful attendant of Sunday services at the Presbyterian Church in Cotulla. While there worshipping the Good Lord, he met Harriet Randolph "Hattie" Burwell, the woman who would become the other constant in his life. Hattie had been born in Jackson County, Texas, on July 29, 1873. Her father, Charles Blair Burwell, ran a successful cattle ranch in La Salle County.

The two courted during the Garza trouble, and married on May 10, 1892. In June, Company F moved its camp south from Cotulla to Realitos in south-central Duval County. With her husband employed elsewhere, Hattie remained at her father's ranch.[28]

Rogers was acknowledged for his work, much of it independent of Brooks, during the Garza war. On January 1, 1893, he was promoted to the rank of captain and assigned to command Company E.[29] Captain McNeel had been forced to resign, which caused all his men to quit in protest. Thus, Rogers was obliged to recruit an entirely new unit. McNeel also spitefully refused to turn over any of the company's papers to his successor. Rogers recruited his cousin Tupper Harris from Company F to serve as first sergeant, as well as his brother Curren, and Harriet's brother, William Merrill Burwell, as privates. The reorganized company was posted to Alice, and Hattie was able to join her husband there.[30]

The new captain went to work almost immediately. On January 11, having been informed bandits were lurking in northern Starr County, Rogers and six Rangers rode to scout the area. They met Brooks at Realitos the next day, and the two captains decided to postpone the patrol for several days while awaiting further information. Rogers returned to Alice on the fourteenth, leaving his men with Brooks, then rejoined them on January 17. Companies E and F together scouted Starr County and arrested a suspected horse thief. Brooks was needed in Laredo, and returned to Realitos on the nineteenth in preparation for the trip. The following day, Rogers, with the assistance of Deputy U.S. Marshal John Ware, learned the main body of *bandidos* had left the county, but a few remained in Julian Guerra's pasture beyond the Bennett Ranch. On January 21, Rogers, his men, and Deputy Ware rode for the pasture. They reached the camp of Captain George Francis Chase, Third Cavalry, who sent a detachment of regulars under First Lieutenant Joseph Theodore Dickman to accompany the Rangers. The state officers and federal troops entered the pasture and divided into small squads to conduct the search. Three soldiers encountered Francisco Benavides and Prudencio González, the highest-ranking leaders of the remaining *Garzistas*, and escorted them back to the rendezvous site. Two Rangers and six cavalrymen took the prisoners back to Chase's camp where Benavides was delivered to

Sheriff Warren Washington "Wash" Shely, and González to military authorities in San Antonio. Rogers and the Rangers returned to Alice on the twenty-third. Five days later, the U.S. commissioner in San Antonio issued an extradition warrant for Benavides to face charges of violating the neutrality laws alongside González. Benavides was convicted and sentenced to thirty-three months at the Iowa state penitentiary at Anamosa.[31]

The first few years of Rogers's captaincy were relatively quiet. Through the beginning of 1893, he and his men continued to scout Starr, Duval, Nueces, McMullen, San Patricio, Live Oak, Bee, and Kimble Counties for fugitives from the Garza troubles, as well as other miscellaneous lawbreakers. Company E often united with Brooks's Company F in making these sweeps. Effecting few personal arrests, Rogers instead attended district court in Oakville and Corpus Christi, and handled the administrative chores incumbent upon any company commander. Six months into his tenure, the captain had to shoulder the unhappy burden of losing a man under his command. Early in the year, Menard County Sheriff Richard Robertson "Dick" Russell requested assistance from Rogers with a series of cattle thefts. Rogers assigned Private J. W. Woods to act as an undercover detective, and the Ranger went to work at a local ranch. Sometime in the month of July, Woods simply vanished. His body was never recovered, but information developed the following March indicated the remains were buried near Fort McKavett. Sergeant Harris periodically searched for evidence of Woods's final fate or whereabouts, but to no avail. Indeed, no clues were ever collected, although the common consensus is that Woods was the victim of foul play.[32]

Even while the Rangers mourned their loss, the dangers of their chosen profession were demonstrated yet again on the evening of October 6, 1893. Privates Burwell and Charles Francis Hiers were searching the northern portion of Duval County that day for suspected rustler Pedro Hinojoso. While on the Flores ranch near San Diego, the two Rangers were confronted by Bonifacio Rivera, who was armed with a Winchester and settling into a shooting stance. The state officers ordered Rivera to surrender or throw up his hands. He refused to comply, and they shot and wounded him in the right arm. Dropping his rifle, the would-be killer escaped into the darkness. The next morning, Burwell and Hiers were joined by Rogers and another

Ranger, and the quartet trailed Rivera to a neighboring ranch. When peacefully taken into custody, the fugitive had no reason for his attempted assault, except that "he was very much intoxicated." Less provocative for Company E was the attempted assassination of prominent Nueces County rancher John Wade on the night of March 17, 1894. Wade had been called to the front gate of his home in Wade City by three Mexicans who engaged him in conversation, then gravely wounded him. Rogers sent four men to the scene to investigate, but the trail had been trampled at the Nueces River by citizens eager to capture the culprits. The Rangers returned to camp on the nineteenth. Rogers continued to work up the case, but Sheriff John J. Seale of Karnes County arrested one of the shooters in early June. The other two would finally be captured the following month by Captain Joe Shely, who was serving as a deputy U.S. marshal. While Rogers ably led his company, he and Hattie were delighted when their daughter Lucile entered the world on August 31, 1893. Their first son, Pleasant Blair, was born on November 14, 1895.[33]

The last half of the nineteenth century bore witness to a growing moral crusade supported by government authority that intruded into the personal sphere. The social reformers opposed certain books, saloons and brothels, gambling, and boxing, among other perceived vices. When sports entrepreneur Daniel Albert Stuart announced his decision to hold a prizefight in Texas, a combination of Governor Charles Allen Culberson, the Twenty-fourth Legislature, President Grover Cleveland, the Forty-third Congress, and various local reformist groups vowed to stop him. Adjutant General Woodford Haywood Mabry and the majority of the Frontier Battalion were sent to El Paso, where the fight was scheduled to occur, in early February 1896. On the third, Rogers dispatched Sergeant Harris and Private Tom M. Ross to report to Captain Hughes in town and attempt to learn the location of the bout. The balance of Company E arrived on February 9, and they breakfasted at the Pierson Hotel while the news of their arrival spread. Legally speaking, pugilistic training and the intent to hold the match were permissible so the Rangers were compelled to watch and wait for Stuart or fighters Robert Prometheus "Ruby Bob" Fitzsimmons and Peter "the Galway Giant" Maher to break the law. Local residents, long accustomed to handling their own affairs, did not universally welcome Austin's focused attention on El Paso. The blatant display of state power to enforce reform was believed by the city fathers to impede the civil liberties of the citizens, and Stuart's financial supporters feared losing their investment. In the meantime, the Rangers patrolled the streets as gamblers and other associates of the sporting crowd streamed into town. On the night of the eighteenth, Rogers, Hiers, and a deputy sheriff pursued a gang that had held up a saloon earlier that evening. They caught the four thieves and lodged them in the county jail. The following day, approximately fifteen hundred visitors—and hundreds of Rangers, American soldiers, Mexican *rurales*, New Mexico militiamen, and federal marshals—were in town to see Fitzsimmons and Maher. The captain and most of his company entrained to Langtry to observe the fight, while the remainder stayed in El Paso to keep the peace.[34]

W. H. Mabry. #1/102–388. Cabinet card photograph by William O. Journeay, Austin, Texas. *Courtesy Texas State Library and Archives Commission, Austin, Texas.*

Following the "fistic carnival" in West Texas, Rogers and Company E returned to Alice by way of San Antonio, and once more settled into their routine duties. The elections of 1896 were a contentious event in South Texas as Democrats vied with Populists and Republicans for political control of the border counties. Due to "election excitement," in late October of the same year, Company E was stretched thin responding to the numerous calls for their presence at voting precincts in Nueces and Duval Counties. On November 2, the day of voting, Rogers assisted the Nueces County sheriff in Corpus Christi. Three Rangers kept order in Alice while another went to San Diego, and a sixth to a rural polling place in Duval County. With the elections concluding peacefully, the Rangers returned to their station on the fourth. In this period of relative quiet, Rogers welcomed his second son, Lapsley Harris, born on January 5, 1898.[35]

The tranquil spell had broken by the summer of 1898. The battleship USS *Maine* had sunk in the harbor of Havana, Cuba, on February 15, following a catastrophic explosion that killed 266 officers and sailors. Fueled by sensationalist "yellow journalism," the United States was swept by a wave of public outrage and patriotism that blamed Spain for the disaster. The William McKinley administration found itself forced into a conflict fittingly described by historian John L. Offner as "an unwanted war." The commencement of hostilities on April 21 pulled federal troops from the Rio Grande. Two companies of the Twenty-third Infantry passed through San Diego the same day on their way from Fort Ringgold to New Orleans, while one troop of the Fifth Cavalry departed Fort Ringgold for the seat of war the following month. On April 22, Rogers went to Largarto and Mathis in response to reports of local uneasiness regarding raids from Mexico. Despite the dire warnings, he found the area quiet and the residents unconcerned, although rumors of potential Spanish filibustering raids from Mexico would continue through the summer. On May 3, the captain and four men commenced scouting Duval, Starr, Zapata, Hidalgo, and Cameron Counties, and offering the prominent local ranchers protection from any lawless element bent on depredations. While on their twenty-two-day tour, the Rangers broke up two rustling gangs, recovered thirty-one head of cattle, and secured evidence against the culprits; one of the thieves was able to escape across the border into Mexico. Heavy rains inundated Alice under two feet of water on June 10, and much of Company E's camp equipage was ruined or lost in the flooding. In response to these difficulties, Rogers and his men were ordered to Cotulla on June 20.[36] The adjutant general would note that Company E conducted an astonishing 411 scouts—more than any other company—and traveled 29,067 miles. The men effected 212 arrests, which included the apprehension of fourteen murderers and fifty-nine thieves.[37]

With a population of approximately fifteen thousand, Laredo fell victim to a smallpox epidemic in early October 1898. In the rush to restrict the contagion, the mayor and the city health officer assumed considerable power in appointing *americano* and *mexicano* health inspectors who were authorized to conduct intrusive examinations and compulsory vaccinations of those affected—usually residents of the poor neighborhood between the railyards and Zacate Creek. Professor John McKiernan-González noted: "The policies associated with smallpox containment became an ideal stage to assert a medically certified, public-spirited, and potentially coercive identity over others in Laredo." Entering this charged atmosphere from Austin on March 16, 1899, Doctor Walter Fraser Blunt, the state health officer, sought to use strong measures to quarantine the sufferers, vaccinate those still not infected, and destroy contaminated homes. He failed to overcome cultural barriers and met opposition from "the Mexican masses" who resented the imperious city and state mandates, even if inoculation could save their lives. Trusting to their personal physicians and time-honored remedies, families often rebuffed efforts to transfer their ailing relatives to the local "pesthouse." Compliance became a matter of public discipline, and refusal a punishable act.[38]

Captain Rogers and Ranger Augustus Yardley "Augie" Old left Cotulla on March 18, and journeyed to Laredo to help enforce the policy to inspect, disinfect, and vaccinate residents. The next morning, the two Rangers and local officers moved patients to the pesthouse; the Mexicans were uneasy but no serious incidents occurred. While eating dinner, Rogers was informed of a shooting affray in the Zacate Creek neighborhood. Together with Private Old, he went to the scene and found the city marshal and his assistant trying to disperse a crowd of hundreds opposing the immunization program. The mob grew so aggressive that shots were exchanged, and the assistant marshal was struck in the head with a stone. The lawmen arrested a few of the protestors, then withdrew to await reinforcements. Rogers summoned Sergeant Harry Gilpin DuBose and the balance of the company. The five Rangers arrived on March 20, and settled at the Hamilton Hotel to await orders.[39]

Once DuBose and the men were in the city, Rogers, Old, and Special Ranger Thomas Ragland accompanied Sheriff Luis R. Ortiz and his deputies in searching houses for caches of firearms and ammunition to be used for armed resistance. The owner of the second home, Agipito Herrera, refused the officers entry while some of his friends began to gather. The sheriff seized Herrera's shoulder and the crowd grew hostile. Two bystanders ran inside the house and reappeared with rifles in hand. The Rangers pulled their pistols and readied themselves for a fight. Escaping the sheriff's grasp, Herrera also ran inside, emerged with a rifle and pointed it at Rogers. The captain responded to the threat, shooting Herrera in the chest. The armed bystanders began firing on the lawmen. A rifleman on a rooftop hit Rogers in the right arm, shattering his humerus near the shoulder, and taking him out of the fight. Old strode over to the prone Herrera and shot him twice in the head. One of Herrera's friends had also received a ranger bullet. Herrera's sister, who had likewise taken part in the shootout, was wounded.[40]

With Old and Ragland covering his withdrawal, Rogers walked away from the fight, cradling his lifeless arm. He commandeered a buggy, which drove him back to the Hamilton. He apprised Sergeant DuBose of the situation, then received medical attention. DuBose led the other four Rangers to the scene, being joined by Old and Ragland. As they turned the corner, they encountered a crowd of between fifty and one hundred irate Mexicans standing around Herrera's corpse. The twenty armed members of the mob opened fire on DuBose's men, which the latter returned. The two sides exchanged gunshots for a half-hour until the crowd finally scattered, ten of them bearing wounds. The following morning, Troop E of the Tenth Cavalry, equipped with a Gatling gun, marched from Fort McIntosh and promptly restored order in town. Health officers again enforced the compulsory regulations, and the epidemic waned. The quarantine was lifted on May 1, at which time DuBose and the company returned to Cotulla.[41]

Meanwhile, Rogers sought medical care from Doctor Amos Maverick Graves at Santa Rosa Hospital in San Antonio. The wound he received from Herrera necessitated the removal of a section of bone from his right arm. With his limb shortened, he could not properly aim his Winchester, so he had one specially made with a bent stock to offset the disability.[42]

Even while the captain recuperated, the Rangers of his company traveled to Columbus in late May 1899 to mitigate a simmering feud between the Townsend and Reese families. Earlier, on May 17, Sheriff William Thomas Burford had placed deputies James Gaither "Jim" Townsend and Andrew Lynn "Step" Yates on the east side of the Colorado River bridge. Their assignment was to watch for the arrival of James Henry "Jim" Coleman, a volatile Reese partisan who had sworn revenge on Marcus Harvey Townsend, leader of the county's political machine. Instead, the officers encountered Burrell Green Whittington "Dick" Reese, the brother of slain ex-sheriff Samuel Houston "Sam" Reese. As Dick Reese drove his carriage up to the bridge, the two deputies opened fire and killed him and his driver Dick Gant. Townsend and Yates were subsequently charged with murder. True to the convoluted nature of the Reese-Townsend feud, Jim Townsend was a first-cousin of the late family patriarch James Light Townsend, and brother-in-law of Sam and Dick Reese.[43]

Captain Lamartine Pemberton "Lam" Sieker, quartermaster of the Frontier Battalion, reached Columbus on May 19, and interviewed the feud's ringleaders. Sergeant DuBose and Privates Old, William L. Wright, and Creed Taylor arrived the following day. General Scurry and Captain McDonald entrained for Columbus and joined their comrades on the twenty-third and twenty-fourth, respectively. With the arrival of the reinforcements, Sieker returned to Austin. The Rangers patrolled the town, disarming belligerents, and persuading those who did not live within city limits to return to their homes. After he had imposed calm on the situation, DuBose left Wright and Taylor in charge, and he and Old returned to Cotulla on May 25. Even though he was not yet ready for active field service, Rogers rejoined his command two days later. Wright stayed in Columbus through the summer, and ensured no further serious incidents occurred. Yates died of natural causes before he was brought to trial, and Deputy Townsend's court date was set for January 15, 1900, in Bastrop.[44]

Throughout the summer of 1899, the town of Orange, in the county of the same name, had been wracked by racial violence. Armed bands, known as "whitecaps," roamed the countryside, forcibly preventing blacks from working in the lumber mills and driving them out of the county. On August 12, one such gang shot up a gambling house patronized by blacks, and Fred Holsten was killed and two other men severely wounded. Rogers and Augie Old arrived in town on August 19, while Wright and Taylor joined the following day. The state officers investigated the incident and gathered testimony. Rogers reported that he found securing evidence to be an "up hill" battle as local sentiment was with the whitecappers, and several key witnesses had left town in fear for their lives. On the twentieth, the captain and Old arrested three area residents for disturbing the peace. They were also suspected in participating in the recent shooting. Old took Will Diggs into custody on August 23, and Frank Weatherford two days later, and charged them both with Holsten's murder. Rogers made several trips to Beaumont to interview witnesses, but no one was willing to talk to the Ranger captain. The next month, Diggs and Weatherford were released, but the latter soon ran afoul of the law. Rogers took him into custody on September 16, but only after Weatherford attempted to resist and had to be wrestled to the ground. In the scuffle, Rogers reinjured his arm and spent the rest of his time in Orange supervising the activities of his Rangers from camp. On September 21, Company E was replaced by Captain Bill McDonald's outfit, and Rogers returned to San Antonio for treatment. The next day, Doctor Graves extracted a piece of bone from his wound, and Rogers was back in Cotulla on September 25.[45]

After a brief stay in Comstock, the company resumed its home station at Cotulla, while detachments operated from Del Rio and Orange for a time. Much of the company's work was routine, as reflected by the scouts made in Webb, La Salle, McMullen, Kinney, Frio, Medina, Dimmit, and Crockett Counties, and arrests for conspiracy to murder, livestock theft, vagrancy, fence cutting, jail breaking, and burglary.[46]

Jim Townsend's trial in Bastrop ended swiftly when his case was granted a continuance. Another shooting in town occurred the same day, with William D. Clements wounded and Arthur Burford, son of the Colorado County sheriff, dead. Already in Bastrop where they were testifying in court,

Wright and Taylor assisted Captain Brooks in subpoenaing witnesses and arresting ten men suspected of being among the shooters. While six of the men were released, John Walter Reese and three accomplices were swiftly indicted for murder and assault with intent; their trial was scheduled for January 22, 1900, although the proceedings were delayed several times. Meanwhile, Captain Rogers, Privates Old and Kid Rogers, three men from Company B, and Special Ranger J. E. Falts were sent to the La Grange train depot on the twenty-third to meet travelers from Columbus, and search the passengers and their luggage for weapons. Walter and Lillian Reese contended in their book, *Flaming Feuds of Colorado County*, that Rogers entered the depot, where Sam Reese's daughter, Mrs. Nuddie Ela Lessing, was waiting for the next train to Bastrop. Despite her objections, the captain allegedly insisted on searching the woman's suitcase, hoping to discover a firearm, but, instead, found a handkerchief covered in her murdered father's dried blood. In his report, Rogers stated the Rangers searched 150 members of the Burford and Townsend party and their valises after the Missouri, Kansas & Texas train had departed La Grange. The party from Columbus was notified of the search beforehand, and the officers found very few pistols aboard the railcars. Once they arrived at Bastrop, the Rangers of Companies B, E, and F kept the two factions under surveillance day and night. Once the case was continued, Rogers and his men accompanied the Burford and Townsend party back to Columbus. They returned to Cotulla on the twenty-seventh.[47]

On February 2, Rogers was ordered to Groveton to attend court and keep the peace between the two factions. He instructed Privates Wright and Gratz Brown to assist him in town on the fourteenth. Augmenting the detachment were Rangers Eugene Bell and Dabney White from Company B. The same day, the captain received orders from General Scurry to proceed to Bastrop. Leaving Brown with the other two privates, Rogers and Wright left on the seventeenth, and arrived in Columbus where they were joined by the rest of the company from Cotulla and Del Rio. The Rangers accompanied the Townsend faction to Bastrop, following the previous month's procedure of disarming the feudists on the train and following them to their hotels. Rogers and his men remained on post until the sixteenth when Walter Reese and his fellow defendants, still under indictment, were granted bail. The state officers made the return trip to Columbus, watching over the Townsends, before reaching Cotulla on February 18.[48]

On October 24, General Scurry ordered Rogers and Private J. T. Armstrong of Company B to Nacogdoches to safeguard prisoner Francis Marion Smith from mob violence. On December 23, 1899, the sixty-six-year-old Smith had murdered Josephine Elmina "Mina" Vawter, his neighbor and sister-in-law, with a shotgun blast to the back after she had allowed a pair of hogs to tear up his garden. Following the killing, Smith calmly walked into town and surrendered to the authorities. The *Houston Daily Post* reported that the suspect claimed, "his head is not right since he was wounded in the head and lost an eye at the battle of Gettysburg." He was found guilty of murder in the first degree early the next year, and spent much of 1900 appealing his conviction. After the court of criminal appeals affirmed the verdict on June 20, Smith was scheduled to be hanged in Nacogdoches on October 27. Instead, Lieutenant Governor James Nathan Browning gave the condemned man a two-week reprieve while the board of pardons considered his case. When the two Rangers arrived on the twenty-fifth, they found an angry mob watching the jail and seemingly determined to keep Smith from being removed to Rusk penitentiary. Rogers tried to reason with the assembled citizens, to no avail. However, the captain arrested Theodore Vawter, the victim's husband and the leader of the mob, removed two pistols from his person, and placed the grief-stricken man in jail. He then ordered a train engine and box car be brought from Lufkin and, with the assistance of county officers and twenty militiamen of the Stone Fort Rifles, safely transported the prisoner to Rusk. On November 5, Governor Sayers declined to commute the sentence, and Smith kept his appointment with the hangman four days later in front of a crowd of five thousand people.[49]

On November 2, 1900, the captain, accompanied by Private Charles Sandherr, traveled to Rio Grande City to monitor the local elections. Twenty-five days later, Rogers returned to Cotulla and shipped the company's state property to the new headquarters at Laredo. He also secured housing in the latter town for his family. On April 11, 1901, Rogers and Creed Taylor traveled to Waco and assisted Sheriff John William Baker in protecting Will King, a black man charged with murdering police officer William Davis Mitchell on October 27 of the previous year. King had already been found guilty once in a court of law. However, the verdict was subsequently set aside, as only white men had been summoned to serve on the jury. Threats were made to lynch the accused, so the Rangers guarded the jail for four days. During that time, King was given a new trial, and convicted and sentenced to death on April 17. Rogers and Taylor returned to Laredo on the nineteenth. In total, operating from Laredo, members of the company scouted 5,031 miles, recovered sixty-six head of stolen cattle, and arrested seventeen men from December 1900 to June 1901.[50]

On June 12, Karnes County Sheriff William Taylor "Brack" Morris, accompanied by Deputies John H. Trimmell and Daniel Boone Choate, rode onto William A. Thulemeyer's ranch and visited the cabin of Gregorio Cortéz y Lira, an allegedly long-time horse thief. The sheriff had been searching for several men, including Cortéz, suspected of stealing horses in Frio and Atascosa Counties. Morris, a veteran of the Frontier Battalion, questioned Cortéz and his older brother Romaldo through Choate, who acted as interpreter. Unfortunately, critical nuances were lost in the translation between Spanish and English. Cortéz was asked about trading to another man *un caballo*—a horse—that had been reported stolen. While "horse" in English does not take into consideration the sex of the animal, the Spanish word has the implicit definition of a male. Accordingly, since Cortéz had traded *una yegua*—a mare, he was perceived as being untruthful in the answers he gave to the sheriff. Unaware of the breakdown in communications, the displeased Morris ordered Choate to apprise Cortéz he was being placed under arrest. When Gregorio demanded to know why, the sheriff replied, "For stealing horses." The interpreter restated Morris's answer in Spanish and Cortéz allegedly cried, "No one can arrest me." Once more, a faulty translation may have caused the tense situation to explode into disastrous violence as Cortéz could have said, "You can't arrest me for nothing." Regardless of the actual words spoken, Romaldo charged the sheriff with a knife. Responding to the imminent threat, Morris stepped back and pulled his pistol. At the same time, Gregorio jerked a gun from his waistband. Morris shot the lunging Romaldo in the mouth, turned his weapon on Gregorio, and fired again. The bullet missed, and Gregorio shot

W. T. Morris. Sketch from *Houston Daily Post*, June 22, 1901.

the sheriff in the right arm and left shoulder. Gregorio then rushed to the incapacitated Morris and fired into his stomach.[51]

Gregorio fled to the east on foot, leaving his mortally wounded brother and the dying Morris behind. Sheriff Richard Martin "Dick" Glover of Gonzales County, an old friend of the fallen officer, raised a posse and tracked Cortéz to a tenant farmhouse near Ottine. During the night of June 14, the weary posse, possibly intoxicated by whiskey, assaulted the house. Bullets flew in all directions, and Henry Schnabel, the farm owner, was accidentally slain by a posseman. Hiding on a nearby hilltop, Cortéz chose not to simply leave, but instead opened fire on the riders, killing Sheriff Glover. The fugitive then slipped away into the brush.[52]

The slaying of two sheriffs in quick succession touched off the second largest manhunt in Texas history. Riding a progression of stolen horses, including the famed *yegua trigueña*—little brown mare—Cortéz eluded pursuers for ten days across three hundred miles of South Texas *brasada*. Posses of local lawmen, Rangers, and citizens killed six horses in the pursuit. In the fashion of Juan Cortina, the local Mexican population celebrated the deeds of Cortéz, who became the subject of numerous *corridos* (folk ballads). On June 22, already on the trail of horse thieves, Rogers was tipped off by a *vaquero* desiring the reward. Along with Bill Merriman, a mounted Customs inspector, the captain quietly arrested the sleeping fugitive at a sheep camp near Laredo, only eight miles from the border. The posse returned to Laredo, then the captain took his prisoner to San Antonio and released him into the custody of Brack Morris's replacement, Sheriff William Charles Hunter. Rogers modestly downplayed his part in the apprehension, and declined his share of the reward. "No especial credit is due to me for the capture," he told the *San Antonio Express*. "Somebody else would have got him if I hadn't." Cortéz was subsequently convicted of murder on October 3, 1903, and sentenced to life imprisonment. Entering Huntsville on January 2, 1905, he received a conditional pardon from Governor Oscar Branch Colquitt on July 14, 1913.[53]

The Cortéz affair cost the lives of four men who need not have died as they did, and "El Corrido de Gregorio Cortez," with equal portions of fact and embellishment, became a popular ballad in the American Southwest and northern Mexico. As Bruce A. Glasrud and Professor Harold J. Weiss commented, "the history and folklore of this man's life and actions continue to reflect tensions along the border."[54] However, even after one hundred years, there exist several pertinent questions that have yet to be definitively addressed. Exactly what kind of lawman was Brack Morris? Could Cortéz have expected firm but fair justice from the sheriff, or a hanging without benefit of due process? Was Cortéz truly the victim of circumstance, or, in spite of the mistranslations, was he actually guilty of horse theft? Regardless of linguistic errors, and Morris's insistence on making an arrest, was there adequate provocation for Romaldo and Gregorio to each use deadly force on law officers? The answers to these queries will require a thoughtful work more comprehensive in scope than can be done in these pages, but the scholar or writer who can cut through the haze of assumptions and preconceived notions will go far in discovering the truth of the matter.

In the wake of the extensive manhunt, the earlier legislation, which had replaced the Frontier Battalion with an expanded Ranger Force, went into effect on July 8, 1901. Granted an authorized strength of eighty-nine men, the new service was formed into four mounted companies of one captain, one sergeant, and twenty privates. Most importantly for the Rangers, the new act unequivocally decreed:

> The officers, non-commissioned officers and privates of this force shall be clothed with all the powers of peace officers, and shall aid the regular civil authorities in the execution of the laws. They shall have authority to make arrests, and to execute process in criminal cases, and in such cases they shall be governed by law regulating and defining the powers and duties of sheriffs when in discharge of similar duties; except that they shall have the power, and shall be authorized to make arrests and to execute all process in criminal cases in any county in the State.[55]

The next day, Rogers was appointed captain of Company C, which was headquartered at Laredo. Some of his most-trusted veterans joined the new outfit, including Sergeant Edwin Morgan DuBose, Will Wright, Creed Taylor,

Will Burwell, Kid Rogers, and James "Jim" Moore (a relative of the Ranger who had been killed by the Conners). Company C covered an immense amount of western Texas, and Rogers personally traveled between Laredo and Fort Hancock. From November 1, 1900, to August 31, 1902, Company C performed 104 scouts, and effected 134 arrests—including eighteen for murder, fourteen for assault with intent to kill, thirty-four for theft, including that of livestock, and two for smuggling. They assisted the district courts on eleven separate occasions, supported various civil authorities forty-nine times, and guarded two jails.[56]

In December 1902, Rogers and his company of seven Rangers were reassigned to Colorado City, the captain's station when he had enlisted in the service twenty years before. Rogers purchased a house that served as not only the family residence, but also the company headquarters. In addition to the four stationed in Colorado City, another quartet were on detached service in Amarillo and Fort Hancock.[57]

Rogers and his men were dispatched to Thurber in early September 1903, at the behest of the Texas & Pacific Coal Company. For years, Colonel Robert Dickey Hunter had successfully resisted efforts by the Knights of Labor and the United Mine Workers of America to organize the company's labor force. After Hunter died on November 3, 1902, William K. Gordon, the general manager, carried on in his stead. In the meantime, the miners had demanded a pay increase and other considerations, all of which the company rejected. In response, union activists encouraged unrest among the miners at a Labor Day picnic, and Adjutant General John Augustus Hulen directed Company E to keep the peace. Observed by the Rangers, all but twenty-five of the eight-hundred-man workforce peacefully walked off the job on September 11. The miners then traveled by train to unionized mines at union expense. By the fourteenth, the diggings were empty, as were ancillary businesses. Gordon attempted to recruit new employees. Eighteen arrived on the train from Pennsylvania and were met by company officials, union organizers, and Rangers. The miners changed their minds, and refused to sign on to the coal company payroll. The company reversed its stance, and the UMW local held its first meeting in Thurber on September 20. Management acquiesced to other demands, and the miners returned to work.[58]

A former member of George "Red Buck" Weightman's outlaw gang, Hillary "Hill" Loftis had been on the run for the last nine years. Following a gun battle with a posse of Texas Rangers and local officers at Suttle Creek in December 1895, he disappeared, and lawmen in the Texas Panhandle and the Indian Territory were unable to pinpoint his whereabouts. By 1904, he was rumored to be living in the southern Staked Plains under the alias "Tom Ross." Throughout the spring, various sheriffs and deputized gunslingers failed to track him, but finally, in June, a man matching his description was reported to be working a roundup on Mayer and Solomon Halff's Mallett Ranch in Gaines County. As would soon be revealed, Loftis, or Ross, had married and settled down on a ranch northwest of Seminole. Captain Rogers entrained west from Colorado City, accompanied by Martin County Sheriff Charles Tom, to confirm the fugitive's presence.[59]

Riding to the Halff spread near the New Mexico line, the two lawmen spotted their quarry on June 17 as he was fleeing into the sand dunes. Rogers's and Tom's exhausted mounts fell behind, and the captain fired once, hoping to hit the fugitive's horse, but he missed. The officers followed Ross into the sand, and Rogers rode some distance ahead of the sheriff. For a few moments, the captain was temporarily out of Tom's sight. Ross suddenly appeared and fired at the Ranger, the bullet grazing the jaw of Rogers's horse and severing the reins. The surprised captain fell to the ground as his horse reared, and he looked up dazedly into the muzzle of the outlaw's rifle. In a calm voice, Rogers warned Ross that the killing of a Texas Ranger would only bring swift and sure vengeance. The outlaw responded by ordering Rogers to hand over his pistol, and the captain carefully complied. At that moment, the sounds of Sheriff Tom's approaching horse could be heard rounding the dune. Ross quickly emptied the cartridges from Rogers's gun and returned the weapon. The outlaw then spurred his horse into the growing darkness. Rogers sent four Rangers into the dunes after Ross three days later, but, by then, the trail had grown cold.[60]

In May 1905, Company C moved from Colorado City to Alpine. While the men transported the camp equipment, official papers, and their personal gear, Hattie and the children traveled with Rogers. The detachment at Fort Hancock continued to operate.[61]

On September 13, Private Thomas Jefferson "Tom" Goff of Company C arrested *tejano* outlaw Augustin Garcia for creating a disturbance in a saloon in the mining village of Big Bend. While being taken to the Terlingua jail, the prisoner managed to unseat the Ranger from his horse and murder him with his own gun. Goff was the first Ranger killed in the line of duty since 1901, and his death the first of a man under Rogers's command. The captain escorted Goff's body home to Throckmorton, and remained for the September 19 funeral in order to pay his respects to the family. Several of Goff's colleagues went after Garcia, who was believed to be heading for El Paso. The killer eventually escaped into Mexico, never to answer for the killing.[62]

In December 1906, Rogers wrote his "Rules and Regulations Governing Company C, Ranger Force" which specified the conduct he required for the men under his command:

1. Men, upon entering the service, are required to procure a good outfit consisting of horse, saddle, Winchester, six-shooter, rope, and bedding. It shall be maintained in good order continuously as long as they remain in the service.
2. Each Ranger is required to perform his full amount of camp duty, such as cooking, herding horses and any and all of the regular routine camp work. This must be strictly observed and any complaint substantiated shall be sufficient grounds for a dismissal from the service.
3. Each member of the Ranger force is expected to look out for and care for and take interest in the preservation of all State property; and especially the pack saddle, pack blankets and pack rope must be kept hanging together and not be molested by the men for their own use in any way, but in some designated place understood by the men it must be kept so that it may be readily found any time even of a dark night when we might be leaving in haste.
4. Men are expected to keep their quarters, at least, in a reasonably clean and neat condition. No one need even apply for a position in this company that is not sober, honest and of a good moral character.[63]

On May 14, 1907, recently appointed Adjutant General James Oscar Newton issued General Orders No. 10, which transferred the headquarters of Company C from Alpine to Austin. Instructed to move his command over the Galveston, Harrisburg & San Antonio and International & Great Northern Railroads to their new station, the captain was to "dismount his company before the movement is made, as no mounts for his men will be furnished with forage here at the expense of the State, except one mount for the commanding officer." He moved his family into their new house at 2406 Lampasas Street, and occupied an office in the capitol building.[64]

Having settled Company C into their latest post, Rogers took a rare day off from work on August 27, and accompanied Hattie and the children to the old Austin dam on the Colorado River. The children were wading in the pool above the dam when nine-year-old Lapsley stepped off the sandbar into deeper water and disappeared. As Hattie watched helplessly, Rogers repeatedly dove into the pool searching for his son. The boy's lifeless body was found nearby an hour later by some youths who were helping in the search. Shattered by grief, the parents held a private funeral ceremony in their home, officiated by Doctor Josephus Johnson of the First Southern Presbyterian Church. Lapsley was buried in Oakwood Cemetery in Austin. The tragedy purportedly strengthened Rogers's faith in God, and he never missed an opportunity to attend church services or teach a Sunday school class. Two weeks after his son's death, the captain returned to duty.[65]

While hunting a noted outlaw in September 1909, Rangers Goff White and Hall Thomas Avriett of Company C were involved in a controversial shooting in Groveton. The two officers related how they encountered a man who fit the description of their quarry. They identified themselves to the suspect, who was armed with a shotgun, and thrice ordered him to drop the weapon. The individual, instead, aimed his shotgun at the Rangers, and they responded by shooting him dead and wounding his seventeen-year-old son. Afterwards, they discovered the man they had killed was not the criminal they were pursuing. White and Avriett were released on bond, and the Trinity County grand jury no-billed the two officers in January 1910. Inexplicably, the panel indicted the pair during the February 1913 session, and the case was later transferred to the Twentieth District Court in Bryan. While the trial was scheduled for the September term, the names of the two men, both having since resigned from the service, do not appear on the docket.[66]

The town of Hempstead, forty miles northwest of Houston, was a rough place that had earned the nickname "Six-shooter Junction" following a deadly gunfight in 1905. On the night of April 28, 1910, a nasty divorce case degenerated into another spectacular shootout that left two men dead, the county sheriff seriously wounded, and several traveling salesmen slightly wounded. Rogers sent Sergeant Joseph Lee Anders and Private Edmund Ledbetter "Ed" Avriett (Hall's brother) to take command of the scene. The two Rangers kept order, but, during the examining trial of the alleged shooters on May 2, the inflamed attitudes of the area forced Anders and Avriett to search everyone entering the courtroom for weapons. The Rangers were able to return to Austin the same day.[67]

Similarly, Galveston had long possessed a reputation as a rowdy town. At the behest of the governor and the adjutant general, Rogers dispatched Rangers Roy Hodge Adams and Robert Marmaduke "Duke" Hudson to the port city to assist a grand jury foreman in investigating illegal gambling. The foreman requested they infiltrate the illicit gaming rooms, gather evidence, and report back to him. He then intended to order raids on the casinos and optimistically arrest between seventy-five and one hundred gamblers. These actions prompted the sportsmen to curtail their rackets until the grand jury adjourned. Having gone back to Austin, the Rangers returned to Galveston when gambling resumed, albeit to a lesser extent. The foreman decided Adams could remain in Austin, while Hudson resumed his undercover assignment. Hudson discovered a large gambling enterprise above the Turk Exchange. He then gained employment with a prominent dry goods store, established himself as a fervent gambler, and began gathering evidence. Captain Rogers assigned another undercover operative, Ranger Levi Davis of Company A, to join Hudson. The two officers raided the gaming room on June 30, but they had such difficulty gaining entry those inside had time to escape. The Rangers were only able to arrest six people, and they turned the prisoners over to the police chief. The district attorney assured Hudson and Davis sufficient evidence existed to successfully prosecute the six suspects for felony gambling.[68]

On July 29, 1910, trouble erupted in the town of Palestine, when rumors spread through Anderson County, and those adjacent, that blacks were preparing a campaign to murder white residents. Terrified whites armed themselves and ran amok, killing eighteen blacks. The governor ordered every available Ranger to gather at Palestine. The first to arrive were Sergeant Anders and Privates Ed and Hall Avriett. After descending from the train that had brought them to town, the Rangers acquired horses and hurried to Slocum, where the worst of the slaughter had occurred. On the morning of the thirty-first, Adjutant General Newton, Captain Rogers, Colonel Robert Henderson Beckham, and two more Texas National Guard officers arrived in Palestine. The same day, the governor ordered in Troop C, First Texas Cavalry, and Company D, Third Texas Infantry. The quick actions of the Rangers in dispersing the mob and saving several blacks made the Guardsmen's arrival the next morning unnecessary.[69]

Rogers and the remainder of the party drove toward Slocum, but they met the Avrietts, a deputy sheriff, and a deputy constable along the way. The lawmen were transporting three of the mob's instigators to the Palestine jail, while Anders lingered in Slocum looking for other suspects. They reported that Slocum was tranquil, as the lawmen had "ordered everyone to disarm themselves and go home, which they promptly did." The prisoners were locked up in Palestine, while several blacks who had agreed to testify were put into protective custody. The jailhouse was placed under a heavy guard to deter any attempts to free the detainees or lynch the witnesses. Anders was unable to locate the men he sought, but they were later captured by the sheriff. Remaining in the area until August 14, Captain Rogers and his Rangers arrested eleven suspects. Four days later, the grand jury indicted seven men on twenty-two counts of murder, including James Spurger, who was believed to be the source of the original rumor.[70]

Rogers sent a man to Atascosa County to keep the peace during the district court session, and personally attended court in Crockett on November 14. He then went to Rocksprings in Edwards County to look into two exceptionally brutal occurrences. The situation began when Effie Eleanor Henderson "spoke roughly" to Antonio Rodríguez when she refused his plea for food. The latter proceeded to rape the woman and fatally shoot her in front of her own children. The murderer was arrested the following day, and he freely admitted to the vicious crime. He was then jailed in Rocksprings.

Enraged over the woman's demise, a mob of approximately fifty citizens, both Anglo and Hispanic, broke into the jailhouse on the night of November 3, and removed Rodríguez from his cell. They dragged the condemned prisoner through town and up a nearby hill. The crowd tied him to a mesquite tree with chains and one by one laid mesquite branches around him. When the funeral pyre was completed, Lemuel Kenneth Henderson, the murdered woman's husband, liberally splashed kerosene from a five-gallon can onto the wood and Rodríguez. A lit match was thrown onto the mesquite, and the vigilantes watched silently as the screaming killer burned to death. The mob members walked back to town in unison.[71]

Following this instance of rough justice, a rumor spread relating how Mexicans were en route to Rocksprings to avenge Rodríguez's impromptu execution. Rogers received his orders to go to Rocksprings on November 16. He took two men and found the town to be quiet. He investigated the death of Rodríguez, and was assured by the sheriff and various citizens the matter was considered closed by the community. Frustrated by the wall of silence, the three Rangers were back in Austin on November 19.[72]

The next day was to be the beginning of Francisco Ignacio Madero González's revolution, the date having been announced earlier in the month. District Attorney John Anthony Valls of the Forty-ninth Judicial District telegraphed the governor and advised him *insurrectos* were reported to be planning to attack Guerrero across the Rio Grande. On November 21, the governor and the adjutant general sent Rogers to Laredo to enforce the neutrality laws. The captain and five of his men arrived the following day and conferred with the district attorney as ordered. Rogers and Valls then crossed the border to consult with the Mexican military commander in Nuevo Laredo. The Ranger captain pledged the general his cooperation in enforcing neutrality. Once back in Laredo, Rogers also extended his support to Francisco Mallen, the Mexican consul, and Calvin George Brewster, the U.S. marshal for the Southern District of Texas. The same day, he learned of a party of revolutionaries encamped on the American side of the Rio Grande, approximately thirty-five miles upriver from Laredo. At first, the number of rebels was estimated at two hundred, but later reports put the number at seventy-five. Rogers alerted Marshal Brewster and the post commander at

Fort McIntosh, both of whom contacted their respective superiors for instructions.[73]

On November 23, Rogers and his five Rangers, the federal marshal, and a company of soldiers traveled by special train to the Minera coal mines, twenty-six miles above Laredo. Since the sun was setting, the troops refused to advance any farther. Rogers led his men, the marshal, and a federal Customs inspector who had joined their party in acquiring horses and riding on toward their destination. Once they drew near to the suspected rebel encampment, they dismounted and waited for daybreak. In the morning, the Americans advanced on foot through the thick *brasada* along the Rio Grande. They located the camp, but it was abandoned. Signs of recent activity suggested the rebels had evacuated in the previous few hours. Rogers believed that sympathizers to the revolutionary cause in Laredo had alerted the camp. They did, however, confirm the number of *insurrectos* to be only fifteen.[74]

Rogers and his companions decided to travel the additional nineteen miles to Palafox. Upon arrival, the captain and the two federal officers crossed the Rio Grande and entered the town of Hidalgo. They exchanged information with the local garrison commander and a captain of the *rurales*, then returned to Texas. The American officers focused on Minera during the next several days, as they believed the mines to be a center for revolutionary activity. One positive accomplishment was the Mexican informant they enlisted, who would report that the previous week Madero himself had been in the area. The lawmen were regrettably unable to develop any solid evidence, and returned to Laredo.[75]

Despite the informant's statement, Madero had quietly left his headquarters in San Antonio, slipped across the border on November 19, and made ready to begin his revolution. Unfortunately, his opening stroke on the symbolic target—Ciudad Porfirio Díaz—went awry when the arms and ammunition he had purchased were absent, as were the soldiers he had expected to lead into battle. Instead of a sweeping victory, the humiliated Madero had to cancel the attack and slink back to San Antonio. With a lack of revolutionary activity, the Mexican consul in Laredo and District Attorney Valls advised the governor that the Rangers were no longer needed in Webb County. The governor agreed, and recalled Rogers and his men to Austin.[76]

The Progressive reform movement that had urged state governments to forbid prizefighting twenty years previously continued to oppose red-light districts and saloons. The moralists campaigned for further expansions of public authority to deter contraceptives, control speech, enact teen curfews and the Mann Act, and push for slow incrementalism toward national prohibition. Indeed, the Anti-Saloon League, formed in 1893, claimed prohibition would lower taxes, break corrupt political machines, assuage poverty, mollify labor unrest, and increase the moral tone of immigrants. Rogers was a loyal Democrat and an ardent prohibitionist, and Oscar Branch Colquitt's gubernatorial victory caused him some concern. As the new governor opposed the banning of liquor in Texas, Rogers resigned from the service on January 29, 1911.[77]

His decision might have been bittersweet, but the family's financial security did not suffer as a result. For over five years, he had been shrewdly putting his income in local real estate investments in El Paso and near Fort Hancock. In the years to come, proceeds from the sale of the land would provide for his children's education and the support of his family long after his death.[78]

The call of duty remained strong, though, and he accepted the offer of a commission from Eugene Nolte, federal marshal of the Western District of Texas. Nolte was an old friend and a Republican, and, regardless of their differing politics, Rogers was sworn into office as a deputy U.S. marshal in El Paso on February 1. Now representing the federal government, Rogers's duties included the enforcement of U.S. neutrality laws and the suppression of revolutionary activities occurring on the American side of the border. The Act of March 26, 1910, provided for the deportation of insurgents and matériel to "prevent the territory of the United States being used as a base for a military expedition against the established government in Mexico." Brigadier-General Joseph Wilson Duncan, department commander in Texas, estimated 80 percent of the Mexicans on both sides of the Rio Grande, and most Anglos, supported the insurgency. In March 1912, Congress passed legislation barring the exportation of arms and munitions to Mexico.[79]

While the federal government was protective of the nation's neutrality, private citizens— both *mexicanos* and Anglos—were active in shipping arms and munitions south across the international boundary. Indeed, hardware store owners in El Paso and Laredo were among those who turned themselves into international weapons traffickers, in violation of federal law. Mexican secret service agents, and American Customs officers and other federal lawmen, diligently toiled to suppress arms dealing, but, in actual practice, the trade proved difficult to shut down. During this period, some two hundred Mexican spies were working for Madero, Orozco, or the highest bidder in El Paso, and the city became a freewheeling center for espionage and revolutionary plots. While the statute allowed merchants and revolutionary agents to purchase firearms, lawmen had to prove the existence of a criminal conspiracy or catch smugglers in the act of crossing the border. Rogers arrested Guadalupe Gonzalez for illegally reentering the country, and Luis Luna Villalobos for smuggling. On March 19, 1912, he detained the De Leon brothers for hiring mercenaries to serve in Mexico. Four days later, he apprehended Allen Rogers (no relation) and John Thomas, who were the leaders of an arms smuggling cartel. By the month's end, he had captured eight additional members of the ring.[80]

Enrique C. Llorente, the Mexican consul, made a complaint regarding Gonzalo G. Enrile, once the financial agent of the revolution, and an arrest warrant was issued by U.S. Commissioner George B. Oliver. Rogers executed the warrant on June 11, 1912. Enrile had previously been stabbed in Chihuahua, and Rogers removed him from the county jail to the Hotel Dieu Hospital on the twenty-third. There, the patient was given an operation to drain his wound. In September, Rogers broke up another gang of smugglers by arresting thirteen late in the month and five more on October 5. Five days later, he apprehended Canuto Leyva for recruiting mercenaries. He escorted a group of prisoners to Fort Leavenworth, Kansas, in November.[81]

After Woodrow Wilson won the 1912 presidential election, the incumbent chief executive William Howard Taft initiated a "policy of reprisal" by sacking office holders who had supported Theodore Roosevelt's "Bull Moose" party. Charged with "pernicious political activity," Eugene Nolte was dismissed on November 30, and replaced with loyalist Bert J. McDowell. Despite having played no role in the intra-party dispute, Rogers was discharged from the El Paso office, and Frank Newnam, ex-police chief in San Antonio, took his place.[82]

The recess appointments of the lame duck president were all replaced as soon as Wilson took office. Indeed, recognizing the inevitable, Marshal McDowell resigned on February 25, 1913. Rogers wanted the permanent appointment for the vacant marshal's post, and he worked hard to secure the office. Charles Allen Culberson and Morris Sheppard, the two U.S. senators from Texas, and Congressman John Nance Garner of Uvalde supported Rogers's nomination. Even more importantly, he attracted the eye of "Colonel" Edward Mandell House, Democratic power broker and trusted advisor to President Wilson. Petitions poured into the Oval Office from across Texas. Numerous sheriffs, chiefs of police, postmasters, mayors, jurists, college professors, ministers, attorneys, physicians, and ordinary citizens wrote to praise Rogers and press for his nomination. Such a diverse outpouring of support had its effect. On March 22, 1913, he was named U.S. Marshal for the Western District of Texas. He received Senate confirmation on April 24, and swore his oath of office in Del Rio.[83] Once he had pinned on the marshal's badge, Rogers wrote a notation on the flyleaf of his Bible:

> After giving due credit to all loyal friends who stood by me so nobly and indorsed me so unqualifiedly, I nevertheless attribute my success to Almighty God, whose servant I am, and whom I serve and to whom I solemnly pledged if He would favor me for this position, I would use the office for His glory, relying upon Him for His help and guidance. It is my desire that what additional influence I have by reason of my office shall be used for Him.[84]

Although initially located in San Antonio, the addition of a fourth federal district to the state curiously caused Rogers's headquarters to be transferred to Waco. By the end of the year, Rogers returned to San Antonio, where he and Chief Deputy Tecumseh Harvell Thompson supervised ten field deputies stationed in the Alamo City, Del Rio, El Paso, Marfa, Eagle Pass, Waco, and Austin. Even with this staff, the marshal was no deskbound bureaucrat. While he was in El Paso for district court, he arrested Clare L. Rogers (no relation) on October 13, 1914, for stealing a registered package containing $25,000. On October 31, Rogers moved his office again, this time to Austin. There, he would purchase a two-story home at 1200 San Antonio Street. The following year, after Clare Rogers was found guilty and sentenced to ten years, Marshal Rogers and Captain John Hughes conveyed him and five other prisoners to Leavenworth. Whether Hughes had been deputized for the excursion or was simply accompanying his old colleague is unknown.[85]

When the United States entered World War I, Rogers's duties as a federal officer increased accordingly. President Wilson nominated him for reappointment, which was confirmed by the Senate, effective April 24, 1917. Three days before, Rogers appeared before the federal district court in El Paso and presented a sworn statement in a *habeas corpus* proceeding. On April 2, the marshal had taken into custody Franz Gottwald, the German-born quartermaster general of the Mexican Constitutionalist Army, on a charge of conspiracy to violate the neutrality laws. Rogers had made the arrest on the instructions of the U.S. attorney general. The president had personally directed Gottwald be held under the Alien Enemy Act of 1798, until such time as Wilson ordered his release. Rogers delivered the prisoner to the stockade at Fort Bliss, but no formal charges were made until the eighteenth. Charles Vowell, Gottwald's lawyer, had submitted a writ seeking his release, arguing the arrest and detention were illegal, but moved for a continuance to obtain additional evidence. Judge Duval West, presiding over the hearing, granted the defense their request. Upon hearing the case on April 24, the judge denied Gottwald's release due to the personal involvement of the president, and suggested counsel contact the attorney general. Instead, Vowell immediately appealed to the U.S. Supreme Court. Unfortunately for Gottwald, while the federal courts did conduct legal reviews to determine the citizenship of defendants, they showed broad deference to the government once the individual in question was demonstrated to be an "enemy" under the relevant legal definition. As Franz Gottwald's name does not appear on the docket of the Supreme Court, the justices likely refused to hear his case. Gottwald was transported to the prisoner of war camp at Fort Douglas near Salt Lake City, Utah, on August 8.[86]

In the wake of the Bandit War of 1915, and the Great War, the Ranger Force had acquired a reputation for brutality and unsavory behavior. On the morning of February 12, 1919, Marshal Rogers appeared before the joint legislative committee investigating the Service. Representative José Canales, the South Texas politician leading a reformist movement, had earlier stated the veteran captain was among "the noblest and best men that I know ... [whose] own conscience was a self-restraint and law." The adjutant general's lawyer similarly wanted to showcase Rogers's status as an example of what the Rangers could become again. On the stand, the marshal was mainly asked mundane questions about the necessity of the Ranger Force. He did testify that placing Rangers under bond, as suggested in House Bill No. 5, would destroy the efficiency of the Service. "I don't think you could get a captain who had any property himself to command a company of Rangers and give bond for their conduct," he argued. When he was asked his opinion of the serving captains, Rogers demurred, saying he did not want to enter into personalities. Since his district encompassed six or seven hundred miles of the border, Rogers needed the continued cooperation of the Rangers.[87]

Rogers agreed with other witnesses that a higher pay scale would attract "good, strong, faithful men" for the Rangers. He also suggested that the Ranger Force had suffered from "divided authority" and needed to reorganize into a "centralized" system under the direction of a "generalissimo" who would supervise separate "squads." This senior officer would nominate men for the commissioned officer slots, subject to the approval of the adjutant general and governor. As the present arrangement made it "practically impossible" for the adjutant general to manage the individual companies, as well as the other assets of the department, the "right man" in such a position would offer better oversight with an improved span of control and render the bonding issue moot.[88]

The Rogers testimony was striking for the personal venom expressed by opposing counsels. While the marshal sat quietly on the witness stand, Canales and the adjutant general's attorneys engaged in a heated exchange of insults. Robert Edward Lee Knight referred to the "vaporous interrogations of counsel" and suggested "obsession or hallucination" guided Canales's crusade. Shortly thereafter, Canales accused Knight of "a misstatement of the facts," which was a genteel way of calling him a liar.[89]

Having served eight years in a Democratic administration, Rogers was not reappointed by newly inaugurated President Warren Gamaliel Harding.

His term ended on April 21, 1921, although he held over to May 25. Following a failed bid for a seat on the Austin Board of City Commissioners, Rogers went to work for the American Railway Express Company as chief of detectives. Working out of San Antonio, he escorted valuable cargo aboard trains across the state, and conducted investigations for the company.[90]

By this time, Hill Loftis, alias Tom Ross, reentered Rogers's life. Two years after fleeing into New Mexico, the outlaw had returned to Texas and surrendered himself to the Martin County sheriff. Once he was cleared of robbery charges in Wilbarger County, he returned to his Gaines County ranch and, except for three misdemeanor convictions, seemed to have gone straight. Appearances may have been deceiving, though, as Ross and Milton Paul "Milt" Good were put on trial for murder in Lubbock and Abilene between June and September 1923. In Seminole, in front of credible eyewitnesses, they had killed William Davis "Dave" Allison and Horace Lorenzo "Hod" Roberson, cattle inspectors for the Texas and Southwestern Cattle Raisers Association. The two dead men had suspected Ross of being the leader of a rustling gang operating along the Texas-New Mexico line, but they lacked hard evidence. Captain Rogers was subpoenaed to testify for the prosecution but, as Loftis had spared him in the sand dunes, the ex-Ranger felt morally obliged not to speak against him. Despite Rogers's refusal, Ross was convicted on two counts of first-degree murder and sentenced to fifty-five years in prison. He soon escaped and committed suicide in Montana in 1929.[91]

In the Austin city election of 1923, Harry W. Nolen won a seat on the city commission. Following his victory, he was given the portfolio of Superintendent of Police and Public Safety, which oversaw the Austin Police Department. The ranking officers of the force were Police Chief Samuel Davis Griffin, Sergeants Robert Edward Nitschke and James Newel Littlepage, and Chief of Detectives Adolphus Love Bugg. In a general reshuffling of jobs that occurred at the same time, Nitschke resigned for health reasons, Bugg replaced him, and Griffin returned to his former post of chief of detectives. Rogers, and his influential allies, successfully lobbied for the vacant office of police chief, and he was appointed on May 1, 1923. With one sergeant, four detectives, three plainclothesmen, five motorcycle officers, one mounted policeman, and ten patrolmen, Rogers went to work cracking down on the narcotics trade, prostitution, violent offences, and property crimes. He also lent support to federal prohibition agents working in the city.[92]

Unfortunately, his greatest impediment would prove to be the police commissioner rather than the criminal element. Both as a matter of duty and principle, Rogers was intent on enforcing the standing Blue Laws that banned certain commercial activities on the Sabbath, including the showing of movies in the cinema and the sale of tobacco products. At first, Nolen and Rogers agreed on this policy and, indeed, the issue was a part of the commissioner's election campaign. On April 22, 1924, Rogers announced a ban, effective May 1, on games of chance and automobile raffles featured at the traveling carnivals that occasionally passed through town. The state's anti-lottery laws would be enforced, the chief declared, and Mayor William "Dick" Yett concurred. Commissioner Nolen found himself in an awkward position as he had already publicly acknowledged the legality of a raffle due to occur at the Odd Fellows-Red Men carnival on May 3. On May 1, Nolen and Rogers held a closed-door meeting concerning the Blue Laws. Nolen later told a *Statesman* reporter that the two had differences on the issue, but they had been resolved. Rogers openly contradicted his supervisor in a statement to the newspapers the same day. The bad publicity proved to be the final straw for Nolen, and he demanded Rogers's resignation that very evening.[93]

The chief's letter was read at the city commission meeting on May 3:

> In accordance with your request of the 1st inst., I hereby tender you my resignation as city marshal, effective immediately. I thank you very heartily for entrusting me with the important position of city marshal for one year and hope the standards and ideals of your police force are none the worse for having come under my supervision. With every good wish for you and your police officers, to whom I have become very attached, and again assuring you of my great appreciation of your favors and courtesies, I am, Yours for law enforcement. J. H. Rogers.[94]

As he was financially comfortable and enjoyed good health, the sixty-year-old Rogers decided to retire and spend his remaining years with Hattie, his children, and his grandchildren. However, God would have other plans for His servant.

By late 1926, the Ranger Force was in disarray. Governor Miriam Amanda "Ma" Ferguson had packed her administration with unqualified political appointees, and the Ranger service was no different. Shortly after his inauguration, Governor Dan Moody decided to clean house. To restore the reputation of the Texas Rangers to their former glory, the executive recruited John Rogers, one of the "Four Captains," to return on May 15, 1927. Originally, his assignment was to serve as commander of Company A at Marfa, but, apparently, either Rogers or Hattie balked at moving to West Texas far from family and friends. Instead, he exchanged places with Captain William L. Wright, once a Ranger private working for Rogers, and commanded Company C in Del Rio. Seeing no reason to uproot his family once more, Rogers maintained his residence in Austin, where Hattie stayed, and took the train home often.[95]

In July 1927, Rogers and several of his men were patrolling the streets of McCamey. The oil town had appeared at the same time as neighboring Borger, a location that would see the Rangers often. Situated in Upton County, McCamey was troubled by the usual lawbreaking that accompanied any boom camp. Almost immediately upon their arrival, though, the crime rate sharply decreased: evidence the veteran Ranger's reputation had preceded him. From the oil fields, Rogers and his men were constantly on the move: suppressing riots, raiding vice rings, and apprehending smugglers, bootleggers, rustlers, deserters, and other less violent offenders. On August 4, they seized 134 quarts of homemade beer and fifteen gallons of mash in Del Rio, and arrested two men. In 1929, Rogers, and Rangers Henry Doyle Glasscock and Robert Yates Secrest (a seventy-seven-year old private), conducted liquor and gaming raids in Hondo, Castroville, Uvalde, and Del Rio.[96]

Having been ill for several weeks, Rogers consulted his doctor, who referred him to Scott and White Hospital in Temple for further tests. The results pointed to the need for gall bladder surgery, which was performed on October 9. The doctors believed his recovery assured, but the captain took a turn for the worse and died on November 11, 1930. The primary cause of death was pronounced as chronic cholecystitis and the secondary as cardiac embolism. His funeral service was held at the First Southern Presbyterian Church in Austin the following day, and Rogers was buried in Oakwood Cemetery.[97]

Early the following year, the *Sheriff's Association of Texas Magazine* paid tribute to the late captain:

> He was the friend of many of the leading sheriffs of this state, and they will miss and mourn him for a long, long time. He did every duty that was ever assigned him, while in the service as a Ranger, a city marshal, a United States marshal or a deputy sheriff. When death called and his commission was returned it was clean and brilliant. He had never left a stain upon it.[98]

Between 1935 and 1940, Hattie relocated to San Antonio and lived with Lucile's family. Having been diagnosed with arteriosclerosis, she died of myocarditis and coronary occlusion on July 5, 1948, at Baptist Memorial Hospital. She was buried next to her husband two days later.[99]

Lucile graduated with honors from the Texas Presbyterian College for Girls at Milford in May 1913, and attended the University of Texas at Austin. She married Charles Mills Reeves, a freight and passenger agent for the Southern Pacific Railroad, on April 30, 1917. They lived in San Antonio, and raised three sons and one daughter. Suffering from a head injury, Reeves died on May 7, 1935, in a Galveston hospital. He was buried at San Jose Burial Park in San Antonio. Lucile died on February 14, 1987. She was laid to rest next to her husband.[100]

Pleasant graduated from Wentworth Military Academy in Lexington, Missouri, in 1915, then attended the University of Texas at Austin. He enlisted in Company E, Second Infantry Regiment of the Texas National Guard on May 10, 1916. The day before, President Wilson had federalized the Guard, and the Second Infantry was assigned to the Sixth Separate Brigade on the lower Rio Grande. Pleas received a commission as a second lieutenant on January 11, 1917. After the Thirty-sixth (Texas-Oklahoma) Division was organized at Camp Bowie in August of the same year, he served in the 141st Infantry Regiment's machine gun company, and later transferred to Headquarters, 71st Infantry Brigade as aide-de-camp to Brigadier-General Henry Hutchins. Pleas married Clara Louise Fink, an old schoolmate from El Paso, on July 3, 1918, in Fort Worth, and she would bear him two daughters. Fifteen days after the wedding, the brigade headquarters sailed from Hoboken, New Jersey, aboard the SS *Rijndam* for France. After General Hutchins was removed from command in August, Pleas transferred to Headquarters Company, 132nd Machine Gun Battalion. Beginning October 6, the brigade was attached to the Second Division near St. Etienne-á-Arnes, and participated in a general attack on the Machault-Cauroy line two days later. On October 11, in conjunction with French forces, the Thirty-sixth Division pursued retreating Germans, and ultimately occupied a front stretching from Fontenille Ferme to Givry. The 71st Brigade made an attack south of Rilly-aux-Oies on the twenty-seventh in order to stabilize the line. The next day, the division was relieved by the French Twenty-second and Sixty-first divisions. Pleas was promoted to captain and a company command on May 19, 1919, and the battalion sailed from Brest aboard the USS *Patricia* four days later. They reached Hoboken on June 4. Deciding on a military career, Pleas entered the Regular Army on September 27, 1920, and served in a variety of infantry and staff assignments. He graduated from the Command and General Staff School at Fort Leavenworth, Kansas, in 1935, and the Army War College, then at Washington Barracks in Washington, D.C., three years later. While a colonel, he was assigned to command the Central Base Section in London from April 1942 to August 1944. Pleas was promoted to the temporary grade of brigadier general on April 2, 1943. He then commanded the Seine Section from August 1944 to November 1945. Reverting to his permanent rank of colonel on May 1, 1946, he served as the senior instructor for the Officer Reserve Corps in New York. His awards and decorations included the Distinguished Service Medal, Legion of Merit, and Bronze Star. He retired on January 31, 1948, as a brigadier, and worked as the manager of the Walter Percy Chrysler estate in Warrenton, Virginia. At some point, he and Clara divorced, and she died in Malvern, Pennsylvania, on March 4, 1966. Pleas died in Charles Town, West Virginia, on December 25, 1974. He was buried in Oakwood Cemetery in Austin.[101]

John H. Rogers believed in his God, his family, and his duty. These were the touchstones of his life. A man of consistent principles, he left the position he loved because he could not support the public policies of his superior. Carrying both a Bible and a gun, he enforced the law in a fair and restrained manner, and only resorted to violence when necessary. In every regard, a brave lawman and a Christian gentleman, he brought integrity and dignity to the Ranger service.

Endnotes

Abbreviations

A&ISD-TSLAC: Archives and Information Services Division, Texas State Library and Archives Commission

AHQ: Arkanas Historical Quaterly

BCAH: Briscoe Center for American History

BLM: Bureau of Land Management

CSR-CGSO: Compiled Service Records of Confederate General and Staff Officers

CSR-CS: Compiled Service Records of Confederate Soldiers

CV: *Confederate Veteran*

CWTI: *Civil War Times Illustrated*

ETHJ: *East Texas Historical Journal*

FTRA: Former Texas Ranger Association

HML&HC: Healey Memorial Library and History Center

MMWH: *Montana: The Magazine of Western History*

MR: Monthly Returns

NARA: National Archives and Records Administration

NOLA Quarterly: *Quarterly of the National Association for Outlaw and Lawman History*

PPHM: Panhandle-Plains Historical Museum

RAG: *Report of the Adjutant General of the State of Texas*

ROS: Record of Scouts

RSR: Ranger Service Records

SHQ: *Southwestern Historical Quarterly*

SJMH: San Jacinto Museum of History

TRF Investigation: Proceedings of the Joint Committee of the Senate and the House in the Investigation of the State Ranger Force, Thirty-sixth Legislature, Regular Session.

TRHF&M: Texas Ranger Hall of Fame and Museum

TSLAC: Texas State Library and Archives Commission

USGLO: United States General Land Office

WTHAY: *West Texas Historical Association Yearbook*

**Note: In order to abbreviate references for sources found in the Texas State Archives, this author has adopted, in part, Robert Utley's method of citing the record group followed by the box number: e.g. 401–178 denotes Record Group 401 (Adjutant General's office), box 178.

Notes for Chapter 1

1. Rick Miller, *Texas Ranger John B. Jones and the Frontier Battalion, 1874–1881* (Denton: University of North Texas Press, 2012), 3, 4, 5; Helen Frances Bonner, "Major John B. Jones: The Defender of the Frontier of Texas" (M.A. thesis, University of Texas, 1950), 1–2, 5; Nancy Timmons Samuels and Barbara Roach Knox, comps., *Old Northwest Texas: Historical—Statistical—Biographical* (Fort Worth: Fort Worth Genealogical Society, 1980), 1-B: 477; William S. Speer and John Henry Brown, eds., *The Encyclopedia of the New West* (Marshall, TX: United States Biographical Publishing Company, 1881), 388, 469.
2. Miller, *Texas Ranger John B. Jones*, 4–6; Bonner, "Major John B. Jones," 2–8; *Texas Sentinel*, June 13, 1840; Tax Rolls, Travis County, 1840–1841, Matagorda County, 1846–1856; Joseph Milton Nance, *Attack and Counterattack: The Texas Military Frontier, 1842* (Austin: University of Texas Press, 1964), 55–56, 67, 94–95; *Telegraph and Texas Register*, November 5, 1845; *Seventh U.S. Census*, Matagorda County, Texas (Slave Schedule); Walter P. Webb, *The Texas Rangers: A Century of Frontier Defense* (Austin: University of Texas Press, 1965), 311; Sidney Smith Johnson, *Texans Who Wore the Gray* (Tyler, TX: self-published, 1907), 161; Speer and Brown, eds., *Encyclopedia of the New West*, 388.
3. Miller, *Texas Ranger John B. Jones*, 7–8; Bonner, "Major John B. Jones," 9–10; Francis Wright Bradley, *A Brief History of the Mount Zion Society: Founded January 29, 1777* (Winnsboro, SC: The News and Herald, 1948), 2, 4; Fitz Hugh McMaster, *History of Fairfield County, South Carolina* (Columbia, SC: State Commercial Printing Company, 1946), 59–60; *Corsicana Semi-Weekly Light*, January 23, 1920; *Corsicana Daily Sun*, May 14, 28, 2002.
4. Miller, *Texas Ranger John B. Jones*, 9; Tax Rolls, Navarro County, 1857; *Corsicana Daily Sun*, May 14, 2002; Bonner, "Major John B. Jones," 10; Samuels and Knox, comps., *Old Northwest Texas*, I-B: 478; Wyvonne Putman, comp., *Navarro County History* (Quanah, TX: Nortex Press, 1975), 200; Annie Carpenter Love, *History of Navarro County* (Dallas: Southwest Press, 1933), 234.
5. Webb, *Texas Rangers*, 309.

6. Miller, *Texas Ranger John B. Jones*, 11; Tax Rolls, Navarro County, 1861; *Eighth U.S. Census*, Navarro County, Texas (Free and Slave Schedules).
7. Miller, *Texas Ranger John B. Jones*, 11; Bonner, "Major John B. Jones," 12–13; Jack Duane Redman, "General Joh B. Jones: Twenty Years of Service to Texas" (M. A. thesis, University of Texas at El Paso, 1983), 105; *Navarro Express*, June 30, 1860.
8. Miller, *Texas Ranger John B. Jones*, 9–10; *Dallas Daily Herald*, December 22, 1877; Webb, *Texas Rangers*, 309 (quotation), 311; Robert M. Utley, *Lone Star Justice: The First Century of the Texas Rangers* (New York: Berkley Books, 2002), 146; Frederick Wilkins, *The Law Comes to Texas: The Texas Rangers, 1870–1901* (Abilene, TX: State House Press, 1999), 43.
9. Miller, *Texas Ranger John B. Jones*, 11, 13; Love, *History of Navarro County*, 104–105; *Navarro Express*, January 21, June 2, 1860.
10. Miller, *Texas Ranger John B. Jones*, 16–17; Bonner, "Major John B. Jones," 18; *Texas State Gazette*, December 14, 1850; Putman, comp., *Navarro County History*, 93; Bruce S. Allardice, *Confederate Colonels: A Biographical Register* (Columbia: University of Missouri Press, 2008), 367. For two examples of Jones's alleged service with Terry, see Speer and Brown, eds., *Encyclopedia of the New West*, 388; and Dan L. Thrapp, *Encyclopedia of Frontier Biography* (Lincoln: University of Nebraska Press, 1991), 2: 742. For more on Terry's regiment, see Jeffery D. Murrah, *None but Texians: A History of Terry's Texas Rangers* (Austin: Eakin Press, 2001); Bryan S. Bush, *Terry's Texas Rangers: A History of the Eighth Texas Cavalry* (New York: Turner Publishing Company, 2002); and Thomas W. Cutrer, ed., *Our Trust Is in the God of Battles: The Civil War Letters of Robert Franklin Bunting, Chaplain, Terry's Texas Rangers* (Knoxville: University of Tennessee Press, 2006).
11. Miller, *Texas Ranger John B. Jones*, 17; CSR-CS, Fifteenth Texas Infantry, John B. Jones, J. W. Speight, Richard Coke; Blake Richard Hamaker, "Making a Good Soldier: A Historical and Quantitative Study of the 15th Texas Infantry, C.S.A." (M.A. thesis, University of North Texas, 1998), 7; Lucy A. Erath, ed., "Memoirs of Major George Bernard Erath," Pt. 2, *SHQ* 27 (October 1923): 158; Allardice, *Confederate Colonels*, 353.
12. Miller, *Texas Ranger John B. Jones*, 17; *The War of the Rebellion: A Compilation of the Official Records of the Union and Confederate Armies*, Series I, XIII: 718, 770, 884, XXII, Pt. 1: 904. Hereafter cited as *OR*, all references are to Series I. Alwyn Barr, *Polignac's Texas Brigade* (College Station: Texas A&M University Press, 1998), 12, 13; Erath, ed.,

"Memoirs of George Bernard Erath," 158; CSR-CS, Fifteenth Texas Infantry, John B. Jones; Allardice, *Confederate Colonels*, 317.
13. *OR*, XIII: 855; Thomas W. Cutrer, *Theater of a Separate War: The Civil War West of the Mississippi River* (Chapel Hill: University of North Carolina Press, 2017), 139–140; Anne J. Bailey, "Henry McCulloch's Texans and the Defense of Arkansas in 1862," *AHQ* 46 (Spring 1987): 53; Joseph Palmer Blessington, *The Campaigns of Walker's Texas Division* (New York: Lange, Little & Co., 1875), 42–43.
14. *OR*, XXII, Pt. 1: 28, Pt. 2: 770–771; Barr, *Polignac's Texas Brigade*, 13; Blessington, *Walker's Texas Division*, 64; CSR-CS, Seventh Texas Cavalry, William Steele. Steele would figure prominently in Jones's life, not to mention scores of other Rangers serving in the 1870s. Astonishingly, no full-length biography of this leading figure has yet been written. For his antebellum military career, see George W. Cullum, *Biographical Register of the Officers and Graduates of the United States Military Academy* (Boston: Houghton, Mifflin and Company, 1891), 1: 613. For his Confederate service, see Ralph A. Wooster, *Lone Star Generals in Gray* (Austin: Eakin Press, 2000), 163–167.
15. Miller, *Texas Ranger John B. Jones*, 18; *OR*, XXII, Pt. 2: 773–774, 775, 776–779, 794–795, 909; Pt. 1: 29; Barr, *Polignac's Texas Brigade*, 13, 14–15, 18; John W. Spencer, *The Confederate Guns of Navarro County* (Corsicana, TX: Texas Press, 1986), 24; CSR-CGSO, John B. Jones; Hamaker, "Making a Good Soldier," 20–21; Mamie Yeary, comp., *Reminiscences of the Boys in Gray, 1861–1865* (Dallas: Smith and Lamar Publishing House, 1912), 587.
16. *OR*, XV: 1083, XXII, Pt. 1: 29–30, 32, 439, Pt. 2: 833–834, 839–840, XXVI, Pt. 2: 6–7, Pt. 1: 331; Jeffrey S. Prushankin, *A Crisis in Confederate Command: Edmund Kirby Smith, Richard Taylor, and the Army of the Trans-Mississippi* (Baton Rouge: Louisiana State University Press, 2005), 43–45, 46; Barr, *Polignac's Texas Brigade*, 18–23; Dudley G. Wooten, ed., *A Comprehensive History of Texas, 1685 to 1897* (Dallas: William G. Scarff, 1898), 2: 640; Hamaker, "Making a Good Soldier," 22–23, 27–29, 30–31.
17. *OR*, XXVI, Pt. 1: 329–330; Cooper K. Ragan, ed., "The Diary of Captain George W, O'Brien, 1863," Pt. 2, *SHQ* 67 (October 1963): 235–236; Thomas Green, "Green to My Dear Wife, October 1, 1863," *Southern Historical Society Papers* 3 (February 1877): 62.
18. Miller, *Texas Ranger John B. Jones*, 19; *OR*, XXVI, Pt. 1: 329–332, 321, 325–326, Pt. 2: 255; Barr, *Polignac's Texas Brigade*, 25–27; Ragan, ed., "Diary of Captain George W. O'Brien," Pt. 2: 237, 240,

242; Green, "Green to My Dear Wife," 62–63; Spencer, *Confederate Guns of Navarro County*, 25–26; *Houston Tri-Weekly Telegraph*, October 9, 30, 1863.
19. *OR*, XXVI, Pt. 1: 331. Reprinted in *Austin Daily Statesman*, April 2, 1881.
20. Harrison to Anderson, October 23, 1863, CSR-CGSO, John B. Jones.
21. Miller, *Texas Ranger John B. Jones*, 24; CSR-CGSO, John B. Jones.
22. Barr, *Polignac's Texas Brigade*, 28–29; Jeff Kinard, *Lafayette of the South: Prince Camille de Polignac and the American Civil War* (College Station: Texas A&M University Press, 2001), 113; Cooper K. Ragan, ed., "The Diary of Captain George W. O'Brien," Pt. 3, *SHQ* 67 (January 1864): 417–418, 420; Gary D. Joiner, ed., *Little to Eat and Thin Mud to Drink: Letters, Diaries, and Memoirs from the Red River Campaigns, 1863–1864* (Knoxville: University of Tennessee Press, 2007), 127–128; CSR-CS, Fifteenth Texas Infantry, James W. Speight and James E. Harrison. The French nobleman and soldier had served in the Crimea and subsequently offered his sword to the Confederacy. He assumed command of his brigade in March 1863. Ella Lonn, *Foreigners in the Confederacy* (Chapel Hill: University of North Carolina Press, 2002), 167–168.
23. *OR*, XXVI, Pt. 2: 392; Stephen A. Dupree, *Planting the Union Flag in Texas: The Campaigns of Major General Nathaniel P. Banks in the West* (College Station: Texas A&M University Press, 2008), 63–64; Mark A. Snell, *From First to Last: The Life of Major William B. Franklin* (New York: Fordham University Press, 2002), 288–289; Richard Lowe, *The Texas Overland Expedition of 1863* (Abilene, TX: McWhiney Foundation Press, 1998), 26, 58, 65; Terry L. Jones, *Historical Dictionary of the Civil War* (Lanham, MD: Scarecrow Press, 2002), 2: 1422.
24. Barr, *Polignac's Texas Brigade*, 30–32; Alwyn Barr, ed., "The Battle of Bayou Bourbeau, November 3, 1863: Colonel Oran M. Roberts' Report," *Louisiana History* 6 (Winter 1965): 85–86 n12; Allardice, *Confederate Colonels*, 228, 324; Richard Lowe, *Walker's Texas Division, C.S.A.: Greyhounds of the Trans-Mississippi* (Baton Rouge: Louisiana State University Press, 2004), 136–144; Dupree, *Planting the Union Flag in Texas*, 67–68; Lowe, *Texas Overland Expedition*, 75–78, 84; Hamaker, "Making a Good Soldier," 49.
25. *OR*, XXXIV, Pt. 2: 212, 934–935, 952–953, 977, Pt. 1: 129–130; *Official Records of the Union and Confederate Navies in the War of the Rebellion*, Series I, XXV: 737; Barr, *Polignac's Texas Brigade*, 36 (first quotation); Kinard, *Lafayette of the South*, 122–123; Lonn, *Foreigners in the Confederacy*, 169 (second quotation), 448; John D. Winters,

The Civil War in Louisiana (Baton Rouge: Louisiana State University Press, 1991), 320, 323.

26. Miller, *Texas Ranger John B. Jones*, 22; *OR*, XXXIV, Pt. 1: 500, 561, 476, 531, 564, Pt. 2: 1072, Pt 3: 764; XLI, Pt. 4: 1142; Bonner, "Major John B. Jones," 23; Kinard, *Lafayette of the South*, 116–118, 133–157; Barr, *Polignac's Texas Brigade*, 38–42; Roy O. Hatton, "Prince Camille de Polignac and the American Civil War, 1863–1865," *Louisiana Studies* 3 (Summer 1964): 173; Richard B. Irwin, *History of the Nineteenth Army Corps* (New York: G. P. Putnam's Sons, 1893), 288; Richard Taylor, *Destruction and Reconstruction: Personal Experiences of the Late War* (New York: D. Appleton and Company, 1879), 154–155; Lester N. Fitzhugh, "Texas Forces in the Red River Campaign," *Texas Military History* 3 (Spring 1963): 18; Shelby Foote, *The Civil War: A Narrative* (New York: Random House, 1986), 3: 44; Yeary, comp., *Reminiscences of the Boys in Gray*, 587, 777; *Houston Daily Telegraph*, April 18, 1864; CSR-CS, Fifteenth Texas Infantry, J. W. Speight and James E. Harrison; Allardice, *Confederate Colonels*, 353. See also Joiner, ed., *Little to Eat and Thin Mud to Drink*, 132–135.

27. *OR*, XXXIV, Pt. 1: 592–595; XLI, Pt. 3: 989–990; "Unpublished After-Action Reports from the Red River Campaign," *Civil War Regiments* 4 (1994): 125, 127; Gary D. Joiner, *Through the Howling Wilderness: The 1864 Red River Campaign and Union Failure in the West* (Knoxville: University of Tennessee Press, 2006), 159–161; Joiner, ed., *Little to Eat and Thin Mud to Drink*, 25, 46 n122; William Riley Brooksher, *War Along the Bayous: The 1864 Red River Campaign in Louisiana* (Washington, D.C.: Brassey's, 1998), 218–219; Spencer, *Confederate Guns of Navarro County*, 31; Hatton, "Polignac and the Civil War," 179; Kinard, *Lafayette of the South*, 164–168; Barr, *Polignac's Texas Brigade*, 44–46; Taylor, *Destruction and Reconstruction*, 191; Yeary, comp., *Reminiscences of the Boys in Gray*, 587, 777.

28. Kinard, *Lafayette of the South*, 173–180; Barr, *Polignac's Texas Brigade*, 49–52; Hatton, "Polignac and the Civil War," 181–183; Spencer, *Confederate Guns of Navarro County*, 33; Clement A. Evans, ed., *Confederate Military History* (Atlanta: Confederate Publishing Company, 1899), 11: 138; CSR-CS, Fifteenth Texas Infantry, John B. Jones and March 1865 Regimental Return.

29. *OR*, XLI, Pt. 4: 1017, 1122, XLVIII, Pt. 1: 1371–1372, 1390, 1391–1392, 1427, 1458, Pt. 2: 1266, 1281, 1286, 1303; CSR-CGSO, John B. Jones; *Dallas Daily Herald*, May 11, 1865; Wooster, *Lone Star Generals in Gray*, 94.

Endnotes **507**

30. Miller, *Texas Ranger John B. Jones*, 24; *OR*, XLVIII, Pt. 2: 1318–1319; CSR-CGSO, John B. Jones; Dumas Malone, ed., *Dictionary of American Biography* (New York: Charles Scribner's Sons, 1933), 10: 182; Johnson, *Texans Who Wore the Gray*, 161.
31. Miller, *Texas Ranger John B. Jones*, 25; Bonner, "Major John B. Jones," 22; Speer and Brown, eds., *Encyclopedia of the New West*, 388; Eugene C. Harter, *The Lost Colony of the Confederacy* (Jackson: University Press of Mississippi, 1985), 11; Andrew Rolle, *The Lost Cause: The Confederate Exodus to Mexico* (Norman: University of Oklahoma Press, 1992), 8–9, 174–175; Todd W. Wahlstrom, *The Southern Exodus to Mexico: Migration Across the Borderlands After the American Civil War* (Lincoln: University of Nebraska Press, 2015), 27–28; Testimony of John B. Jones, January 19, 1878, *Relations of the United States with Mexico*, House Report No. 701, 45th Congress, 2nd Session, Pt. 2: 58.
32. Miller, *Texas Ranger John B. Jones*, 25; Bonner, "Major John B. Jones," 22–24; Harter, *The Lost Colony of the Confederacy*, 22–23, 24, 31, 62–64, 66, 69–70; Thrapp, *Encyclopedia of Frontier Biography*, 2: 742; Speer and Brown, eds., *Encyclopedia of the New West*, 388.
33. Miller, *Texas Ranger John B. Jones*, 25, 27; Tax Rolls, Navarro County, 1866, 1870; Love, *History of Navarro County*, 216–217; *Ninth U.S. Census*, Navarro County, Texas.
34. Miller, *Texas Ranger John B. Jones*, 26; Bonner, "Major John B. Jones," 25; Redman, "General John B. Jones," 105.
35. Miller, *Texas Ranger John B. Jones*, 27–29, 125–126; Love, *History of Navarro County*, 135; *Dallas Daily Herald*, March 6, 1873; *Galveston Daily News*, May 2, 1876.
36. Kenneth W. Howell, ed., *Still the Arena of Civil War: Violence and Turmoil in Reconstruction Texas, 1865–1874* (Denton: University of North Texas Press, 2012), 354, 359.
37. *Governor's Messages, Coke to Ross, 1874–1891* (Austin: Texas State Library, 1916), 14–15.
38. Hans Peter Nielson Gammel, comp., *The Laws of Texas, 1822–1897* (Austin: The Gammel Book Company, 1898), 8: 87 (first quotation), 89 (second quotation), 91 (third quotation); Patsy McDonald Spaw, ed., *The Texas Senate* (College Station: Texas A&M University Press, 1999), 2: 211; Utley, *Lone Star Justice*, 146. Letters from contractors commonly employing the "Frontier Battalion" term can be found in 401–1158, TSLAC.
39. Gammel, comp., *Laws of Texas*, 8: 90–91; *Report of Maj. J. B. Jones, 1876*, 6.

40. Major Horace H. Shelton, "Texas Confederate Generals: General William Steele," *Under Texas Skies* 3 (August 1952): 13–14.
41. Miller, *Texas Ranger John B. Jones*, 36, 39; Thrapp, *Encyclopedia of Frontier Biography*, 2: 742. The *Houston Telegraph* article was reprinted in *Weekly State Gazette*, August 8, 1874, and *Corsicana Observer*, August 12, 1874.
42. RSR, John B. Jones, 401–158, TSLAC.
43. Wilkins, *Law Comes to Texas*, 28–29; William J. Maltby, *Captain Jeff; or, Frontier Life in Texas with the Texas Rangers* (Colorado City, TX: Whipkey Printing Company, 1906), 66 (first quotation), 118 (second quotation).
44. General Order No. 2, May 6, 1874, 401–984, TSLAC (quotation); Wooten, ed., *Comprehensive History of Texas*, 2: 347–350; Utley, *Lone Star Justice*, 147; Special Order No. 24, December 9, 1875, Special Order No. 28, March 15, 1876, Special Order No. 78, November 30, 1876, Special Order No. 39, December 8, 1876, 401–1158, TSLAC.
45. Miller, *Texas Ranger John B. Jones*, 45–47, 50–51; Mike Cox, *The Texas Rangers: Wearing the Cinco Peso, 1821–1900* (New York: Tom Doherty Associates, 2008), 222, 224; Thrapp, *Encyclopedia of Frontier Biography*, 2: 742; Bob Alexander and Donaly E. Brice, *Texas Rangers: Lives, Legend, and Legacy* (Denton: University of North Texas Press, 2017), 123; Wilkins, *Law Comes to Texas*, 42–43.
46. Miller, *Texas Ranger John B. Jones*, 51–56; Jones to Steele, July 14, 1874, 401–392, TSLAC; Wilbur Sturtevant Nye, *Carbine & Lance: The Story of Old Fort Sill* (Norman: University of Oklahoma Press, 1969), 193, 195–197; Allen Lee Hamilton, *Sentinel of the Southern Plains: Fort Richardson and the Northwest Texas Frontier, 1866–1878* (Fort Worth: Texas Christian University Press, 1988), 147–150; Chuck Parsons, ed., "The Memoirs of William Callicott, Texas Ranger," Pt. 1, *The Texas Ranger Dispatch* 3 (Spring 2001), 25–26, 28; Z. T. Wattles, August 22, 1874, unidentified newspaper clipping (likely *Corsicana Observer*), 401–1158, TSLAC; Charles M. Robinson III, "The Tough Little Ranger of Lost Valley," *True West* 38 (August 1991): 20–21; Bob Alexander, *Winchester Warriors: Texas Rangers of Company D, 1874–1901* (Denton: University of North Texas Press, 2009), 42–43. See also Clifford R. Caldwell and Ron DeLord, *Texas Lawmen, 1835–1899: The Good and the Bad* (Charleston, SC: History Press, 2011), 328–330.
47. Miller, *Texas Ranger John B. Jones*, 57–61; Jones to Steele, July 14, 23, 1874, 401–392, TSLAC; Utley, *Lone Star Justice*, 149–150;

Cox, *Wearing the Cinco Peso*, 226–228; Alexander and Brice, *Texas Rangers*, 154; Nye, *Carbine and Lance*, 197–198, 200; Parsons, ed., "Memoirs of William Callicott," Pt. 1: 26; Ed Carnal, "Reminiscences of a Texas Ranger," *Frontier Times* 1 (December 1923): 21–22; Wattles, August 22, 1874, 401–1158, TSLAC (quotations); Walter Robertson, "The Loss [*sic*] Valley Fight, Reminiscences of Walter Robertson," *Frontier Times* 7 (December 1929): 100–104; Hamilton, *Sentinel of the Southern Plains*, 150–151; Andrew Jackson Sowell, *Texas Indian Fighters: Early Settlers and Indian Fighters of Southwest Texas* (Austin: State House Press, 1986), 798–803; Joseph Carroll McConnell, *The West Texas Frontier: or, A Descriptive History of Early Times in Western Texas* (Palo Pinto, TX: Texas Legal Bank & Book Co., 1939), 2: 328; *Galveston Daily News*, July 18, 1874; Alexander, *Winchester Warriors*, 54. *Special RAG, September 1884*, 41: "Probably the greatest benefit derived to the State from this force was the driving back, on July 12, 1874, of a large Indian war party, led by Lone Wolf, that invaded Texas for the purpose of revenge. The loss of life and property which was thus prevented can not be estimated." Jones's report stated his belief that he had faced a combined force of Comanches and Kiowas. Sowell concurs, while Miller, Nye, and Alexander believe it was an exclusively Kiowa war party.
48. Miller, *Texas Ranger John B. Jones*, 61; Jones to Steele, July 14, 23, 1874, 401–392, TSLAC; *Daily Democratic Statesman*, June 10, 1874.
49. Pekka Hämäläinen, *The Comanche Empire* (New Haven: Yale University Press, 2008), 338–339; Special Order No. 12, February 4, 1875, 401–1012, TSLAC. For a concise analysis of the Red River War, see Robert M. Utley, *Frontier Regulars: The United States Army and the Indian, 1866–1891* (Lincoln: University of Nebraska Press, 1984), Ch. 13. For more comprehensive studies, see James L. Haley, *The Buffalo War: The History of the Red River Indian Uprising of 1874* (Abilene, TX: State House Press, 2007); and J. Brett Cruse, *Battles of the Red River War: Archeological Perspectives on the Indian Campaign of 1874* (College Station: Texas A&M University, 2008).
50. Miller, *Texas Ranger John B. Jones*, 70–72; Alexander and Brice, *Texas Rangers*, 123–124; Special Orders No. 5, October 27, 1874, 401–1158, TSLAC (first three quotations); Jones to Steele, October 24, 1874, 401–392, TSLAC (fourth quotation).
51. *Supplemental RAG, 1874*, 10.

52. Miller, *Texas Ranger John B. Jones*, 90, 94; *Daily Democratic Statesman*, November 28, 1874; General Order No. 8, November 25, 1874, 401–392, TSLAC; Message of the Governor, January [12], 1875, *House Journal, Fourteenth Legislature, Second Session*, 43; Jones to Steele, January 3, 1875, Jones to Wilson, January 2, [1875] (quotation), Kenney to Wilson, February 9, 1875, 401–1158, TSLAC; Special Order Nos. 13 and 14, both dated March 17, 1875, 401–1012, TSLAC; RSR, John B. Jones, 401–158, TSLAC; *Report of Maj. J. B. Jones, 1876*, 3.

53. Miller, *Texas Ranger John B. Jones*, 99–101; Jones to Steele, May 9, 1875, 401–393, TSLAC (quotation); *Special RAG, September 1884*, 41; Hamilton, *Sentinel of the Southern Plains*, 166; Robinson, "Tough Little Ranger," 22; *Galveston Daily News*, May 11, 29, 1875; *Daily Democratic Statesman*, June 2, 1875.

54. Utley, *Lone Star Justice*, 153–154; Frederick Nolan, *The Wild West: History, Myth and the Making of America* (Edison, NJ: Chartwell Books, 2004), 74–75; Christopher Knowlton, *Cattle Kingdom: The Hidden History of the Cowboy West* (New York: Houghton Mifflin Harcourt, 2017), 188; Robert Maxwell Brown, *Strain of Violence: Historical Studies of American Violence and Vigilantism* (New York: Oxford University Press, 1975), 247, 250, 254; Frances Mayhugh Holden, *Lambshead Before Interwoven: A Texas Range Chronicle, 1848–1878* (College Station: Texas A&M University Press, 1982), 158; Randolph B. Campbell, *Gone to Texas: A History of the Lone Star State* (New York: Oxford University Press, 2004), 304.

55. David Johnson, *The Mason County "Hoo Doo" War, 1874–1902* (Denton: University of North Texas Press, 2006), 1–2, 15, 19; Dan W. Roberts, *Rangers and Sovereignty* (San Antonio: Wood Printing & Engraving Co., 1914), 86; Mrs. D. W. (Luvenia Conway) Roberts, *A Woman's Reminiscences of Six Years in Camp with the Texas Rangers* (Austin: Von Boeckmann-Jones Co., 1928?), 7; Dave Southworth, *Feuds on the Western Frontier* (Round Rock, TX: Wild Horse Publishing, 1999), 19–20; Wayne Gard, *Frontier Justice* (Norman: University of Oklahoma Press, 1968), 53; Allen G. Hatley, "The Mason County War: Top Texas Feud," *Wild West* 18 (August 2005): 25–26. See also Peter R. Rose and Elizabeth E. Sherry, eds., *The Hoo Doo War: Portraits of a Lawless Time* (Mason, TX: Mason County Historical Commission, 2003).

56. Johnson, *Mason County War*, 55–56, 58–59, 66; Alexander, *Winchester Warriors*, 82; Clifford R. Caldwell and Ron DeLord, *Eternity at the*

End of a Rope: Executions, Lynchings and Vigilante Justice in Texas, 1819–1923 (Santa Fe: Sunstone Press, 2015), 208; Sammy Tise, *Texas County Sheriffs* (Albuquerque: Oakwood Printing, 1989), 357; Edward A. Blackburn Jr., *Wanted: Historic County Jails of Texas* (College Station: Texas A&M University Press, 2006), 225. Hereafter cited as *The County Jails of Texas*. Roberts, *Rangers and Sovereignty*, 88–89; C. L. Douglas, *Famous Texas Feuds* (Austin: State House Press, 1988), 149–150.

57. Johnson, *Mason County War*, 44, 72–74 (quotation on p. 74), 83; C. L. Sonnichsen, *Ten Texas Feuds* (Albuquerque: University of New Mexico Press, 2000), 94, 95; Robert W. Stephens, *Bullets and Buckshot in Texas* (Dallas: Robert W. Stephens, 2002), 18–19; Alexander, *Winchester Warriors*, 92; Hatley, "Mason County War," 28; *Galveston Daily News*, May 29, 1875.

58. Hatley, "The Mason County War," 28; David Johnson, "Scott Cooley— A Byword for Terror," *NOLA Quarterly* 27 (April-June 2003): 5; Stephens, *Bullets and Buckshot*, 19; RSR, W. S. Cooley, 401–148, TSLAC.

59. Johnson, *Mason County War*, 75, 84, 92–93, 95–96, 98–99, 101–102, 105, 107; Sonnichsen, *Ten Texas Feuds*, 95, 97–98; *San Antonio Daily Herald*, August 30, 1875; Roberts, *Rangers and Sovereignty*, 93; Roberts, *A Woman's Reminiscences*, 7–8; Stephens, *Bullets and Buckshot*, 20. Johnny Ringo, sometimes known erroneously as Ringgold, would later figure in the Earp-Clanton feud in Arizona. For more on this shadowy gunman, see David Johnson, *John Ringo, King of the Cowboys: His Life and Times from the Hoo Doo War to Tombstone* (Denton: University of North Texas Press, 2008).

60. *Report of Maj. J. B. Jones, 1876*, 3; *RAG, 1875*, 13; Jones to Roberts, April 30, 1875, Special Order No. 40, May 10, 1875, General Order No. 5, August 5, 1875, Special Order No. 22, August 14, 1875, 401–1158, TSLAC.

61. Miller, *Texas Ranger John B. Jones*, 112–113; Johnson, *Mason County War*, 112–113, 115; Jones to Robert, August 27, 1875, Jones to Roberts, September 6, 1875, 401–1158, TSLAC; Southworth, *Feuds on the Western Frontier*, 22; Sonnichsen, *Ten Texas Feuds*, 100–101; Julius E. DeVos, et al., *The Anthology of the Hoo Doo War: The Participants in the Mason County Texas Cattle War, 1874–1877* (Mason, TX: Mason County Historical Commission, 2006), 66; Chuck Parsons and Donaly E. Brice, *Texas Ranger N. O. Reynolds: The Intrepid* (Denton: University of North Texas Press, 2014), 56.

62. *RAG, 1876*, 5, 6, 7; Johnson, *Mason County War*, 119–121, 147; Roberts, *Rangers and Sovereignty*, 92–93; Special Orders No. 47, October 7, 1875, 401–1158, TSLAC; Wilkins, *Law Comes to Texas*, 74–75; *Galveston Daily News*, January 6, 22, May 23, 1876; Tise, *Texas County Sheriffs*, 357; Johnson, "Scott Cooley," 16–17. See also Parsons and Brice, *Texas Ranger N. O. Reynolds*, 58–59. James B. Gillett incorrectly asserted fifteen Cooley sympathizers quit the Ranger service. *Six Years with the Texas Rangers*, ed. Milton M. Quaife (New Haven: Yale University Press, 1925), 50.

63. Miller, *Texas Ranger John B. Jones*, 117–118; Jones to Roberts, October 16, 1875 (quotation), Roberts to Jones, October 17, 1875, 401–1158, TSLAC; *RAG, 1876*, 5–6; Johnson, *Mason County War*, 158; *Dallas Daily Herald*, June 11, 1876; DeVos, et al., *Anthology of the Hoo Doo War*, 33; Roberts, *A Woman's Reminiscences*, 10; Clifford R. Caldwell, *A Day's Ride from Here: Mountain Home, Texas* (Charleston, SC: History Press, 2011), 72; *Galveston Daily News*, January 6, 22, May 23, 1876; Stephens, *Bullets and Buckshot*, 21, 24.

64. Miller, *Texas Ranger John B. Jones*, 125; Wilkins, *Law Comes to Texas*, 76, 82.; *Report of Maj. J. B. Jones, 1876*, 4–5, 6; General Order No. 6, October 25, 1875, Special Orders No. 50, November 12, 1875, General Order No. 7, November 30, 1875, General Order No. 9, March 1, 1876, General Order No. 10, August 25, 1876, General Order No. 11, August 29, 1876, 401–1158, TSLAC.

65. Miller, *Texas Ranger John B. Jones*, 128, 135, 138, 144–145; Peter Cozzens, *The Earth Is Weeping: The Epic Story of the Indian Wars for the American West* (New York: Alfred A. Knopf, 2016), 161–173; General Order No. 15, March 20, 1877, 401–395, TSLAC; Utley, *Lone Star Justice*, 152, 327.

66. Miller, *Texas Ranger John B. Jones*, 144, 147; Peter R. Rose, *The Reckoning: The Triumph of Order on the Texas Outlaw Frontier* (Lubbock: Texas Tech University Press, 2012), 57, 59, 62; Lee Paul, "Death Faced Straight-Up," *Wild West* 6 (August 1993): 40 (first quotation); Wayne T. Walker, "Major John B. Jones—Ranger Who Tamed the West," *Real West* 24 (April 1981): 10; Utley, *Lone Star Justice*, 179; Cox, *Wearing the Cinco Peso*, 275 (second quotation).

67. Miller, *Texas Ranger John B. Jones*, 144, 147; RSR, H. B. Waddill, 401–175, TSLAC; Parsons and Brice, *Texas Ranger N. O. Reynolds*, 79–80; Alexander and Brice, *Texas Rangers*, 308 (quotation); Wilkins, *Law Comes to Texas*, 126; *Galveston Daily News*, April 11, 26, 1877.

68. Miller, *Texas Ranger John B. Jones*, 148–150; Rose, *The Reckoning*, 66–68; *Galveston Daily News*, May 8, 15, 1877; Redman, "General John B. Jones," 48; Utley, *Lone Star Justice*, 179; Blackburn, *The County Jails of Texas*, 196; Cox, *Wearing the Cinco Peso*, 276; Brown, *Strain of Violence*, 248.

69. Miller, *Texas Ranger John B. Jones*, 150; Alexander and Brice, *Texas Rangers*, 309; Tise, *Texas County Sheriffs*, 307; *Galveston Daily News*, April 29, May 8, 18, 1877; Parsons and Brice, *Texas Ranger N. O. Reynolds*, 86.

70. David Johnson, *The Horrell Wars: Feuding in Texas and New Mexico* (Denton: University of North Texas Press, 2014), 36–41; Frederick Nolan, *Bad Blood: The Life and Times of the Horrell Brothers* (Stillwater, OK: Barbed Wire Press, 1994), 3, 5, 24–27; *RAG, 1873*, 127; Barry A. Crouch and Donaly E. Brice, *The Governor's Hounds: The Texas State Police, 1870–1873* (Austin: University of Texas Press, 2011), 159–160; Allen G. Hatley, *Bringing the Law to Texas: Crime and Violence in Nineteenth Century Texas* (LaGrange, TX: Centex Press, 2002), 62–63; Southworth, *Feuds on the Western Frontier*, 10.

71. Bill O'Neal, *The Bloody Legacy of Pink Higgins: A Half Century of Violence in Texas* (Austin: Eakin Press, 1999), 33, 35, 37–39; Johnson, *The Horrell Wars*, 110–111; Southworth, *Feuds on the Western Frontier*, 11; Douglas, *Famous Texas Feuds*, 136; *Lampasas Dispatch*, September 27, 1877; *Galveston Daily News*, January 30, 1877. For the likely apocryphal story of a cold-blooded Higgins and "a miracle taking place—a cow giving birth to a man," see Clara Watkins, "Rancher-Gunfighter Pink Higgins Survived a Feud and Much More," *Wild West* 22 (February 2010): 18–19.

72. O'Neal, *Pink Higgins*, 41–42; Nolan, *Bad Blood*, 111–112; Wilkins, *Law Comes to Texas*, 130; Gard, *Frontier Justice*, 50; C. L. Sonnichsen, *I'll Die Before I'll Run: The Story of the Great Feuds of Texas* (Lincoln: University of Nebraska Press, 1988), 136–138; *Galveston Daily News*, April 5, 1877.

73. Miller, *Texas Ranger John B. Jones*, 153, 155–156 (quotation); Johnson, *The Horrell Wars*, 122; Nolan, *Bad Blood*, 116–119; O'Neal, *Pink Higgins*, 45–49; Utley, *Lone Star Justice*, 181–182; Jones to Coldwell, July 12, 1877, 401–1158, TSLAC; RSR, N. O. Reynolds, 401–169, TSLAC.

74. Miller, *Texas Ranger John B. Jones*, 156; *Lampasas Dispatch*, August 9, 1877; *San Antonio Daily Express*, August 10, 1877; Gillett,

Six Years, 79; Roberts, *Rangers and Sovereignty*, 168–169; Nolan, *Bad Blood*, 125–127; O'Neal, *Pink Higgins*, 50–51; Parsons and Brice, *Texas Ranger N. O. Reynolds*, 105–107; *Galveston Daily News*, August 14, 1877.

75. Miller, *Texas Ranger John B. Jones*, 157–158; Operations of State Troops, 1 (1876–1881), 401–1082, TSLAC: 76; Johnson, *The Horrell Wars*, 110–111; *Lampasas Dispatch*, August 9, 1877; O'Neal, *Pink Higgins*, 52; Utley, *Lone Star Justice*, 182–183; Redman, "General John B. Jones," 71; Parsons and Brice, *Texas Rangers N. O. Reynolds*, 109. The two letters were reprinted in the *Galveston Daily News*, August 8, 1877, the *Dallas Daily Herald*, August 10, 1877, and the *Daily Democratic Statesman*, August 16, 1877, among other papers.

76. Paul Cool, *Salt Warriors: Insurgency on the Rio Grande* (College Station: Texas A&M University Press, 2008), 3–4 (quotation on p. 3), 26, 58–59, 40–41, 64, 65, 66, 67, 72, 74; Andrew Graybill, *Policing the Great Plains: Rangers, Mounties, and the North American Frontier, 1875–1910* (Lincoln: University of Nebraska Press, 2007), 97; CSR-CS, Eighth Texas Cavalry, Charles H. Howard; C. L. Sonnichsen, *Pass of the North: Four Centuries on the Rio Grande* (El Paso: Texas Western Press, 1968), 1: 179, 193, 195–196, 197–198; Ernest R. Lindley, ed., *Members of the Legislature of the State of Texas from 1846 to 1939* (Austin: State of Texas, 1939), 81, 89.

77. Cool, *Salt Warriors*, 1–2, 9–13, 75–76, 78, 81, 83; Statements of Ward B. Blanchard, January 30, 1878, February 11, 1878, Judge Allen Blacker, March 1878, *El Paso Troubles in Texas*, House Executive Document No. 93, 45th Congress, 2nd Session, 69–70, 122; *Chicago Daily Times*, January 2, 1878; W. H. Timmons, *El Paso: A Borderlands History* (El Paso: Texas Western Press, 2004), 196.

78. Statement of Ward B. Blanchard, February 11, 1878, Affidavit of Sheriff Charles Kerber and Ward P. Blanchard March 6, 1878, Judge Gregorio N. García, March 8, 1878, Report of Captain Thomas Blair, December 19, 1877, Affidavits of Jesus Cobas, February 4, 1878, Vidal García, February 4, 1878, Father Peter Bourgad, March 1, 2, 1878, Judge Gregorio N. García, March 8, 1878, Affidavits of Wesley Owens, February 8, 1878, Jesus Gonzales, February 1, 1878, A. Krakauer, Leopold Sender, Edmond Stine, all dated January 31, 1877, H. H. Harvey, March 8, 1878, *El Paso Troubles*, 71–73, 118, 106–107, 55, 99–100, 59–61, 64; Douglas, *Famous Texas Feuds*, 109; Colonel Martin L. Crimmins, "The Salt War of San Elizario, Texas,"

Frontier Times 8 (April 1931): 297–298; Cool, *Salt Warriors*, 10, 110–111, 116–117; Slade to the Secretary of the Treasury, October 22, 1877, *Relations of the United States with Mexico*, 279–280; Timmons, *El Paso*, 196; *San Antonio Daily Express*, October 30, 1877.

79. Miller, *Texas Ranger John B. Jones*, 167–168; Utley, *Lone Star Justice*, 194; Steele to Jones, October 24, 1877, Jones to Steele, November 3, 1877, Jones to Steele, November 7, 1877, Affidavits of Father Peter Bourgad, March 1, 1878, March 2, 1878, Captain Gregorio García, March 2, 1878, Jones to Steele, November 9, 1877, Minority Report, March 16, 1878, Affidavit of Father Peter Bourgad, March 2, 1878, *El Paso Troubles*, 153, 154, 155, 99–100 (quotation on p. 100), 26; *San Antonio Daily Express*, October 31, November 27, 1877; *Galveston Daily News*, September, October 16, 24, 1877; C. L. Sonnichsen, *The El Paso Salt War [1877]* (El Paso: Texas Western Press, 1961), 36.

80. Miller, *Texas Ranger John B. Jones*, 169; Cool, *Salt Warriors*, 146 (first quotation); Jones to Steele, November 12, 1877, Affidavit of Joseph Magoffin, February 7, 1878, *El Paso Troubles*, 155, 79–80; *Galveston Daily News*, November 17, 1877; Special Order No. 110, November 15, 1877, 401–1158, TSLAC; RSR, John Tays, 401–174, TSLAC; Sonnichsen, *El Paso Salt War*, 38; Charles M. Robinson III, *The Men Who Wear the Star: The Story of the Texas Rangers* (New York: The Modern Library, 2001), 225; Utley, *Lone Star Justice*, 195; Bob Alexander, *Desert Desperadoes: The Banditti of Southwestern New Mexico* (Silver City, NM: Gila Books, 2006), 103 (second quotation).

81. Miller, *Texas Ranger John B. Jones*, 170–171, 180; Steele to Jones, November 13(?), 1877, Jones to Steele, November 18, 1877, Jones to Steele, November 20, 1877, 401–1158, TSLAC; Minority Report, March 22, 1878, Affidavit of Joseph Magoffin, February 7, 1878, Jones to Steele, November 22, 1877, *El Paso Troubles*, 26, 80, 155; Cool, *Salt Warriors*, 148–150; Crimmins, "Salt War," 298.

82. Cool, *Salt Warriors*, 10–11, 163–166, 168–171, 174–175, 193–195; Affidavit of Lieutenant John B. Tays, March 8, 1878, Report of Lieutenant John B. Tays, December 20, 1877, Affidavit of John B. Tays, December 30, 1877, Tays to Jones, two letters dated, December 20, 1877, *El Paso Troubles*, 109, 81–82, 44, 157–158; Utley, *Lone Star Justice*, 198; Jones to Mills, December 20, 1877, Lohman to Jones, December 15, 1877, 401–1158, TSLAC; *Dallas Daily Herald*, December 16, 1877; Graybill, *Policing the Great Plains*, 98; Douglas,

Famous Texas Feuds, 119–121; *Galveston Daily News*, January 1, 3, 6, February 8, 1878; Statement of Lieutenant J. B. Tays, March 25, 1878, 401-1159, TSLAC. Utley wrote Mortimer's first name was Charles, while Alexander, and Caldwell and DeLord, state it was Conrad. Bob Alexander, *Riding Lucifer's Line: Ranger Deaths along the Texas-Mexico Border* (Denton: University of North Texas Press, 2013), 61; Caldwell and DeLord, *Texas Lawmen, 1835–1899*, 332. Mortimer's service records only provide his initials.

83. Cool, *Salt Warriors*, 212–225; Alexander, *Desert Desperadoes*, 112–119; Graybill, *Policing the Great Plains*, 99; Sonnichsen, *El Paso Salt War*, 58–59; Robert N. Mullin, "Here Lies John Kinney," *Journal of Arizona History* 14 (Autumn 1973): 228. Before beginning his reign as a rustling kingpin, Kinney hired out his gun to the Murphy-Dolan faction in the Lincoln County War. Paul Cool, "New Mexico's Rustler King," *Wild West* 26 (April 2014): 40. A lengthy list of affidavits testifying to the reprehensible actions of the civilian gunmen under Sheriff Kerber can be found in *El Paso Troubles*, 85–86, 88–90, 92–94, 95. Others attested to the Rangers' "good and orderly" behavior, ibid., 113–114, 115–116, 117. See also Hubbard to Kerber, December 7, 1877, Hubbard to Kerber, December 15, 1877, Special Order No. 10, November 15, 1877, Kerber to Hubbard, December 25, 1877, Wade to Hatch, December 23, 1877, Ochoa to Hatch, December 28, 1877, Blair to Kerber, January 4, 1878, Steele to Kerber, January 10, 1878, ibid., 144, 145, 116, 79, 88, 91–92, 158; and Slade to the Secretary of the Treasury, December 24, 1877, *Relations of the United States with Mexico*, 282.

84. Minority Report, March 22, 1878, *El Paso Troubles*, 21–22.

85. Miller, *Texas Ranger John B. Jones*, 180, 183; *San Antonio Daily Express*, January 3, 1878, Hubbard to Mills, December 19, 1877, Special Orders No. 2, January 3, 1878, McCrary to Sherman, December 31, 1877, Townsend to Sheridan, December 31, 1877, Drum to King, January 3, 1878, Steele to Jones, February 8, 1878, *El Paso Troubles*, 148, 5, 47–48; Testimony of John B. Jones, January 19, 1878, *Relations of the United States with Mexico*, Pt. 2: 53–62; *Galveston Daily News*, January 24, February 5, 1878.

86. Miller, *Texas Ranger John B. Jones*, 184–187, 189–191; Proceedings of a Board of Investigation, February 19, 27, 1878, Jones to Steele and Steele to Jones, both dated February 19, 1878, Steele to Jones, February 23, 1878, Protest Letter of Major John B. Jones, February 27,

1878, Final Report, March 16, 1878, Minority Report, March 22, 1878, *El Paso Troubles*, 6, 7, 48–49, 13–18, 19–33; Sonnichsen, *Pass of the North*, 1: 210.
87. Miller, *Texas Ranger John B. Jones*, 191; Jones to Tays, January 8, 1878, Affidavit of John C. Ford, February 2, 1878, *El Paso Troubles*, 116–117, 71; *Galveston Daily News*, March 29, 1878; Stine to Commissioners, March 11, 1878, Blacker to Commissioners, n.d., 401–1159, TSLAC; RSR, John Tays and James Tays, both 401–174, TSLAC; Cool, *Salt Warriors*, 262. For two dissimilar critiques of Jones's choices and actions, see Utley, *Lone Star Justice*, 205; and Miller, *Texas Ranger John B. Jones*, 179–180.
88. Rick Miller, *Sam Bass and Gang* (Austin: State House Press, 1999), 1–3. Correcting many of the myths, misconceptions, and outright errors surrounding the outlaw, Miller has written an exhaustive account of Sam Bass. Charley F. Eckhardt, *Tales of Badmen, Bad Women, and Bad Places: Four Centuries of Texas Outlawry* (Lubbock: Texas Tech University Press, 1999), 88–89; J. Frank Dobie, "The Robinhooding of Sam Bass," *MMWH* 5 (Autumn 1955): 34–41 (quotation).
89. Rick Miller, *Sam Bass*, 45–92; James L. Haley, *Passionate Nation: The Epic History of Texas* (New York: Simon and Schuster, 2006), 411; Harry Sinclair Drago, *Road Agents and Train Robbers: Half a Century of Western Banditry* (New York: Dodd, Mead & Company, 1973), 129; "Authentic History of Sam Bass and His Gang, by a Citizen of Denton County," Pt. 1, *Frontier Times* 3 (February 1926): 29–31.
90. Miller, *Sam Bass*, 107, 115, 121–122, 134–136, 150–152, 160–167, 169; Cox, *Wearing the Cinco Peso*, 291–292; *Galveston Daily News*, April 11, 1878; *Dallas Daily Herald*, April 13, 1878.
91. Miller, *Texas Ranger John B. Jones*, 192; Utley, *Lone Star Justice*, 184; Eugene Cunningham, "Sam Bass," *Frontier Times* 4 (May 1927): 12.
92. Miller, *Texas Ranger John B. Jones*, 198; Miller, *Sam Bass*, 201–203; Statement of J. W. Murphy, July 26, 1878, Memorandum of A. J. Evans, May 21, 1878, 401–1159, TSLAC; Haley, *Passionate Nation*, 411; *Galveston Daily News*, July 31, 1878; Redman, "General John B. Jones," 56; "Authentic History of Sam Bass and His Gang," Pt. 3, *Frontier Times* 3 (April 1926): 35–36.
93. Miller, *Sam Bass*, 227–228, 229–230; *Galveston Daily News*, July 31, 1878.
94. Miller, *Sam Bass*, 233–236, 239; *Galveston Daily News*, July 31, 1878; "Authentic History of Sam Bass," Pt. 3: 34.

95. Miller, *Texas Ranger John B. Jones*, 206; Miller, *Sam Bass*, 243–244; *Galveston Daily News*, July 24, 1878; Mike Cox, *Texas Ranger Tales: Stories That Need Telling* (Plano: Republic of Texas Press, 1997), 48–50; Robert W. Stephens, *Texas Ranger Sketches* (Dallas: Robert W. Stephens, 1972), 41; Cunningham, "Sam Bass," 13. George Herold has also been known as Harrell or Herald. His Ranger Service Records bear the first two names. 401–154 and –155, TSLAC.
96. Miller, *Texas Ranger John B. Jones*, 207; Miller, *Sam Bass*, 243–244; Cox, *Texas Ranger Tales*, 60 61; Cunningham, "Sam Bass," 13; Stephens, *Texas Ranger Sketches*, 55.
97. Miller, *Texas Ranger John B. Jones*, 207; Miller, *Sam Bass*, 245–248; *Galveston Daily News*, July 20, 1878.
98. Miller, *Sam Bass*, 248–250; Stephens, *Texas Ranger Sketches*, 57; *Galveston Daily News*, July 25, 1878; Caldwell and DeLord, *Texas Lawmen, 1835–1899*, 236–237.
99. Miller, *Texas Ranger John B. Jones*, 209; Miller, *Sam Bass*, 250–254; *Galveston Daily News*, July 20, 24, 25, 31, 1878; Stephens, *Texas Ranger Sketches*, 59, 60; Wilkins, *Law Comes to Texas*, 165–166; Bill O'Neal, *Encyclopedia of Western Gunfighters* (Norman: University of Oklahoma Press, 1979), 36.
100. Miller, *Texas Ranger John B. Jones*, 210; Miller, *Sam Bass*, 255–264 (quotation on p. 259). In 1927, Jackson was discovered living quietly in New Mexico under an alias. The old indictment for the murder of Deputy Grimes was still valid, and his petition to have the charges quashed was denied by the Williamson County district judge. The case was finally dismissed in December 1936. *Galveston Daily News*, July 19, 1927; *Abilene Reporter-News*, December 25, 1927; *Austin American*, December 22, 1936.
101. Miller, *Sam Bass*, 263–266, 278; Cox, *Wearing the Cinco Peso*, 298; Jones to Campbell, July 25, 1878, Jones to Campbell, August 20, 1878, Murphy to Jones, September 6, 1878, 401–1159, TSLAC; Eckhardt, *Badmen, Bad Women, and Bad Places*, 104–105.
102. Miller, *Texas Ranger John B. Jones*, 226; *Senate Journal, Sixteenth Legislature, First Session*, 112; Redman, "General John B. Jones," 90; *Daily Democratic Statesman*, January 23, 1879; *Galveston Daily News*, January 23, 24, 1879; Jimmy L. Bryan, *More Zeal Than Discretion: The Westward Adventures of Walter P. Lane* (College Station: Texas A&M University Press, 2008), 158–159; Gammel, comp., *Laws of Texas*, 8: 221.

Endnotes

103. Miller, *Texas Ranger John B. Jones*, 226–227; *Galveston Daily News*, January 24, 1879.
104. *Galveston Daily News*, January 26, 1879.
105. Miller, *Texas Ranger John B. Jones*, 227, 233; John B. Jones, Box 2–9/840, Bonds and Oaths of County and State Officials, TSLAC; General Order No. 1, February 8, 1879, Special Order No. 11, May 9, 1879, 401–1012, TSLAC; Wilkins, *Law Comes to Texas*, 175–76; *RAG, 1880*, 25; RSR, Neal Coldwell, 401–147, TSLAC; *Galveston Daily News*, May 31, 1879, April 2, 1880; Redman, "General John B. Jones," 93; Spaw, ed., *Texas Senate*, 2: 269; *San Antonio Daily Express*, February 9, March 2, 1879.
106. Articles 3249–3253, *Revised Civil Statutes of the State of Texas Passed by the Sixteenth Legislature, February 21, 1879*, 471; *RAG, 1880*, 17.
107. Miller, *Texas Ranger John B. Jones*, 236, 230–231; Bonner, "Major John B. Jones," 102; Joseph E. Bennett, "John B. Jones, Masonic Texas Ranger," *The New Age* 97 (February 1989): 30; Speer and Brown, eds., *Encyclopedia of the New West*, 389; *Austin Statesman*, November 26, 1908; *Ninth U.S. Census*, Milam County, Texas.
108. Miller, *Texas Ranger John B. Jones*, 231; Bonner, "Major John B. Jones," 102; Redman, "General John B. Jones," 106; *Galveston Daily News*, February 26, 1879; RSR, R. T. Anderson, 401–141, TSLAC.
109. Miller, *Texas Ranger John B. Jones*, 259; Jones to Roberts, January 12, 1880, Dorman H. Winfrey and James M. Day, eds., *The Indian Papers of Texas and the Southwest* (Austin: Texas State Historical Association, 1995), 4: 436–439; *Galveston Daily News*, January 17, April 2, 1880.
110. *Galveston Daily News*, August 5, 1880; Tise, *Texas County Sheriffs*, 163; *Dallas Daily Herald*, August 5, 1880 (quotation).
111. Miller, *Texas Ranger John B. Jones*, 276–277, 280–281; Frederick W. Rathjen, *The Texas Panhandle Frontier* (Lubbock: Texas Tech University Press, 1998), 188–189; *RAG, 1880*, 3–34; *San Antonio Daily Express*, October 19, 1880; *Galveston Daily News*, October 19, November 17, 1880; *Dallas Daily Herald*, October 20, 1880; *Austin Daily Statesman*, November 17, 19, 1880.
112. *House Journal, Seventeenth Legislature, First Session*, 11; John B. Jones, Box 2–9/840, Bonds and Oaths, TSLAC; *RAG, 1882*, 31; *Dallas Daily Herald*, February 5, 1881; *Austin Daily Statesman*, January 14, 1881; Gammel, comp., *Laws of Texas*, 8: 1458, 9: 181.

113. Miller, *Texas Ranger John B. Jones*, 285, 286; *Galveston Daily News*, September 18, 1879; *RAG, 1882*, 4. Orsay was first employed as clerk in the department in September 1870 and continued, except for a brief period during the tenure of Francis L. Britton, until January 1901. Clarence P. Denman, "The Office of Adjutant General in Texas, 1835–1881," *SHQ* 28 (April 1925): 317 n84. See also "Neal Coldwell, a Gallant Texas Ranger," *Frontier Times* 3 (January 1926): 8–15.
114. Miller, *Texas Ranger John B. Jones*, 293–294, 295–297; Galveston *Daily News*, April 7, 9, July 20, 21, 1881; Bonner, "Major John B. Jones," 104–105; Cox, *Wearing the Cinco Peso*, 320; *Austin Daily Statesman*, July 20, 21 (quotations), 1881. See also Raleigh Maurice Hood, *Early Texas Physicians, 1830–1915* (Austin: State House Press, 1999).
115. Bonner, "Major John B. Jones," 12; Putman, comp., *Navarro County History*, 196; Love, *History of Navarro County*, 217; *Fort Worth Daily Gazette*, December 27, 28, 1888.
116. Bonner, "Major John B. Jones," 136; Bruce S. Allardice, *More Generals in Gray* (Baton Rouge: Louisiana State University Press, 1995), 217–218; *Austin Statesman*, November 26, 1908.
117. *Decennial Register of the Texas Military Institute for 1868 to 1878* (Baltimore: Steam Press of Globe Printing Company, 1878), 31; *Catalogue of the Officers and Students of Roanoke College. Twenty-third Session, 1875–76* (Lynchburg, VA: Bell, Browne, & Co., 1876), 11; *Catalogue of Richmond College. Session 1876–77* (Richmond, OH: Clemitt & Jones, 1877), 5; *Thirteenth U.S. Census*, Tarrant County, Texas; *Fifteenth U.S. Census*, Potter County, Texas; *San Antonio Daily Express*, December 13, 1932; Texas Death Certificate, Reuben T. Anderson, December 16, 1932, Registrar's No. 406.
118. *Thirty-fourth Annual Catalogue of the Officers and Students of Hollins Institute, 1876–1877* (Baltimore: Charles Harvey & Co., 1877), 10–11, 13; *Thirteenth U.S. Census*, Travis, County, Texas; *San Antonio Evening News*, February 11, 1920; *Galveston Daily News*, February 12, 1920; Texas Death Certificates, Lewis Hancock, February 11, 1920, Registrar's No. 82, Attilia Aldridge Hancock, December 11, 1944, File No. 1274.
119. *Thirty-fourth Annual Catalogue, Hollins Institute*, 13; *Austin Daily Statesman*, July 3, December 17, 1884; *Galveston Daily News*, December 18, 1884; *Find A Grave*, s.v. "Elizabeth Anderson Millett."
120. *San Antonio Light*, January 19, 1927; *Twelfth U.S. Census*, Travis County, Texas; *Washington Post*, December 5, 20, 1916; Texas Death

Certificate, Thaddeus Austin Thomson, Registrar No. 3524; *San Antonio Daily Express*, November 20, 1931.
121. "Marriages of St. David's Episcopal Church, Austin, Texas," *Austin Genealogical Society Quarterly* 2 (May 1961): 57; *San Antonio Light*, January 10, 1925; Texas Death Certificates, Walter Bremond Sr., January 23, 1925, Registrar's No. 3198, Mrs. Walter Bremond, June 19, 1951, File No. 32299.
122. *Find A Grave*, s.v. "Matthew Mann Smith"; *Twelfth U.S. Census*, Travis County, Texas; *Fifteenth* and *Sixteenth U.S. Census*, Dallas County, Texas; *Dallas Morning News*, January 1, 2, March 14, 15, 1957; Texas Death Certificates, Eleanor L. Campbell, March 14, 1957, File No. 12539, Grant Gregory Campbell, January 1, 1957, File No. 68861, Stephen Girard Smith, July 5, 1968, File No. 47947.
123. *Galveston Daily News* and *Houston Daily Post*, both dated June 9, 1905.

Notes for Chapter 2

1. Chuck Parsons and Marianne E. Hall Little, *Captain L. H. McNelly—Texas Ranger: The Life and Times of a Fighting Man* (Austin: State House Press, 2001), 3–4; Catherine Lanthrip, "The McNelly Family from Ireland to Virginia to Texas," unpublished MS, n.d., n. pag.; Susan Merle Dotson, comp., *Who's Who of the Confederacy* (San Antonio: Naylor Company, 1966), 171; Annie Maud Knittel Avis, ed., *History of Burton* (Burton: n.p., 1974), 265, 266, 268; *Sixth* and *Seventh U.S. Census*, Brooke County, Virginia.
2. Parsons and Little, *Captain L. H. McNelly*, 4–6; Dotson, comp., *Who's Who of the Confederacy*, 172; *A Proud Heritage: A History of Uvalde County, Texas* (Uvalde, TX: El Progresso Club, 1975), 397; *Civilian and Weekly Gazette*, October 30, 1860; Avis, ed., *History of Burton*, 266; Dan K. Utley and Cynthia J. Beeman, *History Ahead: Stories Beyond the Texas Roadside Markers* (College Station: Texas A&M University Press, 2010), 33. Travis Burton appears in the 1860 census as a member of John M. Burton's household. The elder Burton possessed 507 acres valued at six thousand dollars, six slaves, two horses, and fifty head of cattle. *Eighth U.S. Census*, Washington County, Texas; Tax Rolls, Washington County, 1860.
3. *The War of the Rebellion: A Compilation of the Official Records of the Union and Confederate Armies* (Washington, D.C.: Government Printing Office, 1880–1906), Series I, IV: 93, 107–108, 141–143. Hereafter

cited as *OR*, all references are to Series I. Jerry D. Thompson, *Confederate General of the West: Henry Hopkins Sibley* (College Station: Texas A&M University Press, 1996), 216–219; Donald S. Frazier, *Blood and Treasure: Confederate Empire in the Southwest* (College Station: Texas A&M University Press, 1995), 75–76, 94; John P. Wilson, *When the Texans Came: Missing Records from the Civil War in the Southwest* (Albuquerque: University of New Mexico Press, 2001), 144, 153; Theophilus Noel, *A Campaign from Santa Fe to the Mississippi: Being a History of the Old Sibley Brigade* (Shreveport: Shreveport News Printing Establishment, 1865), 5–6; Thomas W. Cutrer, *Empire of Sand: The Struggle for the Southwest, 1862* (Buffalo Gap, TX: State House Press, 2015), 31–32; Dudley G. Wooten, *A Comprehensive History of Texas, 1685 to 1897* (Dallas: William G. Scarff, 1898), 2: 695–740; Robert Underwood Johnson and Clarence Clough Buel, eds., *Battles and Leaders of the Civil War* (Secaucus, NJ: Castle Books, 1982), 2: 104, 700; *Daily Ledger and Texan*, August 13, 1861; *Texas State Gazette*, September 14, November 9, 1861.

4. Johnson and Buel, eds., *Battles and Leaders*, 2: 700.
5. *OR*, IV: 63–65, 143, 132; Testimony of Colonel B. S. Roberts, July 15, 1862, *Report of the Joint Committee on the Conduct of the War: Miscellaneous*, Senate Report No. 108, Pt. 3, 37th Congress, 3rd Session, 366. Hereafter cited as *JCCW: Miscellaneous*. Paul I. Kliger, "The Confederate Invasion of New Mexico," *Blue and Gray Magazine* 11 (June 1994): 14.
6. Parsons and Little, *Captain L. H. McNelly*, 9, 12; CSR-CS, Fifth Texas Cavalry, L. H. McNelly; Odie Faulk, *General Tom Green: Fightin' Texan* (Waco: Texian Press, 1963), 37; General Marcus J. Wright, comp., *Texas in the War, 1861–1865*, ed. Harold B. Simpson (Hillsboro, Texas: Hill Junior College Press, 1965), 78; *San Antonio Daily Herald*, October 19, 1861. The Fifth Texas was also known as the Second Regiment of the Sibley Brigade. Throughout the various official documents concerning the Confederate Army, McNelly's name can be found frequently misspelled as "McAnelly," "McNalley," or "McNallie."
7. Frazier, *Blood and Treasure*, 86; Charles David Grear, *Why Texans Fought in the Civil War* (College Station: Texas A&M University Press, 2010), 62.
8. Jerry D. Thompson, ed., *Civil War in the Southwest: Recollections of the Sibley Brigade* (College Station: Texas A&M University Press, 2001), 8.

9. *OR*, IV: 111, 157 (quotation), 159, 164; Thompson, *Henry Hopkins Sibley*, 237; Thompson, ed., *Civil War in the Southwest*, xvi, 4–5, 7, 11–14, 19; Cutrer, *Empire of Sand*, 37–39; Noel, *Old Sibley Brigade*, 10–12; Michael L. Tate, ed., "A Johnny Reb in Sibley's New Mexico Campaign: Reminiscences of Pvt. Henry C. Wright, 1861–1862," Pt. 1, *ETHJ* 25 (October 1987): 24; David H. Rosenberg, "Confederate Manifest Destiny in New Mexico," *America's Civil War* 13 (July 2000): 53.
10. CSR-CS, Fifth Texas Cavalry, L. H. McNelly, W. J. Bullard; *Regulations for the Army of the Confederate States: As Adopted by Act of Congress, Approved March 6, 1861*, 85–86; John P. Wilson and Jerry Thompson, eds., *The Civil War in West Texas & New Mexico: The Lost Letterbook of Brigadier General Henry Hopkins Sibley* (El Paso: Texas Western Press, 2001), 103; Frazier, *Blood and Treasure*, 135; Walter A. Faulkner, ed., "With Sibley in New Mexico: The Journal of William Henry Smith," *WTHAY* 27 (October 1951): 124, 126.
11. *OR*, IX: 507, 487–493, IV: 82–83, 142, 89–90, 157–158, L, Pt. 1: 1012, Pt. 2: 151–152; Thompson, ed., *Civil War in the Southwest*, xvi, 18–20, 44–45, 50; Faulkner, ed., "With Sibley in New Mexico," 124–125; Frazier, *Blood and Treasure*, 141–142, 149; Noel, *Old Sibley Brigade*, 12, 15; Rosenberg, "Confederate Manifest Destiny," 54; Kliger, "Confederate Invasion of New Mexico," 14–15.
12. OR, IV: 69–70, 74, 96, 83–84, IX: 488, 630–631; Flint Whitlock, *Distant Bugles, Distant Drums: The Union Response to the Confederate Invasion of New Mexico* (Boulder: University Press of Colorado, 2006), 102; Alvin M. Josephy, Jr., *The Civil War in the American West* (New York: Alfred A. Knopf, 1992), 61, 63.
13. *OR*, IX: 632, 507–508, 487, 489–490, 494–496, 505, 512–14, 518–519, 523, 524, L, Pt. 1: 1013; John Taylor, *Bloody Valverde: A Civil War Battle on the Rio Grande, February 21, 1862* (Albuquerque: University of New Mexico Press, 1995), 41–42, 44, 46–50, 56–58; Thompson, ed., *Civil War in the Southwest*, xvi–xvii, 23–26, 28–29, 31, 45, 46–47, 53–58; Benton Bell Seat, "Memoirs, 1849–1916," MC 799, Florence Cypert Spore Papers, University of Arkansas Libraries, 93; Whitlock, *Distant Bugles, Distant Drums*, 116, 118; Kliger, "Confederate Invasion of New Mexico," 16; Johnson and Buel, eds., *Battles and Leaders*, 2: 104.
14. *OR*, IX: 408, 517, 487, 493, 496, 506, 514–515, 519–520, 521; Thompson, *Henry Hopkins Sibley*, 260–261; Taylor, *Bloody Valverde*, 67–70, 78–79, 84, 85, 91, 104; Thomas W. Cutrer, *Theater of a Separate War: The Civil*

War West of the Mississippi River (Chapel Hill: University of North Carolina Press, 2017), 103–104; Whitlock, *Distant Bugles, Distant Drums*, 125, 126–127, 130–131, 133–136; Thompson, ed., *Civil War in the Southwest*, xvii, 32–36, 47–48, 66–69; Seat, "Memoirs," 94–95; Wooten, ed., *Comprehensive History of Texas*, 2: 698–699; Christine M. Kreiser, "Showdown in New Mexico," *America's Civil War* 25 (January 2013): 47; Wilson, *When the Texans Came*, 254; *San Antonio Herald*, July 12, 1862; *Texas State Gazette*, March 19, 1862; Stewart Sifakis, *Compendium of the Confederate Armies: Texas* (Westminster, MD: Willow Bend Books, 2008), 22.

15. *OR*, IX: 633–634, 636; Thompson, ed., *Civil War in the Southwest*, xvii–xviii, 73–74, 76–78; Frazier, *Blood and Treasure*, 182–184, 191, 196; Tate, ed., "Johnny Reb," Pt. 2: 24; Testimony of Colonel B. S. Roberts, July 15, 1862, *JCCW: Miscellaneous*, 367; Johnson and Buel, eds., *Battles and Leaders*, 103; W. H. Watford, "Confederate Western Ambitions," *SHQ* 44 (October 1940): 172; Wooten, ed., *Comprehensive History of Texas*, 2: 698–699.

16. Andrew E. Masich, *Civil War in the Southwest Borderlands, 1861–1867* (Norman: University of Oklahoma Press, 2017), 94; Frazier, *Blood and Treasure*, 187–188, 205; Robert M. Utley, *Frontiersmen in Blue: The United States Army and the Indian, 1848–1865* (Lincoln: University of Nebraska Press, 1981), 219; Cutrer, *Empire of Sand*, 67; W. H. Watford, "The Far-Flung Wing of the Rebellion, 1861–1865," *California Historical Society Quarterly* 34 (June 1955): 138; Seat, "Memoirs," 97–98; CSR-CS, Fifth Texas Cavalry, G. W. Campbell and B. B. Seat.

17. *OR*, IX: 509, 530–545; Whitlock, *Distant Bugles, Distant Drums*, 173–180; Thompson, ed., *Civil War in the Southwest*, xviii–xix, 80–86, 93–97; Johnson and Buel, eds., *Battles and Leaders*, 2: 104, 111; *Belleville Countryman*, June 7, 1862; Daye H. Molen, "Decision at La Glorieta Pass," *MMWH* 12 (Spring 1962), 23, 26, 27, 28; Wooten, ed., *Comprehensive History of Texas*, 2: 700–701; Tate, ed., "Johnny Reb," Pt. 2: 25. See also Thomas S. Edrington and John Taylor, *The Battle of Glorieta Pass* (Albuquerque: University of New Mexico Press, 1998); and Don E. Alberts, *The Battle of Glorieta: Union Victory in the West* (College Station: Texas A&M University Press, 1998). On November 29, 1864, Chivington led seven hundred Colorado volunteers in a savage attack on a peaceful Cheyenne and Arapaho village located at Sand Creek. For more on this shameful episode, see Ari Kelman, *A Misplaced Massacre: Struggling Over*

the Memory of Sand Creek (Cambridge, MA: Harvard University Press, 2013).
18. *OR*, IX: 510, 714, 716, 717–718, 722, VIII: 627–628, 631, 653–654; Frazier, *Blood and Treasure*, 238, 239–240; Whitlock, *Distant Bugles, Distant Drums*, 225; Tate, ed., "Johnny Reb," Pt. 2: 26; Johnson and Buel, eds., *Battles and Leaders*, 2: 700; Stephen B. Oates, *Confederate Cavalry West of the River* (Austin: University of Texas Press, 1961), 21; Kliger, "Confederate Invasion of New Mexico," 57.
19. *OR*, IX: 510–511; Thompson, *Henry Hopkins Sibley*, 293, 298; Thompson, ed., *Civil War in the Southwest*, xix–xx, 101–117; Frazier, *Blood and Treasure*, 242, 260; Seat, "Memoirs," 99–100; Faulk, *General Tom Green*, 45–46; Curtis W. Milbourn, "'I Have Been Worse Treated than Any Officer': Confederate Colonel Thomas Green's Assessment of the New Mexico Campaign," *SHQ* 105 (October 2001): 236–237; Noel, *Old Sibley Brigade*, 27–28; Testimony of Colonel B. S. Roberts, July 15, 1862, *JCCW: Miscellaneous*, 367–368.
20. *OR*, IX: 714–716, 722; CSR-CS, Fifth Texas Cavalry, L. H. McNelly; Cutrer, *Theater of a Separate War*, 112, 114; Frazier, *Blood and Treasure*, 264, 260–262.
21. *San Antonio Herald*, July 5, 1862.
22. Josephy, *Civil War in the American West*, 89, 90; *San Antonio Herald*, January 11, July 5, 1862; *San Antonio Semi-Weekly News*, June 16, 19, 1862; Utley, *Frontiersmen in Blue*, 231; Wooten, ed., *Comprehensive History of Texas*, 2: 706; *Texas State Gazette*, June 7, 1862; Seat, "Memoirs," 103. The Rebel government in Arizona Territory collapsed with the evacuation of the Confederate Army of New Mexico. The U.S. Congress passed the Arizona Organic Act in February 1863, which created a federal Arizona Territory from the western portion of New Mexico. The act of establishment also abolished slavery in the territory. *The Statutes at Large, Treaties, and Proclamations of the United States*, 12: 664–665.
23. *OR*, XV: 894–895, 968; Thompson, *Henry Hopkins Sibley*, 309–318; Noel, *Old Sibley Brigade*, 40–41; Wooten, ed., *Comprehensive History of Texas*, 2: 706.
24. *OR*, XV: 212, 214, 856–857, 897, 902, 969; Edward T. Cotham, Jr., *Battle on the Bay: The Civil War Struggle for Galveston* (Austin: University of Texas Press, 1998), 108–109; Faulk, *General Tom Green*, 48; Donald S. Frazier, "Sibley's Texans and the Battle of Galveston," *SHQ* 99 (October 1995): 178; Ralph A. Wooster, *Lone Star Generals*

in Gray (Austin: Eakin Press, 2000), 161; Kenneth W. Howell, ed., *The Seventh Star of the Confederacy: Texas during the Civil War* (Denton: University of North Texas Press, 2009), 115, 125.

25. *OR*, XV: 212–214, 902; Noel, *Old Sibley Brigade*, 40–41; Masich, *Civil War in the Southwest Borderlands*, 176; Faulk, *General Tom Green*, 49; Bruce S. Allardice, *Confederate Colonels: A Biographical Register* (Columbia: University of Missouri Press, 2008), 49; *Galveston Daily News*, January 5, 1914. For more on Bagby, see Bruce S. Allardice, *More Generals in Gray* (Baton Rouge: Louisiana State University Press, 1995), 24–25.

26. *OR*, XV: 213, 206, 211; Cotham, *Battle on the Bay*, 108, 112; Robert M. Browning, Jr., *Lincoln's Trident: The West Gulf Blockading Squadron During the Civil War* (Tuscaloosa: University of Alabama Press, 2015), 253; Frazier, "Sibley's Texans," 178–179, 182; Wooten, ed., *Comprehensive History of Texas*, 2: 531–532; *Houston Tri-Weekly Telegraph*, January 19, 1863; Edward B. Williams, ed., "A 'Spirited Account' of the Battle of Galveston, January 1, 1863," *SHQ* 99 (October 1995), 207.

27. Cotham, *Battle on the Bay*, 116–120, 122, 126; Browning, *Lincoln's Trident*, 253–255; Stephen A. Dupree, *Planting the Union Flag in Texas: The Campaigns of Major General Nathaniel P. Banks in the West* (College Station: Texas A&M University Press, 2008), 28–30; S. T. Fontaine, "Battle of Galveston—The Harriet Lane," *CV* 18 (January 1910): 29; Charles C. Cumberland, "The Confederate Loss and Recapture of Galveston, 1862–1863," *SHQ* 51 (October 1947): 123–124; *Houston Weekly Telegraph*, January 7, 1863; Williams, ed., "A 'Spirited Account'," 208, 212–213; "Story of the Harriet Lane," *CV* 17 (October 1909): 516.

Major Alfred Miller Lea, a Confederate engineer on Magruder's staff, boarded the captured *Harriet Lane* and found his dying son, Lieutenant Commander Edward Lea, second-in-command of the Federal craft. The younger Lea's final words were "My father is here." Ralph A. Wooster, *Texas and Texans in the Civil War* (Austin: Eakin Press, 1995), 67. See also W. T. Block, "A Towering East Texas Pioneer: A Biographical Sketch of Colonel Albert Miller Lea," *ETHJ* 31 (October 1993): 23–33.

28. Parsons and Little, *Captain L. H. McNelly*, 27–30; Avis, ed., *History of Burton*, 268 (first quotation); Wooten, ed., *Comprehensive History of Texas*, 2: 709 (second quotation); CSR-CS, Fifth Texas Cavalry, James Carson. N. A. Jennings, *A Texas Ranger* (Norman: University

of Oklahoma Press, 1997), 58: "When Green returned to Texas, he took his regiment to Galveston and captured the Union forces there. McNelly was on the cotton-boat which captured the Harriet Lane, and was the first Confederate to board the Union boat."

29. *OR*, XV: 216, LIII: 849; *Official Records of the Union and Confederate Navies in the War of the Rebellion*, Series I, XIX: 440–443; Browning, *Lincoln's Trident*, 257; Noel, *Old Sibley Brigade*, 44; *Galveston Daily News*, August 6, 1876, January 5, 1914; *Galveston Weekly News*, January 7, 1863; Wooten ed., *Comprehensive History of Texas*, 2: 707–709; Wooster, *Texas and Texans in the Civil War*, 64–67.

30. *OR*, XV: 903–904, 922, 954, 969, 983, XXVI, Pt. 2: 58; Noel, *Old Sibley Brigade*, 44; Richard Taylor, *Destruction and Reconstruction: Personal Experiences of the Late War* (New York: D. Appleton and Company, 1879), 125; Thompson, *Henry Hopkins Sibley*, 321.

31. Donald S. Frazier, *Thunder Across the Swamp: The Fight for the Lower Mississippi, February 1863-May 1863* (Buffalo Gap, TX: State House Press, 2011), 19–21, 108, 113–115; Faulk, *General Tom Green*, 52; Taylor, *Destruction and Reconstruction*, 125–126; Josephy, *Civil War in the American West*, 168; T. Michael Parrish, *Richard Taylor: Soldier Prince of Dixie* (Chapel Hill: University of North Carolina Press, 1992), 269; Robert L. Kerby, *Kirby Smith's Confederacy: The Trans-Mississippi South, 1863–1865* (New York: Columbia University Press, 1972), 98; Alwyn Barr, "Confederate Artillery in Western Louisiana, 1862–1863," *Civil War History* 9 (March 1963): 77.

32. *OR*, XV: 296, 388, 1043; Dupree, *Planting the Union Flag in Texas*, 36; Kerby, *Kirby Smith's Confederacy*, 98; John D. Winters, *The Civil War in Louisiana* (Baton Rouge: Louisiana State University Press, 1991), 222; Taylor, *Destruction and Reconstruction*, 127; Donald S. Frazier, "Texans on the Teche: The Texas Brigade at the Battles of Bisland and Irish Bend, April 12–14, 1863," *Louisiana History* 32 (Autumn 1991): 424–425.

33. *OR*, XV: 296, 388–390, 397; Seat, "Memoirs," 109–110; Noel, *Old Sibley Brigade*, 46–47; Taylor, *Destruction and Reconstruction*, 129–130; Parrish, *Richard Taylor*, 271; Thompson, *Henry Hopkins Sibley*, 325; Winters, *Civil War in Louisiana*, 223; Jack Rudolph, "Battle in the Bayou," *CWTI* 23 (January 1985): 17.

34. Frazier, *Thunder Across the Swamp*, 211–213; Taylor, *Destruction and Reconstruction*, 130–133; Winters, *Civil War in Louisiana*, 224–226;

Dupree, *Planting the Union Flag in Texas*, 36; Faulk, *General Tom Green*, 53; Barr, "Confederate Artillery in Western Louisiana," 81; Thompson, *Henry Hopkins Sibley*, 326.

35. *OR*, XV: 297, 391–394, 399; Seat, "Memoirs," 112; Frazier, *Thunder Across the Swamp*, 259, 342; Taylor, *Destruction and Reconstruction*, 134; Noel, *Old Sibley Brigade*, 47–49; Winters, *Civil War in Louisiana*, 226–229, 231; Rudolph, "Battle in the Bayou," 21.
36. *OR*, XV: 393, 1093–1096; Thompson, *Henry Hopkins Sibley*, 328–331; Ezra J. Warner, *Generals in Gray: Lives of the Confederate Commanders* (Baton Rouge: Louisiana State University Press, 2008), 117.
37. Taylor, *Destruction and Reconstruction*, 136, 137; Kerby, *Kirby Smith's Confederacy*, 109, 112–113; Winters, *Civil War in Louisiana*, 235, 240; Parrish, *Richard Taylor*, 284–285; Dupree, *Planting the Union Flag in Texas*, 45–48.
38. Parsons and Little, *Captain L. H. McNelly*, 35; *OR*, XXVI, Pt. 1: 183, 189, 210–211, 215–219 (quotation on p. 215), 223–226, Pt. 2: 116; Taylor, *Destruction and Reconstruction*, 139–143; Richard B. Irwin, *History of the Nineteenth Army Corps* (New York: G. P. Putnam's Sons, 1893), 236; Kerby, *Kirby Smith's Confederacy*, 115–116; Winters, *Civil War in Louisiana*, 284, 287; *Houston Tri-Weekly Telegraph*, July 6, 1863; Noel, *Old Sibley Brigade*, 52–55, 90; L. Boyd Finch, "Surprise at Brashear City: Sherod Hunter's Sugar Cooler Cavalry," *Louisiana History* 25 (Autumn 1984): 403–426; Faulk, *General Tom Green*, 56–57; Curtis W. Milbourn, "The Lafourche Offensive: Richard Taylor's Attempt to Relieve Port Hudson," *North and South* 7 (August 2004), 76; Augustine Joseph Hickey Duganne, *Camps and Prisons: Twenty Months in the Department of the Gulf* (New York: J. P. Robens, 1865), 170–172, 175.

    Noel claimed McNelly had been made a captain in New Mexico: "For his daring gallantry on many occasions too numerous to mention, he was promoted by that chief of chieftains, Gen. Green, to a captain of scouts. For his intrepid valor, he won the highest confidence of both soldier and officer." *Old Sibley Brigade*, 89–90. The company muster rolls dated October 31, 1862, to January 31, 1863, indicate McNelly held the rank of corporal. The regimental return for February 1864 first notes his promotion to captain. CSR-CS, Fifth Texas Cavalry, L. H. McNelly.
39. *OR*, XXVI, Pt. 1: 183, 190, 216, 225, 226–229; Jeffrey S. Prushankin, *A Crisis in Confederate Command: Edmund Kirby Smith, Richard*

Taylor, and the Army of the Trans-Mississippi (Baton Rouge: Louisiana State University Press, 2005),45; Winters, *Civil War in Louisiana*, 290–291; Taylor, *Destruction and Reconstruction*, 143–144; Kerby, *Kirby Smith's Confederacy*, 118–119, 134; Parrish, *Richard Taylor*, 303–304; Milbourn, "Lafourche Offensive," 77–79; Stephen S. Michot, "In Relief of Port Hudson: Richard Taylor's 1863 Lafourche Offensive," *Military History of the West* 23 (Fall 1993): 120–123.

40. Taylor, *Destruction and Reconstruction*, 145–146. *OR*, XXVI, Pt. 2: 110–111, 117, Pt. 1: 214–215, 222–223, 230–232; Irwin, *Nineteenth Army Corps*, 251–253; Noel, *Old Sibley Brigade*, 59–61; Kerby, *Kirby Smith's Confederacy*, 119–120; Michot, "In Relief of Port Hudson," 130–133.

41. *OR*, XXVI, Pt. 1: 5, 18, 393–395; Stephen A. Townsend, *The Yankee Invasion of Texas* (College: Texas A&M University Press, 2006), 14; Howell, ed., *Seventh Star of the Confederacy*, 140–144; Parrish, *Richard Taylor*, 308; Curtis W. Milbourn, "Brigadier General Thomas Green of Texas," *ETHJ* 32 (March 1994): 7; Cooper K. Ragan, ed., "The Diary of Captain George W. O'Brien, 1863," Pt. 3, *SHQ* 67 (July 1963): 49–50.

42. Parsons and Little, *Captain L. H. McNelly*, 38; Wooster, *Lone Star Generals in Gray*, 105, 111; Winters, *Civil War in Louisiana*, 297; Kerby, *Kirby Smith's Confederacy*, 242–243; Taylor, *Destruction and Reconstruction*, 150; Noel, *Old Sibley Brigade*, 62–67; Mamie Yeary, comp., *Reminiscences of the Boys in Gray, 1861–1865* (Dallas: Smith and Lamar Publishing House, 1912), 107; Wooten, ed., *Comprehensive History of Texas*, 2: 719–720.

43. Parsons and Little, *Captain L. H. McNelly*, 39–40; *OR*, XXXIV, Pt. 2: 1010; Noel, *Old Sibley Brigade*, 89–90; Special Orders No. 21, January 21, 1864, Special Orders No. 221, December 19, 1863, Green to Anderson, November 25, 1863 (quotation), Leander H. McNelly Papers, BCAH. A copy of McNelly's muster roll was reproduced in *Austin Genealogical Society Quarterly* 30 (September 1989): 131–133. See also Janet B. Hewett, ed., *Texas Confederate Soldiers, 1861–1865* (Wilmington, NC: Broadfoot Publishing Company, 1997), 2: 549.

44. *OR*, XXVI, Pt. 1: 385, Pt. 2: 468, 508–509, 519, 565, XXXIV, Pt. 2: 932, 1027; Townsend, *The Yankee Invasion of Texas*, 15–16; Taylor, *Destruction and Reconstruction*, 152, 157–158; Milbourn, "Brigadier

General Thomas Green," 8; Wooten, ed., *Comprehensive History of Texas*, 2: 724; Kerby, *Kirby Smith's Confederacy*, 290.

45. *OR*, XXXIV, Pt. 1: 597, 178, 510–511, 513–515, 518, 524, 561–563, 1075; Winters, *Civil War in Louisiana*, 329, 336; Taylor, *Destruction and Reconstruction*, 157–158.

46. Taylor, *Destruction and Reconstruction*, 160; Ludwell H. Johnson, *Red River Campaign: Politics and Cotton in the Civil War* (Kent, OH: Kent State University Press, 1993), 87; Gary D. Joiner, *Through the Howling Wilderness: The 1864 Red River Campaign and Union Failure in the West* (Knoxville: University of Tennessee Press, 2006), 193–194.

47. *OR*, XXXIV, Pt. 1: 551, 553; Taylor, *Destruction and Reconstruction*, 158; Dupree, *Planting the Union Flag in Texas*, 138; Johnson, *Red River Campaign*, 131.

48. *OR*, XXXIV, Pt. 1: 168, 181, Pt. 2: 895 (quotation); William Riley Brooksher, *War Along the Bayous: The 1864 Red River Campaign in Louisiana* (Washington, D.C.: Brassey's, 1998), 66; Kerby, *Kirby Smith's Confederacy*, 291; Dupree, *Planting the Union Flag in Texas*, 94; Johnson, *Red River Campaign*, 98–99.

49. Parsons and Little, *Captain L. H. McNelly*, 40–41, 42; *OR*, XXXIV, Pt. 1: 182–183, 610, Pt: 782; Gary D. Joiner, ed., *Little to Eat and Thin Mud to Drink: Letters, Diaries, and Memoirs from the Red River Campaigns, 1863–1864* (Knoxville: University of Tennessee Press, 2007), xx–xxi, 18–19, 42 n89, 135–136; Johnson, *Red River Campaign*, 134–135; Johnson and Buel, eds., *Battles and Leaders*, 4: 353; Noel, *Old Sibley Brigade*, 90; Rebecca W. Smith and Marion Mullins, eds., "The Diary of H. C. Medford, Confederate Soldier, 1864," Pt. 2, *SHQ* 34 (January 1931): 218, 225–226, 229; Wright, comp., and Simpson, ed., *Texas in the War*, 79. See also Bruce S. Allardice, "Curious Clash at Blair's Landing," *America's Civil War* 10 (July 1997): 58–64. A contemporary source mistakenly indicated McNelly was standing next to Green when he was killed. *Weekly State Gazette*, April 20, May 4, 1864.

50. Parsons and Little, *Captain L. H. McNelly*, 42; Fredericka Meiners, "Hamilton Bee in the Red River Campaign of 1864," *SHQ* 78 (July 1974): 21–44; Taylor, *Destruction and Reconstruction*, 182; Joiner, *Through the Howling Wilderness*, 144, 146; Joiner, ed., *Little to Eat and Thin Mud to Drink*, 23–24, 44 n109; Winters, *Civil War in Louisiana*, 362–365; Noel, *Old Sibley Brigade*, 90; Avis, ed., *History of Burton*, 267. See also Johnson, *Red River Campaign*, 228–234.

51. Parsons and Little, *Captain L. H. McNelly*, 44; *OR*, XXXIV, Pt. 1: 959, 964; Special Order No. 16, July 6, 1864, McNelly Papers, BCAH; Noel, *Old Sibley Brigade*, 90–91 (quotation on p. 90); *Galveston Weekly News*, July 5, 1864. As chief of cavalry for the XIX Army Corps, Colonel and Reconstruction-era Texas governor Edmund J. Davis was Crebs's direct superior. See also Frederick H. Dyer, *A Compendium of the War of the Rebellion* (De Moines, IA: The Dyer Publishing Company, 1908), 1647.
52. Parsons and Little, *Captain L. H. McNelly*, 45–46; *OR*, XLVIII, Pt. 1: 1457–1458; Noel, *Old Sibley Brigade*, 91 (first quotation); Keagan Lejeune, *Legendary Louisiana Outlaws: The Villains and Heroes of Folk Justice* (Baton Rouge: Louisiana State University Press, 2016), 73–74; Ethel Taylor, "Discontent in Confederate Louisiana," *Louisiana History* 2 (Autumn 1961): 425; Weems to McNelly, April 26, 1865, Unnumbered Special Order, May 23, 1864, McNelly Papers, BCAH; Lois Wood Burkhalter, *Gideon Lincecum, 1793–1874: A Biography* (Austin: University of Texas Press, 1965), 165 (second quotation).
53. Parsons and Little, *Captain L. H. McNelly*, 46–47; Letter of James P. Major, May 28, 1865, McNelly Papers, BCAH.
54. Parsons and Little, *Captain L. H. McNelly*, 49; Tax Rolls, Washington County, 1861–1862, 1865; *Marriage Records of Washington County, 1836–1909* (Brenham, TX: Washington County Genealogical Society, 1999), 2: 269; *Austin American-Statesman*, October 30, 1938; *Eighth U.S. Census*, Washington County, Texas; Widow's Application for a Pension, Mrs. W. T. Wroe, No. 51100, TSLAC; Lanthrip, "McNelly Family," n. pag.; Avis, ed., *History of Burton*, 265, 267, 269, 271; CSR-CS, Twenty-first Texas Cavalry, R. T. Matson.
55. Charles William Ramsdell, *Reconstruction in Texas* (New York: Columbia University Press, 1910), 67; Mrs. R. E. Pennington, *History of Brenham and Washington County, Texas* (Brenham, TX: Washington County Genealogical Society, 1998), 37; James M. Smallwood, et al., *Murder and Mayhem: The War of Reconstruction in Texas* (College Station: Texas A&M University Press, 2003), 3; Kenneth W. Howell, ed., *Still the Arena of Civil War: Violence and Turmoil in Reconstruction Texas, 1865–1874* (Denton: University of North Texas Press, 2012), 190; Allen G. Hatley, "Crime and Violence Made Texas a Dangerous Place to Live After the Civil War," *Wild West* 17 (October 2004): 12; William T. Field, Jr., "The Texas State Police, 1870–1873," *Texas Military History* 5 (Fall 1965): 132.

56. Report of Brevet Major General J. J. Reynolds, *Annual Report of the Secretary of War*, House Executive Document No. 1, 41st Congress, 2nd Session, 144.
57. *Senate Journal, Twelfth Legislature, Regular Session*, 85–86; *House Journal, Twelfth Legislature, Regular Session*, 18, 104–105, 154; Hans Peter Nielson Gammel, comp., *The Laws of Texas, 1822–1897* (Austin: The Gammel Book Company, 1898), 6: 193–195.
58. Ann Patton Baenziger, "The Texas State Police During Reconstruction: A Reexamination," *SHQ* 72 (April 1969), 473–474; Field, "The Texas State Police," 131, 132.
59. Tax Rolls, Washington County, 1870. The federal census for the same year did not calculate the value of McNelly's property.
60. Parsons and Little, *Captain L. H. McNelly*, 51, 55, 56; State Police Service Records, L. H. McNelly, 401–46, TSLAC; *Houston Evening Telegraph*, July 20, 1870; *Flake's Daily Bulletin*, July 21, 1870; Barry A. Crouch and Donaly E. Brice, *The Governor's Hounds: The Texas State Police, 1870–1873* (Austin: University of Texas Press, 2011), 33, 197 n26.
61. Chuck Parsons and Norman Wayne Brown, *A Lawless Breed: John Wesley Hardin, Texas Reconstruction, and Violence in the Wild West* (Denton: University of North Texas Press, 2013), 43; John Wesley Hardin, *The Life of John Wesley Hardin, From the Original Manuscript, As Written By Himself* (Seguin: Smith & Moore, 1896), 25 (quotation).
62. Parsons and Little, *Captain L. H. McNelly*, 56–57; *RAG, 1870*, 10–11; *House Journal, Twelfth Legislature, Regular Session*, 56; *Daily State Journal*, July 26, 1870.
63. Parsons and Little, *Captain L. H. McNelly*, 57–59, 60; *San Antonio Daily Express*, April 30, 1870; *Houston Daily Union*, August 17 (quotation), September 10, 1870; *Daily State Journal*, August 18, September 1, 1870; *Galveston Tri-Weekly News*, August 22, September 7, 1870; *Galveston Daily News*, September 11, 1870, May 26, October 17, 20, 1872; *San Antonio Daily Herald*, October 24, 1872.
64. Chuck Parsons, *The Sutton-Taylor Feud: The Deadliest Blood Feud in Texas* (Denton: University of North Texas Press, 2009), 59–73, 77–91, 95–96; Chuck Parsons, *Captain Jack Helm: A Victim of Texas Reconstruction Violence* (Denton: University of North Texas Press, 2018), 181–182, 214 n2; *Houston Weekly Telegraph*, September 8, 1870, July 31, 1873; *Galveston Daily News*, August 13, 1869, September 7, December 7, 1870,

August 3, 1873; Frederick Nolan, *The Wild West: History, Myth and the Making of America* (Edison, NJ: Chartwell Books, 2004), 99, 102–103; Wayne Gard, *Frontier Justice* (Norman: University of Oklahoma Press, 1968), 42; Baenziger, "Texas State Police," 477–478.
65. Parsons and Little, *Captain L. H. McNelly*, 70–72, 87, 90; *RAG, 1870*, 13 (quotation); *Houston Daily Union*, December 9, 14, 1870; *Galveston Daily News*, December 15, 16, 1870; *Houston Weekly Telegraph*, December 15, 1870.
66. Parsons and Little, *Captain L. H. McNelly*, 73–74; Crouch and Brice, *The Governor's Hounds*, 76–78; *Daily State Journal*, January 27, 1871; *Houston Weekly Telegraph*, December 15, 1870; *Houston Daily Union*, January 16, February 1, 9, 1871; *Galveston Daily News*, January 25, March 9, 1871; Message from the Governor, February 8, 1871, *Senate Journal, Twelfth Legislature, Regular Session*, 188, 204, 206; *Tri-Weekly Houston Union*, January 18, 1871.
67. Parsons and Little, *Captain L. H. McNelly*, 74–75; Howell, ed., *Still the Arena*, 199; Message from the Governor, February 8, 1871, *Senate Journal, Twelfth Legislature, Regular Session*, 204–205; *Houston Daily Journal*, January 16, 24, 1871; *Daily State Journal*, January 27, February 10, 1871; *Galveston Daily News*, March 8, 9, 11, 14, 1871.
68. Parsons and Little, *Captain L. H. McNelly*, 76–77; *Flake's Semi-Weekly Bulletin*, March 8, 1871; Otis A. Singletary, "The Texas Militia During Reconstruction," *SHQ* 60 (July 1956): 29; Message from the Governor, February 8, 1871, *Senate Journal, Twelfth Legislature, Regular Session*, 209, 210; *Galveston Daily News*, February 28, March 7, 22, 1871; Crouch and Brice, *The Governor's Hounds*, 87–88.
69. Parsons and Little, *Captain L. H. McNelly*, 89; *House Journal, Twelfth Legislature, Regular Session*, 56–57; *RAG, 1870*, 11–12, 14–15; Gammel, comp., *Laws of Texas*, 6: 972–974; Davidson to McNelly, May 10, 1871, 401–1032, TSLAC; Crouch and Brice, *The Governor's Hounds*, 48.
70. Parsons and Little, *Captain L. H. McNelly*, 104–107; James V. Reese, "The Early History of Labor Organizations in Texas, 1838–1876," *Texas Labor History*, ed. Bruce A. Glasrud and James C. Maroney (College Station: Texas A&M University Press, 2013), 38–39; *Galveston Daily News*, July 6, 7, 1872.
71. Parsons and Little, *Captain L. H. McNelly*, 107–113; Michael Collins, *A Crooked River: Rustlers, Rangers, and Regulars on the Lower Rio Grande, 1861–1877* (Norman: University of Oklahoma Press, 2018), 122

(quotation); Mary Margaret McAllen Amberson, et al., *I Would Rather Sleep in Texas: A History of the Lower Rio Grande Valley and the People of the Santa Anita Land Grant* (Austin: Texas State Historical Association, 2003), 313–315; *San Antonio Daily Express*, August 11, 1871; Testimony of Levi English, Deposition No. 572, *Depredations on the Frontiers of Texas*, House Executive Document No. 257, 43rd Congress, 1st Session, 11; *Galveston Daily News*, July 13, 14, October 12, 1872; *Daily State Journal*, July 10, 11, 12, 19, 1872; *San Antonio Daily Herald*, July 15, 16, 17, 1872; *Houston Telegraph*, July 18, 25, 1872; Tom Lea, *The King Ranch* (Boston: Little, Brown and Company, 1957), 1: 263–264; Allen G. Hatley, *Bringing the Law to Texas: Crime and Violence in Nineteenth Century Texas* (LaGrange, TX: Centex Press, 2002), 60.

72. *Depredations on the Frontiers of Texas*, House Executive Document No. 39, 42nd Congress, 3rd Session; *Depredations on the Frontiers of Texas*, House Executive Document No. 257.

73. *Reports of the Committee of Investigation Sent in 1873 by the Mexican Government to the Frontier of Texas* (New York: Baker & Goodwin, 1875), 1–5, 12–16, 21–28, 81.

74. Parsons and Little, *Captain L. H. McNelly*, 116–118; *Galveston Daily News*, November 15, 1872; Frederick Wilkins, *The Law Comes to Texas: The Texas Rangers, 1870–1901* (Abilene, TX: State House Press, 1999), 23; *RAG, 1872*, 5. McNelly is thought to have taken a short trip to Canada at this time, possibly to follow up on a clue to Davidson's whereabouts. While in Montreal, he sat for two photographs at James Inglis's studio. The originals are among the collections of the Texas Ranger Hall of Fame and Museum in Waco and the San Jacinto Museum of History in La Porte.

75. Parsons and Little, *Captain L. H. McNelly*, 123–124; Commission, 145.1–05, Leander H. McNelly Papers, SJMH; *Daily Democratic Statesman*, April 23, May 1, 2, July 4, 6, 1873; *Dallas Daily Herald*, April 23, May 2, 1873.

76. Hatley, *Bringing the Law to Texas*, 63.

77. *House Journal, Thirteenth Legislature, Regular Session*, 701, 703; *Senate Journal, Thirteenth Legislature, Regular Session*, 56; Gammel, comp., *Laws of Texas*, 7: 493; *Daily Democratic Statesman*, April 23, 1873; Tax Rolls, Washington County, 1872–1873.

78. Message of the Governor, January [12], 1875, *House Journal, Fourteenth Legislature, Second Session*, 20.

79. Gammel, comp., *Laws of Texas*, 8: 86–87.
80. Ibid., 88–89, 91.
81. Parsons and Little, *Captain L. H. McNelly*, 139, 142–143, 137; Parsons, *The Sutton-Taylor Feud*, 181, 187; Steele to McNelly, Special Order No. 2, July 14, 1874, 401–1012, TSLAC, 73–74; Commission, 145.1–05, McNelly Papers, SJMH; *Daily Democratic Statesman*, July 14 (quotation), 16, 25, 1874; *RAG, 1875*, 14; Steele to Wells, July 24, 1874, 401–621, TSLAC. George Durham recounted that before they left Corpus Christi the following year, the Rangers were loaned thirty-six Sharps carbines, ammunition, and supplies by merchant Sol Lichtenstein. George Durham as told to Clyde Wantland, *Taming the Nueces Strip: The Story of McNelly's Rangers* (Austin: University of Texas Press, 1962), 20.
82. Jennings, *A Texas Ranger*, 44–45 (first two quotations), 59 (third quotation). Jennings enlisted in the company on May 26, 1876, at Laredo. MR, Special State Troops, June 4, 1876.
83. Parsons and Little, *Captain L. H. McNelly*, 144; *Galveston Daily News*, January 13, 1875 (quotation). C. L. Sonnichsen, *I'll Die Before I'll Run: The Story of the Great Feuds of Texas* (Lincoln: University of Nebraska Press, 1988), 83.
84. McNelly to Steele, August 31, 1874, 401–392, TSLAC.
85. Parsons, *The Sutton-Taylor Feud*, 2, 3–4, 6, 7 (third quotation), 38–40, 53–57, 153; Charley F. Eckhardt, *Tales of Badmen, Bad Women, and Bad Places: Four Centuries of Texas Outlawry* (Lubbock: Texas Tech University Press, 1999), 68; McNelly to Steele, August 8, 1874, McNelly to Steele, August 31, 1874, 401–392, TSLAC; James M. Smallwood, *The Feud That Wasn't: The Taylor Ring, Bill Sutton, John Wesley Hardin, and Violence in Texas* (College Station: Texas A&M University Press, 2008), 181 (first two quotations), xviii; Sonnichsen, *I'll Die Before I'll Run*, 83. Parsons and Smallwood, both award-winning writers, agree the struggle was rooted in Reconstruction politics and the general disorder of post-war Texas, but, in the opinion of this author, the feud explanation proves more convincing than the "Taylor ring" theory.
86. Parsons and Little, *Captain L. H. McNelly*, 148–150; McNelly to Steele, August 7, 1874, McNelly to Steele, August 31, 1874, 401–392, TSLAC; Sonnichsen, *I'll Die Before I'll Run*, 85–86; *Daily Democratic Statesman*, August 11, 1874. McNelly to Steele, August 8, 1874, 401–392, TSLAC: Tumlinson "is a man who has always righted his

own wrongs, and he tells me that the only way for this county to have peace is to allow him to kill off the Taylor party."
87. Parsons, *The Sutton-Taylor Feud*, 5, 196, 198, 201–202, 226 (first quotation), 265; McNelly to Steele, August 31, 1874, 401–392, TSLAC; Commission, 145.1–05, McNelly Papers, SJMH; Chuck Parsons, *"Pidge," Texas Ranger* (College Station: Texas A&M University Press, 2013), 37; Nolan, *The Wild West*, 104; Message of the Governor, January 12, 1875, *House Journal, Fourteenth Legislature, Second Session*, 26 (second quotation).
88. Andrew Graybill, *Policing the Great Plains: Rangers, Mounties, and the North American Frontier, 1875–1910* (Lincoln: University of Nebraska Press, 2007), 80; Lea, *The King Ranch*, 1: 261–262, 265; "A Texas Cattle Raid," *Harper's Weekly* 18 (January 31, 1874): 107; Amberson, et al., *I Would Rather Sleep in Texas*, 319, 316; J. Frank Dobie, *The Longhorns* (Boston: Little, Brown and Company, 1941), 240–241; Joseph B. Wilkinson, *Laredo and the Rio Grande Frontier: A Narrative* (Austin: Jenkins Publishing Co., 1975), 328, 333; Testimony of General William Steele, February 9, 1876, Testimony of General E. O. C. Ord, February 12, 1876, *Texas Frontier Troubles*, House Report No. 343, 44th Congress, 1st Session, 27, 30; Testimony of General William Steele, January 17, 1878, Testimony of John S. Ford, January 24, 1878, *Relations of the United States with Mexico*, Pt. 2: 48, 79.
89. J. Frank Dobie and John D. Young, *A Vaquero of the Brush Country: The Life and Times of John D. Young* (Austin: University of Texas Press, 1998), 59; Leopold Morris, "The Mexican Raid of 1875 on Corpus Christi," *SHQ* 4 (October 1900): 128–139.
90. Howell, ed., *Still the Arena*, 319; William M. Hager, "The Nuecestown Raid of 1875: A Border Incident," *Arizona and the West* 1 (Autumn 1959): 261–267; *Galveston Daily News*, March 27, 28, 1875; Report of the Permanent Committee, and Steele to Coke, July 1, *Texas Frontier Troubles*, 52–53, 57, 121–122; Testimony of John S. Ford, January 24, 1878, *Relations of the United States with Mexico*, Pt. 2: 78–79; Clifford R. Caldwell and Ron DeLord, *Eternity at the End of a Rope: Executions, Lynchings and Vigilante Justice in Texas, 1819–1923* (Santa Fe: Sunstone Press, 2015), 210; Arnoldo De León, *They Called Them Greasers: Anglo Attitudes Toward Mexicans in Texas, 1821–1900* (Austin: University of Texas Press, 1983), 99; *San Antonio Daily Express*, April 21, 1875; Dobie, *Vaquero of the Brush Country*, 62.

91. Parsons and Little, *Captain L. H. McNelly*, 160, 163; RSR, L. H. McNelly, 401–30, TSLAC; *RAG, 1875*, 14; Special Order No. 15, April 2, 1875, 401–1012, TSLAC (quotation). On March 13, the legislature appropriated $17,403 for the seven months McNelly's company, as well as the Galveston companies, had been in service. Gammel, comp., *Laws of Texas*, 8: 484.
92. Parsons and Little, *Captain L. H. McNelly*, 176, 181, 185, 189, 191; *San Antonio Daily Express*, April 15, 24, 1875; Testimony of S. H. McNally [*sic*], January 24, 1876, *Texas Frontier Troubles*, 8; McNelly to Steele, August 13, 1875, 401–393, TSLAC; William D. Carrigan and Clive Webb, *Forgotten Dead: Mob Violence against Mexicans in the United States, 1848–1928* (New York: Oxford University Press, 2013), 168; George Durham, as told to Clyde Wantland, "On the Trail of 5100 Outlaws," Pt. 2, *West* 39 (November 1934): 110, Pt. 1 (October 1934): 113; *San Antonio Daily Herald*, May 6, 1875; *Galveston Daily News*, May 4, 1875; Walter Prescott Webb, "McNelly's Rangers," *True West* 9 (January-February 1962): 6; Jennings, *A Texas Ranger*, 65. Jennings's work has been fairly criticized for its loose adherence to facts, and must be applied cautiously. Nonetheless, he did serve in McNelly's company for eight months and was in a position to report on common attitudes. The order for the volunteer companies to disband was not widely hailed. For an example, see *San Antonio Daily Express*, May 8, 1875.
93. Testimony of S. H. McNally [*sic*], January 24, 1876, *Texas Frontier Troubles*, 10.
94. Durham, *Taming the Nueces Strip*, 40; Amberson, et al., *I Would Rather Sleep in Texas*, 330; Wilkins, *Law Comes to Texas*, vii; Jennings, *A Texas Ranger*, 71; Bob Alexander, *Riding Lucifer's Line: Ranger Deaths along the Texas-Mexico Border* (Denton: University of North Texas Press, 2013), 42; Carrigan and Webb, *Forgotten Dead*, 168; Howell, ed., *Still the Arena*, 322–323; Frederic Remington, "How the Law Got into the Chaparral," *Crooked Trails* (New York: Harper and Brothers, 1898), 16. Jerry D. Thompson, *Cortina: Defending the Mexican Name in Texas* (College Station: Texas A&M University Press, 2007), 224: "The Rangers, who had been dispatched to help calm the violence and hysteria, were themselves responsible for numerous executions."
95. Parsons and Little, *Captain L. H. McNelly*, 192, 193–194; Affidavit of Jesus Sandoval, May 3, 1875, *Texas Frontier Troubles*, 83–84 (quotation on p. 84); Collins, *A Crooked River*, 319 n53; *Daily Democratic Statesman*, December 31, 1874, January 27, 1875; RSR, Jesus

Sandoval, 401–170, TSLAC; Leon Metz, "Borderlands," *True West* 47 (September 2000): 36–37.

96. Jennings, *A Texas Ranger*, 75–77; Durham, "On the Trail of 5100 Outlaws," Pt. 2: 113 (quotation); *Seventh U.S. Census*, Cameron, Starr, and Webb Counties, Texas. For examples of the Sandoval legend, see John H. Harrison, "The Day McNelly's 31 Rangers Declared War on Mexico," *Frontier West* 5 (June 1975), 60; and Lynn R. S. Joyce, "Jesus Sandoval: Real-Life 'Lone Ranger' on the Rio Grande," *Real West* 26 (June 1983): 32–37.

97. Durham, *Taming the Nueces Strip*, 31–33; Chuck Parsons, ed., "The Memoirs of William Callicott, Texas Ranger," Pt. 2, *The Texas Ranger Dispatch* 4 (Summer 2001): 33; *Galveston Daily News*, April 20, 1875; Maurice Kildare, "McNelly's Texas Blood Bath," *Westerner* 2 (November 1970): 40; Utley, *Lone Star Justice*, 170. The first mention of multiple Winchester rifles in the company's inventory of public property is found in the monthly return for April 30, 1877. However, King's donations could have been considered personal possessions.

98. Parsons and Little, *Captain L. H. McNelly*, 211; Thompson, *Cortina*, 145–147, 148, 182, 219–222; Milo Kearney and Anthony Knopp, *Boom and Bust: The Historical Cycles of Matamoros and Brownsville* (Austin: Eakin Press, 1991), 136; Lea, *The King Ranch*, 1: 263–264; *RAG, 1875*, 8 (quotation); Testimony of S. H. McNally [sic], January 29, 1876, Affidavit of George A. Hall, June 11, 1875, *Texas Frontier Troubles*, 14, 129. For more on Ford and the Cortina War, see Volume 1 of this trilogy.

99. Parsons and Little, *Captain L. H. McNelly*, 194; *Colorado Citizen*, July 1, 1875; Parsons, *Pidge*, 82; Testimony of S. H. McNally [sic], January 29, 1876, *Texas Frontier Troubles*, 14, 129.

100. Parsons and Little, *Captain L. H. McNelly*, 194–195; *Colorado Citizen*, July 1, 1875 (quotation); Testimony of Captain H. C. Corbin, December 14, 1877, *Texas Border Troubles*, 151; Testimony of S. H. McNally [sic], January 29, 1876, *Texas Frontier Troubles*, 14–15.

101. Parsons and Little, *Captain L. H. McNelly*, 195–199, 201–202; *Colorado Citizen*, July 1, 1875 (quotation); Testimony of S. H. McNally [sic], January 29, 1876, *Texas Frontier Troubles*, 15; *San Antonio Daily Express*, June 14, 1875; *Galveston Daily News*, June 15, 1875; Clifford R. Caldwell and Ron DeLord, *Texas Lawmen, 1835–1899: The Good and the Bad* (Charleston, SC: History Press, 2011), 330–331; Durham, *Taming the Nueces Strip*, 66, 69; Chuck Parsons, ed., "The Memoirs

of William Callicott, Texas Ranger," Pt. 3, *The Texas Ranger Dispatch* 5 (Fall 2001): 21–23; Dobie, *Vaquero of the Brush Country*, 67–68; Parsons, *Pidge*, 84.

102. *Galveston Daily News*, June 13, 1875.
103. Mike Cox, *The Texas Rangers: Wearing the Cinco Peso, 1821–1900* (New York: Tom Doherty Associates, 2008), 250.
104. Jerry D. Thompson, *Juan Cortina and the Texas-Mexico Frontier, 1859–1877* (El Paso: Texas Western Press, 1994), 72, 87, 93; John Mason Hart, *Empire and Revolution: The Americans in Mexico Since the Civil War* (Berkeley: University of California Press, 2002), 66, 76.
105. Parsons and Little, *Captain L. H. McNelly*, 220–225; Testimony of S. H. McNally [sic], January 24, 1876, Randlett to Potter, December 1, 1876, Potter to Adjutant General, November 18, 1876, Clendenin to Potter, December 5, 1876, *Texas Frontier Troubles*, 8–9, 93–95, 91, 88; *Frank Leslie's Illustrated Newspaper*, January 1, 1876.
106. Parsons and Little, *Captain L. H. McNelly*, 229–231; Randlett to Potter, December 1, 1876, Clendenin to Potter, December 5, 1876, *Texas Frontier Troubles*, 94, 91; Durham, "On the Trail of 5100 Outlaws," Pt. 4 (January 1935): 75–77; Walter Prescott Webb, "The Bandits of Las Cuevas," *True West* 10 (September-October 1962): 12; Wilkins, *Law Comes to Texas*, 101; *Galveston Daily News*, December 12, 1875.
107. Parsons and Little, *Captain L. H. McNelly*, 231–232; McNelly to Steele, November 22, 1875, 401–393, TSLAC; Parsons, ed., "Memoirs of William Callicott," Pt. 3: 27; Durham, *Taming the Nueces Strip*, 110–111; Wilkinson, *Laredo and the Rio Grande Frontier*, 344–345.
108. Parsons and Little, *Captain L. H. McNelly*, 233 (quotation); Webb, "Bandits of Las Cuevas," 13; Durham, *Taming the Nueces Strip*, 114; Amberson, et al., *I Would Rather Sleep in Texas*, 331.
109. Parsons and Little, *Captain L. H. McNelly*, 233–235; Potter to Adjutant General, November 18, 1876, Randlett to Potter, December 1, 1876, Clendenin to Potter, December 5, 1876, *Texas Frontier Troubles*, 88, 94, 91; Robert M. Utley, *Frontier Regulars: The United States Army and the Indian, 1866–1891* (Lincoln: University of Nebraska Press, 1984), Ch. 18; Parsons, ed., "Memoirs of William Callicott," Pt. 3: 29.
110. Potter to Adjutant General, November 18, 1876, Randlett to Potter, December 1, 1876, Alexander to Potter, November 29, 1876, Clendenin to Potter, December 5, 1876, *Texas Frontier Troubles*, 88, 95, 90; Webb, *Texas Rangers*, Ch. 13; Durham, *Taming the Nueces Strip*,

115–116; Wilkins, *Law Comes to Texas*, 104; *San Antonio Daily Express*, August 22, 1909.

111. Parsons and Little, *Captain L. H. McNelly*, 236–237, 239, 245; Alexander to Potter, November 29, 1875, *Texas Frontier Troubles*, 90; Webb, "Bandits of Las Cuevas," 73; Durham, "On the Trail of 5100 Outlaws," Pt. 4: 81, Pt. 5: 80–81; Metz, "Borderlands," 37; *Frank Leslie's Illustrated Newspaper*, January 1, 1876; Chuck Parsons, ed., "The Memoirs of William Callicott, Texas Ranger," Pt. 4, *The Texas Ranger Dispatch* 6 (Spring 2002): 13–14; McNelly to Steele, November 22, 1875, 401–393, TSLAC; *RAG, 1876*, 9; Wilkins, *Law Comes to Texas*, 108.

112. *Frank Leslie's Illustrated Newspaper*, January 1, 1876; Hart, *Empire and Revolution*, 76. Stuart N. Lake, "Brush Poppers," *The Saturday Evening Post* 203 (April 11, 1931), 20: "You want to understand that when it came to rounding up criminals, we didn't wait for any political clock to strike the hour for going after 'em, and once we started after an individual or a bunch, we brought 'em in or finished 'em off, no matter who got hurt. We didn't coddle 'em after we caught 'em, either. We kept the outlaws' victims in mind and figured to make it just as tough as possible for thieves and murderers, with no ceremony at all."

Parsons and Little credit Dr. Alexander Manford Headley, American expatriate and spokesman for the Mexican delegation, with keeping the negotiations from turning into a massacre of McNelly's Rangers. *Captain L. H. McNelly*, 243–246. See also Michael G. Webster, "Intrigue on the Rio Grande: The Rio Bravo Affair, 1875," *SHQ* 74 (October 1970): 149–164. On March 8, 2004, a mock trial was held in the Knox Room at the Texas Ranger Hall of Fame and Museum in Waco that inquired into McNelly's actions. For details of the hearing, see Chuck Parsons, "Texas Ranger Leander H. McNelly Stands Trial: Charged with Violating Neutrality Laws," *The Texas Ranger Dispatch* 14 (Summer 2004), 15–19.

113. Testimony of S. H. McNally [sic], January 24, 29, 1876, *Texas Frontier Troubles*, 8–17; *Daily State Gazette*, February 20, 1876.

114. Parsons and Little, *Captain L. H. McNelly*, 257; *RAG, 1876*, 9. Unidentified in the report, the slain *ranchero* may have been Manuel Garcia, who was described on January 21 as being "lately killed by McNelly's men." *Galveston Daily News*, January 21, 1876.

115. Parsons and Little, *Captain L. H. McNelly*, 261–262; *RAG, 1876*, 9; *San Antonio Daily Express*, May 19, 20, 21, 1876; *Galveston Daily News*, May 19, 1876; Amberson, et al., *I Would Rather Sleep in Texas*, 332.

116. Ovie Clark Fisher with Jeff C. Dykes, *King Fisher: His Life and Times* (Norman: University of Oklahoma Press, 1966), ix (quotations), 31–32, 56, 58, 60; Gary P. Fitterer, "Let Justice Be Done Our Western Citizens," *Newsletter of the National Outlaw and Lawman Association* 16 (July, September 1992): 12–14; Judge W. A. Bonnet, "King Fisher, A Noted Character," *Frontier Times* 3 (July 1926): 36. Bill O'Neal calculated Fisher killed five men in four gun battles. *Encyclopedia of Western Gunfighters* (Norman: University of Oklahoma Press, 1979), 5, 108.

117. Parsons and Little, *Captain L. H. McNelly*, 264–265; Fisher with Dykes, *King Fisher*, 64–66, 75–82; *RAG, 1876*, 9; Durham, "On the Trail of 5100 Outlaws," Pt. 6: 108–109; Sammy Tise, *Texas County Sheriffs* (Albuquerque: Oakwood Publishing, 1989), 363; Oath of Office, 145.1-04, McNelly Papers, SJMH; *San Antonio Daily Express*, June 6, 10, 17, 1876. The following year, Sheriff Cook fled into Mexico after having embezzled state and county funds. *Daily Democratic Statesman*, July 17, 1877. Given his demonstrated corruption, one may question whether he released Fisher because of legal obligations or a discreet bribe.

118. Parsons and Little, *Captain L. H. McNelly*, 272; McNelly to Ford, June 8, 1876, TCM94.1.1173a-Box 2, Ford Papers, HML&HC; *Galveston Daily News*, June 22, 1876; *San Antonio Daily Express*, June 25, 1876; Gammel, comp., *Laws of Texas*, 8: 891; RSR, L. H. McNelly, 401-30, TSLAC; Commission, 145.1-05, McNelly Papers, SJMH; *RAG, 1876*, 9; John S. Ford, "Death of Capt. McNelly," MS, n.d., TCM94.1.0175-Box 1, Ford Papers, HML&HC (quotation).

119. Gammel, comp., *Laws of Texas*, 8: 891–892.

120. Steele to Hubbard, March 8, 1877, 301-98, TSLAC; Cox, *Wearing the Cinco Peso*, 254–255; Utley, *Lone Star Justice*, 169–170. McNelly's laxness with report-writing had also earned him numerous reprimands from General Davidson while in the State Police. Parsons and Little, *Captain L. H. McNelly*, Ch. 5–7.

121. *Victoria Advocate*, August 31, 1876; *Daily Democratic Statesman*, October 24, 1876.

122. Parsons and Little, *Captain L. H. McNelly*, 292–295; RSR, L. McNelly, 401-30, TSLAC; Steele to Hubbard, March 8, 1877, 301-98, TSLAC; *Galveston Daily News*, February 6, 1877; *San Antonio Daily Express*, February 9, 1877. Former Rangers who had served under McNelly's leadership wrote an open letter criticizing the adjutant general's decision. *San Antonio Daily Express*, February 11, 1877.

123. Parsons and Little, *Captain L. H. McNelly*, 297; *San Antonio Daily Express*, January 30, July 27, August 15, 1877; *Galveston Daily News*, September 7, October 17, 1877; Ford, "Death of Capt. McNelly," Ford Papers, HML&HC.
124. *Twelfth U. S. Census*, Travis County, Texas; Widow's Application for a Pension, Mrs. W. T. Wroe, No. 51100, Soldier's Application for a Pension, W. T. Wroe, No. 47594, TSLAC; *Brownsville Daily Herald*, September 6, 9, 1895; Texas Death Certificate, Carey Cheek McNelly Wroe, October 30, 1938, File No. 48042; *Austin American-Statesman*, and *Galveston Daily News*, both dated, October 30, 1938; Avis, ed., *History of Burton*, 269; Vivian Adams Rudisill, "History of the Carey McNelly Wroe Chapter of the Children of the Confederacy," *Our Heritage* 34 (Spring 1993): 23–25.
125. Avis, ed., *History of Burton*, 269; *Brenham Weekly Banner*, December 10, 1891; *Galveston Daily News*, January 17, April 8, September 27, 29, 1892; *Brenham Daily Banner*, March 28, April 16, 1893, October 27, 1894; Texas Department of Criminal Justice, Convict Record Ledgers, 1998/038-153, TSLAC, 100; ibid., Conduct Registers, 1998/038-185, TSLAC, 316; Arizona Death Certificate, L. R. McNally, file date unknown, file no. unknown; *Austin Statesman*, January 4, 7, 1907; *Tombstone Epitaph*, January 6, 1907.
126. *Thirty-eighth Annual Catalogue of the Officers and Students of Baylor College, 1884–1885* (*Female Department*) (Brenham, TX: Fred R. Carrick, 1884), 7; *Galveston Daily News*, May 9, 1884.

Notes for Chapter 3

1. Chuck Parsons, *John B. Armstrong, Texas Ranger and Pioneer Ranchman* (College Station: Texas A&M University Press, 2007), 1–2, 115 n1; *Annual Catalogue of the Medical Institute of Louisville, Session 1841–42* (Louisville, KY: Prentice and Weissinger, 1842), 1; Rutherford County Marriage Book (1804–1881), Tennessee Marriage Records, Tennessee State Library and Archives, 64; Diane Solether Smith, *The Armstrong Chronicle: A Ranching History* (San Antonio: Corona Publishing Co., 1986), 115, 331, 333; *Seventh U.S. Census*, Cannon County, Tennessee (free and slave schedules); Walter Womack, *McMinnville at a Milestone, 1810–1960* (McMinnville, TN: Standard Publishing Co., Inc., and Womack Publishing Co., 1960), 107 (quotation); *Southern Standard*, November 14, 1885.

In a telephone conversation with Sara Storey "Sarita" Armstrong Hixon, the current manager of the Armstrong Ranch and a great-granddaughter of John B. Armstrong, this author learned that Tobin Armstrong's extensive collection of family history and genealogical papers disappeared following his death in 2005. Subsequent inquiries to Chuck Parsons, the University of Texas at Corpus Christi, Texas A&M University at Kingsville, TRHFM, FTRA, the King Ranch Museum, and the Kleberg County Historical Commission failed to produce any leads as to their current whereabouts.

The spelling of Armstrong's middle name is frequently found as "Barclay," including on his death certificate. As Parsons has written the definitive biography of John B. Armstrong, and personally found the "Barkley" spelling in the family Bible, this author has chosen to use it as well. *John B. Armstrong*, 115 n3.

Doctor Armstrong died in McMinnville on December 18, 1875, after a lengthy illness, while Maria died on November 9, 1885. *The Tennessean*, December 22, 1875; *Southern Standard*, November 14, 1885.

2. Smith, *Armstrong Chronicle*, 116, 118; Daniel W. Crofts, *Reluctant Confederates: Upper South Unionists in the Secession Crisis* (Chapel Hill: University of North Carolina Press, 1989), 45, 109, 133, 134, 347; Womack, *McMinnville at a Milestone*, 107, 219.
3. *Eighth U.S. Census*, Warren County, Tennessee (free and slave schedules).
4. Johnathan M. Atkins, *Parties, Politics, and the Sectional Conflict in Tennessee, 1832–1861* (Knoxville: University of Tennessee Press, 1997), 239–241, 253–254; *Daily Nashville Patriot*, April 16, 17, May 3, 1861.
5. Womack, *McMinnville at a Milestone*, 271; Mark Mayo Boatner III, *The Civil War Dictionary* (New York: David McKay Company, 1988), 910–911; Smith, *Armstrong Chronicle*, 119; *Nashville Daily Union*, October 4, 1864. John Hunt Morgan's wife, Martha "Mattie" Ready Morgan, was the niece of Maria Armstrong. Monty Wanamaker and Chris Keathley, *McMinnville* (Charleston, SC: Arcadia Publishing, 2009), 45.
6. *The Tennessean*, March 6, 1868; *Memphis Daily Appeal*, June 20, 1870; *Ninth U.S. Census*, Warren County, Tennessee.
7. Parsons, *John B. Armstrong*, 2, 6; Smith, *Armstrong Chronicle*, 119.
8. Parsons, *John B. Armstrong*, 2; *Daily Democratic Statesman*, June 14, August 22, December 27, 1873.

9. Parsons, *John B. Armstrong*, 3–5; *Daily Democratic Statesman*, January 2, 1874; Randolph B. Campbell, *Gone to Texas: A History of the Lone Star State* (New York: Oxford University Press, 2003), 285. The statements of Sheriff Zimpelman and Lieutenant Roberts were included in John S. Ford, *Rip Ford's Texas*, ed. Stephen B. Oates (Austin: University of Texas Press, 1991), 426, 428–429. Sammy Tise, *Texas County Sheriffs* (Albuquerque: Oakwood Publishing, 1989), 494; T. B. Wheeler, "Reminiscences of Reconstruction in Texas," *SHQ* 11 (July 1907): 56. One of the participants, Valentine O. Weed, recorded his memories of the incident for W. S. Reed on November 20, 1930. Archived at the Briscoe Center for American History, this six-page manuscript, entitled "Recollections of V. O. Weed," was unavailable for perusal, but this author was provided a copy of notes courtesy of Chuck Parsons. See also *Austin Statesman*, August 8, 9, 1935.
10. Parsons, *John B. Armstrong*, 6; *Daily Democratic Statesman*, June 23, 24, 25, 1874.
11. Parsons, *John B. Armstrong*, 7, 12–15, 19–22; RSR, J. B. Armstrong, 401–179, TSLAC; Webb, *Texas Rangers*, 238–251; Frederick Wilkins, *The Law Comes to Texas: The Texas Rangers, 1870–1901* (Abilene, TX: State House Press, 1999), 86; *Daily State Gazette*, January 19, 1876; George Durham as told to Clyde Wantland, *Taming the Nueces Strip: The Story of McNelly's Rangers* (Austin: University of Texas Press, 1962), 97–100; R. Bolon, "McNelly's Raiding Rangers," *Big West* 1 (October 1967), 44, 62–64. See also Clyde Wantland, "Taking the Law to the Rio Grande," *Frontier Times* 13 (January 1936): 226–232, (February 1936): 258–263.
12. Frank H. Bushick, "Some Old Texas Ranger Captains," *Frontier Times* 18 (May 1941): 351.
13. Parsons, *John B. Armstrong*, 27; RSR, J. B. Armstrong, 401–179, TSLAC; Keith Guthrie, *The History of San Patricio County* (Austin: Nortex Press, 1986), 24, 265–267; Operations of State Troops, 1 (1876–1881), 401–1082, TSLAC: 2; Tise, *Texas County Sheriffs*, 452; *Goliad Guard*, September 2, 1876; *Galveston Daily News*, September 6, 12, October 10, 19, 1876; *Dallas Daily Herald*, January 23, 1881; 10 *Texas Criminal Reports* 16–25 (1881); Texas Department of Criminal Justice, Convict Record Ledgers, 1998/038–151, TSLAC, 86.
14. Parsons, *John B. Armstrong*, 26–29; *Daily Democratic Statesman*, *Galveston Daily News*, and *San Antonio Daily Express*, all dated October 3, 1876 (quotations); Operations of State Troops, 1: 2; Mike

Cox, *Texas Ranger Tales: Stories That Need Telling* (Plano: Republic of Texas Press, 1997), 41–46; Michael Collins, *A Crooked River: Rustlers, Rangers, and Regulars on the Lower Rio Grande, 1861–1877* (Norman: University of Oklahoma Press, 2018), 263–265; Durham, *Taming the Nueces Strip*, 158–161; Ovie Clark Fisher with Jeff C. Dykes, *King Fisher: His Life and Times* (Norman: University of Oklahoma Press, 1966), 87.

15. Parsons, *John B. Armstrong*, 29–30; *Daily Democratic Statesman*, *Galveston Daily News*, and *San Antonio Daily Express*, all dated October 3, 1876 (quotation); MR, Special State Troops, September 30, 1876.
16. Parsons, *John B. Armstrong*, 32–34; MR, Special State Troops, December 31, 1876; *Daily Democratic Statesman*, January 22, 1874 (first quotation); *San Antonio Daily Express*, December 7, 13 (second quotation), 1876; *Galveston Daily News*, December 12, 1876; *San Antonio Daily Herald*, December 8, 1876.
17. Parsons, *John B. Armstrong*, 37–38; Operations of State Troops, 1: 8–9.
18. Parsons, *John B. Armstrong*, 42–44; Chuck Parsons and Gary P. Fitterer, *Captain C. B. McKinney: The Law in South Texas* (Wolfe City, TX: Henington Publishing Company, 1993), 17–18; *San Antonio Daily Express*, April 21, May 15, 1877; *Galveston Daily News*, May 25, 1877; Hall to Steele, May 14, 1877, 401–1157, TSLAC.
19. *Daily Democratic Statesman*, December 9, 1874 (quotation); John Wesley Hardin, *The Life of John Wesley Hardin, From the Original Manuscript, As Written By Himself* (Seguin: Smith & Moore, 1896); *St. Louis Post-Dispatch*, August 24, 1877; *Galveston Daily News*, August 25, 1877; *Daily Arkansas Gazette*, August 28, 1877; Bill O'Neal, *Encyclopedia of Western Gunfighters* (Norman: University of Oklahoma Press, 1979), 5, 128–130; Chuck Parsons and Norman Wayne Brown, *A Lawless Breed: John Wesley Hardin, Texas Reconstruction, and Violence in the Wild West* (Denton: University of North Texas Press, 2013), 36–37, 55, 63, 67–73, 83, 89, 96–97, 203, 207–208.
20. Parsons and Brown, *A Lawless Breed*, 140–141, 165–172, 201, 209–210; Leon Metz, *John Wesley Hardin: Dark Angel of Texas* (Norman: University of Oklahoma Press, 1998), 34, 101, 109, 112, 137–138, 158–161; Rick Miller, *Bounty Hunter* (College Station: Creative Publishing Company, 1988), 70–71; Charley F. Eckhardt, *Tales of Badmen, Bad Women, and Bad Places: Four Centuries of Texas Outlawry* (Lubbock: Texas Tech University Press, 1999), 72–73; Mollie Moore Godbold, "Comanche and the Hardin Gang," Pt. 1,

SHQ 67 (July 1963): 70; Governors E. J. Davis and Richard Coke, Executive Record Books, 1835–1917, Reel No. 3481, TSLAC, 291, 471; Hans Peter Nielson Gammel, comp., *The Laws of Texas, 1822–1897* (Austin: The Gammel Book Company, 1898), 8: 561 (quotation). Hardin's brother, Joseph Gibson, was lynched by a Brown County mob on June 23, 1874, in retaliation for Webb's killing. Clifford R. Caldwell and Ron DeLord, *Eternity at the End of a Rope: Executions, Lynchings and Vigilante Justice in Texas, 1819–1923* (Santa Fe: Sunstone Press, 2015), 200.

21. Parsons, *John B. Armstrong*, 47–51; Hall to Steele, May 29, 1877, 401–1157, TSLAC; Parsons and Brown, *A Lawless Breed*, 216–219, 221; Metz, *John Wesley Hardin*, 165–167; Robert K. DeArment, *Man-Hunters of the Old West* (Norman: University of Oklahoma Press, 2017), 113–115; Miller, *Bounty Hunter*, 76, 80–86.

22. Parsons, *John B. Armstrong*, 51–52; Parsons and Brown, *A Lawless Breed*, 220–224; Metz, *John Wesley Hardin*, 167–169; DeArment, *Man-Hunters of the Old West*, 115; Miller, *Bounty Hunter*, 86–90; *Daily Democratic Statesman*, August 29, 1877 (quotations); *San Antonio Daily Express*, August 15, 1877; Bob Alexander and Donaly E. Brice, *Texas Rangers: Lives, Legend, and Legacy* (Denton: University of North Texas Press, 2017), 312; Judge Ken Wise, "The Trial of John Wesley Hardin," *Texas Bar Journal* 75 (March 2012): 202; Ann Mendall, "The Texas Rangers," *Great West* 3 (July 1969): 53.

23. DeArment, *Man-Hunters of the Old West*, 116–117; *Dallas Morning News*, August 22, 1895; *Tri-Weekly Herald*, August 28, 1877; *Galveston Daily News*, August 29, 1877; Mike Whittington, "Six Telegrams That Tell the Story: The Arrest of John Wesley Hardin," *The Texas Ranger Dispatch* 3 (Spring 2001), 37 (quotation).

24. Parsons, *John B. Armstrong*, 52; Parsons and Brown, *A Lawless Breed*, 225; Miller, *Bounty Hunter*, 92; Whittington, "Six Telegrams," 39 (quotation).

25. Parsons, *John B. Armstrong*, 52; Parsons and Brown, *A Lawless Breed*, 225–226; Miller, *Bounty Hunter*, 92–93; Whittington, "Six Telegrams," 39 (quotations); Armstrong to Hubbard, August 24, 1877, 401–1157, TSLAC.

26. Whittington, "Six Telegrams," 40 (quotation); *Daily Democratic Statesman*, August 26, 1877.

27. Parsons, *John B. Armstrong*, 56–58, 63, 67; Parsons and Brown, *A Lawless Breed*, 230, 237–238, 251–252; Metz, *John Wesley Hardin*,

173–175, 176–180; Miller, *Bounty Hunter*, 93–94, 96–97, 99; Allen G. Hatley, *Bringing the Law to Texas: Crime and Violence in Nineteenth Century Texas* (LaGrange, TX: Centex Press, 2002), 83; *The Tennessean*, *Daily Arkansas Gazette*, and *Dallas Daily Herald*, all dated August 28, 1877; *Daily Democratic Statesman*, August 29, 1877; Wise, "Trial of John Wesley Hardin," 202.

Discharged from the Rangers in November 1877, Duncan returned to Dallas to open a private detective business. He was later shot in the chest by a prostitute, but continued working until his 1911 death in an automobile accident. DeArment, *Man-Hunters of the Old West*, 120–150.

In Huntsville, Hardin was officially punished eleven times and attempted escape once before he finally became a model prisoner. He read law and studied theology, taught Sunday school, and wrote his autobiography. Pardoned and released on February 17, 1894, he established a law practice in El Paso. However, his old nature soon rose to the surface amid the violence of the border town. On August 19, 1895, Hardin was fatally shot in the back by Constable John Selman (an equally murderous individual) while standing drunk at the Acme Saloon's bar. Robert M. Utley, *Lone Star Justice: The First Century of the Texas Rangers* (New York: Berkley Books, 2002), 174–175.

28. Parsons, *John B. Armstrong*, 5, 67; *Daily Democratic Statesman*, February 16 (quotation), June 6, 1874, February 21, 1878; Lucie Clift Price, *Travis County, Texas Marriage Records, 1840–1882* (Austin: privately published, 1973), 5; Maria Watson, "The Armstrong Ranch: A Documented Narrative History," unpublished MS, 1981, 4. For more on Major Durst, see Stephen L. Moore, *Savage Frontier: Rangers, Riflemen, and Indian Wars in Texas* (Denton: University of North Texas Press, 2006), 2: 88, 106, 108, 110, 147, 151, 245, 274.

29. Parsons, *John B. Armstrong*, 68–69; Rick Miller, *Sam Bass and Gang* (Austin: State House Press, 1999), 246; Armstrong to Steele, December 6, 1878, Armstrong to Steele, December 7, 1878, 401–1157, TSLAC; RSR, John B. Armstrong, 401–179, TSLAC.

30. Parsons, *John B. Armstrong*, 73–74; *Tenth U.S. Census*, Travis County, Texas; *Mooney & Morrison's General Directory of the City of Austin, Texas, for 1877–78* (Austin: Eugene von Boeckmann, 1873), 235; *Morrison & Fourmy's General Directory of the City of Austin, for 1881*

and 1882 (Austin: E. W. Swindells, 1881), 48, 77; Ibid., *1885 and 1886* (Austin: E. W. Swindells, 1885), 63, 100.

31. Parsons, *John B. Armstrong*, 73, 95, 97; Smith, *Armstrong Chronicle*, 124, 127, 132. Smith noted the spelling change of the elder son's middle name was either a deliberate decision by the parents or a clerical error.
32. Parsons, *John B. Armstrong*, 75–76; *Brownsville Daily Herald*, April April 13, 1904; Smith, *Armstrong Chronicles*, 59–61, 125–127; Watson, "Armstrong Ranch," 6; San Patricio District First Class, Kenedy County, File No. 831, TGLO; Galen D. Greaser, et al., *New Guide to Spanish and Mexican Land Grants in South Texas* (Austin: Texas General Land Office, 2009), 155–158. For a review of the legal cases involved, see 73 *Texas Reports* 410–422 (1889); 11 *Southwestern Reporter* 380–385 (1889); 84 *Texas Reports* 159–173 (1892); 19 *Southwestern Reporter* 463–467 (1892); 91 *Texas Reports* 147–149 (1897); 40 *Southwestern Reporter* 315–323 (1897); 98 *Texas Reports* 633 (1905); and 83 *Southwestern Reporter* 1135 (1905).
33. Parsons, *John B. Armstrong*, 76–80; Watson, "Armstrong Ranch," 7–8; Tax Rolls, Cameron County, 1887–1889.
34. Parsons, *John B. Armstrong*, 83–84; Texas Volunteer Guard Service Records, John B. Armstrong, 401–141, TSLAC; *San Antonio Daily Express*, May 3, 1913; RSR, John B. Armstrong, 401–179, TSLAC; Utley, *Lone Star Justice*, 229; Alexander and Brice, *Texas Rangers*, 328.
35. Parsons, *John B. Armstrong*, 80, 97–98; Smith, *Armstrong Chronicles*, 134, 136; Tax Rolls, Cameron County, 1891–1893; Watson, "Armstrong Ranch," 8–9.
36. Parsons, *John B. Armstrong*, 83, 88; Texas Volunteer Guard Service Records, John B. Armstrong, 401–179, RSR, John B. Armstrong, –141, TSLAC; *Galveston Daily News*, May 1, 1891, July 21, 1893, May 11, August 10, 1894, January 4, 1896; *Brownsville Daily Herald*, January 10, 1893; *San Antonio Daily Express*, May 3, 1913. Smith contends Armstrong was appointed to command a Texas volunteer regiment during the Spanish-American War with the rank of major. Whether this was a federalized regiment or one that remained in state service is unclear. The old Ranger was said to have lamented that he saw no action. *Armstrong Chronicles*, 148–149. A review of Francis Heitman's *Historical Register of the United States Army*, the Texas Adjutant General's Spanish-American War service records, and the National Archives' General Index to Compiled Service Records of Volunteer

Soldiers Who Served During the War with Spain failed to produce any mention of Armstrong serving in any capacity in the United States Volunteers. Incidentally, General Smyth was given command of the Third Texas Infantry as a colonel in the USV.

37. Parsons, *John B. Armstrong*, 90–92, 133 n25, 97; *Austin Daily Statesman*, December 28, 1897; Smith, *Armstrong Chronicle*, 147; Watson, "Armstrong Ranch," 10; *Morrison & Fourmy's General Directory of the City of Austin, 1900–1901* (Galveston: Morrison & Fourmy, 1900), 48; *Brownsville Daily Herald*, May 31, 1898.

38. Parsons, *John B. Armstrong*, 92; David Montejano, *Anglos and Mexicans in the Making of Texas, 1836–1986* (Austin: University of Texas Press, 1987), 106–107; Tom Lea, *The King Ranch* (Boston: Little, Brown and Company, 1957), 2: 538–539; *Brownsville Daily Herald*, December 29, 1902; George O. Coalson, "The Building of the Railroad to Brownsville," *South Texas Studies* 1 (1990): 37–38; *Brownsville Daily Herald*, February 2, 1939.

39. J. L. Allhands, *Railroads to the Rio* (Salado, TX: Anson Jones Press, 1960), 48–59; Alicia M. Dewey, *Pesos and Dollars: Entrepreneurs in the Texas-Mexico Borderlands, 1880–1940* (College Station: Texas A&M University Press, 2014), 52; Mary Margaret McAllen Amberson, et al., *I Would Rather Sleep in Texas: A History of the Lower Rio Grande Valley and the People of the Santa Anita Land Grant* (Austin: Texas State Historical Association, 2003), 435; *Brownsville Daily Herald*, January 21, 22, April 9, 14, 1903, July 5, December 20, 1904; Montejano, *Anglos and Mexicans in the Making of Texas*, 107–108; Lea, *The King Ranch*, 2: 541–542, 544, 552. The train stop was later renamed Armstrong and currently has a population of twenty.

40. Parsons, *John B. Armstrong*, 93; Smith, *Armstrong Chronicle*, 147, 155. In a cruel twist of fate, on September 11, 1896, John, Jr.'s horse had fallen on him and broken his thigh bone. *Brownsville Daily Herald*, September 12, 1896.

41. Parsons, *John B. Armstrong*, 95–96; Texas Death Certificate, John Barclay Armstrong, File No. 11310 (quotation); *San Antonio Daily Express*, May 3, 1913.

42. Probate Minutes, Willacy and Kenedy Counties 1 (1913–1950): 3–4.

43. Parsons, *John B. Armstrong*, 98; *Brownsville Daily Herald*, September 30, 1896, June 28, 1897, April 24, 1906; *San Antonio Light*, April 22, 1906; *Ruston Daily Leader*, March 30, 1934; *Lutcher News-Examiner*, October 5, 1972; *Find A Grave*, s.v. "Andrew Stewart" and "Josephine

Stewart." The name of the plantation is derived from the double row of twenty-eight giant live oaks straddling the road that leads to the main house. The trees are estimated to be nearly three hundred years old. J. Frazier Smith, *Plantation Houses and Mansions of the Old South* (New York: Dover Publications, 1993), 191–193. Members of Josephine's family continue to manage the foundation. For more on this historic property, see www.oakalleyplantation.com.

44. Parsons, *John B. Armstrong*, 95, 98; *Brownsville Daily Herald*, September 30, 1896, June 28, 1897, April 29, 1905; *The University of Texas Record* 3 (September 1901): 262, 427; *San Antonio Daily Light*, April 23, 30, 1905; Birth Certificates, John Mirza Bennett, Jr., June 27, 1908, Registrar's No. 8635, Mollie Durst Bennett, March 17, 1910, File No. 8912, Josephine Bennett, April 16, 1913, File No. 96; Texas Death Certificate, Jamie Armstrong Bennett, April 23, 1963, File No. 22050.

45. Parsons, *John B. Armstrong*, 97; *Alumni Directory of Yale University [Graduates and Non-Graduates]* (New Haven: Yale University, 1920), 532; George A. Katzenberger, ed., *Directory of the Legal Fraternity of Phi Delta Phi* (Galesburg, IL: Mail Printing Company, 1909), 228; *Brownsville Daily Herald*, August 28, 1906, July 21, 1908, November 20, 1909; *San Antonio Express*, February 10, 1910; *San Antonio Light*, January 24, 1918; Texas Death Certificate, Charles M. Armstrong, September 14, 1941, File No. 42588. Charles's son, Tobin, was the managing partner of the ranch after Thomas's death. After Tobin's passing in October 2005, his daughter, Sarita Armstrong Hixon, took over the reins. *Corpus Christi Caller-Times*, October 8, 2005.

46. Parsons, *John B. Armstrong*, 97, 98; Smith, *Armstrong Chronicle*, 155, 174; *San Antonio Light*, January 1, 1914; *Fourteenth U.S. Census*, Nassau County, New York; Orleans Parish Marriage Records 53, 3653; *Fifteenth* and *Sixteenth U.S. Census*, Orleans Parish, Louisiana; *New Orleans Times-Picayune*, March 1, 1936, August 2, 1956, December 27, 1991.

47. Parsons, *John B. Armstrong*, 97–98; *Official Register of Harvard University: The Law School* 14 (June 8, 1917): 59; Frederick S. Mead, ed., *Harvard's Military Record in the World War* (Boston: Harvard Alumni Association, 1921), 43; George Sweet Gibb and Evelyn H. Knowlton, *History of Standard Oil Company (New Jersey): The Resurgent Years, 1911–1927* (New York: Harper Brothers, 1956), 385–388; Henrietta M. Larson, et al., *History of Standard Oil (New Jersey): New Horizons,*

1927–1950 (New York: Harper & Row, 1971), 68, 70, 135, 480, 484–485; *San Antonio Light*, June 4, 5, 1949; Lea, *The King Ranch*, 2: 574, 696; John Cypher, *Bob Kleberg and the King Ranch: A Worldwide Sea of Grass* (Austin: University of Texas Press, 1995), 64–65 (quotation); *Corpus Christi Caller-Times*, October 24, 25, 1969; *Corpus Christi Caller*, March 4, 5, 1986.

Notes for Chapter 4

1. James B. Gillett, *Six Years with the Texas Rangers*, ed. Milton M. Quaife (New Haven: Yale University Press, 1925), Ch. 1; *Texas State Gazette*, November 30, 1850; "Ancestors of James Buchanan Gillett" unpublished MS, n.d., n pag.; *The Texas Almanac for 1858* (Galveston: Richardson and Company, 1857), 101–102; Confederate Muster Roll Abstract Records, James S. Gillett, TSLAC. Colonel Gillett died on May 19, 1874, and Bettie died on October 16, 1879. Both were buried in Oak Hill Cemetery in Lampasas. Find A Grave, s.v. "James Shackelford Gillett" and "Elizabeth Jane Harper Gillett."
2. Gillett, *Six Years*, 25–26 (quotation on p. 25), 27 (second quotation); RSR, James B. Gillett, 401–153, TSLAC; Joseph E. Bennett, "Chronicler of the Texas Rangers," *Royal Arch Mason* (Summer 1990): 298; Chuck Parsons and Donaly E. Brice, *Texas Ranger N. O. Reynolds: The Intrepid* (Denton: University of North Texas Press, 2014), 3, 232; Jones to Roberts, June 23, 1875, Roberts to Jones, August 1, 1875, 401–1158, TSLAC.
3. Ed Carnal, "Reminiscences of a Texas Ranger," *Frontier Times* 1 (December 1923): 24: "We rangers, as well as Indians, fought under the black flag. We asked no quarter and gave none. Whenever we met it was simply a case of outfight or outrun 'em, whichever could be done the best. Ours invariably turned out one way—we outfought 'em." For a detailed study of Company D, see Bob Alexander, *Winchester Warriors: Texas Rangers of Company D, 1874–1901* (Denton: University of North Texas Press, 2009). For more on Captain Roberts, see Robert W. Stephens, *Captain Dan Roberts: The Untold Story* (Dallas: Robert W. Stephens, 2009).
4. Gillett, *Six Years*, 33–34 (quotation); MR, Company D, August 31, 1875; Wayne T. Walker, "Jim Gillett—Ranger Diablo," *Real West* 23 (June 1980): 18–19; Calico Jones, "Guns at the Ready," *True Frontier* 4 (July 1971): 24; RSR, N. H. Murray, 401–165, TSLAC. Gillett's

written account of the forthcoming fight was later condensed into the article "Personal Glimpses" for *The Literary Digest* 88 (February 6, 1926): 41. The narrative was reprinted in "'Injun Fighting' with the Texas Rangers," *Frontier Times* 3 (June 1926): 3–6.

5. Gillett, *Six Years*, 34–35, 38, 40–41 (quotation on p. 40); MR, Company D, August 31, 1875; Roberts to Jones, August 26, 1875, 401–1158, TSLAC; *Galveston Daily News*, September 4, 1875; Thomas P. Gillespie, "Fight on the Concho Plains," *True West* 10 (May-June 1963): 32–33.
6. Gillett, *Six Years*, 41–43, 45; MR, Company D, August 31, 1875; Roberts to Jones, August 26, 1875, 401–1158, TSLAC; Gillespie, "Fight on the Concho Plains," 33; Jones, "Guns at the Ready," 25–26. Lehman would write of his experiences in *Nine Years Among the Indians, 1870–1879*, ed. J. Marvin Hunter (Austin: Von Boeckmann-Jones Co., 1927). See also Gregory and Susan Michno, *A Fate Worse Than Death: Indian Captivities in the West, 1830–1885* (Caldwell, ID: Caxton Press, 2009), 412–417.
7. MR, Company D, September 30, 1875-May 31, 1876; ROS, Company D, January 1876.
8. Gillett, *Six Years*, 58–60; MR, Company D, June 30, 1876; *Galveston Daily News*, July 26, 1876; Jones, "Guns at the Ready," 56.
9. Gillett, *Six Years*, 60–61; Alexander, *Winchester Warriors*, 23–24; Special Order No. 33, August 23, 1876, 401–1012, TSLAC.
10. Gillett, *Six Years*, 61.
11. Special Order No. 67, August 29, 1876, Special Order No. 68, September 1, 1876, 401–1158, TSLAC; RSR, James B. Gillett, 401–153, C. L. Nevill, -165, N. O. Reynolds, -169, J. M. Denton, -149, TSLAC; Parsons and Brice, *Texas Ranger N. O. Reynolds*, 70, 71; Robert W. Stephens, *Texas Ranger Sketches* (Dallas: Robert W. Stephens, 1972), 104.
12. Gillett, *Six Years*, 63–64.
13. RSR, J. M. Denton, 401–149, Neal Coldwell, -147, TSLAC; Special Order No. 35, December 6, 1876, Special Order No. 36, December 8, 1876, Special Order No. 82, 401–1012, TSLAC; Special Order No. 79, December 1, 1876, Special Order No. 80, December 5, 1876, December 15, 1876, 401–1158, TSLAC.
14. MR, Company A, December 31, 1876–January 31, 1877; Coldwell to Jones, January 15, 1877, Coldwell to Jones, February 28, 1877, Jones to King, April 12, 1877, Coldwell to Jones, June 30, 1877, 401–1158, TSLAC.

15. Peter R. Rose, *The Reckoning: The Triumph of Order on the Texas Outlaw Frontier* (Lubbock: Texas Tech University Press, 2012), 58; Robert S. Weedle, "The Pegleg Stage Robbers," *Southwest Heritage* 4 (March 1969): 3, 4; *Frontier Echo*, February 2, 1877; "Stage Hold-Up at Pegleg in 1877," *Frontier Times* 4 (February 1927): 50–51; William Curry Holden, "Law and Lawlessness on the Texas Frontier, 1875–1890," *SHQ* 44 (October 1940): 193.
16. Gillett, *Six Years*, 87–88, 103; Operations of State Troops, 1 (1876–1881), 401–1082, TSLAC: 103; Rose, *The Reckoning*, 46–47, 64.
17. Gillett, *Six Years*, 69–70; Operations of State Troops, 1: 102; Frederick Wilkins, *The Law Comes to Texas: The Texas Rangers, 1870–1901* (Abilene, TX: State House Press, 1999), 127–129; Bob Alexander and Donaly E. Brice, *Texas Rangers: Lives, Legend, and Legacy* (Denton: University of North Texas Press, 2017), 309; Rose, *The Reckoning*, 69; Wayne R. Austerman, *Sharps Rifles and Spanish Mules: The San Antonio–El Paso Mail, 1851–1881* (College Station: Texas A&M University Press, 1985), 293.
18. Gillett, *Six Years*, 71; MR, Company A, August 31, 1877; Chuck Parsons and Gary P. Fitterer, *Captain C. B. McKinney: The Law in South Texas* (Wolfe City, TX: Henington Publishing Company, 1993), 19; *Galveston Daily News*, May 30, June 30, July 17, 19, 26, 29, 31, August 8, 12, 14, 1877; Jones to Coldwell, August 7, 1877, 401–1158, TSLAC.
19. Gillett, *Six Years*, 81–84; General Order No. 20, August 24, 1877, 401–1158, TSLAC; RSR, James B. Gillett, 401–153, C. L. Nevill, –165, N. O. Reynolds, -169, TSLAC; Wayne T. Walker, "Jim Gillett, 'Sergeant Diablo' of the Texas Rangers," *Oldtimers Wild West* 1 (February 1978): 49–50.
20. Gillett, *Six Years*, 86; Parsons and Brice, *Texas Ranger N. O. Reynolds*, 1, 129; Chuck Parsons and Norman Wayne Brown, *A Lawless Breed: John Wesley Hardin, Texas Reconstruction, and Violence in the Wild West* (Denton: University of North Texas Press, 2013), 246–249, 252–253; MR, Company E, September 30, 1877; Leon Metz, *John Wesley Hardin: Dark Angel of Texas* (Norman: University of Oklahoma Press, 1998), 180–184; John Wesley Hardin, *The Life of John Wesley Hardin, From the Original Manuscript, As Written by Himself* (Seguin, TX: Smith & Moore, 1896), 122.
21. MR, Company E, October 31-November 30, 1877; *Galveston Daily News*, November 10, 1877.

22. Gillett, *Six Years*, 88–89; Special Order No. 109, November 12, 1877, 401–1158, TSLAC; MR, Company E, November 30-December 31, 1877; *Galveston Daily News*, December 12, 16, 18, 25, 1877; Austerman, *Sharps Rifles and Spanish Mules*, 290–291, 294, 322.
23. Gillett, *Six Years*, 92–95 (quotation on p. 94); ROS, Company E, January 1878; Bill O'Neal, *Encyclopedia of Western Gunfighters* (Norman: University of Oklahoma Press, 1979), 119; Eugene Cunningham, "The Fightin'est Ranger," *Old West* 15 (Fall 1978): 26; MR, Company E, January 31, 1878; *Galveston Daily News*, January 22, 1878; *Dallas Daily Herald*, January 24, 1878; *Lampasas Dispatch*, February 7, 1878.
24. Gillett, *Six Years*, 95–99; MR, Company E, January 31-February 28, 1878; Ovie Clark Fisher, *It Occurred in Kimble* (Houston, TX: Anson Jones Press, 1937), 218–219; George W. Gray, "Quick on the Draw," *The American Magazine* 104 (October 1927): 53 (quotation); Cunningham, "The Fightin'est Ranger," 27; *Galveston Daily News*, February 23, March 1, 1878; *Dallas Daily Herald*, March 5, 1878. Starke Reynolds was remanded to the Tarrant County sheriff and taken to Fort Worth for trial. He evidently escaped, as he was reported to have been seriously wounded and captured in Milam County on April 5, 1879. *Dallas Daily Herald*, March 10, 1878; *Galveston Daily News*, April 6, 24, 1879.
25. ROS, Company E, March-May 1878; *Galveston Daily News*, May 14, 1878.
26. Gillett, *Six Years*, 107, 120–123, 125–126; ROS, Company E, June-July 1878; James B. Gillett, "The Killing of Sam Bass," *Frontier Times* 1 (February 1924): 29–30; MR, Company E, July 31, 1878; *Galveston Daily News*, July 24, 1878.
27. ROS, Company E. August 1878; MR, Company E, August 31, 1878; General Order No. 23, August 4, 1878, 401–1159, TSLAC.
28. Gillett, *Six Years*, 86–87; *Galveston Daily News*, June 6, 1878; ROS, Company E, September 1878; Parsons and Brown, *A Lawless Breed*, 264–267; Metz, *John Wesley Hardin*, 192–194; Parsons and Brice, *Texas Ranger N. O. Reynolds*, 204–207; Charley F. Eckhardt, *Tales of Badmen, Bad Women, and Bad Places: Four Centuries of Texas Outlawry* (Lubbock: Texas Tech University Press, 1999), 76; Jones to Reynolds, September 5, 1878, 401–1159, TSLAC; *Daily Democratic Statesman*, September 18, October 8, 1878; Texas Department of Criminal Justice, Convict Record Ledgers, 1998/038-150, TSLAC, 212; ibid., Conduct Registers, 1998/038-180, TSLAC, 803. For the complete

ruling of the Texas Court of Appeals on Hardin's case, see 4 *Texas Criminal Reports* 355–372 (1878).

29. Gillett, *Six Years*, 102–105; Rose, *The Reckoning*, 74; ROS, Company E, November 1878-January 1879; Fisher, *It Occurred in Kimble*, 193; Parsons and Brice, *Texas Ranger N. O. Reynolds*, 225; Special Order No. 11, November 24, 1878, 401–1159, TSLAC; Weedle, "The Pegleg Stage Robbers," 5; Texas Department of Criminal Justice, Convict Record Ledgers, 1998/038-139, TSLAC, 94; *Galveston Daily News*, July 7, 1878, January 6, August 20, 24, 25, 1880, February 1, 3, 5, 8, 10, 12, March 1, 2, 7, 9, 1882. On April 14, Boyce was arrested in Austin on an outstanding warrant for cattle rustling. *Galveston Daily News*, April 16, 1882.
30. Gillett, *Six Years*, 134; MR, Company E, March 31, 1879; Special Order No. 3, February 19, 1879, 401–1012, TSLAC; Parsons and Brice, *Texas Ranger N. O. Reynolds*, 204–207; RSR, N. O. Reynolds, 401–169, James B. Gillett, -153, TSLAC; *Galveston Daily News*, March 14, 1879.
31. Gillett, *Six Years*, 141–142, 145–148; Bennett, "Chronicler of the Texas Rangers," 299–300.
32. Gillett, *Six Years*, 149.
33. Ibid., 151–160; Operations of State Troops, 1: 187; *El Paso Daily Herald*, January 13, 1900; Andrew Graybill, *Policing the Great Plains: Rangers, Mounties, and the North American Frontier, 1875–1910* (Lincoln: University of Nebraska Press, 2007), 49. The October 10 report Baylor sent to General Jones was reprinted in *Galveston Daily News*, October 23, 1879, and *San Antonio Daily Express*, October 24, 1879. Kathleen P. Chamberlain, *Victorio: Apache Warrior and Chief* (Norman: University of Oklahoma Press, 2007), 175; Cunningham, "The Fightin'est Ranger," 28; *RAG, 1880*, 34.
34. Gillett, *Six Years*, 180–183; Chamberlain, *Victorio*, 176; Jefferson Morgenthaler, *The River Has Never Divided Us: A Border History of La Junta de los Rios* (Austin: University of Texas Press, 2004), 128; Bennett, "Chronicler of the Texas Rangers," 300; Jones, "Guns at the Ready," 57.
35. Gillett, *Six Years*, 183–184; MR, Company A, September 30, 1880; Dan L. Thrapp, *Victorio and the Mimbres Apaches* (Norman: University of Oklahoma Press, 1974), 299; Cecilia Thompson, *History of Marfa and Presidio County, 1535–1946* (Austin: Nortex Press, 1985), 1: 169; Jones, "Guns at the Ready," 58.

36. Gillett, *Six Years*, 186–188; Morgenthaler, *The River Has Never Divided Us*, 128; Chamberlain, *Victorio*, 202; Donald E. Worcester, *The Apaches: Eagles of the Southwest* (Norman: University of Oklahoma Press, 1979), 231; James L. Haley, *Apaches: A History and Culture Portrait* (Norman: University of Oklahoma Press, 1997), 332–334.
37. Eugene Cunningham, *Triggernometry: A Gallery of Gunfighters* (Norman: University of Oklahoma Press, 1996), 198; Bennett, "Chronicler of the Texas Rangers," 301; RSR, James B. Gillett, 401-153, TSLAC.
38. Gillett, *Six Years*, 211–213; MR, Company A, February 28, 1881; Leon Metz, "An Incident at Christmas," *NOLA Quarterly* 14 (1990): 9, 15; Harold L. Edwards, "Trouble in Socorro," *Old West* 27 (Winter 1990): 42–43, 44; Cunningham, "The Fightin'est Ranger," 28.
39. Gillett, *Six Years*, 211–221; RSR, George Lloyd, 401–161, TSLAC; MR, Company A, March 31, 1881; *Las Vegas Gazette*, March 31, April 1, 1881; Walker, "Jim Gillett, 'Sergeant Diablo'," 54–56; Edwards, "Trouble in Socorro," 45, 47; Sam Bloom, "The Christmas that Became a Nightmare," *The West* 16 (January 1973): 48; Leon Metz and Kenneth Goldblatt, "Murdered in Church," *Frontier Times* 43 (October-November 1969): 63.
40. Gillett, *Six Years*, 221; Gray, "Quick on the Draw," 54, 165–167. In both accounts, Gillett incorrectly related the Conklin murder occurred during "Christmas week of 1881." The actual year was 1880 as he had resigned from the Ranger service by the end of December 1881. Keith Milton, "Whistlin' Extradition," *True West* 39 (May 1992): 19; Frederick Wilkins, *The Law Comes to Texas: The Texas Rangers, 1870–1901* (Abilene, TX: State House Press, 1999), 234; *El Paso Herald*, December 20, 1922; *Galveston Daily News*, May 13, 1881; Cunningham, *Triggernometry*, 201.
41. Gillett, *Six Years*, 203–210.
42. *El Paso Times*, September 15, 1974; "Descendants of James Buchanan Gillett" unpublished MS, n.d., n. pag.; *El Paso Daily Times*, September 2, 1883.
43. Gillett, *Six Years*, 230–231, 236–237; Leon C. Metz, *Dallas Stoudenmire* (Norman: University of Oklahoma Press, 1993), 10, 24–28; Cunningham, *Triggernometry*, 202, 174; Colonel Martin L. Crimmins, "Captain Jim Gillett," *Frontier Times* 21 (October 1943): 7. According to the late Bill Stein, director/archivist at the Nesbitt Memorial Library in Columbus, Texas, Cunningham and Metz both misspelled the gunfighter's last

name. He offered as proof Dallas's marriage license and that of his brother's, as well as the latter's headstone in Llano. "Consider the Lily: The Ungilded History of Colorado County, Texas," *Nesbitt Memorial Library Journal* 10 (January 2000): 51. Stoudenmier's Confederate service records support Stein's assertion. CSR-CS, Seventeenth Alabama Infantry, D. Stoudenmier.

44. Gillett, *Six Years*, 234; Metz, *Dallas Stoudenmire*, 3–8; Ben W. Kemp with J. C. Dykes, *Cow Dust and Saddle Leather* (Norman: University of Oklahoma Press, 1968), 19; W. H. Timmons, *El Paso: A Borderlands History* (El Paso: Texas Western Press, 2004), 205; *Austin Daily Stateman*, April 9, 1881. Marshal Campbell was not the same man who had commanded Company B of the Frontier Battalion in Shackelford County.

45. Metz, *Dallas Stoudenmire*, 41–43; C. L. Sonnichsen, *Pass of the North: Four Centuries on the Rio Grande* (El Paso: Texas Western Press, 1968), 1: 221–223; Clifford R. Caldwell and Ron DeLord, *Texas Lawmen, 1835–1899: The Good and the Bad* (Charleston, SC: History Press, 2011), 84–85, 89–90; *El Paso Herald*, January 10, 1906.

46. Metz, *Dallas Stoudenmire*, 51–52, 89; Richard F. Selcer, comp. and ed., *Legendary Watering Holes: The Saloons That Made Texas Famous* (College Station: Texas A&M University Press, 2004), 133, 135; James B. Gillett, "The Killing of Dallas Stoudenmire," *Frontier Times* 1 (July 1924): 24–26; Sonnichsen, *Pass of the North*, 1: 224, 239–240; *Galveston Daily News*, February 15, 1882.

47. Gillett, *Six Years*, 237 (quotation); Cunningham, *Triggernometry*, 183; *Galveston Daily News*, May 31, 1882; James B. Gillett, "An Early Day Sheriff's Experience," *Frontier Times* 1 (February 1924): 2. Reprinted from *El Paso Herald*, August 15, 1917. *El Paso Herald-Post*, January 28, 1956; Mildred Cox Shannon, "James B. Gillett, Indomitable Texan" (M.A. thesis, Sul Ross State College, 1960), 59.

48. Cunningham, *Triggernometry*, 202, 426–428; Mike Cox, *Gunfights and Sites in Texas Ranger History* (Charleston, SC: History Press, 2015), 184; Gray, "Quick on the Draw," 52 (quotation); Walker, "Jim Gillett—Ranger Diablo," 21.

49. Gillett, *Six Years*, 237; Cunningham, *Triggernometry*, 183; *El Paso Times*, July 29, 1882; Selcer, comp. and ed., *Legendary Watering Holes*, 136; Metz, *Dallas Stoudenmire*, 116–120; Kemp with Dykes, *Cow Dust and Saddle Leather*, 20; Gillett, "Killing of Dallas Stoudenmire," 26–27; Sonnichsen, *Pass of the North*, 1: 244–245.

50. Robert M. Utley, "The Range Cattle Industry in the Big Bend of Texas," *SHQ* 69 (April 1966): 429; Ronnie C. Tyler, *The Big Bend: A History of the Last Texas Frontier* (Washington, D.C.: National Park Service, 1975), 140 (quotation); R. D. Holt, "Pioneer Cowman of Brewster County and the Big Ben Area," *The Cattleman* 29 (June 1942): 15.
51. Gillett, *Six Years*, 238; Thompson, *Marfa and Presidio County*, 1: 184, 265–266; Special Order No. 30, November 18, 1882, 401–1159, TSLAC; Sammy Tise, *Texas County Sheriffs* (Albuquerque: Oakwood Publishing, 1989), 424; Holt, "Pioneer Cowman of Brewster County," 26; Tax Rolls, Presidio County, 1884–1885; Joan Bagley, "James B. Gillett, The Man," *The Junior Historian* 14 (May 1969): 7–8; "Descendants of James Buchanan Gillett," n. pag.
52. *El Paso Times*, September 15, 1974; *Galveston Daily News*, March 24, April 2, October 30, December 23, 1883; *El Paso Daily Times*, May 6, 1883; Shannon, "James B. Gillett," 71–72; *Los Angeles Times*, July 19, 1903.
53. Gillett, *Six Years*, 238; J. B. Gillett, "The Old G4 Ranch," *Voice of the Mexican Border* 1 (October 1933), 82 (quotations); Crimmins, "Captain Jim Gillett," 10; Thompson, *Marfa and Presidio County*, 1: 190, 215; J. Marvin Hunter, comp. and ed., *Trail Drivers of Texas* (Austin: University of Texas Press, 1985), 996; Holt, "Pioneer Cowman of Brewster County," 24; Gus L. Ford, ed., *Texas Cattle Brands: A Catalog of the Texas Centennial Exposition Exhibit, 1936* (Dallas: Clyde C. Cockrell Company, 1936), 86. For a brief sketch of Gano's military career, see Ezra J. Warner, *Generals in Gray: Lives of the Confederate Commanders* (Baton Rouge: Louisiana State University Press, 2008), 96.
54. Gillett, *Six Years*, 239; Gillett, "The Old G4 Ranch," 82; Holt, "Pioneer Cowman of Brewster County," 24; Wayne Gard, *Rawhide Texas* (Norman: University of Oklahoma Press, 1965), 11; Will F. Evans, *Border Skylines* (Dallas: Published for the Bloys Camp Meeting Association by Cecil Baugh, 1940), 218.
55. Bagley, "James B. Gillett, The Man," 8; Tax Rolls, Brewster County, 1889; Thompson, *Marfa and Presidio County*, 1: 266, 2: 19.
56. Marshall Hail, *Knight in the Sun: Harper B. Lee, First Yankee Matador* (Boston: Little, Brown and Company, 1962), 26.
57. Shannon, "James B. Gillett," 7; Texas Death Certificate, Lou Chastain Gillett, May 4, 1948, File No. 786; *San Marcos Free Press*, May 2, 1899; *Galveston Daily News*, May 4, 1889.

58. Gillett, *Six Years*, 239; Crimmins, "Captain Jim Gillett," 11; *Fort Worth Daily Gazette*, January 23, 1899; Hunter, comp. and ed., *Trail Drivers of Texas*, 996; Tax Rolls, Brewster County, 1891–1897.
59. Tise, *Texas County Sheriffs*, 65; *Galveston Daily News*, November 14, 19, 1890; *Fort Worth Daily Gazette*, November 19, 1890; ROS, Company D, November 1890; *Austin Daily Statesman*, November 19, 1890; Thompson, *Marfa and Presidio County*, 1: 303, 298; J. B. Gillett, Card Index, Bonds and Oaths of County and State Officials, TSLAC.
60. Alexander, *Winchester Warriors*, 241–242; Thompson, *Marfa and Presidio County*, 1: 303; *Galveston Daily News*, December 21, 1890, February 9, 1891; *Fort Worth Daily Gazette*, December 22, 1890. The Powe-Gilliland episode gave rise to the legend of the "murder calf." For more on this tale, see Byron Browne, *Driving Southwest Texas: On the Road in Big Bend Country* (Charleston, SC: History Press, 2011), 80–85.
61. Tise, *Texas County Sheriffs*, 65; Shannon, "James B. Gillett," 74–75. The U.S. Marshal for the Western District at that time was ex-Ranger Richard C. Ware.
62. Thompson, *Marfa and Presidio County*, 1: 279, 313–315; Bennett, "Chronicler of the Texas Rangers," 302.
63. Bagley, "James B. Gillett, The Man," 1 (quotation); Holt, "Pioneer Cowman of Brewster County," 23; Tax Rolls, Brewster County, 1897.
64. Thompson, *Marfa and Presidio County*, 1: 262 (quotation); Lewis Nordyke, *Great Roundup: The Story of Texas and Southwestern Cowmen* (New York: William Morrow and Company, 1955), 237; Utley, "Range Cattle Industry," 440.
65. Bagley, "James B. Gillett, The Man," 1, 2, 8; Tax Rolls, Brewster County, 1900–1901; Texas Death Certificate, Milton E. Gillett, January 11, 1950, File No. 62602.
66. Bagley, "James B. Gillett, The Man," 2; Thompson, *Marfa and Presidio County*, 2: 19; Shannon, "James B. Gillett," 85; Tax Rolls, Brewster County, 1905.
67. Bagley, "James B. Gillett," 2–3 (quotation on p. 3); *El Paso Herald*, October 1, 1906, April 4, September 12, 1907; *Alpine Avalanche*, August 2, 1907; Thompson, *Marfa and Presidio County*, 1: 316, 2: 31, 26; Evans, *Border Skylines*, 218; Crimmins, "Captain Jim Gillett," 11; Shannon, "James B. Gillett," 11.
68. Bagley, "James B. Gillett, The Man," 4; *El Paso Herald*, June 22, 1909; *San Antonio Daily Express*, August 20, 1908; *Alpine Avalanche*, October 21, 28, 1909; *Galveston Daily News*, October 21, 1909.

69. Shannon, "James B. Gillett," 10, 102; Thompson, *Marfa and Presidio County*, 2: 141, 159–160, 162. See also Capt. J. B. Gillett, "Commanding Leadership Won Against Odds By Herefords," *The American Hereford Journal* 11 (May 15, 1920): 206, 208.
70. William M. Green, "Origin of the Ex-Texas Ranger Association," *Frontier Times* 1 (February 1924): 3; *Dallas Morning News*, August 13, 1921; *Comanche Chief*, August 4, 11, 1922; "Rangers Meet at Menard," *Frontier Times* 1 (October 1923): 19. The original edition of his autobiography was published by the Von Beockmann-Jones Company in Austin, and the second was published by Yale University Press four years later. The book was revised into a school textbook in 1928 for sixth and seventh graders in Indiana, and later became adopted by public schools in at least seventeen states.
71. Bagley, "James B. Gillett, The Man," 7–8. The Barrel Springs Ranch is still in operation today. Thompson, *Marfa and Presidio County*, 2: 227, 250, 282, 296; *Kerrville Daily Times*, October 25, 1928; RSR, James B. Gillett, 401–79, TSLAC.
72. *El Paso Herald-Tribune*, June 12, 1937; Thompson, *Marfa and Presidio County*, 2: 428; Texas Death Certificate, Captain J. B. Gillett, June 11, 1937, Registrar's No. 168; Bennett, "Chronicler of the Texas Rangers," 302.
73. *El Paso Herald-Tribune*, May 4, 1948; Texas Death Certificate, Lou Chastain Gillett, May 4, 1948, File No. 786.
74. Hail, *Knight in the Sun*, 28, 37–216, 221; *El Paso Herald*, May 27, 1909, December 6, 1911; *San Antonio Light*, June 27, 1941, July 18, 1962; Texas Death Certificate, Harper Baylor Gillette, June 27, 1941, File No. 14.
75. Bagley, "James B. Gillett, The Man," 5; *Fourteenth U.S. Census*, Socorro County, New Mexico; *Fifteenth* and *Sixteenth U.S. Census*, Catron County, New Mexico; Birth Certificates, Baby Evans, September 28, 1912, File No. 33278, Pansy Gillette Evans, October 12, 1915, Registrar No. 102, G. W. Evans III, August 1, 1917, File No. 30337; *Albuquerque Journal*, May 4, 6, 1967, October 20, 1988. In 1951, George wrote the book *Slash Ranch Hounds* about his hunting dogs.
76. Bagley, "James B. Gillett, The Man," 5, 6; "Descendants of James Buchanan Gillett," n. pag.; *Albuquerque Tribune*, June 23, 1962; *El Paso Herald-Post*, June 25, 1962; *San Angelo Standard-Times*, July 11, 1988.
77. Bagley, "James B. Gillett, The Man," 5; "Descendants of James Buchanan Gillett," n. pag.; Thompson, *Marfa and Presidio County*, 2: 212;

San Antonio Express, April 26, 1927; Texas Death Certificate, William K. Colquitt, April 21, 1927, Registered No. 489; *Wilmot's Harlingen, Texas, City Directory, 1950* (Harlingen: B. A. Wilmot, 1950), 282; *Corpus Christi Caller-Times*, February 13, 1955; *Odessa American*, November 2, 1973; *San Angelo Standard-Times*, April 21, 1992.

78. Bagley, "James B. Gillett, The Man," 5; Thompson, *Marfa and Presidio County*, 2: 299; Marriage License No. 43668, Marriage Records, Jackson County, Missouri Recorder of Deeds; *El Paso Herald-Post*, March 21, 1940, November 29, 1949; Texas Death Certificate, Milton E. Gillett, January 11, 1950, File No. 62602.

Notes for Chapter 5

1. Dora Neill Raymond, *Captain Lee Hall of Texas* (Norman: University of Oklahoma Press, 1982), 3, 4; Mary Lizzie Hall Adams, *The Hall Family History* (Statesville, NC: n.p., 1949), 318, 337–338; Robert M. Mebane, *History and Genealogy of the Mebane Family of Colonial Pennsylvania and North Carolina* (Alexandria, VA: R. M. Mebane, 1999), 191; Marie L. Hinson, comp., *Marriages of Davidson County, North Carolina: 1822–1880* (Lexington: Genealogical Society of Davidson County, 1992), 89; *Fayetteville Weekly Observer*, January 23, 1849; *Seventh U.S. Census*, Iredell County, North Carolina (Free Schedule); *Eighth U.S. Census*, Guilford County, North Carolina (Free Schedule).

   Dr. Hall died in Greensboro on November 13, 1885. *Greensboro North State*, November 20, 1885. His wife died on August 5, 1913. Both were buried in the First Presbyterian Church Cemetery. *Greensboro Patriot*, August 7, 1913.

2. *Seventh U.S. Census*, Iredell County, North Carolina (Free and Slave Schedules); Adams, *Hall Family History*, 318 (quotation).

3. Raymond, *Captain Lee Hall*, 3–4. Although written in an overly dramatic style, common to the genre at that time, and despite some mistakes, Ms. Raymond's book has remained the authority on Hall's life. One example of an error is that she stated the family moved to the Cotton Grove plantation in Guilford in 1858. In a discussion with Dewey Snider, county genealogist at the Lexington, North Carolina, Public Library, this author discovered the name Cotton Grove belongs to a small village in Davidson County that became a township in 1868. Furthermore, Mr. Snider found no mention of Dr. Hall in county deed

abstracts or the Minutes of the Court of Pleas and Quarter Sessions. Arthur Erickson, genealogy librarian at the Greensboro, North Carolina, Public Library, verified there was no Cotton Grove in Guilford County. Adams, *Hall Family History*, 318; David Stuart, *O. Henry: A Biography of William Sydney Porter* (Chelsea, MI: Scarborough House, 1990), 20; *Greensboro Patriot*, February 4, 1849; *Eighth U.S. Census*, Guilford County, North Carolina (Free and Slave Schedules); CSR-CS, Twenty-second North Carolina Infantry, James K. Hall.

4. Raymond, *Captain Lee Hall*, 5–6; Bill Astoria, "Fighting Lee Hall," *The Junior Historian* 8 (May 1948): 20; Jo White Linn, *First Presbyterian Church, Salisbury, North Carolina, and Its People, 1821–1995* (Salisbury, NC: privately printed, 1996), 19–20.

5. Raymond, *Captain Lee Hall*, 7–8, 11–12; *Ninth U.S. Census*, Grayson County, Texas.

6. Raymond, *Captain Lee Hall*, 13–14; Astoria, "Fighting Lee Hall," 20; Allen G. Hatley, *Texas Constables: A Frontier Heritage* (Lubbock: Texas Tech University Press, 1999), 52–54; Lorie Rubenser and Gloria Priddy, *Constables, Marshals, and More: Forgotten Offices in Teas Law Enforcement* (Denton: University of North Texas Press, 2011), 32; *Galveston Daily News*, July 17, 1872; *Dallas Daily Herald*, January 4, 1873.

7. Raymond, *Captain Lee Hall*, 17–24; Graham Landrum, *Grayson County: An Illustrated History of Grayson County, Texas* (Fort Worth: University Supply & Equipment Company, 1960), 40; *House Journal, Thirteenth Legislature, Regular Session*, 353; Wayne Gard, *Rawhide Texas* (Norman: University of Oklahoma Press, 1965), 168 (first quotation); Jennifer Bridges, "Skiddy Street: Prostitution and Vice in Denison, Texas, 1872–1922" (M.A. thesis, University of North Texas, 2011), 1–2, 19–20; *Sherman Herald Democrat*, October 3, 2009; "The Great South, The New Route to the Gulf," *Scribner's Monthly* 6 (July 1873): 284–285 (second quotation on p. 285); *Denison Daily Cressett*, January 15, 1876; *Denison Weekly News*, January 23, 1873; *Denison Daily News*, April 1 (third quotation), 21, August 3 (fourth quotation), 10, 19, December 2, 1873, February 28, April 21, August 13, September 19, 1874, September 19, 1875; Mollie Stehno, comp., and Jim Fulbright, ed., *Western Lawmen: U.S. Marshals and Their Deputies, 1850–1920* (Goodlettesville, TN: Mid-South Publications, 2015), 201; *Galveston Daily News*, June 10, 1874, October 2, 1875; *Dallas Daily Herald*, March 25, 1876.

8. Raymond, *Captain Lee Hall*, 29, 38–39; Ernest R. Lindley, ed., *Members of the Legislature of the State of Texas from 1846 to 1939* (Austin: State of Texas, 1939), 93; *Galveston Daily News*, April 12, 1876; Robert M. Utley, *Lone Star Justice: The First Century of the Texas Rangers* (New York: Berkley Books, 2002), 169; Petition of July 23, 1876, 401-394, TSLAC; George Durham, as told to Clyde Wantland, "On the Trail of 5100 Outlaws," *West* 40 (March 1935), Pt. 6: 112.
9. Raymond, *Captain Lee Hall*, 39; RSR, J. L. Hall, 401-154, TSLAC. George Durham as told to Clyde Wantland, *Taming the Nueces Strip: The Story of McNelly's Rangers* (Austin: University of Texas Press, 1962), 158. Dudley G. Wooten, ed., *A Comprehensive History of Texas, 1685 to 1897* (Dallas: William G. Scarff, 1898), 2: 352 (quotation).
10. Raymond, *Captain Lee Hall*, 43, 48, 52; Durham, "On the Trail of 5100 Outlaws," Pt. 6: 114.
11. Raymond, *Captain Lee Hall*, 52–54; Hall to Steele, October 4, 1876, 401-394, TSLAC; MR, Special State Troops, October 31, 1876; Chuck Parsons and Gary P. Fitterer, *Captain C. B. McKinney: The Law in South Texas* (Wolfe City, TX: Henington Publishing Company, 1993), 10; Sammy Tise, *Texas County Sheriffs* (Albuquerque: Oakwood Publishing, 1989), 207; Operations of State Troops, 1 (1876–1881), 401-1082, TSLAC: 3; *Victoria Advocate*, August 17, 1876; *Galveston Daily News*, March 22, November 11, 15, 1876.
12. Operations of State Troops, 1: 4; Parsons and Fitterer, *Captain C. B. McKinney*, 12; *Victoria Advocate*, December 2, 1876; *Galveston Daily News*, December 3, 1876; *Daily Democratic Statesman*, December 2, 1876.
13. Raymond, *Captain Lee Hall*, 62–64; Chuck Parsons, "Bill Sutton Avenged: The Death of Jim Taylor," *NOLA Quarterly* 44 (1979): 3–5; *Galveston Daily News*, September 22, October 4, 1876; C. L. Sonnichsen, *I'll Die Before I'll Run: The Story of the Great Feuds of Texas* (Lincoln: University of Nebraska Press, 1988), 98–101, 103; C. L. Douglas, *Famous Texas Feuds* (Austin: State House Press, 1988), 84–85, 88; Durham, *Taming the Nueces Strip*, 164–165. The doctor's name has been spelled as "Brazell" in a variety of sources, but this author has chosen to use the spelling found on the murdered man's gravestone.
14. Raymond, *Captain Lee Hall*, 69–74; Chuck Parsons, *The Sutton-Taylor Feud: The Deadliest Blood Feud in Texas* (Denton: University of North Texas Press, 2009), 234, 235, 239–240, 266; MR, Special State Troops,

December 31, 1876; Frederic Remington, "How the Law Got into the Chaparral," *Crooked Trails* (New York: Harper and Brothers, 1898), 18; Gard, *Rawhide Texas*, 166–167; Hall to Steele, January 4, 1877, 401–395, TSLAC (quotation); Colonel Martin L. Crimmins, "Lee Hall Gets His Men," *Frontier Times* 18 (September 1941): 544–545; Frederick Nolan, *The Wild West: History, Myth and the Making of America* (Edison, NJ: Chartwell Books, 2004), 105; Pat Blackwell, "Judge Henry Clay Pleasants," *The Junior Historian* 16 (May 1956): 18; Beall to Steele, June 5, 1877, 401–1157, TSLAC.

15. *Galveston Daily News*, December 16, 23, 36, 30, 1877; Hall to Steele, June 5, 1877, Hall to Steele, April 17, 1878, 401–1157, TSLAC; 8 *Texas Criminal Reports* 278–279; Parsons and Fitterer, *Captain C. B. McKinney*, 18; Parsons, *The Sutton-Taylor Feud*, 6, 252–253; Sonnichsen, *I'll Die Before I'll Run*, 112–115.

16. Raymond, *Captain Lee Hall*, 81, 91–92, 95; RSR, J. L. Hall, 401–154, TSLAC; Walter P. Webb, *The Texas Rangers: A Century of Frontier Defense* (Austin: University of Texas Press, 1965), 292–293; Operations of State Troops, 1: 10; *Goliad Guard*, May 26, 1877; Galveston *Daily News*, February 2, April 6, 17, June 1, 13, August 2, 1877; Hall to Steele, March 28, 1877, Clarkson and O'Brien to Hubbard, May 26, 1877, Coleman, et. al to Hubbard, May 28, 1877, Threlkeld and Bleberg to Hubbard, n.d., 401–1157, TSLAC; Parsons and Fitterer, *Captain C. B. McKinney*, 17; Astoria, "Fighting Lee Hall," 21.

17. Joseph B. Wilkinson, *Laredo and the Rio Grande Frontier: A Narrative* (Austin: Jenkins Publishing Co., 1975), 331; Michael M. Smith, "General Rafael Benavides and the Texas Border Crisis of 1877," *SHQ* 112 (January 2009): 249–250; William Ray Lewis, "The Hayes Administration and Mexico," ibid. 24 (October 1920): 142–143; Statement of General E. O. C. Ord, December 5, 1877, Testimony of Lieutenant-Colonel William R. Shafter, January 7, 1878, Testimony of Julius G. Tucker, January 26, 1878, *Texas Border Troubles*, House Miscellaneous Document No. 64, 45th Congress, 2nd Session, 89, 111, 157, 262; Testimony of S. H. McNally [sic], January 29, 1876, *Texas Frontier Troubles*, House Report No. 343, 44th Congress, 1st Session, 16, 17; Testimony of Major William R. Price, January 26, 1878, *Relations of the United States with Mexico*, House Report No. 701, 45th Congress, 2nd Session, Pt. 2: 120. *Journal of the Constitutional Convention of the State of Texas, Begun and Held at the City of Austin, September 6, 1875* (Galveston: "News" Office, 1875), 805:

"Mexican officials, civil and military, have been participants in the profits arising from this border war. They have given their sanction to acts of violence and rapine; they have protected perpetrators, and, as far as they could, they have legalized robbery and murder."

18. Shelley Bowen Hatfield, *Chasing Shadows: Indians Along the United States-Mexico Border, 1876–1911* (Albuquerque: University of New Mexico Press, 1998), 23–25; Shafter to Ord, March 9, 1877, Evarts to Foster, March 31, 1877, Secretary of War to Sherman, June 1, 1877, Ogazon to Treviño, June 18, 1877, *Mexican Border Troubles*, House Executive Document No. 13, 45th Congress, 1st Session, 4–5, 14–15 (first quotation on p. 15), 19–20; "Pursuing Raiders into Mexico," *Army and Navy Journal* 15 (May 18, 1878): 666 (second quotation); John W. Foster, *Diplomatic Memoirs* (Boston: Houghton Mifflin Company, 1910), 1: 90 (third quotation). Guy M. Bryan, Confederate officer, Texas legislator and judge, and personal friend of Hayes, advised a similar policy to the president. Ernest William Winkler, ed., "The Bryan-Hayes Correspondence," Pt. 11, *SHQ* 27 (April 1924): 318.

19. Raymond, *Captain Lee Hall*, 88–90; Ovie Clark Fisher with Jeff C. Dykes, *King Fisher: His Life and Times* (Norman: University of Oklahoma Press, 1966), 92–102; Durham, "On the Trail of 5100 Outlaws," Pt. 6: 114; Hall to Steele, May 16, 1877; Transcript of ROS, December 1, 1878, Hall to Jones, September 30, 1879, 401–1157, TSLAC; Parsons and Fitterer, *Captain C. B. McKinney*, 21, 23; *Galveston Daily News*, May 21, 1878; Wilkinson, *Laredo and the Rio Grande Frontier*, 350; Edward A. Blackburn Jr., *Wanted: Historic County Jails of Texas* (College Station: Texas A&M University Press, 2006), 37. For more on Fisher and his violent end, see Charley F. Eckhardt, *Tales of Badmen, Bad Women, and Bad Places: Four Centuries of Texas Outlawry* (Lubbock: Texas Tech University Press, 1999), 110–118.

20. Raymond, *Captain Lee Hall*, 107–108; Operations of State Troops, 1: 13; Parsons and Fitterer, *Captain C. B. McKinney*, 19; *Texas Border Troubles*, 15; Hall to Steele, August 6, 1877, Hall to Steele, August 16, 1877, 401–1157, TSLAC. See also Schofield to Shafter, August 3, 1877, *Mexican Border Troubles*, 214. For more on Arrington, whose real name was John C. Orrick, Jr., see Jerry Sinise, *George Washington Arrington: Civil War Spy, Texas Ranger, Sheriff and Rancher* (Burnet, TX: Eakin Press, 1979).

21. Hubbard to the President, August 13, 1877, Ord to McCrary, August 14, 1877, Ord to Hubbard, August 12, 1877, Marcelli to Hubbard, August 15, 1877, Hubbard to Evarts, October 10, 1877, *Mexican Border Troubles*, 43, 106, 81–82, 77–78; Statement of Brigadier-General E. O. C. Ord, December 7, 1877, Testimony of General William Steele, January 17, 1878, Testimony of Major William R. Price, January 26, 1878, *Relations of the United States with Mexico*, Pt. 2: 9, 50, 116–117, 118; Statement of Lieutenant-General Sheridan, December 12, 1877, *Texas Border Troubles*, 76; Smith, "General Rafael Benavides," 235–236.

22. "Pursuing Raiders into Mexico," 666; Ord to Hubbard, August 24, 1877, *Mexican Border Troubles*, 91; Testimony of Colonel William R. Shafter, January 7, 1878, *Texas Border Troubles*, 163, 164; *Galveston Daily News*, August 14, 1877.

23. Testimony of Major William R. Price, January 26, 1878, *Relations of the United States with Mexico*, Pt. 2: 117–118; Marcelli to Hubbard, August 15, 1877, Hubbard to the President, August 13, 1877, Hubbard to the Governor of Tamaulipas, August 13, 1877, Seward to Hubbard, August 14, 1877, Seward to Foster, August 15, 1877, Foster to Evarts, August 23, 1877, *Mexican Border Troubles*, 83–84, 43–44, 82; *Daily Democratic Statesman*, August 28, 1877; *San Antonio Daily Express*, August 15, 1877; Smith, "General Rafael Benavides," 243–244. The treaty between the United States and Mexico for the extradition of criminals was ratified on May 20, 1862, and proclaimed by President Abraham Lincoln exactly one month later. *The Statutes at Large, Treaties, and Proclamations of the United States*, 12: 1199–1203. According to General Ord, in the twelve years since the war ended, no Mexican who had committed a crime in Texas and fled to Mexico had been punished or extradited by Mexican authorities. Statement of Brigadier-General E. O. C. Ord, December 13, 1877, *Relations of the United States with Mexico*, Pt. 2: 13.

24. Raymond, *Captain Lee Hall*, 115; Smith, "General Rafael Benavides," 245; Testimony of John S. Ford, January 24, 1878, *Relations of the United States with Mexico*, Pt. 2: 68; Testimony of Julius G. Tucker, January 26, 1878, *Texas Border Troubles*, 231; *Galveston Daily News*, August 17, 1877.

25. Raymond, *Captain Lee Hall*, 116–117; Operations of State Troops, 1: 13; Hall to Hubbard, August 22, 1877, *Mexican Border Troubles*, 86; *Daily Democratic Statesman*, August 28, 1877; Statement of Brigadier-General E. O. C. Ord, December 7, 1877, Testimony of General William

Endnotes **567**

Steele, January 17, 1878, *Relations of the United States with Mexico*, Pt. 2: 9, 50–51; Smith, "General Rafael Benavides," 244.
26. Raymond, *Captain Lee Hall*, 117–120; Hall to Hubbard, August 25, 1877, *Mexican Border Troubles*, 92; Sheridan to Townsend, August 24, 1877, Ord to Hubbard, August 24, 1877, Hubbard to Hall, August 24, 1877, *Mexican Border Troubles*, 223–224, 91; *Galveston Daily News*, August 24, 28, 1877.
27. Raymond, *Captain Lee Hall*, 121–122; Hall to Steele, September 10, 1877, 401–1157, TSLAC; Russell to Hubbard, September 12, 1877, Hall to Steele, September 11, 1877, Sheridan to Townsend, September 12, 1877, Hubbard to Evarts, October 10, 1877, *Mexican Border Troubles*, 94, 114, 79. Servando Canales was the son of Antonio Canales, an influential and reviled figure along the border in the 1840s and 1850s.
28. Hall to Steele, September 27, 1877, Hall to Steele, September 29, 1877, 401–1157, TSLAC; Russell to Hubbard, October 3, 1877, *Relations of the United States with Mexico*, Pt. 1: 339; Hubbard to Evarts, October 10, 1877, *Mexican Border Troubles*, 79; *Galveston Daily News*, November 10, 1877.
29. Report of Brigadier-General E. O. C. Ord, October 1, 1879, *Annual Report of the Secretary of War*, House Executive Document No. 1, Pt. 2, 46th Congress, 2nd Session, 93; General Orders No. 4, March 8, 1880, *Army and Navy Journal* 17 (March 27, 1880): 683; Robert Wooster, *The Military and United States Indian Policy, 1865–1903* (Lincoln: University of Nebraska Press, 1995), 95.
30. Raymond, *Captain Lee Hall*, 150, 152; Hall to Steele, November 23, 1877, 401–1157, TSLAC; RSR, J. L. Hall, 401–154, TSLAC; Rick Miller, *Sam Bass and Gang* (Austin: State House Press, 1999), 112–113; Tise, *Texas County Sheriffs*, 213; Hall to Steele, December 7, 1877, 401–1157, TSLAC.
31. Raymond, *Captain Lee Hall*, 152–154; Hall to Steele, December 18, 1877, 401–1157, TSLAC; *Galveston Daily News*, December 19, 1877, February 24, 1878; *Dallas Daily Herald*, December 29, 1877, January 29, February 23, 28, 1878; Miller, *Sam Bass*, 131.
32. *Galveston Daily News*, February 26, 27, March 2, 1878; Operations of State Troops, 1: 15; Mackay to Steele, March 1, 1878, 401–1157, TSLAC.
33. Miller, *Sam Bass*, 170–171; Eckhardt, *Badmen, Bad Women, and Bad Places*, 96, 98; "Authentic History of Sam Bass and His Gang, by a Citizen of Denton County," Pt. 2, *Frontier Times* 3 (March 1926): 32;

Dallas Daily Herald, April 6, 12, 13, 1878; *San Antonio Semi-Weekly Express,* September 13, 1895.
34. Raymond, *Captain Lee Hall,* 160; *Galveston Daily News,* July 18, 23, 1878; Stuart N. Lake, "Brush Poppers," *The Saturday Evening Post* 203 (April 11, 1931), 144; *San Antonio Semi-Weekly Express,* September 13, 1895.
35. Raymond, *Captain Lee Hall,* 161–164; James L. Haley, *Passionate Nation: The Epic History of Texas* (New York: Simon and Schuster, 2006), 411; *San Antonio Semi-Weekly Express,* September 13, 1895; *Galveston Daily News,* July 21, 24, 1878; *El Paso Herald,* August 9, 1902.
36. Raymond, *Captain Lee Hall,* 170, 172; MR, Special State Troops, October 31, 1878, December 1, 1878; *RAG, 1878,* 30, 45; *Daily Democratic Statesman,* October 19, 1878; *Galveston Daily News,* October 23, 24, December 24, 1878.
37. Raymond, *Captain Lee Hall,* 173; Special Order No. 72, December 21, 1878, 401–1012, TSLAC; *Galveston Daily News,* January 1, 1879; *Daily Democratic Statesman,* January 15, 1879; Patsy McDonald Spaw, ed., *The Texas Senate* (College Station: Texas A&M University Press, 1999), 2: 268 (quotation).
38. Message of the Governor, January 14, 1879, *House Journal, Sixteenth Legislature, First Session,* 32–33.
39. Hans Peter Nielson Gammel, comp., *The Laws of Texas, 1822–1897* (Austin: The Gammel Book Company, 1898), 8: 1430–1431.
40. *Galveston Daily News,* May 8, 1879; *House Journal, Sixteenth Legislature, Extra Session,* 366; *San Antonio Daily Express,* August 1, 1879; Hall to Jones, July 16, 1879, 401–1157, TSLAC.
41. Raymond, *Captain Lee Hall,* 176–177; Special Order No. 25, August 1, 1879, 401–1012, TSLAC; RSR, J. L. Hall, 401–154, Thomas Oglesby, 166, TSLAC; *RAG, 1880,* 27–28; *Galveston Daily News,* August 13, 1879; Oglesby to Jones, September 30, 1879, 401–1157, TSLAC.
42. Hall to Jones, October 21, 1879, Hall to Jones, October 29, 1879, 401–1157, TSLAC; *Galveston Daily News,* October 17, 1879; *San Antonio Daily Express,* November 1, 18, 1879.
43. Raymond, *Captain Lee Hall,* 182–183; Hall to Jones, November 5, 1879, 401–1157, TSLAC; Operations of State Troops, 1: 24; MR, Special State Troops, November 30, 1879; *Galveston Daily News,* October 8, 1879; *San Antonio Daily Express,* November 7, 8, 1879; Cyril Leone Patterson, *Atascosa County, Texas: A Progressive and Diversified Agricultural and Livestock Haven* (Pleasanton, TX: Pleasanton Express, 1938), 5–6, 8.

44. Raymond, *Captain Lee Hall*, 187–189; RSR, J. L. Hall, 401–154, TSLAC; Hall to Jones, May 24, 1880, 401–399, Special Order No. 58, May 26, 1880, 401–1012, TSLAC; TSLAC; *Galveston Daily News*, May 1, 1880; *Daily Democratic Statesman*, May 27, 1880. Captain Halter was an officer in the U.S. Coast and Geodetic Survey.
45. Raymond, *Captain Lee Hall*, 183; *Galveston Daily News*, March 5, 6 (quotation), 7, 10, 1880; *Dallas Daily Herald*, March 7, 9, 1880; *National Police Gazette*, March 20, 1880.
46. Raymond, *Captain Lee Hall*, 189; *Galveston Daily News*, May 9, July 23, 29, August 25, October 7, 8, 1880; Hall to Jones, October 19, 1880, 401–1157, TSLAC.
47. *Galveston Daily News*, November 10, 1880, January 4, June 22, December 21, 1881; *Lebanon Daily News*, November 26, 1880; Tax Rolls, La Salle County, 1881.
48. San Patricio Scrip, La Salle and McMullen Counties, File No. 1805, Bexar Donation, La Salle County, File No. 2313, Bexar Scrip, La Salle County, File No. 43807, TGLO; Tax Rolls, La Salle County, 1882–1885; *Galveston Daily News*, June 9, 1882.
49. Raymond, *Captain Lee Hall*, 190–191, 193–196, 198, 206, 217; La Salle County Historical Commission, *La Salle County* (Charleston, SC: Arcadia Publishing, 2010), 7, 9; *Harrisburg Telegraph*, August 24, 1902, April 9, 1914; *Norton's Daily Union Intelligencer*, May 19, 1883; Parsons and Fitterer, *Captain C. B. McKinney*, 55; San Patricio Scrip, McMullen County, File No. 2373, TGLO; Stanley D. Casto, *Settlement of the Cibolo-Nueces Strip: A Partial History of La Salle County* (Hillsboro, TX: Hill Junior College Press, 1969), 10, 14; *Galveston Daily News*, June 15, July 16, 1882, January 27, November 28, 1884, February 22, 23, 1885; *Dallas Daily Herald*, May 5, June 6, 1883; *San Antonio Light*, January 28, 1884; J. Frank Dobie and John D. Young, *A Vaquero of the Brush Country: The Life and Times of John D. Young* (Austin: University of Austin Press, 1998), 84; Stuart, *O. Henry*, 32–33; Adams, *Hall Family History*, 337, 361; Tax Rolls, La Salle County, 1882; Record of Appointment of Postmaster 55, roll 125, M841, RG 28, 494–495.
50. Raymond, *Captain Lee Hall*, 193, 201–206; Tax Rolls, La Salle County, 1882; Stuart, *O. Henry*, 31, 32; Charles Alphonso Smith, *O. Henry Biography* (Garden City, NY: Doubleday, Page and Company, 1916), 93–94, 95, 98, 99; Mike Cox, *Texas Ranger Tales: Stories That Need Telling* (Plano: Republic of Texas Press, 1997), 81–86; Hyder Rollins,

"O. Henry's Texas Days," *The Bookman: A Magazine of Literature and Life* 40 (October 1941): 154–158. For examples of Western influences on Porter's work, see O. Henry, *Heart of the West* (Garden City, NY: Doubleday, Page and Company, 1920), 187–204.

51. Raymond, *Captain Lee Hall*, 218, 223; *Austin Daily Statesman*, May 15, 1884; *San Antonio Light*, May 11, 28, 29, 1885; *Galveston Daily News*, March 26, 1885. The Dull brothers sold their ranch lands to Brazilla L. Naylor and Augustus Harris Jones, Jr., both of San Antonio, in 1901. *San Antonio Express*, April 8, 1913.

52. Raymond, *Captain Lee Hall*, 224; *Galveston Daily News*, July 31, 1885; *Dallas Daily Herald*, August 29, 1885; William T. Hagan, *United States-Comanche Relations: The Reservation Years* (Norman: University of Oklahoma Press, 1990), 168; Annual Report of J. Lee Hall, August 26, 1886, *Annual Report of the Commissioner of Indian Affairs*, House Executive Document No. 1, 49th Congress, 2nd Session, 345. Hereafter cited as *Annual Report of the Commissioner of Indian Affairs, 1886*. J. J. Methvin, *In the Limelight, or History of Anadarko [Caddo County] and Vicinity from the Earliest Days* (Anadarko, OK: Plummer, 1928), 51–53; David La Vere, *Contrary Neighbors: Southern Plains and Removed Indians in Indian Territory* (Norman: University of Oklahoma Press, 2000), 205.

53. F. Todd Smith, *The Caddos, the Wichitas, and the United States, 1846–1901* (College Station: Texas A&M University Press, 1996), 116–118; *Dallas Morning News*, December 31, 1885; Wilbur Sturtevant Nye, *Carbine and Lance: The Story of Old Fort Sill* (Norman: University of Oklahoma Press, 1969), 255.

54. Pekka Hämäläinen, *The Comanche Empire* (New Haven: Yale University Press, 2008), 341; David La Vere, *The Texas Indians* (College Station: Texas A&M University Press, 2004), 217; Morris W. Foster, *Being Comanche: A Social History of an American Indian Community* (Tucson: University of Arizona Press, 1991), 67–69, 80–81, 83, 85, 88–89; *Dallas Morning News*, December 31, 1885; Bill Neal, *From Guns to Gavel: How Justice Grew Up in the Outlaw West* (Lubbock; Texas Tech University Press, 2008), 114; Bill Neeley, *The Last Comanche Chief: The Life and Times of Quanah Parker* (New York: John Wiley & Sons, 1995), 173, 178–196; William T. Hagan, *Quanah Parker, Comanche Chief* (Norman: University of Oklahoma Press, 1993), 36, 32; Lewis Nordyke, *Great Roundup: The Story of Texas and Southwestern Cowmen* (New York: William Morrow and Company, 1955), 198.

Endnotes 571

55. Raymond, *Captain Lee Hall*, 234–235; Foster, *Being Comanche*, 80; Hagan, *Quanah Parker*, 29–30; Nye, *Carbine and Lance*, 259–260; *Fort Worth Daily Gazette*, September 25, 1885; *Galveston Daily News*, September 24, 27, 1885.
56. Raymond, *Captain Lee Hall*, 235, 237; Adams, *Hall Family History*, 337; Methvin, *In the Limelight*, 50.
57. Hagan, *United States-Comanche Relations*, 184, 192, 193; Methvin, *In the Limelight*; 50–51; La Vere, *The Texas Indians*, 217; Foster, *Being Comanche*, 81, 92–95; Annual Report of J. Lee Hall, August 26, 1886, *Annual Report of the Commissioner of Indian Affairs, 1886*, 348; Thomas Constantine Maroukis, *The Peyote Road: Religious Freedom and the Native American Church* (Norman: University of Oklahoma Press, 2010), 32, 25–27.
58. Hagan, *United States-Comanche Relations*, 195–196, 199–200.
59. *Official Opinions of the Attorneys-General of the United States* 20, House Miscellaneous Document No. 44, 53rd Congress, 3rd Session, 561–566 (quotation on p. 566). For Hall's accounts for the fiscal year ending June 30, 1887, see *Letter from the Treasurer of the United States*, House Executive Document No. 15, 50th Congress, 1st Session, 10, 49, 269, 437, 463, 824, 968.
60. Hagan, *Quanah Parker*, 62–63; La Vere, *The Texas Indians*, 220–221; La Vere, *Contrary Neighbors*, 219; Smith, *Caddos, Wichitas, United States*, 146–151; William T. Hagan, *Taking Indian Lands: The Cherokee (Jerome) Commission, 1889–1893* (Norman: University of Oklahoma Press, 2003), 198–203; Francis Paul Prucha, *American Indian Treaties: The History of a Political Anomaly* (Berkeley: University of California Press, 1994), 356, 512; Stanley Noyes and Daniel J. Gelo, *Comanches in the New West, 1895–1908* (Austin: University of Texas Press, 1999), 21–22. See also Blue Clark, *Lone Wolf v. Hitchcock: Treaty Rights and Indian Law at the End of the Nineteenth Century* (Lincoln: University of Nebraska Press, 1999).
61. Lee Irwin, *Native American Spirituality: A Critical Reader* (Lincoln: University of Nebraska Press, 2000), 245; Methvin, *In the Limelight*, 65–66; Hagan, *Quanah Parker*, 41–42; Report of Brigadier-General Wesley Merritt, August 26, 1887, *Annual Report of the Secretary of War*, House Executive Document No. 1, Pt. 2, 50th Congress, 1st Session, 149–150; *Fort Worth Daily Gazette*, April 24, 25, 29, 1887; Returns from U.S. Military Posts, 1800–1916, Fort Sill, March-May 1887, M617, NARA. Hereafter cited as Post Returns.

62. Hagan, *United States-Comanche Relations*, 175; *Fort Worth Daily Gazette*, February 23, 1887; C. C. Painter, *The Condition of Affairs in Indian Territory and California* (Philadelphia: Office of the Indian Rights Association, 1888), 36.
63. Painter, *Condition of Affairs*, 37.
64. Ibid., 44.
65. Raymond, *Captain Lee Hall*, 252–255; Annual Report of J. Lee Hall, n.d., *Annual Report of the Commissioner of Indian Affairs*, House Executive Document No. 1, 50th Congress, 1st Session, 162; Hagan, *United States-Comanche Relations*, 168; Smith, *Caddos, Wichitas, United States*, 119; *Fort Worth Daily Gazette*, October 16, 17, 21, December 9, 1887; *Galveston Daily News*, August 9, 1887.
66. Raymond, *Captain Lee Hall*, 256, 258; Marcum to the Secretary of the Interior, October 18, 1887, *Petition from E. E. White*, Senate Miscellaneous Document No. 203, 53rd Congress, 2nd Session, 1; Hagan, *United States-Comanche Relations*, 168–169; Smith, *Caddos, Wichitas, United States*, 119.
67. Raymond, *Captain Lee Hall*, 256, 262; *Fort Worth Daily Gazette*, February 25, April 22, 1888, July 16, 1889, March 14, 19, 20, 1890; *Galveston Daily News*, February 24, 25, April 22, 1888, May 6, August 23, 1893; Adams, *Hall Family History*, 337.
68. Raymond, *Captain Lee Hall*, 258; *Galveston Daily News*, October 21, 24, 1891, December 28, 1892.
69. Raymond, *Captain Lee Hall*, 262; *San Antonio Daily Express*, January 5, 14, 1892; *Galveston Daily News*, January 5, 7, 1892; *Austin Daily Statesman*, January 5, 1892.
70. Raymond, *Captain Lee Hall*, 263–264; *Twelfth U.S Census*, Lebanon County, Pennsylvania.
71. Raymond, *Captain Lee Hall*, 265–266, 268–271; *San Antonio Daily Light*, April 23, 25, 28, 1898. On April 22, 1898, Congress enacted a bill that temporarily increased the military establishment into a Regular Army and a Volunteer Army. *The Statutes at Large of the United States*, 30: 361.
72. Raymond, *Captain Lee Hall*, 275; James M. McCaffrey, "The Texas Immunes in the Spanish-American War," *Texans and War: New Interpretations of the State's Military History*, ed. Alexander Mendoza and Charles David Grear (College Station: Texas A&M University Press, 2012), 214; *Evening Star*, April 29, May 20, June 2, July 24, 1898; Organization Index to Pension Files of Veterans Who Served Between

Endnotes **573**

1861 and 1900, T289, RG 15, NARA; *Annual Reports of the War Department*, House Executive Document No. 2, 56th Congress, 2nd Session, 1, Pt. 2.: 92. Hereafter cited as *Annual Reports of the War Department, 1900*, all references are to Volume 1.

73. Raymond, *Captain Lee Hall*, 277–278; McCaffrey, "The Texas Immunes," 216; *Galveston Daily News*, June 9, 1898; *Houston Daily Post*, June 16, 1898; Adjutant General's Office, *Official Register of Officers of Volunteers in the Service of the United States*, War Department Document No. 117, 63.

74. Raymond, *Captain Lee Hall*, 278; Corbin to Shafter, July 13, 1898, *Correspondence Relating to the War with Spain* (Washington: Government Printing Office, 1902), 1: 138; *Evening Star*, July 19, 20, August 1, 11, 1898; *New Orleans Daily Picayune*, July 14, 24, 26, 28, 1898.

75. Raymond, *Captain Lee Hall*, 280–294; Corbin to Shafter, August 1, 1898, *Correspondence Relating to the War with Spain*, 1: 191; *New Orleans Daily Picayune*, July 28, 30, 31, August 6, 7, 9, 11, 16, 18, 19, 21, 22, 1898; *Evening Star*, August 20, October 14, 1898; *Annual Reports of the War Department, 1900*, Pt. 2: 92; Organization Index to Pension Files of Veterans, NARA; Max Boot, *The Savage Wars of Peace: Small Wars and the Rise of American Power* (New York: Basic Books, 2002), 106.

76. Brian McAllister Linn, *The Philippine War, 1899–1902* (Lawrence: University Press of Kansas, 2000), 42–55; Boot, *Savage Wars of Peace*, 108–109; Benjamin R. Beede, ed., *The War of 1898 and U.S. Interventions, 1898–1934: An Encyclopedia* (New York: Garland Publishing, 1994), 268, 425; General Orders No. 36, March 4, 1899, *Annual Reports of the War Department*, House Executive Document No. 2, I, Pt. 2, 56th Congress, 1st Session, 57–60. Hereafter cited as *Annual Reports of the War Department, 1899*.

77. Raymond, *Captain Lee Hall*, 297–298; Carded Records Showing Military Service of Soldiers Who Fought in Volunteer Organizations During the Philippine Insurrection, 1899–1927, Thirty-third Regiment, U.S. Volunteer Infantry, Jesse Lee Hall. Hereafter cited as Carded Records … Philippine Insurrection. *Galveston Daily News*, August 8, 1899.

78. Raymond, *Captain Lee Hall*, 299; Brian McAllister Linn, "The Thirty-third Infantry, United States Volunteers: An American Regiment in the Philippine Insurrection, 1899–1901" (M.A. thesis, Ohio State University, 1981), 22, 24; *Army and Navy Journal* 37 (August 19, 1899):

1211, (September 9, 1899): 29; Post Returns, Fort Clark, September 1899, Presidio of San Francisco, September 1899, NARA. For more on Colonel Hare, see Ray Meketa, *Luther Rector Hare, A Texan with Custer: A Biography of an American Hero* (Mattituck, NY: J. M. Carroll, 1983).

79. Raymond, *Captain Lee Hall*, 302; Shafter to Adjutant-General, October 1, 1899, Otis to Agwar, October 27, 1899, *Correspondence Relating to the War with Spain*, 2: 1077, 1090; Linn, "Thirty-third Infantry," 25–26; *Army and Navy Journal* 38 (October 7, 1899): 128; Carded Records ... Philippine Insurrection, Thirty-third Regiment, Jesse Lee Hall.

80. Boot, *Savage Wars of Peace*, 110; Brian McAllister Linn, *The U.S. Army and Counterinsurgency in the Philippine War, 1899–1902* (Chapel Hill: University of North Carolina Press, 1989), 12–13, 14; James H. Blount, *The American Occupation of the Philippines, 1898–1912* (New York: G. P. Putnam's Sons, 1913), 233–234; Major Allan D. Marple, "The Philippine Scouts: A Case Study in the Use of Indigenous Soldiers, Northern Luzon, The Philippine Islands, 1899" (MMAS thesis, Fort Leavenworth, 1983), 5, 104; Beede, ed., *The War of 1898*, 268.

81. Lawton to Schwan, October 18, 1899, Report of First Lieutenant Matthew A. Batson, March 29, 1900, *Annual Reports of the War Department, 1900*, Pt. 4: 41, Pt. 5: 123–125, 129; Marple, "The Philippine Scouts," 5–6, 68, 73; Linn, *U.S. Army and Counterinsurgency*, 17; Beede, ed., *The War of 1898*, 273; Captain Ben H. Chastaine, "Macabebes," *Infantry Journal* 36 (June 1930): 626–27; Captain J. N. Munro, "The Philippine Native Scouts," *Journal of the United States Infantry Association* 2 (July 1, 1905): 180. Perhaps reminded of the Apache scouts he had known in Arizona, Lawton was appreciative of the Macabebes who assisted the U.S. Army in the Philippines: "Macabebe scouts doing excellent services and are proving model soldiers for this service. They are worth twice their number of our inexperienced men." Brigadier-General Frederick Funston, commanding the Macabebes who captured Aguinaldo in 1901, called them "fine little fighters." *Memories of Two Wars: Cuban and Philippine Experiences* (Lincoln: University of Nebraska Press, 2009), 385–418. See also Otis to Agwar, September 29, 1899, *Correspondence Relating to the War with Spain*, 2: 1076.

82. Raymond, *Captain Lee Hall*, 302–303; Starr to Edwards, October 26, 1899, *Annual Reports of the War Department, 1900*, Pt. 4: 79 (quotation);

Edwards to Starr, October 28, 1899, French to Edwards, October 29, 1899, Edwards to Hall, October 29, 1899, Special Orders No. 161, October 30, 1899, Carded Records ... Philippine Insurrection, Thirty-third Regiment, Jesse Lee Hall.

83. The confusion was recorded in two telegrams Edwards sent Hall on October 30. Carded Records ... Philippine Insurrection, Thirty-third Regiment, Jesse Lee Hall. Blount, *American Occupation of the Philippines*, 237–238, 249; Report of Lieutenant Colonel James Parker, December 7, 1899, *Annual Reports of the War Department, 1900*, Pt. 5: 140.

84. Charles R. Howland, "The Philippine Expedition of 1899," *Infantry Journal* 30 (April 1927): 404–05; Edwards to Young, September 18, 1899, Report of Brigadier-General S. B. M. Young, January 6, 1900, Field Orders No. 7, November 6, 1899, *Annual Reports of the War Department, 1900*, Pt. 4: 289, 263–271, 273; David J. Silbey, *A War of Frontier and Empire: The Philippine-American War, 1899–1902* (New York: Hill and Wang, 2007), 117–118; Linn, *U.S. Army and Counterinsurgency*, 69; Beede, ed., *The War of 1898*, 607–608. For a brief biographical sketch of Young, who would become the first army chief of staff in 1903, see William Gardner Bell, *Commanding Generals and Chiefs of Staff, 1775–2005* (Washington, D.C.: U.S. Army Center of Military History, 2005), 96.

85. Report of Brigadier-General S. B. M. Young, January 6, 1900, *Annual Reports of the War Department, 1900*, Pt. 4: 274; Dennis Edward Flake, *Loyal Macabebes: How the Americans Used the Macabebe Scouts in the Annexation of the Philippines* (Angeles City, PI: Juan D. Nepomuceno Center for Kapampangan Studies, Holy Angel University, 2009), 48–49.

86. Raymond, *Captain Lee Hall*, 305; Batson to Parker, November 2, 1899, Report of First Lieutenant Matthew A. Batson, March 29, 1900, *Annual Reports of the War Department, 1900*, Pt. 4: 126–127, Pt. 5: 132–133, 135. Hall was misidentified in Batson's narrative as J. D. Hall, Second Lieutenant, Twenty-first Infantry. See also *Official Register of Officers of Volunteers*, 52, 134; and Otis to Adjutant-General, November 3, 1899, *Correspondence Relating to the War with Spain*, 2: 1093.

87. Raymond, *Captain Lee Hall*, 309; Report of Brigadier-General S. B. M. Young, January 6, 1900, Report of First Lieutenant Matthew A. Batson, March 29, 1900, *Annual Reports of the War Department, 1900*, Pt. 4: 274–275, Pt. 5: 134–135.

88. Report of Brigadier-General S. B. M. Young, January 6, 1900, Report of First Lieutenant Matthew A. Batson, March 29, 1900, *Annual Reports of the War Department, 1900*, Pt. 4: 276–278, Pt. 5: 135.
89. Michael E. Shay, *Henry Ware Lawton: Union Infantryman, Frontier Soldier, Charismatic Warrior* (Columbia: University of Missouri Press, 2016), 220; Report of Brigadier-General S. B. M. Young, January 6, 1900, Young to Otis, November 17, 1899, *Annual Reports of the War Department, 1900*, Pt. 4: 278–279, 161 (quotation); Linn, *U.S. Army and Counterinsurgency*, 69; Boot, *Savage Wars of Peace*, 110–111; Marple, "The Philippine Scouts," 64–65.
90. Linn, *U.S. Army and Counterinsurgency*, 16–17, 20–21, 166; Boot, *Savage Wars of Peace*, 112–113; Beede, ed., *The War of 1898*, 269, 425–426; Silbey, *A War of Frontier and Empire*, 129. The American pacification programs on Luzon met with mixed results, often depending on the regional district and the commander in question. For more on the Army's efforts, see Robert D. Ramsey III, *Savage Wars of Peace: Case Studies of Pacification in the Philippines, 1899–1902* (Fort Leavenworth: Combat Studies Institute Press, 2007).
91. Raymond, *Captain Lee Hall*, 310; Chastaine, "Macabebes," 626, 629; Report of Brigadier-General S. B. M. Young, January 6, 1900, Young to Lawton, November 19, 1899, Report of First Lieutenant Matthew A. Batson, March 29, 1900, *Annual Reports of the War Department, 1900*, Pt. 4: 279, 318; Pt. 5: 136–137; Flake, *Loyal Macabebes*, 51, 53.
92. Raymond, *Captain Lee Hall*, 311–312; Report of Brigadier-General S. B. M. Young, January 6, 1900, *Annual Reports of the War Department, 1900*, Pt. 4: 280–281.
93. Raymond, *Captain Lee Hall*, 312–313; Report of Brigadier-General S. B. M. Young, January 6, 1900, Young to Schwan and Lawton, December 6, 1899, Parker to Lawton, December 7, 1899, Lawton to Chief of Staff, Manila, December 7, 1899, *Annual Reports of the War Department, 1900*, Pt. 4: 281, 230–231; Otis to Adjutant-General, December 7, 1899, *Correspondence Relating to the War with Spain*, 2: 1115; Chastaine, "Macabebes," 629.
94. Raymond, *Captain Lee Hall*, 315–316; Report of Major Peyton C. March, December 8, 1899, *Annual Reports of the War Department, 1900*, Pt. 4: 330–332 (quotation on p. 332); Silbey, *A War of Frontier and Empire*, 124; Carded Records … Philippine Insurrection, Thirty-third Regiment, Jesse Lee Hall. Peyton March served as army chief of staff from 1918 to 1921. For more, see Edward M. Coffman, *The Hilt of the Sword:*

The Career of Peyton C. March (Madison: University of Wisconsin Press, 1966).
95. Shay, *Henry Ware Lawton*, 222–223; Special Orders No. 4, January 4, 1900, *Annual Reports of the War Department, 1900*, Pt. 3: 415; Beede, ed., *The War of 1898*, 41.
96. Raymond, *Captain Lee Hall*, 319–320; Glenn Anthony May, *Battle for Batangas: A Philippine Province at War* (New Haven: Yale University Press, 1991), 95–96; Blount, *American Occupation of the Philippines*, 260–261, 262; Report of Brigadier-General Theodore Schwan, February 8, 1900, Report of First Lieutenant William C. Geiger, n.d., General Orders No. 2, January 4, 1900, Exhibit B, n.d., Field Orders No. 1, January 3, 1900, *Annual Reports of the War Department, 1900*, Pt. 3: 387, 546–547, 415–416.
97. Raymond, *Captain Lee Hall*, 320–321; Report of First Lieutenant William C. Geiger, n.d., Report of Brigadier-General Theodore Schwan, February 8, 1900, *Annual Reports of the War Department, 1900*, Pt. 3: 546, 389–391; May, *Battle for Batangas*, 101–102.
98. Report of Brigadier-General Theodore Schwan, February 8, 1900, Report of First Lieutenant William C. Geiger, n.d., *Annual Reports of the War Department, 1900*, Pt. 3: 391, 546; May, *Battle for Batangas*, 102.
99. Raymond, *Captain Lee Hall*, 321–322; Report of First Lieutenant J. Lee Hall, n.d., Report of Brigadier-General Theodore Schwan, February 8, 1900, *Annual Reports of the War Department, 1900*, Pt. 3: 547, 393.
100. Raymond, *Captain Lee Hall*, 322; Report of First Lieutenant J. Lee Hall, n.d., Report of Major Thomas L. Hartigan, February 21, 1900, *Annual Reports of the War Department, 1900*, Pt. 3: 547, 512.
101. Raymond, *Captain Lee Hall*, 322–322; Report of First Lieutenant William C. Geiger, n.d., Report of Brigadier-General Theodore Schwan, February 8, 1900, *Annual Reports of the War Department, 1900*, Pt. 3: 546–547, 396–397; Otis to Adjutant-General, January 25, 1900, *Correspondence Relating to the War with Spain*, 2: 1138–1139; May, *Battle for Batangas*, 122–123.
102. Raymond, *Captain Lee Hall*, 323; Report of First Lieutenant William C. Geiger, n.d., Report of Brigadier-General Theodore Schwan, February 8, 1900, *Annual Reports of the War Department, 1900*, Pt. 3: 546–547, 396–397, 414 (quotation).
103. Report of Brigadier-General Theodore Schwan, February 8, 1900, Sturgis to Commanding Officer, Santa Cruz, February 8, 1900, *Annual Reports of the War Department, 1900*, Pt. 3: 412 (quotation), 497.

104. Raymond, *Captain Lee Hall*, 324–326; Charles Pelot Summerall, *The Way of Duty, Honor, Country: The Memoirs of Charles Pelot Summerall*, ed. Timothy K. Nenninger (Lexington: University Press of Kentucky, 2010), 47. Summerall served a total of thirty-eight years and retired as army chief of staff in 1930. Miscellaneous Correspondence, Special Orders No. 47, June 8, 1900, Special Orders No. 59, June 9, 1900, Carded Records ... Philippine Insurrection, Thirty-third Regiment, Jesse Lee Hall.
105. Raymond, *Captain Lee Hall*, 326–327; Miscellaneous Correspondence, Special Orders No. 40, Special Orders No. 77, June 30, 1900, Special Orders No. 22, September 20, 1900, General Orders No. 226, September 26, 1900, Carded Records ... Philippine Insurrection, Thirty-third Regiment, Jesse Lee Hall; Organization Index to Pension Files of Veterans, NARA.
106. Raymond, *Captain Hall*, 327; *Lebanon Daily News*, March 31, 1900. This author was provided a copy of Mrs. Weidman's will, written on December 4, 1899, and recorded on April 5, 1900, courtesy of Dawn L. Resanovich, Register of Wills and Clerk of Orphans' Court of Lebanon County, Pennsylvania.
107. Raymond, *Captain Lee Hall*, 331–332; *El Paso Daily Herald*, October 5, 1900; *Evening Star*, May 15, 1902; Beede, *The War of 1898*, 117; Christopher J. Einolf, *America in the Philippines, 1899–1902: The First Torture Scandal* (New York: Palgrave Macmillan, 2014), 58, 144; Testimony of Jesse Lee Hall, *Affairs in the Philippines*, Senate Document No. 331, Pt. 3, 57th Congress, 1st Session, 2428–2440. Andrew J. Birtle, *U.S. Army Counterinsurgency and Contigency Operations Doctrine, 1860–1941* (Washington, D.C.: U.S. Army Center of Military History, 2004), 132: "Only a small percentage of all Filipinos taken prisoner or interrogated by the U.S. Army underwent any form of physical or mental abuse. On the other hand, practices such as forcing large quantities of water down the throats of uncooperative natives ('the water cure'), hanging suspects by ropes ('the rope cure'), denying prisoners food or water, penning prisoners in overcrowded cells, and administering dunkings and beatings occurred more frequently than American authorities cared to admit."
108. Raymond, *Captain Lee Hall*, 332–333.
109. Ibid., 333–335; *Mohave County Miner*, May 8, 1906; *Bisbee Daily Review*, March 18, April 20, June 17, 1906; *Arizona Republic*, April 16, 25, 1906; *Galveston Daily News*, May 18, 31, 1906; *San Antonio Daily Light*, May 23 (quotation), 30, 31, 1906.

Endnotes

110. *Galveston Daily News*, April 17, 1907; *San Antonio Daily Express*, April 15, 1907.
111. Raymond, *Captain Lee Hall*, 336.
112. Ibid., 337, 340; Texas Death Certificate, Jesse Lee Hall, March 18, 1911, Registrar No. 4876.
113. *Thirteenth U.S. Census*, Lebanon County, Pennsylvania; *Lebanon Semi-Weekly News*, October 14, 1926; Virginia Death Certificate, Bessie Weidman Hall, Registration No. 23616.
114. Adams, *Hall Family History*, 361; Marriage License No. 9366, Lebanon County Marriage Records 17 (1906–1907), Lebanon County Register of Wills and Orphans' Court Clerk; *Lebanon Daily News*, October 25, 1906; *Fourteenth* and *Fifteenth U.S. Census*, Fauquier County, Virginia; *Fauquier Democrat*, September 16, 1936, April 4, 1946, September 4, 1958; Helena LeFroy Caperton, *The Social Record of Virginia* (Richmond: The Social Record of Virginia, 1937), 129; *New York Times*, March 31, 1946.
115. *Thirteenth U.S. Census*, Lebanon County, Pennsylvania; *Charleston Daily Mail*, April 22, 1928; *Lebanon Semi-Weekly News*, May 3, 1928; *Sixteenth U.S. Census*, Ohio County, West Virginia; *Charleston Gazette*, October 9, 1951; Pennsylvania Death Certificates, Albert Coudon Whitaker, October 7, 1951, Serial No. 861, Elizabeth Hall Whitaker, September 26, 1959, Serial No. 782.
116. Adams, *The Hall Family History*, 361; *Washington Post*, August 11, 1911, October 27, 1970; Passport Application, Dorothy Hall, M1490, Rolls 389, 574, and 1354, NARA; *Sixteenth U.S. Census*, Washington, D.C.
117. Adams, *Hall Family History*, 361–362; *Thirteenth U.S. Census*, Lebanon County, Pennsylvania; Marriage License No. 12771, Lebanon County Marriage Records 22 (1912–1913), Lebanon County Register of Wills and Orphans' Court Clerk; *Lebanon Daily News*, April 12, 1913, October 13, 1952, April 24, 1963; Frederic A. Godcharles, *Biographical and Genealogical Sketches from Central Pennsylvania* (Baltimore: Clearfield Company, Inc., 1999): 4, 99–100.
118. Adams, *Hall Family History*, 362; The Official Bulletin, 1 (July 28, 1917): 2; Passport Application, Virginia D. Hall, Certificate No. 44783, Roll 626, Virginia H. Pearson, Certificate No. 97573, Roll 836, M1490, NARA; Consular Report of Marriage, May 11, 1919, Marriage Reports in State Department Decimal Files, RG 59, NARA; *Fifteenth* and *Sixteenth U.S. Census*, Coos County, Oregon; *Coquille Valley Sentinel*, September 14, 1939; Oregon Death Certificate, Bert Pearson, April 13, 1964, File No. 3226; Find A Grave, s.v. "Bert Pearson" and "Virginia Pearson."

Notes for Chapter 6

1. "Of a Noted Military Family," *CV* 6 (April 1898): 164; Edward R. Baylor, *A Baylor Genealogy: The Tedious Family History of Some of the Baylors who Lived in the United States in 1989* (Woods Hole, MA: privately printed, 1989), 15–19, 24; Orval Walker Baylor and Henry Bedinger Baylor, *Baylor's History of the Baylors: A Collection of Records and Important Family Data* (Le Roy, IN: Le Roy Journal Publishing Co., 1914), 26, 29–31; Francis B. Heitman, *Historical Register and Dictionary of the United States Army* (Washington, D.C.: Government Printing Office, 1903), 1: 201. The Baylors were to become a renowned family in Texan history, and George's brothers participated in most of Texas's nineteenth-century wars.
2. Baylor, *Baylor Genealogy*, 15, 17, 25; Baylor and Baylor, *Baylor's History of the Baylors*, 31–32; Stan Hoig, *Beyond the Frontier: Exploring the Indian Country* (Norman: University of Oklahoma Press, 1996), 301; *El Paso Herald*, March 23, November 9, 1901; *Arkansas Gazette*, February 24, 1835; Soldier's Application for a Pension, Col. George Wythe Baylor, No. 28182, TSLAC. Dawson served in the Seventh Infantry from June 1, 1821, to December 31, 1835. Heitman, *Historical Register*, 1: 361. See also *Texas State Gazette*, July 6, 1850.
3. L. E. Daniell, comp., *Personnel of the Texas State Government* (Austin: Press of the City Printing Company, 1887), 105; Baylor, *Baylor's History of the Baylors*, 27; *Seventh U.S. Census*, Washington County, Texas, Bexar County, Texas; *San Antonio Ledger*, September 23, 1852; George Wythe Baylor, *Into the Far, Wild Country: True Tales of the Old Southwest*, ed. Jerry D. Thompson (El Paso: Texas Western Press, 1996), 3. See also "First College in Texas," *Frontier Times* 2 (December 1924): 5. Sophie died in San Antonio on August 5, 1862.
4. Baylor, *Into the Far, Wild Country*, 93–99; *New Orleans Crescent*, March 23, 1854; *Daily Alta California*, April 17, 1854; *El Paso Daily Herald*, January 6, December 1, 1900, September 14, 1901; Kenneth A. Goldblatt, "George Wythe Baylor in West Texas, 1848–1865," *WTHAY* 44 (1968), 61; J. S. Holliday, *Rush for Riches: Gold Fever and the Making of California* (Berkeley: University of California Press, 1999), 214; Herbert G. Comfort, *Where Rolls the Kern: A History of Kern County, California* (Moorpark, CA: The Enterprise Press, 1934), 18–20; *Sacramento Daily Union*, February 12, March 1, 1855. Baylor related two contradictory accounts of his trip to California, one claiming

an overland trek and the second by the Nicaraguan route. Both were written late in his life.

5. Robert Maxwell Brown, *Strain of Violence: Historical Studies of American Violence and Vigilantism* (New York: Oxford University Press, 1975), 111–112, 136–137; John L. Waller, "Colonel George Wythe Baylor," *Southwestern Social Science Quarterly* 34 (June 1943): 24; John F. Burns and Richard J. Orsi, eds., *Taming the Elephant: Politics, Government, and Law in Pioneer California* (Berkeley: University of California, 2003), 49–51; Goldblatt, "George Wythe Baylor," 62; *El Paso Herald*, November 8, 1902; *Sacramento Daily Union*, June 23, August 8, 1856. Four years later, Terry would fatally shoot U.S. Senator David Colbreth Broderick in a duel. Philip J. Ethington, *The Public City: The Political Construction of Urban Life in San Francisco, 1850–1900* (Berkeley: University of California Press, 2001), 177.

6. *El Paso Herald*, November 8, 1902; *Sacramento Daily Union*, August 20, 29, 1856; Waller, "Colonel George Wythe Baylor," 24; Goldblatt, "George Wythe Baylor," 62; *Sonoma County Journal*, August 22, October 17, 31, November 7, 1856.

7. Baylor, *Into the Far, Wild Country*, 5; Goldblatt, "George Wythe Baylor," 62; Waller, "Colonel George Wythe Baylor," 24; *Sacramento Daily Union*, July 19, 1858; *Daily Alta California*, November 5, 1858; *New Orleans Daily Picayune*, November 29, 30, December 19, 1858; *New Orleans Crescent*, December 18, 29, 1858; *Civilian and Gazette*, December 21, 1858; Baylor to Ned, July 18, 1859, Box 1, Edward Clifton Wharton Papers, Hill Memorial Library, Louisiana State University. Baylor wrote two conflicting stories of his journey to Texas, one in 1859, and the other in 1901. This author has chosen to utilize the earlier account, which was composed only six months after his return home.

8. Pekka Hämäläinen, *The Comanche Empire* (New Haven: Yale University Press, 2008), 311–312; Thomas W. Kavanagh, *Comanche Political History: An Ethnohistorical Perspective, 1706–1875* (Lincoln: University of Nebraska Press, 1996), 367–368; George Klos, "'Our People Could Not Distinguish One Tribe from Another': The 1859 Expulsion of the Reserve Indians from Texas," *SHQ* 97 (April 1994): 609, 612; Robert Wooster, *The American Military Frontiers: The United States Army in the West, 1783–1900* (Albuquerque: University of New Mexico Press, 2009), 157; "Frontier News—Extra," June 24, 1859, Ross to Neighbors, May 26, 1859, *Annual Report of the Commissioner of Indian Affairs*,

Senate Executive Document No. 2, 36th Congress, 1st Session, 684–685, 645–646; J. Evetts Haley, "Charles Goodnight's Indian Recollections," *Panhandle-Plains Review* 1 (1928): 7–11; Plummer to Withers, May 21, 1859, Plummer to Withers, May 23, 1859, Thomas to Withers, May 26, 1859, Twiggs to Runnels, June 2, 1859, *Annual Report of the Secretary of War*, Senate Executive No. 2, 36th Congress, 1st Session, 371–374; James Buckner Barry, *Buck Barry, Texas Ranger and Frontiersman*, ed. James K. Greer (Lincoln: University of Nebraska Press, 1984), 113–114.
9. *Daily Ledger and Texan*, July 5, 1860; *El Paso Herald*, August 3, 10, 1901; Walker Keith Baylor, "The Paint Creek Fight," *Frontier Times* 2 (April 1925): 37–40; Ty Cashion, *A Texas Frontier: The Clear Fork Country and Fort Griffin, 1849–1887* (Norman: University of Oklahoma Press, 1996), 39–40; Joseph Carroll McConnell, *The West Texas Frontier: or, A Descriptive History of Early Times in Western Texas* (Palo Pinto, TX: Texas Legal Bank & Book Co., 1939), 2: 19–21; Goldblatt, "George Wythe Baylor," 63–64; *Galveston Weekly News*, August 21, 1860; Albert B. Regan, "A Comanche Raid in 1860," *Frontier Times* 9 (December 1931): 139–140; Fannie McAlpine Clarke, "A Chapter in the History of Young Territory," *SHQ* 9 (July 1905): 58; *Eighth U.S. Census*, Parker County, Texas; *White Man*, September 13, 1860.
10. Baylor, *Into the Far, Wild Country*, 173–177; *El Paso Herald*, November 9, 1901; *Galveston Daily News*, March 16, 19, 1861; Goldblatt, "George Wythe Baylor," 64.
11. CSR-CS, Second Texas Mounted Rifles, George Wythe Baylor; Daniell, comp., *Personnel of the Texas State Government*, 105; Bruce S. Allardice, *Confederate Colonels: A Biographical Register* (Columbia: University of Missouri Press, 2008), 57.
12. *The War of the Rebellion: A Compilation of the Official Records of the Union and Confederate Armies*, Series I, I: 577–578. Hereafter cited as *OR*, all references are to Series I unless otherwise indicated. Thomas W. Cutrer, *Theater of a Separate War: The Civil War West of the Mississippi River* (Chapel Hill: University of North Carolina Press, 2017), 94; Donald S. Frazier, *Blood and Treasure: Confederate Empire in the Southwest* (College Station: Texas A&M University Press, 1995), 40–41, 43; Robert Underwood Johnson and Clarence Clough Buel, eds., *Battles and Leaders of the Civil War* (Secaucus, NJ: Castle Books, 1982), 2: 103; CSR-CS, Second Texas Mounted Rifles, George Wythe Baylor; *El Paso Herald*, November 9, 1901.

13. *OR*, I: 604; IV: 45–46, 57–59, 63–64; Andrew E. Masich, *Civil War in the Southwest Borderlands, 1861–1867* (Norman: University of Oklahoma Press, 2017), 43, 47–48; Flint Whitlock, *Distant Bugles, Distant Drums: The Union Response to the Confederate Invasion of New Mexico* (Boulder: University Press of Colorado, 2006), 48; John P. Wilson, *When the Texans Came: Missing Records from the Civil War in the Southwest* (Albuquerque: University of New Mexico Press, 2001), 103–110, 114–116, 147. In 1861, the Territory of New Mexico comprised present-day New Mexico, Arizona, and the southern portion of Nevada.
14. *OR*, IV: 4, 16, 17; Frazier, *Blood and Treasure*, 43, 48, 56–57; Thomas W. Cutrer, *Empire of Sand: The Struggle for the Southwest, 1862* (Buffalo Gap, TX: State House Press, 2015), 20–22; W. H. Watford, "Confederate Western Ambitions," *SHQ* 44 (October 1940): 165; Whitlock, *Distant Bugles, Distant Drums*, 52; David H. Rosenberg, "Confederate Manifest Destiny," *America's Civil War* 13 (July 2000): 51. Baylor's men were soon joined by Captain Bethel Coopwood's "San Elizario Spies and Guides" and Captain George Milton Frazer's "Arizona Rangers." Enrique B. D'Hamel, *The Adventures of a Tenderfoot* (Waco: W. M. Morrison, 1914), 8–16; Martin Hardwick Hall, "Captain George M. Frazer's Arizona Rangers, C.S.A.," *Password* 19 (Summer 1974): 71–77.
15. *OR*, IV: 4–7, 15, 16, 17–23, 64; Frazier, *Blood and Treasure*, 57–58, 59–62; Alvin M. Josephy, Jr., *The Civil War in the American West* (New York: Alfred A. Knopf, 1992), 50; Wilson, *When the Texans Came*, 2, 41, 48–51, 147; Rosenberg, "Confederate Manifest Destiny," 52; Watford, "Confederate Western Ambitions," 165; *El Paso Herald*, November 9, 1901; *Mesilla Times*, July 27, 1861; Martin Hardwick Hall, "The Skirmish at Mesilla," *Arizona and the West* 1 (Winter 1959): 343, 346–351; W. Clement Eaton, "Frontier Life in Southern Arizona, 1858–1861," *SHQ* 36 (January 1933): 191.
16. *OR*, IV: 129, 80–81, 93, 69–70, 74, 132–133; Masich, *Civil War in the Southwest Borderlands*, 48–49; Frazier, *Blood and Treasure*, 103, 117; Wilson, *When the Texans Came*, 3, 134.
17. William Preston Johnston, *The Life of Albert Sidney Johnston: Embracing His Services in the Armies of the United States, the Republic of Texas, and the Confederate States* (Austin: State House Press, 1997), 279–287; Steven E. Woodworth, *Jefferson Davis and His Generals: The Failure of Confederate Command in the West* (Lawrence: University

Press of Kansas, 1990), 50, 51; *El Paso Herald*, November 16, 1901; CSR-CS, Baylor's Regiment, George W. Baylor; "Of a Noted Military Family," 164; Ezra J. Warner, *Generals in Gray: Lives of the Confederate Commanders* (Baton Rouge: Louisiana State University Press, 2008), 160. Johnston was the second-ranking general officer in the Confederate States Army, junior only to Adjutant and Inspector General Samuel Cooper. John H. Eicher and David J. Eicher, *Civil War High Commands* (Stanford: Stanford University Press, 2001), 807. See also Martin H. Hall, "Albert Sidney Johnston's First Confederate Command," *The McNeese Review* 13 (1962): 3–12.

18. Woodworth, *Jefferson Davis and His Generals*, 52, 53, 55, 67–68, 81–83, 85; Timothy B. Smith, *Shiloh: Conquer or Perish* (Lawrence: University Press of Kansas, 2014), 2–4, 24; Larry J. Daniel, *Shiloh: The Battle That Changed the Civil War* (New York: Simon & Schuster, 1997), 24, 65; Stacy D. Allen, "Shiloh! The Campaign and First Day's Battle," *Blue and Gray Magazine* 14 (February 1997): 7–8, 13; Ron Chernow, *Grant* (New York: Penguin Press, 2017), 167–184; Stanley F. Horn, *The Army of Tennessee: A Military History* (Norman: University of Oklahoma Press, 1993), 68–69, 80–98; Clement A. Evans, ed., *Confederate Military History* (Atlanta: Confederate Publishing Company, 1899), 7: 32, 8: 18–27.

19. *OR*, X, Pt. 2: 361, 370–371, Pt. 1: 385, LII, Pt. 1: 26–29; Johnston, *Life of Albert Sidney Johnston*, 539, 549; Winston Groom, *Shiloh, 1862* (Washington, D.C.: National Geographic Society, 2012), 186, 189–190; James McPherson, *Battle Cry of Freedom: The Civil War Era* (New York: Oxford University Press, 1988), 406; Major Thomas K. Hall, "The Confederate High Command at Shiloh" (MMAS thesis, Fort Leavenworth, 1995), 22–23; Eicher and Eicher, *Civil War High Commands*, 887; CSR-CGSO, George W. Baylor; Soldier's Application for a Pension, Col. George Wythe Baylor, No. 28182, TSLAC; George Wythe Baylor, "With Gen. A. S. Johnston at Shiloh," *CV* 5 (December 1897): 609; Earl J. Hess, *Braxton Bragg: The Most Hated Man of the Confederacy* (Chapel Hill: University of North Carolina Press, 2016), 29–30; Bruce Catton, *Terrible Swift Sword* (New York: Fall River Press, 2009), 224. See also Joseph Allan Frank and George A. Reaves, *"Seeing the Elephant": Raw Recruits at the Battle of Shiloh* (Urbana: University of Illinois Press, 2003).

20. *OR*, X, Pt. 2: 390–391, Pt. 1: 403; Daniel, *Shiloh*, 118–119; Allen, "Shiloh! The Campaign and First Day's Battle," 18; Groom, *Shiloh*, 188,

194–195; Johnson and Buel, eds., *Battles and Leaders*, 1: 579; Evans, ed., *Confederate Military History*, 7: 42, 43–44, 8: 35; Catton, *Terrible Swift Sword*, 227; Baylor, "With Gen. A. S. Johnston at Shiloh," 609 (quotation).

21. *OR*, X, Pt. 2: 387, Pt. 1: 397, 392–395; Smith, *Shiloh*, 61–62; Daniel, *Shiloh*, 119–120; Groom, *Shiloh*, 197; Hess, *Braxton Bragg*, 33; Steven E. Woodworth, *Shiloh: Confederate High Tide in the Heartland* (Santa Barbara, CA: Praeger, 2013), 147; Johnson and Buel, eds., *Battles and Leaders*, 1: 554.

22. Baylor, "With Gen. A. S. Johnston at Shiloh," 610; Wiley Sword, *Shiloh: Bloody April* (Dayton, OH: Morningside House, 2001), 147, 148, 222–223; Smith, *Shiloh*, 90; Johnston, *Life of Albert Sidney Johnston*, 586 (quotation); Charles P. Roland, *Albert Sidney Johnston: Soldier of Three Republics* (Lexington: University Press of Kentucky, 2001), 331; Hall, "Confederate High Command at Shiloh," 39, 43; Allen, "Shiloh! The Campaign and First Day's Battle," 20–21.

23. *OR*, X, Pt. 1: 390, 404, 547–556; Baylor, "With Gen. A. S. Johnston at Shiloh," 611 (quotation); Allen, "Shiloh! The Campaign and First Day's Battle," 46, 48, 52; O. Edward Cunningham, *Shiloh and the Western Campaign of 1862*, ed. Gary D. Joiner and Timothy B. Smith (New York: Savis Beatie, 2009), 138, 206, 270, 272–273; Mamie Yeary, comp., *Reminiscences of the Boys in Gray, 1861–1865* (Dallas: Smith and Lamar Publishing House, 1912), 45; Sword, *Shiloh*, 230; McPherson, *Battle Cry of Freedom*, 409–410. Informed the Forty-fifth Tennessee was refusing to attack over open ground, Johnston had inspired the regiment to do their duty. While conceivably a questionable command decision, he personally led a charge on the Union position to their front, which was carried, and came away with bullet holes in his uniform, a flapping boot heel, and a mortal wound. Woodworth, *Shiloh*, 144–145.

24. Baylor, "With Gen. A. S. Johnston at Shiloh," 611; Shelby Foote, *The Civil War: A Narrative* (New York: Random House, 1986), 1: 339–340; Smith, *Shiloh*, 192–193; Daniel, *Shiloh*, 226–227; Groom, *Shiloh*, 299–300. Army commanders did not normally lead regimental charges, but historically battlefield leaders have used displays of personal bravery under fire to embolden their men. Roland, *Albert Sidney Johnston*, 336–338. Johnston was the highest-ranking officer on either side to be killed in action during the entire war. See also Gary W. Gallagher and Joseph T. Glatthaar, eds., *Leaders of the*

Lost Cause: New Perspectives on the Confederate High Command (Mechanicsburg, PA: Stackpole Books, 2004), 153–154.
25. OR, X, Pt. 1: 569–571, 466–470, 409–412; Groom, *Shiloh*, 300; Sword, *Shiloh*, 276, 279–280, 344–345, 361–363, 365; Catton, *Terrible Swift Sword*, 236; Foote, *Civil War*, 1: 341–342; Woodworth, *Shiloh*, 145; Stacy D. Allen, "Shiloh! The Second Day's Battle and Aftermath," *Blue and Gray Magazine* 14 (April 1997): 10.
26. Baylor, "With Gen. A. S. Johnston at Shiloh," 611; Groom, *Shiloh*, 302; Roland, *Albert Sidney Johnston*, 352–353; Chernow, *Grant*, 205–206; Woodworth, *Jefferson Davis and His Generals*, 102; 351, 353–368; Cunningham, *Shiloh and the Western Campaign*, 351–375; Sword, *Shiloh*, 402–403, 413; Evans, ed., *Confederate Military History*, 8: 35; Allen, "Shiloh! The Second Day's Battle," 17, 23, 27. For more on Shiloh, its historiography prior to 2013, and discussions on the four basic schools of interpretation regarding the battle, see Steven E. Woodworth, ed., *The Shiloh Campaign* (Carbondale: Southern Illinois University Press, 2009); and Timothy B. Smith, *The Untold Story of Shiloh: The Battle and the Battlefield* (Knoxville: University of Tennessee Press, 2006), and *Rethinking Shiloh: Myth and Memory* (Knoxville: University of Tennessee Press, 2013).
27. CSR-CS, Baylor's Regiment, George W. Baylor; Special Orders No. 12, April 8, 1862, Unfiled Papers and Slips Belonging in Confederate Compiled Service Records, RG 109, NARA.
28. *OR*, XV: 936, 939, 1000, XXVI, Pt. 2: 57–58, L, Pt. 2: 332–333; James Matthews, "Frontier Commanders in Grey: George Baylor, Alonzo Ridley, and George Madison," *WTHAY* 73 (1997), 145; Marcus J. Wright, comp., *Texas in the War, 1861–1865*, ed. Harold B. Simpson (Hillsboro, TX: Hill Junior College Press, 1965), 30, 124; CSR-CS, Baylor's Regiment, George W. Baylor; Stewart Sifakis, *Compendium of the Confederate Armies: Texas* (Westminster, MD: Willow Bend Books, 2008), 39–40, 44, 49, 52. See also L. Boyd Finch, "Arizona in Exile: Confederate Schemes to Recapture the Far Southwest," *The Journal of Arizona History* 33 (Spring 1992): 57–84.
29. *OR*, XXVI, Pt. 1: 226–227, Pt. 2: 10–11, XV: 1054, 1064; Waller, "Colonel George Wythe Baylor," 35; Earl Wesley Fornell, *The Galveston Era: The Texas Crescent on the Eve of Secession* (Austin: University of Texas Press, 2011), 115, 151; James T. Matthews, "Major's Confederate Cavalry Brigade" (M.A. thesis, Texas Tech University, 1991), 82;

Ralph A. Wooster, *Lone Star Regiments in Gray* (Austin: Eakin Press, 2002), 174–178, 180.

30. *OR*, Series 1, XV: 590–591, XXXIV, Pt. 1: 482–483; John D. Winters, *The Civil War in Louisiana* (Baton Rouge: Louisiana State Press, 1991), 212; Robert L. Kerby, *Kirby Smith's Confederacy: The Trans-Mississippi South, 1863–1865* (New York: Columbia University Press, 1972), 238; Richard B. Irwin, *History of the Nineteenth Army Corps* (New York: G. P. Putnam's Sons, 1893), 95–118; Donald S. Frazier, *Thunder Across the Swamp: The Fight for the Lower Mississippi, February 1863-May 1863* (Buffalo Gap, TX: State House Press, 2011), 275–312; Stephen S. Michot, "In Relief of Port Hudson: Richard Taylor's 1863 Lafourche Offensive," *Military History of the West* 23 (Fall 1993): 103–104; Matthews, "Major's Confederate Cavalry Brigade," 5.

31. Richard Taylor, *Destruction and Reconstruction: Personal Experiences of the Late War* (New York: D. Appleton and Company, 1879), 138, 145–146; Kerby, *Kirby Smith's Confederacy*, 110, 112–113; Winters, *Civil War in Louisiana*, 293; Ralph A. Wooster, *Texas and Texans in the Civil War* (Austin: Eakin Press, 1995), 74.

32. *OR*, XXVI, Pt. 1: 20, 292, 332, 340–341, 357–361, 386–395 (quotation on p. 394), Pt. 2: 291, 294–95, 327, 477–478, XXII, Pt. 2: 1036; Stephen A. Dupree, *Planting the Union Flag in Texas: The Campaigns of Major General Nathaniel P. Banks in the West* (College Station: Texas A&M University Press, 2008), 65; Richard Lowe, *The Texas Overland Expedition of 1863* (Abilene, TX: McWhiney Foundation Press, 1998), 53–56; Ludwell H. Johnson, *Red River Campaign: Politics and Cotton in the Civil War* (Kent, OH: Kent State University Press, 1993), 39; Joseph Palmer Blessington, *The Campaigns of Walker's Texas Division* (New York: Lange, Little & Co., 1875), 139–142; Winters, *Civil War in Louisiana*, 297–299; Kerby, *Kirby Smith's Confederacy*, 245–246; Cooper K. Ragan, ed., "The Diary of Captain George W. O'Brien, 1863," Pt. 3, *SHQ* 67 (July 1963): 419; Taylor, *Destruction and Reconstruction*, 150.

33. *OR*, XXVI, Pt. 2: 512, 527–528, XXXIV, Pt. 2: 895–896, 903–904; *Galveston Weekly News*, January 20, 1864; *Tri-Weekly Telegraph*, January 21, 1864.

34. Kerby, *Kirby Smith's Confederacy*, 284–286, 295–297, 300–301; Gary D. Joiner, *Mr. Lincoln's Brown Water Navy: The Mississippi Squadron* (Lanham, MD: Rowman & Littlefield, 2007), 144–148; Gary D. Joiner, "Up the Red River and Down to Defeat," *America's*

Civil War 17 (March 2004): 22–23, 25–26; Majority Report, Minority Report, Testimony of Major General Nathaniel P. Banks, December 14, 1864, *Report of the Joint Committee on the Conduct of the War: Red River Expedition*, Senate Report No. 142, 38th Congress, 2nd Session, v–vi, xxxiv, xxxvi, 7. Hereafter cited as *JCCW: Red River Expedition*.

35. OR, XXIV, Pt. 1: 516–517; Dupree, *Planting the Union Flag in Texas*, 96, 98, 100, 104, 114; Taylor, *Destruction and Reconstruction*, 158–159; Kerby, *Kirby Smith's Confederacy*, 287, 299; Josephy, *Civil War in the American West*, 199.

36. Matthews, "Major's Confederate Cavalry Brigade," 140–141; Rebecca W. Smith and Marion Mullins, eds., "The Diary of H. C. Medford, Confederate Soldier, 1864," Pt. 1, *SHQ* 34 (October 1930): 126; Gary D. Joiner, "To Defend the Sacred Soil of Texas: Tom Green and the Texas Cavalry in the Red River Campaign," *ETHJ* 46 (March 2008): 13. Some forty years later, Baylor was still trying to recover his saber. "Colonel G. W. Baylor's Sword," *CV* 14 (June 1906): 266.

37. OR, XXXIV, Pt. 1: 520–521, 563, 507; Rebecca W. Smith and Marion Mullins, eds., "The Diary of H. C. Medford, Confederate Soldier, 1864," Pt. 2, *SHQ* 34 (January 1931): 212; Kerby, *Kirby Smith's Confederacy*, 301–302; Richard Lowe, *Walker's Texas Division, C.S.A.: Greyhounds of the Trans-Mississippi* (Baton Rouge: Louisiana State University Press, 2004), 184; Lester N. Fitzhugh, "Texas Forces in the Red River Campaign," *Texas Military History* 3 (Spring 1963): 19–22; Walter P. Lane, *The Adventures and Recollections of General Walter P. Lane: A San Jacinto Veteran, Containing Sketches of the Texan, Mexican, and Late Wars* (Austin: Jenkins Publishing Company, 1970), 108.

38. OR, XXXIV, Pt. 1: 563; William Riley Brooksher, *War Along the Bayous: The 1864 Red River Campaign in Louisiana* (Washington, D.C.: Brassey's, 1998), 80; Curtis W. Milbourn, "Fighting For Time," *North and South* 5 (May 2002): 70; Gary D. Joiner, *Through the Howling Wilderness: The 1864 Red River Campaign and Union Failure in the West* (Knoxville: University of Tennessee Press, 2006), 78; Dupree, *Planting the Union Flag in Texas*, 111–112; Johnson, *Red River Campaign*, 117–120.

39. OR, XXXIV, Pt. 1: 450, 526, 616–617 (quotation on p. 616); Lane, *Adventures and Recollections*, 108–109; Theophilus Noel, *A Campaign from Santa Fe to the Mississippi: Being a History of the Old Sibley Brigade* (Shreveport: Shreveport News Printing Establishment, 1865), 77; Joiner, *Through the Howling Wilderness*, 82; Minority Report;

Testimonies of Brigadier General A. L. Lee, January 11, 1865, Colonel John S. Clark, January 30, 1865, *JCCW: Red River Expedition*, xxxvi–xxxvii, 58–59, 194; Yeary, comp., *Reminiscences of the Boys*, 781; Smith and Mullins, eds., "Medford Diary," Pt. 2: 213–215; Milbourn, "Fighting For Time," 73–75.

40. *OR*, XXXIV, Pt. 1: 258–261, 273, 527, 563–565, 617, Pt. 3: 566; Taylor, *Destruction and Reconstruction*, 162–164; Richard Lowe, ed., *Greyhound Commander: Confederate General John G. Walker's History of the Civil War West of the Mississippi* (Baton Rouge: Louisiana State University Press, 2013), 94–95; Irwin, *Nineteenth Army Corps*, 299–312; Majority Report; Minority Report; Testimonies of Major General William B. Franklin, January 6, 1865, Brigadier General A. L. Lee, January 11, 1865, *JCCW: Red River Expedition*, vi–vii, xxxvii–xxxviii, 31, 60–62; Gary D. Joiner, ed., *Little to Eat and Thin Mud to Drink: Letters, Diaries, and Memoirs from the Red River Campaigns, 1863–1864* (Knoxville: University of Tennessee Press, 2007), 56, 62 n43, n44; Smith and Mullins, eds., "Medford Diary," Pt. 2: 216–218; Yeary, comp., *Reminiscences of the Boys in Gray*, 45, 153; Lane, *Adventures and Recollections*, 110; Curtis W. Milbourn and Steve Bounds, "The Battle of Mansfield," *North and South* 6 (February 2003): 29–30, 32, 34, 39; Pierre Comtois, "Collision at Sabine Crossroads," *Military History* 14 (October 1997): 59–60; Joiner, "Up the Red River and Down to Defeat," 27. Following the battle, the command came to be called "Baylor's Brigade," a name change he protested as Lane had served with Walker Baylor at San Jacinto, and such a revision was a sorry way to reward a gallant soldier. "Of a Noted Military Family," 164–165.

41. *OR*, XXXIV, Pt. 1: 617, 605, 607–608, 617; Joiner, *Through the Howling Wilderness*, 99, 101; Taylor, *Destruction and Reconstruction*, 165–167; Lowe, ed., *Greyhound Commander*, 97; Noel, *Old Sibley Brigade*, 79; Blessington, *Walker's Texas Division*, 193; Curtis W. Milbourn and Steve Bounds, "The Battle of Pleasant Hill," *North and South* 8 (November 2005): 74.

42. *OR*, XXXIV, Pt. 1: 566–567, 602, 608, 617–618 (second quotation on p. 618); Milbourn and Bounds, "Battle of Pleasant Hill," 77, 79 (first quotation), 82, 84; Taylor, *Destruction and Reconstruction*, 167–170; Lowe, *Walker's Texas Division*, 207–209; Lowe, ed., *Greyhound Commander*, 100; Winters, *Civil War in Louisiana*, 349, 353–354; Irwin, *Nineteenth Army Corps*, 318–319; Smith and Mullins, eds.,

"Medford Diary," Pt. 2: 222; Majority Report; Testimonies of Major General Nathaniel P. Banks, December 14, 1864, Major General William B. Franklin, January 6, 1865, *JCCW: Red River Expedition*, vii, 13, 31, 37–38; Brooksher, *War Along the Bayous*, 135.

43. *OR*, XXIV, Pt. 1: 477, 480, 535, 555, 571–589, 618–623; Joiner, *Through the Howling Wilderness*, 118, 143–144; Taylor, *Destruction and Reconstruction*, 180, 186; Josephy, *Civil War in the American West*, 211; Warner, *Generals in Gray*, 332; "Unpublished After-Action Reports from the Red River Campaign," *Civil War Regiments* 4 (1994): 120–121, 124; Joiner, *Mr. Lincoln's Brown Water Navy*, 160–162; Winters, *Civil War in Louisiana*, 370–371; Yeary, comp., *Reminiscences of the Boys in Gray*, 45. See also Odie Faulk, *General Tom Green: Fightin' Texan* (Waco: Texian Press, 1963), 61–64.

44. *OR*, XXXIV, Pt. 1: 320, 329–330, 337, 348, 357, 619, 624, 631; Winters, *Civil War in Louisiana*, 376–377; Joiner, "Up the Red River and Down to Defeat," 28–29; Yeary, comp., *Reminiscences of the Boys in Gray*, 45; "The Battle of Yellow Bayou," *CV* 25 (February 1917): 94–95.

45. Baylor, *Into the Far, Wild Country*, 234–235; *Galveston Daily News*, December 8, 1895. Baylor and his officers were not the only Rebels unhappy with Wharton's leadership. For more, see Anne J. Bailey, *Between the Enemy and Texas: Parsons's Texas Cavalry in the Civil War* (Fort Worth: Texas Christian University, 1989), 189. See also Jerry Bryan Lincecum, et al., eds. *Gideon Lincecum's Sword: Civil War Letters from the Texas Home Front* (Denton: University of North Texas Press, 2001), 322.

46. *OR*, XLI, Pt. 3: 996, 998–999, Pt. 4: 1143, XLVIII, Pt. 2: 1281, Pt. 1: 1351–1352, 1353, 1392–1393; Matthews, "Major's Confederate Cavalry Brigade," 164–168; Baylor, *Into the Far, Wild Country*, 236–237 (quotation on p. 237); *Galveston Daily News*, April 7, 1865; Allardice, *Confederate Colonels*, 367–368. See also William Wharton Groce, "Major General John A. Wharton," *SHQ* 19 (January 1916): 271–278; and Leonidas B. Giles, *Terry's Texas Rangers* (Austin: Von Boeckman-Jones Co., 1911), 14–15, 25.

47. Baylor, *Into the Far, Wild Country*, 19 (first two quotations), 237–239 (third quotation on p. 238); *Galveston Daily News*, April 7, 1865, December 8, 1895; Waller, "Colonel George Wythe Baylor," 25.

48. Baylor, *Into the Far, Wild Country*, 239; *OR*, XLVIII, Pt. 2: 1291; *Galveston Daily News*, April 7, 1865, December 8, 1895; *Dallas Herald*, April 13, 1865; Wright, comp., and Simpson, ed., *Texas in the War*, 96; Ralph A. Wooster, *Lone Star Generals in Gray* (Austin: Eakin Press, 2000), 74. See also Ron Soodalter, "Getting Away with Murder," *America's Civil War* 23 (September 2010): 62–63.
49. *OR*, Series II, VIII: 717; CSR-CS, Baylor's Regiment, George W. Baylor; *Dallas Herald*, May 30, 1868; *Galveston Daily News*, November 14, 29, December 4, 6, 1868; Baylor, *Baylor Genealogy*, 25; "Of a Noted Military Family," 165.
50. *Galveston Daily News*, August 5, 8, 1865, February 1, 1868; Gary Cartwright, *Galveston: A History of the Island* (Fort Worth: Texas Christian University Press, 1991), 118; Kimber Fountain, *Galveston Seawall Chronicles* (Charleston, SC: History Press, 2017), 14; Hans Peter Nielson Gammel, comp., *The Laws of Texas, 1822–1897* (Austin: The Gammel Book Company, 1898), 5: 1572–1574.
51. Henry Wiencek, *The Moodys of Galveston and Their Mansion* (College Station: Texas A&M University Press, 2010), 7–8 (quotation); Cartwright, *Galveston*, 119; Ralph A. Wooster, "Wealthy Texans, 1870," *SHQ* 74 (July 1970): 29.
52. *Galveston Daily News*, December 4, 1869, August 25, 1870; *Dallas Daily Herald*, March 30, 1872, January 16, March 18, April 3, July 25, August 1, September 26, October 6, 1874; Baylor and Baylor, *Baylor's History of the Baylors*, 32.
53. *Daily Democratic Statesman*, August 21, 1875; *Dallas Daily Herald*, January 9, 1875; *El Paso Daily Herald*, January 13, 1900 (quotations); Baylor to Roberts, February 3, 1879, Dorman H. Winfrey and James M. Day, eds., *The Indian Papers of Texas and the Southwest* (Austin: Texas State Historical Association, 1995), 4: 412–414; *San Antonio Daily Express*, July 23, 1879; Baylor, *Into the Far, Wild Country*, 21.
54. Ranger Services Records, George W. Baylor, 401–143, TSLAC; Special Order No. 24, July 26, 1879, 401–1012, TSLAC; Baylor, *Into the Far Wild Country*, 21. As commander of the detachment, Baylor's immediate superior in the chain of command was Captain George Washington Arrington. Jones to Arrington, January 8, 1878, 401–1159, TSLAC.
55. *El Paso Daily Herald*, January 13, 1900; Gillett, *Six Years*, 141, 142 (first two quotations), 143 (third quotation), 198–199; Coldwell to Jones, August 1, 1880, 401–399, TSLAC.

56. Robert M. Utley, *Lone Star Justice: The First Century of the Texas Rangers* (New York: Berkley Books, 2002), 208–209; MR, Company C, September 30, 1879; *San Antonio Light*, June 15, 1930; Walter P. Webb, *The Texas Rangers: A Century of Frontier Defense* (Austin: University of Texas Press, 1965), 396; Baylor, *Into the Far, Wild Country*, 5; *Galveston Daily News*, April 15, 1904; *El Paso Herald*, December 20, 1922; W. H. Timmons, *El Paso: A Borderlands History* (El Paso: Texas Western Press, 2004), 207.

57. Dan L. Thrapp, *Victorio and the Mimbres Apaches* (Norman: University of Oklahoma Press, 1974), 195–251; Donald E. Worcester, *The Apaches: The Eagles of the Southwest* (Norman: University of Oklahoma Press, 1979), 207, 215–222; Robert M. Utley, *Frontier Regulars: The United States Army and the Indian, 1866–1891* (Lincoln: University of Nebraska Press, 1984), 359–360; Peter Cozzens, ed., *Eyewitnesses to the Indian Wars, 1865–1890: The Struggle for Apacheria* (Mechanicsburg, PA: Stackpole Books, 2001), xxv–xxvi, 203. Victorio ranks with Cochise and Mangas Coloradas as one of the greatest leaders of the Apache peoples. His display of generalship in leading his band across an inhospitable landscape of mountains and desert while engaging a better-equipped, numerically superior enemy force in guerilla warfare has few equals in military history. See also Kendall D. Gott, *In Search of an Elusive Enemy: The Victorio Campaign* (Fort Leavenworth: Combat Studies Institute Press, 2004).

58. Gillett, *Six Years*, 162–165; MR, Company C, November 30, 1879; Operations of State Troops, 1: 187; Baylor to Jones, December 3, 1879, Letters Received by the Office of the Adjutant General, M666, RG 94, NARA. Hereafter cited as Letters Received, Adjutant General's Office. *El Paso Daily Herald*, February 17, 1900; Lance R. Blyth, *Chiricahua and Janos: Communities of Violence in the Southwestern Borderlands, 1680–1880* (Lincoln: University of Nebraska Press, 2012), 190–191; Thrapp, *Victorio and the Mimbres Apaches*, 253–256.

59. Baylor, *Into the Far, Wild Country*, 253; Baylor to Jones, August 26, 1880, 401–399, TSLAC (quotation); James L. Haley, *Apaches: A History and Culture Portrait* (Norman: University of Oklahoma Press, 1997), 329–330; *Galveston Daily News*, November 29, 1905, August 26, 1880; *RAG, 1880*, 25; Caldwell to Jones, August 4, 1880, 401–1159, TSLAC; Gillett, *Six Years*, 180–183; Grierson to Assistant Adjutant General, September 20, 1880, *Annual Report of the Secretary of War*, House Executive Document No. 1, Pt. 2, 46th Congress,

Endnotes   **593**

3rd Session, 161–162; *San Antonio Daily Express*, August 12, 15, 1880; Edward L. N. Glass, ed., *The History of the Tenth Cavalry* (Tucson: Acme Printing Company, 1921), 22–23. For more on Byrne's demise, see Richard Selcer, "A Premonition of Death," *Wild West* 27 (August 2014): 60–65.

60. Special Order No. 71, September 8, 1880, 401–1012, TSLAC; RSR, George W. Baylor, 401–143, TSLAC.

61. MR, Company A, September 30, 1880; Thrapp, *Victorio and the Mimbres Apaches*, 299; Haley, *Apaches*, 330–31; Cozzens, ed., *Eyewitnesses to the Indian Wars*, xxvi–xxvii, 236–256; William H. Leckie, with Shirley A. Leckie, *The Buffalo Soldiers: A Narrative of the Black Cavalry in the West* (Norman: University of Oklahoma Press, 2003), 231; Robert Wooster, *The American Military Frontier: The United States Army in the West, 1783–1900* (Albuquerque: University of New Mexico Press, 2009), 249; *RAG, 1880*, 33; Waller, "Colonel George Wythe Baylor," 30.

62. MR, Company A, September 30, 1877; Haley, *Apaches*, 331; Shelley Bowen Hatfield, *Chasing Shadows: Indians Along the United States-Mexico Border, 1876–1911* (Albuquerque: University of New Mexico Press, 1998), 39; Leckie, *Buffalo Soldiers*, 231; *RAG, 1880*, 25; Robert Wooster, *The Military and United States Indian Policy, 1865–1903* (Lincoln: University of Nebraska Press, 1995), 187.

63. Blyth, *Chiricahua and Janos*, 194–196; Thrapp, *Victorio and the Mimbres Apaches*, 300–304; Wooster, *American Military Frontiers*, 249; Leckie, *Buffalo Soldiers*, 231.

64. *Dallas Daily Herald* and *Galveston Daily News*, both dated January 11, 1881; Baylor to Jones, January 16, 1881, 401–400, TSLAC; *El Paso Daily Herald*, August 10, 1900; Andrew Graybill, *Policing the Great Plains: Rangers, Mounties, and the North American Frontier, 1875–1910* (Lincoln: University of Nebraska Press, 2007), 50.

65. ROS, Company A, February 1881; Nevill to Jones, February 6, 1881, Nevill to Jones, February 9, 1881, Baylor to Jones, February 9, 1881, 401–400, TSLAC; George Wythe Baylor, "The Last Fight on Texas Soil Between the Apaches and the Texas Rangers," *A History of the Texas Rangers' Association* 5 (December 1905): 3–8; *San Antonio Daily Express*, February 6, 1881.

66. ROS, Company A, February 1881; Nevill to Jones, February 6, 1881, Nevill to Jones, February 9, 1881, Baylor to Jones, February 9, 1881, 401–400, TSLAC; Baylor, "Last Fight on Texas Soil," 11–13; *El Paso*

Daily Herald, August 11, 13, 1900; *Galveston Daily News*, February 4, 1881; Graybill, *Policing the Great Plains*, 23, 50.

67. ROS, Company A, February 1881; Nevill to Jones, February 6, 1881, Nevill to Jones, February 9, 1881, Baylor to Jones, February 9, 1881, 401–400, TSLAC; Nevill to Jones, February 25, 1881, 401–1159, TSLC; *El Paso Daily Herald*, August 14, 15, 1900; Charles M. Robinson III, *The Men Who Wear the Star: The Story of the Texas Rangers* (New York: The Modern Library, 2001), 243–244; *Galveston Daily News*, February 4, July 16, 1881, June 14, 1883; W. C. Jameson, "Last Stand of the Mescalero Apaches," *True West* 38 (December 1991): 16–19.

68. Hatfield, *Chasing Shadows*, 42; Baylor to Escobar, May 10, 1881, *Foreign Relations*, House Executive Document No. 1, 47th Congress, 1st Session, 830.

69. Timmons, *El Paso*, 198; Walter R. Borneman, *Iron Horses: America's Race to Bring the Railroads West* (New York: Back Bay Books, 2010), 189; Ben W. Kemp with J. C. Dykes, *Cow Dust and Saddle Leather* (Norman: University of Oklahoma Press, 1968), 29–30; *Galveston Daily News*, January 9, 13, 1881; Baylor to Jones, May 8, 1881, 401–1159, TSLAC; *RAG, 1880*, 25–26; ibid., *1882*, 37.

70. *RAG, 1882*, 31, 36; Operations of State Troops, 2 (1882–1885), 401–1083, TSLAC: 1.

71. MR, Company A, March 31, 1883; Waller, "Colonel George Wythe Baylor," 35; *Galveston Daily News*, August 2, September 7, 1882; Sammy Tise, *Texas County Sheriffs* (Albuquerque: Oakwood Publishing, 1989), 172; General Order No. 8, November 18, 1882, Fountain to Baylor, March 15, 1883, Baylor to King, March 18, 1883, Baylor to Johnson, February 21, 1884, 401–1159, TSLAC; Operations of State Troops, 2: 5, 6, 9; *Las Cruces Sun-News*, March 10, 1883; Paul Cool, "New Mexico's Rustler King," *Wild West* 26 (April 2014): 40–41, 43–44; Baylor, *Into the Far, Wild Country*, 27; *RAG, 1883*, 19; ROS, Company A, September 1883. On February 1, 1896, Fountain and his son, Henry, vanished near White Sands. The physical evidence collected at the scene indicated a double homicide, but their bodies were never recovered. For more on this fascinating mystery, see Corey Recko, *Murder on the White Sands: The Disappearance of Albert and Henry Fountain* (Denton: University of North Texas Press, 2007).

72. Jacqueline M. Moore, *Cow Boys and Cattle Men: Class and Masculinities on the Texas Frontier, 1865–1900* (New York: New York University Press, 2010), 27; Christopher Knowlton, *Cattle Kingdom: The Hidden History*

Endnotes **595**

   of the Cowboy West (New York: Houghton Mifflin Harcourt, 2017), 140–141; Jim Lanning and Judy Lanning, *Texas Cowboys: Memories of the Early Days* (College Station: Texas A&M University Press, 1984), 57; Wayne Gard, "The Fence-Cutters," *SHQ* 51 (July 1947), 2 (quotation), 3–4; Lewis Nordyke, *Great Roundup: The Story of Texas and Southwestern Cowmen* (New York: William Morrow and Company, 1955), 86, 90; R. D. Holt, "The Introduction of Barbed Wire into Texas and the Fence Cutting War," *WTHAY* 6 (1930): 70–74; Henry D. and Frances T. McCallum, *The Wire That Fenced the West* (Norman: University of Oklahoma Press, 1965), 156–158, 160–161. The devastating blizzard of 1886 would further convince cattlemen that their continued economic survival required a change to the open range system. For more details, see David L. Wheeler, "The Blizzard of 1886 and Its Effect on the Cattle Range Industry in the Southern Plains," *SHQ* 93 (January 1991): 415–434.

73. *House Journal, Eighteenth Legislature, Called Session*, 11, 13–15, 22, 24; Gammel, comp., *Laws of Texas*, 9: 552, 569, 600–603; Acts 1884, 18th Legislature, 1st Called Session, Ch. 12 and 24, *General and Special Laws of Texas*.
74. Clarence P. Denman, "The Office of Adjutant General in Texas, 1835–1881," *SHQ* 28 (April 1925): 321; Special Order Nos. 53 and 55, both dated March 7, 1884, 401–1012, TSLAC; RSR, George W. Baylor, 401–143, TSLAC; King to Baylor, n.d., 401–631, TSLAC; Dudley G. Wooten, ed., *A Comprehensive History of Texas, 1685 to 1897* (Dallas: William G. Scarff, 1898), 2: 361; *RAG, 1884*, 16–17, 22; ROS, Company A, April 1884.
75. *RAG, 1884*, 21; Operations of State Troops, 2: 11–12; Utley, *Lone Star Justice*, 235–236; RSR, George W. Baylor, 401–143, TSLAC; ROS, Company A, May 1884; King to Baylor, May 12, 1884 (quotation), July 15, 1884, 401–631, TSLAC.
76. ROS, Company A, January 1885; Clifford R. Caldwell and Ron DeLord, *Texas Lawmen, 1835–1899: The Good and the Bad* (Charleston, SC: History Press, 2011), 342; Graybill, *Policing the Great Plains*, 140; *RAG, 1886*, 65.
77. Wilkins, *Law Comes to Texas*, 238, 250; *RAG, 1886*, 49–50; RSR, George W. Baylor, 401–143, TSLAC; General Order No. 21, March 31, 1885, Special Order No. 73, March 31, 1885, 401–1160, TSLAC.
78. *Galveston Daily News*, January 15, 1885; *House Journal, Twentieth Legislature, Regular Session*, 214, 460, 673, 804; Dan L. Thrapp,

Encyclopedia of Frontier Biography (Lincoln: University of Nebraska Press, 1991), 1: 74; Baylor, *Into the Far, Wild Country*, 29; *Austin Daily Statesman*, September 5, 1888.
79. George W. Baylor, "Sentiment, By a Confederate," *CV* 6 (December 1898): 526; *El Paso Daily Herald*, April 20, 22, July 9, 1898.
80. Baylor, *Into the Far, Wild Country*, 25; Candice DuCoin, *Lawmen on the Texas Frontier: Rangers and Sheriffs* (Round Rock, TX: Riata Books, 2007), 124, 130; Robert W. Stephens, *Texas Ranger Sketches* (Dallas: Robert W. Stephens, 1972), 66–68; Marshall Hail, *Knight in the Sun: Harper B. Lee, First Yankee Matador* (Boston: Little, Brown and Company, 1962), 23, 27–28, 36; *El Paso Daily Times*, November 15, 17, 21, 1895; *El Paso Daily Herald*, August 14, 1898.
81. *El Paso Daily Herald*, June 24, 1899; DuCoin, *Lawmen on the Texas Frontier*, 130; Baylor and Baylor, *Baylor's History of the Baylors*, 31–32; Baylor, *Into the Far, Wild Country*, 31–34; *Galveston Daily News*, April 15, 1904; "Wife of Col. G. W. Baylor," *CV* 13 (April 1905): 176; Consular Registration Certificate Nos. 8252 and 8253, RG 59, NARA.
82. Douglas W. Richmond and Sam W. Haynes, eds., *The Mexican Revolution: Conflict and Consolidation, 1910–1940* (College Station: Texas A&M University Press, 2013), 16–17, 62; Michael J. Gonzales, *The Mexican Revolution, 1910–1940* (Albuquerque: University of New Mexico Press, 2003), 92, 97, 98–99; *El Paso Morning Times*, August 28, 1913; Passenger Lists of Vessels Arriving at New Orleans, Louisiana, T905, NARA; *San Antonio Express*, September 30, October 14, 1913.
83. Soldier's Application for a Pension, Col. George Wythe Baylor, No. 28182, TSLAC; *San Antonio Light*, March 28, 1916; Texas Death Certificate, George Wythe Baylor, March 27, 1916, File No. 5813.
84. *Julius A. Appler's General Directory and Household Directory of Greater San Antonio, 1914* (San Antonio: J. A. Appler, 1914), 201; ibid., *1915*, 211; ibid., *1921–1922*, 241; *San Antonio City Directory, 1926* (Dallas: John F. Worley Company, 1926), 345; *Fourteenth* and *Fifteenth U.S. Census*, Bexar County, Texas; *Sixteenth U.S. Census*, Wilson County, Texas; Texas Death Certificate, Mary C. Baylor, February 5, 1942, File No. 3.

Notes for Chapter 7

1. Information from the Texas Ranger Commemorative Commission's files regarding the selection committee, and the nomination and

induction of Bryan Marsh, is scant. As he possessed a healthy measure of personal baggage, and served such a brief tenure as a Ranger captain, the reasons for his inclusion in the Hall of Fame are not readily obvious. This author is indebted to Byron Johnson and Christina Stopka for assistance in establishing the committee's rationale.

2. Bell-Marsh Family Records, H. M. Bell File, Smith County Historical Society Archives, Carnegie History Center; Marilyn Davis Barefield, *Clarke County, Alabama, Records: 1814–1885* (Easley, SC: Southern Historical Press, 1983), 10; *Sixth U.S. Census* and *Seventh U.S. Census*, Sumter County, Alabama (Free and Slave Schedules).

3. P. J. Furse, "Tyler's Distinguished Families," *Tyler Today Magazine* (Fall 1993): 13; Sidney Smith Johnson, *Some Biographies of Old Settlers* (Tyler, TX: self-published, 1900), 160; Tax Rolls, Smith County, 1854; R. S. Burruss, "History of William Tell Lodge No. 27," *Chronicles of Smith County* (Fall 1967): 16–17; *Tyler Reporter*, February 9, 1859.

4. Bryan Marsh, "The Confederate Letters of Bryan Marsh," *Chronicles of Smith County* (Winter 1975): 9; Johnson, *Some Biographies of Old Settlers*, 164 (quotation); Texas Death Certificate, Henry B. Marsh, October 10, 1940, File No. 214.

5. *Eighth U.S. Census*, Smith County, Texas (Free and Slave Schedules); Non-population Census Schedules, Smith County, Texas. Rebecca died on April 15, 1872.

6. John R. Lundberg, *Granbury's Texas Brigade: Diehard Western Confederates* (Baton Rouge: Louisiana State University, 2012), 22; "Report of the Proceedings of Granbury's Brigade Association," *Report of the Proceedings of the Various Associations of Ex-Confederates Held at Dallas, Dallas County, August 6th, 7th, 8th, and 9th, 1884* (Dallas: Dallas Printing House, 1884), 287–288; *Texas State Gazette*, November 16, 1861.

7. *The War of the Rebellion: A Compilation of the Official Records of the Union and Confederate Armies*, Series I, LIII: 800. Hereafter cited as *OR*, all references are to Series I unless otherwise indicated. Norman C. Delaney, ed., "The Diary and Memoirs of Marshall Samuel Pierson, Company C, 17th Reg., Texas Cavalry, 1862–1865," *Military History of Texas and the Southwest* 13 (1976): 25; CSR-CS, Seventeenth Texas Cavalry, Bryan Marsh, George F. Moore, Sterling B. Hendricks, and John McClarty; Bruce S. Allardice, *Confederate Colonels: A Biographical Register* (Columbia: University of Missouri Press, 2008), 277–278; Marcus J. Wright, comp., *Texas in the War, 1861–1865*, ed.

Harold B. Simpson (Hillsboro, Texas: Hill Junior College Press, 1965), 26, 117. Edmund and Darius also enlisted in the Confederate Army. See CSR-CS for E. Marsh, Fortieth Alabama Infantry, and Darius Marsh, Sixth Texas Infantry.

8. Marsh, "Confederate Letters," 10–11; Delaney, ed., "Marshall Samuel Pierson," 25; "Proceedings of Granbury's Brigade Association," 288; Joe R. Wise, ed., "Letters of Lt. Flavius W. Perry, 17th Texas Cavalry—1862–1863," *Military History of Texas and the Southwest* 13 (1976): 12.

9. *OR*, Series IV, I: 1061–1062; CSR-CS, Seventeenth Texas Cavalry, John C. Robertson, James R. Taylor, Bryan Marsh, George F. Moore; Allardice, *Confederate Colonels*, 365; Delaney, ed., "Marshall Samuel Pierson," 25.

10. Marsh, "Confederate Letters," 11–12; *OR*, XIII: 103; Delaney, ed., "Marshall Samuel Pierson," 25–26; *New York Herald*, July 20, 1862.

11. Marsh, "Confederate Letters," 14–15; "Proceedings of Granbury's Brigade Association," 288; Robert M. Collins, *Chapters from the Unwritten History of the War Between the States* (St. Louis, MO: Nixon-Jones Printing Company, 1893), 26–27; Delaney, ed., "Marshall Samuel Pierson," 26–27; Bill O'Neal, ed., "The Civil War Memoirs of Samuel Alonza Cooke," *SHQ* 74 (April 1971): 537. See also Edwin C. Bearss, "The White River Expedition, June 10-July 15, 1862," *AHQ* 21 (Winter 1962): 305–362.

12. Marsh, "Confederate Letters," 14–15; *OR*, XIII: 109–110; O'Neal, ed., "Samuel Alonza Cooke," 537; Delaney, ed., "Marshall Samuel Pierson," 27; William L. Shea, "The Confederate Defeat at Cache River," *AHQ* 52 (Summer 1993): 137, 141–142, 144–146, 148–149; Ralph A. Wooster, *Texas and Texans in the Civil War* (Austin: Eakin Press, 1995), 71.

13. Marsh, "Confederate Letters," 14–15, 17; *OR*, XIII: 36, 38; Delaney, ed., "Marshall Samuel Pierson," 27; Benjamin M. Seaton, *The Bugle Softly Blows: The Confederate Diary of Benjamin M. Seaton*, ed. Colonel Harold B. Simpson (Waco: Texian Press, 1965), 20–21; Dudley G. Wooten, ed., *A Comprehensive History of Texas, 1685 to 1897* (Dallas: William G. Scraff, 1898), 2: 741; Wise, ed., "Letters of Lt. Flavius W. Perry," 15; "Proceedings of Granbury's Brigade Association," 289–290; Lundberg, *Granbury's Texas Brigade*, 44, 46; Wright, comp., and Simpson, ed., *Texas in the War*, 14.

14. James M. McCaffrey, *This Band of Heroes: Granbury's Texas Brigade, C.S.A.* (College Station: Texas A&M University Press, 1996), 25;

Collins, *Unwritten History*, 61–62; Ezra J. Warner, *Generals in Gray: Lives of the Confederate Commanders* (Baton Rouge: Louisiana State University Press, 2008), 223–224, 72; Wise, ed., "Letters of Lt. Flavius W. Perry," 22; *Weekly State Gazette*, October 22, 1862; *OR*, XIII: 883; "Proceedings of Granbury's Brigade Association," 290; CSR-CS, Seventeenth Texas Cavalry, John McClarty.

15. *OR*, XVII, Pt. 1: 705; Barbara Brooks Tomblin, *The Civil War on the Mississippi: Union Sailors, Gunboat Captains, and the Campaign to Control the River* (Lexington: University Press of Kentucky, 2016), 202; Mark K. Christ, *Civil War Arkansas, 1863: The Battle for a State* (Norman: University of Oklahoma Press, 2010), 40; Edwin C. Bearss, "The Battle of the Post of Arkansas," *AHQ* 18 (Autumn 1959): 237, 238–239.

16. Marsh, "Confederate Letters," 19–20; *OR*, XXII, Pt. 1: 902, XIII: 885, 928; McCaffrey, *This Band of Heroes*, 32–33; Seaton, *The Bugle Softly Blows*, 27–28; Delaney, ed., "Marshall Samuel Pierson," 27; "Proceedings of Granbury's Brigade Association," 290; Thomas W. Cutrer, *Theater of a Separate War: The Civil War West of the Mississippi River* (Chapel Hill: University of North Carolina Press, 2017), 159–160; Allardice, *Confederate Colonels*, 158, 136; Mamie Yeary, comp., *Reminiscences of the Boys in Gray, 1861–1865* (Dallas: Smith and Lamar Publishing House, 1912), 145.

17. *OR*, XVII, Pt. 1: 612, 700–701, 709; *Official Records of the Union and Confederate Navies in the War of the Rebellion*, Series I, XXIII: 398. Hereafter cited as *ORN*, all references are to Series I. Bearss, "Post of Arkansas," 244, 246; I. V. Caraway, "The Battle of Arkansas Post," *CV* 14 (March 1906): 127; Snead, "Conquest of Arkansas," 452.

18. *OR*, XVII, Pt. 1: 613, 701–702; Gary D. Joiner, *Mr. Lincoln's Brown Water Navy: The Mississippi Squadron* (Lanham, MD: Rowman & Littlefield, 2007), 105; Christ, *Civil War Arkansas*, 51–52; Bearss, "Post of Arkansas," 247.

19. *OR*, XVII, Pt. 1: 780, 783, 754, 790; *ORN*, XXIV: 107, XXIII: 399; Tomblin, *The Civil War on the Mississippi*, 203; Cutrer, *Theater of a Separate War*, 161–162; William Williston Heartsill, *Fourteen Hundred and 91 Days in the Confederate Army: A Journal Kept by W. W. Heartsill for Four Years, One Month, and One Day*, ed. Bell Irvin Wiley (Jackson, TN: McCowat-Mercer Press, 1953), 90, 91–92; Bearss, "Post of Arkansas," 247–248; R. R. Garland, "Arkansas Post—Its Fall, January 11, 1863," *Southern Historical*

Society Papers 22 (January-December 1894): 10. Hereafter cited as "Fall of Arkansas Post."

20. *OR*, XVII, Pt. 1: 780, 791, 702–704, 783; *ORN*, XXXIII: 399; Joiner, *Mr. Lincoln's Brown Water Navy*, 105; Christ, *Civil War Arkansas*, 55–63; Heartsill, *Fourteen Hundred and 91 Days*, 93, 94; William J. Oliphant, *Only a Private: A Texan Remembers the Civil War: The Memoirs of William J. Oliphant*, ed. James M. McCaffrey (Houston: Halcyon Press, 2004), 26; Delaney, ed., "Marshall Samuel Pierson," 27–28; Seaton, *The Bugle Softly Blows*, 31; Caraway, "Battle of Arkansas Post," 128; "Capture of the Post of Arkansas," *Harper's Weekly* 7 (February 7, 1863): 94.

21. *OR*, XVII, Pt. 1: 699, 706–708, 710, 716–719, 781, 784–785, 793–795, 766–767, 769, 773, 776, 747; *ORN*, XXIV: 107–109, XXIII: 400–401; Joiner, *Mr. Lincoln's Brown Water Navy*, 106, 109; Tomblin, *The Civil War on the Mississippi*, 206–207; Cutrer, *Theater of a Separate War*, 162–163; Delaney, ed., "Marshall Samuel Pierson," 28; Collins, *Unwritten History*, 68; Caraway, "Battle of Arkansas Post," 127–128; S. W. Bishop, "The Battle of Arkansas Post," *CV* 5 (April 1897): 152; Garland, "Fall of Arkansas Post," 121–13; O'Neal, ed., "Samuel Alonza Cooke," 538; Oliphant, *Only a Private*, 27–29 (quotations on p. 28); "Capture of the Post of Arkansas," 94; Clement A. Evans, ed., *Confederate Military History* (Atlanta: Confederate Publishing Company, 1899), 10: 159–160.

22. Marsh, "Confederate Letters," 23; *OR*, Series II, IV: 266–268; CSR-CS, Seventeenth Texas Cavalry, Bryan Marsh; McCaffrey, *This Band of Heroes*, 54; Charles W. Sanders, Jr., *While in the Hands of the Enemy: Military Prisons of the Civil War* (Baton Rouge: Louisiana State University Press, 2005), 115–116, 151–152; James M. McPherson, *Battle Cry of Freedom: The Civil War Era* (New York: Oxford University Press, 1988), 791–792; Roger Pickenpaugh, *Camp Chase and the Evolution of Union Prison Policy* (Tuscaloosa: University of Alabama Press, 2007), 66; Wise, ed., "Letters of Lt. Flavius W. Perry," 30; O'Neal, ed., "Samuel Alonza Cooke," 538–539; Collins, *Unwritten History*, 86–119; Seaton, *The Bugle Softly Blows*, 31–32; Dale Fetzer and Bruce Mowday, *Unlikely Allies: Fort Delaware's Prison Community in the Civil War* (Mechanicsburg, PA: Stackpole Books, 2000), 71; Oliphant, *Only a Private*, 30, 32; Yeary, comp., *Reminiscences of the Boys in Gray*, 145.

Prisoners at Camp Butler and Camp Douglas suffered from inferior housing and poor drainage, all of which created generally unsanitary conditions. By early 1863, when the survivors of Arkansas Post were held there, the latter facility's mortality rate was approximately 10 percent per month, higher than any other prison camp in the Union. The primary causes of death were typhoid fever and pneumonia. Lonnie R. Speer, *Portals to Hell: Military Prisons of the Civil War* (Lincoln: University of Nebraska Press, 2005), 135–137.

Several early accounts mistakenly place Marsh's capture at Fort Donelson, Tennessee, presumably during the battle of February 11–16, 1862. See Sidney Smith Johnson, *Texans Who Wore the Gray* (Tyler: self-published, 1907), 15; Johnson, *Some Biographies of Old Settlers*, 161; and Lucinda Rutherford Douglas, ed., *Douglas's Texas Battery, CSA* (Tyler: Smith County Historical Society, 1966), 67 n77.

23. Marsh, "The Confederate Letters," 22, 23; Lundberg, *Granbury's Texas Brigade*, 87–88; Oliphant, *Only a Private*, 37–38; O'Neal, ed., "Samuel Alonza Cooke," 539; Wooster, *Texas and Texans in the Civil War*, 74; Pickenpaugh, *Camp Chase*, 69–70.

24. Marsh, "Confederate Letters," 24; OR, XXIII, Pt. 2: 868; Wright, comp., and Simpson, ed., *Texas in the War*, 117; CSR-CS, Seventeenth Texas Cavalry, Bryan Marsh, Twenty-fifth Texas Cavalry, Clayton C. Gillespie, Eighteenth Texas Cavalry, John T. Coit, Twenty-fourth Texas Cavalry, William A. Taylor; Allardice, *Confederate Colonels*, 163, 366; O'Neal, ed., "Samuel Alonza Cooke," 539; Norman D. Brown, ed., *One of Cleburne's Command: The Civil War Reminiscences and Diary of Capt. Samuel T. Foster, Granbury's Texas Brigade, CSA* (Austin: University of Texas Press, 1980), 43.

25. Delaney, ed., "Marshall Samuel Pierson," 29; Yeary, comp., *Reminiscences of the Boys in Gray*, 145; CSR-CS, Seventeenth Texas Consolidated (Dismounted) Cavalry, James F. Taylor, Sterling B. Hendricks, Sebron M. Noble, Eighteenth Texas Cavalry, William A. Ryan.

26. OR, XXIII, Pt. 2: 862, Pt. 1: 10, 6 (quotation), 586; Stanley F. Horn, *The Army of Tennessee: A Military History* (Norman: University of Oklahoma Press, 1993), 196–210; Irving A. Buck, *Cleburne and His Command* (New York: Neale Publishing Company, 1908), 99–100; William G. Robertson, et al., *Staff Ride Handbook for the Battle of Chickamauga* (Fort Leavenworth: Combat Studies Institute, 1992), 49. See also Larry J. Daniel, *The Battle of Stones River: The Forgotten Conflict Between the Confederate Army of Tennessee and the Union Army of the Cumberland* (Baton Rouge: Louisiana State University Press, 2012).

27. *OR*, XXIII, Pt. 2: 846, 873, Pt. 1: 10, 403, 586–587; Buck, *Cleburne and His Command*, 106; Thomas Lawrence Connelly, *Autumn of Glory: The Army of Tennessee, 1862–1865* (Baton Rouge: Louisiana State University Press, 2001), 126; Horn, *Army of Tennessee*, 234. Robertson, *Staff Ride Handbook*, 49; Peter Cozzens, *This Terrible Sound: The Battle of Chickamauga* (Urbana: University of Illinois Press, 1992), 18; Robert Underwood Johnson and Clarence Clough Buel, eds., *Battles and Leaders of the Civil War* (Secaucus, NJ: Castle Books, 1982), 3: 636.
28. OR, XXIII, Pt. 1: 402, 583, 618; Earl J. Hess, *Braxton Bragg: The Most Hated Man of the Confederacy* (Chapel Hill: University of North Carolina Press, 2016), 146; Horn, *Army of Tennessee*, 235.
29. Marsh, "Confederate Letters," 25–27; OR, XXIII, Pt. 1: 402, 403, 406, 583–584, 587; Heartsill, *Fourteen Hundred and 91 Days*, 132–133, 136; Robertson, *Staff Ride Handbook*, 49; Cozzens, *This Terrible Sound*, 19; Seaton, *The Bugle Softly Blows*, 35; Shelby Foote, *The Civil War: A Narrative* (New York: Random House, 1986), 2: 671–674; Oliphant, *Only a Private*, 41–42; Collins, *Unwritten History*, 136; CSR-CS, Seventeenth Texas Cavalry, Bryan Marsh. In addition to the abandonment of Middle Tennessee, the month of July would see Confederate reverses at Gettysburg, Port Hudson, and Vicksburg. Mark Mayo Boatner III, *The Civil War Dictionary* (New York: David McKay Company, 1988), 331–340, 663, 876–877.
30. Marsh, "Confederate Letters," 27–28; *OR*, XXX, Pt. 4: 531, 583–584, 599–600, 495, Pt. 2: 21–22, 26–27, 136, XXIII, Pt. 2: 908–909; Robertson, *Staff Ride Handbook*, 50; Hess, *Braxton Bragg*, 153; Cozzens, *This Terrible Sound*, 41–47, 55–57; Collins, *Unwritten History*, 143; Horn, *Army of Tennessee*, 242, 246–248; Connelly, *Autumn of Glory*, 168–169.
31. *OR*, XXX, Pt. 2: 27–31, 138–140, 292–302; Cozzens, *This Terrible Sound*, 64–75, 81–85; Steven E. Woodworth, *Jefferson Davis and His Generals: The Failure of Confederate Command in the West* (Lawrence: University Press of Kansas, 1990), 231–233; Hess, *Braxton Bragg*, 157–158.
32. Marsh, "Confederate Letters," 28; *OR*, XXX, Pt. 2: 24, 32, 140, 153–154, 187–188, 194; Cozzens, *This Terrible Sound*, 89–90, 170–171, 263–266, 271, 274–276, 278–279; Buck, *Cleburne and His Command*, 125–126; Evans, ed., *Confederate Military History*, 8: 100–101; Craig L. Symonds, *Stonewall of the West: Patrick Cleburne and the Civil War* (Lawrence: University of Kansas Press, 1997),

143–146; Major Joseph M. Lance III, "Patrick R. Cleburne and the Tactical Employment of His Division at Chickamauga" (MMAS thesis, Fort Leavenworth, 1996), 64–66; O'Neal, ed., "Samuel Alonza Cooke," 540–541; Oliphant, *Only a Private*, 44–45; W. W. Carnes, "Chickamauga," *Southern Historical Society Papers* 14 (January-December 1886): 400; Bromfield L. Ridley, *Battles and Sketches of the Army of Tennessee* (Mexico, MO: Missouri Printing & Publishing Company, 1906), 220 (quotation); Allardice, *Confederate Colonels*, 395.

33. Cozzens, *This Terrible Sound*, 294, 299–303; Hess, *Braxton Bragg*, 162; Horn, *Army of Tennessee*, 259–260.
34. Marsh, "Confederate Letters," 28; *OR*, XXX, Pt. 2: 24, 33–34, 141–144, 154–156, 188–189, 195; Cozzens, This *Terrible Sound*, 339, 342, 348–349; Oliphant, *Only a Private*, 46 (quotation); McCaffrey, *This Band of Heroes*, 74–76; Heartsill, *Fourteen Hundred and 91 Days*, 153–154; Buck, *Cleburne and His Command*, 132–133; Richard C. Sheridan, "Brigadier General James Deshler, Professional Soldier," *Alabama Historical Quarterly* 26 (Summer 1964): 213–214; Collins, *Unwritten History*, 159; Lance, "Cleburne and the Tactical Employment of His Division," 67–68, 69–70, 99–100.
35. *OR*, XXX, Pt. 2: 22–23, 34, 144–145, 156, 187, 189–190; Johnson and Buel, eds., *Battles and Leaders*, 3: 660–661; Bruce Catton, *Never Call Retreat* (New York: Fall River Press, 2009), 248–249; Buck, *Cleburne and His Command*, 137–139; Brown, ed., *One of Cleburne's Command*, 54; *Galveston Weekly News*, November 25, 1863.
36. *OR*, XXX, Pt. 1: 22, Pt. 2: 26–37; Hess, *Braxton Bragg*, 176, 182; Symonds, *Stonewall of the West*, 153; Wiley Sword, *Mountains Touched with Fire: Chattanooga Besieged, 1863* (New York: St. Martin's Press, 1995), 27; Irving A. Buck, "Cleburne and His Division at Missionary Ridge and Ringgold Gap," *Southern Historical Society Papers* 8 (1880): 464; Lundberg, *Granbury's Texas Brigade*, 113.
37. Marsh, "Confederate Letters," 29; McCaffrey, *This Band of Heroes*, 84; Brown, ed., *One of Cleburne's Command*, 57; *OR*, XXX, Pt. 2: 149, 660, Pt. 4: 752; CSR-CS, Eighteenth Texas Cavalry, John T. Coit, Twenty-fourth Texas Cavalry, William A. Ryan. Coit would remain absent on sick leave until he resigned on May 26, 1864.
38. Catton, *Never Call Retreat*, 255–256, 258; Ron Chernow, *Grant* (New York: Penguin Press, 2017), 305; Sword, *Mountains Touched with Fire*, 52, 56; Hess, *Braxton Bragg*, 190; Horn, *Army of Tennessee*, 292–293; Connelly, *Autumn of Glory*, 254–261.

39. *OR*, XXXI, Pt. 3: 582–583, 767; Buck, "Cleburne and His Division," 465; Horn, *Army of Tennessee*, 296.
40. *OR*, XXXI, Pt. 2: 664, Pt. 3: 745–746; Sword, *Mountains Touched with Fire*, 186–188, 227–230; Chernow, *Grant*, 320, 321–322; Brown, ed., *One of Cleburne's Command*, 58–59; Peter Cozzens, *The Shipwreck of Their Hopes: The Battles for Chattanooga* (Urbana: University of Illinois Press, 1994), 144, 160–194, 197.
41. Cozzens, *Shipwreck of Their Hopes*, 145–148, 151–153; Sword, *Mountains Touched with Fire*, 234–235, 242–243; McCaffrey, *This Band of Heroes*, 88; Craig L. Symonds, "Stonewall of the West: Patrick Cleburne and the Defense of Tunnel Hill," *Civil War Regiments* 7 (2000): 80, 82; Buck, "Cleburne and His Division," 465; Ridley, *Battles and Skirmishes*, 239–241.
42. *OR*, XXXI, Pt. 2: 664–666, 749–751; Chernow, *Grant*, 322; Collins, *Unwritten History*, 180; Brown, ed., *One of Cleburne's Command*, 61–63; Buck, "Cleburne and His Division," 467–469; Peter Cozzens, ed, *Battles and Leaders of the Civil War* (Urbana: University of Illinois Press, 2002), 5: 474–476; CSR-CGSO, Hiram Bronson Granbury; Wright, comp., and Simpson, ed., *Texas in the War*, 5, 78; Symonds, "Cleburne and the Defense of Tunnel Hill," 84–85, 86; Seaton, *The Bugle Softly Blows*, 45 (quotation); Allardice, *Confederate Colonels*, 274–275. Mills, an attorney and legislator in civilian life, was also the brother-in-law of future Frontier Battalion commander John B. Jones. For more on this overlooked statesman, see Alwyn Barr, "The Making of a Secessionist: The Antebellum Career of Roger Q. Mills," *SHQ* 79 (October 1975): 129–144.
43. *OR*, XXXI, Pt. 2: 665–666, 753; Chernow, *Grant*, 322–324; Horn, *Army of Tennessee*, 300–301; McCaffrey, *This Band of Heroes*, 92.
44. Marsh, "Confederate Letters," 30; *OR*, XXXI, Pt. 2: 403–404, 666, 753–756, 773–774, 778 (second quotation), 758, Series II, III: 162; Cozzens, *Shipwreck of Their Hopes*, 370–375, 384; Sword, *Mountains Touched with Fire*, 334–335; Wooten, ed., *Comprehensive History of Texas*, 2: 745; W. W. Gibson, "Reminisces of Ringgold Gap," *CV* 12 (November 1904): 526; Buck, "Cleburne and His Division," 470 (first quotation), 471, 472.
45. Marsh, "Confederate Letters," 9; *OR*, XXXI, Pt. 2: 682, Pt. 3: 764–765, 771, 835–836, 873; Hess, *Braxton Bragg*, 203, 205; John H. Eicher and David J. Eicher, *Civil War High Commands* (Stanford: Stanford University Press, 2001), 890; Seaton, *The Bugle Softly Blows*, 48;

Oliphant, *Only a Private*, 54, 55; Symonds, *Stonewall of the West*, 176; Buck, *Cleburne and His Command*, 209.

46. CSR-CGSO, Hiram Bronson Granbury; Wright, comp., and Simpson, ed., *Texas in the War*, 78; Oliphant, *Only a Private*, 56–57; CSR-CS, Eighteenth Texas Cavalry, George D. Manion, Seventeenth Texas Cavalry, Bryan Marsh. The new Seventeenth and Eighteenth Texas regiment remained separate from the Seventeenth Texas Consolidated Cavalry under Colonel Taylor, and continued to fight east of the Mississippi.

47. Catton, *Never Call Retreat*, 296–299, 301–306; Jay Luvaas and Harold W. Nelson, eds., *Guide to the Atlanta Campaign: Rocky Face Ridge to Kennesaw Mountain* (Lawrence: University Press of Kansas, 2008), 1; Stephen Davis, *A Long and Bloody Task: The Atlanta Campaign from Dalton through Kennesaw to the Chattahoochee, May 5-June 18, 1864* (El Dorado Hills, CA: Savas Beatie, 2016), 12–13; Albert Castel, *Decision in the West: The Atlanta Campaign of 1864* (Lawrence: University Press of Kansas, 1992), 128–186; J. Britt McCarley, *The Atlanta and Savannah Campaigns, 1864* (Washington, D.C.: U.S. Army Center of Military History, 2014), 7–8, 10; Charles A. Leuschner, *The Civil War Diary of Charles A. Leuschner*, ed. Charles D. Spurlin (Austin: Eakin Press, 1992), 30–33; Evans, ed., *Confederate Military History*, 6: 303–308; Brown, ed., *One of Cleburne's Command*, 71–79; Lundberg, *Granbury's Texas Brigade*, 139.

48. *OR*, XXXVIII, Pt. 1: 65; Luvaas and Nelson, eds., *Guide to the Atlanta Campaign*, 173; Robert M. McMurry, *Atlanta 1864: Last Chance for the Confederacy* (Lincoln: University of Nebraska Press, 2000), 85–86; Horn, *Army of Tennessee*, 329; Connelly, *Autumn of Glory*, 353–354; Foote, *Civil War*, 3: 343–347.

49. *OR*, XXXVIII, Pt. 1: 66, 144, Pt. 3: 761; Philip L. Secrist, *Sherman's 1864 Trail of Battle to Atlanta* (Macon, GA: Mercer University Press, 2006), 70–71; Castel, *Decision in the West*, 229; Evans, ed., *Confederate Military History*, 6: 309; Robert M. McMurry, "'The Hell Hole': New Hope Church," *CWTI* 11 (February 1973): 35, 37–38; Seaton, *The Bugle Softly Blows*, 52; Ridley, *Battles and Sketches*, 303–304.

50. *OR*, XXXVIII, Pt. 1: 377–379, Pt. 3: 724–726; Luvaas and Nelson, eds., *Guide to the Atlanta Campaign*, 8, 179, 201–204; Castel, *Decision in the West*, 237, 240; McCarley, *The Atlanta and Savannah Campaigns*, 21–24; McMurry, "'The Hell Hole'," 38–40; Collins, *Unwritten History*, 211–215; Lundberg, *Granbury's Texas Brigade*, 150–152; Oliphant, *Only a Private*, 62–63; Philip L. Secrist, "Scenes

of Awful Carnage," *CWTI* 10 (June 1971): 9, 45–47; Brown, ed., *One of Cleburne's Command*, 85–86; Buck, *Cleburne and His Command*, 248–249; Edward Bourne, "Govan's Brigade at New Hope Church," *CV* 31 (March 1923): 89; O'Neal, ed., "Samuel Alonza Cooke," 542–543; Leuschner, *The Civil War Diary*, 34.

51. *OR*, XXXVIII, Pt. 1: 66–67, Pt. 3: 726, 687; Castel, *Decision in the West*, 240–241, 259–260; Oliphant, *Only a Private*, 66 (second quotation); McMurry, *Atlanta 1864*, 96, 101; Bourne, "Govan's Brigade," 89 (first quotation); Brown, ed., *One of Cleburne's Command*, 89; O'Neal, ed., "Samuel Alonza Cooke," 543; Lundberg, *Granbury's Texas Brigade*, 158. Craig L. Symonds, *Joseph E. Johnston: A Civil War Biography* (New York: W. W. Norton & Company, 1992), 386: "Neither genius nor marplot, Joseph E. Johnston was an old-style Southern solider who fought in a new-style war to the best of his considerable abilities."

52. *OR*, XXXVIII, Pt. 4: 763; Earl J. Hess, *Kennesaw Mountain: Sherman, Johnston, and the Atlanta Campaign* (Chapel Hill: University of North Carolina Press, 2013), 8, 10; Luvaas and Nelson, eds., *Guide to the Atlanta Campaign*, 238; Castel, *Decision in the West*, 267–268; Buck, *Cleburne and His Command*, 256; Evans, ed., *Confederate Military History*, 6: 313.

53. Marsh, "Confederate Letters," 45–46; *OR*, XXXIV, Pt. 1: 564; CSR-CS, Seventeenth Texas Cavalry, Bryan Marsh; Rebecca W. Smith and Marion Mullins, eds., "The Diary of H. C. Medford, Confederate Soldier, 1864," Pt. 2, *SHQ* 34 (January 1931): 219. Regarding Marsh's promotion, Dr. Lundberg generously shared the benefit of his expertise in a series of emails, dated May 15–16, 2017. Artillery officer James P. Douglas also noted Marsh's advancement, but the typescript of his letter bears the date of May 20, 1864. Douglas, ed., *Douglas's Texas Battery*, 88–89.

54. McCarley, *The Atlanta and Savannah Campaigns*, 27–28; Davis, *A Long and Bloody Task*, 67; Secrist, *Sherman's 1864 Trail*, 106–108; Brown, ed., *One of Cleburne's Command*, 95.

55. Marsh, "Confederate Letters," 45–46; Charles Temple, "Marquis de Lafayette Price (1840–1923)," unpublished MS, n.d., n. pag. Price's biographical sketch was prepared by his great-grandson who heard the story of Marsh's rescue from his paternal grandmother, Lottie Frances Price Temple. CSR-CS, Seventeenth Texas Cavalry, Marcus D. L. Price; Brown, ed., *One of Cleburne's Command*, 95–96; Douglas, ed., *Douglas's Texas Battery*, 101, 105.

Endnotes **607**

56. McMurry, *Atlanta 1864*, 103; Davis, *A Long and Bloody Task*, 67–69; Lundberg, *Granbury's Texas Brigade*, 160; Evans, ed., *Confederate Military History*, 6: 314–315. The Atlanta campaign was particularly unpleasant for the Marsh family. Serving as a captain, Edmund was killed at Dalton, Georgia, on May 11, 1864. Darius, a first lieutenant, died at Snake Creek Gap, Georgia, on May 30. CSR-CS, Fortieth Alabama Infantry, E. Marsh, Sixth Texas Infantry, Darius Marsh.
57. *OR*, XXXVIII, Pt. 5: 885, 887, XLI, Pt. 2: 1066, XLVIII, Pt. 2: 311, 533–534; Richard Taylor, "The Last Confederate Surrender," *Southern Historical Society Papers* 3 (March 1877): 156–157; CSR-CS, Seventeenth Texas Cavalry, Bryan Marsh; Johnson, *Texans Who Wore the Gray*, 15.
58. Tax Rolls, Smith County, 1865–1867; Widow's Application for a Pension, Mrs. Lucy Marsh, No. 49090, TSLAC; Johnson, *Some Biographies of Old Settlers*, 164 (quotation); "The Marsh House," *Chronicles of Smith County* 3 (Spring 1964), 14.
59. Sammy Tise, *Texas County Sheriffs* (Albuquerque: Oakwood Printing, 1989), 468; Morris S. Burton, "The Court Houses of Smith County," *Chronicles of Smith County* (Fall 1964), 6.
60. William L. Richter, *The Army in Texas During Reconstruction, 1865–1870* (College Station: Texas A&M University Press, 1987), 120–124; *Galveston Daily News*, November 9, 1867; Tise, *Texas County Sheriffs*, 468.
61. *The South-Western*, July 1, September 2, November 4, 1868, February 23, 1870; Johnson, *Some Biographies of Old Settlers*, 161; *Ouachita Telegraph*, November 6, 1869; Texas Death Certificate, Mitty Rivers Marsh, November 17, 1941, File No. 314.
62. *Shreveport Times*, July 27, August 24, 1872; Andrew L. Leath, "Elected County Officials, 1846–76," *Chronicles of Smith County* 17 (Summer 1978): 59, 61. The Smith County Commissioners Court Minutes covering January to April 1874 are "silent" regarding local elections, while the pages for the day of the election, and for the day after, have been removed entirely. Additionally, election records do not exist in the county clerk's office from March 1867 to November 1878. Randolph B. Campbell, *Grass Roots Reconstruction in Texas, 1865–1880* (Baton Rouge: Louisiaina State University Press, 1997), 23; Docket for Case No. 1923, District Court Minutes Book G, Smith County Records Services, 568–571. Tiffany Wright, archives manager for the Smith County Historical Society, uncovered the details of the Long-Marsh

case. Retired archivist Donaly Brice confirmed that no election returns or election register entries for Smith County's December 1873 contest exist at the Texas State Archives.
63. *Galveston Daily News*, November 1, 1874; Mike Cox, *Gunfights and Sites in Texas Ranger History* (Charleston, SC: History Press, 2015), 46 (first quotation); Zella Lewis, ed., *The Proud Century: Tyler Public Schools 1882–1982* (Tyler, TX: Tyler Independent School System, 1982), Appendix 1–1 (second quotation).
64. *Dallas Daily Herald*, May 29, June 2, 5, 1875; Texas Death Certificate, Mrs. Mary Marsh Crutcher, December 2, 1912, Registrar's No. 298; Tise, *Texas County Sheriffs*, 468; *Galveston Daily News*, February 6, 1875 (quotation), December 4, 1877; Tax Rolls, Smith County, 1880–1882; *Tenth U.S. Census*, Smith County, Texas.
65. Special Order No. 81, November 24, 1880, 401–1012, TSLAC: RSR, Bryan Marsh, 401–163, TSLAC; Dan L. Thrapp, *Encyclopedia of Frontier Biography* (Lincoln: University of Nebraska Press, 1991), 2: 992.
66. *Galveston Daily News*, January 21, 1881.
67. James N. Leiker, *Racial Borders: Black Soldiers Along the Rio Grande* (College Station: Texas A&M University Press, 2002), 90; Patricia E. Lamkin, "Blacks in San Angelo: Relations Between Fort Concho and the City, 1875–1889," *WTHAY* 66 (1990), 26, 28; Frank N. Schubert, "Gunfire at San Angela: When 10th Cavalry Troopers from Fort Concho Retaliated Against Texas Civilians," *Wild West* 16 (February 2004): 14.
68. "Letters of David Williams, 1877–1886," and Grierson to Assistant Adjutant General, February 8, 1881, both in Fort Concho Soldiers Riot, 1881, Tom Green County Historical Society Collection, Angelo State University; William H. Leckie, with Shirley A. Leckie, *The Buffalo Soldiers: A Narrative of the Black Cavalry in the West* (Norman: University of Oklahoma Press, 2003), 239; *Galveston Daily News*, February 2, 3, 1881.
69. Susan Miles, "The Soldiers' Riot," *Fort Concho Report* 13 (Spring 1981): 10–11, 13; Frank N. Schubert, *Voices of the Buffalo Soldier: Records, Reports, and Recollections of Military Life and Service in the West* (Albuquerque: University of New Mexico Press, 2003), 120; *Daily Democratic Statesman*, February 8, 1881; J. Evetts Haley, *Fort Concho and the Texas Frontier* (San Angelo: San Angelo Standard-Times, 1952), 279.
70. *Dallas Daily Herald*, February 5, 1881.

71. Miles, "The Soldiers' Riot," 11, 13–14; *San Antonio Daily Express*, February 11, 1881; *San Angelo Standard*, May 3, 1924; Grierson to Assistant Adjutant General, February 8, 1881, Fort Concho Soldiers Riot; Wooten, ed., *Comprehensive History of Texas*, 2: 356–357.
72. MR, Company B, February 28, 1881; William H. Lessing, Box 2–9/847, Bonds and Oaths of County and State Officials, TSLAC; Marsh to Jones, February 7, 1881, 401–1159, TSLAC; Marsh to Jones, February 11, 1881, RSR, Bryan Marsh, 401–163, TSLAC; *RAG, 1882*, 37; Haley, *Fort Concho*, 280–281; J. Evetts Haley, *Jeff Milton: Good Man with a Gun* (Norman: University of Oklahoma Press, 1948), 37 (quotation). Jeff was the son of John Milton, the Confederate governor of Florida.
73. MR, Company B, February 28, 1881; Marsh to Jones, February 11, 1881, RSR, Bryan Marsh, 401–163, TSLAC (first quotation); Grierson to Assistant Adjutant General, February 8, 1881, Fort Concho Soldiers Riot (second quotation); Haley, *Jeff Milton*, 38 (third quotation); *San Angelo Standard*, May 3, 1924.
74. MR, Company B, February 28, 1881; Marsh to Jones and Falvey to Jones, both dated February 7, 1881, 401–1159, TSLAC; *RAG, 1882*, 33, 37; Miles, "The Soldiers' Riot," 16, 17–18; *San Angelo Standard*, May 3, 1924; *San Antonio Daily Express*, February 22, 1881; *Dallas Daily Herald*, February 26, 1881; Leckie, *Buffalo Soldiers*, 240.
75. Walter R. Borneman, *Iron Horses: America's Race to Bring the Railroads West* (New York: Back Bay Books, 2010), 193; Earle B. Young, *Tracks to the Sea: Galveston and Western Railroad Development, 1866–1900* (College Station: Texas A&M University Press, 1999), 4, 104; Haley, *Jeff Milton*, 42–45; Randolph B. Campbell, *Gone to Texas: A History of the Lone Star State* (New York: Oxford University Press, 2003), 306; Ty Cashion, *A Texas Frontier: The Clear Fork Country and Fort Griffin, 1849–1887* (Norman: University of Oklahoma Press, 1996), 268–270; *Dallas Daily Herald*, June 8, 9, August 26, 1881; Mike Cox, *The Texas Rangers: Wearing the Cinco Peso, 1821–1900* (New York: Tom Doherty Associates, 2008), 317.
76. Robert W. Stephens, *Texas Ranger Sketches* (Dallas: Robert W. Stephens, 1972), 151–152; Haley, *Jeff Milton*, 49–50; Tise, *Texas County Sheriffs*, 378; MR, Company B, April 30-May 31, 1881; Cox, *Wearing the Cinco Peso*, 317; Bob Alexander, *Winchester Warriors: Texas Rangers of Company D, 1874–1901* (Denton: University of North Texas Press, 2009), 166–167; J. Lee Jones, Jr. and Nona C. Jones, comps., and Mac B. McKinnon,

ed., *Lore and Legend: A Compilation of Documents Depicting the History of Colorado City and Mitchell County* (Colorado City, TX: Colorado City Record, 1976), 8, 70, 78, 149; Edward A. Blackburn, Jr., *Wanted: Historic County Jails of Texas* (College Station: Texas A&M University Press, 2006), 242; Dan W. Roberts, *Rangers and Sovereignty* (San Antonio: Wood Printing & Engraving Co., 1914), 64 (quotation). Following his victory at the polls, Ware resigned from the battalion on February 1, 1881. RSR, R. C. Ware, 401–176, TSLAC.

77. MR, Company B, May 31, 1881; Haley, *Jeff Milton*, 50 (quotation); Frederick Wilkins, *The Law Comes to Texas: The Texas Rangers, 1870–1901* (Abilene, TX: State House Press, 1999), 226; *Dallas Daily Herald*, May 18, 1881.

78. Haley, *Jeff Milton*, 52–53 (quotation on p. 52); Roberts, *Rangers and Sovereignty*, 63–65; *Galveston Daily News*, May 27, 1881; *RAG*, 1882, 24; MR, Company B, May 31, 1881; Cox, *Wearing the Cinco Peso*, 323; Patsy McDonald Spaw, ed., *The Texas Senate* (College Station: Texas A&M University Press, 1999), 2:338; *Galveston Daily News*, November 30, December 2, 16, 1883. All three men were transferred to Company E in September 1881. Milton resigned on May 7, 1883, Sedberry was serving as the outfit's first sergeant at the time of the trial, and Wells was a private. RSR, Jeff Milton, 401–164, J. M. Sedberry, 171, L. Wells, -176, TSLAC.

79. Cox, *Wearing the Cinco Peso*, 323; Wilkins, Law Comes to Texas, 229; *RAG, 1882*, 27–28.

80. *Austin Daily Statesman*, June 19, 1881; *Galveston Daily News*, June 19, 1881; MR, Company B, August 31, 1881.

81. *RAG, 1882*, 23; Wilkins, *Law Comes to Texas*, 226; *Galveston Daily News*, May 27, 1881; Michael C. C. Adams, *Living Hell: The Dark Side of the Civil War* (Baltimore: Johns Hopkins University Press, 2014), 109, 120, 129; Shauna Devine, *Learning from the Wounded: The Civil War and the Rise of American Medical Science* (Chapel Hill: University of North Carolina Press, 2014), 159–160, 315 n151, 154–157 (quotation on p. 157); Jacob Mendes Da Costa, "On Irritable Heart: A Clinical Study of a Form of Functional Cardiac Disorder and Its Consequences," *American Journal of the Medical Sciences* 61 (January 1871): 19; Sarah A. M. Ford, "Suffering in Silence: Post-Traumatic Stress Psychological Disorders and Soldiers in the American Civil War," *Journal of Civil War Medicine* 18 (April 2014): 59–66. See also S. Weir Mitchell, *Injuries of Nerves and Their Consequences* (Philadelphia: J. P. Lippincott & Co., 1872).

Endnotes **611**

82. Coldwell to King, June 22, 1881, 401–1159, TSLAC; *RAG, 1882*, 23, 25; *Austin Daily Statesman*, July 26, 1881; *Galveston Daily News*, September 6, 1881; RSR, Bryan Marsh, 401–163, TSLAC; Special Order No. 6, August 22, 1881, 401–1012, TSLAC; Stephens, *Texas Ranger Sketches*, 99–101. King's appointment had not been popular with the rank and file of the Frontier Battalion. While a member of the Seventeenth Legislature, he had advocated reducing appropriations for frontier defense. *Galveston Daily News*, July 23, 24, 1881. There has been some uncertainty over whether Marsh resigned or was dismissed. The official correspondence makes clear the captain was fired.
83. Tax Rolls, Smith County, 1883–1895; *Fort Worth Daily Gazette*, June 16, 1885; Tise, *Texas County Sheriffs*, 468; *Dallas Morning News*, February 22, October 16, December 14, 1887; *Galveston Daily News*, June 8 (quotation), 11, 12, 1885, December 1, 14, 1887, December 14, 1889.
84. *Galveston Daily News*, July 30, 1895, March 26, 1901; Johnson, *Some Biographies of Old Settlers*, 161; *Victoria Daily Advocate*, September 8, 1899 (quotation). See also Timothy B. Smith, *A Chickamauga Memorial: The Establishment of America's First Civil War National Military Park* (Knoxville: University of Tennessee Press, 2009).
85. *Thirteenth* and *Fourteenth U.S. Census*, Smith County, Texas; *City Directory, Tyler, Texas, 1904* (Little Rock, AR: Southern Directory Company, 1904), 1: 174; Widow's Application for a Pension, Mrs. Lucy Marsh, No. 49090, TSLAC; *Worley's City Directory, Tyler, Texas, 1934–1935* (Dallas: John F. Worley Directory Co., 1935), 121, 233; Texas Death Certificate, Lucy Portis Marsh, November 5, 1934, File No. 51294.
86. *Who's Who in the Central States* (Washington, D.C.: Mayflower Publishing Company, 1929), 619; Johnson, *Some Biographies of Old Settlers*, 164; Furse, "Tyler's Distinguished Families," 13–14; Bell-Marsh Family Records; Robert C. Cotner, *James Stephen Hogg: A Biography* (Austin: University of Texas Press, 1959), 106, 124–125; *Worley's Directory of Tyler, Texas, 1913* (Dallas: John F. Worley Directory Co., 1913), 133–134, 138; Texas Death Certificate, Henry B. Marsh, November 2, 1940, File No. 214.
87. *Tyler, Texas, City Directory, 1904*, 1: 179; *Polk's Tyler City Directory, 1927–1928* (Dallas: R. L. Polk & Co., 1927), 180–181; *Sixteenth U.S. Census*, Smith County, Texas; Texas Death Certificate, Mitty Rivers Marsh, November 17, 1941, File No. 314.
88. Smith County Marriage Record 13 (1896–1899): 320; *Thirteenth U.S. Census*, Smith County, Texas; Bell-Marsh Family Records; *City*

Directory, Tyler, Texas, 1904, 1: 85; Texas Death Certificate, Mrs. Mary Marsh Crutcher, December 2, 1912, Registrar's No. 298.
89. Lewis, ed., *The Proud Century*, 30; Robert E. Reed, Jr., *Tyler* (Charleston, SC: Arcadia Publishing, 2009), 44; *Tyler Morning Telegraph*, June 28, 2016.

Notes for Chapter 8

1. Bob Alexander, *Rawhide Ranger, Ira Aten: Enforcing Law on the Texas Frontier* (Denton: University of North Texas Press, 2011), 9–11, 13; Ira Aten interview with Earl Vandale, J. Evetts Haley, and Hervey Chesley at El Centro, California, July 1941, J. Evetts Haley Collection, HML&HC, 2. Hereafter cited as Ira Aten interview, July 1941. Alan J. Lamb, comp., *An Aten Genealogy* (Santa Fe: Alan J. Lamb Publications, 1997), 31–32; John T. Brown, *Churches of Christ* (John P. Morton & Company, 1904), 625; *Find A Grave*, s.v. "Kate Eveline Dunlap Aten" and "Angeline Elizabeth 'Angie' Aten Kimmins"; Robert W. Stephens, *Texas Ranger Sketches* (Dallas: Robert W. Stephens, 1972), 15, 16.
2. Alexander, *Rawhide Ranger*, 11; *Eighth U.S. Census*, Peoria County, Illinois; *Report of the Adjutant General of the State of Illinois*, 6: 22; Frederick H. Dyer, *A Compendium of the War of the Rebellion* (De Moines, IA: The Dyer Publishing Company, 1908), 1079; *The History of Peoria County, Illinois* (Chicago: Johnson & Company, 1880), 385. For two accounts of the regiment written by eyewitnesses, see William H. Bentley, *History of the 77th Illinois Volunteer Infantry, September 2, 1862-July 10, 1865* (Peoria, IL: Edward Hine, 1883); and Terrence J. Winschel, ed., *The Civil War Diary of a Common Soldier: William Wiley of the 77th Illinois Infantry* (Baton Rouge: Louisiana State University Press, 2001).
3. Alexander, *Rawhide Ranger*, 11–12; *Ninth U.S. Census*, Knox County, Illinois; Ira Aten interview, July 1941, 2.
4. Alexander, *Rawhide Ranger*, 16–18; Ira Aten interview, July 1941, 4; *Tenth U.S. Census*, Travis County, Texas; *Galveston Daily News*, August 21, 1889; Stephens, *Texas Ranger* Sketches, 18. Ira's mother Katherine died on February 26, 1897, from injuries sustained in an accidental fire. *Houston Daily Post*, February 28, 1897. The Reverend Aten would serve in later years as minister of the Church of Christ in Round Rock before his death on November 13, 1924. Brown,

Churches of Christ, 625; Texas Death Certificate, Austin Cunningham Aten, December 8, 1924, Registrar No. 132.

5. Alexander, *Rawhide Ranger*, 7–9; Aten to My Darling Wife, November 22, 1936, PPHM; Ira Aten interview, July 1941, 4; Harold Preece, *Lone Star Man: Ira Aten, Last of the Old Texas Rangers* (New York: Hastings House, 1960), 22–23. Written seven years after Ira Aten's death, *Lone Star Man*, the first full-length biography of the Ranger, demonstrates characteristics common among other Western histories of that time: overly dramatic prose, the construction of dialogue "from the recollections of people who heard him speak," the fictionalization of factual persons, and uncited source material. Aten's son, Ira Dunlap Aten, called the work "2 percent fact and 98 percent fiction." He further said his sister was "very hostile" to the book. *Albuquerque Tribune*, December 10, 1960. Standards have changed since then, and readers will have to judge for themselves the book's literary virtues.

6. Alexander, *Rawhide Ranger*, 24, 34–35, 42; MR, Company D, April 30, June 30, 1883; Ira Aten interview, July 1941, 5, 4; Preece, *Lone Star Man*, 26, 27–28; Allen G. Hatley, "Ira Allen, Last of the 'Old Texas Rangers'," *Western Outlaw-Lawman History Association Journal* 14 (Winter 2005): 21; RSR, Ira Aten, 401–141, TSLAC. For a short summary of Lam Sieker's career, see Stephens, *Texas Ranger Sketches*, 144–146.

7. Alexander, *Rawhide Ranger*, 44–46; MR, Company D, January 31-April 30, 1884.

8. Alexander, *Rawhide Ranger*, 47–48; MR, Company D, April 30-May 31, 1884; RSR, J. L. Bargsley, 401–142, TSLAC. The area Aten and Bargsley worked was actually Crockett County, which was administratively attached to Kinney County. Today, the region is in Sutton County. Decades after the fact, Aten incorrectly remembered his duty escorting the tax collector as happening in Val Verde County between the Devil's River and the Pecos. Ira Aten, "Six and One-Half Years in the Ranger Service," Pt. 1, *Frontier Times* 22 (January 1945): 102–104.

9. Alexander, *Rawhide Ranger*, 48–49; Bob Alexander, *Six-Shooters and Shifting Sands: The Wild West Life of Texas Ranger Captain Frank Jones* (Denton: University of North Texas Press, 2015), 132; MR, Company D, June 30-July 31, 1884; RSR, Frank Jones, 401–158, W. W. Collier, -147, J. A. Puckett, -168, TSLAC. Boyce had killed his brother-in-law Robertson Anderson on a Mason County ranch on May 19, 1877. *Galveston Daily News*, May 20, 1877. See also Bob Alexander, *Winchester Warriors: Texas Rangers of Company D,*

1874–1901 (Denton: University of North Texas Press, 2009), 143, 144, 147, 148, 150, 164.

10. Alexander, *Rawhide Ranger*, 49–50; MR, Company D, July 31, September 30, 1884; ROS, Company D, July 1884; *Austin Daily Statesman*, July 27, 1884; Clifford R. Caldwell and Ron DeLord, *Texas Lawmen, 1835–1899: The Good and the Bad* (Charleston, SC: History Press, 2011), 159; Sammy Tise, *Texas County Sheriffs* (Albuquerque: Oakwood Printing, 1989), 363.

11. MR, Company D, September 30, 1884; Operations of State Troops, 2 (1882–1885), 401–1083, TSLAC: 93; Aten, "Six and One-Half Years," Pt. 1: 107–109.

12. Alexander, *Rawhide Ranger*, 53–54; Chuck Parsons, *Captain John R. Hughes, Lone Star Ranger* (Denton: University of North Texas Press, 2011), 25; MR, Company D, November 30, 1884; *Galveston Daily News*, September 14, 1884; Don H. Biggers, comp., *German Pioneers in Texas* (Fredericksburg, TX: Fredericksburg Publishing Company, 1925), 118; *San Antonio Light*, October 10, November 24, 1884; Ira Aten interview with J. Evetts Haley at El Centro, California, February 26, 1928, J. Evetts Haley Collection, HML&HC, 85. Hereafter cited as Ira Aten interview, February 1928. Ira Aten interview, July 1941, 45; Aten, "Six and One-Half Years," Pt. 1: 111; Tise, *Texas County Sheriffs*, 204.

13. Alexander, *Rawhide Ranger*, 67, 70, 55; MR, Company D, November 30, 1884; Operations of State Troops, 2: 94; Parsons, *Captain John R. Hughes*, 25–26; *Galveston Daily News*, November 25, 1884, January 8, 1885; Ira Aten interview, February 1928, 86–87; Ira Aten interview, July 1941, 45; Biggers, comp., *German Pioneers in Texas*, 118; Edward A. Blackburn Jr., *Wanted: Historic County Jails of Texas* (College Station: Texas A&M University Press, 2006), 134.

14. Alexander, *Rawhide Ranger*, 55; MR, Company D, November 30, 1884; RSR, Ira Aten, 401–141, TSLAC. Baird was elected sheriff on November 6, 1888, and served until November 3, 1896. Tise, *Texas County Sheriffs*, 358.

15. Alexander, *Rawhide Ranger*, 71–76; ROS, Company D, July 1885; Ira Aten interview, February 1928, 52; Ira Aten interview, July 1941, 28–29; *RAG, 1886*, 52–53, 60–61; Robert M. Utley, *Lone Star Justice: The First Century of the Texas Rangers* (New York: Berkeley Books, 2002), 244; Alexander, *Winchester Warriors*, 205; Stephens, *Texas Ranger Sketches*, 143.

16. Alexander, *Rawhide Ranger*, 76–78, 80–81, 86–89; MR, Company D, June 30, 1885; ROS, Company D, July 1885; Aten, "Six and One-Half Years," Pt. 1: 99–100; Ira Aten interview, February 1928, 52–53, 58; Ira Aten interview, July 1941, 29, 33; *RAG, 1886*, 53, 61; Alexander, *Winchester Warriors*, 206; Dudley G. Wooten, ed., *A Comprehensive History of Texas, 1685 to 1897* (Dallas: William G. Scarff, 1898), 2: 363; Mike Cox, *The Texas Rangers: Wearing the Cinco Peso, 1821–1900* (New York: Tom Doherty Associates, 2008), 331–332; *Dallas Daily Herald*, June 3, 1885; *Galveston Daily News*, June 19, 1885. For the telegram Captain Sieker sent the adjutant general on June 1 reporting Frank's death, see *Galveston Daily News*, June 2, 1885. The elder Gonzales was characterized as "the best guide and Indian trailer in this country, and [he] owns a large ranch." *El Paso Times*, June 4, 1885. Sheriff Gonzales was removed from office in October 1885, and charged with misappropriation of funds the following year. *Galveston Daily News*, September 29, October 30, 1885; *Fort Worth Daily Gazette*, August 24, October 17, 1886.
17. Alexander, *Rawhide Ranger*, 91; Alexander, *Six-Shooters and Shifting Sands*, 164; *RAG, 1886*, 54, 56; MR, Company D, October 31, 1885; RSR, L. P. Sieker, 401–172, Frank Jones, -158, TSLAC; General Order No. 26, August 15, 1885, 401–1160, TSLAC; Special Order No. 85, October 12, 1885, 401–1012, TSLAC; ROS, Company F, October 1885.
18. Alexander, *Rawhide Ranger*, 92–98; Parsons, *Captain John R. Hughes*, 26–27; Operations of Frontier Battalion, 3 (1885–1892), 401–1084, TSLAC: 84; MR, Company D, September 30, 1885, June 30, 1886; *Galveston Daily News*, September 12, 1885.
19. Alexander, *Rawhide Ranger*, 98–99 (first quotation on p. 99); Parsons, *Captain John R. Hughes*, 28; MR, Company D, June 30, 1886; *RAG, 1886*, 66; *Austin Daily Statesman*, May 28, June 2, 1886; *Fort Worth Daily Gazette, San Antonio Daily Express, Galveston Daily News*, all dated May 26, 1886; Jones to Sieker, May 31, 1886, 401–1160, TSLAC (second quotation).
20. Henry D. McCallum, "Barbed Wire in Texas," *SHQ* 61 (October 1957): 214–215; Henry D. and Frances T. McCallum, *The Wire That Fenced the West* (Norman: University of Oklahoma Press, 1965), 152–154; C. E. Lee, "The Fence-Cutters War in Texas," *Frontier Times* 8 (July 1931): 467–468; Wayne Gard, *Frontier Justice* (Norman: University of Oklahoma Press, 1968), 105–106.

21. Randolph Campbell, *Gone to Texas: A History of the Lone Star State* (New York: Oxford University Press, 2003), 303–304; Wayne Gard, "The Fence-Cutters," *SHQ* 51 (July 1947): 5; McCallum, "Barbed Wire in Texas," 216–217; R. D. Holt, "The Introduction of Barbed Wire into Texas and the Fence Cutting War," *WTHAY* 6 (1930): 76; Samuel Stanley, "The Fence Cutters' War," *Real West* 28 (August 1985): 19, 21; McCallum, *Wire That Fenced the West*, 162; Ira Aten interview, February 1928, 70; *RAG, 1884*, 34–43.
22. Acts 1884, 18th Legislature, Called Session, Ch. 33, *General and Special Laws of Texas*. Hans Peter Nielson Gammel, comp., *The Laws of Texas, 1822–1897* (Austin: The Gammel Book Company, 1898), 9: 566–567; McCallum, *Wire That Fenced the West*, 165; Lewis Nordyke, *Great Roundup: The Story of Texas and Southwestern Cowmen* (New York: William Morrow and Company, 1955), 91.
23. Utley, *Lone Star Justice*, 235; Alexander, *Winchester Warriors*, 192; *Galveston Daily News*, February 11, 1884.
24. Alexander, *Rawhide Ranger*, 103, 107, 108–110; MR, August 31, 1886; Ira Aten interview, February 1928, 70–71; Aten, "Six and One-Half Years," Pt. 2: 128–129; Chuck Parsons and Donaly E. Brice, *Texas Ranger N. O. Reynolds: The Intrepid* (Denton: University of North Texas Press, 2014), 254–255; Walter Prescott Webb, "The Fence-Cutters," *True West* 10 (May-June 1963): 13; Ira Aten, "Fence-Cutting Days," *Frontier Times* 16 (July 1939): 441–442; Hatley, "Last of the 'Old Texas Rangers'," 23. Wilkins asserts that Aten did physically strike the lawyer. *The Law Comes to Texas*, 268. While the Ranger was angry, available sources do not support this notion.
25. Alexander, *Rawhide Ranger*, 114–124; Ira Aten interview, February 1928, 71–72, 77–79; *RAG, 1886*, 53–54; Ira Aten interview, July 1941, 85–87; Aten, "Fence-Cutting Days," 442–443; Aten to King, November 26, 1886, Aten Vertical File, TRHF&M; *Abilene Reporter-News*, June 12, 1938; T. R. Havins, *Something About Brown: A History of Brown County, Texas* (Brownwood, TX, Banner Printing Co., 1958), 39; Operations of Frontier Battalion, 3: 88. See also Ruth Whitehead, "That Bloody Fence-Cutting War," *The West* 17 (November 1973): 60–61; Allen, Last of the 'Old Texas Rangers'," 23; and Wooten, ed., *Comprehensive History of Texas*, 2: 362. The traditional version of the Baugh Ranch shootout argues that "Jim Carmichael" was present. Neither Aten's report, or the record of scouts and the monthly returns for November 1887, name the rank and file participants, but "Frank Carmichael" enlisted in the company on June 1,

1886. MR, Company F, June 30, 1886. The confusion seems to have originated in William Sterling, *Trails and Trials of a Texas Ranger* (Norman: University of Oklahoma Press, 1959), 311.

26. Alexander, *Rawhide Ranger*, 130; Alexander, *Six-Shooters and Shifting Sands*, 195; Ira Aten interview, July 1941, 64–65; MR, Company D, April 30, October 31, 1887; Operations of Frontier Battalion, 3: 90; *Galveston Daily News*, April 20, November 18, 1887; *Fort Worth Daily Gazette*, August 23, 1887.
27. Alexander, *Rawhide Ranger*, 144; ROS, Company D, February 1888 (quotation); MR, Company D, June 30, 1887, March 31, 1888; Operations of Frontier Battalion, 3: 96; RSR, C. G. Aten, 401–141, TSLAC; Stephens, *Texas Ranger Sketches*, 15.
28. Alexander, *Rawhide Ranger*, 151 (quotation); RSR, Ira Aten, 401–141, TSLAC.
29. Alexander, *Rawhide Ranger*, 147, 150–157; Andrew Graybill, *Policing the Great Plains: Rangers, Mounties, and the North American Frontier, 1875–1910* (Lincoln: University of Nebraska Press, 2007), 143; Special Order No. 134, July 30, 1888, 401–1012, TSLAC; *RAG, 1888*, 49; Operations of Frontier Battalion, 3: 99; Aten, "Six and One-Half Years," Pt. 2: 130–131 (first quotation on p. 131); RSR, James W. King, 401–159, TSLAC; Ira Aten interview, February 1928, 79–81; Aten, "Fence-Cutting Days," 444–445; Webb, "The Fence-Cutters," 14–15 (second quotation on p. 14). In his memoirs, Aten recalled the Navarro County episode as occurring in the summer or fall of 1887.
30. Alexander, *Rawhide Ranger*, 160–162; Graybill, *Policing the Great Plains*, 143; Ira Aten interview, February 1928, 81; Ira Aten interview, July 1941, 91; Aten, "Fence-Cutting Days," 445; Webb, "The Fence-Cutters," 50; Hart Stillwell, "Dinamite Aten and His Big Boom," *True Western Adventures* 10 (October 1959): 63.
31. Aten to Sieker, October 8, 1888, 401–412, TSLAC.
32. Alexander, *Rawhide Ranger*, 162–163, 170; Aten, "Six and One-Half Years," Pt. 2: 132; Aten, "Fence-Cutting Days," 445; Utley, *Lone Star Justice*, 237; Stillwell, "Dinamite Aten," 64; MR, Company D, December 31, 1888; Operations of Frontier Battalion, 3: 102, 104. Sterling, *Trails and Trials*, 390: "Aten had no intention of really using the devices, but he wanted to throw a scare into the anti-barbwire group."
33. Alexander, *Rawhide Ranger*, 171–172, 173; Parsons, *Captain John R. Hughes*, 47–48; Clifford R. Caldwell and Ron DeLord, *Eternity at the*

End of a Rope: Executions, Lynchings and Vigilante Justice in Texas, 1819–1923 (Santa Fe: Sunstone Press, 2015), 345; Mike Whittington, "Hughes and Aten Solve the Williamson Family Murders," *The Texas Ranger Dispatch* 12 (Winter 2003): 48 (quotation); J. Marvin Hunter, "The Famous Dick Duncan Murder Case," *Frontier Times* 16 (February 1939): 197. Sheriff Cooke was the son of Texas patriot William Gordon Cooke.

34. Alexander, *Rawhide Ranger*, 173, 174, 170–171; Parsons, *Captain John R. Hughes*, 48; Caldwell and DeLord, *Eternity at the End of a Rope*, 346; Whittington, "Williamson Family Murders," 49. 30; Tise, *Texas County Sheriffs*, 363; 7 *Texas Court of Appeals* 39 (1892); Hunter, "Dick Duncan Murder Case," 197; MR, Company D, March 31, 1889; Operations of Frontier Battalion, 3: 105.

35. Alexander, *Rawhide Ranger*, 174–182; Report of Sergt. Ira Aten, March 22, 1889, 401–1160, TSLAC; Ira Aten interview, July 1941, 71, 74; Parsons, *Captain John R. Hughes*, 48; 11 *Southwestern Reporter* 442 (1889); Hunter, "Dick Duncan Murder Case," 197; Whittington, "Williamson Family Murders," 49–50; Letter from Alexander to author, February 6, 2018; 30 *Texas Criminal Reports* 4 (1892); Caldwell and DeLord, *Eternity at the End of a Rope*, 346; *San Antonio Daily Express*, September 19, 1891; *San Saba News*, March 29, 1889.

36. Alexander, *Rawhide Ranger*, 183–185, 215–216, 182; Ira Aten interview, July 1941, 71–73; Parsons, *Captain John R. Hughes*, 48–50; *Galveston Daily News*, September 19, 1891; "Dick Duncan's Doom," *Frontier Times* 23 (March 1946): 92–95; Whittington, "Williamson Family Murders," 51; 30 *Texas Criminal Reports* 1–42; Hunter, "Dick Duncan Murder Case," 198; *San Antonio Daily Express*, September 19, 1891. Even after more than 125 years, the case of Dick Duncan continues to generate speculation and alternate theories. For more details, see Chet and Kim Brackett, *The Chronicles of Tap* (Three River, ID: Chet and Kim Brackett, 2016).

37. Campbell, *Gone to Texas*, 316; C. L. Douglas, *Famous Texas Feuds* (Austin: State House Press, 1988), 162; Dave Southworth, *Feuds on the Western Frontier* (Round Rock, TX: Wild Horse Publishing, 1999), 101; Clarence R. Wharton, *Wharton's History of Fort Bend County* (Houston: Anson Jones Press, 1950), 176–178, 183, 193–194; Pauline Yelderman, *The Jay Bird Association of Fort Bend County: A White Man's Union* (Waco: Texian Press, 1979), 63–66; Gilbert M. Cuthbertson, "The Jaybird-Woodpecker War," *Texana* 10 (1972):

300–301; C. L. Sonnichsen, *I'll Die Before I'll Run: The Story of the Great Feuds of Texas* (Lincoln: University of Nebraska Press, 1988), 234–235; Robert Maxwell Brown, *Strain of Violence: Historical Studies of American Violence and Vigilantism* (New York: Oxford University Press, 1975), 253, 258.

38. Cuthbertson, "Jaybird-Woodpecker War," 301, 303–304; Douglas, *Famous Texas Feuds*, 165; Sonnichsen, *I'll Die Before I'll Run*, 241–243, 247, 248; Southworth, *Feuds on the Western Frontier*, 103; Brown, *Strain of Violence*, 259; *Galveston Daily News*, November 7, 1888, June 22, 1889; Alwyn Barr, *Reconstruction to Reform: Texas Politics, 1876–1906* (Dallas: Southern Methodist University Press, 2000), 198. Terry was the son of Benjamin Franklin Terry, first colonel of the famed Eighth Texas Cavalry ("Terry's Texas Rangers").

39. Alexander, *Rawhide Ranger*, 195–197; Yelderman, *Jay Bird Association*, 81; Tise, *Texas County Sheriff*, 188; Sonnichsen, *I'll Die Before I'll Run*, 259–260; Candice DuCoin, *Lawmen on the Texas Frontier: Rangers and Sheriffs* (Round Rock, TX: Riata Books, 2007), 122; Ira Aten, "The Jaybird and Woodpecker War," *Frontier Times* 16 (April 1939): 309; Ira Aten interview, February 1928, 44; *RAG, 1889–1890*, 24, 91; Operations of Frontier Battalion, 3: 107; RSR, James Robinson, 401-170, D. S. Roberson, -169, F. Schmid, -171, TSLAC.

40. Alexander, *Rawhide Ranger*, 197–204; Aten, "Six and One-Half Years," Pt. 2: 136–138 (quotation on p. 138); Aten, "Jaybird and Woodpecker War," 310; *Galveston Daily News*, August 17, 1889; MR, Company D, August 31, 1889; Stephens, *Texas Ranger Sketches*, 128; Sonnichsen, *I'll Die Before I'll Run*, 261–265; Southworth, *Feuds on the Western Frontier*, 105–106. Despite being sent to a variety of specialists, Schmid never recovered from his wound and died on June 17, 1893. He was buried in St. Louis, Missouri. *RAG, 1889–1890*, 28–29; *St. Louis Post-Dispatch*, June 18, 1893.

41. Alexander, *Rawhide Ranger*, 204–207; ROS, Company D, August 1889; Douglas, *Famous Texas Feuds*, 172; *Galveston Daily News*, August 18, 1889; Aten, "Six and One-Half Years," 138–139; Ira Aten interview, July 1941, 103; Sonnichsen, *I'll Die Before I'll Run*, 267, 268–270; RSR, Ira Aten, 401–141, TSLAC; Tise, *Texas County Sheriffs*, 188; Ira Aten, Box 2–9/780, Bonds and Oaths of County and State Officials, TSLAC.

42. Alexander, *Rawhide Ranger*, 207, 214; Aten, "Jaybird and Woodpecker War," 312; Ira Aten, Box 2–9/780, Bonds and Oaths, TSLAC;

Yelderman, *Jay Birds of Fort Bend County*, 124, 128–129, 132–136, 323; Wharton, *History of Fort Bend County*, 215, 216; Aten, "Six and One-Half Years," Pt. 2: 139–141; Hatley, "Last of the 'Old Texas Rangers'," 25; Sonnichsen, *I'll Die Before I'll Run*, 272; Cuthbertson, "Jaybird-Woodpecker War," 307.

43. Alexander, *Rawhide Ranger*, 216–217; *Galveston Daily News*, December 25, 26, 1899; *San Antonio Daily Express*, December 27, 1899; Wharton, *History of Fort Bend County*, 218–219.

44. Alexander, *Rawhide Ranger*, 217–219, 223–228; *Galveston Daily News*, December 28, 1899, January 23, April 5, 1890; Aten, "Jaybird and Woodpecker War," 313; Yelderman, *Jay Birds of Fort Bend County*, 140; Cuthbertson, "Jaybird-Woodpecker War," 305; Sonnichsen, *I'll Die Before I'll Run*, 273, 274–275, 277; Southworth, *Feuds on the Western Frontier*, 107; Wharton, *History of Fort Bend County*, 217; Hatley, "Last of the 'Old Texas Rangers'," 23.

45. Alexander, *Rawhide Ranger*, 230–231; *Galveston Daily News*, June 5, 1890; Yelderman, *Jay Birds of Fort Bend County*, 156–157; Tise, *Texas County Sheriffs*, 188; Ira Aten interview, July 1941, 105. Aten, "Six and One-Half Years," Pt. 2: 140: "At the end of my term of office I left the county. It was quiet and peaceful; many of the principals of both factions had left, but those remaining were not entirely reconciled to each other."

46. Alexander, *Rawhide Ranger*, 236–237, 239, 240; Castro County Historical Commission, *Castro County, Texas, 1891–1981* (Dallas: Taylor Publishing Company, 1981), 22, 27; Tax Rolls, Castro County, 1891; Frederick W. Rathjen, *The Texas Panhandle Frontier* (Lubbock: Texas Tech University Press, 1998), 191; RSR, Ira Aten, 140–141, TSLAC; *Fort Worth Daily Gazette*, June 14, August 10, 1891.

47. Alexander, *Rawhide Ranger*, 241–243; Aten, "Six and One-Half Years," Pt. 2: 141–142; Ira Aten interview, February 1928, 7, 8 (quotation), 9; Frederick Nolan, *Tascosa: Its Life and Gaudy Times* (Lubbock; Texas Tech University Press, 2007), 93, 244. Preece ascribed venal motivations to the McClellands when he related how Aten had supposedly sold land near Castro City for reasonable prices, while the brothers had purchased cheap land around Dimmitt, then sold the tracts for inflated amounts. *Lone Star Man*, 212. His assertion is unsupported by the available evidence.

48. Alexander, *Rawhide Ranger*, 243–245; Ira Aten interview, July 1941, 110–113; Ira Aten interview, February 1928, 9–10 (quotation on p. 9); Castro County Historical Commission, *Castro County*, 27, 29. In the

serialized version of Aten's memoirs, J. Marvin Hunter included an article from an Amarillo newspaper, erroneously dated November 28, 1891, that had "Aten ... telling McClelland to shoot, and assuring him that he would catch the bullets." Aten, "Six and One-Half Years," Pt. 2: 141–142. The anecdote may be plausible as Big Ed Connell claimed in a letter to J. Evetts Haley on October 31, 1927, that Aten wore a steel breastplate during the gunfight. J. Evetts Haley Collection, HML&HC.

49. Alexander, *Rawhide Ranger*, 245–247, 250; Ira Aten interview, February 1928, 10–12; Ira Aten interview, July 1941, 113–144; Mark Boardman, "Irate Ira Nails the McClellands," *True West* 56 (July 2009): 52–53; Aten to My Darling Wife, November 7, 1936, PPHM; Castro County Historical Commission, *Castro County*, 29. The exact date of the shooting is unclear. The historical marker on the courthouse lawn places the gunfight on December 23, 1891. The indictment charging Aten gives the date as December 24. On a related note, the January 9, 1892, issue of the *Weimar Mercury* incorrectly reported Aten had killed the brothers.

50. Alexander, *Rawhide Ranger*, 31, 237, 247, 248–249; Ira Aten interview, February 1928, 3; Aten to My Darling Wife, October 31, 1936, PPHM; *Austin Daily Statesmen*, February 4, 1892; Aten, "Six and One-Half Years," Pt. 3: 157; Ira Aten, "Captain Ira Aten's Unique Letter," *Frontier Times* 19 (April 1942): 267.

51. Alexander, *Rawhide Ranger*, 250–251, 253–257; Aten to My Darling Wife, November 7, 1936, October 31, 1936, PPHM; Aten, "Six and One-Half Years," Pt. 3: 157; Ira Aten interview, February 1928, 13; Castro County Historical Commission, *Castro County*, 30; Tax Rolls, Castro County, 1892–1893; Bexar Preemption, Castro County, File No. 8045, TGLO.

52. Alexander, *Rawhide Ranger*, 253, 259–261; Tise, *Texas County Sheriffs*, 94; Ira Aten, Box 2-9/780, Bonds and Oaths, TSLAC; Castro County Historical Commission, *Castro County*, 24; Ira Aten interview, July 1941, 15; Ira Aten interview, February 1928, 3, 6; Aten, "Six and One-Half Years," Pt. 3: 157; Hatley, "Last of the 'Old Texas Rangers'," 25–26.

53. Alexander, *Rawhide Ranger*, 262; Ira Aten interview, July 1941, 114 (second quotation); Castro County Historical Commission, *Castro County*, 24; Aten, "Six and One-Half Years," Pt. 3: 158 (first quotation).

54. Alexander, *Rawhide Ranger*, 262–264; Ira Aten interview, February 1928, 3–4; Castro County Historical Commission, *Castro County*, 24; Tise, *Texas County Sheriffs*, 482.

55. Alexander, *Rawhide Ranger*, 264–265; Aten, "Six and One-Half Years," Pt. 3: 158; Ira Aten interview, July 1941, 16; Ira Aten interview, February 1928, 4; Aten to My Darling Wife, November 9, 1936, PPHM.
56. Alexander, *Rawhide Ranger*, 265; Aten, "Six and One-Half Years," Pt. 3: 158–159; Aten to My Darling Wife, November 9, 1936, PPHM; Ira Aten interview, February 1928, 5.
57. Alexander, *Rawhide Ranger*, 265–266; Aten to My Darling Wife, November 9, 1936, PPHM.
58. Alexander, *Rawhide Ranger*, 267 (second quotation); Aten, "Six and One-Half Years," Pt. 3: 159–160; Ira Aten interview, February 1928, 5 (first quotation), 6; Castro County Historical Commission, *Castro County*, 25.
59. Alexander, *Rawhide Ranger*, 269; Tise, *Texas County Sheriffs*, 94.
60. Alexander, *Rawhide Ranger*, 274, 280–281; J. Marvin Hunter, comp. and ed., *Trail Drivers of Texas* (Austin: University of Texas Press, 1985), 672–673; Ira Aten interview, February 1928, 103; J. Evetts Haley, *The XIT Ranch of Texas* (Norman: University of Oklahoma Press, 1953), 111–112; *Fort Worth Daily Gazette*, November 19, 1895; Ira Aten, "Crossing High Water in a Wagon," *Frontier Times* 18 (May 1941): 367; Castro County Historical Commission, *Castro County*, 18, 25, 34; John E. Boyce, Box 2–9/789, Bonds and Oaths, TSLAC.
61. Haley, *XIT Ranch of Texas*, Ch. 4–5; Christopher Knowlton, *Cattle Kingdom: The Hidden History of the Cowboy West* (New York: Houghton Mifflin Harcourt, 2017), 218; Doug Perkins and Nancy Ward, *Brave Men and Cold Steel: A History of Range Detectives and Their Peacemakers* (For Worth: Texas and Southwestern Cattle Raisers Foundation, 1984), 61; C. L. Douglas, *Cattle Kings of Texas* (Austin: State House Press, 1989), 321–326; Bill O'Neal, *Historic Ranches of the Old West* (Austin: Eakin Press, 1997), 27–29; Gus L. Ford, ed., *Texas Cattle Brands: A Catalog of the Texas Centennial Exposition Exhibit, 1936* (Dallas: Clyde C. Cockrell Company, 1936), 70. For more on Blocker, see Mike Cox, *Legends and Lore of the Texas Capitol* (Charleston, SC: History Press, 2017), 60–64.
62. Alexander, *Rawhide Ranger*, 281, 282, 284, 293; Haley, *XIT Ranch of Texas*, 105 (quotation), 112; Lewis Nordyke, *Cattle Empire: The Fabulous Story of the 3,000,000 Acre XIT* (New York: William Morrow and Company, 1949), 233–235; Ira Aten interview, February 1928, 30–31.
63. Alexander, *Rawhide Ranger*, 284; Stephens, *Texas Ranger Sketches*, 36–38, 124; *The Land and Its People, 1876–1981: Deaf Smith*

County, Texas (Hereford, TX: Deaf Smith County Historical Society, 1982), 9; Haley, *XIT Ranch of Texas*, 111–112 (quotation on p. 111); Douglas, *Cattle Kings of Texas*, 328; Ira Aten interview, February 1928, 34–35, 36; RSR, J. W. Saunders, 401–171, E. F. Connell, –147, TSLAC; Cordia Sloan Duke and Joe B. Frantz, *6,000 Miles of Fence: Life on the XIT Ranch of Texas* (Austin: University of Texas Press, 1961), 111.

64. Alexander, *Rawhide Ranger*, 292, 299; Haley, *XIT Ranch of Texas*, 112; *The Land and Its People*, 10; Douglas, *Cattle Kings of Texas*, 328; Ira Aten interview, February 1928, 31–34; Duke and Frantz, *6,000 Miles of Fence*, 107 (quotation), 111–112, 114.

65. Alexander, *Rawhide Ranger*, 301, 305, 300, 306, 297; Tax Rolls, Castro County, 1895–1898; Castro County Historical Commission, *Castro County*, 25, 39, 139; Bessie Patterson, *A History of Deaf Smith County* (Hereford, TX: Pioneer Publishing, 1964), 5–6, 70–71, 157–158; Duke and Frantz, *6,000 Miles of Fence*, 40; *The Land and Its People*, 86–87, 580.

66. Alexander, *Rawhide Ranger*, 305; *Twelfth U.S. Census*, Deaf Smith County, Texas; Patterson, *History of Deaf Smith County*, 5, 7, 11; Tax Rolls, Deaf Smith County, 1901–1903; Aten to My Darling Wife, November 7, 1936, PPHM.

67. James L. Haley, *Passionate Nation: The Epic History of Texas* (New York: Simon and Schuster, 2006), 381; Nordyke, *Cattle Empire*, 244–246, 248; Douglas, *Cattle Kings of Texas*, 329; O'Neal, *Historic Ranches of the Old West*, 36; Wayne Gard, *Rawhide Texas* (Norman: University of Oklahoma Press, 1965), 86.

68. Alexander, *Rawhide Ranger*, 311–312; Aten, "Six and One-Half in the Ranger Service," 165; Aten, "Crossing High Water in a Wagon," 367; Tax Rolls, Deaf Smith County, 1904–1905; Aten, "Capt. Ira Aten's 'Round Robin'," *Frontier Times* 21 (November 1943): 56; Aten to My Darling Wife, December 6, 1936, PPHM; "Ira Aten to Brothers and Sisters, February 1, 1942," *Frontier Times* 19 (April 1942): 265–269; Robert J. Burdette, ed., *American Biography and Genealogy: California Edition* (Chicago: Lewis Company, n.d.), 2: 945; Otis B. Tout, *The First Thirty Years (1901–1931): Being An Account of the Principal Events in the History of Imperial Valley Southern California, U.S.A.* (San Diego, CA: Otis B. Tout, 1931), 177, 179, 327, 332, 368, 383, 387. Aten was not alone in his success. For more on the region's growth, see Benny J. Andrés, Jr., *Power and Control in the Imperial Valley: Nature,*

Agribusiness, and Workers on the California Borderland, 1900–1940 (College Station: Texas A&M University Press, 2015).

69. Alexander, *Rawhide Ranger*, 312; *Imperial Valley Press*, August 5, 1905 (quotation), June 23, August 4, 1906. The tax rolls for 1906 are the first that do not show Aten owning property in Deaf Smith County. Samuel F. Black, *San Diego and Imperial Counties, California: A Record of Settlement, Organization, Progress, and Achievement* (Chicago: S. J. Clarke Publishing Company, 1913), 2: 560–561, 575; Ira Aten interview, February 1928, 8–9; Burdette, ed., *American Biography and Genealogy*, 2: 945–946; Aten, "Crossing High Water in a Wagon," 368; Tout, *The First Thirty Years*, 180, 186, 191, 326, 328. Fuller had supervised the Tombstone camp on the Escabarda division, worked for Aten as wagon boss, served as the county and district clerk of Deaf Smith County, and functioned as cashier and director of the First National Bank at Hereford.

70. Alexander, *Rawhide Ranger*, 318; *Stanford University Alumni Directory and Ten-Year Book* (Stanford University: published by the university, 1921), 74; *Los Angeles Herald*, May 11, 1917; Tout, *The First Thirty Years*, 206, 221 (quotation); Sergeant-Major Walter W. Weber, *History of the 129th Machine Gun Battalion, 35th Division, A.E.F., 1917–19* (s.l.: n.p., 1920?), 5, 11–12, 15–16, 20, 47–49; Edward G. Lengel, *To Conquer Hell: The Meuse-Argonne, 1918: The Epic Battle That Ended the First World War* (New York: Henry Holt and Company, 2008), 173–177; Aten, "Captain Ira Aten's Unique Letter," 269; *Find A Grave*, s.v. "Lieut Albert Boyce Aten." See also Robert H. Ferrell, *Collapse at Meuse-Argonne: The Failure of the Missouri-Kansas Division* (Columbia: University of Missouri Press, 2004).

71. Alexander, *Rawhide Ranger*, 314; *Imperial Valley Weekly*, August 13, 1953; Tout, *The First Thirty Years*, 116, 127, 248; Aten, "Six and One-Half Years," Pt. 3: 165; Hatley, "Last of the 'Old Texas Rangers'," 26; Aten to My Darling Wife, November 23, 1936, PPHM.

72. Alexander, *Rawhide Ranger*, 321; *Imperial Valley Weekly*, August 13, 1953; Tout, *The First Thirty Years*, 192, 255.

73. *Imperial Valley Weekly*, August 13, 1953; *San Mateo Times*, August 6, 1953.

74. *San Mateo Times*, March 4, 1957.

75. Marion H. Aten, World War I Draft Registration Cards, M1509, RG 163, NARA; Marion H. Aten, Airmen's Records, AIR 79, National

Archives UK; John T. Smith, *Gone to Russia to Fight: The RAF in South Russia, 1918–1920* (Stroud, UK: Amberly Publishing, 2010), 130, 149, 152, 158, 201–202; Derek O'Connor, "Flying Against the Bolsheviks," *Aviation History* 18 (September 2007): 53–57, Aten to My Darling Wife, December 6, 1936, PPHM; Tout, *The First Thirty Years*, 368, 388; *Los Angeles Times*, March 20, 1928; *San Mateo Times*, May 15, 1961, April 7, 1962.

76. Aten, "Crossing High Water in a Wagon," 367; Aten, "Captain Ira Aten's Unique Letter," 269; Tout, *The First Thirty Years*, 388; *San Mateo Times*, March 10, 1934; *Find A Grave*, s.v. "Imogen Aten."
77. *The Badger* (Madison: University of Wisconsin, 1931), 46: 55, 132; *Sixteenth U.S. Census*, San Mateo County, California; *San Mateo Times*, October 8, 1974; *Find A Grave*, s.v. "Eloise Elsie Radder."
78. Alexander, *Rawhide Ranger*, 318–319; Aten to My Darling Wife, December 6, 1936, PPHM; *Stanford University Alumni Directory and Ten-Year Book*, 74; Aten, "Crossing High Water in a Wagon," 367; Tout, *The First Thirty Years*, 387–388; Karen Pillmore Laurie, "History of Vermejo Park," *New Mexico Genealogical Society Guidebook, 27th Field Conference* (Vermejo Park: 1976), 91; Aten, "Capt. Ira Aten's 'Round Robin'," 54; *Fourteenth U.S. Census*, Imperial County, California; *Sixteenth U.S. Census*, Colfax County, New Mexico; Clark County Marriage Book 82, 132360; Record of Appointment of Postmaster 44, roll 84, M841, RG 28, NARA, n. pag.

Notes for Chapter 9

1. Paul N. Spellman, *Captain J. A. Brooks, Texas Ranger* (Denton: University of North Texas Press, 2007), 11–13, 17, 18; Ellis A. Davis and Edwin H. Grobe, comp. and ed., *The New Encyclopedia of Texas* (Dallas: Texas Development Bureau, 1929), 4: 2905; *Kentuckian-Citizen*, June 20, 1944. The article in the newspaper was entitled "Early Bourbon Families" and was drawn from the files of Mrs. William Breckenridge Ardery. Bourbon County, Kentucky Marriage Records 2 (1799–1839), 102; *Catalogue of the Officers and Students of Transylvania University* (Lexington, KY: n. p., January 1825), 5; *Courier-Journal*, December 26, 1897; *Bourbon News*, December 25, 1906; Kentucky Death Certificates, Annie Brooks Kerr, December 20, 1921, File No. 26280, Jennie Brooks Kenney, March 9, 1922, File No. 28676, Sallie K. Brooks, December 27, 1941, File No. 28001, Francis Brooks Nesbitt, April 12, 1926, File No. 11107,

Mrs. Allan Brooks Hudson, October 15, 1947, File No. 21213; Georgia Death Certificate, John C. Brooks, May 22, 1924, File No. 13717; Bourbon County Deed Books, 37: 345, 42: 33; *Eighth U.S. Census*, Bourbon County, Kentucky; *Corpus Christi Caller-Times*, November 20, 1938; Robert Stuart Sanders, *Presbyterianism in Paris and Bourbon County, Kentucky: 1786–1961* (Louisville, KY: Dunne Press, 1961), 232; Mrs. W. H. Whitley, "Hopewell Presbyterian Church: Bourbon County, Kentucky," *Register of the Kentucky Historical Society* 28 (October 1930): 382–85. See also *Tenth* and *Twelfth U.S. Census*, Bourbon County, Kentucky; and *Thirteenth U.S. Census*, Fayette County, Kentucky.

2. Spellman, *Captain J. A. Brooks*, 14; Joshua H. Leet and Karen M. Leet, *Civil War Lexington, Kentucky: Bluegrass Breeding Ground of Power* (Charleston, SC: History Press, 2011), 97; *Find a Grave*, s.v. "Dr. John S. Brooks."

3. Spellman, *Captain J. A. Brooks*, 17; Bourbon County Deed Books, 55: 465–466; *Ninth* and *Twelfth U.S. Census*, Bourbon County, Kentucky. Mary died of a cerebral hemorrhage in Lexington on July 16, 1912. Kentucky Death Certificate, Mrs. Mary Jane Brooks, File No. 16916. For marriage records regarding James and Anne, see Bourbon County Marriage Book 3: 121.

4. Spellman, *Captain J. A. Brooks*, 18–19, 21; *Corpus Christi Caller-Times*, November 20, 1938; Tax Rolls, Collin County, 1878.

5. Spellman, *Captain J. A. Brooks*, 22–24; Davis and Grobe, comp. and ed., *New Encyclopedia of Texas*, 4: 2905.

6. Spellman, *Captain J. A. Brooks*, 25–29; Dora Neill Raymond, *Captain Lee Hall of Texas* (Norman: University of Oklahoma Press, 1982), 197.

7. Spellman, *Captain J. A. Brooks*, 30; RSR, J. A. Brooks, 401–144, C. B. McKinney, -162, J. Shely, -171, TSLAC; Chuck Parsons and Gary P. Fitterer, *Captain C. B. McKinney: The Law in South Texas* (Wolfe City, TX: Henington Publishing Company, 1993), vi, 59; Special Order No. 40, May 4, 1883, 401–1012, TSLAC; Robert W. Stephens, *Texas Ranger Sketches* (Dallas: Robert W. Stephens, 1972), 93. See also Chuck Parsons, "Law and Order in South Texas: The Exploits of Charles Brown McKinney," *South Texas Studies* 6 (1995): 53–87.

8. Spellman, *Captain J. A. Brooks*, 30–33; MR, Company F, April 30–December 31, 1883, June 1, 1884; Stanley D. Casto, *Settlement of the Cibolo-Nueces Strip: A Partial History of La Salle County* (Hillsboro, TX: Hill Junior College Press, 1969), 16; William Warren Sterling, *Trails and Trials of a Texas Ranger* (Norman: University of Oklahoma

Press, 1959), 306–307; ROS, Company F, March-December 1883, May 1884; Shely to Johnson, November 29, 1883, Special Order No. 15, May 15, 1884, 401–1159, TSLAC.
9. Paul N. Spellman, *Captain John H. Rogers, Texas Ranger* (Denton: University of North Texas Press, 2003), x–xv, 33–34; Spellman, *Captain J. A. Brooks*, 5.
10. Spellman, *Captain J. A. Brooks*, 34; MR, Company F, June 1-July 31, December 31, 1884; RSR, J. A. Brooks, 401–144, W. T. Morris, -165, TSLAC; ROS, Company F, June-July 1884, December 1884; Clifford R. Caldwell and Ron DeLord, *Texas Lawmen, 1835-1899: The Good and the Bad* (Charleston, SC: History Press, 2011), 139.
11. ROS, Company F, January 1885.
12. Sammy Tise, *Texas County Sheriffs* (Albuquerque: Oakwood Publishing, 1989), 160; *Galveston Daily News*, January 12, February 8, 10, 1885; *RAG, 1886*, 50–51, 64; Bob Alexander, *Winchester Warriors: Texas Rangers of Company D, 1874–1901* (Denton: University of North Texas Press, 2009), 202.
13. Spellman, *Captain J. A. Brooks*, 34–35; ROS, Company F, February 1885 (second quotation); *RAG, 1886*, 51–52 (first quotation on p. 51); *Dallas Daily Herald*, February 12, 1885; *Wise County Messenger*, February 28, 1885; Ira Aten, "Six and One-Half Years in the Ranger Service," Pt. 1, *Frontier Times* 22 (January 1945): 104; *Galveston Daily News*, February 12, 1885. Parsons and Fitterer correctly illustrate that Shely and Scott were not present at the February 9 meeting. *Captain C. B. McKinney*, 75–76. See also Frederick Wilkins, *The Law Comes to Texas: The Texas Rangers, 1870–1901* (Abilene, TX: State House Press, 1999), 251–252.

Ranger Sergeant George Washington Farrow has been described as accompanying Brooks and McKinney to *Las Ysles*, but his report for the month ending February 28, 1885, details his travels between the Ainsworth ranch, Cotulla, the Votaw spread, and "Live Oak Mott" on San Lorenzo Creek in the same time frame. He does not specifically mention going to the Rio Grande.

Neither Brooks or Aten, or contemporaneous reports, identified "Dr. Pope" by his first name. Spellman asserts the man in question was Benjamin Franklin Pope, a captain and assistant surgeon in the Army's Medical Department. *Captain J. A. Brooks*, 35, 217 n23. However, Pope left Fort Stockton in May 1878, for assignments at Fort Schuyler, New York, at Fort Sully, Dakota Territory, and in the Surgeon General's office. While in Washington, he became entangled in the "Tyler decision" regarding longevity pay and whether he and other officers had been legally appointed by executive order into the Regular Army. The full account is much too complicated to detail here, but, suffice to say, the U.S. Court of Claims, the Supreme Court, and Congress were involved. His commission was finally declared valid, and he received a promotion to major on September 16, 1885. No indications were found that Pope received a leave of absence during this time so he could travel to Mexico. Instead, he remained with the Surgeon General until his assignment to Fort Clark in January 1887. Returns from U.S. Military Posts, 1800–1916, Fort Stockton, May 1878, Fort Clark, January-February 1887, M617, NARA; *Army and Navy Journal* 17–23 (December 20, 1879-April 17, 1886); *New York Times*, February 24, June 27, 1882, August 24, 1883; *Evening Star*, December 10, 1886, January 15, 1887.

On the other hand, O. C. Pope, a doctor of divinity, not medicine, was in Saltillo on a mission trip one week before the parley. *Galveston Daily News*, February 15, 1885.

14. Spellman, *Captain J. A. Brooks*, 34–35; ROS, Company F, February 1885; Operations of State Troops, 2 (1882–1885), 401–1083, TSLAC: 95–96, 181; Parsons and Fitterer, *Captain C. B. McKinney*, 76–77; *RAG, 1886*, 50; *Galveston Daily News*, February 13, 1885.
15. Spellman, *Captain J. A. Brooks*, 35; Parsons and Fitterer, *Captain C. B. McKinney*, 82–84; MR, Company F, March 31, 1885; ROS, Company F, March 1885; *Galveston Daily News*, March 2, 8, 13, 28, 1885; David Montejano, *Anglos and Mexicans in the Making of Texas, 1836–1986* (Austin: University of Texas Press, 1987), 58; Paul S. Taylor, "Historical Note on Dimmit County, Texas," *SHQ* 34 (October 1930): 84.
16. Spellman, *Captain J. A. Brooks*, 36; Special Order No. 75, June 5, 1885, Special Order No. 78, June 12, 1885, 401–1012, TSLAC; RSR, J. Shely, 401–171, TSLAC; MR, Company F, June 30-September 30, 1885; ROS, Company F, June-September 1885; Operations of State Troops, 2: 183–185.
17. Spellman, *Captain J. A. Brooks*, 36; Wilkins, *Law Comes to Texas*, 256; ROS, Company F, November 1885; Operations of Frontier Battalion, 3 (1885–1892), 401–1084, TSLAC: 141.
18. Spellman, *Captain J. A. Brooks*, 37; MR, Company F, April 30, 1886; Operations of Frontier Battalion, 3: 142; Harold Rich, *Fort Worth: Outpost, Cowtown, Boomtown* (Norman: University of Oklahoma Press, 2014), 45–47; Richard F. Selcer and Kevin S. Foster, *Written in*

Blood: The History of Fort Worth's Fallen Lawmen (Denton: University of North Texas Press, 2010), 88 (quotation), 92, 96–100; *Fort Worth Daily Gazette*, April 10, 11, 1886; Robert K. DeArment, *Jim Courtwright of Fort Worth: His Life and Legend* (Fort Worth: Texas Christian University Press, 2004), 194–199.

19. Spellman, *Captain J. A. Brooks*, 37–38; Operations of Frontier Battalion, 3: 142; Robert W. Stephens, *Bullets and Buckshot in Texas* (Dallas: Robert W. Stephens, 2002), 98–99.

20. Spellman, *Captain J. A. Brooks*, 39; Stephens, *Bullets and Buckshot*, 99; Jeffrey Burton, *Indian Territory and the United States, 1866–1906: Courts, Government, and the Movement for Oklahoma Statehood* (Norman: University of Oklahoma Press, 1995), 136–37; *Annual Report of the Commissioner of Indian Affairs*, House Executive Document No. 1, 49th Congress, 2nd Session, 378 (quotation).

21. Spellman, *Captain J. A. Brooks*, 39–40; Burton, *Indian Territory and the United States*, 137; Jacket No. 112, Defendant Jacket Files for Thomas R. Knight and J. A. Brooks, Western District of Arkansas, RG 21, NARA (quotations).

22. Spellman, *Captain J. A. Brooks*, 40–41; MR, Company F, May 31, 1886.

23. Spellman, *Captain J. A. Brooks*, 42; Jacket No. 15, Defendant Jacket Files; Stephens, *Bullets and Buckshot*, 101.

24. Spellman, *Captain J. A. Brooks*, 43–44; MR, Company F, September 30, 1886; ROS, Company F, November 1886.

25. *Austin Daily Statesman*, November 11, 1886.

26. Spellman, *Captain J. A. Brooks*, 44; Andrew Graybill, *Policing the Great Plains: Rangers, Mounties, and the North American Frontier, 1875–1910* (Lincoln: University of Nebraska Press, 2007), 142; T. R. Havins, *Something About Brown: A History of Brown County, Texas* (Brownwood, Tex., Banner Printing Co., 1958), 38–39; Wilkins, *Law Comes to Texas*, 269; ROS, Company F, November 1885; MR, Company F, November 30, 1886-January 31, 1887.

27. Parsons and Fitterer, *Captain C. B. McKinney*, 97–119; Annette Martin Ludeman, *La Salle County: South Texas Brush Country, 1856–1975* (Quanah, TX: Nortex Press, 1975), 112, 115. For a full summary of the case, see 27 *Texas Criminal Reports* 415–437 (1889).

28. Spellman, *Captain J. A. Brooks*, 45; Operations of Frontier Battalion, 3: 146; "The Conner Feud in Sabine County. As Told by W. T. McElroy to Geo. L. Crocket," Box 14, George Louis Crocket Papers, East Texas Research Center, Stephen F. Austin State University, 1.

29. Spellman, *Captain J. A. Brooks*, 46–48; MR, Company F, March 31, 1887; ROS, Company F, March 1887; Operations of Frontier Battalion, 3: 146–147; Sterling, *Trails and Trials*, 310–311.
30. Utley, *Lone Star Justice*, 249–250; *RAG, 1888*, 46, 48; *Galveston Daily News*, November 8, 15, 1887; "The Conner Feud in Sabine County," 2–3; W. S. Adair, "Rangers 40 Years Ago Had No Easy Life," *Frontier Times* 4 (August 1927): 41–43; Joseph F. Combs, *Gunsmoke in the Redlands* (San Antonio: Naylor Company, 1968), 114–116; Henry C. Fuller, *"A Texas Sheriff"* (Nacogdoches, TX: Baker Printing Co., 1931), 58; Texas Department of Criminal Justice, Conduct Registers, 1998/038-182, TSLAC, 1.
31. Spellman, *Captain J. A. Brooks*, 48–49, 51; *Galveston Daily News*, April 3, 8, 1887; *Houston Daily Post*, February 1, 1903.
32. Spellman, *Captain J. A. Brooks*, 52, 53–56; Operations of Frontier Battalion, 3: 149; Stephens, *Bullets and Buckshot*, 103; Burton, *Indian Territory and the United States*, 137; Jacket No. 112, Defendant Jacket Files. The "Hanging Judge" had sat on the federal bench since 1875, and was notorious for his swift and uncompromising verdicts. Before Parker died in 1896, he would send seventy-nine men to the gallows. For more on his life and remarkable career, see Roger Harold Tuller, *"Let No Guilty Man Escape": A Judicial Biography of "Hanging Judge" Isaac C. Parker* (Norman: University of Oklahoma Press, 2001); and Michael J. Brodhead, *Isaac C. Parker: Federal Justice on the Frontier* (Norman: University of Oklahoma Press, 2003).
33. Spellman, *Captain J. A. Brooks*, 57; Burton, *Indian Territory and the United States*, 137; Transcript of Testimony, Defendant Jacket Files.
34. Spellman, *Captain J. A. Brooks*, 57–63; *Annual Report of the Attorney General of the United States*, House Executive Document No. 7, 50th Congress, 2nd Session, 241 (quotation); *Daily Arkansas Gazette*, September 14, 1887.
35. Spellman, *Captain J. A. Brooks*, 63–64; MR, Company F, September 30, November 30, 1887-January 31, 1888; RSR, J. A. Brooks, 401–144, TSLAC; ROS, Company F, December 1887-January 1888.
36. Spellman, *Captain J. A. Brooks*, 65; MR, Company F, March 31, 1888, September 30-October 31, 1889; RSR, J. A. Brooks, 401–144, TSLAC; Special Order No. 126, April 19, 1888, 401–1012, TSLAC; *RAG, 1888*, 42; ROS, Company F, June-September 1888.
37. Spellman, *Captain J. A. Brooks*, 67; MR, Company F, May 31, 1888; *RAG, 1888*, 49; Special Order No. 33, February 16, 1883, 401–1012,

TSLAC; Davis and Grobe, comp. and ed., *New Encyclopedia of Texas*, 4: 2905.
38. William D. Carrigan and Clive Webb, *Forgotten Dead: Mob Violence against Mexicans in the United States, 1848–1928* (New York: Oxford University Press, 2013), 104; Bob Alexander, *Riding Lucifer's Line: Ranger Deaths along the Texas-Mexico Border* (Denton: University of North Texas Press, 2013), 120–121; MR, Company D, May 31, 1888; Arnoldo De León, *They Called Them Greasers: Anglo Attitudes Toward Mexicans in Texas, 1821–1900* (Austin: University of Texas Press, 1983), 93–94; Bob Alexander, *Bad Company and Burnt Powder: Justice and Injustice in the Old Southwest* (Denton: University of North Texas Press, 2014), 10; Mike Cox, *The Texas Rangers: Wearing the Cinco Peso, 1821–1900* (New York: Tom Doherty Associates, 2008), 342; *Galveston Daily News*, September 24, 25, 27, 28, 1888.
39. Elliott Young, *Catarino Garza's Revolution on the Texas-Mexico Border* (Durham, NC: Duke University Press, 2004), 68; *San Antonio Daily Express*, September 22, 1888; *Brownsville Daily Herald*, October 4, 1888; Hernán A. Contreras, "Origins of Boss Rule in Starr County" (M.A. thesis, University of Houston-Clear Lake, 2008), 58–59.
40. Young, *Catarino Garza's Revolution*, 68–70; De León, *They Called Them Greasers*, 94; MR, Companes D and F, October 31, 1888; Contreras, "Origins of Boss Rule," 59–60.
41. *RAG, 1888*, 42; MR, Company F, October 31, 1888, October 31, 1889, May 10, 1890; ROS, Company F, October 1889; *RAG, 1889–1890*, 24, 25 (quotation); Special Order No. 154, May 9, 1889, 401–1012, TSLAC; RSR, J. A. Brooks, 401–144, TSLAC.
42. ROS, Company F, June-July 1891; Operations of Frontier Battalion, 3: 179; *Laredo Times*, June 26, 1891; *Austin Daily Stateman*, June 26, 1891; *Galveston Daily News*, June 5, July 3, 1891.
43. Young, *Catarino Garza's Revolution*, 102–103, 111–112, 118–119, 139; Benjamin Heber Johnson, *Revolution in Texas: How a Forgotten Rebellion and Its Bloody Suppression Turned Mexicans into Americans* (New Haven: Yale University Press, 2003), 25; Graybill, *Policing the Great Plains*, 105; Gilbert M. Cuthbertson, "Catarino E. Garza and the Garza War," *Texana* 12 (1974), 338–340.
44. Graybill, *Policing the Great Plains*, 105; Joseph C. Porter, "'The American Congo': Captain John G. Bourke and the Texas Military Experience," *The Texas Military Experience: From the Texas Revolution Through World War II*, ed. Joseph G. Dawson III (College Station: Texas A&M

University Press, 1995), 118, 120, 121; Young, *Catarino Garza's Revolution*, 120–121, 156, 158–159, 163, 168–174, 176, 189; Richard Harding Davis, *The West from a Car-Window* (New York: Harper & Brothers, 1892), 41.

45. Young, *Catarino Garza's Revolution*, 120, 226; Report of Brigadier-General Frank Wheaton, September 13, 1892, *Annual Report of the Secretary of War*, House Executive Document No. 1, Part 2, 52nd Congress, 2nd Session, 134. Hereafter cited as *Annual Report of the Secretary of War, 1892*. ROS, Company F, December 1891.
46. Cox, *Wearing the Cinco Peso*, 353.
47. Spellman, *Captain J. A. Brooks*, 73; ROS, Company F, December 1891; Letter of First Lieutenant W. D. Beach, January 1, 1892, *The Garza Revolution, 1891–1893: Records of the U.S. Continental Commands, Department of Texas* (Bethesda, MD: LexisNexis, 2009), 6–7; Report of Brigadier-General Frank Wheaton, September 13, 1892, *Annual Report of the Secretary of War, 1892*, 134.
48. Spellman, *Captain J. A. Brooks*, 74, 79; Young, *Catarino Garza's Revolution*, 268–269, 278; ROS, Company F, January 1892; Letter of Captain John G. Bourke, January 6, 1892, *The Garza Revolution*, 7 (first quotation); Utley, *Lone Star Justice*, 255; Davis, *The West from a Car-Window*, 11–14 (second and third quotations on p. 12); Cox, *Wearing the Cinco Peso*, 352–354; Alexander, *Riding Lucifer's Line*, 125–126. Even in exile, Garza continued to involve himself in revolutionary activities. As a leader of the Columbian insurgency, he was killed while assaulting the jail in Bocas del Toro on March 8, 1895. *New York Times*, March 12, 1895; *Evening Star*, March 19, 1895.
49. ROS, Company F, April-September 1892, December 1892, January-February 1893; Operations of Frontier Battalion, 3: 182–189; RSR, D. L. Musgrave, 401–165, TSLAC; Porter, "'The American Congo'," 123.
50. Spellman, *Captain J. A. Brooks*, 83; Chuck Parsons, *Captain John R. Hughes, Lone Star Ranger* (Denton: University of North Texas Press, 2011), 106–108; ROS, Company F, July 1894; Alexander, *Winchester Warriors*, 277–278; Utley, *Lone Star Justice*, 259–260; *Galveston Daily News*, July 14, 15, 18, 1894.
51. Spellman, *Captain J. A. Brooks*, 87.
52. RSR, D. L. Musgrave, 401–165, J. Natus, -165, TSLAC; *RAG, 1895–1896*, 9.
53. Leon N. Miletich, *Dan Stuart's Fistic Carnival* (College Station: Texas A&M University Press, 1994), 11–13, 15–16, 58–59, 220 n23;

Meg Frisbee, *Counterpunch: The Cultural Battles Over Heavyweight Prizefighting in the American West* (Seattle: University of Washington Press, 2016), 52; Jeffrey T. Sammons, *Beyond the Ring: The Role of Boxing in American Society* (Urbana: University of Illinois Press, 1990), 14–15. For more on the two fighters, see Adam J. Pollock, *In the Ring with James J. Corbett* (Iowa City, IA: Win By KO Publications, 2007), and *In the Ring with Bob Fitzsimmons* (Iowa City, IA: Win By KO Publications, 2007).

54. Spellman, *Captain J. A. Brooks*, 89; Miletich, *Dan Stuart's Fistic Carnival*, 20, 22, 26, 28–29, 44–46; Frisbee, *Counterpunch*, 56–57; Elmer M. Million, "History of the Texas Prize Fight Statute," *Texas Law Review* 17 (February 1939): 152–154, 157.

55. Miletich, *Dan Stuart's Fistic Carnival*, 64–66, 69, 89–90; Frisbee, *Counterpunch*, 74–75; Keith R. Robinson, *Fist Fighting Out West: Dan Stuart versus General Mabry and the Texas Rangers* (London: English Westerners' Society, 2010), 12; *El Paso Morning Times*, November 17, 21, 1895; C. L. Sonnichsen, *Pass of the North: Four Centuries on the Rio Grande* (El Paso: Texas Western Press, 1968), 1: 358.

56. Miletich, *Dan Stuart's Fistic Carnival*, 84, 96–97; Frisbee, *Counterpunch*, 66; Robinson, *Fist Fighting Out West*, 6; *Galveston Daily News*, October 23, 1895.

57. Miletich, *Dan Stuart's Fistic Carnival*, 131–132, 135, 145, 177–179, 182; Bill Neal, *From Guns to Gavel: How Justice Grew Up in the Outlaw West* (Lubbock; Texas Tech University Press, 2008), 68; ROS, Company F, February 1896 (quotation); *Austin Daily Statesman*, February 11, 21, 1896; *Chicago Tribune*, February 22, 1896. In additional to his *Tribune* column, Siler was a well-known referee of boxing matches. For more on his story, see George Siler, *Inside Facts on Pugilism* (Chicago: Laird & Lee, 1907).

58. Spellman, *Captain J. A. Brooks*, 95–96; MR, Company F, February 29, April 30, 1896; ROS, Company F, February 1896, April 1896; RSR, W. A. Evetts, 401–151, TSLAC; *Galveston Daily News*, April 7, 11, 1896.

59. Tise, *Texas County Sheriffs*, 321; Stephens, *Texas Ranger Sketches*, 52; Casto, *Settlement of the Cibolo-Nueces Strip*, 20; Parsons and Fitterer, *Captain C. B. McKinney*, 97–99.

60. Spellman, *Captain J. A. Brooks*, 97–101; MR, Company F, January 31-February 28, 1897, January 31-March 31, 1898; Tise, *Texas County Sheriffs*, 321. Devenport would be killed in a 1900 shootout with Texas Ranger Will Wright. See Volume 3 of this series for further details.

61. Spellman, *Captain J. A. Brooks*, 101–102, 104–105 (quotation on p. 105); Mabry to McDonald, Mabry to Hughes, Mabry to Rogers, all dated April 19, 1898, 401–658, TSLAC; MR, Company F, April 30-May 31, 1898; Ludeman, *La Salle County*, 117–118; *Houston Daily Post*, May 22, December 23, 1898.
62. Spellman, *Captain J. A. Brooks*, 105–106 (quotation on p. 105); Davis and Grobe, comp. and ed., *New Encyclopedia of Texas*, 4: 2905.
63. Spellman, *Captain J. A. Brooks*, 106–107; Mary Margaret McAllen Amberson, et al., *I Would Rather Sleep in Texas: A History of the Lower Rio Grande Valley and the People of the Santa Anita Land Grant* (Austin: Texas State Historical Association, 2003), 107–108, 154, 353–354; Evan Anders, *Boss Rule in South Texas: The Progressive Era* (Austin: University of Texas Press, 1982), 43–44; Joe R. Baulch, "Little Tammany," *South Texas Studies* 7 (Spring 1996): 202–206, 208–209; MR, Company F, December 31, 1898.
64. Spellman, *Captain J. A. Brooks*, 112–113; James C. Kearney, et al., *No Hope for Heaven, No Fear of Hell: The Stafford-Townsend Feud of Colorado County, 1871–1911* (Denton: University of North Texas Press, 2016), 95–96; C. L. Sonnichsen, *I'll Die Before I'll Run: The Story of the Great Feuds of Texas* (Lincoln: University of Nebraska Press, 1988), 312; MR, Company F, June 30-August 31, 1899, January 31, 1900; ROS, Company F, August-September 1899, January 1900; *Houston Daily Post*, January 20, 1900; *RAG, 1899–1900*, 24.
65. Spellman, *Captain J. A. Brooks*, 113; Kearney, et al., *No Hope for Heaven, No Fear of Hell*, 100–104; MR, Companies F and E, January 31, 1900; ROS, Company F, January 1900; Sonnichsen, *I'll Die Before I'll Run*, 313; *Bastrop Advertiser*, January 20, 1900; *Colorado County Citizen*, February 25, 1988; *Galveston Daily News*, January 16, 17, 1900; *Houston Daily Post*, January 16, 17, 1900; Sterling, *Trails and Trials*, 319.
66. Spellman, *Captain J. A. Brooks*, 113; Kearney, et al., *No Hope for Heaven, No Fear of Hell*, 106–109; ROS, Company F, February 1900; *Bastrop Advertiser*, January 27, 1900; *Houston Daily Post*, January 19, 20, 21, 23, 24, 25, 26, 1900; Sonnichsen, *I'll Die Before I'll Run*, 313.
67. Kearney, et al., *No Hope for Heaven, No Fear of Hell*, 112–114, 108; *Houston Daily Post*, August 4, 1900; *San Antonio Daily Light*, August 1, 1900; "The Colorado County Feud and Its History," Bill Stein Collection, Nesbitt Memorial Library, n. pag. Mr. Stein was the director/archivist at the library, and he delved into the feud extensively before he passed away in December 2008. *Colorado County Citizen*,

February 25, 1988; John Walter Reese and Lillian Estelle Reese, *Flaming Feuds of Colorado County* (Salado, TX: Anson Jones Press, 1962), 115–116. Written by children of Sheriff Sam Reese, this work suffers from a biased and romanticized interpretation of events, but, once the partisanship is stripped away, offers insight into the complicated motivations and dynamics dominating the feud. *Houston Post*, August 1, 2, 1900.

68. Spellman, *Captain J. A. Brooks*, 121; ROS, Company F, March 1900; *RAG, 1899–1900*, 24–25; RSR, A. Y. Baker, 401–51, TSLAC.

69. Charley F. Eckhardt, *Tales of Badmen, Bad Women, and Bad Places: Four Centuries of Texas Outlawry* (Lubbock: Texas Tech University Press, 1999), 168–170; Gary B. Borders, *A Hanging in Nacogdoches: Murder, Race, Politics, and Polemics in Texas's Oldest Town, 1870–1916* (Austin: University of Texas Press, 2006), 34; Fuller, *"A Texas Sheriff"*, 35–36; Combs, *Gunsmoke in the Redlands*, 12–13.

70. Eckhardt, *Badmen, Bad Women, and Bad Places*, 170; Borders, *A Hanging in Nacogdoches*, 36–37; Thad Sitton, *The Texas Sheriff: Lord of the County Line* (Norman: University of Oklahoma Press, 2000), 11–12; Combs, *Gunsmoke in the Redlands*, 28–30, 33–34, 36, 46–48; Fuller, *"A Texas Sheriff"*, 36–37; *Houston Daily Post*, April 22, 23, May 2, 1900; *San Antonio Daily Express*, June 3, September 5, 1900.

71. Spellman, *Captain J. A. Brooks*, 121–122; Harold J. Weiss, Jr., *Yours to Command: The Life and Legend of Texas Ranger Captain Bill McDonald* (Denton: University of North Texas Press, 2009), 194; MR, Company F, June 30-July 31, 1900; ROS, Company B, June-July 1900, Company E, August-September 1900, Company F, June 1900; Combs, *Gunsmoke in the Redlands*, 37, 51–52, 65–69, 75–77; Fuller, *"A Texas Sheriff"*, 39–43; Allen G. Hatley, *Texas Constables: A Frontier Heritage* (Lubbock: Texas Tech University Press, 1999), 94; *Houston Daily Post*, July 30, 1900, May 31, June 1, October 26, 1901, May 8, 1904; Borders, *A Hanging in Nacogdoches*, 183–184 n24.

72. Bob Alexander and Donaly E. Brice, *Texas Rangers: Lives, Legend, and Legacy* (Denton: University of North Texas Press, 2017), 336–339; *RAG, 1899–1900*, 27; *Houston Daily Post*, May 27, 1900.

73. Christopher J. LaForce, *The Choynski Chronicles: A Biography of Hall of Fame Boxer Jewish Joe Choynski* (Iowa City, IA: Win By KO Publications, 2013), 258–267, 99–110, 389–395; Geoffrey C. Ward, *Unforgivable Blackness: The Rise and Fall of Jack Johnson* (New York: Alfred A. Knopf, 2004), 13, 21, 25, 27–28, 30, 32, 35–36,

208–211; Randy Roberts, "Galveston's Jack Johnson: Flourishing in the Dark," *SHQ* 87 (July 1983): 50–52; Sterling, *Trails and Trials*, 320.
74. Spellman, *Captain J. A. Brooks*, 128; Weiss, *Yours to Command*, 193–194; LaForce, *The Choynski Chronicles*, 439–440; ROS, Companies E and F, February 1901; *Galveston Daily News*, January 19, 20, 1899.
75. Spellman, *Captain J. A. Brooks*, 128; *RAG, 1901–1902*, 31; Ward, *Unforgivable Blackness*, 37–38; LaForce, *The Choynski Chronicles*, 516–518; MR, Company F, February 28, 1901; ROS, Company F, March 1901; Roberts, "Galveston's Jack Johnson," 53, 54–55; *Galveston Daily News*, February 26, 1901; Gary Cartwright, *Galveston: A History of the Island* (Fort Worth: Texas Christian University Press, 1991), 159.
76. Spellman, *Captain J. A. Brooks*, 131, 132; *RAG, 1901–1902*, 28–30, 128–129; *Houston Daily Post*, July 13, 1901; MR, Company A, July 31, 1901.
77. *RAG, 1901–1902*, 33; *Galveston Daily News*, August 20, 1901; Sterling, *Trails and Trials*, 139.
78. Charles H. Harris III and Louis R. Sadler, *The Texas Rangers and the Mexican Revolution: The Bloodiest Decade, 1910–1920* (Albuquerque: University of New Mexico Press, 2007), 57–58.
79. MR, Company A, May 31, 1902; Amberson, et al., *I Would Rather Sleep in Texas*, 442–443; Graybill, *Policing the Great Plains*, 105–106; *RAG, 1901–1902*, 33–34; Sterling, *Trails and Trials*, 322–323. Robuck's surname is often spelled "Roebuck," including in his service records. This author has chosen to use the spelling found on his gravestone.
80. Johnson, *Revolution in Texas*, 22; *Brownsville Daily Herald*, May 19, 21, 26, 29, June 2, 1902.
81. MR, Company A, September 30, 1902; Alexander, *Riding Lucifer's Line*, 205; Amberson, et al., *I Would Rather Sleep in Texas*, 443; Johnson, *Revolution in Texas*, 22; Clifford R. Caldwell and Ron DeLord, *Texas Lawmen, 1900–1940: More of the Good and the Bad* (Charleston, SC: History Press, 2012), 392–393.
82. Spellman, *Captain J. A. Brooks*, 147; Graybill, *Policing the Great Plains*, 106; *RAG, 1901–1902*, 33; MR, Company A, February 28, September 30, 1903; Sterling, *Trails and Trials*, 324–325.
83. Walter P. Webb, *The Texas Rangers: A Century of Frontier Defense* (Austin: University of Texas Press, 1965), 464–465; Utley, *Lone Star Justice*, 276; *RAG, 1901–1902*, 33–34, 40.
84. Spellman, *Captain J. A. Brooks*, 157–158; Paul N. Spellman, *Spindletop Boom Days* (College Station: Texas A&M University Press, 2001), 187–188; MR, Company A, February 29, 1904; *Houston Daily Post*,

February 10, 11, 16, 1904; *Galveston Daily News*, February 10, 1904; Sterling, *Trails and Trials*, 327–328, 330.
85. Spellman, *Captain J. A. Brooks*, 159, 163–164; Utley, *Lone Star Justice*, 278; Webb, *Texas Rangers*, 465–466; MR, Company A, February 29–December 31, 1904; *Houston Daily Post*, March 5, 1904; *Galveston Daily News*, March 6, June 29, 30, 1904.
86. Spellman, *Captain J. A. Brooks*, 152–155; Dale Lasater, *Falfurrias: Ed C. Lasater and the Development of South Texas* (College Station: Texas A&M University Press, 1998), 77, 76.
87. Spellman, *Captain J. A. Brooks*, 166; Spellman, *Spindletop Boom Days*, 208–210; MR, Company A, January 31, 1905.
88. Spellman, *Captain J. A. Brooks*, 167–168; *RAG, 1905–1906*, 32; MR, Company A, June 30, 1904–June 30, 1906.
89. Spellman, *Captain J. A. Brooks*, 169; *Galveston Daily News*, March 7, May 11, June 6, 1905; *Houston Daily Post*, May 10, 12, 13, 1905.
90. Spellman, *Captain J. A. Brooks*, 172, 180; Lasater, *Falfurrias*, 99; Anders, *Boss Rule*, 45–47, 48; Baulch, "Little Tammany," 208, 211; Contreras, "Origins of Boss Rule," 64–65; Tise, *Texas County Sheriffs*, 473.
91. Lasater, *Falfurrias*, 101–102.
92. Ibid., 102; Anders, *Boss Rule*, 47–48; Contreras, "Origins of Boss Rule," 65–68.
93. Anders, *Boss Rule*, 49; Joe R. Baulch, "The Murder of Stanley Welch and the 1906 Starr County Election," *Journal of South Texas* 4 (Spring 1991): 37; *Brownsville Daily Herald*, November 6, 12, 15, 16, December 4, 1906; Contreras, "Origins of Boss Rule," 77–78.
94. Spellman, *Captain J. A. Brooks*, 176–177; *RAG, 1906*, 31.
95. Spellman, *Captain J. A. Brooks*, 182–183; Anders, *Boss Rule*, 58–59; Montejano, *Anglos and Mexicans*, 139; *Brownsville Daily Herald*, July 20, November 12, 1908; *House Journal, Thirty-first Legislature, Regular Session*, 2, 130, 99.
96. Spellman, *Captain J. A. Brooks*, 184; *House Journal, Thirty-first Legislature, Regular Session*, 155, 384, 491, 683–684, 954, 946–947, 1144, 1258; *San Antonio Daily Express*, February 7, 1909; Davis and Grobe, comp. and ed., *New Encyclopedia of Texas*, 4: 2905.
97. Spellman, *Captain J. A. Brooks*, 184; *House Journal, Thirty-first Legislature, Regular Session*, 391–392, 1318.
98. Spellman, *Captain J. A. Brooks*, 186–187; *Galveston Daily News*, July 10, 24, 25, 26, 1910; *House Journal, Thirty-second Legislature, Regular Session*, 147, 433–438, 1222, 1251; Acts 1911, 32nd

Legislature, Regular Session, Ch. 39, *General and Special Laws of Texas*.

99. Spellman, *Captain J. A. Brooks*, 187–188, 196, 190; *Galveston Daily News*, September 3, 1911; Ken Anderson, *Crime in Texas: Your Complete Guide to the Criminal Justice System* (Austin: University of Texas Press, 1997), 21. Brooks County was not the only one to be formed in this period. Willacy County was also established in 1911, Jim Wells County the following year, and Jim Hogg and Kleberg Counties in 1913; despite Brooks's best efforts, the former took nine hundred square miles from Brooks County. Kenedy County came into being in 1921. In addition, the formation of these new counties assisted in the rise of South Texas political bosses, such as Judge Jim Wells, Archie Parr, Ed Lasater, John Closner, and A. Y. Baker. Anders, *Boss Rule*, 139–146, 179–185.

100. Spellman, *Captain J. A. Brooks*, 193–194, 205; Lasater, *Falfurrias*, 132–137, 194–196, 265; Contreras, "Origins of Boss Rule," 83; Davis and Grobe, comp. and ed., *New Encyclopedia of Texas*, 4: 2905.

101. Texas Death Certificate, Mrs. Virginia Brooks, January 3, 1928, Register No. 568.

102. Spellman, *Captain J. A. Brooks*, 205, 207; *Falfurrias Facts*, February 10, 1939; *Sixteenth U.S. Census*, Brooks County, Texas; Texas Death Certificate, James A. Brooks, January 18, 1944, File No. 654.

103. Spellman, *Captain J. A. Brooks*, 197–198; *Falfurrias Facts*, January 30, 1980; Texas Death Certificate, Corrinne Brooks, February 6, 1980, Registrar's File No. 1533.

104. *Corpus Christi Caller*, December 5, 1969; *Falfurrias Facts*, September 10, 1970, March 20, 1986; John M. Brooks, World War I Service Record Cards, Texas Military Force Museum; US Army WWI Transport Service, Passenger Lists, RG 92, NARA; Texas Death Certificate, Gladys S. Brooks, June 16, 1978, Registrar's No. 886.

Notes for Chapter 10

1. Harold J. Weiss, Jr., *Yours to Command: The Life and Legend of Texas Ranger Captain Bill McDonald* (Denton: University of North Texas Press, 2009), 25; Albert Bigelow Paine, *Captain Bill McDonald, Texas Ranger: A Story of Frontier Reform* (New York: J. J. Little & Ives Co., 1909), 16. Dr. Weiss's work has replaced Paine's book as the definitive source on McDonald. Texas Death Certificate, Mrs. M. T. McCauley,

Endnotes **639**

   March 7, 1928, Registered No. 96; Certificate Nos., 40.014, 40.054, 41.087, USGLO Records, BLM; *Seventh* and *Eighth U.S. Census*, Kemper County, Mississippi (Free and Slaves Schedules).
2. *Flag of the Union*, August 22, 1851; Michael Perman, *Pursuit of Unity: A Political History of the American South* (Chapel Hill: University of North Carolina Press, 2009), 44–45 63–64, 66–67, 90–91; *Weekly Mississippian*, July 13, 1859, December 5, 1860; CSR-CS, Fortieth Mississippi Infantry, Enoch McDonald; *The War of the Rebellion: A Compilation of the Official Records of the Union and Confederate Armies*, Series 1, XVII, Pt. 1: 388. For more on the battle, see Timothy B. Smith, *Corinth 1862: Siege, Battle, Occupation* (Lawrence: University Press of Kansas, 2012).
3. Weiss, *Yours to Command*, 28–29; *Ninth U.S. Census*, Rusk County, Texas; *Dallas Daily Herald*, January 19, 1867; Rusk County, 1867 Voters' Registration Lists, Reel VR-10, TSLAC; Tax Rolls, Rusk County, 1867; Paine, *Captain Bill McDonald*, 21–22; *W. A. Dunklin & Co. v. W. J. McDonald, et al.*, Case File M7747, 201–4242, TSLAC, 34, 36, 61–63, 65, 71–72, 77, 81–85.
4. Weiss, *Yours to Command*, 32; Clifford R. Caldwell and Ron DeLord, *Eternity at the End of a Rope: Executions, Lynchings and Vigilante Justice in Texas, 1819–1923* (Santa Fe: Sunstone Press, 2015), 174–175; *Galveston Daily News*, April 10, 14, 21, 23, May 7, December 30, 1869.
5. Weiss, *Yours to Command*, 32–33; Bill Neal, *From Guns to Gavel: How Justice Grew Up in the Outlaw West* (Lubbock: Texas Tech University Press, 2008), 13; Paine, *Captain Bill McDonald*, 26–30.
6. Weiss, *Yours to Command*, 35–36; Paine, *Captain Bill McDonald*, 30–31; Robert C. Reinders, *End of an Era: New Orleans, 1850–1860* (Gretna, LA: Pelican Publishing Company, 1989), 143; Lucille Jones, *History of Mineola, Texas: Gateway to the Pines* (Quanah, TX: Nortex Offset Publications, 1973), 6–7, 99; Mineola Centennial Corporation, *Mineola: The First 100 Years* (Mineola, TX: Mineola Centennial Corporation, 1973), 13, 16; Wood County Historical Society, *Wood County, 1850–1900* (Quitman, TX: Wood County Historical Society, 1979), 116; *Dunklin v. McDonald*, 38, 62, 66–67, 75; Tax Rolls, Wood County, 1875–1877. Eunice died in Wichita Falls in 1885. E. H. Loughery, *Texas State Government: A Volume of Biographical Sketches and Passing Comment* (Austin: McLeod & Jackson Printers, 1897), 19.

7. Weiss, *Yours to Command*, 38–39; *Galveston Daily News*, September 4, 1874, June 9, 1876, June 4, 1878; *Mineola Monitor*, March 26, 1936; Jones, *History of Mineola*, 23; Mineola Centennial Corp., *Mineola*, 14, 16, 19, 46; Wood County Historical Society, *Wood County*, 48.
8. Weiss, *Yours to Command*, 39; *Austin Statesman*, March 10, 1906; Robert C. Cotner, *James Stephen Hogg: A Biography* (Austin: University of Texas Press, 1959), 83; Paine, *Captain Bill McDonald*, 31–32, 41–42; Find A Grave, s.v. "Rhoda Isabel Carter McDonald"; *Eighth U.S. Census*, Wood County, Texas.
9. Weiss, *Yours to Command*, 37–38; *Dunklin v. McDonald*, 1–2, 6, 62, 85; Tax Rolls, Wood County, 1877; *Tenth U.S. Census*, Wood County, Texas. See Weiss, *Yours to Command*, 320 n32 for a summation of the lawsuits and judgments.
10. Weiss, *Yours to Command*, 40; Paine, *Captain Bill McDonald*, 33–35. Several books on the history of Mineola and Wood County maintain McDonald served as deputy to City Marshal George Calhoun Reeves. Jones, *History of Mineola*, 19, 100, 106–107; Mineola Centennial Corp., *Mineola*, 14, 16; Wood County Historical Society, *Wood County*, 132. While he might have carried more than one badge during this time, a not uncommon occurrence, McDonald nevertheless made his reputation as a lawman while serving in the sheriff's office.
11. *Galveston Daily News*, August 17, 1881, August 30, October 26, 1882, May 26, 1883, June 8, 1884; *Dallas Daily Herald*, August 30, 1882, June 6, 7, 1884, June 6, 1885. See also Nyle H. Miller and Joseph W. Snell, *Why the West Was Wild: A Contemporary Look at the Antics of Some Highly Publicized Kansas Cowtown Personalities* (Norman: University of Oklahoma Press, 2003), 57–66. A later account conflated the two episodes into one dramatic tale that ended with McDonald being threatened by Smith County authorities with prosecution for having entered another jurisdiction and executing an illegal arrest using violence. Supposedly, Hogg put an end to the controversy when he informed the grand jury he would refuse to try the case. E. H. Loughery, *Texas State Government*, 19; *Austin Statesman*, March 10, 1906; Paine, *Captain Bill McDonald*, 38–42.
12. Weiss, *Yours to Command*, 42–43, 52; Paine, *Captain Bill McDonald*, 43–55, 149–151; Loughery, *Texas State Government*, 19; Louise Kelly, comp., *Wichita County Beginnings* (Burnet, TX: Eakin Press, 1982), 241; Tax Rolls, Wood County, 1880–1884, Wichita County, 1885–1886, Hardeman County, 1885–1910; Bill Neal, *The Last Frontier:*

The Story of Hardeman County (Austin: Eakin Press, 1996), 81; John Miller Morris, *A Private in the Texas Rangers: A. T. Miller of Company B, Frontier Battalion* (College Station: Texas A&M University Press, 2001), 28, 47, 66–68, 147; Sammy Tise, *Texas County Sheriffs* (Albuquerque: Oakwood Publishing, 1989), 239.

13. Weiss, *Yours to Command*, 44–46; Morris, *A Private in the Texas Rangers*, 16, 37–38, 47, 49, 51, 60, 75, 105–106, 112–115, 130, 132, 147, 175–176 (quotation on p. 175), 182; MR, Company B, February 28, 1887; Robert W. Stephens, *Texas Ranger Sketches* (Dallas: Robert W. Stephens, 1972), 99.
14. Morris, *A Private in the Texas Rangers*, 47 (first quotation), 48 (second quotation), 74, 106, 111–113 (third quotation on p. 112), 148–149, 170, 173, 263; *Fort Worth Daily Gazette*, March 26, April 14, 1887; *Galveston Daily News*, April 10, 1887; MR, Company B, April 30, September 30, 1887; RSR, D. A. Peal, 401-167; Blake Allmendinger, *The Cowboy: Representations of Labor in an American Culture* (New York: Oxford University Press, 1992), 16–17.
15. Weiss, *Yours to Command*, 46–47; Paine, *Captain Bill McDonald*, 66, 55–56, 58–59, 64–68; Morris, *A Private in the Texas Rangers*, 58, 61, 70–72, 75, 78, 112–113, 122–123, 125–127, 134–135, 146, 181–182, 199–201, 208–209, 239–240, 243–244; MR, Company B, December 31, 1887; *Fort Worth Daily Gazette*, January 14, 1887, May 5, 1888; Tise, *Texas County Sheriffs*, 542.
16. Weiss, *Yours to Command*, 47–48, 322 n72.
17. Ibid., 48–49; Paine, *Captain Bill McDonald*, 69–125; Boyce House, *Cowtown Columnist* (San Antonio: Naylor Company, 1946), 233 (quotation); *Fort Worth Daily Gazette*, March 16, 1890.
18. Weiss, *Yours to Command*, 50, 53, 60; RSR, W. J. McDonald, 401-162, TSLAC; Operations of Frontier Battalion, 3 (1885–1892), 401-1084, TSLAC: 5; Morris, *A Private in the Texas Rangers*, 253; Cotner, *James Stephen Hogg*, 211 n48, 300. For more on McMurry, see Stephens, *Texas Ranger Sketches*, 99–102.
19. Weiss, *Yours to Command*, 60–61; *Galveston Daily News*, January 29, 1891; Paine, *Captain Bill McDonald*, 145–148.
20. Eugene Cunningham, *Triggernometry: A Gallery of Gunfighters* (Norman: University of Oklahoma Press, 1996), 315; Morris, *A Private in the Texas Rangers*, 254; Jim Gober, *Cowboy Justice: Tale of a Texas Lawman*, ed. James R. Gober and B. Byron Price (Lubbock: Texas Tech University Press, 1997), 149; Ben H. Procter, *Just One Riot: Episodes*

of the Texas Rangers in the 20th Century (Austin: Eakin Press, 1991), 24; Robert M. Utley, *Lone Star Justice: The First Century of the Texas Rangers* (New York: Berkley Books, 2002), 257.

21. Mike Cox, *The Texas Rangers: Wearing the Cinco Peso, 1821–1900* (New York: Tom Doherty Associates, 2008), 357–358.
22. Weiss, *Yours to Command*, 61–77; Utley, *Lone Star Justice*, 258; MR, Company B, February 28, 1891–May 31, 1894; ROS, Company B, September-November 1893.
23. Weiss, *Yours to Command*, 90–91; MR, Company B, July 31, 1893; Neal, *From Guns to Gavel*, 28–29; Glenn Shirley, *West of Hell's Fringe: Crime, Criminals, and the Federal Peace Officer in Oklahoma Territory, 1889–1907* (Norman: University of Oklahoma Press, 1990), 342; Operations of Frontier Battalion, 4 (1892–1895), 401–1085, TSLAC: 6; *San Saba County News*, August 11, 1893; Michael G. Ehrle, comp., *The Childress County Story* (Childress, TX: Ox Bow Printing, 1971), 58.
24. Weiss, *Yours to Command*, 91; MR, Company B, September 1, 1893; *Galveston Daily News*, August 18, 1893; Neal, *From Guns to Gavels*, 32, 35; Robert W. Stephens, *Bullets and Buckshot in Texas* (Dallas: R. W. Stephens, 2002), 141; Ehrle, comp., *Childress County Story*, 58.
25. Britton to Mabry, December 11, 1893, 401–430, TSLAC; Stephens, *Bullets and Buckshot*, 139–140; Tise, *Texas County Sheriffs*, 102; Neal, *The Last Frontier*, 68; Paine, *Captain Bill McDonald*, 165–169; Ehrle, comp., *Childress County Story*, 61–62, 246–249; Neal, *From Guns to Gavels*, 16.
26. Weiss, *Yours to Command*, 94–97, 98; ROS, Company B, December 1893; Britton to Mabry, December 11, 1893, 401–430, TSLAC; Cox, *Wearing the Cinco Peso*, 438 n26; Clifford R. Caldwell and Ron DeLord, *Texas Lawmen, 1835–1899: The Good and the Bad* (Charleston, SC: History Press, 2011), 52–53; *Fort Worth Daily Gazette*, December 11, 1893; *Galveston Daily News*, December 11, 13, 1893; *Dallas Morning News*, December 31, 1893. Paine recounted McDonald was shot twice in the left arm in addition to his other wounds. *Captain Bill McDonald*, 173. These additional injuries were not mentioned in eyewitness statements. As to who pulled their pistol first, bystanders conflict in their accounts, and the issue cannot be positively resolved.
27. Weiss, *Yours to Command*, 97–98; Moses to McDonald, December 16, 1893, ROS, Company B, 1893; Operations of Frontier Battalion, 4: 12; Neal, *From Guns to Gavels*, 43; *Fort Worth Daily Gazette*, February 10, 1894. George Cook, elected Motley County sheriff late the previous year,

was shot and killed by Beckham on May 29, 1895. Clifford and DeLord, *Texas Lawmen, 1835–1899*, 174.

28. Weiss, *Yours to Command*, 79–80; Operations of Frontier Battalion, 4: 18; Andrew Graybill, *Policing the Great Plains: Rangers, Mounties, and the North American Frontier, 1875–1910* (Lincoln: University of Nebraska Press, 2007), 191–192; Don Woodard, *Black Diamonds! Black Gold!* (Lubbock; Texas Tech University Press, 1998), 42–45; Dick King, "'Rascals' and Rangers," *True West* 22 (April 1975): 11. Captain McMurry and Company B had kept the peace at Thurber during a Knights of Labor strike in December 1888. MR, Company B, December 31, 1888.

29. Woodard, *Black Diamonds! Black Gold!*, 45–46; King, "'Rascals' and Rangers," 11–12; Utley, *Lone Star Justice*, 259; Mary Jane Gentry, *The Birth of a Texas Ghost Town: Thurber, 1886–1933* (College Station: Texas A&M University Press, 2008), 55.

30. Weiss, *Yours to Command*, 81–82; Utley, *Lone Star Justice*, 259–260; Frederick S. Calhoun, *The Lawmen: United States Marshals and Their Deputies, 1789–1989* (Washington, D.C.: Smithsonian Institution Press, 1989), 207, 210; Richard Schneirov, "'From the Ragged Edge of Anarchy': The 1894 Pullman Boycott," *OAH Magazine of History* 13 (Spring 1999): 26, 28; *Austin Daily Statesman*, July 11, 13, 1894; Paine, *Captain Bill McDonald*, 214–220; The best secondary source on the boycott remains Almont Lindsay, *The Pullman Strike: The Story of a Unique Experiment and of a Great Labor Upheaveal* (Chicago: University of Chicago Press, 1964).

31. Weiss, *Yours to Command*, 82; *Fort Worth Gazette*, October 19, 24, 1894, February 28, March 3, 1895; *Galveston Daily News*, October 20, 25, 28, November 1, 1894, February 28, March 5, 1895; ROS, Company B, October 1894; *Austin Daily Statesman*, November 17, 1895.

32. Operations of Frontier Battalion, 4: 20; MR, Company B, October 31, 1894; *Fort Worth Gazette*, November 17, 1894; *Austin Daily Statesman*, November 23, 1894; Bob Alexander, *Lawmen, Outlaws, and S.O.Bs: Gunfighters of the Old Southwest* (Silver City, NM: High-Lonesome Books, 2004), 139; Glenn Shirley, *Law West of Fort Smith: A Tale of Frontier Justice in the Indian Territory, 1834–1896* (New York: Henry Holt and Company, 1957), 111, 119.

33. MR, Company B, January 31, 1895; Robert K. DeArment, *Deadly Dozen: Twelve Forgotten Gunfighters of the Old West* (Norman: University of Oklahoma Press, 2003), 124–126; Tise, *Texas County Sheriffs*, 47, 378; Alexander, *Lawmen, Outlaws, and S.O.Bs*, 141–142; Shirley,

Law West of Fort Smith, 119–120. Sheriff McMurry was the younger brother of former Captain S. A. McMurry.

34. W. John L. Sullivan, *Twelve Years in the Saddle with the Texas Rangers* (Lincoln: University of Nebraska Press, 2001), 99–104; MR, Company B, January 31, 1895.

35. Neal, *From Guns to Gavels*, 51–55, 58; Valerie Owen, *Byrd Cochran of Dead Man's Corner* (Snyder, TX: Feather Press, 1972), 37–38; Robert K. DeArment, *Deadly Dozen: Forgotten Gunfighters of the Old West* (Norman: University of Oklahoma Press, 2010), 3: 279–280; Sullivan, *Twelve Years in the Saddle*, 120–126; Bob Alexander, *Lawmen, Outlaws, and S.O.Bs: Gunfighters of the Old Southwest* (Silver City, NM: High-Lonesome Books, 2007), 2: 257–261; Glenn Shirley, *Six-Gun and Silver Star* (Albuquerque: University of New Mexico Press, 1955), 61, 152–153; Harry Sinclair Drago, *Road Agents and Train Robbers: Half a Century of Western Banditry* (New York: Dodd, Mead & Company, 1973), 234, 243. Weightman would finally be killed by an Oklahoma posse in March 1896. *Wichita Daily Eagle*, March 12, 1896.

36. Leon N. Miletich, *Dan Stuart's Fistic Carnival* (College Station: Texas A&M University Press, 1994), 91–92, 102, 104; Keith R. Robinson, *Fist Fighting Out West: Dan Stuart versus General Mabry and the Texas Rangers* (London: English Westerners' Society, 2010), 4; Neal, *From Guns to Gavel*, 66; Steve Bogener, "The World Heavyweight Boxing Championship Bout, 1896, at Langtry, Texas," *WTHAY* 74 (1998), 47.

37. Weiss, *Yours to Command*, 109; Elliott J, Gorn, *The Manly Art: Bare-Knuckle Prize Fighting in America* (Ithaca, NY: Cornell University Press, 2010), 166, 202, 204–205; Hans Peter Nielson Gammel, comp., *The Laws of Texas, 1822–1897* (Austin: The Gammel Book Company, 1898), 10: 1051; Miletich, *Dan Stuart's Fistic Carnival*, 136, 138, 141, 148; *RAG, 1895–1896*, 11; Bogener, "The World Heavyweight Boxing Championship Bout," 48; Sullivan, *Twelve Years in the Saddle*, 146 (first quotation), 148 (second quotation); *Austin Daily Statesman*, February 6, 10, 1896.

38. Weiss, *Yours to Command*, 110–116; Miletich, *Dan Stuart's Fistic Carnival*, 151, 161, 163, 167, 173–174, 175, 188; Meg Frisbee, *Counterpunch: The Cultural Battles Over Heavyweight Prizefighting in the American West* (Seattle: University of Washington Press, 2016), 72, 90, 99; C. L. Sonnischen, *Pass of the North: Four Centuries on the Rio Grande* (El Paso: Texas Western Press, 1968), 1: 345–378; Sullivan, *Twelve Years in the Saddle*, 148; Dan L. Thrapp, *Encyclopedia of*

Endnotes

Frontier Biography (Lincoln: University of Nebraska Press, 1991), 1: 79–80; Cox, *Wearing the Cinco Peso*, 362–364; *Chicago Dispatch*, February 22, 1896. See also Robert Fitzsimmons, *Physical Culture and Self-Defense* (Philadelphia: Drexell Biddle, 1901).

39. Paine, *Captain Bill McDonald*, 198 (second, third, and fourth quotations); Robinson, *Fist Fight Out West*, 23; *San Francisco Chronicle*, February 22, 1896 (first quotation).
40. For examples, see House, *Cowtown Columnist*, 234; Robert K. DeArment, *Bat Masterson, The Man and the Legend* (Norman: University of Oklahoma, 1979), 348–349; and Miletich, *Dan Stuart's Fistic Carnival*, 177.
41. Robert K. DeArment, *Gunfighter in Gotham* (Norman: University of Oklahoma, 2013), 27–28.
42. "Incident of Capt. Bill McDonald," *Frontier Times* 2 (August 1925): 15.
43. Weiss, *Yours to Command*, 121–125; Caldwell and DeLord, *Eternity at the End of a Rope*, 387–388; Bill Neal, *Getting Away with Murder on the Texas Frontier: Notorious Killings and Celebrated Trials* (Lubbock: Texas Tech University Press, 2006), 52–56; *Dallas Morning News*, February 26, 27, 28, 1896; *Austin Daily Statesman*, February 26, 1896; Kelly, comp., *Wichita County Beginnings*, 43–44, 221; Glenn Shirley, *West of Hell's Fringe: Crime, Criminals, and the Federal Peace Officer in Oklahoma Territory, 1889–1907* (Norman: University of Oklahoma Press, 1990), 347–348; Robert K. DeArment, *Deadly Dozen: Forgotten Gunfighters of the Old West* (Norman: University of Oklahoma Press, 2007), 2: 148.
44. Weiss, *Yours to Command*, 125–130; Caldwell and DeLord, *Eternity at the End of a Rope*, 388; Neal, *From Guns to Gavels*, 78–86, 93; Kelly, comp., *Wichita County Beginnings*, 44; *Fort Worth Gazette*, February 26, 27, 28, 1896; *Galveston Daily News*, February 26, 27, 28, 1896; *Houston Daily Post*, February 26, 1896; *Wichita Daily Times*, June 24, July 1, 1951; MR, Company B, February 28, 1896; Sullivan, *Twelve Years in the Saddle*, 151; Cox, *Wearing the Cinco Peso*, 364–365.
45. Weiss, *Yours to Command*, 126, 128; Neal, *From Guns to Gavels*, 93–94, 98–101; Neal, *Getting Away with Murder*, 67–70, 259 n48, n50, n51; Kelly, comp., *Wichita County Beginnings*, 161.
46. C. L. Sonnichsen, *Ten Texas Feuds* (Albuquerque: University of New Mexico Press, 2000), 6; Ross J. Cox, Sr., *The Texas Rangers and the San Saba Mob* (San Saba, TX: C & S Farm Press, 2005), 1: 4–5, 8–10, 12, 44; C. L. Sonnichsen, *I'll Die Before I'll Run: The Story of the*

Great Feuds of Texas (Lincoln: University of Nebraska Press, 1988), 210–219; Ross McSwain, *See No Evil, Speak No Evil: A History of Mob Violence in the Texas Heartland, 1869–1904* (San Angelo, TX: Shadetree Enterprises, 2008), 32–33, 64, 140–141; Robert Maxwell Brown, *Strain of Violence: Historical Studies of American Violence and Vigilantism* (New York: Oxford University Press, 1975), 249, 250, 292; MR, Company F, May 31, 1888.

47. Weiss, *Yours to Command*, 137–138; Cox, *Texas Rangers and the San Saba Mob*, 1: 11–12, 13; MR, Companies B and E, August 31, 1896; ROS, Company E, August 1896; Sonnichsen, *I'll Die Before I'll Run*, 219–221; Sullivan, *Twelve Years in the Saddle*, 161–162; Stephens, *Texas Ranger Sketches*, 22.

48. Cox, *Texas Rangers and the San Saba Mob*, 1: 16, 17–20, 24, 27; MR, Company B, November 30, 1896; ROS, Company E, January 1897; Sonnichsen, *I'll Die Before I'll Run*, 223–226; McSwain, *See No Evil, Speak No Evil*, 147–149, 151; Sullivan, *Twelve Years in the Saddle*, 163; Cox, *Wearing the Cinco Peso*, 368; *Houston Daily Post*, February 22, 28, June 8, 17, 21, 24, 1897; *Austin Daily Statesman*, March 6, June 9, 10, 11, 15, 16, 18, 1897.

49. Weiss, *Yours to Command*, 142–144; MR, Company B, May 31, 1897; Cox, *Texas Rangers and the San Saba Mob*, 1: 24–26, 21–22, 27; Sonnichsen, *I'll Die Before I'll Run*, 226.

50. Weiss, *Yours to Command*, 145; MR, Company B, July 31-November 30, 1897; Cox, *Texas Rangers and the San Saba Mob*, 1: 27–28, 33; Sonnichsen, *I'll Die Before I'll Run*, 227.

51. Weiss, *Yours to Command*, 145–148; MR, Company B, December 31, 1897; Cox, *Texas Rangers and the San Saba Mob*, 1: 29, 31–36, 43; *Autin Daily Statesman*, May 31, 1899; Texas Department of Criminal Justice, Convict Record Ledgers, 1998/038–139, TSLAC, 132; Brown, *Strain of Violence*, 293. Ogle received a pardon from Governor Thomas M. Campbell on December 20, 1909. *San Antonio Daily Express*, December 31, 1909.

52. Weiss, *Yours to Command*, 148; Cox, *Texas Rangers and the San Saba Mob*, 1: 37–38, 52 (quotation); McSwain, *See No Evil, Speak No Evil*, 154–155; Sonnichsen, *I'll Die Before I'll Run*, 227–230; Brown, *Strain of Violence*, 293–294.

53. James C. Kearney, et al., *No Hope for Heaven, No Fear of Hell: The Stafford-Townsend Feud of Colorado County, 1871–1911* (Denton: University of North Texas Press, 2016), 6–7, 54–56; John Walter Reese

and Lillian Estelle Reese, *Flaming Feuds of Colorado County* (Salado, TX: Anson Jones Press, 1962), 30; *Colorado County Chronicles* (Colorado County Historical Commission, comp., 1986), 1: 193; Sonnichsen, *I'll Die Before I'll Run*, 302–303.

54. Kearney, et al., *No Hope for Heaven, No Fear of Hell*, 9–11, 15–16; *Colorado County Chronicles*, 1: 196; Sonnichsen, *I'll Die Before I'll Run*, 304–306; "The Colorado County Feud and Its History," Bill Stein Collection, Nesbitt Memorial Library, n. pag. In addition to his manuscript, Stein also wrote a series of well-researched articles about the quarrel for the *Colorado County Citizen*. According to the Reeses, the killing of the two Staffords had actually been the result of a murder plot hatched by Light Townsend and other members of his family. Reese and Reese, *Flaming Feuds of Colorado County*, 33–34.

55. Kearney, et al., *No Hope for Heaven, No Fear of Hell*, 34–36, 70–71, 109, 137; *Colorado County Chronicles*, 1: 208; "The Colorado County Feud and Its History," n. pag.; *Colorado County Citizen*, February 4, 11, 1988; Sonnichsen, *I'll Die Before I'll Run*, 307–309. Light Townsend died in 1894 after fourteen years in office, and Chief Deputy Reese, who had married the sheriff's first cousin, filled his unexpired term. Reese then won election to the office in 1896.

56. Kearney, et al., *No Hope for Heaven, No Fear of Hell*, 81–82; Sonnichsen, *I'll Die Before I'll Run*, 308, 309–310; "The Colorado County Feud and Its History," n. pag.; *Colorado County Citizen*, February 11, 1988, March 23, 1899, February 18, 1988; Reese and Reese, *Flaming Feuds of Colorado County*, 80; *Galveston Daily News*, March 17, 24, 25, 29, 1899; *Houston Daily Post*, March 17, 19, 24, 1899.

57. Weiss, *Yours to Command*, 156–158; Kearney, et al., *No Hope for Heaven, No Fear of Hell*, 83, 85–86; MR, Company B, March 31, 1899; *RAG, 1900*, 21 (quotation); *Galveston Daily News*, March 22, 23, 24, 29, 1899; *Houston Daily Post*, March 29, 1899; Earl Mayo, "The Texas Rangers: The Most Efficient Police Force in the World," *Frank Leslie's Popular Monthly* 52 (October 1901): 536; Sonnichsen, *I'll Die Before I'll Run*, 310–311; Frederick Wilkins, *The Law Comes to Texas: The Texas Rangers, 1870–1901* (Abilene, TX: State House Press, 1999), 335. See also Brown, *Strain of Violence*, 252–255.

58. Caldwell and DeLord, *Eternity at the End of a Rope*, 415; Mark Busby, "An East Texas Lynching: The Humphries/Wilkinson-Greenhaw Feud," *Corners of Texas*, ed. Francis Edward Abernathy (Denton: University of North Texas Press, 1993), 147–148, 152; *Dallas Morning*

News, May 26, 27, 29, June 27, 28, 29, 1899; *San Antonio Daily Express*, May 30, 1899; *Houston Daily Post*, June 9, 10, 23, 27, 28, 29, 30, 1899; *Galveston Daily News*, May 29, 30, June 4, 7, 10, 12, 13, 15, 22, 23, 25, 26, 27, 28, 29, 30, July 13, 14, 15, August 9, 10, 11, 12, 13, September 5, 29, 1899.

59. J. L. Wilkinson, *The Trans-Cedar Lynching and the Texas Penitentiary*, ed. Bertha E. Drager (New York: Carlton Press, 1974), 26–32; Busby, "An East Texas Lynching," 149, 152, 157; Jim Monaghan, *The Trans-Cedar Tragedy: Triple Lynching in Henderson County, Texas* (Dallas, TX: Homemade Publishers, 1989), 258; *Dallas Morning News*, May 27, 28, 29, June 7, 8, 12, 27, 28, 29, 30, August 10, 11, 12, December 17, 18, 19, 20, 1899, January 14, August 3, 1900; *Houston Daily Post*, May 27, 1899.

60. Weiss, *Yours to Command*, 178–179; ROS, Company E, June-July 1899; Caldwell and DeLord, *Eternity at the End of a Rope*, 415; Busby, "An East Texas Lynching," 150; *Dallas Morning News*, May 30, 31, June 1, 4, 8, 12, 1899; *Galveston Daily News*, June 7, 1899; *RAG, 1899–1900*, 21–22. Ranger Old transferred to Company B on August 1. Special Order No. 13, August 1, 1899, 401–1013, TSLAC.

61. MR, Company B, June 30, 1899; Busby, "An East Texas Lynching," 151; Wilkinson, *The Trans-Cedar Lynching*, 34; *Dallas Morning News*, June 29, December 17, 1899, August 2, 1900.

62. Weiss, *Yours to Command*, 179–184; *Dallas Morning News*, June 27, 28, 29, 30, August 9, 10, December 22, 23, 1899, January 14, August 22, 1900; MR, Company B, June 30, 1899-August 30, 1900. After receiving calls for clemency from judges, attorneys, prison officials, the advisory board of pardons, and respected citizens, Governor Campbell pardoned the eight convicted lynchers between 1908 and 1911. *Houston Daily Post*, June 27, December 10, 1908, December 22, 1909, November 30, 1910, April 11, 1911.

63. Weiss, *Yours to Command*, 197–199; Paine, *Captain Bill McDonald*, 407; MR, Company B, September 30-December 31, 1899; ROS, Company E, August-September 1899.

64. Weiss, *Yours to Command*, 202–203; *Austin Daily Statesman*, December 22, 24, 1899; *Houston Daily Post*, October 1, December 22, 23, 24, 1899; January 14, May 22, 1900; *Galveston Daily News*, December 22, 1899; MR, Company B, December 31, 1899-January 31, April 30, 1900.

65. Mike Cox, *Time of the Rangers: From 1900 to the Present* (New York: Tom Doherty Books, 2009), 20; *El Paso Daily Herald*, May 28, 1900;

Patsy McDonald Spaw, ed., *The Texas Senate* (College Station: Texas A&M University Press, 1999), 2: 338; *Austin Daily Statesman*, February 2, May 27, 1900; Utley, *Lone Star Justice*, 272; Wilkins, *Law Comes to Texas*, 345; Walter P. Webb, *The Texas Rangers: A Century of Frontier Defense* (Austin: University of Texas Press, 1965), 453 (quotation).

66. *RAG, 1899–1900*, 127–130; Special Orders No. 67, July 3, 1900, 401–1013, TSLAC; Cox, *Time of the Rangers*, 20–21; Utley, *Lone Star Justice*, 273; Webb, *Texas Rangers*, 457.

67. Weiss, *Yours to Command*, 201; MR, Company B, October 31, 1900; *Galveston Daily News*, October 17, 1900; *Houston Daily Post*, October 16, 1900; *RAG, 1899–1900*, 23; Paine, *Captain Bill McDonald*, 261–262; William Warren Sterling, *Trails and Trials of a Texas Ranger* (Norman: University of Oklahoma Press, 1959), 339.

68. Weiss, *Yours to Command*, 201; Sterling, *Trials and Trials*, 339; Clifford R. Caldwell and Ron DeLord, *Texas Lawmen, 1900–1940: More of the Good & the Bad* (Charleston, SC: History Press, 2012), 293–94, 392; *Houston Daily Post*, March 13, May 13, 1902. George was killed in a labor race riot near Shreveport on March 16, 1908. *Austin Statesman*, March 17, 1908.

69. Weiss, *Yours to Command*, 210–218; RSR, W. J. McDonald, 401–162, TSLAC; Webb, *Texas Rangers*, 457–458; *RAG, 1901–1902*, 127–128, 32–33, 40; MR, Company B, July 31, 1901-December 31, 1902.

70. Weiss, *Yours to Command*, 219–220; *Galveston Daily News*, December 5, 6, 15, 17, 1903, January 12, April 3, 1904; MR, Company B, December 31, 1903-March 31, 1904; Paine, *Captain Bill McDonald*, 266–267; 79 *Southwestern Reporter* 1198 (1904); *RAG, 1903–1904*, 158.

71. Weiss, *Yours to Command*, 220–221; MR, Company B, February 29–March 31, 1904; Bob Alexander, *Bad Company and Burnt Powder: Justice and Injustice in the Old Southwest* (Denton: University of North Texas Press, 2014), 227; *Twelfth U.S. Census*, Trinity County, Texas; Texas Death Certificate, Mary Jane Thomas, September 11, 1903, File No. 1019. Suzanne Waller of the Trinity County Historical Commission has taken on the daunting task of researching the murder. Unfortunately, despite her best efforts, little new material has been uncovered.

72. Weiss, *Yours to Command*, 221; MR, Company B, February 29–April 30, August 31, 1904; *Houston Post*, February 24, 1904; Paine, *Captain Bill McDonald*, 270; *RAG, 1903–1904*, 158; Texas Department of Criminal Justice, Convict Record Ledgers, 1998/038-156, TSLAC, 128; ibid., Conduct Registers, 1998/038-193, TSLAC, 319.

73. Neal, *From Guns to Gavel*, 116–118; Kelly, comp., *Wichita County Beginnings*, 50; *Austin Statesman*, April 2, 3, 4, 5, 6, 7, 8, 9, 10, 11, 1905; *San Antonio Daily Light*, April 2, 6, 1905; Bill Neeley, *The Last Comanche Chief: The Life and Times of Quanah Parker* (New York: John Wiley & Sons, 1995), 219–220; Edward H. Phillips, "Teddy Roosevelt in Texas, 1905," *WTHAY* 56 (1980), 58–67.
74. Weiss, *Yours to Command*, 225; MR, Company B, April 30, 1905; *Austin Statesman*, April 15, 16, 1905; Paine, *Captain Bill McDonald*, 278–289; Theodore Roosevelt, "A Wolf Hunt in Oklahoma," *Scribner's Magazine* 38 (November 1905): 513–532 (quotation on p. 513). See also John R. (Jack) Abernathy, *In Camp with Theodore Roosevelt, or the Life of John R. (Jack) Abernathy* (Oklahoma City: Times-Journal Publishing Co., 1933); Frederick S. Barde, "Story of John Abernathy and His Famous Wolf Hunts," unpublished MS, n.d., Frederick S. Barde Collection, Oklahoma Historical Society; Foster Harris, "T. R. and the Great Wolf Hunt," *Oklahoma Today* 8 (Fall 1958); Theodore Roosevelt, *Theodore Roosevelt's Letters to His Children*, ed. Joseph Bucklin Bishop (New York: Charles Scribner's Sons, 1919); and Brian Lee Smith, "Theodore Roosevelt Visits Oklahoma," *The Chronicles of Oklahoma* 51 (Fall 1973): 263–279.
75. Weiss, *Yours to Command*, 226; MR, Company B, July 31, 1905; *RAG, 1905–1906*, 170–171.
76. Harold J. Weiss, "The Texas Rangers and Captain Bill McDonald in General—And the Conditt Murder Case in Particular," *South Texas Studies* 9 (1998): 56–57; 110 *Southwestern Reporter* 42 (1908).
77. Weiss, *Yours to Command*, 230–232; Weiss, "Conditt Murder Case," 57–58; *Brownsville Daily Herald*, October 3, 6, 10, 1905; *RAG, 1905–1906*, 28.
78. Weiss, *Yours to Command*, 232; Weiss, "Conditt Murder Case," 58; *Victoria Daily Advocate*, October 21, 1905; MR, Company B, October 31, 1905; Paine, *Captain Bill McDonald*, 298–303; Sterling, *Trails and Trials*, 345; *Brownsville Daily Herald*, October 19, 1905.
79. *Houston Daily Post*, December 11, 13, 14, 15, 16, 17, 19, 20, 21, 22, 23, 1905; *Brownsville Daily Herald*, December 20, 21, 23, 26, 1905. For more on the use of fingerprints as a means of identification, see Henry Faulds and William J. Herschel, *Dactylography and the Origin of Finger-Printing* (Cambridge, UK: Cambridge University Press, 2015).

80. Weiss, *Yours to Command*, 234–236; Weiss, "Conditt Murder Case," 60–61, 63; Sterling, *Trails and Trials*, 346; 99 *Southwestern Reporter* 1005–06, 1007, 1008 (1907).
81. Weiss, *Yours to Command*, 236–239; Weiss, "Conditt Murder Case," 61–64; MR, Company B, December 31, 1906; *Victoria Daily Advocate*, December 8, 10, 11, 12, 13, 15, 1906, March 2, 1907, July 4, 1908; 99 *Southwestern Reporter* 1005, 1009; 110 *Southwestern Reporter* 41–54; See also 50 *Texas Criminal Reports* 592–99 (1907); and 53 *Texas Criminal Reports* 349–72 (1907).
82. Weiss, *Yours to Command*, 227–228; Paine, *Captain Bill McDonald*, 304–307; Texas Death Certificate, Mrs. W. J. McDonald, May 26, 1906, File No. 4863.
83. Mary Margaret McAllen Amberson, et al., *I Would Rather Sleep in Texas: A History of the Lower Rio Grande Valley and the People of the Santa Anita Land Grant* (Austin: Texas State Historical Association, 2003), 447; Quintard Taylor, *In Search of the Racial Frontier: African Americans in the American West, 1528–1990* (New York: W. W. Norton & Company, 1998), 177; James N. Leiker, *Racial Borders: Black Soldiers Along the Rio Grande* (College Station: Texas A&M University Press, 2002), 119 (second quotation); Charles D. Thompson, Jr., *Border Odyssey: Travels Along the U.S./Mexico Divide* (Austin: University of Texas Press, 2015), 70; Jovita González, *Life Along the Border: A Landmark Tejana Thesis* (College Station: Texas A&M University Press, 2006), 7–8; David Montejano, *Anglos and Mexicans in the Making of Texas, 1836–1986* (Austin: University of Texas Press, 1987), 109 (first quotation), 111.
84. Leiker, *Racial Borders*, 131, 133, 134 (quotation), 135, 137–138; William H. Leckie, with Shirley A. Leckie, *The Buffalo Soldiers: A Narrative of the Black Cavalry in the West* (Norman: University of Oklahoma Press, 2003), 286; Karin L. Sandford, ed., *If We Must Die: African-American Voices on War and Peace* (Lanham, MD: Rowman & Littlefield, 2008), 87; Taylor, *In Search of the Racial Frontier*, 177; Richard Young, "The Brownsville Affray," *American History Illustrated* 21 (October 1986): 11; Ricardo Purnell Malbrew, "Brownsville Revisited" (M.A. thesis, Louisiana State University, 2007), 8, 10.

The federal government amassed an immense amount of official correspondence and testimony concerning the Brownsville Affair. This collection of primary documentation can be found in *Summary*

Discharge or Mustering Out of Regiments or Companies, Senate Document No. 155, 59th Congress, 2nd Session; *Affray at Brownsville,* Senate Document No. 402, Pts. 1–6, 60th Congress, 1st Session; and *Report of Brownsville Court of Inquiry,* Senate Document No. 701, Pts. 1–12, 61st Congress, 3rd Session.

Examples of the extensive secondary sources that reference or examine the event and its outcome include studies of President Theodore Roosevelt's administration written by H. W. Brands, Edmund Morris, Kathleen Dalton, and Harry Lembeck, as well as Texas Ranger histories authored by Robert Utley, Mike Cox, and Bob Alexander and Donaly Brice. The five works that offer the best overview of the Brownsville incident are Leiker, *Racial Borders*; Garna L. Christian, *Black Soldiers in Jim Crow Texas, 1899–1917* (College Station: Texas A&M University Press, 1995); Ann J. Lane, *The Brownsville Affair: National Crisis and Black Reaction* (Port Washington, NY: Kennikat Press, 1971); and John D. Weaver, *The Brownsville Raid* (College Station: Texas A&M University Press, 1992), and *The Senator and the Sharecropper's Son: Exoneration of the Brownsville Soldiers* (College Station: Texas A&M University Press, 1997). See also James A. Tinsley, "Roosevelt, Foraker, and the Brownsville Affray," *Journal of Negro History* 41 (January 1956): 43–65; John H. Nankivell, *Buffalo Soldier Regiment: History of the Twenty-fifth United States Infantry, 1869–1926* (Lincoln: University of Nebraska Press, 2001); and Walter Pierce, "The Brownsville Raid: A Historiographical Assessment," and Antonio N. Zavaleta, "The Twin Cities: A Historical Synthesis of the Socio-Economic Interdependence of the Brownsville-Matamoros Border Community," both in *Studies in Brownsville History,* ed. Milo Kearney (Brownsville: Pan-American University at Brownsville, 1986).

85. *Summary Discharge or Mustering Out,* 33, 61, 69, 90, 440–453; *Affray at Brownsville,* Pt. 6, 2138–2155, 2224–2241, 2564–2565, 3293–3299; Weaver, *The Brownsville Raid,* 15, 35–41, 44, 47–50, 55–57, 62–63, 66, 71, 75–76, 87, 154–156, 162–164, 166–169, 255, 257–258; Lane, *The Brownsville Affair,* 5, 17–18, 19; Christian, *Black Soldiers in Jim Crow Texas,* 73–75; *Brownsville Daily Herald,* August 14, 15, 1906; *San Antonio Express,* August 15, 1906; Leiker, *Racial Borders,* 135; Utley, *Lone Star Justice,* 279; Amberson, et al., *I Would Rather Sleep in Texas,* 449.

86. Weiss, *Yours to Command,* 256; Procter, *Just One Riot,* 35; *Brownsville Daily Herald,* August 15, 16, 17, 18, 20, 21, 22, 1906; Christian, *Black*

Soldiers in Jim Crow Texas, 75, 76; Lane, *The Brownsville Affair*, 19; Young, "The Brownsville Affray," 13, 14; Utley, *Lone Star Justice*, 279–280.

87. Weiss, *Yours to Command*, 256–258; William J. McDonald, "Report of the Brownsville Outrage," 401–496, TSLAC, 1–2 (quotation on p. 1); *Brownsville Daily Herald*, August 22, 1906; MR, Company B, August 31, 1906; Procter, *Just One Riot*, 36–37; Paine, *Captain Bill McDonald*, 322–325; *San Antonio Express*, August 17, 18, 21, 22, 1906; Weaver, *The Brownsville Raid*, 80–81, 255–256.

88. Weiss, *Yours to Command*, 258–260; McDonald, "Report of the Brownsville Outrage," 3; Paine, *Captain Bill McDonald*, 327–328, 329–338 (second quotation on p. 335); Procter, *Just One Riot*, 37–39; Weaver, *The Brownsville Raid*, 65, 82–83, 116, 157–160, 238–241; Lane, *The Brownsville Affair*, 19–20, 30; Christian, *Black Soldiers in Jim Crow Texas*, 77–78; Bob Alexander and Donaly E. Brice, *Texas Rangers: Lives, Legend, and Legacy* (Denton: University of North Texas Press, 2017), 349; Letter from Alexander to author, February 6, 2018; *Summary Discharge and Mustering Out*, 56 (third quotation), 65 (first quotation); *Browning Daily Herald*, August 23, 1906; MR, Company B, August 31, 1906. The famous phrase involving hell and water has been wrongly ascribed to Major Penrose. Sterling, *Trails and Trials*, 351. Likewise, McDonald's obituary in *San Antonio Express*, January 16, 1918, incorrectly credited President Roosevelt or an unnamed Texas congressman.

89. Weiss, *Yours to Command*, 263–264; McDonald, "Report of the Brownsville Outrage," 9–10; Weaver, *The Brownsville Raid*, 44, 84–86, 128, 146–147; Utley, *Lone Star Justice*, 280–281; Leiker, *Racial Borders*, 136; *Affray at Brownsville*, 435 (quotation).

90. Weiss, *Yours to Command*, 263–268; *Summary Discharge and Mustering Out*, 47–53, 103–104, 70, 65 (quotation), 53–54, 54–58, 59, 107–108; Paine, *Captain Bill McDonald*, 341–342, 346–347, 344, 345–355, 355–359; Weaver, *The Brownsville Raid*, 78, 84–86, 90–92; Lane, *The Brownsville Affair*, 20; Christian, *Black Soldiers in Jim Crow Texas*, 78–79; Procter, *Just One Riot*, 40–42; *Brownsville Daily Herald*, August 25, 28, September 4, 28, October 2, 1906; *San Antonio Express*, August 25, 1906.

91. Weiss, *Yours to Command*, 269; Weaver, *The Brownsville Raid*, 88 (first quotation), 93, 95, 97–99, 103–108, 133, 145–185 (fourth quotation on p. 160); Lane, *The Brownsville Affair*, 20–23, 34–52, 70–71; Christian,

Black Soldiers in Jim Crow Texas, 79–80; Leiker, *Racial Borders*, 138, 143–144; Weaver, *The Senator and the Sharecropper's Son*, 129–131; Young, "The Brownsville Affray," 15; Malbrew, "Brownsville Revisited," 17–21; Louis R. Harland, *Booker T. Washington: The Wizard of Tuskegee, 1901–1915* (New York: Oxford University Press, 1983), 323 (second quotation); *Summary Discharge and Mustering Out*, 178–185; *Brownsville Daily Herald*, October 19, November 7, 8, 12, 14, 1906; *Army and Navy Journal* 44 (March 30, 1907): 848 (third quotation); *New York Times*, March 9, 1907. See also Oliver to Garlington, October 4, 1906, *Brownsville Affray*, 3. For the distinction between a discharge without honor and a dishonorable discharge, see George Breckenridge Davis, *A Treatise on the Military Law of the United States: Together with the Purchase and Procedure of Courts-martial and Other Military Tribunals* (Clark, NJ: Lawbook Exchange, 2007), 183–185. For more on Booker T. Washington and President Roosevelt, see Raymond W. Smock, *Booker T. Washington: Black Leadership in the Age of Jim Crow* (Chicago: Ivan R. Dee, 2009). For a defense of the garrison, see Joseph Benson Foraker, "A Review of the Testimony in the Brownsville Investigation," *North American Review* 187 (April 1908): 550–558.
92. Weaver, *The Brownsville Raid*, 258.
93. Lane, *The Brownsville Affair*, 166.
94. Weaver, *The Senator and the Sharecropper's Son*, xiv, xvi, xix (quotation); *New York Times*, September 29, 1972, February 12, August 5, 1973, January 11, 1974; Thompson, *Border Odyssey*, 71; Lane, *The Brownsville Affair*, 18.
95. *Summary Discharge and Mustering Out*, 66; Lane, *The Brownsville Affair*, 166; Christian, *Black Soldiers in Jim Crow Texas*, 86; Leiker, *Racial Borders*, 143–145; Young, "The Brownsville Affray," 16.
96. Weiss, *Yours to Command*, 279–281; Paine, *Captain Bill McDonald*, 364–365, 365–372, 393–394; Joe R. Baulch, "The Murder of Stanley Welch and the 1906 Starr County Election," *Journal of South Texas* 4 (Spring 1991): 33, 38; *Brownsville Daily Herald*, November 7, 8, 9, 13, 1906; MR, Company B, November 30, 1906; Sterling, *Trails and Trials*, 352, 353–354, 356–358.
97. Weiss, *Yours to Command*, 282; *Brownsville Daily Herald*, November 10, 13, 1906; MR, Company B, November 30, 1906.
98. Weiss, *Yours to Command*, 284; *Austin Statesman*, January 17, 1907; W. J. McDonald, *Biennial Report of the State Revenue Agent, 1906–08*, 3; Paine, *Captain Bill McDonald*, 373–376, 383–384 (quotation);

Hans Peter Nielson Gammel, comp., *The Laws of Texas, 1903–1905* (Austin: Gammel's Book Store, 1906), 1307.

99. Weiss, *Yours to Command*, 289; McDonald, *Biennial Report of the State Revenue Agent, 1906–08*, 7, 9–24, 25–29, 31; *Austin Statesman*, July 2, September 12, 13, 14, 17, 18, 24, 30, October 5, 9, 29, November 15, 1907.

100. Weiss, *Yours to Command*, 289–290; *Austin Statesman*, October 30, 1907, September 14, November 29, 1908, February 21, April 29, 1909; 120 *Southwestern Reporter* 267 (1909).

101. Weiss, *Yours to Command*, 295–296; Charles Seymour, ed., *Intimate Papers of Colonel House* (Boston: Houghton Mifflin Company, 1926), 1: 20–21; *Austin Statesman*, February 23, 1909, June 2, 4, 1908. William Sidney Porter (more famously known as O. Henry) had not replied to House's letter in time to write McDonald's memoirs. Paine published his biography of the captain and portions of the book were presented as serial installments in *Pearson's Magazine* from October 1908 to October 1909. See also Paine, *Captain Bill McDonald*, 394–395.

102. Weiss, *Yours to Command*, 293–295, 297; W. J. McDonald, *Report of the State Revenue Agent, 1908–1910*, 1–17; *Austin Statesman*, January 23, September 14, October 14, November 10, 28, 1909, February 19, 22, April 22, August 28, September 11, 24, 29, 30, October 5, 15, 20, 29, 31, November 27, December 8, 1910, January 20, 1911.

103. Weiss, *Yours to Command*, 297–298; Michael R. Botson, Jr., *Labor, Civil Rights, and the Hughes Tool Company* (College Station: Texas A&M University Press, 2005), 30–32; *Houston Daily Post*, April 15, March 20, September 30, October 1, 3, 4, 1911.

104. Weiss, *Yours to Command*, 298–299; *Austin Statesman*, August 20, 22, 1911; Seymour, *Intimate Papers of Colonel House*, 1: 78–80 (first four quotations); *El Paso Morning Times*, November 7, 1912 (fifth quotation). The Secret Service began providing protection for U.S. presidents in 1902, after the assassination of William McKinley. The service expanded its responsibilities to include presidents-elect in 1908, and presidential candidates in 1968. For more, see Ronald Kessler, *In the President's Secret Service: Behind the Scenes with Agents in the Line of Fire and the Presidents They Protect* (New York: Crown Publishers, 2009).

105. Weiss, *Yours to Command*, 301–302; Seymour, *Intimate Papers of Colonel House*, 1: 80–81; *New York Sun*, November 7, 1912; Virgil D. White, *Index of U.S. Marshals, 1789–1960* (Waynesboro, TN: National

Historical Publishing, 1988), 58. According to Dave Turk, Historian of the U.S. Marshals Service, McDonald was given a recess appointment on March 28, while his commission date was April 24. The latter day is given in *Register of the Department of Justice and the Courts of the United States*, 22nd Edition (1914), 183.

106. Weiss, *Yours to Command*, 302–303; *Thirteenth U.S. Census*, Hardeman County, Texas; *Wichita Daily Times*, December 28, 1914; *Report of the Attorney General, 1915*, 230; White, *Index of U.S. Marshals*, 58.
107. Weiss, *Yours to Command*, 305; *Austin Statesman*, January 15, 16, 1918.
108. Texas Death Certificate, Louis Alva Williams, November 7, 1925, Register No. 2423; *Fifteenth U.S. Census*, Dallas County Texas; *Sixteenth U. S. Census*, Harris County, Texas; Find A Grave, s.v. "Pearl Wilkirson Williams."

Notes for Chapter 11

1. Chuck Parsons, *Captain John R. Hughes: Lone Star Ranger* (Denton: University of North Texas Press, 2011), 2–3; *Linn County Republic*, January 1, 1892; Butler County, Ohio Marriage Records 2 (1835–1847), 209; *Salem Weekly Advocate*, May 3, 1860, May 1, 1862; *Leavenworth Times*, May 13, 1874; Missouri Death Certificate, Bond Hughes, August 4, 1919, File No. 29473; Find A Grave, s.v. "Louise Hughes Kincaid" and "Em S. Hughes"; *1875 Kansas State Census*, Linn County; *Ninth U.S. Census*, Linn County, Kansas; Mrs. Clifton Hughes Taylor, Hughes-Bond-Sargent Family Tree, Linn County Historical Museum & Genealogy Library. See also *Lawrence Daily Journal*, June 1, 1880.

   Thomas was struck with "apoplexy of the brain" in June 1890, and he died on December 26, 1891. Jennie died from heart failure on December 3, 1903. They were both buried in Woodland Cemetery in Mound City. *Linn County Republic*, January 1, 1892, December 11, 1903; Thomas Hughes obituary, Wickham Scrapbook Collection 15: 99–100; Jane Bond Hughes obituary, ibid. 4: 14. While in Linn County, this author also traveled to Woodland Cemetery and visited the graves of Thomas, Jennie, Nellie, and Bond.

2. Parsons, *Captain John R. Hughes*, 6, 7–8; *San Antonio Express*, October 11, 1925; *El Paso Herald-Post*, April 12, 1938; William Cx Hancock, "Ranger's Ranger," *True West* 8 (March-April 1961): 24; *El Paso Herald*, January 13–14, 1923 (Sunday edition). Henry N. Ferguson

related the story about Hughes and his purported fight with the Indian in "Zane Grey's Original 'Lone Star Ranger'," *Old West* 14 (Spring 1978): 11, 28. Jack Martin claimed Hughes's injury occurred when he stepped in between Art Rivers, his boss at the Choctaw Agency, and a disgruntled Indian wielding a clubbed rifle. Hughes supposedly "threw up his arm to deflect the blow. The weapon shattered the bones in his arm, but he thus saved himself from more critical injuries." While a widely recounted story, no evidence of Art Rivers has been found in the historical record. *Border Boss: Captain John R. Hughes—Texas Ranger* (Austin: State House Press, 1990), 3. Incidentally, Mrs. Alice Jack (Dolan) Shipman was the daughter of Captain Pat Dolan, who commanded Company F in the Frontier Battalion.

3. Parsons, *Captain John R. Hughes*, 6–7; Wilbur Sturtevant Nye, *Carbine and Lance: The Story of Old Fort Sill* (Norman: University of Oklahoma Press, 1969), 101, 102, 292; Hancock, "Ranger's Ranger," 24.

4. Parsons, *Captain John R. Hughes*, 9–11; William B. Shillingberg, *Dodge City: The Early Years, 1872–1886* (Norman, OK: Arthur H. Clark Company, 2009), 160–161, 182; Craig Miner, *West of Wichita: Settling the High Plains of Kansas, 1865–1890* (Lawrence: University Press of Kansas, 1986), 176–177; *Dodge City Times*, May 12 (first quotation), June 2, 16, 1877, January 26, 1878; *Ellis County Star*, May 24, 1877; *Hays City Sentinel*, June 8 (second quotation), 22, 1877; Bonnie Haas and Joyce J. Bender, "Major Andrew Drumm: Cowman, Businessman, and Visionary," *Chronicles of Oklahoma* 79 (Spring 2001): 22; Meade L. McClure, "Major Andrew Drumm, 1828–1919," unpublished MS, 11–13. See also *Leavenworth Times*, October 22, 1884, January 11, 1907.

Eugene Cunningham wrote that Hughes drove cattle for the "Cross-P" outfit, but no mention of this ranch could be found in any primary source material. *Triggernometry: A Gallery of Gunfighters* (Norman: University of Oklahoma Press, 1996), 220. The brand most similar, the Cross P Connected, was recorded in Colorado and Austin Counties by George Prause & Son in 1945. Jane Pattie, *Cattle Brands: Ironclad Signatures* (Albany, TX: Bright Sky Press, 2002), 107. Parsons cited a mention in an undated Mound City newspaper that noted Hughes worked for the "well known Drum[m] & Snider Cattle Co." Although he speculated "Snider" was a reference to highly successful Texas ranchers Dudley Hiram Snyder and John Wesley Snyder, A. J. Snider seems more likely the herd's co-owner. He and Drumm jointly operated the "U" Ranch from 1874 to 1891. *Captain John R. Hughes*, 11, 304 n36; Tim Zwick and Donovan Reichenberger, *Ranchlands to Railroads: An Illustrated Sketch of M County's Pre-Territorial History* (Alva, OK: Alva Centennial Commission, 1986), 11–12.

5. Parsons, *Captain John R. Hughes*, 15–18; J. Marvin Hunter, "The Outstanding Texas Ranger," *Frontier Times* 22 (December 1944): 76; Hughes Brothers' Horse Record, TRHF; Tax Rolls, Travis County, 1883; *San Antonio Express*, January 17, 1915; Paul Havens, "Border Boss: The Saga of Captain John R. Hughes, Texas Ranger," Pt. 1, *True Detective Mysteries* 34 (June 1940): 43–44; *Black Range*, July 11, 1884; *Galveston Daily News*, August 27, 1884. The ranch was in Travis County while the nearest post office was in Liberty Hill. As well as Moscow, the horses stolen were Flossie, Bee Creek, Dinah, Bessie, Matilda, Fraulein, Diamond, Quarter Horse, Sam, Kurg, Lee, Nancy, Magnolia, Elias, and Satilla.

6. Parsons, *Captain John R. Hughes*, 19–23; Transcript of John R. Hughes interview with Vera P. Elliott at El Paso, Texas, undated, Federal Writers Project, Works Progress Administration (quotation); Robert K. DeArment, *Man-Hunters of the Old West* (Norman: University of Oklahoma Press, 2018), 2: 190–192; *Black Range*, June 13, July 4, 11, 18, August 22, 1884; *Galveston Daily News*, August 27, 1884.

7. *Houston Chronicle*, December 27, 1914. The Doña Ana County Stock Association employed Colonel Albert Jennings Fountain to assist in the prosecution of Toppy Johnson, the Cravens, and the other defendants. After a failed escape attempt, John and Jim Craven were convicted in April 1885, and sentenced to five years in prison. *Las Cruces Sun-News*, August 23, November 15, 29, December 6, 1884, April 25, 1885.

8. Parsons, *Captain John R. Hughes*, xxii; G. W. Ogden, "The Watch on the Rio Grande," *Everybody's Magazine* 24 (September 1911): 357, 360.

9. Cunningham, *Triggernometry*, 221; Dane Coolidge, *Fighting Men of the West* (New York: Bantam Books, 1952), 120; Havens, "Border Boss," Pt 1: 45; Martin, *Border Boss*, 30–32; Larry D. Ball, *Desert Lawmen: The High Sheriffs of New Mexico and Arizona, 1846–1912* (Albuquerque: University of New Mexico Press, 1992), 345–372. See also Enos Jurgens, "The Most Wanted Corpse in Texas," *America's Frontier West* 1 (July 1974), 37; and Ferguson, "Zane Grey's Original 'Lone Star Ranger'," 29.

10. *Black Range*, July 11, 1884. See also DeArment, *Man-Hunters of the Old West*, 2: 211–214.

11. Parsons, *Captain John R. Hughes*, 27; Hughes Brothers' Horse Record; *Pioneers in God's Hills: A History of Fredericksburg and Gillespie County People and Events* (Fredericksburg, TX: Gillespie County Historical Society, 1974): 2, 10–11 (quotation); MR, Company D, January 31-March 31, 1886.
12. Aten, "Six and One-Half Years in the Ranger Service," Pt. 1, *Frontier Times* 22 (January 1945): 112.
13. Parsons, *Captain John R. Hughes*, 27–28; MR, Company D, June 30, 1886 (first quotation); DeArment, *Man-Hunters of the Old West*, 2: 194; Haven, "Border Boss," Pt. 1, 45: 121–122; Martin, *Border Boss*, 34 (second quotation). Other authors have also disregarded available evidence and continued the fallacy of Judd Roberts, which unfortunately has made its way into both the Aten and Hughes stories. For examples, see Preece, *Lone Star Man*, and Allen G. Hatley, "Ira Allen, Last of the 'Old Texas Rangers'," *Western Outlaw-Lawman History Association Journal* 14 (Winter 2005): 23.
14. Parsons, *Captain John R. Hughes*, 31; RSR, John R. Hughes, 401-156, TSLAC; MR, Company D, August 31, October 31-November 30, 1887; ROS, Company D. February 1888; Bob Alexander, *Rawhide Ranger, Ira Aten: Enforcing Law on the Texas Frontier* (Denton: University of North Texas Press, 2011), 136; Ogden, "The Watch on the Rio Grande," 356 (quotation). Hughes's brother, William, had previously served in the Frontier Battalion as a private in Company E from September 1 to November 30, 1877. RSR, W. P. Hughes, 401-156, TSLAC.
15. Parsons, *Captain John R. Hughes*, 39, 41–42; Bob Alexander, *Whiskey River Ranger: The Old West Life of Baz Outlaw* (Denton: University of North Texas Press, 2016), 93–96; Special Order No. 129, May 12, 1888, 401-1012, TSLAC; ROS, Company D, March-September 1888 (first quotation); Wyvonne Putman, comp., *Navarro County History* (Quanah, TX: Nortex Press, 1975), 196; MR, Company D, June 30, 1888 (second quotation).
16. Parsons, *Captain John R. Hughes*, 43; MR, Company D, May 31, August 31, 1888; Operations of Frontier Battalion, 3 (1885–1892), 401-1084, TSLAC: 99; Bob Alexander, *Bad Company and Burnt Powder: Justice and Injustice in the Old Southwest* (Denton: University of North Texas Press, 2014), 8–9; Elliott Young, *Catarino Garza's Revolution on the Texas-Mexico Border* (Durham, NC: Duke University Press, 2004), 65–66; Clifford R. Caldwell and Ron DeLord, *Eternity at the End of a Rope: Executions, Lynchings and Vigilante Justice in Texas,*

1819–1923 (Santa Fe: Sunstone Press, 2015), 311; Hernán A. Contreras, "Origins of Boss Rule in Starr County" (M.A. thesis, University of Houston-Clear Lake, 2008), 57–58. Martin allotted twelve paragraphs to Garza's arrest and continued to embellish the facts with a thrilling tale of two titans facing one another like gunfighters at high noon. As Martin relates the story, Garza went for his pistol but Hughes was faster and "With a quick wrench he got it away from the startled editor, and in another instant had him and his companions covered. The fight was over without a shot being fired." Martin, *Border Boss*, 44–47.

17. Parsons, *Captain John R. Hughes*, 182–183, 261; Aten, "Six and One-Half Years," Pt. 2: 135–136; Martin, *Border Boss*, 66, 75, 207 (quotation); Hancock, "Ranger's Ranger," 25.

18. Parsons, *Captain John R. Hughes*, 183–185; Maude T. Gilliland, *Wilson County Texas Rangers, 1837–1977* (Brownsville, TX: Springman-King Company, 1968), 116; Maude T. Gilliland, *Horsebackers of the Brush Country: A Story of the Texas Rangers and the Mexican Liquor Smugglers* (Brownsville, TX: Springman-King Company, 1968), 166; *Thirteenth*, *Fourteenth*, and *Fifteenth U.S. Census*, El Paso County, Texas; *Sixteenth U.S. Census*, Yuma County, Arizona; *Yuma Daily Sun*, July 20, 1956; *Tucson Daily Citizen*, May 14, 16, 1973. Writing under his pen name, Martin first identified Hughes's fiancée as "Mary Todd." Paul Havens, "Border Boss: The Saga of Captain John R. Hughes, Texas Ranger," Pt. 2, *True Detective Mysteries* 34 (July 1940): 34.

19. Mary A. Sutherland, *The Story of Corpus Christi* (Corpus Christi Chapter, Daughters of the Confederacy, 1916).

20. Parsons, *Captain John R. Hughes*, 50; Alexander, *Whiskey River Ranger*, 123–124; MR, Company D, May 31, 1889; RSR, B. L. Outlaw, 401–166, John R. Hughes, -156, and J. W. Durbin, -150, TSLAC; Robert W. Stephens, *Walter Durbin: Texas Ranger and Sheriff* (Clarendon: Clarendon Press, 1970), 77–78 (quotation). When the three Rangers were hired, John A. Gowan was the superintendent of Fronteriza. *Wood River Times*, May 29, 1889.

21. Parsons, *Captain John R. Hughes*, 51–52; Alexander, *Whiskey River Ranger*, 127–134; *Southern Mercury*, May 30, 1889; Stephens, *Walter Durbin*, 77–81; MR, Company D, September 30, December 31, 1889; RSR, B. L. Outlaw, 401–166, John R. Hughes, –156, TSLAC. Martin tells the story of how an intoxicated Outlaw killed a Mexican workman who had allegedly confronted him with a knife. Hughes and Durbin were in their quarters when they heard the gunshot. The three Texans

barricaded themselves in their room and readied for the potentially enraged Mexicans to attack. Instead the miners assured the Americans they bore no grudge as the slain man was unpopular and "deserved to go." *Border Boss*, 79–81.

22. Parsons, *Captain John R. Hughes*, 53–56; MR, Company D, December 31, 1889; ROS, Company D, December 1889; *RAG, 1889–1890*, 91; DeArment, *Man-Hunters of the Old West*, 2: 196; Alexander, *Winchester Warriors*, 227–228; Alexander, *Whiskey River Ranger*, 149–154; Bill O'Neal, *Encyclopedia of Western Gunfighters* (Norman: University of Oklahoma Press, 1979), 162; Ira Aten interview with Earl Vandale, J. Evetts Haley, and Hervey Chesley at El Centro, California, July 1941, J. Evetts Haley Collection, HML&HC, 65.

23. Bob Alexander, *Riding Lucifer's Line: Ranger Deaths along the Texas-Mexico Border* (Denton: University of North Texas Press, 2013), 105–107; ROS, Company D, April 1890; Robert Ernst, *Deadly Affrays: The Violent Deaths of the United States Marshals* (Lafayette, IN: Scarlet Mask, 2006), 97–98; Alexander, *Winchester Warriors*, 233 (quotation); *RAG, 1889–1890*, 24–25, 91; Robert W. Stephens, *Texas Ranger Sketches* (Dallas: Robert W. Stephens, 1972), 59, 60, 61; *El Paso Times*, April 18, 19, 1890; Rick Miller, *Sam Bass and Gang*, 373 n15; C. L. Sonnichsen, *Pass of the North: Four Centuries on the Rio Grande* (El Paso: Texas Western Press, 1968), 1: 312.

24. Parsons, *Captain John R. Hughes*, 60–61; ROS, Company D, April 1890; Mike Cox, *The Texas Rangers: Wearing the Cinco Peso, 1821–1900* (New York: Tom Doherty Associates, 2008), 356; Alexander, *Whiskey River Ranger*, 160.

25. Parsons, *Captain John R. Hughes*, 63; Frederick Jackson Turner, *The Frontier in American History* (Tucson: University of Arizona Press, 1986), Ch. 1 (quotation on p. 1); MR, Company D, May 31-June 30, October 31, 1890; ROS, Company D, August 1890; Cox, *Wearing the Cinco Peso*, 357–358; *RAG, 1889–1890*, 91. In response to the Census Bureau's statement, historian Frederick Jackson Turner delivered his landmark paper "The Significance of the Frontier in American History" three years later to the American Historical Association in Chicago. Turner's "Frontier Thesis" influenced the teaching of American history for the next eighty-odd years until the emergence of the New Western History movement. For a vigorous defense of the frontier thesis, see Ray Allen Billington and Martin Ridge, *Westward Expansion: A History of the American Frontier* (Albuquerque: University of

New Mexico Press, 2001). For the leading example of New West interpretation, see Patricia Nelson Limerick, *The Legacy of Conquest: The Unbroken Past of the American West* (New York: W. W. Norton & Co., 1987).

26. Frederick Wilkins, *The Law Comes to Texas: The Texas Rangers, 1870–1901* (Abilene, TX: State House Press, 1999), 308–309; Operations of Frontier Battalion, 3: 127; MR, Company D, August 31, November 30, 1891; Martin, *Border Boss*, 94–95; Stephens, *Texas Ranger Sketches*, 149.

27. Parsons, *Captain John R. Hughes*, 71; MR, Company D, January 31, 1892; Operations of Frontier Battalion, 3: 130; DeArment, *Man-Hunters of the Old West*, 2: 197; O'Neal, *Encyclopedia of Western Gunfighters*, 243–244. Martin placed St. Leon at the scene of the gunfight, although his name does not appear in Hughes's report. Possibly, the corporal had meant to conceal the identity of his informant. *Border Boss*, 96–100.

28. Parsons, *Captain John R. Hughes*, 72–74; Ann Jensen, ed., *Texas Ranger's Diary and Scrapbook* (Dallas: Kaleidograph Press, 1936), 59; MR, Company D, June 30, 1892; Operations of Frontier Battalion, 3: 132. The third Carrasco brother, Antonino, who was wanted for killing a Presidio County deputy sheriff, fled south of the border, where he was outlawed by the Mexican government. He joined Francisco Madero's insurrection, but was court-martialed for treason and executed in 1911. *El Paso Daily Herald*, April 24, 1900, April 6, 1911.

29. Parsons, *Captain John R. Hughes*, 75; Alexander, *Whiskey River Ranger*, 235–236; MR, Company D, September 30, 1892; RSR, B. L. Outlaw, 401–166, John R. Hughes, -156, TSLAC; Jones to Mabry, January 17, 1893, 401–427, TSLAC.

30. Parsons, *Captain John R. Hughes*, 81; MR, Company D, June 30, 1893; ROS, Company D, June 1893; Operations of Frontier Battalion, 4 (1892–1895), 401–1085, TSLAC: 77.

31. Alexander, *Six-Shooters and Shifting Sands*, 350–353; *RAG, 1893–1894*, 66, 67, 68; Operations of Frontier Battalion, 4: 77; Baylor to Mabry, July 9, 1893, 401–428, TSLAC; Hughes to Mabry, September 4, 1893, Hughes to Mabry, September 6, 1893, 401–429, TSLAC; *Galveston Daily News*, July 1, 1893; W. C. Jameson, "Incident at Pirate Island," *True West* 35 (November 1988): 43; Stephens, *Texas Ranger Sketches*, 18–19, 33, 68–69, 78.

32. Alexander, *Six-Shooters and Shifting Sands*, 353–357; *RAG, 1893–1894*, 67–68; Baylor to Mabry, July 9, 1893, 401–428, TSLAC (quotations);

Galveston Daily News, July 1, 2, 1893; J. Marvin Hunter, "The Killing of Captain Frank Jones," *Frontier Times* 6 (January 1929): 146–147; Sonnichsen, *Pass of the North*, 1: 314.

33. Parsons, *Captain John R. Hughes*, 87, 90–94; Alexander, *Six-Shooters and Shifting Sands*, 357–359; MR, Company D, June 30, 1893; Kirchner to Mabry, two telegrams dated June 30, 1893, Hughes to Mabry, July 1, 1893, Kirchner to Mabry, July 5, 1893 (quotation), Hughes to Mabry, July 8, 1893, 401–428, TSLAC; Special Order No. 105, July 4, 1893, 401–1012, TSLAC; *Galveston Daily News*, July 1, 2, 1893; Alexander, *Winchester Warriors*, 263; Cox, *Wearing the Cinco Peso*, 359–360; RSR, John R. Hughes, 401–156, Carl Kirchner, -159, TSLAC.
34. "Captain Hughes, of the Texas Rangers," *Frontier Times* 5 (October 1927): 4.
35. Alexander, *Whiskey River Ranger*, 277–281 (quotation on p. 279); Alexander, *Riding Lucifer's Line*, 139–145; Jensen, ed., *Texas Ranger's Diary and Scrapbook*, 40–41, 76; MR, Company D, April 30, 1894; Stephens, *Texas Ranger Sketches*, 92, 110–111; *El Paso Daily Times*, April 6, 8, 1894; *Austin Daily Statesman*, April 7, 1894; Stephens, *Bullets and Buckshot*, 43, 45.
36. Parsons, *Captain John R. Hughes*, 123; Utley, *Lone Star Justice*, 267; MR, Company D, July 31, 1895.
37. Leon N. Miletich, *Dan Stuart's Fistic Carnival* (College Station: Texas A&M University Press, 1994), 19, 35; Jeffrey T. Sammons, *Beyond the Ring: The Role of Boxing in American Society* (Urbana: University of Illinois Press, 1990), 20; Elmer M. Million, "History of the Texas Prize Fight Statute," *Texas Law Review* 17 (February 1939): 158; Steve Bogener, "The World Heavyweight Boxing Champion Bout, 1896, at Langtry, Texas," *WTHAY* 74 (1998), 47.
38. Miletich, *Dan Stuart's Fistic Carnival*, 55–56; Meg Frisbee, *Counterpunch: The Cultural Battles Over Heavyweight Prizefighting in the American West* (Seattle: University of Washington Press, 2016), 59 (quotation), 98; *House Journal, Twenty-fourth Legislature, Called Session*, 6–7, 8, 10–12. See also Proclamation by the Governor, October 1, 1895, ibid., 1–5.
39. Parsons, *Captain John R. Hughes*, 125–126; Hughes to Mabry, November 4, 1895, November 8, 1895, Hughes to Mabry, December 27, 1895, 401–437, TSLAC; Miletich, *Dan Stuart's Fistic Carnival*, 101; Keith R. Robinson, *Fist Fighting Out West: Dan Stuart versus General Mabry and the Texas Rangers* (London: English Westerners' Society,

2010), 8. For more on Maher, see Matt Donnellon, *The Irish Champion Peter Maher: The Untold Story of Ireland's Only World Heavyweight Champion and the Records of the Men He Fought* (Victoria, BC: Trafford, 2008).

40. Parsons, *Captain John R. Hughes*, 127; MR, Company D, February 29, 1896; Miletich, *Dan Stuart's Fistic Carnival*, 136, 152–153, 163, 170; Frisbee, *Counterpunch*, 88; Robinson, *Fist Fighting Out West*, 17; *The Statutes at Large and Treaties of the United States*, 29: 5; Larry D. Ball, *The United States Marshals of New Mexico and Arizona Territories, 1846–1912* (Albuquerque: University of New Mexico Press, 1978), 145–146; Sonnichsen, *Pass of the North*, 1: 360.

41. Parsons, *Captain John R. Hughes*, 130–134; C. L. Sonnichsen, *Roy Bean: Law West of the Pecos* (Albuquerque: University of New Mexico Press, 1986), 184–185, 187–189; Miletich, *Dan Stuart's Fistic Carnival*, 184–186; Bogener, "World Heavyweight Boxing Champion Bout," 54, 55; *RAG, 1895–1896*, 10–12; Utley, *Lone Star Justice*, 268–269; *Austin Daily Statesman*, February 22, 1896. For more on Bean, see Jack Skiles, *Judge Roy Bean Country* (Lubbock: Texas Tech University Press, 1996).

42. Parsons, *Captain John R. Hughes*, 137–138; MR, Company D, March 31, 1896 (quotation); *Galveston Daily News*, March 12, 20, 1896.

43. Parsons, *Captain John R. Hughes*, 142–146; Hughes to Mabry, September 29, 1896, Hughes to Mabry, October 4, 1896, 401–440, TSLAC; MR, Company D, September 30, 1896; Wilkins, *Law Comes to Texas*, 332–33.

44. Parsons, *Captain John R. Hughes*, 146–147; St. Leon to Mabry, September 30, 1896, Hughes to Mabry, October 13, 1896, 401–440, TSLAC; Hughes to Mabry, December 20, 1896, Hughes to Mabry, December 31, 1896, 401–441, TSLAC.

45. Parsons, *Captain John R. Hughes*, 99, 108, 118, 162–163; Baylor to Mabry, July 9, 1893, 401–428, TSLAC; Hughes to Mabry, September 6, 1893, 401–429, TSLAC; Ernst, *Deadly Affrays*, 98; DeArment, *Man-Hunters of the Old West*, 2: 201–202; *Galveston Daily News*, October 9, 1893; *Brownsville Daily Herald*, October 12, 1893; *El Paso Daily Herald*, November 4, 1898; *El Paso Times*, January 6, 1900; Utley, *Lone Star Justice*, 266.

46. Parsons, *Captain John R. Hughes*, 163–166; Application for Requisition No. 539, Box 2–10/403, Texas Secretary of State Fugitive Records, TSLAC; Hughes to Scurry, March 9, 1899, 401-668, TSLAC;

MR, Company D, March 31, 1899; *El Paso Daily Herald*, November 7, 1898; *Houston Daily Post* and *El Paso Times*, both dated January 6, 1900; Sonnichsen, *Pass of the North*, 1: 313.

In *Border Boss*, Martin relates how Hughes struck a bargain with Garrett in October 1898 at Ysleta. Garrett, the killer of Billy the Kid, offered to facilitate Parra facing Texas justice if the Ranger captain would track down outlaw Pat Agnew, who was wanted in Garrett's jurisdiction. Hughes found and delivered the fugitive to Garrett and soon took custody of Parra. While a good story, there is no supporting evidence that either Pat Agnew or a *quid pro quo* between Hughes and Garrett ever existed. Martin, *Border Boss*, 146–150. See also Leon C. Metz, *Pat Garrett: The Story of a Western Lawman* (Norman: University of Oklahoma Press, 1974), 216–17; and Douglas V. Meed, "Daggers on the Gallows: The Revenge of Texas Ranger Captain 'Boss' Hughes," *True West* 46 (May 1999): 44–49.

47. *House Journal, Twenty-seventh Legislature, Regular Session*, 23–24 (first quotation), 72; *House Journal, Twenty-seventh Legislature, Regular Session*, 37 (second quotation); Acts 1901, 27th Regular Session, Ch. 34, *General and Special Laws of Texas*.
48. Parsons, *Captain John R. Hughes*, 173; General Order No. 62, July 3, 1901, 401-1183, TSLAC. The order can also be found in Military Orders Ledger, 401–984, TSLAC. *RAG, 1901–1902*, 32, 40, 126–127.
49. MR, Company D, December 31, 1902.
50. Parsons, *Captain John R. Hughes*, 188–190; MR, Company D, February 29, 1904; Martin, *Border Boss*, 166–169; Arthur Train, "The Fall of Hummel," *Cosmopolitan Magazine* 44 (May 1908): 594, 596–602, 45 (June 1908): 32–37.
51. Parsons, *Captain John R. Hughes*, 192–193 (first quotation on p. 193); *El Paso Daily Herald*, May 18, 1903; MR, Company D, June 30, 1905; *RAG, 1905–1906*, 30 (second quotation).
52. Parsons, *Captain John R. Hughes*, 193–194; MR, Company D, July 31-October 31, 1905, January 31, 1906; Bob Alexander, *Lawmen, Outlaws, and S.O.Bs: Gunfighters of the Old Southwest* (Silver City, NM: High-Lonesome Books, 2004), 258; *Houston Daily Post*, January 24, 1906. After his stint with the Rangers, "Doc" White served as a federal agent with the Prohibition Unit and the U.S. Division of Investigation (later renamed the Federal Bureau of Investigation). Karl G. Hastedt, "White Brothers of Texas Had Notable FBI Careers," *The Grapevine* (February 1960): 16–17.

53. Parsons, *Captain John R. Hughes*, 199; James C. Kearney, et al., *No Hope for Heaven, No Fear of Hell: The Stafford-Townsend Feud of Colorado County, 1871–1911* (Denton: University of North Texas Press, 2016), 128–131; *Colorado County Chronicles*, 1: 210–214; John Walter Reese and Lillian Estelle Reese, *Flaming Feuds of Colorado County* (Salado, TX: Anson Jones Press, 1962), 140–142; *Colorado County Citizen*, March 3, 10, 1988; *Galveston Daily News* and *San Antonio Light*, both dated July 1, 1906; *Weimar Mercury*, July 21, 1906 (quotation); MR, Company D, July 31, 1906.

54. Parsons, *Captain John R. Hughes*, 200; MR, Company D, July 31-October 31, 1906; *San Antonio Light*, May 18, 1907.

55. Parsons, *Captain John R. Hughes*, 200–201; MR, Company D, November 30-December 31, 1906; ROS, Company D, January 1907; *RAG, 1906*, 29; Joe R. Baulch, "The Murder of Stanley Welch and the 1906 Starr County Election," *Journal of South Texas* 4 (Spring 1991): 39; Contreras, "Origins of Boss Rule," 81.

56. Parsons, *Captain John R. Hughes*, 203, 204–207; ROS, Company D, May 1907, March 1908, June 1908; Baulch, "The Murder of Stanley Welch," 39–42; Contreras, "Origins of Boss Rule," 81–82; MR, Company D, June 30, December 31, 1907, March 31, June 30, 1908; *Brownsville Daily Herald*, July 15, November 27, 1907, January 13, 15, March 20, 21, May 19, July 4, 6, 1908, August 31, 1915; *Victoria Advocate*, July 26, 1908; RSR, John R. Hughes, 401–57, –156, TSLAC.

57. Gilbert M. Joseph and Jürgen Buchenau, *Mexico's Once and Future Revolution: Social Upheaval and the Challenge of Rule since the Late Nineteenth Century* (Durham, NC: Duke University Press, 2013), 19, 38; W. H. Timmons, *El Paso: A Borderlands History* (El Paso: Texas Western Press, 2004), 248; Chris Frazer, *Bandit Nation: A History of Outlaws and Cultural Struggle in Mexico, 1810–1920* (Lincoln: University of Nebraska Press, 2006), 55–56; Tomas T. Smith, *The Old Army in Texas: A Research Guide to the U.S. Army in Nineteenth-Century Texas* (Austin: Texas State Historical Association, 2000), 55, 59, 72, 67, 78, 80, 56.

58. Parsons, *Captain John R. Hughes*, 212–214; Timmons, *El Paso*, 235; MR, Company D, October 31, 1909; Scout Reports, Company A, October 1909; Charles H. Harris III and Louis R. Sadler, *The Texas Rangers and the Mexican Revolution: The Bloodiest Decade, 1910–1920* (Albuquerque: University of New Mexico Press, 2007), 26; Paul N. Spellman, *Captain John H. Rogers, Texas Ranger* (Denton: University of North Texas Press, 2003), 150–151.

59. Parsons, *Captain John R. Hughes*, 215–217; Utley, *Lone Star Justice*, 284; *El Paso Daily Herald*, October 30, 1909; *Houston Daily Post*, October 31, 1909; MR, Company D, November 30-December 31, 1909, March 31-July 31, 1910.
60. Parsons, *Captain John R. Hughes*, 222–223; Charles Dudley Eaves and Cecil Allen Hutchinson, *Post City, Texas: C.W. Post's Colonizing Activities in West Texas* (Austin: Texas State Historical Association, 1952), 58–59, 88–89; *Abilene Semi-Weekly Farm Reporter*, August 21, 1910.
61. Parsons, *Captain John R. Hughes*, 223–224; Scout Reports, Company A, August 1910; Eaves and Hutchinson, *Post City*, 89–90; *San Antonio Daily Express*, September 2, 1910; MR, Company D, August 31, 1910.
62. Parsons, *Captain John R. Hughes*, 224; Scout Reports, Company A, September 1910; *Houston Daily Post*, September 29, 1910, April 30, 1912; *Galveston Daily News*, September 29, October 20, 1910; MR, Company D, October 31, 1910.
63. *RAG, 1908*, 14; *Houston Daily Post*, October 3, 1910.
64. Parsons, *Captain John R. Hughes*, 225–226; Scout Reports, Company A, October 1910; *Galveston Daily News*, October 4, 1910; Alexander, *Riding Lucifer's Line*, 220.
65. Harris and Sadler, *Texas Rangers and the Mexican Revolution*, 47–48; *Galveston Daily News*, November 5, 1910; *Houston Daily Post*, October 22, November 5, 1910; *El Paso Daily Herald*, August 2, 1910; Clifford R. Caldwell and Ron DeLord, *Texas Lawmen, 1900–1940: More of the Good and the Bad* (Charleston, SC: History Press, 2012), 396–397.
66. Parsons, *Captain John R. Hughes*, 226; *El Paso Herald*, October 4 (first quotation), November 19 (second quotation), 1910; Scout Reports, Company A, November 1910.
67. Harris and Sadler, *Texas Rangers and the Mexican Revolution*, 50–51; Scout Reports, Company A, November 1910; Evan Anders, *Boss Rule in South Texas: The Progressive Era* (Austin: University of Texas Press, 1982), 148–151.
68. Michael J. Gonzales, *The Mexican Revolution, 1910–1940* (Albuquerque: University of New Mexico Press, 2002), 60, 71, 72–74; Jefferson Morgenthaler, *The River Has Never Divided Us: A Border History of La Junta de los Rios* (Austin: University of Texas Press, 2004), 143–144; David Dorado Romo, *Ringside Seat to a Revolution, An Underground Cultural History of El Paso and Juárez: 1893–1923* (El Paso, TX: Cinco Puntos Press, 2005), 61; Sonnichsen, *Pass of the North*, 1: 388.
69. F. Arturo Rosales, *¡Pobre Raza! Violence, Justice, and Mobilization among México Lindo Immigrants, 1900–1936* (Austin: University of

Texas Press, 1999), 11; William D. Carrigan and Clive Webb, *Forgotten Dead: Mob Violence against Mexicans in the United States, 1848–1928* (New York: Oxford University Press, 2013), 142; Travis Taylor, "Lynching on the Border: The Death of Antonio Rodríguez and the Rise of Anti-Americanism during the Mexican Revolution" (M.A. thesis, Angelo State University, 2012), 1–2, 9, 10–11, 20–21; Romo, *Ringside Seat to a Revolution*, 64–65; MR, Company C, November 30, 1910.

70. Scout Reports, Company A, November 1910; Morgenthaler, *The River Has Never Divided Us*, 146; Rosales, *¡Pobre Raza!*, 11; Romo, *Ringside Seat to a Revolution*, 66–67.
71. Mike Cox, *Time of the Rangers: From 1900 to the Present* (New York: Tom Doherty Books, 2009), 48–49; Gonzales, *The Mexican Revolution*, 78–80; Harris and Sadler, *Texas Rangers and the Mexican Revolution*, 55; MR, Company D, November 30, December 31, 1910; Raymond Caballero, *Orozco: The Life and Death of a Mexican Revolutionary* (Norman: University of Oklahoma Press, 2017), 80, 83; Friedrich Katz, *The Life and Times of Pancho Villa* (Stanford, CA: Sandford University Press, 1998), 76, 100–101.
72. Parsons, *Captain John R. Hughes*, 230–231; *RAG, 1911–1912*, 8; Stephen W. Schuster, "The Modernization of the Texas Rangers: 1933–1936," *WTHAY* 43 (1967): 65–66.
73. Parsons, *Captain John R. Hughes*, 226–227; Charles H. Harris III and Louis R. Sadler, *The Secret War in El Paso: Mexican Revolutionary Intrigue, 1906–1920* (Albuquerque: University of New Mexico Press, 2009), 33, 39, 55; Morgenthaler, *The River Has Never Divided Us*, 150; Timmons, *El Paso*, 250; Caballero, *Orozco*, 84–85.
74. Harris and Sadler, *Texas Rangers and the Mexican Revolution*, 68–69; Romo, *Ringside Seat to a Revolution*, 74; Morgenthaler, *The River Has Never Divided Us*, 151–152; Timmons, *El Paso*, 251; *El Paso Daily Herald*, February 14, 15, 1911.
75. Harris and Sadler, *Texas Rangers and the Mexican Revolution*, 69–70; MR, Company D, April 30, 1911; Scout Reports, Company A, April 1911.
76. Utley, *Lone Star Lawmen*, 12; Scout Reports, Company A, May 1911; Hughes to Hutchings, May 9, 1911, 401–530, TSLAC; Douglas W. Richmond and Sam W. Haynes, eds., *The Mexican Revolution: Conflict and Consolidation, 1910–1940* (College Station: Texas A&M University Press, 2013), 38; Romo, *Ringside Seat to a Revolution*, 97, 103–106; MR, Company D, April 30, May 31, 1911; *El Paso Daily Herald*, May 8, 9, 1911.

77. Richmond and Haynes, eds., *The Mexican Revolution*, 38; Harris and Sadler, *Texas Rangers and the Mexican Revolution*, 71–72; Colquitt to Hughes, May 15, 1911, Box 2E138, Oscar Branch Colquitt Papers, BCAH.
78. Gonzales, *The Mexican Revolution*, 80; Joseph and Buchenau, *Mexico's Once and Future Revolution*, 45 (quotation).
79. MR, Company A, June 30-July 31, 1911; Caldwell and DeLord, *Eternity at the End of a Rope*, 520; *Houston Daily Post*, July 25, 30, 1911; *El Paso Daily Herald*, July 27, 29, 1911; *Galveston Daily News*, July 28, 29, 30, 1911. See also 66 *Texas Reports* 1–122 (1912), and 145 *Southwestern Reporter* 959–1023 (1912).
80. MR, Company A, July 31-August 31, 1911; Alexander, *Lawmen, Outlaws, and S.O.Bs*, 259.
81. *RAG, 1911–1912*, 8; Richmond and Haynes, eds., *The Mexican Revolution*, 39; Harris and Sadler, *Texas Rangers and the Mexican Revolution*, 75–77; Utley, *Lone Star Lawmen*, 10; *El Paso Herald*, November 9, 1911.
82. Parsons, *Captain John R. Hughes*, 234; MR, Company A, September 1, 1909-June 30, 1911.
83. MR, Company D, November 30-December 31, 1911; Harris and Sadler, *Secret War in El Paso*, 63–66; George T. Díaz, "Smugglers in Dangerous Times: Revolution and Communities in the Tejano Borderlands," *War Along the Border: The Mexican Revolution and Tejano Communities*, ed. Arnoldo de León (College Station: Texas A&M University Press, 2012), 278–279; Joseph B. Wilkinson, *Laredo and the Rio Grande Frontier: A Narrative* (Austin: Jenkins Publishing Co., 1975), 382–383. Agent Ross was compelled to resign in October 1912, when it was revealed he had been selling seized ammunition. He was quickly hired by the *maderista* secret service. *El Paso Morning Times*, October 14, 19, 1912, February 22, 1913.
84. Harris and Sadler, *Texas Rangers and the Mexican Revolution*, 87–88; Richmond and Haynes, eds., *The Mexican Revolution*, 39; Taft to Colquitt, January 22, 1912, Colquitt to Taft, February 27, 1912, *Expense of Patrolling the Boundary in Texas*, Senate Document No. 404, 62nd Congress, 2nd Session, 2.
85. Harris and Sadler, *Secret War in El Paso*, 67–68; Richmond and Haynes, eds., *The Mexican Revolution*, 39; Romo, *Ringside Seat to a Revolution*, 108.

86. Harris and Sadler, *Texas Rangers and the Mexican Revolution*, 88–89; Caballero, *Orozco*, 138, 142; *El Paso Daily Herald*, February 3, 1912.
87. Gonzales, *The Mexican Revolution*, 88–90; Morgenthaler, *The River Has Never Divided Us*, 158; Rosales, ¡*Pobre Raza!*, 12; *El Paso Herald*, February 21, 22 (quotation), 1912; *El Paso Morning Times*, May 4, 1912; Timmons, *El Paso*, 253; MR, Company D, February 29, 1912.
88. Joseph and Buchenau, *Mexico's Once and Future Revolution*, 51; Harris and Sadler, *Texas Rangers and the Mexican Revolution*, 92–93; Richmond and Haynes, eds., *The Mexican Revolution*, 39, 41; Romo, *Ringside Seat to a Revolution*, 108; Harris and Sadler, *Secret War in El Paso*, 72; Morgenthaler, *The River Has Never Divided Us*, 158.
89. Harris and Sadler, *Texas Rangers and the Mexican Revolution*, 93–94; Romo, *Ringside Seat to a Revolution*, 110; *El Paso Herald*, March 11, 1912.
90. Harris and Sadler, *Secret War in El Paso*, 87–89, 91–92, 111, 153–154; Romo, *Ringside Seat to a Revolution*, 109; *El Paso Herald*, September 28, 1912.
91. Harris and Sadler, *Texas Rangers and the Mexican Revolution*, 95–96; MR, Company D, April 30, 1912.
92. Cox, *Time of the Rangers*, 54–55 (quotation on p. 54); Utley, *Lone Star Lawmen*, 16; Harris and Sadler, *Texas Rangers and the Mexican Revolution*, 98–99; MR, Companies A and B, May 31, 1912.
93. Morgenthaler, *The River Has Never Divided Us*, 158; Harris and Sadler, *Texas Rangers and the Mexican Revolution*, 100–101; Richmond and Haynes, eds., *The Mexican Revolution*, 41.
94. Morgenthaler, *The River Has Never Divided Us*, 158, 160, 162; Harris and Sadler, *Texas Rangers and the Mexican Revolution*, 102–103; Caballero, *Orozco*, 160–167; Morgenthaler, *The River Has Never Divided Us*, 158, 160, 162; *El Paso Herald*, June 4, August 8, 1912; MR, Company D, August 31, 1912 (quotation).
95. Harris and Sadler, *Texas Rangers and the Mexican Revolution*, 115; *El Paso Herald*, January 28, 30, 1913.
96. *El Paso Herald*, January 31, 1913 (first quotation); Cox, *Time of the Rangers*, 55; Colquitt to Hughes, February 3, 1913, Box 2E153, Colquitt Papers, BCAH (second quotation).
97. Harris and Sadler, *Texas Rangers and the Mexican Revolution*, 116–118; Gonzales, *The Mexican Revolution*, 97, 98–99, 112–113, 114–115, 124; Morgenthaler, *The River Has Never Divided Us*, 163, 168; Katz, *Life and Times of Pancho Villa*, 208–210; Timmons, *El Paso*, 255.

98. Harris and Sadler, *Texas Rangers and the Mexican Revolution*, 119; Joseph and Buchenau, *Mexico's Once and Future Revolution*, 57; Gonzales, *The Mexican Revolution*, 103–104, 106–107, 122; Wilkinson, *Laredo and the Rio Grande Frontier*, 384.
99. Mike Cox, *Texas Ranger Tales: Stories That Need Telling* (Plano: Republic of Texas Press, 1997), 120–121, 124; Andrew Graybill, *Policing the Great Plains: Rangers, Mounties, and the North American Frontier, 1875–1910* (Lincoln: University of Nebraska Press, 2007), 17; Ferguson, "Zane Grey's Original 'Lone Star Ranger'," 30. For Zane Grey's fictional Texas Rangers, see *The Lone Star Ranger* (New York: Pinnacle Books, 2013).
100. *RAG, 1913–1914*, 10; *El Paso Herald*, June 24, 1913; Caldwell and DeLord, *Texas Lawmen, 1900–1940*, 398–99.
101. Harris and Sadler, *Texas Rangers and the Mexican Revolution*, 125–127; Caldwell and DeLord, *Texas Lawmen, 1900–1940*, 399; *El Paso Herald*, June 25, 1913.
102. Harris and Sadler, *Texas Rangers and the Mexican Revolution*, 128; Joseph and Buchenau, *Mexico's Once and Future Revolution*, 59; Morgenthaler, *The River Has Never Divided Us*, 185.
103. Harris and Sadler, *Texas Rangers and the Mexican Revolution*, 130.
104. Ibid., 132–133, 135–136; Katz, *Life and Times of Pancho Villa*, 224; Gonzales, *The Mexican Revolution*, 129; Romo, *Ringside Seat to a Revolution*, 109; *El Paso Herald*, November 27, 1913.
105. Parsons, *Captain John R. Hughes*, 236–239; Harris and Sadler, *Texas Rangers and the Mexican Revolution*, 164; *RAG, 1913–1914*, 10; *Brownsville Daily Herald*, June 8, 11, 13, 1914.
106. Parsons, *Captain John R. Hughes*, 239–240; *San Antonio Light*, December 15, 1914; *El Paso Herald*, April 20, 28, 1915.
107. Parsons, *Captain John R. Hughes*, 242; *Austin Statesman*, June 4, 1947.
108. Parsons, *Captain John R. Hughes*, 256, 260–261; *El Paso Herald-Post*, December 8, 1934, September 3, 1936.
109. Parsons, *Captain John R. Hughes*, 247, 251–254, 257, 274, 281; *El Paso Herald-Post*, March 23, 28, 1936. The latest edition of *Triggernometry* was published by the University of Oklahoma Press in 1996. The introduction was written by the English-born historian and Wild Bill Hickok scholar, Joseph G. Rosa. Hughes's two stints as grand marshal were covered in *El Paso Herald-Post*, December 19, 1935, December 30, 1941. Martin's book was originally published by the Naylor Company of San Antonio. Original copies are extremely

rare and valuable, which led State House Press to reprint the book in 1990. Former DPS spokesman and Texas historian Mike Cox wrote the introduction.
110. Parsons, *Captain John R. Hughes*, 284; House Special Resolution No. 238, *House Journal, Fiftieth Legislature, Regular Session*, 2778–2779; Senate Resolution No. 113, *Senate Journal, Fiftieth Legislature, Regular Session*, 1115.
111. Parsons, *Captain John R. Hughes*, 285–289; Texas Death Certificate, John R. Hughes, June 5, 1947, Registrar No. 27427; *Austin American*, June 4, 5, 1947; J. Marvin Hunter, "The Passing of Capt. John H. Hughes," *Frontier Times* 24 (June 1947): 427.

Notes for Chapter 12

1. Paul N. Spellman, *Captain John H. Rogers, Texas Ranger* (Denton: University of North Texas Press, 2003), 3–4, 7–8, 11–12; Curren Rogers McLane, "The Rogers Family Genealogy," 18, 42, 56, and Family Pedigree Chart No. 1, both in Rogers Vertical File, TRHF&M; *Seventh U.S. Census*, De Soto County, Mississippi; Tax Rolls, Guadalupe County, 1856–1875; *Ninth U.S. Census*, Guadalupe County, Texas; CSR-CS, Third Texas Infantry and Thirty-sixth Texas Cavalry, Pleasant Rogers. See similar rolls for Fourth Texas Cavalry, Martin Rogers; Thirty-sixth Texas Cavalry, Richard Rogers; Fourth Texas Infantry, Michael Rogers; and Fourth Texas Infantry, John Rogers; *The War of the Rebellion: A Compilation of the Official Records of the Union and Confederate Armies*, Series I, VI: 378–390.
2. Spellman, *Captain John H. Rogers*, 12, 14; Jim Lanning and Judy Lanning, *Texas Cowboys: Memories of the Early Days* (College Station: Texas A&M University Press, 1984), 151; Tax Rolls, Guadalupe County, 1876–1877; *Tenth U.S. Census*, Guadalupe County, Texas. Mary passed away on March 23, 1918, in Del Rio, where she and Crier had moved years before to be closer to John and his family. Crier died on January 7, 1941. Both were buried in City Cemetery #6 in San Antonio. McLane, "Rogers Family Genealogy," TRHF&M, 40; *San Antonio Express*, March 24, 1918; *Del Rio News-Herald*, January 9, 1941.
3. Spellman, *Captain John H. Rogers*, 17; Harry Van Demark, "Religion and Bullets: Two Factors Which Have Figured Prominently in the

Making of a Famous Texas Ranger," *Texas Monthly* 3 (March 1929): 349; Webb, *The Texas Rangers*, 460.
4. Spellman, *Captain John H. Rogers*, 17–18, 21, 24–25; RSR, J. H. Rogers, 401–170, TSLAC; MR, Company B, October 31, 1882-October 31, 1883.
5. Spellman, *Captain John H. Rogers*, 25–26; Frederick Wilkins, *The Law Comes to Texas: The Texas Rangers, 1870–1901* (Abilene, TX: State House Press, 1999), 236; MR, Company B, October 31, 1883; RSR, J. H. Rogers, 401–170, TSLAC; ROS, Company F, April 1884; *RAG, 1884*, 21, 28.
6. Spellman, *Captain John H. Rogers*, 27; MR, Company F, September 1, 1884.
7. Spellman, *Captain John H. Rogers*, 27–28; MR, Company F, September 30, December 31, 1884; ROS, Company F, September, December 1884.
8. Spellman, *Captain John H. Rogers*, 29, 31; MR, Company F, January 31, July 31, November 30, 1885; *RAG, 1886*, 49; RSR, John H. Rogers, 401–170, Joseph Shely and William Scott, both -171, TSLAC; ROS, Company F, July 1885.
9. Utley, *Lone Star Justice*, 249; Joseph F. Combs, *Gunsmoke in the Redlands* (San Antonio: Naylor Company, 1968), 105–106, 108–110; "The Conner Feud in Sabine County. As Told by W. T. McElroy to Geo. L. Crocket," Box 14, George Louis Crocket Papers, East Texas Research Center, Stephen F. Austin State University, 1–2; Texas Department of Criminal Justice, Convict Record Ledgers, 1998/038-152, TSLAC, 2; Mark Dugan, *Tales Never Told Around the Campfire* (Athens: Swallow Press/Ohio University Press, 1992), 114–115; Henry C. Fuller, *"A Texas Sheriff"* (Nacogdoches, TX: Baker Printing Co., 1931), 55–56; William Warren Sterling, *Trails and Trials of a Texas Ranger* (Norman: University of Oklahoma Press, 1959), 309. Nine of the conspirators in the breakout were convicted by the fall of 1887 and served prison terms.
10. Spellman, *Captain John H. Rogers*, 36; Utley, *Lone Star Justice*, 249; Fuller, *"A Texas Sheriff"*, 56–57; RSR, William Scott, 401–171, TSLAC; *RAG, 1886*, 56; MR, Company F, March 31, July 31, 1886. Burrows had assisted Sheriff Milton Mast in apprehending desperado William Preston "Bill" Longley in 1877. For more on the outlaw-gunfighter and his capture, see Rick Miller, *Bloody Bill Longley: The Mythology of a Gunfighter* (Denton: University of North Texas Press, 2011).

11. Spellman, *Captain John H. Rogers*, 36–41; MR, Company F, August 31-September 30, 1886; *RAG, 1886*, 55–56, 66; Texas Department of Criminal Justice, Convict Record Ledgers, 1998/038-148, TSLAC, 122; ibid., Conduct Registers, 1998/038-178, TSLAC, 171.
12. Spellman, *Captain John H. Rogers*, 43, 45–46; "The Conner Feud in Sabine County," 2; Combs, *Gunsmoke in the Redlands*, 110–111.
13. Spellman, *Captain John H. Rogers*, 46–49; Combs, *Gunsmoke in the Redlands*, 111–113; L. E. Daniell, *Texas—The Country and Its Men* (Austin: L. E. Daniell, n.d.), 484–487; Mike Cox, *The Texas Rangers: Wearing the Cinco Peso, 1821–1900* (New York: Tom Doherty Associates, 2008), 339–340; Mike Cox, *Texas Ranger Tales II* (Plano: Republic of Texas Press, 1999), 137–139; Sarah Ellen Davidge, "Texas Rangers Were Rough and Ready Fighters," *Frontier Times* 13 (November 1935): 125; *Austin Daily Statesmen*, April 3, 1887; Robert W. Stephens, *Bullets and Buckshot in Texas* (Dallas: R. W. Stephens, 2002), 102; Wilkins, *Law Comes to Texas*, 261; "The Texas Rangers Brought Law and Order," *Frontier Times* 12 (July 1935): 425.
14. Spellman, *Captain John H. Rogers*, 53; RSR, C. L. Rogers, 401–170, TSLAC.
15. Spellman, *Captain John H. Rogers*, 55; MR, Company F, April 30, June 30, 1887; John Miller Morris, *A Private in the Texas Rangers: A. T. Miller of Company B, Frontier Battalion* (College Station: Texas A&M University Press, 2001), 69, 79.
16. Spellman, *Captain John H. Rogers*, 54–55; *San Antonio Daily Express*, June 19, 1887; *Galveston Daily News*, June 19, 21, 23, 1887; *Fort Worth Daily Gazette*, June 19, 22, 23, 24, 28, 1887; MR, Company F, July 31, 1887.
17. Spellman, *Captain John H. Rogers*, 56; MR, Company F, August 31, 1887; Operations of Frontier Battalion, 3 (1885–1892), 401–1084, TSLAC: 149.
18. Spellman, *Captain John H. Rogers*, 56; MR, Company F, October 31, 1887; *San Saba News*, October 7, 1887; Opertions of Frontier Battalion, 3: 150.
19. Spellman, *Captain John H. Rogers*, 57; MR, Company F, November 30, 1887; ROS, Company F, December 1887.
20. Spellman, *Captain John H. Rogers*, 60; *Galveston Daily News*, February 14, 16, September 24, 27, 1888; Beatriz de la Garza, *A Law for the Lion: A Tale of Crime and Injustice in the Borderlands* (Austin: University of Texas Press, 2003), 34–35; Annette Martin Ludeman, *La Salle County:*

South Texas Brush County, 1856–1975 (Quanah, TX: Nortex Press, 1975), 116–117; Glenn Shirley, *Heck Thomas, Frontier Marshal* (Norman: University of Oklahoma Press, 1981), 122–123.
21. Spellman, *Captain John H. Rogers*, 60, 62, 64; MR, Company F, May 31-October 31, 1888, May 31-June 30, 1889, January 31, 1900; RSR, John H. Rogers, 401–170, TSLAC; ROS, Company F, June-July 1888.
22. Spellman, *Captain John H. Rogers*, 64, 65; *RAG, 1889–1890*, 28–29, 93; MR, Company F, May 31-December 31, 1890; ROS, Company F, May-August 1890.
23. Elliott Young, *Catarino Garza's Revolution on the Texas-Mexico Border* (Durham, NC: Duke University Press, 2004), 1 (quotation), 112–115, 129–130, 145, 155, 157.
24. Spellman, *Captain John H. Rogers*, 69; Young, *Catarino Garza's Revolution*, 160, 176; ROS, Company F, December 1891; Operations of Frontier Battalion, 3: 184; Wilkins, *Law Comes to Texas*, 303–304; Sterling, *Trails and Trials*, 373.
25. Letter of James O. Luby, March 28, 1892, Letter of Captain John G. Bourke, April 2, 1892, *The Garza Revolution, 1891–1893: Records of the U.S. Continental Commands, Department of Texas* (Bethesda, MD: LexisNexis, 2009), 11.
26. Spellman, *Captain John H. Rogers*, 69–71; MR, Company F, March 31, 1892; ROS, Company F, March-April 1892; *Laredo Times*, April 4, 1892.
27. Spellman, *Captain John H. Rogers*, 70–71; MR, Company F, April 30, 1892; ROS, Company F, April 1892; Young, *Catarino Garza's Revolution*, 177–178.
28. Spellman, *Captain John H. Rogers*, 67–68, 71; McLane, "Rogers Family Genealogy," 22, and Family Pedigree Chart No. 1, both in Rogers Vertical File, TRHF&M.
29. Spellman, *Captain John H. Rogers*, 72; Utley, *Lone Star Justice*, 256; RSR, John H. Rogers, 401–170, TSLAC.
30. Spellman, *Captain John H. Rogers*, 72–73; MR, Companies E and F, January 31-February 28, 1893; ROS, Companies E and F, January 1893; RSR, Tupper Harris, 401–154, C. L. Rogers, -170, and W. M. Burwell, -145, TSLAC.
31. ROS, Company E, January 1893; Operations of Frontier Battalion, 4 (1892–1896), 401–1805, TSLAC: 150; Francis B. Heitman, *Historical Register and Dictionary of the United States Army* (Washington, D.C.: Government Printing Office, 1903), 1: 297, 373; *Brownsville Daily*

Herald, January 23, 25, 1893; *Austin Daily Statesman*, February 2, May 26, 1893.

32. Spellman, *Captain John H. Rogers*, 74–75; MR, Company E, February 28, 1893-February 28, 1895; ROS, Company E, February 1893-February 1896; Sammy Tise, *Texas County Sheriffs* (Albuquerque: Oakwood Publishing, 1989), 371; Clifford R. Caldwell and Ron DeLord, *Texas Lawmen, 1835–1899: The Good and the Bad* (Charleston, SC: History Press, 2011), 352–353.

33. Spellman, *Captain John H. Rogers*, 75–76; ROS, Company E, October 1893 (quotation), March-April 1894, June-July 1894: *RAG, 1893–1894*, 66; *Galveston Daily News*, October 10, 1893, March 19, 20, July 20, 22, 23, 1894; *Brownsville Daily Herald*, March 22, July 16, 17, 1894; McLane, "Rogers Family Genealogy," TRHF&M, 22; Daniell, *Texas—The Country and Its Men*, 489.

34. Spellman, *Captain John H. Rogers*, 81, 82–83, 86–88; James A. Monroe, *Hellfire Nation: The Politics of Sin in American History* (New Haven: Yale University Press, 2003), 219–220; Meg Frisbee, *Counterpunch: The Cultural Battles Over Heavyweight Prizefighting in the American West* (Seattle: University of Washington Press, 2016), 91, 99; Keith R. Robinson, *Fist Fighting Out West: Dan Stuart versus General Mabry and the Texas Rangers* (London: English Westerners' Society, 2010), 14–15; MR, Company E, February 29, 1896; ROS, Company E, February 1896; *RAG, 1896*, 12.

35. Spellman, *Captain John H. Rogers*, 88–90; ROS, Company E, February 1896, October-November 1896; Evan Anders, *Boss Rule in South Texas: The Progressive Era* (Austin: University of Texas Press, 1982), 30, 70, 105, 171, 173; McLane, "Rogers Family Genealogy," TRFH&M, 22.

36. Spellman, *Captain John H. Rogers*, 91–92; John A. Britton, *Cables, Crises, and the Press: The Geopolitics of the New International Information System in the Americas, 1866–1903* (Albuquerque: University of New Mexico Press, 2013), 199–200, 215–226; ROS, Company E, April 1898, June 1898; *Houston Daily Post*, April 22, 26, May 23, June 12, 1898. See also John L. Offner, *An Unwanted War: The Diplomacy of the United States and Spain over Cuba, 1895–1898* (Chapel Hill: University of North Carolina Press, 1992). The exact cause of the explosion that sank the *Maine* remains unknown. The prevailing theories point to the external detonation of a mine or a spontaneous internal combustion in the coal bunkers. For more, see Jim Leeke, *Manila and Santiago: The New Steel*

Navy in the Spanish-American War (Annapolis, MD: Naval Institute Press, 2009), 23–34.
37. *RAG, 1897–1898*, 13.
38. John McKiernan-González, *Fevered Measures: Public Health and Race at the Texas-Mexico Border, 1848–1942* (Durham, NC: Duke University Press, 2012), 127–130 (first quotation on p. 130), 132, 136 (second quotation), 141; Joseph B. Wilkinson, *Laredo and the Rio Grande Frontier: A Narrative* (Austin: Jenkins Publishing Co., 1975), 377; Arnoldo De León, *They Called Them Greasers: Anglo Attitudes Toward Mexicans in Texas, 1821–1900* (Austin: University of Texas Press, 1983), 95.
39. Spellman, *Captain John H. Rogers*, 98–99; McKiernan-González, *Fevered Measures*, 142; Utley, *Lone Star Justice*, 269–270; ROS, Company E, March 1899; *RAG, 1899–1900*, 22; Wilkinson, *Laredo and the Rio Grande Frontier*, 377.
40. Spellman, *Captain John H. Rogers*, 99–101; ROS, Company E, March 1899; McKiernan-González, *Fevered Measures*, 142; *RAG, 1899–1900*, 22; Cox, *Texas Ranger Tales II*, 142; Earl Mayo, "The Texas Rangers: The Most Efficient Police Force in the World," *Frank Leslie's Popular Monthly* 52 (October 1901): 535–536; De León, *They Called Them Greasers*, 96; Daniell, *Texas—The Country and Its Men*, 490–492.
41. Spellman, *Captain John H. Rogers*, 101–102; ROS, Company E, March 1899; Webb, *Texas Rangers*, 450–451. Utley, *Lone Star Justice*, 270; *RAG, 1899–1900*, 22; James N. Leiker, *Racial Borders: Black Soldiers Along the Rio Grande* (College Station: Texas A&M University Press, 2002), 118.
42. Spellman, *Captain John H. Rogers*, 102–103; ROS, Company E, May 1899; Cox, *Texas Ranger Tales* II, 142–143; Daniell, *Texas—The Country and Its Men*, 493.
43. Spellman, *Captain John H. Rogers*, 104; James C. Kearney, et al., *No Hope for Heaven, No Fear of Hell: The Stafford-Townsend Feud of Colorado County, 1871–1911* (Denton: University of North Texas press, 2016), 88–89; *Colorado County Citizen*, February 18, 1988; *Galveston Daily News*, May 19, 1899; "The Colorado County Feud and Its History," Bill Stein Collection, Nesbitt Memorial Library, n. pag. See also John Walter Reese and Lillian Estelle Reese, *Flaming Feuds of Colorado County* (Salado, TX: Anson Jones Press, 1962), 94–97.
44. Spellman, *Captain John H. Rogers*, 104–105; Kearney, et al., *No Hope for Heaven, No Fear of Hell*, 89, 95; ROS, Company E, May-June 1899; MR, Company E, May 31-September 30, 1899; Reese and Reese,

Flaming Feuds of Colorado County, 100–101. According to the accepted story, Rogers commanded the detachment in Columbus. In the course of events, he disarmed Light Townsend when he rode in to take up his kinfolk's fight. Townsend, a cousin in the extended family who shared the same name as the deceased sheriff, was supposedly impressed by Rogers and promised to refrain from participation in any further feuding. Indeed, he became a Ranger captain himself. While Townsend did command Company C of the Ranger Force in 1931, Rogers did not leave the hospital and return to duty until May 27. C. L. Sonnichsen, *I'll Die Before I'll Run: The Story of the Great Feuds of Texas* (Lincoln: University of Nebraska Press, 1988), 312–313; Sterling, *Trails and Trials*, 376–377; RSR, L. Townsend, 401–64, TSLAC.

45. Spellman, *Captain John H. Rogers*, 106–107; MR, Company E, August 31-September 30, 1899; ROS, August-September 1899; *Houston Daily Post*, August 14, 18, 19, 20, 21, 24, 26, 1899; *Austin Daily Statesman*, August 19, 20, 1899; *RAG, 1899–1900*, 9–10, 22–23.

46. Spellman, *Captain John H. Rogers*, 107–108; MR, Company E, October 31-November 30, 1899; ROS, Company E, October 1899-January 1900.

47. Kearney, et al., *No Hope for Heaven, No Fear of Hell*, 106–107; ROS, Company E, January 1900; Reese and Reese, *Flaming Feuds of Colorado County*, 100–101.

48. ROS, Company E, February 1900; Kearney, et al., *No Hope for Heaven, No Fear of Hell*, 112; *Houston Daily Post*, February 8, 22, 23, 1900.

49. Spellman, *Captain John H. Rogers*, 109; ROS, Company E, October 1900; 58 *Southwestern Reporter* (1900) 101–102; Gary B. Borders, *A Hanging in Nacogdoches: Murder, Race, Politics, and Polemics in Texas's Oldest Town, 1870–1916* (Austin: University of Texas Press, 2006), 137–138; *Houston Daily Post*, December 24 (quotation), 26, 1899, November 6, 1900; *Brownsville Daily Herald*, November 13, 1900.

50. Spellman, *Captain John H. Rogers*, 110; ROS, Company E, November 1900-June 1901; Special Orders No. 97, November 24, 1900, 401–1013, TSLAC; *San Antonio Daily Express*, April 18, 1901; Clifford R. Caldwell and Ron De Lord, *Texas Lawmen, 1900–1940: More of the Good & the Bad* (Charleston, SC: History Press, 2012), 362–363; Tise, *Texas County Sheriffs*, 365.

51. *Kenedy Times*, October 31, 1963; Américo Paredes, *"With His Pistol in His Hand": A Border Ballad and Its Hero* (Austin: University of Texas Press, 1958), 58–64 (quotations on p. 62); Charley F. Eckhardt, *Tales of Badmen, Bad Women, and Bad Places: Four Centuries of Texas*

Outlawry (Lubbock: Texas Tech University Press, 1999), 156–157; William D. Carrigan and Clive Webb, *Forgotten Dead: Mob Violence against Mexicans in the United States, 1848–1928* (New York: Oxford University Press, 2013), 174; Richard J. Mertz, "'No One Can Arrest Me': The Story of Gregorio Cortez," *Journal of South Texas* 1 (1974): 1–2, 6–7; Annette Martin Ludeman, *La Salle County: South Texas Brush County, 1856–1975* (Quanah, TX: Nortex Press, 1975), 122.

52. Mertz, "'No One Can Arrest Me'," 7–8; Utley, *Lone Star Justice*, 274–275; Cox, *Texas Ranger Tales II*, 143; Benjamin Heber Johnson, *Revolution in Texas: How a Forgotten Rebellion and Its Bloody Suppression Turned Mexicans into Americans* (New Haven: Yale University Press, 2003), 21.

53. Spellman, *Captain John H. Rogers*, 114–116; *RAG, 1901–1902*, 32; ROS, Company E, June 1901; Paredes, *"With His Pistol in His Hand,"* 79–83, 97–100; Eckhardt, *Badmen, Bad Women, and Bad Places*, 161; Stanley D. Casto, *Settlement of the Cibolo-Nueces Strip: A Partial History of La Salle County* (Hillsboro, TX: Hill Junior College Press, 1969), 39; Sterling, *Trails and Trials*, 507–511; *San Antonio Daily Express*, June 23, 25 (quotation), 1901; Texas Department of Criminal Justice, Convict Record Ledgers, 1998/038-156, TSLAC, 144. The Cortez pursuit has been eclipsed in size only by the July 1986 search for murderer and rapist Jerry Walter "Animal" McFadden in the Big Sandy area. *Austin American-Statesman*, July 10–13, 1986.

54. Bruce A. Glasrud and Harold J. Weiss, Jr., eds., *Tracking the Texas Rangers: The Twentieth Century* (Denton: University of North Texas Press, 2013), 2.

55. Hans Peter Nielson Gammel, comp., *The Laws of Texas, 1897–1902* (Austin: Gammel's Book Store, 1902), 748–750 (quotation on pp. 749–750).

56. Spellman, *Captain John H. Rogers*, 118; MR, Company C, July 31, 1901; *RAG, 1901–1902*, 40.

57. Spellman, *Captain John H. Rogers*, 122; MR, Company C, December 31, 1902.

58. Spellman, *Captain John H. Rogers*, 123–125; *RAG, 1903–1904*, 161; Andrew Graybill, *Policing the Great Plains: Rangers, Mounties, and the North American Frontier, 1875–1910* (Lincoln: University of Nebraska Press, 2007), 193–194; Don Woodard, *Black Diamonds! Black Gold!* (Lubbock; Texas Tech University Press, 1998), 76–84; Dick King, "'Rascals' and Rangers," *True West* 22 (April 1975): 44; Utley, *Lone Star Justice*, 278.

59. Spellman, *Captain John H. Rogers*, 127; Bill Neal, *From Guns to Gavel: How Justice Grew Up in the Outlaw West* (Lubbock; Texas Tech University Press, 2008), 169, 173–174; Valerie Owen, *Byrd Cochran of Dead Man's Corner* (Snyder, TX: Feather Press, 1972), 43; James Fenton, "Tom Ross: Ranger Nemesis," *National Association for Outlaw and Lawmen History Quarterly* 4 (Summer 1990); Robert K. DeArment, *Deadly Dozen: Forgotten Gunfighters of the Old West* (Norman: University of Oklahoma Press, 2010), 3: 283.
60. Spellman, *Captain John H. Rogers*, 127–129; Fenton, "Tom Ross," 19–20; *RAG, 1903–1904*, 161–162; Cox, *Texas Ranger Tales II*, 143–144.
61. Spellman, *Captain John H. Rogers*, 130; MR, Company C, June 30, 1905.
62. Bob Alexander, *Riding Lucifer's Line: Ranger Deaths along the Texas-Mexico Border* (Denton: University of North Texas Press, 2013), 216–218; Caldwell and DeLord, *Texas Lawmen, 1900–1940*, 393–94; *El Paso Daily Herald*, October 3, December 27, 1905.
63. Spellman, *Captain John H. Rogers*, 137.
64. Ibid., 139, 140; *RAG, 1907–1908*, 38 (quotation).
65. Spellman, *Captain John H. Rogers*, 140–144; *Galveston Daily News*, *San Antonio Daily Express*, and *Laredo Times*, all dated August 28, 1907.
66. Spellman, *Captain John H. Rogers*, 150; *Galveston Daily News*, September 10, 11, 15, 1909; *Houston Daily Post*, April 1, 1913; *Bryan Daily Eagle*, August 25, 1913.
67. Spellman, *Captain John H. Rogers*, 152; Charles H. Harris III and Louis R. Sadler, *The Texas Rangers and the Mexican Revolution: The Bloodiest Decade, 1910–1920* (Albuquerque: University of New Mexico Press, 2007), 35; *Austin Statesman*, April 30, May 1, 1910.
68. Harris and Sadler, *Texas Rangers and the Mexican Revolution*, 35–36; MR, Company C, June 30, 1910; *Houston Daily Post*, July 2, 1910.
69. Clifford R. Caldwell and Ron DeLord, *Eternity at the End of a Rope: Executions, Lynchings and Vigilante Justice in Texas, 1819–1923* (Santa Fe: Sunstone Press, 2015), 501; *RAG, 1910*, 8; *Palestine Daily Herald*, July 30, 31, August 1, 1910; *Austin Statesman*, August 1, 1910.
70. *Palestine Daily Herald*, August 1, 10, 15, 18, 1910; MR, Company C, July 31–August 31, 1910 (quotation); *Houston Daily Post*, August 1, 1910.

71. Spellman, *Captain John H. Rogers*, 153–155; *Galveston Daily News*, November 15, 1910; William D. Carrigan and Clive Webb, *Forgotten Dead: Mob Violence against Mexicans in the United States, 1848–1928* (New York: Oxford University Press, 2013), 81, 141; Travis Taylor, "Lynching on the Border: The Death of Antonio Rodríguez and the Rise of Anti-Americanism during the Mexican Revolution" (M.A. thesis, Angelo State University, 2012), 8–9; De la Garza, *A Law for the Lion*, 82.
72. Spellman, *Captain John H. Rogers*, 154; *Houston Daily Post*, November 16, 22, 1910; *Galveston Daily News*, November 17, 22, 1910.
73. Spellman, *Captain John H. Rogers*, 155–156; Frederick S. Calhoun, *The Lawmen: United States Marshals and Their Deputies, 1789–1989* (Washington, D.C.: Smithsonian Institution Press, 1989), 216; *Galveston Daily News*, November 22, 1910.
74. Spellman, *Captain John H. Rogers*, 156; *Galveston Daily News*, November 24, 27, 1910; *Houston Daily Post*, November 24, 27, 1910.
75. Spellman, *Captain John H. Rogers*, 156; Harris and Sadler, *Texas Rangers and the Mexican Revolution*, 52–53; *Laredo Times*, November 27, 1910; *Galveston Daily News*, November 26, 1910.
76. Harris and Sadler, *Texas Rangers and the Mexican Revolution*, 54; F. Arturo Rosales, *¡Pobre Raza! Violence, Justice, and Mobilization among México Lindo Immigrants, 1900–1936* (Austin: University of Texas Press, 1999), 11; *Houston Daily Post*, November 29, 1910; Wilkinson, *Laredo and the Rio Grande Frontier*, 381.
77. Spellman, *Captain John H. Rogers*, 157–158; Monroe, *Hellfire Nation*, 278, 290; RSR, J. H. Rogers, 401-170, TSLAC; MR, Company C, January 31, 1911; *El Paso Herald*, January 19, August 28, 1911.
78. McLane, "Rogers Family Genealogy," TRHF&M, 33; Cox, *Texas Ranger Tales II*, 144.
79. Spellman, *Captain John H. Rogers*, 158; *El Paso Herald*, January 31, August 28, 1911; Calhoun, *The Lawmen*, 215–216, 217, 219 (quotation); W. H. Timmons, *El Paso: A Borderlands History* (El Paso: Texas Western Press, 2004), 254–255; *Galveston Daily News*, March 16, 1912.
80. Spellman, *Captain John H. Rogers*, 165–166; George T. Díaz, "Smugglers in Dangerous Times: Revolution and Communities in the Tejano Borderlands," *War Along the Border: The Mexican Revolution and Tejano Communities*, ed. Arnoldo de León (College Station: Texas A&M University Press, 2012), 277–278, 281; David Dorado Romo, *Ringside Seat to a Revolution, An Underground Cultural History of El Paso and Juárez:*

1893–1923 (El Paso, TX: Cinco Puntos Press, 2005), 110; *El Paso Herald*, October 6, 1911, March 19, 21, 1912. The number of indicted men brought before the federal court was quite large. *El Paso Herald*, April 7, 1911.

81. Spellman, *Captain John H. Rogers*, 165–166; *El Paso Herald*, April 10, 14, June 11, 24, November 22, 1912.
82. Spellman, *Captain John H. Rogers*, 169–170; *El Paso Herald*, November 30, December 13, 18, 1912; *New York Times*, December 1, 1912. The Taft administration also dismissed Robert Winston Dowe, customs collector at Eagle Pass; Sloan Simpson, postmaster of Dallas; and Dupont Bayard Lyon, U.S. marshal of the Eastern District. *El Paso Herald*, December 2, 1912.
83. Spellman, *Captain John H. Rogers*, 170–172; *El Paso Herald*, November 6, 8, 22, 1912, March 24, April 3, 1913; Virgil D. White, *Index of U.S. Marshals, 1789–1960* (Waynesboro, TN: National Historical Publishing, 1988), 73. See also Charles E. Neu, *Colonel House: A Biography of Woodrow Wilson's Silent Partner* (New York: Oxford University Press, 2015).
84. Demark, "Religion and Bullets," 349.
85. Spellman, *Captain John H. Rogers*, 172, 175; Attorney General's Office, *Register of the Department of Justice and the Courts of the United States*, Twenty-second Edition (1914), 188, Twenty-third Edition (1915), 190, Twenty-sixth Edition (1918), 188; *El Paso Herald*, October 12, 1914, May 1, 1915, April 18, 1917; *Houston Daily Post*, November 1, 1914, May 2, 1915.
86. Spellman, *Captain John H. Rogers*, 175; *El Paso Herald*, April 17, 20, 21, 24, 25, 1917; Stephen L. Vladeck, "Enemy Aliens, Enemy Property, and Access to the Courts," *Lewis and Clark Law Review* 11 (Winter 2007): 965, 970–973.
87. Spellman, *Captain John H. Rogers*, 190–192; Mike Cox, *Time of the Rangers: From 1900 to the Present* (New York: Tom Doherty Books, 2009), 87–91; Testimony of José Canales, February 10, 1919, Testimony of Captain J. H. Rogers, February 12, 1919, TRF Investigation, 857 (first quotation), 1233–1235, 1246 (second quotation); *Galveston Daily News*, February 13, 1919.
88. Spellman, *Captain John H. Rogers*, 193–194; Testimony of Captain J. H. Rogers, February 12, 1919, TRF Investigation, 1235–1238; *Floresville Chronicle-Journal*, February 14, 1919.
89. Testimony of Captain J. H. Rogers, February 12, 1919, TRF Investigation, 1247–1248 (quotations). The 1919 investigation into the Ranger Force will be covered in greater detail in Volume 3 of this trilogy.

Endnotes **683**

90. Spellman, *Captain John H. Rogers*, 205–206; *Austin Statesman*, May 6, 22, 24, 25, 1921; Cox, *Texas Ranger Tales II*, 146.
91. Spellman, *Captain John H. Rogers*, 129; Neal, *From Guns to Gavels*, 177, 178–182, 209–213, 218–220, 241, 244–246, 250; DeArment, *Deadly Dozen*, 3: 287; Bob Alexander, *Lawmen, Outlaws, and S.O.Bs: Gunfighters of the Old Southwest* (Silver City, NM: High-Lonesome Books, 2004), 233–234; Owen, *Byrd Cochran of Dead Man's Corner*, 47–48; Doug Perkins and Nancy Ward, *Brave Men and Cold Steel: A History of Range Detectives and Their Peacemakers* (Fort Worth: Texas and Southwestern Cattle Raisers Foundation, 1984), 22–27. Martha Plummer "Mattie" Roberson witnessed her husand's murder, and she responded by shooting both killers, although their wounds proved non-fatal. For more on this formidable lady, see Jan Devereaux, "Gentle Woman, Tough Medicine," *NOLA Quarterly* 27 (April-June 2003): 21–33.
92. Spellman, *Captain John H. Rogers*, 210, 212; *Austin American*, May 1, 4, 1923, January 24, 27, April 4, 1924; *Austin Statesman*, May 1, 2, 1923.
93. Spellman, *Captain John H. Rogers*, 211–213; *Austin American*, May 3, 15, 20, June 1, July 10, November 19, 23, 24, 1923, April 24, May 2, 3, 1924; *Austin Statesman*, May 1, 1924; Cox, *Texas Ranger Tales II*, 146.
94. *Austin Statesman*, May 2, 1924.
95. Spellman, *Captain John H. Rogers*, 218–219; RSR, John H. Rogers, 401-62, TSLAC; Special Orders No. 8, May 14, 1927, Rogers Vertical File, TRHF&M; *San Antonio Express*, May 20, 1927.
96. Spellman, *Captain John H. Rogers*, 220–221; *San Antonio Express*, August 6, 1927.
97. Spellman, *Captain John H. Rogers*, 221–222; Texas Death Certificate, J. H. Rogers, November 15, 1930, File No. 47704; *Austin American*, *Austin Statesman*, and *San Antonio Express*, all dated November 12, 1930.
98. "Many Brilliant Exploits Manifest Courage of Captain Rogers," *Sheriff's Association of Texas Magazine* 1 (March 1931), 11.
99. *Sixteenth Federal Census*, Bexar County, Texas; Texas Death Certificate, Harriet Burwell Rogers, July 6, 1948, File No. 28765; Family Pedigree Chart No. 1, TRHF&M; *San Antonio Express*, July 6, 1948.
100. Daniell, *Texas—the Country and Its Men*, 489; Family Group Record-146, Rogers Vertical File, TRHF&M, 1; *Fifteenth U.S. Census*, Bexar County, Texas; Texas Death Certificate, C. M. Reeves, May 7, 1935, File No. 23379; *San Antonio Express*, May 8, 1935; *Find A Grave*, s.v. "Lucile Rogers Reeves."

101. *Wentworth Military Academy Annual Catalog 1913–1914* (Lexington, MO: The Academy, 1914), 31, 39, 45, 68, 76, 83, 88, 90; R. Manning Ancell with Christine M. Miller, *The Biographical Dictionary of World War II Generals and Flag Officers* (Westport, CT: Greenwood Press, 1996), 278; Lonnie J. White, *Panthers to Arrowheads: The 36th (Texas-Oklahoma) Division in World War I* (Austin: Presidial Press, 1984), 2–3, 25, 127, 133–143, 151–155, 164–167, 210; *Houston Daily Post*, October 9, 1917; US Army WWI Transport Service, Passenger Lists, RG 92, NARA; American Battle Monuments Commission, *36th Division Summary of Operations in the World War* (Washington, D.C.: Government Printing Office, 1944), 1, 4, 7–18; *El Paso Herald*, July 8, 1918; *Official Army Register for July 1, 1921* (Washington, D.C.: Government Printing Office, 1922), 868; *Official Army Register for January 1, 1949* (Washington, D.C.: Government Printing Office, 1949): I, 785; *El Paso Herald-Post*, March 7, 1966.

Bibliography

Archive and Manuscript Collections

1867 Voters' Registration Lists. Reel VR-10. A&ISD-TSLAC, Austin, Texas. Online at Ancestry.com.

Aten, Ira. Interview with Earl Vandale, J. Evetts Haley, and Hervey Chesley at El Centro, California, July 1941. Typescript. J. Evetts Haley Collection, HML&HC, Midland, Texas.

———. Interview with J. Evetts Haley at El Centro, California, February 26, 1928. Typescript. J. Evetts Haley Collection, HML&HC, Midland, Texas.

———. "Love Letters to My Wife." Nine letters. PPHM, Canyon, Texas.

Bell-Marsh Family Records. H. M. Bell File. Smith County Historical Society Archives. Carnegie History Center, Tyler, Texas.

"The Colorado County Feud and Its History." Bill Stein Collection. Nesbitt Memorial Library, Columbus, Texas.

Confederate Muster Roll Abstract Records. Texas Adjutant General's Department. A&ISD-TSLAC, Austin, Texas.

"The Conner Feud in Sabine County. As Told by W. T. McElroy to Geo. L. Crocket." Box 14, George Louis Crocket Papers. East Texas Research Center, Stephen F. Austin State University, Nacogdoches, Texas.

Fort Concho Soldiers Riot, 1881. Tom Green County Historical Society Collection. West Texas Collection, Angelo State University, San Angelo, Texas.

Hughes Brothers' Horse Record. Armstrong Research Center, TRHF&M, Waco, Texas.

Hughes, John R. Interview with Vera P. Elliott at El Paso, Texas, n.d. Transcript. Federal Writers Project, Works Progress Administration. Copy provided to author by the Library of Congress, Washington, D.C.

Kansas State Censuses, 1875. Microfilm reel K-1. Kansas State Historical Society, Topeka, Kansas. Online at Ancestry.com.

McNelly, Leander H., Papers. MC084. Manuscript Collection. Herzstein Library, SJMH, La Porte, Texas.

Report of Maj. J. B. Jones, Commanding the Frontier Battalion, Texas State Troops. March, 1876. Houston: A. C. Gray, 1876.

Seat, Benton Bell. "Memoirs, 1849–1916." MC 799. Florence Cypert Spore Papers. Special Collections, University of Arkansas Libraries, Fayetteville, Arkansas.

Taylor, Mrs. Clifton Hughes. Hughes-Bond-Sargent Family Tree. Mrs. Taylor of Houston, Texas, whose husband was a grandson of Emery S. Hughes, researched and compiled the tree. A copy is archived at the Linn County Historical Museum & Genealogy Library in Pleasanton, Kansas.

Texas Adjutant General's Department. Record Group 401. A&ISD-TSLAC, Austin, Texas.

———. World War I Service Record Cards. Texas Military Force Museum, Camp Mabry, Texas.

Texas Adjutant General's Office Records, 1838–1889. Transcripts from the Office of the Adjutant-General of Texas, 1870–1876. Research and Collections Division, BCAH, The University of Texas at Austin.

Texas Comptroller's Office. Confederate Pension Applications, 1899–1975. A&ISD-TSLAC, Austin, Texas. Online at Ancestry.com.

———. Texas County Tax Rolls. A&ISD-TSLAC, Austin, Texas. Online at FamilySearch.org.

Texas Department of Criminal Justice. Convict Record Ledgers, 1849–1954. Twenty-nine ledgers. A&ISD-TSLAC, Austin, Texas. Online at Ancestry.com.

———. Conduct Registers, 1875–1945. Sixty ledgers. A&ISD-TSLAC, Austin, Texas. Online at Ancestry.com.

Texas General Land Office. Land Grants. Archives and Records Program, General Land Office, Austin, Texas. Online at www.glo.texas.gov.

Texas Governors' Papers and Records. Record Group 301. A&ISD-TSLAC, Austin, Texas.

Texas Secretary of State. Bonds and Oaths of County and State Officials, 1846–1920. A&ISD-TSLAC, Austin, Texas. Online at Ancestry.com.

———. Executive Clemency Records. A&ISD-TSLAC, Austin, Texas.

———. Extradition Records, Fugitive Records. A&ISD-TSLAC, Austin, Texas.

United Kingdom. Air Ministry. Airmen's Records. Series AIR 79: Department of the Master-General of Personnel. The National Archives, Kew, London. Online at Fold3.com.

United States Army. WWI Transport Service, Passenger Lists. Record Group 92: Records of the Office of the Quartermaster General. NARA, Washington, D. C. Online at Ancestry.com.

———. World War I Draft Registration Cards. Record Group 163: Records of the Selective Service System, Microfilm Publication M1509. NARA, Washington, D. C. Online at Fold3.com.

United States Bureau of the Census. *Third* through *Sixteenth Census of the United States*. Record Group 29: Records of the Bureau of the Census, Microfilm Publications M252, M33, M19, M704, M432, M653, M593, T9, T623, T624, T625, T626, T627, T1134. NARA, Washington, D.C. Online at Ancestry.com.

United States Department of Commerce and Labor. Passenger Lists of Vessels Arriving at New Orleans, Louisiana, 1903–1945. Record Group 85: Records of the Immigration and Naturalization Service, T905. NARA, Washington, D.C. Online at Ancestry.com.

United States Department of State. Consular Registration Certificates, compiled 1907–1918. Record Group 59: General Records of the Department of State, 1763–2002. NARA, Washington, D.C. Online at Ancestry.com.

———. Marriage Reports in State Department Decimal Files, 1910–1949. Record Group: 59: General Records of the Department of State, 1763–2002. NARA, Washington, D.C. Online at Ancestry.com.

———. Passport Applications, January 2, 1906-March 31, 1925. Record Group 59: General Records of the Department of State, Microfilm Publication M1490. NARA, Washington D.C. Online at Ancestry.com.

United States Department of War. Carded Records Showing Military Service of Soldiers Who Fought in Volunteer Organizations During the Philippine Insurrection, 1899–1927. Record Group 94: Records of the Adjutant General's Office, 1780s–1917. NARA, Washington, D. C.

———. Compiled Service Records of Confederate General and Staff Officers. Record Group 109: War Department Collection of Confederate Records, Microfilm Publication M331. NARA, Washington, D. C. Online at Fold3.com.

———. Compiled Service Records of Confederate Soldiers Who Served in Organizations from the State of Texas. Record Group 109: War Department Collection of Confederate Records, Microfilm Publication M323. National Archives and Records Service, Washington, D. C. Material accessed at the Historical Research Center, Texas Heritage Museum, Hill College, Hillsboro, Texas.

———. Letters Received by the Office of the Adjutant General, 1805–1889. Record Group 94: Records of the Adjutant General's Office, 1780s–1917, Microfilm Publication M666. NARA, Washington, D. C. Online at Fold3.com.

———. Organization Index to Pension Files of Veterans Who Served Between 1861 and 1900, T289. Record Group 15: Records of the Department of Veterans Affairs, 1773–2007. NARA, Washington, D. C. Online at Fold3.com.

———. Returns from U.S. Military Posts, 1800–1916. Record Group 94: Records of the Adjutant General's Office, 1780's–1917, Microfilm Publication M617. NARA, Washington, D.C. Online at Ancestry.com.

———. Unfiled Papers and Slips Belonging in Confederate Compiled Service Records. Record Group 109: War Department Collection of Confederate Records, Microfilm Publication M347. NARA, Washington, D. C. Online at Fold3.com.

United States District Court for Western District of Arkansas, Fort Smith Division. Defendant Jacket Files. Record Group 21: Records of District Courts of the United States. NARA, Fort Worth, Texas. Online at Ancestry.com.

United States Post Office Department. Record of Appointment of Postmaster, 1832–1971. Record Group 28: Records of the Post Office Department, Microfilm Publication M841. NARA, Washington, D.C. Online at Ancestry.com.

Vertical Files. Armstrong Texas Ranger Research Center. TRHF&M, Waco, Texas.

W. A. Dunklin & Co. v. W. J. McDonald, et al. Case File M7747, Box 201–4242. Texas Supreme Court Records. A&ISD-TSLAC, Austin, Texas.

Wharton, Edward Clifton, Papers. Louisiana and Lower Mississippi Valley Collections. Hill Memorial Library, Louisiana State University, Baton Rouge, Louisiana.

Wickham, Hannah. Scrapbook Collection. Mrs. Wickham assembled nineteen notebooks filled with newspaper clippings of occurrences and individuals in Linn County, Kansas. She collected these articles from various newspapers for fifty years before her death in 1935. The originals are housed in the archives of the Sommerville Free Library in Mound City, Kansas, photocopies are stored at the Linn County Historical Museum & Genealogy Library.

Articles

Adair, W. S. "Rangers 40 Years Ago Had No Easy Life." *Frontier Times* 4, no. 11 (August 1927).

Allen, Stacy D. "Shiloh! The Campaign and First Day's Battle." *Blue and Gray Magazine* 14, no. 3 (February 1997).

———. "Shiloh! The Second Day's Battle and Aftermath." *Blue and Gray Magazine* 14, no. 4 (April 1997).
Astoria, Bill. "Fighting Lee Hall." *The Junior Historian* 8, no. 6 (May 1948).
Aten, Ira. "Capt. Ira Aten's 'Round Robin'." *Frontier Times* 21, no. 2 (November 1943).
———. "Captain Ira Aten's Unique Letter." *Frontier Times* 19, no. 7 (April 1942).
———. "Crossing High Water in a Wagon." *Frontier Times* 18, no. 18 (May 1941).
———. "Fence-Cutting Days in Texas." *Frontier Times* 16, no. 10 (July 1939).
———. "The Jaybird and Woodpecker War." *Frontier Times* 16, no. 7 (April 1939).
———. "Six and One-Half Years in the Ranger Service: Memoirs of Ira Aten, Sergeant Co. D, Texas Rangers." Four parts. *Frontier Times* 22, no. 4 (January 1945), no. 5 (February 1945), no. 6 (March 1945), no. 7 (April 1945).
"A Texas Cattle Raid." *Harper's Weekly* 18, no. 892 (January 31, 1874).
"Authentic History of Sam Bass and His Gang, by a Citizen of Denton County." Three parts. *Frontier Times* 3, no. 5 (February 1926), no. 6 (March 1926), no. 7 (April 1926).
Baenziger, Ann Patton. "The Texas State Police During Reconstruction: A Reexamination." *SHQ* 72, no. 4 (April 1969).
Bagley, Joan. "James B. Gillett, The Man." *The Junior Historian* 14, no. 6 (May 1969).
Bailey, Anne J. "Henry McCulloch's Texans and the Defense of Arkansas in 1862." *AHQ* 46, no. 1 (Spring 1987).
Barr, Alwyn. "Confederate Artillery in Western Louisiana, 1862–1863." *Civil War History* 9, no. 1 (March 1963).
———, editor. "The Battle of Bayou Bourbeau, November 3, 1863: Colonel Oran M. Roberts' Report." *Louisiana History* 6, no. 1 (Winter 1965).
"The Battle of Yellow Bayou." *CV* 25, no. 2 (February 1917).
Baulch, Joe R. "Little Tammany." *South Texas Studies* 7 (Spring 1996).
———. "The Murder of Stanley Welch and the 1906 Starr County Election." *Journal of South Texas* 4, no. 1 (Spring 1991).
Baylor, George Wythe. "Sentiment, By a Confederate." *CV* 6, no. 11 (December 1898).
———. "The Last Fight on Texas Soil Between the Apaches and the Texas Rangers." *A History of the Texas Rangers' Association* 5 (December 1905).

———. "With Gen. A. S. Johnston at Shiloh." *CV* 5, no. 12 (December 1897).
Baylor, Walker Keith. "The Paint Creek Fight." *Frontier Times* 2, no. 7 (April 1925).
Bearss, Edwin C. "The Battle of the Post of Arkansas." *AHQ* 18, no. 3 (Autumn 1959).
Bennett, Joseph E. "Chronicler of the Texas Rangers." *Royal Arch Mason* (Summer 1990).
———. "John B. Jones, Masonic Texas Ranger." *The New Age* 97, no. 2 (February 1989).
Bishop, S. W. "The Battle of Arkansas Post." *CV* 5, no. 4 (April 1897).
Blackwell, Pat. "Judge Henry Clay Pleasants." *The Junior Historian* 16, no. 6 (May 1956).
Bloom, Sam. "The Christmas that Became a Nightmare." *The West* 16, no. 6 (January 1973).
Boardman, Mark. "Irate Ira Nails the McClellands." *True West* 56, no. 7 (July 2009).
Bogener, Steve. "The World Heavyweight Boxing Championship Bout, 1896, at Langtry, Texas." *WTHAY* 74 (1998).
Bolon, R. "McNelly's Raiding Rangers." *Big West* 1, no. 2 (October 1967).
Bonnet, Judge W. A. "King Fisher, A Noted Character." *Frontier Times* 3, no. 10 (July 1926).
Bourne, Edward. "Govan's Brigade at New Hope Church." *CV* 31, no. 3 (March 1923).
Buck, Irving A. "Cleburne and His Division at Missionary Ridge and Ringgold Gap." *Southern Historical Society Papers* 8, nos. 10–12 (October-December 1880).
Burruss, R. S. "Dick." "History of William Tell Lodge No. 27." *Chronicles of Smith County* 6, no. 2 (Fall 1967).
Burton, Morris S. "The Court Houses of Smith County." *Chronicles of Smith County* 3, no. 2 (Fall 1964).
Bushick, Frank H. "Some Old Texas Ranger Captains." *Frontier Times* 18, no. 8 (May 1941).
"Capt. John W. Dunnington." *CV* 4, no. 3 (March 1896).
"Captain Hughes, of the Texas Rangers." Frontier Times 5, no. 1 (October 1927).
"Capture of the Post of Arkansas." *Harper's Weekly* 7, no. 1840 (February 7, 1863).
Caraway, I. V. "The Battle of Arkansas Post." *CV* 14, no. 3 (March 1906).
Carnal, Ed. "Reminiscences of a Texas Ranger." *Frontier Times* 1, no. 3 (December 1923).

Carnes, W. W. "Chickamauga." *Southern Historical Society Papers* 14 (January-December 1886).
Chastaine, Captain Ben H. "Macabebes." *Infantry Journal* 36, no. 6 (June 1930).
Clarke, Fannie McAlpine. "A Chapter in the History of Young Territory." *SHQ* 9, no. 1 (July 1905).
Coalson, George O. "The Building of the Railroad to Brownsville." *South Texas Studies* 1 (1990).
"Colonel G. W. Baylor's Sword." *CV* 14, no. 6 (June 1906).
Comtois, Pierre. "Collision at Sabine Crossroads." *Military History* 14, no. 4 (October 1997).
Cool, Paul. "New Mexico's Rustler King." *Wild West* 26, no. 6 (April 2014).
Crimmins, Colonel Martin L. "Captain Jim Gillett." *Frontier Times* 21, no. 1 (October 1943).
———. "Lee Hall Gets His Men." *Frontier Times* 18, no. 12 (September 1941).
———. "The Salt War of San Elizario, Texas." *Frontier Times* 8, no. 7 (April 1931).
Cumberland, Charles C. "The Confederate Loss and Recapture of Galveston, 1862–1863." *SHQ* 51, no. 2 (October 1947).
Cunningham, Eugene. "The Fightin'est Ranger." *Old West* 15, no. 1 (Fall 1978).
———. "Sam Bass." *Frontier Times* 4, no. 8 (May 1927).
Cuthbertson, Gilbert M. "Catarino E. Garza and the Garza War." *Texana* 12, no. 4 (1974).
———. "The Jaybird-Woodpecker War." *Texana* 10, no. 4 (1972).
Da Costa, Jacob Mendes. "On Irritable Heart: A Clinical Study of a Form of Functional Cardiac Disorder and Its Consequences." *American Journal of the Medical Sciences* 61 (January 1871).
Davidge, Sarah Ellen. "Texas Rangers Were Rough and Ready Fighters." *Frontier Times* 13, no. 2 (November 1935).
Delaney, Norman C. editor. "The Diary and Memoirs of Marshall Samuel Pierson, Company C, 17th Reg., Texas Cavalry, 1862–1865." *Military History of Texas and the Southwest* 13, no. 3 (1976).
Denman, Clarence P. "The Office of Adjutant General in Texas, 1835–1881." *SHQ* 28, no. 4 (April 1925).
"Dick Duncan's Doom." *Frontier Times* 23, no. 6 (March 1946).
Dobie, J. Frank. "The Robinhooding of Sam Bass." *MMWH* 5, no. 4 (Autumn 1955).
Durham, George, as told to Clyde Wantland. "On the Trail of 5100 Outlaws." Seven parts. *West* 39, no. 2 (October 1934), no. 3 (November 1934), no. 4

(December 1934), no. 5 (January 1935), no. 6 (February 1935); 40, no. 1 (March 1935), no. 2 (April 1935).

Eaton, W. Clement. "Frontier Life in Southern Arizona." *SHQ* 34, no. 3 (January 1933).

Edwards, Harold L. "Trouble in Socorro." *Old West* 27, no. 2 (Winter 1990).

Erath, Lucy A., ed., "Memoirs of Major George Bernard Erath." Part Four. *SHQ* 27, no. 2 (October 1923).

Faulkner, Walter A., editor. "With Sibley in New Mexico: The Journal of William Henry Smith." *WTHAY* 27 (October 1951).

Fenton, James. "Tom Ross: Ranger Nemesis." *National Association for Outlaw and Lawmen History Quarterly* 14 (Summer 1990).

Ferguson, Henry N. "Zane Grey's Original 'Lone Star Ranger'." *Old West* 14, no. 3 (Spring 1978).

Field, William T, Jr. "The Texas State Police, 1870–1873." *Texas Military History* 5, no. 3 (Fall 1965).

Finch, L. Boyd. "Surprise at Brashear City: Sherod Hunter's Sugar Cooler Cavalry." *Louisiana History* 25, no. 4 (Autumn 1984).

Fitterer, Gary P. "Let Justice Be Done Our Western Citizens." *Newsletter of the National Outlaw and Lawman Association* 16, no. 3 (July, September 1992).

Fitzhugh, Lester N. "Texas Forces in the Red River Campaign." *Texas Military History* 3, no. 1 (Spring 1963).

Fontaine, S. T. "Battle of Galveston—The Harriet Lane." *CV* 18, no. 1 (January 1910).

Ford, Sarah A. M. "Suffering in Silence: Post-Traumatic Stress Psychological Disorders and Soldiers in the American Civil War." *Journal of Civil War Medicine* 18, no. 2 (April-June 2014). Reprinted from *Armstrong Undergraduate Journal of History* 3, no. 2 (April 2013).

Frazier, Donald S. "Sibley's Texans and the Battle of Galveston." *SHQ* 99, no. 2 (October 1995).

———. "Texans on the Teche: The Texas Brigade at the Battles of Bisland and Irish Bend, April 12–14, 1863." *Louisiana History* 32, no. 4 (Autumn 1991).

Furse, P. J. "Tyler's Distinguished Families Part I: The Marsh Family." *Tyler Today Magazine* (Fall 1993).

Gard, Wayne. "The Fence-Cutters." *SHQ* 51, no. 1 (July 1947).

Garland, R. R. "Arkansas Post—Its Fall, January 11, 1863." *Southern Historical Society Papers* 22 (January-December 1894).

Gibson, W. W. "Reminisces of Ringgold Gap." *CV* 12, no. 11 (November 1904).

Gillett, James B. "An Early Day Sheriff's Experience." *Frontier Times* 1, no. 5 (February 1924).

———. "The Old G4 Ranch." *Voice of the Mexican Border* 1, no. 2 (October 1933).

———. "The Killing of Dallas Stoudenmire." *Frontier Times* 1, no. 10 (July 1924)

———. "The Killing of Sam Bass." *Frontier Times* 1, no. 5 (February 1924).

Gillespie, Thomas P. "Fight on the Concho Plains." *True West* 10, no. 5 (May/June 1963).

Godbold, Mollie Moore. "Comanche and the Hardin Gang." *SHQ* 67, no. 1 (July 1963), no. 2 (October 1963).

Goldblatt, Kenneth A. "George Wythe Baylor in West Texas, 1848–1865." *WTHAY* 44 (1968).

Gray, George W. "Quick on the Draw!" *The American Magazine* 104, no. 4 (October 1927).

"The Great South, The New Route to the Gulf." *Scribner's Monthly* 6, no. 3 (July 1873).

Green, Thomas. "Battle of Atchafalaya River—Letter from General Thomas Green." Edited by V. O. King. *Southern Historical Society Papers* 3, no. 2 (February 1877).

———. "Green to My Dear Wife, October 1, 1863." *Southern Historical Society Papers* 3, no. 2 (February 1877).

Green, William M. "Origin of the Ex-Texas Ranger Association." *Frontier Times* 1, no. 5 (February 1924).

Haas, Bonnie, and Joyce J. Bender. "Major Andrew Drumm: Cowman, Businessman, and Visionary." *Chronicles of Oklahoma* 79, no. 1 (Spring 2001).

Hager, William M. "The Nuecestown Raid of 1875: A Border Incident." *Arizona and the West* 1, no. 3 (Autumn 1959).

Haley, J. Evetts. "Charles Goodnight's Indian Recollections." *Panhandle-Plains Review* 1, no. 1 (1928).

Hall, Martin Hardwick. "Captain George M. Frazer's Arizona Rangers, C.S.A." *Password* 19, no. 2 (Summer 1974).

———. "The Skirmish at Mesilla." *Arizona and the West* 1, no. 4 (Winter 1959).

Hancock, William Cx. "Ranger's Ranger." *True West* 8, no. 4 (March-April 1961).

Hastedt, Karl G. "White Brothers of Texas Had Notable FBI Careers." *The Grapevine* (February 1960). A copy of the article was provided to the author by retired FBI Special Agent Larry Wack. Mr. Wack is the owner/editor of the fascinating website *Faded Glory: Dusty Roads of an FBI Era* (historicalgmen.squarespace.com).

Hatley, Allen G. "Crime and Violence Made Texas a Dangerous Place to Live After the Civil War." *Wild West* 17, no. 3 (October 2004).

———. "The Mason County War: Top Texas Feud." *Wild West* 18, no. 2 (August 2005).

———. "Ira Aten, Last of the 'Old Texas Rangers'." *Western Outlaw-Lawman History Association Journal* 14, no. 4 (Winter 2005).

Hatton, Roy O. "Prince Camille de Polignac and the American Civil War, 1863–1865." *Louisiana Studies* 3, no. 2 (Summer 1964).

Havens, Paul. "Border Boss: The Saga of Captain John R. Hughes, Texas Ranger." Four parts. *True Detective Mysteries* 34, no. 3 (June 1940), no. 4 (July 1940), no.5 (August 1940), no. 6 (September 1940).

Holden, William Curry. "Law and Lawlessness on the Texas Frontier, 1875–1890." *SHQ* 44, no. 2 (October 1940).

Holt, R. D. "The Introduction of Barbed Wire into Texas and the Fence Cutting War." *WTHAY* 6 (1930).

———. "Pioneer Cowman of Brewster County and the Big Bend Area." *The Cattleman* 29, no. 1 (June 1942).

Howland, Charles R. "The Philippine Expedition of 1899." *Infantry Journal* 30, no. 4 (April 1927).

Hunter, J. Marvin. "The Famous Dick Duncan Murder Case." *Frontier Times* 16, no. 5 (February 1939).

———. "Incident of Capt. Bill McDonald." *Frontier Times* 2, no. 11 (August 1925).

———. "The Killing of Captain Frank Jones," *Frontier Times* 6, no. 4 (January 1929).

———. "The Outstanding Texas Ranger." *Frontier Times* 22, no. 3 (December 1944).

———. "The Passing of Capt. John H. Hughes." *Frontier Times* 24, no 9 (June 1947).

Jameson, W. C. "Incident at Pirate Island." *True West* 35, no. 11 (November 1988).

———. "Last Stand of the Mescalero Apaches." *True West* 38, no. 12 (December 1991).

Johnson, David. "Scott Cooley—A Byword for Terror." *NOLA Quarterly* 27, no. 2 (April-June 2003).

Joiner, Gary D. "To Defend the Sacred Soil of Texas: Tom Green and the Texas Cavalry in the Red River Campaign." *ETHJ* 46, no. 1 (March 2008).

———. "Up the Red River and Down to Defeat." *America's Civil War* 17, no. 1 (March 2004).
Jones, Calico. "Guns at the Ready." *True Frontier* 4, no. 4 (July 1971).
Kildare, Maurice. "McNelly's Texas Blood Bath." *Westerner* 2, no. 7 (November 1970).
King, Dick. "'Rascals' and Rangers." *True West* 22, no. 4 (April 1975).
Kliger, Paul I. "The Confederate Invasion of New Mexico." *Blue and Gray Magazine* 11, no. 5 (June 1994).
Klos, George. "'Our People Could Not Distinguish One Tribe from Another': The 1859 Expulsion of the Reserve Indians from Texas." *SHQ* 97, no. 4 (April 1994).
Kreiser, Christine M. "Showdown in New Mexico." *America's Civil War* 25, no. 6 (January 2013).
Lake, Stuart N. "Brush Poppers." *The Saturday Evening Post* 203, no. 41 (April 11, 1931).
Lamkin, Patricia E. "Blacks in San Angelo: Relations Between Fort Concho and the City, 1875–1889." *WTHAY* 66 (1990).
Laurie, Karen Pillmore. "History of Vermejo Park." *New Mexico Genealogical Society Guidebook, 27th Field Conference*. Vermejo Park: 1976.
Leath, Andrew L. "Elected County Officials, 1846–76." *Chronicles of Smith County* 17, no. 1 (Summer 1978).
McCallum, Henry D. "Barbed Wire in Texas." *SHQ* 61, no. 2 (October 1957).
McMurry, Robert M. "'The Hell Hole': New Hope Church." *CWTI* 11, no. 10 (February 1973).
"Many Brilliant Exploits Manifest Courage of Captain Rogers." *Sheriff's Association of Texas Magazine* 1, no. 12 (March 1931).
"Marriages of St. David's Episcopal Church, Austin, Texas." *Austin Genealogical Society Quarterly* 2, no. 2 (May 1961).
Marsh, Bryan. "The Confederate Letters of Bryan Marsh." *Chronicles of Smith County* 14, no. 2 (Winter 1975).
"The Marsh House." *Chronicles of Smith County* 3, no. 1 (Spring 1964).
Matthews, James. "Frontier Commanders in Grey: George Baylor, Alonzo Ridley, and George Madison." *WTHAY* 73 (1997).
Mayo, Earl. "The Texas Rangers: The Most Efficient Police Force in the World." *Frank Leslie's Popular Monthly* 52, no. 6 (October 1901).
Meiners, Fredericka. "Hamilton Bee in the Red River Campaign of 1864." *SHQ* 78, no. 1 (July 1974).
Mendall, Ann. "The Texas Rangers." *Great West* 3, no. 3 (July 1969).

Mertz, Richard J. "'No One Can Arrest Me': The Story of Gregorio Cortez." *Journal of South Texas* 1 (1974).
Metz, Leon. "An Incident at Christmas." *NOLA Quarterly* 14, no. 1 (1990).
———. "Borderlands." *True West* 47, no. 9 (September 2000)
———, and Kenneth Goldblatt. "Murdered in Church." *Frontier Times* 43, no. 6 (October-November 1969).
Michot, Stephen S. "In Relief of Port Hudson: Richard Taylor's 1863 Lafourche Offensive." *Military History of the West* 23, no. 2 (Fall 1993).
Milbourn, Curtis W. "Brigadier General Thomas Green of Texas." *ETHJ* 32, no. 1 (March 1994).
———. "Fighting for Time." *North and South* 5, no. 4 (May 2002).
———. "'I Have Been Worse Treated than Any Officer': Confederate Colonel Thomas Green's Assessment of the New Mexico Campaign." *SHQ* 105, no. 2 (October 2001).
———. "The Lafourche Offensive: Richard Taylor's Attempt to Relieve Port Hudson." *North and South* 7, no. 5 (August 2004).
———, and Steve Bounds. "The Battle of Mansfield." *North and South* 6, no. 2 (February 2003).
———. "The Battle of Pleasant Hill." *North and South* 8, no. 6 (November 2005).
Miles, Susan. "The Soldiers' Riot." *Fort Concho Report* 13, no. 1 (Spring 1981).
Million, Elmer M. "History of the Texas Prize Fight Statute." *Texas Law Review* 17, no. 2 (February 1939).
Milton, Keith. "Whistlin' Extradition." *True West* 39, no. 5 (May 1992).
Molen, Daye H. "Decision at La Glorieta Pass." *MMWH* 12, no. 2 (Spring 1962).
Morris, Leopold. "The Mexican Raid of 1875 on Corpus Christi." *SHQ* 4, no. 2 (October 1900).
Mullin, Robert N. "Here Lies John Kinney." *Journal of Arizona History* 14, no. 3 (Autumn 1973).
Munro, Captain J. N. "The Philippine Native Scouts." *Journal of the United States Infantry Association* 2, no. 1 (July 1, 1905).
"Muster Roll of McNelly's Scouts." *Austin Genealogical Society Quarterly* 30, no. 3 (September 1989).
O'Connor, Derek. "Flying Against the Bolsheviks." *Aviation History* 18, no. 1 (September 2007).
"Of a Noted Military Family." *CV* 6, no. 4 (April 1898).
Ogden, G. W. "The Watch on the Rio Grande." *Everybody's Magazine* 25, no. 3 (September 1911).

O'Neal, Bill, editor. "The Civil War Memoirs of Samuel Alonza Cooke." *SHQ* 74, no. 4 (April 1971).
Parsons, Chuck. "Bill Sutton Avenged: The Death of Jim Taylor." *NOLA Quarterly* 4, no. 3 (1979).
———, editor. "The Memoirs of William Callicott, Texas Ranger." Four parts. *The Texas Ranger Dispatch* 3 (Spring 2001); 4 (Summer 2001); 5 (Fall 2001); 6 (Spring 2002). Online at www.texasranger.org.
Paul, Lee. "Death Faced Straight Up." *Wild West* 6, no. 2 (August 1993).
Phillips, Edward H. "Teddy Roosevelt in Texas, 1905." *WTHAY* 56 (1980).
Ragan, Cooper K., editor. "The Diary of Captain George W. O'Brien, 1863." *SHQ* 67, no. 1 (July 1963), no. 2 (October 1963), no. 3 (January 1964).
"Rangers Meet at Menard." *Frontier Times* 1, no. 1 (October 1923).
Regan, Albert B. "A Comanche Raid in 1860." *Frontier Times* 9, no. 3 (December 1931).
Rippy, J. Fred. "Mexican Projects of the Confederates." *SHQ* 22, no. 4 (April 1919).
Roberts, Randy. "Galveston's Jack Johnson: Flourishing in the Dark." *SHQ* 87, no. 1 (July 1983).
Robertson, Walter. "The Loss [sic] Valley Fight, Reminiscences of Walter Robertson." *Frontier Times* 7, no. 3 (December 1929).
Robinson, Charles M., III. "The Tough Little Ranger of Lost Valley." *True West* 38, no. 8 (August 1991).
Rollins, Hyder. "O. Henry's Texas Days." *The Bookman: A Magazine of Literature and Life* 40, no. 2 (October 1941).
Roosevelt, Theodore. "A Wolf Hunt in Oklahoma." *Scribner's Magazine* 38, no. 5 (November 1905).
Rosenberg, David H. "Confederate Manifest Destiny in New Mexico." *America's Civil War* 13, no. 3 (July 2000).
Rudisill, Vivian Adams. "History of the Carey McNelly Wroe Chapter of the Children of the Confederacy." *Our Heritage* 34, no. 3 (Spring 1993).
Rudolph, Jack. "Battle in the Bayou." *CWTI* 23, no. 9 (January 1985).
Schneirov, Richard. "'From the Ragged Edge of Anarchy': The 1894 Pullman Boycott." *OAH Magazine of History* 13, no. 3 (Spring 1999).
Schubert, Frank N. "Gunfire at San Angela: When 10th Cavalry Troopers from Fort Concho Retaliated Against Texas Civilians." *Wild West* 16, no. 5 (February 2004).
Schuster, Stephen W. "The Modernization of the Texas Rangers: 1933–1936." *WTHAY* 43 (1967).
Secrist, Philip L. "Scenes of Awful Carnage." *CWTI* 10, no. 3 (June 1971).

Shea, William L. "The Confederate Defeat at Cache River." *AHQ* 52, no. 2 (Summer 1993).
Shelton, Major Horace H. "Texas Confederate Generals: General William Steele, West Pointer, Indian Fighter, Mexican War Hero, Confederate Leader, Re-Organizer of the Texas Rangers and Restorer of Law and Order in Texas After Reconstruction Days." *Under Texas Skies* 3, no. 4 (August 1952).
Sheridan, Richard C. "Brigadier General James Deshler, Professional Soldier." *Alabama Historical Quarterly* 24, no. 2 (Summer 1964).
Singletary, Otis A. "The Texas Militia During Reconstruction." *SHQ* 60, no. 1 (July 1956).
Smith, Michael M. "General Rafael Benavides and the Texas Border Crisis of 1877." *SHQ* 113, no. 3 (January 2009).
Smith, Rebecca W., and Marion Mullins, editors. "The Diary of H. C. Medford, Confederate Soldier, 1864." Two parts. *SHQ* 34, no. 2 (October 1930), no. 3 (January 1931).
"Stage Hold-Up at Pegleg in 1877." *Frontier Times* 4, no. 5 (February 1927).
Stanley, Samuel. "The Fence Cutters' War." *Real West* 28, no. 204 (August 1985).
Stein, Bill. "Consider the Lily: The Ungilded History of Colorado County, Texas." *Nesbitt Memorial Library Journal* 10, no. 1 (January 2000).
Stillwell, Hart. "Dinamite Aten and His Big Boom." *True Western Adventures*, no. 10 (October 1959).
"Story of the Harriet Lane." *CV* 17, no. 10 (October 1909).
Symonds, Craig L. "Stonewall of the West: Patrick Cleburne and the Defense of Tunnel Hill." *Civil War Regiments: A Journal of the American Civil War* 7, no. 1 (2000).
Tate, Michael L., editor. "A Johnny Reb in Sibley's New Mexico Campaign: Reminiscences of Pvt. Henry C. Wright, 1861–1862." Three parts. *ETHJ* 25, no. 2 (October 1987); 26, no. 1 (March 1988), no. 2 (October 1988).
Taylor, Ethel. "Discontent in Confederate Louisiana." *Louisiana History* 2, no. 4 (Autumn 1961).
Taylor, Paul S. "Historical Note on Dimmit County, Texas." *SHQ* 34, no. 2 (October 1930).
Taylor, Richard. "The Last Confederate Surrender." *Southern Historical Society Papers* 3, no. 3 (March 1877).
"The Texas Rangers Brought Law and Order." *Frontier Times* 12, no. 10 (July 1935).
Train, Arthur. "The Fall of Hummel." *Cosmopolitan Magazine* 44, no. 6 (May 1908); 45, no. 1 (June 1908).

"Unpublished After-Action Reports from the Red River Campaign." *Civil War Regiments: A Journal of the American Civil War* 4, no. 2 (1994).

Utley, Robert M. "The Range Cattle Industry in the Big Bend of Texas." *SHQ* 69, no. 4 (April 1966).

Van Demark, Harry. "Religion and Bullets: Two Factors Which Have Figured Prominently in the Making of a Famous Texas Ranger." *Texas Monthly* 3, no. 2 (March 1929).

Vladeck, Stephen L. "Enemy Aliens, Enemy Property, and Access to the Courts." *Lewis and Clark Law Review* 11, no. 4 (Winter 2007).

Walker, Wayne T. "Jim Gillett—Ranger Diablo." *Real West* 23, no. 170 (June 1980).

———. "Jim Gillett, 'Sergeant Diablo' of the Texas Rangers." *Oldtimers Wild West*, no. 1, February 1978.

———. "Major John B. Jones—Ranger Who Tamed the West." *Real West* 24, no. 176 (April 1981).

Waller, John L. "Colonel George Wythe Baylor." *Southwestern Social Science Quarterly* 34, no. 1 (June 1943).

Watford, W. H. "Confederate Western Ambitions." *SHQ* 44, no. 2 (October 1940).

———. "The Far-Flung Wing of the Rebellion, 1861–1865." *California Historical Society Quarterly* 34, no. 2 (June 1955).

Webb, Walter Prescott. "The Bandits of Las Cuevas." *True West* 10, no. 1 (September-October 1962).

———. "The Fence-Cutters." *True West* 10, no. 5 (May-June 1963).

———. "McNelly's Rangers." *True West* 9, no. 3 (January-February 1962).

Weedle, Robert S. "The Pegleg Stage Robbers." *Southwest Heritage* 4, no. 1 (March 1969).

Weiss, Harold J., Jr. "The Texas Rangers and Captain Bill McDonald in General—And the Conditt Murder Case in Particular." *South Texas Studies* 9 (1998).

Wheeler, T. B. "Reminiscences of Reconstruction in Texas." *SHQ* 11, no. 1 (July 1907).

Whitehead, Ruth. "That Bloody Fence-Cutting War." *The West* 17, no. 4 (November 1973).

Whitley, W. H. "Hopewell Presbyterian Church: Bourbon County, Kentucky." *Register of the Kentucky Historical Society* 28, no. 85 (October 1930).

Whittington, Mike. "Hughes and Aten Solve the Williamson Family Murders." *Texas Ranger Dispatch* 12 (Winter 2003). Online at www.texasranger.org.

———. "Six Telegrams That Tell the Story: The Arrest of John Wesley Hardin." *Texas Ranger Dispatch* 3 (Spring 2001). Online at www.texasranger.org.

Williams, Edward B., editor. "A 'Spirited Account' of the Battle of Galveston, January 1, 1863." *SHQ* 99, no. 2 (October 1995).

"Wife of Col. G. W. Baylor." *CV* 13, no. 4 (April 1905).

Winkler, Ernest William, editor. "The Bryan-Hayes Correspondence." Part Eleven. *SHQ* 27, no. 4 (April 1924).

Wise, Joe R, editor. "Letters of Lt. Flavius W. Perry, 17th Texas Cavalry—1862–1863." *Military History of Texas and the Southwest* 13, no. 2 (1976).

Wise, Judge Ken. "The Trial of John Wesley Hardin." *Texas Bar Journal* 75, no. 3 (March 2012).

Wooster, Ralph A. "Wealthy Texans, 1870." *SHQ* 74, no. 1 (July 1970).

Young, Richard. "The Brownsville Affray." *American History Illustrated* 21, no. 6 (October 1986).

Books

11 *Southwestern Reporter* (April 1–August 19, 1889). St. Paul: West Publishing Company, 1889.

79 *Southwestern Reporter* (March 30–April 27, 1904). St. Paul: West Publishing Company, 1904.

99 *Southwestern Reporter* (February 13–March 27, 1907). St. Paul: West Publishing Company, 1907.

110 *Southwestern Reporter* (June 10–July 1, 1908). St. Paul: West Publishing Company, 1908.

Adams, Mary Lizzie Hall. *The Hall Family History*. Statesville, NC: n.p., 1949.

Adams, Michael C. C. *Living Hell: The Dark Side of the Civil War*. Baltimore: Johns Hopkins University Press, 2014.

Alexander, Bob. *Bad Company and Burnt Powder: Justice and Injustice in the Old Southwest*. Denton: University of North Texas Press, 2014.

———. *Desert Desperadoes: The Banditti of Southwestern New Mexico*. Silver City, NM: Gila Books, 2006.

———. *Lawmen, Outlaws, and S.O.Bs: Gunfighters of the Old Southwest*. Two volumes. Silver City, NM: High-Lonesome Books, 2004–2007.

———. *Rawhide Ranger, Ira Aten: Enforcing Law on the Texas Frontier*. Denton: University of North Texas Press, 2011.

———. *Riding Lucifer's Line: Ranger Deaths along the Texas-Mexico Border*. Denton: University of North Texas Press, 2013.

———. *Six-Shooters and Shifting Sands: The Wild West Life of Texas Ranger Captain Frank Jones*. Denton: University of North Texas Press, 2015.

———. *Whiskey River Ranger: The Old West Life of Baz Outlaw*. Denton: University of North Texas Press, 2016.

———. *Winchester Warriors: Texas Rangers of Company D, 1874–1901*. Denton: University of North Texas Press, 2009.

———, and Donaly E. Brice. *Texas Rangers: Lives, Legend, and Legacy*. Denton: University of North Texas Press, 2017.

Allardice, Bruce S. *Confederate Colonels: A Biographical Register*. Columbia: University of Missouri Press, 2008.

———. *More Generals in Gray*. Baton Rouge: Louisiana State University Press, 1995.

Allhands, J. L. *Railroads to the Rio*. Salado, TX: Anson Jones Press, 1960.

Allmendinger, Blake. *The Cowboy: Representations of Labor in an American Culture*. New York: Oxford University Press, 1992.

Alumni Directory of Yale University [Graduates and Non-Graduates]. New Haven: Yale University, 1920.

Amberson, Mary Margaret McAllen, et al. *I Would Rather Sleep in Texas: A History of the Lower Rio Grande Valley and the People of the Santa Anita Land Grant*. Austin: Texas State Historical Association, 2003.

Ancell, R. Manning, with Christine M. Miller. *The Biographical Dictionary of World War II Generals and Flag Officers*. Westport, CT: Greenwood Press, 1996.

Anders, Evan. *Boss Rule in South Texas: The Progressive Era*. Austin: University of Texas Press, 1982.

Annual Catalogue of the Medical Institute of Louisville, Session 1841–42. Louisville, KY: Prentice and Weissinger, 1842.

A Proud Heritage: A History of Uvalde County, Texas. Uvalde, TX: El Progresso Club, 1975.

Atkins, Johnathan M. *Parties, Politics, and the Sectional Conflict in Tennessee, 1832–1861*. Knoxville: University of Tennessee Press, 1997.

Austerman, Wayne R. *Sharps Rifles and Spanish Mules: The San Antonio–El Paso Mail, 1851–1881*. College Station: Texas A&M University Press, 1985.

Avis, Annie Maud Knittel, editor. *History of Burton*. Burton: n.p., 1974.

The Badger. Volume Forty-six. Madison: University of Wisconsin, 1931.

Ball, Larry D. *Desert Lawmen: The High Sheriffs of New Mexico and Arizona, 1846–1912*. Albuquerque: University of New Mexico Press, 1992.

———. *The United States Marshals of New Mexico and Arizona Territories, 1846–1912*. Albuquerque: University of New Mexico Press, 1978.

Barefield, Marilyn Davis. *Clarke County, Alabama, Records: 1814–1885*. Easley, SC: Southern Historical Press, 1983.

Barr, Alwyn. *Polignac's Texas Brigade*. College Station: Texas A&M University Press, 1998.

———. *Reconstruction to Reform: Texas Politics, 1876–1906*. Austin: University of Texas Press, 1971; rpt. Dallas: Southern Methodist University Press, 2000.

Barry, James Buckner. *Buck Barry, Texas Ranger and Frontiersman*. Edited by James K. Greer. Waco: Friends of the Moody Texas Ranger Library, 1978; rpt. Lincoln: University of Nebraska Press, 1984.

Baylor, Edward R. *A Baylor Genealogy: The Tedious Family History of Some of the Baylors who Lived in the United States in 1989*. Woods Hole, MA: privately printed, 1989.

Baylor, George Wythe. *Into the Far, Wild Country: True Tales of the Old Southwest*. Edited by Jerry D. Thompson. El Paso: Texas Western Press, 1996. This book features a collection of articles Baylor wrote for the *El Paso Herald* from 1899 to 1906.

Baylor, Orval Walker, and Henry Bedinger Baylor. *Baylor's History of the Baylors: A Collection of Records and Important Family Data*. Le Roy, IN: Le Roy Journal Publishing Co., 1914.

Beede, Benjamin R., editor. *The War of 1898 and U.S. Interventions, 1898–1934: An Encyclopedia*. New York: Garland Publishing, 1994.

Biggers, Don H., compiler. *German Pioneers in Texas: A Brief History of their Hardships, Struggles and Accomplishments*. Fredericksburg, TX: Fredericksburg Publishing Company, 1925.

Birtle, Andrew J. *U.S. Army Counterinsurgency and Contigency Operations Doctrine, 1860–1941*. Washington, D.C.: U.S. Army Center of Military History, 2004.

Black, Samuel F. *San Diego and Imperial Counties, California: A Record of Settlement, Organization, Progress, and Achievement*. Chicago: S. J. Clarke Publishing Company, 1913.

Blackburn, Edward A., Jr. *Wanted: Historic County Jails of Texas*. College Station: Texas A&M University Press, 2006.

Blessington, Joseph Palmer. *The Campaigns of Walker's Texas Division*. New York: Lange, Little & Co., 1875.

Blount, James H. *The American Occupation of the Philippines, 1898–1912*. New York: G. P. Putnam's Sons, 1913.

Blyth, Lance R. *Chiricahua and Janos: Communities of Violence in the Southwestern Borderlands, 1680–1880*. Lincoln: University of Nebraska Press, 2012.

Boatner, Mark Mayo, III. *The Civil War Dictionary*. Revised Edition. New York: David McKay Company, 1988.

Boot, Max. *The Savage Wars of Peace: Small Wars and the Rise of American Power*. New York: Basic Books, 2002.

Borders, Gary B. *A Hanging in Nacogdoches: Murder, Race, Politics, and Polemics in Texas's Oldest Town, 1870–1916*. Austin: University of Texas Press, 2006.

Borneman, Walter R. *Iron Horses: America's Race to Bring the Railroads West*. New York: Back Bay Books, 2010.

Botson. Michael R., Jr. *Labor, Civil Rights, and the Hughes Tool Company*. College Station: Texas A&M University Press, 2005.

Bradley, Francis Wright. *A Brief History of the Mount Zion Society: Founded January 29, 1777*. Winnsboro, SC: The News and Herald, 1948.

Britton, John A. *Cables, Crises, and the Press: The Geopolitics of the New International Information System in the Americas, 1866–1903*. Albuquerque: University of New Mexico Press, 2013.

Brooksher, William Riley. *War Along the Bayous: The 1864 Red River Campaign in Louisiana*. Washington, D.C.: Brassey's, 1998.

Brown, John T. *Churches of Christ*. John P. Morton & Company, 1904.

Brown, Norman D., editor. *One of Cleburne's Command: The Civil War Reminiscences and Diary of Capt. Samuel T. Foster, Granbury's Texas Brigade, CSA*. Austin: University of Texas Press, 1980.

Brown, Robert Maxwell. *Strain of Violence: Historical Studies of American Violence and Vigilantism*. New York: Oxford University Press, 1975.

Browning, Robert M., Jr. *Lincoln's Trident: The West Gulf Blockading Squadron During the Civil War*. Tuscaloosa: University of Alabama Press, 2015.

Bryan, Jimmy L. *More Zeal Than Discretion: The Westward Adventures of Walter P. Lane*. College Station: Texas A&M University Press, 2008.

Buck, Irving A. *Cleburne and His Command*. New York: Neale Publishing Company, 1908.

Burdette, Robert J., editor. *American Biography and Genealogy: California Edition*. Volume Two. Chicago: Lewis Company, n.d.

Burkhalter, Lois Wood. *Gideon Lincecum, 1793–1874: A Biography*. Austin: University of Texas Press, 1965.

Burns, John F., and Richard J. Orsi, editors. *Taming the Elephant: Politics, Government, and Law in Pioneer California.* Berkeley: University of California, 2003.

Burton, Jeffrey. *Indian Territory and the United States, 1866–1906: Courts, Government, and the Movement for Oklahoma Statehood.* Norman: University of Oklahoma Press, 1995.

Busby, Mark. "An East Texas Lynching: The Humphries/Wilkinson-Greenhaw Feud." *Corners of Texas.* Edited by Francis Edward Abernathy. Denton: University of North Texas Press, 1993.

Caballero, Raymond. *Orozco: The Life and Death of a Mexican Revolutionary.* Norman: University of Oklahoma Press, 2017.

Caldwell, Clifford R. *A Day's Ride from Here: Mountain Home, Texas.* Charleston, SC: History Press, 2011.

———, and Ron DeLord. *Eternity at the End of a Rope: Executions, Lynchings and Vigilante Justice in Texas, 1819–1923.* Santa Fe: Sunstone Press, 2015.

———. *Texas Lawmen, 1835–1899: The Good and the Bad.* Charleston, SC: History Press, 2011.

———. *Texas Lawmen, 1900–1940: More of the Good & the Bad.* Charleston, SC: History Press, 2012.

Calhoun, Frederick S. *The Lawmen: United States Marshals and Their Deputies, 1789–1989.* Washington, D.C.: Smithsonian Institution Press, 1989.

Campbell, Randolph B. *Gone to Texas: A History of the Lone Star State.* New York: Oxford University Press, 2003.

———. *Grass Roots Reconstruction in Texas, 1865–1880.* Baton Rouge: Louisiaina State University Press, 1997.

Caperton, Helena LeFroy. *The Social Record of Virginia.* Richmond: The Social Record of Virginia, 1937.

Cardwell, John. *Fifteenth Legislature: Sketches of Legislators and State Officers, 1876–1878.* Austin: Democratic Statesman Steam Print, 1876.

Carrigan, William D., and Clive Webb. *Forgotten Dead: Mob Violence against Mexicans in the United States, 1848–1928.* New York: Oxford University Press, 2013.

Cartwright, Gary. *Galveston: A History of the Island.* Fort Worth: Texas Christian University Press, 1991.

Cashion, Ty. *A Texas Frontier: The Clear Fork Country and Fort Griffin, 1849–1887.* Norman: University of Oklahoma Press, 1996.

Castel, Albert. *Decision in the West: The Atlanta Campaign of 1864.* Lawrence: University Press of Kansas, 1992.

Bibliography   **705**

Casto, Stanley D. *Settlement of the Cibolo-Nueces Strip: A Partial History of La Salle County*. Hillsboro, TX: Hill Junior College Press, 1969.
Castro County Historical Commission. *Castro County, Texas, 1891–1981*. Dallas: Taylor Publishing Company, 1981.
Catalogue of the Officers and Students of Transylvania University. Lexington, KY: n. p., January 1825.
Catalogue of the Officers and Students of Roanoke College. Twenty-third Session, 1875–76. Lynchburg, VA: Bell, Browne, & Co., 1876.
Catalogue of Richmond College. Session 1876–77. Richmond, OH: Clemitt & Jones, 1877.
Catton, Bruce. *Never Call Retreat*. Garden City, NY: Doubleday and Company, 1963; rpt. New York: Fall River Press, 2009.
——. *Terrible Swift Sword*. Garden City, NY: Doubleday and Company, 1963; rpt. New York: Fall River Press, 2009.
Chamberlain, Kathleen P. *Victorio: Apache Warrior and Chief*. Norman: University of Oklahoma Press, 2007.
Chernow, Ron. *Grant*. New York: Penguin Press, 2017.
Christ, Mark K. *Civil War Arkansas, 1863: The Battle for a State*. Norman: University of Oklahoma Press, 2010.
Christian, Garna L. *Black Soldiers in Jim Crow Texas, 1899–1917*. College Station: Texas A&M University Press, 1995.
City Directory, Tyler, Texas, 1904. Volume One. Little Rock, AR: Southern Directory Company, 1904.
Collins, Michael. *A Crooked River: Rustlers, Rangers, and Regulars on the Lower Rio Grande, 1861–1877*. Norman: University of Oklahoma Press, 2018.
Collins, Robert M. *Chapters from the Unwritten History of the War Between the States*. St. Louis, MO: Nixon-Jones Printing Company, 1893.
Combs, Joseph F. *Gunsmoke in the Redlands*. San Antonio: Naylor Company, 1968.
Comfort, Herbert G. *Where Rolls the Kern: A History of Kern County, California*. Moorpark, CA: The Enterprise Press, 1934.
Connelly, Thomas Lawrence. *Autumn of Glory: The Army of Tennessee, 1862–1865*. Baton Rouge: Louisiana State University Press, 1971; rpt. 2001.
Cool, Paul. *Salt Warriors: Insurgency on the Rio Grande*. College Station: Texas A&M University Press, 2008.
Coolidge, Dane. *Fighting Men of the West*. New York: E. P. Dutton & Co., 1932; rpt. New York: Bantam Books, 1952.

Cotham, Edward T., Jr. *Battle on the Bay: The Civil War Struggle for Galveston.* Austin: University of Texas Press, 1998.

Cotner, Robert C. *James Stephen Hogg: A Biography.* Austin: University of Texas Press, 1959.

Cox, Mike. *Gunfights and Sites in Texas Ranger History.* Charleston, SC: History Press, 2015.

———. *Texas Ranger Tales: Stories That Need Telling.* Plano: Republic of Texas Press, 1997.

———. *Texas Ranger Tales II.* Plano: Republic of Texas Press, 1999

———. *The Texas Rangers: Wearing the Cinco Peso, 1821–1900.* New York: Tom Doherty Associates, 2008.

———. *Time of the Rangers: From 1900 to the Present.* New York: Tom Doherty Books, 2009.

Cox, Ross J., Sr. *The Texas Rangers and the San Saba Mob.* Two volumes. San Saba, TX: C & S Farm Press, 2005.

Cozzens, Peter. *The Earth is Weeping: The Epic Story of the Indian Wars for the American West.* New York: Alfred A. Knopf, 2016.

———. *The Shipwreck of Their Hopes: The Battles for Chattanooga.* Urbana: University of Illinois Press, 1994.

———. *This Terrible Sound: The Battle of Chickamauga.* Urbana: University of Illinois Press, 1992.

———, editor. *Eyewitnesses to the Indian Wars, 1865–1890: The Struggle for Apacheria.* Mechanicsburg, PA: Stackpole Books, 2001.

———. *Battles and Leaders of the Civil War.* Volume Five. Urbana: University of Illinois Press, 2002.

Crofts, Daniel W. *Reluctant Confederates: Upper South Unionists in the Secession Crisis.* Chapel Hill: University of North Carolina Press, 1989.

Crouch, Barry A., and Donaly E. Brice. *The Governor's Hounds: The Texas State Police, 1870–1873.* Austin: University of Texas Press, 2011.

Cunningham, Eugene. *Triggernometry: A Gallery of Gunfighters.* Revised edition. Norman: University of Oklahoma Press, 1996.

Cunningham, O. Edward. *Shiloh and the Western Campaign of 1862.* Edited by Gary D. Joiner and Timothy B. Smith. New York: Savas Beatie, 2009.

Cutrer, Thomas W. *Empire of Sand: The Struggle for the Southwest, 1862.* Buffalo Gap, TX: State House Press, 2015.

———. *Theater of a Separate War: The Civil War West of the Mississippi River.* Chapel Hill: University of North Carolina Press, 2017.

Cypher, John. *Bob Kleberg and the King Ranch: A Worldwide Sea of Grass.* Austin: University of Texas Press, 1995.

Daniel, Larry J. *Shiloh: The Battle That Changed the Civil War.* New York: Simon & Schuster, 1997.
Daniell, L. E., compiler. *Personnel of the Texas State Government.* Austin: Press of the City Printing Company, 1887.
——. *Texas—The Country and Its Men.* Austin: L. E. Daniell, n.d.
Davis, Ellis A., and Edwin H. Grobe, compilers and editors. *The New Encyclopedia of Texas.* Volume Four. Dallas: Texas Development Bureau, 1929.
Davis, Richard Harding. *The West from a Car-Window.* New York: Harper & Brothers, 1892.
Davis, Stephen. *A Long and Bloody Task: The Atlanta Campaign from Dalton through Kennesaw to the Chattahoochee, May 5-June 18, 1864.* El Dorado Hills, CA: Savas Beatie, 2016.
DeArment, Robert K. *Deadly Dozen: Forgotten Gunfighters of the Old West.* Three volumes. Norman: University of Oklahoma Press, 2003–2010.
——. *Gunfighter in Gotham.* Norman: University of Oklahoma, 2013.
——. *Jim Courtwright of Fort Worth: His Life and Legend.* Fort Worth: Texas Christian University Press, 2004.
——. *Man-Hunters of the Old West.* Two volumes. Norman: University of Oklahoma Press, 2017–2018.
Decennial Register of the Texas Military Institute for 1868 to 1878. Baltimore: Steam Press of Globe Printing Company, 1878.
De La Garza, Beatriz. *A Law for the Lion: A Tale of Crime and Injustice in the Borderlands.* Austin: University of Texas Press, 2003.
De León, Arnoldo. *They Called Them Greasers: Anglo Attitudes Toward Mexicans in Texas, 1821–1900.* Austin: University of Texas Press, 1983.
Devine, Shauna. *Learning from the Wounded: The Civil War and the Rise of American Medical Science.* Chapel Hill: University of North Carolina Press, 2014.
DeVos, Julius E., et al. *The Anthology of the Hoo Doo War: The Participants in the Mason County Texas Cattle War, 1874–1877.* Mason, TX: Mason County Historical Commission, 2006.
Dewey, Alicia M. *Pesos and Dollars: Entrepreneurs in the Texas-Mexico Borderlands, 1880–1940.* College Station: Texas A&M University Press, 2014.
D'Hamel, Enrique B. *The Adventures of a Tenderfoot.* Waco: W. M. Morrison, 1914.
Díaz, George T. "Smugglers in Dangerous Times: Revolution and Communities in the Tejano Borderlands." *War Along the Border: The Mexican Revolution and Tejano Communities.* Edited by Arnoldo de León. College Station: Texas A&M University Press, 2012.

Dobie, J. Frank. *The Longhorns*. Boston: Little, Brown and Company, 1941.

———, and John D. Young. *A Vaquero of the Brush Country: The Life and Times of John D. Young*. Dallas: Southwest Press, 1929; rpt. Austin: University of Texas Press, 1998.

Dotson, Susan Merle, compiler. *Who's Who of the Confederacy*. San Antonio: Naylor Company, 1966.

Douglas, C. L. *Cattle Kings of Texas*. Dallas: C. Baugh, 1939; rpt. Austin: State House Press, 1989.

———. *Famous Texas Feuds*. Dallas: Turner Co., 1936; rpt. Austin: State House Press, 1988.

Douglas, Lucia Rutherford. *Douglas's Texas Battery, CSA*. Tyler: Smith County Historical Society, 1966.

Drago, Harry Sinclair. *Road Agents and Train Robbers: Half a Century of Western Banditry*. New York: Dodd, Mead & Company, 1973.

DuCoin, Candice. *Lawmen on the Texas Frontier: Rangers and Sheriffs*. Round Rock, TX: Riata Books, 2007.

Dugan, Mark. *Tales Never Told Around the Campfire*. Athens: Swallow Press/Ohio University Press, 1992.

Duganne, Augustine Joseph Hickey. *Camps and Prisons: Twenty Months in the Department of the Gulf*. New York: J. P. Robens, 1865.

Duke, Cordia Sloan, and Joe B. Frantz. *6,000 Miles of Fence: Life on the XIT Ranch of Texas*. Austin: University of Texas Press, 1961.

Dupree, Stephen A. *Planting the Union Flag in Texas: The Campaigns of Major General Nathaniel P. Banks in the West*. College Station: Texas A&M University Press, 2008.

Durham, George, as told to Clyde Wantland. *Taming the Nueces Strip: The Story of McNelly's Rangers*. Austin: University of Texas Press, 1962.

Dyer, Frederick H. *A Compendium of the War of the Rebellion*. De Moines, IA: The Dyer Publishing Company, 1908.

Eaves, Charles Dudley, and Cecil Allen Hutchinson. *Post City, Texas: C.W. Post's Colonizing Activities in West Texas*. Austin: Texas State Historical Association, 1952.

Eckhardt, Charley F. *Tales of Badmen, Bad Women, and Bad Places: Four Centuries of Texas Outlawry*. Lubbock: Texas Tech University Press, 1999.

Ehrle, Michael G., compiler. *The Childress County Story*. Childress, TX: Ox Bow Printing, 1971.

Eicher, John H., and David J. Eicher, *Civil War High Commands*. Stanford: Stanford University Press, 2001.

Einolf, Christopher J. *America in the Philippines, 1899–1902: The First Torture Scandal*. New York: Palgrave Macmillan, 2014.

Ernst, Robert. *Deadly Affrays: The Violent Deaths of the United States Marshals*. Lafayette, IN: Scarlet Mask, 2006.
Ethington, Philip J. *The Public City: The Political Construction of Urban Life in San Francisco, 1850–1900*. Berkeley: University of California Press, 2001.
Evans, Clement A., editor. *Confederate Military History*. Twelve volumes. Atlanta: Confederate Publishing Company, 1899.
Evans, Will F. *Border Skylines*. Dallas: Published for the Bloys Camp Meeting Association by Cecil Baugh, 1940.
Faulk, Odie. *General Tom Green: Fightin' Texan*. Waco: Texian Press, 1963.
Fetzer, Dale, and Bruce Mowday. *Unlikely Allies: Fort Delaware's Prison Community in the Civil War*. Mechanicsburg, PA: Stackpole Books, 2000.
Fisher, Ovie Clark. *It Occurred in Kimble*. Houston, TX: Anson Jones Press, 1937.
———, with Jeff C. Dykes. *King Fisher: His Life and Times*. Norman: University of Oklahoma Press, 1966.
Flake, Dennis Edward. *Loyal Macabebes: How the Americans Used the Macabebe Scouts in the Annexation of the Philippines*. Angeles City, PI: Juan D. Nepomuceno Center for Kapampangan Studies, Holy Angel University, 2009.
Ford, John S. *Rip Ford's Texas*. Edited by Stephen B. Oates. Austin: University of Texas Press, 1963; rpt. 1991.
Fornell, Earl Wesley. *The Galveston Era: The Texas Crescent on the Eve of Secession*. Austin: University of Texas Press, 2011.
Foote, Shelby. *The Civil War: A Narrative*. Three volumes. New York: Random House, 1958; rpt. 1986.
Ford, Gus L., editor. *Texas Cattle Brands: A Catalog of the Texas Centennial Exposition Exhibit, 1936*. Dallas: Clyde C. Cockrell Company, 1936.
Foster, John W. *Diplomatic Memoirs*. Volume One. Boston: Houghton Mifflin Company, 1910.
Foster, Morris W. *Being Comanche: A Social History of an American Indian Community*. Tucson: University of Arizona Press, 1991.
Fountain, Kimber. *Galveston Seawall Chronicles*. Charleston, SC: History Press, 2017.
Frazer, Chris. *Bandit Nation: A History of Outlaws and Cultural Struggle in Mexico, 1810–1920*. Lincoln: University of Nebraska Press, 2006.
Frazier, Donald S. *Blood and Treasure: Confederate Empire in the Southwest*. College Station: Texas A&M University Press, 1995.
———. *Thunder Across the Swamp: The Fight for the Lower Mississippi, February 1863-May 1863*. Buffalo Gap, TX: State House Press, 2011.

Frisbee, Meg. *Counterpunch: The Cultural Battles Over Heavyweight Prizefighting in the American West*. Seattle: University of Washington Press, 2016.
Fuller, Henry C. *"A Texas Sheriff"*. Nacogdoches, TX: Baker Printing Co., 1931.
Funston, Frederick. *Memories of Two Wars: Cuban and Philippine Experiences*. New York: Charles Scribner's Sons, 1911; rpt. Lincoln: University of Nebraska Press, 2009.
Gammel, Hans Peter Nielson, compiler. *The Laws of Texas, 1822–1897*. Ten volumes. Austin: The Gammel Book Company, 1898.
———. *The Laws of Texas, 1897–1902*. Austin: Gammel's Book Store, 1902.
———. *The Laws of Texas, 1903–1905*. Austin: Gammel's Book Store, 1906.
Gard, Wayne. *Frontier Justice*. Norman: University of Oklahoma Press, 1949; rpt. 1968.
———. *Rawhide Texas*. Norman: University of Oklahoma Press, 1965.
The Garza Revolution, 1891–1893: Records of the U.S. Continental Commands, Department of Texas. Bethesda, MD: LexisNexis, 2009.
Gentry, Mary Jane. *The Birth of a Texas Ghost Town: Thurber, 1886–1933*. College Station: Texas A&M University Press, 2008.
Gibb, George Sweet, and Evelyn H. Knowlton. *History of Standard Oil Company (New Jersey): The Resurgent Years, 1911–1927*. New York: Harper Brothers, 1956.
Gilliland, Maude T. *Horsebackers of the Brush Country: A Story of the Texas Rangers and the Mexican Liquor Smugglers*. Brownsville, TX: Springman-King Company, 1968.
———. *Wilson County Texas Rangers, 1837–1977*. Brownsville, TX: Springman-King Company, 1977.
Gillett, James B. *Six Years with the Texas Rangers, 1875–1881*. Edited by Milton M. Quaife. Austin: Von Boeckmann-Jones Co., 1921; rpt. New Haven: Yale University Press, 1925.
Glasrud, Bruce A., and Harold J. Weiss, Jr., editors. *Tracking the Texas Rangers: The Twentieth Century*. Denton: University of North Texas Press, 2013.
Glass, Edward L. N., editor. *The History of the Tenth Cavalry, 1866–1921*. Tucson: Acme Printing Company, 1921.
Gober, Jim. *Cowboy Justice: Tale of a Texas Lawman*. Edited by James R. Gober and B. Byron Price. Lubbock: Texas Tech University Press, 1997.
Godcharles, Frederic A. *Biographical and Genealogical Sketches from Central Pennsylvania: Excerpted from Chronicles of Central Penn-*

sylvania, Volume 4: Personal and Family History. New York: Lewis Historical Publishing Company, Inc., 1944; rpt. Baltimore: Clearfield Company, Inc., 1999.

Gonzales, Michael J. *The Mexican Revolution, 1910–1940*. Albuquerque: University of New Mexico Press, 2002.

González, Jovita. *Life Along the Border: A Landmark Tejana Thesis*. College Station: Texas A&M University Press, 2006.

Gorn, Elliott J, *The Manly Art: Bare-Knuckle Prize Fighting in America*. Updated Edition. Ithaca, NY: Cornell University Press, 1986; rpt. 2010.

Governor's Messages, Coke to Ross, 1874–1891. Edited by and for the Archive and History Department. Austin: Texas State Library, 1916.

Graybill, Andrew. *Policing the Great Plains: Rangers, Mounties, and the North American Frontier, 1875–1910*. Lincoln: University of Nebraska Press, 2007.

Grear, Charles David. *Why Texans Fought in the Civil War*. College Station: Texas A&M University Press, 2010.

Greaser, Galen D., et al. *New Guide to Spanish and Mexican Land Grants in South Texas*. Austin: Texas General Land Office, 2009.

Groom, Winston. *Shiloh, 1862*. Washington, D.C.: National Geographic Society, 2012.

Guthrie, Keith. *The History of San Patricio County*. Austin: Nortex Press, 1986.

Hagan, William T. *Quanah Parker, Comanche Chief*. Norman: University of Oklahoma Press, 1993.

———. *Taking Indian Lands: The Cherokee (Jerome) Commission, 1889–1893*. Norman University of Oklahoma Press, 2003.

———. *United States-Comanche Relations: The Reservation Years*. New Haven: Yale University Press, 1976; rpt. Norman: University of Oklahoma Press, 1990.

Hail, Marshall. *Knight in the Sun: Harper B. Lee, First Yankee Matador*. Boston: Little, Brown and Company, 1962.

Haley, J. Evetts. *Fort Concho and the Texas Frontier*. San Angelo: San Angelo Standard-Times, 1952.

———. *Jeff Milton: Good Man with a Gun*. Norman: University of Oklahoma Press, 1948.

———. *The XIT Ranch of Texas and the Early Days of the Llano Estacado*. Chicago: Capitol Reservation Lands, 1929; rpt. Norman: University of Oklahoma Press, 1953.

Haley, James L. *Apaches: A History and Culture Portrait*. Garden City, NY: Doubleday & Company, 1981; rpt. Norman: University of Oklahoma Press, 1997.

———. *Passionate Nation: The Epic History of Texas*. New York: Simon and Schuster, 2006.

Hämäläinen, Pekka. *The Comanche Empire*. New Haven: Yale University Press, 2008.

Hamilton, Allen Lee. *Sentinel of the Southern Plains: Fort Richardson and the Northwest Texas Frontier, 1866–1878*. Fort Worth: Texas Christian University Press, 1988.

Hardin, John Wesley. *The Life of John Wesley Hardin, From the Original Manuscript, As Written by Himself*. Seguin, TX: Smith & Moore, 1896.

Harland, Louis R. *Booker T. Washington: The Wizard of Tuskegee, 1901–1915*. New York: Oxford University Press, 1983.

Harris, Charles H., III, and Louis R. Sadler. *The Secret War in El Paso: Mexican Revolutionary Intrigue, 1906–1920*. Albuquerque: University of New Mexico Press, 2009.

———. *The Texas Rangers and the Mexican Revolution: The Bloodiest Decade, 1910–1920*. Albuquerque: University of New Mexico Press, 2007.

Hart, John Mason. *Empire and Revolution: The Americans in Mexico Since the Civil War*. Berkeley: University of California Press, 2002.

Harter, Eugene C. *The Lost Colony of the Confederacy*. Jackson: University Press of Mississippi, 1985.

Hatfield, Shelley Bowen. *Chasing Shadows: Indians Along the United States-Mexico Border, 1876–1911*. Albuquerque: University of New Mexico Press, 1998.

Hatley, Allen G. *Bringing the Law to Texas: Crime and Violence in Nineteenth Century Texas*. LaGrange, TX: Centex Press, 2002.

———. *Texas Constables: A Frontier Heritage*. Lubbock: Texas Tech University Press, 1999.

Havins, T. R. *Something About Brown: A History of Brown County, Texas*. Brownwood, TX: Banner Printing Company, 1958.

Heartsill, William Williston. *Fourteen Hundred and 91 Days in the Confederate Army: A Journal Kept by W. W. Heartsill for Four Years, One Month, and One Day; or, Camp Life, Day by Day, of the W. P. Lane Rangers from April 10, 1861, to May 20, 1865*. Edited by Bell Irvin Wiley. Jackson, TN: McCowat-Mercer Press, 1953.

Heitman, Francis B. *Historical Register and Dictionary of the United States Army from its Organization, September 29 1789, to March 2 1903*. Two volumes. Washington, D.C.: Government Printing Office, 1903.

Hess, Earl J. *Braxton Bragg: The Most Hated Man of the Confederacy*. Chapel Hill: University of North Carolina Press, 2016.

———. *Kennesaw Mountain: Sherman, Johnston, and the Atlanta Campaign*. Chapel Hill: University of North Carolina Press, 2013.

Hinson, Marie L., compiler. *Marriages of Davidson County, North Carolina: 1822–1880*. Lexington, NC: Genealogical Society of Davidson County, 1992.

The History of Peoria County, Illinois. Chicago: Johnson & Company, 1880.

Hoig, Stan. *Beyond the Frontier: Exploring the Indian Country*. Norman: University of Oklahoma Press, 1996.

Holden, Frances Mayhugh. *Lambshead Before Interwoven: A Texas Range Chronicle, 1848–1878*. College Station: Texas A&M University Press, 1982.

Holliday, J. S. *Rush for Riches: Gold Fever and the Making of California*. Berkeley: University of California Press, 1999.

Horn, Stanley F. *The Army of Tennessee: A Military History*. Indianapolis, IN: Bobbs-Merrill Company, 1941; rpt. Norman: University of Oklahoma Press, 1993.

House, Boyce. *Cowtown Columnist*. San Antonio: Naylor Company, 1946.

Howell, Kenneth W., editor. *The Seventh Star of the Confederacy: Texas during the Civil War*. Denton: University of North Texas Press, 2009.

———. *Still the Arena of Civil War: Violence and Turmoil in Reconstruction Texas, 1865–1874*. Denton: University of North Texas Press, 2012.

Hunter, John Marvin, compiler and editor. *Trail Drivers of Texas*. Nashville: Cokesbury Press, 1925; rpt. Austin: University of Texas Press, 1985.

Irwin, Lee. *Native American Spirituality: A Critical Reader*. Lincoln: University of Nebraska Press, 2000.

Irwin, Richard B. *History of the Nineteenth Army Corps*. New York: G. P. Putnam's Sons, 1893.

Jennings, Napoleon Augustus. *A Texas Ranger*. New York: Charles Scribners Sons, 1899; rpt. Norman: University of Oklahoma Press, 1997.

Jensen, Ann, editor. *Texas Ranger's Diary and Scrapbook*. Dallas: Kaleidograph Press, 1936.

Johnson, Benjamin Heber. *Revolution in Texas: How a Forgotten Rebellion and Its Bloody Suppression Turned Mexicans into Americans*. New Haven: Yale University Press, 2003.

Johnson, David. *The Horrell Wars: Feuding in Texas and New Mexico*. Denton: University of North Texas Press, 2014.

———. *The Mason County "Hoo Doo" War, 1874–1902*. Denton: University of North Texas Press, 2006.

Johnson, Ludwell H. *Red River Campaign: Politics and Cotton in the Civil War*. Baltimore: The Johns Hopkins Press, 1958; rpt. Kent, OH: Kent State University Press, 1993.

Johnson, Robert Underwood, and Clarence Clough Buel. *Battles and Leaders of the Civil War*. Four volumes. New York: Century Company, 1884–1888; rpt. Secaucus, NJ: Castle Books, 1982.

Johnson, Sidney Smith. *Some Biographies of Old Settlers. Historical, Personal and Reminiscent*. Tyler: self-published, 1900.

———. *Texans Who Wore the Gray*. Tyler, TX: self-published, 1907.

Johnston, William Preston. *The Life of Albert Sidney Johnston: Embracing His Services in the Armies of the United States, the Republic of Texas, and the Confederate States*. New York: D. Appleton and Company, 1878; rpt. Austin: State House Press, 1997.

Joiner, Gary D. *Through the Howling Wilderness: The 1864 Red River Campaign and Union Failure in the West*. Knoxville: University of Tennessee Press, 2006.

———. *Mr. Lincoln's Brown Water Navy: The Mississippi Squadron*. Lanham, MD: Rowman & Littlefield, 2007.

———, editor. *Little to Eat and Thin Mud to Drink: Letters, Diaries, and Memoirs from the Red River Campaigns, 1863–1864*. Knoxville: University of Tennessee Press, 2007.

Jones, Lucille. *History of Mineola, Texas: Gateway to the Pines*. Quanah, TX: Nortex Offset Publications, 1973.

Jones, J. Lee, Jr., and Nona C. Jones, compilers, and Mac B. McKinnon, editor. *Lore and Legend: A Compilation of Documents Depicting the History of Colorado City and Mitchell County*. Colorado City, TX: Colorado City Record, 1976.

Jones, Terry L. *Historical Dictionary of the Civil War*. Volume Two. Lanham, MD: Scarecrow Press, 2002.

Joseph, Gilbert M., and Jürgen Buchenau. *Mexico's Once and Future Revolution: Social Upheaval and the Challenge of Rule since the Late Nineteenth Century*. Durham, NC: Duke University Press, 2013.

Josephy, Alvin M., Jr. *The Civil War in the American West*. New York: Alfred A. Knopf, 1992.

Julius A. Appler's General Directory and Household Directory of Greater San Antonio. San Antonio: J. A. Appler, 1914–1922.

Katz, Friedrich. *The Life and Times of Pancho Villa*. Stanford, CA: Sandford University Press, 1998.

Katzenberger, George A., editor. *Directory of the Legal Fraternity of Phi Delta Phi*. Galesbrg, IL: Mail Printing Company, 1909.

Kavanagh, Thomas W. *Comanche Political History: An Ethnohistorical Perspective, 1706–1875*. Lincoln: University of Nebraska Press, 1996.

Kearney, James C., et al. *No Hope for Heaven, No Fear of Hell: The Stafford-Townsend Feud of Colorado County, 1871–1911*. Denton: University of North Texas Press, 2016.

Kearney, Milo, and Anthony Knopp. *Boom and Bust: The Historical Cycles of Matamoros and Brownsville*. Austin: Eakin Press, 1991.

Kelly, Louise, compiler. *Wichita County Beginnings*. Burnet, TX: Eakin Press, 1982.

Kemp, Ben W., with J. C. Dykes. *Cow Dust and Saddle Leather*. Norman: University of Oklahoma Press, 1968.

Kerby, Robert L. *Kirby Smith's Confederacy: The Trans-Mississippi South, 1863–1865*. New York: Columbia University Press, 1972.

Kinard, Jeff. *Lafayette of the South: Prince Camille de Polignac and the American Civil War*. College Station: Texas A&M University Press, 2001.

Knowlton, Christopher. *Cattle Kingdom: The Hidden History of the Cowboy West*. New York: Houghton Mifflin Harcourt, 2017.

LaForce, Christopher J. *The Choynski Chronicles: A Biography of Hall of Fame Boxer Jewish Joe Choynski*. Iowa City, IA: Win By KO Publications, 2013.

Lamb, Alan J., compiler. *An Aten Genealogy*. Santa Fe: Alan J. Lamb Publications, 1997.

The Land and Its People, 1876–1981: Deaf Smith County, Texas. Hereford, TX: Deaf Smith County Historical Society, 1982.

Landrum, Graham. *Grayson County: An Illustrated History of Grayson County, Texas*. Fort Worth: University Supply & Equipment Company, 1960.

Lane, Ann J. *The Brownsville Affair: National Crisis and Black Reaction*. Port Washington, NY: Kennikat Press, 1971.

Lane, Walter P. *The Adventures and Recollections of General Walter P. Lane: A San Jacinto Veteran, Containing Sketches of the Texan, Mexican, and Late Wars*. Marshall, TX: Tri-Weekly Herald Job Print, 1887; rpt. Austin: Jenkins Publishing Company, 1970.

Lanning, Jim, and Judy Lanning. *Texas Cowboys: Memories of the Early Days*. College Station: Texas A&M University Press, 1984.

Larson, Henrietta M., et al. *History of Standard Oil (New Jersey): New Horizons, 1927–1950*. New York: Harper & Row, 1971.

La Salle County Historical Commission. *La Salle County*. Charleston, SC: Arcadia Publishing, 2010.

Lasater, Dale. *Falfurrias: Ed C. Lasater and the Development of South Texas*. College Station: Texas A&M University Press, 1998.

La Vere, David. *Contrary Neighbors: Southern Plains and Removed Indians in Indian Territory*. Norman: University of Oklahoma Press, 2000.

———. *The Texas Indians*. College Station: Texas A&M University Press, 2004.

Lea, Tom. *The King Ranch*. Two volumes. Boston: Little, Brown and Company, 1957.

Leckie, William H, with Shirley A. Leckie. *The Buffalo Soldiers: A Narrative of the Black Cavalry in the West*. Revised Edition. Norman: University of Oklahoma Press, 1967; rpt. 2003.

Leet, Joshua H., and Karen M. Leet. *Civil War Lexington, Kentucky: Bluegrass Breeding Ground of Power*. Charleston, SC: History Press, 2011.

Leiker, James N. *Racial Borders: Black Soldiers Along the Rio Grande*. College Station: Texas A&M University Press, 2002.

Lejeune, Keagan. *Legendary Louisiana Outlaws: The Villains and Heroes of Folk Justice*. Baton Rouge: Louisiana State University Press, 2016.

Lengel, Edward G. *To Conquer Hell: The Meuse-Argonne, 1918: The Epic Battle That Ended the First World War*. New York: Henry Holt and Company, 2008.

Leuschner, Charles A. *The Civil War Diary of Charles A. Leuschner*. Edited by Charles D. Spurlin. Austin: Eakin Press, 1992.

Lewis, Zella, editor. *The Proud Century: Tyler Public Schools 1882–1982*. Tyler, TX: Tyler Independent School System, 1982.

Lindley, Ernest R., editor. *Members of the Legislature of the State of Texas from 1846 to 1939*. Austin: State of Texas, 1939.

Linn, Brian McAllister. *The Philippine War, 1899–1902*. Lawrence: University Press of Kansas, 2000.

———. *The U.S. Army and Counterinsurgency in the Philippine War, 1899–1902*. Chapel Hill: University of North Carolina Press, 1989.

Linn, Jo White. *First Presbyterian Church, Salisbury, North Carolina, and Its People, 1821–1995*. Salisbury, NC: privately printed, 1996.

Lonn, Ella. *Foreigners in the Confederacy*. Chapel Hill: University of North Carolina Press, 1940; rpt. 2002.

Loughery, E. H. *Texas State Government: A Volume of Biographical Sketches and Passing Comment*. Austin: McLeod & Jackson Printers, 1897.

Love, Annie Carpenter. *History of Navarro County*. Dallas: Southwest Press, 1933.

Lowe, Richard. *The Texas Overland Expedition of 1863*. Abilene, TX: McWhiney Foundation Press, 1998.

―――――. *Walker's Texas Division, C.S.A.: Greyhounds of the Trans-Mississippi*. Baton Rouge: Louisiana State University Press, 2004.

―――――, editor. *Greyhound Commander: Confederate General John G. Walker's History of the Civil War West of the Mississippi*. Baton Rouge: Louisiana State University Press, 2013.

Lundberg, John R. *Granbury's Texas Brigade: Diehard Western Confederates*. Baton Rouge: Louisiana State University, 2012.

Ludeman, Annette Martin. *La Salle County: South Texas Brush County, 1856–1975*. Quanah, TX: Nortex Press, 1975.

Luvaas, Jay, and Harold W. Nelson, editors. *Guide to the Atlanta Campaign: Rocky Face Ridge to Kennesaw Mountain*. Lawrence: University Press of Kansas, 2008.

McCaffrey, James M. "The Texas Immunes in the Spanish-American War." *Texans and War: New Interpretations of the State's Military History*. Edited by Alexander Mendoza and Charles David Grear. College Station: Texas A&M University Press, 2012.

―――――. *This Band of Heroes: Granbury's Texas Brigade, C.S.A.* College Station: Texas A&M University Press, 1996.

McCallum, Henry D., and Frances T. *The Wire That Fenced the West*. Norman: University of Oklahoma Press, 1965.

McCarley, J. Britt. *The Atlanta and Savannah Campaigns, 1864*. Washington, D.C.: U.S. Army Center of Military History, 2014.

McConnell, Joseph Carroll. *The West Texas Frontier: or, A Descriptive History of Early Times in Western Texas*. Volume Two. Palo Pinto, TX: Texas Legal Bank & Book Co., 1939.

McKiernan-González, John. *Fevered Measures: Public Health and Race at the Texas-Mexico Border, 1848–1942*. Durham, NC: Duke University Press, 2012.

McMaster, Fitz Hugh. *History of Fairfield County, South Carolina*. Columbia, SC: State Commercial Printing Company, 1946.

McMurry, Richard M. *Atlanta 1864: Last Chance for the Confederacy*. Lincoln: University of Nebraska Press, 2000.

McPherson, James. *Battle Cry of Freedom: The Civil War Era*. New York: Oxford University Press, 1988.

McSwain, Ross. *See No Evil, Speak No Evil: A History of Mob Violence in the Texas Heartland, 1869–1904*. San Angelo, TX: Shadetree Enterprises, 2008.

Malone, Dumas, editor. *Dictionary of American Biography*. Volume Ten. New York: Charles Scribner's Sons, 1933.

Maltby, William J. *Captain Jeff; or, Frontier Life in Texas with the Texas Rangers*. Colorado City, TX: Whipkey Printing Company, 1906.

Maroukis, Thomas Constantine. *The Peyote Road: Religious Freedom and the Native American Church*. Norman: University of Oklahoma Press, 2010.

Marriage Records of Washington County, 1836–1909. Brenham, TX: Washington County Genealogical Society, 1999.

Martin, Jack. *Border Boss: Captain John R. Hughes—Texas Ranger*. San Antonio: Naylor Co., 1942; rpt. Austin: State House Press, 1990.

Masich, Andrew E. *Civil War in the Southwest Borderlands, 1861–1867*. Norman: University of Oklahoma Press, 2017.

May, Glenn Anthony. *Battle for Batangas: A Philippine Province at War*. New Haven: Yale University Press, 1991.

Mebane, Robert M. *History and Genealogy of the Mebane Family of Colonial Pennsylvania and North Carolina*. Alexandria, VA: R. M. Mebane, 1999.

Methvin, J. J. *In the Limelight, or History of Anadarko [Caddo County] and Vicinity from the Earliest Days*. Anadarko, OK: Plummer, 1928.

Metz, Leon C. *Dallas Stoudenmire*. Norman: University of Oklahoma Press, 1969; rpt. 1993.

———. *John Wesley Hardin: Dark Angel of Texas*. Norman: University of Oklahoma Press, 1996; rpt. 1998.

Miletich, Leon N. *Dan Stuart's Fistic Carnival*. College Station: Texas A&M University Press, 1994.

Miller, Rick. *Bounty Hunter*. College Station: Creative Publishing Company, 1988.

———. *Sam Bass and Gang*. Austin: State House Press, 1999.

———. *Texas Ranger John B. Jones and the Frontier Battalion, 1874–1881*. Denton: University of North Texas Press, 2012.

Mineola Centennial Corporation. *Mineola: The First 100 Years*. Mineola: Mineola Centennial Corporation, 1973.

Miner, Craig. *West of Wichita: Settling the High Plains of Kansas, 1865–1890*. Lawrence: University Press of Kansas, 1986.

Monaghan, Jim. *The Trans-Cedar Tragedy: Triple Lynching in Henderson County, Texas*. Dallas, TX: Homemade Publishers, 1989.

Monroe, James A. *Hellfire Nation: The Politics of Sin in American History.* New Haven: Yale University Press, 2003.
Montejano, David. *Anglos and Mexicans in the Making of Texas, 1836–1986.* Austin: University of Texas Press, 1987.
Mooney & Morrison's General Directory of the City of Austin, Texas, for 1877–78. Austin: Eugene von Boeckmann, 1877.
Moore, Jacqueline M. *Cow Boys and Cattle Men: Class and Masculinities on the Texas Frontier, 1865–1900.* New York: New York University Press, 2010.
Morgenthaler, Jefferson. *The River Has Never Divided Us: A Border History of La Junta de los Rios.* Austin: University of Texas Press, 2004.
Morris, John Miller. *A Private in the Texas Rangers: A. T. Miller of Company B, Frontier Battalion.* College Station: Texas A&M University Press, 2001.
Morrison & Fourmy's General Directory of the City of Austin, 1885 and 1886. Austin: E. W. Swindells, 1885.
Morrison & Fourmy's General Directory of the City of Austin, 1889–90. Galveston: Morrison & Fourmy, 1889.
Morrison & Fourmy's General Directory of the City of Austin, 1897–98. Galveston: Morrison & Fourmy, 1897.
Morrison & Fourmy's General Directory of the City of Austin, 1900–1901. Galveston: Morrison & Fourmy, 1900.
Morrison & Fourmy's General Directory of the City of Austin, for 1881 and 1882. Austin: E. W. Swindells, 1881.
Nance, Joseph Milton. *Attack and Counterattack: The Texas Military Frontier, 1842.* Austin: University of Texas Press, 1964.
Neal, Bill. *From Guns to Gavel: How Justice Grew Up in the Outlaw West.* Lubbock; Texas Tech University Press, 2008.
———. *Getting Away with Murder on the Texas Frontier: Notorious Killings and Celebrated Trials.* Lubbock: Texas Tech University Press, 2006.
———. *The Last Frontier: The Story of Hardeman County.* Quanah, TX: Quanah Tribune Chief, 1966; rpt. Austin: Eakin Press, 1996.
Neeley, Bill. *The Last Comanche Chief: The Life and Times of Quanah Parker.* New York: John Wiley & Sons, 1995.
Noel, Theophilus. *A Campaign from Santa Fe to the Mississippi: Being a History of the Old Sibley Brigade.* Shreveport: Shreveport News Printing Establishment, 1865.
Nolan, Frederick W. *Bad Blood: The Life and Times of the Horrell Brothers.* Stillwater, OK: Barbed Wire Press, 1994.

———. *Tascosa: Its Life and Gaudy Times*. Lubbock; Texas Tech University Press, 2007.

———. *The Wild West: History, Myth and the Making of America*. Edison, NJ: Chartwell Books, 2004.

Nordyke, Lewis. *Cattle Empire: The Fabulous Story of the 3,000,000 Acre XIT*. New York: William Morrow and Company, 1949.

———. *Great Roundup: The Story of Texas and Southwestern Cowmen*. New York: William Morrow and Company, 1955.

Noyes, Stanley, and Daniel J. Gelo. *Comanches in the New West, 1895–1908*. Austin: University of Texas Press, 1999.

Nye, Wilbur Sturtevant. *Carbine and Lance: The Story of Old Fort Sill*. Norman: University of Oklahoma Press, 1937; rpt. 1969.

Oates, Stephen B. *Confederate Cavalry West of the River*. Austin: University of Texas Press, 1961.

Official Register of Harvard University: The Law School 14, No. 32 (June 8, 1917).

Oliphant, William J. *Only a Private: A Texan Remembers the Civil War: The Memoirs of William J. Oliphant*. Edited by James M. McCaffrey. Houston: Halcyon Press, 2004.

O'Neal, Bill. *The Bloody Legacy of Pink Higgins: A Half Century of Violence in Texas*. Austin: Eakin Press, 1999.

———. *Encyclopedia of Western Gunfighters*. Norman: University of Oklahoma Press, 1979.

———. *Historic Ranches of the Old West*. Austin: Eakin Press, 1997.

Owen, Valerie. *Byrd Cochran of Dead Man's Corner*. Snyder, TX: Feather Press, 1972.

Paine, Albert Bigelow. *Captain Bill McDonald, Texas Ranger: A Story of Frontier Reform*. New York: J. J. Little & Ives Co., 1909.

Painter, C. C. *The Condition of Affairs in Indian Territory and California*. Philadelphia: Office of the Indian Rights Association, 1888.

Paredes, Américo. *"With His Pistol in His Hand": A Border Ballad and Its Hero*. Austin: University of Texas Press, 1958.

Parrish, T. Michael. *Richard Taylor: Soldier Prince of Dixie*. Chapel Hill: University of North Carolina Press, 1992.

Parsons, Chuck. *Captain Jack Helm: A Victim of Texas Reconstruction Violence*. Denton: University of North Texas Press, 2018.

———. *Captain John R. Hughes, Lone Star Ranger*. Denton: University of North Texas Press, 2011.

———. *John B. Armstrong, Texas Ranger and Pioneer Ranchman*. College Station: Texas A&M University Press, 2007.

———. *"Pidge," Texas Ranger.* College Station: Texas A&M University Press, 2013.

———. *The Sutton-Taylor Feud: The Deadliest Blood Feud in Texas.* Denton: University of North Texas Press, 2009.

———, and Donaly E. Brice. *Texas Ranger N. O. Reynolds: The Intrepid.* Honolulu: Talei Publishers, 2005; rpt. Denton: University of North Texas Press, 2014.

———, and Gary P. Fitterer, *Captain C. B. McKinney: The Law in South Texas.* Wolfe City, TX: Henington Publishing Company, 1993.

———, and Norman Wayne Brown. *A Lawless Breed: John Wesley Hardin, Texas Reconstruction, and Violence in the Wild West.* Denton: University of North Texas Press, 2013.

———, with Marianne E. Hall Little. *Captain L. H. McNelly—Texas Ranger: The Life and Times of a Fighting Man.* Austin: State House Press, 2000.

Patterson, Bessie. *A History of Deaf Smith County.* Hereford, TX: Pioneer Publishing, 1964.

Patterson, Cyril Leone. *Atascosa County, Texas: A Progressive and Diversified Agricultural and Livestock Haven.* Pleasanton, TX: Pleasanton Express, 1938.

Pattie, Jane. *Cattle Brands: Ironclad Signatures.* Albany, TX: Bright Sky Press, 2002.

Pennington, Mrs. R. E. *History of Brenham and Washington County, Texas.* n.p.: Mrs. R. E. Pennington, 1915; rpt. Brenham, TX: Washington County Genealogical Society, 1998.

Perkins, Doug, and Nancy Ward. *Brave Men and Cold Steel: A History of Range Detectives and Their Peacemakers.* Fort Worth: Texas and Southwestern Cattle Raisers Foundation, 1984.

Perman, Michael. *Pursuit of Unity: A Political History of the American South.* Chapel Hill: University of North Carolina Press, 2009.

Pickenpaugh, Roger. *Camp Chase and the Evolution of Union Prison Policy.* Tuscaloosa: University of Alabama Press, 2007.

Pioneers in God's Hills: A History of Fredericksburg and Gillespie County People and Events. Fredericksburg, TX: Gillespie County Historical Society, 1974.

Polk's Tyler City Directory, 1927–1928. Dallas: R. L. Polk & Co., 1927.

Porter, Joseph C. "'The American Congo': Captain John G. Bourke and the Texas Military Experience." *The Texas Military Experience: From the Texas Revolution Through World War II.* Edited by Joseph G. Dawson III. College Station: Texas A&M University Press, 1995.

Preece, Harold. *Lone Star Man: Ira Aten, Last of the Old Texas Rangers*. New York: Hastings House, 1960.

Price, Lucie Clift. *Travis County, Texas Marriage Records, 1840–1882*. Austin: privately published, 1973.

Procter, Ben H. *Just One Riot: Episodes of the Texas Rangers in the 20th Century*. Austin: Eakin Press, 1991.

Prucha, Francis Paul. *American Indian Treaties: The History of a Political Anomaly*. Berkeley: University of California Press, 1994.

Prushankin, Jeffrey S. *A Crisis in Confederate Command: Edmund Kirby Smith, Richard Taylor, and the Army of the Trans-Mississippi*. Baton Rouge: Louisiana State University Press, 2005.

Putman, Wyvonne, compiler. *Navarro County History*. Quanah, TX: Nortex Press, 1975.

Ramsdell, Charles William. *Reconstruction in Texas*. New York: Columbia University Press, 1910.

Rathjen, Frederick W. *The Texas Panhandle Frontier*. Revised Edition. Lubbock: Texas Tech University Press, 1973; rpt. 1998.

Raymond, Dora Neill. *Captain Lee Hall of Texas*. Norman: University of Oklahoma Press, 1940; rpt. 1982.

Reed, Robert E., Jr. *Tyler*. Charleston, SC: Arcadia Publishing, 2009.

Reese, James V. "The Early History of Labor Organizations in Texas, 1838–1876." *Texas Labor History*. Edited by Bruce A. Glasrud and James C. Maroney. College Station: Texas A&M University Press, 2013.

Reese, John Walter, and Lillian Estelle Reese. *Flaming Feuds of Colorado County*. Salado, TX: Anson Jones Press, 1962.

Reinders, Robert C. *End of an Era: New Orleans, 1850–1860*. Gretna, LA: Pelican Publishing Company, 1964; rpt. 1989.

Remington, Frederic. "How the Law Got into the Chaparral." *Crooked Trails*. New York: Harper and Brothers, 1898.

Report of the Proceedings of the Various Associations of Ex-Confederates Held at Dallas, Dallas County, August 6th, 7th, 8th, and 9th, 1884. Dallas: Dallas Printing House, 1884.

Rich, Harold. *Fort Worth: Outpost, Cowtown, Boomtown*. Norman: University of Oklahoma Press, 2014.

Richmond, Douglas W., and Sam W. Haynes, editors. *The Mexican Revolution: Conflict and Consolidation, 1910–1940*. College Station: Texas A&M University Press, 2013.

Richter, William L. *The Army in Texas During Reconstruction, 1865–1870*. College Station: Texas A&M University Press, 1987.

Ridley, Bromfield L. *Battles and Sketches of the Army of Tennessee*. Mexico, MO: Missouri Printing & Publishing Company, 1906.

Roberts, Dan W. *Rangers and Sovereignty*. San Antonio: Wood Printing & Engraving Co., 1914.

Roberts, Mrs. D. W. (Luvenia Conway). *A Woman's Reminiscences of Six Years in Camp with the Texas Rangers*. Austin: Von Boeckmann-Jones Co., 1928?

Robertson, William G., et al. *Staff Ride Handbook for the Battle of Chickamauga*. Fort Leavenworth: Combat Studies Institute, 1992.

Robinson, Charles M., III. *The Men Who Wear the Star: The Story of the Texas Rangers*. New York: Random House, 2000; rpt. New York: The Modern Library, 2001.

Robinson, Keith R. *Fist Fighting Out West: Dan Stuart versus General Mabry and the Texas Rangers*. London: English Westerners' Society, 2010.

Roland, Charles P. *Albert Sidney Johnston: Soldier of Three Republics*. Austin: University of Texas Press, 1964; rpt. Lexington: University Press of Kentucky, 2001.

Rolle, Andrew. *The Lost Cause: The Confederate Exodus to Mexico*. University of Oklahoma Press, 1992.

Romo, David Dorado. *Ringside Seat to a Revolution, An Underground Cultural History of El Paso and Juárez: 1893–1923*. El Paso, TX: Cinco Puntos Press, 2005.

Rosales, F. Arturo. *¡Pobre Raza! Violence, Justice, and Mobilization among México Lindo Immigrants, 1900–1936*. Austin: University of Texas Press, 1999.

Rose, Peter R. *The Reckoning: The Triumph of Order on the Texas Outlaw Frontier*. Lubbock: Texas Tech University Press, 2012.

Rubenser, Lorie, and Gloria Priddy. *Constables, Marshals, and More: Forgotten Offices in Teas Law Enforcement*. Denton: University of North Texas Press, 2011.

Samuels, Nancy Timmons, and Barbara Roach Knox, compilers. *Old Northwest Texas: Historical—Statistical—Biographical*. Fort Worth: Fort Worth Genealogical Society, 1980.

San Antonio City Directory, 1926. Dallas: John F. Worley Company, 1926.

Sanders, Charles W., Jr. *While in the Hands of the Enemy: Military Prisons of the Civil War*. Baton Rouge: Louisiana State University Press, 2005.

Sanders, Robert Stuart. *Presbyterianism in Paris and Bourbon County, Kentucky: 1786–1961*. Louisville, KY: Dunne Press, 1961.

Sandford, Karin L. editor. *If We Must Die: African-American Voices on War and Peace*. Lanham, MD: Rowman & Littlefield, 2008.

Sammons, Jeffrey T. *Beyond the Ring: The Role of Boxing in American Society.* Urbana: University of Illinois Press, 1990.

Schubert, Frank N. *Voices of the Buffalo Soldier: Records, Reports, and Recollections of Military Life and Service in the West.* Albuquerque: University of New Mexico Press, 2003.

Seaton, Benjamin M. *The Bugle Softly Blows: The Confederate Diary of Benjamin M. Seaton.* Edited by Colonel Harold B. Simpson. Waco: Texian Press, 1965.

Secrist, Philip L. *Sherman's 1864 Trail of Battle to Atlanta.* Macon, GA: Mercer University Press, 2006.

Selcer, Richard F., compiler and editor. *Legendary Watering Holes: The Saloons That Made Texas Famous.* College Station: Texas A&M University Press, 2004.

Selcer, Richard F., and Kevin S. Foster. *Written in Blood: The History of Fort Worth's Fallen Lawmen.* Denton: University of North Texas Press, 2010.

Seymour, Charles, editor. *Intimate Papers of Colonel House.* Volume One. Boston: Houghton Mifflin Company, 1926.

Shay, Michel E. *Henry Ware Lawton: Union Infantryman, Frontier Soldier, Charismatic Warrior.* Columbia: University of Missouri Press, 2016.

Shillingberg, William B. *Dodge City: The Early Years, 1872–1886.* Norman, OK: Arthur H. Clark Company, 2009.

Shirley, Glenn. *Heck Thomas, Frontier Marshal.* Philadelphia: Chilton Company, 1962; rpt. Norman: University of Oklahoma Press, 1981.

———. *Law West of Fort Smith: A Tale of Frontier Justice in the Indian Territory, 1834–1896.* New York: Henry Holt and Company, 1957.

———. *West of Hell's Fringe: Crime, Criminals, and the Federal Peace Officer in Oklahoma Territory, 1889–1907.* Norman: University of Oklahoma Press, 1978; rpt. 1990.

Sifakis, Stewart. *Compendium of the Confederate Armies: Texas.* Westminster, MD: Willow Bend Books, 2008.

Silbey, David J. *A War of Frontier and Empire: The Philippine-American War, 1899–1902.* New York: Hill and Wang, 2007.

Sitton, Thad. *The Texas Sheriff: Lord of the County Line.* Norman: University of Oklahoma Press, 2000.

Smallwood, James M. *The Feud That Wasn't: The Taylor Ring, Bill Sutton, John Wesley Hardin, and Violence in Texas.* College Station: Texas A&M University Press, 2008.

———, et al. *Murder and Mayhem: The War of Reconstruction in Texas.* College Station: Texas A&M University Press, 2003.

Smith, Charles Alphonso. *O. Henry Biography*. Garden City, NY: Doubleday, Page and Company, 1916.

Smith, Diane Solether. *The Armstrong Chronicle: A Ranching History*. San Antonio: Corona Publishing Co., 1986.

Smith, F. Todd. *The Caddos, the Wichitas, and the United States, 1846–1901*. College Station: Texas A&M University Press, 1996.

Smith, J. Frazier. *Plantation Houses and Mansions of the Old South*. New York: Dover Publications, 1993.

Smith, Thomas T. *The Old Army in Texas: A Research Guide to the U.S. Army in Nineteenth-Century Texas*. Austin: Texas State Historical Association, 2000.

Smith, Timothy B. *Shiloh: Conquer or Perish*. Lawrence: University Press of Kansas, 2014.

Snell, Mark A. *From First to Last: The Life of Major William B. Franklin*. New York: Fordham University Press, 2002.

Sonnichsen, C. L. *The El Paso Salt War [1877]*. El Paso: Texas Western Press, 1961. The chapters of this slim volume originally appeared in *Ten Texas Feuds*.

———. *I'll Die Before I'll Run: The Story of the Great Feuds of Texas*. New York: Harper and Bros., 1951; rpt. Lincoln: University of Nebraska Press, 1988.

———. *Roy Bean: Law West of the Pecos*. Albuquerque: University of New Mexico Press, 1943; rpt. 1986.

———. *Pass of the North: Four Centuries on the Rio Grande*. Two volumes. El Paso: Texas Western Press, 1968.

———. *Ten Texas Feuds*. Albuquerque: University of New Mexico Press, 1957; rpt. 2000.

Southworth, Dave. *Feuds on the Western Frontier*. Round Rock, TX: Wild Horse Publishing, 1999.

Sowell, Andrew Jackson. *Texas Indian Fighters: Early Settlers and Indian Fighters of Southwest Texas*. Austin: Ben C. Jones & Co., 1900; rpt. Austin: State House Press, 1986.

Spaw, Patsy McDonald. *The Texas Senate*. Volume Two. College Station: Texas A&M University Press, 1999.

Speer, Lonnie R. *Portals to Hell: Military Prisons of the Civil War*. Lincoln: University of Nebraska Press, 2005.

Speer, William S., and John Henry Brown, editors. *The Encyclopedia of the New West*. Marshall, TX: United States Biographical Publishing Company, 1881.

Spellman, Paul N. *Captain J. A. Brooks, Texas Ranger*. Denton: University of North Texas Press, 2007.

———. *Captain John H. Rogers, Texas Ranger*. Denton: University of North Texas Press, 2003.

———. *Spindletop Boom Days*. College Station: Texas A&M University Press, 2001.

Spencer, John W. *The Confederate Guns of Navarro County*. Corsicana, TX: Texas Press, 1986.

Stanford University Alumni Directory and Ten-Year Book. Stanford University: published by the university, 1921.

Stehno, Mollie, compiler, and Jim Fulbright, editor. *Western Lawmen: U.S. Marshals and Their Deputies, 1850–1920*. Goodlettesville, TN: Mid-South Publications, 2015.

Stephens, Robert W. *Bullets and Buckshot in Texas*. Dallas: Robert W. Stephens, 2002.

———. *Texas Ranger Sketches*. Dallas: Robert W. Stephens, 1972.

———. *Walter Durbin: Texas Ranger and Sheriff*. Clarendon: Clarendon Press, 1970.

Sterling, William Warren. *Trails and Trials of a Texas Ranger*. Norman: University of Oklahoma Press, 1959.

Stuart, David. *O. Henry: A Biography of William Sydney Porter*. Chelsea, MI: Scarborough House, 1990.

Sullivan, W. John L. *Twelve Years in the Saddle with the Texas Rangers*. Austin: Von Boeckmann-Jones Co., 1909; rpt. Lincoln: University of Nebraska Press, 2001. Pagination follows the 2001 edition.

Summerall, Charles Pelot. *The Way of Duty, Honor, Country: The Memoirs of Charles Pelot Summerall*. Edited by Timothy K. Nenninger. Lexington: University Press of Kentucky, 2010.

Sutherland, Mary A. *The Story of Corpus Christi*. Corpus Christi Chapter, Daughters of the Confederacy, 1916.

Sword, Wiley. *Mountains Touched with Fire: Chattanooga Besieged, 1863*. New York: St. Martin's Press, 1995.

———. *Shiloh: Bloody April*. New York: William Morrow & Co., 1974; rpt. Dayton, OH: Morningside House, 2001.

Symonds, Craig L. *Joseph E. Johnston: A Civil War Biography*. New York: W. W. Norton & Company, 1992.

———. *Stonewall of the West: Patrick Cleburne and the Civil War*. Lawrence: University Press of Kansas, 1997.

Taylor, John. *Bloody Valverde: A Civil War Battle on the Rio Grande, February 21, 1862*. Albuquerque: University of New Mexico Press, 1995.

Taylor, Quintard. *In Search of the Racial Frontier: African Americans in the American West, 1528–1990.* New York: W. W. Norton & Company, 1998.

Taylor, Richard. *Destruction and Reconstruction: Personal Experiences of the Late War.* New York: D. Appleton and Company, 1879.

The Texas Almanac for 1858. Galveston: Richardson and Company, 1857.

Thirty-eighth Annual Catalogue of the Officers and Students of Baylor College, 1884–1885 (Female Department). Brenham: Fred R. Carrick, 1884.

Thirty-fourth Annual Catalogue of the Officers and Students of Hollins Institute, 1876–1877. Baltimore: Charles Harvey & Co., 1877.

Thompson, Cecilia. *History of Marfa and Presidio County, 1535–1946.* Two volumes. Austin: Nortex Press, 1985.

Thompson, Charles D., Jr. *Border Odyssey: Travels Along the U.S./Mexico Divide.* Austin: University of Texas Press, 2015.

Thompson, Jerry D. *Confederate General of the West: Henry Hopkins Sibley.* Natchitoches: Northwestern State University Press, 1987; rpt. College Station: Texas A&M University Press, 1996.

———. *Cortina: Defending the Mexican Name in Texas.* College Station: Texas A&M University Press, 2007.

———. *Juan Cortina and the Texas-Mexico Frontier, 1859–1877.* El Paso: Texas Western Press, 1994.

———, editor. *Civil War in the Southwest: Recollections of the Sibley Brigade.* College Station: Texas A&M University Press, 2001.

Thrapp, Dan L. *Encyclopedia of Frontier Biography.* Four volumes. Glendale, CA: Arthur H. Clark Company, 1988; rpt. Lincoln: University of Nebraska Press, 1991.

———. *Victorio and the Mimbres Apaches.* Norman: University of Oklahoma Press, 1974.

Tise, Sammy. *Texas County Sheriffs.* Albuquerque: Oakwood Printing, 1989.

Timmons, W. H. *El Paso: A Borderlands History.* El Paso: Texas Western Press, 1990; rpt. 2004.

Tomblin, Barbara Brooks. *The Civil War on the Mississippi: Union Sailors, Gunboat Captains, and the Campaign to Control the River.* Lexington: University Press of Kentucky, 2016.

Tout, Otis B. *The First Thirty Years (1901–1931): Being An Account of the Principal Events in the History of Imperial Valley, Southern California, U.S.A.* San Diego, CA: Otis B. Tout, 1931.

Townsend, Stephen A. *The Yankee Invasion of Texas.* College: Texas A&M University Press, 2006.

Turner, Frederick Jackson. *The Frontier in American History*. New York: Henry Holt and Company, 1921; rpt. Tucson: University of Arizona Press, 1986.

Tyler, Ronnie C. *The Big Bend: A History of the Last Texas Frontier*. Washington, D.C.: National Park Service, 1975.

The University of Texas Record 3, no. 3 (September 1901).

Utley, Dan K., and Cynthia J. Beeman. *History Ahead: Stories Beyond the Texas Roadside Markers*. College Station: Texas A&M University Press, 2010.

Utley, Robert M. *Frontier Regulars: The United States Army and the Indian, 1866–1891*. New York: Macmillan Press, 1974; rpt. Lincoln: University of Nebraska Press, 1984.

———. *Frontiersmen in Blue: The United States Army and the Indian, 1848–1865*. New York: Macmillan Press, 1967; rpt. Lincoln: University of Nebraska Press, 1981.

———. *Lone Star Justice: The First Century of the Texas Rangers*. New York: Berkley Books, 2002.

Wahlstrom, Todd W. *The Southern Exodus to Mexico: Migration Across the Borderlands After the American Civil War*. Lincoln: University of Nebraska Press, 2015.

Wanamaker, Monty, and Chris Keathley. *McMinnville*. Charleston, SC: Arcadia Publishing, 2009.

Ward, Geoffrey C. *Unforgivable Blackness: The Rise and Fall of Jack Johnson*. New York: Alfred A. Knopf, 2004.

Warner, Ezra J. *Generals in Gray: Lives of the Confederate Commanders*. Baton Rouge: Louisiana State University Press, 1959; rpt. 2008.

Weaver, John D. *The Brownsville Raid*. New York: W. W. Norton & Company, 1970; rpt. College Station: Texas A&M University Press, 1992.

———. *The Senator and the Sharecropper's Son: Exoneration of the Brownsville Soldiers*. College Station: Texas A&M University Press, 1997.

Webb, Walter Prescott. *The Texas Rangers: A Century of Frontier Defense*. Second Edition. Austin: University of Texas Press, 1965.

Weber, Sergeant-Major Walter W. *History of the 129th Machine Gun Battalion, 35th Division, A.E.F., 1917–19*. s.l.: n.p., 1920?

Weiss, Harold J., Jr. *Yours to Command: The Life and Legend of Texas Ranger Captain Bill McDonald*. Denton: University of North Texas Press, 2009.

Wentworth Military Academy Annual Catalog 1913–1914. Lexington, MO: The Academy, 1914.

Wharton, Clarence R. *Wharton's History of Fort Bend County*. San Antonio: The Naylor Company, 1939; rpt. Houston: Anson Jones Press, 1950.
White, Virgil D. *Index of U.S. Marshals, 1789–1960*. Waynesboro, TN: National Historical Publishing Company, 1988.
Whitlock, Flint. *Distant Bugles, Distant Drums: The Union Response to the Confederate Invasion of New Mexico*. Boulder: University Press of Colorado, 2006.
Wiencek, Henry. *The Moodys of Galveston and Their Mansion*. College Station: Texas A&M University Press, 2010.
Wilkins, Frederick. *The Law Comes to Texas: The Texas Rangers, 1870–1901*. Abilene, TX: State House Press, 1999.
Wilkinson, J. L. *The Trans-Cedar Lynching and the Texas Penitentiary*. Edited by Bertha E. Drager. New York: Carlton Press, 1974.
Wilkinson, Joseph B. *Laredo and the Rio Grande Frontier: A Narrative*. Austin: Jenkins Publishing Co., 1975.
Wilmot's Harlingen, Texas, City Directory, 1950. Harlingen: B. A. Wilmot, 1950.
Wilson, John P. *When the Texans Came: Missing Records from the Civil War in the Southwest*. Albuquerque: University of New Mexico Press, 2001.
———, and Jerry Thompson, editors. *The Civil War in West Texas & New Mexico: The Lost Letterbook of Brigadier General Henry Hopkins Sibley*. El Paso: Texas Western Press, 2001.
Winfrey, Dorman H., and James M. Day, editors. *The Indian Papers of Texas and the Southwest*. Austin: Texas State Historical Association, 1995.
Winters, John D. *The Civil War in Louisiana*. Baton Rouge: Louisiana State Press, 1963; rpt. 1991.
Womack, Walter. *McMinnville at a Milestone, 1810–1960*. McMinnville, TN: Standard Publishing Co., Inc., and Womack Publishing Co., 1960.
Woodard, Don. *Black Diamonds! Black Gold!* Lubbock; Texas Tech University Press, 1998.
Wood County Historical Society. *Wood County, 1850–1900*. Quitman, TX: Wood County Historical Society, 1979.
Woodworth, Steven E. *Jefferson Davis and His Generals: The Failure of Confederate Command in the West*. Lawrence: University Press of Kansas, 1990.
———. *Shiloh: Confederate High Tide in the Heartland*. Santa Barbara, CA: Praeger, 2013.
Wooster, Ralph A. *Lone Star Generals in Gray*. Austin: Eakin Press, 2000.
———. *Lone Star Regiments in Gray*. Austin: Eakin Press, 2002.
———. *Texas and Texans in the Civil War*. Austin: Eakin Press, 1995.

Wooster, Robert. *The American Military Frontiers: The United States Army in the West, 1783–1900.* Albuquerque: University of New Mexico Press, 2009.

———. *The Military and United States Indian Policy, 1865–1903.* New Haven: Yale University Press, 1988; rpt. Lincoln: University of Nebraska Press, 1995

Wooten, Dudley C., editor. *A Comprehensive History of Texas, 1685–1897.* Volume Two. Dallas: William G. Scarff, 1898.

Worcester, Donald E. *The Apaches: The Eagles of the Southwest.* Norman: University of Oklahoma Press, 1979.

Worley's City Directory, Tyler, Texas, 1934–1935. Dallas: John F. Worley Directory Co., 1935.

Worley's Directory of Tyler, Texas, 1913. Dallas: John F. Worley Directory Co., 1913.

Wright, General Marcus J., compiler. *Texas in the War, 1861–1865.* Edited by Harold B. Simpson. Hillsboro, TX: Hill Junior College Press, 1965.

Yeary, Mamie, compiler. *Reminiscences of the Boys in Gray, 1861–1865.* Dallas: Smith and Lamar Publishing House, 1912.

Yelderman, Pauline. *The Jay Bird Association of Fort Bend County: A White Man's Union.* Waco: Texian Press, 1979.

Young, Earle B. *Tracks to the Sea: Galveston and Western Railroad Development, 1866–1900.* College Station: Texas A&M University Press, 1999.

Young, Elliott. *Catarino Garza's Revolution on the Texas-Mexico Border.* Durham, NC: Duke University Press, 2004.

White, Lonnie J. *Panthers to Arrowheads: The 36th (Texas-Oklahoma) Division in World War I.* Austin: Presidial Press, 1984.

Zwick, Tim, and Donovan Reichenberger. *Ranchlands to Railroads: An Illustrated Sketch of M County's Pre-Territorial History.* Alva, OK: Alva Centennial Commission, 1986.

Internet Sources

Find A Grave. Online at http://www.findagrave.com.

Newspapers

Abilene Reporter-News
Abilene Semi-Weekly Farm Reporter
Albuquerque Journal

Bibliography

Albuquerque Tribune
Alpine Avalanche
Arizona Daily Star (Tucson)
Arizona Republic (Phoenix)
Arkansas Gazette (Arkansas Post)
Austin American
Austin American-Statesman
Austin Daily Statesman
Austin Statesman
Bastrop Advertiser
Belleville Countryman
Bisbee Daily Review
Black Range (Robinson, NM)
Bourbon News (Paris, KY)
Brenham Daily Banner
Brenham Weekly Banner
Brownsville Daily Herald
Charleston Daily Mail
Charleston Gazette
Chicago Daily Times
Chicago Dispatch
Chicago Tribune
Civilian and Weekly Gazette (Galveston)
Colorado Citizen (Columbus, TX)
Comanche Chief (TX)
Coquille Valley Sentinel (OR)
Corpus Christi Caller
Corpus Christi Caller-Times
Courier-Journal (Louisville, KY)
Corsicana Observer
Corsicana Semi-Weekly Light
Daily Alta California (San Francisco)
Daily Arkansas Gazette (Little Rock)
Daily Ledger and Texan (San Antonio)
Daily Nashville Patriot
Daily State Gazette (Austin)
Daily State Journal (Austin)
Dallas Daily Herald
Dallas Morning News

Denison Daily Cressett
Denison Daily News
Dodge City Times
Ellis County Star (Ellis, KS)
El Paso Daily Times
El Paso Herald
El Paso Herald-Post
El Paso Morning Times
El Paso Times
Evening Star (Washington, D.C.)
Falfurrias Facts
Fauquier Democrat (Warrenton, VA)
Fayetteville Weekly Observer
Flag of the Union (Jackson, MS)
Flake's Daily Bulletin (Galveston)
Flake's Semi-Weekly Bulletin (Galveston)
Floresville Chronicle-Journal
Fort Worth Daily Gazette
Frank Leslie's Illustrated Newspaper (New York)
Frontier Echo (Jacksboro, TX)
Galveston Daily News
Galveston Tri-Weekly News
Galveston Weekly News
Goliad Guard
Greensboro North State (NC)
Greensboro Patriot (NC)
Hays City Sentinel
Houston Daily Journal
Houston Daily Post
Houston Daily Telegraph
Houston Daily Union
Houston Evening Telegraph
Houston Tri-Weekly Telegraph
Houston Tri-Weekly Union
Houston Weekly Telegraph
Imperial Valley Weekly (El Centro, CA)
Kenedy Times
Kentuckian-Citizen (Paris)
Kerrville Daily Times

Lampasas Dispatch
Laredo Times
Las Cruces Sun-News
Las Vegas Gazette
Leavenworth Times
Lebanon Daily News (PA)
Lebanon Semi-Weekly News (PA)
Linn County Republic (Mound City, KS)
Los Angeles Herald
Los Angeles Times
Lutcher News-Examiner
Memphis Daily Appeal
Mineola Monitor
Mohave County Miner (Kingman, AZ)
Nashville Daily Union
National Police Gazette (New York City)
Navarro Express
New Orleans Crescent
New Orleans Daily Picayune
New Orleans Times-Picayune
New York Herald
New York Sun
New York Times
Norton's Daily Union Intelligencer (Dallas, TX)
Odessa American
Palestine Daily Herald
Ruston Daily Leader
St. Louis Post-Dispatch
Sacramento Daily Union
Salem Weekly Advocate
San Angelo Standard-Times
San Antonio Daily Express
San Antonio Daily Herald
San Antonio Daily Light
San Antonio Ledger
San Antonio Light
San Antonio Semi-Weekly Express
San Antonio Semi-Weekly News
San Francisco Chronicle

San Marcos Free Press
San Mateo Times
San Saba County News
San Saba News
Sherman Herald Democrat
Shreveport Times
Sonoma County Journal (Petaluma, CA)
Southern Standard (McMinnville, TN)
The South-Western (Shreveport, LA)
Statesville Record and Landmark
Telegraph and Texas Register (Houston)
The Tennessean (Nashville)
Texas Sentinel (Austin)
Texas State Gazette (Austin)
Tri-Weekly Herald (Marshall, TX)
Tri-Weekly Houston Union
Tucson Daily Citizen
Tyler Morning Telegraph
Tyler Reporter
Victoria Advocate
Victoria Daily Advocate
Washington Post
Weekly Mississippian (Jackson, MS)
Weekly State Gazette (Austin)
Weekly State Journal (Austin)
White Man (Weatherford, TX)
Wichita Daily Eagle (KS)
Wichita Daily Times (KS)
Wise County Messenger
Yuma Daily Sun

Public and Official Documents

Arizona Office of Vital Records. Death Certificates. Department of Health Services, Phoenix, Arizona. Copy in the possession of the author.

American Battle Monuments Commission. *36th Division Summary of Operations in the World War*. Washington, D.C.: Government Printing Office, 1944.

Bourbon County, Kentucky. Deed Books. Office of the Clerk of the Circuit Court. Paris, Kentucky. Copies in the possession of the author.

———. Marriage Records 2 (1799–1839). Office of the Clerk of the Circuit Court. Paris, Kentucky. Copy in the possession of the author.

Butler County, Ohio. Marriage Records 2 (1835–1847). Office of the Clerk of the County Court. Hamilton, Ohio. Copy in the possession of the author.

Clark County, Nevada. Marriage Book 82. Clark County Recorder's Office. Las Vegas, Nevada. Copy in the possession of the author.

Confederate States Army. *Regulations for the Army of the Confederate States: As Adopted by Act of Congress, Approved March 6, 1861.* New Orleans: Henry P. Lanthrop, 1861.

Georgia Department of Public Health. Death Certificates. Office of Vital Records, Atlanta, Georgia. Copy in the possession of the author.

Illinois Adjutant General's Department. *Report of the Adjutant General of the State of Illinois.* Volume Six. Springfield: Baker, Bailhache & Co., 1867.

Jackson County, Missouri. Marriage Records. Office of the County Recorder of Deeds, Independence, Missouri. Copies in the possession of the author.

Kenedy County. Probate Minutes (Willacy and Kenedy Counties). Volume 1 (1913–1950). Office of the Clerk of the County Court. Sarita, Texas. Copies in the possession of the author.

Kentucky Department for Public Health. Death Certificates. Office of Vital Statistics, Frankfort, Kentucky. Copies in the possession of the author.

Lebanon County, Pennsylvania. County Marriage Records. Office of the Register of Wills and Clerk of Orphans' Court, Lebanon, Pennsylvania. Copies in the possession of the author.

McDonald, W. J. *Biennial Report of the State Revenue Agent, 1906–08.* Austin: Von Boeckmann-Jones Company, 1908.

McDonald, W. J. *Biennial Report of the State Revenue Agent, 1908–1910.* Austin: Austin Printing Company, 1910.

México. Comisión Pesquisidora de la Frontera del Norte. *Reports of the Committee of Investigation Sent in 1873 by the Mexican Government to the Frontier of Texas.* New York: Baker & Godwin, 1875.

Rutherford County Marriage Book (1804–1881). Tennessee Marriage Records. Tennessee State Library and Archives, Nashville, Tennessee. Copies in the possession of the author.

Texas Adjutant General's Department. *Annual and Biennial Reports of the Adjutant-General of the State of Texas, 1870–1916.* Austin: State Printers, 1870–1917.

Texas Bureau of Vital Statistics. Death Certificates. Department of Health, Austin, Texas. Copies in the possession of the author.

———. Birth Certificates. Department of Health, Austin, Texas. Copies in possession of author.

Texas Constitutional Convention. *Journal of the Constitutional Convention of the State of Texas, Begun and Held at the City of Austin, September 6, 1875.* Galveston: "News" Office, 1875.

Texas Court of Criminal Appeals. 8–10, 30 *Texas Criminal Reports* (1880–1881, 1892). St. Louis: F. H. Thomas and Company, 1880; St. Louis: Gilbert Book Company, 1881; Austin: State of Texas, 1892.

Texas Legislature. *General and Special Laws of Texas.*

———. Proceedings of the Joint Committee of the Senate and the House in the Investigation of the State Ranger Force. Thirty-sixth Legislature, Regular Session. Copies provided to the author by A&ISD-TSLAC, Austin, Texas.

———. *Revised Civil Statutes of the State of Texas Passed by the Sixteenth Legislature, February 21, 1879.* Austin: State Printing Office, 1887.

Texas Legislature. House. *House Journal of the Twelfth Legislature, State of Texas. First [Called] Session.* Austin: Tracy, Siemering & Co., 1870.

———. *Journal of the House of Representatives: Being the First Session of the Seventeenth Legislature of the State of Texas.* Galveston: A. H. Belo & Co., 1881.

———. *Journal of the House of Representatives. Fourteenth Legislature—Second Session.* Austin: n.p., 1875.

———. *Journal of the House of Representatives of the Regular Session of the Fiftieth Legislature of the State of Texas.* Austin: Von Boeckmann-Jones, 1947.

———. *Journal of the House of Representatives of the Regular Session of the Thirty-first Legislature of Texas.* Austin: Von Boeckmann-Jones, 1909.

———. *Journal of the House of Representatives of the Regular Session of the Thirty-second Legislature of Texas.* Austin: Austin Printing Company, 1911.

———. *Journal of the House of Representatives of the Sixteenth Legislature of the State of Texas (Extra Session).* Galveston: News Book and Job Establishment, 1879.

———. *Journal of the House of Representatives of the State of Texas, Being the Called Session of the Eighteenth Legislature.* Austin: E. W. Swindells, 1884.

———. *Journal of the House of Representatives of the State of Texas, Being the Called Session of the Twenty-fourth Legislature.* Austin: Ben C. Jones & Co., 1895.

———. *Journal of the House of Representatives of the State of Texas: Being the [First] Session of the Fourteenth Legislature.* Austin: n.p., 1874–1875.

———. *Journal of the House of Representatives of the State of Texas, Being the First Session of the Sixteenth Legislature.* Galveston: A. H. Belo & Co., 1879.

———. *Journal of the House of Representatives of the State of Texas: Being the Session of the Thirteenth Legislature.* Austin: John Cardwell, 1873.

———. *Journal of the House of Representatives of Texas, Being the Regular Session of the Twenty-seventh Legislature.* Austin: Von Boeckmann, Schutze & Co., 1901.

———. *Journal of the House of Representatives of the Twelfth Legislature. Regular Session.* Austin: J. G. Tracy, 1871.

———. *Journal of the House of Representatives of the Twentieth Legislature, State of Texas. Regular Session.* Austin: Triplett & Hutchings, 1887.

Texas Legislature. Senate. *Journal of the Senate of Texas: Being the Session of the Thirteenth Legislature.* Austin: John Cardwell, 1873.

———. *Journal of the Senate of the State of Texas, Being the First Session of the Sixteenth Legislature.* Galveston: A. H. Belo & Co., 1879.

———. *Journal of the Senate of the State of Texas, Regular Session of the Fiftieth Legislature.* Austin: Von Boeckmann-Jones Co., 1901.

———. *Journal of the Senate of Texas, Being the Regular Session of the Twenty-seventh Legislature.* Austin: Von Boeckmann, Schutze & Co., 1901.

———. *Senate Journal of the Twelfth Legislature of the State of Texas. [Regular Session].* Austin: J. G. Tracy, 1871.

United States Army. *Army and Navy Journal: Gazette of the Regular and Volunteer Forces.* New York: Army and Navy Journal, Inc., 1878–1880, 1899–1900.

———. *Correspondence Relating to the War with Spain.* Two volumes. Washington, D.C.: Government Printing Office, 1902.

———. *Official Army Register for January 1, 1949.* Washington, D.C.: Government Printing Office, 1949.

———. *Official Army Register for July 1, 1921.* Washington, D.C.: Government Printing Office, 1922.

———. *Official Register of Officers of Volunteers in the Service of the United States.* War Department Document No. 117. Washington, D.C.: Government Printing Office, 1900.

United States Attorney General's Office. *Register of the Department of Justice and the Courts of the United States*. Twenty-second–Twenty-sixth Editions. Washington, D.C.: Government Printing Office, 1914–1918.

United States Committee on Public Information. Official Bulletin.

United States Congress. *The United States Statutes at Large*. 125 volumes. Boston: Little, Brown and Company, 1848–1874; Washington: Government Printing Office, 1875–2011.

United States Congress. House of Representatives. *Annual Report of the Attorney General of the United States*. House Executive Document No. 7. 50th Congress, 2nd Session. Serial No. 2645.

———. *Annual Report of the Commissioner of Indian Affairs*. House Executive Document No. 1. 49th Congress, 2nd Session. Serial No. 2467.

———. *Annual Report of the Commissioner of Indian Affairs*. House Executive Document No. 1. 50th Congress, 1st Session. Serial No. 2542.

———. *Annual Report of the Secretary of War*. House Executive Document No. 1. 41st Congress, 2nd Session. Serial No. 1412.

———. *Annual Report of the Secretary of War*. House Executive Document No. 1, Part. 2. 46th Congress, 2nd Session. Serial No. 1903.

———. *Annual Report of the Secretary of War*. House Executive Document No. 1, Part. 2. 46th Congress, 3rd Session. Serial No. 1952.

———. *Annual Report of the Secretary of War*. House Executive Document No. 1, Pt. 2. 50th Congress, 1st Session. Serial No. 2533.

———. *Annual Report of the Secretary of War*, House Executive Document No. 1, Part 2. 52nd Congress, 2nd Session. Serial No. 3077.

———. *Annual Reports of the War Department*. House Executive Document No. 2, Volume 1, Part 2. 56th Congress, 1st Session. Serial Nos. 3900.

———. *Annual Reports of the War Department*. House Executive Document No. 2, Volume 1, Parts 3–5. 56th Congress, 2nd Session. Serial Nos. 4074–4076.

———. *Depredations on the Frontiers of Texas*. House Executive Document No. 39. 42nd Congress, 3rd Session. Serial No. 1565.

———. *Depredations on the Frontiers of Texas*. House Executive Document No. 257. 43rd Congress, 1st Session. Serial No. 1615.

———. *Foreign Relations*. House Executive Document No. 1. 47th Congress, 1st Session. Serial No. 2009.

———. *Mexican Border Troubles*. House Executive Document No. 13. 45th Congress, 1st Session. Serial No. 1773.

———. *Official Opinions of the Attorneys-General of the United States* 20. House Miscellaneous Document No. 44. 53rd Congress, 3rd Session. Serial No. 3331.

Bibliography

———. *Relations of the United States with Mexico*. Two Parts. House Report No. 701. 45th Congress, 2nd Session. Serial No. 1824.

———. *Texas Frontier Troubles*. House Report No. 343. 44th Congress, 1st Session. Serial 1709.

United States Congress. Senate. *Affairs in the Philippines*. Senate Document No. 331, Pt. 3. 57th Congress, 1st Session. Serial No. 4244.

———. *Affray at Brownsville*. Senate Document No. 402, Parts 1–6. 60th Congress, 1st Session. Serial Nos. 5252–5256.

———. *Annual Report of the Commissioner of Indian Affairs*. Senate Executive Document No. 2. 36th Congress, 1st Session. Serial No. 1023.

———. *Annual Report of the Secretary of War*. Senate Executive No. 2. 36th Congress, 1st Session. Serial No. 1024.

———. *Expense of Patrolling the Boundary in Texas*. Senate Document No. 404. 62nd Congress, 2nd Session. Serial No. 6175.

———. *Petition from E. E. White*. Senate Miscellaneous Document No. 203. 53rd Congress, 2nd Session. Serial No. 3171.

———. *Report of Brownsville Court of Inquiry*, Senate Document No. 701, Parts 1–12, 61st Congress, 3rd Session. Serial No. 5888-5891.

———. *Report of the Joint Committee on the Conduct of the War: Miscellaneous*. Senate Report No. 108, Part 3. 37th Congress, 3rd Session. Serial No. 1154

———. *Report of the Joint Committee on the Conduct of the War: Red River Expedition*. Senate Report No. 142. 38th Congress, 2nd Session. Serial No. 1213.

———. *Summary Discharge or Mustering Out of Regiments or Companies*. Senate Document No. 155. 59th Congress, 2nd Session. Serial No. 5078.

United States Department of the Navy. *Official Records of the Union and Confederate Navies in the War of the Rebellion*. Thirty volumes. Washington, D.C.: Government Printing Office, 1894–1914.

United States Department of War. *The War of the Rebellion: A Compilation of the Official Records of the Union and Confederate Armies*. 128 volumes. Washington, D.C.: Government Printing Office, 1880–1901.

West Virginia Division of Vital Statistics. Death Certificates. State Department of Health, Charleston, West Virginia. Copy in possession of author.

Theses and Dissertations

Bonner, Helen Frances. "Major John B. Jones: The Defender of the Frontier of Texas." M.A. thesis, University of Texas at Austin, 1950.

Bridges, Jennifer. "Skiddy Street: Prostitution and Vice in Denison, Texas, 1872–1922." M.A. thesis, University of North Texas, 2011.

Contreras, Hernán A. "Origins of Boss Rule in Starr County." M.A. thesis, University of Houston-Clear Lake, 2008.

Hall, Major Thomas K. "The Confederate High Command at Shiloh." MMAS thesis, Fort Leavenworth, 1995.

Hamaker, Blake Richard. "Making a Good Soldier: A Historical and Quantitative Study of the 15th Texas Infantry, C.S.A." M.A. thesis, University of North Texas, 1998.

Lance, Major Joseph M., III. "Patrick R. Cleburne and the Tactical Employment of His Division at Chickamauga." MMAS thesis, Fort Leavenworth, 1996.

Linn, Brian McAllister. "The Thirty-third Infantry, United States Volunteers: An American Regiment in the Philippine Insurrection, 1899–1901." M.A. thesis, Ohio State University, 1981.

Malbrew, Ricardo Purnell. "Brownsville Revisited." M.A. thesis, Louisiana State University, 2007.

Marple, Major Allan D. "The Philippine Scouts: A Case Study in the Use of Indigenous Soldiers, Northern Luzon, The Philippine Islands, 1899." MMAS thesis, Fort Leavenworth, 1983.

Matthews, James T. "Major's Confederate Cavalry Brigade." M.A. thesis, Texas Tech University, 1991.

Redman, Jack Duane. "General John B. Jones: Twenty Years of Service to Texas." M. A. thesis, University of Texas at El Paso, 1983.

Shannon, Mildred Cox. "James B. Gillett, Indomitable Texan." M.A. thesis, Sul Ross State College, 1960.

Taylor, Travis. "Lynching on the Border: The Death of Antonio Rodríguez and the Rise of Anti-Americanism during the Mexican Revolution." M.A. thesis, Angelo State University, 2012.

Unpublished Material

Alexander, Bob. Letter to author. Maypearl, Texas. 6 February 2018.

"Ancestors of James Buchanan Gillett." MS, n.d. Copy provided to the author by James M. McCrae.

"Descendants of James Buchanan Gillett." MS, n.d. Copy provided to the author by James M. McCrae.

Lanthrip, Catherine. "The McNelly Family from Ireland to Virginia to Texas." MS, n.d. Copy provided to the author by the Family History Library, Salt Lake City, Utah.

McClure, Meade L. "Major Andrew Drumm, 1828–1919." MS. McClure's paper was read before the Missouri Valley Historical Society on May 31, 1919.

"Marquis de Lafayette Price (1840–1923)." MS, n.d. Copy provided to the author by Charles Temple.

Watson, Maria. "The Armstrong Ranch: A Documented Narrative History." MS, 1981. Copy provided to the author by the Texas Historical Commission, Austin, TX.

Index

A

Abernathy, John R. "Jack," 394
Abilene, Texas, 235, 275, 300, 353, 430, 459, 496
Adair, Ab, 275
Adams, John W., 269
Adams, Roy Hodge, 487
Addington, James Preston, 174
Adobe Walls, second battle of, 20
Aguinaldo y Famy, Emilio, 184–185, 188–191
Ainsworth Ranch, 320–321
Albuquerque, New Mexico, 56–58, 149, 313
Albuquerque, Texas, 74
Alexander, Andrew Jackson, 91–92
Alexander, William Vinson "Red," 324
Alexander, Bob, viii, 34, 297, 411
Alexandria, Louisiana, 10–11, 62, 64, 67–69, 215–217
Alice, Texas, 114, 341, 344–345, 348, 350, 394, 396, 432, 468–469, 472
Allee, Alfred Young, 332, 464
Allee, James Milton, 366
Allison, William "Bill," 127–128, 130, 134, 285–286
Allison, William Mack, 381–382, 384
Allison, William Davis "Dave," 496
Alpine, Texas, 144–146, 148, 423, 484, 486
Altuda Ranch, 146
Amarillo, Texas, 46, 301, 305, 368–369, 371, 391–392, 436–439, 483
American Expeditionary Forces, 118
Anahuac, Texas, 459
Anders, Joseph Lee, 437, 487–488
Anderson, Anna Eloise, 43, 47
Anderson, Attilia Aldridge, 43, 46–47
Anderson, Eleanor Lena, 43, 47
Anderson, Elizabeth, 43, 47
Anderson, Mary E., 43, 47
Anderson, Reuben T., 43–44, 46
Anderson, Samuel Smith, 8
Anderson, Texas, 73
Anderson, Thomas J. H. (father), 43
Anderson, Thomas J. H. (son), 43, 47
Anderson County, Texas, 72–73, 365, 487
Angelina County, Texas, 72
Angle, Albert "Ab," 393
Anthony, Milton, 327

Apache Indians, 136, 174, 226, 228, 230–231; Lipans, 124–125, 130, 160; Chihennes (or Mimbres), 135–136, 138, 226, 229–231; Mescaleros, 135–136, 226, 231; Chiricahuas, 226
Apache Reservation (Ojo Caliente), 226
Apache Reservation (San Carlos), 135, 226
Apache Reservation (Tularosa), 228
Appomattox Court House, Virginia, 266
Aransas County, Texas, 419–420
Arapaho Indians, 317
Arizona Brigade (CSA), 6, 214
Arkansas Post, Arkansas, 5, 248, 250–252; battle of, 249–250
Armstrong, Betavia Jane "Beta," 100
Armstrong, Charles Mitchell, 112, 117, 118
Armstrong, Elliott Ropes "Tim," 113, 114
Armstrong, Jamie Durst, 112, 117
Armstrong, John Barclay, Jr. (IV), 112, 115, 548 n31, 549 n40
Armstrong, John Barkley, III: and Las Cuevas War, 90, 103; birth of, 99; education, 100; travels to Texas, 101; and Travis Rifles, 102; and Coke-Davis dispute, 102; as city marshal candidate, 102; enlists in McNelly's company, 103–104; and Second Battle of Palo Alto, 103; as Ranger sergeant, 103; personality, characteristics, and motivations, 104; and Espantosa Lake fight, 104–105; and John Mayfield, 105; as Ranger lieutenant, 106, 111; and John Wesley Hardin, 106, 108–110, 159; marries Mollie, 111; and Round Rock fight, 111, 166–167; resigns from Special State Troops, 111; as businessman, 111, 113–115, 350; as cattle rancher, 112–113; and Brownsville Rifles, 113; as Special Ranger, 113; and Texas Volunteer Guard, 113–114; and death of Mollie, 114; and deaths of children, 114, 115; and railroad project, 114–115; death of, 115; and Brassel murders, 159
Armstrong, John Barkley, Jr., 99–101, 543 n1
Armstrong, J. T., 343, 478
Armstrong, Julia Katherine, 113, 117
Armstrong, Laura Maria, 100
Armstrong, Lavanda Martin "Van," 100
Armstrong, Maria Susannah (Ready), 99, 543 n1
Armstrong, Mary Helena "Mollie" (Durst), 111–112, 114, 116
Armstrong, Mary Ready "Mollie," 100
Armstrong, Thomas Reeves, 113, 117–118
Armstrong, Thomas Temple, 100
Armstrong, William Francis, 100
Armstrong, Maria Josephine, 112, 117
Armstrong County, Texas, 304–305
Armstrong Ranch, 112–113, 341
Arrington, George Washington, 128, 161, 269, 591 n54
Atascosa County, Texas, 106, 169–170, 433, 479, 488
Atchison, Topeka & Santa Fe Railroad, 138

Index

Aten, Albert Boyce, 305, 310
Aten, Austin Cunningham, 281–282, 303, 612 n4
Aten, Austin Ira: birth of, 281; and Sam Bass, 282; enlists in Frontier Battalion, 282; and tax collecting, 283; and Wesley Collier, 285, 289–290, 416–417; as Ranger corporal, 286; and San Ambrosia Creek fight, 286, 288; and John R. Hughes, 289, 293, 416–418; and fence-cutting, 291–292, 294–295, 325; and Odle brothers, 292–293; and train robbers, 293; as Ranger sergeant, 294; and Williamson family murders, 296–297; and Jaybird-Woodpecker War, 298–299; as Fort Bend County sheriff, 299; as cattle rancher, 301, 303, 308–309; as Special Ranger, 301; as businessman, 301, 308–309; and dispute with McClelland brothers, 301–303, 620–621 n48; marries Imogen, 302; as Castro County sheriff, 303–305; as XIT division superintendent, 306–307; and civic affairs, 308–311; moves to California, 309; death of, 311; and Las Ysles parley, 319–320
Aten, Calvin Grant "Cal," 282, 294, 421
Aten, Clara Isabell "Belle," 282
Aten, Edwin Dunlap "Ed," 282, 424, 426
Aten, Eloise, 310, 312
Aten, Frank Lincoln, 282
Aten, Imogen, 308, 312
Aten, Imogen (Boyce), 302–303, 305, 309, 311
Aten, Ira Dunlap, 308, 312
Aten, Katherine Eveline (Dunlap), 281, 612 n4
Aten, Margaret Angeline Elizabeth "Angie," 281–282
Aten, Marion Hughes, 303, 311–312
Aten, Thomas Quinn, 281–282
Athens, Texas, 388
Atkinson, John G., 35
Atlanta, Georgia, 255, 262, 266
Austin, Arkansas, 5, 246
Austin, Texas, 2, 31–32, 34, 38, 43, 45–47, 79, 89, 92, 95–96, 102–103, 108, 110–112, 114, 116, 121–122, 130–134, 157, 165, 168, 170, 172, 282–283, 285, 291, 301–303, 337–338, 341, 350–351, 356, 372, 382, 393, 399, 406, 433–435, 449, 454–455, 470, 473, 475, 486–487, 489–490, 493–494, 496, 498–500
Avriett, Edmund Ledbetter "Ed," 487–488
Avriett, Hall Thomas, 486, 488

B

Baca, Enofre, 136–137
Baca, José, 138
Bader, Karl, 25
Bader, Peter, 25–26
Bagby, Arthur Pendleton, 11, 60, 66–68, 218

Bagdad, Mexico, 83, 87
Bailey, David W. H., 20
Bailey, Marvin Eugene, 439
Baird, John R., 25–26
Baird, Philip Cuney, 285–286
Baird, Spruce McCoy, 214
Baker, Anderson Yancey "Ancey," 343–344, 348–350, 432, 435
Baker, John William, 478
Baker, Sam, 374
Ballinger, Texas, 329, 464–465
Bandera County, Texas, 433
Banks, Nathaniel Prentice, 10–11, 62–64, 67, 215–216
Barber, John, 293, 417, 463, 465
Barela, Francisco "Chico," 33, 35
Barker, Dudley Snyder "Dud," 381
Barker, W. N., 367
Barksdale, Texas, 296, 329, 465
Barnes, John H., 421
Barnes, Seaborn "Sebe," 38, 40–41, 165, 167, 273
Barnes, Thomas Harris, 328
Barrel Springs Ranch, 146–147, 148, 149, 150
Bass, Sam, 37–38, 40–42, 111, 133, 165–167, 282, 373, 421
Bastrop County, Texas, 73, 75, 82
Bastrop, Texas, 160, 343–344, 475–477
Bates, John Coalter, 191
Bates, Lonnie, 434
Bates, Winfred Finas, 343–344, 346, 348, 351
Baton Rouge, Louisiana, 6, 215
Batson, Matthew Arlington, 186–190
Batson, Texas, 351–352
Baugh, Levin Powell, 292, 325
Baugh, Washington Morgan, 292, 325
Bay City, Texas, 115
Baylor, Charles Gano, 204
Baylor, Frances Norton "Fanny," 204
Baylor, George Wythe: as lieutenant of Detachment C, Frontier Battalion, 134–135, 225, 227–228; as captain of Company A, Frontier Battalion, 135–138, 229, 232–233; and Sierra Diablo fight, 138, 230–231; birth of, 203; education, 204; and California gold rush, 204–205, 580–581 n4; and Vigilance Committee, 205; returns from California, 205–206, 581 n7; as Indian fighter, 206–207; as adjutant of Second Texas Mounted Rifles, 207; and invasion of New Mexico, 208–209; as Johnston's aide-de-camp, 209–210; and Battle of Shiloh, 212–213; as colonel of Second Texas Cavalry, Arizona Brigade, 214; marries Sallie, 214; and Battle of Bayou Bourbeau, 216; and Wilson's Farm skirmish, 218; and Battle of Mansfield, 218–219; and Battle of Pleasant Hill, 219; as brigade commander,

Index

219–220; and Battle of Yellow Bayou, 220–221; and John A. Wharton, 221–223; as businessman, 223–225; personality, characteristics, and motivation, 225–226; and relations with Mexicans, 228, 229; and Victorio, 228–229; as temporary commander of Frontier Battalion, 235; and fence-cutting, 235–236; discharged from Frontier Battalion, 236; as legislator, 236–237; as expatriate in Mexico, 238; and Mexican Revolution, 238–239; death of, 239
Baylor, Henry Weidner, 204
Baylor, John Robert, 50, 53, 204, 206–209, 214
Baylor, John Walker (father), 203, 209
Baylor, John Walker (son), 203
Baylor, John William, 206, 467
Baylor, Mary Courtenay, 224–225, 238–239
Baylor, Mary Jane, 204
Baylor, Robert Emmett Bledsoe, 204
Baylor, Sallie Garland (Sydnor), 214, 221, 223–226, 238
Baylor, Sophie Elizabeth, 203
Baylor, Sophie Marie, 224
Baylor, Sophie Marie (Weidner), 203–204, 580 n3
Baylor, Walker Keith, 206
Bayou Bourbeau, battle of, 10, 66, 216
Beam, Jackson "Jack," 285, 289
Bean, Edward "Ed," 365
Bean, James "Jim," 365
Bean, Robert, 16
Bean, Roy, 377, 379, 429
Beauregard, Pierre Gustave Toutant, 210–211, 213–214
Beckham, Joseph Preston "Joe," 370–372, 375, 642 n27
Beckham, Robert Henderson, 488
Bee, Hamilton Prioleau, 67–69, 218–220
Bee County, Texas, 158, 469
Bell, Charles S., 74
Bell County, Texas, 75, 293, 326
Bell, Eugene, 389, 477
Bell, Peter Hansbrough, 121
Bellevue, Texas, 374, 379
Belton, Texas, 38
Benavides, Francisco, 468–469
Benavides, Santos, 170
Ben Ficklin, Texas, 271–272
Benham, Calhoun, 212
Bennett Ranch, 336, 468
Bexar County, Texas, 172, 395, 463
Beyers, Joseph K., 412
Big Bend, Texas, 485
Big Spring, Nebraska, 37

Big Spring, Texas, 276, 437, 443, 448, 459
Bishop, Bob, 304
Blackburn, William Allen, 28–29, 130, 292
Blakely, Jacob W. "Jake," 299
Blanco County, Texas, 284
Blocker, Abner Pickens, Sr., 19
Blocker, Abner Pickens "Ab," Jr., 306
Blocksom, Augustus Perry, 399–400, 402
Blount, James H., 192
Blunt, Walter Fraser, 473
Boerne, Texas, 298
Bolza Ranch, Mexico, 169
Bonham, Texas, 155
Boone, Hannibal Honestus, 8–9, 42, 66, 73, 96
Booth, Richard R., 79
Borajo, Antonio Severo, 32
Borden County, Texas, 374
Border, C. Lycurgus "Curg," 345–346
Borger, Texas, 498
Boring, Samuel Watson, 142
Boudinot, Elias Cornelius, 328
Bourke, John Gregory, 333, 335, 467
Bowen, Neill, 108
Bowen, Walter C., 332
Bowen, William Jerry, 341
Boyce, Albert Gallatin, 305, 307
Boyce, John Ely, 303, 306
Boyce, Reuben Hornsby "Rube," 125, 131, 134, 283, 555 n29, 613 n9
Brackettville, Texas, 78, 170, 435
Brady City, Texas, 284
Braeutigam, Johann Wolfgang, 285, 289, 416
Bragg, Braxton, 210–213, 252–259, 261
Brashear City, Louisiana, 62, 65–66, 215; battle of, 65, 215
Brassell, George, 158–159
Brassell, Phillip H., 158–159, 165
Brazoria County, Texas, 72
Brazos County, Texas, 72, 75, 365
Brazos Reservation, 206
Breckinridge, John Cabell, 210, 258
Brenham, Texas, 67, 70, 72, 95
Brewster, Calvin George, 407, 489
Brewster County, Texas, 142, 144, 237
Bridge, Walter Eldridge "Dickie," 433–434
Bridges, Arthur, 238–239
Briscoe County, Texas, 304

Index

Britton, Francis L. "Frank," 78, 102
Broocks, Benjamin Carlo, 346
Brooken, Bill, 367
Brooken, Bood, 367
Brooks, Adeline "Ada," 316
Brooks, Annie E., 316
Brooks, Corrinne Kenny, 342, 357
Brooks County, Texas, 356
Brooks, Francis Breckinridge "Fannie," 316
Brooks, James Abijah: as first sergeant of Company F, 292, 322, 329, 464; birth of, 315; education, 316; moves to Texas, 316; as farmer, 317; as trail driver, 317; and business failures, 317; and alcoholism, 317, 342, 357; enlists in Company F, Frontier Battalion, 317; and John H. Rogers, 318; as corporal of Company F, 318; and Las Ysles parley, 319–321; and labor strikes, 323, 336–337, 351–352; and Albert St. John, 323–324; and fence-cutting, 325–326; and legal troubles, 325, 328, 463; and Conner fight, 326–327; and presidential pardon, 328–329; as lieutenant of Company F, 329, 465; marries Virginia, 329; as captain of Company F, 331, 336, 468; and Garza War, 333, 335–336, 467–468; personality, characteristics, and motivations, 336–337, 342; and Fitzsimmons-Maher prizefight, 338–339, 376; and William Bowen murder, 341; and Reese-Townsend feud, 343–344, 387, 477; and Broocks-Border feud, 346; and Choynski-Johnson prizefight, 347–348; as captain of Company A, Ranger Force, 348; and Baker-de la Cerda feud, 350; and oil boom towns, 351–352; and Ed Lasater, 352–353, 355; resigns from Ranger Force, 354; as state legislator, 355–356; as Brooks County judge, 356–358; death of Virginia, 357; death of, 357
Brooks, Jane Marie "Jennie," 316
Brooks, John Clarence, 316
Brooks, John Morgan, 342, 357–358
Brooks, John Strode, 315–316
Brooks, Lillie Belle, 316
Brooks, Mary Adeline "Ada," 316
Brooks, Mary Jane (Kerr), 315–316, 626 n3
Brooks, Mary Vernon, 337
Brooks, Sally Kenny, 316
Brooks, Virginia (Willborn), 329, 337, 342, 357
Brown County, Texas, 75, 108, 235, 291–294, 326, 381, 417, 462, 464
Brown, Emma, 443
Brown, George S., 365
Brown, John R., 317
Browning, James Nathan, 478
Brownsville Affair, 397, 399, 402–404, 651–652 n84
Brownsville Rifles, 113
Brownsville, Texas, 76, 78, 85–87, 103, 113–115, 117, 157, 167, 341–343, 350, 353, 392, 396, 399, 402–404, 432, 438–439, 449, 454, 465–466
Brownwood, Texas, 292, 325, 462

Brushy Creek, battle of, 2
Brushy, Texas, 308
Bryan, Texas, 486
Bryan, William Jennings, 345
Bryant, Robert Edward "Ed," 424, 429–431
Buckingham, Edwin J., 352
Buckley, Edward, 170
Buell, Don Carlos, 211, 213
Buell, George Pearson, 213, 229
Bugg, Adolphus Love, 496
Bulkley, Fernando Cortez, 413
Bullard, W. J., 54
Burford, Arthur, 343, 476
Burford, Frank Walker "Red," 344
Burford, William Thomas, 343, 386, 475
Burkett, William "Bill," 304
Burleson County, Texas, 75
Burleson, Edward, 2
Burnet County, Texas, 25, 27, 133, 285, 292–293, 420
Burnett, James Russell, 74
Burnett, Samuel Burk, 174
Burnham, Frederick Russell, 435
Burrell, Isaac S., 61
Burrows, William Muckleroy, 461, 673 n10
Burton, Texas, 50, 76, 80, 95
Burton, Travis J., 50
Burwell, William Merrill, 341, 468–470, 483
Butterfield, Daniel, 265
Byrne, James J., 228

C

Cabrera, Alberto, 434–435
Caddo Indians, 174, 206
Caddo Jake, 178
Caldwell, Dee, 323
Caldwell, Kansas, 317
Calhoun County, Texas, 166
Calhoun, George, 406
Calhoun, James Henry, 275
Calipatria, California, 309
Calipatria Ranch, 309, 312
Callahan County, Texas, 463
Callison, Frank, 158
Camargo, Mexico, 83, 87, 89–92, 163–164, 332
Cambridge, Illinois, 411

Index

Camden, Arkansas, 12, 245
Cameron County, Texas, 85, 90, 113–114, 330, 342, 401, 438–439, 454, 472
Camp Allyn, Texas, 184
Camp Barton, Texas, 133
Camp Bayou Meto, Arkansas, 5
Camp Bear Creek, Texas, 131
Campbell, A. M., 393
Campbell, George Washington (marshal), 138, 140
Campbell, George Washington (soldier), 51, 56
Campbell, Thomas Mitchell, 405, 407, 440
Camp Bisland, Louisiana, 10, 62, 64, 66, 215; battle of, 62–63, 215
Camp Bowie, Texas, 499
Camp Bragg, Arkansas, 12
Camp Butler, Illinois, 250, 600 n22
Camp Chase, Ohio, 250–251
Camp Contrary, Texas, 134
Camp Crystal Hill, Arkansas, 247
Camp Doniphan, Oklahoma, 310
Camp Douglas, Illinois, 250, 600–601 n22
Camp Groce, Texas, 12
Camp Hawley, Texas, 183
Camp Hogg, Texas, 423
Camp Hope, Arkansas, 247
Camp Hubbard, Texas, 127
Camp Johnson, Texas, 283
Camp Jones, Texas, 125
Camp Kiamichi, Indian Territory, 6
Camp King, Texas, 282
Camp Las Moras, Texas, 122, 124–125
Camp Leona, Texas, 282–285, 295
Camp Manassas, Texas, 51
Camp McKnight, Texas, 245
Camp Nelson, Arkansas, 5, 247–248
Camp Rogers, Texas, 13
Camp Ross, Texas, 417
Camp Savage, Texas, 293
Camp Shely, Texas, 417
Camp Sieker, Texas, 292
Camp Speight, Texas, 4
Camp Stockbridge, Texas, 133
Camp Swenson, Texas, 134
Camp Travis, Texas, 149
Canales, José, 495
Canales, Servando, 164
Canby, Edward Richard Sprigg, 51, 54–58, 208–209

Cardis, Luis, 32–33, 36
Carencro Bayou, battles of, 215–216
Carleton, James Henry, 56, 57, 59
Carlton, William, 235
Carmichael, Francis Powell "Frank," 292, 325, 327, 464, 616–617 n25
Carnes, Herff Alexander, 419, 433–434, 443
Carnes, Quirl Bailey, 438
Carr, Eugene Asa, 229
Carranza, Venustiano, 450–451
Carrasco, Florencio, 423
Carrasco, Matildo, 423
Carrington, William H. D., 122
Carrizal, Mexico, 136, 226
Carrizo Springs, Texas, 104, 168, 228, 234, 288, 319, 352, 467
Carroll, John, 325
Carson, Christopher "Kit," 55
Carter, Ben F., 131–132
Caruthers, Lavoizare Blair, 230–231
Castro City, Texas, 301
Castro County, Texas, 301–303, 305, 308
Castroville, Texas, 161, 163, 165, 498
Cathey, Lewis "Luke," 128
Cavius, Henry, 293
Center, Texas, 346
Center Point, Texas, 329
Centerville, Louisiana, 62, 64; skirmish at, 64
Chadwick, Harry R., 188
Chalmers, James Roland, 212
Chambers County, Texas, 72, 459
Chase, George Francis, 188, 468
Chattanooga, Tennessee, 251, 253–255, 257–258
Chavez, Guintino, 423
Cheatham, Benjamin Franklin, 257
Cherokee County, Texas, 72
Cheyenne and Arapaho Reservation (Darlington), 180, 317
Cheyenne Indians, 20, 317
Chicago, Illinois, 250, 291, 301, 306, 316, 339, 347, 373, 412
Chicago, Rock Island & Pacific Railroad, 196
Chicago Ranch, 113
Chickamauga, battle of, 256–257
Chickasaw Indians, 323
Childress County, Texas, 370–371
Childress, Texas, 370
Chilton, Horace, 237
Chivington, John Milton, 57, 524–525 n17

Index

Choate, Daniel Boone, 479
Choctaw Indians, 6
Choynski, Joseph Bartlett "Chrysanthemum Joe," 347–348
Christian, Grana L., 404
Christi Corpus, Texas, 420
Churchill, Thomas James, 68, 219–220, 248–250, 252, 254–255
Cisco, Texas, 293, 329, 414, 463
Clark, John, 24–26
Clarksville, Texas, 245
Clay County, Texas, 20, 235, 374, 433
Cleburne, Patrick Ronayne, 252, 255–257, 259–263, 265–266
Clements, Emanuel "Mannen," 108
Clements, Hiram, 433
Clements, Jim, 344
Clements, William D., 343–344, 386–387, 433, 476
Cleveland, Grover, 328, 373, 429, 470
Cline, A. B., 424
Clinkscales, Francis Brownlee "Frank," 278
Clinton, Texas, 80–82, 159
Closner, John, 342
Coahoma, Texas, 437, 448
Cockrell, Albert, 144
Cody, William Frederick "Buffalo Bill," 406
Coffer, Richard Poteet, 371
Coit, John Taylor, 252, 256, 258
Coke County, Texas, 235
Coke, Richard, 5, 10, 16–17, 28, 42, 79–80, 84, 89, 102, 105, 108, 157, 297
Cold Springs, Texas, 25–26, 355
Coldwell, Cornelius Vernon "Neal," 19, 25, 43, 45, 122, 127–128, 161, 225, 277, 329
Coleman County, Texas, 28, 34, 122, 128, 235
Coleman, James Henry "Jim," 343–344, 386, 434, 475
Coleman, Texas, 292
Coleman, William, 205
Collier, Charles Wesley, 285, 289–290, 417
Collier, William Wallace, 283
Collin County, Texas, 316–317
Collin, Texas, 316
Collingsworth County, Texas, 304
Collins, Michael, 49
Collins, Texas, 167
Colorado City, Texas, 273, 277, 483–484
Colorado County, Texas, 343, 385, 387, 433–434, 476
Colorow Ranch, 335
Colquitt, Oscar Branch, 356, 407, 440–445, 447, 449–451, 453, 481, 491
Columbus, Texas, 214, 344, 385, 387, 433–434, 475, 477–478

Comanche and Kiowa Reservation (Fort Sill), 174, 412
Comanche County, Texas, 75, 130, 235, 381, 413
Comanche Indians, 20–21, 174–175, 177, 206–207
Comanche, Kiowa, and Wichita Reservation (Anadarko), 173–175, 177–181, 323, 394
Comanche, Texas, 108, 110, 130, 133–134
Combs, Joseph F., 345
Comstock, Texas, 476
Concho County, Texas, 326
Conditt, Joseph Fagan, 394
Conditt, Lora, 394
Confederate Army of Mississippi, 210–211, 213
Confederate Army of New Mexico, 53, 58
Confederate Army of Northern Virginia, 256–257, 262
Confederate Army of Tennessee, 251, 254, 258–261, 264, 266
Confederate Army of the West, 362
Confederate States, Arizona Territory of, 53, 209; Congress, 61; War Department, 214, 245
Conklin, A. M., 136
Connell, Edward Fulton "Big Ed," 307
Connelly, Barney, 465
Conner, Alfred Horton "Alfie," 326, 462
Conner, Charles Wilson, 326–327, 461
Conner, Frederick M. "Fed," 326–327, 461
Conner, John Willis, 326–327, 461
Conner, Leander Jackson, 327
Conner, William E. "Bill," 326–327, 461
Conner, Willis Jackson "Uncle Willis," 326–327, 403, 461–462
Connor, Christopher Reyzor, 39–40, 167
Cook, C. J., 93, 541 n117
Cook, George W., 370
Cook, Thalis Tucker, 145, 422, 424, 429–430
Cook, William Tuttle "Bill," 374
Cooke County, Texas, 165
Cooke, William Navarro, 296–297
Cool, Paul, 32
Cooley, William Scott, 25–27
Coolidge, Dane, 415
Coopwood, Bethel, 112
Copeland, Joe, 292, 464
Corbett, James John "Gentleman Jim," 337–339, 347, 426–427
Corbin, Henry Clark, 183–184
Cordel, Fred, 304–305
Cordel, Oscar, 304–305
Corinth, Mississippi, 210–211, 213–214; battle of, 362
Corn, Lee, 19

Index

Cornett, Braxton "Brack," 464
Corpus Christi & South American Railway, 113
Corpus Christi, Texas, 78, 84–85, 115, 147, 157, 161, 167, 169–170, 335, 344–345, 396, 418–419, 454, 466, 469, 472
Corsicana, Texas, 3, 15, 388
Cortéz y Lira, Gregorio, 479, 481–482
Cortéz y Lira, Romaldo, 479, 482
Cortina, Juan Nepomuceno "Cheno," 76, 87, 89–90, 481
Coryell County, Texas, 75, 366
Cottle County, Texas, 366
Cotulla, Texas, 317–319, 331–332, 336–337, 339, 341–343, 459–460, 465–468, 473–478
Courtright, Timothy Isaiah "Longhaired Jim," 323
Cox, Dee W., 438
Cox, Perry G., 303
Cox's Plantation, battle of, 66
Coy, Antonio Paulino Santos, 467
Craighead, Charles Archer, 438, 443
Craighead, James Patterson Nelson "Pat," 438
Craven, James, 414–416, 658 n7
Craven, John, 414–416, 658 n7
Crawford, Foster "Bill," 379–380
Crawford, William Lyne, 181
Crebs, John Montgomery, 69
Crenshaw, George W. "Bud," 326
Crier, Haywood, 458
Crier, Maggie Amanda, 458
Crier, William Carey, 458, 672 n2
Crockett County, Texas, 150, 170, 322, 351, 476
Crockett, Texas, 488
Cronin, Marcus Daniel, 195
Crook, Jeremiah Mitchum, 388
Crowder, T. S., 464
Cuero, Texas, 159, 165, 167, 182, 318–319, 396, 435, 458–459
Culberson, Charles Allen, 237, 278, 338, 376, 380, 426–427, 429, 470, 493
Culberson County, Texas, 144
Culmanaris, Mariano, 228
Cummings, Stanley M. "Doc," 140
Cunningham, Eugene, 369
Curtis, Samuel Ryan, 247
Cypress City, Texas, 59

Da Costa, Jacob Mendes, 276
Dale, W. O., 433

Dallas County, Texas, 143
Dallas, Texas, 37–38, 47, 165–166, 181, 224, 268, 337–338, 393, 399, 409, 426–427, 455
Dalton, Mike, 413
Daniel, John W., 5
Daniels, Thomas Barnette, 343
Darden, Stephen Heard, 42
Davidson, James, 72, 74–75, 78
Davidson, William Lott, 51
Davis, C. C., 284
Davis, Charles, 429
Davis, Edmund Jackson, 71, 73–76, 78–79, 102
Davis, George W., 343
Davis, Jefferson, 50, 68, 221, 261
Davis, Levi, 487
Davis, Richard Harding, 335–336
Davis, Thomas C. "Tom," 346
Day, James P., 26
Deaf Smith County, Texas, 305, 307–309
Debray, Xavier Blanchard, 11, 60
Debs, Eugene Victor, 373
Deggs, T. W., 105
DeJarnette, Francis William "Frank," 235
de la Cerda, Ramón, 349–350
de la Cerda, Alfredo, 350
Delaware Indians, 174, 251
Delling, Manoah George "Blaze," 392–393, 399, 405
del Pilar, Gregorio, 191
Del Rio, Texas, 284, 476–477, 493, 498
Denison, Texas, 155–156
Denton County, Texas, 143
Denton, John M., 126–127
Des Arc, skirmish at, 247
Deshler, James, 248–249, 252, 255, 257
Devenport, James Richard, 341, 633 n60
Devine, Shauna, 277
DeWitt County, Texas, 74, 80–83, 108, 158–159, 165, 167, 318–319, 458–459
Díaz, Porfirio, 90, 160–161, 163–164, 332, 418, 429, 435, 439–440, 442, 444, 466
Dickens County, Texas, 370, 372, 448
Dickens, Texas, 453
Dickerson, James Jones, 300
Dickman, Joseph Theodore, 468
Diggs, Will, 476
Dillard, Jim, 330, 418

Index

Dimmit County, Texas, 76, 319–321, 351, 476
Dimmitt, Texas, 301, 303–305, 308
Dix, John Adams, 250
Dixon, Bob, 304–305
Dixon, John, 30
Doaty, Robert E., 336
Dodge, Charles Foster, 432
Dodge City, Kansas, 413
Domínguez, M. Ygnacio "José," 399
Doña Ana, New Mexico Territory, 54, 58
Donegan, Joe B., 321
Donley County, Texas, 304–305
Doolin, William "Bill," 375
Doss, R. C., 79
Dresden, Texas, 14
Driscoll, Robert, Sr., 115
Drumm, Andrew, 413
Dublin, James "Jimmy," 127
Dublin, James Roland "Roll," 127–128
Dublin, John Sheldon "Dell," 128, 131–132
Dublin, Richard "Dick," 128, 131
DuBois, W. E. B., 402
Dubose, Edwin Morgan, 482
Dubose, Harry Gilpin, 474–475
Duffy, Gregorio, 354, 405
Dull, Andrew Jackson, 171, 173
Dull, James Junkin, 171, 173
Dull Ranch, 171–173
Duncan, George Taplin "Tap," 296–297
Duncan, John Riley "Jack," 108–110, 547 n27
Duncan, Joseph Wilson, 491
Duncan, Richard H. "Dick," 296–297
Dunn, John Francis, 344
Dunnington, John William, 248
Durán, Desedario, 423
Durbin, Joseph Walter, 417, 420
Durham, George, 86
Durham, Paul, 26
Durham, Thomas J., 362
Durst, James H., 111–112
Durst, James William, 112
Durst, Mary Josephine (Atwood), 111–112, 114
Duval County, Texas, 44, 164, 168, 294, 298, 317, 336, 342, 355, 468–469, 472
Dwyer, Edward, 395
Dykes, Cal, 371

E

Eagle Ford, Texas, 166
Eagle Lake, Texas, 353
Eagle Pass, Texas, 76, 78, 83, 93, 106, 128, 157, 161, 163, 168, 284–285, 296–297, 429, 435, 440, 466, 493
Edinburg, Texas, 84, 92–93, 465
Edna, Texas, 394–396, 433
Edstrom, Charles H., 333, 467
Edwards, Clarence Ransom, 186
Edwards County, Texas, 28, 238, 292–293, 296, 322, 329, 417, 420, 440, 460–461, 488
Edwards, Samuel Vaughan "Pet," 341
Egg, Albert, 395
Eighteenth Louisiana Infantry (CSA), 63
Eighteenth Texas Cavalry (CSA), 245, 247, 251–252, 261; and consolidation as Seventeenth, Eighteenth, Twenty-fourth, and Twenty-fifth Texas Cavalry (Dismounted), 251; and Seventeenth, Eighteenth, Twenty-fourth, and Twenty-fifth Texas Cavalry (Dismounted), 260; and consolidation as Seventeenth and Eighteenth Texas Cavalry (Dismounted), 261, 605 n46
Eighteenth Texas Infantry (CSA), 10
Eighth Arkansas Infantry (CSA), 263
Eighth Texas Cavalry (CSA), 4, 32, 254
Eighth U.S. Cavalry, 90, 93, 163, 187
El Centro, California, 309–310, 312
Electra, Texas, 375
Eleventh Texas Infantry (CSA), 10
Eleventh U.S. Volunteer Cavalry, 188, 192
Ellis, Charles E., 34
Ellis, Kansas, 413
El Paso County, Texas, 32, 135, 225, 230, 232, 425, 431, 443
El Paso, Texas, 31–37, 53, 58, 138, 140–142, 148–149, 208, 225–226, 232, 338–339, 375–377, 379, 419, 421, 424, 426–427, 429–431, 435, 440–442, 444–445, 447–454, 458, 470–471, 485, 491–494, 499
El Sauz Ranch, 349
Emory, William Hemsley, 69
Encinal County, Texas, 84, 466
Encinal, Texas, 320–321, 331–332, 336
English, Levi, Sr., 76
Ennis, Texas, 38
Enrile, Gonzalo G., 492
Erath County, Texas, 235, 372, 374, 433
Escobedo, Mariano, 93, 163
Espronceda, Rudolfo, 163
Estado Land and Cattle Company, 142
Evans, Andrew Jackson, 38

Index **759**

Evans, John S., 412
Everheart, William Calvin, 165
Evetts, W. A., 339

F

Falfurrias, Texas, 352–353, 355, 357
Falls County, Texas, 75
False River, skirmish at, 69
Falts, J. E., 477
Falvey, Thomas A., 272
Farnsworth, Henry Joseph, 93
Farrell's Commercial Detective Agency, 235, 291
Farrow, George Washington, 74, 627 n13
Faulk, Stephen, 388
Fayette County, Texas, 2, 75, 204
Ferguson, James Edward, 454
Ferguson, Miriam Amanda "Ma," 498
Fernandez, Victoriano, 397
Fifteenth Texas Cavalry (CSA), 245, 247, 252, 260
Fifteenth Texas Infantry (CSA), 5–6, 8–10, 12–13, 260
Fifteenth U.S. Infantry, 229
Fifth Texas Mounted Rifles/Fifth Texas Cavalry (CSA), 51–53, 55, 57–59, 61, 63–64, 67–68, 95, 218
Fifth U.S. Artillery, 195
Fifth U.S. Cavalry, 472
Fifth U.S. Infantry, 54
Finley, Newton Webster, 338
First Colorado Volunteers (USV), 56, 58
First New Mexico Volunteers (USV), 55
First Texas Artillery (CSA), 208
First Texas Cavalry, Arizona Brigade (CSA), 13, 214
First Texas Cavalry (CSA), 220
First Texas Cavalry (TVG), 341, 488
First Texas Heavy Artillery (CSA), 60
First Texas Partisan Rangers (CSA), 215
First U.S. Army, 310
First U.S. Cavalry, 54
First U.S. Infantry, 206
First U.S. Volunteer Cavalry ("Rough Riders"), 182–183, 393
First U.S. Volunteer Infantry ("Immunes"), 183–184
Fisher, John J., 412
Fisher, John King, 93–94, 104, 158, 161, 304, 541 n116
Fitzhugh, William, 247
Fitzsimmons, Robert Prometheus "Ruby Bob," 337–339, 347, 375–377, 426–427, 429, 470–471

Flatonia, Texas, 463–464
Fleming, James Richard, 110, 130, 133
Flores, Pablo, 349
Flores Salinas, Juan, 90–91
Floresville, Texas, 465
Flournoy, George M., 247
Follansbee, Virginia, 50
Foraker, Joseph Benson, 402
Ford, John C., 37
Ford, John Salmon "Rip," 42, 67, 87, 92, 94–95, 207–208
Ford, William Madison "Matt," 381–382, 384
Forrest, Nathan Bedford, 254
Fort Belknap, Texas, 19
Fort Bend County, Texas, 72, 297, 299–300, 344
Fort Bliss, Texas, 36, 58, 208–209, 435, 449, 494
Fort Breckinridge, New Mexico Territory, 208
Fort Brown, Texas, 89, 164, 350, 397, 399–400, 435
Fort Buchanan, New Mexico Territory, 208
Fort Butler, battle of, 65
Fort Chadbourne, Texas, 235
Fort Clark, Texas, 78, 160, 165, 185, 435
Fort Concho, Texas, 269, 271
Fort Craig, New Mexico Territory, 51, 54–58, 208–209
Fort Davis, Texas, 145, 149, 208, 226, 231, 426
Fort Delaware, Delaware, 251
Fort Donelson, Tennessee, 210, 248
Fort Douglas, Utah, 494
Fort Duncan, Texas, 435
Fort Elliott, Texas, 44, 170
Fort Fillmore, New Mexico Territory, 208–209
Fort Gibson, Indian Territory, 203–204
Fort Hancock, Texas, 392, 426, 432, 435–436, 453, 483–484, 491
Fort Henry, Tennessee, 210, 248
Fort Huachuca, Arizona, 435
Fort Lancaster, Texas, 125, 208
Fort Leavenworth, Kansas, 492, 494, 500
Fort Martin Scott, Texas, 416
Fort McIntosh, Texas, 435, 474, 490
Fort McKavett, Texas, 127–128, 132, 469
Fort McLane, New Mexico Territory, 208
Fort Meade, South Dakota, 441
Fort Quitman, Texas, 53, 228, 435
Fort Reno, Oklahoma Territory, 401
Fort Richardson, Texas, 20
Fort Riley, Kansas, 57

Fort Sam Houston, Texas, 357, 401
Fort Sill, Indian Territory, 20, 174–175, 178–179, 325, 412
Fort Smith, Arkansas, 5–6, 180, 325, 328, 374, 463
Fort Stanton, New Mexico Territory, 209, 226, 228, 231
Fort Stockton, Texas, 226, 422, 426, 450
Fort Sumner, New Mexico Territory, 374
Fort Sumter, South Carolina, 4, 101
Fort Thorn, New Mexico Territory, 54, 58–59
Fort Union, New Mexico Territory, 50–51, 54, 56–57, 208
Fort Worth & Denver Railway, 368, 371, 375
Fort Worth, Texas, 37, 143, 165–166, 323, 370, 372–373, 379–380, 394, 499
Forty-second Massachusetts Infantry (USV), 60–61
Forty-sixth U.S. Volunteer Infantry, 192
Foster, John Watson, 163
Fountain, Albert Jennings, 232–233, 594 n71
Fourteenth Texas Cavalry (CSA), 245
Fourteenth U.S. Infantry, 192
Fourth Texas Cavalry, Arizona Brigade (CSA), 214
Fourth Texas Mounted Rifles/Fourth Texas Cavalry (CSA), 53, 55, 58–60, 68, 218
Fourth U.S. Cavalry, 15, 186–187, 192
Francklyn Land & Cattle Company, 174
Franklin, William Buel, 10, 215
Franks, Joseph, 128
Fredericksburg, Texas, 24, 27, 29, 285–286, 416
Freestone County, Texas, 72, 75
Frier, Arthur, 430
Frier, Jube, 430
Frio City, Texas, 161, 165
Frio County, Texas, 106, 127, 169, 336, 465, 476, 479
Frost, Henry H., 298–299
Frost, Samuel Romulus, 417
Fuller, T. Lawrence, 389–391
Fulton, Texas, 166
Fusselman, Charles Henry Vanvalkenburg "Charley," 421, 430–431

G

G4 Ranch, 142–143, 144
Gaines County, Texas, 484, 496
Gaines, J. H., 165
Gainesville, Texas, 336
Galveston County, Texas, 72, 74, 159, 347
Galveston, Houston & Henderson Railroad, 59
Galveston, Houston & San Antonio Railroad, 429, 486
Galveston, Texas, 4, 50, 67, 171, 173, 183–184, 206, 217, 223–224, 300, 336, 347–348, 373, 448, 487; battle of, 60–61

Gano, Richard Montgomery, 142
Gant, Dick, 475
Garcia, Augustin, 485
García, Encarnacion, 87
García Osuña, Estévan, 349
García, Gregorio Nacianceno, 33
Garcia, Santiago, 344
Gard, Wayne, 155
Gardener, Cornelius, 193–194
Gardiner, Floyd, 331
Garland, Augustus Hill, 328
Garland, Robert Rice, 248–250
Garlick, William Henry, 451
Garner, Edward Rufus, 104
Garner, John Nance, 493
Garrett, Patrick Floyd "Pat," 430–431
Garvey, James Thomas, 298–300
Garza, Catarino Erasmo, 330–333, 335–336, 418, 466, 632 n48; and Victor Sebree, 330; and *Garzistas*, 332–333, 335, 466–467; abandons revolution, 336, 467; arrest by John R. Hughes, 418
Garza County, Texas, 436
Garza, Encarnacion, 349–350
Garza, Rafael, 163
Garza, Segundo, 163
Gaston, Alabama, 243
Geary, John, 265
Geiger, William C., 192–194
Georgetown, Texas, 30, 38, 293, 417
Gibson, Guilford, 299
Gibson, Henry "Monk," 394–396, 433
Gibson, Levi Eden "Ned," 298, 300
Gibson, Volney M., 298–300
Gilgal Church, battle of, 265–266
Gillespie, Clayton Crawford, 252, 256
Gillespie County, Texas, 285, 433
Gillespie, J. T., 236
Gillett, Baylor, 138
Gillett, Beulah, 144, 147, 149
Gillett, Elizabeth Jane "Bettie" (Harper), 121–122, 551 n1
Gillett, Eva, 122
Gillett, Helen (Baylor), 134, 138, 142–143, 224–225, 237–238
Gillett, James Buchanan: birth of, 121; education, 122; as cowhand, 122; enlists in Company D, Frontier Battalion, 122; personality, characteristics, and motivations, 122; and Nelson O. Reynolds, 122; as Indian fighter, 122, 124–125, 135–136; and Jones's escort, 126, 128; and Pegleg Crossing gang, 127–128,

Index **763**

131–132, 134; transfers to Company E, Frontier Battalion, 128; and Dick Dublin, 131; and Round Rock fight, 133; and John Wesley Hardin, 133–134; as Ranger corporal, 134; as first sergeant of Detachment C, Frontier Battalion, 134–135, 225; as first sergeant of Company A, Frontier Battalion, 135; and Enofre Baca, 137–138; marriages, 138, 143–144, 237; as railroad guard, 138; as assistant marshal of El Paso, 138, 142; as city marshal of El Paso, 140–142; as cattle rancher, 142–147; as manager of G4 Ranch, 142–144; and civic affairs, 143, 145, 147–148; as Brewster County sheriff, 144; as deputy U.S. marshal, 145; as Mason, 145; as farmer, 146; and deaths of children, 147; as author, 147; as Special Ranger, 148; death of, 148; and train robbers, 429; honors and accolades, 455
Gillett, James Harper, 142, 143, 148–149
Gillett, James Shackleford, 121–122, 551 n1
Gillett, James Stuart "Jeb," 144, 147
Gillett, Leota, 144, 149–150
Gillett, Lucile Chastain "Lou," 144, 149
Gillett, Mary Eva, 144
Gillett, Mary Harper, 122
Gillett, Mary Lou (Chastain), 144, 146, 148
Gillett, Milton E., 146, 148, 150
Gillett, Pansy Elizabeth, 144, 147
Gilliland, Finus "Fine," 144–145
Gladden, George W., 25–26
Glasrud, Bruce A., 482
Glass, William A. "Billy," 19
Glasscock, Henry Doyle, 498
Gloriéta Pass, battle of, 57
Glover, Eugene A., 3, 11, 13, 15, 42, 44
Glover, Richard Martin "Dick," 481
Gober, James Ransler "Jim," 369
Goff, Thomas Jefferson "Tom," 485
Goliad County, Texas, 106, 158, 319
Goliad, Texas, 158, 160
Gómez, Emilio Vázquez, 445
Gomez, José Maria, 164
Gonzales, Apolonio, 288
Gonzales County, Texas, 74, 82, 108, 318, 481
Gonzales, Dario, 288, 615 n16
González, Prudencio, 468–469
Good, Milton Paul "Milt," 496
Goodnight, Charles, 174, 370
Gordon, Texas, 374
Gordon, William K., 483
Gottwald, Franz, 494
Gould, Jason "Jay," 323

Graham, Texas, 181
Granbury, Hiram Bronson, 260–266
Granbury's Texas Brigade, 261–262, 264
Grand Ecore, Louisiana, 6, 12, 69, 216–217, 220
Grant, Ulysses S., 102, 210–211, 213, 215, 248, 258–259, 261
Graves, Amos Maverick, 475, 476
Graydon, James "Paddy," 55
Grayson County, Texas, 16, 154–156, 165, 284
Grear, Charles David, 51
Green, Charles M., 363
Green, Elihu H., 388
Green, Peter V., 363
Green, Thomas, 6, 8, 10, 13, 51, 53–55, 57, 59–61, 63–68, 215–218, 220
Greenhaw, Arthur, 389
Greenhaw, John, 388–389
Greer County, Texas, 304, 366–367, 370
Gregg County, Texas, 363, 365
Grey, Zane, 451, 455
Grierson, Benjamin Henry, 228–229, 269, 271–272
Griffin, Samuel Davis, 496
Grimes, Alijah W. "Caige," 40–41, 72, 167
Grimes County, Texas, 73
Groce, Helen Halbert, 3
Groos, Carl Frederick, 352
Groveton, Texas, 392, 433, 477, 486
Guadalajara, Mexico, 148, 238
Guadalupe County, Texas, 457–459
Guadalupe, Mexico, 135–136, 453
Guaderrama, Juan, 452
Guaderrama, Manuel, 451–452
Guaderrama, Marina, 452
Guerra, Deodoro, 354, 435
Guerra, Manuel, 353–354
Guerrero, Mexico, 332, 489
Gulf, Colorado & Santa Fe Railroad, 336
Guthrie, Oklahoma Territory, 304–305

H

Hale, John, 140
Halff, Mayer, 484
Halff, Solomon, 484
Hall, Charles Wharton, 154
Hall County, Texas, 368, 390
Hall, Elizabeth Cook "Bessie" (Weidman), 169, 172, 182, 183, 195–198
Hall, Frances Mebane (Rankin), 153–154, 561 n1

Hall, Francis Rankin "Frank," 154, 173
Hall, Frank Kerr, 199
Hall, George A., 87
Hall, James King, 153–154, 561 n1
Hall, James King, Jr., 154
Hall, Jesse Lee: and Round Rock fight, 40; as lieutenant of Special State Troops, 94, 106, 157, 159–160; as captain of Special State Troops, 128, 168; birth of, 153; education, 154; as schoolteacher in Texas, 154; as constable in Sherman, 155; as Grayson County deputy sheriff, 155–157; as deputy U.S. marshal, 156; as sergeant-at-arms, 157, 166; and Nueces Strip, 157, 161, 163–164, 168; and Sutton-Taylor feud, 159, 165; and King Fisher, 161, 304; and Sam Bass, 165–167; resigns from Special State Troops, 170; as sheep raiser, 170–171; marries Bessie, 171; as cattle rancher, 171, 173; as manager of Dull Ranch, 171–173; and O. Henry, 173; as Indian agent, 173, 177, 179–180; and relations with agency Indians, 175, 178–179; and alcoholism, 175, 177, 182; and legal troubles, 177–178, 180–181; and misfortunes, 181–182, 195–197; as strikebreaker, 182; as captain in First U.S. Volunteer Infantry, 183–184; and health issues, 183, 191, 195; as lieutenant in Thirty-third U.S. Volunteer Infantry, 184–185, 187; and Macabebe Scouts, 186, 188, 190–195; discharged from U.S. Army, 195; testimony before Lodge Committee, 196; as mine guard, 196–197; death of, 198; as volunteer on Rio Grande, 320, 336, 467
Hall, Jessie Lee, 172, 198–199
Hall, Jim, 347
Hall, Martha Dorothy Kline, 175, 197, 199
Hall, Mary Weidman, 181, 197, 199
Hall, Richard Moore, 154, 167, 173, 181
Hall, Sarah Elizabeth, 172, 197, 198–199
Hall, Virginia Derr, 181, 196, 197, 199
Hall, William Paisley, 154
Halleck, Henry Wager, 210, 254
Hallettsville, Texas, 395
Halsey, William, 204
Halter, Captain Richard E., 169
Hamilton County, Texas, 75, 235, 381, 433
Hamilton, Mack, 400
Hamner, Harris A., 207
Hardee, William Joseph, 210–211, 252, 254–255, 258, 260–262, 264, 266
Hardeman County, Texas, 366–368, 370–371
Hardeman, Peter, 13, 214
Hardesty, Frank B., 379
Hardie, Francis Hunter, 333, 335, 466
Hardin, Bud, 375
Hardin County, Texas, 72, 351
Hardin, Jane, 108

Hardin, John Wesley, 72, 83, 130; killings of, 72, 74, 106–108; capture of, 106, 108–110, 130; as fugitive, 108, 159; trial of, 110, 130, 133; as prisoner, 134, 547 n27; death of, 426, 547 n27
Harding, Warren Gamaliel, 495
Hare, Luther Rector, 185
Harkey, Jefferson Davis, 370
Harkey, Martin Luther, 436–437
Harley, James Aloysius, 495
Harlingen, Texas, 150, 433
Harriman, Edward Henry, 407
Harris, Henry, 327
Harris, Tupper, 332, 468–470
Harrisburg, Texas, 11, 59–60
Harris County, Texas, 72, 74, 352, 463
Harrison, James Edward, 5–6, 8, 9, 10, 11–12, 13, 221, 223
Harrison, Nat, 230
Harrold & Ikard Ranch, 174
Harrold, Texas, 366, 375
Harry, James B., 327
Hart, William, 249
Harwood, Texas, 465
Hatley, Allen G., 281
Hawkins, Andrew Jackson, 382, 384
Hay, Silas, 320
Hayes, Rutherford Birchard, 36, 160, 163, 229
Haynes, James Leal, 342
Haynes, Robert Anderson, 335
Hays County, Texas, 75, 431
Hays, John Coffee "Jack," 121
Hazelwood, Robert R., 180
Hebbronville, Texas, 343, 450, 453
Hébert, Paul Octave, 4
Helena, Arkansas, 5, 248
Helena, Texas, 235, 318–319
Helm, John Jackson Marshal "Jack," 73
Hemphill, Texas, 217, 326–327, 461–462
Hempstead, Texas, 12, 59, 61, 69, 73, 76, 221, 351, 434, 487
Henderson County, Texas, 387–388
Henderson, Lemuel Kenneth, 288, 489
Henderson, Texas, 362–363
Henderson, Thomas Elijah "Lige," 381
Hendricks, Sterling Brown, 245, 252
Hereford, Texas, 308
Herff, Ferdinand Ludwig, 46
Herold, George, 39–40, 167, 421

Index   **767**

Herrera, Agipito, 474–475
Herrera, Pendincia, 286, 288
Herriman, A. A., 158
Herrin, John W., 268
Herring, Cornelius Taylor, 174
Herring, Marcus Delafayette, 4
Hidalgo County, Texas, 113–114, 164, 330, 336, 342, 355–356, 472
Hidalgo, Texas, 342, 490
Hiers, Charles Francis, 469–471
Higgins, John Calhoun Pinkney "Pink," 29–31
Highsmith, Henry, 40
Hill County, Texas, 79, 157
Hill, Daniel Harvey, 250, 255
Hillsboro, New Mexico Territory, 414
Hindman, Thomas Carmichael, 5
Hoerster, Daniel, 26
Hogg, James Stephen, 96, 181, 237, 279, 297, 305, 333, 338, 364–365, 368, 371
Holden, Frances Mayhugh, 23
Holmes, John P., 20
Holmes, Levonia Williamson, 296
Holmes, Theophilus Hunter "Granny," 5, 247–248
Hondo, Texas, 498
Hood, John Bell, 257, 262, 264, 266
Hooker, Joseph "Fighting Joe," 263, 265
Hope, Larkin Secrest, 385–386
Hope, Samuel Marion, 385–386, 433–434
Horrell, Benjamin Franklin, 29
Horrell, James Martin "Mart," 29–31
Horrell, Merritt, 29–30
Horrell, Samuel Houston, Jr., 29, 31
Horrell, Thomas, 30–31
Hot Springs, Arkansas, 427, 454
House, Edward Mandell, 406–407, 493
Houston & Texas Central Railroad, 4, 75, 165, 181, 268
Houston County, Texas, 72
Houston, George Smith, 110
Houston, Texas, 13, 15, 60, 67, 76, 115, 118, 165–166, 199, 214, 221, 223, 338, 344, 348, 371, 406–407, 409, 432–433, 487
Houston Light Guard, 299
Howard, Charles Henry, 32–37
Howard, Sewell B., 296
Hubbard, Richard Bennett, 33, 35–38, 42, 94–95, 110, 163–166
Hudson, James Wilson, 2
Hudson, Robert Marmaduke "Duke," 487
Hudson, Robert Weir, 332

Hudspeth County, Texas, 230
Huerta, Victoriano, 238, 449–451
Hughes, Ben, 374
Hughes, Bond, 412
Hughes, Ellen "Nellie," 412
Hughes, Emery H., 455
Hughes, Emery Sargent, 412–414, 416, 455
Hughes, Jane Augusta "Jennie" (Bond), 411, 656 n1
Hughes, John Reynolds: and Williamson family murders, 296; and labor strikes, 336–337; and Reese-Townsend feud, 344, 433–434; and Fitzsimmons-Maher prizefight, 376, 426–427, 429, 470; and Monk Gibson, 395, 433; and Judge Welch murder, 405, 434–435; birth of, 411; and sojourn in Indian Territory, 412, 657 n2; as trail driver, 413, 657–658 n4; as horse rancher, 413–414, 416; and pursuit of horse thieves, 414–416; and Ira Aten, 416; and Wesley Collier, 416–417; enlists in Company D, Frontier Battalion, 417; personality, characteristics, and motivations, 417, 425–426, 454; and fence-cutters, 417; and Catarino Garza, 418, 660 n16; and "Elizabeth Todd," 418–420; as mine guard, 420; rejoins Company D, 420; and Odle fight, 420–421; and Charley Fusselman, 421, 430; as corporal of Company D, 421–422; and Shafter mines, 423; and Florencio Carrasco, 423; as first sergeant of Company D, 423; as captain of Company D, 425–426, 432–433; and deaths of McKidrict and Outlaw, 426; and Star pasture fight, 429–430; and Gerónimo Parra, 430–431, 665 n46; as captain of Company D, Ranger Force, 432–433; and Taft-Díaz summit, 435; and Mexican Revolution, 440–442, 444–445, 447–448, 450, 452–453; as captain of Company A, Ranger Force, 440, 444, 450, 453–454; and Zane Grey, 451; and death of Russell, 452; dismissed from Ranger Force, 454; in retirement, 454–455; honors and accolades, 455; death of, 455; and John H. Rogers, 494
Hughes, Louis Bond, 419
Hughes, Louise, 412
Hughes, Thomas Forster, Jr., 412
Hughes, Thomas Forster, Sr., 411, 656 n1
Hughes, William Parker, 412, 659 n14
Hulen, John Augustus, 352, 354, 399, 401, 405, 432–433, 483
Humble, Texas, 352, 433
Humphreys, Burke, 430
Humphries, George Washington, 387–388
Humphries, James Knox Polk, 387–388
Humphries, John Samuel, 387–388
Hunter, Robert Dickey, 372–373, 483
Hunter, Sherod, 54, 65, 214
Hunter, William Charles, 481
Huntsville, Texas, 74, 96, 104, 134, 326, 384, 392, 424, 481
Hurt, James Mann, 338
Hutchings, Henry, 442, 445, 449–450, 499–500

Index

Hutchinson, Kansas, 443
Hutchinson, William Henry "Hutch," 108–109

I

Ikard, Elisha Floyd, 19–20
Indianola, Texas, 82, 206
International & Great Northern Railroad, 39, 317, 486
Ireland, John, 104, 234, 236, 288, 291, 319, 323, 326, 459, 461
Irion County, Texas, 352
Irish Bend, battle of, 64, 215
Isaacks, Samuel Jackson, 443

J

Jack County, Texas, 19, 156, 235, 374, 433
Jackson County, Texas, 394, 467
Jackson, Francis M. "Frank," 38, 40–41, 133, 167, 518 n100
Jackson, John King, 212
Jackson, Wayman Crow, 328
James, William Alexander, 381–382
Jamestown, Texas, 245
Jasper County, Texas, 72
Jeanerette, skirmish at, 64
Jeff Davis County, Texas, 237
Jefferson County, Texas, 72
Jefferson, Texas, 363
Jeffries, James Jackson, 347
Jenkins, Sam, 74–75
Jennings, Napoleon Augustus, 80–81, 84–85
Jett, James A., 391
Jim Wells County, Texas, 394
Johnson, Albert, 331
Johnson, Byron, vii–viii, xiv
Johnson, Charles, 326
Johnson City, Texas, 284
Johnson, Frank, 436
Johnson, John Arthur "Jack," 347–348
Johnson, Middleton Tate, 245–246
Johnson, Toppy, 414
Johnston, Albert Sidney, 209–213, 585 n23, n24
Johnston, Joseph Eggleston, 261–262, 264, 266
Jones, Ann Eloise (Holliday) Anderson, 43, 46
Jones, Ann P., 2
Jones, Benoni Robertson, 2
Jones, Caroline Robertson "Carrie," 2

Jones, Carroll, 11, 67, 218
Jones, Ed, 286
Jones, Francis E. "Fannie," 2, 11
Jones, Frank, 144, 237, 283–284, 288, 290, 292–293, 296, 298, 320, 417, 420–425, 430, 448
Jones, Frank Baylor, 237–238
Jones, Henry, 1–4, 14, 17, 46
Jones: John B., birth of, 1; education, 2; as horse rancher, 3, 14; personality, characteristics, and motivations, 3–4, 17; as slaveowner, 3; as Mason, 3, 14–15, 43; and secession, 4; as adjutant of Fifteenth Texas Infantry, 4–5; as brigade adjutant, 6, 8, 13; and Battle of Stirling's Plantation, 8–9; and Battle of Bayou Bourbeau, 10; and health issues, 13, 31, 45, 277; and colonization proposals, 13–14; as businessman, 15; as commander of Frontier Battalion, 17, 19, 21–22, 25, 27–28, 125–127; and Lost Valley fight, 19–20; and Mason County War, 23, 25–26; and Kimble County Cleanup, 28–29, 106, 128; and Horrell-Higgins feud, 31, 128; and El Paso Salt War, 33–36; testimony before Senate Committee on Foreign Affairs, 36; and Sam Bass, 37–38, 41, 166; and Round Rock fight, 38–40, 133, 166; as adjutant general, 41–45, 168, 171, 225, 230, 232, 272, 275; marries Ann, 43; as step-father, 44; death of, 46, 276–277
Jones, Mickle C., 2
Jones, Nancy Elizabeth (Robertson), 1–2
Jones, Nat B. "Kiowa," 389
Jones, "Picnic" (aka H. Walter Landers), 296–297
Jones, Polly R., 2
Jones, Walter W., 144
Junction, Texas, 29, 131–132, 273

K

Kansas Pacific Railway, 413
Karnes County, Texas, 82, 318, 459, 470, 479
Katherine, Texas, 115
Keating, Paul, 142
Keese, Tom, 74
Kelly, Henry, 73
Kelly, William, 73
Kelso, Winchester, 297
Kenedy County, Texas, 112
Kenedy, John Gregory, 115
Kenedy, Mifflin, 112
Kenney, Martin McHenry, 19, 22, 41–42
Kent County, Texas, 352
Kent, Texas, 441
Kerber, Charles, 34–35
Kerr County, Texas, 125, 329, 433, 465
Kerrville, Texas, 293, 329

Kichai Indians, 174
Kickapoo Indians, 125, 160
Kimble County, Texas, 28–29, 34, 106, 125, 127–128, 130–132, 134, 285, 352, 469
King County, Texas, 372
King, James W., 294
King, John Haskell, 36
King Ranch, 118, 349
King, Richard, 86, 118, 350
King, Richard, II, 115
King, Wilburn Hill, 10, 12, 113, 157, 232, 235–236, 276–277, 288–294, 319–321, 328, 331, 341, 417, 459–460, 611 n82
King, Will, 478–479
Kingsbury, Texas, 457
Kinney County, Texas, 283, 351, 476
Kinney, John, 35, 233–234
Kiowa Indians, 19–21, 174–175, 177–179
Kirchner, Carl, 424–426
Kirwim, James Martin, 198
Kleberg, Caesar, 115
Kleberg, Robert Justus "Bob," Jr., 118
Kleberg, Robert Justus, Sr., 115
Kleiber, John I., 354
Knight, Denton Gibbon, 424
Knight, George A., 367
Knight, Robert Edward Lee, 495
Knight, Thomas Rogers, 323–325, 328–329
Komal-ty, 175
Kountze, Texas, 351
Kozlowski's Ranch, 57
Krempkau, Gus, 140

L

La Grange, Texas, 2–3, 67, 204, 214, 477
La Havana Ranch, 335
Lambert, Alexander, 394
Lampasas County, Texas, 27, 29, 75, 122, 235, 326, 381
Lampasas, Texas, 29–31, 38, 122, 128, 433
Landers, Charley, 375
Lane, Ann J., 403
Lane, Walter Paye, 215, 217–219, 221
Lang, Willis, 55
Langford, Ace, 131
Langtry, Texas, 339, 341, 377, 429, 471
Lanham, Samuel Willis Tucker, 351, 395, 399, 401, 432–433
La Porte, Texas, 409

Laredo, Texas, 78, 92, 161, 288, 329, 333, 335, 339, 341, 350–353, 432, 435, 444, 447, 466, 468, 473, 478–479, 481–483, 489–490, 492
Largarto, Texas, 472
La Salle County, Texas, 106, 171–173, 317, 331, 336, 341, 351, 459, 466, 468, 476
Lasater, Edward Cunningham, 352–356
Las Cruces, New Mexico Territory, 427, 430–431
Las Cucharas, skirmish at, 90
Las Cuevas, Mexico, 467, skirmish at, 91
Latham, James V., 285
Lavaca County, Texas, 74, 82
Lawrence, Henry Boomer, 438
Lawton, Henry Ware, 185–187, 189, 191
Leakey, Texas, 293, 465
Leary, Edgar, 318–319
Lebanon, Pennsylvania, 171, 181, 182, 198–199
Lee, Fitzhugh, 237
Lee, Robert Edward, 266
Leet, Joshua, 316
Leet, Karen, 316
Lehman, Herman, 125
Lehmberg, Karl Friedrich "Charley," 24
Leiker, James N., 397
Leon County, Texas, 72, 75, 365
Lerdo de Tejada, Sebastián, 90, 160
Lerma, Camillo, 87
Lessing, Joseph Franklin, 434
Lessing, William Herman, 272
Lewis, Elmore "Kid," 375, 379–380
Lewis, William Henry, 36
Lexington, North Carolina, 153
Liberty County, Texas, 72
Liberty Hill, Texas, 289, 413, 417
Ligon, Dave L., 132
Limestone County, Texas, 72, 74–75, 130
Lincecum, Gideon, 69
Lincoln, Abraham, 101, 215, 258
Linden, Walter Courtney, 382, 384–385
Lindsey, Benjamin Dennis, 286, 288
Littlepage, James Newel, 496
Little Rock, Arkansas, 5, 110, 156, 204, 245–246, 427
Live Oak County, Texas, 167, 433, 469
Livingston, Alonzo W. "Lon," 344, 346, 348
Llano County, Texas, 24–26, 131, 235, 283–284, 384
Llano, Texas, 283–284
Llorente, Enrique C., 447, 492

Index

Lloyd, George, 137
Lockridge, Samuel A., 51, 56
Lodge, Henry Cabot, 196
Loftis, Hillary "Hill," 375, 484, 496
Logan, John Alexander, Jr., 185
Lone Wolf (Gui-päh-go), 19, 175, 178
Long Hollow Ranch, 289, 413
Long, Ira, 22, 25, 125, 269
Long, Minas, 102
Long Mott, Texas, 166
Long, Richard Brown, 268
Longorio, Sisto, 335
Longstreet, James, 256–257
Longview, Texas, 110
Lonn, Ella, 11
Lookout Mountain, battle of, 259
Lopez, Federico, 330
Los Angeles, California, 309, 313
Los Angeles, Texas, 466
Lost Valley, battle of, 19–20
Lott, Uriah, 114–115
Love, Thomas Decatur, 374
Lovejoy, John, 348
Lovell, Jim, 292, 325
Lovenskiold, Charles George, 112
Loving, James Carroll, 20
Loving Ranch, 22
Lowe, Marcellus French, 332
Loyas Ranch, 286
Lubbock, Texas, 496
Lucy, James E., 165, 167
Ludwick, Marcus Humphrey, 226
Lufkin, Texas, 478
Lundberg, John R., 262, 265
Lynch, D. L., 346
Lynde, Isaac, 208–209

M

Mabry, Woodford Haywood, 113, 332–333, 335, 337–339, 372–373, 376, 380–382, 384, 424–425, 427, 470
Macabebes, 186, 188–192, 196; and Macabebe Scouts, 186, 188–194, 574 n81
Mackay, A. S., 166
Mackay, James Ormond, 335
Mackay, John W., 112
Mackenzie, Murdo, 370

Maddox, Allen R., 381
Madero González, Francisco Ignacio, 238, 439–442, 444–445, 447, 449–450, 489–490, 492
Madison County, Texas, 72
Magruder, John Bankhead "Prince John," 12, 59–61, 67, 217, 221–223
Maher, Peter "the Galway Giant," 338–339, 347, 375–377, 427, 470–471
Major, James Patrick, 6, 11, 64–68, 70, 214–218
Mallett Ranch, 484
Maltby, William Jeff, 17, 19
Maman-ti, 19
Manila, Philippines, 184–185, 191, 194–195
Manion, George D., 261
Mann, James W. "Jim," 109
Manning, Frank, 140
Manning, George Felix, 141
Manning, James, 140–141
Manning, John, 140
Mansfield (Sabine Crossroads), battle of, 11, 68, 217–218, 264
Mansura, battle of, 11–12
Marathon, Texas, 145, 339
March, Peyton Conway, 191
Marcum, Thomas Damron, 180
Marfa, Texas, 144–150, 422–423, 426, 435, 440, 450, 452, 493, 498
Marion, Texas, 111
Marsden, Crosby, 405
Marsh, Araminta "Mittie" (Shuart), 244, 261
Marsh, Bryan, III: birth of, 243; as businessman, 244–245, 267–269; as farmer, 244–245, 267; marries Mittie, 244; as slaveowner, 245; as captain of Company C, Seventeenth Texas Cavalry, 245; and Battle of Arkansas Post, 249–250; as prisoner of war, 250–251; released from captivity and returns to duty, 251; as acting regimental commander, 251, 261, 264; as captain of Company I, Seventeenth, Eighteenth, Twenty-fourth, and Twenty-fifth Texas Cavalry, 252; and Tullahoma Campaign, 254; and Chickamauga Campaign, 255–257; and Battle of Chickamauga, 256–257; and Chattanooga Campaign, 257–260; and Battle of Tunnel Hill, 259–260; and Battle of Ringgold Gap, 260; and death of Mittie, 261; and Atlanta Campaign, 262–266; and Battle of New Hope Church, 263; and promotion to colonel, 264–265; and Battle of Gilgal Church, 265; returns to duty, 266; marries Lucy, 267; as Smith County sheriff, 267–269, 278; as captain of Company B, Frontier Battalion, 269, 458; and San Angelo Riot, 272; policing railroad towns, 273, 276; and Patterson shooting, 275; and alcoholism, 276–278; and allegations of unfitness, 276–277; personality, characteristics, and motivations, 276; and post-traumatic stress, 277; discharged from Frontier Battalion, 278; as Smith County deputy sheriff, 278; and honors and accolades, 278, 279; death of, 278
Marsh, Bryan, Jr., 243–244

Index

Marsh, Darius, 244, 598 n7, 607 n56
Marsh, Edmund, 244, 598 n7, 607 n56
Marsh, Henry Bryan, 244, 279
Marsh, Isabella, 244
Marsh, Lucy Mary (Portis), 267, 278–279
Marsh, Martha, 244
Marsh, Mary, 269, 279
Marsh, Mitty Rivers, 267, 279
Marsh, Peter, 244–245
Marsh, Rebecca Waller (Jones), 244, 597 n5
Marsh, Sarah E., 244
Marsh, William, 244
Martin County, Texas, 484, 496
Martin, Jack, 417–419
Martínez, Leon Cárdenas, 443
Martinez, Manuel, 170
Mason County, Texas, 23–26, 125, 130, 283, 286, 289, 433
Mason, Texas, 24, 26–27, 124, 416
Masterson, William Barclay "Bat," 376–377, 379
Matador, Texas, 370–371
Matagorda County, Texas, 2
Matagorda, Texas, 2, 4
Matamoros, Mexico, 83, 87, 164, 167, 451
Mather, M. D., 102
Mathewson, William "Buffalo Bill," 412
Mathis, Texas, 472
Matthews, John, 326
Matthews, John Pearce, 370–372
Maury, Matthew Fontaine, 14
Maverick County, Texas, 93, 169, 284–285, 292, 296, 320
Maxey, Samuel Bell, 13
Mayfield, John Lewis, 105–106
McBee, Bob, 30
McBride, Charles, 35
McBride, John, 32
McCamey, Texas, 498
McCampbell, John Solomon, 112
McCarty, John, 271
McCarty, Thomas J., 270–273
McCaskey William Spencer, 400, 403
McCauley, William J., 374, 389, 395, 399–400, 405
McClarty, John, 245, 248, 264
McClelland, Andrew, 301–302
McClelland, Hugh, 301–302
McClernand, John Alexander, 248–249

McClure, Robert B., 370–371, 382
McCoy, James Eli, 326
McCulloch County, Texas, 125, 235, 283, 326, 381
McCulloch, Henry Eustice, 5
McDonald, Enoch, 361–362
McDonald, Eunice (Durham), 361–362, 363, 639 n6
McDonald, Mary, 361–362
McDonald, Pearl (Wilkirson), 408
McDonald, Rhoda Isabel (Carter), 364–365, 405
McDonald, William Jesse: and Reese-Townsend feud, 343–344, 385, 387, 475; and Choynski-Hall prizefight, 347; birth of, 361; and Charles Green, 363; as businessman, 363–364; education, 363; and civic affairs, 364; as Mason, 364, 366; and James S. Hogg, 364, 368, 371; marries Rhoda, 364; as cattle rancher, 365–366, 407; as deputy sheriff, 365–368; as Special Ranger, 367; as deputy U.S. marshal, 367–368, 656 n105; as captain of Company B, Frontier Battalion, 368, 370; personality, characteristics, and motivations, 369, 380, 384, 400; and John P. Matthews, 370–372; and labor strikes, 372–373; and Red Buck gang, 375; and Fitzsimmons-Maher prizefight, 376, 427; and Bat Masterson, 377, 379; and Wichita Falls bank robbery, 379–380; and San Saba Mob, 381–382, 384; and Humphries lynching, 388–389; and racial strife, 389, 476; as captain of Company B, Ranger Force, 391–392; and death of Fuller, 391; and Touchstone/Thomas murder, 392–393; and Theodore Roosevelt, 394, 406; and Conditt family murders, 395–396; and death of Rhoda, 396, 405; as sergeant-at-arms, 399, 407; and Brownsville Affair, 399–403; and Casitas road fight, 405; and Judge Welch murder, 405; as state revenue agent, 405–407; and Edward M. House, 406–407; and Mark Twain, 406; as strikebreaker, 407; and Woodrow Wilson, 407–408; as U.S. marshal, 408; marries Pearl, 408; death of, 408
McDowell, Bert J., 492–493
McDowell, Clyde, 351
McDowell, J. C., 156
McKenzie, Samuel, 395, 399, 405
McKidrict, Joseph W. "Joe," 426
McKiernan-González, John, 473
McKinley, William, 184, 237, 472
McKinney, Charles Brown, 170, 172, 317, 320–321, 326, 341
McKinney, Texas, 166
McLennan County, Texas, 75
McMahan, Francis Marion "Frank," 426
McMaster, Arthur, 430
McMillan, Albert C., 188
McMinnville, Tennessee, 99–101
McMullen County, Texas, 106, 167, 171–172, 469, 476
McMurry, Samuel Alexander "Soft Voice," 278, 366–369, 643 n28
McMurry, Young Douglas, 374
McNeel, James S., 333, 335, 467, 468

Index

McNeill, Henry Cameron, 51, 67
McNelly, Carey Cheek (Matson), 70, 95
McNelly, Charles B., 61
McNelly, Clarinda, 50
McNelly, Irene Mary, 70
McNelly, James, 50
McNelly, John, 463
McNelly, Leander Harvey: as captain of Special State Troops, 45, 94, 157, 317; birth of, 50; and health issues, 50, 94–95, 157; as sheepherder, 50; enlists in Fifth Texas Mounted Rifles, 51; personality, characteristics, and motivations, 51, 72, 80–81, 85; as escort for Sibley, 53–54, 58; and Battle of Valverde, 55–56; and Battle of Galveston, 60–61; and Bayou Teche Campaign, 62–64; and Battle of Bayou Boeuf, 65; as Green's aide-de-camp, 65; and Second Battle of Donaldsonville, 65; and Battle of Stirling's Plantation, 66; as captain of Confederate scouts, 66–67, 69, 528 n38; honors and accolades, 66–67, 70; and Battle of Mansfield, 68; as farmer, 70, 72, 79; marries Carey, 70; as captain of Texas State Police, 72–73, 75, 385; and Walker County Rebellion, 74–75; and labor strikes, 75–76; and Rio Grande Expedition, 76; and James Davidson, 78; as deputy U.S. marshal, 78–79; as captain of Company A, Washington County Volunteer Militia, 80, 103; and Sutton-Taylor feud, 81–83; and intelligence network, 83, 84, 87; testifies before House Committee on Foreign Affairs, 85, 92; and Juan Cortina, 87; and Second Battle of Palo Alto, 87, 89; and Las Cuevas War, 90–92; and King Fisher, 93, 104, 161; and John S. Ford, 94; and dismissal from Special State Troops, 95, 106; death of, 95
McNelly, Leander Rebel, 70, 96
McNelly, Margaret, 50
McNelly, Mary, 50
McNelly, Mary Katherine (Killian), 50
McNelly, Owen, 50
McNelly, Owen, Jr., 50
McNelly, Peter John, 50
McNelly, Thomas, 50
McPherson, James Birdseye, 262, 264
Meade, George Gordon, 262
Means, John Helms, 104
Meansville, Texas, 104
Medina County, Texas, 433, 476
Mellette, William Moore, 328
Memphis & El Paso Railroad, 32
Memphis, Tennessee, 110, 210, 248, 267, 390
Memphis, Texas, 390
Menard County, Texas, 25, 27–28, 44, 122, 125, 131–132, 235, 283, 352, 469
Menardville, Texas, 26, 122, 125, 130, 283, 288
Meridian, Mississippi, 266, 362
Merriman, Bill, 481

Mesilla, New Mexico Territory, 33, 58, 209
Mesquite, Texas, 166
Methvin, John Jasper, 175, 177
Metz, Leon, 121
Mexico: and colonization schemes, 13; and El Paso Salt War, 32–33, 36; national government, 36, 78, 332, 425; and extradition treaty, 37, 163, 566 n23; border officials, 37, 160, 163, 565 n17; and cross-border depredations, 76, 78, 83–84, 157, 160, 165, 319, 435; and "hot pursuit" order, 160–161; French occupation, 215; Mexican Revolution, 238, 441–442, 447, 451, 491–492; and Garza War, 332–333, 466; and Spanish-American War, 341, 472; and *Porfiriato*, 418, 435, 439–440, 442; and Pirate Island, 424; Constitutionalist Army, 450–451, 453, 494
Middleton, Charles M., 82
Midland County, Texas, 352
Midland, Texas, 353, 443, 459
Mier, Mexico, 83, 332, 466
Milam County, Texas, 43, 75
Miles, C. P., 158
Miles, Martin Emmett, 115
Millbrook, Illinois, 281
Miller, George E., 380
Miller, Jesse, 349–350
Mills County, Texas, 381–382, 465
Mills, Roger Quarles, 260, 264, 604 n42
Millville, Texas, 363
Milton, Jefferson Davis "Jeff," 243, 272–273, 275
Mineola, Texas, 363–365
Minera, Texas, 351, 490
Missionary Ridge, battle of, 259–260
Missouri, Kansas & Texas Railroad, 155, 323, 477
Missouri Pacific Railroad, 196
Mitchell County, Texas, 273, 276, 352, 374, 458
Mitchell, Frank, 30–31
Mitchell, Robert, 30–31
Mitchell, Silas Weir, 277
Mitchell, William Davis, 478
Monaghan, Jim, 388
Monett's Ferry, battle of, 69, 220
Monroe, John R., 353
Montague County, Texas, 235
Monterrey, Mexico, 90, 238
Montgomery, Alabama, 108, 109–110
Moody, Dan, 498
Moore, Charles R., 435, 437, 443, 445, 448–450
Moore, George, 19
Moore, George Fleming, 245

Index

Moore, Harry, 437, 443
Moore, James H. "Jim," 327, 462, 483
Moore, Maurice B., 39–40, 167
Morgan, John Hunt, 101
Morgan's Ferry, battle of, 66
Morrill, Wells Clifford, 173, 175
Morris, John Milton, 367
Morris, Ned Bradford, 388, 393
Morris, Wade Allen, 45
Morris, William Taylor "Brack," 318, 479, 481–482
Mortimer, C. E., 34
Moses, William, 372
Motley County, Texas, 370, 372
Mound City, Kansas, 412
Mouton, Jean Jacques Alfred Alexandre, 6, 9, 11, 62, 64–65, 68, 217–218
Mullen, John W., 214
Murchison, Ivan, 434
Murfreesboro (Stones River), second battle of, 252
Murphy, James "Jim," 38, 40–41, 166
Murphysville, Texas, 234–236
Murray, Newton Harris "Plunk," 124
Musgrave, Daniel Lynch, 336–337
Muskogee, Indian Territory, 323

N

Nacogdoches County, Texas, 72, 461
Nacogdoches, Texas, 346, 478
Nana, 136
Nashville, Tennessee, 101, 210
Nasworthy, John Richard "Sarge," 272
Natchitoches, Louisiana, 64, 67, 69, 216, 220
Natus, Frank, 399
Natus, John, 337
Navarro County, Texas, 3, 11, 13, 15, 42, 44, 294, 296, 417
Navasota, Texas, 434
Neal, Edgar Thomas, 381–382
Neely, Adolphus Asbury, 336
Neighbors, Robert Simpson, 206
Nelson, Allison, 247–248
Nevill, Charles Liborn, 41, 126–128, 131–134, 142–143, 230–231
Newcomb, James Pearson, 71, 78
New Hope Church, battle of, 263
New Iberia, Louisiana, 62, 66, 215; skirmish at, 64
New Madrid, Missouri, 248
New Mexico Volunteers, 232

Newnam, Frank, 492
New Orleans, Louisiana, 6, 50, 64, 117–118, 183, 204–206, 210, 213, 215–216, 239, 248, 291, 363, 408, 432, 472
Newton County, Texas, 72
Newton, James Allen, 292, 325, 327
Newton, James Oscar, 436–437, 439, 485, 488
New York City, New York, 78, 118, 198, 406, 408, 432
Nicholson, E. G., 19, 126
Ninth U.S. Cavalry, 20, 35
Ninth U.S. Infantry, 36
Nitschke, Robert Edward, 496
Nixon, Richard, 403
Noakes, Thomas John, 84
Noble, Sebron Miles, 252, 264
Nolan County, Texas, 235, 288
Nolan, Nicholas, 228
Nolen, Harry W., 496–497
Nolte, Eugene, 491–492
Noyola, Valentín, 438
Nueces County, Texas, 84, 86, 104, 112–114, 167, 355, 435, 467, 469–470, 472
Nuecestown, Texas, 84
Nuevo Laredo, Mexico, 451, 489

O

Oakville, Texas, 157, 469
Oatmanville, Texas, 285
O'Bannon, James B., 284
Ochiltree, Thomas Peck, 54, 56
Ochoa, ———, 140
Oden, Alonzo W. "Lon," 344, 423
Odessa, Texas, 353
Odle, Alvin C., 292–293, 420
Odle, Walter P. "Will," 292–293, 420
Odom, Thomas Lawson, 235–236
Ogle, William Alvin "Bill," 384
Oglesby, Thomas Lindsey "Bose," 44, 168, 170, 284, 292, 320
O'Grady, William "Bill," 420
Ojinaga, Mexico, 440, 451
Old, Augustus Yardley "Augie," 388–389, 473, 475–477
Oldham County, Texas, 301
Olguin, Antonio, 424
Olguin, Jesús María, 424–425
Olguín, José Maria, 87
Olguin, Severo, 424–425
Olive, John Thomas, 293

Oliver, George B., 492
Opelousas, Louisiana, 10, 61, 68, 215–216
Orange County, Texas, 72, 389
Orange, Texas, 391, 476
Ord, Edward Otho Cresap, 160, 163–164
Orozco, Pascual, 440–442, 445, 447, 449, 492
Orsay, Henry, 45, 520 n113
Ortiz, Luis R., 474
Otero, Miguel Antonio, 430
Otis, Elwell Stephen, 184, 186, 191
Outlaw, Nathaniel A., 74–75
Outlaw, Bazzell Lamar "Baz," 417, 420–421, 423, 426
Overstreet, Rufus, 30
Owen, Robert Latham, 323
Ozona, Texas, 150

P

Paine, Albert Bigelow, 400, 405
Pa-ingya, 178–179
Painter, Charles Cornelius, 179
Palafox, Texas, 490
Palestine, Texas, 365, 487–488
Palito Blanco, Texas, 348
Palo Alto, second battle of, 87, 89, 103
Palo Blanco, Texas, 467
Palo Duro Canyon, battle of, 21
Palo Pinto County, Texas, 207, 372, 374, 433
Pardue, William Merritt, Jr., 390
Paris, Kentucky, 315
Paris, Texas, 121
Parish, John McKinley, 74–75
Parker County, Texas, 105–106, 206–207, 235
Parker, Isaac Charles, 328, 630 n32
Parker, James Weston, 298–299
Parks, Fred, 74
Parra, Gerónimo, 421, 430–431
Parrott, A. L., 106, 165–166
Parsons, Chuck, 82
Parsons, Mosby Monroe, 68, 219
Parsons, William Henry, 220, 247
Paso del Norte/Ciudad Juárez, Mexico, 136, 226, 375–376, 427, 430, 435, 441–442, 445, 447–449, 453
Patterson, James, 388
Patterson, W. P., 273, 275
Peal, Dennis A., 366

Pearre, Charles Baer, 181
Pearsall, Texas, 235, 318, 332
Pease, Elisha Marshall, 121
Pecos & Northern Texas Railroad, 308
Pecos County, Texas, 351
Pecos, Texas, 234, 276, 426, 443
Penrose, Charles Wilkinson, 399, 401–402
Pensacola, Florida, 108–109, 210
Peralta, New Mexico Territory, 58
Perez, Desiderio, 434
Perez, Segundo, 344
Perry, Christopher Columbus "Charley," 374
Perry, Rufus Cicero "Rufe," 19
Pershing, John Joseph "Black Jack," 310
Petersburg, Virginia, 251
Pflugerville, Texas, 282
Philip, John G., 54
Philippine Army of Liberation, 185, 189
Philippines, 184–185, 187, 196–197, 397; and Filipino independence movement, 189; and Lodge Committee, 196
Phillip, Joseph, 214
Pickett, Tom, 375
Piedras Negras/Ciudad Porfirio Díaz, Mexico, 106, 238, 440, 490
Pierce, Edward "Ed," 73
Pilot Grove, Texas, 156
Pinkerton's National Detective Agency, 38, 108, 166, 291
Pirate Island, 424–425, 448, 450
Pitts, Thomas T., 68
Pittsburg Landing, Tennessee, 211–213
Placerville, California, 204
Pleasant Hill, battle of, 11, 68, 219
Pleasanton, Texas, 106, 169
Pleasants, Henry Clay, 159
Plum Creek, battle of, 2
Plummer, Joseph Bennett, 206
Poindexter, James Waller, 100
Polant, 175
Polignac, Prince de (Camille Armand Jules Marie), 9–13, 220
Polignac's Texas Brigade, 9–12
Polk County, Texas, 72
Polk, Leonidas, 210–211, 254, 257–258, 262, 264
Polk, Lucius Eugene, 264, 266
Polly, James, 327
Pool, Jim, 430
Poole, George Franklin, 390

Index

Poole, George H., 391
Poole, Oscar, 390
Poole, Thomas F., 391
Pope, Owen Clinton, 320, 628 n13
Porter, Algernon Sidney, 154
Porter, David Dixon, 216–217, 248
Porter, Mel, 20
Porter, William Sydney ("O. Henry"), 154, 173
Port Hudson, battle of, 6, 62, 64–66, 215, 248
Port Lavaca, Texas, 433
Post, Charles William "C. W.," 436
Post City, Texas, 436–437
Poteet, A. J., 341
Potter County, Texas, 369, 436
Potter, Mack, 128, 132, 134
Potter, Thomas, 131
Potter, William, 29
Powe, Henry Harrison, 145
Powell, Felix, 395–396
Powell Ranch, 145
Powers, David Whitehead, 413
Powers, Stephen, 342
Prairie Grove, battle of, 5
Prentiss, Benjamin Mayberry, 211
Presidio County, Texas, 142, 147, 236, 421, 424, 430
Presidio of San Francisco, 185, 310
Presidio, Texas, 422, 426, 440–441
Price, Archibald "Arch," 345
Price, Marquis de Lafayette "Pal," 266
Price, Sterling, 362
Price, William Redwood, 163–164
Procter, Ben H., 369
Puckett, J. A., 283
Pueblo Indians, 228, 230
Putman, James Mitchell "Jim," 145, 423
Putz, Henry, 323–325, 328–329
Pyron, Charles Lynn, 54–55, 57

##

Quanah, Texas, 366, 369–371, 396, 407–408
Quanah Parker, 174, 177, 394, 412–413
Queen, Samuel Dawson "Kep," 465
Queen, Victor, 465
Quinlan, Dennis Patrick, 188, 190
Quitman, Texas, 364

R

Radder, Roland William, 312
Ragland, Thomas, 474
Raguet, Henry, 55
Ramirez, José, 467
Ramirez, Pancho, 467
Ramsey, Alexander, 165
Rancho Las Cucharas (Rancho Cachattus), skirmish at, 90–91
Rancho Las Cuevas, skirmish at, 90–91
Randal, Horace, 5
Randlett, James Franklin, 90–91
Randolph, George Wythe, 214
Rankin, Jesse, 154
Rankin, John, 463
Raymondville, Texas, 453
Realitos, Texas, 298, 336, 418, 467–468
Recéndez, Abram, 329–330, 418
Reese, Burrell Green Whittington "Dick," 343, 475
Reese, John Walter, 343–344, 433–434, 477
Reese, Leslie Wilkinson "Les," 343
Reese, Lillian, 477
Reese, Samuel Houston "Sam," 386, 475, 477, 647 n55
Reese, Spencer Herbert "Hub," 433
Reeves County, Texas, 234
Reinbolt, Edward, 331
Remington, Frederic, 85, 153
Rendado Ranch, skirmish at, 335
Renfrow, William Cary, 304–305
Renshaw, William Bainbridge, 61
Reyes, Bernardo, 444
Reynolds, J. M., 28–29, 125
Reynolds, Joseph Jones, 71, 74, 267
Reynolds, Nelson Orcelus "Mage," 25–26, 31, 38–41, 122, 126–128, 130–134, 291
Reynolds, Starke, 131–132
Reynosa, Mexico, 93, 332
Rhodes, John, 388
Richardson, Knox, 388
Riché, Charles Swift, 183
Richland, Texas, 294
Richland Springs, Texas, 384
Richmond, Texas, 13, 297–298, 300, 344
Richmond, Virginia, 50, 56, 59, 208–209, 251, 261, 264
Riel, Crisostomo, 193
Riley, Ben C., 286, 288
Riley, James, 60–61

Ringgold Barracks/Fort Ringgold, Texas, 78, 330, 335, 435, 472
Ringgold Gap, battle of, 260–261
Ringo, John Peters, 25
Rio Grande City, Texas, 163–165, 235, 330–331, 353, 405, 417–418, 434, 465, 478
Robb, Howard Leonidas, 393
Robbins, Arthur Ferris, 15
Roberson, David Seth, 298–299
Roberson, Horace Lorenzo "Hod," 496
Roberts, Albert S., 102
Roberts, Amos, 292, 325–326
Roberts, Daniel Webster, 24–26, 122, 124, 126–127, 275
Roberts, Felix, 346
Roberts, Noel Gill, 346
Roberts, Oran Milo, 10, 41–42, 44–46, 137, 168, 170, 225, 272
Roberts, R. A., 301
Roberts, Sidney, 346
Robertson County, Texas, 43, 72, 74–75, 365
Robertson, Jerome Bonaparte, 223
Robertson, John Charles, 245
Robertson, Sterling Clack, 271
Robinson, James R. "Jim," 298
Robinson, Julius A., 268
Robinson, Thomas C. "Pidge," 87
Robstown, Texas, 115
Robuck, William Emmett, 349–350
Rockport, Texas, 419–420
Rocksprings, Texas, 238, 440, 488–489
Rodríguez, Antonio, 238, 439–440, 488–489
Rogers, Curren Lee "Kid," 458, 463, 468, 477, 483
Rogers, G. W., 46
Rogers, Harriet Randolph "Hattie" (Burwell), 467–468, 470, 484, 486, 497, 498, 499
Rogers, John Harris: and fence-cutters, 292, 325; and train robbers, 293, 463; and James A. Brooks, 318; and Conner fight, 327, 462; as first sergeant of Company F, 332, 465; as captain of Company E, Frontier Battalion, 336, 468–469, 473; and Fitzsimmons-Maher prizefight, 338, 376, 470–471; and Reese-Townsend feud, 343–344, 387, 475, 477, 678 n44; and Wall-Broocks-Border feud, 346; and San Saba Mob, 381; and Christian faith, 425, 458, 467, 486, 493; as deputy U.S. marshal, 444, 491, 494; birth of, 457; education, 458; enlists in Company B, Frontier Battalion, 458; personality, characteristics, and motivations, 458, 466, 491; discharged from Frontier Battalion, 459; enlists in Company F, Frontier Battalion, 459; and Garza War, 466–469; and Laredo smallpox riot, 473–474; and racial strife, 476, 488; and vigilantes, 478, 489; and Gregorio Cortéz, 481; as captain of Company C, Ranger Force, 482–483, 485, 498; and labor strikes, 483; and Hillary "Hill" Loftis, 484, 496; and death of Lapsley, 486; and Mexican Revolution, 489–490, 492; resigns from

Ranger Force, 491; discharged from federal service, 492, 495; as U.S. marshal, 493–494; and Ranger Force investigation, 495; as Austin police chief, 496–497; as express company detective, 496; and oil boom towns, 498; death of, 498
Rogers, Lapsley Harris, 472, 486
Rogers, Laura Henrietta, 458
Rogers, Lucile, 470, 499
Rogers, Mary Amanda (Harris), 457–458, 672 n2
Rogers, Pleasant Blair, 457, 470, 499–500
Rogers, Pleasant William Miles, 457–458
Roosevelt, Theodore, 182, 393–394, 399, 401–402, 406–407, 492
Rosecrans, William Starke, 253, 258
Rosenburg, Texas, 344
Ross, Bob, 421
Ross, Lawrence Sullivan "Sul," 294, 298–299, 327–328
Ross, Louis E., 444
Ross, Tom M., 336–337, 434–436, 470
Roswell, New Mexico Territory, 146
Round Rock, Texas, 38–41, 111, 133, 166–167, 273, 282–283, 421
Rudd, William Lawrence, 166–168
Ruidosa, Texas, 440
Runnels City, Texas, 235
Runnels County, Texas, 130, 235, 329, 461, 464
Rusk County, Texas, 362–363
Rusk, Texas, 389, 462, 478
Russell, Grover Scott, 451–452
Russell, Richard Robertson "Dick," 469
Russell, William, 271
Rust, Albert, 246–247
Ryan, Carl T., 395
Ryan, Samuel, 399
Ryan, William Aurelius, 252, 265

S

Sabin, Chauncey Brewer, 300
Sabine County, Texas, 72, 327, 461–462
Sabine Pass, second battle of, 66
Salennia Ranch, 333
Salinas, Rafael, 87
Salisbury, Texas, 368
San Ambrosia, Texas, 288
San Angelo, Texas, 149–150, 269–273, 329, 353, 430, 464
San Antonio & Aransas Pass Railroad, 114, 182
San Antonio, Texas, 46–47, 50–51, 53, 57–59, 78, 94–95, 105, 117, 125, 127, 134, 149–150, 157–158, 161, 167, 170–173, 181, 183, 196–198, 204, 206–207, 209, 225, 239, 285, 293, 317, 338–339, 344, 386, 393, 395–396, 401–402,

Index 787

406, 434, 439, 441, 444, 447, 451, 453, 463, 467, 469, 472, 475–476, 481, 490, 492–493, 496, 499
San Augustine County, Texas, 72, 345, 461
San Augustine, Texas, 327, 346, 461, 463
San Augustín Springs, New Mexico Territory, 209
San Benito, Texas, 438
Sandels, Monte Hines, 325, 328
Sanders, John Jesse, 348–349
Sanderson, Texas, 339, 377
Sandherr, Charles, 478
San Diego, California, 309, 435
San Diego, Texas, 78, 84, 168–169, 194, 235, 335, 469, 472
Sandoval, Jesús "Old Casuse," 85–87
Sandoval, José, 434–435
San Elizario, Texas, 32–34, 136, 424–425
San Francisco, California, 185, 195, 204–205, 212, 221, 311, 426; Committee of Vigilance, 205
San Ignacio, Mexico, 136
San José, Mexico, 136
San Luis Potosí, Mexico, 439
San Marcos, Texas, 144, 453
San Patricio County, Texas, 104, 167, 330, 342, 433, 469
San Saba County, Texas, 75, 133, 235, 283, 326, 381, 384, 387, 407, 433
San Saba, Texas, 40, 133, 296, 382, 384, 387
Santa Fe, New Mexico Territory, 50, 56–58, 121, 137, 430
Santa Gertrudis Ranch, 78
Santa María, Texas, 90, 92, 169, 331, 465
Saragosa, Texas, 443
Saunders, Jonathan Woodard "Wood," 307, 424
Saxon, Andrew Lawrence "Lou," 390–391
Sayers, Joseph Draper, 56, 159, 237, 346–347, 350, 387–388, 390, 431, 478
Schmid, Frank Louis, 298–299, 619 n40
Schmitt, George Heinrich, 326
Schnabel, Henry, 481
Schofield, John McAllister, 262, 264, 266
Schutz, Solomon, 33
Schwan, Theodore, 191–194
Scott, Frank W., 304
Scott, William, 292, 318, 320–322, 325–329, 459–465
Scurry, Thomas, 343–344, 347–348, 350, 387, 390–391, 431, 475, 477–478
Scurry, Will, 343
Scurry, William Read "Dirty Shirt," 55–60
Seale, John J., 470
Searcy, Arkansas, 246
Seat, Benton Bell, 57, 64

Sebree, Victor, 330–331, 418
Second Colorado Infantry (USV), 55
Second New Mexico Volunteers (USV), 55
Second Texas Cavalry, Arizona Brigade (CSA), 214, 218, 221
Second Texas Infantry (CSA), 212
Second Texas Mounted Rifles/Second Texas Cavalry (CSA), 54, 60, 207–208, 214
Second Texas Partisan Rangers (CSA), 215
Secrest, Robert Yates, 498
Sedberry, James Martin "Jim," 145, 273, 275
Selcer, Richard F., 323
Selman, John, 426, 547 n27
Seminole, Texas, 484, 496
Seventeenth Texas Cavalry (CSA), 245–247, 251–252, 261, 264–265; and Seventeenth Texas Consolidated Cavalry (Dismounted), 9, 12–13, 252, 605 n46; and consolidation as Seventeenth, Eighteenth, Twenty-fourth, and Twenty-fifth Texas Cavalry (Dismounted), 251; and Seventeenth, Eighteenth, Twenty-fourth, and Twenty-fifth Texas Cavalry (Dismounted), 260–261; and consolidation as Seventeenth and Eighteenth Texas Cavalry (Dismounted), 261, 605 n46
Seventh Texas Infantry (CSA), 260
Seventh Texas Mounted Rifles/Seventh Texas Cavalry (CSA), 53, 55, 58, 60, 67–68
Seventh U.S. Artillery, 192
Seventh U.S. Infantry, 54, 203, 209
Seventy-seventh Illinois Infantry (USV), 282
Seward, Frederick William, 163
Shackelford, William, 155
Shafter, Texas, 317, 423–424, 426, 454
Shafter, William Rufus "Pecos Bill," 160, 183
Shamblin, James Madison, 298
Sharp, James, 81
Shelby County, Texas, 72
Shelbyville, Tennessee, 254
Sheldon, Lionel Allen, 232
Shely, Abraham Lincoln, 318
Shely, Josephus "Joe," 317, 319–322, 330, 459–460, 470
Shely, Warren Washington "Wash," 330, 335, 353, 418, 469
Sheppard, Morris, 493
Sheridan, Philip Henry, 15
Sherman, Texas, 155–156, 165, 175
Sherman, William Tecumseh, 248–249, 259, 262–265
Shiloh, battle of, 211–213
Shiloh, Texas, 158
Shreveport, Louisiana, 6, 217, 245, 267, 372, 393
Shropshire, John Samuel, 57
Sibley, Henry Hopkins, 50–51, 53–59, 62–64, 209, 729

Sibley Brigade (CSA), 51, 58, 61, 209
Sieker, Edward Armon, 124–125
Sieker, Frank Edward, 286, 288
Sieker, Lamartine Pemberton "Lam," 28, 122, 124, 282–284, 288, 295, 321, 328, 475
Sierra Blanca, Texas, 273
Siler, George, 339
Silver City, New Mexico Territory, 35
Simmons, Frank B., 425
Sinks, Edward R., 343
Sitter, Joseph Russell "Joe," 429
Sixteenth Texas Cavalry (CSA), 245, 246
Sixth Texas Infantry (CSA), 249, 252, 260; and consolidation as Sixth and Tenth Texas Infantry, 251
Sixth U.S. Cavalry, 15, 229
Slocum, Texas, 488
Slough, John Potts, 57
Smallwood, James M., 82
Smeltertown, Texas, 451–452
Smith, ———, 275
Smith County, Texas, 244, 268, 365
Smith, D. S., 371
Smith, Edmund Kirby, 6, 8, 67–68, 216–217, 221, 223, 252
Smith, Francis Marion, 478
Smith, James Argyle, 258–260, 264
Smith, L. B. ("Berry"), 89
Smith, Leon, 59–61
Smith, Thomas Slater, 347, 390;
Smyth, Rawleigh Portues, 114
Snider, Andy J., 413
Socorro, New Mexico Territory, 35, 56, 134, 136–137
Socorro, Texas, 136
Soledad Ranch, 335
Southern Pacific Railroad, 114, 141, 184, 197, 232, 273, 377, 407, 429, 463, 499
Southwestern Railroad, 101
Sparks John C., 30, 269
Spears, James Daniel, 270, 272
Speight, Joseph Warren, 4–6, 8–9, 11, 66
Spellman, Paul N., 341, 361
Spivey, William F., 66
Spradley, Andrew Jackson "John," 461
Stafford, John, 385–386
Stafford, Robert Earl "Bob," 385–386
Stafford, Warren Decatur, 385
Starr County, Texas, 86, 163, 329, 336, 342, 352–356, 405, 418, 434–435, 467–469, 472

Steele, William, 5, 16–18, 21–22, 28, 34, 40–42, 81, 84, 87, 89, 95, 108–110, 160, 163, 220, 504 n14
Sterling, William Warren, 461
Stevens, George Washington, 19, 20
Stevenson, George Bushrod, 234
Stewart, Charles, 41–42
Stirling's Plantation, battle of, 8, 66
St. John, Albert, 324, 328
St. Leon, Ernest "Diamond Dick," 423
St. Louis, Brownsville & Mexico Railroad, 115
St. Louis, Missouri, 47, 196
Stone, Benton Warren, 12, 215
Stone, Robert Dillard, 11
Stone, William D., 68
Stone Fort Rifles, 346, 478
Stoneman, George, 251
Stonewall County, Texas, 372
Stoudenmier, Dallas, 138, 140–141, 556–557 m43
Stuart, Daniel Albert, 337–338, 375–377, 426–427, 429, 470–471
Stumbling Bear, 178
Sugg, Eli Calvin, 174
Sullivan, John Lawrence, 337
Sullivan, William John L., 372, 374–376, 381–382, 384
Sulphur Springs, Texas, 364
Summerall, Charles Pelot, 195
Sunset, Texas, 365
Sutton, John Schuyler, 55
Sutton, William "Bill," 81–82, 158
Sweetwater, Texas, 236, 448
Swisher County, Texas, 303–305

T

Taft, William Howard, 435, 443, 445, 447, 492
Talley, George W., 158
Taovaya Indians, 174
Tascosa, Texas, 301
Tawakoni Indians, 174
Taylor, Charles, 81
Taylor, Creed, 343, 348, 475, 482
Taylor County, Texas, 461
Taylor, Felix, 321
Taylor, James Creed "Jim," 74, 83, 158
Taylor, James Rather, 245–247, 251–252, 264, 605 n46
Taylor, John Milam, 82
Taylor, Pitkin Barnes, 73

Index **791**

Taylor Ranch, 329
Taylor, Richard, 6, 61–64, 67, 215–216, 266
Taylor, William A., 252, 258
Taylor, William P. "Buck," 82
Taylor, William Riley "Bill," 158
Tays, James Alexander, 37
Tays, John Bernard, 33–37
Teal, Trevanion Theodore, 51
Temple, Texas, 148, 336–337, 498
Tenth Texas Infantry (CSA), 247, 252, 260; and consolidation as Sixth and Tenth Texas Infantry, 252
Tenth U.S. Cavalry, 228, 269, 271, 474
Tenth U.S. Infantry, 54
Terlingua, Texas, 426, 485
Terrazas, Joaquín, 136, 229
Terrell, Alexander Watkins, 46, 221
Terry, Ben, 30
Terry, Benjamin Franklin, 4
Terry, David Smith, 205, 221
Terry, Jefferson Kyle, 298, 300
Terry, Will, 421
Terry, William, 460–461
Texas: Indian depredations, 15, 76; legislature, 15–16, 79, 157, 168, 234, 355, 427, 431, 455, 470; vigilantism, 23–24, 84–85, 380–381, 385, 387–389, 395, 436, 489; feuds, 24–25, 29–33, 35, 386–387, 434, 437, 475, 478; racial strife, 71, 321, 330, 389, 397, 404, 418, 440, 476, 487–489; and cross-border depredations, 76, 78, 83, 157; Reconstruction, 82, 267, 297; and Nueces Strip, 83, 93, 157; and open range, 234, 458, 461, 595 n72; politics, 342, 349, 439, 472; formal end of frontier, 422
Texas & Pacific Railroad, 141, 144, 166, 228, 232, 273, 323, 370, 374, 459
Texas National Guard, 395, 399, 449, 488, 499
Texas Rangers: Frontier Battalion, 16, 19, 21–22, 27–28, 43–45, 80, 133, 232, 236, 276, 288, 322, 337, 346–348, 369, 390–391, 431, 459, 465, 482; heritage and traditions, 16; challenges, 22–23, 29, 290–291; and shift to law enforcement, 28; El Paso Salt War, 36, 135, 225–226; Special State Troops (Hall's), 45, 160, 168, 171; and firearms, 80, 86, 535 n81; Washington County Volunteer Militia, Company A, 80, 83, 94, 103; Special State Troops (McNelly's), 92, 94, 104, 157, 276; Special Rangers, 113, 391; and fence-cutting, 234–235, 290–291, 294–295, 325, 465; arrest powers, 346–347, 390, 482; Ranger Force, 347–348, 355, 391, 431–432, 440, 443, 453, 482, 485, 494–495, 498, 682 n89; and politics, 441, 454, 498
Texas State Police, 71–72, 74–75, 78–79, 385
Texas Volunteer Guard, 113–114, 299, 320
Thatcher, Howard, 304–305
Third New Mexico Volunteers (USV), 55

Third Texas Cavalry, Arizona Brigade (CSA), 6, 214–215
Third Texas Infantry (CSA), 458
Third Texas Infantry (TVG), 488
Third U.S. Artillery, 188
Third U.S. Cavalry, 54, 179, 188, 330, 333, 335, 467–468
Thirteenth Texas Cavalry Battalion (CSA), 68
Thirteenth Texas Infantry (CSA), 66
Thirtieth U.S. Volunteer Infantry, 188, 192–193
Thirty-fifth (Missouri-Kansas) Division, 310
Thirty-first Texas Cavalry (CSA), 5; and Thirty-first Texas Cavalry (Dismounted), 10
Thirty-first Texas Infantry (CSA), 6
Thirty-fourth Texas Cavalry (Dismounted) (CSA), 5–6, 10
Thirty-seventh U.S. Volunteer Infantry, 187
Thirty-sixth Texas Cavalry (CSA), 458
Thirty-third U.S. Volunteer Infantry, 184–185, 187, 191
Thomas, George Henry, 257–258, 262
Thompson, Tecumseh Harvell, 493
Thorne, Joe, 414
Throckmorton County, Texas, 27
Throckmorton, James Webb, 15
Throckmorton, Texas, 485
Thulemeyer, William A., 479
Thurber, Texas, 372, 483
Thurman, Mace, 455
Tiernan, Patrick, 300
Tirad Pass, battle of, 191
Tom, Charles, 484
Tom Green County, Texas, 269, 329, 352, 430, 464
Tompkins, William O. "Bill," 172
Toole, John, 327
Touchstone/Thomas, Mary Jane, 392–393
Townsend, Howard Asa, 343
Townsend, James Gaither "Jim," 343–344, 475–476
Townsend, James Light, 343, 385–386, 434, 475, 647 n55
Townsend, Light (cousin), 678 n44
Townsend, Marcus Harvey, 344, 386–387, 475
Townsend, Richard W. "Dick," 323, 475
Townsend, Sumner, 385
Toyah, Texas, 143, 234–236
Trainer, James, 24
Travis County, Texas, 2, 32, 39, 73, 75, 80, 108, 110, 121, 130, 132–134, 272, 282, 285, 289, 406, 413
Travis Rifles, 102, 111
Treadwell, William "Billy," 292, 325, 327
Trent, Jim, 331

Index

Tres Jacales, Mexico, 136, 424
Trimmell, John H., 479
Trinity County, Texas, 72, 392–393, 486
Trowbridge, George Washington, 382, 384
Tucker, Thomas F., 265
Tucson, Arizona, 54, 57, 419
Tulia, Texas, 303
Tumlinson, Joseph, 319
Tumlinson, Joseph "Old Joe," 82
Tumlinson, Lott, 351
Tunnel Hill, battle of, 259
Turnbo, Lycurgus S. "Kirk," 234–235
Turner, James R., 382
Turney, William Ward, 431
Twain, Mark, 406
Twelfth Texas Cavalry (CSA), 220, 246
Twentieth Texas Infantry (CSA), 12, 60
Twenty-fifth Texas Cavalry (CSA), 251–252, 261; and consolidation as Seventeenth,
    Eighteenth, Twenty-fourth, and Twenty-fifth Texas Cavalry (Dismounted), 251;
    and Seventeenth, Eighteenth, Twenty-fourth, and Twenty-fifth Texas Cavalry
    (Dismounted), 260; and consolidation as Twenty-fourth and Twenty-fifth Texas
    Cavalry (Dismounted), 261
Twenty-fifth U.S. Infantry, 397, 399–401, 403
Twenty-first Texas Infantry Battalion (CSA), 60
Twenty-fourth Louisiana Infantry (CSA), 63
Twenty-fourth Texas Cavalry (CSA), 251–252, 256; and consolidation as Seventeenth,
    Eighteenth, Twenty-fourth, and Twenty-fifth Texas Cavalry (Dismounted), 251;
    and Seventeenth, Eighteenth, Twenty-fourth, and Twenty-fifth Texas Cavalry
    (Dismounted), 260; and consolidation as Twenty-fourth and Twenty-fifth Texas
    Cavalry (Dismounted), 261
Twenty-fourth U.S. Infantry, 160, 187
Twenty-ninth U.S. Volunteer Infantry, 192
Twenty-second North Carolina Infantry (CSA), 154
Twenty-second Texas Cavalry (CSA), 5–6, 9
Twenty-second Texas Infantry (CSA), 11
Twenty-sixth Texas Cavalry (CSA), 60
Twenty-third U.S. Infantry, 472
Twohig, Texas, 326
Tyler County, Texas, 72
Tyler, Texas, 244–245, 267–269, 278–279

U

Union Agency (Muskogee), 323
Union Army of the Cumberland, 253, 255, 257–258, 262
Union Army of the Gulf, 10, 216

Union Army of the Mississippi, 248
Union Army of the Ohio, 262
Union Army of the Potomac, 258, 262
Union Army of the Tennessee, 262
Union Pacific Railroad, 37, 165
United States: War Department, 71, 182, 199, 208, 216, 251, 403, 441; Congress, 78, 86, 178, 183, 238, 403, 429, 443, 445, 470, 491; Dawes Severalty Act, 178, 394; Bureau of Indian Affairs, 180; Lodge Committee, 196; Dix-Hill cartel, 251
United States Army, 28, 36, 80, 161, 183–184, 310, 357, 425, 435; and Red River War, 28; and Philippine War, 185, 189
Upton County, Texas, 422, 498
U Ranch, 413
U.S. VIII Corps, 184–185
U.S. First Army, 310
U.S. Regiment of Mounted Riflemen, 208
Utley, Robert M., 315
Utter, Charles H. "Colorado Charlie," 140
Uvalde County, Texas, 28, 143, 169, 322, 330, 460
Uvalde, Texas, 78, 165, 225, 282, 284, 288, 293, 322, 453, 461, 493, 498

V

Vaden, James Williamson, 156
Valdés, Pedro Advíncula, 128, 161
Valentine, Texas, 341, 423, 443, 450, 452–453
Valls, John Alexander, 489–490
Valverde, battle of, 55–56
Valverde Battery (CSA), 56, 58, 65
Val Verde County, Texas, 351
Van Buren, Arkansas, 121
Vance, Texas, 421
Vandegriff, E. L., 144
Van Dorn, Earl, 208
Van Horn, Texas, 144, 429, 441
Van Riper, William H., 335, 463
Vásquez Invasion, 2
Vaughan, John, 160
Vawter, Josephine Elmina "Mina," 478
Vawter, Theodore, 478
Velasco, Marguerita, 238–239
Veleta, José, 423
Veracruz, Mexico, 239
Vermilion Bayou, skirmish at, 64
Vernon, Texas, 305, 322, 375, 461
Vicksburg, Mississippi, 65, 215, 248
Victoria, Texas, 206, 319, 396

Index

795

Victorio, 135–136, 226, 228–229, 592 n57
Vidalia, Louisiana, raid on, 10
Villa, Francisco "Pancho," 440, 445, 450
Virginia Point, Texas, 60, 67, 214, 216
Votaw Ranch, 320
Votaw, William, 320–321

W

Waco, Texas, 38, 174, 181, 289, 294, 314, 478, 493
Waddill, H. B., 28
Wade City, Texas, 470
Wade, William T., 299
Waelder, Texas, 235
Waggoner, Daniel, 174
Waggoner Ranch, 375
Waldrup, Jim "Buck," 31
Walker County, Texas, 72, 74–75, 392–393
Walker, John George, 67, 69–70, 216, 218
Walker, William Henry Talbot, 257
Walker, William Robert "Bob," 386
Walker's Texas Division, 68, 216–218, 220
Wall, Brune, 345–346
Wall, Eugene Beauharnais, 345–346
Wall, George Washington, 345–346
Wall, Lopez "Pez," 345–346
Wall, Ney, 345
Wall, W. A. "Uncle Buck," 345–346
Wallace, Lewis "Lew," 137
Waller County, Texas, 12, 351
Waller, Edwin, Jr., 208
Waller, Edwin, Sr., 73
Waller, John R., 19
Wallis, Harry, 349
Walter, John, 285–286
Ware, John, 468
Ware, Richard Clayton "Dick," 39–41, 132, 273, 275–276
Warren, Benjamin Goodin, 235–236
Washington, Booker T., 402
Washington County, Texas, 2, 50, 69–70, 75, 80, 122
Washington, D.C., 36, 92, 118, 178, 182, 184, 196–197, 199, 229, 333, 399–400, 406, 444, 451, 500
Washington, Louisiana, 10, 66
Washington, Texas, 96
Watkins, William, 270–272
Waugh, William Alexander, 172

Weatherford, Frank, 476
Weatherford, Texas, 165, 206–207, 463
Weatherred, William Wallace, 327
Weaver, John Downing, 403
Webb, Charles M., 108, 110
Webb County, Texas, 164, 286, 288, 336, 342, 351, 476, 490
Webb, Walter Prescott, 99, 291, 458
Webster, Charles H., 443, 448, 450
Weeks, Polk, 389
Weightman, George "Red Buck," 375, 484
Weisiger, William Jordan, 80
Weiss, Harold J., Jr., viii, 1, 482
Welch, Stanley, 354, 400–401, 405, 434–435
Wellington, Kansas, 365
Wells, James Babbage, Jr., 112, 115, 333, 342, 405, 434, 438
Wells, Louis Benjamin, 273, 275
West, Duval, 494
West, Earl, 438
West, Henry Clay, 6
West, Stephen P., 390
Western & Atlantic Railroad, 262
Whaley Ranch, 105
Wharton County, Texas, 214, 298
Wharton, John Austin, 12, 69, 101, 220–223
Wharton, Texas, 298, 417
Wheat, Ira Lewis, 420, 461
Wheaton, Lloyd, 187, 189, 191–192, 194
Wheeler County, Texas, 44
Wheeler, Joseph, 101, 254, 262
White, Dabney, 477
White, Eugene E., 180–181
White, Gideon, 465
White, Goff, 486
White, Ham, 160
White, James Campbell "Doc," 433–434
Whitley, William Henry "Bill," 293, 417, 465
Wichita, Kansas, 173
Wichita Agency (Fort Cobb), 206
Wichita County, Texas, 365, 375
Wichita Falls, Texas, 235, 365–366, 373, 379–380, 408
Wichita Indians, 174, 206
Wichita Reservation (Anadarko), 174
Wilbarger County, Texas, 235, 322, 367, 375, 461, 496
Wilder, Wilbur Elliott, 190
Wilkes, Franklin Collett, 256–258

Wilkins, Frederick, 85
Wilkinson, Joseph L., 387–389
Wilkinson, Leslie "Les," 343
Wilkinson, Walter, 388–389
Williams, Johnny, 375, 387
Williams, M. H. "Polly," 104–105
Williams, Thomas Howard, 30
Williamson, Ben, 296
Williamson, Beulah, 296
Williamson County, Texas, 30, 40, 75, 282–283, 289, 293, 305, 308, 413
Williamson, Mary Ann, 296
Williamson, Timothy P., 24–25
Willis, Dorsie W., 403
Wilson County, Texas, 105, 170
Wilson, Ellen Axson, 408
Wilson, James C., 395–396
Wilson, J. Thomas "Tom," 19, 22
Wilson, Vernon Coke, 38
Wilson, Woodrow, 238, 407–408, 492–494, 499
Wilson's Farm, skirmish at, 218
Winkler, Clinton McKamy, 17
Winnsboro, South Carolina, 1–2
Wise County, Texas, 365
Wohrle, Johann Anton "John," 24–25
Wood County, Texas, 363, 365
Wood, Thomas James, 263
Woods, J. W., 469
Wooldridge, Augustus Bruce "Gunger," 344, 386
Wooten, Thomas Dudley, 46
Wozencraft, Alfred Prior, 473
Wren, William R., 30–31
Wright, John, 74
Wright, Milam Harper, 433–434
Wright, Nathaniel A., 74–75
Wright, William Lee, 343, 434, 475–477, 482, 498
Wuerschmidt, Elfrieda Gertrude, 419

X

XIT Ranch, 305–308

Y

Yaqui Indians, 196–197
Yates, Andrew Lynn "Step," 475
Yellow Bayou, battle of, 12, 69, 220–221

Yett, William "Dick," 497
Yoakum, Benjamin Franklin, 114, 116
Yoakum, Texas, 182
Yorktown, Texas, 82, 319, 459
Young County, Texas, 20, 207, 374
Young, Samuel Baldwin Marks, 187–191
Ysleta, Texas, 34–35, 134, 136–138, 142, 226–229, 232–233, 235, 237, 419, 424–425, 427, 429, 432, 435–436, 438, 442–443, 448–450, 452–454

Z

Zapata County, Texas, 335–336, 356, 434, 472
Zavala County, Texas, 352
Zimpelman, George B., 32, 37, 102